HAMMOND

New Century World Atlas

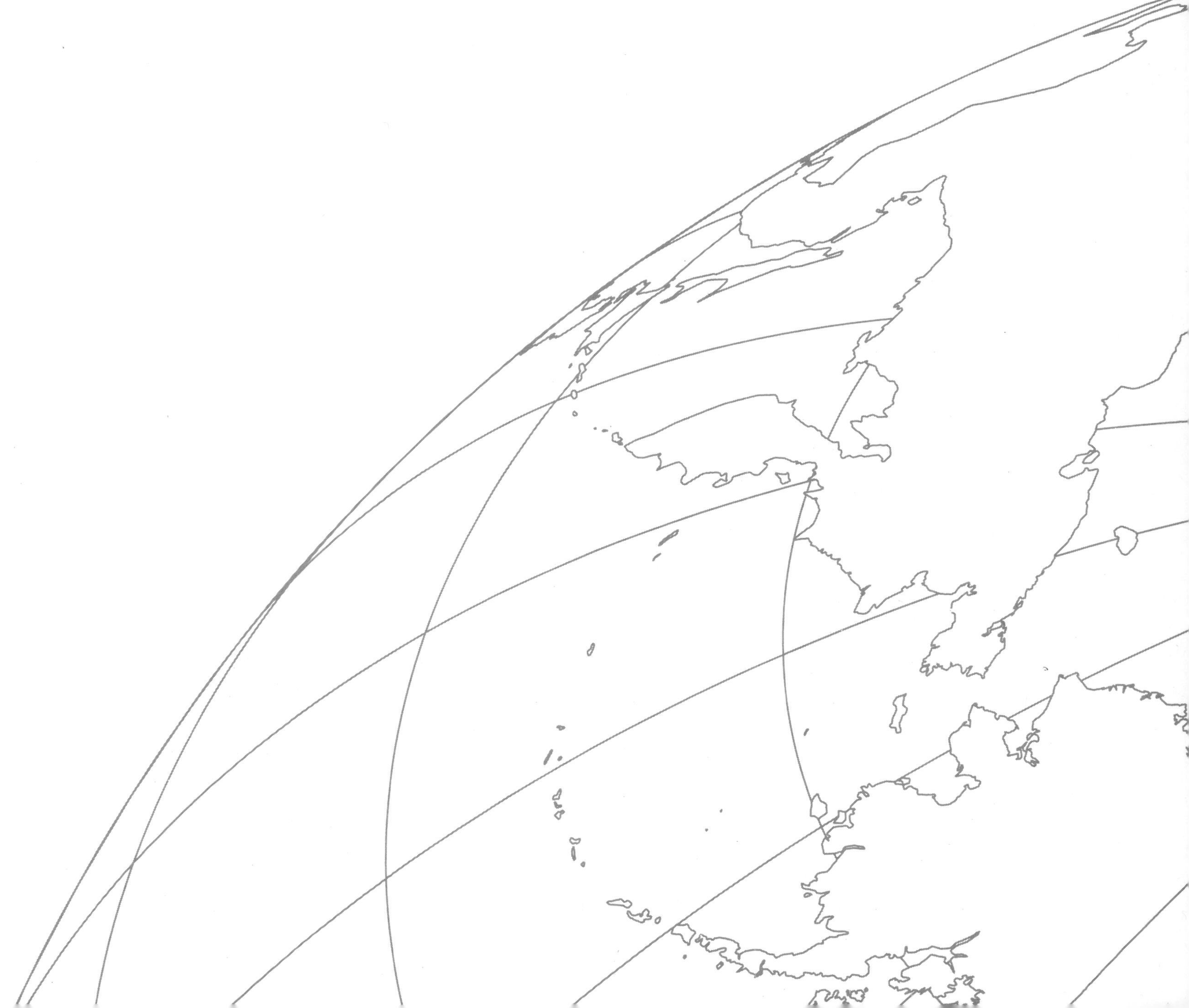

Contents

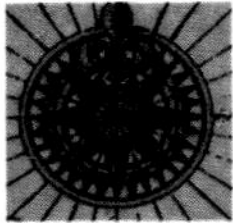

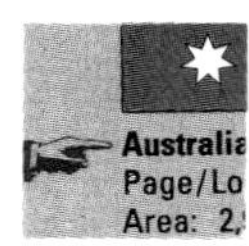

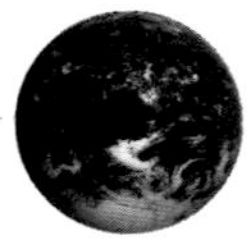

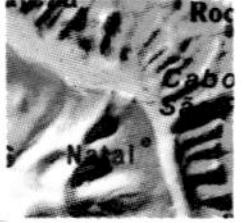

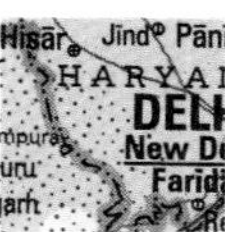

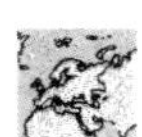

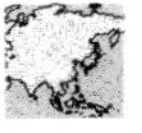

LIBRARY OF CONGRESS
CATALOGING-IN-PUBLICATION DATA

Hammond Incorporated.
  Hammond new century world atlas
      p. cm.
  Includes index.
  ISBN 0-8437-1196-5
  ISBN 0-8437-1197-3 (pbk.)
  1. Atlases. I. Title.
G1021. H2735   1995   <G&M>
912--dc20   95-9638
                                  CIP
                                  MAP

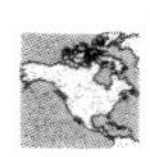

Map Projections

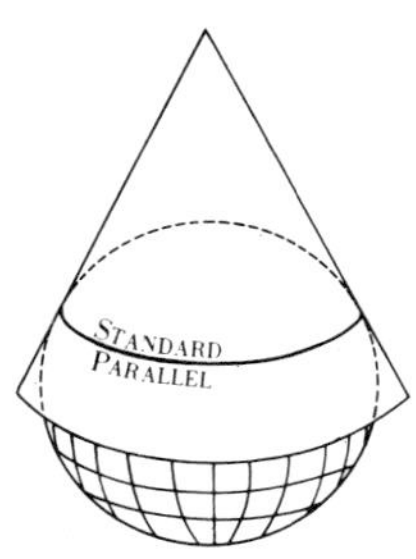

FIGURE 3
Conic Projection

The original idea of a conic projection is to cap the globe with a cone, and then project onto the cone from the planet's center the lines of latitude and longitude (the parallels and meridians). To produce a working map, the cone is simply cut open and laid flat. The conic projection used here is a modification of this idea. A cone can be made tangent to any standard parallel you choose. One popular version of a conic projection, the Lambert Conformal Conic, uses two standard parallels near the top and bottom of the map to further reduce errors of scale.

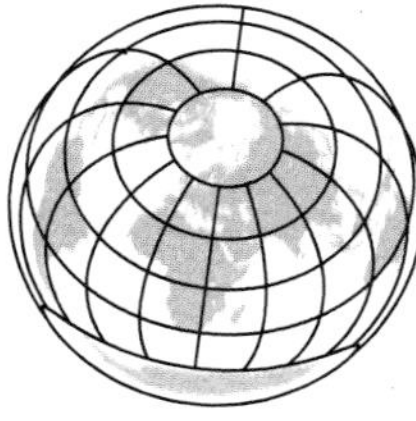

FIGURE 4
Lambert Azimuthal Equal-Area Projection

Because this projection shows correct areas with relatively little distortion of shapes, it is commonly used to plot maps of the continents. However, because of improved accuracy, the Optimal Conformal projection was used for all of the continent maps in this atlas.

Simply stated, the mapmaker's challenge is to project the earth's curved surface onto a flat plane. To achieve this elusive goal, cartographers have developed map projections — equations which govern this conversion of geographic data.

This section explores some of the most widely used projections. It also introduces a new projection, Hammond's Optimal Conformal.

GENERAL PRINCIPLES AND TERMS

The earth rotates around its axis once a day. Its end points are the North and South poles; the line circling the earth midway between the poles is the equator. The arc from the equator to either pole is divided into 90 degrees of latitude. The equator represents 0° latitude. Circles of equal latitude, called parallels, are traditionally shown at every fifth or tenth degree.

The equator is divided into 360 degrees. Lines circling the globe from pole to pole through the degree points on the equator are called meridians, or great circles. All meridians are equal in length, but by international agreement the meridian passing through the Greenwich Observatory near London has been chosen as the prime meridian or 0° longitude. The distance in degrees from the prime meridian to any point east or west is its longitude.

While meridians are all equal in length, parallels become shorter as they approach the poles. Whereas one degree of latitude represents approximately 69 miles (112 km.) anywhere on the globe, a degree of longitude varies from 69 miles (112 km.) at the equator to zero at the poles. Each degree of latitude and longitude is divided into 60 minutes. One minute of latitude equals one nautical mile (1.15 land miles or 1.85 km.).

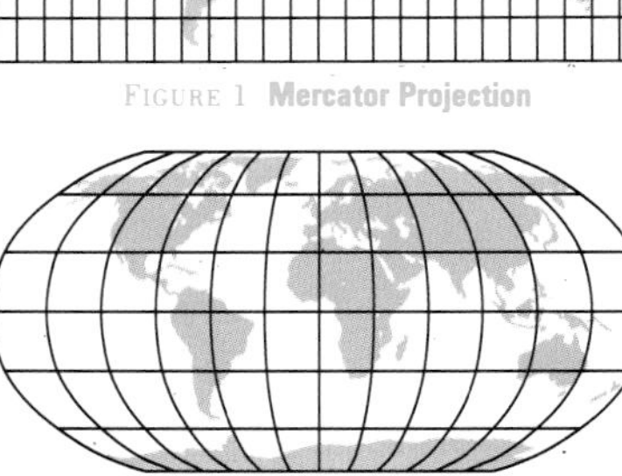

HOW TO FLATTEN A SPHERE: THE ART OF CONTROLLING DISTORTION

There is only one way to represent a sphere with absolute precision: on a globe. All attempts to project our planet's surface onto a plane unevenly stretch or tear the sphere as it flattens, inevitably distorting shapes, distances, area (sizes appear larger or smaller than actual size), angles or direction.

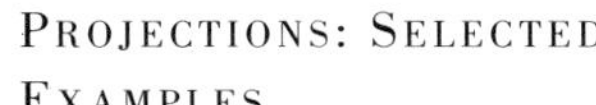

FIGURE 1 Mercator Projection

FIGURE 2 Robinson Projection

Since representing a sphere on a flat plane always creates distortion, only the parallels or the meridians (or some other set of lines) can maintain the same length as on a globe of corresponding scale. All other lines must be either too long or too short. Accordingly, the scale on a flat map cannot be true everywhere; there will always be different scales in different parts of a map. On world maps or very large areas, variations in scale may be extreme. Most maps seek to preserve either true area relationships (equal area projections) or true angles and shapes (conformal projections); some attempt to achieve overall balance.

PROJECTIONS: SELECTED EXAMPLES

Mercator (Fig. 1): This projection is especially useful because all compass directions appear as straight lines, making it a valuable navigational tool. Moreover, every small region conforms to its shape on a globe — hence the name conformal. But because its meridians are evenly-spaced vertical lines which never converge (unlike the globe), the horizontal parallels must be drawn farther and farther apart at higher latitudes to maintain a correct relationship. Only the equator is true to scale, and the size of areas in the higher latitudes is dramatically distorted.

Robinson (Fig. 2): To create the thematic maps in Global Relationships and the two-page world map in the Maps of the World section, the Robinson projection was used. It combines elements of both conformal and equal area projections to show the whole earth with relatively true shapes and reasonably equal areas.

Conic (Fig. 3): This projection has been used frequently for air navigation charts and to create most of the national and regional maps in this atlas. (See text in margin at left).

HAMMOND'S OPTIMAL CONFORMAL

As its name implies, this new conformal projection presents the optimal view of an area by reducing shifts in scale over an entire region to the minimum degree possible. While conformal maps generally preserve all small shapes, large shapes can become very distorted because of varying scales, causing considerable inaccuracy in distance measurements. The concept underlying the Optimal Conformal is that for any region on the globe, there is an ideal projection for which scale variation can be made as small as possible. Consequently, unlike other projections, the Optimal Conformal does not use one standard formula to construct a map. Each map is a unique projection — the optimal projection for that particular area.

In practice, the cartographer first defines the map subject, then, working on a computer, draws a band around the region to be mapped. Next, a sophisticated software program evaluates the size and shape of the region to determine the most accurate way to project it. The result is the most distortion-free conformal map possible, and the most

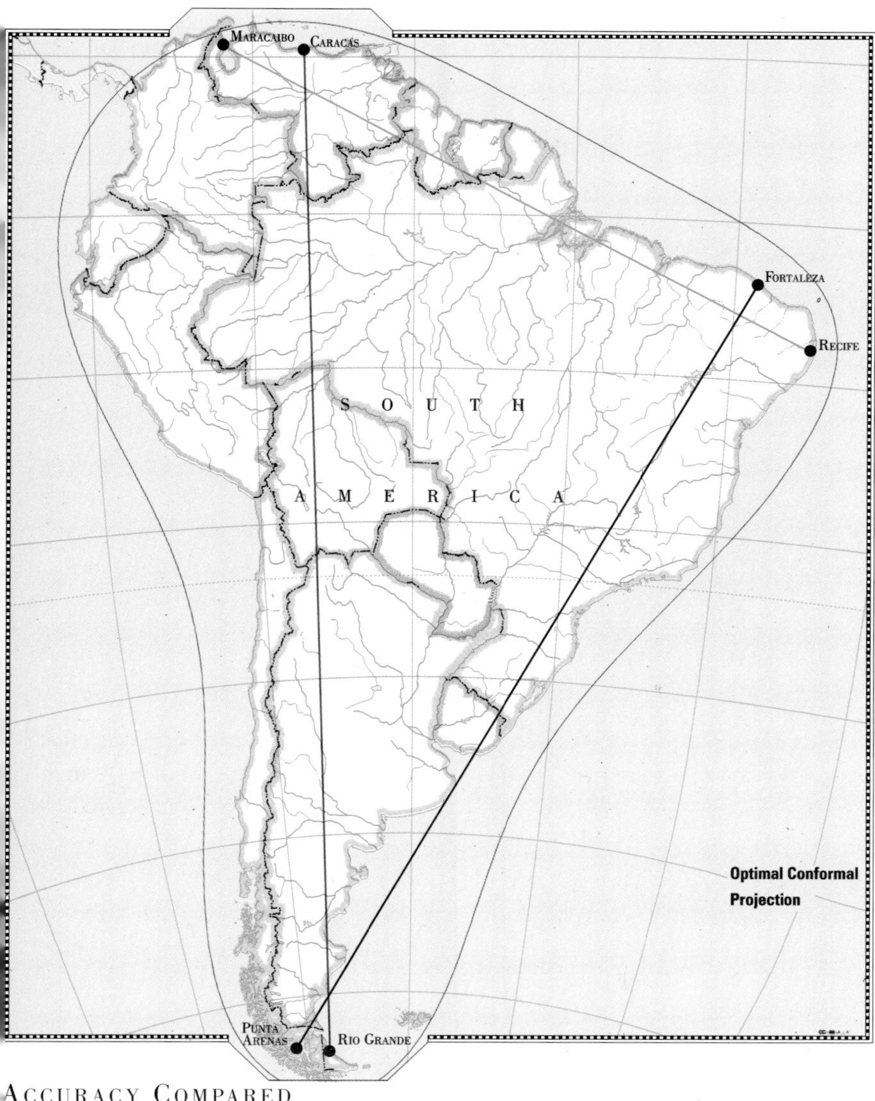

Optimal Conformal
Projection

ACCURACY COMPARED

CITIES	SPHERICAL (TRUE) DISTANCE	OPTIMAL CONFORMAL DISTANCE	LAMBERT AZIMUTHAL DISTANCE
CARACAS TO RIO GRANDE	4,443 MI. (7,149 KM.)	4,429 MI. (7,126 KM.)	4,316 MI. (6,944 KM.)
MARACAIBO TO RECIFE	2,834 MI. (4,560 KM.)	2,845 MI. (4,578 KM.)	2,817 MI. (4,533 KM.)
FORTALEZA TO PUNTA ARENAS	3,882 MI. (6,246 KM.)	3,907 MI. (6,266 KM.)	3,843 MI. (6,163 KM.)

Continent maps drawn using the Lambert Azimuthal Equal Area projection (Fig. 4) contain distortions ranging from 2.3 percent for Europe up to 15 percent for Asia. The Optimal Conformal cuts that distortion in half, improving distance measurements on these continent maps. Less distortion means greater visual fidelity, so the shape of a continent on an Optimal projection more closely represents its True shape. The table above compares measurements on the Optimal projection to those of the Lambert Azimuthal Equal Area projection for selected cities.

accurate projections that have ever been made. All of the continents maps in this atlas (with the exception of Antarctica) have been drawn using this projection.

PROJECTIONS COMPARED

Because the true shapes of earth's landforms are unfamiliar to most people, distinguishing between various projections can be difficult. The following diagrams reveal the distortions introduced by several commonly used projections. By using a simple face with familiar shapes as the starting point (The Plan), it is easy to see the benefits — and drawbacks — of each. Think of the facial features as continents. Note that distortion appears not only in the features themselves, but in the changing shapes, angles and areas of the background grid, or graticule.

Figure 5: The Plan
The Plan indicates that the continents are either perfect concentric circles

or are true straight lines *on the earth.* They should appear that way on a "perfect" map.

Figure 6: Orthographic Projection
This view shows the continents on the earth as seen from space. The facial features occupy half of the earth, which is all that you can see from this perspective. As you move outward towards the edge, note how the eyes become elliptical, the nose appears larger and less straight, and the mouth is curved into a smile.

Figure 7: Mercator
This cylindrical projection preserves angles exactly, but the mouth is now smiling broadly, and shows extreme distortion at the map's outer edge. This rapid expansion as you move away from the map's center is typified by the extreme enlargement of Greenland found on Mercator world maps (also see Fig. 1).

Figure 8: Peters
The Peters projection is a square equal area projection elongated, or stretched vertically, by a factor of two. While representing areas in their correct proportions, it does not closely resemble the Plan, and angles, local shapes and global relations are significantly distorted.

Figure 9: Hammond's Optimal Conformal
As you can see, this projection minimizes inaccuracies between the angles and shapes of the Plan, yielding a near-perfect map of the given area, up to a complete hemisphere. Like all conformal maps, the Optimal projection preserves every angle exactly, but it is more successful than previous projections at spreading the inevitable curvature across the entire map. Note that the sides of the triangle appear almost straight while correctly containing more than 180°. And though the eyes are slightly too large, it is the only map with eyes which appear concentric. Both mathematically and visually, it offers the best conformal map that can be made of the ideal Plan. All continent maps in this atlas are drawn on this projection.

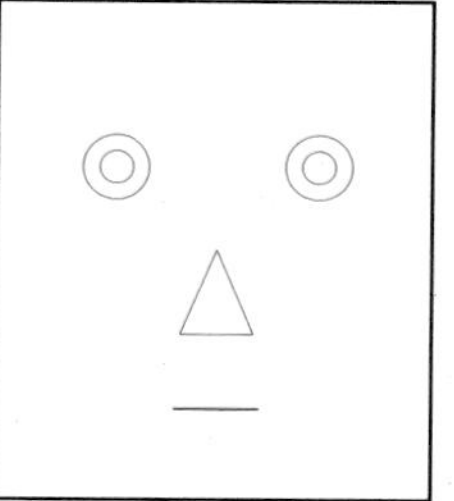

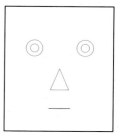

FIGURE 5
The Plan

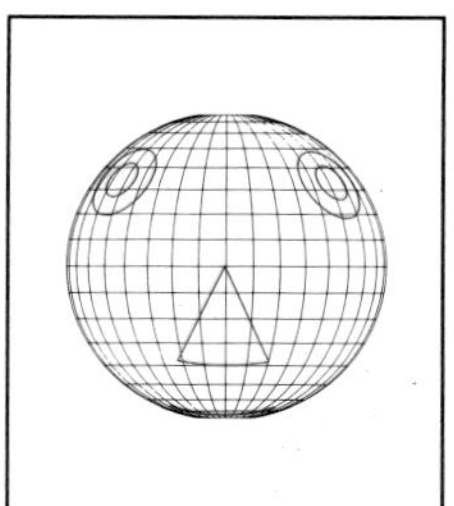

FIGURE 6
Orthographic Projection

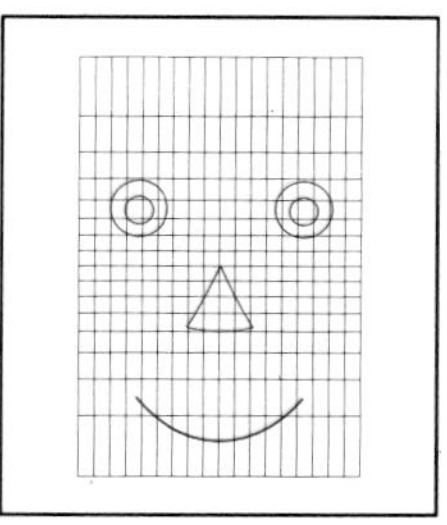

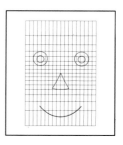

FIGURE 7
Mercator Projection

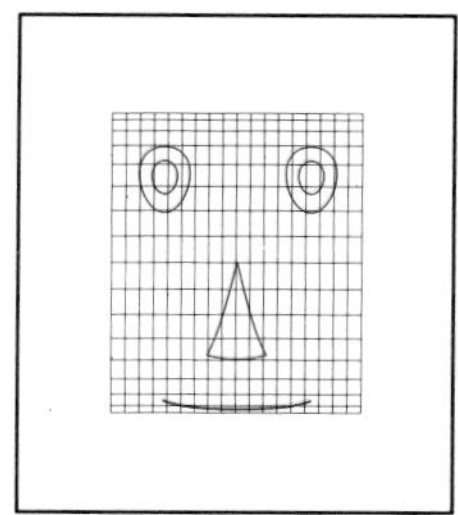

FIGURE 8
Peters Projection

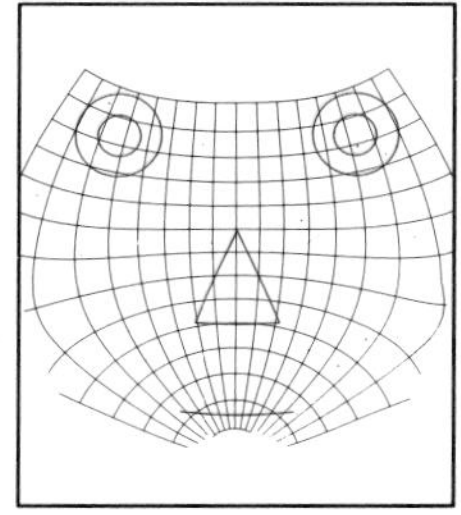

FIGURE 9
Optimal Conformal
Projection

Using This Atlas

How to Locate Information Quickly
Our Maps of the World section is organized by continent. If you're looking for a major region of the world, consult the Contents on page two.

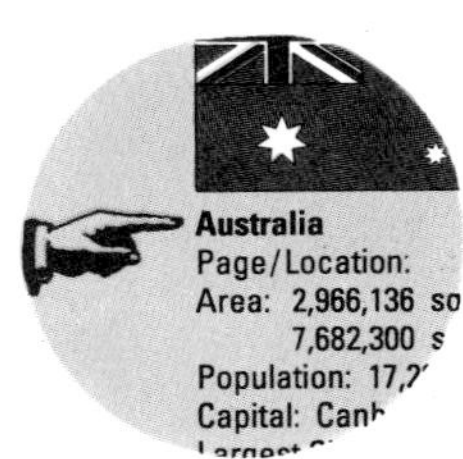

Australia
Page/Location:
Area: 2,966,136 sq
7,682,300 s
Population: 17,7
Capital: Canb

World Reference Guide
This concise guide lists the countries of the world alphabetically. If you're looking for the largest scale map of any country, you'll find a page and alpha-numeric reference at a glance, as well as information about each country, including its flag.

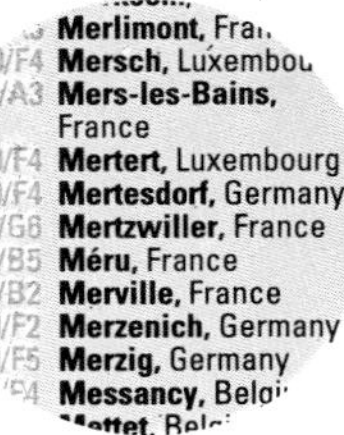

Merlimont, Fran...
/F4 Mersch, Luxembou
68/A3 Mers-les-Bains, France
69/F4 Mertert, Luxembourg
69/F4 Mertesdorf, Germany
69/G6 Mertzwiller, France
68/B5 Méru, France
68/B2 Merville, France
69/F2 Merzenich, Germany
69/F5 Merzig, Germany
Messancy, Belo...
attet, Belo...

Master Index
When you're looking for a specific place or physical feature, your quickest route is the Master Index. This 45,000-entry alphabetical index lists both the page number and alpha-numeric reference for major places and features in Maps of the World.

T his completely new atlas has been thoughtfully designed for easy, enjoyable use. It is organized as both a general reference atlas and as a comparative tour of the world and its regions. A short time spent familiarizing yourself with its arrangement will help you to benefit fully from its use.

WORLD FLAGS AND REFERENCE GUIDE
This colorful section portrays each nation of the world with its flag and important geographical data including area, population, capital, largest city, highest point and monetary unit. The guide also serves as a quick reference to page and location in the detailed Maps of the World section.

GLOBAL RELATIONSHIPS
World thematic maps highlight important social, cultural, economic and geographic factors affecting today's world. Here, readers can explore complex relationships among such topics as population growth, environmental problems and land utilization or compare worldwide standards of living, energy, resources and manufacturing. Chapters on the Solar System and Structure of the Earth complete this thematic unit.

THE PHYSICAL WORLD
These relief maps of the continents are actual photographs of three-dimensional TerraScape™ models. They present the relationships of land and sea forms with startling realism.

MAPS OF THE WORLD
The largest part of the atlas, this section is subdivided into continental groupings. Each division is introduced with facing-page thematic and political maps of each continent, making topical relationships easier to compare. The thematic maps include topography, population distribution, land use and mineral resources.

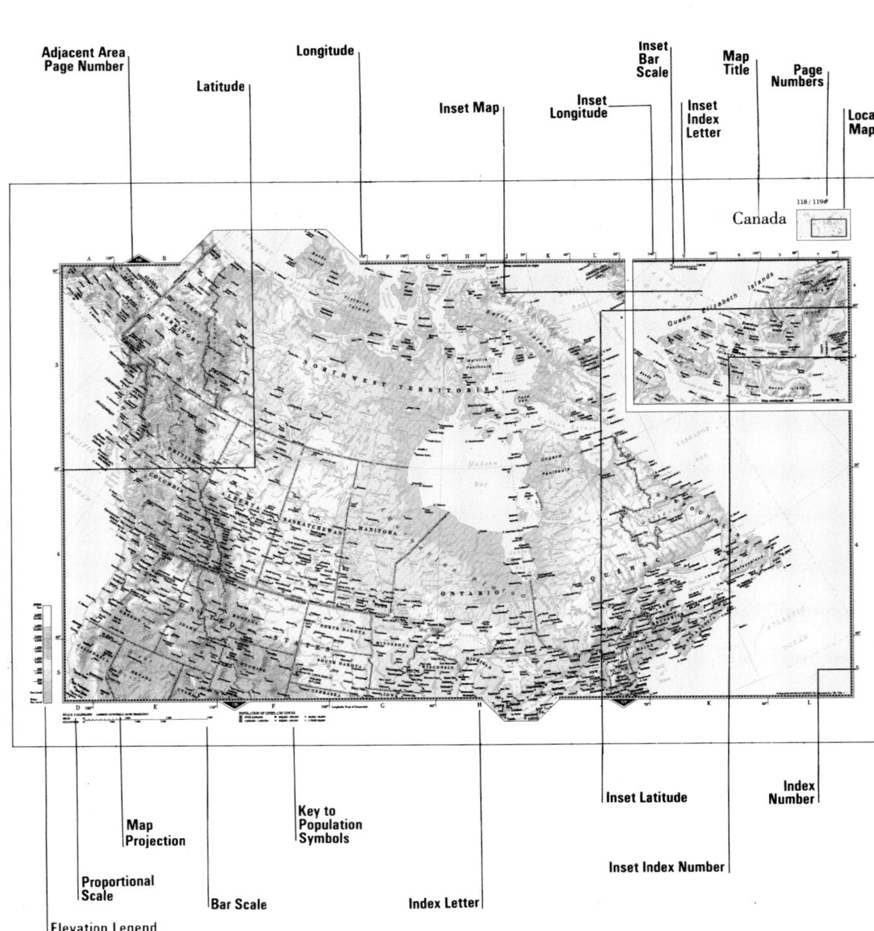

SYMBOLS USED ON MAPS OF THE WORLD

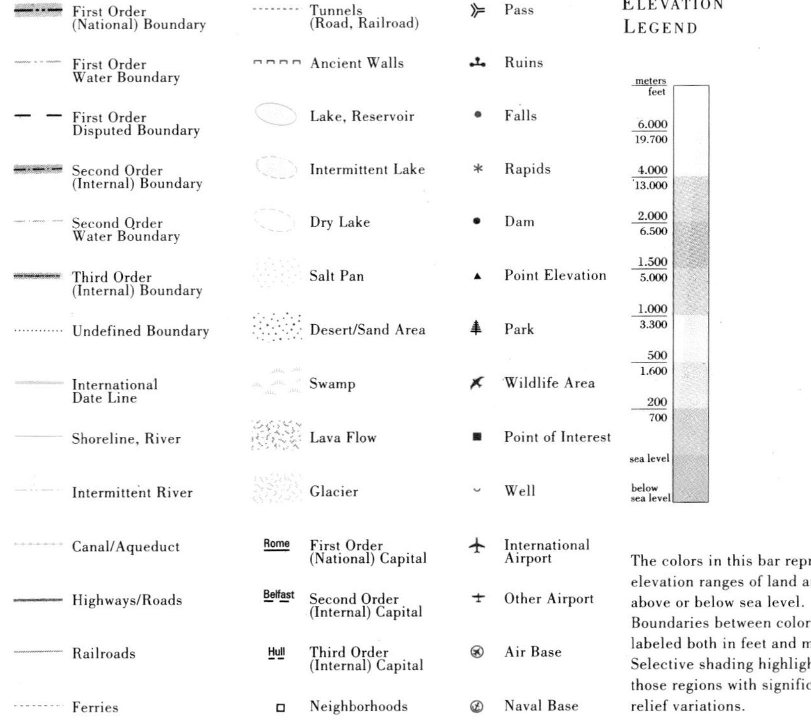

First Order (National) Boundary	Tunnels (Road, Railroad)	Pass
First Order Water Boundary	Ancient Walls	Ruins
First Order Disputed Boundary	Lake, Reservoir	Falls
Second Order (Internal) Boundary	Intermittent Lake	Rapids
Second Order Water Boundary	Dry Lake	Dam
Third Order (Internal) Boundary	Salt Pan	Point Elevation
Undefined Boundary	Desert/Sand Area	Park
International Date Line	Swamp	Wildlife Area
Shoreline, River	Lava Flow	Point of Interest
Intermittent River	Glacier	Well
Canal/Aqueduct	Rome First Order (National) Capital	International Airport
Highways/Roads	Belfast Second Order (Internal) Capital	Other Airport
Railroads	Hull Third Order (Internal) Capital	Air Base
Ferries	Neighborhoods	Naval Base

ELEVATION LEGEND

meters / feet
6.000 / 19.700
4.000 / 13.000
2.000 / 6.500
1.500 / 5.000
1.000 / 3.300
500 / 1.600
200 / 700
sea level
below sea level

The colors in this bar represent elevation ranges of land areas above or below sea level. Boundaries between colors are labeled both in feet and meters. Selective shading highlights those regions with significant relief variations.

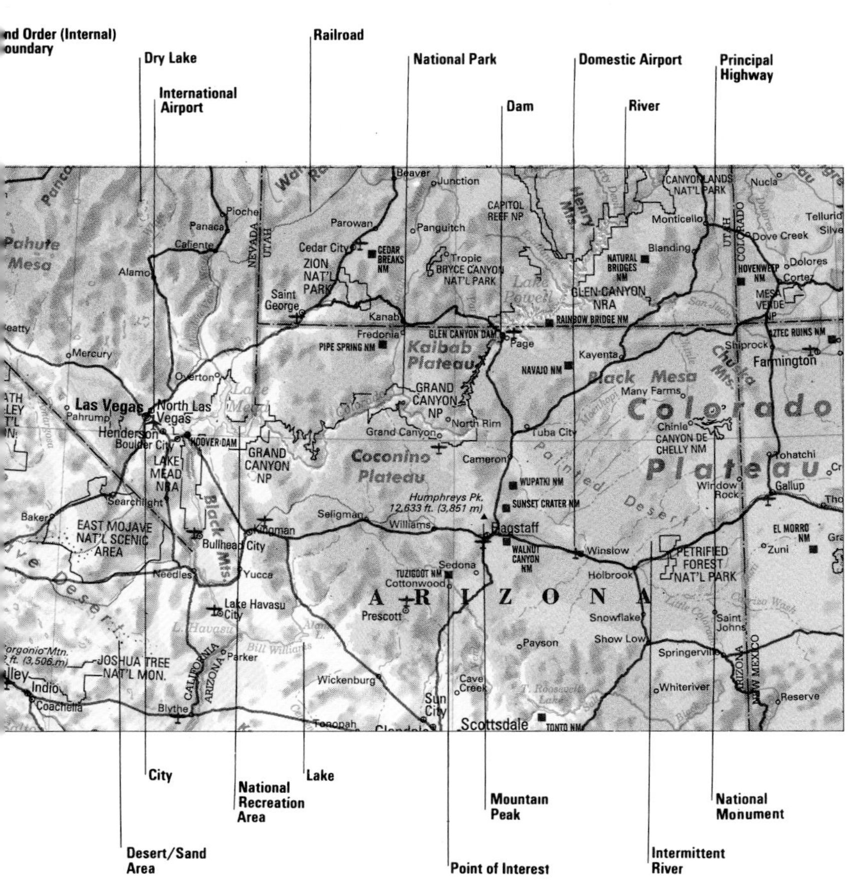

Map legend labels: Land Order (Internal) Boundary, Dry Lake, Railroad, National Park, Domestic Airport, Principal Highway, International Airport, Dam, River, City, National Recreation Area, Lake, Mountain Peak, National Monument, Desert/Sand Area, Point of Interest, Intermittent River

PRINCIPAL MAP ABBREVIATIONS

ABOR. RSV.	ABORIGINAL RESERVE	IND. RES.	INDIAN RESERVATION	NWR	NATIONAL WILDLIFE RESERVE
ADMIN.	ADMINISTRATION	INT'L	INTERNATIONAL		
AFB	AIR FORCE BASE	IR	INDIAN RESERVATION	OBL.	OBLAST
AMM. DEP.	AMMUNITION DEPOT	ISTH.	ISTHMUS	OCC.	OCCUPIED
ARCH.	ARCHIPELAGO	JCT.	JUNCTION	OKR.	OKRUG
ARPT.	AIRPORT	L.	LAKE	PAR.	PARISH
AUT.	AUTONOMOUS	LAG.	LAGOON	PASSG.	PASSAGE
	BAY	LAKESH.	LAKESHORE	PEN.	PENINSULA
BFLD.	BATTLEFIELD	MEM.	MEMORIAL	PK.	PEAK
BK.	BROOK	MIL.	MILITARY	PLAT.	PLATEAU
BOR.	BOROUGH	MISS.	MISSILE	PN	PARK NATIONAL
BR.	BRANCH	MON.	MONUMENT	PREF.	PREFECTURE
	CAPE	MT.	MOUNT	PROM.	PROMONTORY
CAN.	CANAL	MTN.	MOUNTAIN	PROV.	PROVINCE
CAP.	CAPITAL	MTS.	MOUNTAINS	PRSV.	PRESERVE
CG.	COAST GUARD	NAT.	NATURAL	PT.	POINT
CHAN.	CHANNEL	NAT'L	NATIONAL	R.	RIVER
CO.	COUNTY	NAV.	NAVAL	RA	RECREATION AREA
CR.	CREEK	NB	NATIONAL BATTLEFIELD	RA.	RANGE
CTR.	CENTER			REC.	RECREATION(AL)
DEP.	DEPOT	NBP	NATIONAL BATTLEFIELD PARK	REF.	REFUGE
DEPR.	DEPRESSION			REG.	REGION
DEPT.	DEPARTMENT	NBS	NATIONAL BATTLEFIELD SITE	REP.	REPUBLIC
DES.	DESERT			RES.	RESERVOIR, RESERVATION
DIST.	DISTRICT	NHP	NATIONAL HISTORICAL PARK		
DMZ	DEMILITARIZED ZONE			RVWY.	RIVERWAY
DPCY.	DEPENDENCY	NHPP	NATIONAL HISTORICAL PARK AND PRESERVE	SA.	SIERRA
ENG.	ENGINEERING			SD.	SOUND
EST.	ESTUARY	NHS	NATIONAL HISTORIC SITE	SEASH.	SEASHORE
F.	FIORD, FJORD			SO.	SOUTHERN
FED.	FEDERAL	NL	NATIONAL LAKESHORE	SP	STATE PARK
FK.	FORK	NM	NATIONAL MONUMENT	SPR., SPRS.	SPRING, SPRINGS
FD.	FIELD	NMEMP	NATIONAL MEMORIAL PARK	ST.	STATE
FOR.	FOREST			STA.	STATION
FT.	FORT	NMILP	NATIONAL MILITARY PARK	STM.	STREAM
	GULF			STR.	STRAIT
GOV.	GOVERNOR	NO.	NORTHERN	TERR.	TERRITORY
GOVT.	GOVERNMENT	NP	NATIONAL PARK	TUN.	TUNNEL
GD.	GRAND	NPP	NATIONAL PARK AND PRESERVE	TWP.	TOWNSHIP
GT.	GREAT			VAL.	VALLEY
HAR.	HARBOR	NPRSV	NATIONAL PRESERVE	VILL.	VILLAGE
HD.	HEAD	NRA	NATIONAL RECREATION AREA	VOL.	VOLCANO
HIST.	HISTORIC(AL)			WILD.	WILDLIFE, WILDERNESS
HTS.	HEIGHTS	NRSV	NATIONAL RESERVE		
Is.	ISLAND(S)	NS	NATIONAL SEASHORE	WTR.	WATER

Completing the continental coverage, in-depth regional maps offer abundant detail including boundaries, cities, transportation networks, rivers and major mountain peaks. Map backgrounds are shown in a pleasing combination of elevation coloration and relief shading, with boundary bands identifying the extent of each country's national and internal limits.

In place of relief, colors on metropolitan area inset maps highlight cities, parks and other bounded areas. Population legends accompany all maps.

WORLD STATISTICS

These tables list the dimensions of the earth's principal mountains, islands, rivers and lakes, along with other useful geographical information.

MASTER INDEX

This is an A to Z listing of names found on the political maps in the Maps of the World section. It has its own abbreviation list which, along with an introduction, appears on page 138.

MAP SCALES

A map's scale is the relationship of any length on that map to an identical length on the earth's surface. A scale of 1:7,000,000 means that one inch on the map represents 7,000,000 inches (110 miles, 178 kilometers) on the earth's surface. Thus, a 1:7,000,000 scale is larger than a 1:14,000,000 scale just as 1/7 is larger than 1/14.

In addition to these proportional scales, each map is accompanied by a linear (bar) scale, useful in making accurate measurements between places on the maps.

In this atlas, the most densely populated areas are shown at a scale of 1:1,170,000. Other populous areas are presented at 1:3,500,000 and 1:7,000,000, allowing you to accurately compare areas and distances of similar regions. Remaining regions are scaled at 1:10,500,000. The continent maps, as well as the United States, Canada, Russia, Pacific and World have smaller scales.

Boundary Policies
This atlas observes the boundary policies of the U.S. Department of State. Boundary disputes are customarily handled with a special symbol treatment, but de facto boundaries are favored if they seem to have any degree of permanence, in the belief that boundaries should reflect current geographic and political realities. The portrayal of independent nations in the atlas follows their recognition by the United Nations and/or the United States government.

Hammond also uses
accepted conventional names for certain major foreign places. Usually, space permits the inclusion of the local form in parentheses. To make the maps more readily understandable to English-speaking readers, many foreign physical features are translated into more recognizable English forms.

A Word About Names
Our source for all foreign names and physical names in the United States is the decision lists of the U.S. Board of Geographic Names, which contain hundreds of thousands of place names. If a place is not listed, the Atlas follows the name form appearing on official foreign maps or in official gazetteers of the country concerned. For rendering domestic city, town and village names, this atlas follows the forms and spelling of the U.S. Postal Service.

World Flags and Reference Guide

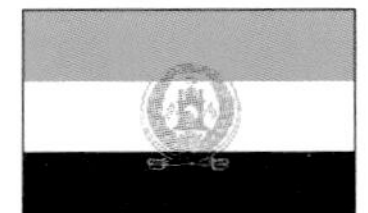

Afghanistan
Page/Location: 73/H2
Area: 250,775 sq. mi.
    649,507 sq. km.
Population: 16,903,000
Capital: Kabul
Largest City: Kabul
Highest Point: Noshaq
Monetary Unit: afghani

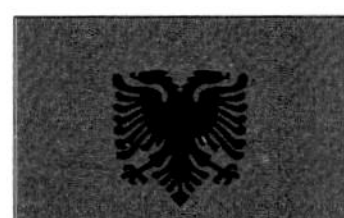

Albania
Page/Location: 61/F2
Area: 11,100 sq. mi.
    28,749 sq. km.
Population: 3,374,000
Capital: Tiranë
Largest City: Tiranë
Highest Point: Korab
Monetary Unit: lek

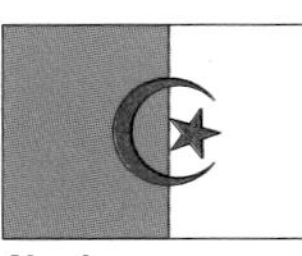

Algeria
Page/Location: 96/F2
Area: 919,591 sq. mi.
    2,381,740 sq. km.
Population: 27,895,000
Capital: Algiers
Largest City: Algiers
Highest Point: Tahat
Monetary Unit: Algerian dinar

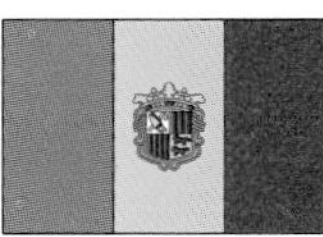

Andorra
Page/Location: 59/F1
Area: 188 sq. mi.
    487 sq. km.
Population: 64,000
Capital: Andorra la Vella
Largest City: Andorra la Vella
Highest Point: Coma Pedrosa
Monetary Unit: Fr. franc, Sp. peseta

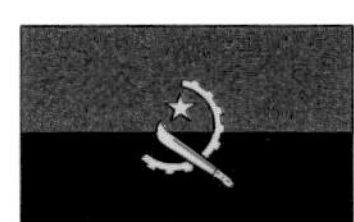

Angola
Page/Location: 104/C3
Area: 481,351 sq. mi.
    1,246,700 sq. km.
Population: 9,804,000
Capital: Luanda
Largest City: Luanda
Highest Point: Morro de Môco
Monetary Unit: kwanza

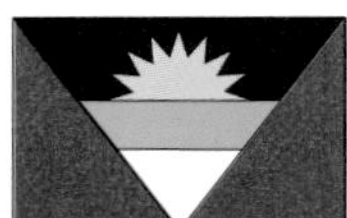

Antigua and Barbuda
Page/Location: 117/J4
Area: 171 sq. mi.
    443 sq. km.
Population: 65,000
Capital: St. John's
Largest City: St. John's
Highest Point: Boggy Peak
Monetary Unit: East Caribbean dollar

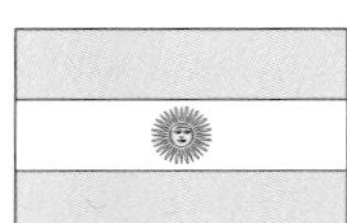

Argentina
Page/Location: 111/C4
Area: 1,072,070 sq. mi.
    2,776,661 sq. km.
Population: 33,913,000
Capital: Buenos Aires
Largest City: Buenos Aires
Highest Point: Cerro Aconcagua
Monetary Unit: Argentine peso

Armenia
Page/Location: 67/H5
Area: 11,506 sq. mi.
    29,800 sq. km.
Population: 3,522,000
Capital: Yerevan
Largest City: Yerevan
Highest Point: Alagez
Monetary Unit: dram

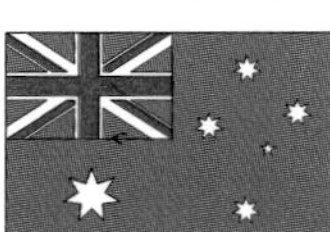

Australia
Page/Location: 89
Area: 2,966,136 sq. mi.
    7,682,300 sq. km.
Population: 18,077,000
Capital: Canberra
Largest City: Sydney
Highest Point: Mt. Kosciusko
Monetary Unit: Australian dollar

Austria
Page/Location: 57/L3
Area: 32,375 sq. mi.
    83,851 sq. km.
Population: 7,955,000
Capital: Vienna
Largest City: Vienna
Highest Point: Grossglockner
Monetary Unit: schilling

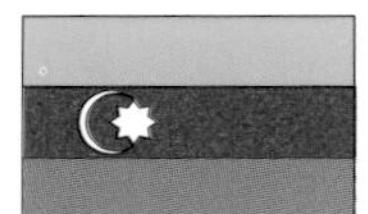

Azerbaijan
Page/Location: 67/H4
Area: 33,436 sq. mi.
    86,600 sq. km.
Population: 7,684,000
Capital: Baku
Largest City: Baku
Highest Point: Bazardyuzyu
Monetary Unit: manat

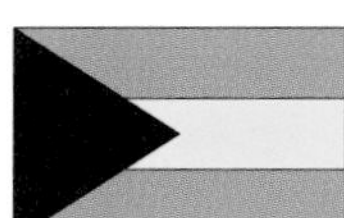

Bahamas
Page/Location: 117/F2
Area: 5,382 sq. mi.
    13,939 sq. km.
Population: 273,000
Capital: Nassau
Largest City: Nassau
Highest Point: 207 ft. (63 m)
Monetary Unit: Bahamian dollar

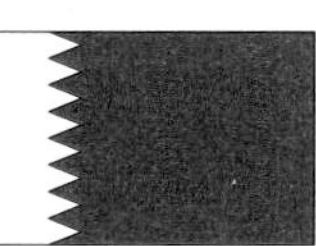

Bahrain
Page/Location: 72/F3
Area: 240 sq. mi.
    622 sq. km.
Population: 586,000
Capital: Manama
Largest City: Manama
Highest Point: Jabal Dukhān
Monetary Unit: Bahraini dinar

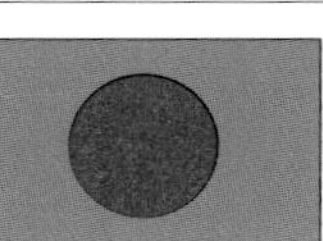

Bangladesh
Page/Location: 84/E3
Area: 55,126 sq. mi.
    142,776 sq. km.
Population: 125,149,000
Capital: Dhākā
Largest City: Dhākā
Highest Point: Keokradong
Monetary Unit: taka

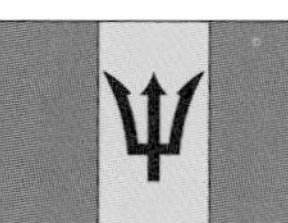

Barbados
Page/Location: 117/J5
Area: 166 sq. mi.
    430 sq. km.
Population: 256,000
Capital: Bridgetown
Largest City: Bridgetown
Highest Point: Mt. Hillaby
Monetary Unit: Barbadian dollar

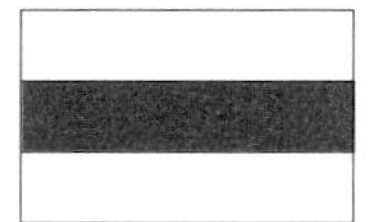

Belarus
Page/Location: 41/G3
Area: 80,154 sq. mi.
    207,600 sq. km.
Population: 10,405,000
Capital: Minsk
Largest City: Minsk
Highest Point: Dzerzhinskaya
Monetary Unit: Belarusian ruble

Belgium
Page/Location: 52/C2
Area: 11,781 sq. mi.
    30,513 sq. km.
Population: 10,063,000
Capital: Brussels
Largest City: Brussels
Highest Point: Botrange
Monetary Unit: Belgian franc

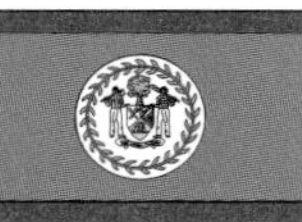

Belize
Page/Location: 116/D4
Area: 8,867 sq. mi.
    22,966 sq. km.
Population: 209,000
Capital: Belmopan
Largest City: Belize City
Highest Point: Victoria Peak
Monetary Unit: Belize dollar

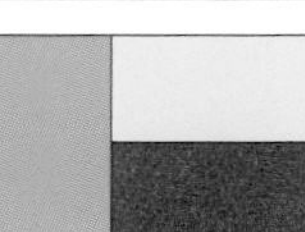

Benin
Page/Location: 99/F4
Area: 43,483 sq. mi.
    112,620 sq. km.
Population: 5,342,000
Capital: Porto-Novo
Largest City: Cotonou
Highest Point: Nassoukou
Monetary Unit: CFA franc

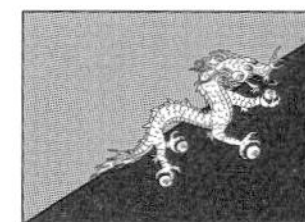

Bhutan
Page/Location: 84/E2
Area: 18,147 sq. mi.
    47,000 sq. km.
Population: 1,739,000
Capital: Thimphu
Largest City: Thimphu
Highest Point: Kula Kangri
Monetary Unit: ngultrum

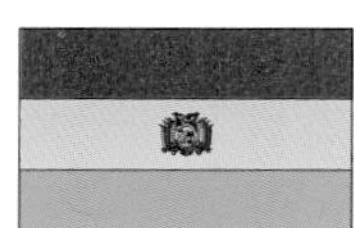

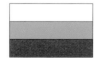

Bolivia
Page/Location: 108/F7
Area: 424,163 sq. mi.
    1,098,582 sq. km.
Population: 7,719,000
Capital: La Paz; Sucre
Largest City: La Paz
Highest Point: Nevado Ancohuma
Monetary Unit: Bolivian peso

Bosnia and Herzegovina
Page/Location: 62/C3
Area: 19,940 sq. mi.
    51,645 sq. km.
Population: 4,651,000
Capital: Sarajevo
Largest City: Sarajevo
Highest Point: Maglič
Monetary Unit: —

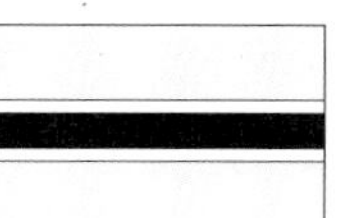

Botswana
Page/Location: 104/D5
Area: 224,764 sq. mi.
    582,139 sq. km.
Population: 1,359,000
Capital: Gaborone
Largest City: Gaborone
Highest Point: Tsodilo Hills
Monetary Unit: pula

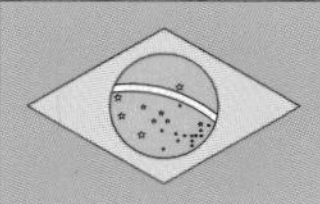

Brazil
Page/Location: 107/D3
Area: 3,284,426 sq. mi.
    8,506,663 sq. km.
Population: 158,739,000
Capital: Brasília
Largest City: São Paulo
Highest Point: Pico da Neblina
Monetary Unit: cruzeiro real

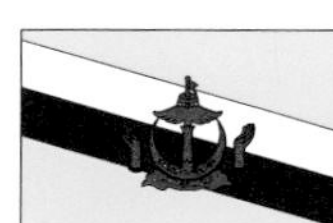

Brunei
Page/Location: 86/D2
Area: 2,226 sq. mi.
    5,765 sq. km.
Population: 285,000
Capital: Bandar Seri Begawan
Largest City: Bandar Seri Begawan
Highest Point: Bukit Pagon
Monetary Unit: Brunei dollar

Bulgaria
Page/Location: 63/G4
Area: 42,823 sq. mi.
    110,912 sq. km.
Population: 8,800,000
Capital: Sofia
Largest City: Sofia
Highest Point: Musala
Monetary Unit: lev

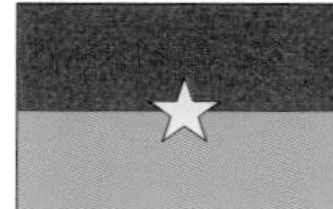

Burkina Faso
Page/Location: 99/E3
Area: 105,869 sq. mi.
    274,200 sq. km.
Population: 10,135,000
Capital: Ouagadougou
Largest City: Ouagadougou
Highest Point: 2,405 ft. (733 m)
Monetary Unit: CFA franc

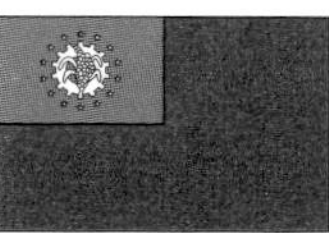

Burma
Page/Location: 85/G3
Area: 261,789 sq. mi.
    678,034 sq. km.
Population: 44,277,000
Capital: Rangoon
Largest City: Rangoon
Highest Point: Hkakabo Razi
Monetary Unit: kyat

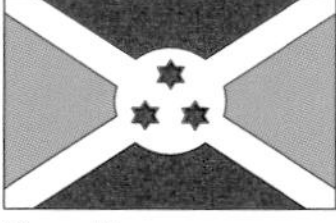

Burundi
Page/Location: 101/A3
Area: 10,747 sq. mi.
    27,835 sq. km.
Population: 6,125,000
Capital: Bujumbura
Largest City: Bujumbura
Highest Point: 8,760 ft. (2,670 m)
Monetary Unit: Burundi franc

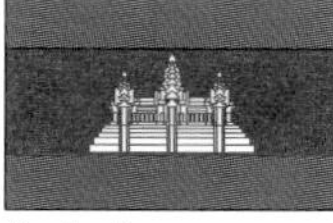

Cambodia
Page/Location: 83/D3
Area: 69,898 sq. mi.
    181,036 sq. km.
Population: 10,265,000
Capital: Phnom Penh
Largest City: Phnom Penh
Highest Point: Phnum Aoral
Monetary Unit: riel

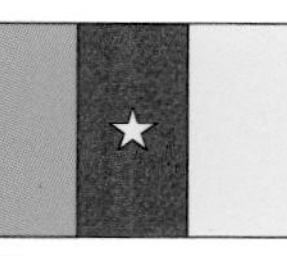

ameroon
age/Location: 96/H7
ea: 183,568 sq. mi.
475,441 sq. km.
opulation: 13,132,000
apital: Yaoundé
rgest City: Douala
ghest Point: Mt. Cameroon
onetary Unit: CFA franc

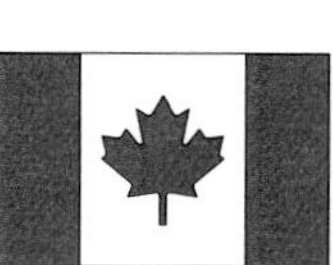

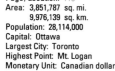

Canada
Page/Location: 118
Area: 3,851,787 sq. mi.
9,976,139 sq. km.
Population: 28,114,000
Capital: Ottawa
Largest City: Toronto
Highest Point: Mt. Logan
Monetary Unit: Canadian dollar

Cape Verde
Page/Location: 38/H5
Area: 1,557 sq. mi.
4,033 sq. km.
Population: 423,000
Capital: Praia
Largest City: Praia
Highest Point: 9,282 ft. (2,829 m)
Monetary Unit: Cape Verde escudo

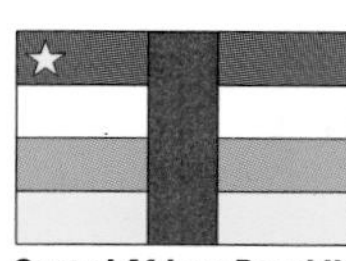

Central African Republic
Page/Location: 97/J6
Area: 242,000 sq. mi.
626,780 sq. km.
Population: 3,142,000
Capital: Bangui
Largest City: Bangui
Highest Point: Mt. Kayagangiri
Monetary Unit: CFA franc

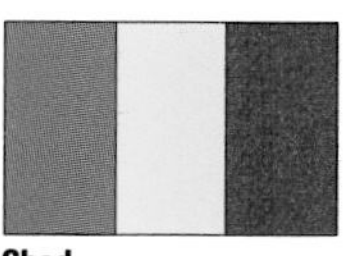

Chad
Page/Location: 97/J4
Area: 495,752 sq. mi.
1,283,998 sq. km.
Population: 5,467,000
Capital: N'Djamena
Largest City: N'Djamena
Highest Point: Emi Koussi
Monetary Unit: CFA franc

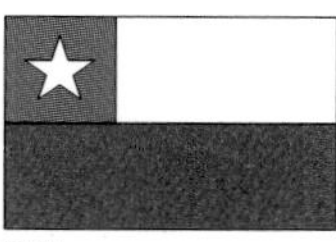

Chile
Page/Location: 111/B3
Area: 292,257 sq. mi.
756,946 sq. km.
Population: 13,951,000
Capital: Santiago
Largest City: Santiago
Highest Point: Nevado Ojos del Salado
Monetary Unit: Chilean peso

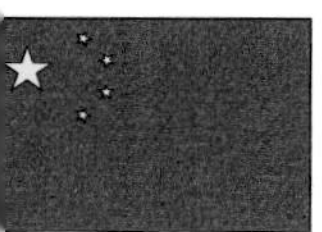

ina
age/Location: 71/J6
ea: 3,691,000 sq. mi.
9,559,690 sq. km.
opulation: 1,190,431,000
apital: Beijing
rgest City: Shanghai
ghest Point: Mt. Everest
onetary Unit: yuan

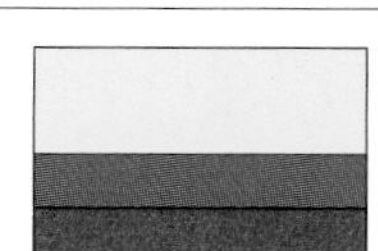

Colombia
Page/Location: 108/D3
Area: 439,513 sq. mi.
1,138,339 sq. km.
Population: 35,578,000
Capital: Bogotá
Largest City: Bogotá
Highest Point: Pico Cristóbal Colón
Monetary Unit: Colombian peso

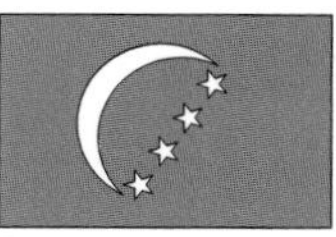

Comoros
Page/Location: 103/G5
Area: 719 sq. mi.
1,862 sq. km.
Population: 530,000
Capital: Moroni
Largest City: Moroni
Highest Point: Karthala
Monetary Unit: Comorian franc

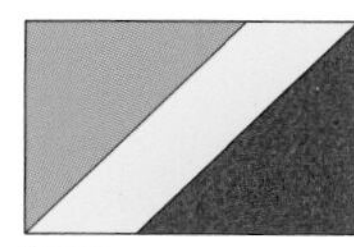

Congo
Page/Location: 95/D4
Area: 132,046 sq. mi.
342,000 sq. km.
Population: 2,447,000
Capital: Brazzaville
Largest City: Brazzaville
Highest Point: Lékéti Mts.
Monetary Unit: CFA franc

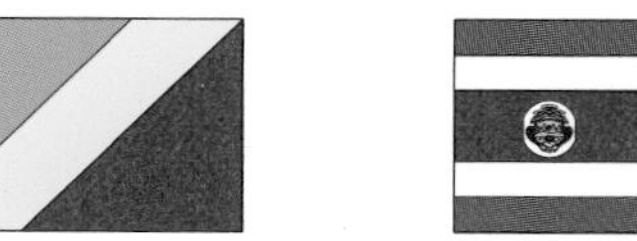

Costa Rica
Page/Location: 116/E5
Area: 19,575 sq. mi.
50,700 sq. km.
Population: 3,342,000
Capital: San José
Largest City: San José
Highest Point: Cerro Chirripó Grande
Monetary Unit: Costa Rican colón

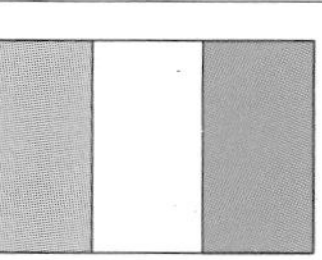

Côte d'Ivoire
Page/Location: 98/D5
Area: 124,504 sq. mi.
322,465 sq. km.
Population: 14,296,000
Capital: Yamoussoukro
Largest City: Abidjan
Highest Point: Mt. Nimba
Monetary Unit: CFA franc

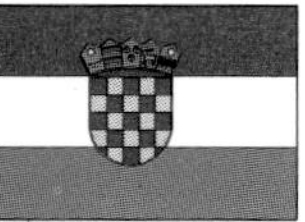
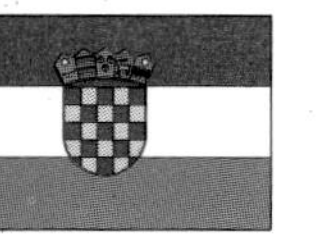

oatia
age/Location: 62/C3
ea: 22,050 sq. mi.
57,110 sq. km.
opulation: 4,698,000
apital: Zagreb
rgest City: Zagreb
ghest Point: Veliki Troglav
onetary Unit: Kuna

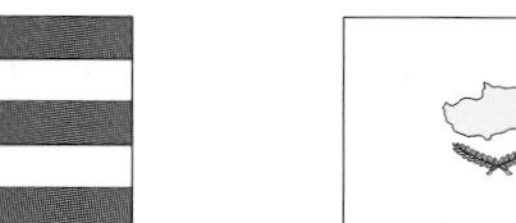

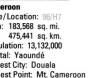

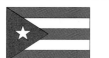

Cuba
Page/Location: 117/F3
Area: 44,206 sq. mi.
114,494 sq. km.
Population: 11,064,000
Capital: Havana
Largest City: Havana
Highest Point: Pico Turquino
Monetary Unit: Cuban peso

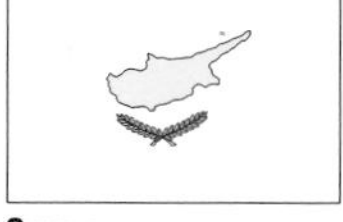

Cyprus
Page/Location: 72/B1
Area: 3,473 sq. mi.
8,995 sq. km.
Population: 730,000
Capital: Nicosia
Largest City: Nicosia
Highest Point: Olympus
Monetary Unit: Cypriot pound

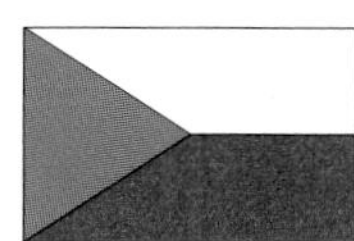

Czech Republic
Page/Location: 49/H4
Area: 30,449 sq. mi.
78,863 sq. km.
Population: 10,408,000
Capital: Prague
Largest City: Prague
Highest Point: Sněžka
Monetary Unit: Czech koruna

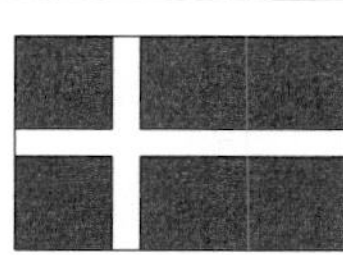

Denmark
Page/Location: 42/C5
Area: 16,629 sq. mi.
43,069 sq. km.
Population: 5,188,000
Capital: Copenhagen
Largest City: Copenhagen
Highest Point: Yding Skovhøj
Monetary Unit: Danish krone

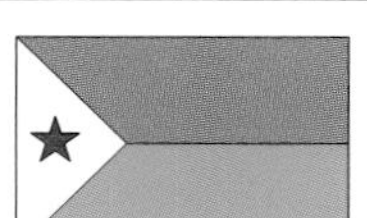

Djibouti
Page/Location: 97/P5
Area: 8,880 sq. mi.
23,000 sq. km.
Population: 413,000
Capital: Djibouti
Largest City: Djibouti
Highest Point: Moussa Ali
Monetary Unit: Djibouti franc

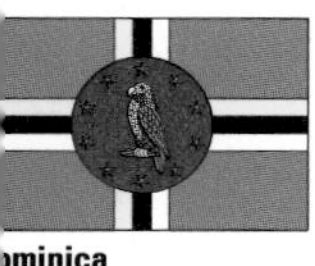

ominica
age/Location: 117/J4
ea: 290 sq. mi.
751 sq. km.
opulation: 88,000
apital: Roseau
rgest City: Roseau
ghest Point: Morne Diablotin
onetary Unit: Dominican dollar

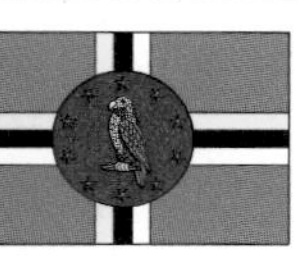

Dominican Republic
Page/Location: 117/H4
Area: 18,704 sq. mi.
48,443 sq. km.
Population: 7,826,000
Capital: Santo Domingo
Largest City: Santo Domingo
Highest Point: Pico Duarte
Monetary Unit: Dominican peso

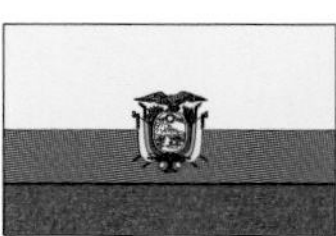

Ecuador
Page/Location: 108/C4
Area: 109,483 sq. mi.
283,561 sq. km.
Population: 10,677,000
Capital: Quito
Largest City: Guayaquil
Highest Point: Chimborazo
Monetary Unit: sucre

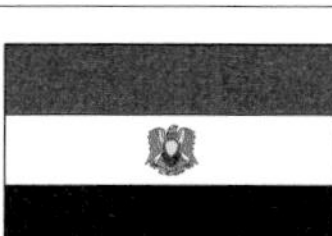

Egypt
Page/Location: 100/L2
Area: 386,659 sq. mi.
1,001,447 sq. km.
Population: 60,765,000
Capital: Cairo
Largest City: Cairo
Highest Point: Mt. Catherine
Monetary Unit: Egyptian pound

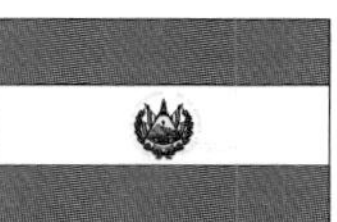

El Salvador
Page/Location: 116/C5
Area: 8,260 sq. mi.
21,393 sq. km.
Population: 5,753,000
Capital: San Salvador
Largest City: San Salvador
Highest Point: Santa Ana
Monetary Unit: Salvadoran colón

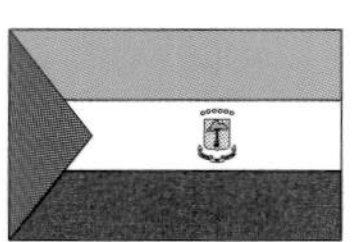

Equatorial Guinea
Page/Location: 96/G7
Area: 10,831 sq. mi.
28,052 sq. km.
Population: 410,000
Capital: Malabo
Largest City: Malabo
Highest Point: Pico de Santa Isabel
Monetary Unit: CFA franc

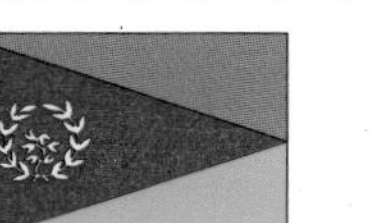

itrea
age/Location: 97/N5
ea: 36,170 sq. mi.
93,679 sq. km.
opulation: 3,783,000
apital: Asmara
rgest City: Asmara
ghest Point: Soira
onetary Unit: birr

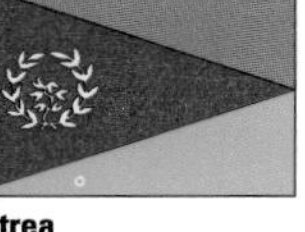

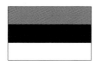

Estonia
Page/Location: 64/E4
Area: 17,413 sq. mi.
45,100 sq. km.
Population: 1,617,000
Capital: Tallinn
Largest City: Tallinn
Highest Point: Munamägi
Monetary Unit: kroon

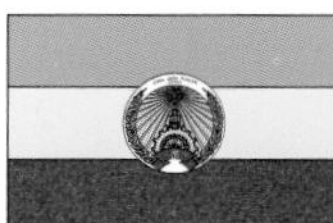

Ethiopia
Page/Location: 97/N5
Area: 435,606 sq. mi.
1,128,220 sq. km.
Population: 54,927,000
Capital: Addis Ababa
Largest City: Addis Ababa
Highest Point: Ras Dashen Terara
Monetary Unit: birr

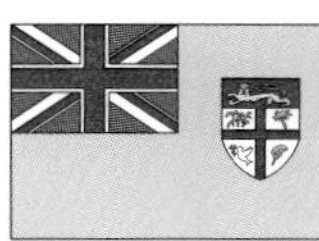

Fiji
Page/Location: 92/G6
Area: 7,055 sq. mi.
18,272 sq. km.
Population: 764,000
Capital: Suva
Largest City: Suva
Highest Point: Tomaniivi
Monetary Unit: Fijian dollar

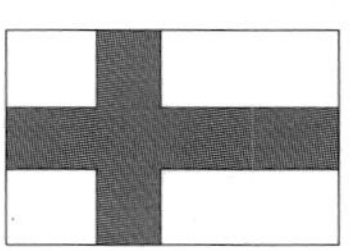

Finland
Page/Location: 42/H2
Area: 130,128 sq. mi.
337,032 sq. km.
Population: 5,069,000
Capital: Helsinki
Largest City: Helsinki
Highest Point: Kahperusvaara
Monetary Unit: markka

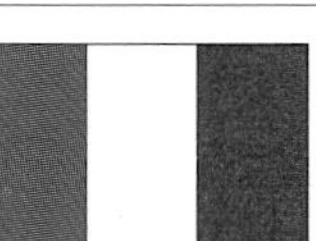

France
Page/Location: 56/D3
Area: 210,038 sq. mi.
543,998 sq. km.
Population: 57,840,000
Capital: Paris
Largest City: Paris
Highest Point: Mont Blanc
Monetary Unit: French franc

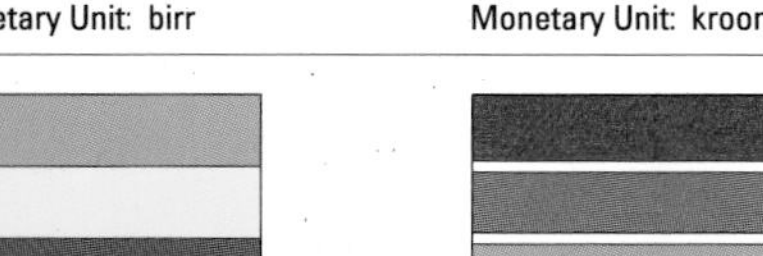

abon
age/Location: 96/H7
ea: 103,346 sq. mi.
267,666 sq. km.
opulation: 1,139,000
pital: Libreville
rgest City: Libreville
ghest Point: Mt. Iboundji
onetary Unit: CFA franc

Gambia
Page/Location: 98/B3
Area: 4,127 sq. mi.
10,689 sq. km.
Population: 959,000
Capital: Banjul
Largest City: Banjul
Highest Point: 98 ft. (30 m)
Monetary Unit: dalasi

Georgia
Page/Location: 67/G4
Area: 26,911 sq. mi.
69,700 sq. km.
Population: 5,681,000
Capital: Tbilisi
Largest City: Tbilisi
Highest Point: Kazbek
Monetary Unit: lari

Germany
Page/Location: 48/E3
Area: 137,753 sq. mi.
356,780 sq. km.
Population: 81,088,000
Capital: Berlin
Largest City: Berlin
Highest Point: Zugspitze
Monetary Unit: Deutsche mark

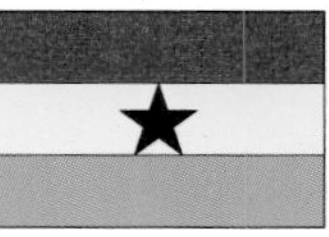

Ghana
Page/Location: 99/E4
Area: 92,099 sq. mi.
238,536 sq. km.
Population: 17,225,000
Capital: Accra
Largest City: Accra
Highest Point: Afadjoto
Monetary Unit: cedi

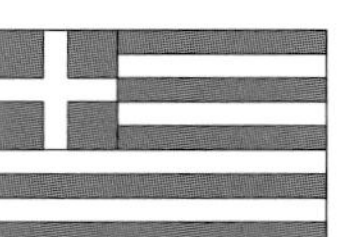

Greece
Page/Location: 61/G3
Area: 50,944 sq. mi.
131,945 sq. km.
Population: 10,565,000
Capital: Athens
Largest City: Athens
Highest Point: Mt. Olympus
Monetary Unit: drachma

World Flags and Reference Guide

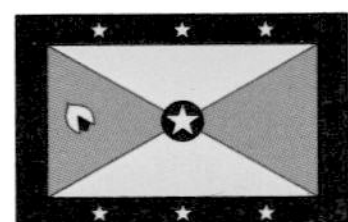

Grenada
Page/Location: 117/J5
Area: 133 sq. mi.
    344 sq. km.
Population: 94,000
Capital: St. George's
Largest City: St. George's
Highest Point: Mt. St. Catherine
Monetary Unit: East Caribbean dollar

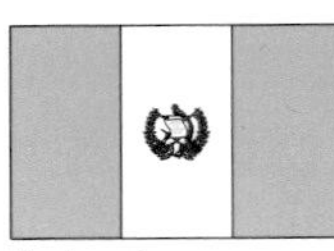

Guatemala
Page/Location: 116/C4
Area: 42,042 sq. mi.
    108,889 sq. km.
Population: 10,721,000
Capital: Guatemala
Largest City: Guatemala
Highest Point: Tajumulco
Monetary Unit: quetzal

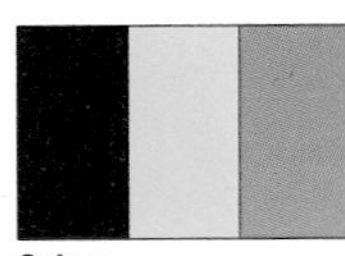

Guinea
Page/Location: 98/C4
Area: 94,925 sq. mi.
    245,856 sq. km.
Population: 6,392,000
Capital: Conakry
Largest City: Conakry
Highest Point: Mt. Nimba
Monetary Unit: Guinea franc

Guinea-Bissau
Page/Location: 98/B3
Area: 13,948 sq. mi.
    36,125 sq. km.
Population: 1,098,000
Capital: Bissau
Largest City: Bissau
Highest Point: 689 ft. (210 m)
Monetary Unit: Guinea-Bissau peso

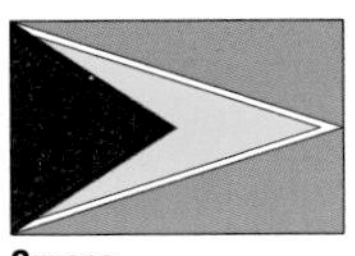

Guyana
Page/Location: 108/G3
Area: 83,000 sq. mi.
    214,970 sq. km.
Population: 729,000
Capital: Georgetown
Largest City: Georgetown
Highest Point: Mt. Roraima
Monetary Unit: Guyana dollar

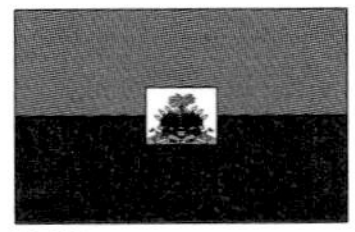

Haiti
Page/Location: 117/G4
Area: 10,694 sq. mi.
    27,697 sq. km.
Population: 6,491,000
Capital: Port-au-Prince
Largest City: Port-au-Prince
Highest Point: Pic la Selle
Monetary Unit: gourde

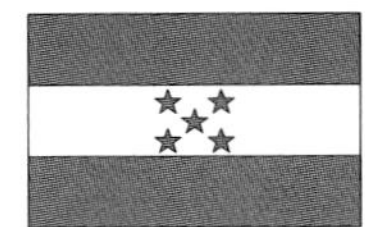

Honduras
Page/Location: 116/D4
Area: 43,277 sq. mi.
    112,087 sq. km.
Population: 5,315,000
Capital: Tegucigalpa
Largest City: Tegucigalpa
Highest Point: Cerro de las Minas
Monetary Unit: lempira

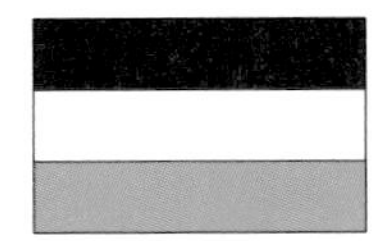

Hungary
Page/Location: 62/D2
Area: 35,919 sq. mi.
    93,030 sq. km.
Population: 10,319,000
Capital: Budapest
Largest City: Budapest
Highest Point: Kékes
Monetary Unit: forint

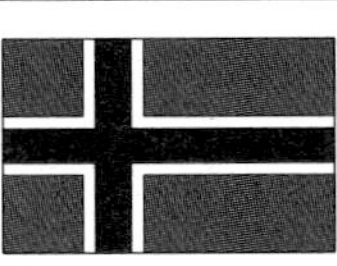

Iceland
Page/Location: 42/N7
Area: 39,768 sq. mi.
    103,000 sq. km.
Population: 264,000
Capital: Reykjavík
Largest City: Reykjavík
Highest Point: Hvannadalshnúkur
Monetary Unit: króna

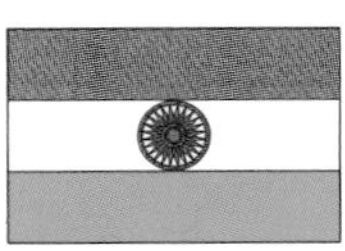

India
Page/Location: 84/C3
Area: 1,269,339 sq. mi.
    3,287,588 sq. km.
Population: 919,903,000
Capital: New Delhi
Largest City: Calcutta
Highest Point: Nanda Devi
Monetary Unit: Indian rupee

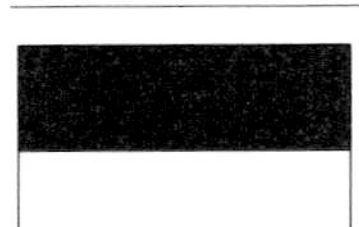

Indonesia
Page/Location: 87/E4
Area: 788,430 sq. mi.
    2, 042,034 sq. km.
Population: 200,410,000
Capital: Jakarta
Largest City: Jakarta
Highest Point: Puncak Jaya
Monetary Unit: rupiah

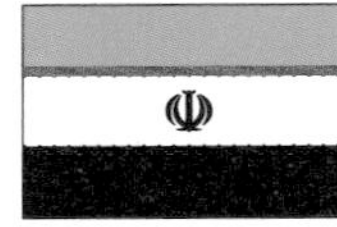

Iran
Page/Location: 72/F2
Area: 636,293 sq. mi.
    1,648,000 sq. km.
Population: 65,615,000
Capital: Tehrān
Largest City: Tehrān
Highest Point: Qolleh-ye Damāvand
Monetary Unit: Iranian rial

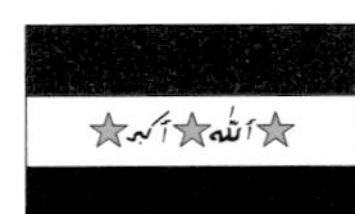

Iraq
Page/Location: 72/D2
Area: 172,476 sq. mi.
    446,713 sq. km.
Population: 19,890,000
Capital: Baghdad
Largest City: Baghdad
Highest Point: Haji Ibrahim
Monetary Unit: Iraqi dinar

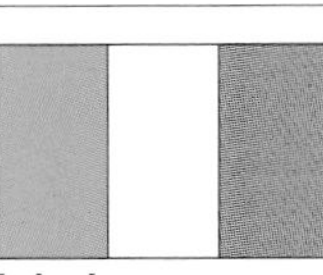

Ireland
Page/Location: 43/A4
Area: 27,136 sq. mi.
    70,282 sq. km.
Population: 3,539,000
Capital: Dublin
Largest City: Dublin
Highest Point: Carrantuohill
Monetary Unit: Irish pound

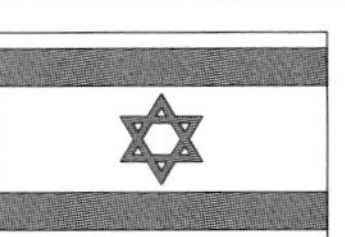

Israel
Page/Location: 74/J5
Area: 7,847 sq. mi.
    20,324 sq. km.
Population: 5,051,000
Capital: Jerusalem
Largest City: Tel Aviv-Yafo
Highest Point: Har Meron
Monetary Unit: shekel

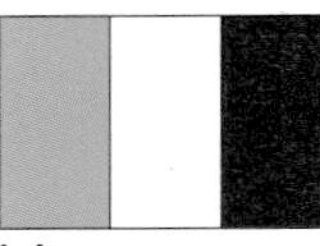

Italy
Page/Location: 41/F4
Area: 116,303 sq. mi.
    301,225 sq. km.
Population: 58,138,000
Capital: Rome
Largest City: Rome
Highest Point: Monte Rosa
Monetary Unit: Italian lira

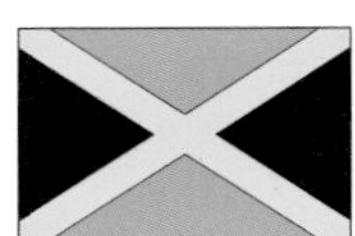

Jamaica
Page/Location: 117/F4
Area: 4,411 sq. mi.
    11,424 sq. km.
Population: 2,555,000
Capital: Kingston
Largest City: Kingston
Highest Point: Blue Mountain Pk.
Monetary Unit: Jamaican dollar

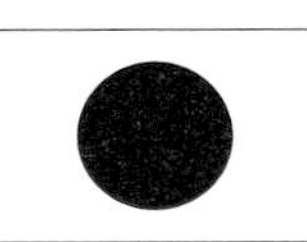

Japan
Page/Location: 77/M4
Area: 145,730 sq. mi.
    377,441 sq. km.
Population: 125,107,000
Capital: Tokyo
Largest City: Tokyo
Highest Point: Fujiyama
Monetary Unit: yen

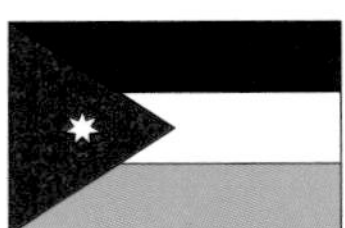

Jordan
Page/Location: 72/C2
Area: 35,000 sq. mi.
    90,650 sq. km.
Population: 3,961,000
Capital: Ammān
Largest City: Ammān
Highest Point: Jabal Ramm
Monetary Unit: Jordanian dinar

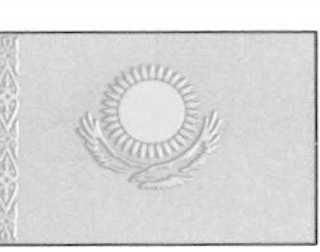

Kazakhstan
Page/Location: 68/G5
Area: 1,048,300 sq. mi.
    2,715,100 sq. km.
Population: 17,268,000
Capital: Aqmola
Largest City: Alma-Ata
Highest Point: Khan-Tengri
Monetary Unit: tenge

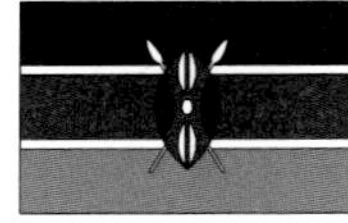

Kenya
Page/Location: 101/C2
Area: 224,960 sq. mi.
    582,646 sq. km.
Population: 28,241,000
Capital: Nairobi
Largest City: Nairobi
Highest Point: Mt. Kenya
Monetary Unit: Kenya shilling

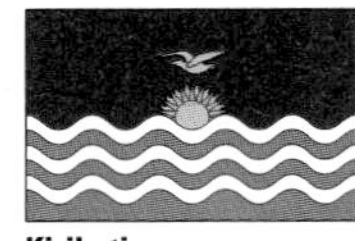

Kiribati
Page/Location: 92/H5
Area: 291 sq. mi.
    754 sq. km.
Population: 78,000
Capital: Bairiki
Largest City: —
Highest Point: Banaba Island
Monetary Unit: Australian dollar

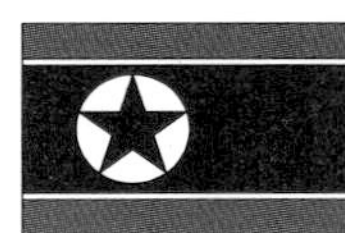

Korea, North
Page/Location: 80/D2
Area: 46,540 sq. mi.
    120,539 sq. km.
Population: 23,067,000
Capital: P'yŏngyang
Largest City: P'yŏngyang
Highest Point: Paektu-san
Monetary Unit: North Korean won

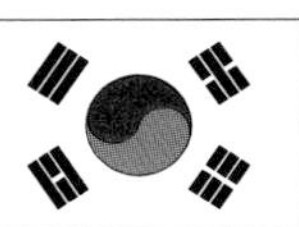

Korea, South
Page/Location: 80/D4
Area: 38,175 sq. mi.
    98,873 sq. km.
Population: 45,083,000
Capital: Seoul
Largest City: Seoul
Highest Point: Halla-san
Monetary Unit: South Korean won

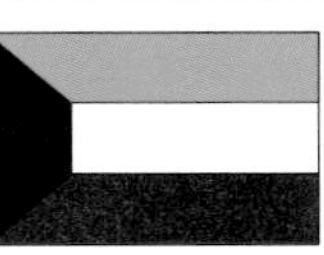

Kuwait
Page/Location: 72/E3
Area: 6,532 sq. mi.
    16,918 sq. km.
Population: 1,819,000
Capital: Al Kuwait
Largest City: Al Kuwait
Highest Point: 951 ft. (290 m)
Monetary Unit: Kuwaiti dinar

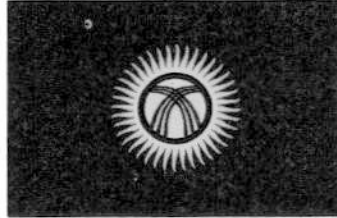

Kyrgyzstan
Page/Location: 75/B3
Area: 76,641 sq. mi.
    198,500 sq. km.
Population: 4,698,000
Capital: Bishkek
Largest City: Bishkek
Highest Point: Pik Pobedy
Monetary Unit: som

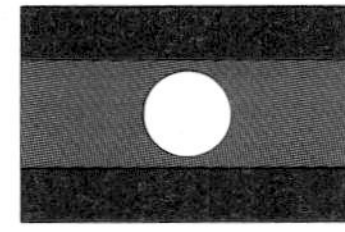

Laos
Page/Location: 83/C2
Area: 91,428 sq. mi.
    236,800 sq. km.
Population: 4,702,000
Capital: Vientiane
Largest City: Vientiane
Highest Point: Phou Bia
Monetary Unit: kip

Latvia
Page/Location: 64/E4
Area: 24,595 sq. mi.
    63,700 sq. km.
Population: 2,749,000
Capital: Riga
Largest City: Riga
Highest Point: Gaizina Kalns
Monetary Unit: lats

Lebanon
Page/Location: 74/K5
Area: 4,015 sq. mi.
    10,399 sq. km.
Population: 3,620,000
Capital: Beirut
Largest City: Beirut
Highest Point: Qurnat as Sawdā'
Monetary Unit: Lebanese pound

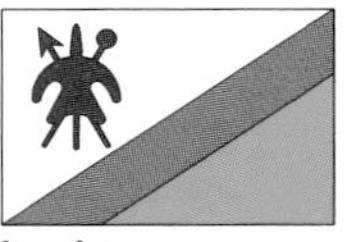

Lesotho
Page/Location: 102/D3
Area: 11,720 sq. mi.
    30,355 sq. km.
Population: 1,944,000
Capital: Maseru
Largest City: Maseru
Highest Point: Thabana-Ntlenyana
Monetary Unit: loti

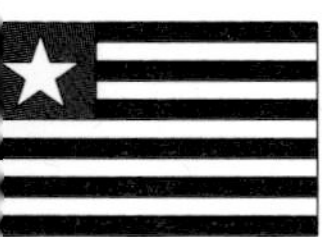

Liberia
Page/Location: 98/C5
Area: 43,000 sq. mi.
111,370 sq. km.
Population: 2,973,000
Capital: Monrovia
Largest City: Monrovia
Highest Point: Mt. Wuteve
Monetary Unit: Liberian dollar

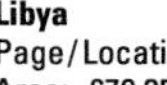

Libya
Page/Location: 97/J2
Area: 679,358 sq. mi.
1,759,537 sq. km.
Population: 5,057,000
Capital: Tripoli
Largest City: Tripoli
Highest Point: Picco Bette
Monetary Unit: Libyan dinar

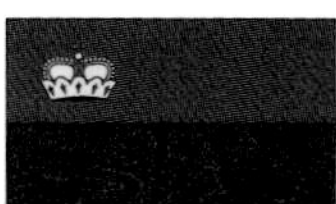

Liechtenstein
Page/Location: 55/F3
Area: 61 sq. mi.
158 sq. km.
Population: 30,000
Capital: Vaduz
Largest City: Vaduz
Highest Point: Grauspitz
Monetary Unit: Swiss franc

Lithuania
Page/Location: 64/D5
Area: 25,174 sq. mi.
65,200 sq. km.
Population: 3,848,000
Capital: Vilnius
Largest City: Vilnius
Highest Point: Nevaišių
Monetary Unit: litas

Luxembourg
Page/Location: 53/E4
Area: 999 sq. mi.
2,587 sq. km.
Population: 402,000
Capital: Luxembourg
Largest City: Luxembourg
Highest Point: Ardennes Plateau
Monetary Unit: Luxembourg franc

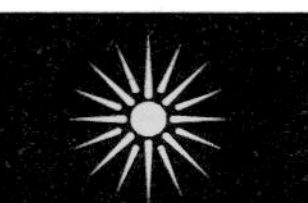

Macedonia
Page/Location: 61/G2
Area: 9,889 sq. mi.
25,612 sq. km.
Population: 2,214,000
Capital: Skopje
Largest City: Skopje
Highest Point: Korab
Monetary Unit: denar

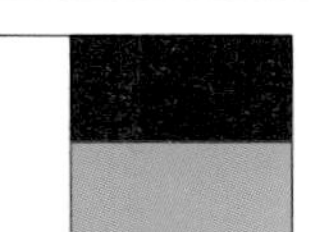

Madagascar
Page/Location: 103/H8
Area: 226,657 sq. mi.
587,041 sq. km.
Population: 13,428,000
Capital: Antananarivo
Largest City: Antananarivo
Highest Point: Maromokotro
Monetary Unit: Malagasy franc

Malawi
Page/Location: 104/F3
Area: 45,747 sq. mi.
118, 485 sq. km.
Population: 9,732,000
Capital: Lilongwe
Largest City: Blantyre
Highest Point: Mulanje Mts.
Monetary Unit: Malawi kwacha

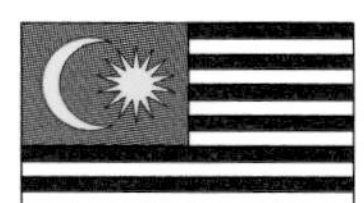

Malaysia
Page/Location: 86/C2
Area: 128,308 sq. mi.
332,318 sq. km.
Population: 19,283,000
Capital: Kuala Lumpur
Largest City: Kuala Lumpur
Highest Point: Gunung Kinabalu
Monetary Unit: ringgit

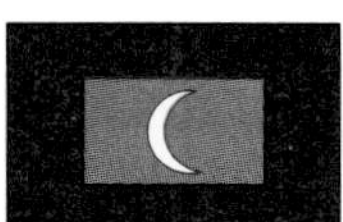

Maldives
Page/Location: 71/G9
Area: 115 sq. mi.
298 sq. km.
Population: 252,000
Capital: Male
Largest City: Male
Highest Point: 20 ft. (6 m)
Monetary Unit: rufiyaa

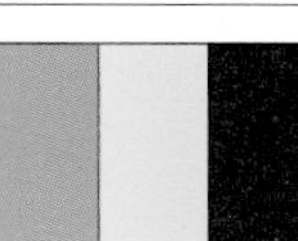

Mali
Page/Location: 96/E4
Area: 464,873 sq. mi.
1,204,021 sq. km.
Population: 9,113,000
Capital: Bamako
Largest City: Bamako
Highest Point: Hombori Tondo
Monetary Unit: CFA franc

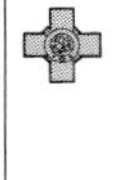

Malta
Page/Location: 60/D5
Area: 122 sq. mi.
316 sq. km.
Population: 367,000
Capital: Valletta
Largest City: Sliema
Highest Point: 830 ft. (253 m)
Monetary Unit: Maltese lira

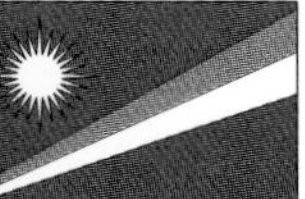

Marshall Islands
Page/Location: 92/G3
Area: 70 sq. mi.
181 sq. km.
Population: 54,000
Capital: Majuro
Largest City: —
Highest Point: 20 ft. (6 m)
Monetary Unit: U.S. dollar

Mauritania
Page/Location: 96/C4
Area: 419,229 sq. mi.
1,085, 803 sq. km.
Population: 2,193,000
Capital: Nouakchott
Largest City: Nouakchott
Highest Point: Kediet Ijill
Monetary Unit: ouguiya

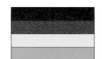

Mauritius
Page/Location: 103/S15
Area: 790 sq. mi.
2,046 sq. km.
Population: 1,117,000
Capital: Port Louis
Largest City: Port Louis
Highest Point: 2,713 ft. (827 m)
Monetary Unit: Mauritian rupee

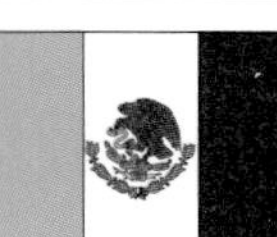

Mexico
Page/Location: 116/A3
Area: 761,601 sq. mi.
1,972,546 sq. km.
Population: 92,202,000
Capital: Mexico City
Largest City: Mexico City
Highest Point: Citlaltépetl
Monetary Unit: Mexican peso

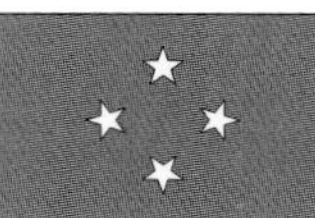

Micronesia
Page/Location: 92/D4
Area: 271 sq. mi.
702 sq. km.
Population: 120,347
Capital: Kolonia
Largest City: —
Highest Point: —
Monetary Unit: U.S. dollar

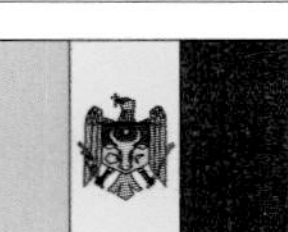

Moldova
Page/Location: 63/H2
Area: 13,012 sq. mi.
33,700 sq. km.
Population: 4,473,000
Capital: Chişinău
Largest City: Chişinău
Highest Point: 1,408 ft. (429 m)
Monetary Unit: leu

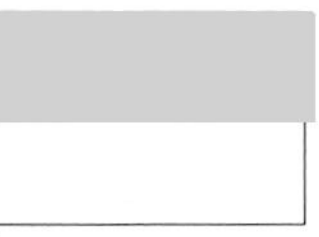

Monaco
Page/Location: 57/G5
Area: 368 acres
149 hectares
Population: 31,000
Capital: Monaco
Largest City: —
Highest Point: —
Monetary Unit: French franc

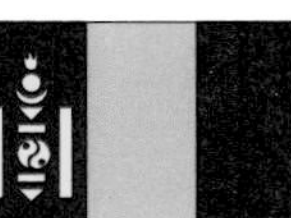

Mongolia
Page/Location: 76/D2
Area: 606,163 sq. mi.
1,569, 962 sq. km.
Population: 2,430,000
Capital: Ulaanbaatar
Largest City: Ulaanbaatar
Highest Point: Tavan Bogd Uul
Monetary Unit: tughrik

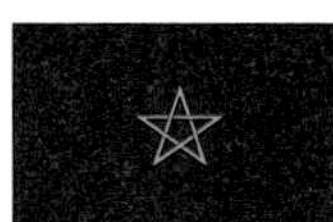

Morocco
Page/Location: 96/C1
Area: 172,414 sq. mi.
446,550 sq. km.
Population: 28,559,000
Capital: Rabat
Largest City: Casablanca
Highest Point: Jebel Toubkal
Monetary Unit: Moroccan dirham

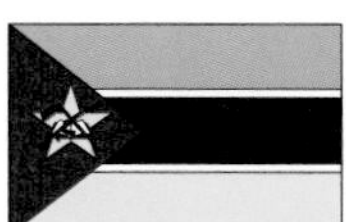

Mozambique
Page/Location: 104/G4
Area: 303,769 sq. mi.
786,762 sq. km.
Population: 17,346,000
Capital: Maputo
Largest City: Maputo
Highest Point: Monte Binga
Monetary Unit: metical

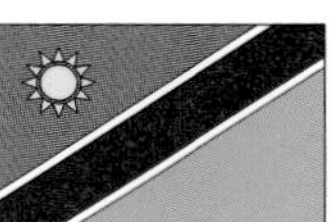

Namibia
Page/Location: 104/C5
Area: 317,827 sq. mi.
823,172 sq. km.
Population: 1,596,000
Capital: Windhoek
Largest City: Windhoek
Highest Point: Brandberg
Monetary Unit: rand

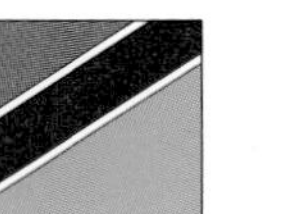

Nauru
Page/Location: 92/F5
Area: 7.7 sq. mi.
20 sq. km.
Population: 10,000
Capital: Yaren (district)
Largest City: —
Highest Point: 230 ft. (70 m)
Monetary Unit: Australian dollar

Nepal
Page/Location: 84/D2
Area: 54,663 sq. mi.
141,577 sq. km.
Population: 21,042,000
Capital: Kāthmāndu
Largest City: Kāthmāndu
Highest Point: Mt. Everest
Monetary Unit: Nepalese rupee

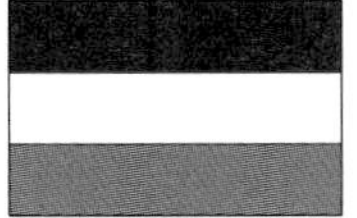

Netherlands
Page/Location: 50/B5
Area: 15,892 sq. mi.
41,160 sq. km.
Population: 15,368,000
Capital: The Hague; Amsterdam
Largest City: Amsterdam
Highest Point: Vaalserberg
Monetary Unit: Netherlands guilder

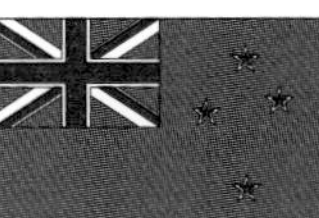

New Zealand
Page/Location: 89/H6
Area: 103,736 sq. mi.
268,676 sq. km.
Population: 3,389,000
Capital: Wellington
Largest City: Auckland
Highest Point: Mt. Cook
Monetary Unit: New Zealand dollar

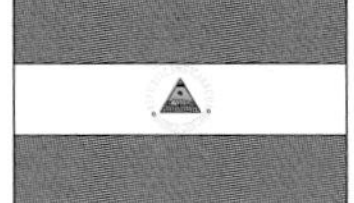

Nicaragua
Page/Location: 116/D5
Area: 45,698 sq. mi.
118,358 sq. km.
Population: 4,097,000
Capital: Managua
Largest City: Managua
Highest Point: Pico Mogotón
Monetary Unit: córdoba

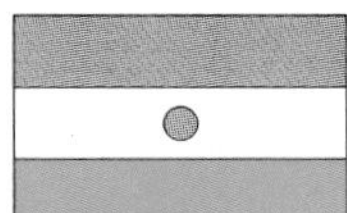

Niger
Page/Location: 96/G4
Area: 489,189 sq. mi.
1,267,000 sq. km.
Population: 8,972,000
Capital: Niamey
Largest City: Niamey
Highest Point: Bagzane
Monetary Unit: CFA franc

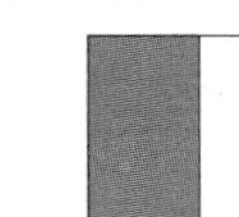

Nigeria
Page/Location: 96/G6
Area: 357,000 sq. mi.
924,630 sq. km.
Population: 98,091,000
Capital: Abuja
Largest City: Lagos
Highest Point: Dimlang
Monetary Unit: naira

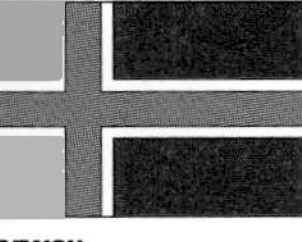

Norway
Page/Location: 42/C3
Area: 125,053 sq. mi.
323,887 sq. km.
Population: 4,315,000
Capital: Oslo
Largest City: Oslo
Highest Point: Glittertjnden
Monetary Unit: Norwegian krone

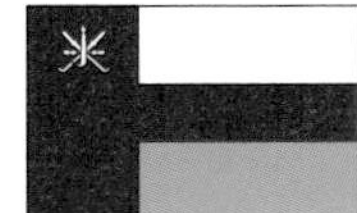

Oman
Page/Location: 73/G4
Area: 120,000 sq. mi.
310,800 sq. km.
Population: 1,701,000
Capital: Muscat
Largest City: Muscat
Highest Point: Jabal ash Shām
Monetary Unit: Omani rial

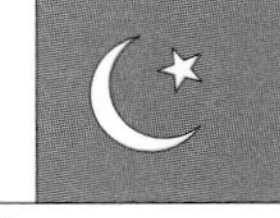

Pakistan
Page/Location: 73/H3
Area: 310,403 sq. mi.
803,944 sq. km.
Population: 128,856,000
Capital: Islāmābād
Largest City: Karāchi
Highest Point: K2 (Godwin Austen)
Monetary Unit: Pakistani rupee

Palau
Page/Location: 92/C4
Area: 177 sq. mi.
458 sq. km.
Population: 15,122
Capital: Koror
Largest City: Koror
Highest Point: 699 ft. (213m)
Monetary Unit: U.S. dollar

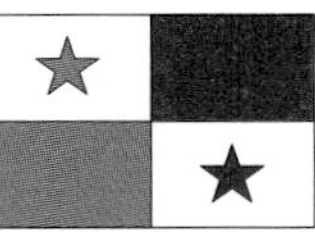

Panama
Page/Location: 116/E6
Area: 29,761 sq. mi.
77,082 sq. km.
Population: 2,630,000
Capital: Panamá
Largest City: Panamá
Highest Point: Barú
Monetary Unit: balboa

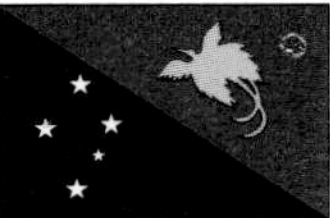

Papua New Guinea
Page/Location: 92/D5
Area: 183,540 sq. mi.
475,369 sq. km.
Population: 4,197,000
Capital: Port Moresby
Largest City: Port Moresby
Highest Point: Mt. Wilhelm
Monetary Unit: kina

World Flags and Reference Guide

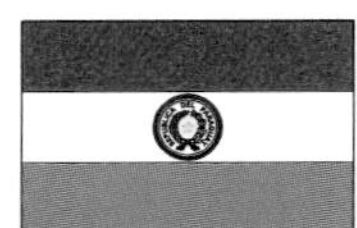

Paraguay
Page/Location: 107/D5
Area: 157,047 sq. mi.
   406,752 sq. km.
Population: 5,214,000
Capital: Asunción
Largest City: Asunción
Highest Point: Sierra de Amambay
Monetary Unit: guaraní

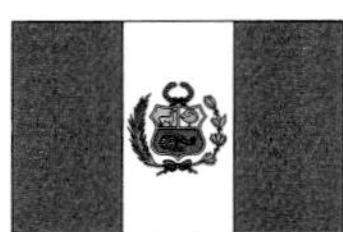

Peru
Page/Location: 108/C5
Area: 496,222 sq. mi.
   1,285,215 sq. km.
Population: 23,651,000
Capital: Lima
Largest City: Lima
Highest Point: Nevado Huascarán
Monetary Unit: nuevo sol

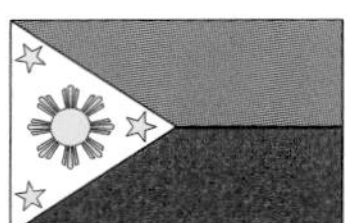

Philippines
Page/Location: 82/D5
Area: 115,707 sq. mi.
   299,681 sq. km.
Population: 69,809,000
Capital: Manila
Largest City: Manila
Highest Point: Mt. Apo
Monetary Unit: Philippine peso

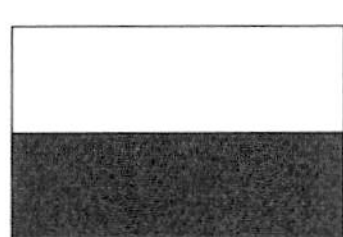

Poland
Page/Location: 49/K2
Area: 120,725 sq. mi.
   312,678 sq. km.
Population: 38,655,000
Capital: Warsaw
Largest City: Warsaw
Highest Point: Rysy
Monetary Unit: zloty

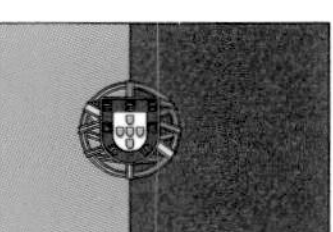

Portugal
Page/Location: 58/A3
Area: 35,549 sq. mi.
   92,072 sq. km.
Population: 10,524,000
Capital: Lisbon
Largest City: Lisbon
Highest Point: Serra da Estrela
Monetary Unit: Portuguese escudo

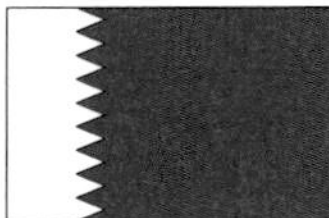

Qatar
Page/Location: 72/F3
Area: 4,247 sq. mi.
   11,000 sq. km.
Population: 513,000
Capital: Doha
Largest City: Doha
Highest Point: Dukhān Heights
Monetary Unit: Qatari riyal

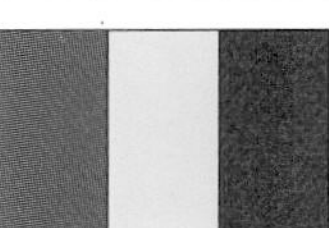

Romania
Page/Location: 63/F3
Area: 91,699 sq. mi.
   237,500 sq. km.
Population: 23,181,000
Capital: Bucharest
Largest City: Bucharest
Highest Point: Moldoveanul
Monetary Unit: leu

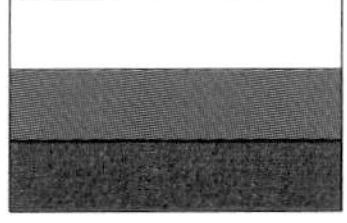

Russia
Page/Location: 68/H3
Area: 6,592,812 sq. mi.
   17,075,400 sq. km.
Population: 149,609,000
Capital: Moscow
Largest City: Moscow
Highest Point: El'brus
Monetary Unit: Russian ruble

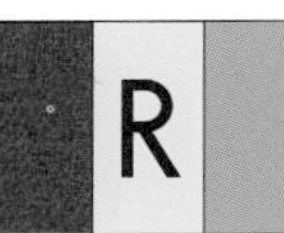

Rwanda
Page/Location: 101/A3
Area: 10,169 sq. mi.
   26,337 sq. km.
Population: 8,374,000
Capital: Kigali
Largest City: Kigali
Highest Point: Karisimbi
Monetary Unit: Rwanda franc

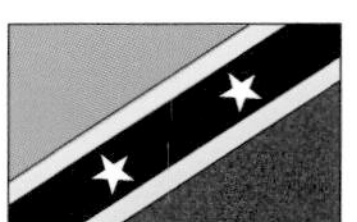

Saint Kitts and Nevis
Page/Location: 117/J4
Area: 104 sq. mi.
   269 sq. km.
Population: 41,000
Capital: Basseterre
Largest City: Basseterre
Highest Point: Mt. Misery
Monetary Unit: East Caribbean doll

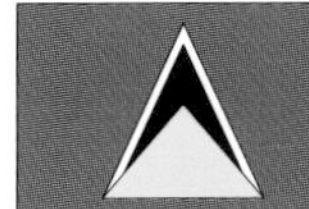

Saint Lucia
Page/Location: 117/J5
Area: 238 sq. mi.
   616 sq. km.
Population: 145,000
Capital: Castries
Largest City: Castries
Highest Point: Mt. Gimie
Monetary Unit: East Caribbean dollar

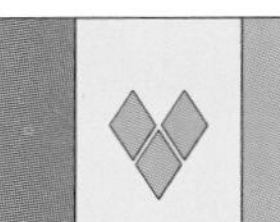

Saint Vincent and the Grenadines
Page/Location: 117/J5
Area: 150 sq. mi.
   388 sq. km.
Population: 115,000
Capital: Kingstown
Largest City: Kingstown
Highest Point: Soufrière
Monetary Unit: East Caribbean dollar

San Marino
Page/Location: 57/K5
Area: 23.4 sq. mi.
   60.6 sq. km.
Population: 24,000
Capital: San Marino
Largest City: San Marino
Highest Point: Monte Titano
Monetary Unit: Italian lira

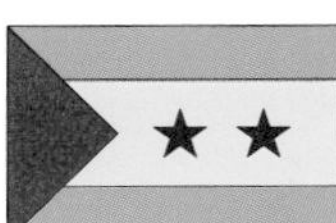

São Tomé and Príncipe
Page/Location: 96/F7
Area: 372 sq. mi.
   963 sq. km.
Population: 137,000
Capital: São Tomé
Largest City: São Tomé
Highest Point: Pico de São Tomé
Monetary Unit: dobra

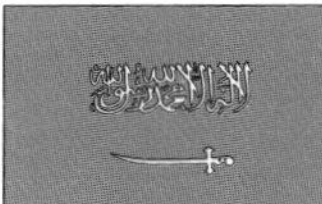

Saudi Arabia
Page/Location: 72/D4
Area: 829,995 sq. mi.
   2,149,687 sq. km.
Population: 18,197,000
Capital: Riyadh
Largest City: Riyadh
Highest Point: Jabal Sawdā'
Monetary Unit: Saudi riyal

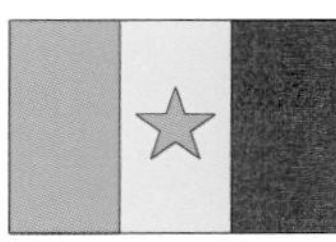

Senegal
Page/Location: 98/B3
Area: 75,954 sq. mi.
   196,720 sq. km.
Population: 8,731,000
Capital: Dakar
Largest City: Dakar
Highest Point: Fouta Djallon
Monetary Unit: CFA franc

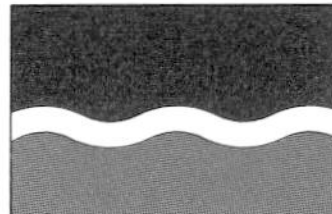

Seychelles
Page/Location: 39/M6
Area: 145 sq. mi.
   375 sq. km.
Population: 72,000
Capital: Victoria
Largest City: Victoria
Highest Point: Morne Seychellois
Monetary Unit: Seychellois rupee

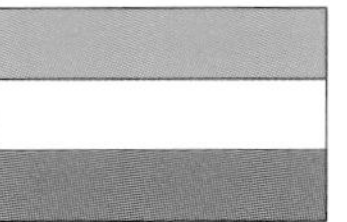

Sierra Leone
Page/Location: 98/B4
Area: 27,925 sq. mi.
   72,325 sq. km.
Population: 4,630,000
Capital: Freetown
Largest City: Freetown
Highest Point: Loma Mansa
Monetary Unit: leone

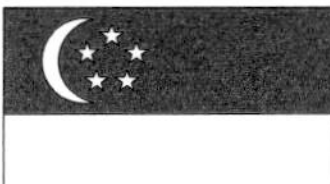

Singapore
Page/Location: 86/B3
Area: 226 sq. mi.
   585 sq. km.
Population: 2,859,000
Capital: Singapore
Largest City: Singapore
Highest Point: Bukit Timah
Monetary Unit: Singapore dollar

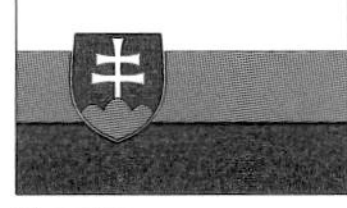

Slovakia
Page/Location: 49/K4
Area: 18,924 sq. mi.
   49,013 sq. km.
Population: 5,404,000
Capital: Bratislava
Largest City: Bratislava
Highest Point: Gerlachovský Štít
Monetary Unit: Slovak koruna

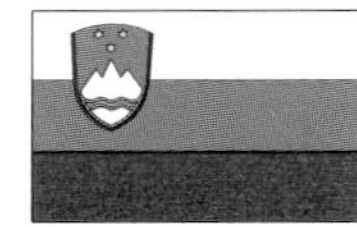

Slovenia
Page/Location: 62/B3
Area: 7,898 sq. mi.
   20,456 sq. km.
Population: 1,972,000
Capital: Ljubljana
Largest City: Ljubljana
Highest Point: Triglav
Monetary Unit: tolar

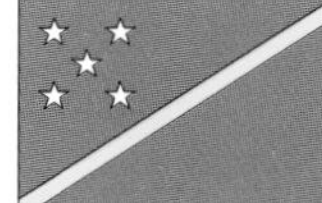

Solomon Islands
Page/Location: 92/E6
Area: 11,500 sq. mi.
   29,785 sq. km.
Population: 386,000
Capital: Honiara
Largest City: Honiara
Highest Point: Mt. Makarakomburu
Monetary Unit: Solomon Islands dollar

Somalia
Page/Location: 97/Q6
Area: 246,200 sq. mi.
   637,658 sq. km.
Population: 6,667,000
Capital: Mogadishu
Largest City: Mogadishu
Highest Point: Shimber Berris
Monetary Unit: Somali shilling

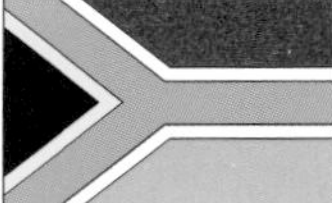

South Africa
Page/Location: 102/C3
Area: 455,318 sq. mi.
   1,179,274 sq. km.
Population: 43,931,000
Capital: Cape Town; Pretoria
Largest City: Johannesburg
Highest Point: Injasuti
Monetary Unit: rand

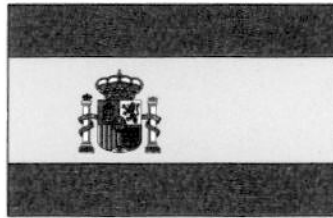

Spain
Page/Location: 58/C2
Area: 194,881 sq. mi.
   504,742 sq. km.
Population: 39,303,000
Capital: Madrid
Largest City: Madrid
Highest Point: Pico de Teide
Monetary Unit: peseta

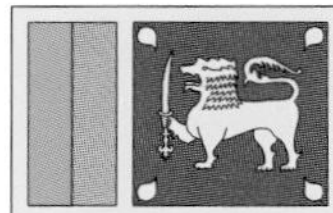

Sri Lanka
Page/Location: 84/D6
Area: 25,332 sq. mi.
   65,610 sq. km.
Population: 18,130,000
Capital: Colombo
Largest City: Colombo
Highest Point: Pidurutalagala
Monetary Unit: Sri Lanka rupee

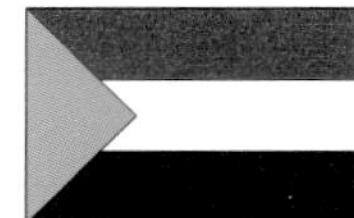

Sudan
Page/Location: 97/L5
Area: 967,494 sq. mi.
   2,505,809 sq. km.
Population: 29,420,000
Capital: Khartoum
Largest City: Omdurman
Highest Point: Jabal Marrah
Monetary Unit: Sudanese pound

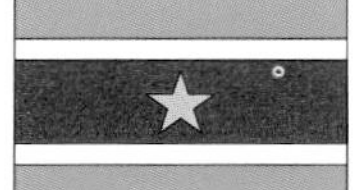

Suriname
Page/Location: 109/G3
Area: 55,144 sq. mi.
   142,823 sq. km.
Population: 423,000
Capital: Paramaribo
Largest City: Paramaribo
Highest Point: Juliana Top
Monetary Unit: Suriname guilder

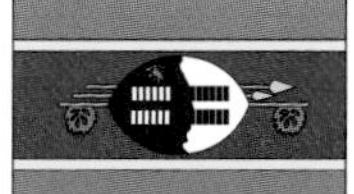

Swaziland
Page/Location: 103/E2
Area: 6,705 sq. mi.
   17,366 sq. km.
Population: 936,000
Capital: Mbabane
Largest City: Mbabane
Highest Point: Emlembe
Monetary Unit: lilangeni

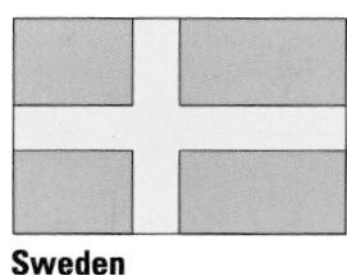

Sweden
Page/Location: 42/E3
Area: 173,665 sq. mi.
   449,792 sq. km.
Population: 8,778,000
Capital: Stockholm
Largest City: Stockholm
Highest Point: Kebnekaise
Monetary Unit: krona

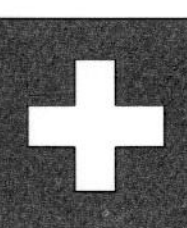

Switzerland
Page/Location: 54/D4
Area: 15,943 sq. mi.
41,292 sq. km.
Population: 7,040,000
Capital: Bern
Largest City: Zürich
Highest Point: Dufourspitze
Monetary Unit: Swiss franc

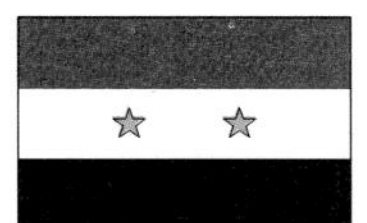

Syria
Page/Location: 72/C1
Area: 71,498 sq. mi.
185,180 sq. km.
Population: 14,887,000
Capital: Damascus
Largest City: Damascus
Highest Point: Jabal ash Shaykh
Monetary Unit: Syrian pound

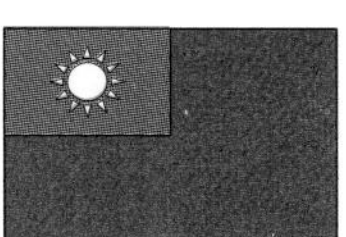

Taiwan
Page/Location: 82/D3
Area: 13,971 sq. mi.
36,185 sq. km.
Population: 21,299,000
Capital: Taipei
Largest City: Taipei
Highest Point: Yü Shan
Monetary Unit: new Taiwan dollar

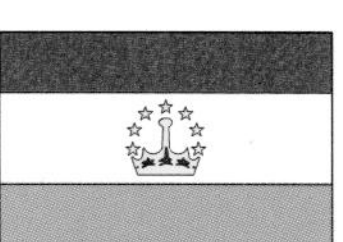

Tajikistan
Page/Location: 68/H6
Area: 55,251 sq. mi.
143,100 sq. km.
Population: 5,995,000
Capital: Dushanbe
Largest City: Dushanbe
Highest Point: Communism Peak
Monetary Unit: Tajik ruble

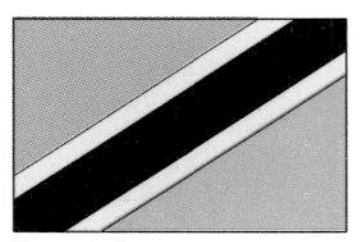

Tanzania
Page/Location: 101/B4
Area: 363,708 sq. mi.
942,003 sq. km.
Population: 27,986,000
Capital: Dar es Salaam
Largest City: Dar es Salaam
Highest Point: Kilimanjaro
Monetary Unit: Tanzanian shilling

Thailand
Page/Location: 83/C3
Area: 198,455 sq. mi.
513,998 sq. km.
Population: 59,510,000
Capital: Bangkok
Largest City: Bangkok
Highest Point: Doi Inthanon
Monetary Unit: baht

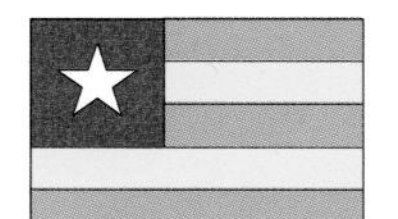

Togo
Page/Location: 99/F4
Area: 21,622 sq. mi.
56,000 sq. km.
Population: 4,255,000
Capital: Lomé
Largest City: Lomé
Highest Point: Mt. Agou
Monetary Unit: CFA franc

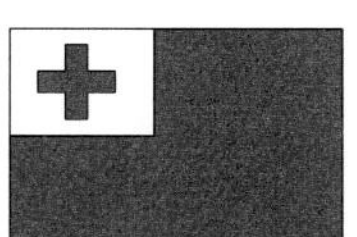

Tonga
Page/Location: 93/H7
Area: 270 sq. mi.
699 sq. km.
Population: 105,000
Capital: Nuku'alofa
Largest City: Nuku'alofa
Highest Point: Kao Island
Monetary Unit: pa'anga

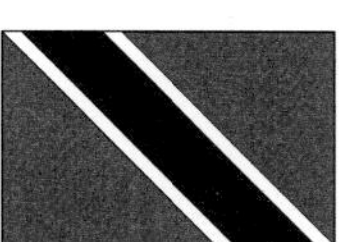

Trinidad and Tobago
Page/Location: 117/J5
Area: 1,980 sq. mi.
5,128 sq. km.
Population: 1,328,000
Capital: Port-of-Spain
Largest City: Port-of-Spain
Highest Point: El Cerro del Aripo
Monetary Unit: Trin. & Tobago dollar

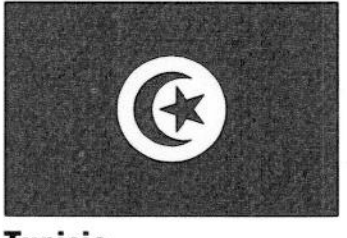

Tunisia
Page/Location: 96/G1
Area: 63,378 sq. mi.
164,149 sq. km.
Population: 8,727,000
Capital: Tūnis
Largest City: Tūnis
Highest Point: Jabal ash Sha'nabī
Monetary Unit: Tunisian dinar

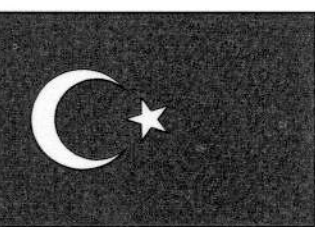

Turkey
Page/Location: 74/C2
Area: 300,946 sq. mi.
779,450 sq. km.
Population: 62,154,000
Capital: Ankara
Largest City: Istanbul
Highest Point: Mt. Ararat
Monetary Unit: Turkish lira

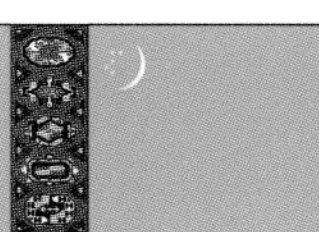

Turkmenistan
Page/Location: 68/F6
Area: 188,455 sq. mi.
488,100 sq. km.
Population: 3,995,000
Capital: Ashkhabad
Largest City: Ashkhabad
Highest Point: Rize
Monetary Unit: manat

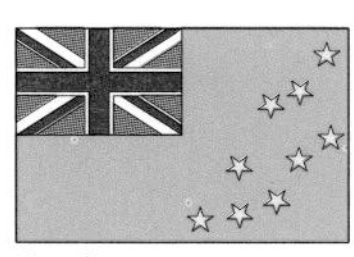

Tuvalu
Page/Location: 92/G5
Area: 9.78 sq. mi.
25.33 sq. km.
Population: 10,000
Capital: Funafuti
Largest City: —
Highest Point: 16 ft. (5 m)
Monetary Unit: Australian dollar

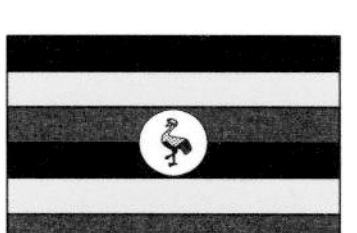

Uganda
Page/Location: 101/B2
Area: 91,076 sq. mi.
235,887 sq. km.
Population: 19,859,000
Capital: Kampala
Largest City: Kampala
Highest Point: Margherita Peak
Monetary Unit: Ugandan shilling

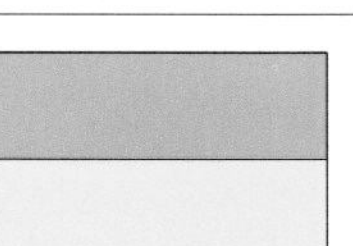

Ukraine
Page/Location: 66/D2
Area: 233,089 sq. mi.
603,700 sq. km.
Population: 51,847,000
Capital: Kiev
Largest City: Kiev
Highest Point: Goverla
Monetary Unit: karbovanet

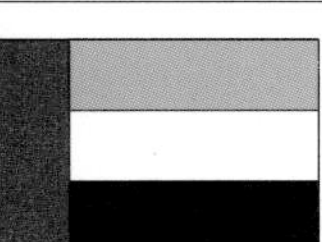

United Arab Emirates
Page/Location: 72/F4
Area: 32,278 sq. mi.
83,600 sq. km.
Population: 2,791,000
Capital: Abu Dhabi
Largest City: Dubayy
Highest Point: Hajar Mts.
Monetary Unit: Emirian dirham

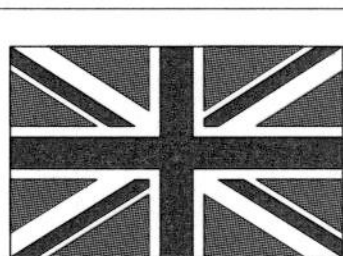

United Kingdom
Page/Location: 43
Area: 94,399 sq. mi.
244,493 sq. km.
Population: 58,135,000
Capital: London
Largest City: London
Highest Point: Ben Nevis
Monetary Unit: pound sterling

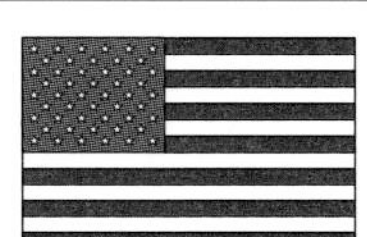

United States
Page/Location: 120
Area: 3,540,542 sq. mi.
9,170,002 sq. km.
Population: 260,714,000
Capital: Washington
Largest City: New York
Highest Point: Mt. McKinley
Monetary Unit: U.S. dollar

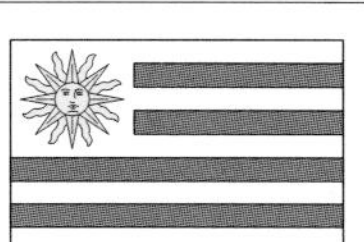

Uruguay
Page/Location: 111/E3
Area: 72,172 sq. mi.
186,925 sq. km.
Population: 3,199,000
Capital: Montevideo
Largest City: Montevideo
Highest Point: Cerro Catedral
Monetary Unit: Uruguayan peso

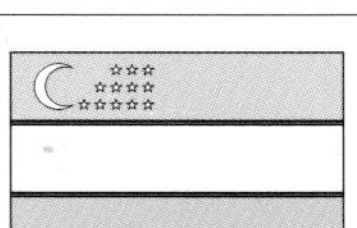

Uzbekistan
Page/Location: 68/G5
Area: 173,591 sq. mi.
449,600 sq. km.
Population: 22,609,000
Capital: Tashkent
Largest City: Tashkent
Highest Point: Khodzha-Pir'yakh
Monetary Unit: som

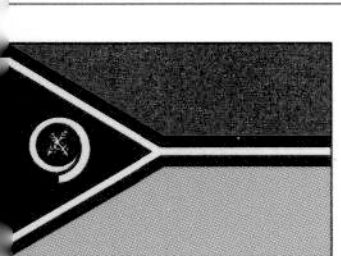

Vanuatu
Page/Location: 92/F6
Area: 5,700 sq. mi.
14,763 sq. km.
Population: 170,000
Capital: Vila
Largest City: Vila
Highest Point: Tabwemasana
Monetary Unit: vatu

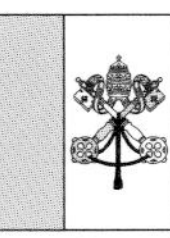

Vatican City
Page/Location: 60/C2
Area: 108.7 acres
44 hectares
Population: 821
Capital: —
Largest City: —
Highest Point: —
Monetary Unit: Italian lira

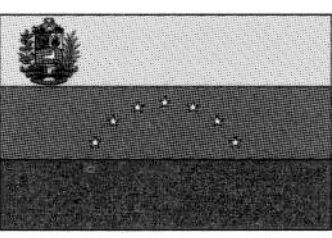

Venezuela
Page/Location: 108/E2
Area: 352,143 sq. mi.
912,050 sq. km.
Population: 20,562,000
Capital: Caracas
Largest City: Caracas
Highest Point: Pico Bolívar
Monetary Unit: bolívar

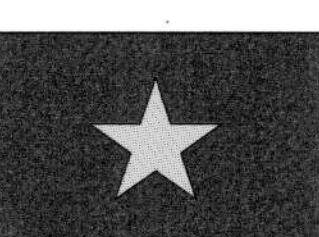

Vietnam
Page/Location: 83/D2
Area: 128,405 sq. mi.
332,569 sq. km.
Population: 73,104,000
Capital: Hanoi
Largest City: Ho Chi Minh City
Highest Point: Fan Si Pan
Monetary Unit: dong

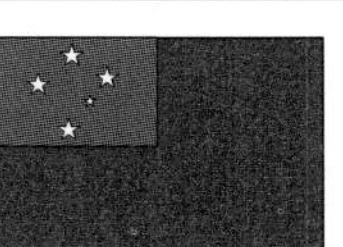

Western Samoa
Page/Location: 93/H6
Area: 1,133 sq. mi.
2,934 sq. km.
Population: 204,000
Capital: Apia
Largest City: Apia
Highest Point: Mt. Silisili
Monetary Unit: tala

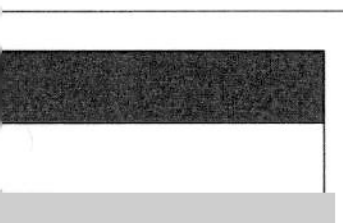

Yemen
Page/Location: 72/E5
Area: 188,321 sq. mi.
487,752 sq. km.
Population: 11,105,000
Capital: Sanaa
Largest City: Aden
Highest Point: Nabī Shu'ayb
Monetary Unit: Yemeni rial

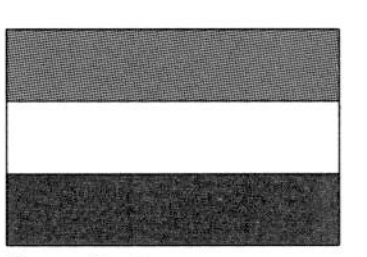

Yugoslavia
Page/Location: 62/E3
Area: 38,989 sq. mi.
100,982 sq. km.
Population: 10,760,000
Capital: Belgrade
Largest City: Belgrade
Highest Point: Đaravica
Monetary Unit: Yugoslav new dinar

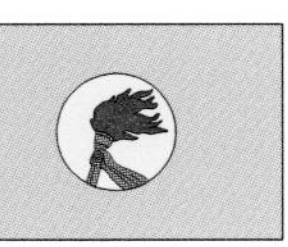

Zaire
Page/Location: 95/E5
Area: 905,063 sq. mi.
2,344,113 sq. km.
Population: 42,684,000
Capital: Kinshasa
Largest City: Kinshasa
Highest Point: Margherita Peak
Monetary Unit: zaire

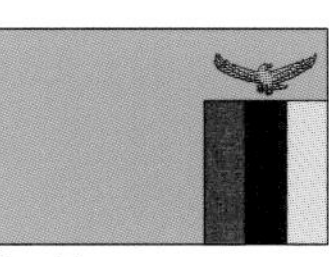

Zambia
Page/Location: 104/E3
Area: 290,586 sq. mi.
752,618 sq. km.
Population: 9,188,000
Capital: Lusaka
Largest City: Lusaka
Highest Point: Sunzu
Monetary Unit: Zambian kwacha

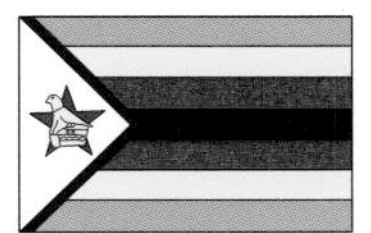

Zimbabwe
Page/Location: 104/E4
Area: 150,803 sq. mi.
390,580 sq. km.
Population: 10,975,000
Capital: Harare
Largest City: Harare
Highest Point: Inyangani
Monetary Unit: Zimbabwe dollar

The Solar System

Pluto

Neptune

Uranus

Jupiter

Sun

Mercury

Venus

Mercury

Mean Distance from Sun:
35,990,000 miles
Period of Revolution
around Sun: 87.97 days
Period of Rotation
on Axis: 59 days
Equatorial Diameter:
3,032 miles
Surface Gravity
(Earth = 1): 0.38
Mass (Earth = 1): 0.055
Mean Density:
(Water = 1): 5.5
Satellites: 0

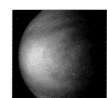

Venus

Mean Distance from Sun:
67,240,000 miles
Period of Revolution
around Sun: 224.70 days
Period of Rotation
on Axis: 243 days†
Equatorial Diameter:
7,523 miles
Surface Gravity
(Earth = 1): 0.90
Mass (Earth = 1): 0.815
Mean Density:
(Water = 1): 5.25
Satellites: 0
† retrograde motion

Earth

Mean Distance from Sun:
93,000,000 miles
Period of Revolution
around Sun: 365.26 days
Period of Rotation
on Axis: 23h 56m
Equatorial Diameter:
7,926 miles
Surface Gravity
(Earth = 1): 1.00
Mass (Earth = 1): 1.00
Mean Density:
(Water = 1): 5.5
Satellites: 1

Mars

Mean Distance from Sun:
141,730,000 miles
Period of Revolution
around Sun: 687.00 days
Period of Rotation
on Axis: 24h 37m
Equatorial Diameter:
4,220 miles
Surface Gravity
(Earth = 1): 0.38
Mass (Earth = 1): 0.107
Mean Density:
(Water = 1): 4.0
Satellites: 2

Jupiter

Mean Distance from Sun:
483,880,000 miles
Period of Revolution
around Sun: 11.86 years
Period of Rotation
on Axis: 9h 50m
Equatorial Diameter:
88,750 miles
Surface Gravity
(Earth = 1): 2.87
Mass (Earth = 1): 317.9
Mean Density:
(Water = 1): 1.3
Satellites: 16

Saturn

Mean Distance from Sun:
887,130,000 miles
Period of Revolution
around Sun: 29.46 years
Period of Rotation
on Axis: 10h 39m
Equatorial Diameter:
74,580 miles
Surface Gravity
(Earth = 1): 1.32
Mass (Earth = 1): 95.2
Mean Density:
(Water = 1): 0.7
Satellites: 23

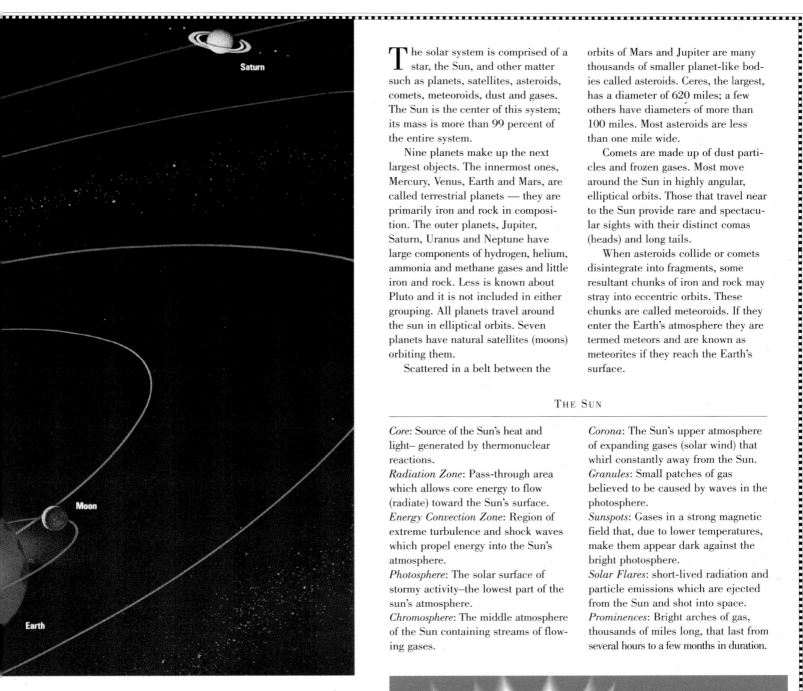

Saturn

Moon

Earth

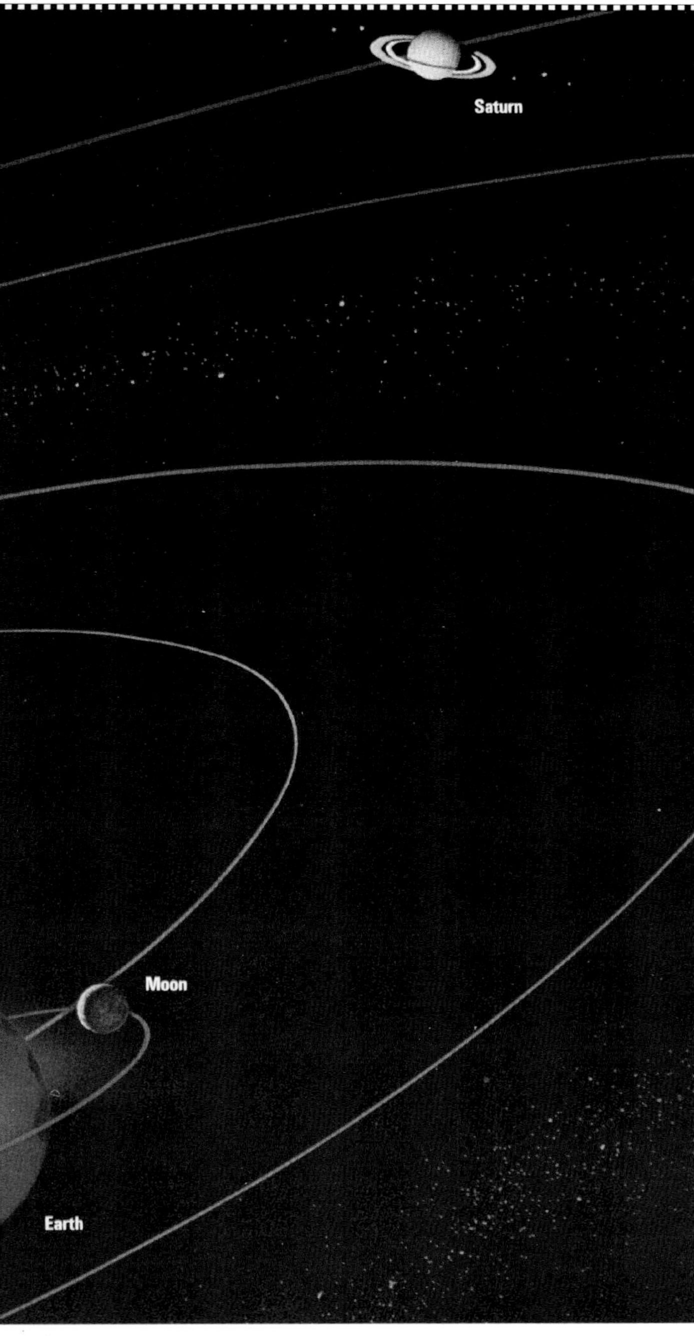

The solar system is comprised of a star, the Sun, and other matter such as planets, satellites, asteroids, comets, meteoroids, dust and gases. The Sun is the center of this system; its mass is more than 99 percent of the entire system.

Nine planets make up the next largest objects. The innermost ones, Mercury, Venus, Earth and Mars, are called terrestrial planets — they are primarily iron and rock in composition. The outer planets, Jupiter, Saturn, Uranus and Neptune have large components of hydrogen, helium, ammonia and methane gases and little iron and rock. Less is known about Pluto and it is not included in either grouping. All planets travel around the sun in elliptical orbits. Seven planets have natural satellites (moons) orbiting them.

Scattered in a belt between the orbits of Mars and Jupiter are many thousands of smaller planet-like bodies called asteroids. Ceres, the largest, has a diameter of 620 miles; a few others have diameters of more than 100 miles. Most asteroids are less than one mile wide.

Comets are made up of dust particles and frozen gases. Most move around the Sun in highly angular, elliptical orbits. Those that travel near to the Sun provide rare and spectacular sights with their distinct comas (heads) and long tails.

When asteroids collide or comets disintegrate into fragments, some resultant chunks of iron and rock may stray into eccentric orbits. These chunks are called meteoroids. If they enter the Earth's atmosphere they are termed meteors and are known as meteorites if they reach the Earth's surface.

THE SUN

Core: Source of the Sun's heat and light– generated by thermonuclear reactions.

Radiation Zone: Pass-through area which allows core energy to flow (radiate) toward the Sun's surface.

Energy Convection Zone: Region of extreme turbulence and shock waves which propel energy into the Sun's atmosphere.

Photosphere: The solar surface of stormy activity–the lowest part of the sun's atmosphere.

Chromosphere: The middle atmosphere of the Sun containing streams of flowing gases.

Corona: The Sun's upper atmosphere of expanding gases (solar wind) that whirl constantly away from the Sun.

Granules: Small patches of gas believed to be caused by waves in the photosphere.

Sunspots: Gases in a strong magnetic field that, due to lower temperatures, make them appear dark against the bright photosphere.

Solar Flares: short-lived radiation and particle emissions which are ejected from the Sun and shot into space.

Prominences: Bright arches of gas, thousands of miles long, that last from several hours to a few months in duration.

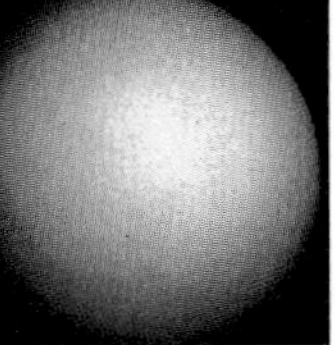

anus

ean Distance from Sun:
?83,700,000 miles
riod of Revolution
und Sun: 84.01 years
riod of Rotation
Axis: 17h 24m†
uatorial Diameter:
,600 miles
rface Gravity
arth = 1): 0.93
ass (Earth = 1): 14.6
ean Density:
Vater = 1): 1.3
tellites: 15
etrograde motion

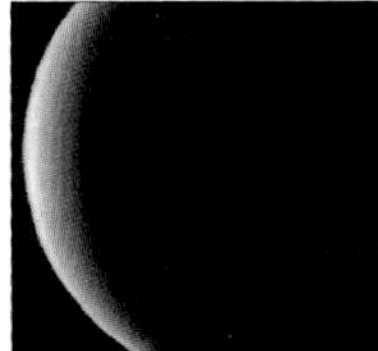

Neptune

Mean Distance from Sun:
2,795,500,000 miles
Period of Revolution
around Sun: 164.79 years
Period of Rotation
on Axis: 17h 50m
Equatorial Diameter:
30,200 miles
Surface Gravity
(Earth = 1): 1.23
Mass (Earth = 1): 17.2
Mean Density:
(Water = 1): 1.8
Satellites: 8

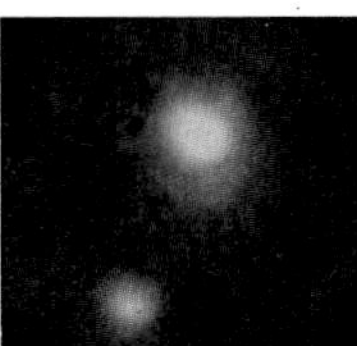

Pluto

Mean Distance from Sun:
3,667,900,000 miles
Period of Revolution
around Sun: 247.70 years
Period of Rotation
on Axis: 6.39 days (?)
Equatorial Diameter:
1,500 miles
Surface Gravity
(Earth = 1): 0.03(?)
Mass (Earth = 1): 0.01(?)
Mean Density:
(Water = 1): 0.7(?)
Satellites: 1

Granular surface

Corona (up to 2,000,000°F)

Solar Flares

Chromosphere

Sunspots

Photosphere (7,000–11,000°F)

Energy Convection Zone

Prominences

Radiation Zone

Core (30,000,000°F)

Equitorial Diameter: 850,000 miles

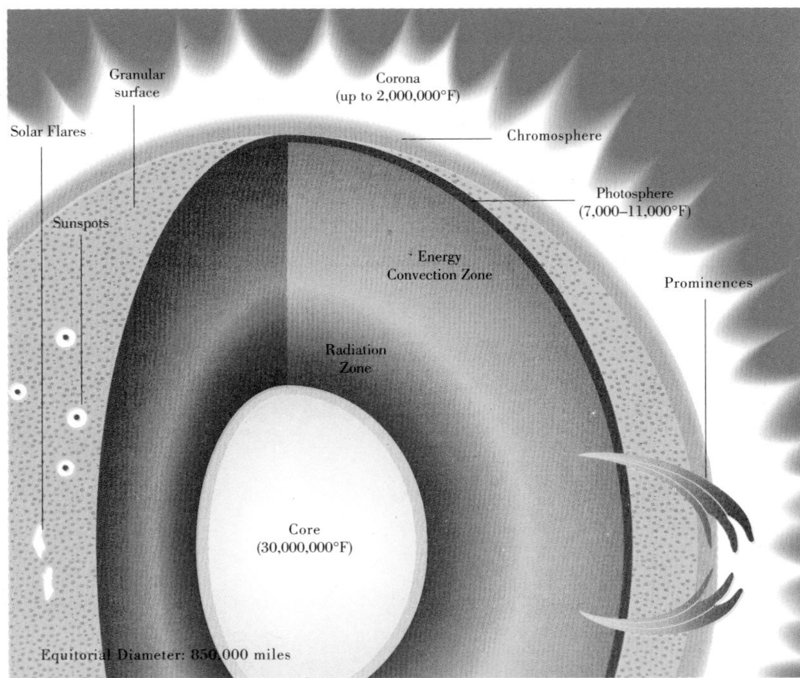

Structure of the

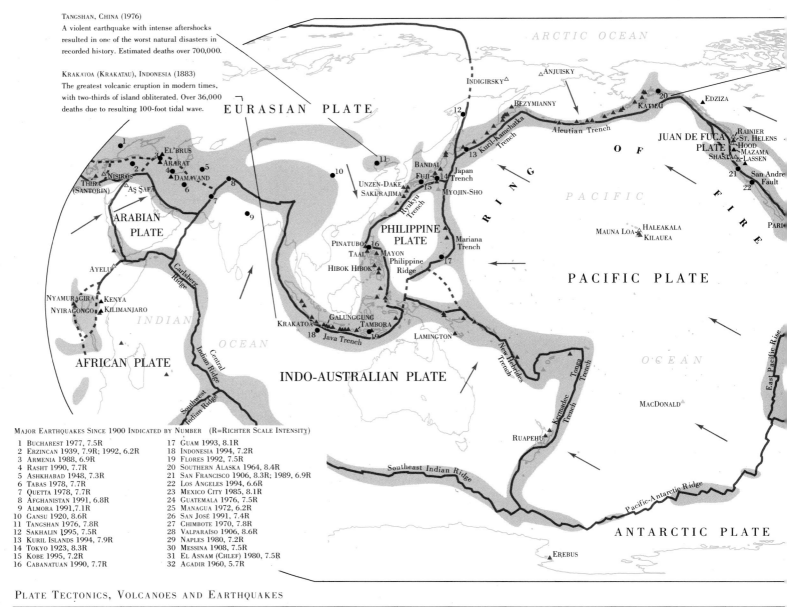

TANGSHAN, CHINA (1976)
A violent earthquake with intense aftershocks resulted in one of the worst natural disasters in recorded history. Estimated deaths over 700,000.

KRAKATOA (KRAKATAU), INDONESIA (1883)
The greatest volcanic eruption in modern times, with two-thirds of island obliterated. Over 36,000 deaths due to resulting 100-foot tidal wave.

EURASIAN PLATE

ARABIAN PLATE

AFRICAN PLATE

PHILIPPINE PLATE

INDO-AUSTRALIAN PLATE

JUAN DE FUCA PLATE

PACIFIC PLATE

ANTARCTIC PLATE

RING OF FIRE

ARCTIC OCEAN

INDIAN OCEAN

MAJOR EARTHQUAKES SINCE 1900 INDICATED BY NUMBER   (R=RICHTER SCALE INTENSITY)

1 BUCHAREST 1977, 7.5R
2 ERZINCAN 1939, 7.9R; 1992, 6.2R
3 ARMENIA 1988, 6.9R
4 RASHT 1990, 7.7R
5 ASHKHABAD 1948, 7.3R
6 TABAS 1978, 7.7R
7 QUETTA 1978, 7.7R
8 AFGHANISTAN 1991, 6.8R
9 ALMORA 1991,7.1R
10 GANSU 1920, 8.6R
11 TANGSHAN 1976, 7.8R
12 SAKHALIN 1995, 7.5R
13 KURIL ISLANDS 1994, 7.9R
14 TOKYO 1923, 8.3R
15 KOBE 1995, 7.2R
16 CABANATUAN 1990, 7.7R

17 GUAM 1993, 8.1R
18 INDONESIA 1994, 7.2R
19 FLORES 1992, 7.5R
20 SOUTHERN ALASKA 1964, 8.4R
21 SAN FRANCISCO 1906, 8.3R; 1989, 6.9R
22 LOS ANGELES 1994, 6.6R
23 MEXICO CITY 1985, 8.1R
24 GUATEMALA 1976, 7.5R
25 MANAGUA 1972, 6.2R
26 SAN JOSÉ 1991, 7.4R
27 CHIMBOTE 1970, 7.8R
28 VALPARAÍSO 1906, 8.6R
29 NAPLES 1980, 7.2R
30 MESSINA 1908, 7.5R
31 EL ASNAM (CHLEF) 1980, 7.5R
32 AGADIR 1960, 5.7R

PLATE TECTONICS, VOLCANOES AND EARTHQUAKES

▲ ACTIVE VOLCANOES   △ DORMANT VOLCANOES   ▲ EXTINCT VOLCANOES   ⬚ SUBMARINE VOLCANOES   ● EARTHQUAKES   ▭ EARTHQUAKE ZONES   ▬▬ PLATE BO

The making of continents began more than 200 million years ago with the splitting of a gigantic landmass known as Pangaea. Two super continents, Laurasia and Gondwana, were formed by the initial division. Over a period of many millions of years these landmasses further subdivided into smaller parts and drifted across a single great ocean, forming the oceans and continents of today. In terms of current theory, called plate tectonics, the earth's crust is divided into at least 15 rigid rock segments, known as plates, that float on a semi-molten layer of upper mantle. Seven plates are of major size and, except for the vast Pacific

CONTINENTAL DRIFT

180 MILLION YEARS AGO

70 MILLION YEARS AGO

PRESENT TIME

Earth

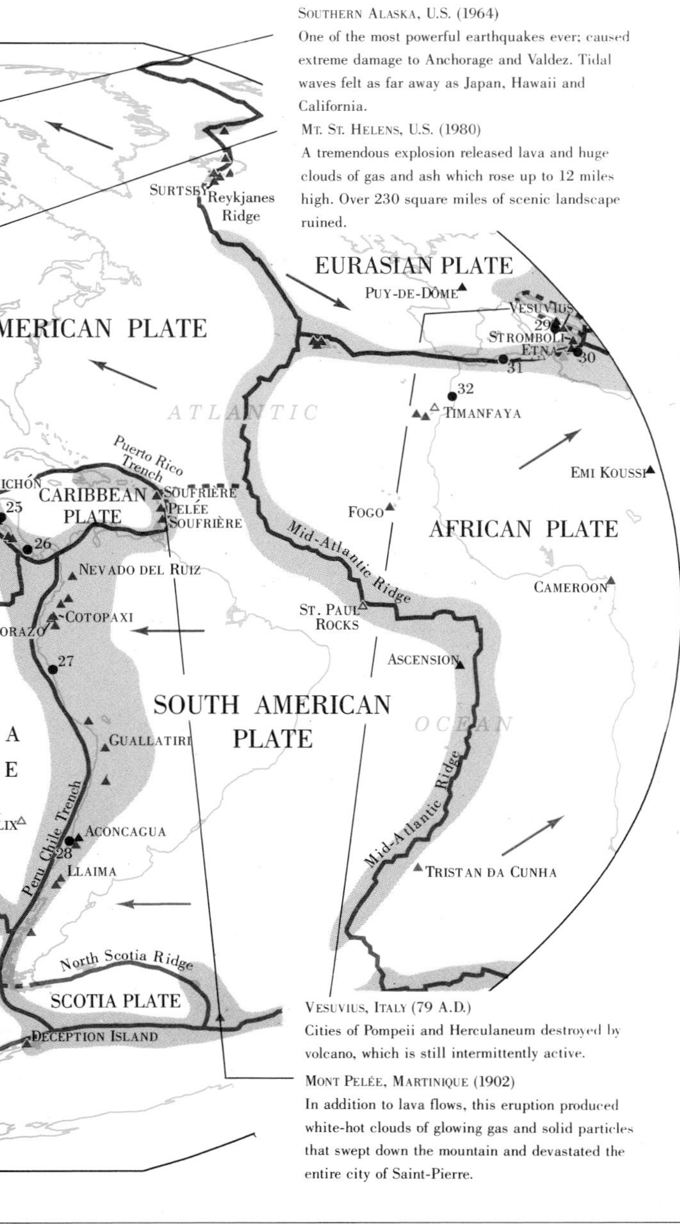

SOUTHERN ALASKA, U.S. (1964)
One of the most powerful earthquakes ever; caused extreme damage to Anchorage and Valdez. Tidal waves felt as far away as Japan, Hawaii and California.

MT. ST. HELENS, U.S. (1980)
A tremendous explosion released lava and huge clouds of gas and ash which rose up to 12 miles high. Over 230 square miles of scenic landscape ruined.

VESUVIUS, ITALY (79 A.D.)
Cities of Pompeii and Herculaneum destroyed by volcano, which is still intermittently active.

MONT PELÉE, MARTINIQUE (1902)
In addition to lava flows, this eruption produced white-hot clouds of glowing gas and solid particles that swept down the mountain and devastated the entire city of Saint-Pierre.

--- UNCERTAIN BOUNDARIES   ◀— DIRECTION OF PLATE MOVEMENT

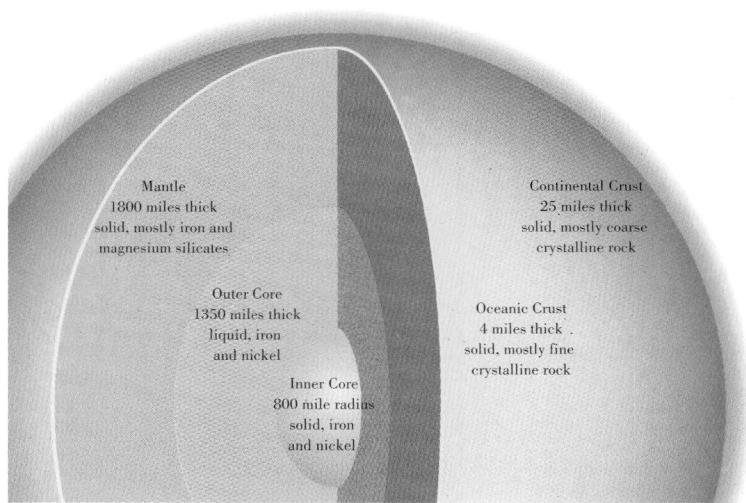

INTERIOR AND CRUST OF THE EARTH

By studying records of earthquakes, scientists have developed a fairly reasonable picture (cross section) of the earth's principal layers, including their composition. The inner core is a very dense, highly-pressurized, extremely hot (about 9,000° F.) sphere. Moving outward toward the crust, densities, pressures and temperatures decrease significantly.

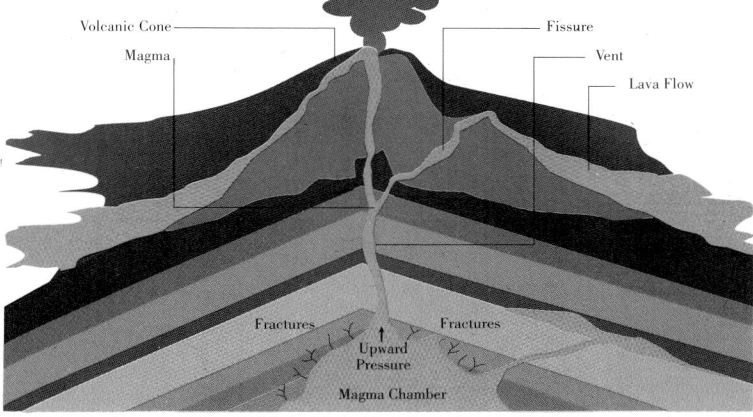

VOLCANOES

One of the earth's most dynamic and colorful builders is the volcano. In the mantle, magma—molten rock containing compressed gases—probes for weak spots in the earth's crust and bursts forth through the ground in an eruption of fiery lava, ash, gas and steam. After a period of eruption, lasting from a few days to many years, the magma ceases to push upward and the volcano becomes dormant.

Plate, carry a continental landmass with surrounding ocean floor and island areas. The plates are slow-moving, driven by powerful forces within the mantle. At their boundaries they are either slowly separating with new material added from the mantle, converging, with one plate being forced down (subducted) and consumed under another, or sliding past each other. Almost all earthquake, volcanic and mountain-building activity closely follows these boundaries and is related to movements between them. Although these movements may be no more than inches per year, the destructive power unleashed can be cataclysmic.

PLATE TECTONICS

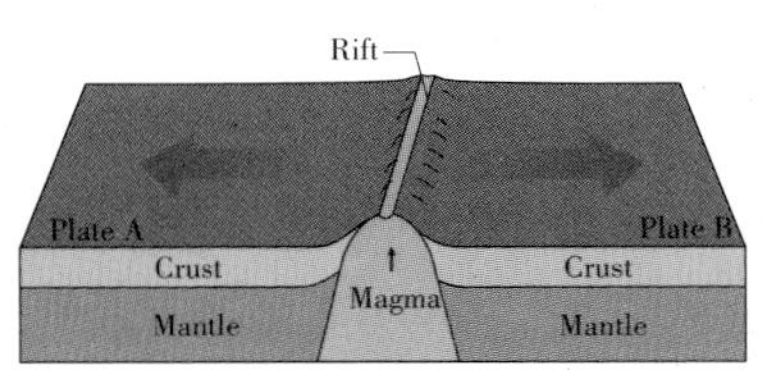

SEPARATING PLATES

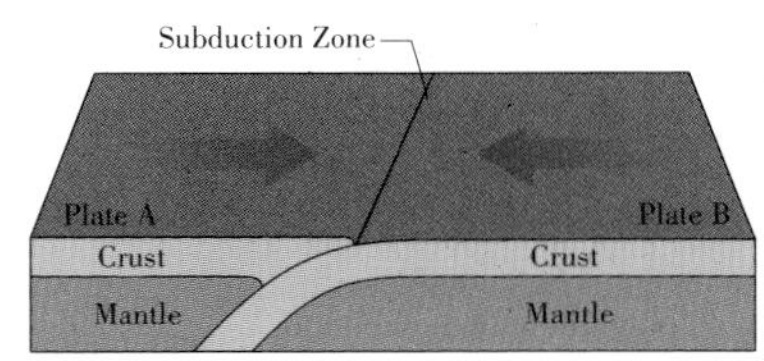

CONVERGING PLATES

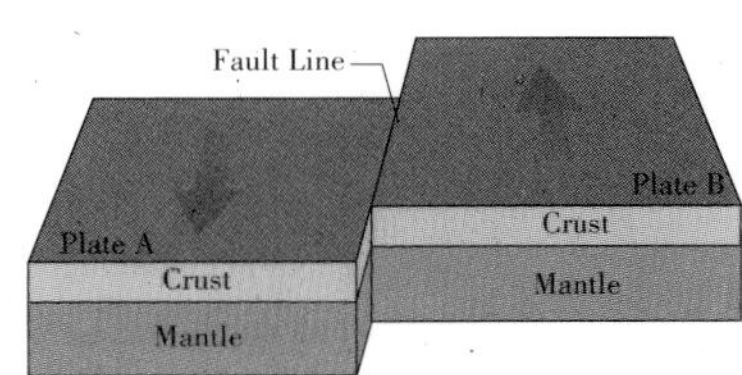

SLIDING PLATES

Environmental Concerns

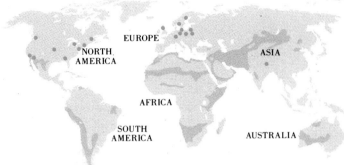

EUROPE

NORTH AMERICA

ASIA

AFRICA

SOUTH AMERICA

AUSTRALIA

DESERTIFICATION AND ACID RAIN DAMAGE

AREAS OF PRODUCTIVE DRYLANDS DESERTIFIED BY EARLY 1980'S

● AREAS OF DAMAGE FROM ACID RAIN AND OTHER AIRBORNE POLLUTANTS

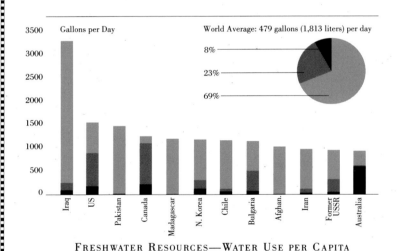

Gallons per Day

World Average: 479 gallons (1,813 liters) per day

8%
23%
69%

3500
3000
2500
2000
1500
1000
500
0

Iraq · US · Pakistan · Canada · Madagascar · N. Korea · Chile · Bulgaria · Afghan. · Iran · Former USSR · Australia

FRESHWATER RESOURCES—WATER USE PER CAPITA

■ DOMESTIC ■ INDUSTRY ■ AGRICULTURE

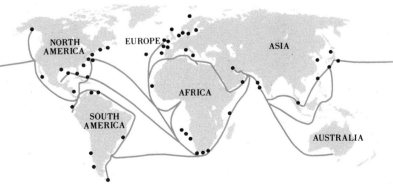

NORTH AMERICA

EUROPE

ASIA

AFRICA

SOUTH AMERICA

AUSTRALIA

MAIN TANKER ROUTES AND MAJOR OIL SPILLS

—— ROUTES OF VERY LARGE CRUDE OIL CARRIERS ● MAJOR OIL SPILLS

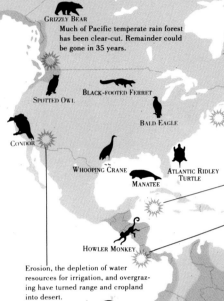

GRIZZLY BEAR
Much of Pacific temperate rain forest has been clear-cut. Remainder could be gone in 35 years.

WOODLAND CARIBOU

HUMPBACK

Hydroelectric power p[…] and development in Qu[…] are disrupting wildlife habitats.

Commercial fishing ha[…] in the northwest Atlant[…] declined over 30 perce[…] since 1970.

SPOTTED OWL

BLACK-FOOTED FERRET

BALD EAGLE

CONDOR

Fragile barrier beaches of the Atla[…] coast have been damaged by agric[…] tural runoff, sewage and overdeve[…] ment.

WHOOPING CRANE

MANATEE

ATLANTIC RIDLEY TURTLE

Ecological balance in coral reefs […] Gulf and Caribbean area is being upset by a booming tourist indust[…]

At the present rate of clearing, h[…] Central America's rain forest wil[…] appear by the year 2000.

One-third of Guinea's tropical fo[…] expected to disappear in the nex[…] decade.

HOWLER MONKEY

Erosion, the depletion of water resources for irrigation, and overgraz-ing have turned range and cropland into desert.

GALÁPAGOS TORTOISE

BLACK CAIMAN

JAGUAR

VICUNA

Every year over 5000 square miles (13,000 sq km) of rain forest is destroyed in Brazil's Amazon Basin.

CHINCHILLA

GOLDEN LION TAMARIN

GIANT ARMADILLO

The Atlantic waters of Patagonia have suffere[…] over-fishing and oil sp[…]

Southern Chile's rain forest is threat-ened by development.

BLUE WHALE

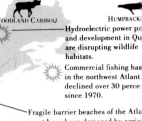

Acid Rain

Acid rain of nitric and sulfuric acids has killed all life in thousands of lakes, and over 15 million acres (6 million hectares) of virgin forest in Europe and North America are dead or dying.

Deforestation

Each year, 50 million acres (20 million hectares) of tropical rainforests are be-ing felled by loggers. Trees remove carbon-dioxide from the atmosphere and are vital to the prevention of soil erosion.

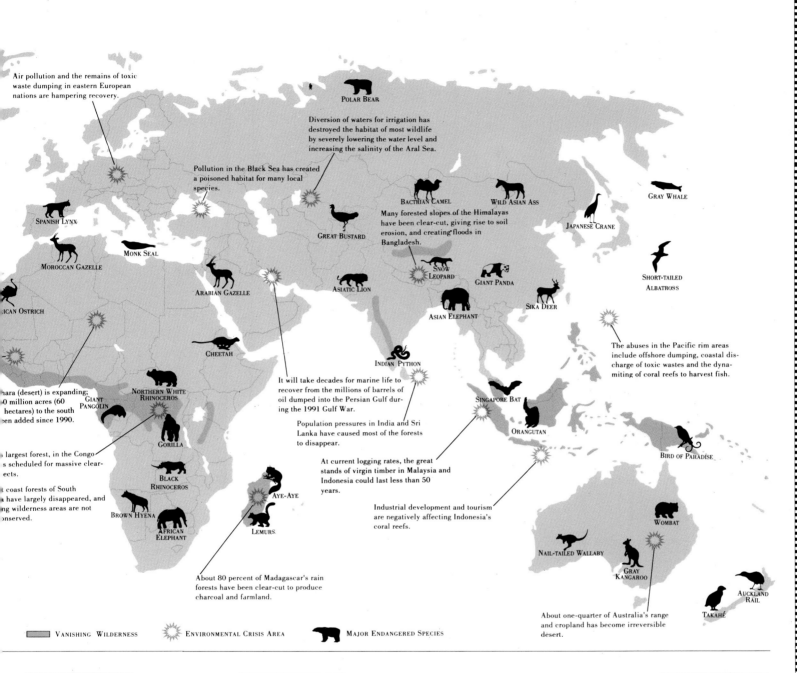

Air pollution and the remains of toxic waste dumping in eastern European nations are hampering recovery.

Diversion of waters for irrigation has destroyed the habitat of most wildlife by severely lowering the water level and increasing the salinity of the Aral Sea.

Pollution in the Black Sea has created a poisoned habitat for many local species.

Many forested slopes of the Himalayas have been clear-cut, giving rise to soil erosion, and creating floods in Bangladesh.

POLAR BEAR

GRAY WHALE

SPANISH LYNX

JAPANESE CRANE

MONK SEAL

MOROCCAN GAZELLE

GREAT BUSTARD

BACTRIAN CAMEL

WILD ASIAN ASS

ARABIAN GAZELLE

ASIATIC LION

SNOW LEOPARD

GIANT PANDA

SHORT-TAILED ALBATROSS

ICAN OSTRICH

SIKA DEER

ASIAN ELEPHANT

CHEETAH

INDIAN PYTHON

The abuses in the Pacific rim areas include offshore dumping, coastal discharge of toxic wastes and the dynamiting of coral reefs to harvest fish.

It will take decades for marine life to recover from the millions of barrels of oil dumped into the Persian Gulf during the 1991 Gulf War.

SINGAPORE BAT

hara (desert) is expanding; 0 million acres (60 hectares) to the south een added since 1990.

GIANT PANGOLIN

NORTHERN WHITE RHINOCEROS

Population pressures in India and Sri Lanka have caused most of the forests to disappear.

ORANGUTAN

BIRD OF PARADISE

largest forest, in the Congo s scheduled for massive clear-ects.

GORILLA

At current logging rates, the great stands of virgin timber in Malaysia and Indonesia could last less than 50 years.

coast forests of South a have largely disappeared, and ng wilderness areas are not onserved.

BLACK RHINOCEROS

AYE-AYE

Industrial development and tourism are negatively affecting Indonesia's coral reefs.

WOMBAT

BROWN HYENA

AFRICAN ELEPHANT

LEMURS

NAIL-TAILED WALLABY

GRAY KANGAROO

AUCKLAND RAIL

TAKAHÉ

About 80 percent of Madagascar's rain forests have been clear-cut to produce charcoal and farmland.

About one-quarter of Australia's range and cropland has become irreversible desert.

VANISHING WILDERNESS   ENVIRONMENTAL CRISIS AREA   MAJOR ENDANGERED SPECIES

Extinction

Biologists estimate that over 50,000 plant and animal species inhabiting the world's rain forests are disappearing each year due to pollution, unchecked hunting and the destruction of natural habitats.

Air Pollution

Billions of tons of industrial emissions and toxic pollutants are released into the air each year, depleting our ozone layer, killing our forests and lakes with acid rain and threatening our health.

Water Pollution

Only 3 percent of the earth's water is fresh. Pollution from cities, farms and factories has made much of it unfit to drink. In the developing world, most sewage flows untreated into lakes and rivers.

Ozone Depletion

The layer of ozone in the stratosphere shields earth from harmful ultraviolet radiation. But man-made gases are destroying this vital barrier, increasing the risk of skin cancer and eye disease.

Population

EACH AREA'S SIZE IS PROPORTIONATE TO ITS POPULATION

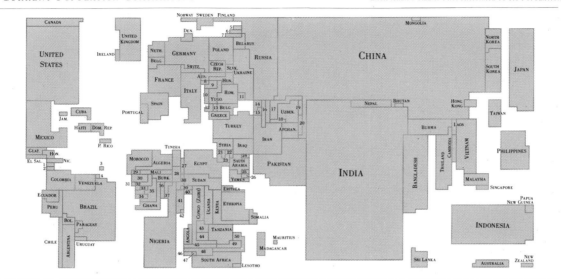

COUNTRIES INDICATED BY NUMBER

1	COSTA RICA	10	BOSNIA AND	20	TAJIKISTAN	30	SENEGAL	40	CONGO	51	CYPRUS
2	PANAMA		HERZEGOVINA	21	LEBANON	31	GUINEA-BISSAU	41	CAMEROON	52	CAPE VERDE
3	TRINIDAD AND	11	MOLDOVA	22	JORDAN	32	GUINEA	42	GABON	53	GAMBIA
	TOBAGO	12	ALBANIA	23	ISRAEL	33	SIERRA LEONE	43	RWANDA	54	EQUATORIAL GUINEA
4	GUYANA	13	MACEDONIA	24	KUWAIT	34	LIBERIA	44	BURUNDI	55	BAHRAIN
5	ESTONIA	14	GEORGIA	25	UNITED ARAB	35	CÔTE D'IVOIRE	45	ZAMBIA	56	QATAR
6	LATVIA	15	ARMENIA		EMIRATES	36	TOGO	46	NAMIBIA	57	BRUNEI
7	LITHUANIA	16	AZERBAIJAN	26	OMAN	37	BENIN	47	BOTSWANA	58	SOLOMON ISLANDS
8	SLOVENIA	17	KAZAKHSTAN	27	LIBYA	38	CHAD	48	ZIMBABWE		
9	CROATIA	18	TURKMENISTAN	28	NIGER	39	CENTRAL AFRICAN	49	MOZAMBIQUE		
		19	KYRGYZSTAN	29	MAURITANIA		REPUBLIC	50	MALAWI		

EACH AREA'S SIZE IS PROPORTIONATE TO ITS POPULATION

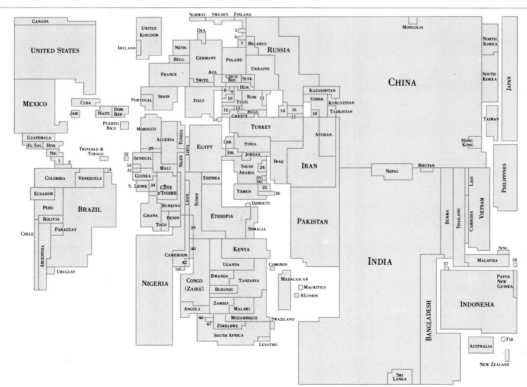

ALASKA

3.5 PERCENT OR

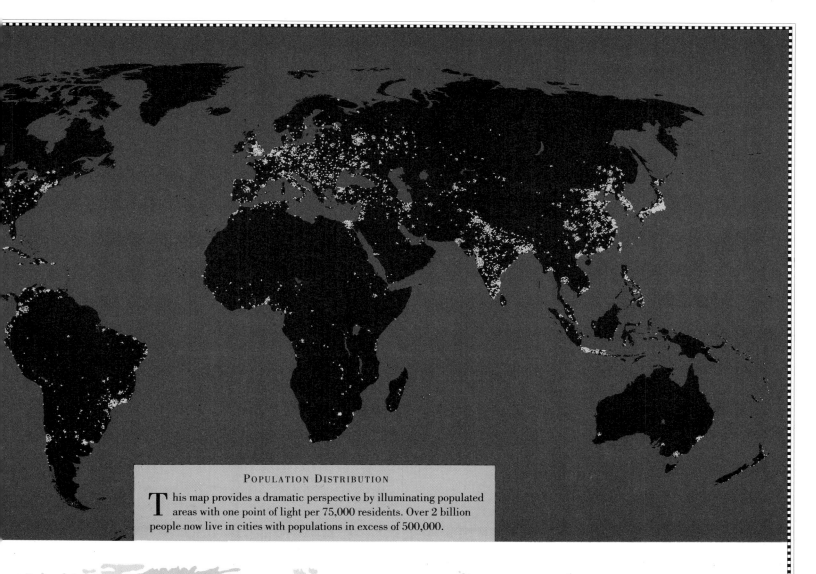

POPULATION DISTRIBUTION

This map provides a dramatic perspective by illuminating populated areas with one point of light per 75,000 residents. Over 2 billion people now live in cities with populations in excess of 500,000.

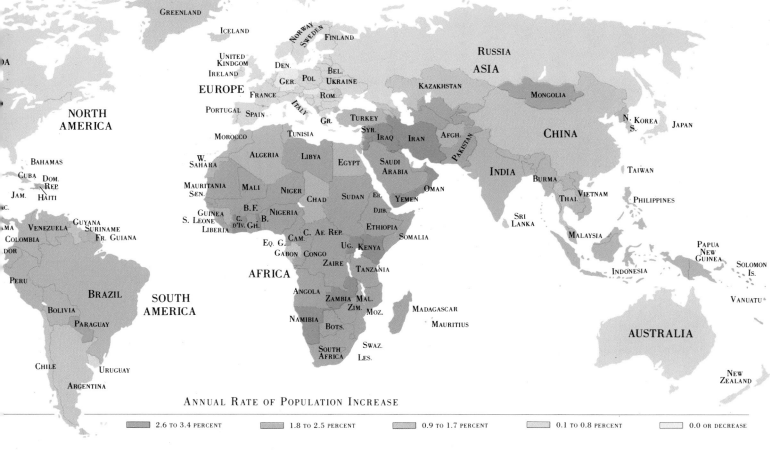

ANNUAL RATE OF POPULATION INCREASE

| 2.6 TO 3.4 PERCENT | 1.8 TO 2.5 PERCENT | 0.9 TO 1.7 PERCENT | 0.1 TO 0.8 PERCENT | 0.0 OR DECREASE |

Languages
& Religions

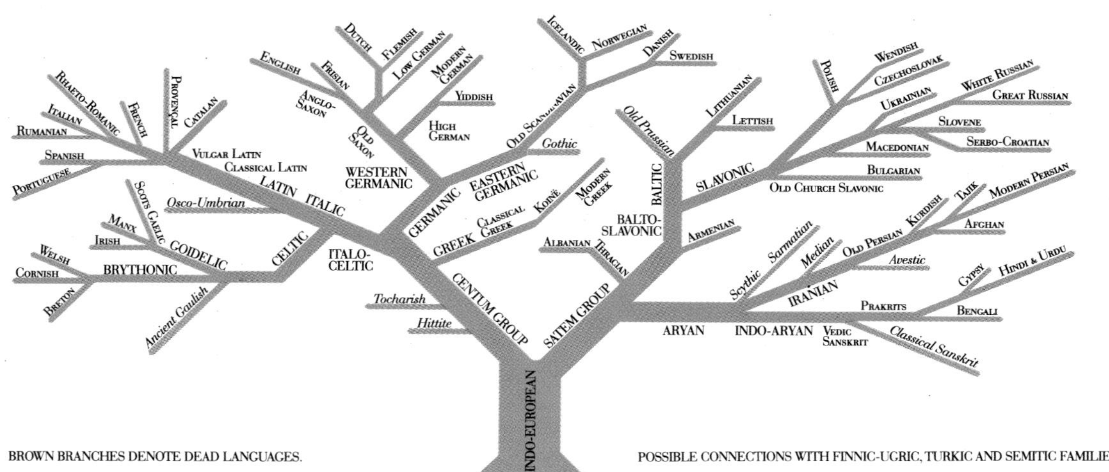

BROWN BRANCHES DENOTE DEAD LANGUAGES.

POSSIBLE CONNECTIONS WITH FINNIC-UGRIC, TURKIC AND SEMITIC FAMILIES

THE INDO-EUROPEAN LANGUAGE TREE

The most well-established family tree is Indo-European. Spoken by more than 2.5 billion people, it contains dozens of languages. Some linguists theorize that all people - and all languages - are descended from a tiny population that lived in Africa some 200,000 years ago.

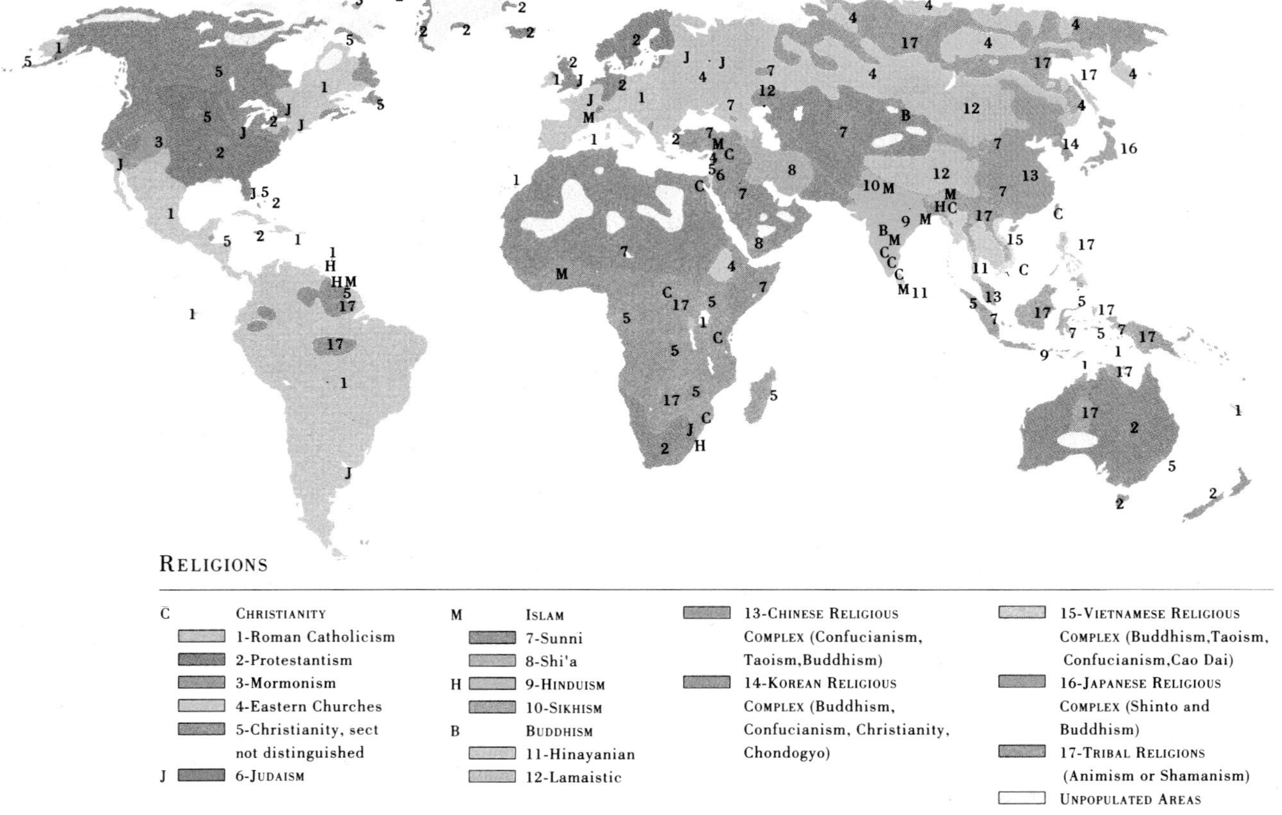

RELIGIONS

C	CHRISTIANITY	M	ISLAM		13-CHINESE RELIGIOUS COMPLEX (Confucianism, Taoism,Buddhism)	15-VIETNAMESE RELIGIOUS COMPLEX (Buddhism,Taoism, Confucianism,Cao Dai)
	1-Roman Catholicism		7-Sunni			
	2-Protestantism		8-Shi'a			
	3-Mormonism	H	9-Hinduism		14-KOREAN RELIGIOUS COMPLEX (Buddhism, Confucianism, Christianity, Chondogyo)	16-JAPANESE RELIGIOUS COMPLEX (Shinto and Buddhism)
	4-Eastern Churches		10-Sikhism			
	5-Christianity, sect not distinguished	B	BUDDHISM			17-TRIBAL RELIGIONS (Animism or Shamanism)
J	6-JUDAISM		11-Hinayanian			UNPOPULATED AREAS
			12-Lamaistic			

Important Local Minorities are Indicated by Letter

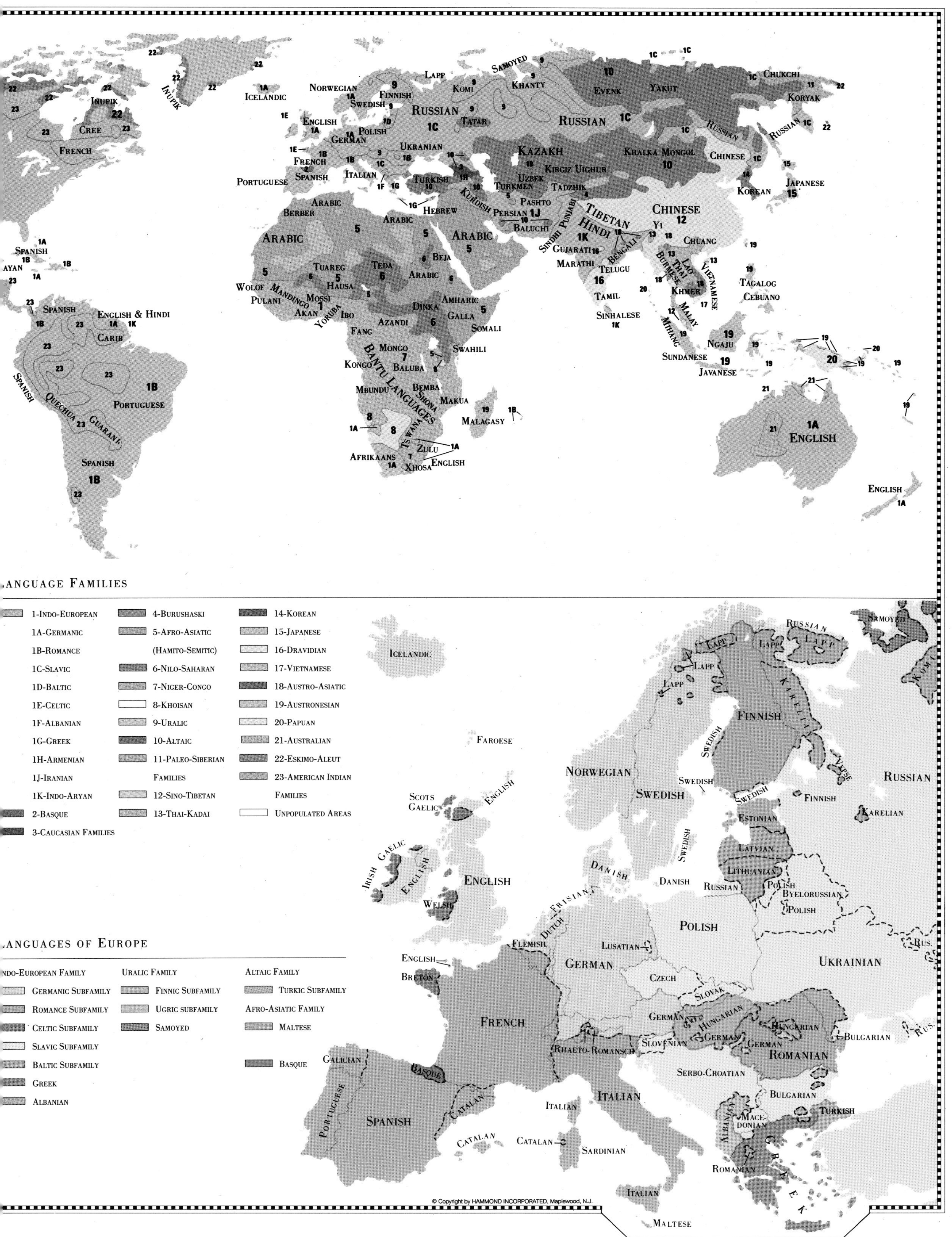
ICELANDIC
NORWEGIAN
SWEDISH
FINNISH
LAPP
KOMI
SAMOYED
KHANTY
RUSSIAN
EVENK
YAKUT
CHUKCHI
KORYAK
INUPIK
CREE
FRENCH
ENGLISH
GERMAN
POLISH
UKRANIAN
TATAR
KAZAKH
KHALKA MONGOL
CHINESE
KOREAN
JAPANESE
PORTUGUESE
SPANISH
ITALIAN
TURKISH
KIRGIZ UIGHUR
UZBEK
TURKMEN
TADZHIK
PASHTO
PERSIAN
BALUCHI
KURDISH
HEBREW
ARABIC
BERBER
TIBETAN
HINDI
SINDHI
PUNJABI
GUJARATI
BENGALI
MARATHI
TELUGU
TAMIL
SINHALESE
YI
CHUANG
LAO
THAI
BURMESE
KHMER
VIETNAMESE
MALAY
MIHANG
TAGALOG
CEBUANO
NGAJU
SUNDANESE
JAVANESE
TUAREG
TEDA
BEJA
HAUSA
WOLOF
MANDINGO
PULANI
MOSSI
AKAN
YORUBA
IBO
AMHARIC
DINKA
GALLA
SOMALI
AZANDI
FANG
MONGO
KONGO
BALUBA
SWAHILI
BANTU LANGUAGES
MBUNDU
BEMBA
SHONA
MAKUA
MALAGASY
TSWANA
ZULU
XHOSA
AFRIKAANS
CARIB
QUECHUA
GUARANI
ENGLISH & HINDI
LANGUAGE FAMILIES
1-INDO-EUROPEAN
1A-GERMANIC
1B-ROMANCE
1C-SLAVIC
1D-BALTIC
1E-CELTIC
1F-ALBANIAN
1G-GREEK
1H-ARMENIAN
1J-IRANIAN
1K-INDO-ARYAN
2-BASQUE
3-CAUCASIAN FAMILIES
4-BURUSHASKI
5-AFRO-ASIATIC (HAMITO-SEMITIC)
6-NILO-SAHARAN
7-NIGER-CONGO
8-KHOISAN
9-URALIC
10-ALTAIC
11-PALEO-SIBERIAN FAMILIES
12-SINO-TIBETAN
13-THAI-KADAI
14-KOREAN
15-JAPANESE
16-DRAVIDIAN
17-VIETNAMESE
18-AUSTRO-ASIATIC
19-AUSTRONESIAN
20-PAPUAN
21-AUSTRALIAN
22-ESKIMO-ALEUT
23-AMERICAN INDIAN FAMILIES
UNPOPULATED AREAS
LANGUAGES OF EUROPE
INDO-EUROPEAN FAMILY
GERMANIC SUBFAMILY
ROMANCE SUBFAMILY
CELTIC SUBFAMILY
SLAVIC SUBFAMILY
BALTIC SUBFAMILY
GREEK
ALBANIAN
URALIC FAMILY
FINNIC SUBFAMILY
UGRIC SUBFAMILY
SAMOYED
ALTAIC FAMILY
TURKIC SUBFAMILY
AFRO-ASIATIC FAMILY
MALTESE
BASQUE
FAROESE
SCOTS GAELIC
IRISH GAELIC
WELSH
BRETON
DANISH
FRISIAN
DUTCH
FLEMISH
KARELIA
KARELIAN
VEPSE
ESTONIAN
LATVIAN
LITHUANIAN
BYELORUSSIAN
LUSATIAN
CZECH
SLOVAK
HUNGARIAN
ROMANIAN
BULGARIAN
SLOVENIAN
RHAETO-ROMANSCH
SERBO-CROATIAN
GALICIAN
CATALAN
SARDINIAN
MACEDONIAN
GREEK
RUS.
© Copyright by HAMMOND INCORPORATED, Maplewood, N.J.

Standards of Living

ALASKA

CANADA

UNITED STATES

GREE

MEXICO

BAHAMAS

CUBA

JAM.   DOM. REP.

HAITI

BEL.   HON.

GUAT.   NIC.

EL SAL

C R.

PANAMA

VENEZUELA   GUYANA

SURINAME

COLOMBIA   FR. GUIANA

ECUADOR

PERU

BRAZIL

BOLIVIA

PARAGUAY

CHILE

URUGUAY

ARGENTINA

UNITED STATES
The economic and political influence
of women has risen substantially. In a
number of fields, women's salaries are
now nearly equal to men's.

SOUTH AMERICA
Political unrest, rising inflation and
slow economic growth continue to
thwart efforts to bring unity and pro-
perity to the nations of South Ameri

LATIN AMERICA
The gulf between rich and poor continues to widen, despite efforts to reform
oppressive governments, increase lit-
eracy and relieve overburdened cities.

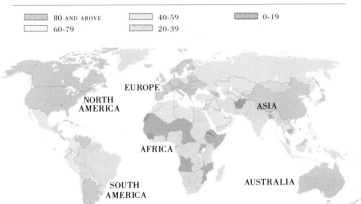

EUROPE

NORTH
AMERICA

ASIA

AFRICA

SOUTH
AMERICA

AUSTRALIA

LITERATE PERCENT OF POPULATION

80 AND ABOVE	40-59	0-19
60-79	20-39	

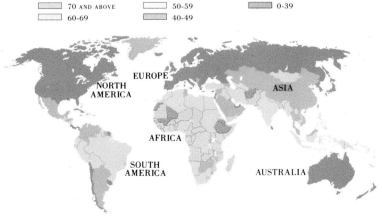

EUROPE

NORTH
AMERICA

ASIA

AFRICA

SOUTH
AMERICA

AUSTRALIA

YEARS OF LIFE EXPECTANCY (MEN AND WOMEN)

70 AND ABOVE	50-59	0-39
60-69	40-49	

EUROPE

NORTH
AMERICA

ASIA

AFRICA

SOUTH
AMERICA

AUSTRALIA

INFANT DEATHS PER 1,000 LIVE BIRTHS

150 AND MORE	50-99	0-24
100-149	25-49	

COMPARISON OF EUROPEAN, U.S. AND JAPANESE WORKERS

COUNTRY	SCHEDULED WEEKLY HOURS	ANNUAL LEAVE DAYS/HOLIDAYS	ANNUAL HOURS WORKED
GERMANY	39	42	1708
NETHERLANDS	40	43.5	1740
BELGIUM	38	31	1748
AUSTRIA	39.3	38	1751
FRANCE	39	34	1771
ITALY	40	39	1776
UNITED KINGDOM	39	33	1778
LUXEMBOURG	40	37	1792
FINLAND	40	37	1792
SWEDEN	40	37	1792
SPAIN	40	36	1800
DENMARK	40	34	1816
NORWAY	40	30	1848
GREECE	40	28	1864
IRELAND	40	28	1864
UNITED STATES	40	22	1912
SWITZERLAND	41.5	30.5	1913
PORTUGAL	45	36	2025
JAPAN	44	23.5	2116

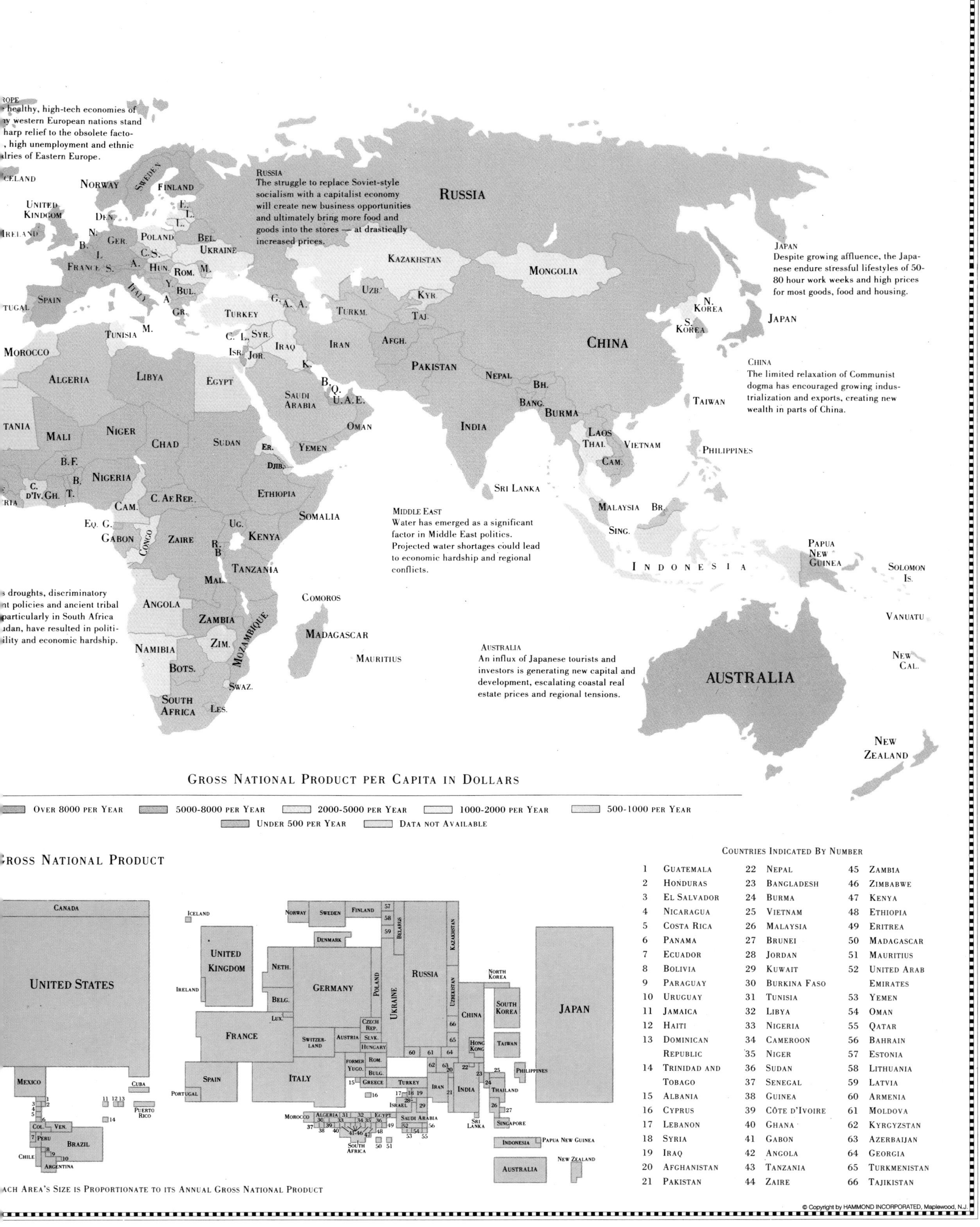

ROPE
healthy, high-tech economies of
y western European nations stand
harp relief to the obsolete facto-
, high unemployment and ethnic
alries of Eastern Europe.

ICELAND

NORWAY SWEDEN FINLAND

UNITED KINGDOM DEN. E.

IRELAND L.

N. GER. POLAND BEL.
B. L. UKRAINE
C.S.
FRANCE S. A. HUN. ROM. M.
Y. BUL.
ITALY A GR.
SPAIN M.
TUGAL TUNISIA M.

MOROCCO

ALGERIA LIBYA EGYPT

TANIA MALI NIGER CHAD SUDAN

B.F.
B.
C. NIGERIA
D'IV. GH. T.
CAM.
EQ. G.
GABON CONGO ZAIRE R. UG. KENYA
B
TANZANIA
MAL.

ANGOLA

ZAMBIA
ZIM.
NAMIBIA MOZAMBIQUE
BOTS.
SWAZ.
SOUTH
AFRICA LES.

s droughts, discriminatory
nt policies and ancient tribal
particularly in South Africa
udan, have resulted in politi-
ility and economic hardship.

RUSSIA
The struggle to replace Soviet-style
socialism with a capitalist economy
will create new business opportunities
and ultimately bring more food and
goods into the stores — at drastically
increased prices.

RUSSIA

KAZAKHSTAN

MONGOLIA

UZB. KYR.
G. A. A.
TURKM. TAJ.
TURKEY
C. L. SYR. AFGH.
ISR. JOR. IRAQ IRAN
K.
B.
Q. PAKISTAN
SAUDI U.A.E.
ARABIA NEPAL
OMAN BH.
YEMEN BANG. BURMA
ER.
DJIB.
INDIA

N. KOREA
S. KOREA

JAPAN
Despite growing affluence, the Japanese endure stressful lifestyles of 50-
80 hour work weeks and high prices
for most goods, food and housing.

JAPAN

CHINA

TAIWAN

CHINA
The limited relaxation of Communist
dogma has encouraged growing indus-
trialization and exports, creating new
wealth in parts of China.

LAOS
THAI. VIETNAM
CAM.
PHILIPPINES

ETHIOPIA

SOMALIA

SRI LANKA

MIDDLE EAST
Water has emerged as a significant
factor in Middle East politics.
Projected water shortages could lead
to economic hardship and regional
conflicts.

MALAYSIA BR.

SING.

INDONESIA

COMOROS

MADAGASCAR

MAURITIUS

AUSTRALIA
An influx of Japanese tourists and
investors is generating new capital and
development, escalating coastal real
estate prices and regional tensions.

PAPUA
NEW
GUINEA

SOLOMON
IS.

VANUATU

NEW
CAL.

AUSTRALIA

NEW
ZEALAND

GROSS NATIONAL PRODUCT PER CAPITA IN DOLLARS

OVER 8000 PER YEAR   5000-8000 PER YEAR   2000-5000 PER YEAR   1000-2000 PER YEAR   500-1000 PER YEAR

UNDER 500 PER YEAR   DATA NOT AVAILABLE

GROSS NATIONAL PRODUCT

CANADA

UNITED STATES

MEXICO

CUBA

MEXICO

COL. VEN.
PERU
CHILE BRAZIL
ARGENTINA

PUERTO
RICO

ICELAND

NORWAY SWEDEN FINLAND 57
58
59
BELARUS

UNITED
KINGDOM DENMARK

IRELAND NETH.

BELG.

LUX.

FRANCE

SPAIN

PORTUGAL ITALY

GERMANY

SWITZER-
LAND

FORMER
YUGO.

MOROCCO ALGERIA

POLAND

UKRAINE

CZECH
REP.
AUSTRIA SLVK.
HUNGARY
ROM.
BULG.
GREECE TURKEY

ISRAEL

EGYPT

RUSSIA

KAZAKHSTAN

UZBEKISTAN

CHINA

NORTH
KOREA

SOUTH
KOREA

HONG
KONG

TAIWAN

IRAN

INDIA

SAUDI ARABIA

SRI
LANKA

JAPAN

PHILIPPINES

THAILAND

SINGAPORE

INDONESIA PAPUA NEW GUINEA

NEW ZEALAND

SOUTH
AFRICA

AUSTRALIA

EACH AREA'S SIZE IS PROPORTIONATE TO ITS ANNUAL GROSS NATIONAL PRODUCT

COUNTRIES INDICATED BY NUMBER

1	GUATEMALA	22	NEPAL	45	ZAMBIA
2	HONDURAS	23	BANGLADESH	46	ZIMBABWE
3	EL SALVADOR	24	BURMA	47	KENYA
4	NICARAGUA	25	VIETNAM	48	ETHIOPIA
5	COSTA RICA	26	MALAYSIA	49	ERITREA
6	PANAMA	27	BRUNEI	50	MADAGASCAR
7	ECUADOR	28	JORDAN	51	MAURITIUS
8	BOLIVIA	29	KUWAIT	52	UNITED ARAB
9	PARAGUAY	30	BURKINA FASO		EMIRATES
10	URUGUAY	31	TUNISIA	53	YEMEN
11	JAMAICA	32	LIBYA	54	OMAN
12	HAITI	33	NIGERIA	55	QATAR
13	DOMINICAN	34	CAMEROON	56	BAHRAIN
	REPUBLIC	35	NIGER	57	ESTONIA
14	TRINIDAD AND	36	SUDAN	58	LITHUANIA
	TOBAGO	37	SENEGAL	59	LATVIA
15	ALBANIA	38	GUINEA	60	ARMENIA
16	CYPRUS	39	CÔTE D'IVOIRE	61	MOLDOVA
17	LEBANON	40	GHANA	62	KYRGYZSTAN
18	SYRIA	41	GABON	63	AZERBAIJAN
19	IRAQ	42	ANGOLA	64	GEORGIA
20	AFGHANISTAN	43	TANZANIA	65	TURKMENISTAN
21	PAKISTAN	44	ZAIRE	66	TAJIKISTAN

Energy & Resources

TOP FIVE WORLD PRODUCERS OF SELECTED MINERAL COMMODITIES

MINERAL FUELS	1	2	3	4	5
CRUDE OIL	RUSSIA	UNITED STATES	SAUDI ARABIA	CHINA	IRAQ
REFINED OIL	UNITED STATES	RUSSIA	JAPAN	CHINA	UNITED KINGDOM
NATURAL GAS	RUSSIA	UNITED STATES	CANADA	NETHERLANDS	UNITED KINGDOM
COAL (ALL GRADES)	CHINA	UNITED STATES	GERMANY	RUSSIA	POLAND
MINE URANIUM	CANADA	SOUTH AFRICA	UNITED STATES	AUSTRALIA	NAMIBIA

METALS	1	2	3	4	5
CHROMITE	SOUTH AFRICA	KAZAKHSTAN	ALBANIA	FINLAND	INDIA
IRON ORE	BRAZIL	UKRAINE	RUSSIA	CHINA	AUSTRALIA
MANGANESE ORE	FORMER USSR	SOUTH AFRICA	CHINA	GABON	AUSTRALIA
MINE NICKEL	CANADA	RUSSIA	NEW CALEDONIA	AUSTRALIA	INDONESIA
MINE SILVER	MEXICO	UNITED STATES	PERU	FORMER USSR	CANADA
BAUXITE	AUSTRALIA	GUINEA	BRAZIL	JAMAICA	FORMER USSR
ALUMINIUM	UNITED STATES	FORMER USSR	CANADA	AUSTRALIA	BRAZIL
GOLD	SOUTH AFRICA	FORMER USSR	UNITED STATES	AUSTRALIA	CANADA
MINE COPPER	CHILE	UNITED STATES	CANADA	FORMER USSR	ZAIRE
MINE LEAD	AUSTRALIA	FORMER USSR	UNITED STATES	CANADA	CHINA
MINE TIN	BRAZIL	INDONESIA	MALAYSIA	CHINA	FORMER USSR
MINE ZINC	CANADA	FORMER USSR	AUSTRALIA	CHINA	PERU

NONMETALS	1	2	3	4	5
NATURAL DIAMOND	AUSTRALIA	ZAIRE	BOTSWANA	FORMER USSR	SOUTH AFRICA
POTASH	FORMER USSR	CANADA	GERMANY	UNITED STATES	FRANCE
PHOSPHATE ROCK	UNITED STATES	FORMER USSR	MOROCCO	CHINA	TUNISIA
ELEMENTAL SULFUR	UNITES STATES	FORMER USSR	CANADA	POLAND	CHINA

Names in Black Indicate More Than 10% of Total World Production

NUCLEAR POWER PRODUCTION

PERCENTAGE OF WORLD TOTAL

United States	27.4
France	15.1
Japan	11.4
Germany	8.6
Canada	4.6
Sweden	4.1
United Kingdom	3.3
Belgium	2.5
Spain	2.5
South Korea	2.4
Czech Republic	1.3
Switzerland	1.3
Finland	1.2

COMMERCIAL ENERGY CONSUMPTION/PRODUCTION

PERCENTAGE OF WORLD TOTAL
□ 0.0 PRODUCTION ■ 0.0 CONSUMPTION

	Production / Consumption
Former USSR	23.2 / 19.3
United States	19.8 / 24.1
China	8.8 / 8.3
Canada	3.3 / 2.7
United Kingdom	3.3 / 3.0
Saudi Arabia	3.3 / 0.8
Mexico	2.5 / 1.5
Germany	2.5 / 4.9
India	2.1 / 2.3
Australia	1.9 / 1.1
Iran	1.9 / 0.7
Poland	1.8 / 1.9
Venezuela	1.7 / 0.6

Map Legend

- Oil Fields
- Natural Gas Fields
- Major Coal Deposits
- Oil Sands
- Oil Shale
- Major Uranium Deposits
- Important Peat Deposits

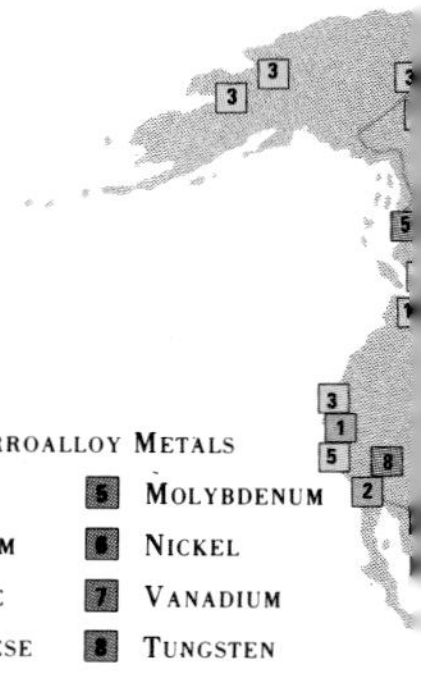

IRON AND FERROALLOY METALS
1	COBALT	5	MOLYBDENUM
2	CHROMIUM	6	NICKEL
3	IRON ORE	7	VANADIUM
4	MANGANESE	8	TUNGSTEN

OTHER METALS
1	SILVER	7	PLATINUM
2	BAUXITE	8	ANTIMONY
3	GOLD	9	TIN
4	COPPER	10	TITANIUM
5	MERCURY	11	ZINC
6	LEAD		

NONMETALS
1	ASBESTOS	10	MICA
2	BORAX	11	NITRATES
3	DIAMONDS	12	OPALS
4	EMERALDS	13	PHOSPHATES
5	FLUORSPAR	14	PEARLS
6	GRAPHITE	15	RUBIES
7	IODINE	16	SULFUR
8	JADE	17	SAPPHIRES
9	POTASH		

ALASKA

UNIT

ME

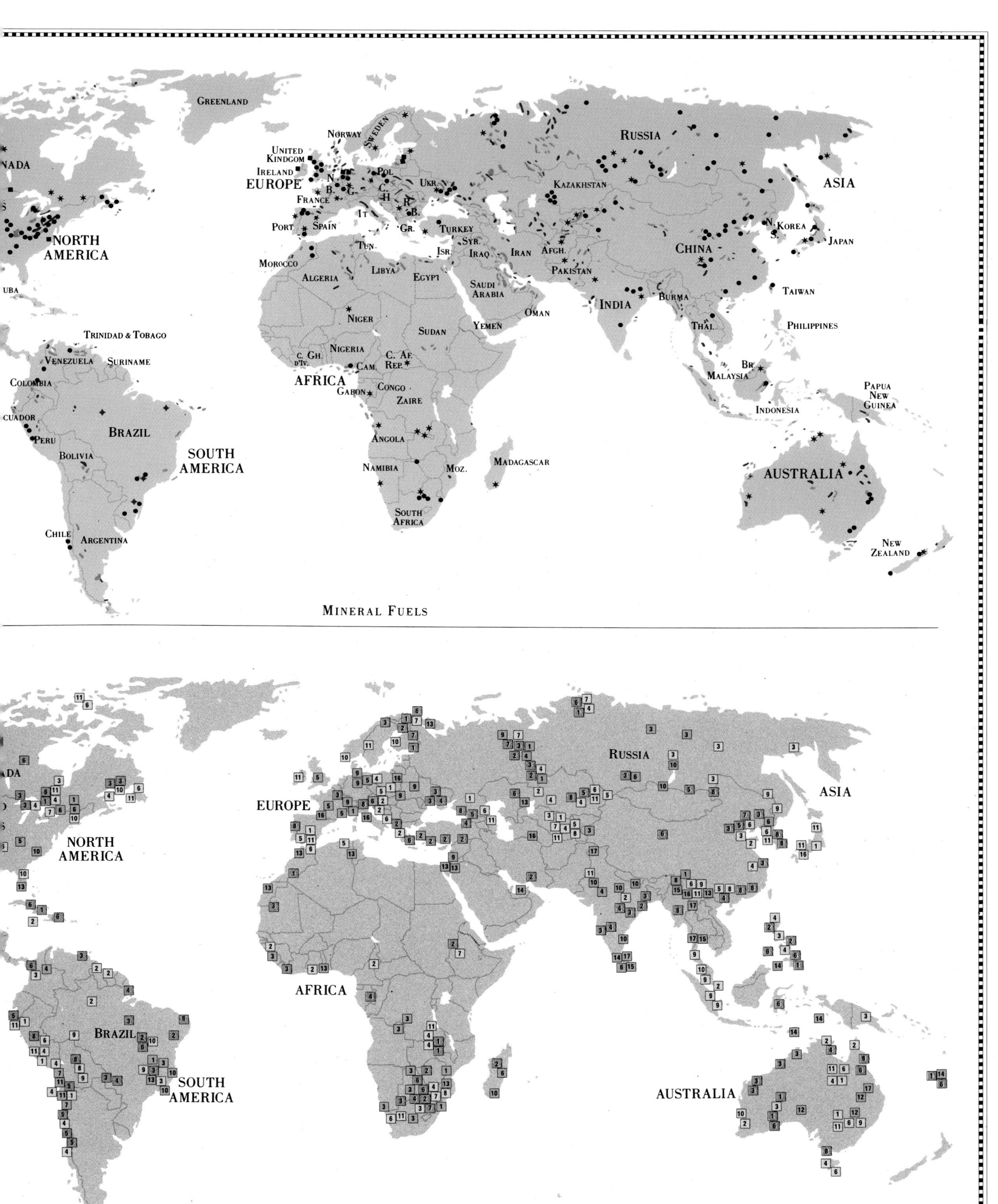
GREENLAND
NORWAY
SWEDEN
UNITED KINGDOM
IRELAND
EUROPE
FRANCE
PORT.
SPAIN
RUSSIA
KAZAKHSTAN
ASIA
N. KOREA
JAPAN
CHINA
TURKEY
SYR.
IRAQ
IRAN
AFGH.
PAKISTAN
ISR.
MOROCCO
ALGERIA
LIBYA
EGYPT
SAUDI ARABIA
OMAN
YEMEN
INDIA
BURMA
THAI.
TAIWAN
PHILIPPINES
NIGER
SUDAN
NIGERIA
C. AF. REP.
CAM.
AFRICA
GABON
CONGO
ZAIRE
ANGOLA
NAMIBIA
MOZ.
MADAGASCAR
SOUTH AFRICA
BR.
MALAYSIA
INDONESIA
PAPUA NEW GUINEA
AUSTRALIA
NEW ZEALAND
NORTH AMERICA
TRINIDAD & TOBAGO
VENEZUELA
SURINAME
COLOMBIA
PERU
BRAZIL
BOLIVIA
SOUTH AMERICA
CHILE
ARGENTINA
MINERAL FUELS
RUSSIA
EUROPE
ASIA
NORTH AMERICA
AFRICA
BRAZIL
SOUTH AMERICA
AUSTRALIA
METALS AND NONMETALS

Agriculture & Manufacturing

Top Five World Producers of Selected Agricultural Commodities

	1	2	3	4	5
Wheat	China	Former USSR	United States	India	France
Rice	China	India	Indonesia	Bangladesh	Thailand
Oats	Former USSR	United States	Canada	Germany	Poland
Corn (Maize)	United States	China	Brazil	Romania	Former USSR
Soybeans	United States	Brazil	China	Argentina	Canada
Potatoes	Russia	Poland	China	Germany	Ukraine
Coffee	Brazil	Colombia	Indonesia	Mexico	Côte d'Ivoire
Tea	India	China	Sri Lanka	Kenya	Former USSR
Tobacco	China	United States	India	Brazil	Former USSR
Cotton	China	United States	Former USSR	Pakistan	India
Cattle	Australia	Brazil	United States	China	Russia
Sheep	Australia	China	New Zealand	Russia	India
Hogs	China	United States	Russia	Germany	Brazil
Cow's Milk	United States	Germany	Russia	France	Poland
Hen's Eggs	China	United States	Russia	Japan	Brazil
Wool	Australia	Former USSR	New Zealand	China	Argentina
Roundwood	United States	Russia	China	India	Brazil
Natural Rubber	Malaysia	Indonesia	Thailand	China	India
Fish Catches	Japan	Former USSR	China	United States	Chile

Names in Black Indicate More Than 10% of Total World Production

Percent of Total Employment in Agriculture, Manufacturing and Other Industries

- Agriculture (Includes Forestry and Fishing)
- Manufacturing
- Construction
- Trade and Commerce
- Finance, Insurance, Real Estate
- Services
- Other (Includes Mining, Utilities, Transportation)

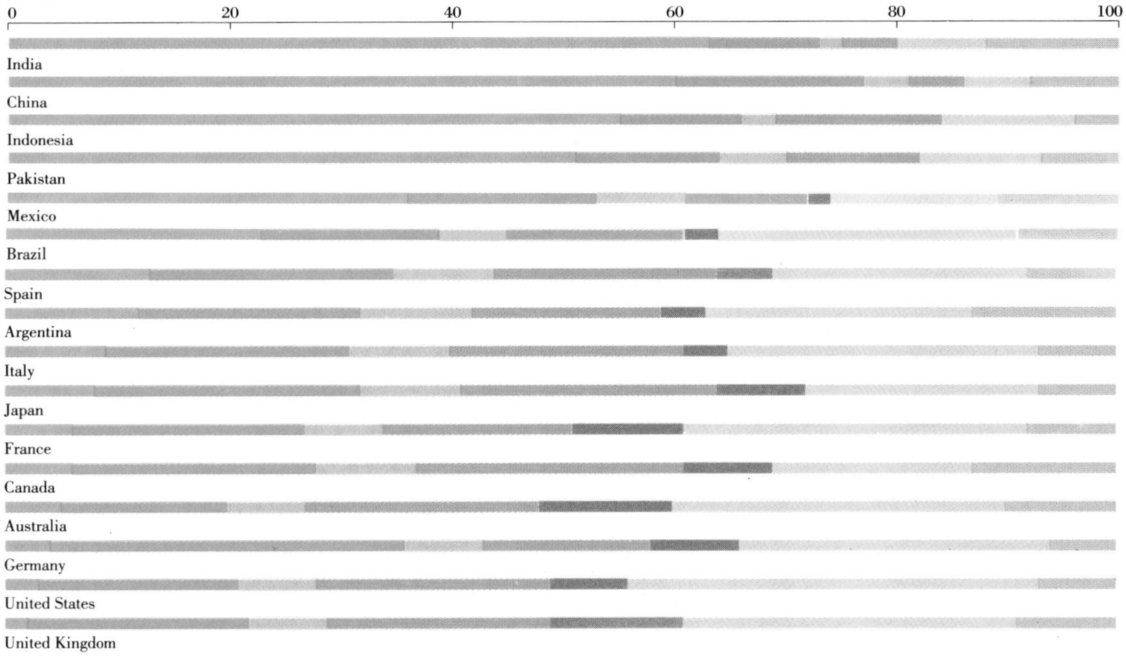

0   20   40   60   80   100

India
China
Indonesia
Pakistan
Mexico
Brazil
Spain
Argentina
Italy
Japan
France
Canada
Australia
Germany
United States
United Kingdom

Finance, Insurance, Real Estate Data Included With "Other" for India, China, Indonesia and Pakistan

Cereals, Livestock

Livestock Ranching and

Seattle - Tacoma
Chicago
San Francisco - San Jose
Southern California
St
Mexico City - Puebla

Santiago - Va

▲ Aircraft
△ Motor Vehicles
▽ Shipbuilding

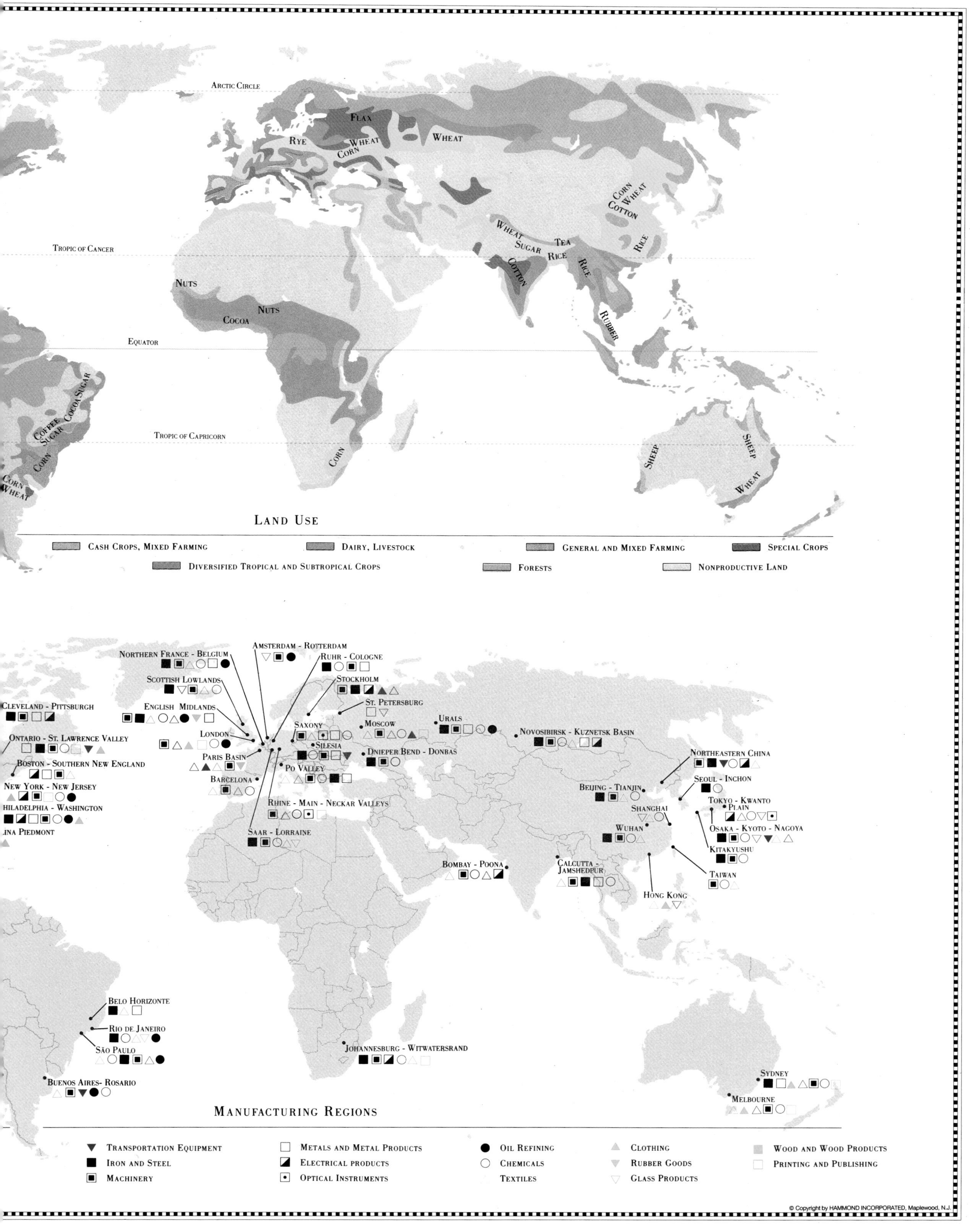

ARCTIC CIRCLE

FLAX

RYE
CORN WHEAT WHEAT
WHEAT

CORN WHEAT COTTON

TROPIC OF CANCER

WHEAT SUGAR TEA RICE
COTTON RICE RICE

NUTS

CORN WHEAT COTTON

RUBBER

NUTS
COCOA NUTS

EQUATOR

COFFEE SUGAR COCOA SUGAR

SHEEP SHEEP

CORN WHEAT

TROPIC OF CAPRICORN

CORN

SHEEP

WHEAT

LAND USE

CASH CROPS, MIXED FARMING		DAIRY, LIVESTOCK		GENERAL AND MIXED FARMING		SPECIAL CROPS
DIVERSIFIED TROPICAL AND SUBTROPICAL CROPS			FORESTS		NONPRODUCTIVE LAND	

AMSTERDAM - ROTTERDAM
NORTHERN FRANCE - BELGIUM
RUHR - COLOGNE
SCOTTISH LOWLANDS
STOCKHOLM
CLEVELAND - PITTSBURGH
ENGLISH MIDLANDS
ST. PETERSBURG
ONTARIO - ST. LAWRENCE VALLEY
SAXONY
MOSCOW
URALS
NOVOSIBIRSK - KUZNETSK BASIN
LONDON
BOSTON - SOUTHERN NEW ENGLAND
SILESIA
PARIS BASIN
NEW YORK - NEW JERSEY
DNIEPER BEND - DONBAS
NORTHEASTERN CHINA
PO VALLEY
PHILADELPHIA - WASHINGTON
BARCELONA
SEOUL - INCHON
LINA PIEDMONT
BEIJING - TIANJIN
RHINE - MAIN - NECKAR VALLEYS
TOKYO - KWANTO PLAIN
SHANGHAI
SAAR - LORRAINE
OSAKA - KYOTO - NAGOYA
WUHAN
KITAKYUSHU
BOMBAY - POONA
CALCUTTA - JAMSHEDPUR
TAIWAN
HONG KONG

BELO HORIZONTE
RIO DE JANEIRO
SÃO PAULO
JOHANNESBURG - WITWATERSRAND
BUENOS AIRES - ROSARIO

SYDNEY

MELBOURNE

MANUFACTURING REGIONS

▼ TRANSPORTATION EQUIPMENT	☐ METALS AND METAL PRODUCTS	● OIL REFINING	▲ CLOTHING	▨ WOOD AND WOOD PRODUCTS
■ IRON AND STEEL	◪ ELECTRICAL PRODUCTS	○ CHEMICALS	▼ RUBBER GOODS	☐ PRINTING AND PUBLISHING
▣ MACHINERY	⊡ OPTICAL INSTRUMENTS	TEXTILES	▽ GLASS PRODUCTS	

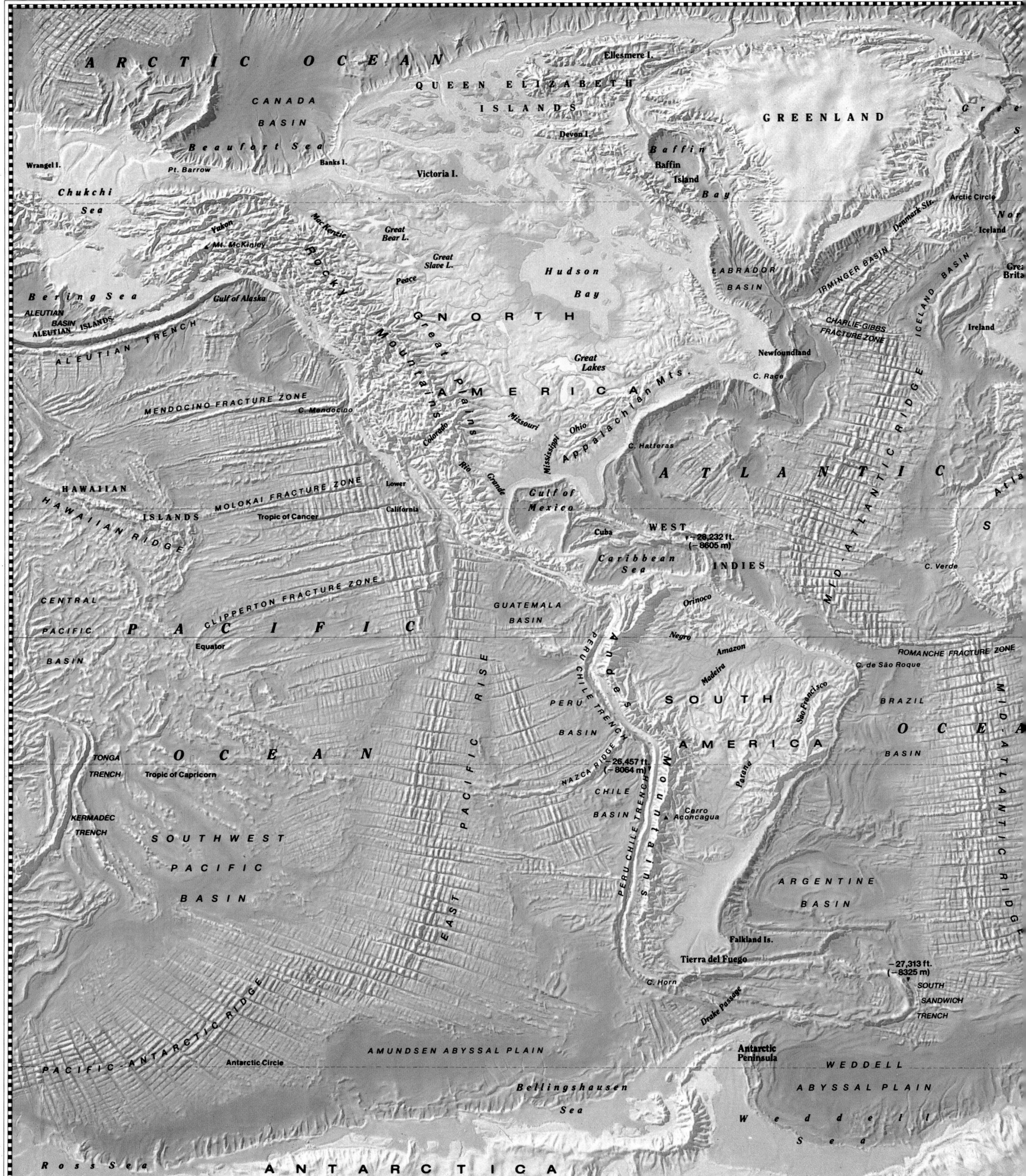

ARCTIC OCEAN
CANADA BASIN
Beaufort Sea
QUEEN ELIZABETH ISLANDS
Ellesmere I.
Devon I.
GREENLAND
Wrangel I.
Pt. Barrow
Banks I.
Victoria I.
Baffin Island
Baffin Bay
Chukchi Sea
Arctic Circle
Denmark Str.
Iceland
Yukon
Mt. McKinley
MacKenzie
Great Bear L.
Great Slave L.
Rocky Mountains
Peace
Hudson Bay
LABRADOR BASIN
IRMINGER BASIN
ICELAND BASIN
Bering Sea
Gulf of Alaska
ALEUTIAN BASIN
ALEUTIAN ISLANDS
ALEUTIAN TRENCH
NORTH AMERICA
Great Plains
CHARLIE-GIBBS FRACTURE ZONE
Ireland
Great Lakes
Newfoundland
C. Race
MENDOCINO FRACTURE ZONE
C. Mendocino
Missouri
Ohio
Appalachian Mts.
Colorado
Mississippi
C. Hatteras
Rio Grande
ATLANTIC
MID-ATLANTIC RIDGE
HAWAIIAN ISLANDS
HAWAIIAN RIDGE
MOLOKAI FRACTURE ZONE
Lower California
Tropic of Cancer
Gulf of Mexico
Cuba
WEST INDIES
28,232 ft. (−8605 m)
Caribbean Sea
C. Verde
CENTRAL PACIFIC BASIN
CLIPPERTON FRACTURE ZONE
PACIFIC
Equator
GUATEMALA BASIN
Orinoco
Negro
Amazon
Madeira
Andes Mountains
PERU CHILE TRENCH
ROMANCHE FRACTURE ZONE
C. de São Roque
EAST PACIFIC RISE
PERU BASIN
SOUTH AMERICA
São Francisco
BRAZIL BASIN
OCEAN
TONGA TRENCH
Tropic of Capricorn
NAZCA RIDGE
−26,457 ft. (−8064 m)
Paraná
CHILE BASIN
Cerro Aconcagua
KERMADEC TRENCH
SOUTHWEST PACIFIC BASIN
ARGENTINE BASIN
Falkland Is.
Tierra del Fuego
−27,313 ft. (−8325 m)
SOUTH SANDWICH TRENCH
C. Horn
Drake Passage
PACIFIC-ANTARCTIC RIDGE
AMUNDSEN ABYSSAL PLAIN
Antarctic Circle
Antarctic Peninsula
WEDDELL ABYSSAL PLAIN
Bellingshausen Sea
Weddell Sea
Ross Sea
ANTARCTICA

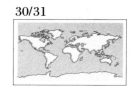

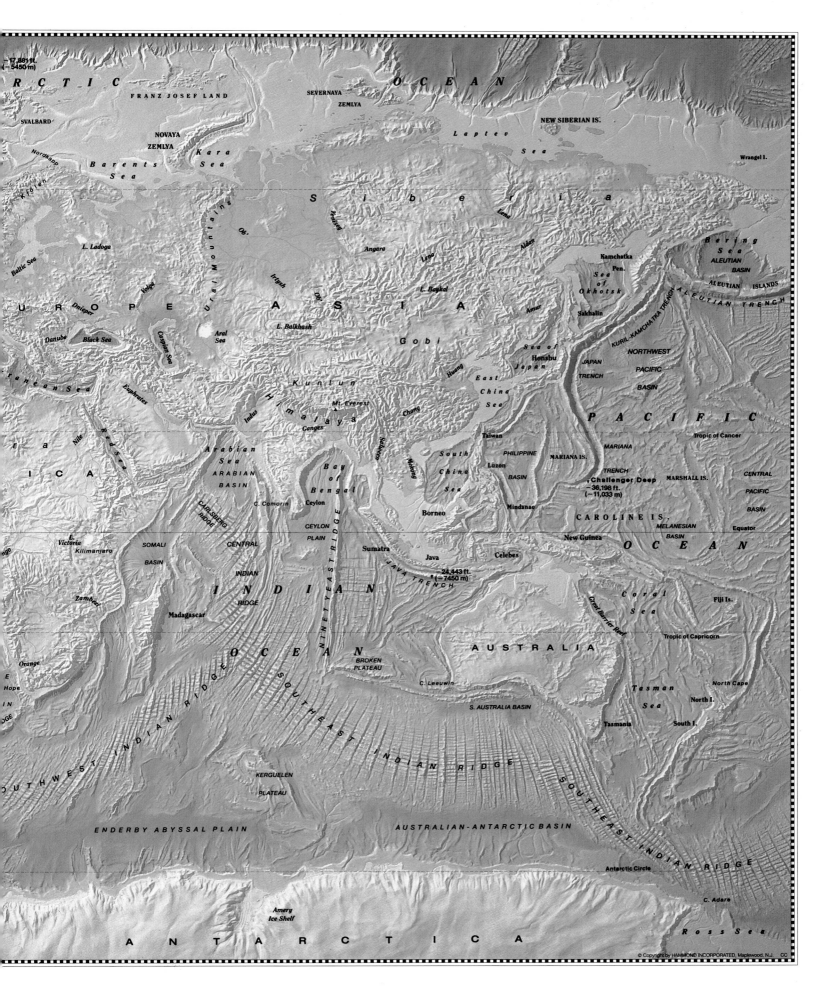

−17,881 ft.
(−5450 m)

R · C · T · I · C   O C E A N

FRANZ JOSEF LAND

SVALBARD

SEVERNAYA
ZEMLYA

NEW SIBERIAN IS.

Nordkapp

NOVAYA
ZEMLYA

Kara
Sea

Laptev
Sea

Wrangel I.

Kildin

B a r e n t s
S e a

S   i   b   e   r   i   a

Baltic Sea

L. Ladoga

Ural Mountains

Ob.

Yenisey

Angara

Lena

Aldan

B e r i n g
S e a
ALEUTIAN
BASIN

Kamchatka
Pen.

ALEUTIAN   ISLANDS

U R O P E

Volga

Dnieper

Irtysh

Ob

Lena

L. Baykal

Sea of
Okhotsk

KURIL-KAMCHATKA TRENCH

ALEUTIAN TRENCH

Danube

Black Sea

Caspian Sea

Aral
Sea

L. Balkhash

Gobi

Amur

Sakhalin

NORTHWEST

A S I A

Sea of
Japan

JAPAN
TRENCH

PACIFIC
BASIN

ranean Sea

Euphrates

Kunlun

Huang

Honshu
Japan

East
China
Sea

Nile

Red Sea

Himalaya

Mt. Everest

Chang

P A C I F I C

I C A

Indus

Ganges

Salween

Mekong

Taiwan

Tropic of Cancer

Arabian
Sea
ARABIAN
BASIN

Bay
of
Bengal

South
China
Sea

PHILIPPINE

Luzon

MARIANA IS.

MARIANA

TRENCH

MARSHALL IS.

CENTRAL

C. Comorin

Ceylon

BASIN

Challenger Deep
−36,198 ft.
(−11,033 m)

PACIFIC

CARLSBERG
RIDGE

CEYLON
PLAIN

Mindanao

CAROLINE IS.

BASIN

L.
Victoria

Kilimanjaro

SOMALI
BASIN

CENTRAL

Sumatra

Borneo

Java

Celebes

New Guinea

MELANESIAN
BASIN

Equator

O C E A N

ugo

INDIAN

−24,443 ft.
(−7450 m)

Zambezi

RIDGE

I N D I A N

Coral
Sea

Fiji Is.

Madagascar

Great Barrier Reef

Tropic of Capricorn

O C E A N

BROKEN
PLATEAU

A U S T R A L I A

Orange

Hope

C. Leeuwin

Tasman
Sea

North Cape

IN

RIDGE

S. AUSTRALIA BASIN

North I.

OUTHWEST   INDIAN   RIDGE

SOUTHEAST   INDIAN   RIDGE

Tasmania

South I.

KERGUELEN

PLATEAU

SOUTHEAST INDIAN RIDGE

Antarctic Circle

ENDERBY ABYSSAL PLAIN

AUSTRALIAN-ANTARCTIC BASIN

C. Adare

Amery
Ice Shelf

Ross Sea

A N T A R C T I C A

Europe

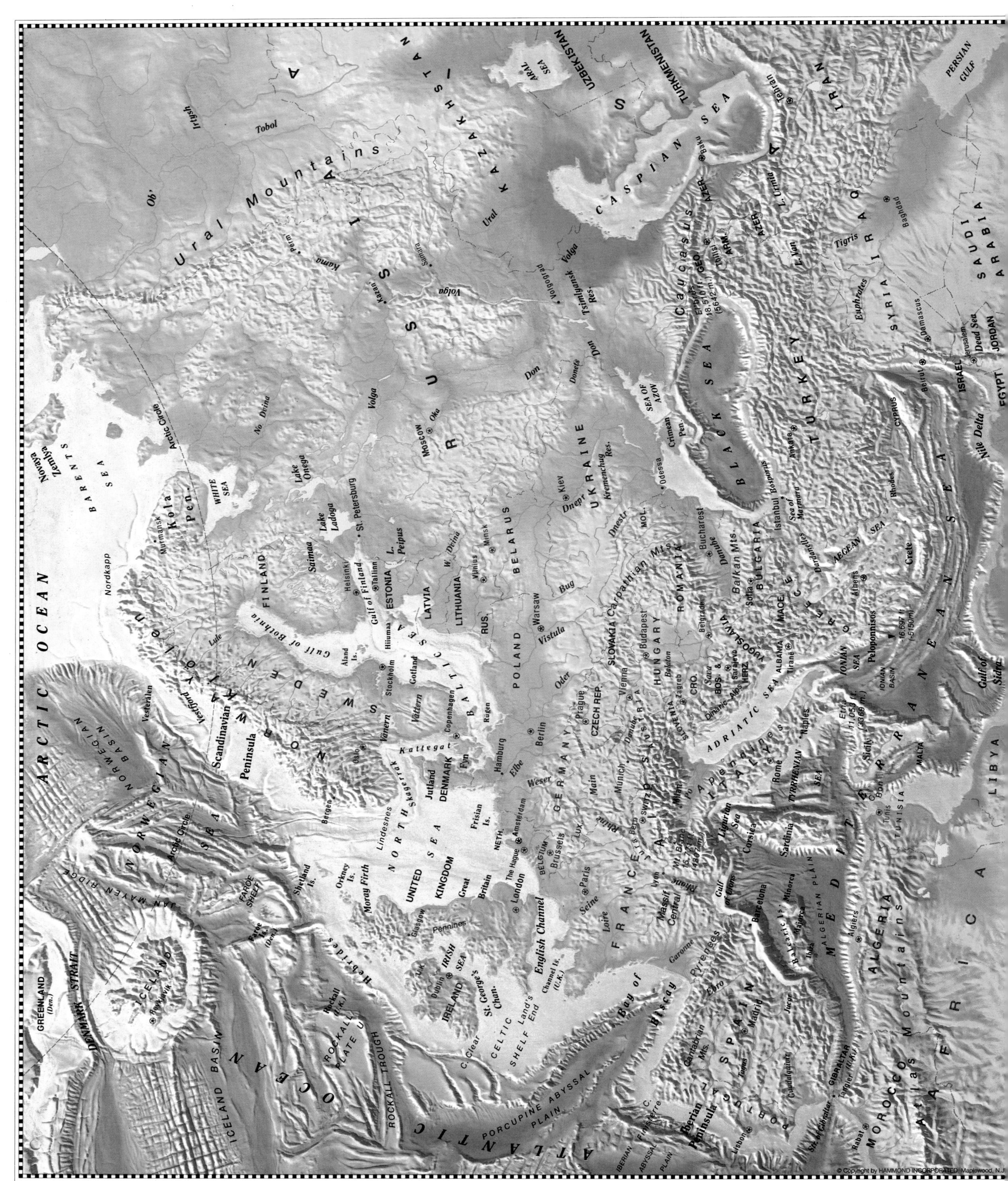

ARCTIC OCEAN
BARENTS SEA
Novaya Zemlya
WHITE SEA
Kola Pen.
Murmansk
Nordkapp
Arctic Circle
NORWEGIAN SEA
NORWEGIAN BASIN
JAN MAYEN RIDGE
ICELAND
Reykjavík
GREENLAND (Den.)
DENMARK STRAIT
FAROE SHELF
Faroe Is. (Den.)
ICELAND BASIN
ROCKALL PLATEAU
Rockall (U.K.)
ROCKALL TROUGH
ATLANTIC OCEAN
PORCUPINE ABYSSAL PLAIN
IBERIAN ABYSSAL PLAIN
CELTIC SHELF
C. Clear
Scandinavian Peninsula
Vesterålen
Vestfjord
Lule
Bergen
Oslo
Stockholm
Gulf of Bothnia
Åland Is.
Hiiumaa
Gotland
Vänern
Vättern
Kattegat
Skagerrak
Lindesnes
FINLAND
Helsinki
Gulf of Finland
Saimaa
Lake Ladoga
Lake Onega
St. Petersburg
Tallinn
ESTONIA
L. Peipus
LATVIA
LITHUANIA
Vilnius
RUS.
BELARUS
Minsk
W. Dvina
BALTIC SEA
Copenhagen
DENMARK
Jutland
Fyn
Rügen
NORTH SEA
Shetland Is.
Orkney Is.
Moray Firth
Hebrides
UNITED KINGDOM
Great Britain
Glasgow
Pennines
IRISH SEA
IRELAND
Dublin
St. George's Chan.
Land's End
London
English Channel
Channel Is. (U.K.)
Frisian Is.
NETH.
Amsterdam
The Hague
BELGIUM
Brussels
LUX.
Paris
Seine
Loire
FRANCE
Massif Central
Lyon
Rhône
Garonne
Bay of Biscay
Pyrenees
Gulf of Lions
Barcelona
Ebro
SPAIN
Madrid
Cantabrian Mts.
Tagus
Guadalquivir
Iberian Peninsula
PORTUGAL
Lisbon
C. Finisterre
Str. of Gibraltar
GIBRALTAR
Tangier
Rabat
MOROCCO
Atlas Mountains
ALGERIA
Algiers
Balearic Is.
Majorca
Minorca
Ibiza
ALGERIAN PLAIN
Corsica
Sardinia
Ligurian Sea
TUNISIA
Tunis
C. Bon
MALTA
LIBYA
Gulf of Sidra
AFRICA
MEDITERRANEAN SEA
IONIAN BASIN
IONIAN SEA
Sicily
Etna
TYRRHENIAN SEA
Rome
Naples
ITALY
Apennines
Po
Milan
Alps
SWITZ.
AUSTRIA
Vienna
Munich
Rhine
Main
Weser
Elbe
Hamburg
GERMANY
Berlin
Prague
CZECH REP.
Oder
POLAND
Warsaw
Vistula
Bug
SLOVAKIA
Carpathian Mts.
Budapest
HUNGARY
Balaton
Danube
SLOVENIA
Zagreb
CRO.
BOS. & HERZ.
Sarajevo
Sava
Dinaric Alps
Belgrade
YUGOSLAVIA
ADRIATIC SEA
ALBANIA
Tiranë
MACE.
GREECE
Athens
Peloponnisos
Crete
AEGEAN SEA
Rhodes
Sofia
BULGARIA
Balkan Mts.
ROMANIA
Bucharest
MOL.
Dnestr
Odessa
Dnepr
Kiev
UKRAINE
Kremenchug Res.
Crimean Pen.
SEA OF AZOV
BLACK SEA
Bosporus
Istanbul
Sea of Marmara
Dardanelles
Ankara
TURKEY
CYPRUS
Beirut
Damascus
Jerusalem
Dead Sea
ISRAEL
JORDAN
EGYPT
Nile Delta
SYRIA
Euphrates
Tigris
IRAQ
Baghdad
SAUDI ARABIA
PERSIAN GULF
IRAN
Tehran
L. Urmia
L. Van
ARM.
Yerevan
Tbilisi
GEO.
AZER.
Baku
Caucasus
Elbrus
CASPIAN SEA
TURKMENISTAN
UZBEKISTAN
ARAL SEA
KAZAKHSTAN
Ural
Volga
Volgograd
Tsimlyansk Res.
Don
Donets
RUSSIA
Moscow
Oka
Kazan'
Samara
Kama
Perm
Ural Mountains
No. Dvina
Ob'
Irtysh
Tobol
ASIA

Asia

ARCTIC OCEAN

GREENLAND (Den.)

Pt. Barrow A l a s k a UNITED STATES

LOMONOSOV RIDGE

MENDELEYEV RIDGE

North Pole MAKAROV BASIN

AMUNDSEN BASIN

−17,881 ft. (−5450 m)

Bering C. Dezhnev Str. Alaska Pen.

ALEUTIAN TRENCH

NANSEN BASIN

Svalbard (Nor.)

Franz Josef Ld.

BISCAY ABYSSAL PLAIN

CELTIC SHELF

IRELAND

FAROE SHELF

NORWEGIAN SHELF

NORWEGIAN SEA

VORING PLATEAU

BARENTS SEA

Severnaya Zemlya

New Siberian Is.

C. Chelyuskin

BERING SEA

ALEUTIAN BASIN

Kamchatka Peninsula

Koryak Ra.

PORTUGAL

English Chan.

UNITED KINGDOM

London NORTH SEA

Nordkapp

Novaya Zemlya

KARA SEA

LAPTEV SEA

BOWERS RIDGE

Paris

FRANCE BELG. NETH.

GERMANY Berlin

Rhine

DEN.

BALTIC SEA

NORWAY

SWEDEN

FINLAND

Norilsk

Arctic Circle

Lena

Yakutsk

Vilyuy

Aldan

SEA OF OKHOTSK

Sakhalin

KAMCHATKA TRENCH

Volga

POLAND

Russ. LITH.

LAT.

EST.

Moscow

Ob'

Yenisey

S i b e r i a

Kolyma

KURIL BASIN

Kuril Is.

KURIL-KAMCHATKA TRENCH

URALS

UKRAINE

BELARUS

Don

Caspian Sea

Ural Mountains

Yekaterinburg

Chelyabinsk

Tobol

Irtysh

Omsk

R U S S I A

Krasnoyarsk

Angara

Lake Baykal

Amur

Khabarovsk

Hokkaido

JAPAN BASIN

Romania

BLACK SEA

Caucasus Mts.

KAZAKHSTAN

Aqmola

Karaganda

Novosibirsk

Irkutsk

Yablonovyy Ra.

Ulaanbaatar

Great Khingan Ra.

Harbin

Shenyang

Vladivostok

SEA OF JAPAN

Honshu

TURKEY

TURKMENISTAN

Ashkhabad

UZBEKISTAN

Tashkent

Syrdar'ya

Balkhash

Alma-Ata

KYRGYZSTAN

T i e n S h a n

Ürümqi

A l t a i M t s.

MONGOLIA

G o b i

Beijing

Dalian

N. KOREA

Seoul

S. KOREA

Nagoya

Tokyo

Osaka

JAPAN

MEDITERRANEAN SEA

IRAN

Zagros Mountains

Amudar'ya

AFGHANISTAN

Kabul

Hindu Kush

K2 (Godwin Austen) 28,250 ft. (8611 m)

Taklimakan

K u n l u n

Tarim

Lanzhou

Xi'an

Taiyuan

Tianjin

Huang

YELLOW SEA

EAST CHINA SEA

RYUKYU TRENCH

IRAQ

Baghdad

Euphrates

KUWAIT

BAHRAIN

QATAR

U.A.E.

Gulf of Oman

PAKISTAN

Islamabad

Lahore

Indus

H i m a l a y a

T i b e t

C H I N A

Chengdu

Chang

Wuhan

Nanjing

Shanghai

SAUDI ARABIA

Riyadh

Mecca

Helmand

Delhi

New Delhi

NEPAL

Mt. Everest 29,028 ft. (8848 m)

BHUTAN

Brahmaputra

Chongqing

Xi

Guangzhou

HONG KONG (U.K.)

Taipei

Taiwan

Tropic of Cancer

KYUSHU-PALAU RIDGE

PARECE VELA BASIN

RED SEA

YEMEN

Aden

Gulf of Aden

Muscat

OMAN

Karachi

OWEN FRACTURE ZONE

INDUS CONE

Ahmadabad

Narbada

Bombay

Godavari

INDIA

Kanpur

Ganges

Jumna

Calcutta

BANGLADESH

Dhaka

BURMA

Hanoi

Hainan

LAOS

Guangzhou

C. Engano

PHILIPPINE BASIN

PHILIPPINE SEA

SOMALIA

Ras Asir

ARABIAN BASIN

CARLSBERG RIDGE

Hyderabad

Kistna

Madras

Bangalore

BAY OF BENGAL

GANGES CONE

Rangoon

THAILAND

Bangkok

VIETNAM

CAMBODIA

Ho Chi Minh City

SOUTH CHINA SEA

Manila

PHILIPPINES

34,440 ft. (−10,497 m)

ETHIOPIA

SOMALI BASIN

Equator

SEYCHELLES

CHAGOS-LACCADIVE RIDGE

CENTRAL INDIAN RIDGE

Comorin

Madurai

SRI LANKA (CEYLON)

Colombo

Dondra Head

MALDIVES

Andaman Is.

ANDAMAN SEA

ANDAMAN BASIN

−13,773 ft. (−4198 m)

Nicobar Is.

Gulf of Thailand

Palawan

SULU SEA

BRUNEI

Mindanao

SULU BASIN

CELEBES SEA

New Guinea

PALAU TRENCH

COMOROS

MADAGASCAR

I N D I A N O C E A N

MASCARENE BASIN

MASCARENE PLATEAU

BRITISH INDIAN OCEAN TERR.

CEYLON PLAIN

MID-INDIAN OCEAN BASIN

NINETYEAST RIDGE

COCOS BASIN

INVESTIGATOR RIDGE

JAVA TRENCH

SUNDA TRENCH

S u n d a I s l a n d s

Kuala Lumpur

MALAYSIA

SINGAPORE

SUNDA SHELF

Sumatra

Borneo

Celebes

FLORES SEA

SAVU BASIN

TIMOR TROUGH

TIMOR SEA

I N D O N E S I A

Jakarta

Java

Surabaya

LOMBOK BASIN

24,443 ft. (−7450 m)

NORTH AUSTRALIA BASIN

AUSTRALIA

PACIFIC OCEAN

© Copyright by HAMMOND INCORPORATED, Maplewood, N.J.

Africa

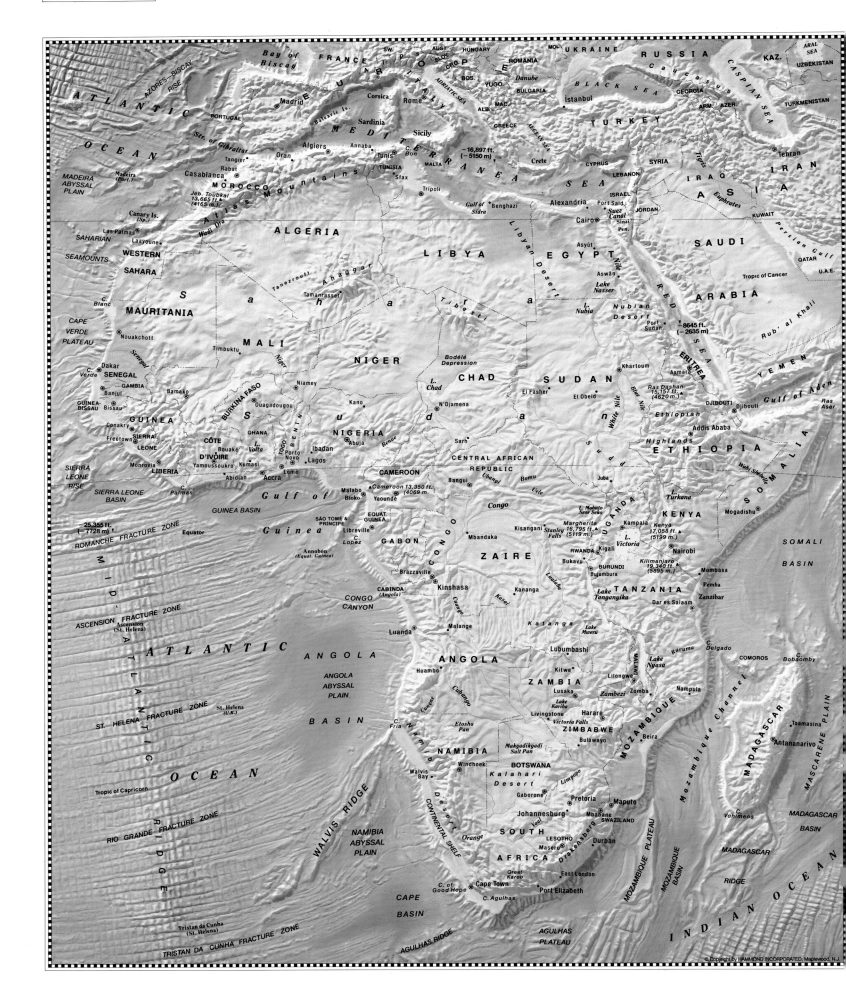

South America

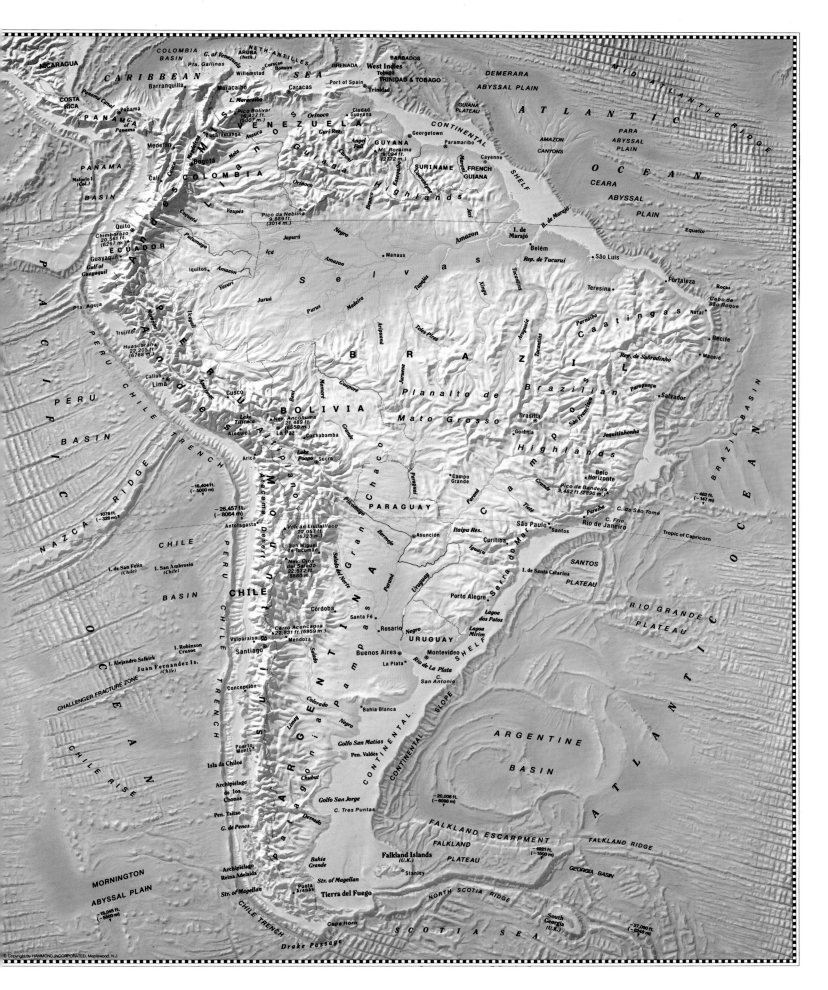

North America

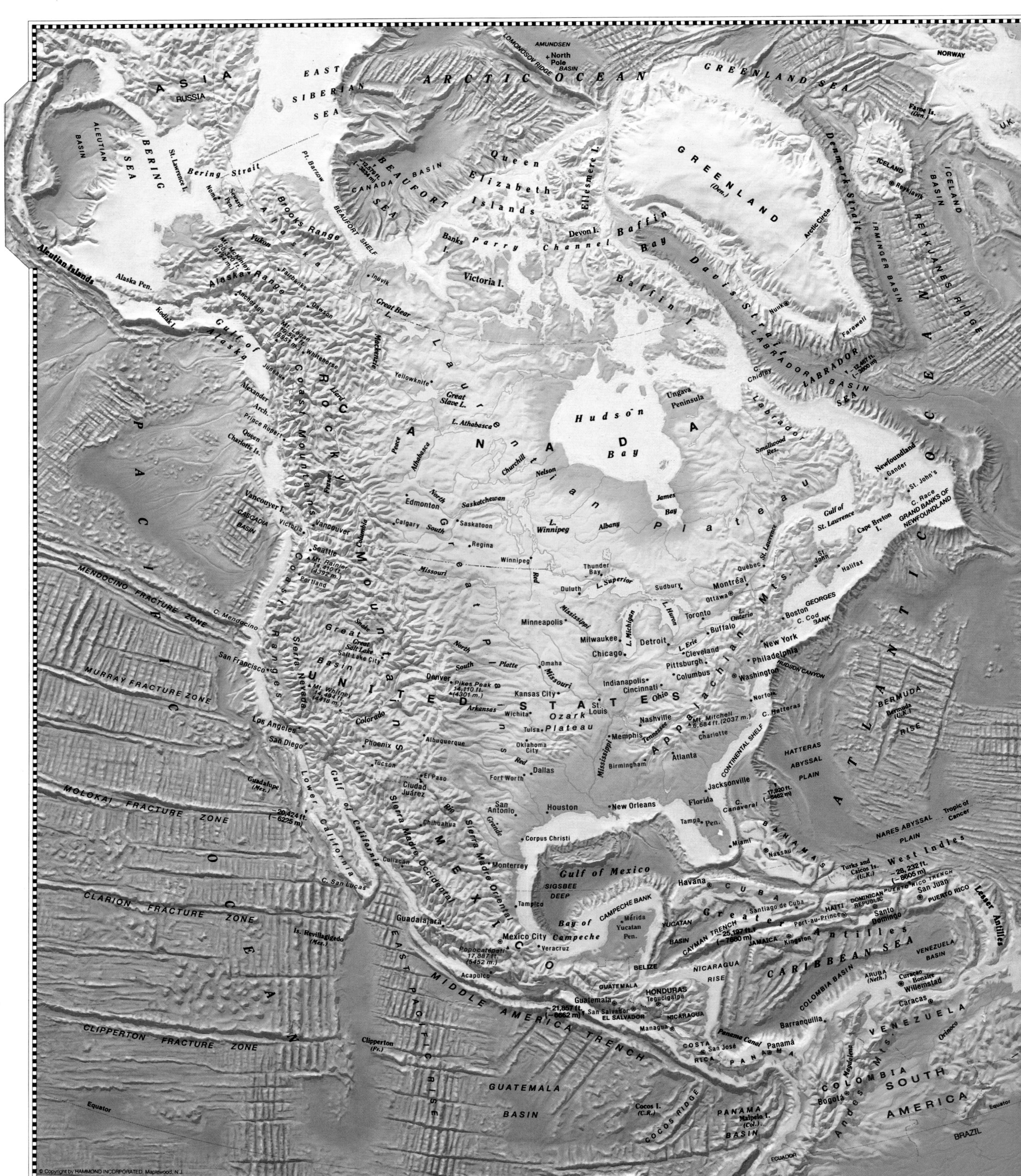

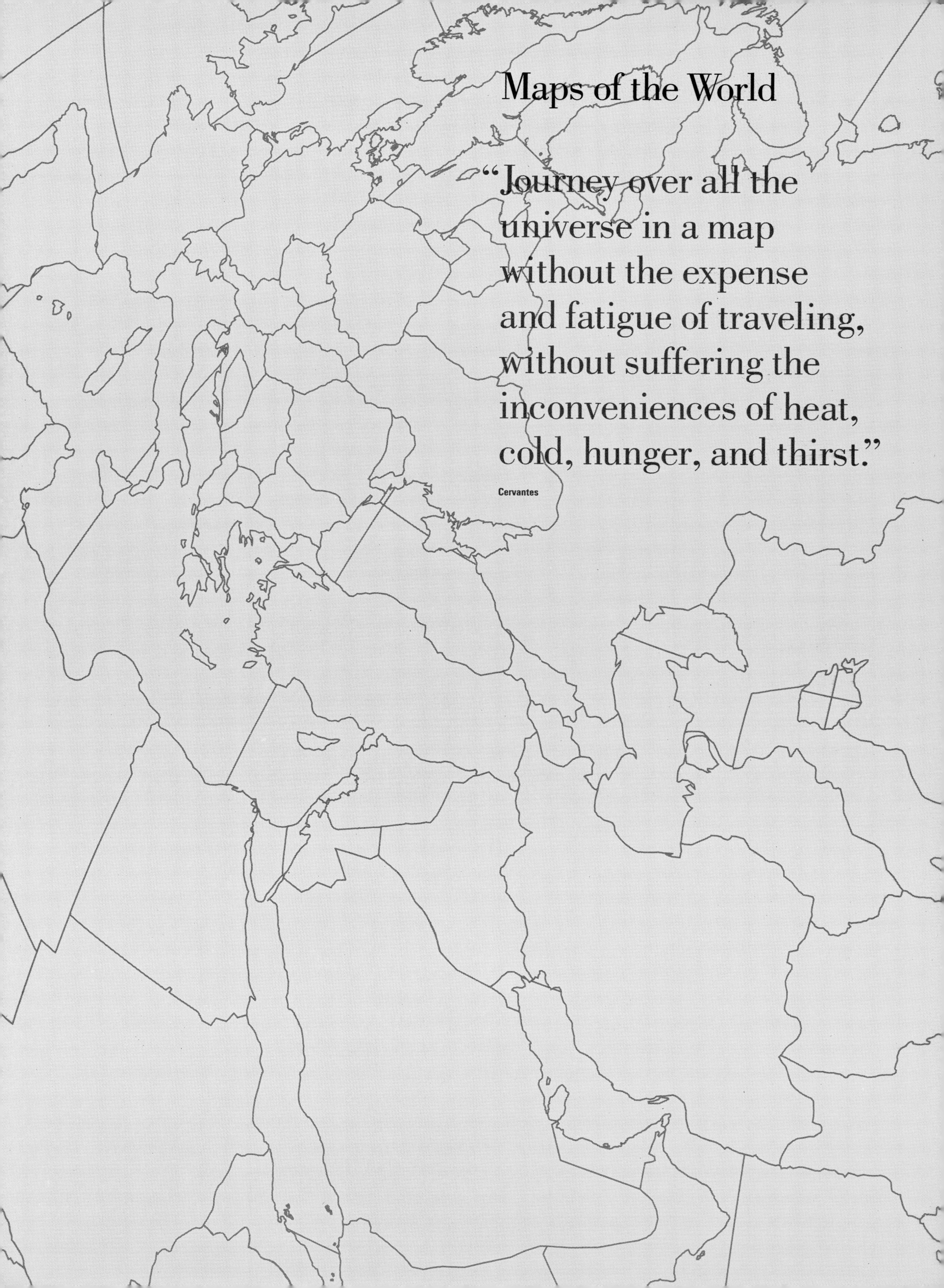

Maps of the World

"Journey over all the universe in a map without the expense and fatigue of traveling, without suffering the inconveniences of heat, cold, hunger, and thirst."

Cervantes

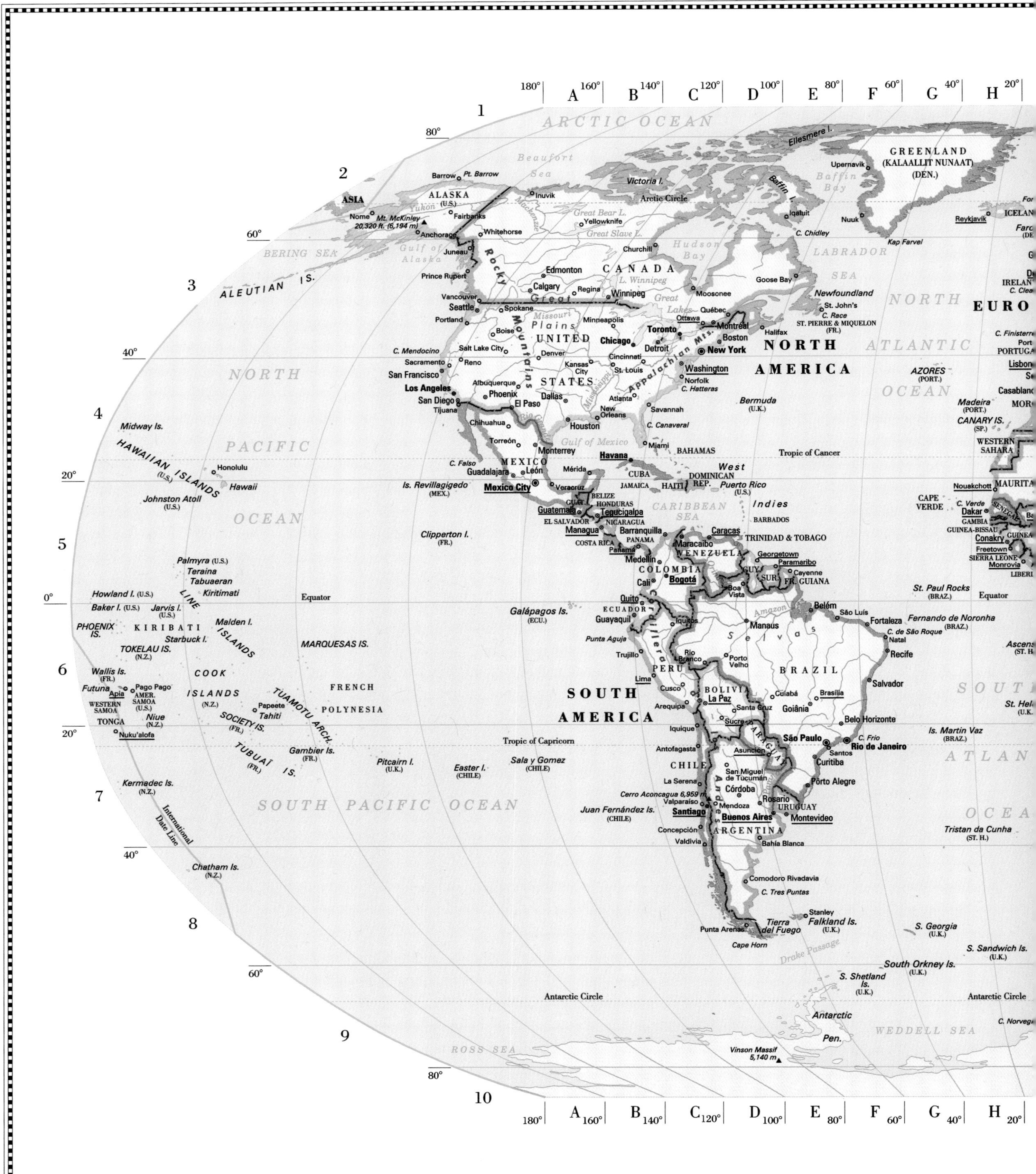

180°
A 160°
B 140°
C 120°
D 100°
E 80°
F 60°
G 40°
H 20°
1
2
3
4
5
6
7
8
9
10
80°
60°
40°
20°
0°
ARCTIC OCEAN
Ellesmere I.
GREENLAND
(KALAALLIT NUNAAT)
(DEN.)
Upernavik
Baffin Bay
Baffin I.
Beaufort Sea
Barrow
Pt. Barrow
ASIA
ALASKA
(U.S.)
Yukon
Inuvik
Victoria I.
Arctic Circle
Nome
Mt. McKinley
20,320 ft. (6,194 m)
Fairbanks
Mackenzie
Great Bear L.
Yellowknife
Great Slave L.
Iqaluit
C. Chidley
Nuuk
Reykjavík
ICELAND
Anchorage
Whitehorse
BERING SEA
Gulf of Alaska
Juneau
Rocky
Churchill
Hudson Bay
LABRADOR SEA
Kap Farvel
Edmonton
CANADA
Prince Rupert
L. Winnipeg
Goose Bay
ALEUTIAN IS.
Calgary
Regina
Winnipeg
Moosonee
Newfoundland
IRELAND
Vancouver
Seattle
Spokane
Great
Great Lakes
Québec
St. John's
C. Race
NORTH
EURO
Portland
Missouri
Plains
Minneapolis
Ottawa
Montréal
ST. PIERRE & MIQUELON
(FR.)
Boise
UNITED
Toronto
Halifax
C. Finisterre
C. Mendocino
Salt Lake City
Chicago
Detroit
Boston
NORTH
ATLANTIC
Sacramento
Reno
Denver
Appalachian Mts.
New York
Kansas City
Cincinnati
Washington
AMERICA
Lisbon
San Francisco
Mountains
St. Louis
Norfolk
AZORES
(PORT.)
NORTH
Albuquerque
STATES
C. Hatteras
OCEAN
Los Angeles
Phoenix
Dallas
Atlanta
Bermuda
(U.K.)
Madeira
(PORT.)
San Diego
El Paso
Mississippi
New Orleans
Savannah
Tijuana
CANARY IS.
(SP.)
Midway Is.
Chihuahua
Houston
C. Canaveral
PACIFIC
Torreón
Gulf of Mexico
WESTERN SAHARA
HAWAIIAN ISLANDS
(U.S.)
Monterrey
Miami
BAHAMAS
Tropic of Cancer
MEXICO
Havana
West
C. Falso
Honolulu
Guadalajara
León
Mérida
CUBA
DOMINICAN REP.
Hawaii
Is. Revillagigedo
(MEX.)
Mexico City
Veracruz
JAMAICA
HAITI
Puerto Rico
(U.S.)
Nouakchott
Johnston Atoll
(U.S.)
BELIZE
Indies
CAPE VERDE
C. Verde
Dakar
HONDURAS
CARIBBEAN SEA
OCEAN
Guatemala
Tegucigalpa
BARBADOS
GAMBIA
EL SALVADOR
NICARAGUA
Managua
Barranquilla
Caracas
GUINEA-BISSAU
Clipperton I.
(FR.)
COSTA RICA
PANAMA
TRINIDAD & TOBAGO
Conakry
Panamá
Maracaibo
VENEZUELA
Freetown
SIERRA LEONE
Palmyra (U.S.)
Georgetown
Monrovia
Teraina
Medellín
Paramaribo
Tabuaeran
COLOMBIA
GUY.
SUR.
Cayenne
Kiritimati
Cali
Bogotá
FR. GUIANA
Howland I. (U.S.)
LINE
St. Paul Rocks
(BRAZ.)
Equator
Quito
Baker I. (U.S.)
Jarvis I.
(U.S.)
Galápagos Is.
(ECU.)
ECUADOR
Belém
São Luís
Guayaquil
Amazon
Fortaleza
Fernando de Noronha
(BRAZ.)
PHOENIX IS.
KIRIBATI
Malden I.
ISLANDS
Iquitos
Manaus
C. de São Roque
Natal
Starbuck I.
Selvas
Punta Aguja
TOKELAU IS.
(N.Z.)
MARQUESAS IS.
Recife
Trujillo
Rio Branco
Porto Velho
Wallis Is.
(FR.)
COOK
PERU
BRAZIL
Futuna
Apia
Pago Pago
AMER. SAMOA
(U.S.)
FRENCH
SOUTH
Lima
Salvador
WESTERN SAMOA
ISLANDS
(N.Z.)
Papeete
POLYNESIA
AMERICA
Cusco
BOLIVIA
Cuiabá
Brasília
Niue
(N.Z.)
SOCIETY IS.
(FR.)
Tahiti
TUAMOTU ARCH.
Arequipa
La Paz
Santa Cruz
Goiânia
St. Helena
TONGA
Nuku'alofa
Sucre
Belo Horizonte
Iquique
PARAGUAY
São Paulo
C. Frio
Is. Martín Vaz
(BRAZ.)
TUBUAI IS.
(FR.)
Gambier Is.
(FR.)
Tropic of Capricorn
Antofagasta
Asunción
Rio de Janeiro
Santos
ATLANTIC
Pitcairn I.
(U.K.)
Easter I.
(CHILE)
Sala y Gomez
(CHILE)
CHILE
Curitiba
Kermadec Is.
(N.Z.)
La Serena
San Miguel de Tucumán
Córdoba
Pôrto Alegre
Cerro Aconcagua 6,959 m
Andes
SOUTH PACIFIC OCEAN
Valparaíso
Rosario
International Date Line
Juan Fernández Is.
(CHILE)
Santiago
Mendoza
URUGUAY
Buenos Aires
Montevideo
OCEAN
Tristan da Cunha
(ST. H.)
Concepción
ARGENTINA
Valdivia
Bahía Blanca
Chatham Is.
(N.Z.)
Comodoro Rivadavia
C. Tres Puntas
Stanley
Falkland Is.
(U.K.)
Tierra del Fuego
S. Georgia
(U.K.)
Punta Arenas
Cape Horn
S. Sandwich Is.
(U.K.)
Drake Passage
South Orkney Is.
(U.K.)
S. Shetland Is.
(U.K.)
Antarctic Circle
Antarctic Circle
Antarctic
Pen.
WEDDELL SEA
C. Norvegia
ROSS SEA
Vinson Massif
5,140 m

World

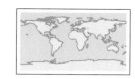

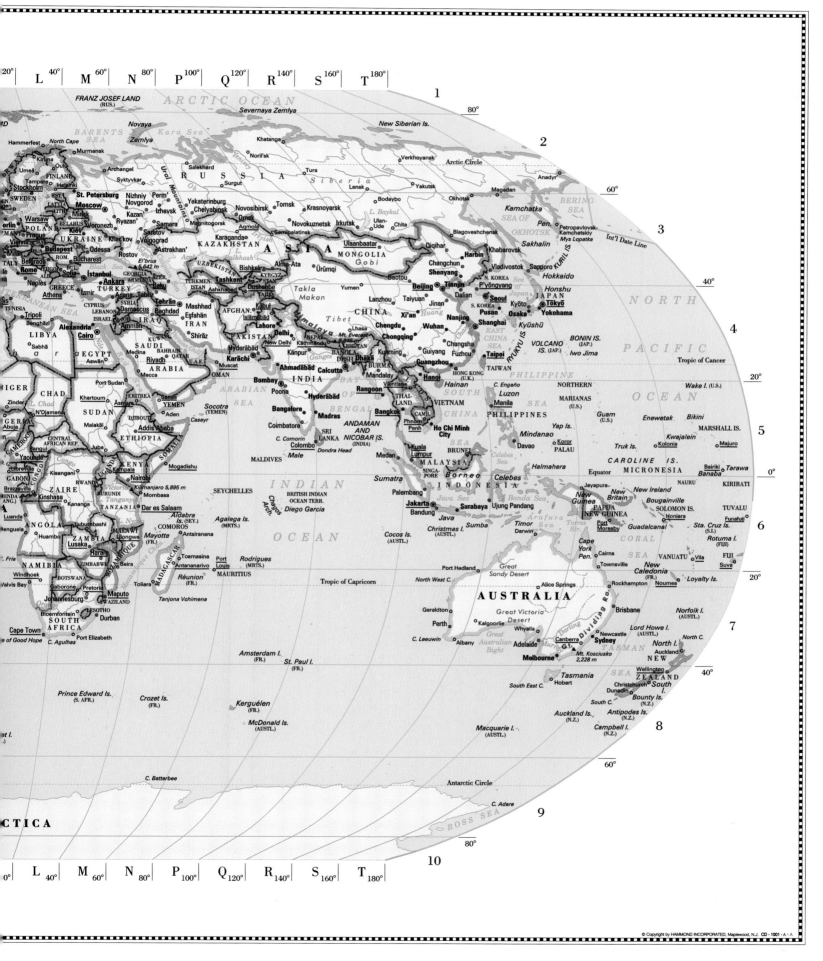

1

2

3

4

5

6

7

8

9

10

ARCTIC OCEAN

FRANZ JOSEF LAND (RUS.)

Severnaya Zemlya

80°

New Siberian Is.

BARENTS SEA

Novaya Zemlya

Kara Sea

Khatanga

Verkhoyansk

Arctic Circle

Hammerfest

North Cape

Murmansk

Archangel

Noril'sk

Tura

60°

Anadyr

Kiruna

Umeå

Oulu

FINLAND

Salekhard

Yakutsk

Magadan

Kamchatka

BERING SEA

Tampere

Helsinki

St. Petersburg

Nizhniy Novgorod

Perm'

Yekaterinburg

Chelyabinsk

Novosibirsk

Tomsk

Krasnoyarsk

Lensk

Bodaybo

L. Baykal

Irkutsk

Ulan-Ude

Chita

Blagoveshchensk

Okhotsk

SEA OF OKHOTSK

Petropavlovsk-Kamchatskiy

Mys Lopatka

Int'l Date Line

3

SWEDEN

Stockholm

Moscow

Kazan

Izhevsk

Omsk

Novokuznetsk

Semipalatinsk

Khabarovsk

Sakhalin

KURIL IS.

Warsaw

Minsk

Voronezh

Ryazan'

Samara

Saratov

Volgograd

Magnitogorsk

Aqmola

Karaganda

Ulaanbaatar

Qiqihar

Harbin

Vladivostok

Sapporo

Hokkaido

40°

POLAND

Kiev

BELARUS

Rostov

Astrakhan'

KAZAKHSTAN

ASIA

MONGOLIA

Gobi

Changchun

Shenyang

N. KOREA

P'yongyang

Honshu

JAPAN

Tokyo

Yokohama

Vienna

Budapest

ROM.

Bucharest

Odessa

UKRAINE

Kharkov

El'brus 5,642 m

Balkhash

L. Balkhash

Baotou

Beijing

Tianjin

Dalian

S. KOREA

Seoul

Pusan

Kyoto

Osaka

Kyūshū

Milan

Belgrade

Sofia

Black Sea

GEORGIA

Alma-Ata

Bishkek

KYRGYZ

Ürümqi

Lanzhou

Taiyuan

Jinan

Nanjing

Shanghai

Rome

ITALY

Istanbul

Ankara

ARMENIA

AZER.

Baku

UZBEKISTAN

Tashkent

TAJIK.

Yumen

CHINA

Xi'an

Huang

Wuhan

EAST CHINA SEA

VOLCANO IS. (JAP.)

BONIN IS. (JAP.)

Iwo Jima

Naples

GREECE

Athens

Izmir

TURKEY

Adana

SYRIA

Damascus

Tehrān

Mashhad

TURKMEN.

Ashkhabad

Dushanbe

Takla Makan

Tibet

Lhasa

Chengdu

Chongqing

Changsha

Guiyang

Fuzhou

RYUKYU IS.

Tropic of Cancer

20°

Tripoli

CYPRUS

LEBANON

ISRAEL

Baghdad

Eşfahān

AFGHAN.

Kābul

Islāmābād

Mt. Everest 8,848 m

BHUTAN

Kāthmāndu

Kunming

Guangzhou

HONG KONG (U.K.)

TAIWAN

Taipei

PHILIPPINE

Wake I. (U.S.)

Alexandria

Cairo

JOR.

Amman

IRAQ

KUWAIT

IRAN

Shirāz

PAKISTAN

Lahore

Delhi

NEPAL

BANGLA-DESH

BURMA

Mandalay

Hanoi

Hainan

C. Engaño

Luzon

NORTHERN MARIANAS (U.S.)

OCEAN

LIBYA

Sabhā

EGYPT

Aswān

SAUDI

Medina

BAHRAIN

QATAR

U.A.E.

Hyderābād

New Delhi

Kānpur

Ganges

Ahmadābād

Calcutta

Dhāka

Rangoon

Vientiane

THAI-LAND

Bangkok

CAMB.

VIETNAM

SOUTH CHINA SEA

Manila

PHILIPPINES

Guam (U.S.)

Enewetak

Bikini

MARSHALL IS.

NIGER

CHAD

Zinder

Port Sudan

Riyadh

Mecca

OMAN

Muscat

INDIA

Bombay

Poona

Hyderābād

Bangalore

Madras

Ho Chi Minh City

Yap I.

Mindanao

Davao

Koror

PALAU

Truk Is.

Kwajalein

Kolonia

Majuro

N'Djamena

Khartoum

SUDAN

ERITREA

Asmara

Sansa

YEMEN

Aden

Socotra (YEMEN)

ARABIAN SEA

Caseyr

Coimbatore

SRI LANKA

ANDAMAN AND NICOBAR IS. (INDIA)

Phnom Penh

CAROLINE IS.

MICRONESIA

Bairiki

Tarawa

NIGERIA

Abuja

CAMEROON

CENTRAL AFRICAN REP.

Juba

ETHIOPIA

Addis Ababa

Malakāl

KENYA

Mogadishu

SEYCHELLES

MALDIVES

Male

C. Comorin

Colombo

Dondra Head

Medan

Kuala Lumpur

BRUNEI

Celebes Sea

Halmahera

Equator

Jayapura

New Guinea

New Ireland

NAURU

Banaba

KIRIBATI

0°

GABON

Yaoundé

Libreville

Bangui

Kisangani

ZAIRE

Kampala

RWANDA

BURUNDI

Nairobi

Kilimanjaro 5,895 m

TANZANIA

L. Tanganyika

Mombasa

Dar es Salaam

BRITISH INDIAN OCEAN TERR.

Diego Garcia

Chagos Arch.

Sumatra

MALAYSIA

SINGA-PORE

Borneo

INDONESIA

Celebes

Palembang

Java Sea

Banda Sea

New Britain

Bougainville

SOLOMON IS.

Honiara

TUVALU

Brazzaville

Kinshasa

Luanda

Kananga

Lubumbashi

Victoria

L. Nyasa

Aldabra Is. (SEY.)

COMOROS

Agalega Is. (MRTS.)

Jakarta

Bandung

Java

Surabaya

Ujung Pandang

Sumba

Timor

Arafura Sea

PAPUA NEW GUINEA

Port Moresby

Guadalcanal

Sta. Cruz Is. (S.I.)

Rotuma I. (FIJI)

Funafuti

6

ANGOLA

Huambo

ZAMBIA

MALAWI

Lusaka

Lilongwe

Harare

Mayotte (FR.)

Antananarivo

MADAGASCAR

Toamasina

Christmas I. (AUSTL.)

Cocos Is. (AUSTL.)

Darwin

Torres Str.

Cape York Pen.

Cairns

CORAL SEA

VANUATU

Vila

FIJI

Suva

Benguela

L. Fria

NAMIBIA

ZIMBABWE

MOZAMBIQUE

Beira

Réunion (FR.)

MAURITIUS

Port Louis

Rodrigues

Tropic of Capricorn

North West C.

Port Hedland

Great Sandy Desert

Alice Springs

Townsville

Rockhampton

New Caledonia (FR.)

Noumea

Loyalty Is.

20°

Windhoek

BOTSWANA

Gaborone

Pretoria

Johannesburg

SWAZILAND

Maputo

Toliara

Tanjona Vohimena

Geraldton

Perth

AUSTRALIA

Great Victoria Desert

Whyalla

Great Australian Bight

Brisbane

Newcastle

Lord Howe I. (AUSTL.)

Norfolk I. (AUSTL.)

North C.

7

Walvis Bay

SOUTH AFRICA

Bloemfontein

LESOTHO

Durban

Port Elizabeth

Cape Town

of Good Hope

C. Agulhas

Amsterdam I. (FR.)

St. Paul I. (FR.)

C. Leeuwin

Kalgoorlie

Albany

Adelaide

Canberra

Sydney

Mt. Kosciusko 2,228 m

Melbourne

Murray

Darling

Great Dividing Ra.

Auckland I.

North I.

NEW ZEALAND

Wellington

40°

Prince Edward Is. (S. AFR.)

Crozet Is. (FR.)

Kerguélen (FR.)

McDonald Is. (AUSTL.)

Macquarie I. (AUSTL.)

Tasmania

Hobart

South East C.

TASMAN SEA

Christchurch

South I.

Dunedin

Auckland Is. (N.Z.)

Antipodes Is. (N.Z.)

Campbell I. (N.Z.)

Bounty Is. (N.Z.)

South C.

8

C. Batterbee

Antarctic Circle

60°

C. Adare

ROSS SEA

9

80°

10

ANTARCTICA

POPULATION OF CITIES AND TOWNS

◉ OVER 5,000,000   ⊙ 500,000 - 1,999,999

● 2,000,000 - 4,999,999   ○ UNDER 500,000

SCALE 1:81,700,000   ROBINSON PROJECTION   STANDARD PARALLELS 38°N AND 38°S

MILES 0 ___ 1000 ___ 2000 ___ 3000 ___ 4000

KILOMETERS 0 ___ 1000 ___ 2000 ___ 3000 ___ 4000

Europe - Comparisons

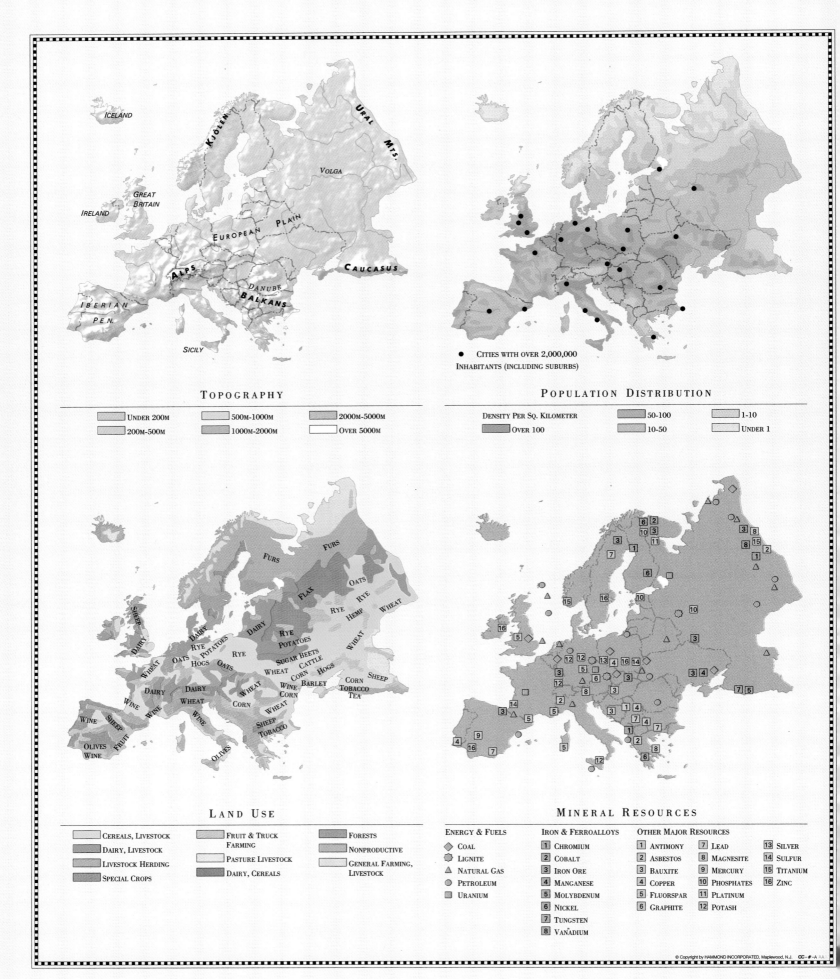

TOPOGRAPHY

UNDER 200M	500M-1000M	2000M-5000M
200M-500M	1000M-2000M	OVER 5000M

POPULATION DISTRIBUTION

● CITIES WITH OVER 2,000,000
INHABITANTS (INCLUDING SUBURBS)

DENSITY PER SQ. KILOMETER	50-100	1-10
OVER 100	10-50	UNDER 1

LAND USE

CEREALS, LIVESTOCK	FRUIT & TRUCK FARMING	FORESTS
DAIRY, LIVESTOCK	PASTURE LIVESTOCK	NONPRODUCTIVE
LIVESTOCK HERDING	DAIRY, CEREALS	GENERAL FARMING, LIVESTOCK
SPECIAL CROPS		

MINERAL RESOURCES

ENERGY & FUELS
◇ COAL
◉ LIGNITE
△ NATURAL GAS
○ PETROLEUM
▢ URANIUM

IRON & FERROALLOYS
1 CHROMIUM
2 COBALT
3 IRON ORE
4 MANGANESE
5 MOLYBDENUM
6 NICKEL
7 TUNGSTEN
8 VANADIUM

OTHER MAJOR RESOURCES
1 ANTIMONY
2 ASBESTOS
3 BAUXITE
4 COPPER
5 FLUORSPAR
6 GRAPHITE
7 LEAD
8 MAGNESITE
9 MERCURY
10 PHOSPHATES
11 PLATINUM
12 POTASH
13 SILVER
14 SULFUR
15 TITANIUM
16 ZINC

Europe

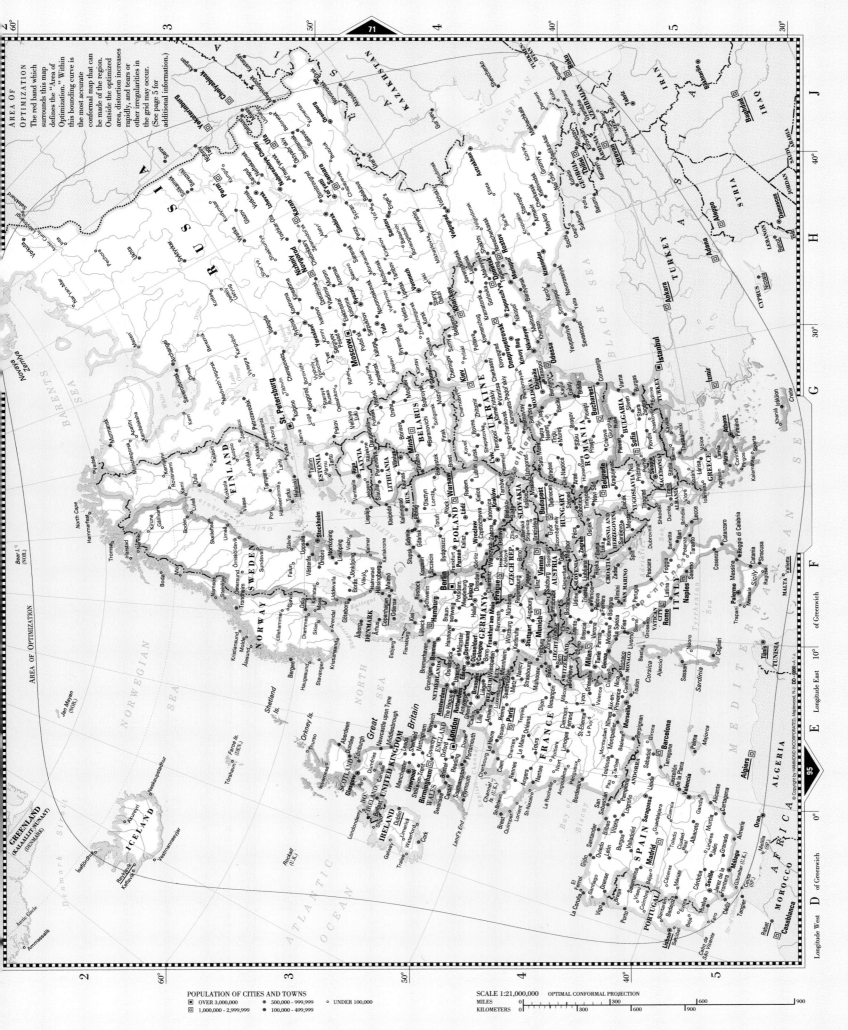

POPULATION OF CITIES AND TOWNS

- ▣ OVER 3,000,000
- ▣ 1,000,000 - 2,999,999
- ● 500,000 - 999,999
- ● 100,000 - 499,999
- ○ UNDER 100,000

SCALE 1:21,000,000   OPTIMAL CONFORMAL PROJECTION

MILES 0   300   600   900

KILOMETERS 0   300   600   900

© Copyright by HAMMOND INCORPORATED, Maplewood, N.J.

Scandinavia and Finland, Iceland

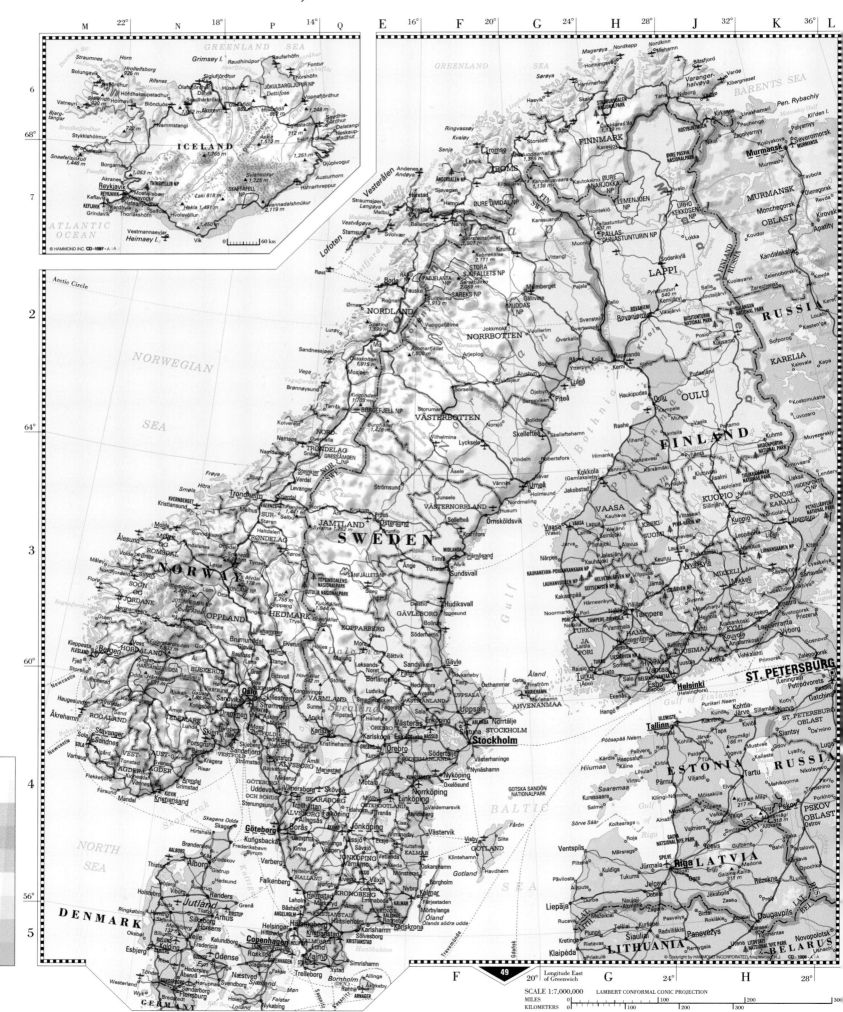

United Kingdom, Ireland

SCOTLAND

NORTHERN IRELAND

IRELAND

ENGLAND

WALES

ATLANTIC OCEAN

CELTIC SEA

IRISH SEA

NORTH SEA

ENGLISH CHANNEL

Great Britain

FRANCE

48

56

2° Longitude West of Greenwich

0° Longitude East of Greenwich

SCALE 1:3,500,000 LAMBERT CONFORMAL CONIC PROJECTION

MILES 0 50 100 150

KILOMETERS 0 50 100 150

meters	feet
6,000	19,700
4,000	13,000
2,000	6,500
1,500	5,000
1,000	3,300
500	1,600
200	700
Sea Level	
Below Sea Level	

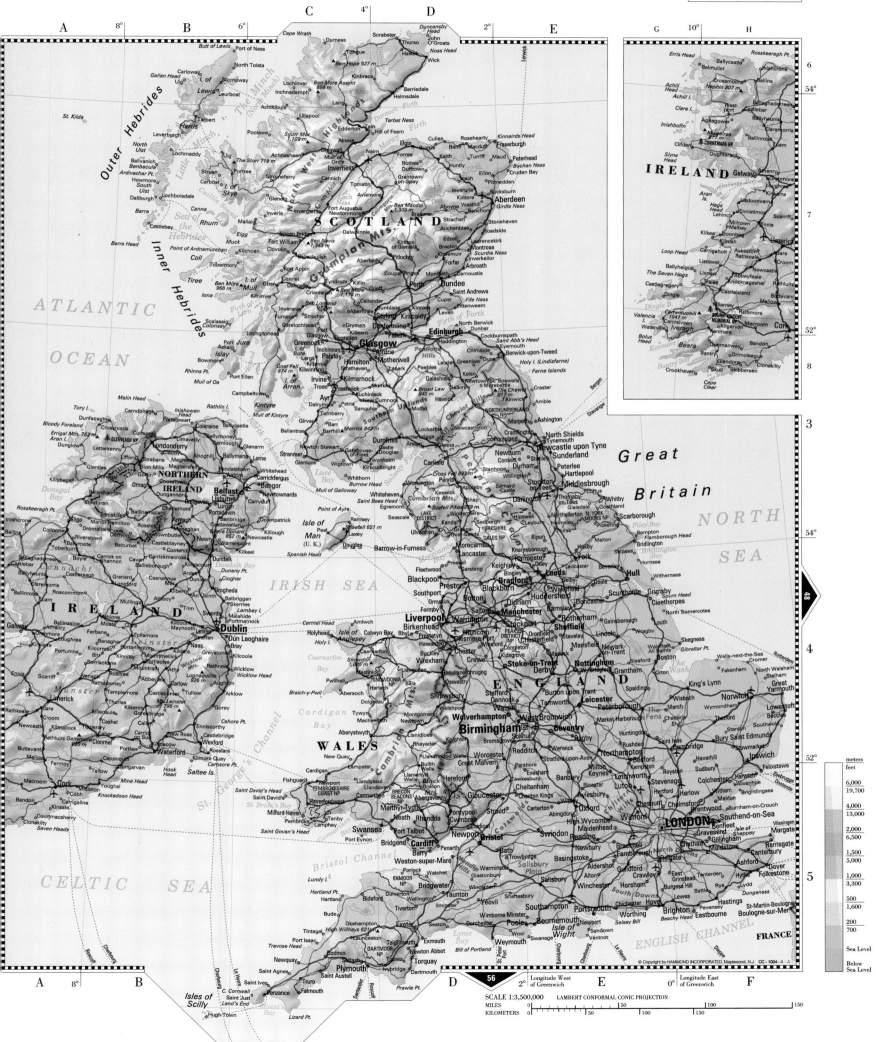

7°
B
6°
C
5°
D
4°
43
55°
2
54° 30′
3
54°
4
53° 30′
5
53°
6
A
meters
feet
4,000
13,000
3,000
9,900
2,000
6,500
1,000
3,300
500
1,600
200
700
100
330
Sea Level
Below Sea Level
NORTHERN IRELAND
IRELAND
SCOTLAND
IRISH SEA
Isle of Man
(U.K.)
UNITED KINGDOM
IRELAND
Ulster
Leinster
North Channel
Firth of Clyde
St. George's Channel
Southern
Cambrian Mts.
Inishowen Pen.
DONEGAL
Malin
Ballyliffin
Clonmany
Raghtin More 505 m
Carndonagh
Culdaff
Inishowen Head
Slieve Snaght 615 m
Greencastle
Moville
Magilligan Point
Magilligan
Castlerock
Carrowkeel
Lough Foyle
Muff
Culmore
LONDONDERRY (EGLINTON)
Limavady
Ballykelly
Eglinton
Londonderry
LONDONDERRY
New Buildings
LIMAVADY
Round Knowe 384 m
Macosquin
COLERAINE
Coleraine
Portrush
Portstewart
Bushmills
GIANT'S CAUSEWAY
Benbane Head
Dunseverick
Ballintoy
Ballycastle
MOYLE
Moss-side
Armoy
Dervock
Stranocum
Ballymoney
Kilraghts
BALLYMONEY
Agivey
Ringsend
Garvagh
Kilrea
Dunloy
Rasharkin
Cloughmills
BALLYMENA
Rathlin I.
Bull Point
Rue Point
Fair Head
Torr Head
Runabay Head
Carnanmore 379 m
Knocklayd 517 m
Cushendall
Red Bay
Garron Point
Trostan 551 m
Antrim Mts.
Carnlough
Glenarm
LARNE
Carncastle
Larne
Island Magee
Glynn
Kilwaughter
Broughshane
Cullybackey
Portglenone
Upperlands
Ahoghill
Galgorm
Ballymena
Maghera
Knockcloghrim
Tobermore
MAGHERAFELT
Draperstown
Swatragh
Glenshane Pass
Mullaghmore 555 m
Sperrin Mts.
Sawel Mtn. 678 m
Feeny
Dungiven
Claudy
Dunnamanagh
STRABANE
Plumbridge
Newtownstewart
Gortin
ULSTER AMERICAN FOLK PARK
OMAGH
Killyclogher
Omagh
Drumnakilly
Carrickmore
Sixmilecross
Beragh
Fintona
Castledawson
Bellaghy
Magherafelt
Moneymore
Dunnamore
Gulladuff
Cookstown
COOKSTOWN
Pomeroy
Coagh
The Loup
Lough Neagh
Stewartstown
Coalisland
Donaghmore
Dungannon
DUNGANNON
Castlecaulfield
Moygashel
Ballygawley
Augher
Aughnacloy
Charlemont
Moy
Benburb
Caledon
Emyvale
Fivemiletown
Slieve Beagh 382 m
FERMANAGH
Rosslea
Scotstown
Monaghan
MONAGHAN
Clones
Newbliss
Ballybay
Rockcorry
Castleblayney
Cootehill
Ballyhaise
Shercock
Carrickmacross
Cavan
CAVAN
Bailieborough
Kingscourt
Ballyjamesduff
Kilnaleck
Virginia
Mullagh
Lough Ramor
Oldcastle
Sliabh na Caillighe 278 m
Castlepollard
Clonmellon
Delvin
Athboy
WESTMEATH
Rathwire
Killucan
Kinnegad
Randalstown
ANTRIM
Antrim
Ballyclare
Ballyeaston
Parkgate
Templepatrick
Muckamore Abbey
Aldergrove
BELFAST (ALDERGROVE)
Crumlin
Glenavy
Divis 480 m
Dunmurry
Lambeg
Lisburn
LISBURN
Hillsborough
Dromore
Newtownabbey
Mallusk
Mossley
Greenisland
Ballycarry
Ballynure
Woodburn
CARRICKFERGUS
Carrickfergus
Whitehead
Black Head
Belfast Lough
Grey Pt.
Holywood
Cultra
Craigavad
Bangor
Copeland I.
NORTH DOWN
Donaghadee
Conlig
Millisle
Newtownards
Ballyferis Point
Carrowdore
Grey Abbey
Ballywalter
Ballyhalbert
Comber
ARDS
Ards Pen.
Kircubbin
Portavogie
Ringboy Point
Cloghy
Portaferry
Kearny Point
Strangford
Strangford Lough
Ballyquintin Point
BELFAST (CITY)
Belfast
BELFAST
STORMONT
Moneyreagh
Carryduff
Ballygowan
Killinchy
Derryboy
Crossgar
Killyleagh
Saintfield
Ballynahinch
Drumaness
Aghagallon
CRAIGAVON
Craigavon
Lurgan
Portadown
Waringstown
Loughgall
Richhill
Laurelvale
Tandragee
Gilford
Banbridge
BANBRIDGE
Loughbrickland
Annaclone
Slieve Croob 535 m
Lawrencetown
DOWN
Downpatrick
Ardglass
Killough
Saint John's Point
Seaforde
Castlewellan
Dundrum
Dundrum Bay
Newcastle
Armagh
ARMAGH
Milford
Middletown
Markethill
Keady
Carrigatuke 366 m
Bessbrook
Newtownhamilton
Newry
Rathfriland
Hilltown
Belleek
Slieve Gullion 577 m
MOURNE
Mourne Mts.
Slieve Donard 852 m
Slieve Binnian 746 m
Annalong
Jonesborough
Forkhill
Warrenpoint
Rostrevor
Omeath
Crossmaglen
Kilkeel
Lisnacree
Greenore
Carlingford Mtn. 587 m
Carlingford
Carlingford Lough
Ballagan Point
Cooley Point
Dundalk
Dundalk Bay
LOUTH
Louth
Tallanstown
Dromiskin
Castlebellingham
Drumcar
Dunany Point
Dunleer
Ardee
Nobber
Drumcondra
Moynalty
Collon
Clogher Head
Clogherhead
Termonfeckin
Ceanannus Mór (Kells)
Kilberry
Slane
Drogheda
Baltray
Mornington
Betaghstown
Laytown
Gormanstown
Navan (An Uaimh)
Duleek
MEATH
HILL OF TARA
Stamullen
Balbriggan
Skerries
Ballivor
Trim
Laracor
Dunshaughlin
Ratoath
Ashbourne
Lusk
Rush
Donabate
Lambay I.
Swords
Malahide
Portmarnock
Ireland's Eye
DUBLIN (COLLINSTOWN)
DUBLIN
Dunboyne
Blanchardstown
PHOENIX PARK
Drumleck Point
Dublin
Dublin Bay
Dún Laoghaire
Lucan
Clondalkin
Tallaght
Leixlip
Celbridge
Maynooth
Kilcock
Straffan
Newcastle
Rathcoole
Saggart
Rochfortbridge
Rhode
Carbury
Edenderry
Bog of Allen
Philipstown
OFFALY
Clonbullogue
Prosperous
Clane
Robertstown
Sallins
Rathangan
KILDARE
Kill
Droichead Nuadh
Naas
Rathmore
Bracknagh
Kildare
Portarlington
Monasterevin
THE CURRAGH
Kilcullen
Ballymore Eustace
Blessington
Poulaphouca
Kippure 754 m
Enniskerry
Stepaside
Bray
Bray Head
Kilmacanoge
Greystones
Sally Gap
Delgany
Djouce Mtn. 726 m
Mullaghcleevaun 850 m
Kilcoole
Newtown Mt. Kennedy
Wicklow Mts.
Togher
Wicklow Gap
Dunlavin
Stradbally
Ballitore
Athy
LAOIS (LEIX)
Baltinglass
Lugnaquillia 926 m
Rathnew
Wicklow
Wicklow Head
Glenealy
Rathdrum
WICKLOW
Castledermot
Rathvilly
Hacketstown
Aughrim
Avoca
Mizen Head
Woodenbridge
Clogh
Carlow
CARLOW
Castlecomer
Tullow
Tinahely
Croghan Mtn. 607 m
Arklow
Oldleighlin
Leighlinbridge
Shillelagh
Carnew
WEXFORD
Kilmichael Point
KILKENNY
Clonegall
Kintyre
Southend
Sanda I.
Mull of Kintyre
Maidens
Turnberry
Maybole
Crosshill
Patna
Dalmellington
Dailly
Girvan
Ailsa Craig
STRATHCLYDE
Barr
Blackcraig Hill 700 m
Cairnsmore of Carsphairn 797 m
Carsphairn
Loch Doon
Sanquhar
Colt Hill 598 m
Penpont
Thornhill
Queensberry 697 m
Closeburn
Lowther Hills
DUMFRIES
Moniaive
Corserine 813 m
Bogrie Hill 432 m
Dunscore
Lochar
Bennane Head
Ballantrae
Colmonell
Barrhill
Beneraid 439 m
Glentrool
Lamachan Hill 716 m
New Galloway
Crocketford
Milleur Point
Corsewall Point
Kirkcolm
Cairnryan
Minnigaff
Newton Stewart
Laurieston
Crossmichael
New Abbey
Criffell 596 m
Leswalt
Stranraer
Castle Kennedy
Dunragit
Glenluce
Kirkcowan
Creetown
Castle Douglas
Dalbeattie
Cairn Pat 182 m
Portpatrick
Lochans
The Rhinns
The Machars
Wigtown
Kirkinner
Gatehouse-of-Fleet
Twynholm
Palnackie
Auchencairn
Kirkcudbright
Balcary Point
Sandhead
Garlieston
Port William
Wigtown Bay
Whithorn
Luce Bay
Money Head
Mull of Logan
Abbey Head
Isle of Whithorn
Burrow Head
Drummore
Mull of Galloway
Solway
Workington
Whitehaven
Saint Bees Head
Saint Bees
Point of Ayre
Jurby Head
Bride
Ramsey Bay
Ramsey
Ballaugh
North Barrule 565 m
Maughold
Maughold Head
Kirkmichael
Snaefell 621 m
Laxey
Peel
Invermoriston
Onchan
Clay Head
South Barrule 483 m
Douglas
Bradda Head
Port Erin
Port St. Mary
ISLE OF MAN (RONALDSWAY)
Castletown
Calf of Man
Carmel Head
Amlwch
Point Lynas
Llanerchymedd
Benllech
Puffin I.
Holyhead Mtn. 220 m
Holyhead
Anglesey
Penrhyn Mawr
Holy I.
Beaumaris
Menai Bridge
Llanfair-Pwllgwyngyll
Bangor
Pen-y-Gogarth
Llandudno
Deganwy
Colwyn Bay
Conwy
Penmaenmawr
Llanfairfechan
Aber
Abergele
Bethesda
Carnedd Llewelyn 1,062 m
Carnedd Dafydd 1,044 m
Llanrwst
Caernarfon
CAERNARFON CASTLE
Llanberis
Pass of Llanberis
Capel-Curig
Betws-y-Coed
Caernarfon Bay
Snowdon 1,085 m
GWYNEDD
SNOWDONIA
Llanllyfni
Beddgelert
Blaenau Ffestiniog
Cerrig-y-Druid
Yr Eifl 564 m
Garreg
Ffestiniog
Carreg Ddu
Nefyn
Porthmadog
Criccieth
Trawsfynydd
Arenig Fawr 854 m
Lleyn Pen.
Pwllheli
Harlech
Tremadoc Bay
NAT'L PARK
Penrhyn Mawr
Abersoch
Y Llethr 754 m
Llanenddwyn
Aran 905 m
Braich-y-Pwll
Aberdaron
Trwyn Cilan
Dyffryn
Llanelltyd
Dolgellau
Bardsey I.
Cardigan Bay

Northeastern Ireland, Northern England and Wales

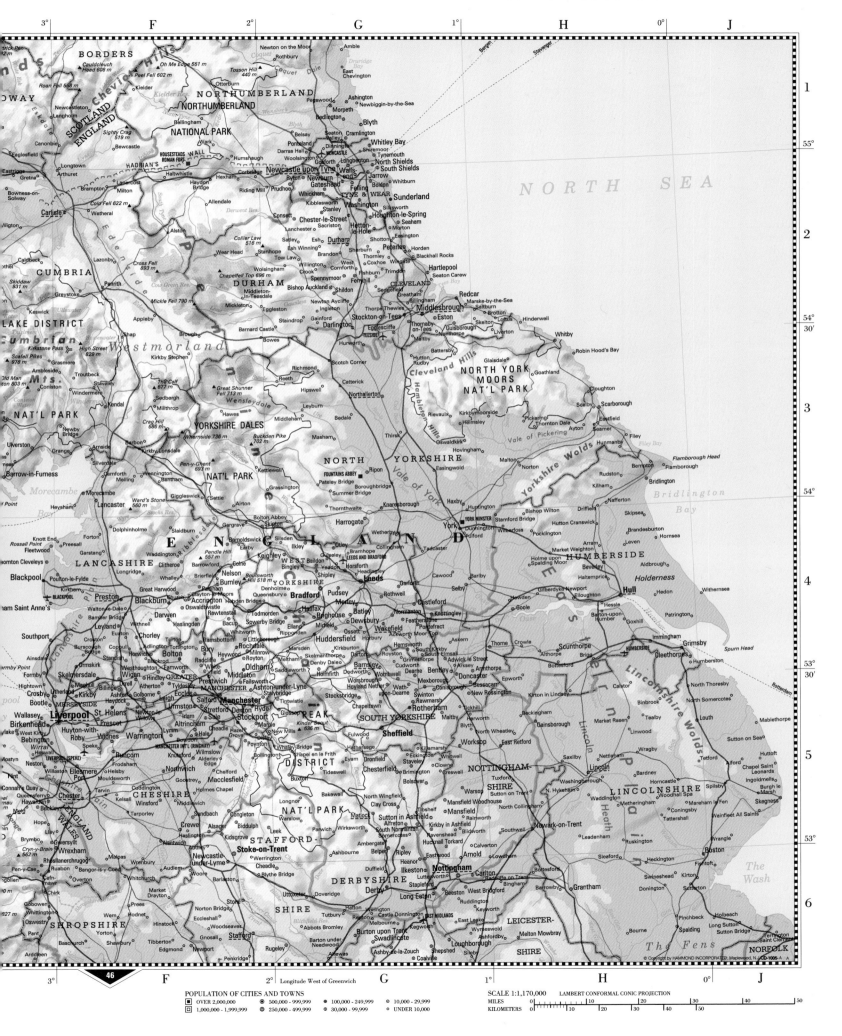

Southern England and Wales

POPULATION OF CITIES AND TOWNS

- ■ OVER 2,000,000
- ▣ 1,000,000 - 1,999,999
- ● 500,000 - 999,999
- ◉ 250,000 - 499,999
- ◉ 100,000 - 249,999
- ◎ 30,000 - 99,999
- ○ 10,000 - 29,999
- ○ UNDER 10,000

SCALE 1:1,170,000   LAMBERT CONFORMAL CONIC PROJECTION

MILES   0   10   20   30   40   50
KILOMETERS 0 10 20 30 40 50

Longitude West of Greenwich

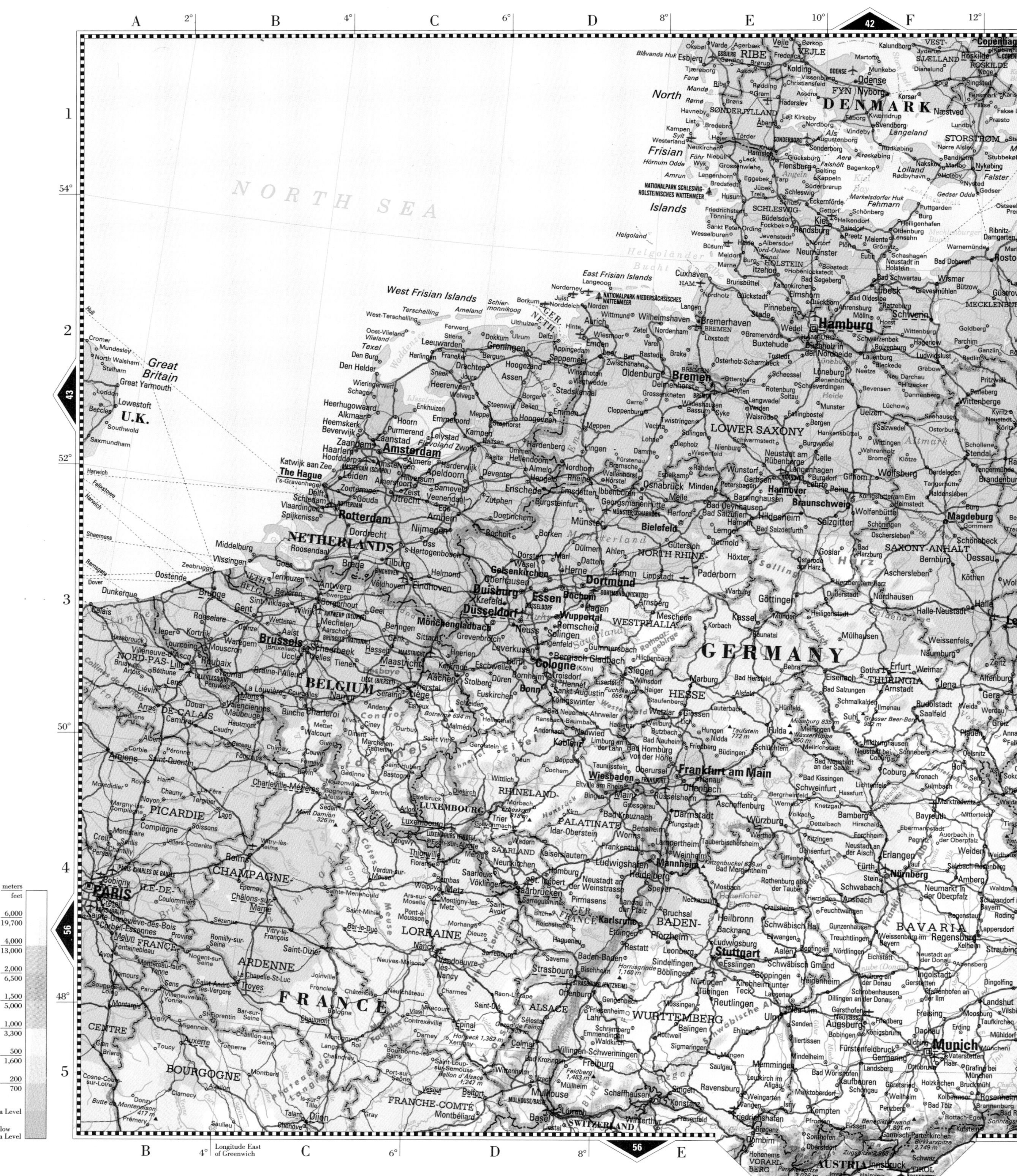

A
B
C
D
E
F
2°
4°
6°
8°
10°
12°
42
43
56
1
2
3
4
5
54°
52°
50°
48°
NORTH SEA
North
Frisian
Islands
West Frisian Islands
East Frisian Islands
DENMARK
U.K.
Great Britain
NETHERLANDS
BELGIUM
LUXEMBOURG
GERMANY
FRANCE
SWITZERLAND
AUSTRIA
LOWER SAXONY
SAXONY-ANHALT
NORTH RHINE-WESTPHALIA
HESSE
THURINGIA
RHINELAND-PALATINATE
SAARLAND
BADEN-WURTTEMBERG
BAVARIA
NORD-PAS-DE-CALAIS
PICARDIE
CHAMPAGNE-ARDENNE
ÎLE-DE-FRANCE
LORRAINE
ALSACE
BOURGOGNE
FRANCHE-COMTÉ
CENTRE
SCHLESWIG-HOLSTEIN
PARIS
Amsterdam
The Hague
Rotterdam
Brussels
Hamburg
Bremen
Hannover
Cologne
Düsseldorf
Essen
Dortmund
Frankfurt am Main
Stuttgart
Munich
Copenhagen
Odense
Magdeburg
Braunschweig
Bielefeld
Mönchengladbach
Nürnberg
Mannheim
Wiesbaden
Karlsruhe
Strasbourg
Dijon
Metz
Luxembourg
Longitude East of Greenwich
meters
feet
6,000
19,700
4,000
13,000
2,000
6,500
1,500
5,000
1,000
3,300
500
1,600
200
700
Sea Level
Below Sea Level

North Central Europe

BALTIC SEA

SWEDEN
DENMARK

RUSSIA **LITHUANIA**

Kaunas
KAUNAS

Vilnius

Kaliningrad

RUSSIA
POLAND

Gdynia
Sopot
Gdańsk

SŁUPSK
Słupsk
GDAŃSK

Koszalin
KOSZALIN

SUWAŁKI

Grodno
GRODNO OBLAST

Białystok
BIAŁYSTOK

Szczecin
SZCZECIN

BYDGOSZCZ
TORUŃ
Bydgoszcz

OLSZTYN

ŁOMŻA

BELARUS

CIECHANÓW
OSTROŁĘKA

PIŁA

GORZÓW
Gorzów Wielkopolski

WŁOCŁAWEK
Włocławek

PŁOCK
Płock

Warsaw
WARSAW

SIEDLCE
Siedlce

BRZEŚĆ OBLAST
Brzeć

POZNAŃ
Poznań

POLAND

ŁÓDŹ
Łódź

SKIERNIEWICE

LUBLIN
Lublin

BIAŁA
PODLASKA

ZIELONA
GÓRA
Zielona Góra

LESZNO

KONIN
Konin

RADOM
Radom

CHEŁM

VOLYNO
OBLAST

KALISZ

SIERADZ

PIOTRKÓW

LEGNICA
Legnica

WROCŁAW
Wrocław

KIELCE
Kielce

TARNOBRZEG

ZAMOŚĆ

Dresden

WAŁBRZYCH
Wałbrzych

OPOLE

CZĘSTOCHOWA
Częstochowa

RZESZÓW
Rzeszów

Prague

Katowice
KATOWICE
Sosnowiec

Kraków
KRAKÓW

Tarnów

PRZEMYŚL

L'viv
L'VIV OBLAST

CZECH
REPUBLIC

Ostrava

NOWY SĄCZ

KROSNO

UKRAINE

Brno

SLOVAKIA

Košice

TRANS-CARPATHIAN
OBLAST

Vienna
Bratislava
BRATISLAVA

AUSTRIA

HUNGARY

ROMANIA

BUDAPEST

SATU MARE
Satu Mare

POPULATION OF CITIES AND TOWNS

■ OVER 2,000,000	● 500,000 - 999,999	● 100,000 - 249,999	○ 10,000 - 29,999
▣ 1,000,000 - 1,999,999	◉ 250,000 - 499,999	○ 30,000 - 99,999	∘ UNDER 10,000

SCALE 1:3,500,000   LAMBERT CONFORMAL CONIC PROJECTION

MILES 0 ___ 50 ___ 100 ___ 150
KILOMETERS 0 ___ 50 ___ 100 ___ 150

Netherlands, Northwestern Germany

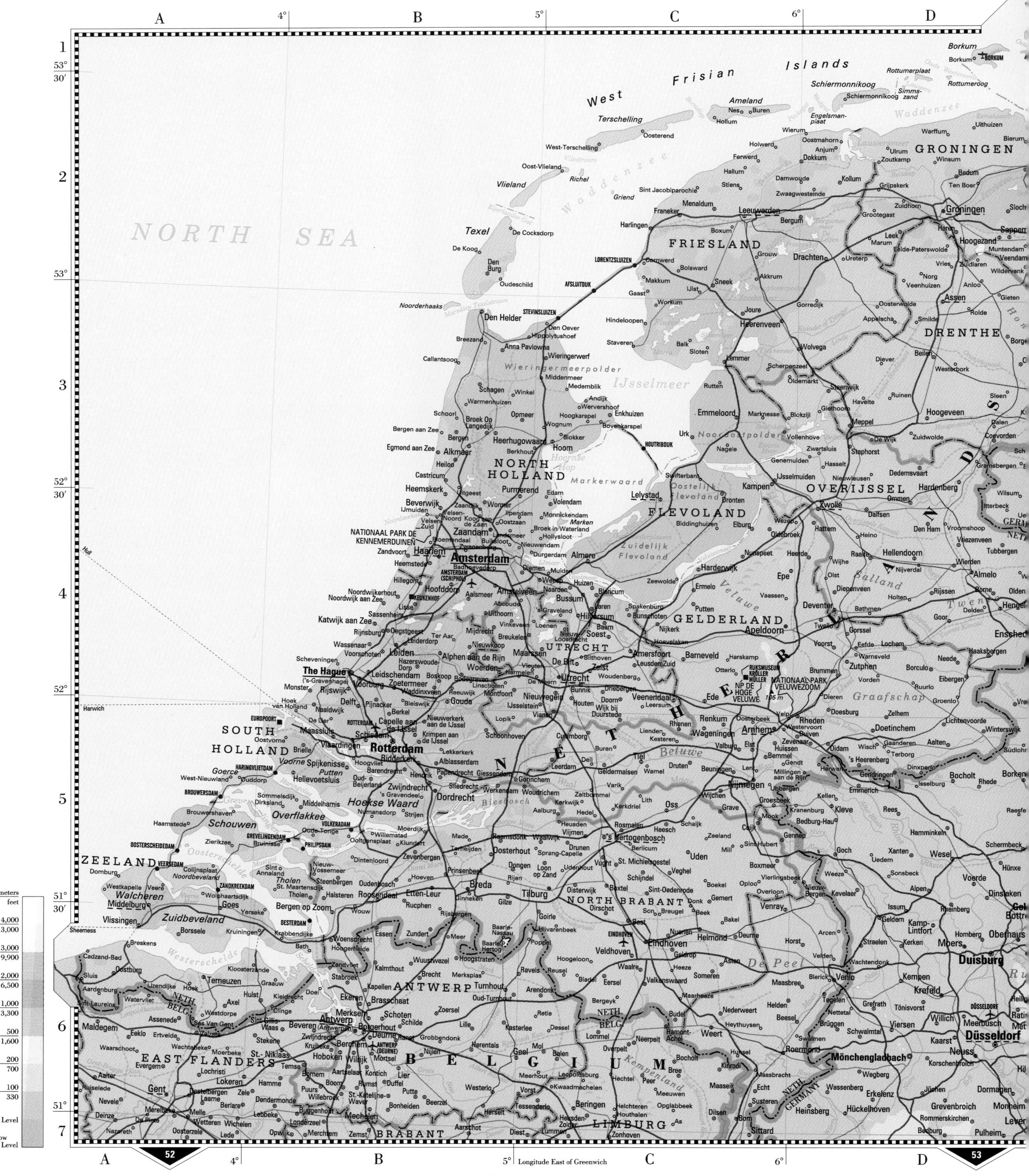

GERMANY · **LOWER SAXONY**

Frisian Islands / Ostfriesland region

Islands · Wangerooge · Wangerooge · Minsener Oog · Mellum · Oldoog · Spiekeroog · Langeoog · Baltrum · Norderney · Juist

Helgoländer Bucht · Grosser Knechtsand · Scharhörn (To Hamburg) · Neuwerk (To Hamburg) · Cuxhaven

Wilster · Brunsbüttel · Glückstadt · Freiburg · Wischhafen · Elmshorn · Bramstedt · Quickborn · Bargfeld-Stegen · Bargteheide · Ahrensburg

Nordholz · Otterndorf · Cadenberge · Osten · Drochtersen · Uetersen · Pinneberg · HAMBURG (FUHLSBÜTTEL) · Grosshansdorf · Trittau

Midlum · Dorum · Hemmoor · Hechthausen · Himmelpforten · Stade · Wedel · Blankenese · Altona · Sankt Pauli · Wandsbek · Glinde · Aumühle · SCHLESWIG-HOLSTEIN · Gudow · Zarrentin

Wremen · Langen · Bederkesa · Lamstedt · Harsefeld · Apensen · Buxtehude · Hollenstedt · **Hamburg** · Wilhelmsburg · Fischbek · Geesthacht · Büchen · MECKLENBURG-WESTERN POMERANIA

Westerholt · Wittmund · Jever · Schortens · Wilhelmshaven · Nordenham · **BREMEN** · Bremerhaven · Geestemünde · BREMERHAVEN · Bremervörde · Kutenholz · Ahlerstedt · Stelle · Winsen · Lauenburg · Hohnstorf · Boizenburg

Aurich · Friedeburg · Zetel · Bockhorn · Varel · Loxstedt · Beverstedt · Selsingen · Zeven · Tostedt · Handeloh · Hanstedt · Salzhausen · Lüneburg · Deutsch Evern · Dahlenburg · Neu Darchau

Ostfriesland · Leer · Filsum · Detern · Apen · Rastede · Oldenburg · Wiefelstede · Westerstede · Blumenthal · Schwanewede · Osterholz-Scharmbeck · Worpswede · Tarmstedt · Gyhum · Elsdorf · Heeslingen · Sittensen · Jesteburg · Brackel · Adendorf · Scharnebeck · Neetze · Bleckede

Weener · Ihrhove · Barssel · Edewecht · Elsfleth · Lemwerder · Ritterhude · Grasberg · Wilstedt · Reessum · Sottrum · Scheessel · Fintel · Schneverdingen · Bispingen · Amelinghausen · Bienenbüttel · Embsen · Melbeck · Bad Bevensen · Zernien

Papenburg · Friesoythe · Wardenburg · Hude · Ganderkesee · Delmenhorst · **BREMEN** · **Bremen** · Achim · Oyten · Ottersberg · Rotenburg · Visselhövede · Soltau · Munster · Uelzen · Rosche

Dörpen · Surwold · Esterwegen · Garrel · Dötlingen · Syke · Riede · Langwedel · Verden · Kirchlinteln · Neuenkirchen · Wietzendorf · Unterlüss · Suhlendorf · Wieren · Bodenteich

Meppen · Herzlake · Löningen · Cloppenburg · Lindern · Lastrup · Molbergen · Werlte · Visbek · Wildeshausen · Harpstedt · Bassum · Morsum · Blender · Martfeld · Hilgermissen · Hoya · Hassel · Rethem · Hodenhagen · Schwarmstedt · Hermannsburg · Eschede · Hankensbüttel · Wittingen

Haselünne · Quakenbrück · Badbergen · Dinklage · Lohne · Steinfeld · Diepholz · Kirchdorf · Landesbergen · Stolzenau · Nienburg · Steimbke · Winsen · Hambühren · Müden · Sassenburg · Wahrenholz

LOWER SAXONY · **GERMANY**

Lingen · Fürstenau · Ankum · Bersenbrück · Neuenkirchen · Bramsche · Damme · Rahden · Espelkamp · Uchte · Rehburg-Loccum · Neustadt am Rübenberge · Wedemark · Adelheidsdorf · Eicklingen · Celle · Lachendorf · Gross Oesingen

Freren · Lünne · Hopsten · Recke · Westerkappeln · Belm · Ostercappeln · Preussisch Oldendorf · Lübbecke · Minden · Stadthagen · Wunstorf · **HANNOVER** · Langenhagen · Burgwedel · Isernhagen · Burgdorf · Meinersen · Meine · Wolfsburg

Rheine · Emsdetten · Mettingen · Wallenhorst · Bad Essen · Rödinghausen · Hüllhorst · Porta Westfalica · Bückeburg · Sachsenhagen · Lindhorst · Bad Nenndorf · Ronnenberg · Gehrden · Laatzen · Sehnde · Peine · Vechelde · Edemissen · Lehrte · **BRAUNSCHWEIG** · **Braunschweig** · Königslutter am Elm · Cremlingen

Wettringen · Ibbenbüren · Lotte · **Osnabrück** · Bissendorf · Melle · Bünde · Kirchlengern · Löhne · Vlotho · Rinteln · Bad Münder am Deister · Springe · Bad Salzdetfurth · Sarstedt · Salzgitter · Schellerten · Lengede · Ilsede · Wolfenbüttel · Schöppenstedt · Remlingen

Borghorst · Horstmar · Laer · Nordwalde · Greven · Hagen a.T.W. · Georgsmarienhütte · Dissen a.T.W. · Hilter a.T.W. · Hiddenhausen · Enger · Herford · Kalletal · Extertal · Hameln · Coppenbrügge · Elze · Gronau · Hildesheim · Baddeckenstedt · Bockenem · Hornburg · Hessen

NORTH RHINE-WESTPHALIA · Münster · Havixbeck · Telgte · Münsterland · Nottuln · Dülmen · Ascheberg · Senden · Drensteinfurt · Ahlen · Beckum · Wadersloh · Lippstadt · Geseke · Büren · Paderborn · **PADERBORN** · Lichtenau · Willebadessen · Borgentreich · Warburg

Emskirchen · Burgsteinfurt · Steinfurt · Ochtrup · Metelen · Ladbergen · Lienen · Bad Iburg · Bad Rothenfelde · Halle · Werther · **Bielefeld** · Steinhagen · Brackwede · Lage · Detmold · Leopoldshöhe · Dörentrup · Barntrup · Bad Pyrmont · Blomberg · Schieder-Schwalenberg · Steinheim · Nieheim · Höxter · Dassel · Einbeck · Northeim · Katlenburg-Lindau · Osterode · Goslar · Seesen · Bad Gandersheim · Kreiensen · Alfeld · Duingen · Delligsen · Eschershausen · Holzminden · Bad Grund · Clausthal-Zellerfeld · Altenau · Wernigerode · **SAXONY-ANHALT** · Osterwieck · Vienenburg · Langelsheim · Bad Harzburg · Harz · Brocken 1,142 m · Braunlage · Benneckenstein

Havixbeck · Nordkirchen · Olfen · Selm · Werne an der Lippe · Lünen · Bergkamen · Kamen · Unna · Werl · Soest · Bad Sassendorf · Erwitte · Anröchte · Rüthen · Warstein · Brilon · Marsberg · Trendelburg · Beverungen · Lauenförde · Uslar · Hardegsen · Nörten-Hardenberg · Göttingen · Rosdorf · Duderstadt · Worbis · Bleicherode · Wipperdorf · Gebra-Hainleite

Castrop-Rauxel · **Dortmund** · DORTMUND (WICKEDE) · Holzwickede · Wickede · Neheim-Hüsten · Arnsberg · Bestwig · Olsberg · Winterberg · Medebach · Hallenberg · Korbach · Waldeck · Vöhl · Volkmarsen · Wolfhagen · Zierenberg · Calden · Breuna · Grebenstein · Immenhausen · Münden · Hannoversch Münden · Witzenhausen · Bad Sooden-Allendorf · Heiligenstadt · Leinefelde · Breitenworbis

WESTPHALIA · Witten · Schwerte · Menden · Iserlohn · Balve · Sundern · Meschede · Schmallenberg · Hagen · Hemer · Neuenrade · Werdohl · Altena · Lennestadt · Finnentrop · Eslohe · Willingen · Frankenau · Frankenberg-Eder · Battenberg · Allendorf · Haina · Wildungen · Bad Wildungen · Fritzlar · Borken · Homberg · Felsberg · Melsungen · Spangenberg · Sontra · **THURINGIA** · Mühlhausen · Menteroda · Ebeleben · Schlotheim · Körner · Bad Langensalza · Nägelstedt

Ennepetal · Breckerfeld · Lüdenscheid · Herscheid · Plettenberg · Attendorn · Schmallenberg · Hatzfeld · Wüstegarten 675 m · Jesberg · Gilserberg · Neustadt · Wabern · Guxhagen · Baunatal · **Kassel** · Niestetal · Kaufungen · Grossalmerode · Hessisch Lichtenau · Eschwege · Wanfried · Treffurt · Creuzburg · Eisenach · Gotha

Halver · Kierspe · Meinerzhagen · Marienheide · Bergneustadt · Olpe · Lindlar · Drolshagen · Hilchenbach · Bromskirchen · Hallenberg · Medebach · Korbach · Hünfeld · Rotenburg an der Fulda · Bebra · Herleshausen · Gerstungen

POPULATION OF CITIES AND TOWNS
- ■ OVER 2,000,000
- ◙ 1,000,000 - 1,999,999
- ◉ 500,000 - 999,999
- ● 250,000 - 499,999
- ● 100,000 - 249,999
- ◉ 30,000 - 99,999
- ○ 10,000 - 29,999
- ○ UNDER 10,000

SCALE 1:1,170,000 · LAMBERT CONFORMAL CONIC PROJECTION

MILES 0 10 20 30 40 50
KILOMETERS 0 10 20 30 40 50

CD-1011-A

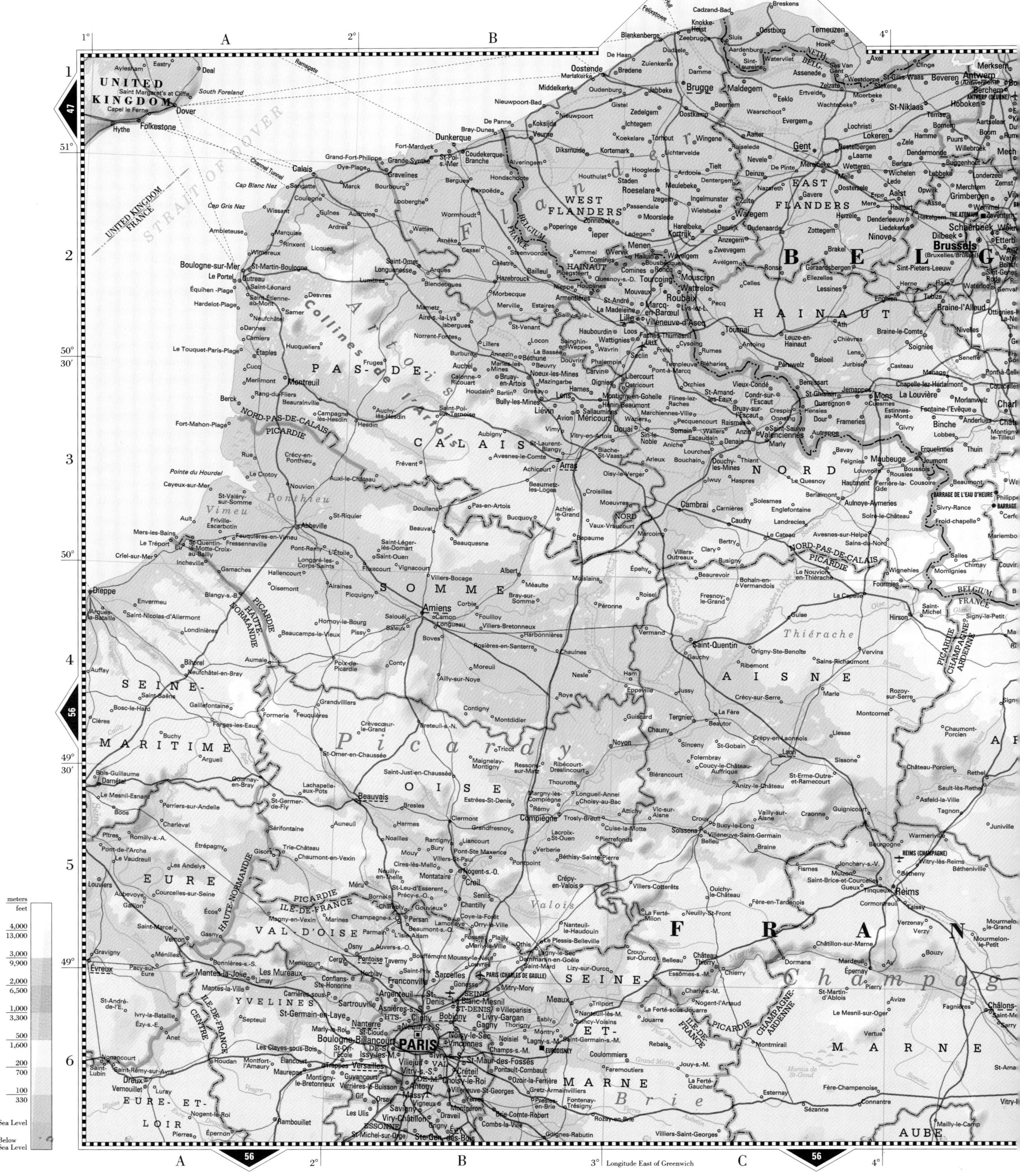

A
B
C
1°
2°
3°
4°
Longitude East of Greenwich
51°
50° 30′
50°
49° 30′
49°
1
2
3
4
5
6
47
56
UNITED KINGDOM
STRAIT OF DOVER
Channel Tunnel
BELGIUM
FRANCE
UNITED KINGDOM FRANCE
NETH.
BELG.
Flanders
WEST FLANDERS
EAST FLANDERS
HAINAUT
NORD-PAS-DE-CALAIS
PICARDIE
HAUTE-NORMANDIE
ILE-DE-FRANCE
CHAMPAGNE-ARDENNE
CENTRE
PAS-DE-CALAIS
NORD
SOMME
AISNE
OISE
SEINE-MARITIME
EURE
VAL-D'OISE
YVELINES
SEINE-ET-MARNE
MARNE
EURE-ET-LOIR
ESSONNE
AUBE
Artois
Collines de l'Artois
Picardy
Ponthieu
Vimeu
Thiérache
Valois
Brie
Champagne
FRANCE
BELG
Dover
Folkestone
Deal
Hythe
South Foreland
Cap Blanc Nez
Cap Gris Nez
Pointe du Hourdel
Calais
Dunkerque
Oostende
Brugge
Gent
Antwerp
Brussels
Kortrijk
Ieper
Lille
Roubaix
Tourcoing
Boulogne-sur-Mer
Saint-Omer
Montreuil
Le Touquet-Paris-Plage
Berck
Abbeville
Amiens
Arras
Douai
Lens
Béthune
Cambrai
Valenciennes
Mons
Tournai
Maubeuge
Saint-Quentin
Laon
Soissons
Reims
Compiègne
Beauvais
Dieppe
Évreux
Senlis
Meaux
Épernay
Châlons-
Château-Thierry
PARIS
PARIS (CHARLES DE GAULLE)
EURODISNEY
Versailles
Saint-Denis
Nanterre
Créteil
Évry
Massy
Rambouillet
Dreux
Mantes-la-Jolie
Pontoise
Cergy
Argenteuil
Sarcelles
Melun
meters
feet
4,000
13,000
3,000
9,900
2,000
6,500
1,000
3,300
500
1,600
200
700
100
330
Sea Level
Below Sea Level

Belgium, Northern France, Western Germany

POPULATION OF CITIES AND TOWNS

■ OVER 2,000,000	● 500,000 - 999,999	● 100,000 - 249,999	○ 10,000 - 29,999
□ 1,000,000 - 1,999,999	● 250,000 - 499,999	● 30,000 - 99,999	○ UNDER 10,000

SCALE 1:1,170,000   LAMBERT CONFORMAL CONIC PROJECTION

MILES 0   10   20   30   40   50

KILOMETERS 0   10   20   30   40   50

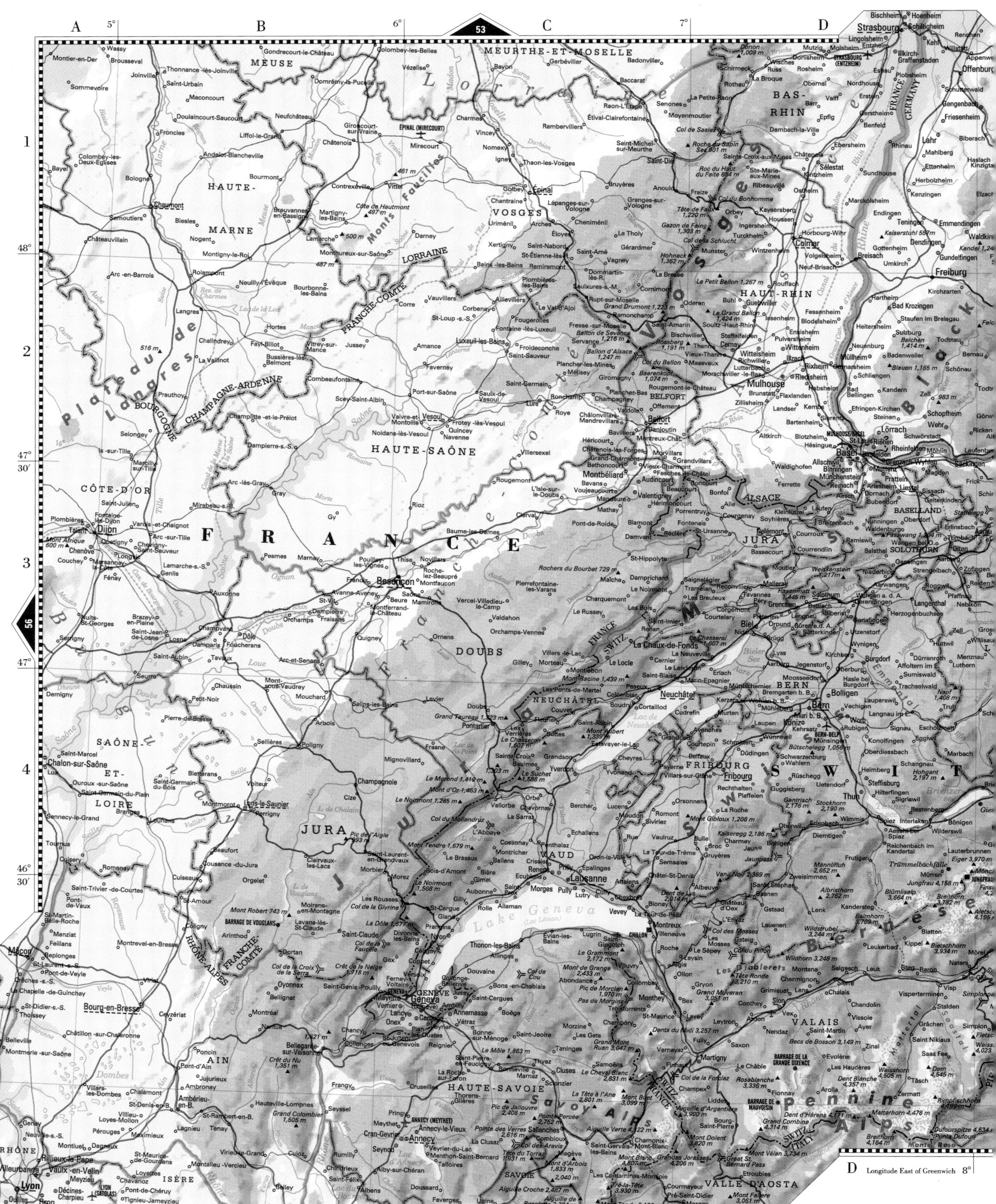

A
5°
B
6°
53
C
7°
D
1
2
3
4
48°
47° 30′
47°
46° 30′
56
D Longitude East of Greenwich 8°
MEUSE
MEURTHE-ET-MOSELLE
Lorraine
HAUTE-MARNE
VOSGES
LORRAINE
FRANCHE-COMTÉ
CHAMPAGNE-ARDENNE
BOURGOGNE
Plateau de Langres
HAUTE-SAÔNE
CÔTE-D'OR
FRANCE
Franche-Comté
DOUBS
JURA
SAÔNE-ET-LOIRE
Bourgogne
AIN
RHÔNE
ISÈRE
SAVOIE
HAUTE-SAVOIE
RHÔNE-ALPES
FRANCHE-COMTÉ
BAS-RHIN
HAUT-RHIN
ALSACE
Vosges
Monts Faucilles
FRANCE
GERMANY
Black
BASELLAND
SOLOTHURN
JURA
NEUCHÂTEL
BERN
FRIBOURG
VAUD
VALAIS
SWITZ.
SWITZ
Swiss
Jura
Lake Geneva
(Lac Léman)
Lac de Neuchâtel
Bieler See
Savoy Alps
Bernese
Pennine Alps
VALLE D'AOSTA
ITALY
Strasbourg
Colmar
Mulhouse
Freiburg
Basel
Belfort
Montbéliard
Épinal
Vesoul
Besançon
Dijon
Chaumont
Langres
Dole
Lons-le-Saunier
Chalon-sur-Saône
Mâcon
Bourg-en-Bresse
Lyon
Villeurbanne
Annecy
Genève
Geneva
Lausanne
Neuchâtel
Bern
Biel
Fribourg
Solothurn
Thun
Sion
Montreux
Vevey
La Chaux-de-Fonds
Pontarlier
Chamonix-Mont-Blanc
Martigny
Lörrach
Mont Blanc 4,807 m
Grandes Jorasses 4,206 m
Matterhorn 4,478 m
Dent d'Hérens 4,171 m
Grand Combin 4,314 m
Dufourspitze 4,634 m
Jungfrau 4,158 m
Eiger 3,970 m
Crêt de la Neige 1,718 m
Le Grand Ballon 1,424 m
Ballon d'Alsace 1,247 m
Hohneck 1,362 m
Le Chasseral 1,607 m
Mont Tendre 1,679 m
La Dôle 1,677 m

Central Alps Region

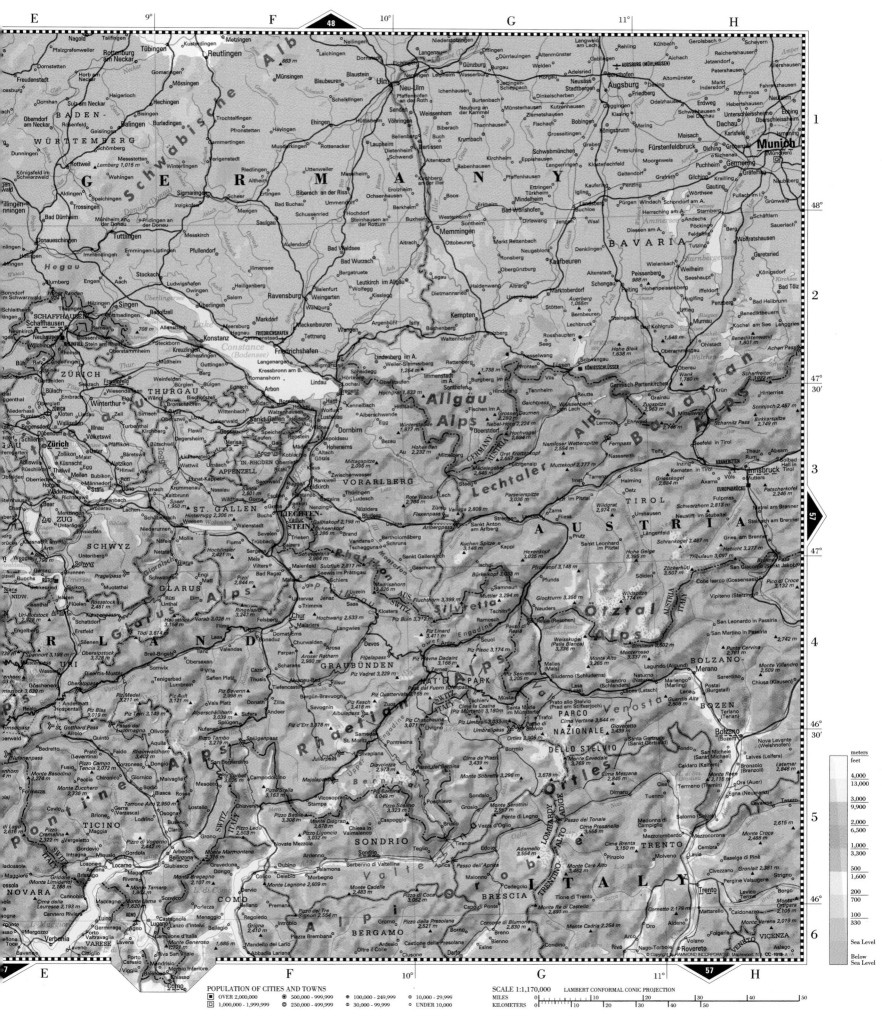

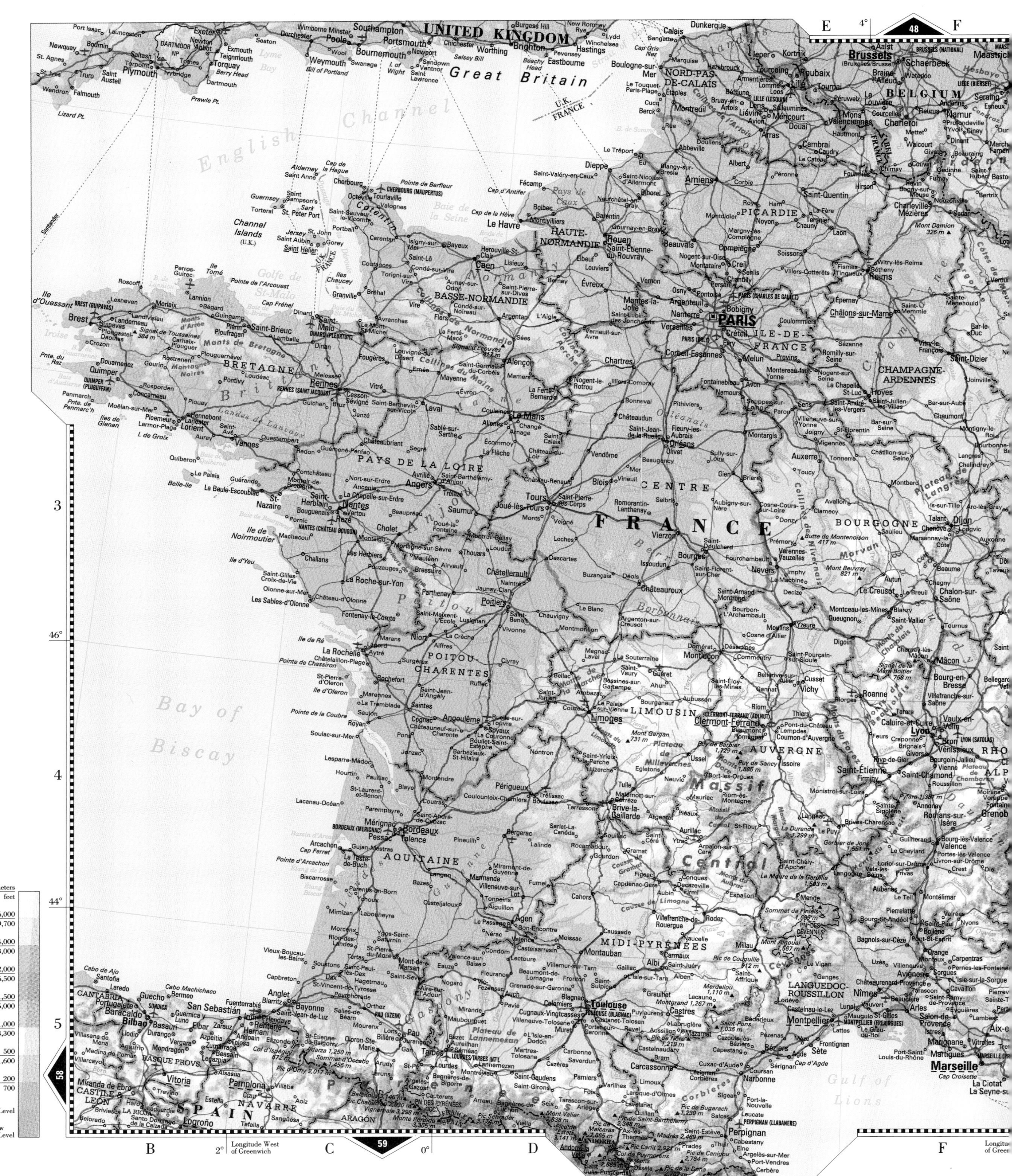

West Central Europe

POPULATION OF CITIES AND TOWNS

■ OVER 2,000,000   ● 500,000 - 999,999   ● 100,000 - 249,999   ○ 10,000 - 29,999

□ 1,000,000 - 1,999,999   ● 250,000 - 499,999   ● 30,000 - 99,999   ○ UNDER 10,000

SCALE 1:3,500,000   LAMBERT CONFORMAL CONIC PROJECTION

MILES   0   50   100   150

KILOMETERS   0   50   100   150

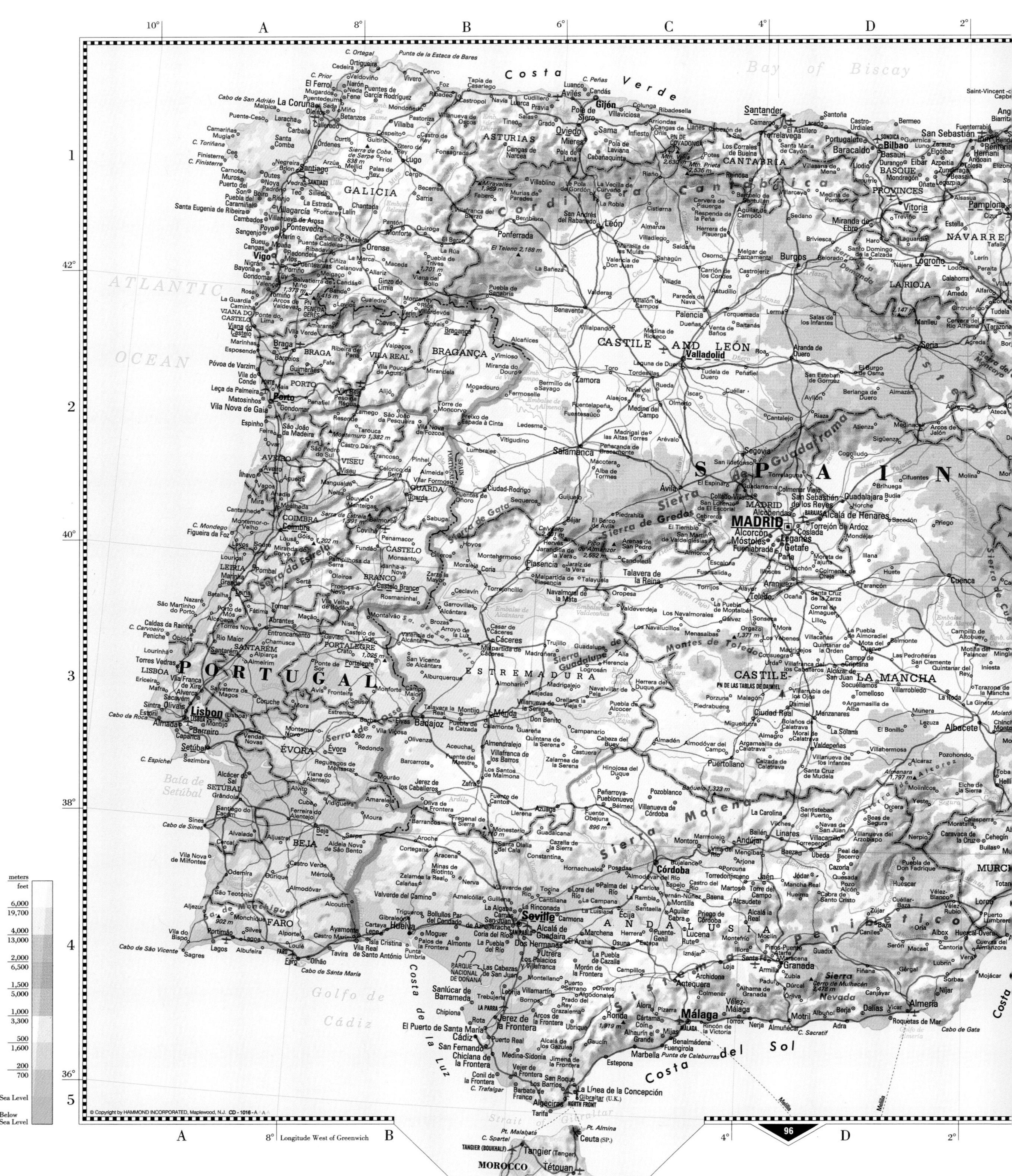
10°
A
8°
B
6°
C
4°
D
2°
1
2
3
4
5
42°
40°
38°
36°
Bay of Biscay
Costa Verde
ATLANTIC
OCEAN
GALICIA
ASTURIAS
CANTABRIA
BASQUE PROVINCES
NAVARRE
LA RIOJA
CASTILE AND LEÓN
S P A I N
MADRID
CASTILE-LA MANCHA
ESTREMADURA
ANDALUSIA
PORTUGAL
Cordillera Cantábrica
Sierra de Guadarrama
Sierra de Gredos
Sierra de Gata
Serra da Estrela
Montes de Toledo
Sierra Morena
Sistema Penibético
Sierra Nevada
La Coruña
El Ferrol
Santiago
Lugo
Orense
Vigo
Oviedo
Gijón
Avilés
Santander
Bilbao
San Sebastián
Vitoria
Pamplona
Logroño
Burgos
León
Palencia
Valladolid
Soria
Segovia
Ávila
Salamanca
Zamora
Madrid
Guadalajara
Alcalá de Henares
Toledo
Cuenca
Albacete
Ciudad Real
Cáceres
Badajoz
Mérida
Córdoba
Jaén
Granada
Málaga
Almería
Seville
Huelva
Cádiz
Jerez de la Frontera
Algeciras
Gibraltar (U.K.)
La Línea de la Concepción
Ceuta (SP.)
Tangier (Tanger)
Tétouan
MOROCCO
Strait of Gibraltar
Costa del Sol
Costa de la Luz
Golfo de Cádiz
Baía de Setúbal
Porto
Braga
Viana do Castelo
Bragança
Vila Real
Viseu
Guarda
Aveiro
Coimbra
Leiria
Castelo Branco
Santarém
Portalegre
Lisbon
Setúbal
Évora
Beja
Faro
Cabo de São Vicente
Cabo da Roca
C. Finisterre
C. Ortegal
C. Trafalgar
Cabo de Gata
meters
feet
6,000
19,700
4,000
13,000
2,000
6,500
1,500
5,000
1,000
3,300
500
1,600
200
700
Sea Level
Below Sea Level
Longitude West of Greenwich
© Copyright by HAMMOND INCORPORATED, Maplewood, N.J.
96

Spain, Portugal

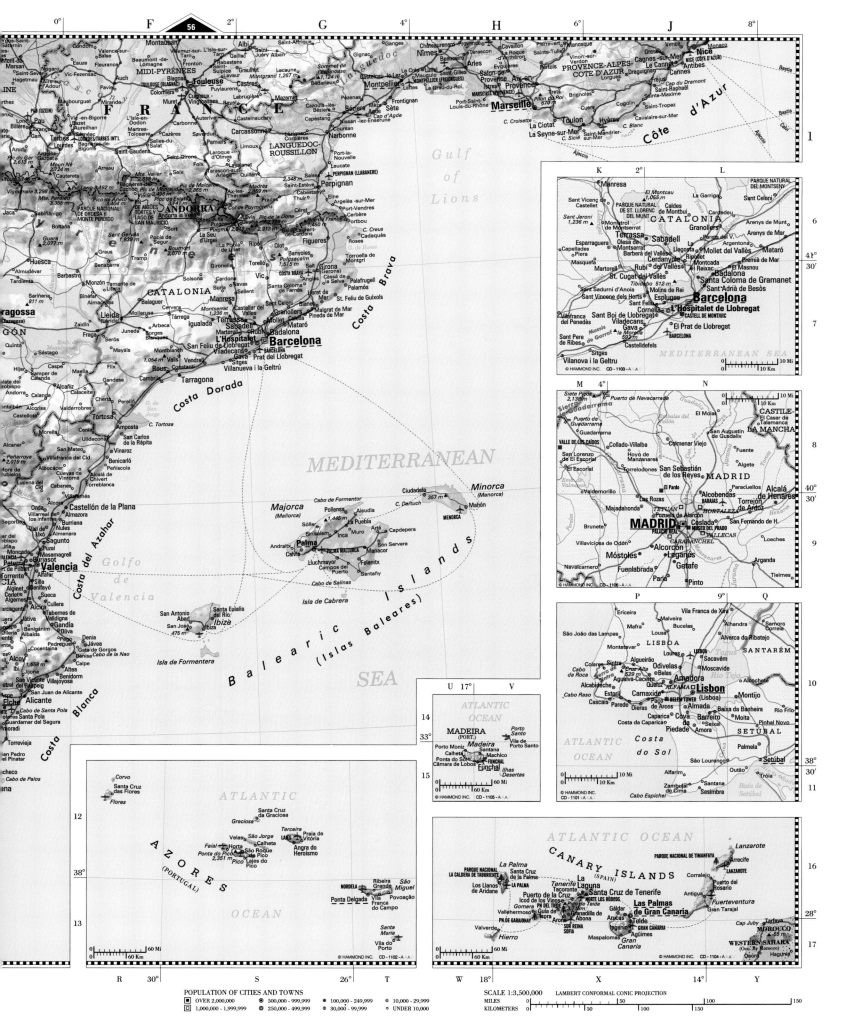

POPULATION OF CITIES AND TOWNS

■ OVER 2,000,000	● 500,000 - 999,999	● 100,000 - 249,999	○ 10,000 - 29,999
▣ 1,000,000 - 1,999,999	● 250,000 - 499,999	○ 30,000 - 99,999	○ UNDER 10,000

SCALE 1:3,500,000   LAMBERT CONFORMAL CONIC PROJECTION

MILES   0   50   100   150

KILOMETERS   0   50   100   150

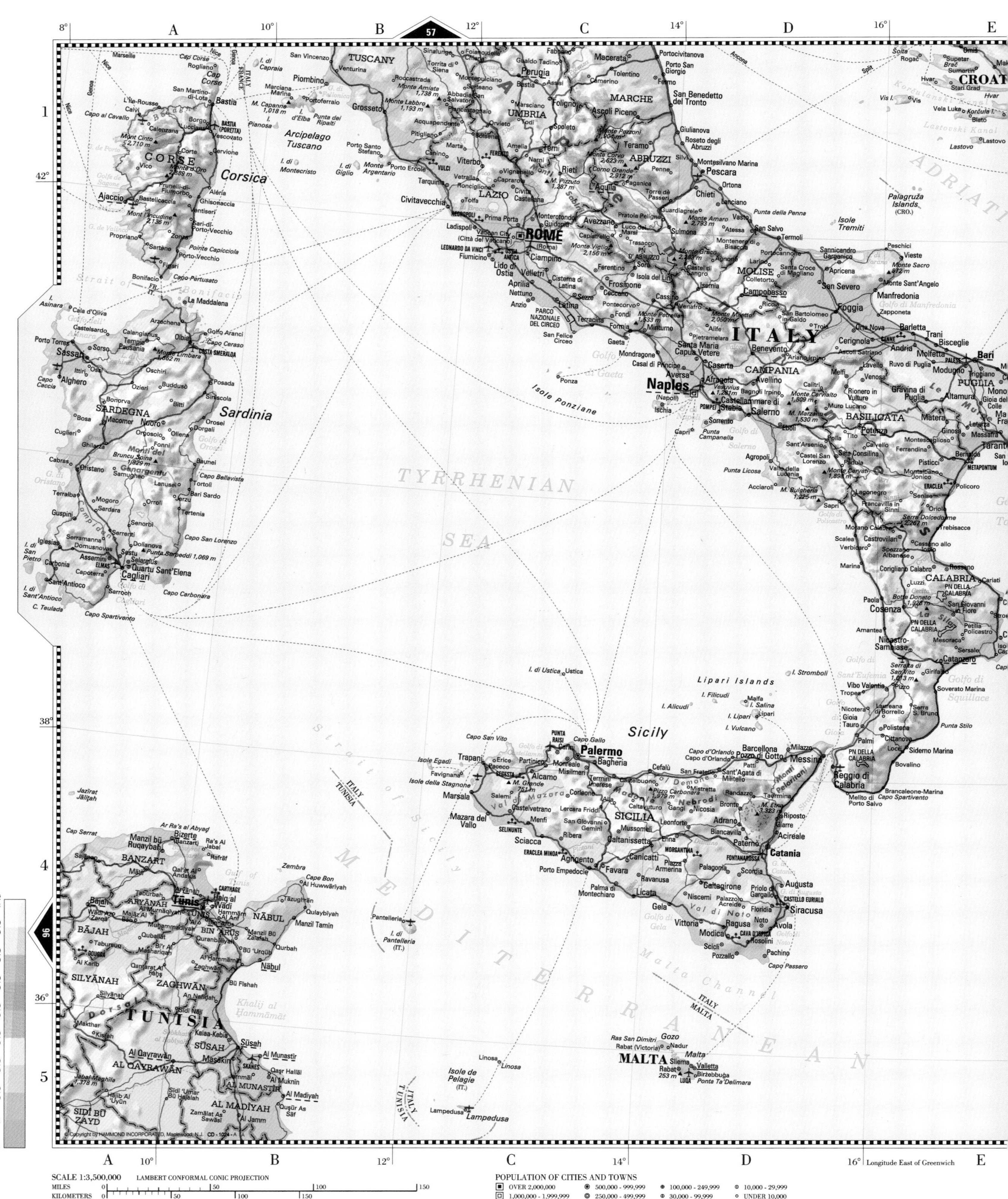

96

SCALE 1:3,500,000   LAMBERT CONFORMAL CONIC PROJECTION

MILES
KILOMETERS

0   50   100   150
0   50   100   150

POPULATION OF CITIES AND TOWNS

| ■ OVER 2,000,000 | ● 500,000 - 999,999 | ● 100,000 - 249,999 | ○ 10,000 - 29,999 |
| □ 1,000,000 - 1,999,999 | ◉ 250,000 - 499,999 | ● 30,000 - 99,999 | ○ UNDER 10,000 |

meters
feet

6,000
19,700

4,000
13,000

2,000
6,500

1,500
5,000

1,000
3,300

500
1,600

200
700

Sea Level

Below
Sea Level

Southern Italy, Albania, Greece

MILES   0   50   100   150
KILOMETERS   0   50   100   150

POPULATION OF CITIES AND TOWNS

■ OVER 2,000,000   ● 500,000 - 999,999   ● 100,000 - 249,999   ● 10,000 - 29,999
□ 1,000,000 - 1,999,999   ● 250,000 - 499,999   ● 30,000 - 99,999   ○ UNDER 10,000

* WHILE THERE IS NO OTHER OFFICIALLY RECOGNIZED NAM
AREA, THE NAME 'MACEDONIA' DERIVES FROM ITS FORMEF
A YUGOSLAV REPUBLIC, AND IS NOT RECOGNIZED BY MANY

Hungary, Northern Balkan States

24°   48°

UKRAINE

IVANO-FRANKOVSK
OBLAST

Chernovtsy

CHERNOVTSY
OBLAST

VINNITSA
OBLAST

KIRKOVGRAD
OBLAST

Krivoy Rog

DNEPROPETROVSK
OBLAST

BOTOŞANI

UKRAINE
ROMANIA

MOLDOVA

NIKOLAYEV
OBLAST

SUCEAVA

MARAMUREŞ

BISTRIŢA-
NĂSĂUD

Botoşani

Suceava

IAŞI

Iaşi

Nikolayev

ODESSA OBLAST

NEAMŢ

MOLDOVA
ROMANIA

Chişinău

Tiraspol

Bendery

KHERSON OBLAST

Kherson

Novaya Kakhovka

2

MUREŞ

HARGHITA

Tîrgu Mureş

BACĂU

Bacău

VASLUI

66

Odessa

B L A C K   S E A

Kartinitsk
Gulf

ROMANIA

SIBIU

Sibiu

COVASNA

BRAŞOV

Braşov

VRANCEA

GALAŢI

Galaţi

Crimean
Peninsula

Mys Tarkhankut

CRIMEAN
OBLAST

46°

PRAHOVA

BUZĂU

Buzău

BRĂILA

Brăila

Măcin

TULCEA

Tulcea

Delta of the
Danube

3

VÎLCEA

ARGEŞ

DÎMBOVIŢA

Tîrgovişte

Ploieşti

Sfîntu
Gheorghe

IALOMIŢA

Mouths of the Danube

Yalta

44°

Bucharest
(Bucureşti)

CĂLĂRAŞI

OLT

GIURGIU

Giurgiu

CONSTANŢA

Constanţa

B L A C K

Alexandria

TELEORMAN

ROMANIA
BULGARIA

Ruse

RAZGRAD

Silistra

Mangalia

S E A

4

Pleven

LOVECH

Razgrad

Shumen

VARNA

Varna

Sreda Mts.

Veliko Tŭrnovo

BULGARIA

Stara Zagora

BURGAS

Burgas

42°

Plovdiv

PLOVDIV

KHASKOVO

74

Zonguldak

ZONGULDAK

Edirne

KIRKLARELI

İstanbul

ISTANBUL

Üsküdar

KOCAELI

SAKARYA

BOLU

5

BULGARIA
GREECE

BULGARIA
TURKEY

EDİRNE

TEKİRDAĞ

TURKEY

Sea of
Marmara

BURSA

BİLECİK

ANKARA

Thracian
Sea

8° A 12° B 16° C 20° D 24° E 28° F 32° G 36° H 40°
2
3
4
5
64°
60°
56°
NORWEGIAN SEA
Arctic Circle
NORWAY
SWEDEN
FINLAND
LAPPI
OULU
VAASA
KUOPIO
POHJOIS-KARJALA
NORRBOTTEN
VÄSTERBOTTEN
JAMTLAND
VÄSTERNORRLAND
GAVLEBORG
KOPPARBERG
FINNMARK
TROMS
NORDLAND
Kola Peninsula
MURMANSK OBLAST
KARELIAN AUT. REPUBLIC
ARCHANG
VOLOGDA
SAINT PETERSBURG OBLAST
NOVGOROD OBL.
PSKOV OBLAST
T'VER OBLAST
SMOLENSK OBLAST
YAROSLAVL' OBL.
IVANOVO OBL.
VLADIMIR OBL.
MOSCOW OBL.
KALUGA OBL.
RYAZAN' OBL.
ESTONIA
LATVIA
LITHUANIA
RUSSIA
KALININGRAD OBLAST
POLAND
BELARUS
VITEBSK
GRODNO OBL.
MINSK OBL.
MOGILEV OBL.
BALTIC SEA
Gulf of Bothnia
Gulf of Finland
Gulf of Riga
Lake Ladoga
Lake Onega
Onega Bay
Dvina Bay
White Sea
Kandalaksha Gulf
Åland
AHVENANMAA
Stockholm
Helsinki (Helsingfors)
Tallinn
Riga
ST. PETERSBURG
MOSCOW (Moskva)
Minsk
Vilnius
Kaunas
Kaliningrad
Gdańsk
Gdynia
Białystok
Murmansk
Petrozavodsk
Novgorod
Pskov
Tartu
Turku (Åbo)
Tampere
Oulu
Luleå
Umeå
Uppsala
Vologda
Cherepovets
Yaroslavl'
Kostroma
Ivanovo
Vladimir
T'ver
Smolensk
Kaluga
Ryazan'
Rybinsk
Vitebsk
Mogilev
Grodno
Archangel'sk
meters feet
6,000 19,700
4,000 13,000
2,000 6,500
1,500 5,000
1,000 3,300
500 1,600
200 700
Sea Level
Below Sea Level
42
49
66
20° D 24° E 28° Longitude East of Greenwich F 32° G 36° H 40° J

Northeastern Europe

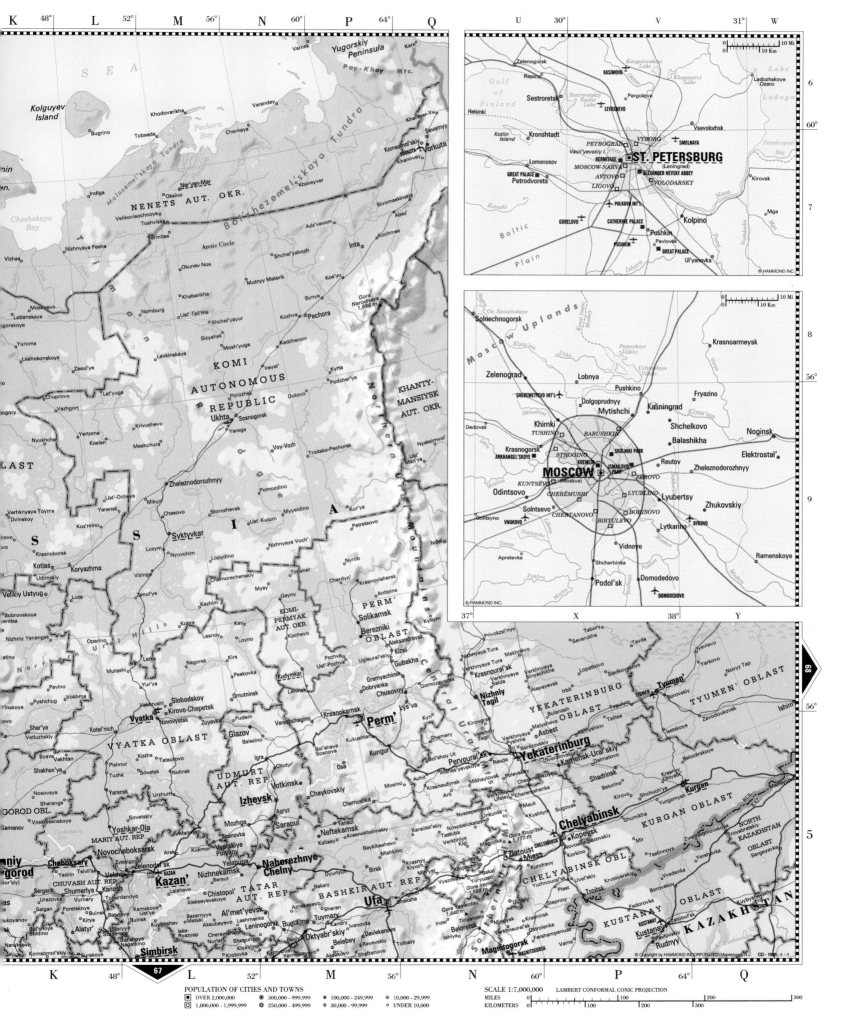

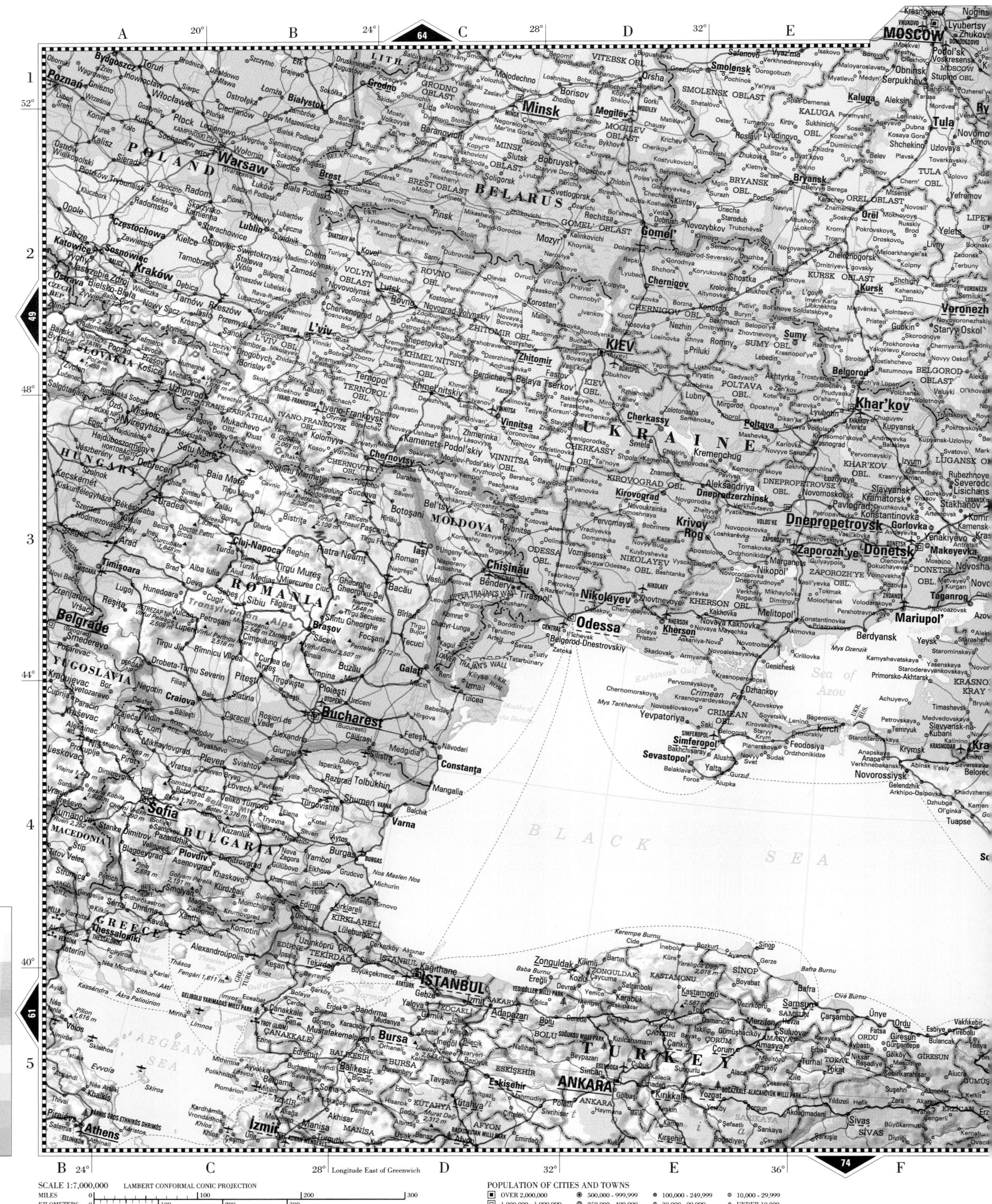

66/67

Southeastern Europe

65
68
73

RUSSIA
KAZAKHSTAN
UZBEKISTAN
TURKMENISTAN
AZERBAIJAN
ARMENIA
GEORGIA
IRAN
CASPIAN SEA
Aral Sea
URAL'SK OBLAST
GUR'YEV OBLAST
AKTYUBINSK OBLAST
MANGISTAUZ OBLAST
KARAKALPAK AUT. REP.
TASHAUZ OBLAST
BALKHAN OBLAST
KUSTANAY OBLAST
ORENBURG OBLAST
SAMARA OBLAST
SARATOV OBLAST
PENZA OBLAST
VOLGOGRAD OBLAST
ASTRAKHAN' OBL.
KALMYK AUTONOMOUS REPUBLIC
STAVROPOL' KRAY
DAGESTAN AUT. REP.
CHECHEN-INGUSH AUT. REP.
KABARDIN-BALKAR AUT. REP.
NORTH OSSETIAN AUT. REP.
SOUTH OSSETIAN AUT. OBL.
BASHKIR AUT. REP.
TATAR AUT. REP.
CHUVASH AUT. REP.
MORDVIAN AUT. REP.
NIZHEGOROD OBL.
SIMBIRSK OBL.
CHELYABINSK OBLAST
Ustyurt Plateau
Mugodzharskoye Mts.
Caspian Lowland

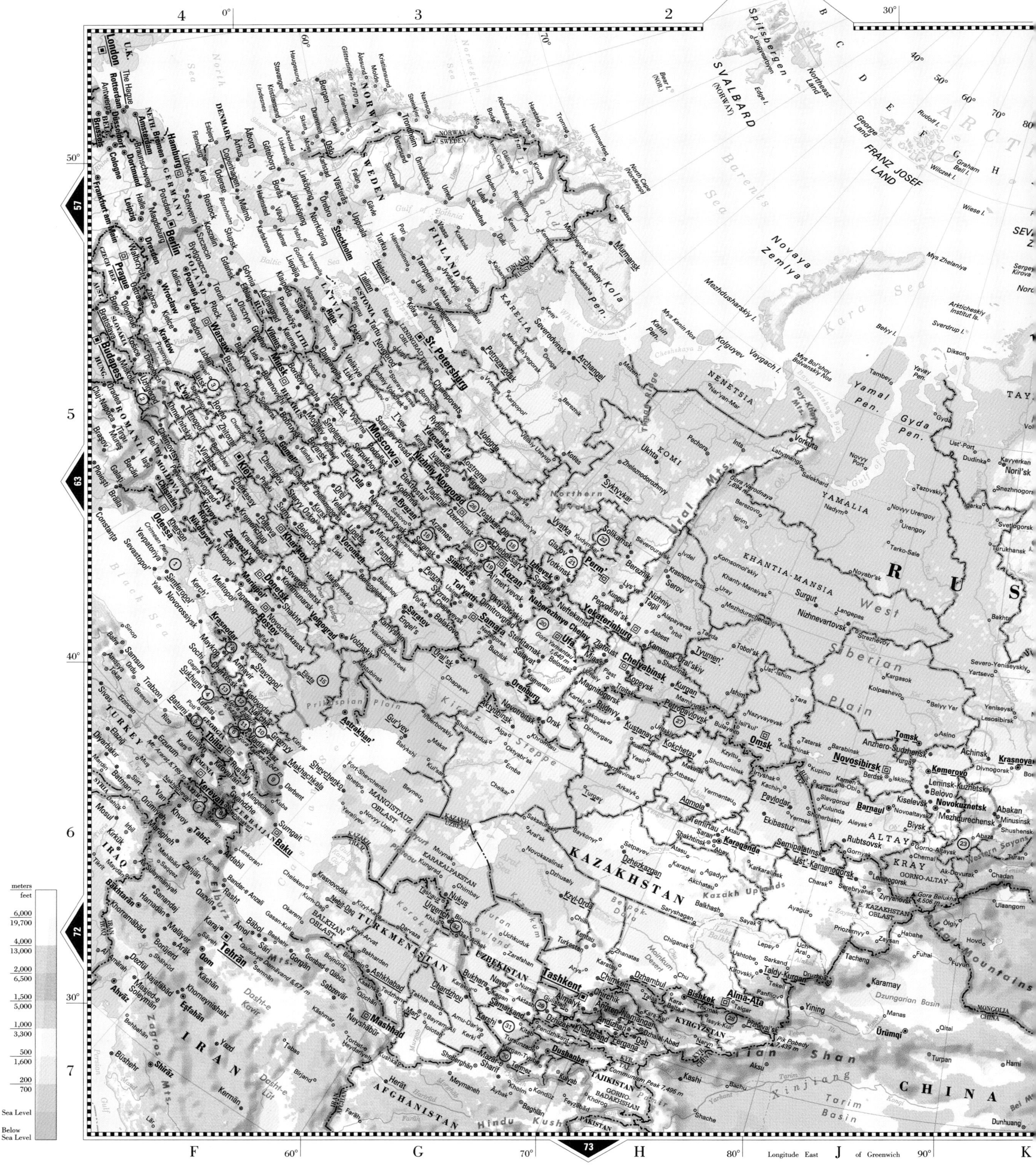

meters
feet
6,000
19,700
4,000
13,000
2,000
6,500
1,500
5,000
1,000
3,300
500
1,600
200
700
Sea Level
Below Sea Level
4
3
2
5
6
7
0°
30°
40°
50°
60°
70°
80°
90°
F
G
H
J
K
Longitude East of Greenwich
57
63
72
73
RUSSIA
KAZAKHSTAN
IRAN
CHINA
TURKMENISTAN
AFGHANISTAN
Moscow
St. Petersburg

Russia and Neighboring Countries

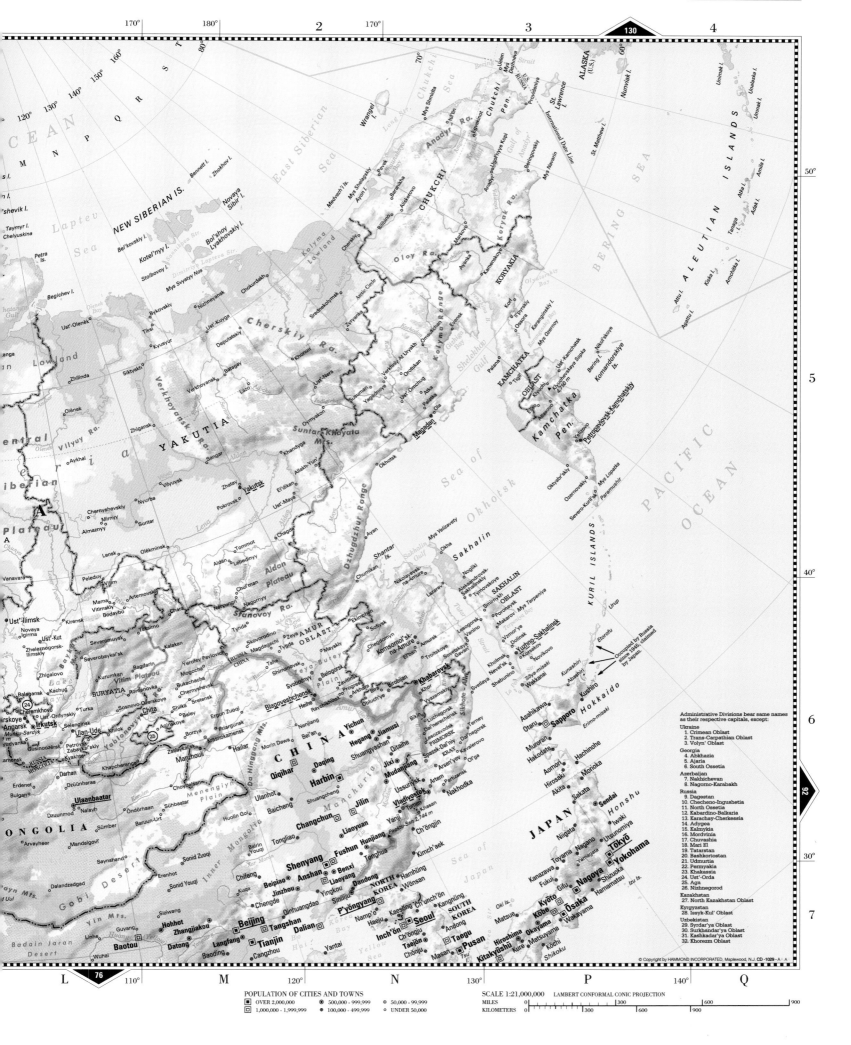

Administrative Divisions bear same names
as their respective capitals, except:
Ukraine
 1. Crimean Oblast
 2. Trans-Carpathian Oblast
 3. Volyn' Oblast
Georgia
 4. Abkhazia
 5. Ajaria
 6. South Ossetia
Azerbaijan
 7. Nakhichevan
 8. Nagorno-Karabakh
Russia
 9. Dagestan
 10. Checheno-Ingushetia
 11. North Ossetia
 12. Kabardino-Balkaria
 13. Karachay-Cherkessia
 14. Adygea
 15. Kalmykia
 16. Mordvinia
 17. Chuvashia
 18. Mari El
 19. Tatarstan
 20. Bashkortostan
 21. Udmurtia
 22. Permyakia
 23. Khakassia
 24. Ust'-Orda
 25. Aga
 26. Nizhnegorod
Kazakhstan
 27. North Kazakhstan Oblast
Kyrgyzstan
 28. Issyk-Kul' Oblast
Uzbekistan
 29. Syrdar'ya Oblast
 30. Surkhandar'ya Oblast
 31. Kashkadar'ya Oblast
 32. Khorezm Oblast

© Copyright by HAMMOND INCORPORATED, Maplewood, N.J. CD -1029 - A - A

POPULATION OF CITIES AND TOWNS

| ■ OVER 2,000,000 | ● 500,000 - 999,999 | ⊙ 50,000 - 99,999 |
| ▣ 1,000,000 - 1,999,999 | ● 100,000 - 499,999 | ○ UNDER 50,000 |

SCALE 1:21,000,000   LAMBERT CONFORMAL CONIC PROJECTION

MILES   0   300   600   900
KILOMETERS 0   300   600   900

Asia - Comparisons

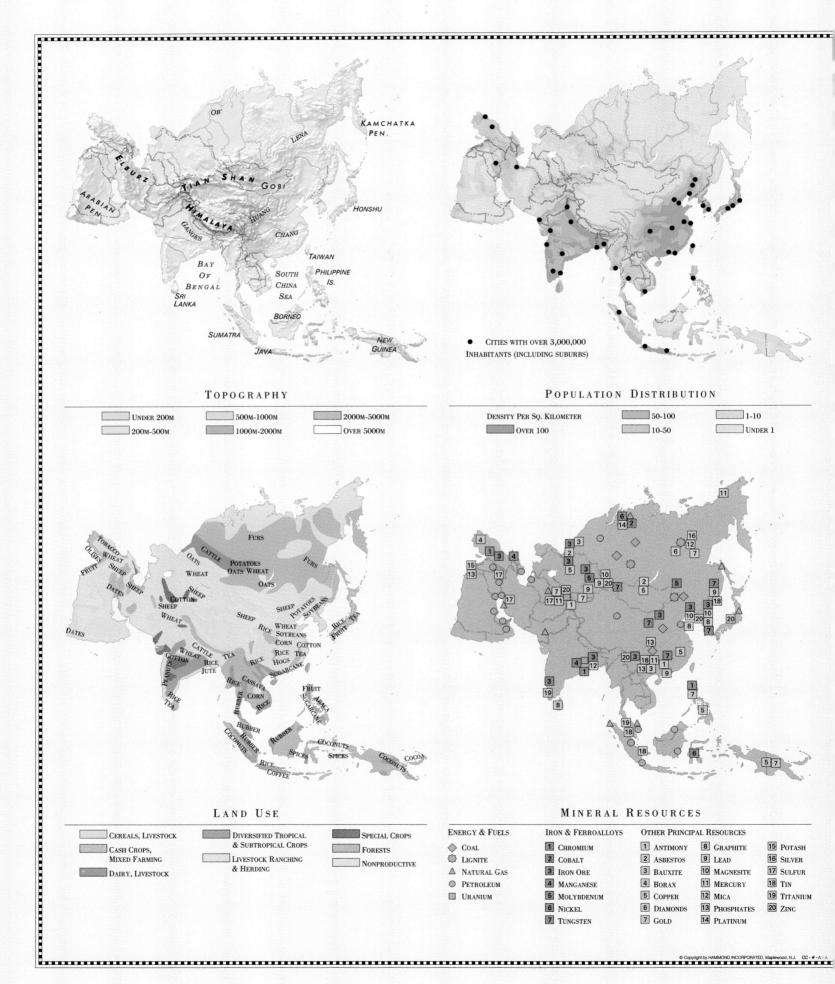

TOPOGRAPHY

UNDER 200M	500M-1000M	2000M-5000M
200M-500M	1000M-2000M	OVER 5000M

Topography labels: OB', LENA, KAMCHATKA PEN., ELBURZ, TIAN SHAN, GOBI, ARABIAN PEN., HIMALAYA, HUANG, HONSHU, GANGES, CHANG, TAIWAN, BAY OF BENGAL, SOUTH CHINA SEA, PHILIPPINE IS., SRI LANKA, BORNEO, SUMATRA, NEW GUINEA, JAVA

POPULATION DISTRIBUTION

● CITIES WITH OVER 3,000,000
INHABITANTS (INCLUDING SUBURBS)

DENSITY PER SQ. KILOMETER	50-100	1-10
OVER 100	10-50	UNDER 1

LAND USE

Land use labels: TOBACCO, WHEAT, OLIVES, FRUIT, SHEEP, DATES, CATTLE, POTATOES, OATS, WHEAT, FURS, FURS, OATS, SHEEP, COTTON, SHEEP, WHEAT, SHEEP, SOYBEANS, POTATOES, RICE, FRUIT, TEA, DATES, CATTLE, WHEAT, RICE, TEA, WHEAT, SOYBEANS, CORN, RICE, COTTON, TEA, PEANUTS, COTTON, RICE, JUTE, HOGS, SUGARCANE, RICE, CASSAVA, CORN, RICE, FRUIT, SUGARCANE, ABACA, RICE, TEA, RUBBER, RUBBER, RUBBER, RUBBER, COCONUTS, SPICES, SPICES, COCONUTS, COCOA, COCONUTS, RICE, COFFEE

CEREALS, LIVESTOCK	DIVERSIFIED TROPICAL & SUBTROPICAL CROPS	SPECIAL CROPS
CASH CROPS, MIXED FARMING	LIVESTOCK RANCHING & HERDING	FORESTS
DAIRY, LIVESTOCK		NONPRODUCTIVE

MINERAL RESOURCES

ENERGY & FUELS	IRON & FERROALLOYS	OTHER PRINCIPAL RESOURCES	
◇ COAL	1 CHROMIUM	1 ANTIMONY · 8 GRAPHITE	15 POTASH
⬡ LIGNITE	2 COBALT	2 ASBESTOS · 9 LEAD	16 SILVER
△ NATURAL GAS	3 IRON ORE	3 BAUXITE · 10 MAGNESITE	17 SULFUR
○ PETROLEUM	4 MANGANESE	4 BORAX · 11 MERCURY	18 TIN
☐ URANIUM	5 MOLYBDENUM	5 COPPER · 12 MICA	19 TITANIUM
	6 NICKEL	6 DIAMONDS · 13 PHOSPHATES	20 ZINC
	7 TUNGSTEN	7 GOLD · 14 PLATINUM	

Asia

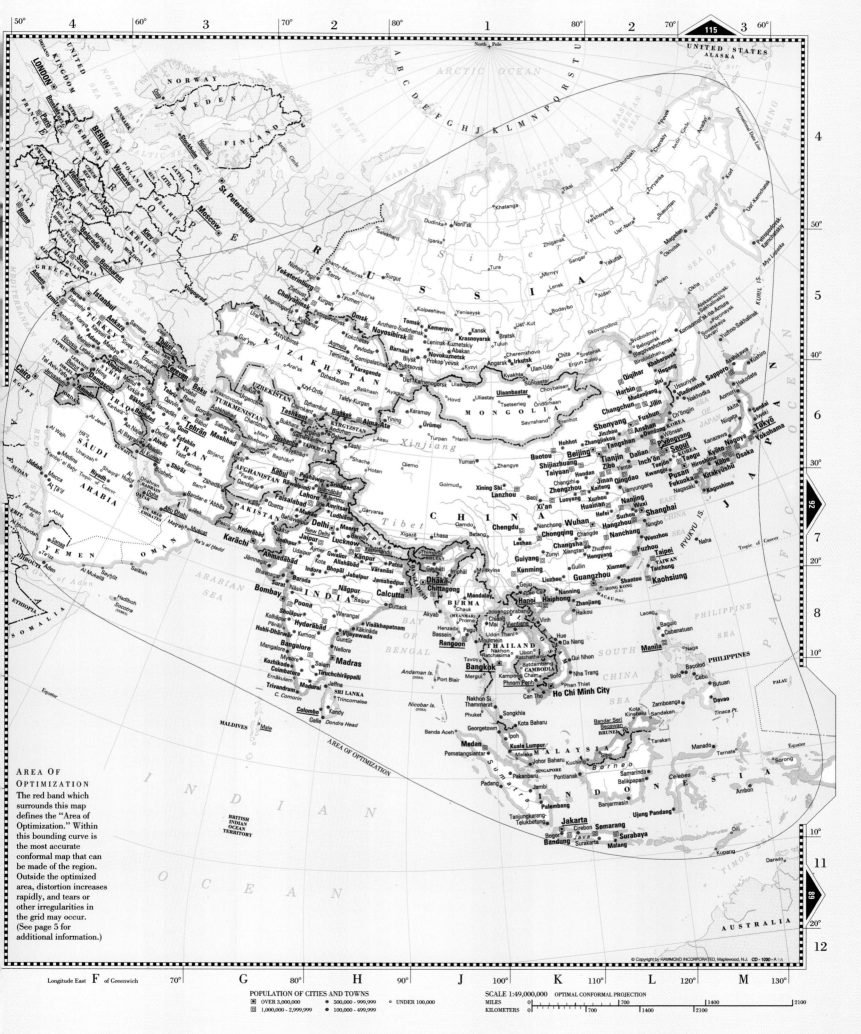

© Copyright by HAMMOND INCORPORATED, Maplewood, N.J. CD-1030-A-A

AREA OF
OPTIMIZATION
The red band which
surrounds this map
defines the "Area of
Optimization." Within
this bounding curve is
the most accurate
conformal map that can
be made of the region.
Outside the optimized
area, distortion increases
rapidly, and tears or
other irregularities in
the grid may occur.
(See page 5 for
additional information.)

Longitude East **F** of Greenwich   70°   **G**   80°   **H**   90°   **J**   100°   **K**   110°   **L**   120°   **M**   130°

POPULATION OF CITIES AND TOWNS

| ▣ OVER 3,000,000 | ● 500,000 - 999,999 | ○ UNDER 100,000 |
| ▣ 1,000,000 - 2,999,999 | ● 100,000 - 499,999 | |

SCALE 1:49,000,000   OPTIMAL CONFORMAL PROJECTION

MILES   0   700   1400   2100
KILOMETERS 0   700   1400   2100

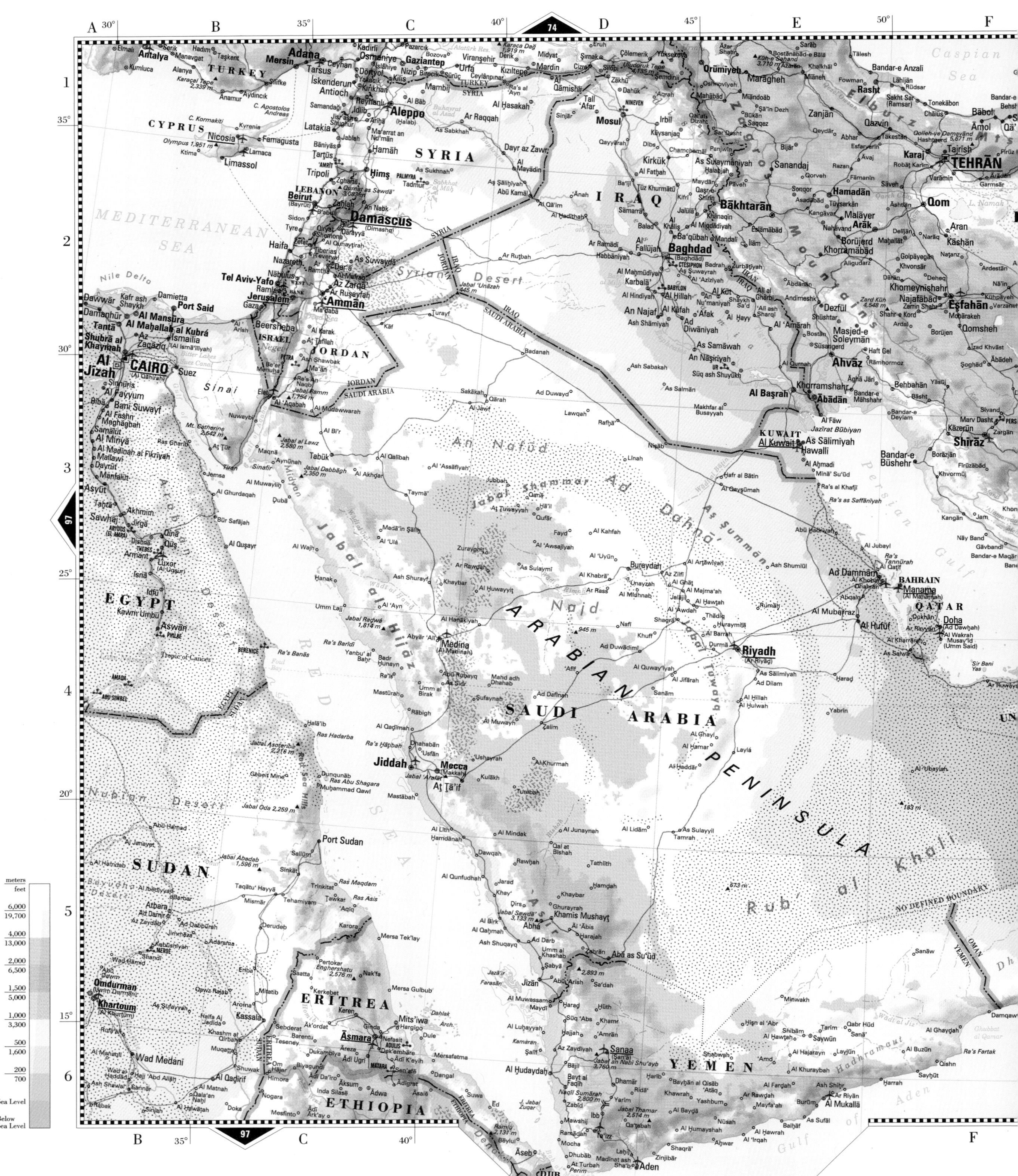

74
97
A
B
C
D
E
F
30°
35°
40°
45°
50°
1
2
3
4
5
6
15°
20°
25°
30°
35°
TURKEY
Antalya
Manavgat
Alanya
Anamur
Mersin
Adana
Tarsus
Ceyhan
Osmaniye
Gaziantep
İskenderun
Antioch
Kilis
Şanlıurfa
Urfa
Viranşehir
Mardin
Kızıltepe
Midyat
Cizre
Şırnak
Yüksekova
Karacal Tepe 2,339 m
CYPRUS
Nicosia
Famagusta
Larnaca
Limassol
Kyrenia
Olympus 1,951 m
SYRIA
Aleppo
Ar Raqqah
Al Hasakah
Al Qamishli
Latakia
Bāniyās
Ţarţūs
Tripoli
Ḩamāh
Ḩimş
Palmyra
Tadmur
Dayr az Zawr
Al Mayādin
Abū Kamāl
LEBANON
Beirut
(Bayrūt)
Zahlah
Damascus
(Dimashq)
Sidon
Tyre
Haifa
Nazareth
Tel Aviv-Yafo
Jerusalem
Gaza
Ramla
Nābulus
WEST BANK
Beersheba
ISRAEL
JORDAN
Amman
Az Zarqā'
Ar Ruşayfah
Mādabā
Al Karak
Aţ Ţafīlah
Ash Shawbak
Ma'ān
PETRA
Al 'Aqabah
Elat
MEDITERRANEAN SEA
Nile Delta
Damietta
Port Said
Dawwār
Damanhūr
Tanţā
Al Manşūrah
Al Maḩallah al Kubrá
Shubrā al Khaymah
Az Zaqāzīq
Ismailia
(Al Ismā'īlīyah)
Bitter Lakes
Suez Canal
CAIRO
(Al Qāhirah)
Al Jīzah
Suez
Sinai
Al 'Arīsh
Negev
Nuwaybi'
Mt. Catherine 2,642 m
Aţ Ţūr
Sinnūris
Al Fayyūm
Banī Suwayf
Al Fashn
Maghāghah
Samālūţ
Al Minyā
Mallawī
Dayrūţ
Manfalūţ
Asyūţ
Ţahţā
Sawhāj
Akhmīm
Jirjā
Qinā
Qūş
Luxor
(Al Uqşur)
THEBES
Armant
Isnā
Idfū
Kawm Umbū
Aswān
PHILAE
EGYPT
Arabian Desert
Al Ghurdaqah
Būr Safājah
Al Quşayr
BERENICE
Ra's Banās
Foul Bay
Tropic of Cancer
ABU SIMBEL
AMADA
Nubian Desert
SUDAN
Abū Hamad
Port Sudan
Sawākin
Sinkāt
Jabal Abadab 1,596 m
Jabal Oda 2,259 m
Atbara
Ad Dāmir
Shandī
MEROE
Omdurman
(Umm Durman)
Khartoum
(Al Kharţūm)
Wad Medanī
Kassala
Al Qaḑārif
Sannār
ERITREA
Keren
Asmara
Mits'iwa
Assab
ETHIOPIA
Aksum
Ādīgrat
Mek'ele
Dahlak Arch.
RED SEA
Ra's Abu Shagara
Muḩammad Qawl
Ḩalā'ib
Ras Hadarba
Jabal Asotériba 2,216 m
Dunqunāb
IRAQ
Mosul
Irbil
Kirkūk
As Sulaymānīyah
Tall 'Afar
NINEVEH
Sāmarrā'
Baghdad
(Baghdād)
CTESIPHON
Ba'qūbah
Al Fallūjah
Ar Ramādī
Al Ḩadīthah
Ar Ruţbah
Karbalā'
Al Ḩillah
BABYLON
An Najaf
Al Kūfah
Ad Dīwānīyah
Al Kūt
Al 'Amārah
As Samāwah
An Nāşirīyah
UR
Al Başrah
Syrian Desert
Jabal 'Unāzah 445 m
KUWAIT
Al Kuwayt
Ḩawallī
Al Aḩmadī
IRAN
Orūmīyeh
Marāgheh
Tabrīz
Zanjān
Qazvīn
Rasht
Bandar-e Anzalī
Caspian Sea
Elburz Mts.
Damāvand 5,671 m
Karaj
TEHRĀN
Qom
Hamadān
Bākhtarān
Sanandaj
Arāk
Malāyer
Borūjerd
Khorramābād
Kāshān
Eşfahān
Khomeynīshahr
Najafābād
Zard Kūh 4,548 m
Dezfūl
Shūshtar
Masjed-e Soleymān
Ahvāz
Khorramshahr
Ābādān
Behbahān
Bandar-e Būshehr
Kāzerūn
Shīrāz
Zagros Mountains
Persian Gulf
BAHRAIN
Manama
(Al Manāmah)
QATAR
Doha
(Ad Dawḩah)
Al Wakrah
Umm Said
SAUDI ARABIA
ARABIAN PENINSULA
An Nafūd
Ad Dahnā'
Aş Şummān
Jabal Shammar
Najd
Jabal Ţuwayq
Al Ḩijāz
Ḩā'il
Al Jawf
Sakākah
Tabūk
Taymā'
Buraydah
'Unayzah
Ar Rass
Riyadh
(Ar Riyāḑ)
Al Kharj
Ad Dammām
Al Hufūf
Al Mubarraz
Al Jubayl
Ra's Tannūrah
Ra's al Khafjī
Medina
(Al Madīnah)
Yanbu' al Baḩr
Jiddah
Mecca
(Makkah)
Aţ Ţā'if
Al Līth
Al Qunfudhah
Abhā
Khamīs Mushayţ
Jīzān
Najrān
Rub' al Khālī
Sulayyil
Badanah
Rafḩā'
Ḩafar al Bāţin
Al Qayşūmah
Mastūrah
Rābigh
Al Wajh
Ḑubā
Jabal al Lawz 2,580 m
Jabal Dabbāgh 2,350 m
Jabal Raḑwá 1,814 m
Jabal Sawdā' 3,133 m
NO DEFINED BOUNDARY
YEMEN
Sanaa
(Şan'ā')
Al Ḩudaydah
Dhamār
Ibb
Ta'izz
Aden
Al Mukallā
Shabwah
Hadhramaut
Mocha
Jabal an Nabī Shu'ayb 3,760 m
Gulf of Aden
OMAN
Ra's Fartak
Qishn
DJIB.
meters
feet
6,000
19,700
4,000
13,000
2,000
6,500
1,500
5,000
1,000
3,300
500
1,600
200
700
Sea Level
Below Sea Level

Kara-Kala • Nokhur • Bakherden
Gora-Lagaryia 2,246 m. • Gök-Tepe • Firyuza
Ashkhabad
Gifan • Bajgiran
Bojnūrd • Shirvān • Lotfābād • Kirovsk
Chārjew • Bāghrān
Gharmeh • Chaman Bid • Ravnina • Ueli-Adzhi
Tappeh • Kaakhka • Tedzhen
Esfarāyen • Jājarm • Kūshka • Gowghān • Dushak • Takhta-Bazar
TURKMENISTAN
Nāy Band

TAJIKISTAN
CHINA

Dangara • Kulyab • Taxkorgan
Kurgan-Tyube • Khorog • Pik Karla Marksa 6,726 m • Shaymak
Kolkhozabad • Pyandzh • Pik Mayakovskogo 6,096 m • Mintaka Pass • Kunjirap Daban
Feyzābād • Vrang • Yasin • Rakaposhi 7,788 m • K2(Godwin-Austen) 8,611 m • Dehoglluatang

AFGHANISTAN

Mashhad
Neyshābūr • Sabzevār

Herāt
Kabul (Kābol)

Kandahār

PAKISTAN
Quetta

Baluchistān

Central Makrān Range

Zāhedān

Kermān • Bam

OMAN
Muscat (Masqat)

Gulf of Oman

Makran Coast

KARACHI
Hyderābād

Mouths of the Indus

ARABIAN SEA

Gulf of Masira

Gulf of Cambay

BOMBAY
Poona

Sholāpur

Kolhāpur • Sāngli • Miraj

Belgaum

Hubli-Dhārwār

GOA

INDIA
DELHI
New Delhi

Jaipur

Jodhpur • Ajmer

Indian Thar Desert

RAJASTHAN

AHMADĀBĀD
Baroda
Surat

Srīnagar
Peshāwar • Rāwalpindi • Islāmābad

LAHORE • Amritsar • Ludhiāna • Chandīgarh
Faisalābād • Jullundur

Multān

GUJARĀT

POPULATION OF CITIES AND TOWNS
■ OVER 2,000,000
▣ 1,000,000 - 1,999,999
◉ 500,000 - 999,999
◎ 250,000 - 499,999
● 100,000 - 249,999
⊙ 30,000 - 99,999
○ 10,000 - 29,999
· UNDER 10,000

SCALE 1:10,500,000   LAMBERT CONFORMAL CONIC PROJECTION
MILES   0   150   300   450
KILOMETERS   0   150   300   450

Eastern Mediterranean Region

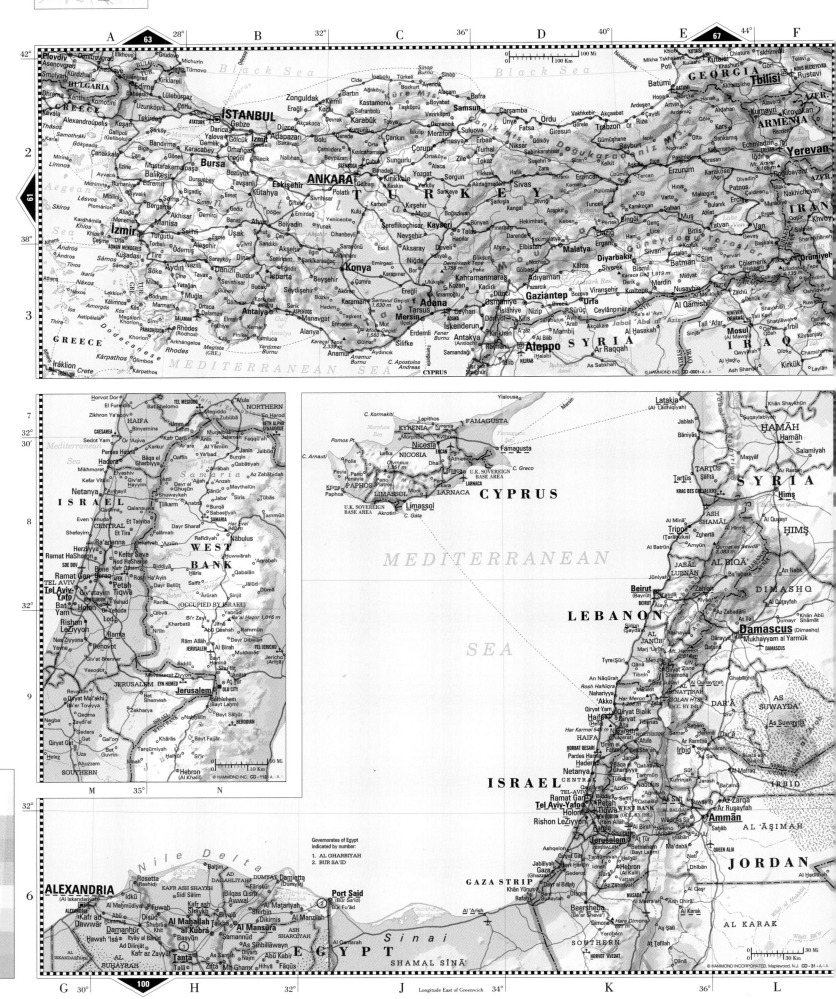

POPULATION OF CITIES AND TOWNS

■ OVER 2,000,000	⊛ 500,000 - 999,999	● 100,000 - 249,999	◦ 10,000 - 29,999
▣ 1,000,000 - 1,999,999	◉ 250,000 - 499,999	◎ 30,000 - 99,999	◦ UNDER 10,000

Longitude East of Greenwich

Central Asia

POPULATION OF CITIES AND TOWNS

Symbol	Range	Symbol	Range
■ OVER 2,000,000		● 500,000 - 999,999	● 100,000 - 249,999
□ 1,000,000 - 1,999,999		● 250,000 - 499,999	● 30,000 - 99,999
			● 10,000 - 29,999
			○ UNDER 10,000

SCALE 1:10,500,000   LAMBERT CONFORMAL CONIC PROJECTION

Longitude East of Greenwich

MILES   0   150   300   450
KILOMETERS   0   150   300   450

meters / feet elevation legend

meters	feet
6,000	19,700
4,000	13,000
2,000	6,500
1,500	5,000
1,000	3,300
500	1,600
200	700
Sea Level	Sea Level
Below	Below
Sea Level	Sea Level

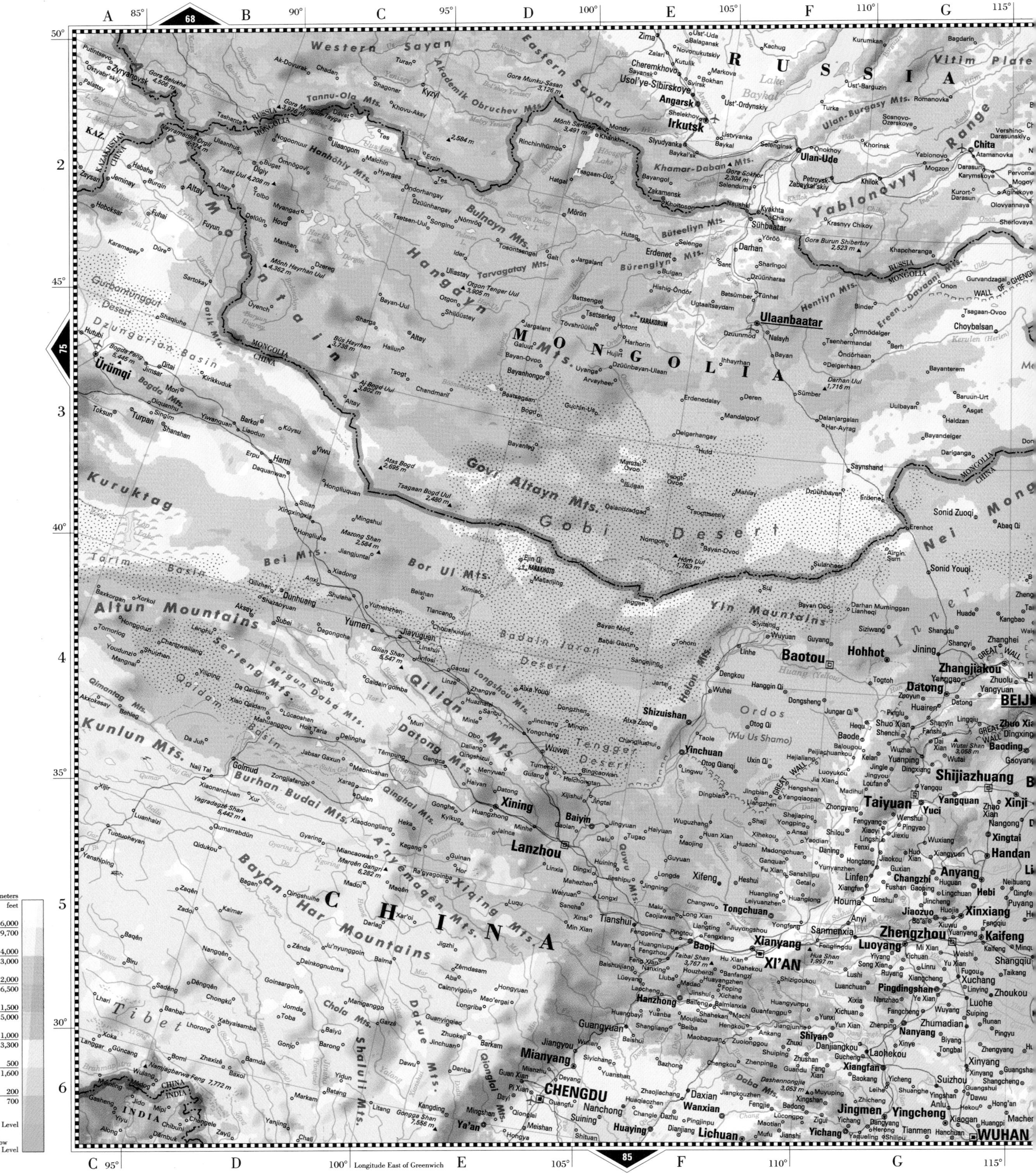

A
85°
68
B
90°
C
95°
D
100°
E
105°
F
110°
G
115°
50°
45°
40°
35°
30°
2
3
4
5
6
75
85
Longitude East of Greenwich
R U S S I A
M O N G O L I A
C H I N A
Western Sayan
Eastern Sayan
Tannu-Ola Mts.
Akademik Obruchev Mts.
Khamar-Daban Mts.
Ulan-Burgasy Mts.
Yablonovyy Range
Vitim Plateau
Baykal Lake
Irkutsk
Angarsk
Ulan-Ude
Chita
Kyzyl
Hanhöhiy Mts.
Bulnayn Mts.
Hangayn Mts.
Tarvagatay Mts.
Büteeliyn Mts.
Bürengiyn Mts.
Hentiyn Mts.
Mongolian Altai Mountains
Ulaanbaatar
Darhan
Erdenet
Sühbaatar
Choybalsan
KARAKORUM
Gurbantünggüt Desert
Dzungarian Basin
Bogda Mts.
Ürümqi
Turpan
Hami
Kuruktag
Tarim Basin
Bei Mts.
Bor Ul Mts.
Govi Altayn Mts.
Gobi Desert
Yin Mountains
Inner Mongolia
Nei Mongol
Altun Mountains
Serteng Mts.
Tergun Daba Mts.
Qaidam Basin
Qilian Mts.
Longshou Mts.
Datong Mts.
Kunlun Mts.
Burhan Budai Mts.
Qinghai Mts.
A'nyêmaqên Mts.
Xiqing Mts.
Bayan Har Mountains
Badain Jaran Desert
Tengger Desert
Ordos (Mu Us Shamo)
Helan Mts.
Daba Mts.
Chola Mts.
Daxue Mts.
Shaluli Mts.
Qionglai Mts.
Tibet
Dunhuang
Yumen
Jiayuguan
Golmud
Xining
Lanzhou
Baotou
Hohhot
Datong
Zhangjiakou
Yinchuan
Shizuishan
Taiyuan
Shijiazhuang
Handan
Anyang
Xinxiang
Zhengzhou
Kaifeng
Luoyang
Xianyang
XI'AN
Baoji
Tianshui
Hanzhong
Mianyang
CHENGDU
Ya'an
Nanchong
Daxian
Wanxian
Shiyan
Xiangfan
Yichang
Jingmen
Yingcheng
WUHAN
Gongga Shan 7,556 m
Namjagbarwa Feng 7,772 m
INDIA
meters
feet
6,000
19,700
4,000
13,000
2,000
6,500
1,500
5,000
1,000
3,300
500
1,600
200
700
Sea Level
Below Sea Level

Eastern Asia

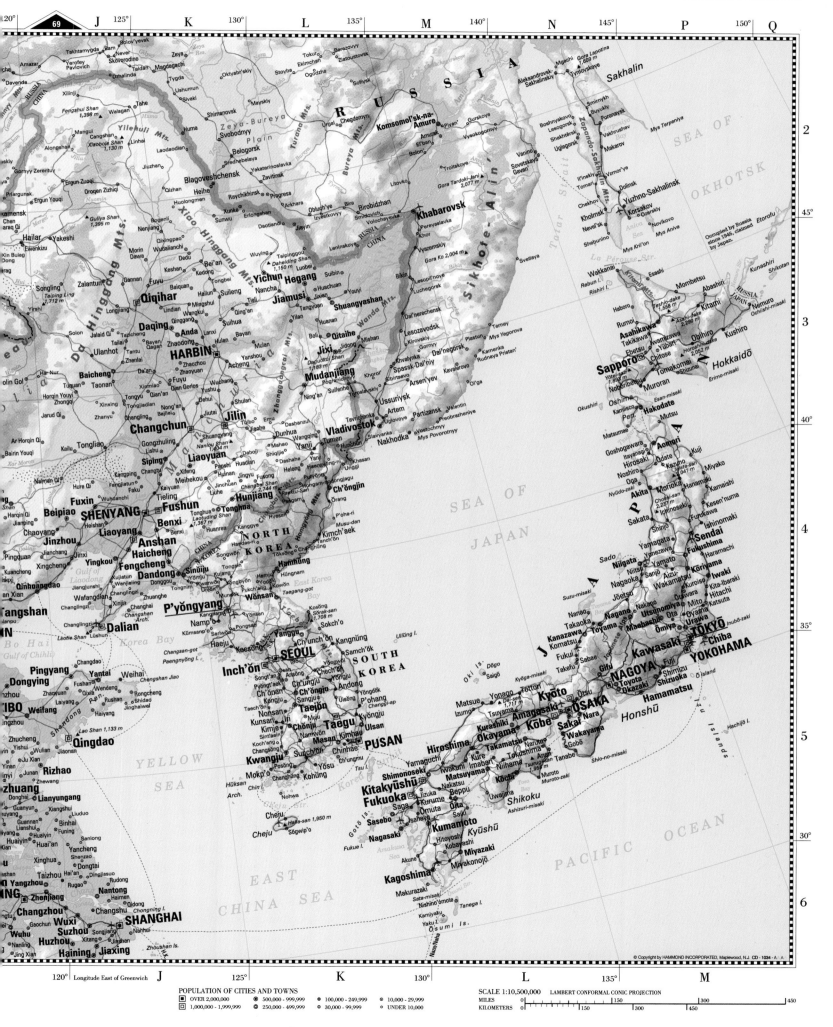

RUSSIA

Komsomol'sk-na-Amure

SEA OF OKHOTSK

Sakhalin

Khabarovsk

Yuzhno-Sakhalinsk

Occupied by Russia since 1945, claimed by Japan.

Sikhote-Alin' Mts.

SEA OF JAPAN

Qiqihar

Yichun Hegang

Jiamusi

Shuangyashan

Daqing

HARBIN

Baicheng

Mudanjiang

Jilin

Changchun

Vladivostok

Ussuriysk

Nakhodka

Ch'ŏngjin

Asahikawa

Sapporo

Hokkaidō

Hakodate

Aomori

Akita

Morioka

Siping

Liaoyuan

Tonghua

Hunjiang

Sendai

Fukushima

Kōriyama

Iwaki

Fuxin

SHENYANG

Fushun

Benxi

Liaoyang

Anshan

Haicheng

Fengcheng

Dandong

Sinŭiju

NORTH KOREA

Hamhŭng

Wŏnsan

Niigata

Nagaoka

Yamagata

Utsunomiya

Mito

TOKYO

Kawasaki

YOKOHAMA

Chiba

Jinzhou

Yingkou

Beipiao

Chaoyang

Jinzhou

Qinhuangdao

Tangshan

Dalian

P'yŏngyang

Namp'o

Nagano

Toyama

Kanazawa

NAGOYA

Shizuoka

Hamamatsu

Pingyang

Yantai

Weihai

Dongying

Weifang

SEOUL

Inch'ŏn

SOUTH KOREA

Taejŏn

Taegu

PUSAN

Kwangju

Kyōto

OSAKA

Kōbe

Sakai

Nara

Honshū

Qingdao

Rizhao

YELLOW SEA

Mokp'o

Cheju

Hiroshima

Okayama

Takamatsu

Shikoku

Kitakyūshū

Fukuoka

Shimonoseki

Matsuyama

Kōchi

Nagasaki

Kumamoto

Kyūshū

Miyazaki

Kagoshima

EAST CHINA SEA

PACIFIC OCEAN

Nantong

Changzhou

Wuxi

Suzhou

SHANGHAI

Huzhou

Haining   Jiaxing

POPULATION OF CITIES AND TOWNS

▣ OVER 2,000,000	● 500,000 - 999,999	● 100,000 - 249,999	• 10,000 - 29,999
▢ 1,000,000 - 1,999,999	● 250,000 - 499,999	● 30,000 - 99,999	○ UNDER 10,000

SCALE 1:10,500,000   LAMBERT CONFORMAL CONIC PROJECTION

MILES

KILOMETERS

SEA OF JAPAN

PACIFIC OCEAN

EAST CHINA SEA

SOUTH KOREA

KOREA

JAPAN

Kyūshū

Shikoku

Longitude East of Greenwich

meters

feet	
6,000	19,700
4,000	13,000
2,000	6,500
1,500	5,000
1,000	3,300
500	1,600
200	700

Sea Level

Below Sea Level

Central and Southern Japan

FUJI-HAKONE-IZU NATIONAL PARK

0 10 Mi
0 10 Km

© HAMMOND INC. CD - 1114 - A A

© HAMMOND INC. CD - 1115 - A A

POPULATION OF CITIES AND TOWNS

- OVER 2,000,000
- 1,000,000 - 1,999,999
- 500,000 - 999,999
- 250,000 - 499,999
- 100,000 - 249,999
- 30,000 - 99,999
- 10,000 - 29,999
- UNDER 10,000

SCALE 1:3,500,000 LAMBERT CONFORMAL CONIC PROJECTION

MILES 0 50 100 150

KILOMETERS 0 50 100 150

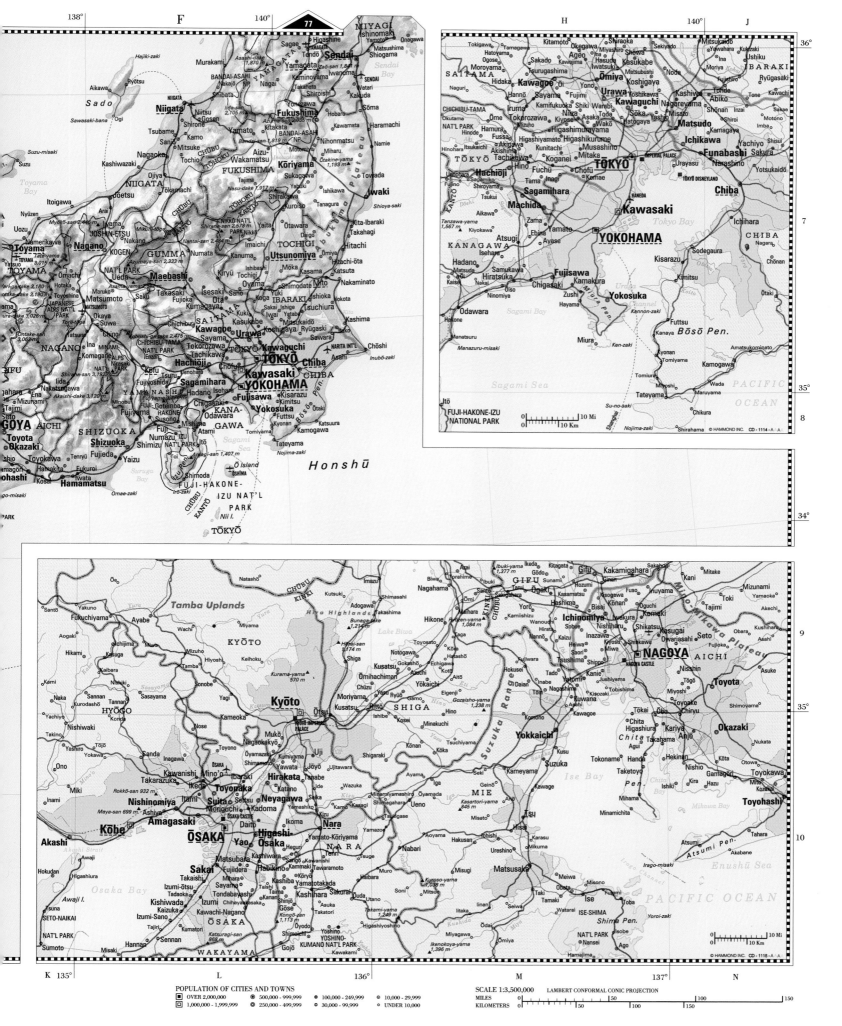

Korea

NORTH KOREA
SOUTH KOREA
CHINA
JAPAN
LIAONING
JILIN
Manchuria
KOREA BAY
YELLOW SEA
SEA OF JAPAN
East Korea Bay
Gulf of Liaodong
Liaodong Peninsula
SHENYANG
Fushun
Fuxin
Anshan
Liaoyang
Haicheng
Yingkou
Fengcheng
Dandong
Dalian
Weihai
SHANDONG
Tieling
Hunjiang
Tonghua
P'yŏngyang
Sinŭiju
Namp'o
Wŏnsan
Hamhŭng
Kimch'aek
Ch'ŏngjin
Haeju
Kaesŏng
SEOUL
Inch'ŏn
Suwŏn
Ch'unch'ŏn
Taejŏn
Ch'ŏngju
Chŏnju
Kwangju
Taegu
Ulsan
PUSAN
Masan
Mokp'o
YANGGANG-DO
CHAGANG-DO
HAMGYŎNG-BUKTO
HAMGYŎNG-NAMDO
P'YŎNGAN-BUKTO
P'YŎNGAN-NAMDO
HWANGHAE-NAMDO
HWANGHAE-BUKTO
KANGWŎN-DO
KYŎNGGI-DO
CH'UNGCH'ŎNG-BUKTO
CH'UNGCH'ŎNG-NAMDO
CHŎLLA-BUKTO
CHŎLLA-NAMDO
KYŎNGSANG-BUKTO
KYŎNGSANG-NAMDO
Armistice Line, 1953
Demilitarized Zone
Paektu-San (Changbai Shan) 2,744 m
Kangnam Mts.
Nangnim Mts.
T'aebaek Mts.
Hamgyŏng Mts.
Changbai Mts.
Qian Mts.
Changshan Arch.
Tŏkchŏk Arch.
Hŭksan Arch.
Cheju
Tsushima
© Copyright by HAMMOND INCORPORATED, Maplewood, N.J.
SCALE 1:3,500,000
LAMBERT CONFORMAL CONIC PROJECTION
MILES 0 50 100 150
KILOMETERS 0 50 100 150
Longitude East of Greenwich
POPULATION OF CITIES AND TOWNS
OVER 2,000,000
1,000,000 - 1,999,999
500,000 - 999,999
250,000 - 499,999
100,000 - 249,999
30,000 - 99,999
10,000 - 29,999
UNDER 10,000
meters
feet
6,000 19,700
4,000 13,000
2,000 6,500
1,500 5,000
1,000 3,300
500 1,600
200 700
Sea Level
Below Sea Level

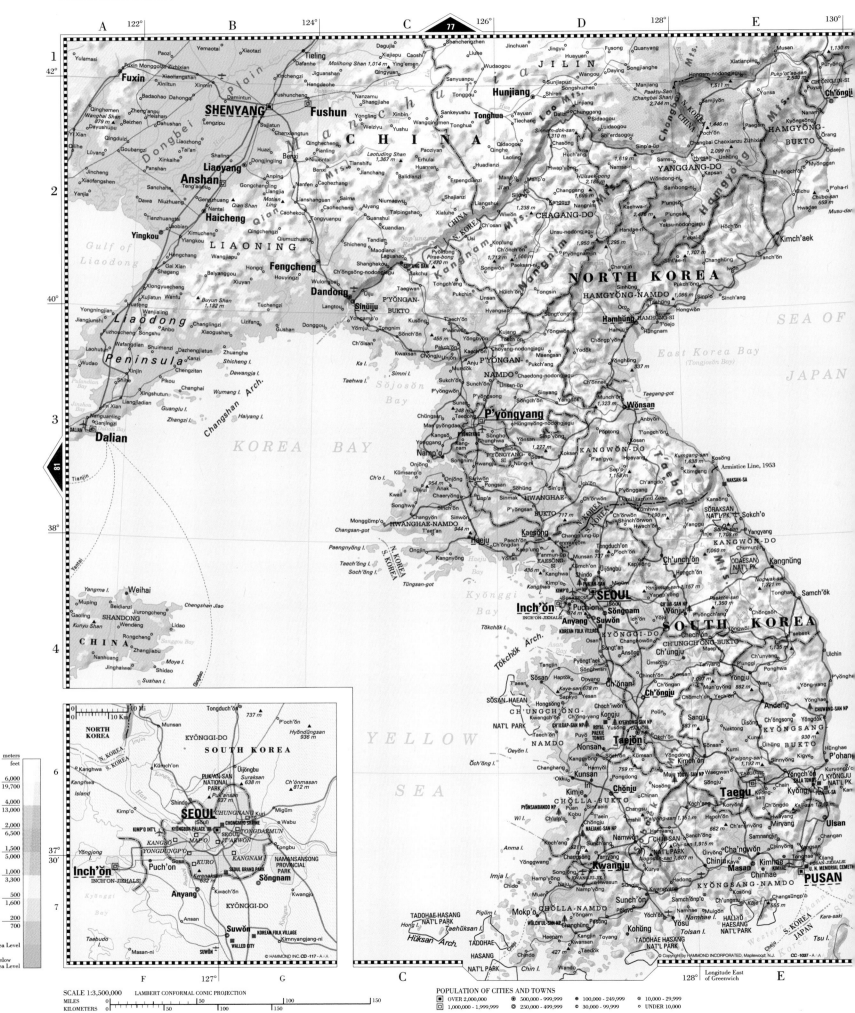

Northeastern China

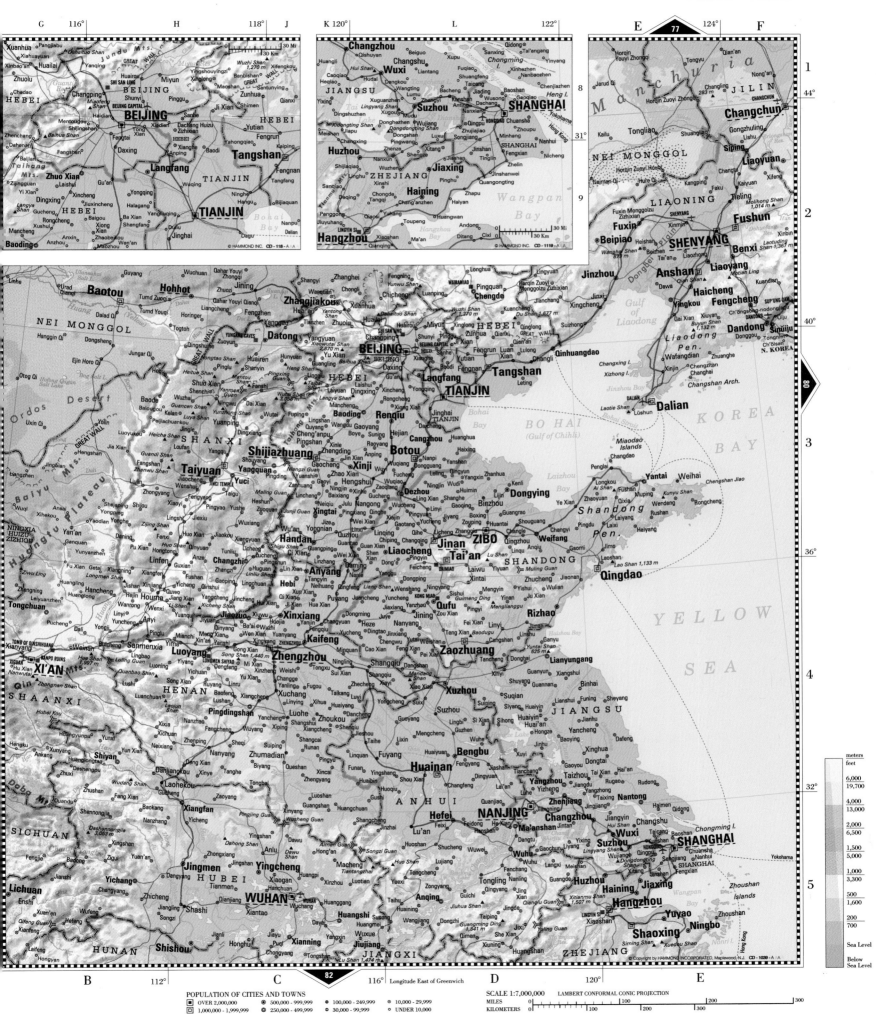

POPULATION OF CITIES AND TOWNS

- ◼ OVER 2,000,000
- ◉ 500,000 - 999,999
- ● 100,000 - 249,999
- ○ 10,000 - 29,999
- ◻ 1,000,000 - 1,999,999
- ◉ 250,000 - 499,999
- ● 30,000 - 99,999
- ∘ UNDER 10,000

SCALE 1:7,000,000   LAMBERT CONFORMAL CONIC PROJECTION

MILES   0   100   200   300

KILOMETERS   0   100   200   300

Longitude East of Greenwich

meters / feet
6,000 / 19,700
4,000 / 13,000
2,000 / 6,500
1,500 / 5,000
1,000 / 3,300
500 / 1,600
200 / 700
Sea Level
Below Sea Level

© Copyright by HAMMOND INCORPORATED, Maplewood, N.J.

Southeastern China, Taiwan, Philippines

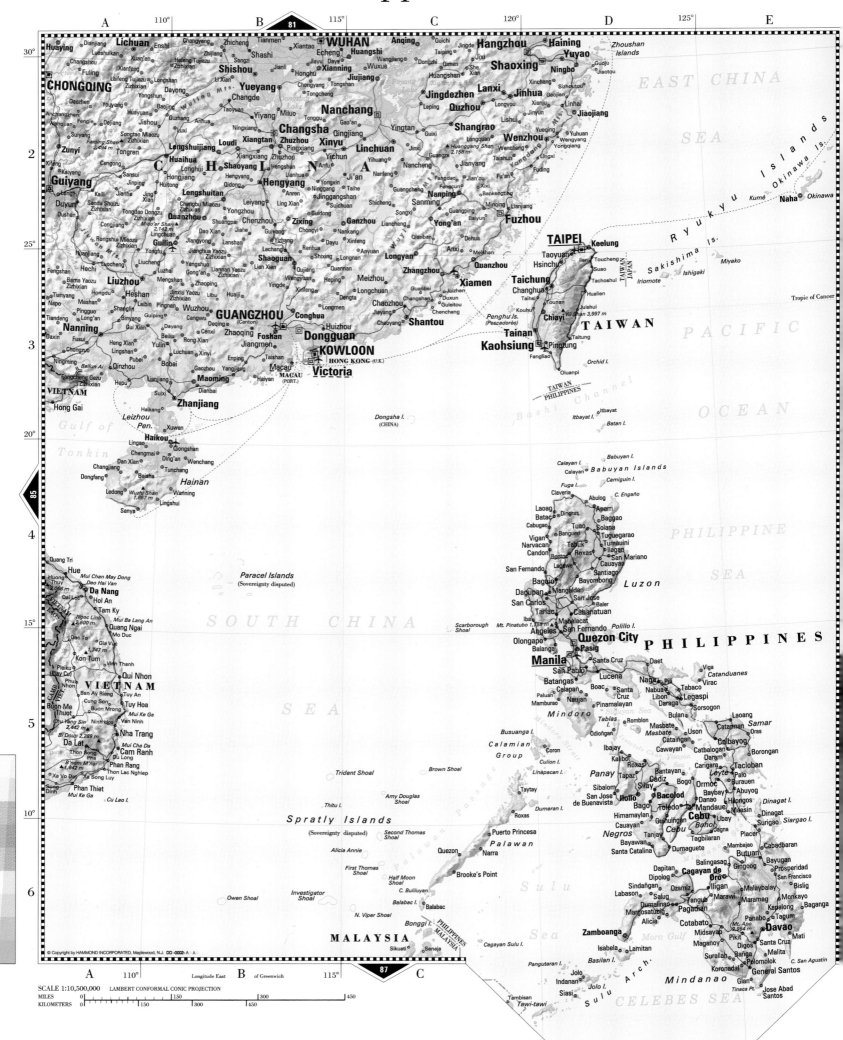

SCALE 1:10,500,000   LAMBERT CONFORMAL CONIC PROJECTION

MILES

KILOMETERS

Longitude East   of Greenwich

meters
feet

6,000
19,700

4,000
13,000

2,000
6,500

1,500
5,000

1,000
3,300

500
1,600

200
700

Sea Level

Below
Sea Level

Eastern Burma, Thailand, Indochina

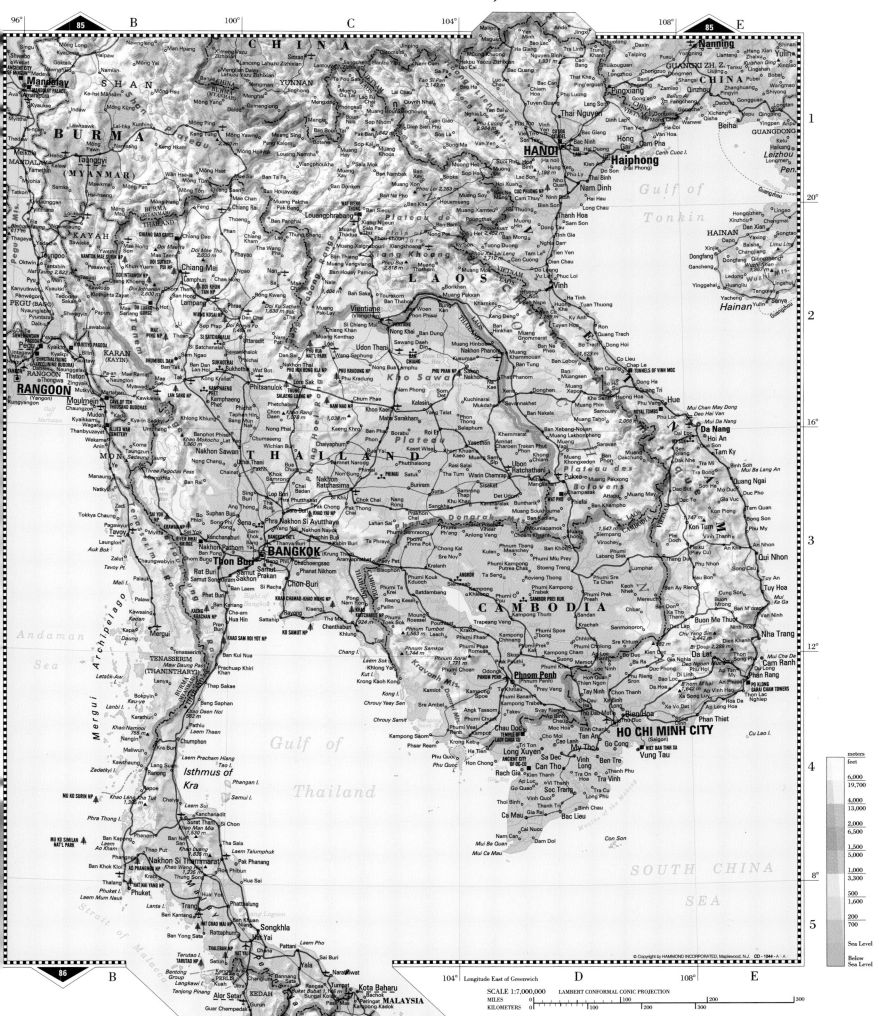

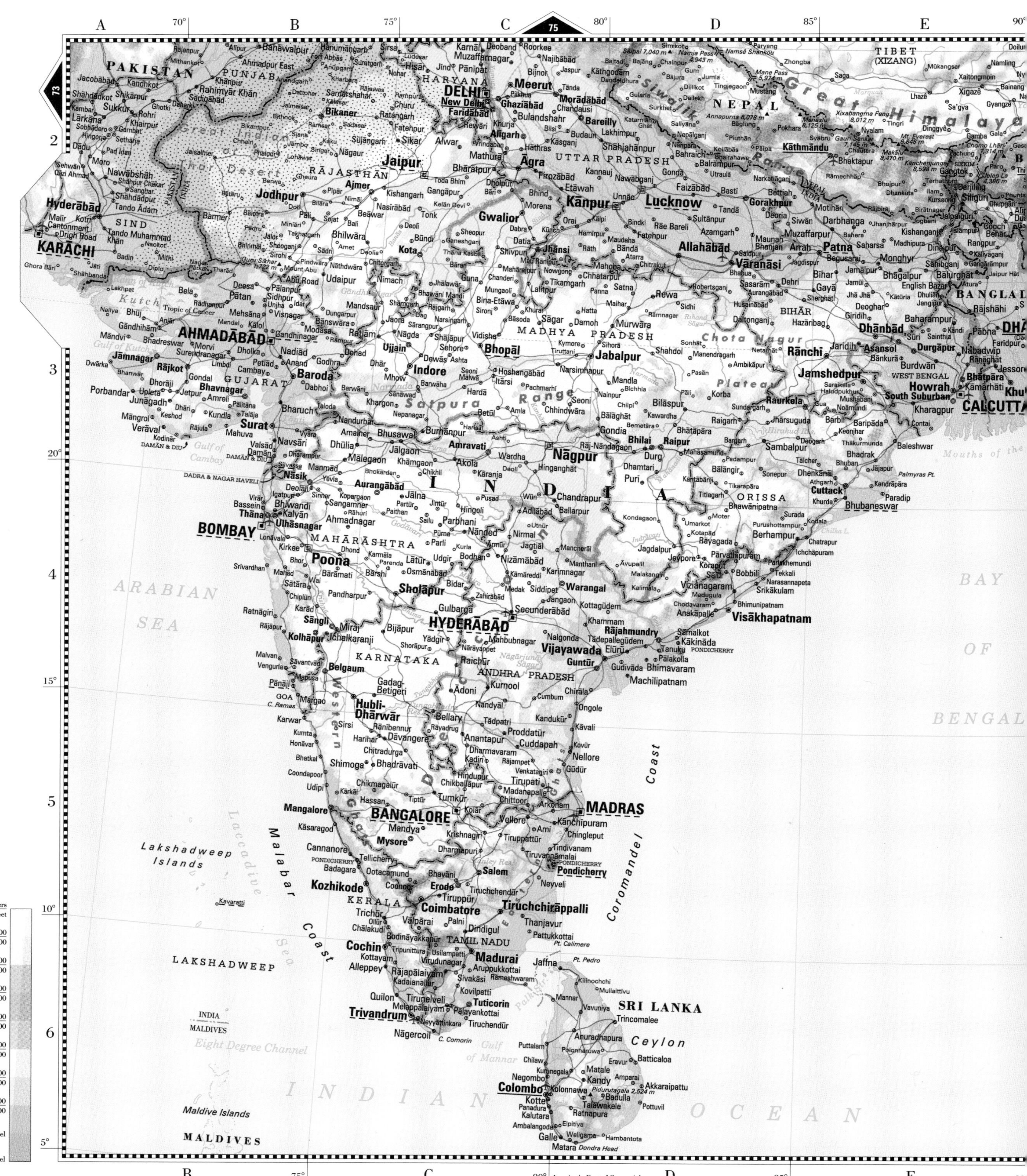
A
B
C
D
E
70°
75°
80°
85°
90°
75
73
2
3
4
5
6
20°
15°
10°
5°
PAKISTAN
PUNJAB
SIND
KARĀCHI
Hyderābād
TIBET
(XIZANG)
NEPAL
Kāthmāndu
Great Himalaya
HARYANA
DELHI
New Delhi
Farīdābād
UTTAR PRADESH
Meerut
Ghaziābād
Morādābād
Bareilly
Alīgarh
Āgra
Mathura
Jaipur
RĀJASTHĀN
Great Indian or Thar Desert
Jodhpur
Ajmer
Bīkaner
Kānpur
Lucknow
Allahābād
Vārānasi
Gorakhpur
Patna
Gwalior
Jhānsi
Kota
Udaipur
BIHĀR
Rānchī
Jamshedpur
Dhanbād
Asansol
Durgāpur
WEST BENGAL
Howrah
South Suburban
CALCUTTA
BANGLA
AHMADĀBĀD
GUJARAT
Kutch
Gulf of Kutch
Rājkot
Jāmnagar
Bhavnagar
Baroda
Surat
Gulf of Cambay
DAMĀN & DIU
DADRA & NAGAR HAVELI
MADHYA PRADESH
Bhopāl
Indore
Ujjain
Jabalpur
Sāgar
Satpura Range
Chota Nagpur Plateau
Raipur
Bhilai
Durg
Nāgpur
Amravati
Akola
Nāsik
Aurangābād
Bombay
Thāna
Kalyān
Ulhāsnagar
Poona
Ahmadnagar
MAHĀRĀSHTRA
Sholāpur
INDIA
ORISSA
Cuttack
Bhubaneswar
Berhampur
Visākhapatnam
Rājahmundry
Kākināda
Vijayawada
Guntūr
HYDERĀBĀD
Secunderābād
Warangal
Gulbarga
Bijāpur
Kolhāpur
Sāngli
Belgaum
Hubli-Dhārwār
GOA
Pānāji
KARNATAKA
ANDHRA PRADESH
Kurnool
Bellary
Dāvangere
Shimoga
Nellore
Tirupati
MADRAS
Kānchipuram
Vellore
BANGALORE
Mysore
Mangalore
Western Ghats
Eastern Ghats
Deccan
Salem
Pondicherry
Coimbatore
Tiruchchirāppalli
Thanjavur
Madurai
TAMIL NADU
KERALA
Kozhikode
Cochin
Alleppey
Quilon
Trivandrum
Tuticorin
Nāgercoil
C. Comorin
Malabar Coast
Coromandel Coast
ARABIAN SEA
Laccadive Sea
BAY OF BENGAL
INDIAN OCEAN
Lakshadweep Islands
LAKSHADWEEP
Kavaratti
INDIA
MALDIVES
Eight Degree Channel
Maldive Islands
MALDIVES
Gulf of Mannar
Palk Strait
Jaffna
SRI LANKA
Ceylon
Trincomalee
Anuradhapura
Batticaloa
Kandy
Colombo
Kotte
Galle
Matara
Dondra Head
Pt. Pedro
Pt. Calimere
Longitude East of Greenwich
meters
feet
6,000
19,700
4,000
13,000
2,000
6,500
1,500
5,000
1,000
3,300
500
1,600
200
700
Sea Level
Below Sea Level

Southern Asia

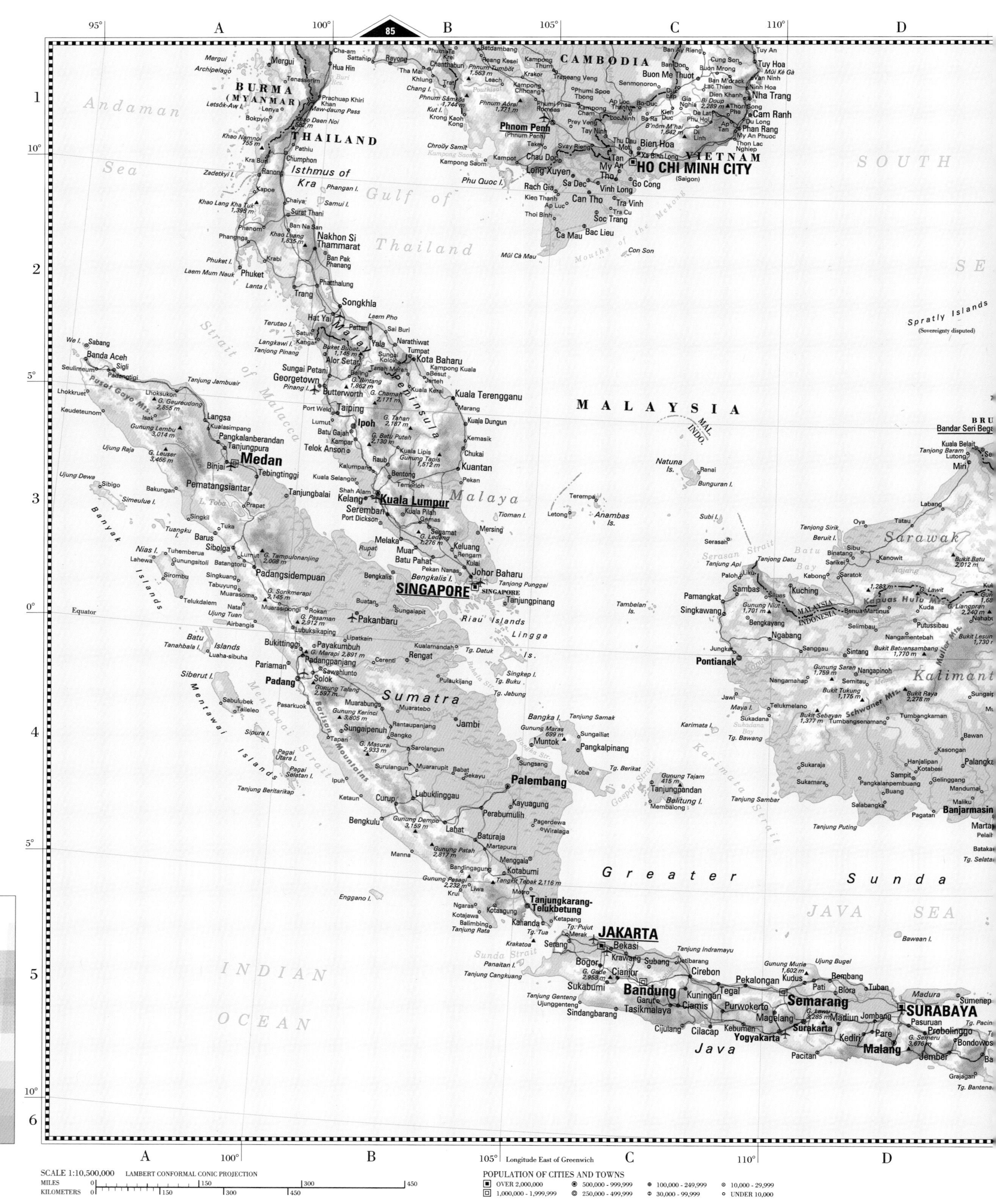

SCALE 1:10,500,000   LAMBERT CONFORMAL CONIC PROJECTION

MILES
KILOMETERS

POPULATION OF CITIES AND TOWNS

■ OVER 2,000,000	⊙ 500,000 - 999,999
▣ 1,000,000 - 1,999,999	⊙ 250,000 - 499,999

◉ 100,000 - 249,999   ⊙ 10,000 - 29,999
● 30,000 - 99,999   ○ UNDER 10,000

Southeastern Asia

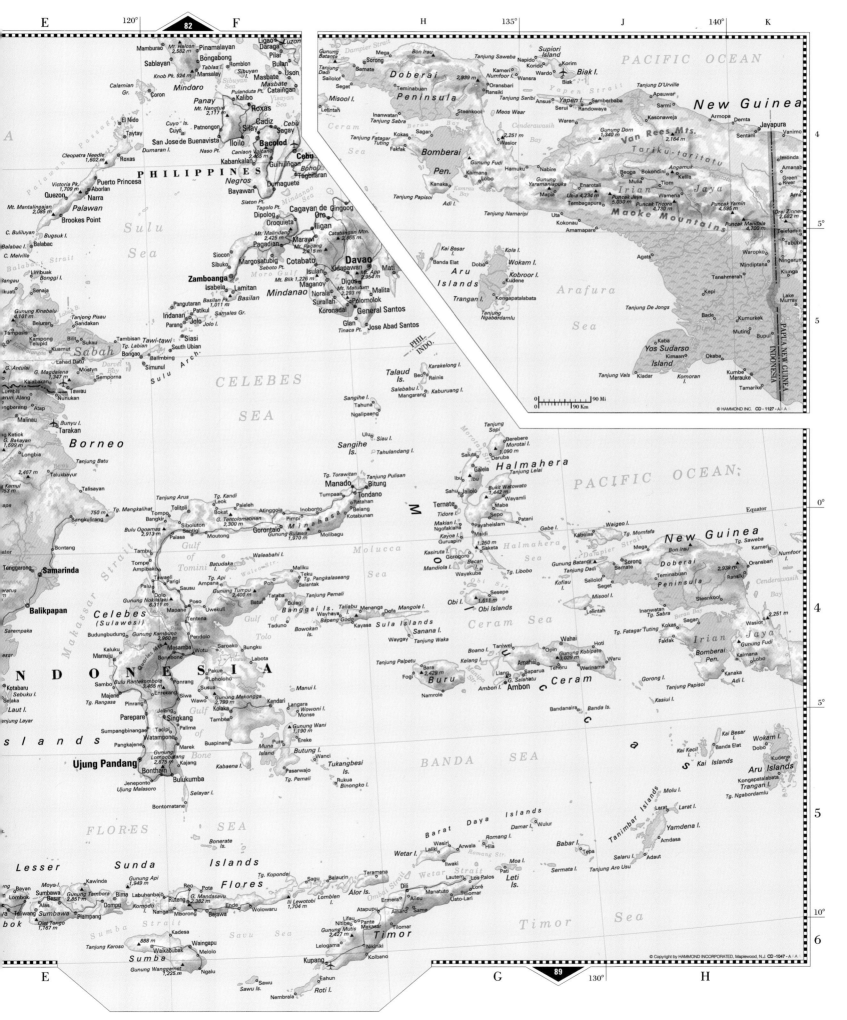

Australia and New Zealand - Comparisons

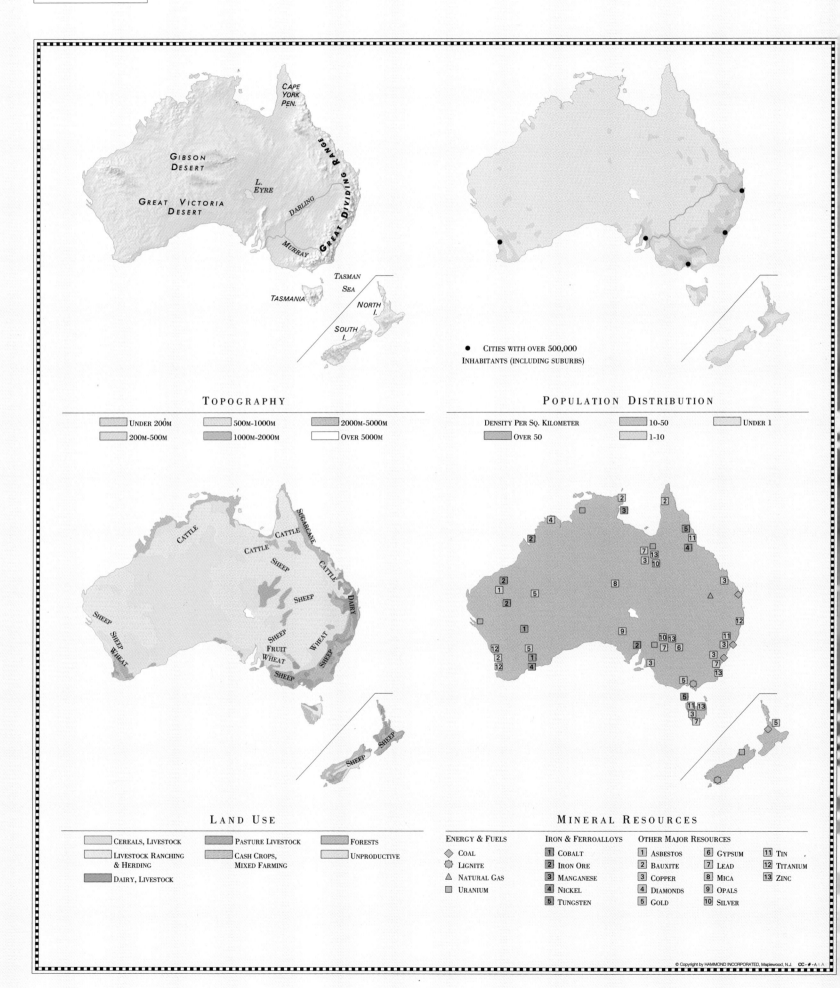

TOPOGRAPHY

UNDER 200M	500M-1000M	2000M-5000M
200M-500M	1000M-2000M	OVER 5000M

POPULATION DISTRIBUTION

● CITIES WITH OVER 500,000
INHABITANTS (INCLUDING SUBURBS)

DENSITY PER SQ. KILOMETER | 10-50 | UNDER 1
OVER 50 | 1-10

LAND USE

CEREALS, LIVESTOCK	PASTURE LIVESTOCK	FORESTS
LIVESTOCK RANCHING & HERDING	CASH CROPS, MIXED FARMING	UNPRODUCTIVE
DAIRY, LIVESTOCK		

MINERAL RESOURCES

ENERGY & FUELS
◇ COAL
⬡ LIGNITE
△ NATURAL GAS
▢ URANIUM

IRON & FERROALLOYS
1 COBALT
2 IRON ORE
3 MANGANESE
4 NICKEL
5 TUNGSTEN

OTHER MAJOR RESOURCES
1 ASBESTOS
2 BAUXITE
3 COPPER
4 DIAMONDS
5 GOLD
6 GYPSUM
7 LEAD
8 MICA
9 OPALS
10 SILVER
11 TIN
12 TITANIUM
13 ZINC

Australia, New Zealand

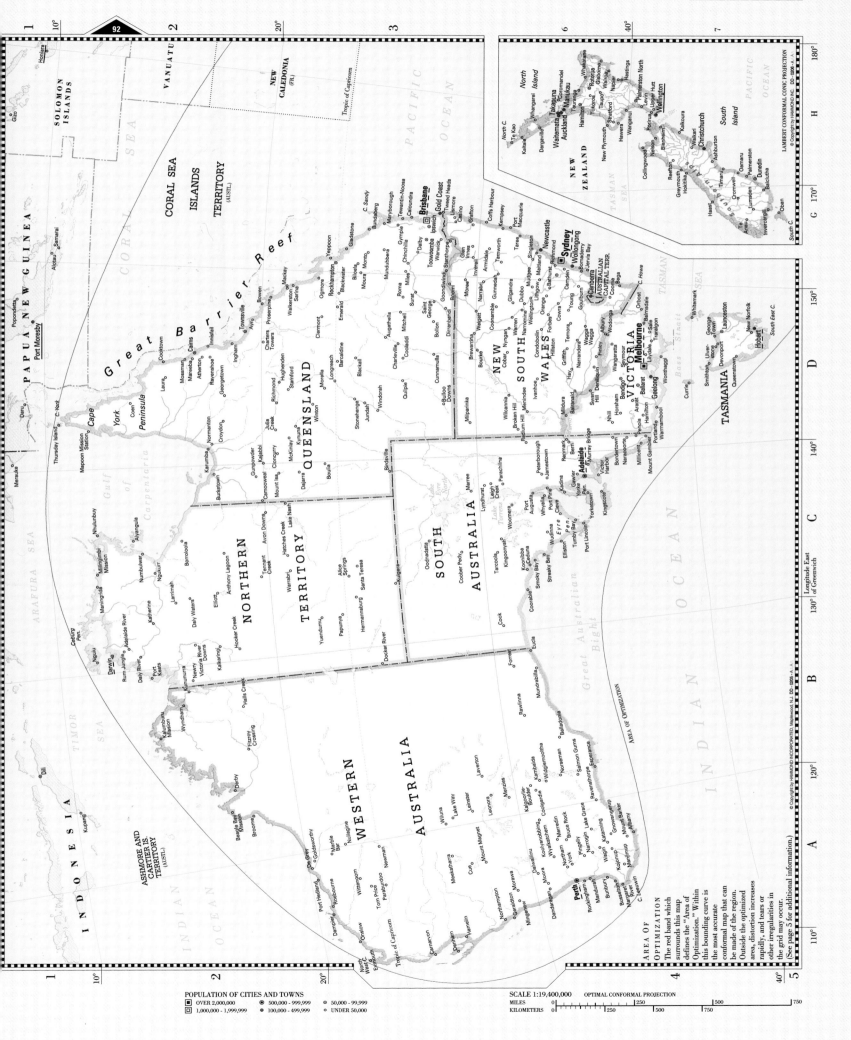

POPULATION OF CITIES AND TOWNS

- ■ OVER 2,000,000
- ⊡ 1,000,000 - 1,999,999
- ◉ 500,000 - 999,999
- ◉ 100,000 - 499,999
- ○ 50,000 - 99,999
- ○ UNDER 50,000

SCALE 1:19,400,000   OPTIMAL CONFORMAL PROJECTION

MILES 0   250   500   750

KILOMETERS 0   250   500   750

© Copyright by HAMMOND INCORPORATED, Maplewood, N.J. DD-0205-A-A

AREA OF OPTIMIZATION

The red band which surrounds this map defines the "Area of Optimization." Within this bounding curve is the most accurate conformal map that can be made of the region. Outside the optimized area, distortion increases rapidly, and tears or other irregularities in the grid may occur.
(See page 5 for additional information.)

LAMBERT CONFORMAL CONIC PROJECTION
© Copyright by HAMMOND INC. DD-0205-A-A

Northeastern Australia

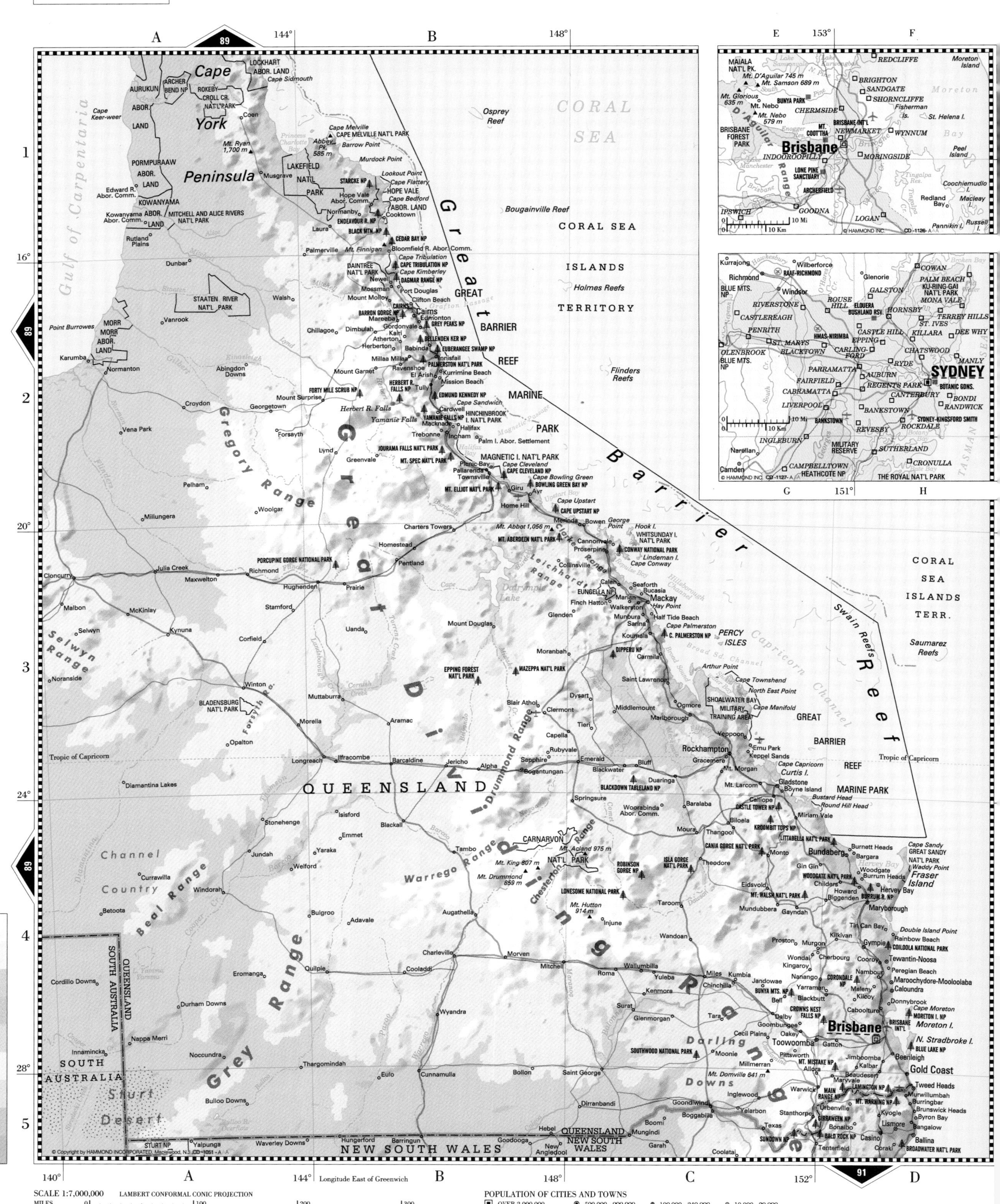

SCALE 1:7,000,000 LAMBERT CONFORMAL CONIC PROJECTION

MILES 0   100   200   300
KILOMETERS 0   100   200   300

POPULATION OF CITIES AND TOWNS

■ OVER 2,000,000	◉ 500,000 - 999,999
□ 1,000,000 - 1,999,999	◉ 250,000 - 499,999

● 100,000 - 249,999	○ 10,000 - 29,999
● 30,000 - 99,999	○ UNDER 10,000

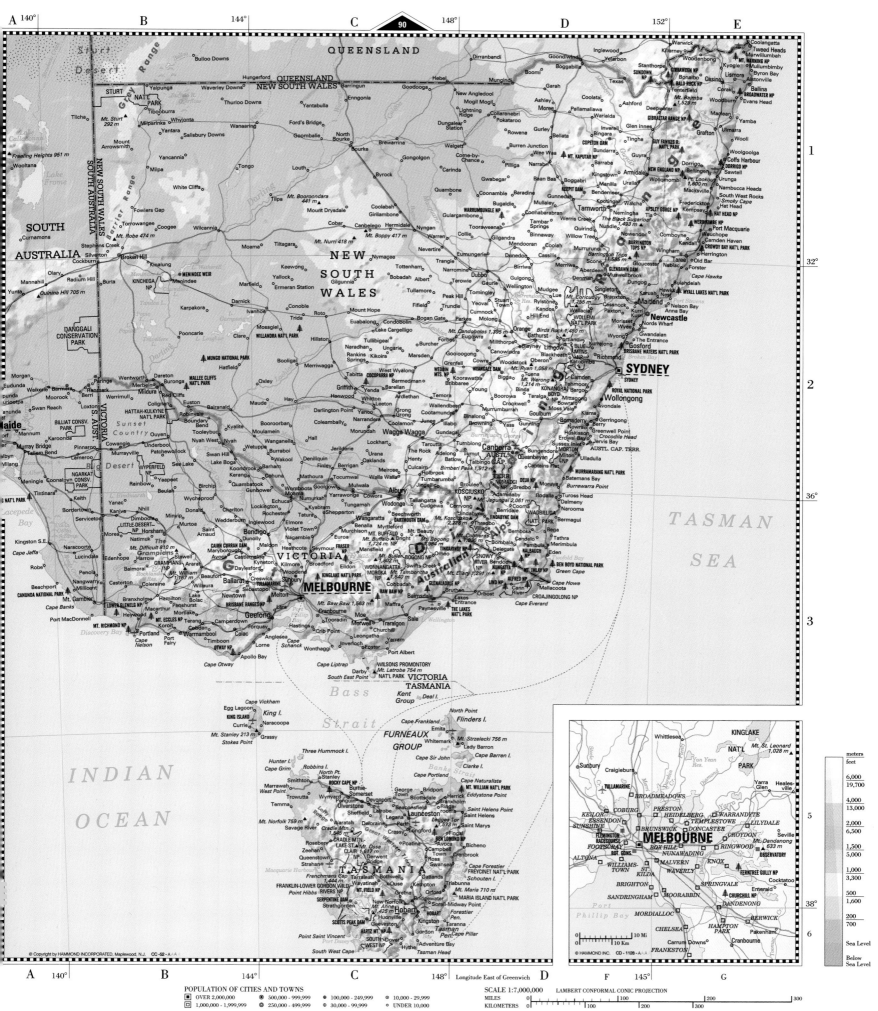

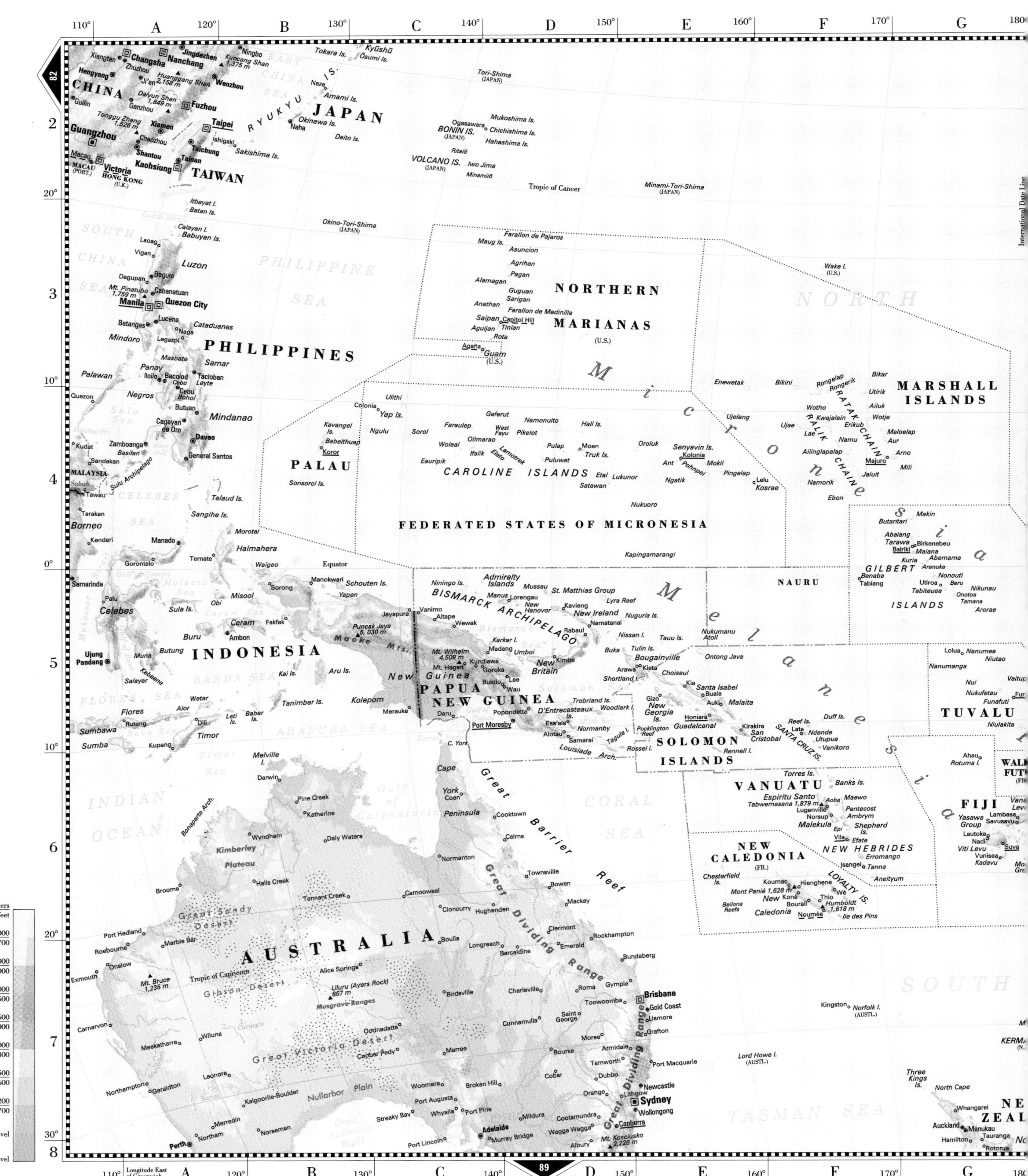

110° A 120° B 130° C 140° D 150° E 160° F 170° G 180°

CHINA

Xiangtan Zhuzhou Changsha Jingdezhen Nanchang Ningbo
Hengyang Huanggang Shan Kuocang Shan Tokara Is. Kyūshū
Guilin Ji'an 2,158 m 1,375 m Ōsumi Is.
Dayun Shan Ganzhou Wenzhou Naze Amami Is. Tori-Shima
Tonggu Zhang 1,849 m Fuzhou (JAPAN)
1,526 m Xiamen JAPAN
Guangzhou Chaozhou Taipei RYUKYU IS. Ogasawara Mukoshima Is.
Macau Shantou Taichung Ishigaki Okinawa Chichishima Is. BONIN IS.
MACAU Victoria Kaohsiung Tainan Naha Sakishima Is. Daito Is. Ritaiō Hahashima Is. (JAPAN)
(PORT.) HONG KONG TAIWAN VOLCANO IS. Iwo Jima
(U.K.) (JAPAN) Minamiiō Minami-Tori-Shima
Tropic of Cancer (JAPAN)

20°

Itbayat I. Batan Is. Okino-Tori-Shima Farallon de Pajaros
Calayan I. (JAPAN) Maug Is. Asuncion
Laoag Babuyan Is. Agrihan Wake I.
Vigan Luzon Pagan (U.S.)
Dagupan Baguio Alamagan NORTHERN
Mt. Pinatubo Cabanatuan Guguan
1,759 m Sarigan MARIANAS
Manila Quezon City Anathan Farallon de Medinilla
Batangas Lucena Cataduanes Saipan Capitol Hill (U.S.)
Naga Aguijan Tinian
Mindoro Legazpi Rota
Masbate Agaña Guam
PHILIPPINES Panay Iloilo (U.S.)
Palawan Bacolod Cebu Tacloban Enewetak Bikini Rongelap Rongerik Bikar
Negros Bohol Leyte Ujelang Utirik Ailuk MARSHALL
Quezon Cebu Ulithi Wotho ISLANDS
Butuan Colonia Yap Is. Gaferut Namonuito Hall Is. Ujae Kwajalein Erikub
Cagayan Mindanao Ngulu Faraulep West Pikelot Lae Namu Maloelap
Kudat de Oro Kavangel Sorol Fayu Senyavin Is. Ailinglapalap Aur
Zamboanga Davao Babelthuap Woleai Olimarao Oroluk Ant Pohnpei Mokil Namorik Majuro Arno
MALAYSIA Basilan General Santos PALAU Eauripik Ifalik Elato Puluwat Truk Is. Ngatik Pingelap Jaluit Mili
Sabah Koror Lamotrek Etal Lukunor Lelu Ebon
Tawau Sonsorol Is. CAROLINE ISLANDS Satawan Kosrae
Sangihe Is. Nukuoro Butaritari Makin
Tarakan FEDERATED STATES OF MICRONESIA Abaiang Tarawa Birkenebeu
Borneo Talaud Is. Bairiki Maiana Abemama
Kendari Manado Morotai Kuria Aranuka GILBERT
Gorontalo Ternate Halmahera Kapingamarangi Banaba Nonouti Beru
Samarinda Waigeo Equator NAURU Tabiteuea Tamana ISLANDS
Palu Celebes Sorong Manokwari Schouten Is. Admiralty Mussau St. Matthias Group Onotoa Arorae
Ujung Sula Is. Obi Yapen Islands Manus Lorengau New Lyra Reef
Pandang Buru Ceram Fakfak BISMARCK ARCHIPELAGO Nanovor New Ireland Nuguria Is.
Butung Ambon Puncak Jaya Jayapura Vanimo Kavieng Namatanai
INDONESIA 5,030 m Maoke Mts. Altape Wewak Bismarck Sea Karkar I. Rabaul Nissan I.
Muna Kai Is. Mt. Wilhelm Madang Umboi Teuu Is. Nukumanu
Salayar Kabaena Aru Is. 4,509 m Kundiawa New Kimbe Buka Tulin Is. Atoll
Flores Wetar Tanimbar Is. Mt. Hagen Goroka New Britain Bougainville Ontong Java
Sumbawa Alor Ruteng New Guinea Bulolo Lae Kieta
Sumba Kupang Leti Babar Kolepom PAPUA Trobriand Is. Arawa Shortland I. Choiseul
Timor Is. Merauke NEW GUINEA D'Entrecasteaux Woodlark I. Santa Isabel
Dili Daru Popondetta Buala Malaita
Timor Gulf of Normanby Gizo New Auki
Port Moresby Alotau Samarai Taguia I. Georgia Honiara
Louisiade Arch. Pocklington Is. Guadalcanal Kirakira San Reef Is. Duff Is.
C. York Rossel I. Reef Cristobal Lata Ndende Utupua
SOLOMON Rennell I. Santa Cruz Is. Vanikoro
ISLANDS

VANUATU Torres Is. Banks Is.
Cape Espiritu Santo Maewo
York Tabwemasana 1,879 m Aoba Pentecost
Peninsula Luganville Ambrym
Norsup Shepherd Is.
Malekula Epi Vila Efate NEW HEBRIDES Erromango
NEW Isangel Aneityum
CALEDONIA Mont Panié 1,628 m Koumac (FR.) LOYALTY IS.
Chesterfield New Koné Hienghene Wé
Bellona Thio Humboldt
Reefs Bourail 1,618 m
Caledonia Nouméa Ile des Pins

FIJI
Viti Levu

FInal lower right labels: TUVALU, GILBERT ISLANDS

AUSTRALIA

Melville I. Darwin
Pine Creek
Katherine
Daly Waters
Kimberley Wyndham
Plateau Halls Creek
Broome
Great Sandy Desert Tennant Creek Camooweal
Marble Bar Normanton Hughenden Townsville
Port Hedland Mackay
Roebourne Daly Waters Cloncurry Bowen
Onslow Alice Springs Longreach Barcaldine
Exmouth Mt. Bruce Clermont Rockhampton
1,235 m Tropic of Capricorn Birdsville Emerald
Gibson Desert Uluru (Ayers Rock) Boulia Bundaberg
Carnarvon 867 m Charleville Roma Gympie
Musgrave Ranges Saint Toowoomba Brisbane
Meekatharra Wiluna Oodnadatta George Gold Coast
Coober Pedy Marree Cunnamulla Lismore
Great Victoria Desert Bourke Moree Grafton
Northampton Leonora Armidale Lord Howe I.
Geraldton Tamworth Port Macquarie (AUSTL.)
Kalgoorlie-Boulder Woomera Cobar Dubbo
Nullarbor Plain Broken Hill Orange Newcastle Three
Merredin Port Augusta Mildura Lithgow Kings Is. North Cape
Norseman Whyalla Port Pirie Cootamundra Sydney
Perth Streaky Bay Port Lincoln Adelaide Wagga Wagga Canberra Wollongong Whangarei
Northam Murray Bridge Mt. Kosciusko Auckland Manukau
Albury 2,228 m Hamilton Tauranga
Rotorua

KERMA (N.)

NE ZEAL

TASMAN SEA SOUTH

INDIAN OCEAN

CORAL SEA

PHILIPPINE SEA

SOUTH CHINA SEA

CELEBES SEA

BANDA SEA

FLORES SEA

ARAFURA SEA

meters / feet
6,000 / 19,700
4,000 / 13,000
2,000 / 6,500
1,500 / 5,000
1,000 / 3,300
500 / 1,600
200 / 700
Sea Level
Below Sea Level

110° Longitude East 120° B 130° C 140° D 150° E 160° F 170° G 180°
of Greenwich A

Central Pacific Ocean

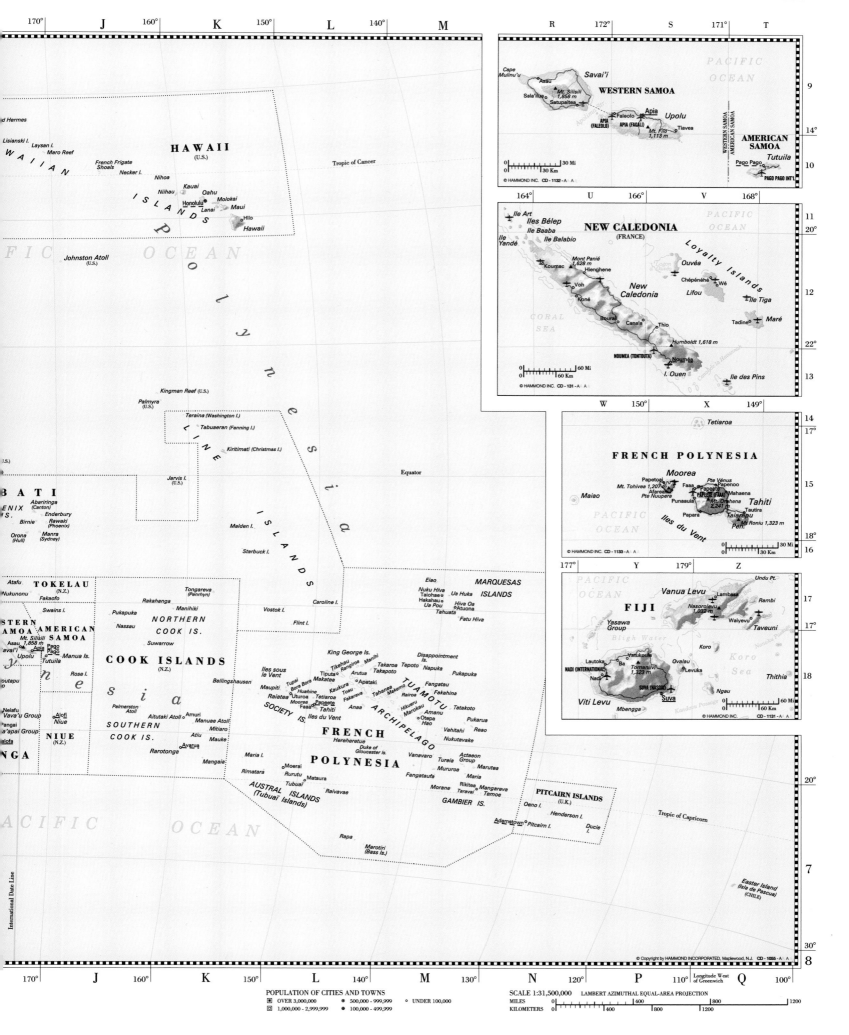

WESTERN SAMOA

Cape Mulinu'u
Asau
Savai'i
Sala'ilua
Mt. Silisili 1,858 m
Setupaitea
Faleolo
APIA (FALEOLO)
Apia
APIA (FAGALI)
Upolu
Tiavea
Mt. Fito 1,113 m

WESTERN SAMOA
AMERICAN SAMOA

AMERICAN SAMOA
Tutuila
Pago Pago
PAGO PAGO INT'L

PACIFIC OCEAN

0 ... 30 Mi
0 ... 30 Km

© HAMMOND INC. CD-1132-A-A

NEW CALEDONIA
(FRANCE)

PACIFIC OCEAN

Ile Art
Iles Bélep
Ile Baaba
Ile Yandé
Ile Balabio

Koumac
Mont Panié 1,628 m
Hienghene
Voh
Koné
Loyalty Islands
Ouvéa
Chépénéhé
Wé
Lifou
Ile Tiga

New Caledonia
Bourail
Canala
Thio
Tadine
Maré
Humboldt 1,618 m

CORAL SEA

NOUMEA (TONTOUTA)
Nouméa
I. Ouen
Ile des Pins

0 ... 60 Mi
0 ... 60 Km

© HAMMOND INC. CD-131-A-A

FRENCH POLYNESIA

Tetiaroa

Moorea
Papetoai
Mt. Tohivea 1,207 m
Afareaitu
Pte Nuupere
Maiao
Maiao
Punaauia
Papara
Papeete
PAPEETE (FAAA)
Faaa
Pte Vénus
Papenoo
Mahaena
Mt. Orohena 2,241 m
Tautira
Taiarapu Pen.
Mt. Roniu 1,323 m
Tahiti
Iles du Vent

PACIFIC OCEAN

0 ... 30 Mi
0 ... 30 Km

© HAMMOND INC. CD-1133-A-A

FIJI

PACIFIC OCEAN

Vanua Levu
Lambasa
Undu Pt.
Nasorolevu 1,032 m
Rambi
Yasawa Group
Waiyevu
Taveuni
Koro
Blight Water
Lautoka
Vatukoula
Koro
Koro Sea
Ba
NADI (INTERNATIONAL)
Nadi
Tomanivi 1,323 m
Ovalau
Levuka
Thithia
Viti Levu
SUVA (NASORI)
Suva
Ngau
Mbengga
Kandavu Passage

0 ... 60 Mi

© HAMMOND INC. CD-1131-A-A

HAWAII (U.S.)

French Frigate Shoals
Necker I.
Nihoa
Kauai
Niihau
Oahu
Honolulu
Lanai
Molokai
Maui
Hilo
Hawaii

Pearl and Hermes
Lisianski I.
Laysan I.
Maro Reef

WAIIAN ISLANDS

Tropic of Cancer

Johnston Atoll (U.S.)

PACIFIC OCEAN

Kingman Reef (U.S.)
Palmyra (U.S.)
Teraina (Washington I.)
Tabuaeran (Fanning I.)
Kiritimati (Christmas I.)
Jarvis I. (U.S.)

Equator

LINE ISLANDS

Malden I.
Starbuck I.
Vostok I.
Caroline I.
Flint I.

BATI
PHOENIX IS.
Abariringa (Canton)
Enderbury
Birnie
Rawaki (Phoenix)
Orona (Hull)
Manra (Sydney)

P o l y n e s i a

TOKELAU (N.Z.)
Atafu
Nukunonu
Fakaofo
Swains I.

WESTERN SAMOA
AMERICAN SAMOA
Mt. Silisili 1,858 m
Asau
Apia
Pago Pago
Upolu
Tutuila
Manua Is.
Rose I.

Tongareva (Penrhyn)
Rakahanga
Manihiki
Pukapuka
Nassau
NORTHERN COOK IS.
Suwarrow

COOK ISLANDS (N.Z.)
Bellingshausen
Palmerston Atoll
Aitutaki Atoll
Manuae Atoll
Amuri
SOUTHERN COOK IS.
Atiu
Mitiaro
Mauke
Avarua
Rarotonga
Mangaia

MARQUESAS ISLANDS
Eiao
Nuku Hiva
Taiohae
Ua Huka
Hakahau
Ua Pou
Hiva Oa
Atuona
Tahuata
Fatu Hiva

Iles sous le Vent
King George Is.
Tikehau
Rangiroa
Manihi
Takaroa
Tepoto
Napuka
Pukapuka
Maupiti
Bora Bora
Tupai
Makatea
Arutua
Apataki
Kaukura
Toau
Fangatau
Fakahina
Raiatea
Huahine
Tetiaroa
Takapoto
Fakarava
Raroia
Rioroa
Faaa
Moorea
Tahanea
Makemo
Tahiti
Anaa
Hikueru
Marokau
Amanu
Hao
Tatakoto
SOCIETY IS.
Iles du Vent
Vahitahi
Pukarua
Reao
Nukutavake

TUAMOTU ARCHIPELAGO

FRENCH POLYNESIA
Hereheretue
Duke of Gloucester Is.
Vanavaro
Tureia
Actaeon Group
Marutea
Maria I.
Moerai
Mururoa
Fangataufa
Morane
Rikitea
Taravai
Mangareva
Temoe
GAMBIER IS.

AUSTRAL ISLANDS (Tubuai Islands)
Rimatara
Rurutu
Mataura
Tubuai
Raivavae
Rapa
Marotiri (Bass Is.)

PITCAIRN ISLANDS (U.K.)
Oeno I.
Adamstown
Pitcairn I.
Henderson I.
Ducie I.

Tropic of Capricorn

PACIFIC OCEAN

Easter Island (Isla de Pascua) (CHILE)

Wallis and Hermes

TONGA
Neiafu
Vava'u Group
Alofi
Niue
'apai Group
NIUE (N.Z.)
alofa

International Date Line

Longitude West of Greenwich

© Copyright by HAMMOND INCORPORATED, Maplewood, N.J. CD-1055-A-A

POPULATION OF CITIES AND TOWNS
⊡ OVER 3,000,000
⊡ 1,000,000 - 2,999,999
● 500,000 - 999,999
● 100,000 - 499,999
○ UNDER 100,000

SCALE 1:31,500,000 LAMBERT AZIMUTHAL EQUAL-AREA PROJECTION
MILES 0 ... 400 ... 800 ... 1200
KILOMETERS 0 ... 400 ... 800 ... 1200

Africa - Comparisons

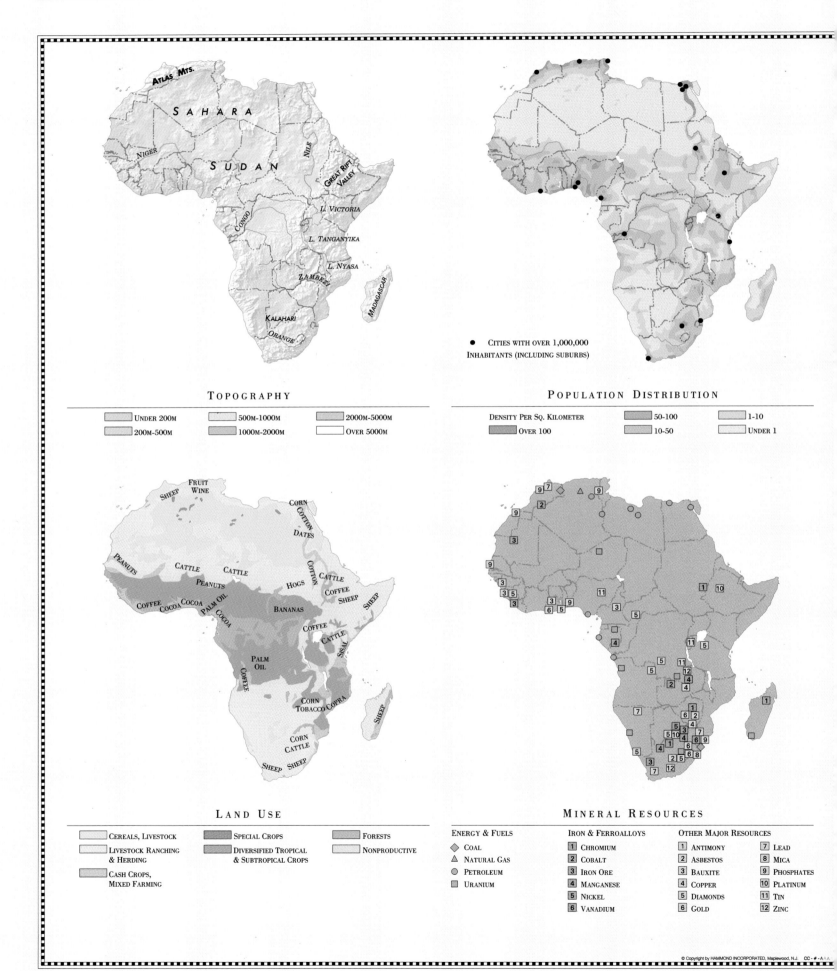

TOPOGRAPHY

	UNDER 200M		500M-1000M		2000M-5000M
	200M-500M		1000M-2000M		OVER 5000M

POPULATION DISTRIBUTION

● CITIES WITH OVER 1,000,000
INHABITANTS (INCLUDING SUBURBS)

DENSITY PER SQ. KILOMETER | | 50-100 | | 1-10
| | OVER 100 | | 10-50 | | UNDER 1

LAND USE

	CEREALS, LIVESTOCK		SPECIAL CROPS		FORESTS
	LIVESTOCK RANCHING & HERDING		DIVERSIFIED TROPICAL & SUBTROPICAL CROPS		NONPRODUCTIVE
	CASH CROPS, MIXED FARMING				

MINERAL RESOURCES

ENERGY & FUELS
◆ COAL
△ NATURAL GAS
○ PETROLEUM
▢ URANIUM

IRON & FERROALLOYS
1 CHROMIUM
2 COBALT
3 IRON ORE
4 MANGANESE
5 NICKEL
6 VANADIUM

OTHER MAJOR RESOURCES
1 ANTIMONY   7 LEAD
2 ASBESTOS   8 MICA
3 BAUXITE   9 PHOSPHATES
4 COPPER   10 PLATINUM
5 DIAMONDS   11 TIN
6 GOLD   12 ZINC

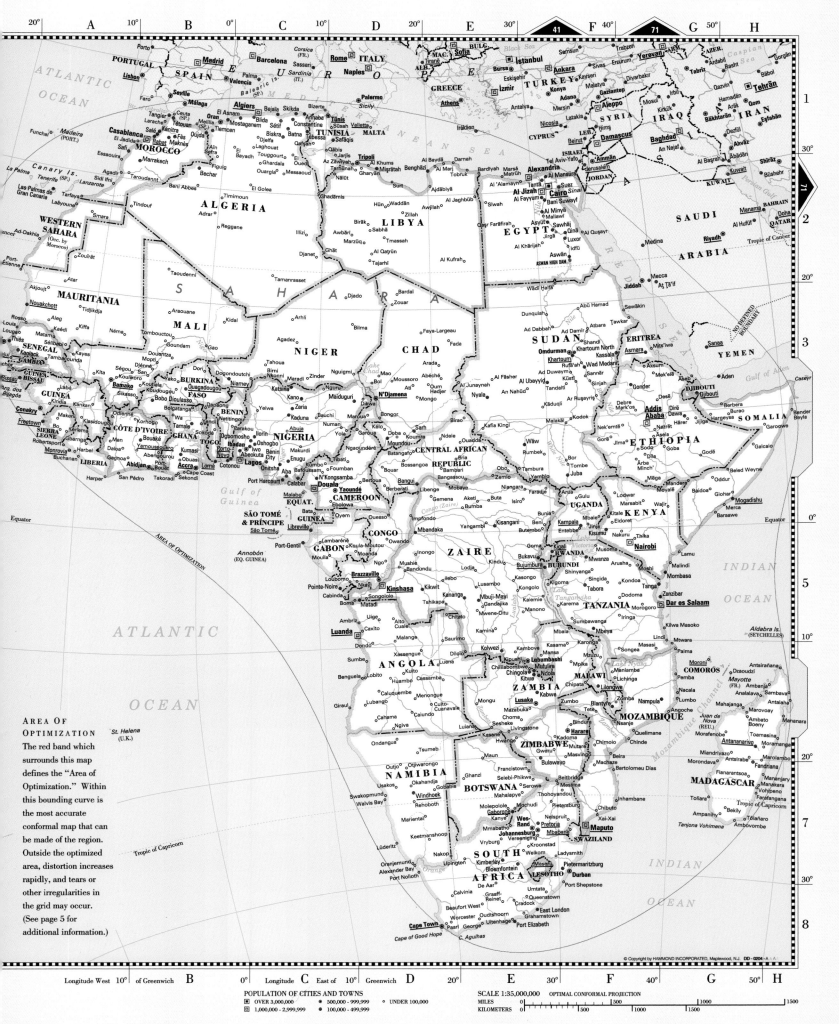

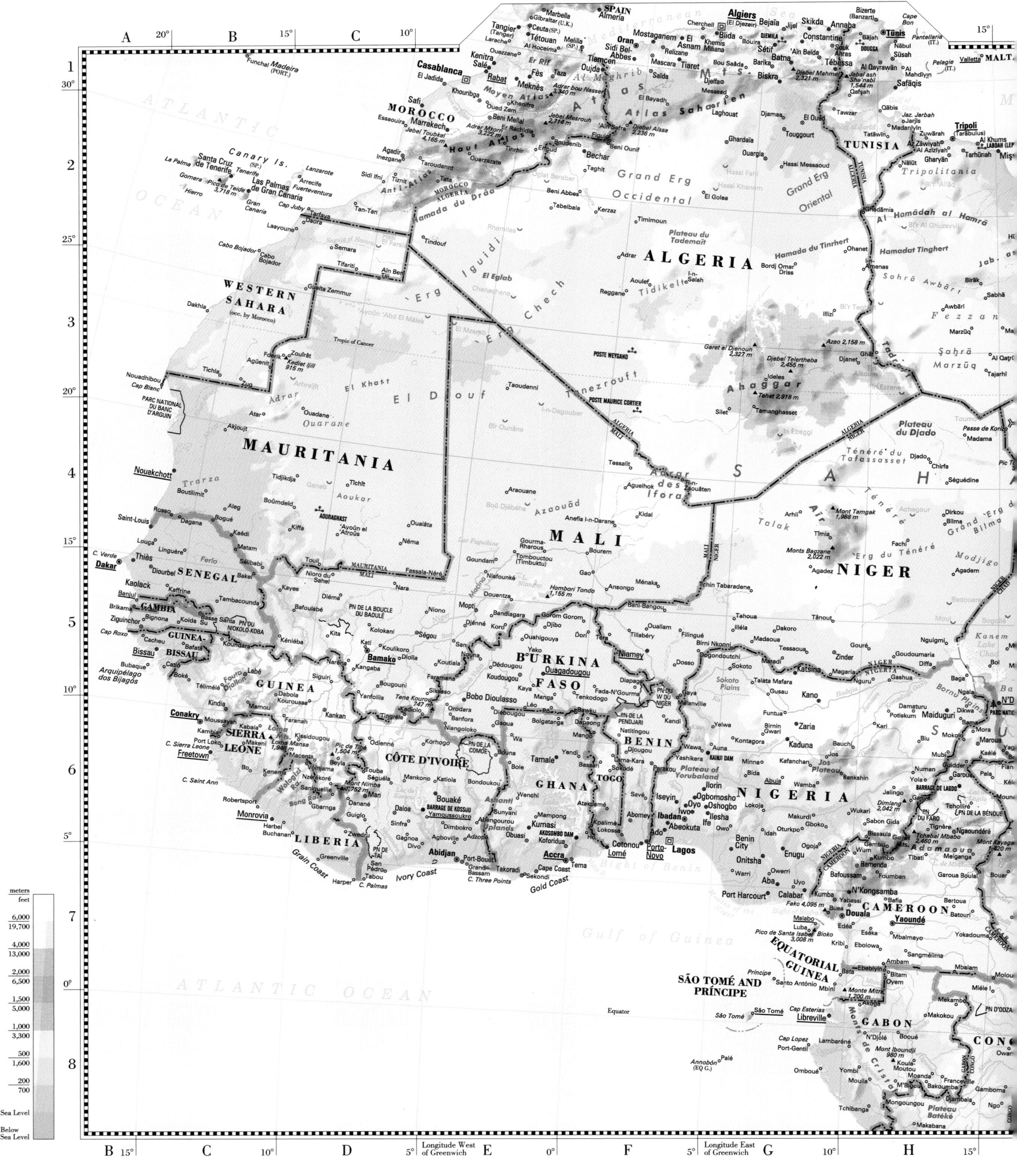

ATLANTIC OCEAN
MOROCCO
ALGERIA
TUNISIA
WESTERN SAHARA
(occ. by Morocco)
MAURITANIA
MALI
NIGER
SENEGAL
GAMBIA
GUINEA-BISSAU
GUINEA
SIERRA LEONE
LIBERIA
CÔTE D'IVOIRE
BURKINA FASO
GHANA
TOGO
BENIN
NIGERIA
CAMEROON
EQUATORIAL GUINEA
SÃO TOMÉ AND PRÍNCIPE
GABON
Canary Is. (SP.)
Madeira (PORT.)
Algiers
Tunis
Tripoli
Rabat
Casablanca
Nouakchott
Dakar
Banjul
Bissau
Conakry
Freetown
Monrovia
Bamako
Ouagadougou
Niamey
Accra
Lomé
Porto-Novo
Lagos
Yaoundé
Malabo
Libreville
São Tomé
Grand Erg Occidental
Grand Erg Oriental
Ahaggar
Tanezrouft
El Djouf
Gulf of Guinea
Bight of Benin
Ivory Coast
Gold Coast
Grain Coast
Tropic of Cancer
Equator
Longitude West of Greenwich
Longitude East of Greenwich
meters
feet
6,000
19,700
4,000
13,000
2,000
6,500
1,500
5,000
1,000
3,300
500
1,600
200
700
Sea Level
Below Sea Level

Northern Africa

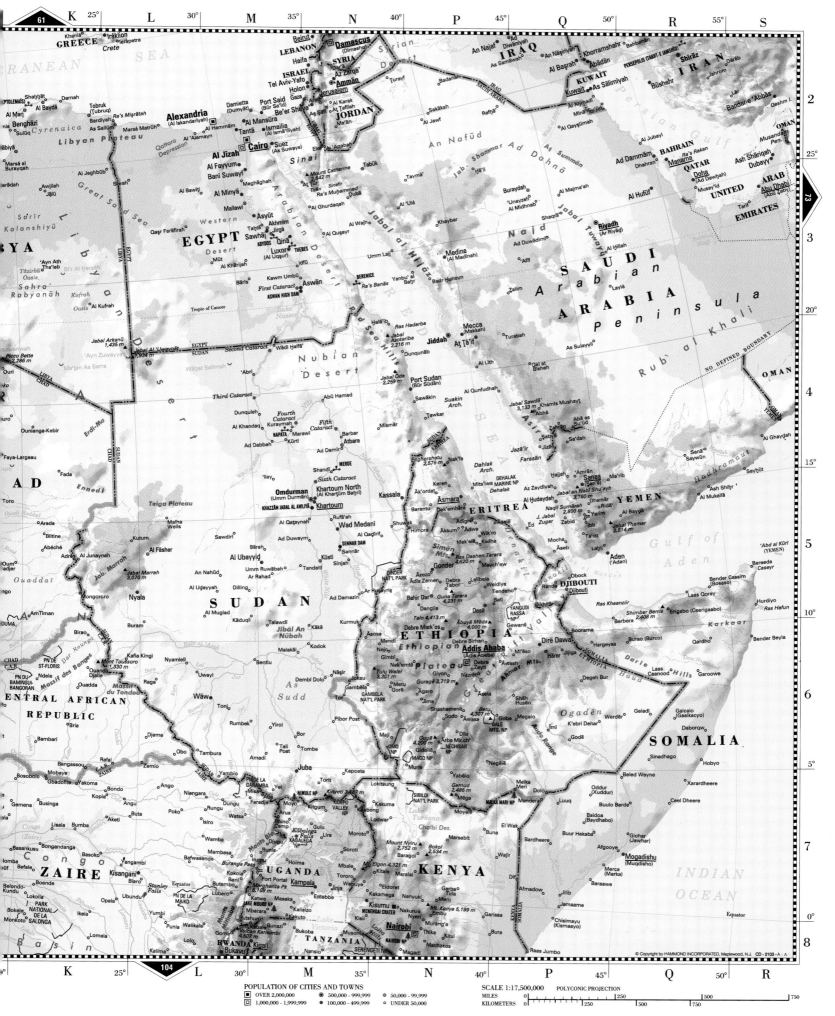

POPULATION OF CITIES AND TOWNS

- ■ OVER 2,000,000
- ◻ 1,000,000 - 1,999,999
- ⦿ 500,000 - 999,999
- ⊙ 100,000 - 499,999
- ◉ 50,000 - 99,999
- ∘ UNDER 50,000

SCALE 1:17,500,000   POLYCONIC PROJECTION

MILES 0   250   500   750

KILOMETERS 0   250   500   750

© Copyright by HAMMOND INCORPORATED, Maplewood, N.J.   CD - 2103 - A - A

A · 16° · B · 12° · C · 8° · D · 4°

1

20°

DAKHLET
NOUADHIBOU

B. d'Arguin

Cap Ioulik Ioulik
Ile Tidra

INCHIRI

Cap Timiris
Nouâmghâr

PN DU
BANC
D'ARGUIN

Benichchab
Akjoujt

Tijirit

Akchâr

Dhar de Chinguetti

Chinguetti

Atar

Adrar

Oujeft

Aguilal Fai

Jreïda

TRARZA

Tâmassoumit

Tidikdja

Lekhcheb
Tichit
Arhrijit

ADRAR

MAURITANIA

Nierquent

El Djouf

El Mreyyé

Nouakchott

NOUAKCHOTT
Ouad Nâga

TAGANT

Arbjij

S

TOMBOUCT

SA

2

16°

Boutilimit

Mederdra

Bir
Aleg

BRAKNA

Moudjéria

Aoukar

HODH
ECH
CHARGUI

Ras el
Mâ

Keur Massène
Tiguent

Boûmdeid

Kiffa

Nema

Richard Toll

Rosso Tékane
Dagana
Podor
Dar el
Barka
Bogué

Mal

AOUDAGHAST

Tamchaket

464 m▲
Guérou

Barkéwol el
Abiod

El Djoueni

Adel Bagrou

Fassala-Néré

Nara

Léré

Niafounké

Gou

Saint-Louis

Ndiago
Mpal

SAINT-
LOUIS

Mbagne
Kaédi

M'Bout

GORGOL

EL
'ACÂBA

Ayoûn el
Atroûs

HODH EL
GHARBI

Djiguéni

KOUMBI SALEH

Goumbou

Nampala

Macina

Mo

Louga

Kébémer

LOUGA

Dahra
Linguère

Ranérou

Maghama
Sivé
Matam

GUIDIMAKA

Ould Yenje
Hamoud

Touil
Kobenni

Bassikounou

Sokolo

Ténenkou
Ouro Modi

Mopti

M

DAKAR
DAKAR (YOFF)
Dakar
M'Bour

Thiès
Rufisque
Tivaouane
THIÈS
DIOURBEL
Diourbel
Mbacké
Touba

SENEGAL

Vélingara
Namari
Wompou

Sélibaby
Gouraye
Bakel

Yélimané
Tambakara
Sandaré

Nioro du
Sahel

Ké Macina

Niono
Manimpé
Diabaly

SÉGOU
Ségou

Djenné

MO

S

Fatick

Gossas
Guinguineo

KAOLACK
Kaolack

Birkelane

Goudiri
Kidira
Kayes
Lonétou

Ambidédi
Maréna
Lakamané

Diéma
Mourdiah

Doura Kolongotomo

San

Tominian

3

Bakau
M'Bour
Foundiougne
FATICK

Nioro-du-
Rip

Kaffrine
Koungheul

GAMBIA

C. Saint Mary
Yundum
Brikama

BANJUL
BANJUL (INT'L)
YUNDUM

Banjul
Mansa Konko

Kuntaur
Georgetown
Basse Santa Su

Fatoto

TAMBACOUNDA

Tambacounda

Goudiri
Sadiola
Bafoulabé

KAYES

584 m▲

Didiéni

Kolokani
Banamba

Farako

BAMAKO
Katiéra

SÉGOU

Katé

Niakassola

Koutiala

KOSSI

Déd

NOU

Diouloulou
ZIGUINCHOR

KOLDA

Diaroumé
Sédhiou

Vélingara
Kolda

Médina
Gonassé

PN DU
NIOKOLO
KOBA

Saraya

Koundian

Kotofata

Kita

Sébékoro

RÉSERVE DE
KÉNIÉBAOULÉ

Kéniéba

Satadougou Tintiba

656 m▲

Niagassola

BAMAKO (SENOU)

Koulikoro

Banamba

Kati
Bamako

Fana

Koulikoro
Konobougou
Mpessoba

Kémparana

Yorosso

Nouna

KOSSI

Bignona
Oussouye
Ziguinchor

Cap Roxo

GUINEA
BISSAU

Cacheu
São Domingos

Susana

Teixeira Pinto

Farim

SENEGAL
G.-BISSAU

Sâmbailo
Koundara

Guingan

MALI
GUINEA

Naréna

Siguiri

Kangaba

Kouremalé
Kangaré

Bougouni

Kolondiéba

Garalo

Blinndio

Nkourala

Kadiana
Tingréla

409 m▲

Niélé

KÉNÉ-
DOUGOU

SIKASSO
Sikasso

733 m▲

Orodara

HOUET

Bobo Dioulasso

BORGO

BO

Ilha de Jeta

Ponta de Pelindá

Ilha Caravela

Arq. dos
Bijagós

I. de
Orango

I. Roxa

Bissorã
Mansôa
Bafatá

BISSAU (BIPINT)
Bolama

Fulacunda
Buba

Xitole

Nova
Lamego

Koumbia

LABÉ

Linsan

Gaoual

Wendou Borou
Touba

Koubia
Tougué

1,245 m▲
Labé

Mali

Tambéring

Dinguiraye

Norassoba

Kalinko
Seloumba

Yanfolila

Kouroussa

GUINEA

Kankan

Baro

KANKAN

Mandiana
Kankan

Samatigila

Kadiolo

Tiéfinzo

587 m▲

Samoradougou

Niangoloko

Bounouna

Banfora

Sidéradougou

COMOÉ

Formosa

Catió
Cacine

Bubaque

Télémélé

Dubréka

Sansale
BOKÉ
Boké
Victoria

Kamsar

Bintimodiaya
Koliya
Tormélou
Tondon

Mitti
Timbo
Dalaba

Massif
du Fouta
Djallon

Dabola
Sifray

Konindou

Kouroussa

708 m▲

Koumban

Moribaya

Komodougou

Kani

Mankono

Tiéningboé

4

Cap Verga

Boffa

Wassou
Tatéma

Félissédou

KINDIA
Kindia
Friguiagbé

Sougéta
Kourala Konkouré
Kolenté

Mamou

FARANAH

Kaba

1,119 m▲
Faranah

Banian

Tokonou

Kérouané

Koumandougou

Odienné

Tyémé
Ségéla-Koro

Boundiali

Ferkéssédougou

Korhogo

PARC NATION
DE LA
COMOÉ

Conakry

Cité de
Kassa

CONAKRY
Forécariah

Kamsar
Benti

Moussayah

Kambia

Fadugu
Loma Mansa
1,948 m▲

Kamakwie

Falaba
Kabala

Loma
Mts.

Sangardo

Kissidougou

1,439 m▲
Koumandougou

Beyla

1,656 m▲

Touba

Kabala

PN DU
MONT
SANGBÉ

Sifié

Séguéla

Mankono

Katiola

Bwandougou

NORTHERN
Bumbuna

Binkolo

Pointe Sallatouk

Makeni
Port Loko

Benkunya
Sankanbiriwa
1,853 m▲

Yende Millimou

Kissi
Kailahun

Diomandou
Nionsamoridougou
Macenta

Koundou
1,346 m▲

Pic de Tibé
1,504 m▲

Koyama

Boola

1,257 m▲

Koyama

Lola

Nimba
1,752 m▲

Mont Tonkoui
1,189 m▲

Man

Biankouma

PN DE
LA MARAOUE

Vavoua

623 m▲
Bouaflé

Sinfra

Zuénoula

Tiébissou

BARRAGE DE KOSSOU

Yamoussoukro

COTE D'IVOIRE

Bouaké

Mbahiakro

Bocanda

Dimbokro

Bongouanou

8°

FREETOWN (LUNGI INT'L)
Lungi
Pepel

Freetown
WESTERN
AREA
Banana Is.

C. Sierra Leone

Hastings
Rokupr
Kissy
Moyamba

Tingi
Mts.

Yonibana
Talama

Jaiama

Koidu

SIERRA
LEONE

Panguma

EASTERN

Kenema
Blama
Daru

Pendembu

Fangamandou

Slela

Guéckédou

Kolahun

Voinjama

Zelimai
Zorzor

NZÉRÉKORÉ

Nzérékoré

Koulé

Yomou

Yekepa

Séniquélie

Danané

Toulépleu

Guiglo

Duékoué

Issia

Daloa

Gagnoa

PN DU
MONT
PEKO

BARRAGE DE TAABO

Oumé

Divo

Grand Afén

Adzopé

Agboville

Sinfra

Akoupé

Turtle Is.
C. Saint Ann

Bonthe
Sherbro
Island

Sumbuya

Pujehun

SOUTHERN

Potoru

Gbangbatok

Sembehun

Bo
Bojbal

Mano

S. LEONE
LIBERIA

Mount Wuteve
1,381 m▲

Koyama

LOFA

Bella
Yella

Zwedru

Bondougou

5

ATLANTIC

OCEAN

Robertsport

Robertsport

Bopolu

Gbarnga

645 m▲
Totota

Salala

NIMBA

Gbanga

Zia Town

Dirou

Kahnple

Gahnpa

BONG

Tota

Belefuanai

Tapeta

CÔTE D'IVOIRE

PN DE
TAÏ

Chutes
Néaoua

Mont Nienokoué
396 m▲

Sinfra

Lakota

Divo

Ndouci

BARRAGE D

Sikinssa

GRAND CAPE
MOUNT
Tubmanburg

Brewerville
C. Mesurado

Monrovia

MONTSERRADO
Kakata

Mt. Barclay
Harbel

Marshall
Edina

Buchanan

GRAND
BASSA

Hartford

Dolobli

LIBERIA

Guigio

Guibéroua

Soubre

Guiri

Soubre

PN
D'ASNAGY

Abidjan

Dabou
Port-Bouët

ABIDJAN
(PORT BOUET)

GRAND

Bingerv

MARYLAND

Plibo

SINO

Dodwekon

Kahnwia

Diroutou

Mont Kope 424 m▲

Fresco

Grand-Lahou

Grand Cess

Sassandra

Ivory

Coast

River
Cess

GRAND
JIDE

Bafu

Greenville

Sasstown

Nyaake

Harper
C. Palmas

Basa

San Pédro

Tabou

A · 16° · B · 12° · Longitude West of Greenwich · C

SCALE 1:7,000,000 · LAMBERT CONFORMAL CONIC PROJECTION

MILES 0 · 100 · 200 · 300

KILOMETERS 0 · 100 · 200 · 300

© Copyright by HAMMOND INCORPORATED, Maplewood, N.J. · CC-5B-A-A

meters
feet

6,000
19,700

4,000
13,000

2,000
6,500

1,500
5,000

1,000
3,300

500
1,600

200
700

Sea Level

Below
Sea Level

Grain Coast

Putu Ra.

Bong Ra.

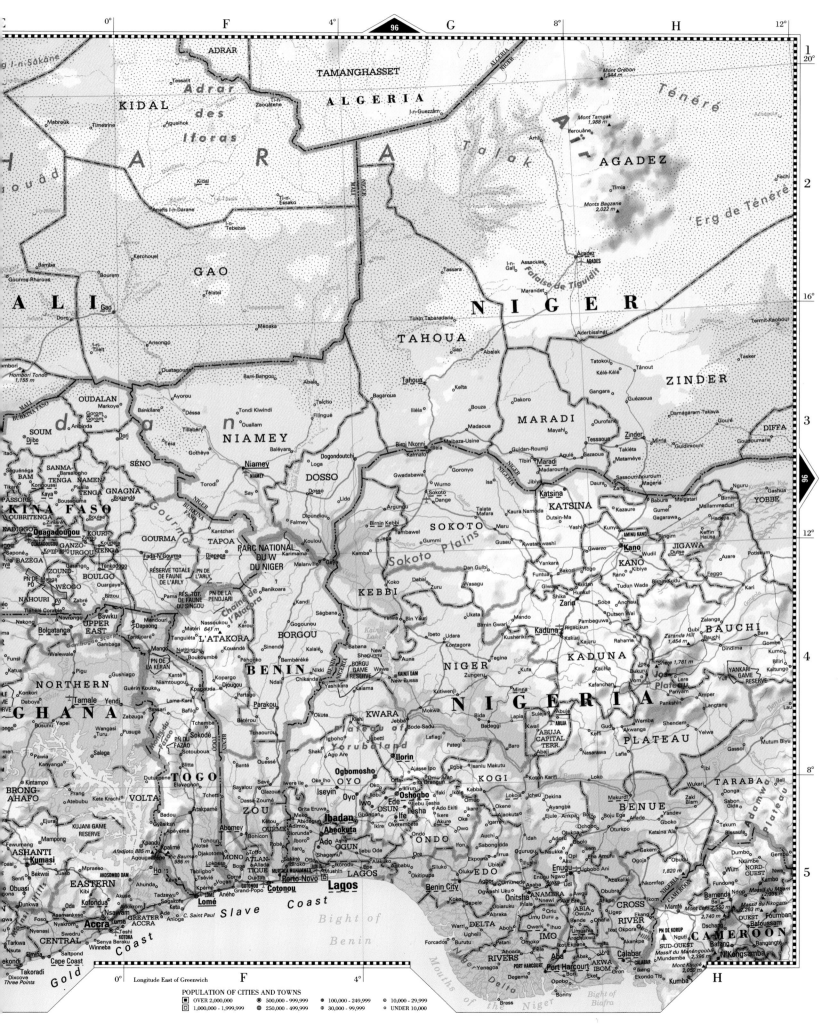

POPULATION OF CITIES AND TOWNS

Symbol	Population	Symbol	Population	Symbol	Population
■	OVER 2,000,000	◉	500,000 - 999,999	◉	100,000 - 249,999	⊙	10,000 - 29,999
▣	1,000,000 - 1,999,999	◉	250,000 - 499,999	◉	30,000 - 99,999	○	UNDER 10,000

Longitude East of Greenwich

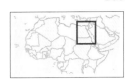

Northeastern Africa

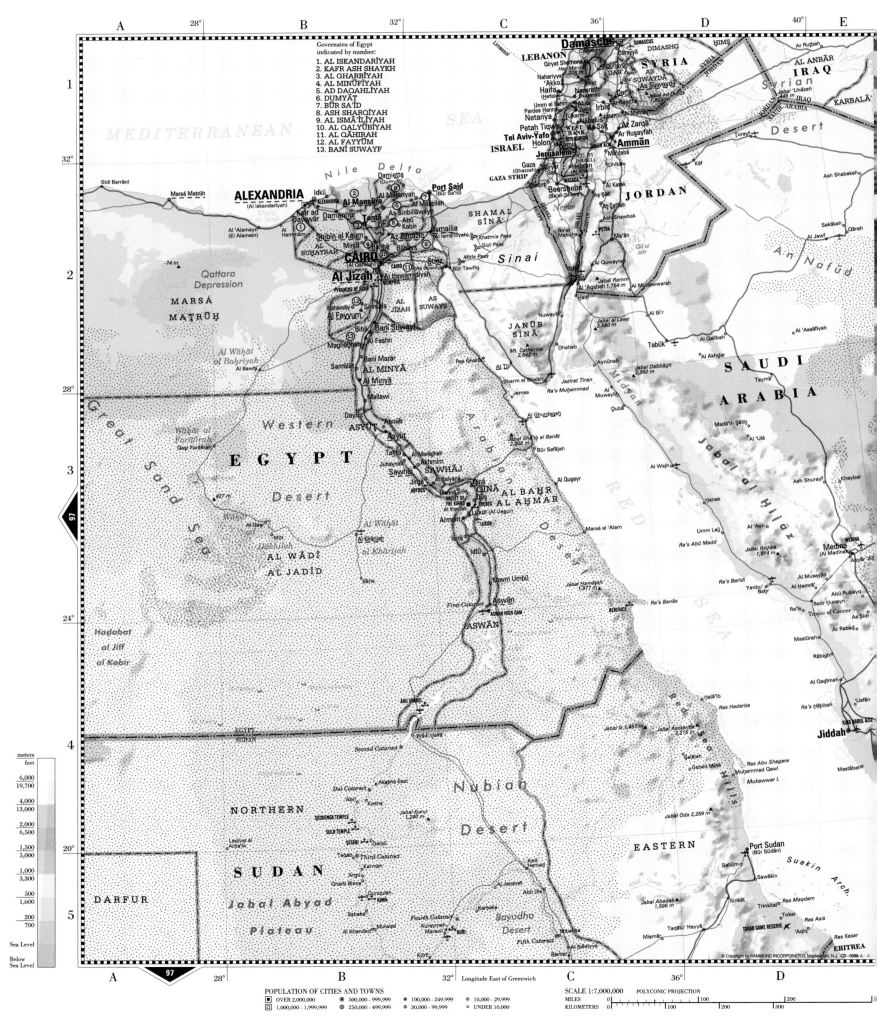

Governates of Egypt
indicated by number:

1. AL ISKANDARĪYAH
2. KAFR ASH SHAYKH
3. AL GHARBĪYAH
4. AD DAQAHLĪYAH
5. DUMYĀT
6. BŪR SA'ĪD
7. ASH SHARQĪYAH
8. AL ISMĀ'ĪLĪYAH
9. AL QALYŪBĪYAH
10. AL QĀHIRAH
11. AL FAYYŪM
12. BANĪ SUWAYF

Longitude East of Greenwich

POPULATION OF CITIES AND TOWNS

▣ OVER 2,000,000	◉ 500,000 - 999,999
▢ 1,000,000 - 1,999,999	◉ 250,000 - 499,999

⊛ 100,000 - 249,999   ⊙ 10,000 - 29,999
⊙ 30,000 - 99,999   ○ UNDER 10,000

SCALE 1:7,000,000   POLYCONIC PROJECTION

MILES
KILOMETERS

East Africa

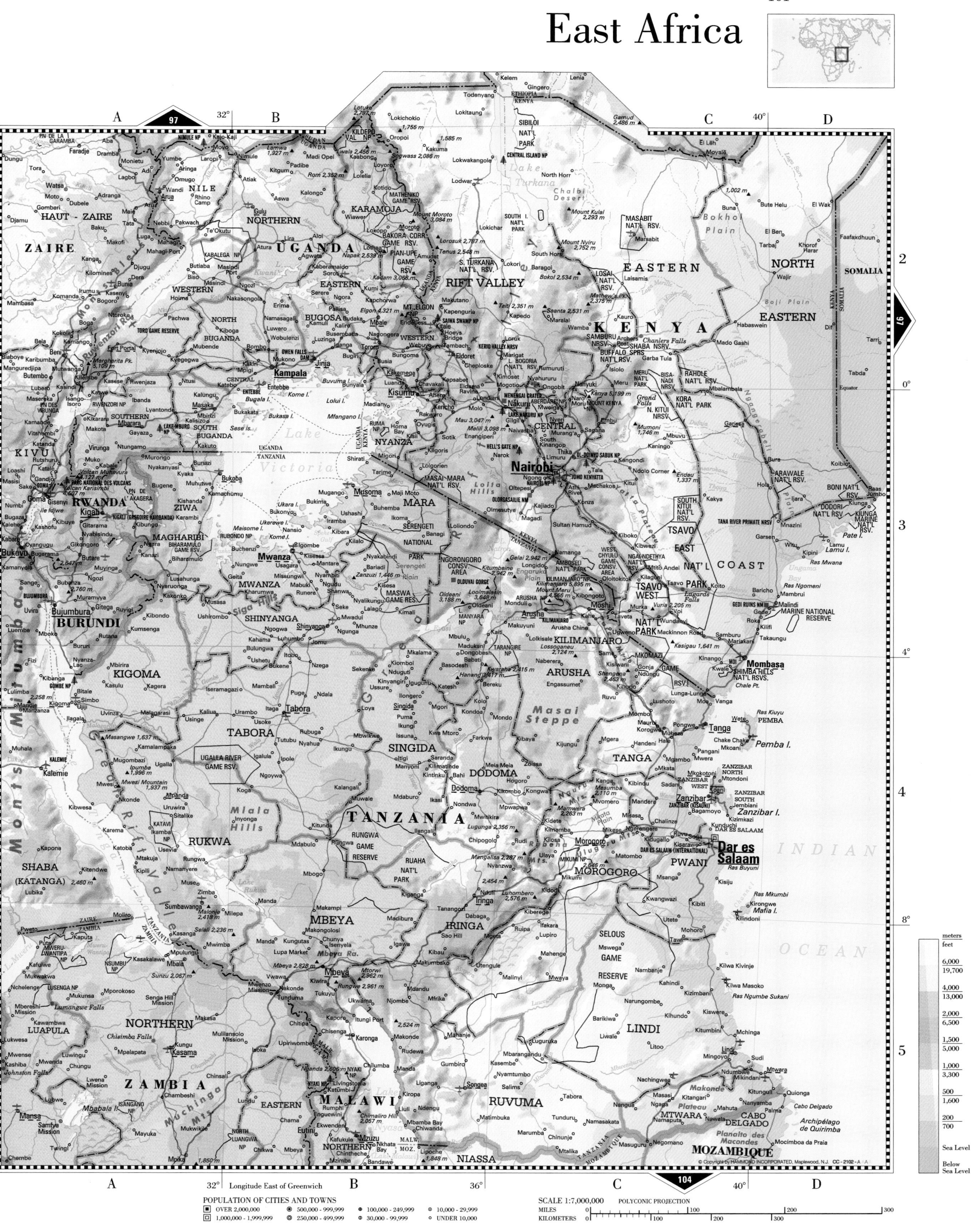

POPULATION OF CITIES AND TOWNS
- ■ OVER 2,000,000
- ◉ 500,000 - 999,999
- ⊕ 100,000 - 249,999
- ○ 10,000 - 29,999
- ▣ 1,000,000 - 1,999,999
- ⊙ 250,000 - 499,999
- ⊕ 30,000 - 99,999
- ○ UNDER 10,000

SCALE 1:7,000,000 POLYCONIC PROJECTION

MILES 0 ... 100 ... 200 ... 300
KILOMETERS 0 ... 100 ... 200 ... 300

Longitude East of Greenwich

meters / feet
- 6,000 / 19,700
- 4,000 / 13,000
- 2,000 / 6,500
- 1,500 / 5,000
- 1,000 / 3,300
- 500 / 1,600
- 200 / 700
- Sea Level
- Below Sea Level

© Copyright by HAMMOND INCORPORATED, Maplewood, N.J. CC-2102-A

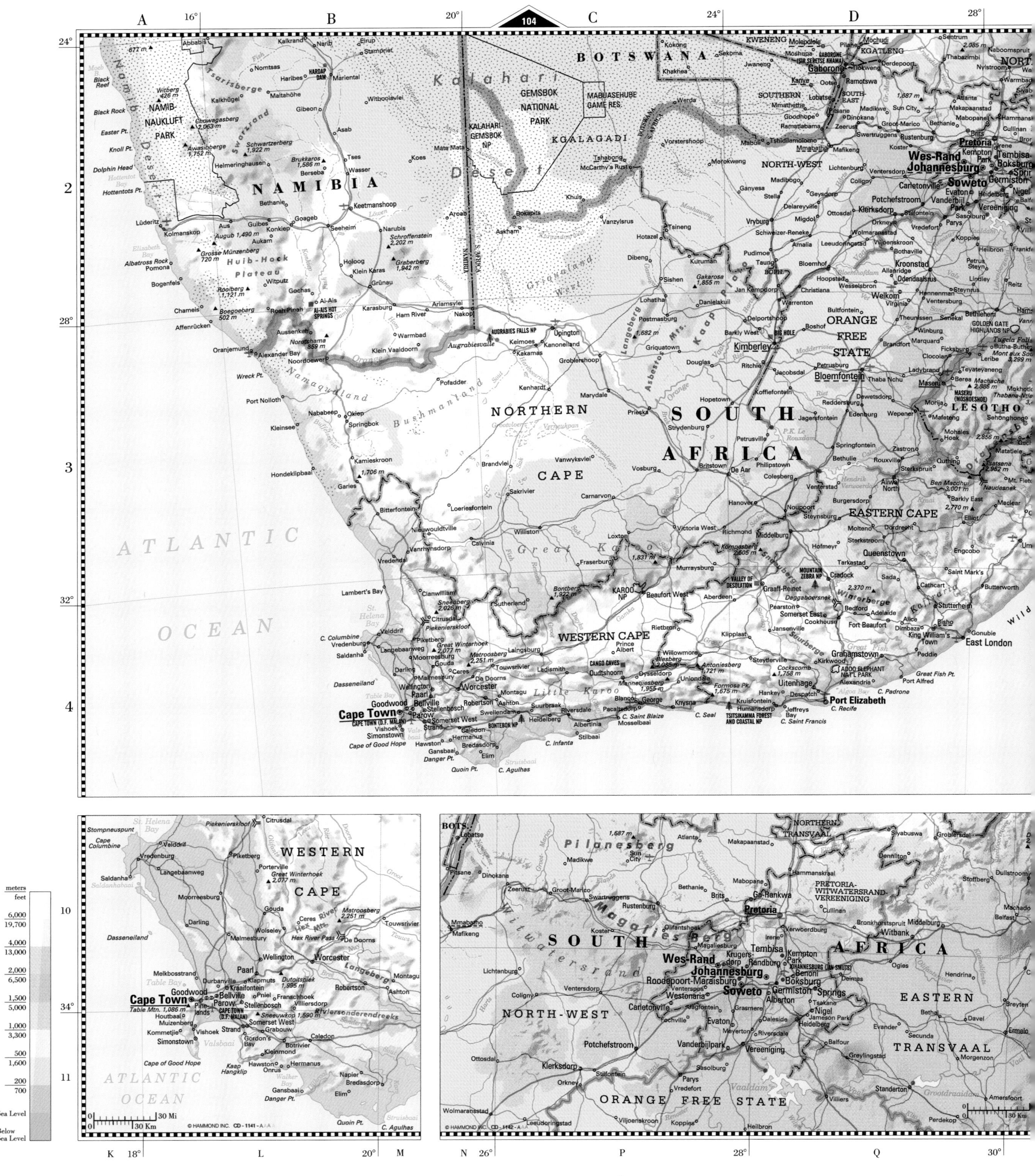
104
A
B
C
D
16°
20°
24°
28°
BOTSWANA
NAMIBIA
Kalahari Desert
Namib Desert
GEMSBOK NATIONAL PARK
KALAHARI-GEMSBOK NP
MABUASEHUBE GAME RES.
KGALAGADI
NAMIB-NAUKLUFT PARK
Huib-Hock Plateau
NORTH-WEST
SOUTH AFRICA
NORTHERN CAPE
WESTERN CAPE
EASTERN CAPE
ORANGE FREE STATE
LESOTHO
Namaqualand
Bushmanland
Great Karoo
Little Karoo
ATLANTIC OCEAN
Windhoek
Gaborone
Pretoria
Wes-Rand
Johannesburg
Soweto
Kimberley
Bloemfontein
Lüderitz
Keetmanshoop
Upington
Beaufort West
Port Elizabeth
East London
Cape Town
Cape of Good Hope
C. Agulhas
WESTERN CAPE
ATLANTIC OCEAN
Table Bay
Stellenbosch
Worcester
Paarl
Bellville
meters
feet
6,000
19,700
4,000
13,000
2,000
6,500
1,500
5,000
1,000
3,300
500
1,600
200
700
Sea Level
Below Sea Level
Pilanesberg
Magaliesberg
Witwatersrand
SOUTH AFRICA
NORTH-WEST
EASTERN TRANSVAAL
ORANGE FREE STATE
NORTHERN TRANSVAAL
PRETORIA-WITWATERSRAND-VEREENIGING
Vereeniging
Krugersdorp
Randburg
Benoni
Boksburg
Germiston
Roodepoort-Maraisburg
Potchefstroom
Klerksdorp
Vanderbijlpark
K
18°
L
20°
M
N
26°
P
28°
Q
30°
© HAMMOND INC. CD-1141
© HAMMOND INC. CD-1142

South Africa

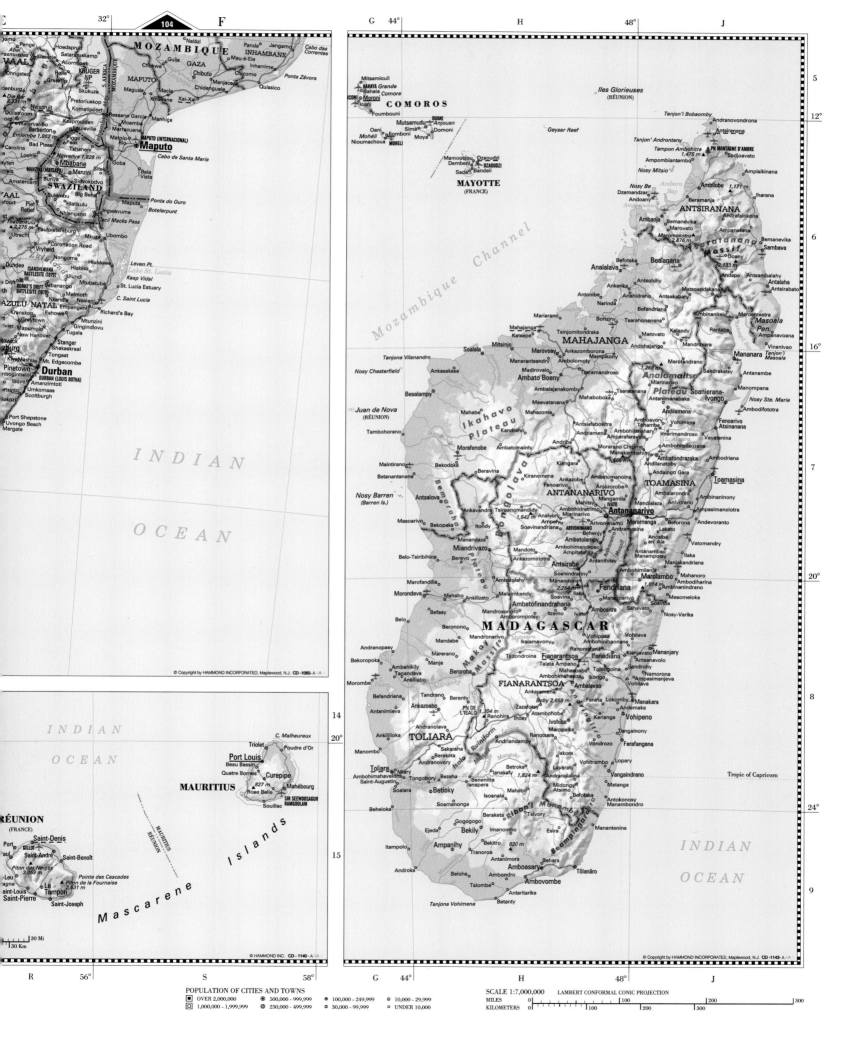

POPULATION OF CITIES AND TOWNS

■ OVER 2,000,000	● 500,000 - 999,999	● 100,000 - 249,999	○ 10,000 - 29,999
□ 1,000,000 - 1,999,999	● 250,000 - 499,999	○ 30,000 - 99,999	∘ UNDER 10,000

SCALE 1:7,000,000   LAMBERT CONFORMAL CONIC PROJECTION

MILES   0   100   200   300

KILOMETERS   0   100   200   300

Southern Africa

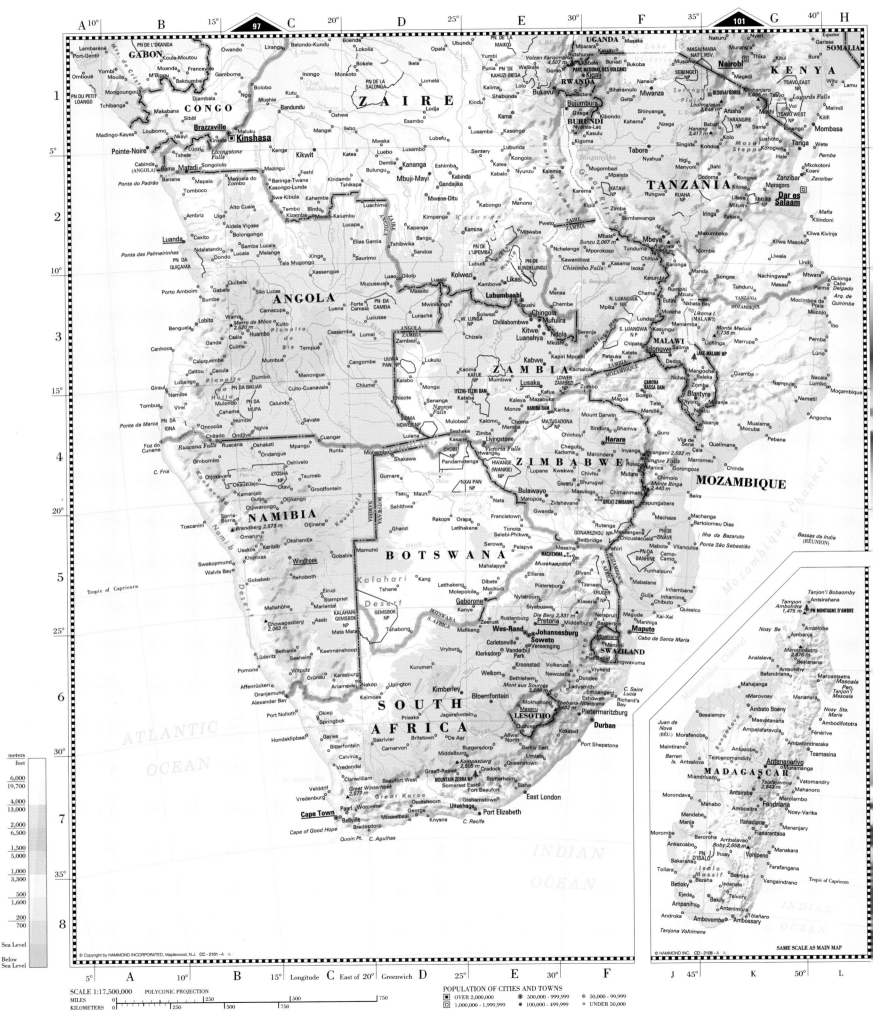

SCALE 1:17,500,000   POLYCONIC PROJECTION

MILES

KILOMETERS

POPULATION OF CITIES AND TOWNS

■ OVER 2,000,000   ● 500,000 - 999,999   ● 50,000 - 99,999
◻ 1,000,000 - 1,999,999   ● 100,000 - 499,999   ○ UNDER 50,000

© Copyright by HAMMOND INCORPORATED, Maplewood, N.J.   CC -2101 - A   A

Antarctica

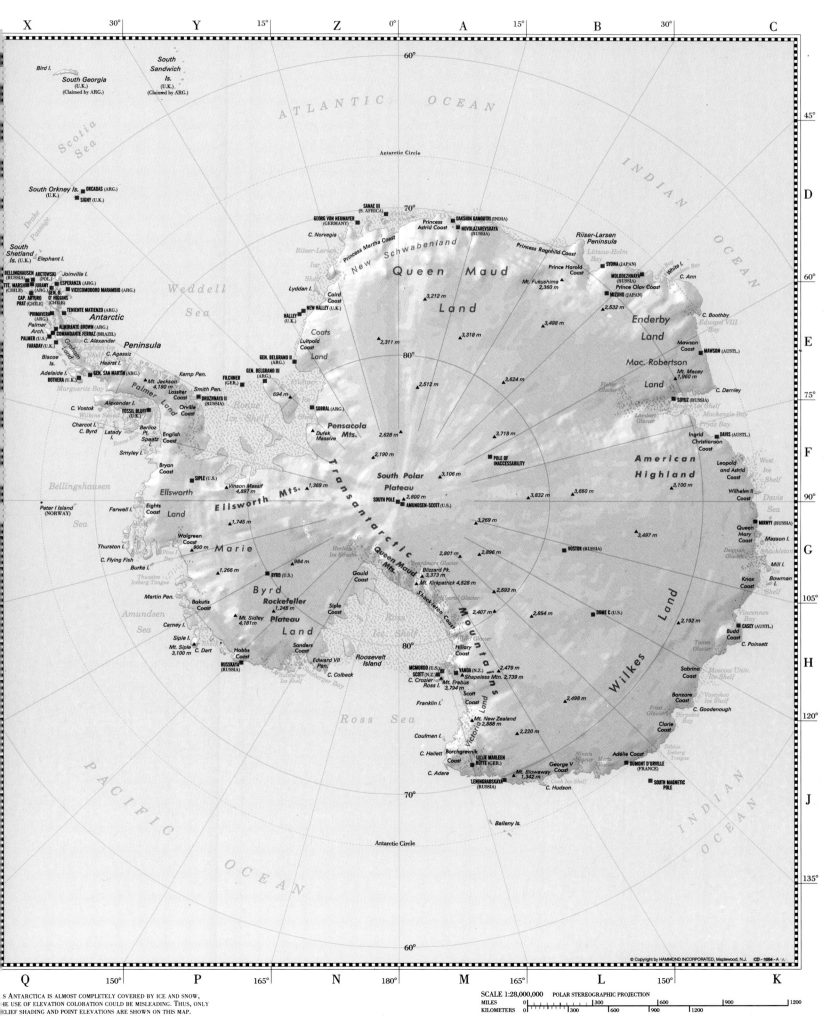

S ANTARCTICA IS ALMOST COMPLETELY COVERED BY ICE AND SNOW,
HE USE OF ELEVATION COLORATION COULD BE MISLEADING. THUS, ONLY
ELIEF SHADING AND POINT ELEVATIONS ARE SHOWN ON THIS MAP.

SCALE 1:28,000,000   POLAR STEREOGRAPHIC PROJECTION

MILES 0 300 600 900 1200
KILOMETERS 0 300 600 900 1200

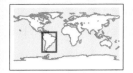

South America - Comparisons

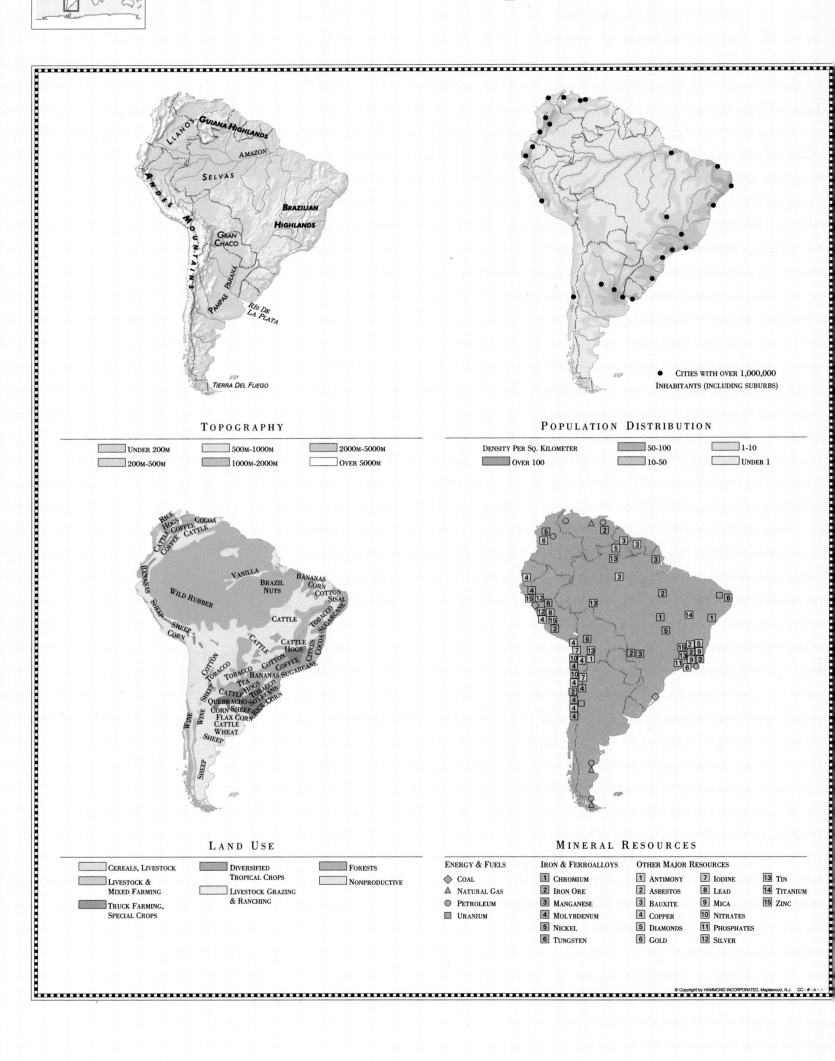

Guiana Highlands
Llanos
Amazon
Selvas
Brazilian Highlands
Gran Chaco
Andes Mountains
Pampas Parana
Río de la Plata
Tierra del Fuego

TOPOGRAPHY

Under 200m	500m-1000m	2000m-5000m
200m-500m	1000m-2000m	Over 5000m

• Cities with over 1,000,000 Inhabitants (including suburbs)

POPULATION DISTRIBUTION

Density Per Sq. Kilometer

Over 100	50-100	1-10
	10-50	Under 1

Rice
Hogs
Cattle Coffee Cocoa
Coffee Cattle
Vanilla
Brazil Nuts
Bananas Corn Cotton Sisal
Bananas
Wild Rubber
Sheep
Cattle
Sheep
Corn
Cattle
Cattle Hogs
Tobacco Cotton Coffee Citrus Cocoa Sugarcane
Cotton
Tobacco
Tea Bananas Sugarcane
Sheep Hogs Tobacco
Cattle Hogs Soybeans
Quebracho Rice Corn
Corn Sheep
Flax Corn
Wine Cattle
Wine Wheat
Sheep
Sheep

LAND USE

Cereals, Livestock	Diversified Tropical Crops	Forests
Livestock & Mixed Farming	Livestock Grazing & Ranching	Nonproductive
Truck Farming, Special Crops		

MINERAL RESOURCES

ENERGY & FUELS
◆ Coal
△ Natural Gas
● Petroleum
▢ Uranium

IRON & FERROALLOYS
1 Chromium
2 Iron Ore
3 Manganese
4 Molybdenum
5 Nickel
6 Tungsten

OTHER MAJOR RESOURCES
1 Antimony
2 Asbestos
3 Bauxite
4 Copper
5 Diamonds
6 Gold
7 Iodine
8 Lead
9 Mica
10 Nitrates
11 Phosphates
12 Silver
13 Tin
14 Titanium
15 Zinc

South America

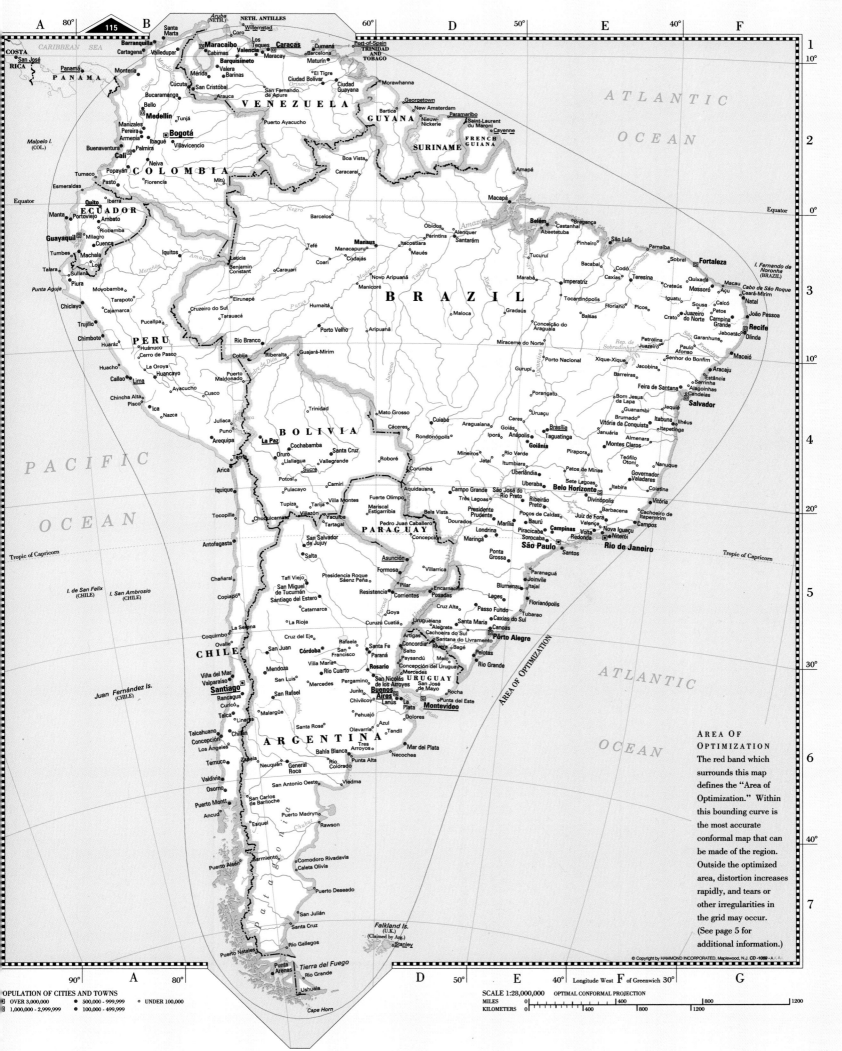

ATLANTIC OCEAN

PACIFIC OCEAN

ATLANTIC OCEAN

CARIBBEAN SEA

VENEZUELA

GUYANA

SURINAME

FRENCH GUIANA

COLOMBIA

ECUADOR

PERU

BRAZIL

BOLIVIA

PARAGUAY

CHILE

ARGENTINA

URUGUAY

Equator

Tropic of Capricorn

AREA OF OPTIMIZATION

The red band which surrounds this map defines the "Area of Optimization." Within this bounding curve is the most accurate conformal map that can be made of the region. Outside the optimized area, distortion increases rapidly, and tears or other irregularities in the grid may occur. (See page 5 for additional information.)

© Copyright by HAMMOND INCORPORATED, Maplewood, N.J. CD -1089 -A -A

POPULATION OF CITIES AND TOWNS
⊙ OVER 3,000,000   ● 500,000 - 999,999   ○ UNDER 100,000
⊡ 1,000,000 - 2,999,999   ● 100,000 - 499,999

SCALE 1:28,000,000   OPTIMAL CONFORMAL PROJECTION
MILES 0 — 400 — 800 — 1200
KILOMETERS 0 — 400 — 800 — 1200

Longitude West F of Greenwich 30°

CARIBBEAN SEA
SAINT VINCENT AND THE GRENADINES
Kingstown
NETH. ANTILLES
Aruba (NETH.)
Oranjestad
Willemstad
Curaçao
Bonaire
GRENADA
TRINIDAD AND TOBAGO
Port-of-Spain
Caracas
Maracaibo
Barquisimeto
Valencia
Maracay
VENEZUELA
Ciudad Guayana
Ciudad Bolívar
Delta del Orinoco
Barranquilla
Santa Marta
Cartagena
Medellín
Bogotá
Cali
Cúcuta
Bucaramanga
COLOMBIA
Llanos
NICARAGUA
COSTA RICA
San José
PANAMA
Panamá
Isthmus of Panama
Isla del Coco (COSTA RICA)
I. de Malpelo (COLOMBIA)
Equator
Quito
ECUADOR
Guayaquil
Gulf of Guayaquil
Manta
Cuenca
Iquitos
Manaus
Amazon
Selvas
PERU
Cordillera Central
Cordillera Oriental
Chiclayo
Trujillo
Chimbote
Lima
Callao
Huancayo
Cusco
Arequipa
La Montaña
Rio Branco
Porto Velho
BOLIVIA
La Paz
Cochabamba
Oruro
Santa Cruz
Sucre
Potosí
Arica
Iquique
CHILE
ARGENTINA
Atacama Desert
Gran Chaco
PARAG
Tropic of Capricorn
PACIFIC OCEAN
B R
GUY
meters
feet
6,000
19,700
4,000
13,000
2,000
6,500
1,500
5,000
1,000
3,300
500
1,600
200
700
Sea Level
Below Sea Level
A
B
C
D
E
F
85°
80°
Longitude West of Greenwich
75°
70°
65°
60°
10°
5°
0°
5°
10°
15°
20°
1
2
3
4
5
6
7
8
116
111

Northern South America

ATLANTIC OCEAN

ATLANTIC OCEAN

FRENCH GUIANA

SURINAME

Paramaribo
Nieuw-Amsterdam
Albina
Saint-Laurent du Maroni
Sinnamary
Kourou
Cayenne
Devil's I.
Iles du Salut
Pointe Béhague
Cabo Orange
Oiapoque
PN DO CABO ORANGE

Macapá
Mazagão
I. Janaucu
I. Caviana
I. Mexiana
Cabo do Norte

Belém
Castanhal
Abaetetuba
Igarapé-Miri
Bragança
Capanema

São Luís
Rosário
Teresina
Fortaleza
Sobral
Caucaia
Maranguape
Cascavel

Natal
João Pessoa
Campina Grande
Recife
Olinda
Jaboatão
Caruaru

Imperatriz
Marabá
Araguaína

Maceió
Aracaju

Salvador

Mossoró

Juazeiro do Norte

Brasília
Goiânia
Anápolis
Taguatinga

Planalto Central

Planalto de Mato Grosso

Campo Grande

Uberlândia
Uberaba

Vitória da Conquista
Itabuna
Ilhéus

Montes Claros

Governador Valadares
Ipatinga

Belo Horizonte
Contagem
Divinópolis

Vitória
Vila Velha

Ribeirão Preto
Campinas
São José do Rio Preto
Sorocaba

Rio de Janeiro
Niterói
Petrópolis
Nova Iguaçu
Volta Redonda
Campos
Juiz de Fora

São Paulo
Santo André
Santos
Osasco

St. Peter and St. Paul Rocks (BRAZIL)

Fernando de Noronha (BRAZIL)

Rocas

Equator

Trinidade (BRAZIL)
Martin Vaz (BRAZIL)

POPULATION OF CITIES AND TOWNS
- ■ OVER 2,000,000
- ◉ 500,000 - 999,999
- ◎ 50,000 - 99,999
- ▣ 1,000,000 - 1,999,999
- ● 100,000 - 499,999
- ○ UNDER 50,000

SCALE 1:15,000,000   LAMBERT CONFORMAL CONIC PROJECTION
MILES
KILOMETERS

Southeastern Brazil

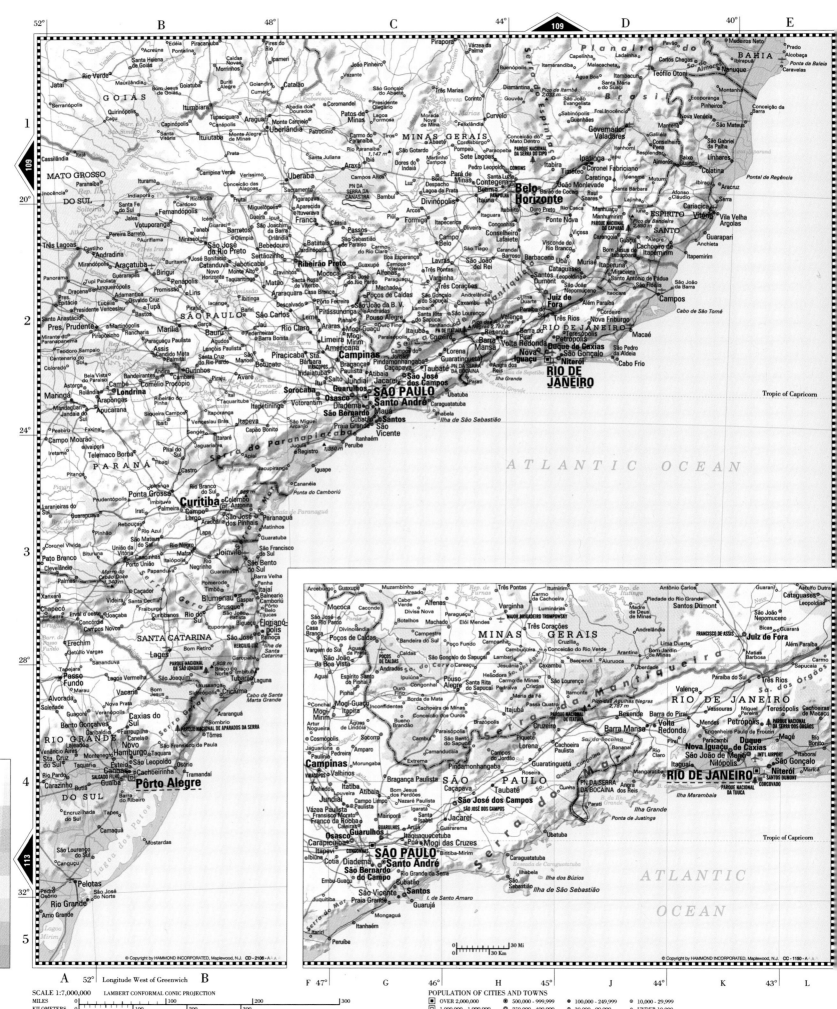

SCALE 1:7,000,000   LAMBERT CONFORMAL CONIC PROJECTION

Longitude West of Greenwich

MILES
KILOMETERS

POPULATION OF CITIES AND TOWNS

■ OVER 2,000,000	● 500,000 - 999,999	● 100,000 - 249,999	○ 10,000 - 29,999
◻ 1,000,000 - 1,999,999	◉ 250,000 - 499,999	◦ 30,000 - 99,999	◦ UNDER 10,000

Southern South America

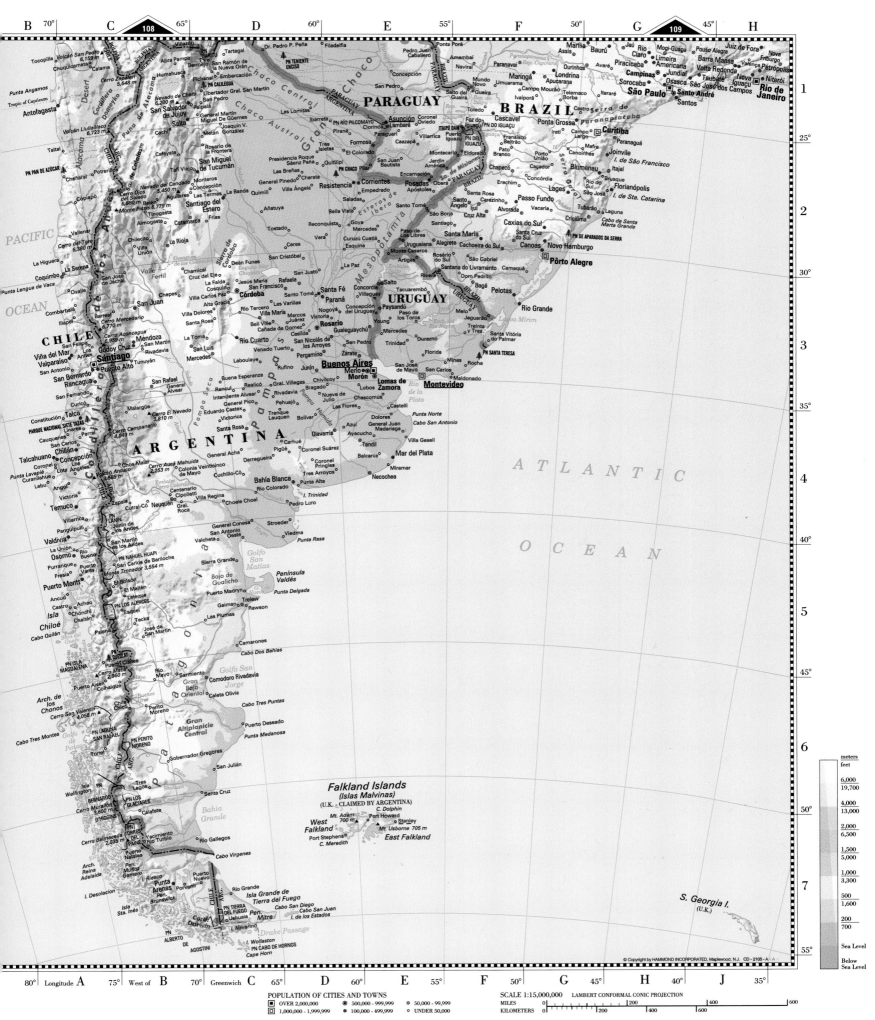

Map grid references (top): B 70° | C 108 | 65° | D 60° | E 55° | F 50° | G 109 | 45° | H

Map grid references (bottom): 80° Longitude A | 75° West of B | 70° Greenwich C | 65° D | 60° E | 55° F | 50° G | 45° H | 40° J | 35°

PACIFIC OCEAN

ATLANTIC OCEAN

CHILE

ARGENTINA

PARAGUAY

URUGUAY

BRAZIL

Buenos Aires
Santiago
Montevideo
Asunción
São Paulo
Rio de Janeiro

Falkland Islands
(Islas Malvinas)
(U.K. - CLAIMED BY ARGENTINA)
West Falkland
East Falkland
Mt. Adam 700 m
Mt. Usborne 705 m
C. Dolphin
Port Howard
Stanley
Port Stephens
C. Meredith

S. Georgia I.
(U.K.)

Cape Horn

POPULATION OF CITIES AND TOWNS
- ▣ OVER 2,000,000
- ◙ 1,000,000-1,999,999
- ◉ 500,000-999,999
- ● 100,000-499,999
- ◦ 50,000-99,999
- ◦ UNDER 50,000

SCALE 1:15,000,000   LAMBERT CONFORMAL CONIC PROJECTION
MILES 0 ... 200 ... 400 ... 600
KILOMETERS 0 ... 200 ... 400 ... 600

meters / feet
6,000 / 19,700
4,000 / 13,000
2,000 / 6,500
1,500 / 5,000
1,000 / 3,300
500 / 1,600
200 / 700
Sea Level
Below Sea Level

© Copyright by HAMMOND INCORPORATED, Maplewood, N.J. CD - 2105 - A - A

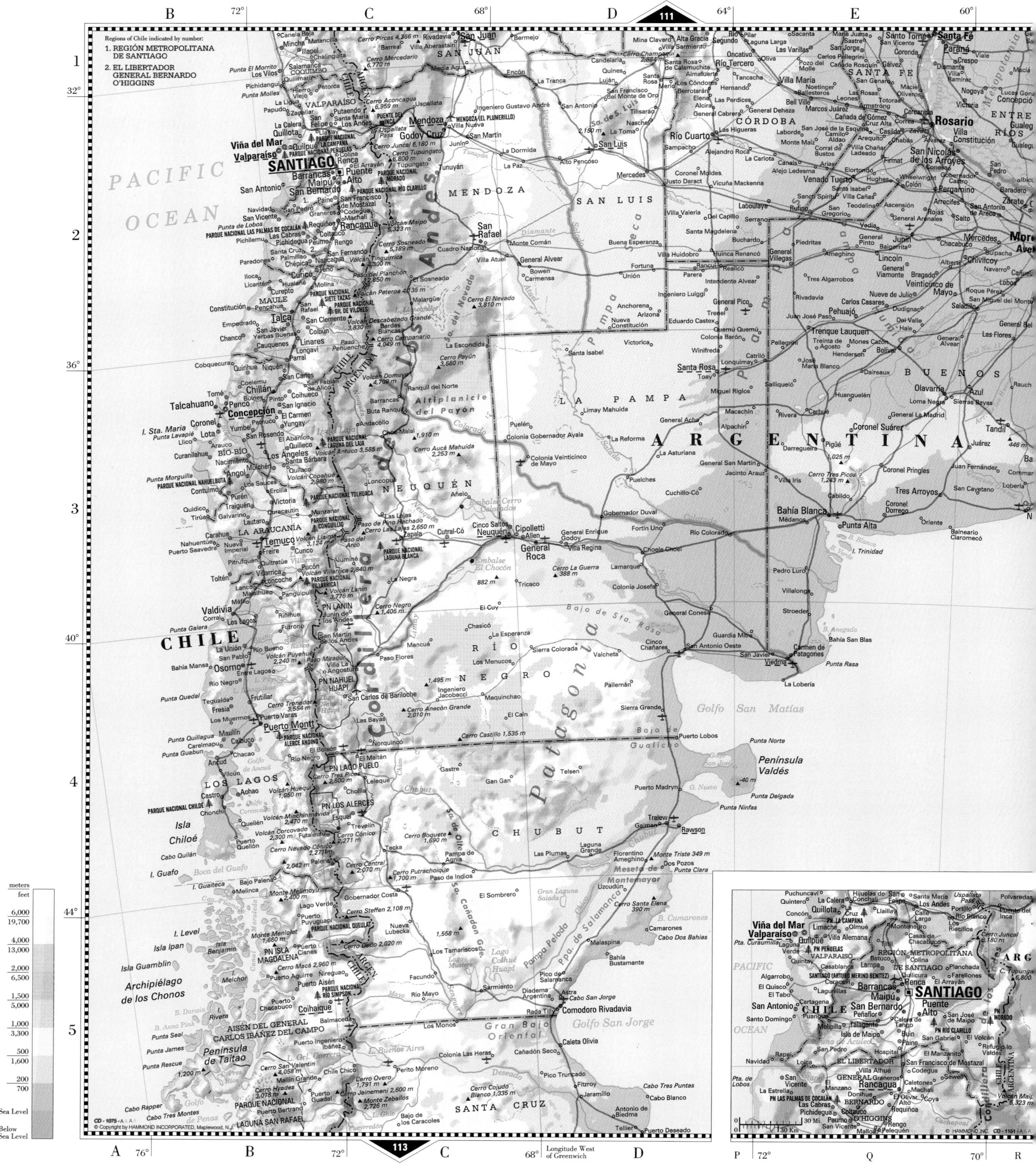

111
Regions of Chile indicated by number:
1. REGIÓN METROPOLITANA DE SANTIAGO
2. EL LIBERTADOR GENERAL BERNARDO O'HIGGINS
PACIFIC OCEAN
CHILE
ARGENTINA
SAN JUAN
MENDOZA
SAN LUIS
CÓRDOBA
SANTA FE
ENTRE RÍOS
BUENOS AIRES
LA PAMPA
NEUQUÉN
RÍO NEGRO
CHUBUT
SANTA CRUZ
VALPARAÍSO
MAULE
BÍO-BÍO
LA ARAUCANÍA
LOS LAGOS
AISÉN DEL GENERAL CARLOS IBAÑEZ DEL CAMPO
Cordillera de Los Andes
Patagonia
Pampa
Altiplanicie del Payún
SANTIAGO
Viña del Mar
Valparaíso
Rancagua
Talca
Chillán
Concepción
Talcahuano
Los Angeles
Temuco
Valdivia
Osorno
Puerto Montt
Coihaique
Mendoza
San Juan
San Luis
Río Cuarto
Rosario
Santa Fe
Paraná
Santa Rosa
Neuquén
Bahía Blanca
Viedma
Rawson
Trelew
Puerto Madryn
Comodoro Rivadavia
San Rafael
General Roca
Península Valdés
Golfo San Matías
Golfo San Jorge
Isla Chiloé
Archipiélago de los Chonos
Península de Taitao
Cerro Aconcagua 6,959 m
meters / feet
6,000 / 19,700
4,000 / 13,000
2,000 / 6,500
1,500 / 5,000
1,000 / 3,300
500 / 1,600
200 / 700
Sea Level
Below Sea Level
CD-1075-A A A
© Copyright by HAMMOND INCORPORATED, Maplewood, N.J.
Longitude West of Greenwich
113
A B C D E
1 2 3 4 5
76° 72° 68° 64° 60°
32° 36° 40° 44°
SANTIAGO
REGIÓN METROPOLITANA DE SANTIAGO
EL LIBERTADOR GENERAL BERNARDO O'HIGGINS
San Bernardo
Puente Alto
Maipú
San Antonio
0 30 Mi
0 30 Km
© HAMMOND INC.
CD-1151-A A A
P Q R
72° 70°

Southern Chile and Argentina

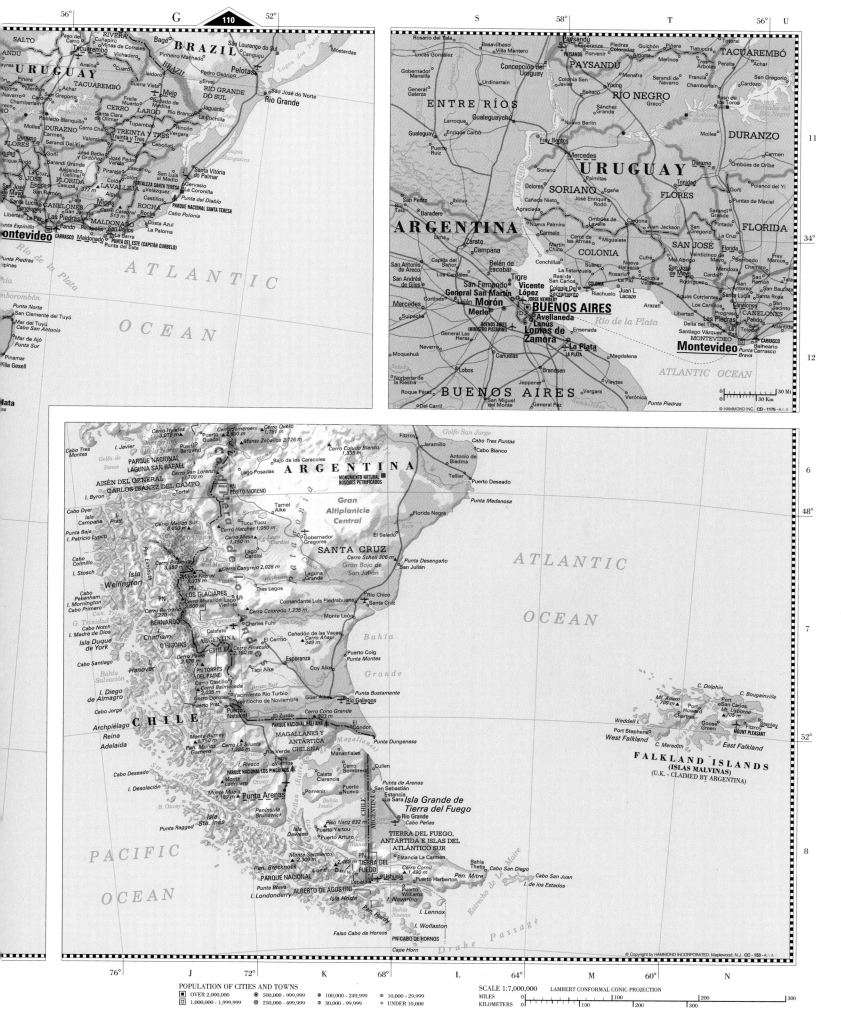

POPULATION OF CITIES AND TOWNS

- ■ OVER 2,000,000
- ⊡ 1,000,000 - 1,999,999
- ◉ 500,000 - 999,999
- ◉ 250,000 - 499,999
- ◉ 100,000 - 249,999
- ◉ 30,000 - 99,999
- ○ 10,000 - 29,999
- ○ UNDER 10,000

SCALE 1:7,000,000   LAMBERT CONFORMAL CONIC PROJECTION

MILES   0   100   200   300
KILOMETERS   0   100   200   300

North America - Comparisons

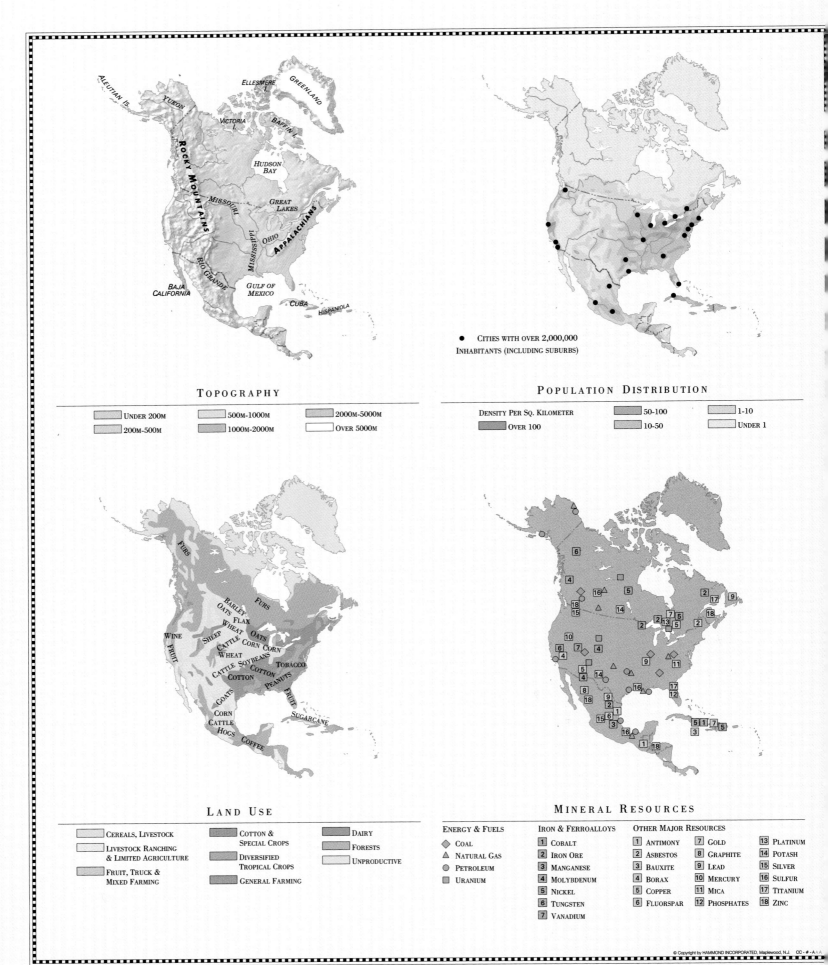

TOPOGRAPHY

UNDER 200M	500M-1000M	2000M-5000M
200M-500M	1000M-2000M	OVER 5000M

POPULATION DISTRIBUTION

● CITIES WITH OVER 2,000,000
INHABITANTS (INCLUDING SUBURBS)

DENSITY PER SQ. KILOMETER

OVER 100	50-100	1-10
	10-50	UNDER 1

LAND USE

CEREALS, LIVESTOCK	COTTON & SPECIAL CROPS	DAIRY
LIVESTOCK RANCHING & LIMITED AGRICULTURE	DIVERSIFIED TROPICAL CROPS	FORESTS
FRUIT, TRUCK & MIXED FARMING	GENERAL FARMING	UNPRODUCTIVE

MINERAL RESOURCES

ENERGY & FUELS

◆ COAL
△ NATURAL GAS
○ PETROLEUM
▢ URANIUM

IRON & FERROALLOYS

1 COBALT
2 IRON ORE
3 MANGANESE
4 MOLYBDENUM
5 NICKEL
6 TUNGSTEN
7 VANADIUM

OTHER MAJOR RESOURCES

1 ANTIMONY
2 ASBESTOS
3 BAUXITE
4 BORAX
5 COPPER
6 FLUORSPAR
7 GOLD
8 GRAPHITE
9 LEAD
10 MERCURY
11 MICA
12 PHOSPHATES
13 PLATINUM
14 POTASH
15 SILVER
16 SULFUR
17 TITANIUM
18 ZINC

North America

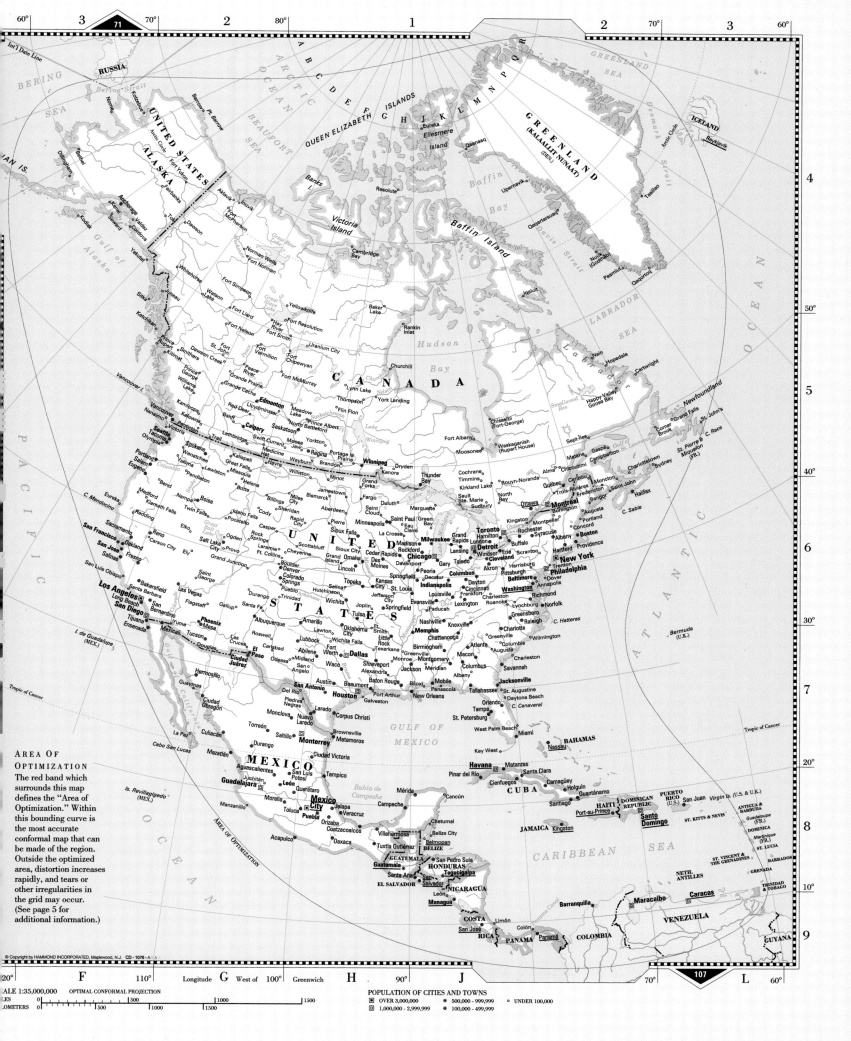

AREA OF
OPTIMIZATION
The red band which
surrounds this map
defines the "Area of
Optimization." Within
this bounding curve is
the most accurate
conformal map that can
be made of the region.
Outside the optimized
area, distortion increases
rapidly, and tears or
other irregularities in
the grid may occur.
(See page 5 for
additional information.)

SCALE 1:35,000,000   OPTIMAL CONFORMAL PROJECTION

MILES 0 [scale] 500   1000   1500
KILOMETERS 0 [scale] 500   1000   1500

POPULATION OF CITIES AND TOWNS

| ▣ OVER 3,000,000 | ● 500,000 - 999,999 | ○ UNDER 100,000 |
| ▢ 1,000,000 - 2,999,999 | ● 100,000 - 499,999 | |

Middle America and Caribbean

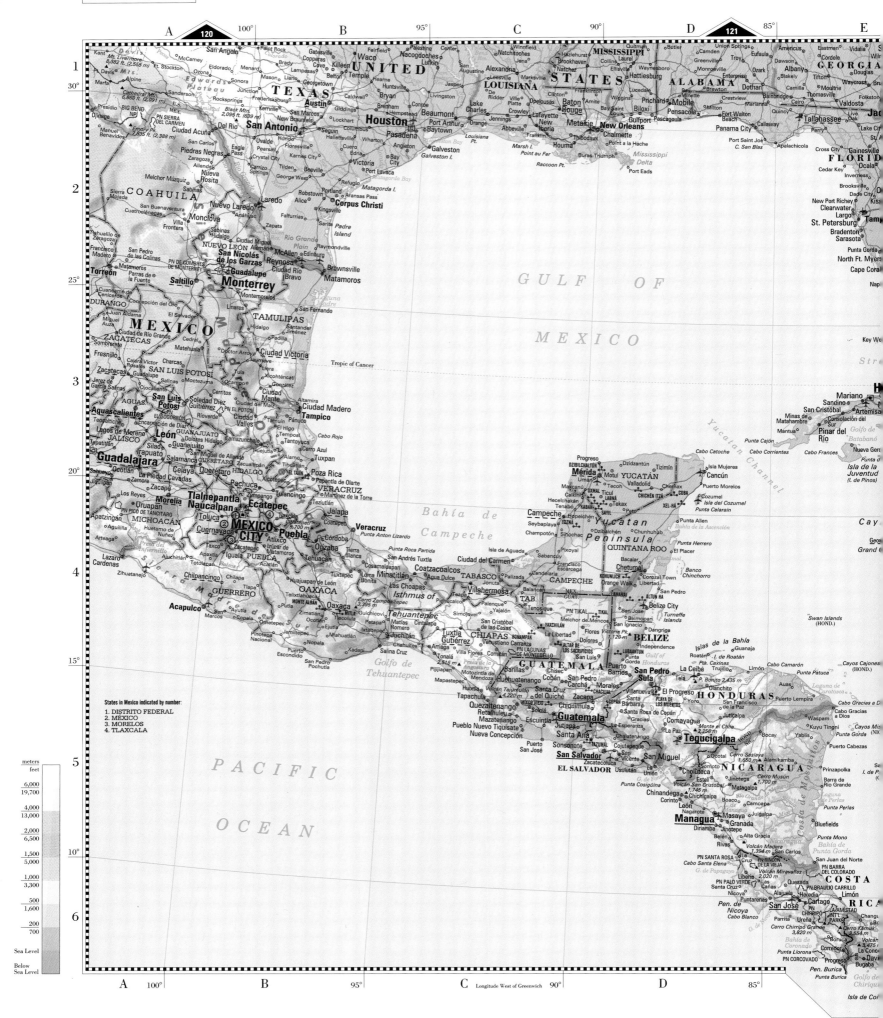

States in Mexico indicated by number:
1. DISTRITO FEDERAL
2. MÉXICO
3. MORELOS
4. TLAXCALA

meters feet
6,000 19,700
4,000 13,000
2,000 6,500
1,500 5,000
1,000 3,300
500 1,600
200 700
Sea Level
Below Sea Level

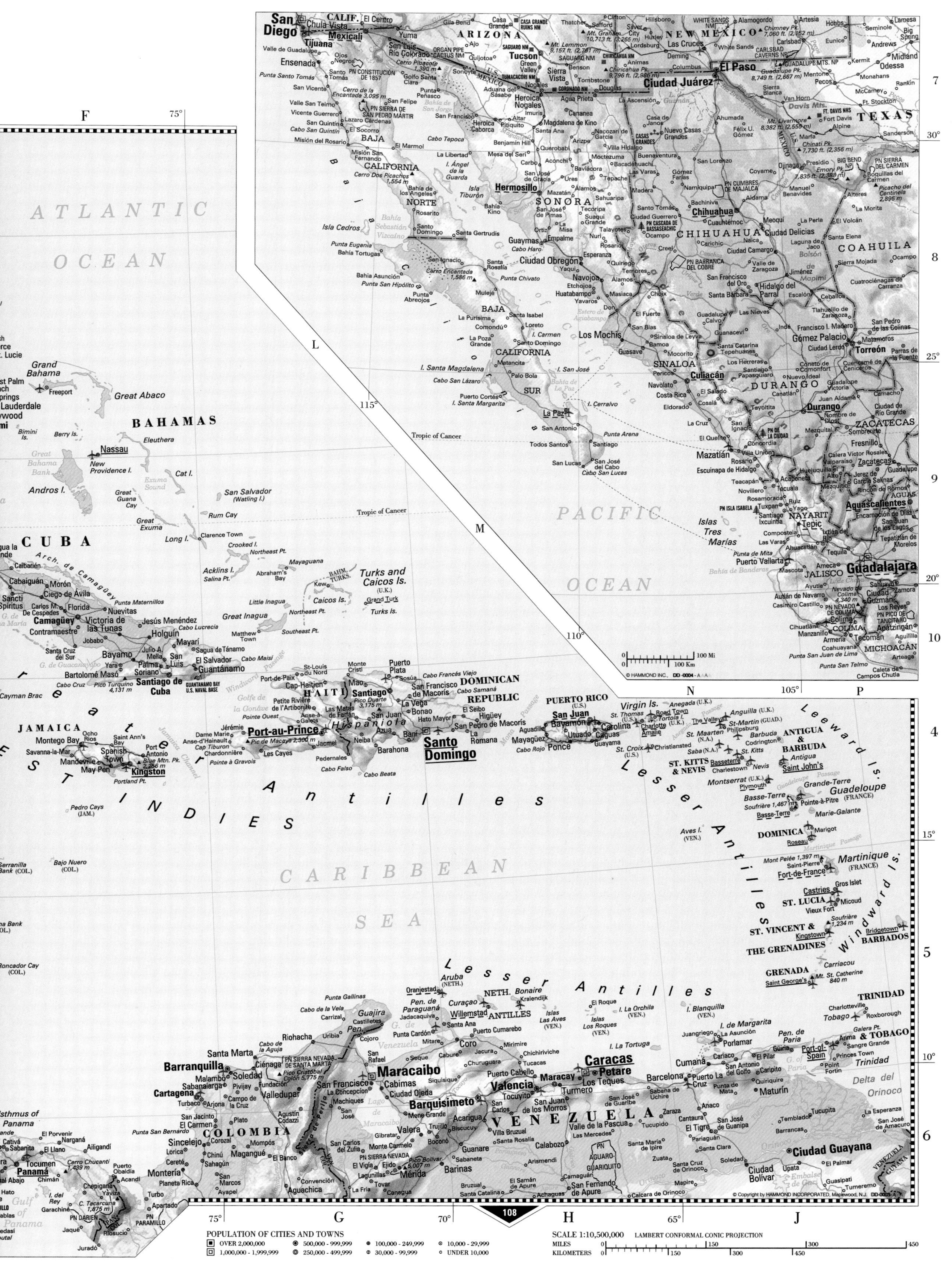

ATLANTIC OCEAN
PACIFIC OCEAN
CARIBBEAN SEA
ARIZONA
NEW MEXICO
TEXAS
CALIF.
BAJA CALIFORNIA
BAJA CALIFORNIA NORTE
BAJA CALIFORNIA SUR
SONORA
CHIHUAHUA
COAHUILA
SINALOA
DURANGO
ZACATECAS
NAYARIT
JALISCO
MICHOACÁN
AGUAS.
San Diego
Tijuana
Mexicali
Tucson
El Paso
Ciudad Juárez
Hermosillo
Chihuahua
Ciudad Obregón
Los Mochis
Culiacán
Torreón
Gómez Palacio
Durango
Mazatlán
Aguascalientes
Tepic
Guadalajara
La Paz
Tropic of Cancer
Islas Tres Marías
BAHAMAS
Nassau
Grand Bahama
Great Abaco
Andros I.
Eleuthera
CUBA
Camagüey
Holguín
Santiago de Cuba
Guantánamo
JAMAICA
Kingston
Montego Bay
HAITI
Port-au-Prince
Cap-Haïtien
DOMINICAN REPUBLIC
Santo Domingo
Santiago
Hispaniola
PUERTO RICO (U.S.)
San Juan
Ponce
Turks and Caicos Is. (U.K.)
Virgin Is.
Anguilla (U.K.)
ANTIGUA & BARBUDA
Saint John's
ST. KITTS & NEVIS
Basseterre
Montserrat (U.K.)
Guadeloupe (FRANCE)
DOMINICA
Roseau
Martinique (FRANCE)
Fort-de-France
ST. LUCIA
Castries
ST. VINCENT & THE GRENADINES
Kingstown
BARBADOS
Bridgetown
GRENADA
Saint George's
TRINIDAD & TOBAGO
Port-of-Spain
Aruba (NETH.)
NETH. ANTILLES
Curaçao
Willemstad
Bonaire
Greater Antilles
WEST INDIES
Lesser Antilles
Leeward Is.
Windward Is.
VENEZUELA
Caracas
Maracaibo
Valencia
Barquisimeto
Ciudad Guayana
Ciudad Bolívar
COLOMBIA
Barranquilla
Cartagena
Panamá
Isthmus of Panama
Gulf of Panama
© HAMMOND INC.
© Copyright by HAMMOND INCORPORATED, Maplewood, N.J.
108
POPULATION OF CITIES AND TOWNS
OVER 2,000,000
1,000,000 - 1,999,999
500,000 - 999,999
250,000 - 499,999
100,000 - 249,999
30,000 - 99,999
10,000 - 29,999
UNDER 10,000
SCALE 1:10,500,000
LAMBERT CONFORMAL CONIC PROJECTION
MILES 0 150 300 450
KILOMETERS 0 150 300 450

SCALE 1:14,000,000 LAMBERT CONFORMAL CONIC PROJECTION

MILES 0 | 200 | 400 | 600

KILOMETERS 0 | 200 | 400 | 600

POPULATION OF CITIES AND TOWNS

- OVER 2,000,000
- 1,000,000 - 1,999,999
- 500,000 - 999,999
- 100,000 - 499,999
- 50,000 - 99,999
- UNDER 50,000

Canada

Map continued at right

Baffin Bay

Davis Strait

Baffin Island

Foxe Basin

Hudson Strait

Ungava Peninsula

Ungava Bay

LABRADOR SEA

NEWFOUNDLAND

Labrador

QUÉBEC

James Bay

Gulf of St. Lawrence

Cabot Strait

PRINCE EDWARD ISLAND

NEW BRUNSWICK

NOVA SCOTIA

MAINE

VT.

N.H.

NEW YORK

MASS.

PA.

OHIO

ATLANTIC OCEAN

Gulf of Maine

GREENLAND (KALAALLIT NUNAAT) (DEN.)

AUYUITTUQ NATIONAL PARK

ST. PIERRE & MIQUELON (FR.)

ARCTIC OCEAN

Queen Elizabeth Islands

Ellesmere Island

Axel Heiberg Island

Sverdrup Islands

Parry Islands

Melville Island

Banks Island

Devon Island

Bathurst I.

Victoria Island

NORTH MAGNETIC POLE

Viscount Melville Sd.

Jones Sound

ELLESMERE ISLAND NP

Map continued at left

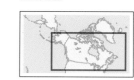

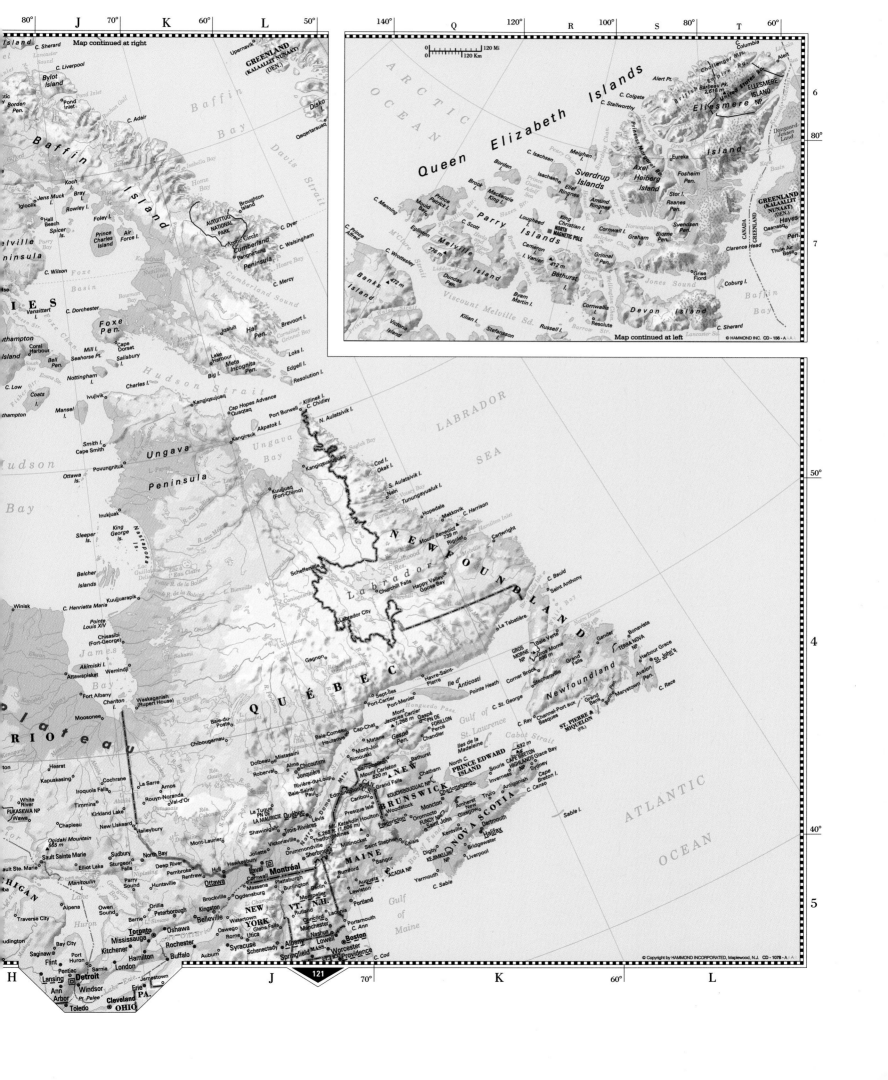

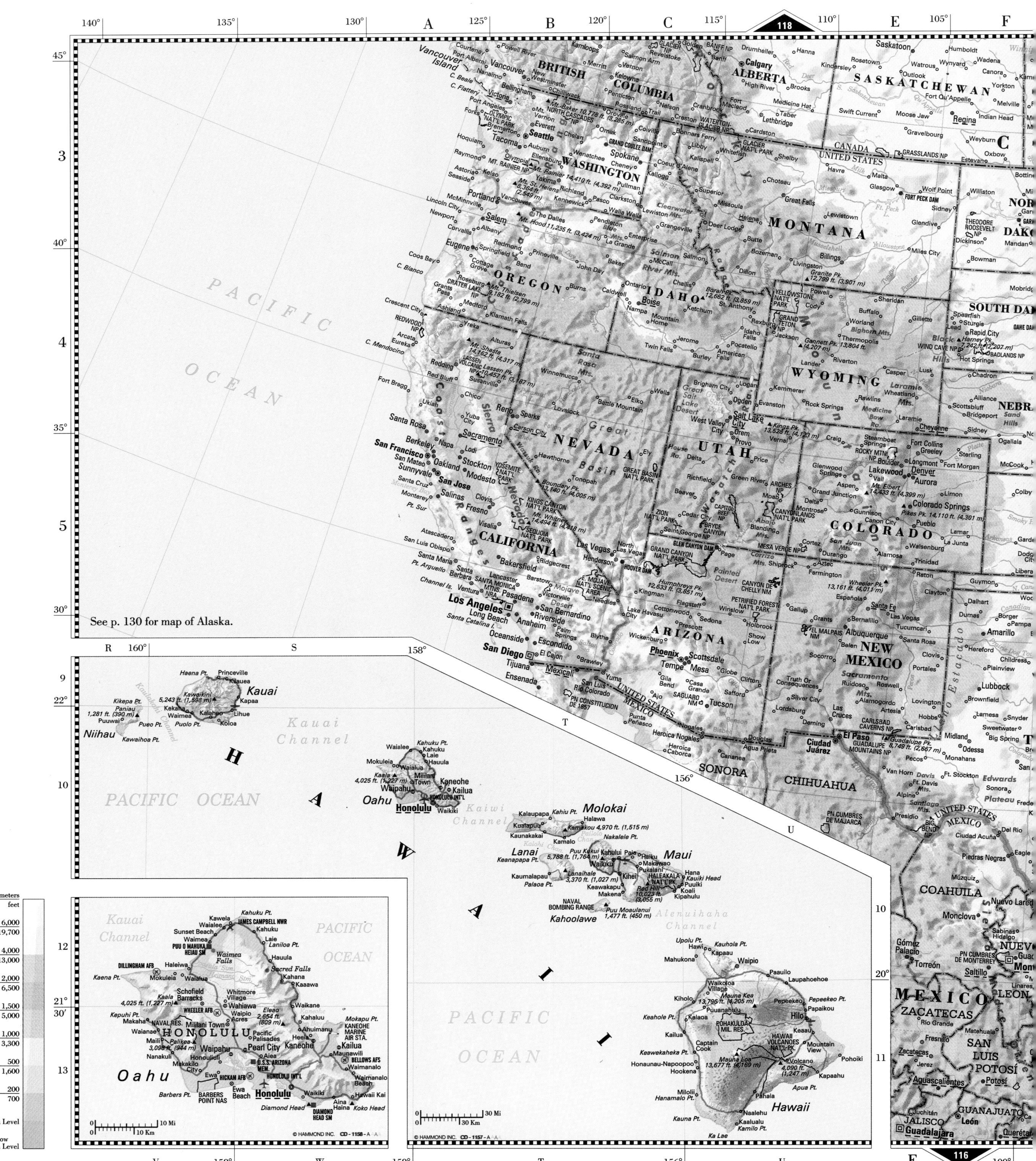

United States

POPULATION OF CITIES AND TOWNS

| ■ OVER 2,000,000 | ⊛ 500,000 - 999,999 | ◉ 50,000 - 99,999 |
| ▣ 1,000,000 - 1,999,999 | ● 100,000 - 499,999 | ○ UNDER 50,000 |

SCALE 1:14,000,000   LAMBERT CONFORMAL CONIC PROJECTION

MILES 0 —————— 200 —————— 400 —————— 600

KILOMETERS 0 —————— 200 —————— 400 —————— 600

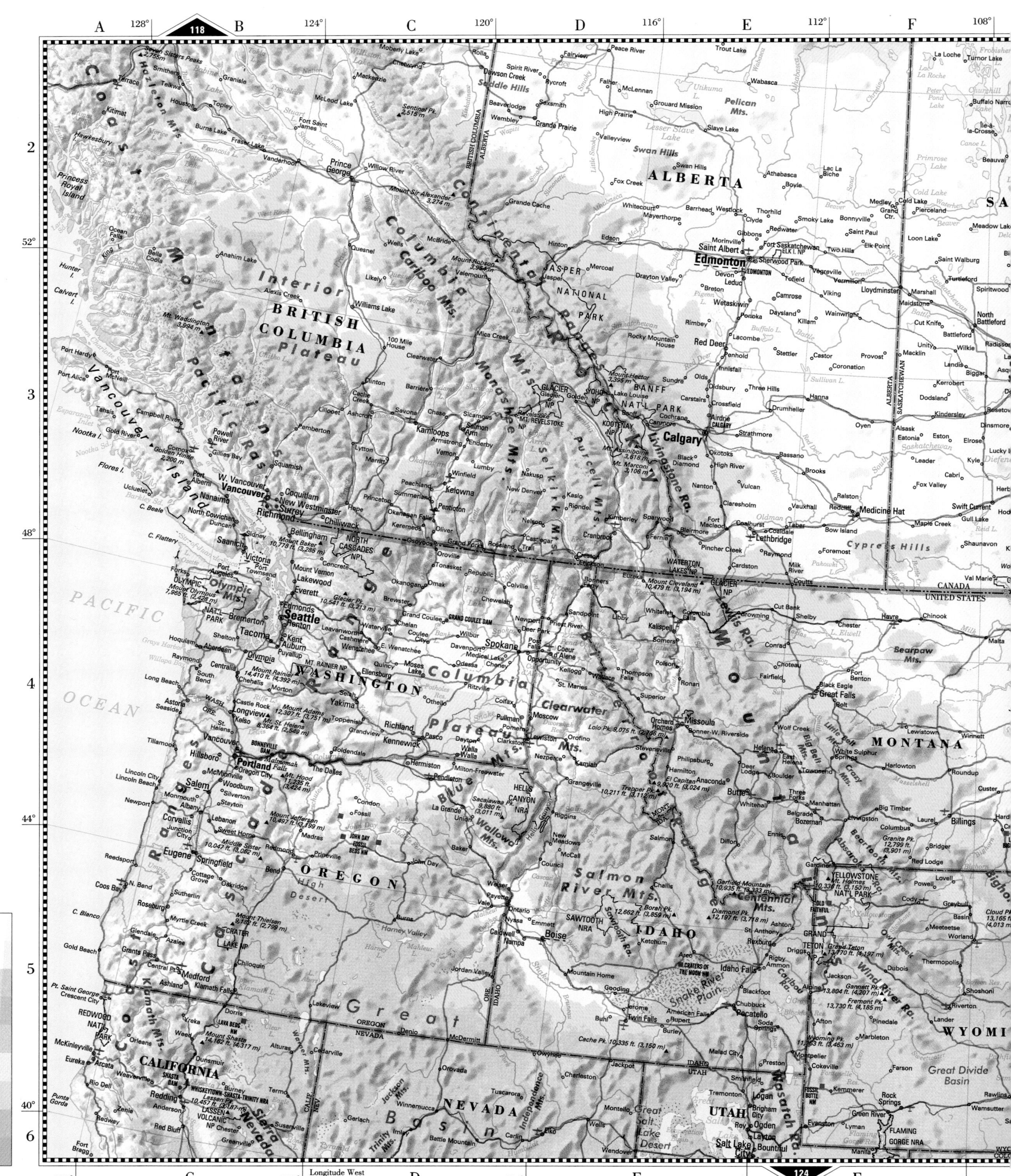

A
B
C
D
E
F
128°
124°
120°
116°
112°
108°
118
124
2
3
4
5
6
52°
48°
44°
40°
Longitude West of Greenwich
PACIFIC
OCEAN
BRITISH COLUMBIA
ALBERTA
WASHINGTON
OREGON
IDAHO
MONTANA
NEVADA
UTAH
CALIFORNIA
WYOMI
CANADA
UNITED STATES
Coast Mountains
Interior
Plateau
Columbia Mts.
Cariboo Mts.
Continental Ranges
Rocky Mts.
Monashee Mts.
Selkirk Mts.
Purcell Mts.
Hazelton Mts.
Pacific Ras.
Vancouver Island
Olympic Mts.
Cascade Ra.
Coast Ranges
Klamath Mts.
Columbia Plateau
Blue Mts.
Wallowa Mts.
Clearwater Mts.
Salmon River Mts.
Sawtooth Ra.
Bitterroot Range
Lewis Ra.
Centennial Mts.
Snake River Plain
Great Basin
High Desert
Wasatch Ra.
Wind River Ra.
Great Divide Basin
Great Salt Lake Desert
Sierra Nevada
Swan Hills
Pelican Mts.
Saddle Hills
Cypress Hills
Bearpaw Mts.
Lesser Slave Lake
JASPER NATIONAL PARK
BANFF NAT'L PARK
GLACIER NP
YELLOWSTONE NAT'L PARK
CRATER LAKE NP
HELLS CANYON NRA
SAWTOOTH NRA
Edmonton
Calgary
Vancouver
Victoria
Seattle
Tacoma
Olympia
Spokane
Portland
Salem
Eugene
Boise
Missoula
Helena
Butte
Billings
Great Falls
Lethbridge
Medicine Hat
Red Deer
Kamloops
Kelowna
Prince George
Salt Lake City
Ogden
Idaho Falls
Pocatello
Twin Falls
Medford
Redding
Mt. Rainier 14,410 ft. (4,392 m)
Mt. Hood 11,235 ft. (3,424 m)
Mt. Shasta 14,162 ft. (4,317 m)
Mount Robson 3,954 m
Grand Teton 13,770 ft. (4,197 m)
Borah Pk. 12,662 ft. (3,859 m)
meters
feet
6,000
19,700
4,000
13,000
2,000
6,500
1,500
5,000
1,000
3,300
500
1,600
200
700
Sea Level
Below Sea Level

Southwestern Canada, Northwestern United States

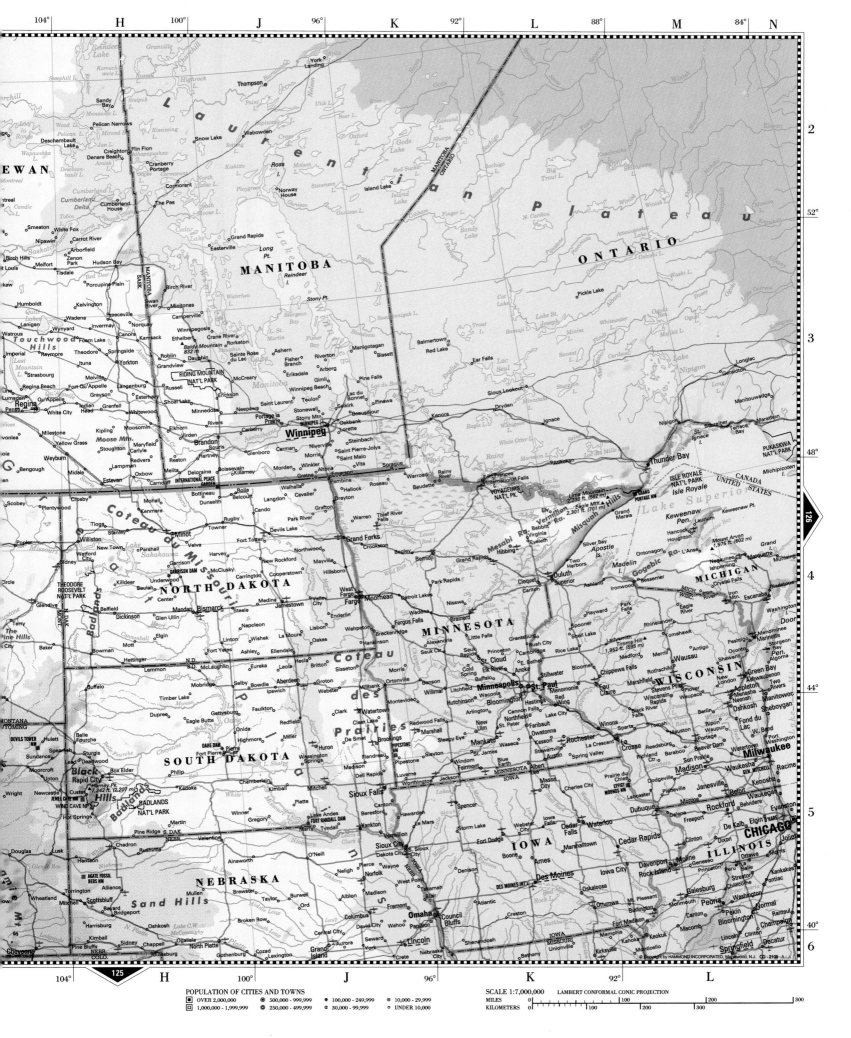

A 124° B 120° C 122 116° D 112° E 108°

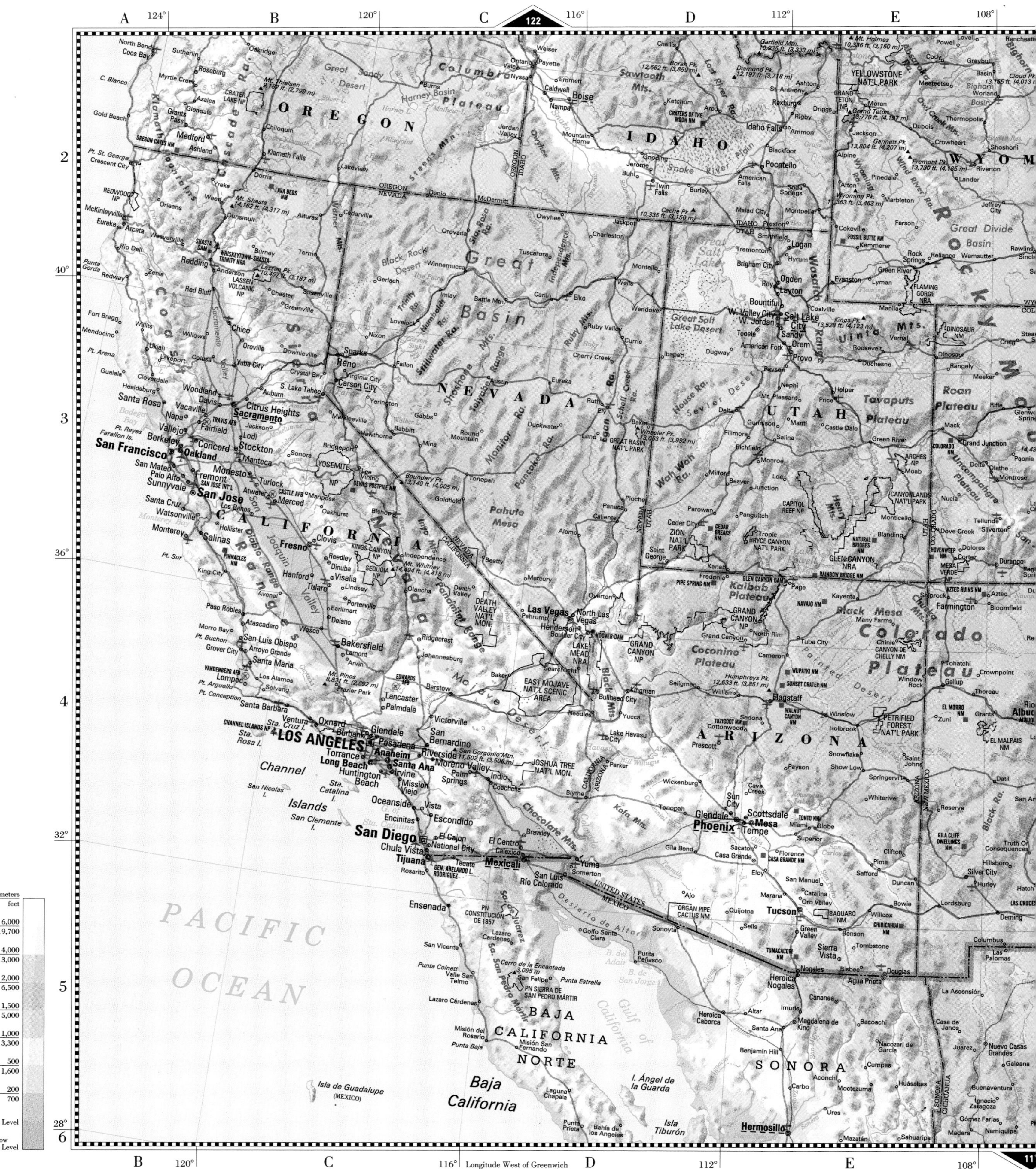

meters / feet
6,000 / 19,700
4,000 / 13,000
2,000 / 6,500
1,500 / 5,000
1,000 / 3,300
500 / 1,600
200 / 700
Sea Level
Below Sea Level

40° 36° 32° 28°

2 3 4 5 6

B 120° C 116° Longitude West of Greenwich D 112° E 108°

Southwestern United States

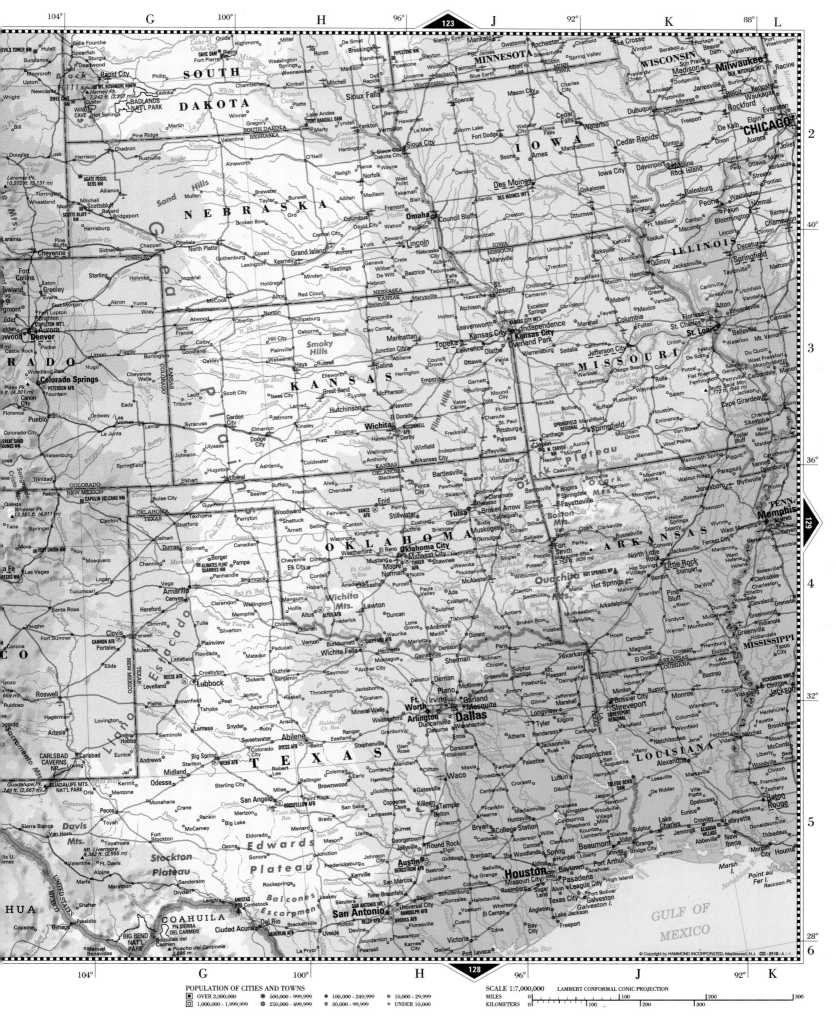

POPULATION OF CITIES AND TOWNS

■ OVER 2,000,000
▣ 1,000,000 - 1,999,999
● 500,000 - 999,999
● 250,000 - 499,999
● 100,000 - 249,999
● 30,000 - 99,999
○ 10,000 - 29,999
○ UNDER 10,000

SCALE 1:7,000,000 LAMBERT CONFORMAL CONIC PROJECTION
MILES 0 | 100 | 200 | 300
KILOMETERS 0 | 100 | 200 | 300

© Copyright by HAMMOND INCORPORATED, Maplewood, N.J. CD-2110-A

Southeastern Canada, Northeastern United States

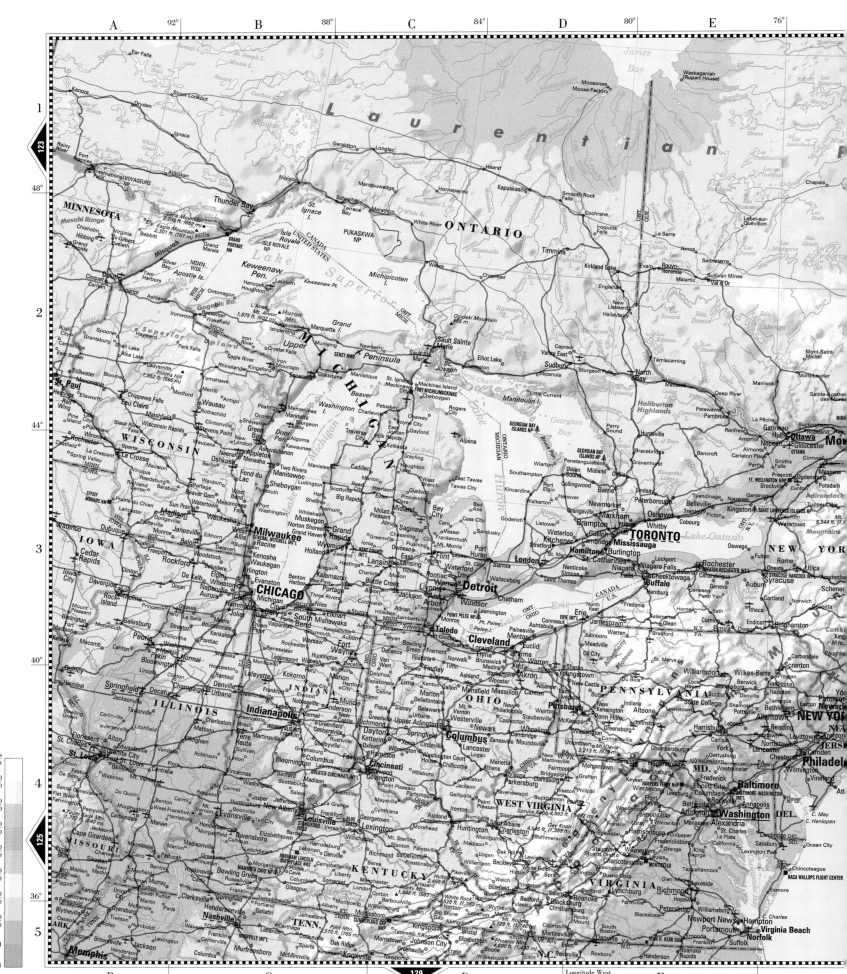

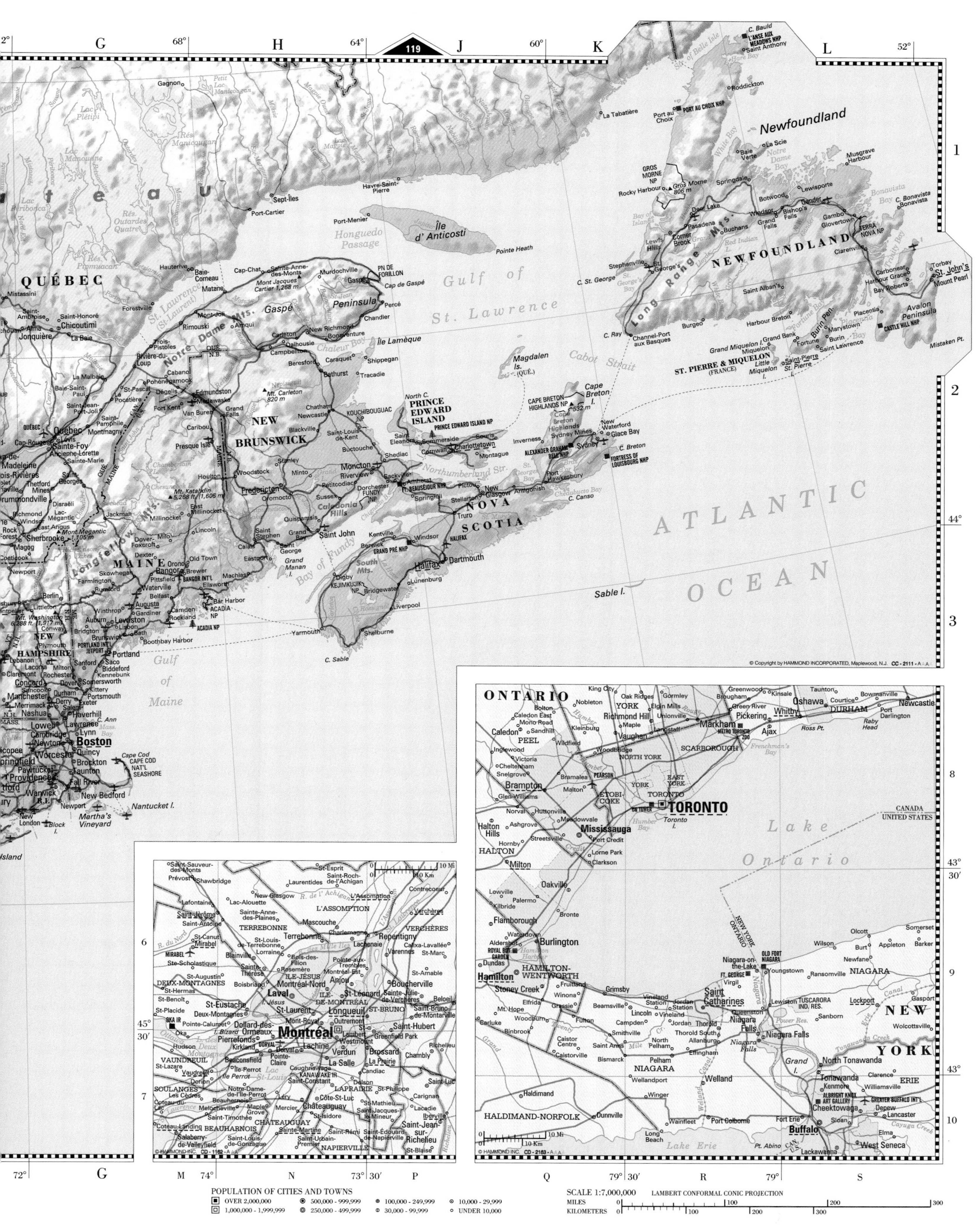

QUÉBEC

Mistassini
Saint-Ambroise
Chicoutimi
Jonquière
Alma
La Baie
Saint-Honoré
Sept-Îles
Havre-Saint-Pierre
Port-Cartier
Port-Menier
Baie-Comeau
Hauterive
Matane
Forestville
Gagnon
Sainte-Anne-des-Monts
Murdochville
Cap-Chat
Mont Jacques-Cartier 1,268 m
Gaspé
Cap de Gaspé
PN DE FORILLON
Percé
Baie-du-Loup
Trois-Pistoles
Rivière-du-Loup
Cabano
Carleton
Nouvelle
New Richmond
Bonaventure
Chandler

Gaspé Peninsula

Rimouski
Amqui
Dalhousie
Chaleur Bay
Île Lamèque
Caraquet
Shippegan
Tracadie
Beresford
Bathurst

Gulf of St. Lawrence

Île d'Anticosti
Pointe Heath
Honguedo Passage

NEWFOUNDLAND

Long Range Mts.

C. Bauld
L'ANSE AUX MEADOWS NHP
Saint Anthony
Roddickton
Port au Choix NHP
La Tabatière
Port au Choix
La Scie
Baie Verte
Notre Dame Bay
Musgrave Harbour
GROS MORNE NP
Rocky Harbour
Gros Morne 806 m
Springdale
Botwood
Lewisporte
Bonavista Bay
C. Bonavista
Bonavista
Bay of Islands
Corner Brook
Pasadena
Deer Lake
Buchans
Windsor
Grand Falls
Bishop's Falls
Gambo
Glovertown
TERRA NOVA NP
Lewis Hills
Red Indian L.
Stephenville
St. George's
Clarenville
C. St. George
St. George's Bay
Saint Alban's
Torbay
St. John's
Mount Pearl

C. Ray
Channel-Port aux Basques
Burgeo
Grand Miquelon I.
Grand Bank
Fortune
Harbour Breton
Burin Pen.
Burin
Placentia Bay
Avalon Peninsula
Carbonear
Harbour Grace
Bay Roberts
Placentia
CASTLE HILL NHP
Marystown
Saint Lawrence
ST. PIERRE & MIQUELON (FRANCE)
Little Miquelon
St. Pierre
Mistaken Pt.

Magdalen Is. (QUÉ.)

Cabot Strait

PRINCE EDWARD ISLAND

KOUCHIBOUGUAC NP
North C.
PRINCE EDWARD ISLAND NP
Summerside
Charlottetown
Souris
Cornwall
Montague
Inverness
ALEXANDER GRAHAM BELL NHP
Cape Breton Highlands NP
Cape Breton I.
1,532 m
Cape Breton
Baddeck
New Waterford
Glace Bay
Sydney
Sydney Mines
FORTRESS OF LOUISBOURG NHP

Chatham
Newcastle
Blackville
Saint-Louis-de-Kent
Rexton
Buctouche
Shediac
Sackville
Moncton
Riverview
Dorchester
FUNDY NP
Petitcodiac
Sussex
Amherst
Springhill
Pictou
Antigonish
Port Hawkesbury
C. Canso
Chedabucto Bay

NEW BRUNSWICK

Mt. Carleton 820 m
Campbellton
Bartibog
Stanley
Minto
Oromocto
Fredericton
Woodstock
Grand Falls
Van Buren
Caribou
Presque Isle
Edmundston
Madawaska
Fort Kent

NOVA SCOTIA

Stellarton
New Glasgow
Truro
BEAUBOURS NHP
Caledonia Hills
Quispamsis
Saint John
Saint Stephen
Calais
Saint George
Eastport
Grand Manan I.
Kentville
BERWICK
GRAND PRÉ NHP
Windsor
HALIFAX
Dartmouth
South Mts.
KEJIMKUJIK NP
Bridgewater
Liverpool
Lunenburg
Digby
Annapolis Royal
North Mts.
Yarmouth
C. Sable
Shelburne

Sable I.

ATLANTIC OCEAN

© Copyright by HAMMOND INCORPORATED, Maplewood, N.J. CC-2111-A-A

MAINE

Mt. Katahdin 5,268 ft / 1,606 m
Medway
Lincoln
Old Town
Orono
Bangor
Brewer
Ellsworth
Machias
Bar Harbor
ACADIA NP
Rockland
Camden
Belfast
Waterville
Augusta
Gardiner
Bath
Boothbay Harbor
Skowhegan
Farmington
Rumford
Dexter
Dover-Foxcroft
Millinocket
East Millinocket
Jackman
Mont-Mégantic 1,105 m
Sherbrooke
Lac-Mégantic
Rock Forest
Magog
Coaticook
Newport
Berlin
Littleton
Mt. Washington 6,288 ft / 1,917 m
Conway
Plymouth
Bridgton
Auburn
Lewiston
Brunswick
Portland
PORTLAND INT'L JETPORT
Saco
Sanford
Biddeford
Kennebunk

NEW HAMPSHIRE

Lebanon
Claremont
Concord
Manchester
Nashua
Laconia
Milton
Rochester
Dover
Durham
Somersworth
Exeter
Portsmouth
Derry
Merrimack

Gulf of Maine

Ann
MASS.
Lowell
Lawrence
Haverhill
Lynn
Newton
Cambridge
Boston
Quincy
Brockton
Cape Cod
CAPE COD NAT'L SEASHORE
Worcester
Taunton
Fall River
New Bedford
Providence
R.I.
Newport
Pawtucket
Warwick
Springfield
Hartford
New London
Block I.
Martha's Vineyard
Nantucket I.

Bay of Fundy

ONTARIO

King City
Nobleton
Oak Ridges
Gormley
Greenwood
Taunton
Bolton
Caledon East
Brougham
Kinsale
Oshawa
Courtice
Bowmanville
Richmond Hill
Unionville
Green River
Pickering
Whitby
DURHAM
Newcastle
Caledon
Mono Road
Sandhill
Kleinburg
Maple
Vaughan
Woodbridge
SCARBOROUGH
Ajax
Ross Pt.
Raby Head
Port Darlington
Inglewood
Victoria
Wildfield
NORTH YORK
Frenchman's Bay

PEEL

Cheltenham
Snelgrove
Bramalea
PEARSON
YORK
EAST YORK
Brampton
Malton
ETOBI-COKE
CN TOWER
TORONTO
Glen Williams
Norval
Ashgrove
Meadowvale
Toronto I.
Huttonville

Mississauga
Streetsville
Port Credit
Lorne Park
Clarkson
CANADA
UNITED STATES

HALTON

Halton Hills
Hornby
Milton
Lowville
Palermo
Oakville
Kilbride
Bronte
Lake Ontario

Flamborough
Waterdown
Aldershot
ROYAL BOTANICAL GARDEN
Burlington
Dundas
Hamilton
HAMILTON-WENTWORTH
Stoney Creek
Elfrida
Winona
Grimsby
Vineland Station
Jordan
Beamsville
Lincoln
Vineland
NEW YORK
Olcott
Somerset
Wilson
Burt
Appleton
Barker
Newfane
NIAGARA
Niagara-on-the-Lake
OLD FORT NIAGARA
FT. GEORGE
Virgil
Saint Catharines
Queenston
Niagara Falls
Lewiston
TUSCARORA IND. RES.
Youngstown
Ransomville
Lockport
Gasport

Mt. Hope
Woodburn
Grassie
Fulton
Campden
Smithville
Jordan
Thorold
Niagara Falls
Sanborn
Thorold South
Pelham
North Pelham
Allanburg
Power Res.
NEW YORK
Wolcottsville

Caledonia
Binbrook
Caistor Centre
Saint Anns
Bismarck
Caistorville
Welland
Effingham
Niagara Falls
North Tonawanda
Clarence
Elma

NIAGARA

Wellandport
Welland
Winger
ERIE
Tonawanda
Kenmore
Williamsville

HALDIMAND-NORFOLK

Haldimand
Dunnville
Wainfleet
Port Colborne
Long Beach
Fort Erie
Lake Erie
Pt. Abino
GREATER BUFFALO INT'L
ALBRIGHT-KNOX ART GALLERY
Cheektowaga
Depew
Lancaster
Sloan
Buffalo
West Seneca
Lackawanna
Cayuga Creek

© HAMMOND INC.   CD-2163-A-A

Montréal inset

Saint-Sauveur-des-Monts
Prévost
Shawbridge
St-Esprit
St-Roch-de-l'Achigan
Laurentides
L'Assomption
Contrecœur
Lafontaine
New Glasgow
Lac-Alouette
Saint-Jérôme
Saint-Anne-des-Plaines
Mascouche
Charlemagne
Repentigny
VERCHÈRES
Verchères
TERREBONNE
St-Antoine
St-Canut
Mirabel
MIRABEL
St-Louis-de-Terrebonne
Lorraine
Blainville
Terrebonne
Lachenaie
Calixa-Lavallée
St-Marc
Ste-Scholastique
St-Augustin
Ste-Thérèse
Bois-des-Filion
Rosemère
Pointe-aux-Trembles
Varennes
DEUX-MONTAGNES
Boisbriand
ÎLE-JÉSUS
Montréal-Nord
Anjou
St-Bruno
de-Montarville
St-Benoît
St-Eustache
ÎLE-JÉSUS
Laval
St-Léonard
Sainte-Julie-de-Verchères
Beloeil
St-Placide
Deux-Montagnes
St-Laurent
ÎLE-DE-MONTRÉAL
St-Bruno
de-Montarville
OKA IR
Pointe-Calumet
I. Bizard
Ormeaux
Dollard-des-
Montréal
Longueuil
ST-BRUNO
VAUDREUIL
Kirkland
DORVAL
Lachine
St-Lambert
Greenfield Park
St-Lazare
Beaconsfield
Pointe-Claire
Verdun
Westmount
Richelieu
Vaudreuil
Île-Perrot
Dorval
La Salle
Brossard
Chambly
Coteau-du-Lac
Notre-Dame-de-l'Île-Perrot
Caughnawaga
KANAWAKE IR
Candiac
St-Amable
SOULANGES
Les Cèdres
Maple Grove
LAPRAIRIE
St-Philippe
Saint-Rémi
Coteau-Landing
BEAUHARNOIS
Beauharnois
Mercier
St-Mathieu
Lacadie
Carignan
Coteau-Station
Melocheville
St-Isidore
St-Mineur
CHÂTEAUGUAY
St-Timothée
Châteauguay
St-Jacques
St-Édouard
Saint-Jean-sur-Richelieu
Salaberry-de-Valleyfield
St-Louis-de-Gonzague
Saint-Martine
Ste-Clotilde
St-Urbain-Premier
St-Rémi
St-Édouard-de-Napierville
St-Blaise
NAPIERVILLE

0 10 Mi
0 10 Km

© HAMMOND INC.

POPULATION OF CITIES AND TOWNS

- ■ OVER 2,000,000
- ☑ 1,000,000 - 1,999,999
- ● 500,000 - 999,999
- ◉ 250,000 - 499,999
- ⊙ 100,000 - 249,999
- ⊙ 30,000 - 99,999
- ⊙ 10,000 - 29,999
- ○ UNDER 10,000

SCALE 1:7,000,000   LAMBERT CONFORMAL CONIC PROJECTION

MILES 0   100   200   300
KILOMETERS 0   100   200   300

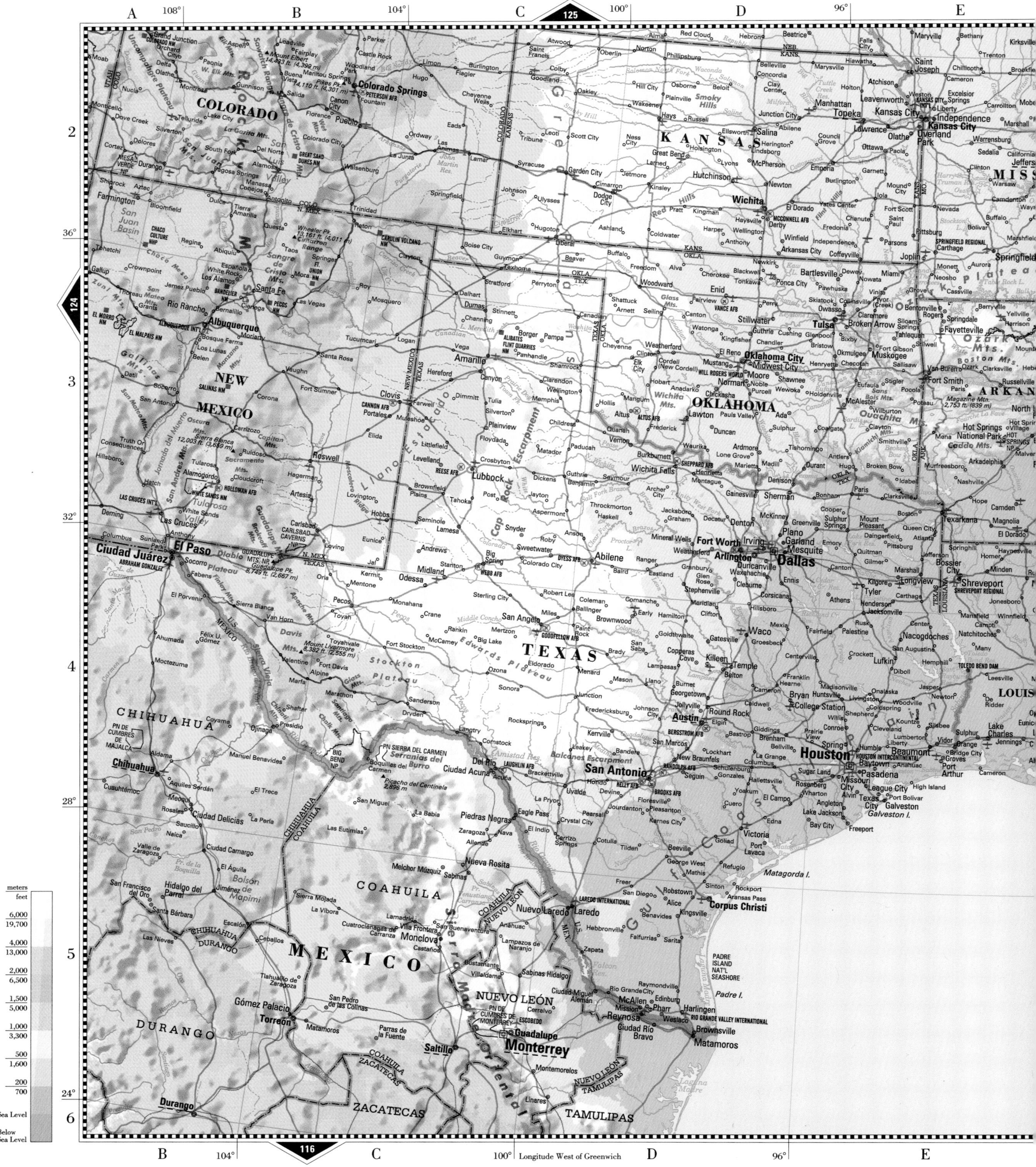

A
108°
B
104°
C
125
100°
D
96°
E
124
2
3
4
5
6
36°
32°
28°
24°
COLORADO
KANSAS
OKLAHOMA
NEW MEXICO
TEXAS
CHIHUAHUA
COAHUILA
MEXICO
DURANGO
NUEVO LEÓN
ZACATECAS
TAMULIPAS
ARKANSAS
LOUISIANA
Rocky Mts.
Colorado Springs
Pueblo
Denver
Wichita
Topeka
Kansas City
Oklahoma City
Tulsa
Amarillo
Lubbock
Albuquerque
Santa Fe
El Paso
Ciudad Juárez
Abilene
Fort Worth
Dallas
Austin
San Antonio
Houston
Corpus Christi
Monterrey
Saltillo
Chihuahua
Torreón
Durango
Nuevo Laredo
Laredo
Brownsville
Matamoros
Edwards Plateau
Llano Estacado
Gulf Coastal Plain
Sierra Madre Oriental
Matagorda I.
Padre I.
Galveston I.
meters
feet
6,000
19,700
4,000
13,000
2,000
6,500
1,500
5,000
1,000
3,300
500
1,600
200
700
Sea Level
Below Sea Level
B
104°
116
C
100°
Longitude West of Greenwich
D
96°
E

Southeastern United States

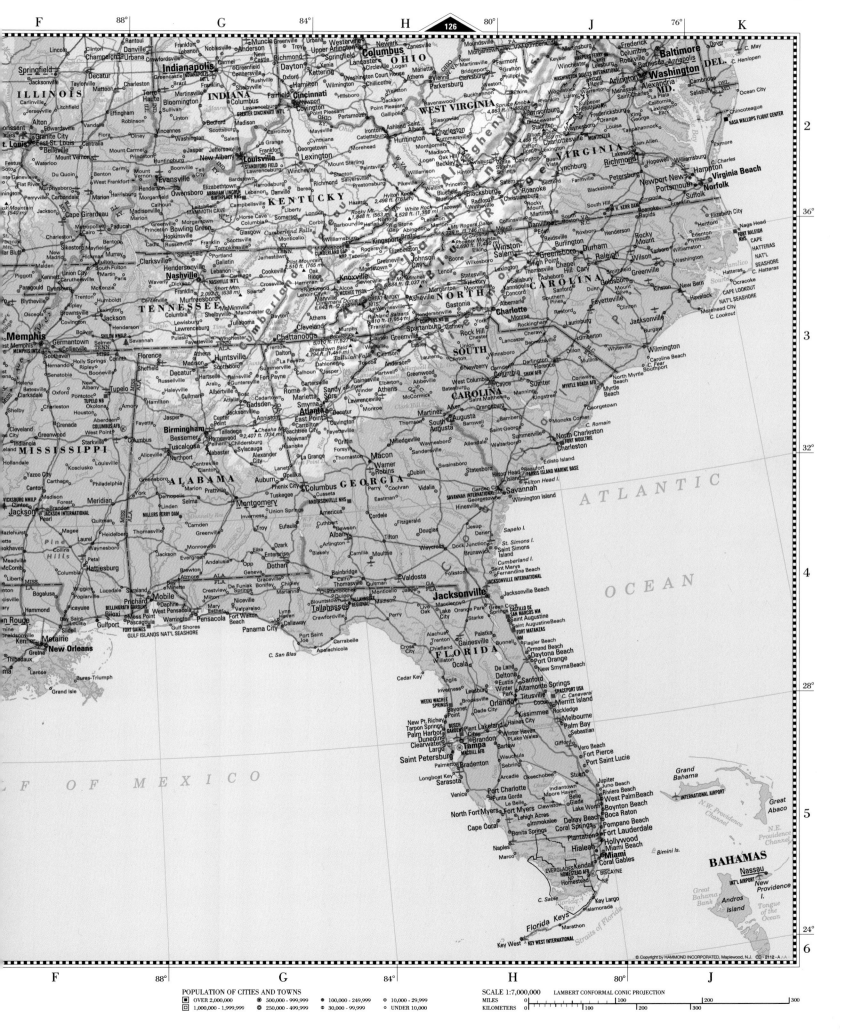

Alaska

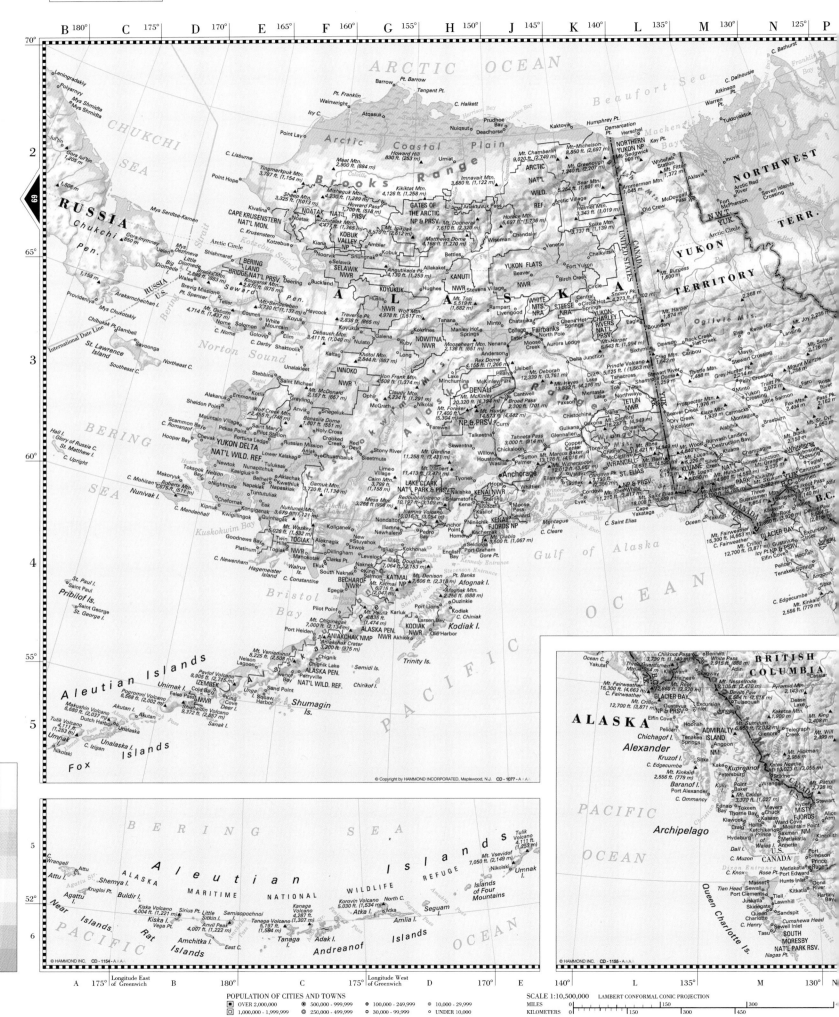

POPULATION OF CITIES AND TOWNS

■ OVER 2,000,000	● 500,000 - 999,999
▣ 1,000,000 - 1,999,999	● 250,000 - 499,999

● 100,000 - 249,999
● 10,000 - 29,999
● 30,000 - 99,999
● UNDER 10,000

SCALE 1:10,500,000   LAMBERT CONFORMAL CONIC PROJECTION

MILES   0   150   300

KILOMETERS   0   150   300   450

Los Angeles, New York-Philadelphia-Washington

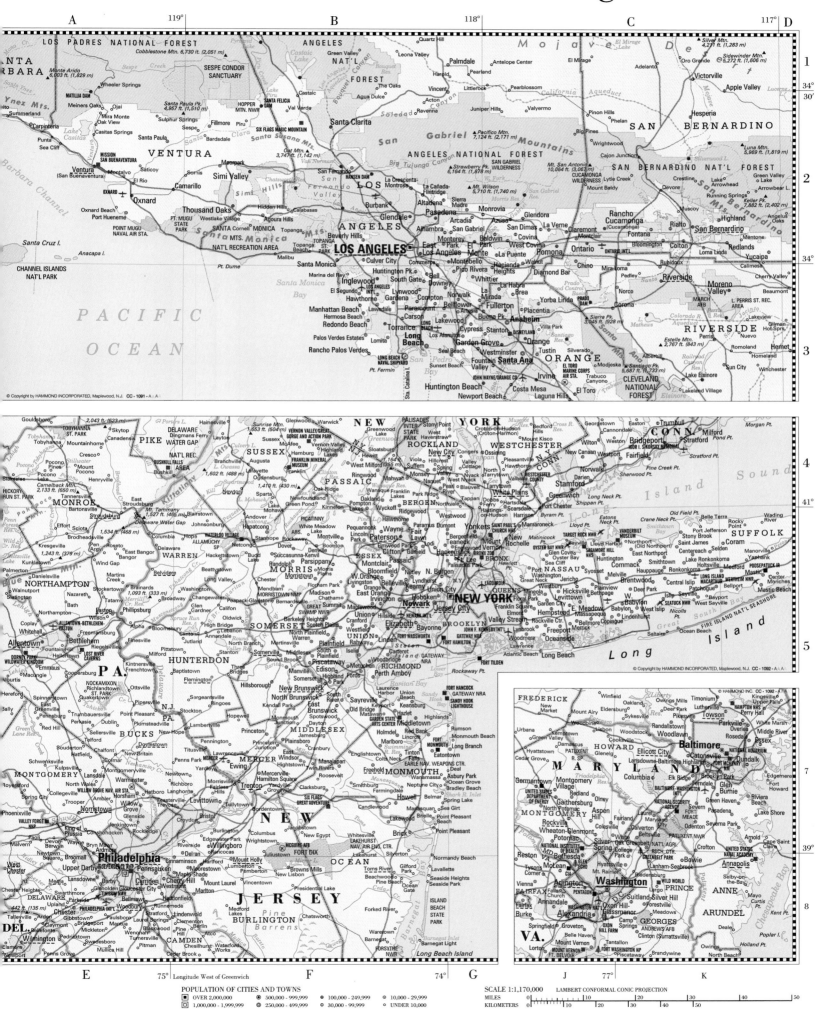

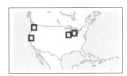

Seattle, San Francisco, Detroit, Chicago

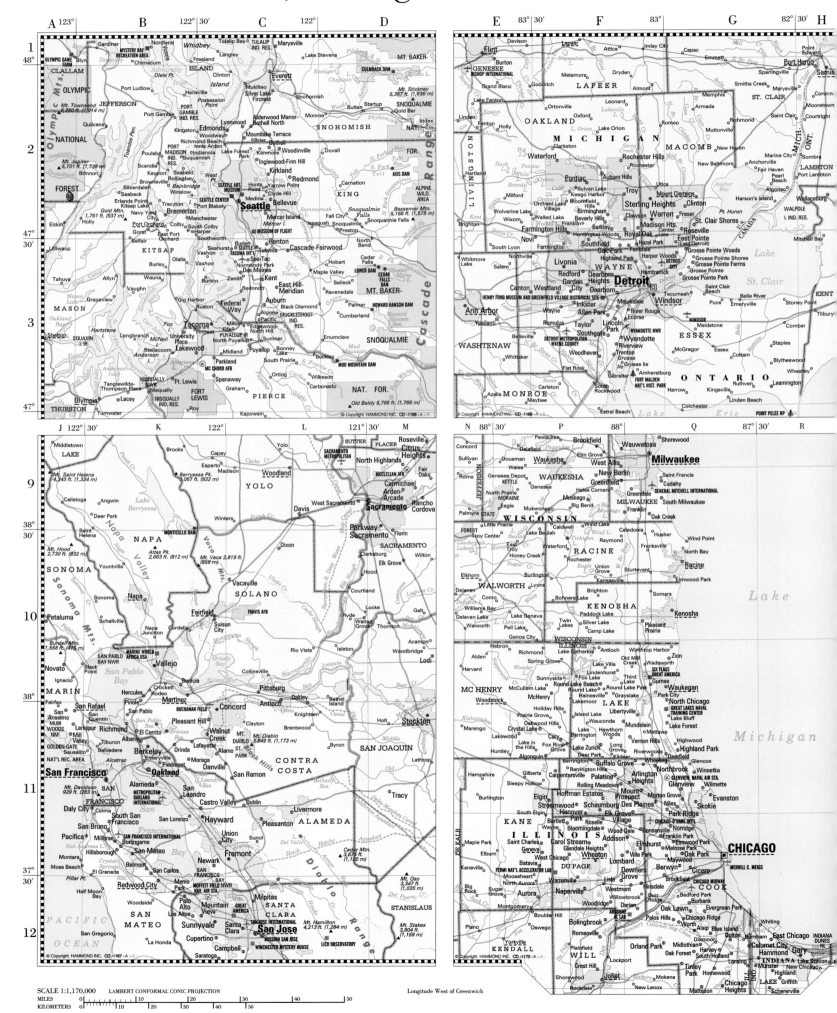

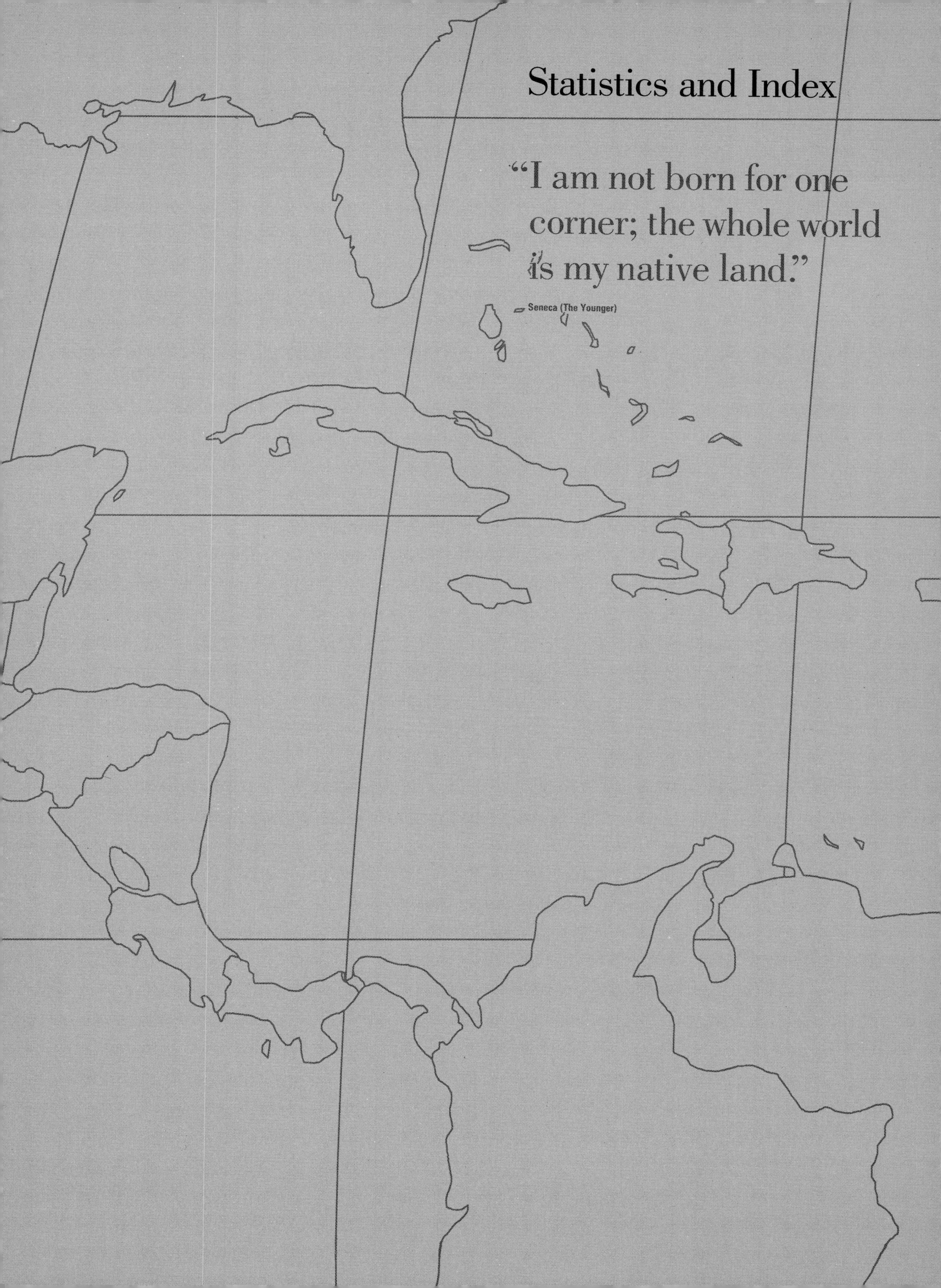

Statistics and Index

"I am not born for one corner; the whole world is my native land."

— Seneca (The Younger)

Time Zones of the World

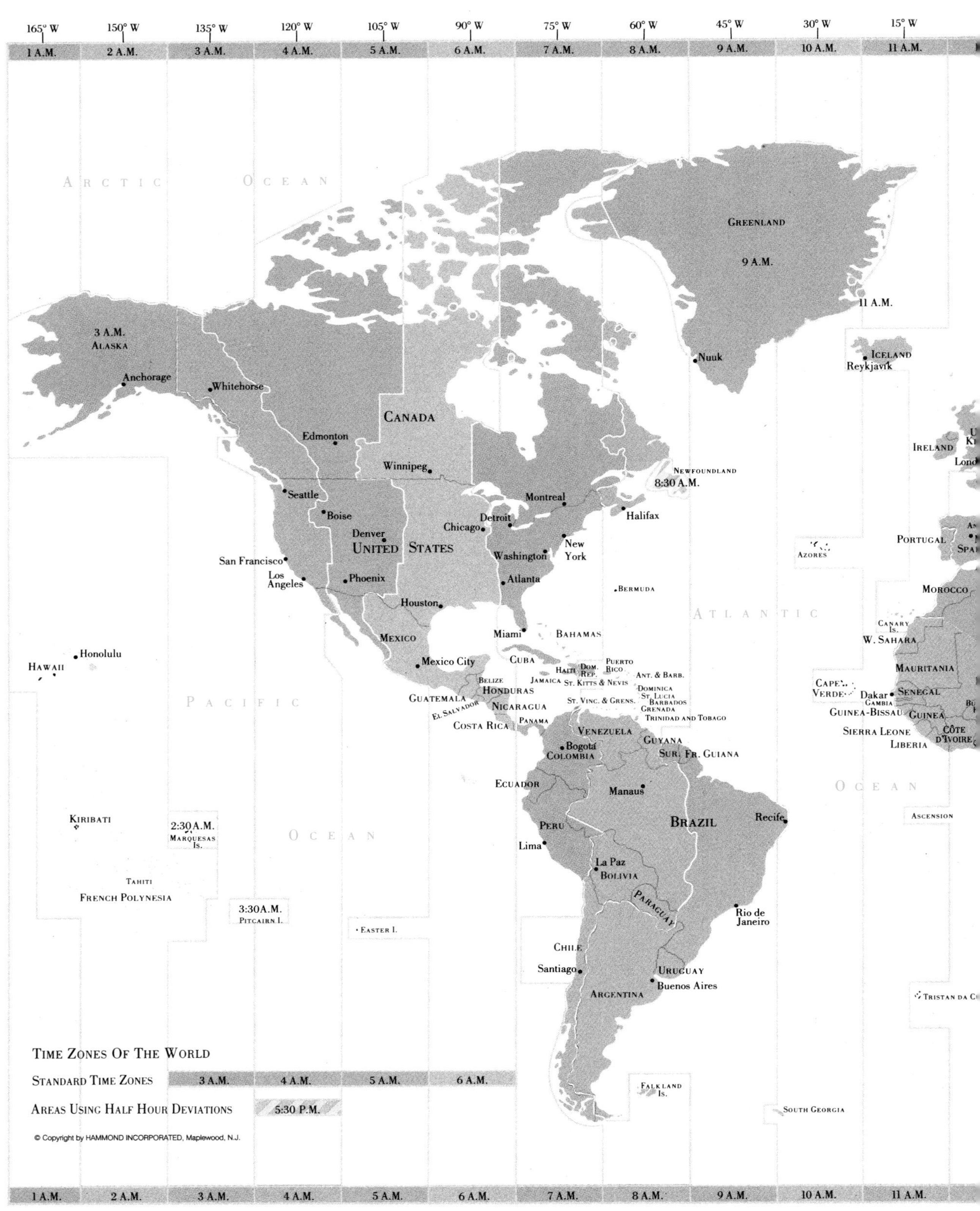

165° W	150° W	135° W	120° W	105° W	90° W	75° W	60° W	45° W	30° W	15° W
1 A.M.	2 A.M.	3 A.M.	4 A.M.	5 A.M.	6 A.M.	7 A.M.	8 A.M.	9 A.M.	10 A.M.	11 A.M.

ARCTIC OCEAN

GREENLAND
9 A.M.

11 A.M.

ICELAND
Reykjavík

3 A.M.
ALASKA

Anchorage

Nuuk

Whitehorse

CANADA

IRELAND
London

Edmonton

Winnipeg

Seattle

Boise

Montreal

NEWFOUNDLAND
8:30 A.M.

Detroit

Chicago

Halifax

Denver

UNITED STATES

San Francisco

Washington

New York

PORTUGAL
SPAIN

AZORES

Los Angeles

Phoenix

Atlanta

MOROCCO

Houston

BERMUDA

ATLANTIC

Honolulu

MEXICO

Miami

BAHAMAS

CANARY Is.
W. SAHARA

HAWAII

Mexico City

CUBA

DOM.
HAITI REP. PUERTO RICO
JAMAICA ST. KITTS & NEVIS ANT. & BARB.

MAURITANIA

PACIFIC

GUATEMALA
EL SALVADOR
Costa Rica

BELIZE
HONDURAS
NICARAGUA
PANAMA

DOMINICA
ST. LUCIA
ST. VINC. & GRENS. BARBADOS
GRENADA
TRINIDAD AND TOBAGO

CAPE VERDE
Dakar SENEGAL
GAMBIA
GUINEA-BISSAU GUINEA

SIERRA LEONE
LIBERIA

CÔTE D'IVOIRE

VENEZUELA
Bogotá
COLOMBIA

GUYANA
SUR. FR. GUIANA

OCEAN

ECUADOR

Manaus

KIRIBATI

2:30 A.M.
MARQUESAS Is.

OCEAN

PERU
Lima

BRAZIL

Recife

ASCENSION

TAHITI
FRENCH POLYNESIA

La Paz
BOLIVIA

3:30 A.M.
PITCAIRN I.

· EASTER I.

PARAGUAY

Rio de Janeiro

CHILE

Santiago

URUGUAY
Buenos Aires

ARGENTINA

TRISTAN DA C

TIME ZONES OF THE WORLD

STANDARD TIME ZONES	3 A.M.	4 A.M.	5 A.M.	6 A.M.

AREAS USING HALF HOUR DEVIATIONS   5:30 P.M.

FALKLAND Is.

SOUTH GEORGIA

© Copyright by HAMMOND INCORPORATED, Maplewood, N.J.

1 A.M.	2 A.M.	3 A.M.	4 A.M.	5 A.M.	6 A.M.	7 A.M.	8 A.M.	9 A.M.	10 A.M.	11 A.M.

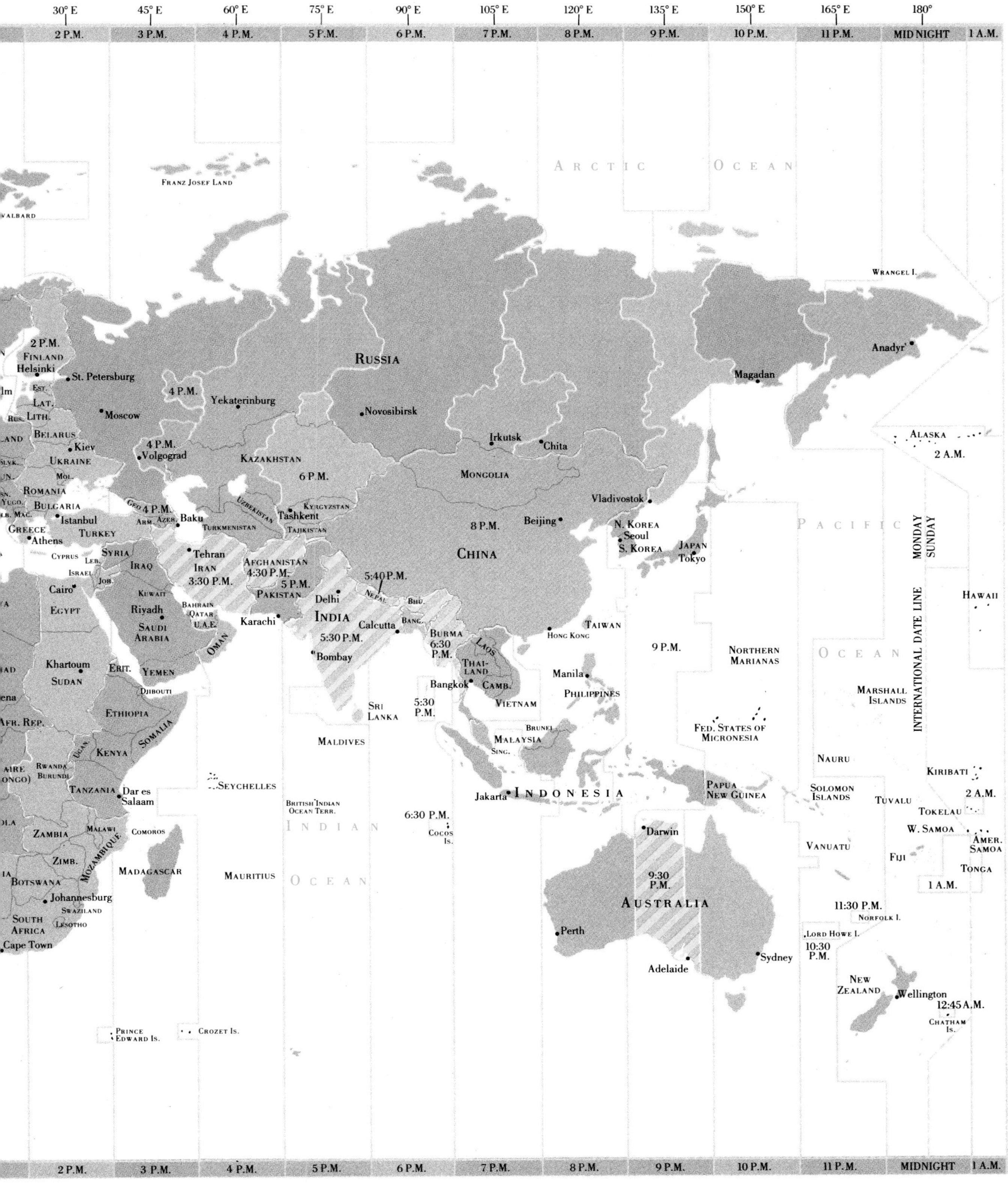

30° E
45° E
60° E
75° E
90° E
105° E
120° E
135° E
150° E
165° E
180°
2 P.M.
3 P.M.
4 P.M.
5 P.M.
6 P.M.
7 P.M.
8 P.M.
9 P.M.
10 P.M.
11 P.M.
MIDNIGHT
1 A.M.
ARCTIC OCEAN
FRANZ JOSEF LAND
WRANGEL I.
2 P.M.
FINLAND
Helsinki
St. Petersburg
RUSSIA
Anadyr'
Magadan
EST.
LAT.
LITH.
Moscow
4 P.M.
Yekaterinburg
Novosibirsk
BELARUS
Kiev
UKRAINE
4 P.M.
Volgograd
KAZAKHSTAN
Irkutsk
Chita
ALASKA
2 A.M.
MOL.
ROMANIA
BULGARIA
6 P.M.
MONGOLIA
Vladivostok
4 P.M.
Baku
Istanbul
GREECE
Athens
TURKEY
UZBEKISTAN
KYRGYZSTAN
Tashkent
TURKMENISTAN
TAJIKISTAN
8 P.M.
Beijing
N. KOREA
Seoul
S. KOREA
JAPAN
Tokyo
PACIFIC
MONDAY
SUNDAY
CYPRUS
SYRIA
IRAQ
Tehran
IRAN
3:30 P.M.
AFGHANISTAN
4:30 P.M.
5 P.M.
PAKISTAN
CHINA
ISRAEL
Cairo
EGYPT
KUWAIT
Riyadh
SAUDI ARABIA
BAHRAIN
QATAR
U.A.E.
OMAN
Karachi
Delhi
INDIA
5:40 P.M.
NEPAL
BHU.
BANG.
Calcutta
5:30 P.M.
Bombay
BURMA
6:30 P.M.
LAOS
HONG KONG
TAIWAN
HAWAII
INTERNATIONAL DATE LINE
9 P.M.
NORTHERN MARIANAS
OCEAN
Khartoum
SUDAN
ERIT.
YEMEN
DJIBOUTI
ETHIOPIA
SOMALIA
THAI-LAND
CAMB.
Bangkok
VIETNAM
Manila
PHILIPPINES
MARSHALL ISLANDS
SRI LANKA
5:30 P.M.
BRUNEI
MALAYSIA
SING.
FED. STATES OF MICRONESIA
KENYA
MALDIVES
NAURU
RWANDA
BURUNDI
TANZANIA
Dar es Salaam
SEYCHELLES
Jakarta
INDONESIA
PAPUA NEW GUINEA
SOLOMON ISLANDS
TUVALU
KIRIBATI
2 A.M.
TOKELAU
BRITISH INDIAN OCEAN TERR.
6:30 P.M.
COCOS IS.
ZAMBIA
MALAWI
COMOROS
INDIAN OCEAN
Darwin
W. SAMOA
AMER. SAMOA
VANUATU
FIJI
TONGA
ZIMB.
MOZAMBIQUE
MADAGASCAR
MAURITIUS
9:30 P.M.
1 A.M.
BOTSWANA
Johannesburg
SWAZILAND
LESOTHO
SOUTH AFRICA
Cape Town
AUSTRALIA
11:30 P.M.
NORFOLK I.
Perth
LORD HOWE I.
10:30 P.M.
Sydney
Adelaide
NEW ZEALAND
Wellington
12:45 A.M.
CHATHAM IS.
PRINCE EDWARD IS.
CROZET IS.

World Statistics

Elements of the Solar System

	Mean Distance from Sun: in Miles	in Kilometers	Period of Revolution around Sun	Period of Rotation on Axis	Equatorial Diameter in Miles	in Kilometers	Surface Gravity (Earth = 1)	Mass (Earth = 1)	Mean Density (Water = 1)	Number of Satellites
Mercury	35,990,000	57,900,000	87.97 days	59 days	3,032	4,880	0.38	0.055	5.5	0
Venus	67,240,000	108,200,000	224.70 days	243 days†	7,523	12,106	0.90	0.815	5.25	0
Earth	93,000,000	149,700,000	365.26 days	23h 56m	7,926	12,755	1.00	1.00	5.5	1
Mars	141,730,000	228,100,000	687.00 days	24h 37m	4,220	6,790	0.38	0.107	4.0	2
Jupiter	483,880,000	778,700,000	11.86 years	9h 50m	88,750	142,800	2.87	317.9	1.3	16
Saturn	887,130,000	1,427,700,000	29.46 years	10h 39m	74,580	120,020	1.32	95.2	0.7	23
Uranus	1,783,700,000	2,870,500,000	84.01 years	17h 24m†	31,600	50,900	0.93	14.6	1.3	15
Neptune	2,795,500,000	4,498,800,000	164.79 years	17h 50m	30,200	48,600	1.23	17.2	1.8	8
Pluto	3,667,900,000	5,902,800,000	247.70 years	6.39 days(?)	1,500	2,400	0.03(?)	0.01(?)	0.7(?)	1

† Retrograde motion

Dimensions of the Earth

	Area in: Sq. Miles	Sq. Kilometers
Superficial area	196,939,000	510,073,000
Land surface	57,506,000	148,941,000
Water surface	139,433,000	361,132,000

	Distance in: Miles	Kilometers
Equatorial circumference	24,902	40,075
Polar circumference	24,860	40,007
Equatorial diameter	7,926.4	12,756.4
Polar diameter	7,899.8	12,713.6
Equatorial radius	3,963.2	6,378.2
Polar radius	3,949.9	6,356.8

Volume of the Earth	2.6×10^{11} cubic miles	10.84×10^{11} cubic kilometers
Mass or weight	6.6×10^{21} short tons	6.0×10^{21} metric tons
Maximum distance from Sun	94,600,000 miles	152,000,000 kilometers
Minimum distance from Sun	91,300,000 miles	147,000,000 kilometers

Oceans and Major Seas

	Area in: Sq. Miles	Sq. Kms.	Greatest Depth in: Feet	Meters
Pacific Ocean	64,186,000	166,241,700	36,198	11,033
Atlantic Ocean	31,862,000	82,522,600	28,374	8,648
Indian Ocean	28,350,000	73,426,500	25,344	7,725
Arctic Ocean	5,427,000	14,056,000	17,880	5,450
Caribbean Sea	970,000	2,512,300	24,720	7,535
Mediterranean Sea	969,000	2,509,700	16,896	5,150
South China Sea	895,000	2,318,000	15,000	4,600
Bering Sea	875,000	2,266,250	15,800	4,800
Gulf of Mexico	600,000	1,554,000	12,300	3,750
Sea of Okhotsk	590,000	1,528,100	11,070	3,370
East China Sea	482,000	1,248,400	9,500	2,900
Yellow Sea	480,000	1,243,200	350	107
Sea of Japan	389,000	1,007,500	12,280	3,740
Hudson Bay	317,500	822,300	846	258
North Sea	222,000	575,000	2,200	670
Black Sea	185,000	479,150	7,365	2,245
Red Sea	169,000	437,700	7,200	2,195
Baltic Sea	163,000	422,170	1,506	459

The Continents

	Area in: Sq. Miles	Sq. Kms.	Percent of World's Land
Asia	17,128,500	44,362,815	29.5
Africa	11,707,000	30,321,130	20.2
North America	9,363,000	24,250,170	16.2
South America	6,875,000	17,806,250	11.8
Antarctica	5,500,000	14,245,000	9.5
Europe	4,057,000	10,507,630	7.0
Australia	2,966,136	7,682,300	5.1

Major Ship Canals

	Length in: Miles	Kms.	Minimum Depth in: Feet	Meters
Volga-Baltic, Russia	225	362	–	–
Baltic-White Sea, Russia	140	225	16	5
Suez, Egypt	100.76	162	42	13
Albert, Belgium	80	129	16.5	5
Moscow-Volga, Russia	80	129	18	6
Volga-Don, Russia	62	100	–	–
Göta, Sweden	54	87	10	3
Kiel (Nord-Ostsee), Germany	53.2	86	38	12
Panama Canal, Panama	50.72	82	41.6	13
Houston Ship, U.S.A.	50	81	36	11

Largest Islands

	Area in: Sq. Miles	Sq. Kms.
Greenland	840,000	2,175,600
New Guinea	305,000	789,950
Borneo	290,000	751,100
Madagascar	226,400	586,376
Baffin, Canada	195,928	507,454
Sumatra, Indonesia	164,000	424,760
Honshu, Japan	88,000	227,920
Great Britain	84,400	218,896
Victoria, Canada	83,896	217,290
Ellesmere, Canada	75,767	196,236
Celebes, Indonesia	72,986	189,034
South I., New Zealand	58,393	151,238
Java, Indonesia	48,842	126,501
North I., New Zealand	44,187	114,444
Newfoundland, Canada	42,031	108,860
Cuba	40,533	104,981
Luzon, Philippines	40,420	104,688
Iceland	39,768	103,000
Mindanao, Philippines	36,537	94,631
Ireland	31,743	82,214
Sakhalin, Russia	29,500	76,405
Hispaniola, Haiti & Dom. Rep.	29,399	76,143

	Area in: Sq. Miles	Sq. Kms.
Hokkaido, Japan	28,983	75,066
Banks, Canada	27,038	70,028
Ceylon, Sri Lanka	25,332	65,610
Tasmania, Australia	24,600	63,710
Svalbard, Norway	23,957	62,049
Devon, Canada	21,331	55,247
Novaya Zemlya (north isl.), Russia	18,600	48,200
Marajó, Brazil	17,991	46,597
Tierra del Fuego, Chile & Argentina	17,900	46,360
Alexander, Antarctica	16,700	43,250
Axel Heiberg, Canada	16,671	43,178
Melville, Canada	16,274	42,150
Southhampton, Canada	15,913	41,215
New Britain, Papua New Guinea	14,100	36,519
Taiwan, China	13,836	35,835
Kyushu, Japan	13,770	35,664
Hainan, China	13,127	33,999
Prince of Wales, Canada	12,872	33,338
Spitsbergen, Norway	12,355	31,999
Vancouver, Canada	12,079	31,285
Timor, Indonesia	11,527	29,855
Sicily, Italy	9,926	25,708

	Area in: Sq. Miles	Sq. Kms.
Somerset, Canada	9,570	24,786
Sardinia, Italy	9,301	24,090
Shikoku, Japan	6,860	17,767
New Caledonia, France	6,530	16,913
Nordaustlandet, Norway	6,409	16,599
Samar, Philippines	5,050	13,080
Negros, Philippines	4,906	12,707
Palawan, Philippines	4,550	11,785
Panay, Philippines	4,446	11,515
Jamaica	4,232	10,961
Hawaii, United States	4,038	10,458
Viti Levu, Fiji	4,010	10,386
Cape Breton, Canada	3,981	10,311
Mindoro, Philippines	3,759	9,736
Kodiak, Alaska, U.S.A.	3,670	9,505
Cyprus	3,572	9,251
Puerto Rico, U.S.A.	3,435	8,897
Corsica, France	3,352	8,682
New Ireland, Papua New Guinea	3,340	8,651
Crete, Greece	3,218	8,335
Anticosti, Canada	3,066	7,941
Wrangel, Russia	2,819	7,301

Principal Mountains

	Height in : Feet	Meters		Height in : Feet	Meters		Height in : Feet	Meters
rest, Nepal-China	29,028	8,848	Llullaillaco, Chile-Argentina	22,057	6,723	Blanc, France	15,771	4,807
(Godwin Austen), Pakistan-China	28,250	8,611	Nevada Ancohuma, Bolivia	21,489	6,550	Klyuchevskaya Sopka, Russia	15,584	4,750
kalu, Nepal-China	27,789	8,470	Chimborazo, Ecuador	20,561	6,267	Fairweather, Br. Col., Canada	15,300	4,663
ulagiri, Nepal	26,810	8,172	McKinley, Alaska	20,320	6,194	Dufourspitze (Mte. Rosa), Italy-Switzerland	15,203	4,634
ga Parbat, Pakistan	26,660	8,126	Logan, Yukon, Canada	19,524	5,951	Ras Dashen, Ethiopia	15,157	4620
apurna, Nepal	26,504	8,078	Cotopaxi, Ecuador	19,347	5,897	Matterhorn, Switzerland	14,691	4,478
aposhi, Pakistan	25,550	7,788	Kilimanjaro, Tanzania	19,340	5,895	Whitney, California, U.S.A.	14,494	4,418
gur Shan, China	25,325	7,719	El Misti, Peru	19,101	5,822	Elbert, Colorado, U.S.A.	14,433	4,399
ch Mir, Pakistan	25,230	7,690	Pico Cristóbal Colón, Colombia	18,947	5,775	Rainier, Washington, U.S.A.	14,410	4,392
gga Shan, China	24,790	7,556	Huila, Colombia	18,865	5,750	Shasta, California, U.S.A.	14,162	4,317
mmunism Peak, Tajikistan	24,590	7,495	Citlaltépetl (Orizaba), Mexico	18,701	5,700	Pikes Peak, Colorado, U.S.A.	14,110	4,301
edy Peak, Kyrgyzstan	24,406	7,439	Damavand, Iran	18,606	5,671	Finsteraarhorn, Switzerland	14,022	4,274
mo Lhari, Bhutan-China	23,997	7,314	El'brus, Russia	18,510	5,642	Mauna Kea, Hawaii, U.S.A.	13,796	4,205
rtag, China	23,891	7,282	St. Elias, Alaska, U.S.A.-Yukon, Canada	18,008	5,489	Mauna Loa, Hawaii, U.S.A.	13,677	4,169
ro Aconcagua, Argentina	22,831	6,959	Dykh-tau, Russia	17,070	5,203	Jungfrau, Switzerland	13,642	4,158
s del Salado, Chile-Argentina	22,572	6,880	Batian (Kenya), Kenya	17,058	5,199	Grossglockner, Austria	12,457	3,797
ete, Chile-Argentina	22,546	6,872	Ararat, Turkey	16,946	5,165	Fujiyama, Japan	12,389	3,776
ungato, Chile-Argentina	22,310	6,800	Vinson Massif, Antarctica	16,864	5,140	Cook, New Zealand	12,349	3,764
sis, Argentina	22,241	6,779	Margherita (Ruwenzori), Africa	16,795	5,119	Etna, Italy	10,902	3,323
rcedario, Argentina	22,211	6,770	Kazbek, Georgia-Russia	16,558	5,047	Kosciusko, Australia	7,310	2,228
scarán, Peru	22,205	6,768	Puncak Jaya, Indonesia	16,503	5,030	Mitchell, North Carolina, U.S.A.	6,684	2,037

Longest Rivers

	Length in : Miles	Kms.		Length in : Miles	Kms.		Length in : Miles	Kms.
, Africa	4,145	6,671	Indus, Asia	1,800	2,897	Don, Russia	1,222	1,967
azon, S. America	3,915	6,300	Danube, Europe	1,775	2,857	Red, U.S.A.	1,222	1,966
ng Jiang (Yangtze), China	3,900	6,276	Salween, Asia	1,770	2,849	Columbia, U.S.A.-Canada	1,214	1,953
sissippi-Missouri-Red Rock, U.S.A.	3,741	6,019	Brahmaputra, Asia	1,700	2,736	Saskatchewan, Canada	1,205	1,939
Irtysh-Black Irtysh, Russia-Kazakhstan	3,362	5,411	Euphrates, Asia	1,700	2,736	Peace-Finlay, Canada	1,195	1,923
isey-Angara, Russia	3,100	4,989	Tocantins, Brazil	1,677	2,699	Tigris, Asia	1,181	1,901
ng He (Yellow), China	2,877	4,630	Xi (Si), China	1,650	2,601	Darling, Australia	1,160	1,867
ur-Shilka-Onon, Asia	2,744	4,416	Amudar'ya, Asia	1,616	2,601	Angara, Russia	1,135	1,827
a, Russia	2,734	4,400	Nelson-Saskatchewan, Canada	1,600	2,575	Sungari, Asia	1,130	1,819
go (Zaire), Africa	2,718	4,374	Orinoco, S. America	1,600	2,575	Pechora, Russia	1,124	1,809
ckenzie-Peace-Finlay,Canada	2,635	4,241	Zambezi, Africa	1,600	2,575	Snake, U.S.A.	1,038	1,670
ong, Asia	2,610	4,200	Paraguay, S. America	1,584	2,549	Churchill, Canada	1,000	1,609
souri-Red Rock, U.S.A.	2,564	4,125	Kolyma, Russia	1,562	2,514	Pilcomayo, S. America	1,000	1,609
er, Africa	2,548	4,101	Ganges, Asia	1,550	2,494	Uruguay, S. America	994	1.600
aná-La Plata, S. America	2,450	3,943	Ural, Russia-Kazakhstan	1,509	2,428	Platte-N. Platte, U.S.A.	990	1,593
sissippi, U.S.A.	2,348	3,778	Japurá, S. America	1,500	2,414	Ohio, U.S.A.	981	1,578
rray-Darling, Australia	2,310	3,718	Arkansas, U.S.A.	1,450	2,334	Magdalena, Colombia	956	1,538
ga, Russia	2,194	3,531	Colorado, U.S.A.-Mexico	1.450	2,334	Pecos, U.S.A.	926	1,490
deira, S. America	2,013	3,240	Negro, S. America	1,400	2,253	Oka, Russia	918	1,477
us, S. America	1,995	3,211	Dnieper, Russia-Belarus-Ukraine	1,368	2,202	Canadian, U.S.A.	906	1,458
on, Alaska-Canada	1,979	3,185	Orange, Africa	1,350	2,173	Colorado, Texas, U.S.A.	894	1,439
Lawrence, Canada-U.S.A.	1,900	3,058	Irrawaddy, Burma	1,325	2,132	Dniester, Ukraine-Moldova	876	1,410
Grande, Mexico-U.S.A.	1,885	3,034	Brazos, U.S.A.	1,309	2,107	Fraser, Canada	850	1,369
dar'ya-Naryn, Asia	1,859	2,992	Ohio-Allegheny, U.S.A.	1,306	2,102	Rhine, Europe	820	1,319
Francisco, Brazil	1,811	2,914	Kama, Russia	1,252	2,031	Northern Dvina, Russia	809	1,302

Principal Natural Lakes

	Area in: Sq. Miles	Sq. Kms.	Max. Depth in: Feet	Meters		Area in: Sq. Miles	Sq. Kms.	Max. Depth in: Feet	Meters
pian Sea, Asia	143,243	370,999	3,264	995	Lake Eyre, Australia	3,500-0	9,000-0	–	–
e Superior, U.S.A.-Canada	31,820	82,414	1,329	405	Lake Titicaca, Peru-Bolivia	3,200	8,288	1,000	305
e Victoria, Africa	26,724	69,215	270	82	Lake Nicaragua, Nicaragua	3,100	8,029	230	70
e Huron, U.S.A.-Canada	23,010	59,596	748	228	Lake Athabasca, Canada	3,064	7,936	400	122
e Michigan, U.S.A.	22,400	58,016	923	281	Reindeer Lake, Canada	2,568	6,651	–	–
l Sea, Kazakhstan-Uzbekistan	15,830	41,000	213	65	Lake Turkana (Rudolf), Africa	2,463	6,379	240	73
e Tanganyika, Africa	12,650	32,764	4,700	1,433	Issyk-Kul', Kyrgyzstan	2,425	6,281	2,303	702
e Baykal, Russia	12,162	31,500	5,316	1,620	Lake Torrens, Australia	2,230	5,776	–	–
at Bear Lake, Canada	12,096	31,328	1,356	413	Vänern, Sweden	2,156	5,584	328	100
e Nyasa (Malawi), Africa	11,555	29,928	2,320	707	Nettilling Lake, Canada	2,140	5,543	–	–
at Slave Lake, Canada	11,031	28,570	2,015	614	Lake Winnipegosis, Canada	2,075	5,374	38	12
e Erie, U.S.A.-Canada	9,940	25,745	210	64	Lake Mobutu Sese Seko (Albert), Africa	2,075	5,374	160	49
e Winnipeg, Canada	9,417	24,390	60	18	Kariba Lake, Zambia-Zimbabwe	2,050	5,310	295	90
e Ontario, U.S.A.-Canada	7,540	19,529	775	244	Lake Nipigon, Canada	1,872	4,848	540	165
e Ladoga, Russia	7,104	18,399	738	225	Lake Mweru, Zaire-Zambia	1,800	4,662	60	18
e Balkhash, Kazakhstan	7,027	18,200	87	27	Lake Manitoba, Canada	1,799	4,659	12	4
e Maracaibo, Venezuela	5,120	13,261	100	31	Lake Taymyr, Russia	1,737	4,499	85	26
e Chad, Africa	4,000 –	10,360 –			Lake Khanka, China-Russia	1,700	4,403	33	10
	10,000	25,900	25	8	Lake Kioga, Uganda	1,700	4,403	25	8
e Onega, Russia	3,710	9,609	377	115	Lake of the Woods, U.S.A.-Canada	1,679	4,349	70	21

Index of the World

This index is a comprehensive listing of the places and geographic features found in the atlas. Names are arranged in strict alphabetical order, without regard to hyphens or spaces. Every name is followed by the country or area to which it belongs. Except for cities, towns, countries and cultural areas, all entries include a reference to feature type, such as province, river, island, peak, and so on. The page number and alpha-numeric code appear in green to the left of each listing, The page number directs you to the largest scale map on which the name can be found. The code refers to the grid squares formed by the horizontal and vertical lines of latitude and longitude on each map. Following the letters from left to right and the numbers from top to bottom helps you to locate quickly the square containing the place or feature. Inset maps have their own alpha-numeric codes. Names that are accompanied by a point symbol are indexed to the symbol's location on the map. Other names are indexed to the initial letter of the name. When a map name contains a subordinate or alternate name both names are listed in the index. To conserve space and provide room for more entries, many abbreviations are used in this index. The primary abbreviations are listed below.

Index Abbreviations

A Ab,Can	Alberta	**Cap. Terr.**	Capital Territory	**Gha.**	Ghana	**Me,US**	Maine	**PE,Can**	Prince Edward Island	**Sval.**	Svalbard
Acad.	Academy	**Cay.**	Cayman Islands	**Gib.**	Gibraltar	**Mem.**	Memorial			**Swaz.**	Swaziland
ACT	Australian Capital Territory	**C.G.**	Coast Guard	**Glac.**	Glacier	**Mex.**	Mexico	**Pen.**	Peninsula	**Swe.**	Sweden
		Chan.	Channel	**Gov.**	Governorate	**Mi,US**	Michigan	**Phil.**	Philippines	**Swi.**	Switzerland
A.F.B.	Air Force Base	**Chl.**	Channel Islands	**Govt.**	Government	**Micr.**	Micronesia, Federated States of	**Phys. Reg.**	Physical Region	**T Tah.**	Tahiti
Afld.	Airfield	**Co.**	County	**Gre.**	Greece			**Pitc.**	Pitcairn Islands	**Tai.**	Taiwan
Afg.	Afghanistan	**Co,US**	Colorado	**Grld.**	Greenland	**Mil.**	Military	**Plat.**	Plateau	**Taj.**	Tajikistan
Afr.	Africa	**Col.**	Colombia	**Gren.**	Grenada	**Mn,US**	Minnesota	**PNG**	Papua New Guinea	**Tanz.**	Tanzania
Ak,US	Alaska	**Com.**	Comoros	**Grsld.**	Grassland	**Mo,US**	Missouri			**Ter.**	Terrace
Al,US	Alabama	**Cont.**	Continent	**Guad.**	Guadeloupe	**Mol.**	Moldova	**Pol.**	Poland	**Terr.**	Territory
Alb.	Albania	**CpV.**	Cape Verde Islands	**Guat.**	Guatemala	**Mon.**	Monument	**Port.**	Portugal	**Thai.**	Thailand
Alg.	Algeria			**Gui.**	Guinea	**Mona.**	Monaco	**Poss.**	Possession	**Tn,US**	Tennessee
Amm. Dep.	Ammunition Depot	**CR**	Costa Rica	**Guy.**	Guyana	**Mong.**	Mongolia	**Pkwy.**	Parkway	**Tok.**	Tokelau
		Cr.	Creek			**Monts.**	Montserrat	**PR**	Puerto Rico	**Trg.**	Training
And.	Andorra	**Cro.**	Croatia	**H Har.**	Harbor	**Mor.**	Morocco	**Pref.**	Prefecture	**Trin.**	Trinidad and Tobago
Ang.	Angola	**CSea.**	Coral Sea Islands Territory	**Hi,US**	Hawaii	**Moz.**	Mozambique	**Prov.**	Province		
Angu.	Anguilla			**Hist.**	Historic(al)	**Mrsh.**	Marshall Islands	**Prsv.**	Preserve	**Trkm.**	Turkmenistan
Ant.	Antarctica	**Ct,US**	Connecticut	**HK**	Hong Kong			**Pt.**	Point	**Trks.**	Turks and Caicos Islands
Anti.	Antigua and Barbuda	**Ctr.**	Center	**Hon.**	Honduras	**Mrta.**	Mauritania				
		Ctry.	Country	**Hts.**	Heights	**Mrts.**	Mauritius	**Q Qu,Can**	Quebec	**Tun.**	Tunisia
Ar,US	Arkansas	**Cyp.**	Cyprus	**Hun.**	Hungary	**Ms,US**	Mississippi			**Tun.**	Tunnel
Arch.	Archipelago	**Czh.**	Czech Republic			**Mt.**	Mount	**R Rec.**	Recreation(al)	**Turk.**	Turkey
Arg.	Argentina			**I Ia,US**	Iowa	**Mt,US**	Montana	**Ref.**	Refuge	**Tuv.**	Tuvalu
Arm.	Armenia	**D DC,US**	District of Columbia	**Ice.**	Iceland	**Mtn., Mts.**	Mountain, Mountains	**Reg.**	Region	**Twp.**	Township
Arpt.	Airport			**Id,US**	Idaho			**Rep.**	Republic	**Tx,US**	Texas
Aru.	Aruba	**De,US**	Delaware	**Il,US**	Illinois	**Mun. Arpt.**	Municipal Airport	**Res.**	Reservoir, Reservation		
ASam.	American Samoa	**Den.**	Denmark	**IM**	Isle of Man					**U UAE**	United Arab Emirates
Ash.	Ashmore and Cartier Islands	**Depr.**	Depression	**In,US**	Indiana	**N NAm.**	North America	**Reun.**	Réunion		
		Dept.	Department	**Ind. Res.**	Indian Reservation	**Namb.**	Namibia	**RI,US**	Rhode Island	**Ugan.**	Uganda
Aus.	Austria	**Des.**	Desert			**NAnt.**	Netherlands Antilles	**Riv.**	River	**UK**	United Kingdom
Austl.	Australia	**DF**	Distrito Federal	**Indo.**	Indonesia			**Rom.**	Romania	**Ukr.**	Ukraine
Aut.	Autonomous	**Dist.**	District	**Int'l**	International	**Nat'l**	National	**Rsv.**	Reserve	**Uru.**	Uruguay
Az,US	Arizona	**Djib.**	Djibouti	**Ire.**	Ireland	**Nav.**	Naval	**Rus.**	Russia	**US**	United States
Azer.	Azerbaijan	**Dom.**	Dominica	**Isl., Isls.**	Island, Islands	**NB,Can**	New Brunswick	**Rvwy.**	Riverway	**USVI**	U.S. Virgin Islands
Azor.	Azores	**Dpcy.**	Dependency	**Isr.**	Israel	**Nbrhd.**	Neighborhood	**Rwa.**	Rwanda		
		DRep.	Dominican Republic	**Isth.**	Isthmus	**NC,US**	North Carolina			**Ut,US**	Utah
B Bahm.	Bahamas			**It.**	Italy	**NCal.**	New Caledonia	**S SAfr.**	South Africa	**Uzb.**	Uzbekistan
Bahr.	Bahrain	**E Ecu.**	Ecuador	**IvC.**	Côte d'Ivoire	**ND,US**	North Dakota	**SAm.**	South America		
Bang.	Bangladesh	**Emb.**	Embankment			**Ne,US**	Nebraska	**SaoT.**	São Tomé and Príncipe	**V Va,US**	Virginia
Bar.	Barbados	**Eng.**	Engineering	**J Jam.**	Jamaica	**Neth.**	Netherlands			**Val.**	Valley
BC,Can	British Columbia	**Eng,UK**	England	**Jor.**	Jordan	**Nf,Can**	Newfoundland	**SAr.**	Saudi Arabia	**Van.**	Vanuatu
Bela.	Belarus	**EqG.**	Equatorial Guinea			**Nga.**	Nigeria	**Sc,UK**	Scotland	**VatC.**	Vatican City
Belg.	Belgium			**K Kaz.**	Kazakhstan	**NH,US**	New Hampshire	**SC,US**	South Carolina	**Ven.**	Venezuela
Belz.	Belize	**Erit.**	Eritrea	**Kiri.**	Kiribati	**NI,UK**	Northern Ireland	**SD,US**	South Dakota	**Viet.**	Vietnam
Ben.	Benin	**ESal.**	El Salvador	**Ks,US**	Kansas	**Nic.**	Nicaragua	**Seash.**	Seashore	**Vill.**	Village
Berm.	Bermuda	**Est.**	Estonia	**Kuw.**	Kuwait	**NJ,US**	New Jersey	**Sen.**	Senegal	**Vol.**	Volcano
Bfld.	Battlefield	**Eth.**	Ethiopia	**Ky,US**	Kentucky	**NKor.**	North Korea	**Sey.**	Seychelles	**Vt,US**	Vermont
Bhu.	Bhutan	**Eur.**	Europe	**Kyr.**	Kyrgyzstan	**NM,US**	New Mexico	**SGeo.**	South Georgia and Sandwich Islands		
Bol.	Bolivia					**NMar.**	Northern Mariana Islands			**W Wa,US**	Washington
Bor.	Borough	**F Falk.**	Falkland Islands	**L La,US**	Louisiana			**Sing.**	Singapore	**Wal,UK**	Wales
Bosn.	Bosnia and Hercegovina			**Lab.**	Laboratory	**Nor.**	Norway	**Sk,Can**	Saskatchewan	**Wall.**	Wallis and Futuna
		Far.	Faroe Islands	**Lag.**	Lagoon	**NS,Can**	Nova Scotia	**SKor.**	South Korea		
Bots.	Botswana	**Fed. Dist.**	Federal District	**Lakesh.**	Lakeshore	**Nv,US**	Nevada	**SLeo.**	Sierra Leone	**WBnk.**	West Bank
Braz.	Brazil	**Fin.**	Finland	**Lat.**	Latvia	**NW,Can**	Northwest Territories	**Slov.**	Slovenia	**Wi,US**	Wisconsin
Brln.	British Indian Ocean Territory	**Fl,US**	Florida	**Lcht.**	Liechtenstein			**Slvk.**	Slovakia	**Wild.**	Wildlife, Wilderness
		For.	Forest	**Ldg.**	Landing	**NY,US**	New York	**SMar.**	San Marino		
Bru.	Brunei	**Fr.**	France	**Leb.**	Lebanon	**NZ**	New Zealand	**Sol.**	Solomon Islands	**WSah.**	Western Sahara
Bul.	Bulgaria	**FrAnt.**	French Southern and Antarctic Lands	**Les.**	Lesotho			**Som.**	Somalia	**WSam.**	Western Samoa
Burk.	Burkina			**Libr.**	Liberia	**O Obl.**	Oblast	**Sp.**	Spain	**WV,US**	West Virginia
Buru.	Burundi			**Lith.**	Lithuania	**Oh,US**	Ohio	**Spr., Sprs.**	Spring, Springs	**Wy,US**	Wyoming
BVI	British Virgin Islands	**FrG.**	French Guiana	**Lux.**	Luxembourg	**Ok,US**	Oklahoma	**SrL.**	Sri Lanka		
		FrPol.	French Polynesia			**On,Can**	Ontario	**Sta.**	Station	**Y Yem.**	Yemen
C Ca,US	California			**M Ma,US**	Massachusetts	**Or,US**	Oregon	**StH.**	Saint Helena	**Yk,Can**	Yukon Territory
CAfr.	Central African Republic	**G Ga,US**	Georgia	**Macd.**	Macedonia			**Str.**	Strait	**Yugo.**	Yugoslavia
		Galp.	Galapagos Islands	**Madg.**	Madagascar	**P Pa,US**	Pennsylvania	**StK.**	Saint Kitts and Nevis		
Camb.	Cambodia			**Madr.**	Madeira	**PacUS**	Pacific Islands, U.S.			**Z Zam.**	Zambia
Camr.	Cameroon	**Gam.**	Gambia	**Malay.**	Malaysia			**StL.**	Saint Lucia	**Zim.**	Zimbabwe
Can.	Canada	**Gaza**	Gaza Strip	**Mald.**	Maldives	**Pak.**	Pakistan	**StP.**	Saint Pierre and Miquelon		
Can.	Canal	**GBis.**	Guinea-Bissau	**Malw.**	Malawi	**Pan.**	Panama				
Canl.	Canary Islands	**Geo.**	Georgia	**Mart.**	Martinique	**Par.**	Paraguay	**StV.**	Saint Vincent and the Grenadines		
Cap.	Capital	**Ger.**	Germany	**May.**	Mayotte	**Par.**	Parish				
Cap. Dist.	Capital District			**Mb,Can**	Manitoba			**Sur.**	Suriname		
				Md,US	Maryland						

A

52/B2 Aa (riv.), Fr.
50/D5 Aa (riv.), Ger.
51/G5 Aa (riv.), Ger.
53/F2 Aachen, Ger.
50/C5 Aalburg, Neth.
57/J2 Aalen, Ger.
50/B4 Aalsmeer, Neth.
52/D2 Aalst, Belg.
50/D5 Aalten, Neth.
52/C1 Aalter, Belg.
54/E3 Aarau, Swi.
54/D3 Aare (riv.), Swi.
54/E3 Aargau (canton), Swi.
53/D2 Aarschot, Belg.
52/D1 Aartselaar, Belg.
76/E5 Aba, China
99/G5 Aba, Nga.
101/A2 Aba, Zaire
72/D5 Abā as Su'ūd, SAr.
108/G5 Abacaxis (riv.), Braz.
100/C5 Abadab, Jabal (peak), Sudan
72/E2 Ābādān, Iran
72/F2 Ābādeh, Iran
110/C1 Abaeté, Braz.
109/J4 Abaetetuba, Braz.
92/G4 Abaiang (atoll), Kiri.
120/D4 Abajo (mts.), Ut,US
68/K4 Abakan, Rus.
108/D6 Abancay, Peru
76/G3 Abaq Qi, China
58/E3 Abarán, Sp.
93/H5 Abariringa (Canton) (atoll), Kiri.
72/F2 Abar Kūh, Iran
77/N3 Abashiri, Japan
68/H5 Abay, Kaz.
97/N6 Ābaya Hayk' (lake), Eth.
75/F1 Abaza, Rus.
60/B1 Abbadia San Salvatore, It.
52/A3 Abbeville, Fr.
128/E4 Abbeville, La,US
129/H3 Abbeville, SC,US
44/E2 Abbey Head (pt.), Sc,UK
90/B3 Abbot (mt.), Austl.
105/T Abbot Ice Shelf, Ant.
45/G6 Abbots Bromley, Eng,UK
46/D5 Abbotsbury, Eng,UK
73/K2 Abbottābād, Pak.
50/B4 Abcoude, Neth.
74/E3 'Abd al 'Azīz, Jabal (mts.), Syria
67/K1 Abdulino, Rus.
97/K5 Abéché, Chad
103/E2 Abel Erasmuspas (pass), SAfr.
92/G4 Abemama (atoll), Kiri.
98/E5 Abengourou, IvC.
48/E1 Åbenrå, Den.
57/J2 Abens (riv.), Ger.
99/F5 Abeokuta, Nga.
44/D5 Aber, Wal,UK
46/B2 Aberaeron, Wal,UK
46/C1 Aberangell, Wal,UK
46/B2 Aberath, Wal,UK
46/C3 Abercarn, Wal,UK
46/C3 Aberdare, Wal,UK
44/D6 Aberdaron, Wal,UK
118/G2 Aberdeen (lake), NW,Can
43/D2 Aberdeen, Sc,UK
129/F3 Aberdeen, Ms,US
123/J4 Aberdeen, SD,US
122/C4 Aberdeen, Wa,US
46/B1 Aberdyfi, Wal,UK
43/D2 Aberfeldy, Sc,UK
43/C2 Aberfoyle, Sc,UK
46/C3 Abergavenny, Wal,UK
44/E5 Abergele, Wal,UK
46/B2 Aberporth, Wal,UK
44/D6 Abersoch, Wal,UK
46/C3 Abersychan, Wal,UK
124/B2 Abert (lake), Or,US
46/C3 Abertillery, Wal,UK
46/B2 Aberystwyth, Wal,UK
72/D5 Abhá, SAr.
72/E1 Abhar, Iran
97/P5 Abhe Bad (lake), Djib., Eth.
98/D5 Abidjan, IvC.
79/J7 Abiko, Japan
125/H3 Abilene, Ks,US
128/D3 Abilene, Tx,US
47/E3 Abingdon, Eng,UK
126/D4 Abingdon, Va,US
127/R10 Abino (pt.), On,Can
125/F3 Abiquiu, NM,US
126/E1 Abitibi (lake), On,Can
126/D1 Abitibi (riv.), On,Can
67/G4 Abkhaz Aut. Rep., Geo.
100/B3 Abnūb, Egypt
98/E5 Aboisso, IvC.
99/F5 Abomey, Ben.
62/E2 Abony, Hun.
87/E2 Aborlan, Phil.
42/G3 Åbo (Turku), Fin.
43/D2 Aboyne, Sc,UK
82/D4 Abra (riv.), Phil.
117/G3 Abraham's Bay, Bahm.
58/A3 Abrantes, Port.
111/C1 Abra Pampa, Arg.
100/B4 'Abrī, Sudan
62/F2 Abrud, Rom.
60/C1 Abruzzi (reg.), It.
60/C2 Abruzzo Nat'l Park, It.
122/F4 Absaroka (range), Mt, Wy,US
72/F4 Abū al Abyaḑ (isl.), UAE
73/F4 Abu Dhabi (Abū Ẓaby) (cap.), UAE
100/C5 Abū Dīs, Sudan
100/B4 Abu el-Husein, Bîr (well), Egypt
100/C5 Abū Hamad, Sudan
100/C4 Abu Hashim, Bi'r (well), Egypt
74/H6 Abū Ḩummuş, Egypt
99/G4 Abuja (cap.), Nga.
99/G4 Abuja Cap. Terr., Nga.
74/H6 Abū Kabīr, Egypt
72/D2 Abū Kamāl, Syria
79/G2 Abukuma (hills), Japan
79/G2 Abukuma (riv.), Japan
82/D4 Abulog, Phil.
100/A3 Abu Minqâr, Bîr (well), Egypt
108/E6 Abuná (riv.), Bol.
108/E5 Abunã (riv.), Braz.
84/B3 Abu Road, India
100/D4 Abu Shagara, Ras (cape), Sudan
100/B4 Abu Simbel (ruins), Egypt
97/N5 Ābuyē Mēda (peak), Eth.
82/E5 Abuyog, Phil.
73/F4 Abū Ẓaby (Abu Dhabi) (cap.), UAE
60/A4 Abyaḑ, Ar Ra's al (cape), Tun.
100/B3 Abydos (ruins), Egypt
127/G2 Acadia Nat'l Park, Me,US
117/N9 Acaponeta, Mex.
116/B4 Acapulco, Mex.
108/G5 Acari (riv.), Braz.
117/H6 Acarigua, Ven.
116/B4 Acatlán, Mex.
99/E5 Accra (cap.), Gha.
45/F4 Accrington, Eng,UK
112/B4 Achao, Chile
99/H2 Achegour (well), Niger
77/K2 Acheng, China
52/B3 Achicourt, Fr.
52/B3 Achiel-le-Grand, Fr.
127/N6 Achigan (riv.), Qu,Can
68/K4 Achinsk, Rus.
98/D2 Achmîm (well), Mrta.
43/C2 Achnasheen, Sc,UK
53/G3 Acht, Hohe (peak), Ger.
60/D4 Acireale, It.
117/G3 Acklins (isl.), Bahm.
45/G4 Ackworth Moor Top, Eng,UK
90/C4 Acland (peak), Austl.
47/H1 Acle, Eng,UK
112/C2 Aconcagua, Cerro (peak), Arg.
109/L5 Acopiara, Braz.
57/H4 Acqui Terme, It.
108/E6 Acre (riv.), Braz., Peru
110/B1 Acreúna, Braz.
61/L7 Acropolis, Gre.
93/M7 Actaeon Group (isls.), FrPol.
131/B2 Acton, Ca,US
109/L5 Açu, Braz.
112/Q9 Aculeo (lake), Chile
126/D3 Ada, Oh,US
125/H4 Ada, Ok,US
62/E3 Ada, Yugo.
119/J1 Adair (cape), NW,Can
58/C2 Adaja (riv.), Sp.
130/C6 Adak (isl.), Ak,US
130/C6 Adak (str.), Ak,US
113/M7 Adam (peak), Falk.
110/B2 Adamantina, Braz.
99/H5 Adamawa (plat.), Camr., Nga.
122/D3 Adams (lake), BC,Can
122/C4 Adams (peak), Wa,US
74/C3 Adana, Turk.
63/K5 Adapazarı, Turk.
105/M Adare (cape), Ant.
56/C5 Adarza (mtn.), Fr.
57/H4 Adda (riv.), It.
97/M4 Ad Dabbah, Sudan
72/D3 Ad Dahnā' (des.), SAr.
97/M5 Ad Damazin, Sudan
97/M4 Ad Dāmir, Sudan
72/F3 Ad Dammām, SAr.
74/H6 Ad Daqahlīyah (gov.), Egypt
72/F3 Ad Dawḩah (Doha) (cap.), Qatar
74/H6 Ad Dilinjāt, Egypt
97/N6 Addis Ababa (cap.), Eth.
132/Q16 Addison, Il,US
72/D2 Ad Dīwānīyah, Iraq
102/D4 Addo Elephant Nat'l Park, SAfr.
97/M5 Ad Duwaym, Sudan
105/V Adelaide (isl.), Ant.
91/A2 Adelaide, Austl.
118/G2 Adelaide (pen.), NW,Can
102/D4 Adelaide, SAfr.
131/C1 Adelanto, Ca,US
51/G5 Adelebsen, Ger.
105/K Adélie (coast), Ant.
97/Q5 Aden (gulf), Afr., Asia
72/D6 Aden, Yem.
51/H2 Adendorf, Ger.
87/H4 Adi (isl.), Indo.
57/J4 Adige (Etsch) (riv.), It.
97/N5 Ādīgrat, Eth.
84/C4 Adilābād, India
99/E2 Adiora (well), Mali
126/F2 Adirondack (mts.), NY,US
97/N6 Ādīs Ābeba (Addis Ababa) (cap.), Eth.
97/N5 Ādīs Zemen, Eth.
72/C6 Ādī Ugri, Erit.
74/D3 Adıyaman, Turk.
63/H2 Adjud, Rom.
116/B3 Adjuntas (res.), Mex.
45/F4 Adlington, Eng,UK
119/H1 Admiralty (inlet), NW,Can
92/D5 Admiralty (isls.), PNG
132/B2 Admiralty (inlet), Wa,US
130/M4 Admiralty I. Nat'l Mon., Ak,US
79/L9 Ado (riv.), Japan
99/F5 Ado, Nga.
79/M9 Adogawa, Japan
84/C4 Ādoni, India
56/C5 Adour (riv.), Fr.
58/D4 Adra, Sp.
60/D4 Adrano, It.
96/E2 Adrar, Alg.
98/B1 Adrar (reg.), Mrta.
96/E1 Adrar bou Nasser (peak), Mor.
99/F1 Adrar des Iforas (mts.), Mali
97/K5 Adré, Chad
57/K4 Adria, It.
126/C3 Adrian, Mi,US
47/F5 Adur (riv.), Eng,UK
97/N5 Ādwa, Eth.
45/G4 Adwick le Street, Eng,UK
69/P3 Adycha (riv.), Rus.
67/G4 Adzhar Aut. Rep., Geo.
65/N2 Adz'va (riv.), Rus.
61/J3 Aegean (sea), Gre., Turk.
48/F1 Aerø (isl.), Den.
46/B2 Aeron (riv.), Wal,UK
44/E1 Ae, Water of (riv.), Sc,UK
99/F5 Afadjoto (peak), Gha.
93/X15 Afareaitu, FrPol.
74/M8 Afek Nat'l Park, Isr.
56/B3 Aff (riv.), Fr.
73/H2 Afghanistan
97/Q7 Afgooye, Som.
130/H4 Afognak (isl.), Ak,US
130/H4 Afognak (mtn.), Ak,US
98/C2 Afollé (reg.), Mrta.
110/D2 Afonso Cláudio, Braz.
60/D2 Afragola, It.
95/* Africa
74/D2 Afşin, Turk.
50/C2 Afsluitdijk (IJsselmeer) (dam), Neth.
51/F5 Afte (riv.), Ger.
122/F5 Afton, Wy,US
74/K5 'Afula, Isr.
74/B2 Afyon, Turk.
96/H4 Agadem, Niger
99/G2 Agadez, Niger
99/H2 Agadez (dept.), Niger
98/D2 Agâdîr, Mor.
39/M6 Agalega (isls.), Mrts.
99/F2 Agamor (well), Mali
92/D3 Agaña (cap.), Guam
79/F2 Agano (riv.), Japan
97/N6 Āgaro, Eth.
85/F3 Agartala, India
105/V Agassiz (cape), Ant.
119/T6 Agassiz (ice field), NW,Can
125/G2 Agate Fossil Beds Nat'l Mon., Ne,US
130/A5 Agattu (isl.), Ak,US
130/A5 Agattu (str.), Ak,US
99/G5 Agbor, Nga.
98/D5 Agboville, IvC.
67/H5 Ağdam, Azer.
56/E5 Agde, Fr.
56/E5 Agde, Cap d' (cape), Fr.
56/D4 Agen, Fr.
79/H7 Ageo, Japan
48/E1 Agerbæk, Den.
51/E6 Agger (riv.), Ger.
62/E1 Aggteleki Nat'l Park, Hun.
44/B3 Aghagallon, NI,UK
72/E2 Āghā Jārī, Iran
117/N8 Agiabampo, Estero de (bay), Mex.
76/G1 Aginskoye, Rus.
44/B1 Agivey, NI,UK
56/E5 Agly (riv.), Fr.
63/G3 Agnita, Rom.
79/M10 Ago, Japan
57/H4 Agogna (riv.), It.
131/B2 Agoura Hills, Ca,US
56/D5 Agout (riv.), Fr.
84/C2 Āgra, India
60/E2 Agri (riv.), It.
67/H5 Ağri (Ararat) (peak), Turk.
60/C4 Agrigento, It.
92/D3 Agrihan (isl.), NMar.
61/G3 Agrínion, Gre.
112/C3 Agrio (riv.), Arg.
60/D2 Agropoli, It.
65/M4 Agryz, Rus.
117/G6 Aguachica, Col.
117/H4 Aguadilla, PR
116/C4 Agua Dulce, Mex.
117/E6 Aguadulce, Pan.
110/F7 Aguaí, Braz.
59/P10 Agualva-Cacém, Port.
116/D4 Aguan (riv.), Hon.
110/B2 Aguapeí (riv.), Braz.
117/N7 Agua Prieta, Mex.
117/H6 Aguaro-Guariquito Nat'l Park, Ven.
110/H6 Águas (hills), Braz.
116/A3 Aguascalientes, Mex.
116/A3 Aguascalientes (state), Mex.
110/G6 Águas da Prata, Braz.
110/G7 Águas de Lindóia, Braz.
110/B1 Aguavermelha (res.), Braz.
110/B2 Agudos, Braz.
58/A2 Águeda, Port.
58/B2 Águeda (riv.), Sp.
96/C3 Agüenit, WSah.
79/M10 Agui, Japan
92/D3 Aguijan (isl.), NMar.
58/C4 Aguilar, Sp.
58/C1 Aguilar de Campóo, Sp.
111/C2 Aguilares, Arg.
58/E4 Águilas, Sp.
117/P10 Aguililla de Iturbide, Mex.
59/X17 Agüimes, Canl.,Sp.
117/G5 Aguja (cape), Col.
102/M11 Agulhas (cape), SAfr.
110/C2 Agulhas Negras (peak), Braz.
87/E5 Agung (vol.), Indo.
82/E6 Agusan (riv.), Phil.
117/G5 Agustín Codazzi, Col.
96/G3 Ahaggar (plat.), Alg.
50/E4 Ahaus, Ger.
53/F3 Ahbach (riv.), Ger.
74/E2 Ahlat, Turk.
51/E5 Ahlen, Ger.
84/B3 Ahmadābād, India
84/B4 Ahmadnagar, India
73/K3 Ahmadpur East, Pak.
97/P6 Ahmar (mts.), Eth.
44/B2 Ahoghill, NI,UK
53/F3 Ahr (riv.), Ger.
51/H1 Ahrensburg, Ger.
51/F5 Ahse (riv.), Ger.
117/P9 Ahuacatlán, Mex.
120/W13 Ahuimanu, Hi,US
117/M7 Ahumada, Mex.
72/E2 Ahvāz, Iran
42/F4 Ahvenanmaa (prov.), Fin.
102/B2 Ai-Ais Hot Springs, Namb.
81/B2 Aibag Gol (riv.), China
79/E3 Aichi (pref.), Japan
120/W13 Aiea, Hi,US
56/E4 Aigoual (mtn.), Fr.
56/F4 Aigues (riv.), Fr.
59/F1 Aigues Tortes y Lago de San Mauricio Nat'l Park, Sp.
79/F1 Aikawa, Japan
129/H3 Aiken, SC,US
117/F6 Ailigandí, Pan.
92/F4 Ailinglapalap (atoll), Mrsh.
44/C1 Ailsa Craig (isl.), Sc,UK
92/G3 Ailuk (atoll), Mrsh.
81/C5 Aimen Guan (pass), China
110/D1 Aimorés, Braz.
54/B5 Ain (dept.), Fr.
56/F4 Ain (riv.), Fr.
96/G1 'Aïn Beïda, Alg.
96/D2 Aïn Ben Tili, Mrta.
61/G3 Aínos (peak), Gre.
61/G3 Ainos Nat'l Park, Gre.
45/E4 Ainsdale, Eng,UK
96/E1 'Aïn Sefra, Alg.
125/H2 Ainsworth, Ne,US
99/G2 Aïr (plat.), Niger
122/E3 Airdrie, Ab,Can
43/D3 Airdrie, Sc,UK
52/D5 Aire (riv.), Fr.
45/G4 Aire (riv.), Eng,UK
52/B2 Aire, Canal de (can.), Fr.
45/E5 Aire, Point of (pt.), Wal,UK
52/B2 Aire-sur-la-Lys, Fr.
119/J2 Air Force (isl.), NW,Can
45/F3 Airton, Eng,UK
57/J2 Aisch (riv.), Ger.
52/D3 Aiseau-Presles, Belg.
112/B5 Aisén del General Carlos Ibáñez del Campo (reg.), Chile
81/E3 Ai Shan (mtn.), China
130/L3 Aishihik, Yk,Can
53/E3 Aisne (riv.), Belg.
52/C4 Aisne (dept.), Fr.
52/C5 Aisne (riv.), Fr.
96/E1 Aïssa (peak), Alg.
79/M9 Aitō, Japan
93/J6 Aitutaki (atoll), CookIs.
63/F2 Aiud, Rom.
110/J7 Aiuruoca (riv.), Braz.
56/F5 Aix-en-Provence, Fr.
56/F4 Aix-les-Bains, Fr.
61/H4 Aiyina, Gre.
61/H3 Aiyion, Gre.
79/F2 Aizu-Wakamatsu, Japan
85/F3 Aīzwal, India
60/A2 Ajaccio, Fr.
60/A2 Ajaccio (gulf), Fr.
127/R8 Ajax, On,Can
76/D3 Aj Bogd (peak), Mong.
96/K1 Ajdābiyā, Libya
100/C5 Aj Janayet, Sudan
62/C2 Ajka, Hun.
84/B2 Ajmer, India
124/D4 Ajo, Az,US
58/D1 Ajo, Cabo de (cape), Sp.
116/A4 Ajuchitlán, Mex.
79/F1 Aka (riv.), Japan
79/N10 Akabane, Japan
75/F1 Akademik Obruchev (mts.), Rus.
79/F3 Akaishi-dake (mtn.), Japan
100/B4 Akasha East, Sudan
78/D3 Akashi, Japan
79/K10 Akashi (str.), Japan
75/B4 Akbaytal (pass), Taj.
74/D2 Akçaabat, Turk.
74/D3 Akçakale, Turk.
63/K5 Akçakoca, Turk.
98/B2 Akchâr (reg.), Mrta.
74/C2 Akdağmadeni, Turk.
72/G4 Akdar, Al Jabal (mts.), Oman
79/N9 Akechi, Japan
42/D3 Akershus (co.), Nor.
97/K7 Aketi, Zaire
67/G4 Akhaltsikhe, Geo.
61/H3 Akharnaí, Gre.
61/G3 Akhelóos (riv.), Gre.
74/A2 Akhisar, Turk.
100/B3 Akhmīm, Egypt
67/H3 Akhtuba (riv.), Rus.
67/H2 Akhtubinsk, Rus.
66/E2 Akhtyrka, Ukr.
78/C4 Aki, Japan
79/H7 Aki (riv.), Japan
79/H7 Akigawa, Japan
119/H3 Akimiski (isl.), NW,Can
79/H7 Akishima, Japan
77/N4 Akita, Japan
98/B2 Akjoujt, Mrta.
84/D6 Akkaraipattu, SrL.
74/K5 'Akko, Isr.
98/D2 'Aklé 'Aouâna (dune), Mali, Mrta.
78/D3 Akō, Japan
96/H7 Akoga, Gabon
84/C3 Akola, India
97/N4 Āk'ordat, Erit.
99/F5 Akosombo (dam), Gha.
119/K2 Akpatok (isl.), NW,Can
75/C3 Akqi, China
61/J2 Akrathos, Ákra (cape), Gre.
42/C4 Åkrehamn, Nor.
61/G4 Akritas, Ákra (cape), Gre.
125/G2 Akron, Co,US
126/D3 Akron, Oh,US
75/C4 Aksai Chin (reg.), China, India
74/C2 Aksaray, Turk.
76/C4 Aksay, China
67/K2 Aksay, Kaz.
74/B2 Akşehir, Turk.
74/B2 Akşehir (lake), Turk.
75/C2 Aksoran (peak), Kaz.
75/D3 Aksu, China
75/C3 Aksu (riv.), China
75/C2 Aksu (riv.), Kaz.
97/N5 Āksum, Eth.
61/J2 Aktí (pen.), Gre.
67/L2 Aktyubinsk, Kaz.
67/L3 Aktyubinsk Obl., Kaz.
78/B4 Akune, Japan
42/N6 Akureyri, Ice.
130/E5 Akutan (isl.), Ak,US
130/E5 Akutan (passg.), Ak,US
99/G5 Akwa Ibom (state), Nga.
85/F3 Akyab (Sittwe), Burma
67/L2 Ak"yar, Rus.
63/K5 Akyazı, Turk.
76/B3 Ala (riv.), China
129/G3 Alabama (state), US
129/G4 Alabama (riv.), Al,US
129/G3 Alabaster, Al,US
74/C2 Alaca, Turk.
74/C2 Alaçam, Turk.
129/H4 Alachua, Fl,US
67/H4 Alagir, Rus.
56/E4 Alagnon (riv.), Fr.
109/L6 Alagoinhas, Braz.
58/B2 Alagón (riv.), Sp.
42/G3 Alajärvi, Fin.
116/E5 Alajuela, CR
75/D2 Alakol' (lake), Kaz.
100/B2 Al 'Alamayn (El Alamein), Egypt
92/D3 Alamagan (isl.), NMar.
72/E2 Al 'Amārah, Iraq
72/F3 'Alāmarvdasht (riv.), Iran
132/K11 Alameda, Ca,US
116/E5 Alamikamba, Nic.
116/B3 Alamo, Mex.
124/D4 Alamo (lake), Az,US
132/K11 Alamo, Ca,US
124/D3 Alamo, Nv,US
125/F4 Alamogordo, NM,US
117/N8 Álamos, Mex.
125/F3 Alamosa, Co,US
42/G3 Åland (isls.), Fin.
48/F2 Aland (riv.), Ger.
74/C3 Alanya, Turk.
103/J7 Alaotra (lake), Madg.
129/H4 Alapaha (riv.), Ga,US
63/K5 Alaplı, Turk.
58/D3 Alarcón (res.), Sp.
74/B2 Alaşehir, Turk.
74/L6 Al 'Āsimah (gov.), Jor.
130/* Alaska (state), US
130/J4 Alaska (gulf), Ak,US
130/F4 Alaska (pen.), Ak,US
130/H3 Alaska (range), Ak,US
130/B5 Alaska Maritime Nat'l Wild. Ref., Ak,US
130/G4 Alaska Pen. Nat'l Wild. Ref., Ak,US
57/H5 Alassio, It.
65/K5 Alatyr', Rus.
67/H4 Alaverdi, Arm.
42/G3 Alavus, Fin.
44/D5 Alaw (riv.), Wal,UK
44/D5 Alaw, Llyn (lake), Wal,UK
75/B4 Alayskiy (mts.), Kyr.
69/R3 Alazeya (riv.), Rus.
72/E2 Al 'Azīzīyah, Iraq
96/H1 Al 'Azīzīyah, Libya
57/H4 Alba, It.
63/F2 Alba (co.), Rom.
74/D3 Al Bāb, Syria
58/E3 Albacete, Sp.
100/C3 Al Baḩr al Aḩmar (gov.), Egypt
63/F2 Alba Iulia, Rom.
74/K5 Al Balqā' (gov.), Jor.
100/C3 Al Balyanā, Egypt
127/F1 Albanel (lake), Qu,Can
61/F2 Albania
89/A4 Albany, Austl.
119/H3 Albany (riv.), On,Can
132/K11 Albany, Ca,US
129/G4 Albany, Ga,US
126/C4 Albany, Ky,US
126/F3 Albany (cap.), NY,US
122/C4 Albany, Or,US
72/E2 Al Başrah, Iraq
102/A2 Albatross (pt.), Namb.
100/B2 Al Bawīţī, Egypt
97/K1 Al Bayḑā, Libya
129/H3 Albemarle, NC,US
129/J2 Albemarle (sound), NC,US
57/H4 Albenga, It.
58/C2 Alberche (riv.), Sp.
91/A2 Albert (inlet), Austl.
53/E2 Albert (can.), Belg.
52/B4 Albert, Fr.
101/A2 Albert (lake), Ugan., Zaire
118/E3 Alberta (prov.), Can.
112/E2 Alberti, Arg.
62/D2 Albertirsa, Hun.
123/K5 Albert Lea, Mn,US
101/A2 Albert Nile (riv.), Ugan.
113/J8 Alberto de Agostini Nat'l Park, Chile
102/Q13 Alberton, SAfr.
57/G4 Albertville, Fr.
129/G3 Albertville, Al,US
56/E5 Albi, Fr.
57/H4 Albino, It.
126/C3 Albion, Mi,US
125/H2 Albion, Ne,US
74/L4 Al Biqā' (gov.), Leb.
74/K5 Al Biqā' (Bekaa) (val.), Leb.
74/K6 Al Bīrah, WBnk.
50/B5 Alblasserdam, Neth.
42/D4 Ålborg, Den.
58/D4 Albox, Sp.
46/D1 Albrighton, Eng,UK
58/A4 Albufeira, Port.
74/H6 Al Buḩayrah (gov.), Egypt
55/F4 Albula (riv.), Swi.
124/F4 Albuquerque, NM,US
58/B3 Alburquerque, Sp.
91/C3 Albury, Austl.
59/P10 Alcabideche, Port.
58/A3 Alcácer do Sal, Port.
58/C4 Alcalá de Guadaira, Sp.
58/D2 Alcalá de Henares, Sp.
58/D4 Alcalá la Real, Sp.
60/C4 Alcamo, It.
59/E2 Alcanadre (riv.), Sp.
59/E2 Alcanar, Sp.
59/E2 Alcañiz, Sp.
58/B3 Alcántara (res.), Sp.
58/E4 Alcantarilla, Sp.
58/D3 Alcaraz (range), Sp.
58/C4 Alcaudete, Sp.
58/D3 Alcázar de San Juan, Sp.
47/E2 Alcester, Eng,UK
59/E3 Alcira, Sp.
129/H3 Alcoa, Tn,US
58/D2 Alcobendas, Sp.
59/Q10 Alcochete, Port.
59/E2 Alcora, Sp.
58/D2 Alcorcón, Sp.
129/H3 Alcovy (riv.), Ga,US
59/E3 Alcoy, Sp.
95/G5 Aldabra (isls.), Sey.
128/B4 Aldama, Mex.
69/N4 Aldan, Rus.
69/N4 Aldan (plat.), Rus.
69/P3 Aldan (riv.), Rus.
75/G2 Aldarhaan, Mong.
47/E4 Aldbourne, Eng,UK
45/H4 Aldbrough, Eng,UK
47/H2 Alde (riv.), Eng,UK
47/H2 Aldeburgh, Eng,UK
104/B2 Aldeia Viçosa, Ang.
53/F2 Aldenhoven, Ger.
44/B2 Aldergrove, NI,UK
45/F5 Alderley Edge, Eng,UK
47/F4 Aldermaston, Eng,UK
127/Q9 Aldershot, On,Can
47/F4 Aldershot, Eng,UK
132/C2 Alderwood Manor-Bothell North, Wa,US
128/E4 Aldine, Tx,US
47/E1 Aldridge, Eng,UK
98/B2 Aleg, Mrta.
110/D2 Alegre, Braz.
111/E2 Alegrete, Braz.
107/A6 Alejandro Selkirk (isl.), Chile
66/E2 Aleksandriya, Ukr.
64/H4 Aleksandrov, Rus.
65/N4 Aleksandrovsk, Rus.
77/N1 Aleksandrovsk-Sakhalinskiy, Rus.
49/K2 Aleksandrów Kujawski, Pol.
49/K3 Aleksandrów Łódzki, Pol.
75/B1 Alekseyevka, Kaz.
66/F2 Alekseyevka, Rus.
64/H5 Aleksin, Rus.
62/E4 Aleksinac, Yugo.
110/L6 Além Paraíba, Braz.
56/D2 Alençon, Fr.
109/H4 Alenquer, Braz.
120/T10 Alenuihaha (chan.), Hi,US
74/D3 Aleppo (Ḩalab), Syria
112/B4 Alerce Andino Nat'l Park, Chile
119/S6 Alert (pt.), NW,Can
62/F2 Aleşd, Rom.
57/H4 Alessandria, It.
42/C3 Ålesund, Nor.
130/E5 Aleutian (isls.), Ak,US
130/G4 Aleutian (range), Ak,US
105/V Alexander (cape), Ant.
105/V Alexander (isl.), Ant.
130/L4 Alexander (arch.), Ak,US
129/G3 Alexander City, Al,US
61/H2 Alexándria, Gre.
63/G4 Alexandria, Rom.
128/E4 Alexandria, La,US
123/K4 Alexandria, Mn,US
131/J8 Alexandria, Va,US
74/G6 Alexandria (Al Iskandarīyah), Egypt
91/A2 Alexandrina (lake), Austl.
61/J2 Alexandroúpolis, Gre.
122/C2 Alexis Creek, BC,Can
75/D1 Aley (riv.), Rus.
75/D1 Aleysk, Rus.
59/E3 Alfafar, Sp.
72/D2 Al Fallūjah, Iraq
59/P10 Alfama, Port.
59/P11 Alfarim, Port.
58/E1 Alfaro, Sp.
97/L5 Al Fāsher, Sudan
100/B2 Al Fashn, Egypt
72/D1 Al Fatḩah, Iraq
72/E3 Al Fāw, Iraq
100/B2 Al Fayyum, Egypt
53/F3 Alfbach (riv.), Ger.
51/G5 Alfeld, Ger.
110/H6 Alfenas, Braz.
61/G4 Alfiós (riv.), Gre.
45/J5 Alford, Eng,UK
91/D3 Alfred Nat'l Park, Austl.
45/G5 Alfreton, Eng,UK
47/G5 Alfriston, Eng,UK
53/G2 Alfter, Ger.
67/L2 Alga, Kaz.
42/D3 Ålgård, Nor.
58/C4 Algeciras, Sp.
59/E3 Algemesí, Sp.
96/F2 Algeria
51/G4 Algermissen, Ger.
59/N8 Algete, Sp.
100/B2 Al Gharbīyah (gov.), Egypt
60/A2 Alghero, It.
100/C3 Al Ghurdaqah, Egypt
96/F1 Algiers (cap.), Alg.
59/E3 Alginet, Sp.
102/D4 Algoa (bay), SAfr.
108/D4 Algodón (riv.), Peru
132/P15 Algonquin, Il,US
59/P10 Algueirão, Port.
72/D2 Al Ḩadīthah, Iraq
74/E3 Al Ḩaḑr, Iraq
73/G4 Al Ḩajar ash Sharqī (mts.), Oman
73/G5 Al Ḩallānīyah (isl.), Oman
58/D4 Alhama de Granada, Sp.
58/E4 Alhama de Murcia, Sp.
131/B2 Alhambra, Ca,US
100/B2 Al Ḩammām, Egypt
59/Q10 Alhandra, Port.
74/E3 Al Ḩasakah, Syria
58/C4 Alhaurín el Grande, Sp.
100/B2 Al Ḩawāmidīyah, Egypt
72/E2 Al Ḩayy, Iraq
72/D2 Al Ḩillah, Iraq
72/D2 Al Hindīyah, Iraq
96/E1 Al Hoceima, Mor.
72/E3 Al Hufūf, SAr.
74/A2 Aliağa, Turk.
61/G2 Aliákmon (riv.), Gre.
61/G2 Aliákmonos (lake), Gre.
72/E2 'Alī al Gharbī, Iraq
72/E2 'Alī ash Sharqī, Iraq
128/C3 Alibates Flint Quarries Nat'l Mon., Tx,US
67/J5 Ali-Bayramly, Azer.
100/C5 Al Ibēdiyya, Sudan
63/J5 Alibeyköy, Turk.
59/E3 Alicante, Sp.
90/A1 Alice (riv.), Austl.
60/E3 Alice (pt.), It.
128/D5 Alice, Tx,US
89/C3 Alice Springs, Austl.
129/F3 Aliceville, Al,US
82/D6 Alicia, Phil.
82/C6 Alicia Annie (shoal)
60/D3 Alicudi (isl.), It.
84/C2 Alīgarh, India
72/E2 Alīgudarz, Iran
96/J8 Alima (riv.), Congo
42/E4 Alingsås, Swe.
84/B2 Alīpur, Pak.
84/E2 Alīpur Duār, India
74/G6 Al Iskandarīyah (gov.), Egypt
74/G6 Al Iskandarīyah (Alexandria), Egypt
100/C2 Al Ismā'īlīyah (gov.), Egypt
100/C2 Al Ismā'īlīyah (Ismalia), Egypt
102/D3 Aliwal North, SAfr.
97/K2 Al Jaghbūb, Libya
60/B5 Al Jamm, Tun.
74/K5 Al Janūb (gov.), Leb.
100/B2 Al Jīzah, Egypt
100/B2 Al Jīzah (gov.), Egypt
97/K5 Al Junaynah, Sudan
58/A4 Aljustrel, Port.
74/K6 Al Karak, Jor.
74/L6 Al Karak (gov.), Jor.
100/C3 Al Karnak, Egypt
53/E2 Alken, Belg.
73/G4 Al Khābūrah, Oman
74/K6 Al Khalīl (Hebron), WBnk.
72/D2 Al Khāliş, Iraq
100/B5 Al Khandaq, Sudan
100/B3 Al Khārijah, Egypt
97/M4 Al Kharţūm Baḩrī (Khartoum North), Sudan
72/F3 Al Khobar, SAr.
96/H1 Al Khums, Libya
50/B3 Alkmaar, Neth.
96/H3 Alkoum (well), Alg.
72/D2 Al Kūfah, Iraq
97/K3 Al Kufrah, Libya
72/E2 Al Kūt, Iraq
72/E3 Al Kuwait (Kuwait) (cap.), Kuw.
74/K4 Al Lādhiqīyah (Latakia), Syria
84/D2 Allahābād, India
123/G3 Allan, Sk,Can
123/G3 Allan (hills), Sk,Can
127/R9 Allanburg, On,Can
85/G4 Allanmyo, Burma
123/L3 Allan Water (riv.), On,Can
96/H1 'Allāq (well), Libya
100/C4 'Allāqī, Wādī al (dry riv.), Egypt
126/C3 Allegan, Mi,US
121/K4 Allegheny (mts.), US
126/E3 Allegheny (plat.), Pa,US
126/E3 Allegheny (riv.), Pa,US
112/D3 Allen, Arg.
46/B5 Allen (riv.), Eng,UK
44/B5 Allen, Bog of (swamp), Ire.
45/F2 Allendale, Eng,UK
129/H3 Allendale, SC,US
116/A2 Allende, Mex.
132/F7 Allen Park, Mi,US
131/E5 Allentown, Pa,US
84/C6 Alleppey, India
51/G3 Aller (riv.), Ger.
51/H4 Allerkanal (can.), Ger.
55/G3 Allgäu (mts.), Aus., Ger.
125/G2 Alliance, Ne,US
126/D3 Alliance, Oh,US
56/E3 Allier (riv.), Fr.
56/D3 Allones, Fr.
127/G1 Alma, Qu,Can
126/C3 Alma, Mi,US
125/H2 Alma, Ne,US
75/C3 Alma-Ata, Kaz.
58/A3 Almada, Port.
58/C3 Almadén, Sp.
72/B3 Al Madīnah al Fikrīyah, Egypt
60/B5 Al Madīyah, Tun.
60/B5 Al Madīyah (gov.), Tun.
74/L5 Al Mafraq, Jor.
112/D2 Almafuerte, Arg.
96/E1 Al Maghrib (reg.), Alg., Mor.
58/D3 Almagro, Sp.
74/H6 Al Maḩallah al Kubrá, Egypt
74/H6 Al Maḩmūdīyah, Egypt
72/D2 Al Maḩmūdīyah, Iraq
74/E3 Al Mālikīyah, Syria
75/A3 Almalyk, Uzb.
72/F3 Al Manāmah (Manama) (cap.), Bahr.
124/B2 Almanor (lake), Ca,US
59/E3 Almansa, Sp.
74/H6 Al Manşūra, Egypt
74/H6 Al Manzilah, Egypt
58/D4 Almanzora (riv.), Sp.
58/C2 Almanzor, Pico de (peak), Sp.
100/B3 Al Marāghah, Egypt
96/K1 Al Marj, Libya
109/J6 Almas (riv.), Braz.

74/J6 **Al Maţarīyah,** Egypt
74/E3 **Al Mawşil** (Mosul), Iraq
72/D1 **Al Mayādin,** Syria
59/E3 **Almazora,** Sp.
51/F5 **Alme** (riv.), Ger.
58/A3 **Almeirim,** Port.
50/D4 **Almelo,** Neth.
109/K7 **Almenara,** Braz.
58/D3 **Almenara** (mtn.), Sp.
58/B2 **Almendra** (res.), Sp.
58/B3 **Almendralejo,** Sp.
50/C4 **Almere,** Neth.
58/D4 **Almería,** Sp.
59/D4 **Almeria** (gulf), Sp.
65/M5 **Al'met'yevsk,** Rus.
42/E4 **Älmhult,** Swe.
58/C5 **Almina** (pt.), Sp.
100/B2 **Al Minūfīyah** (gov.), Egypt
100/B2 **Al Minyā,** Egypt
100/B3 **Al Minyā** (gov.), Egypt
72/D2 **Al Miqdādiyah,** Iraq
113/J7 **Almirante Montt** (gulf), Chile
61/H3 **Almirós,** Gre.
61/J5 **Almiroú** (gulf), Gre.
58/C3 **Almodóvar del Campo,** Sp.
58/C4 **Almodóvar del Río,** Sp.
43/D2 **Almond** (riv.), Sc,UK
126/E2 **Almonte,** On,Can
58/B4 **Almonte,** Sp.
59/E3 **Almoradí,** Sp.
110/D1 **Almores** (range), Braz.
72/E3 **Al Mubarraz,** SAr.
97/L5 **Al Muglad,** Sudan
60/B5 **Al Muknīn,** Tun.
60/B5 **Al Munastīr,** Tun.
60/B5 **Al Munastīr** (gov.), Tun.
58/D4 **Almuñécar,** Sp.
43/C2 **Alness,** Sc,UK
93/J6 **Alofi** (cap.), Niue
92/H6 **Alofi** (isl.), Wall.
85/G2 **Along,** India
61/H3 **Alónnisos** (isl.), Gre.
87/F5 **Alor** (isls.), Indo.
58/C4 **Álora,** Sp.
86/B2 **Alor Setar,** Malay.
92/E6 **Alotau,** PNG
50/D5 **Alpen,** Ger.
126/D2 **Alpena,** Mi,US
109/J5 **Alpercatas** (mts.), Braz.
50/B4 **Alphen aan de Rijn,** Neth.
58/A3 **Alpiarça,** Port.
128/C4 **Alpine,** Tx,US
122/F5 **Alpine,** Wy,US
58/B4 **Alportel,** Port.
41/E4 **Alps** (mts.), Eur.
79/F3 **Alps-Minami Nat'l Park,** Japan
73/G4 **Al Qābil,** Oman
97/N5 **Al Qadīrif,** Sudan
100/B2 **Al Qāhirah** (Cairo) (cap.), Egypt
74/E3 **Al Qāmishlī,** Syria
100/B3 **Al Qaşr,** Egypt
97/M5 **Al Qaţaynah,** Sudan
96/H3 **Al Qaţrūn,** Libya
60/A5 **Al Qayrawān,** Tun.
60/A5 **Al Qayrawān** (gov.), Tun.
74/K5 **Al Qunayţirah** (prov.), Syria
100/C3 **Al Quşayr,** Egypt
74/L4 **Al Quşayr,** Syria
74/L5 **Al Quţayfah,** Syria
47/E1 **Alrewas,** Eng,UK
48/F1 **Als** (isl.), Den.
54/D2 **Alsace** (reg.), Fr.
54/C2 **Alsace, Ballon d'** (mtn.), Fr.
45/F5 **Alsager,** Eng,UK
122/F3 **Alsask,** Sk,Can
58/D1 **Alsasua,** Sp.
53/F2 **Alsdorf,** Ger.
48/E3 **Alsfeld,** Ger.
132/Q16 **Alsip,** Il,US
51/H1 **Alster** (riv.), Ger.
45/F2 **Alston,** Eng,UK
45/F4 **Alt** (riv.), Eng,UK
42/G1 **Alta,** Nor.
131/B2 **Altadena,** Ca,US
109/G5 **Alta Floresta,** Braz.
112/D1 **Alta Gracia,** Arg.
116/D5 **Alta Gracia,** Nic.
75/D1 **Altai** (mts.), Asia
129/H4 **Altamaha** (riv.), Ga,US
109/H4 **Altamira,** Braz.
116/B3 **Altamira,** Mex.
129/H4 **Altamonte Springs,** Fl,US
60/E2 **Altamura,** It.
116/C4 **Altar de los Sacrificios** (ruins), Guat.
76/B2 **Altay,** China
68/J4 **Altay** (kray), Rus.
55/E4 **Altdorf,** Swi.
57/J2 **Altdorf bei Nürnberg,** Ger.
59/E3 **Altea,** Sp.
51/E6 **Altena,** Ger.
51/F5 **Altenau** (riv.), Ger.
51/F5 **Altenbeken,** Ger.
48/G3 **Altenburg,** Ger.
49/G2 **Altentreptow,** Ger.
117/P8 **Alteres,** Mex.
50/D5 **Alter Rhein** (riv.), Ger.
51/G1 **Altes Land** (reg.), Ger.
45/H4 **Althorpe,** Eng,UK
108/E7 **Altiplano** (plat.), Bol., Peru
48/F2 **Altmark** (reg.), Ger.
57/J2 **Altmühl** (riv.), Ger.
57/K3 **Altmünster,** Aus.
109/J6 **Alto** (peak), Braz.
109/H7 **Alto Araguaia,** Braz.
104/C2 **Alto Cuale,** Ang.
47/F4 **Alton,** Eng,UK
126/B4 **Alton,** Il,US
91/F5 **Altona,** Austl.
123/J3 **Altona,** Mb,Can
126/E3 **Altoona,** Pa,US
108/D6 **Alto Purús** (riv.), Peru
109/K5 **Altos,** Braz.
45/F5 **Altrincham,** Eng,UK
76/C4 **Altun** (mts.), China
116/D4 **Altun Ha** (ruins), Belz.
124/B2 **Alturas,** Ca,US
125/H4 **Altus,** Ok,US
125/H4 **Altus** (res.), Ok,US
125/H4 **Altus A.F.B.,** Ok,US
97/M5 **Al Ubayyiḑ,** Sudan
97/L5 **Al Uḑayyah,** Sudan
44/E5 **Alun** (riv.), Wal,UK
100/C3 **Al Uqşur** (Luxor), Egypt
66/E3 **Alushta,** Ukr.
97/L3 **Al 'Uwaynāt** (peak), Sudan
125/H3 **Alva,** Ok,US
47/E2 **Alvechurch,** Eng,UK
58/A3 **Alverca,** Port.
59/P10 **Alverca do Ribatejo,** Port.
42/E4 **Alvesta,** Swe.
46/D4 **Alveston,** Eng,UK
128/E4 **Alvin,** Tx,US
42/F3 **Älvkarleby,** Swe.
42/E4 **Älvsborg** (co.), Swe.
42/G2 **Älvsbyn,** Swe.
100/B3 **Al Wādī al Jadīd** (gov.), Egypt
84/C2 **Alwar,** India
76/E4 **Alxa Youqi,** China
76/F4 **Alxa Zuoqi,** China
49/N1 **Alytus,** Lith.
57/K2 **Alz** (riv.), Ger.
57/H4 **Alzano Lombardo,** It.
53/F4 **Alzette** (riv.), Lux.
100/C2 **Al `Aqabah,** Jor.
108/D4 **Amacayacú Nat'l Park,** Col.
72/B4 **Amada** (ruins), Egypt
97/M6 **Amadi,** Sudan
119/J2 **Amadjuak** (lake), NW,Can
58/A3 **Amadora,** Port.
79/L10 **Amagasaki,** Japan
78/B4 **Amagi,** Japan
79/F3 **Amagi-san** (mtn.), Japan
87/G4 **Amahai,** Indo.
78/A4 **Amakusa** (sea), Japan
42/E4 **Åmål,** Swe.
76/G1 **Amalat** (riv.), Rus.
61/G4 **Amaliás,** Gre.
84/C3 **Amalner,** India
111/E1 **Amambaí,** Braz.
109/H8 **Amambaí** (riv.), Braz.
92/B2 **Amami** (isls.), Japan
60/E3 **Amantea,** It.
93/L6 **Amanu** (atoll), FrPol.
58/A2 **Amarante,** Port.
83/B1 **Amarapura,** Burma
124/C3 **Amargosa** (dry riv.), Ca, Nv,US
128/C3 **Amarillo,** Tx,US
60/D1 **Amaro** (peak), It.
74/C2 **Amasya,** Turk.
79/J7 **Amatsukominato,** Japan
53/E2 **Amay,** Belg.
109/H4 **Amazon** (riv.), SAm.
109/G4 **Amazônia** (Tapajós) Nat'l Park, Braz.
84/C4 **Ambajogai,** India
73/L2 **Ambāla,** India
84/D6 **Ambalangoda,** SrL.
103/H8 **Ambalavao,** Madg.
103/J6 **Ambanja,** Madg.
103/H6 **Ambaro** (bay), Madg.
108/C4 **Ambato,** Ecu.
103/H7 **Ambato Boeny,** Madg.
103/H8 **Ambatofinandrahana,** Madg.
103/H7 **Ambatolampy,** Madg.
103/J7 **Ambatondrazaka,** Madg.
61/H4 **Ámbelos, Ákra** (cape), Gre.
57/J2 **Amberg,** Ger.
45/G5 **Ambergate,** Eng,UK
84/D3 **Ambikāpur,** India
103/J6 **Ambilobe,** Madg.
103/J7 **Ambinaninony,** Madg.
45/G1 **Amble,** Eng,UK
131/E5 **Ambler,** Pa,US
45/F3 **Ambleside,** Eng,UK
52/A2 **Ambleteuse,** Fr.
53/F3 **Amblève** (riv.), Belg.
103/H9 **Amboasary,** Madg.
103/J6 **Ambohitra, Tampon** (peak), Madg.
87/G4 **Ambon,** Indo.
87/G4 **Ambon** (isl.), Indo.
103/H8 **Ambositra,** Madg.
103/H9 **Ambovombe,** Madg.
104/B2 **Ambriz,** Ang.
92/F6 **Ambrym** (isl.), Van.
130/B6 **Amchitka** (isl.), Ak,US
130/B6 **Amchitka** (passg.), Ak,US
117/P9 **Ameca,** Mex.
53/F3 **Amel,** Belg.
50/C2 **Ameland** (isl.), Neth.
50/B5 **Amer** (chan.), Neth.
105/F **American** (highland), Ant.
132/M9 **American** (riv.), Ca,US
132/B3 **American** (lake), Wa,US
110/C2 **Americana,** Braz.
122/E5 **American Falls,** Id,US
124/D2 **American Falls** (res.), Id,US
124/E2 **American Fork,** Ut,US
93/J6 **American Samoa** (terr.), US
129/G3 **Americus,** Ga,US
57/L3 **Ameringkogel** (peak), Aus.
50/C4 **Amersfoort,** Neth.
47/F3 **Amersham,** Eng,UK
105/E **Amery Ice Shelf,** Ant.
123/K5 **Ames,** Ia,US
47/E4 **Amesbury,** Eng,UK
61/H3 **Ámfissa,** Gre.
69/N3 **Amga** (riv.), Rus.
69/T3 **Amguema** (riv.), Rus.
77/M1 **Amgun'** (riv.), Rus.
127/H2 **Amherst,** NS,Can
132/F7 **Amherstburg,** On,Can
60/B1 **Amiata** (peak), It.
52/B4 **Amiens,** Fr.
69/U4 **Amila** (isl.), Ak,US
39/M6 **Amirante** (isls.), Sey.
123/H2 **Amisk** (lake), Sk,Can
128/C4 **Amistad** (res.), Mex., US
125/G5 **Amistad Nat'l Rec. Area,** Tx,US
125/K5 **Amite** (riv.), La,US
84/C3 **Amla,** India
130/D6 **Amlia** (isl.), Ak,US
44/D5 **Amlwch,** Wal,UK
74/K6 **'Ammān** (cap.), Jor.
46/C3 **Amman** (riv.), Wal,UK
46/C3 **Ammanford,** Wal,UK
42/E2 **Ammarfjället** (peak), Swe.
130/K2 **Ammerman** (mtn.), Yk,Can
55/H2 **Ammersee** (lake), Ger.
122/F5 **Ammon,** Id,US
83/D3 **Amnat Charoen,** Thai.
53/F5 **Amnéville,** Fr.
72/F1 **Āmol,** Iran
59/P10 **Amora,** Port.
61/J4 **Amorgós** (isl.), Gre.
129/F3 **Amory,** Ms,US
126/E1 **Amos,** Qu,Can
103/J8 **Ampangalana** (can.), Madg.
103/H9 **Ampanihy,** Madg.
84/D6 **Amparai,** SrL.
110/G7 **Amparo,** Braz.
103/J6 **Ampasindava** (bay), Madg.
59/F2 **Amposta,** Sp.
47/F2 **Ampthill,** Eng,UK
127/H1 **Amqui,** Qu,Can
84/C3 **Amravati,** India
84/B3 **Amreli,** India
72/C2 **'Amrīt** (ruins), Syria
73/K2 **Amritsar,** India
48/E1 **Amrun** (isl.), Ger.
50/B4 **Amstel** (riv.), Neth.
50/B4 **Amstelveen,** Neth.
39/N7 **Amsterdam** (isl.), FrAnt.
50/B4 **Amsterdam** (cap.), Neth.
126/F3 **Amsterdam,** NY,US
50/C5 **Amsterdam-Rijnkanaal** (can.), Neth.
57/L2 **Amstetten,** Aus.
97/K5 **Am Timan,** Chad
71/F5 **Amudar'ya** (riv.), Asia
130/D5 **Amukta** (passg.), Ak,US
119/S7 **Amund Rignes** (isl.), NW,Can
105/D **Amundsen** (bay), Ant.
105/S **Amundsen** (sea), Ant.
118/D1 **Amundsen** (gulf), NW,Can
105/A **Amundsen-Scott,** Ant.
77/M1 **Amur** (riv.), China, Rus.
93/K6 **Amuri,** CookIs.
69/N4 **Amur Obl.,** Rus.
58/D1 **Amurrio,** Sp.
77/M1 **Amursk,** Rus.
100/C5 **'Amur, Wādī** (dry riv.), Sudan
82/C5 **Amy Douglas** (shoal)
74/K4 **Amyūn,** Leb.
93/L6 **Anaa** (atoll), FrPol.
69/L3 **Anabar** (riv.), Rus.
131/A2 **Anacapa** (isl.), Ca,US
117/J6 **Anaco,** Ven.
122/E4 **Anaconda,** Mt,US
125/H4 **Anadarko,** Ok,US
69/T3 **Anadyr',** Rus.
69/U3 **Anadyr'** (gulf), Rus.
69/T3 **Anadyr'** (range), Rus.
71/S3 **Anadyr'** (riv.), Rus.
61/J4 **Anáfi** (isl.), Gre.
72/D2 **'Ānah,** Iraq
131/C3 **Anaheim,** Ca,US
122/B2 **Anahim Lake,** BC,Can
116/A2 **Anáhuac,** Mex.
128/E4 **Anahuac,** Tx,US
84/D4 **Anakāpalle,** India
103/H6 **Analalava,** Madg.
103/J7 **Analamaitso** (plat.), Madg.
117/F3 **Ana María** (gulf), Cuba
86/C3 **Anambas** (isls.), Indo.
99/G5 **Anambra** (state), Nga.
74/C3 **Anamur,** Turk.
74/C3 **Anamur** (pt.), Turk.
78/D4 **Anan,** Japan
84/B3 **Anand,** India
84/C5 **Anantapur,** India
73/L2 **Anantnag,** India
75/C3 **Anan'yevo,** Kyr.
66/F3 **Anapa,** Rus.
113/K7 **Añapi** (peak), Arg.
109/J7 **Anápolis,** Braz.
109/H4 **Anapu** (riv.), Braz.
109/G8 **Anastácio,** Braz.
92/D3 **Anathan** (isl.), NMar.
74/B2 **Anatolia** (reg.), Turk.
111/D2 **Añatuya,** Arg.
108/F3 **Anauá** (riv.), Braz.
127/Q9 **Ancaster,** On,Can
82/A2 **Anchangzhen,** China
132/G6 **Anchor** (bay), Mi,US
130/J3 **Anchorage,** Ak,US
127/G2 **Ancienne-Lorette,** Qu,Can
108/E7 **Ancohuma** (peak), Bol.
57/K5 **Ancona,** It.
112/B4 **Ancud,** Chile
112/B4 **Ancud** (gulf), Chile
77/K2 **Anda,** China
108/D6 **Andahuaylas,** Peru
103/J7 **Andaingo Gara,** Madg.
42/C3 **Åndalsnes,** Nor.
58/C4 **Andalusia** (aut. comm.), Sp.
129/G4 **Andalusia,** Al,US
85/F5 **Andaman** (sea), Asia
85/F5 **Andaman** (isls.), India
85/F5 **Andaman & Nicobar Is.** (terr.), India
103/J6 **Andapa,** Madg.
52/A4 **Andelle** (riv.), Fr.
42/F1 **Andenes,** Nor.
53/E3 **Andenne,** Belg.
42/F1 **Ånderdalen Nat'l Park,** Nor.
52/D3 **Anderlues,** Belg.
53/G3 **Andernach,** Ger.
130/N2 **Anderson** (riv.), NW,Can
124/B2 **Anderson,** Ca,US
126/C3 **Anderson,** In,US
129/H3 **Anderson,** SC,US
128/E4 **Anderson,** Tx,US
132/B3 **Anderson** (isl.), Wa,US
107/C4 **Andes** (mts.), SAm.
42/F1 **Andfjorden** (fjord), Nor.
84/C4 **Andhra Pradesh** (state), India
61/H5 **Andikíthira** (isl.), Gre.
103/J7 **Andilamena,** Madg.
72/E2 **Andīmeshk,** Iran
61/J4 **Andíparos** (isl.), Gre.
110/B2 **Andira,** Braz.
75/B3 **Andizhan,** Uzb.
58/D1 **Andoain,** Sp.
80/E4 **Andong,** SKor.
80/E4 **Andong** (lake), SKor.
59/F1 **Andorra**
59/E2 **Andorra,** Sp.
59/F1 **Andorra la Vella** (cap.), And.
47/E4 **Andover,** Eng,UK
131/F5 **Andover,** NJ,US
42/E1 **Andøya** (isl.), Nor.
110/G7 **Andradas,** Braz.
110/B2 **Andradina,** Braz.
59/G3 **Andraitx,** Sp.
103/H7 **Andranomavo** (riv.), Madg.
130/C6 **Andreanof** (isls.), Ak,US
110/J6 **Andrelândia,** Braz.
128/C3 **Andrews,** Tx,US
60/E2 **Andria,** It.
103/H8 **Andringitra** (mts.), Madg.
103/J6 **Androntany** (cape), Madg.
117/F3 **Andros** (isl.), Bahm.
61/J4 **Ándros** (isl.), Gre.
126/G2 **Androscoggin** (riv.), Me, NH,US
58/C3 **Andújar,** Sp.
112/C4 **Anecón Grande** (peak), Arg.
112/E4 **Anegada** (bay), Arg.
117/J4 **Anegada** (isl.), BVi.
117/J4 **Anegada** (passage), NAm.
99/F5 **Anécho,** Togo
92/G7 **Aneityum** (isl.), Van.
59/F1 **Aneto, Pico de** (peak), Sp.
82/B2 **Anfu,** China
111/B1 **Angamos** (pt.), Chile
76/E1 **Angara** (riv.), Rus.
76/E1 **Angarsk,** Rus.
42/E3 **Ånge,** Swe.
51/E5 **Angel** (riv.), Ger.
117/M8 **Ángel de la Guarda** (isl.), Mex.
82/D4 **Angeles,** Phil.
131/B2 **Angeles Nat'l Forest,** Ca,US
128/E4 **Angelina** (riv.), Tx,US
48/E1 **Angeln** (reg.), Ger.
108/F2 **Angel, Salto** (falls), Ven.
132/F6 **Angelus** (lake), Mi,US
87/J4 **Angemuk** (mtn.), Indo.
42/E2 **Ångermanälven** (riv.), Swe.
49/H2 **Angermünde,** Ger.
56/C3 **Angers,** Fr.
83/C3 **Angkor** (ruins), Camb.
83/D4 **Angk Tasaom,** Camb.
44/D5 **Anglesey** (isl.), Wal,UK
56/C5 **Anglet,** Fr.
128/E4 **Angleton,** Tx,US
56/D3 **Anglin** (riv.), Fr.
83/C2 **Ang Nam Ngum** (lake), Laos
97/L7 **Ango,** Zaire
112/B3 **Angol,** Chile
104/C3 **Angola**
126/C3 **Angola,** In,US
116/C4 **Angostura** (res.), Mex.
56/D4 **Angoulême,** Fr.
59/S12 **Angra do Heroísmo,** Azor.,Port.
110/J8 **Angra dos Reis,** Braz.
75/B3 **Angren,** Uzb.
83/C3 **Ang Thong,** Thai.
97/K7 **Angu,** Zaire
117/J4 **Anguilla** (isl.), UK
130/G2 **Angutikada** (peak), Ak,US
109/H8 **Anhanduí** (riv.), Braz.
53/D3 **Anhée,** Belg.
85/K2 **Anhua,** China
81/D4 **Anhui** (prov.), China
130/G4 **Aniakchak** (crater), Ak,US
130/G4 **Aniakchak Nat'l Mon. & Prsv.,** Ak,US
52/C3 **Aniche,** Fr.
124/F3 **Animas** (riv.), Co, NM,US
62/E3 **Anina,** Rom.
77/N2 **Aniva** (bay), Rus.
42/H3 **Anjalamkoski,** Fin.
84/B3 **Anjār,** India
79/N10 **Anjō,** Japan
127/N6 **Anjou,** Qu,Can
56/C3 **Anjou** (hist. reg.), Fr.
103/H6 **Anjouan** (isl.), Com.
74/C2 **Ankara** (cap.), Turk.
103/H7 **Ankaratra, Massif** (plat.), Madg.
128/C2 **Ankaree** (riv.), Co,US
103/H8 **Ankazoabo,** Madg.
83/E3 **An Khe,** Viet.
49/G2 **Anklam,** Ger.
83/D3 **Anlong Veng,** Camb.
50/D2 **Anloo,** Neth.
81/C5 **Anlu,** China
105/D **Ann** (cape), Ant.
127/G3 **Ann** (cape), Ma,US
126/E4 **Anna** (lake), Va,US
96/G1 **Annaba,** Alg.
57/K1 **Annaberg-Buchholz,** Ger.
74/L4 **An Nabk,** Syria
44/B3 **Annaclone,** NI,UK
72/C3 **An Nafūd** (des.), SAr.
97/L5 **An Nahūd,** Sudan
72/D2 **An Najaf,** Iraq
43/B3 **Annalee** (riv.), Ire.
44/C3 **Annalong,** NI,UK
83/D2 **Annamitique, Chaine** (mts.), Laos, Viet.
45/E2 **Annan,** Sc,UK
43/D3 **Annan** (riv.), Sc,UK
131/J8 **Annandale,** Va,US
50/B3 **Anna Pavlowna,** Neth.
112/B5 **Anna Pink** (bay), Chile
131/K8 **Annapolis** (cap.), Md,US
84/D2 **Annapurna** (mtn.), Nepal
72/C3 **An Naqb, Ra's,** Jor.
132/E7 **Ann Arbor,** Mi,US
72/E2 **An Nāşirīyah,** Iraq
91/C4 **Anne** (peak), Austl.
57/G4 **Annecy,** Fr.
83/E3 **An Nhon,** Viet.
129/G3 **Anniston,** Al,US
96/F8 **Annobón** (isl.), EqG.
56/F4 **Annonay,** Fr.
72/E2 **An Nu'manīyah,** Iraq
79/M10 **Anō,** Japan
59/K7 **Anoia** (riv.), Sp.
123/K4 **Anoka,** Mn,US
103/J7 **Anosibe an' Ala,** Madg.
99/G2 **Ânou-Zeggarene** (wadi), Niger
83/E4 **An Phuoc,** Viet.
81/D5 **Anqing,** China
51/F5 **Anröchte,** Ger.
53/E2 **Ans,** Belg.
57/J2 **Ansbach,** Ger.
117/G4 **Anse-d'Hainault,** Haiti
57/L2 **Ansfelden,** Aus.
85/J2 **Anshun,** China
128/D3 **Anson,** Tx,US
80/D4 **Ansŏng,** SKor.
92/E4 **Ant** (atoll), Micr.
47/H1 **Ant** (riv.), Eng,UK
74/D3 **Antakya** (Antioch), Turk.
103/J6 **Antalaha,** Madg.
74/B3 **Antalya,** Turk.
74/B3 **Antalya** (gulf), Turk.
103/H7 **Antananarivo** (cap.), Madg.
103/H7 **Antananarivo** (prov.), Madg.
105/W **Antarctic** (pen.), Ant.
105/* **Antarctica**
110/B4 **Antas** (riv.), Braz.
52/D5 **Ante** (riv.), Fr.
58/C4 **Antequera,** Sp.
125/H3 **Anthony,** Ks,US
124/F4 **Anthony,** NM,US
96/D2 **Anti-Atlas** (mts.), Mor.
57/G5 **Antibes,** Fr.
127/J1 **Anticosti** (isl.), Qu,Can
56/D2 **Antifer, Cap d'** (cape), Fr.
126/B2 **Antigo,** Wi,US
127/J2 **Antigonish,** NS,Can
117/J4 **Antigua** (isl.), Ant. & Barb.
117/J4 **Antigua and Barbuda**
74/K5 **Anti-Lebanon** (mts.), Leb.
132/L10 **Antioch,** Ca,US
132/P15 **Antioch,** Il,US
74/D3 **Antioch** (Antakya), Turk.
39/T8 **Antipodes** (isls.), NZ
125/J4 **Antlers,** Ok,US
111/B1 **Antofagasta,** Chile
52/C2 **Antoing,** Belg.
103/J6 **Antongil** (bay), Madg.
102/C4 **Antoniesberg** (peak), SAfr.
110/B3 **Antonina,** Braz.
125/F3 **Antonito,** Co,US
116/B4 **Anton Lizardo** (pt.), Mex.
52/B6 **Antony,** Fr.
44/B2 **Antrim,** NI,UK
44/B2 **Antrim** (dist.), NI,UK
44/B1 **Antrim** (mts.), NI,UK
103/H7 **Antsalova,** Madg.
103/H7 **Antsirabe,** Madg.
103/J6 **Antsiranana,** Madg.
103/J6 **Antsiranana** (prov.), Madg.
103/H6 **Antsohihy,** Madg.
112/C3 **Antuco** (vol.), Chile
53/E1 **Antwerp** (prov.), Belg.
52/D1 **Antwerp** (Antwerpen), Belg.
84/D6 **Anuradhapura,** SrL.
130/B6 **Anvil** (vol.), Ak,US
82/C2 **Anxi,** China
81/C3 **Anyang,** China
76/D4 **A'nyêmaqên** (mts.), China
81/B4 **Anyi,** China
77/M2 **Anyuy** (riv.), Rus.
52/C2 **Anzegem,** Belg.
68/J4 **Anzhero-Sudzhensk,** Rus.
52/C3 **Anzin,** Fr.
60/C2 **Anzio,** It.
79/L9 **Aogaki,** Japan
83/B4 **Ao Kham** (pt.), Thai.
77/N3 **Aomori,** Japan
61/G2 **Aóos** (riv.), Gre.
83/B4 **Ao Phangnga Nat'l Park,** Thai.
83/D3 **Aoral** (peak), Camb.
57/G4 **Aosta,** It.
98/C2 **Aoudaghost** (ruins), Mrta.
97/K5 **Aouk** (riv.), CAfr., Chad
98/C2 **Aoukar** (reg.), Mrta.
96/F2 **Aoulef,** Alg.
79/M10 **Aoyama,** Japan
96/J3 **Aozou,** Chad
128/B4 **Apache** (mts.), Tx,US
129/G4 **Apalachicola,** Fl,US
110/B4 **Aparados da Serra Nat'l Park,** Braz.
110/C2 **Aparecida,** Braz.
110/B2 **Aparecida do Taboado,** Braz.
82/D4 **Aparri,** Phil.
117/F6 **Apartado,** Col.
93/L6 **Apataki,** FrPol.
62/D3 **Apatin,** Yugo.
64/G2 **Apatity,** Rus.
117/P10 **Apatzingán,** Mex.
116/B4 **Apaxtla,** Mex.
83/D4 **Ap Binh Chau,** Viet.
50/C4 **Apeldoorn,** Neth.
50/D4 **Apeldoornsch** (can.), Neth.
51/E2 **Apen,** Ger.
41/F4 **Apennines** (mts.), It.
86/C3 **Api** (cape), Indo.
87/E5 **Api** (peak), Indo.
75/D5 **Api** (mtn.), Nepal
93/H6 **Apia** (cap.), WSam.
109/G6 **Apiacás** (mts.), Braz.
110/B3 **Apiaí,** Braz.
83/D4 **Ap Loc Thanh,** Viet.
83/E4 **Ap Long Hoa,** Viet.
83/D4 **Ap Luc,** Viet.
82/E6 **Apo** (mt.), Phil.
93/R9 **Apolima** (str.), WSam.
110/B1 **Aporé** (riv.), Braz.
126/B2 **Apostle** (isls.), Wi,US
111/E2 **Apóstoles,** Arg.
74/C3 **Apostolos Andreas** (cape), Cyp.
121/K4 **Appalachian** (mts.), US
55/F3 **Appenzell Ausser Rhoden** (canton), Swi.
55/F3 **Appenzell Inner Rhoden** (canton), Swi.
50/D2 **Appingedam,** Neth.
45/F2 **Appleby,** Eng,UK
47/E1 **Appleby Magna,** Eng,UK
127/S9 **Appleton,** NY,US
126/B2 **Appleton,** Wi,US
131/C1 **Apple Valley,** Ca,US
60/D2 **Apricena,** It.
60/C2 **Aprilia,** It.
66/F3 **Apsheronsk,** Rus.
91/E1 **Apsley Gorge Nat'l Park,** Austl.
83/E4 **Ap Tan My,** Viet.
120/U11 **Apua** (pt.), Hi,US
57/J4 **Apuane** (mts.), It.
110/B2 **Apucarana,** Braz.
117/H6 **Apure** (riv.), Ven.
108/D6 **Apurímac** (riv.), Peru
83/E4 **Ap Vinh Hao,** Viet.
100/C2 **Aqaba** (gulf), Asia
72/B3 **Aqaba** (gulf), Egypt, SAr.
100/D5 **'Aqīq,** Sudan
75/B1 **Aqmola** (cap.), Kaz.
80/D4 **Ch'ungch'ŏng-Bukto** (prov.), SKor.
80/D4 **Ch'ungch'ŏng-Namdo** (prov.), SKor.
75/E4 **Aqqikkol** (lake), China
72/D1 **'Aqrah,** Iraq
109/G8 **Aquidauana,** Braz.
109/G8 **Aquidauana** (riv.), Braz.
56/C4 **Aquitaine** (reg.), Fr.
76/D4 **Ar** (riv.), China
79/F2 **Ara** (riv.), Japan
97/L5 **'Arab** (riv.), Sudan
129/G3 **Arab,** Al,US
100/C2 **'Arabah, Wādī** (dry riv.), Egypt
72/D3 **Arabian** (pen.), Asia
73/H5 **Arabian** (sea), Asia
100/C3 **Arabian** (des.), Egypt
74/L5 **'Arab, Jabal al** (mts.), Syria
100/B2 **'Arab, Kalīj al** (gulf), Egypt
66/E4 **Araç** (riv.), Turk.
109/L6 **Aracaju,** Braz.
109/L4 **Aracati,** Braz.
110/B2 **Araçatuba,** Braz.
58/B4 **Aracena,** Sp.
110/D1 **Aracruz,** Braz.
109/K7 **Araçuaí,** Braz.
62/E2 **Arad,** Rom.
62/E2 **Arad** (co.), Rom.
97/K4 **Arada,** Chad
72/F1 **Ārādān,** Iran
72/D4 **'Arafāt, Jabal** (mtn.), SAr.
92/C5 **Arafura** (sea), Austl., Indo.
109/H7 **Aragarças,** Braz.
67/H4 **Aragats, Gora** (peak), Arm.
59/E2 **Aragon** (aut. comm.), Sp.
58/E1 **Aragón** (riv.), Sp.
109/J5 **Araguaia** (riv.), Braz.
109/H5 **Araguaia Nat'l Park,** Braz.
109/J5 **Araguaína,** Braz.
110/B1 **Araguari,** Braz.
109/H3 **Araguari** (riv.), Braz.
109/J7 **Araguari** (riv.), Braz.
110/C1 **Araguari** (Valhas) (riv.), Braz.
109/J5 **Araguatins,** Braz.
79/F2 **Arai,** Japan
72/E2 **Arāk,** Iran
130/D3 **Arakamchechan** (isl.), Rus.
85/F3 **Arakan** (mts.), Burma
61/G3 **Árakhthos** (riv.), Gre.
67/H5 **Araks (Aras)** (riv.), Eur., Asia
68/G5 **Aral** (sea), Uzb., Kaz.
68/G5 **Aral'sk,** Kaz.
67/H2 **Aralsor** (lake), Kaz.
72/F2 **Ārān,** Iran
43/H7 **Aran** (isl.), Ire.
43/A4 **Aran** (isls.), Ire.
58/D2 **Aranda de Duero,** Sp.
62/E3 **Arandelovac,** Yugo.
58/D2 **Aranjuez,** Sp.
44/E6 **Aran Mawddwy** (mtn.), Wal,UK
128/D5 **Aransas Pass,** Tx,US
92/G4 **Aranuka** (atoll), Kiri.
109/L5 **Arapiraca,** Braz.
74/D2 **Arapkir,** Turk.
110/B2 **Arapongas,** Braz.
110/B4 **Araranguá,** Braz.
110/B2 **Araraquara,** Braz.
110/C2 **Araras,** Braz.
91/B3 **Ararat,** Austl.
109/K5 **Araripina,** Braz.
67/H5 **Aras** (riv.), Asia
98/C2 **Aratane** (well), Mrta.
108/F4 **Arauá** (riv.), Braz.
108/D2 **Arauca,** Col.
110/B3 **Araucária,** Braz.
92/E5 **Arawa,** PNG
110/C1 **Araxá,** Braz.
97/N6 **Ārba Minch',** Eth.
123/H2 **Arborfield,** Sk,Can
123/J3 **Arborg,** Mb,Can
43/D2 **Arbroath,** Sc,UK
56/F5 **Arc** (riv.), Fr.
57/G4 **Arc** (riv.), Fr.
56/C4 **Arcachon,** Fr.
56/C4 **Arcachon** (lag.), Fr.
56/C4 **Arcachon, Pointe d'** (pt.), Fr.
131/B2 **Arcadia,** Ca,US
129/H5 **Arcadia,** Fl,US
124/A2 **Arcata,** Ca,US
64/J2 **Archangel** (Arkhangel'sk), Rus.
64/H3 **Archangel Obl.,** Rus.
58/E3 **Archena,** Sp.
90/A1 **Archer** (riv.), Austl.
90/A1 **Archer Bend Nat'l Park,** Austl.
128/D3 **Archer City,** Tx,US
124/E3 **Arches Nat'l Park,** Ut,US
58/C4 **Archidona,** Sp.
112/C3 **Arco** (pass), Arg.
57/J4 **Arco,** It.
122/E5 **Arco,** Id,US
110/C2 **Arcos,** Braz.
58/C4 **Arcos de la Frontera,** Sp.
109/L5 **Arcoverde,** Braz.
38/A1 **Arctic** (ocean)
130/F2 **Arctic** (coast. pl.), Ak,US
130/J2 **Arctic Nat'l Wild. Ref.,** Ak,US
130/M2 **Arctic Red River,** NW,Can
63/G5 **Arda** (riv.), Bul.
74/E2 **Ardahan,** Turk.
72/F2 **Ardakān,** Iran
42/C3 **Årdalstangen,** Nor.
74/E2 **Ardanuç,** Turk.
45/E6 **Arddleen,** Wal,UK
56/F4 **Ardèche** (riv.), Fr.
132/M9 **Arden-Arcade,** Ca,US
53/E4 **Ardennes** (for.), Eur.
52/D4 **Ardennes** (dept.), Fr.
53/D4 **Ardennes, Canal des** (can.), Fr.
74/E2 **Ardeşen,** Turk.
44/C3 **Ardglass,** NI,UK
58/B3 **Ardila** (riv.), Sp.
125/H4 **Ardmore,** Ok,US
131/E5 **Ardmore,** Pa,US
52/C2 **Ardooie,** Belg.
44/C2 **Ards** (dist.), NI,UK
44/C3 **Ards** (pen.), NI,UK
42/E3 **Åre,** Swe.
110/G6 **Areado,** Braz.
109/L4 **Areia Branca,** Braz.
117/N9 **Arena** (pt.), Mex.
124/B3 **Arena** (pt.), Ca,US
109/G6 **Arenápolis,** Braz.
58/C2 **Arenas de San Pedro,** Sp.
113/K8 **Arenas, Punta de** (pt.), Arg.
42/D4 **Arendal,** Nor.
50/C6 **Arendonk,** Belg.
44/E6 **Arenig Fawr** (mtn.), Wal,UK
59/L6 **Arenys de Mar,** Sp.
59/L6 **Arenys de Munt,** Sp.
108/D7 **Arequipa,** Peru
58/C2 **Arévalo,** Sp.
57/J5 **Arezzo,** It.
56/C5 **Arga** (riv.), Sp.
58/D3 **Argamasilla de Alba,** Sp.
58/C3 **Argamasilla de Calatrava,** Sp.
59/N9 **Arganda,** Sp.
57/G5 **Argens** (riv.), Fr.
56/C2 **Argentan,** Fr.
57/G4 **Argentera** (peak), It.
52/B6 **Argenteuil,** Fr.
111/C4 **Argentina**
113/J7 **Argentino** (lake), Arg.
59/L6 **Argentona,** Sp.
63/G3 **Argeş** (co.), Rom.
63/G3 **Argeş** (riv.), Rom.
73/J2 **Arghandab** (riv.), Afg.
100/B5 **Argo,** Sudan
61/H4 **Argolis** (gulf), Gre.
53/E5 **Argonne** (for.), Fr.
61/H4 **Árgos,** Gre.
61/G3 **Argostólion,** Gre.
52/A4 **Argueil,** Fr.
124/B4 **Arguello** (pt.), Ca,US
98/A1 **Arguin** (bay), Mrta.
77/H1 **Argun** (riv.), China, Rus.
75/E2 **Argut** (riv.), Rus.
96/C3 **Arhreijīt** (well), Mrta.
42/D4 **Århus,** Den.
60/D2 **Ariano Irpino,** It.
58/C1 **Arianza** (riv.), Sp.
108/D7 **Arica,** Chile
78/D3 **Arida,** Japan
131/A1 **Arido** (mt.), Ca,US
56/D5 **Ariège** (riv.), Fr.
63/K5 **Arifiye,** Turk.
74/K6 **Arīḩā** (Jericho), WBnk.
125/G3 **Arikaree** (riv.), Co,US
117/J5 **Arima,** Trin.
109/G6 **Arinos** (riv.), Braz.
108/F5 **Aripuanã** (riv.), Braz.
108/F5 **Ariquemes,** Braz.
100/C2 **'Arīsh, Wādī al** (dry riv.), Egypt
103/H7 **Arivonimamo,** Madg.
59/F1 **Arize** (riv.), Fr.
124/D4 **Arizona** (state), US
117/F5 **Arjona,** Col.
58/C4 **Arjona,** Sp.
128/E3 **Arkadelphia,** Ar,US
43/C2 **Arkaig, Loch** (lake), Sc,UK
75/A1 **Arkalyk,** Kaz.
125/K4 **Arkansas** (riv.), US
128/E3 **Arkansas** (state), US
129/F3 **Arkansas City,** Ar,US
125/H3 **Arkansas City,** Ks,US
97/K3 **Arkanū** (peak), Libya
64/J2 **Arkhangel'sk** (Archangel), Rus.
44/B6 **Arklow,** Ire.
49/G1 **Arkona, Kap** (cape), Ger.
84/C5 **Arkonam,** India
45/G4 **Arksey,** Eng,UK
68/H2 **Arkticheskiy Institut** (isls.), Rus.
58/C1 **Arlanza** (riv.), Sp.
58/C1 **Arlazón** (riv.), Sp.
56/F5 **Arles,** Fr.
52/C3 **Arleux,** Fr.
129/G4 **Arlington,** Ga,US
123/K4 **Arlington,** Mn,US

141

Arlin – Balei

128/D3 **Arlington,** Tx,US
131/J8 **Arlington,** Va,US
132/Q15 **Arlington Heights,** Il,US
53/E4 **Arlon,** Belg.
99/F4 **Arly Nat'l Park,** Burk.
132/G6 **Armada,** Mi,US
44/B3 **Armagh,** NI,UK
44/B3 **Armagh** (dist.), NI,UK
56/F3 **Armançon** (riv.), Fr.
110/B2 **Armando Laydner** (res.), Braz.
100/C3 **Armant,** Egypt
67/G3 **Armavir,** Rus.
57/G5 **Arme, Cap d'** (cape), Fr.
67/H4 **Armenia**
108/C3 **Armenia,** Col.
52/B2 **Armentières,** Fr.
117/P10 **Armería,** Mex.
91/D1 **Armidale,** Austl.
58/D4 **Armilla,** Sp.
44/B1 **Armoy,** NI,UK
112/E2 **Armstrong,** Arg.
122/D3 **Armstrong,** BC,Can
45/G4 **Armthorpe,** Eng,UK
84/C4 **Ārmūr,** India
119/J3 **Arnaud** (riv.), Qu,Can
74/J4 **Arnauti** (cape), Cyp.
47/E3 **Arncott,** Eng,UK
58/D1 **Arnedo,** Sp.
52/B2 **Arnèke,** Fr.
125/H3 **Arnett,** Ok,US
50/C5 **Arnhem,** Neth.
84/C5 **Arni,** India
57/J5 **Arno** (riv.), It.
92/G4 **Arno** (atoll), Mrsh.
45/G5 **Arnold,** Eng,UK
57/K3 **Arnoldstein,** Aus.
56/E3 **Arnon** (riv.), Fr.
126/E2 **Arnprior,** On,Can
51/F6 **Arnsberg,** Ger.
45/F3 **Arnside,** Eng,UK
48/F3 **Arnstadt,** Ger.
51/G6 **Arolsen,** Ger.
56/E3 **Aron** (riv.), Fr.
59/X16 **Arona,** Canl.
52/B4 **Aronde** (riv.), Fr.
92/G5 **Arorae** (atoll), Kiri.
87/H5 **Aro Usu** (cape), Indo.
52/B2 **Arques,** Fr.
84/D2 **Arrah,** India
97/M5 **Ar Rahad,** Sudan
109/H6 **Arraias** (riv.), Braz.
45/H4 **Arram,** Eng,UK
72/D2 **Ar Ramādī,** Iraq
74/L5 **Ar Ramthā,** Jor.
43/C3 **Arran** (isl.), Sc,UK
74/D3 **Ar Raqqah,** Syria
52/B3 **Arras,** Fr.
74/L4 **Ar Rastan,** Syria
59/F1 **Arrats** (riv.), Fr.
59/Y16 **Arrecife,** Canl.
112/E2 **Arrecifes,** Arg.
56/B2 **Arrée** (mts.), Fr.
116/C4 **Arriaga,** Mex.
110/A5 **Arrio Grande,** Braz.
72/E4 **Ar Riyāḑ** (Riyadh) (cap.), SAr.
56/F3 **Arroux** (riv.), Fr.
58/B3 **Arroyo de la Luz,** Sp.
124/B4 **Arroyo Grande,** Ca,US
74/L5 **Ar Ruşayfah,** Jor.
97/M5 **Ar Ruşayriş,** Sudan
72/F4 **Ar Ruways,** SAr.
77/L3 **Arsen'yev,** Rus.
93/T11 **Art** (isl.), NCal.
61/G3 **Árta,** Gre.
61/G3 **Árta** (gulf), Gre.
58/A1 **Arteijo,** Sp.
77/L3 **Artem,** Rus.
116/E3 **Artemisa,** Cuba
131/B3 **Artesia,** Ca,US
125/F4 **Artesia,** NM,US
90/C3 **Arthur** (pt.), Austl.
111/E3 **Artigas,** Uru.
52/A2 **Artois** (reg.), Fr.
52/B2 **Artois, Collines de l'** (hills), Fr.
110/F7 **Artur Nogueira,** Braz.
75/C4 **Artux,** China
74/E2 **Artvin,** Turk.
87/H5 **Aru** (isls.), Indo.
101/A2 **Arua,** Ugan.
117/H5 **Aruba** (isl.), Neth.
110/B3 **Arujá,** Braz.
47/F5 **Arun** (riv.), Eng,UK
85/F2 **Arunachal Pradesh** (state), India
47/F5 **Arundel,** Eng,UK
84/C6 **Aruppukkottai,** India
87/F3 **Arus** (cape), Indo.
101/C3 **Arusha,** Tanz.
101/C4 **Arusha** (prov.), Tanz.
93/L6 **Arutua** (atoll), FrPol.
97/L7 **Aruwimi** (riv.), Zaire
76/E2 **Arvayheer,** Mong.
42/F2 **Arvidsjaur,** Swe.
42/E4 **Arvika,** Swe.
124/C4 **Arvin,** Ca,US
126/B2 **Arvon** (peak), Mi,US
60/A4 **Aryānah** (gov.), Tun.
75/A3 **Arys',** Kaz.
56/B3 **Arz** (riv.), Fr.
65/J5 **Arzamas,** Rus.
51/G4 **Arzen,** Ger.
53/F3 **Arzfeld,** Ger.
58/A1 **Arzúa,** Sp.
53/E1 **As,** Belg.
57/K1 **Aš,** Czh.
42/D4 **Ås,** Nor.
72/E2 **Asadābād,** Iran
98/D5 **Asagny Nat'l Park,** IvC.
86/A3 **Asahan** (riv.), Indo.
78/C3 **Asahi** (riv.), Japan
79/G2 **Asahi-Bandai Nat'l Park,** Japan
77/N3 **Asahi-dake** (mtn.), Japan
77/N3 **Asahikawa,** Japan
79/H7 **Asaka,** Japan
79/M9 **Asake** (riv.), Japan
97/P5 **Āsalē,** Erit.
79/F2 **Asama-yama** (mtn.), Japan
84/E3 **Asansol,** India
96/J3 **Asawanwah** (well), Libya
65/P4 **Asbest,** Rus.
102/C3 **Asbestos** (mts.), SAfr.
131/F5 **Asbury Park,** NJ,US
116/D4 **Ascención** (bay), Mex.
38/J6 **Ascension** (isl.), StH.
51/E5 **Ascheberg,** Ger.
48/F3 **Aschersleben,** Ger.
60/A1 **Asco** (riv.), Fr.
60/C1 **Ascoli Piceno,** It.
60/D2 **Ascoli Satriano,** It.
47/F4 **Ascot,** Eng,UK
97/P5 **Āseb,** Erit.
97/N6 **Āsela,** Eth.
63/G4 **Asenovgrad,** Bul.
76/G2 **Asgat,** Mong.
47/G4 **Ash,** Eng,UK
47/F4 **Ashampstead,** Eng,UK
99/E5 **Ashanti** (reg.), Gha.
99/E5 **Ashanti** (uplands), Gha.
45/G5 **Ashbourne,** Eng,UK
89/H7 **Ashburton,** NZ
46/C5 **Ashburton,** Eng,UK
47/E1 **Ashby** (can.), Eng,UK
45/G6 **Ashby-de-la-Zouch,** Eng,UK
46/D3 **Ashchurch,** Eng,UK
122/C3 **Ashcroft,** BC,Can
129/J3 **Asheboro,** NC,US
123/J3 **Ashern,** Mb,Can
129/H3 **Asheville,** NC,US
123/M2 **Asheweig** (riv.), On,Can
47/F1 **Ashfordby,** Eng,UK
127/Q8 **Ashgrove,** On,Can
45/G1 **Ashington,** Eng,UK
79/L10 **Ashiya,** Japan
78/C4 **Ashizuri-misaki** (cape), Japan
73/G1 **Ashkhabad** (cap.), Trkm.
125/H3 **Ashland,** Ks,US
124/D4 **Ashland,** Ky,US
126/D3 **Ashland,** Oh,US
122/C5 **Ashland,** Or,US
126/B2 **Ashland,** Wi,US
123/J4 **Ashley,** ND,US
89/B2 **Ashmore and Cartier Is.** (terr.), Austl.
74/L4 **Ash Shamāl** (gov.), Leb.
72/D2 **Ash Shāmīyah,** Iraq
73/G3 **Ash Shāriqah,** UAE
74/E3 **Ash Sharqāt,** Iraq
74/H6 **Ash Sharqīyah** (gov.), Egypt
42/D3 **Ashta,** India
126/D3 **Ashtabula,** Oh,US
122/F4 **Ashton,** Id,US
45/F5 **Ashton-in-Makerfield,** Eng,UK
45/F5 **Ashton-under-Lyne,** Eng,UK
126/B2 **Ashwaubenon,** Wi,US
47/F2 **Ashwell,** Eng,UK
71/* **Asia**
60/A2 **Asinara** (gulf), It.
60/A2 **Asinara** (isl.), It.
68/J4 **Asino,** Rus.
72/D5 **'Asīr** (mts.), SAr., Yemen
100/D5 **Asis, Ras** (cape), Sudan
74/E2 **Aşkale,** Turk.
45/E3 **Askam in Furness,** Eng,UK
42/D4 **Asker,** Nor.
45/G4 **Askern,** Eng,UK
42/D4 **Askim,** Nor.
61/G2 **Áskion** (peak), Gre.
42/P6 **Askja** (crater), Ice.
97/N4 **Asmara** (cap.), Erit.
52/B6 **Asnières-sur-Seine,** Fr.
78/B4 **Aso Nat'l Park,** Japan
97/M5 **Āsosa,** Eth.
78/B4 **Aso-san** (mtn.), Japan
100/D4 **Asoteriba, Jabal** (peak), Sudan
45/E2 **Aspatria,** Eng,UK
59/E3 **Aspe,** Sp.
124/F3 **Aspen,** Co,US
131/J7 **Aspen Hill,** Md,US
128/C3 **Aspermont,** Tx,US
59/F1 **Aspin, Col d'** (pass), Fr.
61/H3 **Asprópirgos,** Gre.
122/G2 **Asquith,** Sk,Can
98/C2 **'Assâba, Massif de l'** (reg.), Mrta.
74/D3 **As Sabkhah,** Syria
74/K6 **Aş Şāfī,** Jor.
72/E3 **As Sālimīyah,** Kuw.
72/E4 **As Sālimīyah,** SAr.
97/L1 **As Sallūm,** Egypt
74/K5 **As Salţ,** Jor.
85/F2 **Assam** (state), India
72/E2 **As Samāwah,** Iraq
74/H6 **As Santah,** Egypt
74/K5 **Aş Şarīḩ,** Jor.
52/D2 **Asse,** Belg.
60/A3 **Assemini,** It.
50/D2 **Assen,** Neth.
52/C1 **Assenede,** Belg.
96/J1 **As Sidr,** Libya
74/H6 **As Sinbillāwayn,** Egypt
123/G3 **Assiniboia,** Sk,Can
122/E3 **Assiniboine** (peak), BC,Can
123/J3 **Assiniboine** (riv.), Mb,Can
126/F1 **Assinika** (lake), Qu,Can
110/B2 **Assis,** Braz.
59/G1 **Assou** (riv.), Fr.
97/M6 **As Sudd** (reg.), Sudan
72/E1 **As Sulaymānīyah,** Iraq
72/E3 **Aş Şummān** (mts.), SAr.
74/L5 **As Suwaydā',** Syria
74/L5 **As Suwaydā'** (dist.), Syria
72/D2 **Aş Şuwayrah,** Iraq
100/C2 **As Suways** (gov.), Egypt
100/C2 **As Suways** (Suez), Egypt
50/C6 **Asten,** Neth.
57/H4 **Asti,** It.
110/L6 **Astolfo Dutra,** Braz.
47/E2 **Aston,** Eng,UK
46/D2 **Aston on Clun,** Eng,UK
110/B2 **Astorga,** Braz.
122/C4 **Astoria,** Or,US
67/J3 **Astrakhan',** Rus.
67/H3 **Astrakhan Obl.,** Rus.
58/B1 **Asturias** (aut. comm.), Sp.
47/E2 **Astwood Bank,** Eng,UK
79/L10 **Asuka,** Japan
79/N9 **Asuke,** Japan
92/D3 **Asuncion** (isl.), NMar.
111/E2 **Asunción** (cap.), Par.
116/B4 **Asunción Ixtaltepec,** Mex.
101/B2 **Aswa** (riv.), Ugan.
100/C3 **Aswān,** Egypt
100/C4 **Aswān** (gov.), Egypt
100/C4 **Aswan High** (dam), Egypt
100/B3 **Asyūt,** Egypt
100/B3 **Asyūt** (gov.), Egypt
100/C2 **Asyūţī, Wādī al** (dry riv.), Egypt
111/C2 **Atacama** (des.), Chile
111/C1 **Atacama, Puna de** (plat.), Arg.
99/F4 **Atacora** (range), Ben.
93/H5 **Atafu** (atoll), Tok.
99/F5 **Atakpamé,** Togo
79/F3 **Atami,** Japan
98/B1 **Atar,** Mrta.
58/D4 **Atarfe,** Sp.
84/D2 **Atarra,** India
76/D3 **Atas Bogd** (peak), Mong.
124/B4 **Atascadero,** Ca,US
74/D3 **Atatürk** (res.), Turk.
97/M4 **Atbara,** Sudan
97/M4 **Atbara** (Atbarah) (riv.), Eth., Sudan
75/A1 **Atbasar,** Kaz.
125/K5 **Atchafalaya** (bay), La,US
129/F4 **Atchafalaya** (riv.), La,US
125/J3 **Atchison,** Ks,US
99/E5 **Atebubu,** Gha.
42/G1 **Ateelva** (riv.), Nor.
117/P9 **Atengo** (riv.), Mex.
60/C1 **Aterno** (riv.), It.
52/C2 **Ath,** Belg.
122/E2 **Athabasca,** Ab,Can
118/E3 **Athabasca** (riv.), Ab,Can
118/F3 **Athabasca** (lake), Ab, Sk,Can
123/H2 **Athapapuskow** (lake), Mb,Can
96/K1 **Athār Ţulmaythah** (Ptolemais) (ruins), Libya
129/G3 **Athens,** Al,US
129/H3 **Athens,** Ga,US
126/D4 **Athens,** Oh,US
129/G3 **Athens,** Tn,US
128/E3 **Athens,** Tx,US
61/L7 **Athens** (Athínai) (cap.), Gre.
47/E1 **Atherstone,** Eng,UK
45/F4 **Atherton,** Eng,UK
43/B4 **Athlone,** Ire.
61/J2 **Áthos** (peak), Gre.
96/J5 **Ati,** Chad
110/G8 **Atibaia,** Braz.
110/G7 **Atibaia** (riv.), Braz.
126/B1 **Atikokan,** On,Can
93/K7 **Atiu** (isl.), CookIs.
130/C5 **Atka** (isl.), Ak,US
67/H2 **Atkarsk,** Rus.
130/M2 **Atkinson** (pt.), NW,Can
129/G3 **Atlanta** (cap.), Ga,US
128/E3 **Atlanta,** Tx,US
38/G3 **Atlantic** (ocean)
123/K5 **Atlantic,** Ia,US
131/G5 **Atlantic Beach,** NY,US
99/F5 **Atlantique** (prov.), Ben.
96/E2 **Atlas** (mts.), Afr.
132/K10 **Atlas** (peak), Ca,US
96/E1 **Atlas Saharien** (mts.), Alg., Mor.
130/M4 **Atlin** (lake), BC,Can
116/B4 **Atlixco,** Mex.
129/G4 **Atmore,** Al,US
96/B3 **Atoui** (dry riv.), Mrta.
73/G1 **Atrak** (riv.), Iran
108/C2 **Atrato** (riv.), Col.
79/H7 **Atsugi,** Japan
79/N10 **Atsumi,** Japan
79/N10 **Atsumi** (pen.), Japan
74/K6 **Aţ Ţafīlah,** Jor.
72/D4 **Aţ Ţā'if,** SAr.
74/L5 **At Tall,** Syria
129/G3 **Attalla,** Al,US
119/H3 **Attawapiskat** (riv.), On,Can
51/E6 **Attendorn,** Ger.
57/K3 **Attersee** (lake), Aus.
52/C5 **Attichy,** Fr.
47/E2 **Attleborough,** Eng,UK
47/H2 **Attleborough,** Eng,UK
130/A5 **Attu** (isl.), Ak,US
100/C2 **Aţ Ţūr,** Egypt
74/K6 **Aţ Ţūr,** WBnk.
72/D6 **At Turbah,** Yem.
112/D2 **Atuel** (riv.), Arg.
42/F4 **Åtvidaberg,** Swe.
124/B3 **Atwater,** Ca,US
125/G3 **Atwood,** Ks,US
116/E4 **Auas,** Hon.
53/E4 **Aubange,** Belg.
52/D6 **Aube** (dept.), Fr.
56/F2 **Aube** (riv.), Fr.
56/F4 **Aubenas,** Fr.
52/C6 **Aubetin** (riv.), Fr.
52/A5 **Aubette** (riv.), Fr.
56/E4 **Aubin,** Fr.
56/E4 **Aubrac** (mts.), Fr.
129/G3 **Auburn,** Al,US
124/B3 **Auburn,** Ca,US
126/C3 **Auburn,** In,US
127/G2 **Auburn,** Me,US
125/J2 **Auburn,** Ne,US
126/E3 **Auburn,** NY,US
132/C3 **Auburn,** Wa,US
132/F6 **Auburn Hills,** Mi,US
112/C3 **Aucá Mahuida** (peak), Arg.
56/D5 **Auch,** Fr.
52/B3 **Auchel,** Fr.
43/D2 **Auchenblae,** Sc,UK
44/E2 **Auchencairn,** Sc,UK
43/C3 **Auchinleck,** Sc,UK
89/H6 **Auckland,** NZ
39/S8 **Auckland** (isls.), NZ
56/E5 **Aude** (riv.), Fr.
52/D2 **Auderghem,** Belg.
56/A3 **Audierne** (bay), Fr.
45/F6 **Audlem,** Eng,UK
45/F5 **Audley,** Eng,UK
97/P6 **Audo** (range), Eth.
53/E5 **Audun-le-Tiche,** Fr.
57/K1 **Aue,** Ger.
51/E2 **Aue** (riv.), Ger.
51/F3 **Aue** (riv.), Ger.
57/K1 **Auerbach,** Ger.
57/J2 **Auerbach in der Oberpfalz,** Ger.
44/A3 **Augher,** NI,UK
44/B3 **Aughnacloy,** NI,UK
102/C3 **Augrabies Falls Nat'l Park,** SAfr.
102/C3 **Augrabiesvalle** (falls), SAfr.
55/G1 **Augsburg,** Ger.
102/A2 **Augub** (peak), Namb.
60/D4 **Augusta,** It.
60/D4 **Augusta** (gulf), It.
129/H3 **Augusta,** Ga,US
127/G2 **Augusta** (cap.), Me,US
51/F5 **Augustdorf,** Ger.
49/M2 **Augustów,** Pol.
83/B3 **Auk Bok** (isl.), Burma
55/M9 **Aulencia** (riv.), Sp.
56/B2 **Aulne** (riv.), Fr.
52/C3 **Aulnoye-Aymeries,** Fr.
52/B5 **Aunette** (riv.), Fr.
102/B2 **Auob** (dry riv.), Namb.
102/C2 **Auobrivier** (dry riv.), SAfr.
92/G4 **Aur** (atoll), Mrsh.
84/C4 **Aurangābād,** India
84/D3 **Aurangābād,** India
56/B3 **Auray,** Fr.
56/D5 **Aureilhan,** Fr.
51/E2 **Aurich,** Ger.
110/B2 **Auriflama,** Braz.
56/E4 **Aurillac,** Fr.
125/F3 **Aurora,** Co,US
132/P16 **Aurora,** Il,US
125/J3 **Aurora,** Mo,US
125/H2 **Aurora,** Ne,US
90/A1 **Aurukun Abor. Land,** Austl.
126/C2 **Au Sable** (riv.), Mi,US
49/K3 **Auschwitz** (Oświęcim), Pol.
56/E5 **Aussillon,** Fr.
42/C4 **Aust-Agder** (co.), Nor.
118/G2 **Austin** (isl.), NW,Can
123/K5 **Austin,** Mn,US
124/C3 **Austin,** Nv,US
128/D4 **Austin** (cap.), Tx,US
89/* **Australia**
91/C3 **Australian Alps** (mts.), Austl.
91/D3 **Australian Cap. Terr.,** Austl.
57/L3 **Austria**
42/P7 **Austurhorn** (pt.), Ice.
52/B3 **Authie** (riv.), Fr.
117/P10 **Autlán de Navarro,** Mex.
52/B5 **Automne** (riv.), Fr.
56/F3 **Autun,** Fr.
56/E4 **Auvergne** (reg.), Fr.
52/B5 **Auvers-sur-Oise,** Fr.
56/D4 **Auvézère** (riv.), Fr.
56/E3 **Auxerre,** Fr.
54/B3 **Auxonne,** Fr.
126/D2 **Aux Sables** (riv.), On,Can
119/K2 **Auyuittuq Nat'l Park,** NW,Can
108/D6 **Auzangate** (peak), Peru
56/E3 **Avallon,** Fr.
127/K2 **Avalon** (pen.), Nf,Can
110/B2 **Avaré,** Braz.
47/E4 **Avebury,** Eng,UK
58/A2 **Aveiro,** Port.
58/A2 **Aveiro** (dist.), Port.
52/C2 **Avelgem,** Belg.
112/F2 **Avellaneda,** Arg.
60/D2 **Avellino,** It.
52/A4 **Avelon** (riv.), Fr.
124/B3 **Avenal,** Ca,US
52/A58 **Aver** (riv.), Fr.
60/D2 **Aversa,** It.
117/J4 **Aves** (isl.), Ven.
42/F3 **Avesta,** Swe.
56/D4 **Aveyron** (riv.), Fr.
60/C1 **Avezzano,** It.
43/D2 **Aviemore,** Sc,UK
56/F5 **Avignon,** Fr.
58/C2 **Ávila de los Caballeros,** Sp.
58/C1 **Avilés,** Sp.
52/B3 **Avion,** Fr.
58/B3 **Avis,** Port.
44/B6 **Avoca,** Ire.
44/B6 **Avoca** (riv.), Ire.
60/D4 **Avola,** It.
56/E2 **Avon,** Fr.
46/D4 **Avon** (co.), Eng,UK
46/C6 **Avon** (riv.), Eng,UK
46/D4 **Avon** (riv.), Eng,UK
47/E2 **Avon** (riv.), Eng,UK
47/E5 **Avon** (riv.), Eng,UK
44/B6 **Avonbeg** (riv.), Ire.
123/G3 **Avonlea,** Sk,Can
44/B6 **Avonmore** (riv.), Ire.
46/D4 **Avonmouth,** Eng,UK
56/C2 **Avranches,** Fr.
52/B4 **Avre** (riv.), Fr.
56/C3 **Avrillé,** Fr.
79/L10 **Awaji,** Japan
78/D3 **Awaji** (isl.), Japan
74/L5 **A'waj, Nahr al** (riv.), Syria
53/E2 **Awans,** Belg.
97/N6 **Āwasa,** Eth.
97/P5 **Āwash Wenz** (riv.), Eth.
102/A2 **Awasibberge** (peak), Namb.
96/H2 **Awbārī,** Libya
43/C2 **Awe, Loch** (lake), Sc,UK
97/K2 **Awjilah,** Libya
42/P6 **Axarfjördhur** (bay), Ice.
46/D4 **Axbridge,** Eng,UK
46/D4 **Axe** (riv.), Eng,UK
46/D5 **Axe** (riv.), Eng,UK
50/A6 **Axel,** Neth.
119/S7 **Axel Heiberg** (isl.), NW,Can
99/E5 **Axim,** Gha.
61/H2 **Axios** (riv.), Gre.
46/D5 **Axminster,** Eng,UK
65/N5 **Ay** (riv.), Rus.
78/D3 **Ayabe,** Japan
112/F3 **Ayacucho,** Arg.
108/D6 **Ayacucho,** Peru
75/D2 **Ayaguz,** Kaz.
75/D2 **Ayaguz** (riv.), Kaz.
75/E4 **Ayakkum** (lake), China
79/M10 **Ayama,** Japan
98/E5 **Ayamé, Barrage d'** (dam), IvC.
58/B4 **Ayamonte,** Sp.
74/C2 **Ayancık,** Turk.
117/F6 **Ayapel,** Col.
79/H7 **Ayase,** Japan
108/D6 **Ayaviri,** Peru
73/J1 **Āybak,** Afg.
74/N8 **'Aybāl, Jabal** (Har Eval) (mtn.), WBnk.
74/A3 **Aydın,** Turk.
74/C3 **Aydıncık,** Turk.
92/C7 **Ayers Rock** (Uluru) (peak), Austl.
61/J3 **Áyios Evstrátios** (isl.), Gre.
61/J5 **Áyios Ioánnis, Ákra** (cape), Gre.
61/J5 **Áyios Nikólaos,** Gre.
47/F3 **Aylesbury,** Eng,UK
47/G4 **Aylesford,** Eng,UK
47/H4 **Aylesham,** Eng,UK
118/F2 **Aylmer** (lake), NW,Can
47/H1 **Aylsham,** Eng,UK
74/D3 **'Ayn al 'Arab,** Syria
97/K2 **'Ayn Ath Tha'lab,** Libya
72/D1 **'Ayn, Ra's al,** Syria
97/K3 **'Ayn Zuwayyah** (well), Libya
69/S3 **Ayon** (isl.), Rus.
59/E3 **Ayora,** Sp.
96/D3 **'Ayoûn 'Abd el Mâlek** (well), Mrta.
90/B2 **Ayr,** Austl.
43/C3 **Ayr,** Sc,UK
43/C3 **Ayr** (riv.), Sc,UK
44/D3 **Ayre, Point of** (pt.), Eng,UK
45/H3 **Ayton,** Eng,UK
63/H4 **Aytos,** Bul.
116/B4 **Ayutla,** Mex.
83/C3 **Ayutthaya** (ruins), Thai.
74/A2 **Ayvacık,** Turk.
74/A2 **Ayvalık,** Turk.
53/E3 **Aywaille,** Belg.
59/F3 **Azahar** (coast), Sp.
79/M9 **Azaj,** Japan
122/C5 **Azalea,** Or,US
84/D2 **Azamgarh,** India
108/D6 **Azángaro,** Peru
96/G2 **Azao** (peak), Alg.
99/E2 **Azaouād** (reg.), Mali
99/G2 **Azaouak, Vallée de l'** (wadi), Mali, Niger
74/D3 **A'zāz,** Syria
67/H4 **Azerbaijan**
97/N5 **Āzezo,** Eth.
75/E1 **Azhu-Tayga, Gora** (peak), Rus.
108/C4 **Azogues,** Ecu.
59/R12 **Azores** (aut. reg.), Port.
59/R12 **Azores** (isls.), Port.
66/F3 **Azov,** Rus.
66/E3 **Azov** (sea), Rus., Ukr.
58/D1 **Azpeitia,** Sp.
124/F3 **Aztec,** NM,US
124/E3 **Aztec Ruins Nat'l Mon.,** NM,US
117/G4 **Azua,** DRep.
58/C3 **Azuaga,** Sp.
79/M9 **Azuchi,** Japan
117/F6 **Azuero** (pen.), Pan.
112/F3 **Azul,** Arg.
79/G2 **Azuma-san** (mtn.), Japan
79/F2 **Azumaya-san** (mtn.), Japan
57/G5 **Azur, Côte d'** (coast), Fr.
131/C2 **Azusa,** Ca,US
74/L5 **Az Zabadānī,** Syria
100/B2 **Az Zagāzīg,** Egypt
57/K4 **Azzano Decimo,** It.
74/L5 **Az Zarqā',** Jor.
96/H1 **Az Zāwiyah,** Libya

B

93/Y18 **Ba,** Fiji
83/E3 **Ba** (riv.), Viet.
93/U11 **Baaba** (isl.), NCal.
74/N9 **Ba'al Hazor** (Tall 'Āşūr) (mtn.), WBnk.
55/E3 **Baar,** Swi.
50/C4 **Baarn,** Neth.
76/D2 **Baatsagaan,** Mong.
73/J2 **Baba** (mts.), Afg.
63/F4 **Baba** (peak), Bul.
66/D4 **Baba Burnu** (pt.), Turk.
63/J3 **Babadag,** Rom.
63/H5 **Babaeski,** Turk.
108/C4 **Babahoyo,** Ecu.
87/G5 **Babar** (isl.), Indo.
101/B4 **Babati,** Tanz.
46/C5 **Babbacombe** (bay), Eng,UK
123/L4 **Babbitt,** Mn,US
124/C3 **Babbitt,** Nv,US
97/P5 **Bab el Mandeb** (str.), Afr., Asia
92/C4 **Babelthuap** (isl.), Palau
66/A2 **Babia Gora** (peak), Pol.
85/H3 **Babian** (riv.), China
122/B2 **Babine** (lake), BC,Can
118/D3 **Babine** (riv.), BC,Can
72/F1 **Bābol,** Iran
82/D4 **Babuyan** (isls.), Phil.
72/D2 **Babylon** (ruins), Iraq
131/G5 **Babylon,** NY,US
109/J4 **Bacabal,** Braz.
109/H4 **Bacajá** (riv.), Braz.
87/G4 **Bacan** (isl.), Indo.
63/H2 **Bacău,** Rom.
63/H2 **Bacău** (co.), Rom.
83/D1 **Bac Can,** Viet.
83/D1 **Bac Giang,** Viet.
118/G2 **Back** (riv.), NW,Can
126/E2 **Back** (lake), On,Can
131/K7 **Back** (riv.), Md,US
62/D3 **Bačka** (reg.), Yugo.
62/D3 **Bačka Palanka,** Yugo.
62/D3 **Bačka Topola,** Yugo.
57/H2 **Backnang,** Ger.
46/D4 **Backwell,** Eng,UK
83/D4 **Bac Lieu,** Viet.
83/D1 **Bac Ninh,** Viet.
82/D5 **Bacolod,** Phil.
83/D1 **Bac Quang,** Viet.
62/D2 **Bácsalmás,** Hun.
62/D2 **Bács-Kiskun** (co.), Hun.
47/H1 **Bacton,** Eng,UK
45/F4 **Bacup,** Eng,UK
123/H4 **Bad** (riv.), SD,US
84/C5 **Badagara,** India
76/E3 **Badain Jaran** (des.), China
58/B3 **Badajoz,** Sp.
59/L7 **Badalona,** Sp.
126/D3 **Bad Axe,** Mi,US
51/F6 **Bad Berleburg,** Ger.
53/G2 **Bad Breisig,** Ger.
48/F1 **Bad Doberan,** Ger.
51/G5 **Bad Driburg,** Ger.
57/M2 **Baden,** Aus.
57/H2 **Baden-Baden,** Ger.
55/E1 **Baden-Württemberg** (state), Ger.
51/F4 **Bad Essen,** Ger.
49/H2 **Bad Freienwalde,** Ger.
51/H5 **Bad Gandersheim,** Ger.
57/K3 **Bad Goisern,** Aus.
51/H5 **Bad Harzburg,** Ger.
48/E3 **Bad Hersfeld,** Ger.
57/H1 **Bad Homburg vor der Höhe,** Ger.
53/G2 **Bad Honnef,** Ger.
73/J4 **Badīn,** Pak.
57/K3 **Bad Ischl,** Aus.
57/G2 **Bad Kreuznach,** Ger.
54/D2 **Bad Krozingen,** Ger.
123/H4 **Badlands** (uplands), ND,US
123/H5 **Badlands** (hills), SD,US
123/H5 **Badlands Nat'l Park,** SD,US
51/H6 **Bad Langensalza,** Ger.
51/H5 **Bad Lauterberg,** Ger.
51/F5 **Bad Lippspringe,** Ger.
57/H2 **Bad Mergentheim,** Ger.
51/G4 **Bad Munder am Deister,** Ger.
53/F2 **Bad Münstereifel,** Ger.
57/H1 **Bad Nauheim,** Ger.
51/G4 **Bad Nenndorf,** Ger.
53/G2 **Bad Neuenahr-Ahrweiler,** Ger.
57/J1 **Bad Neustadt an der Saale,** Ger.
51/F4 **Bad Oeynhausen,** Ger.
48/F2 **Bad Oldesloe,** Ger.
51/G5 **Bad Pyrmont,** Ger.
73/J3 **Bādrāh,** Pak.
48/G5 **Bad Reichenhall,** Ger.
51/H5 **Bad Sachsa,** Ger.
51/H4 **Bad Salzdetfurth,** Ger.
51/F4 **Bad Salzuflen,** Ger.
48/F3 **Bad Salzungen,** Ger.
51/F5 **Bad Sassendorf,** Ger.
48/F2 **Bad Schwartau,** Ger.
48/F2 **Bad Segeberg,** Ger.
51/G6 **Bad Sooden-Allendorf,** Ger.
55/H2 **Bad Tölz,** Ger.
84/D6 **Badulla,** SrL.
57/M3 **Bad Vöslau,** Aus.
51/G6 **Bad Wildungen,** Ger.
51/E2 **Bad Zwischenahn,** Ger.
58/C4 **Baena,** Sp.
110/J6 **Baependi,** Braz.
53/F2 **Baesweiler,** Ger.
58/D4 **Baeza,** Sp.
99/H5 **Bafang,** Camr.
119/H1 **Baffin** (isl.), NW,Can
119/K1 **Baffin** (bay), Can.,Grld.
128/D5 **Baffin** (bay), Tx,US
96/H7 **Bafia,** Camr.
98/D4 **Bafing** (riv.), Gui., IvC.
98/C3 **Bafing** (riv.), Gui., Mali
99/H5 **Bafoussam,** Camr.
74/C2 **Bafra,** Turk.
98/B2 **Bafrechié** (well), Mrta.
97/L7 **Bafwasende,** Zaire
81/B3 **Bag** (salt lake), China
96/H5 **Baga,** Nga.
82/E6 **Baganga,** Phil.
99/G3 **Bagaroua,** Niger
75/E3 **Bagda** (mts.), China
113/G1 **Bagé,** Braz.
82/D4 **Baggao,** Phil.
46/B4 **Baggy** (pt.), Eng,UK
72/D2 **Baghdād** (Baghdād) (cap.), Iraq
60/C3 **Bagheria,** It.
73/J1 **Baghlān,** Afg.
46/C3 **Baglan,** Wal,UK
123/K4 **Bagley,** Mn,US
56/D5 **Bagnères-de-Bigorre,** Fr.
56/F4 **Bagnols-sur-Cèze,** Fr.
82/D5 **Bago,** Phil.
98/D3 **Bagoe** (riv.), IvC., Mali
83/B2 **Bago** (Pegu) (div.), Burma
82/D4 **Baguio,** Phil.
96/J5 **Baguirmi** (reg.), Chad
99/H2 **Bagzane** (peak), Niger
117/F2 **Bahamas**
84/E3 **Baharampur,** India
75/B6 **Bahāwalnagar,** Pak.
73/K3 **Bahāwalpur,** Pak.
101/B4 **Bahi,** Tanz.
116/D4 **Bahía** (isls.), Hon.
117/M8 **Bahía Asunción,** Mex.
112/E3 **Bahía Blanca,** Arg.
117/M8 **Bahía de los Angeles,** Mex.
84/D3 **Bahía Honda,** Cuba
117/M8 **Bahía Kino,** Mex.
117/M8 **Bahía Tortugas,** Mex.
97/N5 **Bahir Dar,** Eth.
73/G4 **Bahlah,** Oman
84/D2 **Bahraich,** India
72/F3 **Bahrain**
72/F3 **Bahrain** (gulf), Bahr., SAr.
72/D2 **Baḩr al Milḩ** (lake), Iraq
97/K6 **Bahr Aouk** (riv.), CAfr., Chad
100/B2 **Baḩrīyah, Al Wāḩāt al** (oasis), Egypt
81/C2 **Bai** (riv.), China
81/C4 **Bai** (riv.), China
63/F2 **Baia Mare,** Rom.
63/F2 **Baia Sprie,** Rom.
96/J6 **Baïbokoum,** Chad
77/J2 **Baicheng,** China
75/D3 **Baicheng,** China
63/G3 **Băicoi,** Rom.
97/P7 **Baidoa,** Som.
81/D5 **Baidong** (lake), China
127/G1 **Baie-Comeau,** Qu,Can
119/J3 **Baie-du-Poste,** Qu,Can
127/G2 **Baie-Saint-Paul,** Qu,Can
127/K1 **Baie Verte,** Nf,Can
81/G7 **Baigou** (riv.), China
81/C3 **Baihua Shan** (mtn.), China
72/D2 **Ba'ījī,** Iraq
69/L4 **Baikal** (Baykal) (lake), Rus.
45/G4 **Baildon,** Eng,UK
58/D3 **Bailén,** Sp.
63/F3 **Băileşti,** Rom.
52/B2 **Bailleul,** Fr.
76/E5 **Bailong** (riv.), China
81/C4 **Bailu** (riv.), China
45/H5 **Bain** (riv.), Eng,UK
129/G4 **Bainbridge,** Ga,US
132/B2 **Bainbridge** (isl.), Wa,US
75/D4 **Bairab** (lake), China
130/F3 **Baird** (inlet), Ak,US
128/D3 **Baird,** Tx,US
92/G4 **Bairiki** (cap.), Kiri.
91/C3 **Bairnsdale,** Austl.
74/L6 **Bā'ir, Wādī** (riv.), Jor.
56/D5 **Baïse** (riv.), Fr.
84/D2 **Baitadi,** Nepal
83/D2 **Bai Thuong,** Viet.
59/P10 **Baixa de Banheira,** Port.
110/D1 **Baixo Guandu,** Braz.
76/E4 **Baiyin,** China
81/B3 **Baiyu** (mts.), China
82/C2 **Baiyun,** China
113/J7 **Baja** (pt.), Chile
62/D2 **Baja,** Hun.
117/L8 **Baja California** (pen.), Mex.
117/L7 **Baja California Norte** (state), Mex.
117/M8 **Baja California Sur** (state), Mex.
60/A4 **Bājah,** Tun.
60/A4 **Bājah** (gov.), Tun.
87/F5 **Bajawa,** Indo.
62/D4 **Bajina Bašta,** Yugo.
91/E1 **Bajmba** (peak), Austl.
62/D3 **Bajmok,** Yugo.
117/F4 **Bajo Nuero** (isl.), Col.
75/C2 **Bakanas** (riv.), Kaz.
87/E3 **Bakayan** (peak), Indo.
98/B3 **Bakel,** Sen.
118/G2 **Baker** (lake), NW,Can
113/J6 **Baker** (riv.), Chile
93/H4 **Baker** (isl.), PacUS
124/C4 **Baker,** Ca,US
123/G4 **Baker,** Mt,US
124/D3 **Baker,** Nv,US
122/D4 **Baker,** Or,US
122/C3 **Baker** (peak), Wa,US
124/C4 **Bakersfield,** Ca,US
45/G5 **Bakewell,** Eng,UK
66/E3 **Bakhchisaray,** Ukr.
66/E2 **Bakhmach,** Ukr.
72/E2 **Bākhtarān,** Iran
72/F3 **Bakhtegān** (lake), Iran
42/P6 **Bakkaflói** (bay), Ice.
104/B1 **Bakoumba,** Gabon
98/C4 **Bakoye** (riv.), Gui., Mali
67/J4 **Baku** (cap.), Azer.
105/S **Bakutis** (coast), Ant.
108/E6 **Bala** (mts.), Bol.
44/E6 **Bala,** Wal,UK
87/E2 **Balabac** (str.), Malay., Phil.
82/C6 **Balabac,** Phil.
82/C6 **Balabac** (isl.), Phil.
74/L5 **Ba'labakk,** Leb.
93/U12 **Balabio** (isl.), NCal.
72/D2 **Balad,** Iraq
84/D3 **Bālāghāt,** India
60/A1 **Balagne** (range), Fr.
59/F2 **Balaguer,** Sp.
56/C5 **Balaïtous** (mtn.), Fr.
104/F3 **Balaka,** Malw.
67/H1 **Balakovo,** Rus.
73/H1 **Bālā Morghab,** Afg.
63/G2 **Bălan,** Rom.
116/C4 **Balancán,** Mex.
82/D5 **Balanga,** Phil.
83/E3 **Ba Lang An** (cape), Viet.
84/D3 **Bālāngīr,** India
65/X9 **Balashikha,** Rus.
67/G2 **Balashov,** Rus.
62/D1 **Balassagyarmat,** Hun.
62/C2 **Balaton** (lake), Hun.
62/C2 **Balatonfüred,** Hun.
112/F3 **Balcarce,** Arg.
44/E2 **Balcary** (pt.), Sc,UK
63/J4 **Balchik,** Bul.
89/G7 **Balclutha,** NZ
47/F4 **Balcombe,** Eng,UK
128/D4 **Balcones Escarpment** (plat.), Tx,US
129/H2 **Bald** (peak), Va,US
47/F3 **Baldock,** Eng,UK
91/E1 **Bald Rock Nat'l Park,** Austl.
131/C2 **Baldwin Park,** Ca,US
123/H3 **Baldy** (peak), Mb,Can
59/F3 **Balearic** (Baleares) (isls.), Sp.
110/E1 **Baleia, Ponta da** (pt.), Braz.

Balei – Beloe

143
Belog – Bogo

77/K1 Belogorsk, Rus.
62/F4 Belogradchik, Bul.
110/D1 Belo Horizonte, Braz.
125/H3 Beloit, Ks,US
126/B3 Beloit, Wi,US
109/L5 Belo Jardim, Braz.
64/G2 Belomorsk, Rus.
104/C1 Belondo-Kundu, Zaire
66/F3 Belorechensk, Rus.
65/N5 Beloretsk, Rus.
62/E4 Beloševac, Yugo.
63/H4 Beloslav, Bul.
68/J4 Belovo, Rus.
64/H3 Beloye (lake), Rus.
45/G5 Belper, Eng,UK
45/G1 Belsay, Eng,UK
122/F4 Belt, Mt,US
50/D3 Belterwijde (lake), Neth.
47/H1 Belton, Eng,UK
128/D4 Belton, Tx,US
131/K7 Beltsville, Md,US
63/H2 Bel'tsy, Mol.
131/E5 Beltzville (lake), Pa,US
75/E2 Belukha, Gora (peak), Rus.
126/B3 Belvidere, Il,US
90/B3 Belyando (riv.), Austl.
68/G2 Belyy (isl.), Rus.
48/G2 Belzig, Ger.
49/M3 Bełżyce, Pol.
103/H7 Bemaraha (plat.), Madg.
103/H7 Bemarivo (riv.), Madg.
58/B1 Bembibre, Sp.
47/E5 Bembridge, Eng,UK
123/K4 Bemidji, Mn,US
50/C5 Bemmel, Neth.
45/H3 Bempton, Eng,UK
91/C3 Benalla, Austl.
58/C4 Benalmádena, Sp.
58/C2 Benavente, Sp.
128/D5 Benavides, Tx,US
44/B1 Benbane Head (pt.), NI,UK
91/D3 Ben Boyd Nat'l Park, Austl.
44/B3 Benburb, NI,UK
122/C4 Bend, Or,US
99/G5 Bendel (state), Nga.
130/F2 Bendeleben (mtn.), Ak,US
63/J2 Bendery, Mol.
91/C3 Bendigo, Austl.
74/M8 Bene Beraq, Isr.
119/L3 Benedict (mtn.), Nf,Can
44/D1 Beneraird (hill), Sc,UK
57/L2 Benešov, Czh.
60/D2 Benevento, It.
47/G3 Benfleet, Eng,UK
84/E4 Bengal (bay), Asia
81/D4 Bengbu, China
97/K1 Benghāzī, Libya
83/D3 Ben Giang, Viet.
86/B3 Bengkalis, Indo.
86/B3 Bengkalis (isl.), Indo.
86/C3 Bengkayang, Indo.
86/B4 Bengkulu, Indo.
123/G3 Bengough, Sk,Can
42/E4 Bengtsfors, Swe.
104/B3 Benguela, Ang.
101/A5 Bengweulu (lake), Zam.
108/E6 Beni (riv.), Bol.
101/A2 Beni, Zaire
96/E1 Beni Abbes, Alg.
59/F2 Benicarló, Sp.
132/K10 Benicia, Ca,US
59/E3 Benidorm, Sp.
59/E3 Benifayó, Sp.
96/D1 Beni Mellal, Mor.
99/F4 Benin
99/F5 Benin (bight), Ben., Nga.
99/G5 Benin City, Nga.
96/E1 Beni Ounif, Alg.
59/F3 Benisa, Sp.
112/B5 Benjamin (isl.), Chile
128/D3 Benjamin, Tx,US
108/D4 Benjamin Constant, Braz.
117/M7 Benjamín Hill, Mex.
125/G2 Benkelman, Ne,US
44/D5 Benllech, Wal,UK
43/C2 Ben Lomond (mtn.), Sc,UK
91/C4 Ben Lomond Nat'l Park, Austl.
43/D2 Ben Macdui (mtn.), Sc,UK
43/C2 Ben More (mtn.), Sc,UK
44/C1 Bennane Head (pt.), Sc,UK
69/R2 Bennett (isl.), Rus.
129/J3 Bennettsville, SC,US
43/C2 Ben Nevis (mtn.), Sc,UK
127/F3 Bennington, Vt,US
102/Q13 Benoni, SAfr.
103/J6 Be, Nosy (isl.), Madg.
96/H6 Bénoué Nat'l Park, Camr.
83/D2 Ben Quang, Viet.
132/Q16 Bensenville, Il,US
57/H2 Bensheim, Ger.
124/E5 Benson, Az,US
123/K4 Benson, Mn,US
45/F3 Bentham, Eng,UK
51/E4 Bentheim, Ger.
97/L6 Bentiu, Sudan
45/G4 Bentley, Eng,UK
110/B4 Bento Gonçalves, Braz.
128/E3 Benton, Ar,US
126/B4 Benton, Il,US
126/B4 Benton, Ky,US
86/B3 Bentong, Malay.
126/C3 Benton Harbor, Mi,US
128/E2 Bentonville, Ar,US
83/D4 Ben Tre, Viet.
99/G4 Benue (riv.), Nga.
99/G5 Benue (state), Nga.
62/D3 Beočin, Yugo.
62/E3 Beograd (Belgrade) (cap.), Yugo.
78/B4 Beppu, Japan
78/B4 Beppu (bay), Japan
96/E1 Beraber (well), Alg.
44/A2 Beragh, NI,UK
61/F2 Berat, Alb.
87/E4 Beratus (peak), Indo.
87/H4 Berau (bay), Indo.
87/E3 Berau (riv.), Indo.
97/Q5 Berbera, Som.
96/J7 Berberati, CAfr.
108/G2 Berbice (riv.), Guy.
52/D1 Berchem, Belg.
57/K3 Berchtesgaden, Ger.
57/K3 Berchtesgaden Nat'l Park, Ger.
52/A3 Berck, Fr.
66/D2 Berdichev, Ukr.
68/J4 Berdsk, Rus.
66/F3 Berdyansk, Ukr.
126/C4 Berea, Ky,US
66/B2 Beregovo, Ukr.
99/E5 Berekum, Gha.
100/C4 Berenice (ruins), Egypt
46/D5 Bere Regis, Eng,UK
127/H2 Beresford, NB,Can
123/J5 Beresford, SD,US
62/E2 Berettyo (riv.), Hun.
62/E2 Berettyóújfalu, Hun.
66/D1 Berezina (riv.), Bela.
65/N4 Berezniki, Rus.
102/B4 Berg (riv.), SAfr.
74/A2 Bergama, Turk.
57/H4 Bergamo, It.
50/B3 Bergen, Neth.
42/C3 Bergen, Nor.
51/G3 Bergen-Belsen, Ger.
131/F5 Bergenfield, NJ,US
50/B6 Bergen op Zoom, Neth.
56/D4 Bergerac, Fr.
50/C6 Bergeyk, Neth.
53/F2 Bergheim, Ger.
51/E6 Bergisch Gladbach, Ger.
51/E5 Bergkamen, Ger.
51/E6 Bergneustadt, Ger.
50/C2 Bergum, Neth.
50/D2 Bergumermeer (lake), Neth.
84/D4 Berhampur, India
86/C4 Berikat (cape), Indo.
69/S4 Bering (isl.), Rus.
130/E3 Bering (str.), Rus., Ak,US
53/E1 Beringen, Belg.
130/E2 Bering Land Bridge Nat'l Prsv., Ak,US
86/B4 Beritarikap (cape), Indo.
58/D4 Berja, Sp.
50/D4 Berkel (riv.), Ger.
50/B5 Berkel, Neth.
46/D3 Berkeley, Eng,UK
132/K11 Berkeley, Ca,US
131/F5 Berkeley Heights, NJ,US
47/F3 Berkhamsted, Eng,UK
132/F6 Berkley, Mi,US
105/W Berkner (isl.), Ant.
63/F4 Berkovitsa, Bul.
47/E4 Berkshire (co.), Eng,UK
47/E4 Berkshire Downs (uplands), Eng,UK
52/C1 Berlare, Belg.
50/C5 Berlicum, Neth.
49/G2 Berlin (cap.), Ger.
127/G2 Berlin, NH,US
105/V Berlioz (pt.), Ant.
107/C5 Bermejo (riv.), Arg.
111/D1 Bermejo, Bol.
58/D1 Bermeo, Sp.
115/L6 Bermuda (isl.), UK
54/D3 Bern (canton), Swi.
54/D4 Bern (cap.), Swi.
108/B5 Bernal, Peru
60/E2 Bernalda, It.
124/F4 Bernalillo, NM,US
118/D1 Bernard (riv.), NW,Can
113/J7 Bernardo O'Higgins Nat'l Park, Chile
131/G5 Bernardsville, NJ,US
56/D2 Bernay, Fr.
48/F3 Bernburg, Ger.
51/F2 Berne (riv.), Ger.
54/D5 Bernese Alps (range), Swi.
118/G1 Bernier (bay), NW,Can
55/G5 Bernina, Passo del (pass), Swi.
52/C3 Bernissart, Belg.
53/G4 Bernkastel-Kues, Ger.
103/H8 Beroroha, Madg.
57/L2 Beroun, Czh.
57/K2 Berounka (riv.), Czh.
62/F5 Berovo, Macd.
56/F5 Berre (lag.), Fr.
46/C1 Berriew, Wal,UK
117/F2 Berry (isls.), Bahm.
56/D3 Berry (hist. reg.), Fr.
132/K9 Berryessa (lake), Ca,US
132/K9 Berryessa (peak), Ca,US
46/C6 Berry Head (pt.), Wal,UK
128/E2 Berryville, Ar,US
96/H7 Bertoua, Camr.
113/J7 Bertrand (peak), Arg.
53/E4 Bertrix, Belg.
92/G5 Beru (atoll), Kiri.
86/D3 Beruit (isl.), Malay.
91/G5 Berwick, Austl.
127/H2 Berwick, NB,Can
43/D3 Berwick-upon-Tweed, Eng,UK
44/E6 Berwyn (mts.), Wal,UK
132/Q16 Berwyn, Il,US
131/E5 Berwyn-Devon, Pa,US
56/E4 Bès (riv.), Fr.
103/H7 Besalampy, Madg.
54/B3 Besançon, Fr.
87/E4 Besar (peak), Indo.
56/E3 Besbre (riv.), Fr.
68/F6 Beshahr, Iran
62/E3 Beška, Yugo.
49/K4 Beskids (mts.), Pol.
67/H4 Beslan, Rus.
62/F4 Besna Kobila (peak), Yugo.
123/G2 Besnard (lake), Sk,Can
45/G4 Bessacarr, Eng,UK
63/J2 Bessarabia (reg.), Mol.
44/B3 Bessbrook, NI,UK
129/G3 Bessemer, Al,US
126/B2 Bessemer, Mi,US
132/D2 Bessemer (mtn.), Wa,US
67/K3 Besshoky, Gora (peak), Kaz.
50/C6 Best, Neth.
51/F6 Bestwig, Ger.
58/A1 Betanzos, Sp.
74/N7 Beth Alpha Synagogue Nat'l Park, Isr.
125/J2 Bethany, Mo,US
44/D5 Bethesda, Wal,UK
131/J8 Bethesda, Md,US
102/E3 Bethlehem, SAfr.
131/E5 Bethlehem, Pa,US
74/K6 Bethlehem (Bayt Laḩm), WBnk.
131/G5 Bethpage, NY,US
123/G3 Bethune, Sk,Can
52/B2 Béthune, Fr.
52/A4 Béthune (riv.), Fr.
110/C1 Betim, Braz.
103/H8 Betioky, Madg.
75/A2 Betpak-Dala (des.), Kaz.
53/G6 Betschdorf, Fr.
74/K5 Bet She'an, Isr.
74/M9 Bet Shemesh, Isr.
127/G1 Betsiamites (riv.), Qu,Can
103/H7 Betsiboka (riv.), Madg.
97/J3 Bette (peak), Libya
53/F4 Bettembourg, Lux.
84/D2 Bettiah, India
84/C3 Betūl, India
50/C5 Betuwe (reg.), Neth.
44/E5 Betws-y-Coed, Wal,UK
53/G2 Betzdorf, Ger.
123/H4 Beulah, ND,US
50/D3 Beulakerwijde (lake), Neth.
47/G4 Beult (riv.), Eng,UK
50/C5 Beuningen, Neth.
56/D3 Beuvron (riv.), Fr.
52/B2 Beuvry, Fr.
51/H2 Bevensen, Ger.
51/E4 Bever (riv.), Ger.
52/D1 Beveren, Belg.
45/H4 Beverley, Eng,UK
131/B2 Beverly Hills, Ca,US
132/F6 Beverly Hills, Mi,US
51/G5 Beverungen, Ger.
50/B4 Beverwijk, Neth.
45/F1 Bewcastle, Eng,UK
46/D2 Bewdley, Eng,UK
47/G4 Bewl Bridge (res.), Eng,UK
53/G5 Bexbach, Ger.
47/G5 Bexhill, Eng,UK
63/J5 Beykoz, Turk.
53/E2 Beyne-Heusay, Belg.
63/K5 Beypazarı, Turk.
74/B3 Beyşehir, Turk.
74/B3 Beyşehir (lake), Turk.
62/D3 Bezdan, Yugo.
57/L1 Bezděz (peak), Czh.
64/H4 Bezhetsk, Rus.
56/E5 Béziers, Fr.
84/D2 Bhabua, India
84/E3 Bhadrak, India
84/C5 Bhadrāvati, India
84/A3 Bhadreswar, India
84/E2 Bhāgalpur, India
73/K2 Bhakkar, Pak.
84/E2 Bhaktapur, Nepal
85/G3 Bhamo, Burma
84/C2 Bharātpur, India
84/B3 Bharuch, India
84/D3 Bhātāpāra, India
73/K2 Bhatinda, India
84/B5 Bhatkal, India
84/E3 Bhātpāra, India
84/C5 Bhavāni, India
84/B3 Bhavnagar, India
84/C3 Bhawāni Mandi, India
84/D4 Bhawānipatna, India
84/D3 Bhilai, India
84/B2 Bhīlwāra, India
84/C4 Bhīma (riv.), India
84/D4 Bhīmavaram, India
84/D4 Bhimunipatnam, India
84/C2 Bhind, India
84/B3 Bhīnmāl, India
84/B4 Bhiwandi, India
84/E2 Bhojpur, Nepal
84/C3 Bhopāl, India
84/B4 Bhor, India
84/E3 Bhuban, India
84/E3 Bhubaneswar, India
84/A3 Bhuj, India
83/B2 Bhumibol (dam), Thai.
84/C3 Bhusawal, India
84/E2 Bhutan
75/F5 Bi (riv.), China
108/E4 Biá (riv.), Braz.
98/E5 Bia (riv.), Gui., IvC.
52/B3 Biache-Saint-Vaast, Fr.
96/G7 Biafra (bight), Afr.
87/J4 Biak (isl.), Indo.
49/M2 Biała Podlaska, Pol.
49/M3 Biała Podlaska (prov.), Pol.
49/L3 Białobrzegi, Pol.
49/J2 Białogard, Pol.
49/K4 Białowieski Nat'l Park, Pol.
49/M2 Białystok, Pol.
49/M2 Białystok (prov.), Pol.
55/G4 Bianca (peak), It.
60/D4 Biancavilla, It.
97/L7 Biaro, Zaire
56/C5 Biarritz, Fr.
100/B2 Bibā, Egypt
110/K6 Bicas, Braz.
63/H2 Bicaz, Rom.
47/E3 Bicester, Eng,UK
62/D2 Bicske, Hun.
98/D5 Bidaga (rapids), IvC.
84/C4 Bīdar, India
127/G3 Biddeford, Me,US
45/F5 Biddulph, Eng,UK
46/B4 Bideford, Eng,UK
46/B4 Bideford (Barnstaple) (bay), Eng,UK
47/E2 Bidford on Avon, Eng,UK
83/E3 Bi Doup (peak), Viet.
59/E1 Bidouze (riv.), Fr.
104/B4 Bié (plat.), Ang.
49/M2 Biebrza (riv.), Pol.
54/D3 Biel, Swi.
49/J3 Bielawa, Pol.
51/F4 Bielefeld, Ger.
119/J1 Bieler (lake), NW,Can
49/K4 Bielsko (prov.), Pol.
49/K4 Bielsko-Biała, Pol.
49/M2 Bielsk Podlaski, Pol.
83/D4 Bien Hoa, Viet.
83/D1 Bien Son, Viet.
119/J3 Bienville (lake), Qu,Can
50/B5 Biesbosch (reg.), Neth.
50/D5 Biesme (riv.), Fr.
54/D5 Bietschhorn (peak), Swi.
60/D2 Biferno (riv.), It.
91/B2 Big (des.), Austl.
119/J2 Big (isl.), NW,Can
118/D1 Big (riv.), NW,Can
63/H5 Biga, Turk.
74/B2 Bigadiç, Turk.
122/F4 Big Belt (mts.), Mt,US
128/C4 Big Bend Nat'l Park, Tx,US
125/K4 Big Black (riv.), Ms,US
125/H2 Big Blue (riv.), Ks, Ne,US
46/C6 Bigbury (bay), Eng,UK
130/D2 Big Diomede (isl.), Rus.
123/K4 Big Fork (riv.), Mn,US
122/G2 Biggar, Sk,Can
53/G1 Biggasee (lake), Ger.
51/E6 Bigge (riv.), Ger.
51/E6 Biggesee (res.), Ger.
47/F2 Biggleswade, Eng,UK
102/D3 Big Hole, SAfr.
122/E4 Big Hole (riv.), Mt,US
122/F4 Bighorn (lake), Mt, Wy,US
122/G4 Bighorn (mts.), Mt, Wy,US
122/G4 Bighorn (riv.), Mt, Wy,US
124/E1 Bighorn (basin), Wy,US
118/F4 Bighorn Canyon Nat'l Rec. Area, Mt,US
128/C4 Big Lake, Tx,US
124/D2 Big Lost (riv.), Id,US
132/P14 Big Muskego (lake), Wi,US
98/A3 Bignona, Sen.
126/C3 Big Rapids, Mi,US
122/G2 Big River, Sk,Can
132/N16 Big Rock (cr.), Il,US
129/H4 Big Saltilla (cr.), Ga,US
125/G3 Big Sandy (cr.), Co,US
129/F2 Big Sandy (riv.), Tn,US
124/E2 Big Sandy (riv.), Wy,US
123/J5 Big Sioux (riv.), Ia, SD,US
128/C3 Big Spring, Tx,US
123/J4 Big Stone (lake), Mn, SD,US
126/D4 Big Stone Gap, Va,US
122/F4 Big Timber, Mt,US
118/H3 Big Trout (lake), On,Can
131/B2 Big Tujunga (canyon), Ca,US
110/B3 Biguaçu, Braz.
124/D2 Big Wood (riv.), Id,US
62/B3 Bihać, Yugo.
84/E2 Bihār, India
84/D3 Bihār (state), India
62/F2 Bihor (co.), Rom.
52/A4 Bihorel, Fr.
98/A4 Bijagós (isls.), GBis.
84/C4 Bijāpur, India
72/E1 Bījār, Iran
62/D3 Bijeljina, Bosn.
62/D4 Bijelo Polje, Yugo.
84/C2 Bijnor, India
84/B2 Bīkaner, India
92/G3 Bikar (atoll), Mrsh.
77/L2 Bikin, Rus.
77/M2 Bikin (riv.), Rus.
92/F3 Bikini (atoll), Mrsh.
104/C4 Bikuar Nat'l Park, Moz.
83/B3 Bilauktaung (range), Burma, Thai.
58/D1 Bilbao, Sp.
100/B2 Bilbays, Egypt
62/D4 Bileća, Bosn.
74/B2 Bilecik, Turk.
63/K5 Bilecik (prov.), Turk.
49/M3 Biłgoraj, Pol.
69/S3 Bilibino, Rus.
91/B3 Bilin (riv.), Burma
91/C2 Billabong (cr.), Austl.
51/H1 Bille (riv.), Ger.
51/E5 Billerbeck, Ger.
56/C5 Billère, Fr.
47/G3 Billericay, Eng,UK
91/B2 Billiat Consv. Park, Austl.
45/F5 Billinge, Eng,UK
45/G2 Billingham, Eng,UK
122/F4 Billings, Mt,US
47/F4 Billingshurst, Eng,UK
71/K10 Billiton (isl.), Indo.
124/D4 Bill Williams (riv.), Az,US
90/C4 Biloela, Austl.
129/F4 Biloxi, Ms,US
84/C2 Bilsi, India
53/E2 Bilzen, Belg.
87/E5 Bima, Indo.
91/D2 Bimberi (peak), Austl.
117/F2 Bimini (isls.), Bahm.
84/C3 Bina-Etāwa, India
60/B4 Bin 'Arūs (gov.), Tun.
127/Q9 Binbrook, On,Can
45/H5 Binbrook, Eng,UK
52/D3 Binche, Belg.
76/G2 Binder, Mong.
84/D2 Bindki, India
104/C2 Bindu, Zaire
104/F4 Bindura, Zim.
59/F2 Binéfar, Sp.
47/F4 Binfield, Eng,UK
104/F4 Binga (mtn.), Moz.
57/G2 Bingen, Ger.
98/E5 Bingerville, IvC.
45/H6 Bingham, Eng,UK
126/F3 Binghamton, NY,US
45/G4 Bingley, Eng,UK
74/E2 Bingöl, Turk.
81/D4 Binhai, China
83/D4 Binh Chanh, Viet.
83/D4 Binh Chau, Viet.
85/G4 Binhon (peak), Burma
83/E3 Binh Son, Viet.
86/A3 Binjai, Indo.
87/F5 Binongko (isl.), Indo.
86/B2 Bintang (peak), Malay.
85/J3 Binyang, China
81/D3 Binzhou, China
112/B3 Bío-Bío (reg.), Chile
112/B3 Bío-Bío (riv.), Chile
62/B4 Biograd, Cro.
62/D4 Biogradska Nat'l Park, Yugo.
96/G7 Bioko (isl.), EqG.
84/C4 Bīr, India
96/H2 Birāk, Libya
96/H2 Bi'r al Ghuzayyil (well), Libya
97/K2 Bi'r al Ḩarash (well), Libya
84/E2 Birātnagar, Nepal
118/E3 Birch (mts.), Ab,Can
123/G2 Birch Hills, Sk,Can
123/H2 Birch River, Mb,Can
105/X Bird (isl.), Ant.
91/D2 Birds Rock (peak), Austl.
74/D3 Birecik, Turk.
110/B2 Birigui, Braz.
110/G8 Biritiba-Mirim, Braz.
73/G2 Bīrjand, Iran
92/G4 Birkenebeu, Kiri.
45/E5 Birkenhead, Eng,UK
55/H3 Birkkarspitze (peak), Aus.
63/H2 Bîrlad, Rom.
63/H2 Bîrlad (riv.), Rom.
75/B3 Birlik, Kaz.
47/E2 Birmingham, Eng,UK
129/G3 Birmingham, Al,US
132/F6 Birmingham, Mi,US
57/K3 Birnhorn (peak), Aus.
93/H5 Birnie (isl.), Kiri.
99/G3 Birni Nkonni, Niger
77/L2 Birobidzhan, Rus.
96/E3 Bīr Ounâne (well), Mali
54/D3 Birs (riv.), Swi.
65/M5 Birsk, Rus.
64/E4 Biržai, Lith.
63/F4 Bis (lake), Rom.
79/M9 Bisai, Japan
124/E5 Bisbee, Az,US
56/C4 Biscarrosse, Fr.
56/C4 Biscarrosse (lag.), Fr.
56/B4 Biscay (bay), Eur.
129/H5 Biscayne Nat'l Park, Fl,US
60/E2 Bisceglie, It.
54/D1 Bischheim, Fr.
57/K3 Bischofshofen, Aus.
53/G6 Bischwiller, Fr.
105/V Biscoe (isls.), Ant.
117/H6 Biscucuy, Ven.
72/D4 Bīshah (dry riv.), SAr.
75/B3 Bishkek (cap.), Kyr.
124/C3 Bishop, Ca,US
45/G2 Bishop Auckland, Eng,UK
46/D2 Bishops Castle, Eng,UK
46/D3 Bishops Cleeve, Eng,UK
127/L1 Bishop's Falls, Nf,Can
47/G3 Bishop's Stortford, Eng,UK
47/E5 Bishops Waltham, Eng,UK
45/H4 Bishop Wilton, Eng,UK
96/G1 Biskra, Alg.
49/L2 Biskupiec, Pol.
82/E6 Bislig, Phil.
127/Q9 Bismarck, On,Can
92/D5 Bismarck (arch.), PNG
92/D5 Bismarck (sea), PNG
123/H4 Bismarck (cap.), ND,US
74/E3 Bismil, Turk.
98/B4 Bissau (cap.), GBis.
51/F4 Bissendorf, Ger.
123/K3 Bissett, Mb,Can
63/G2 Bistrița, Rom.
63/G2 Bistrița-Năsăud (co.), Rom.
108/E2 Bita (riv.), Col.
96/H7 Bitam, Gabon
53/F4 Bitburg, Ger.
53/G5 Bitche, Fr.
96/J5 Bitkin, Chad
74/E2 Bitlis, Turk.
62/E5 Bitola, Macd.
62/C5 Bitonto, It.
63/G2 Bitrița (riv.), Rom.
100/C2 Bitter (lakes), Egypt
122/E4 Bitterroot (range), Id, Mt,US
87/G3 Bitung, Indo.
96/H5 Biu, Nga.
79/M9 Biwa, Japan
78/E3 Biwa (lake), Japan
125/J4 Bixby, Ok,US
74/H6 Biyalā, Egypt
75/E1 Biysk, Rus.
127/N7 Bizard (isl.), Qu,Can
60/A4 Bizerte (Banzart), Tun.
42/M6 Bjargtangar (pt.), Ice.
48/G1 Bjärred, Swe.
62/C3 Bjelovar, Cro.
119/S7 Bjorne (pen.), NW,Can
47/E1 Blaby, Eng,UK
49/K3 Blachownia, Pol.
66/D4 Black (sea), Asia, Eur.
126/B1 Black (bay), On,Can
123/L2 Black (riv.), On,Can
130/M3 Black (mtn.), Yk,Can
83/C1 Black (riv.), China
66/D4 Black (sea), Eur.
54/D2 Black (for.), Ger.
102/A2 Black (pt.), Namb.
46/A6 Black (pt.), Eng,UK
46/C3 Black (mtn.), Wal,UK
46/C3 Black (mts.), Wal,UK
125/K3 Black (riv.), Ar, Mo,US
124/D4 Black (mts.), Az,US
124/E4 Black (riv.), Az,US
132/L11 Black (hills), Ca,US
132/G5 Black (riv.), Mi,US
124/F4 Black (range), NM,US
126/F3 Black (riv.), NY,US
123/H5 Black (hills), SD, Wy,US
123/L4 Black (riv.), Wi,US
47/E3 Black Bourton, Eng,UK
45/F4 Blackburn, Eng,UK
44/D1 Blackcraig (hill), Sc,UK
83/C1 Black (Da) (riv.), Viet.
122/E3 Black Diamond, Ab,Can
47/F4 Blackdown (hill), Eng,UK
46/C5 Blackdown (hills), Eng,UK
90/C3 Blackdown Tableland Nat'l Park, Austl.
122/F4 Black Eagle, Mt,US
122/E5 Blackfoot, Id,US
122/F5 Blackfoot (res.), Id,US
45/G2 Blackhall Rocks, Eng,UK
44/C2 Black Head (pt.), NI,UK
124/E3 Black Mesa (upland), Az,US
46/B6 Blackmoor (upland), Eng,UK
90/B1 Black Mountain Nat'l Park, Austl.
45/E4 Blackpool, Eng,UK
102/A2 Black Reef (pt.), Namb.
126/B2 Black River Falls, Wi,US
124/C2 Black Rock (des.), Nv,US
45/F4 Blackrod, Eng,UK
126/D4 Blacksburg, Va,US
129/H3 Blackshear (lake), Ga,US
126/E4 Blackstone, Va,US
91/D1 Black Sugarloaf (peak), Austl.
90/G8 Blacktown, Austl.
127/H2 Blackville, NB,Can
98/E4 Black Volta (riv.), Afr.
129/G3 Black Warrior (riv.), Al,US
90/C3 Blackwater, Austl.
44/B4 Blackwater (riv.), Ire.
43/A4 Blackwater (riv.), Ire.
47/G3 Blackwater (riv.), Eng,UK
44/B3 Blackwater (riv.), NI,UK
125/J3 Blackwater (riv.), Mo,US
125/H3 Blackwell, Ok,US
46/C3 Blackwood, Wal,UK
131/K8 Bladensburg, Md,US
90/A3 Bladensburg Nat'l Park, Austl.
44/D2 Bladnoch (riv.), Sc,UK
44/E6 Blaenau-Ffestiniog, Wal,UK
46/C3 Blaenavon, Wal,UK
56/D5 Blagnac, Fr.
63/F4 Blagoevgrad, Bul.
77/K1 Blagoveshchensk, Rus.
122/G2 Blaine Lake, Sk,Can
127/N6 Blainville, Qu,Can
125/H2 Blair, Ne,US
122/E3 Blairmore, Ab,Can
131/F5 Blairstown, NJ,US
54/A1 Blaise (riv.), Fr.
63/F2 Blaj, Rom.
129/G4 Blakely, Ga,US
96/B3 Blanc (cape), Mrta.
112/E3 Blanca (bay), Arg.
108/C5 Blanca (range), Peru
58/E3 Blanca, Sp.
59/E4 Blanca (coast), Sp.
125/F4 Blanca (peak), NM,US
57/G4 Blanc, Mont (mtn.), Fr., It.
52/A2 Blanc Nez (cape), Fr.
113/K6 Blanco (riv.), Arg.
113/K8 Blanco (lake), Chile
112/C1 Blanco (riv.), Chile
116/D6 Blanco (cape), CR
108/B4 Blanco (cape), Peru
122/B5 Blanco (cape), Or,US
125/H5 Blanco (riv.), Tx,US
46/D5 Blandford Forum, Eng,UK
124/E3 Blanding, Ut,US
52/C2 Blanes, Sp.
59/G1 Blanes, Serre de (mtn.), Fr.
49/G4 Blanice (riv.), Czh.
52/C1 Blankenberge, Belg.
53/F3 Blankenheim, Ger.
117/J5 Blanquilla (isl.), Ven.
49/J4 Blansko, Czh.
104/G4 Blantyre, Malw.
56/F3 Blanzy, Fr.
50/C4 Blaricum, Neth.
48/E1 Blåvands Huk (pt.), Den.
56/B2 Blavet (riv.), Fr.
51/H2 Bleckede, Ger.
53/E2 Blégny, Belg.
52/C2 Bléharies, Belg.
62/B2 Bleiburg, Aus.
51/H6 Bleicherode, Ger.
50/B4 Bleiswijk, Neth.
42/E4 Blekinge (co.), Swe.
89/H7 Blenheim, NZ
47/E3 Blenheim Palace, Eng,UK
57/G4 Bléone (riv.), Fr.
52/C4 Blérancourt, Fr.
102/C4 Blesberg (peak), SAfr.
47/F2 Bletchley, Eng,UK
101/A2 Bleus (mts.), Zaire
47/E3 Blewbury, Eng,UK
96/F1 Blida, Alg.
45/G5 Blidworth, Eng,UK
53/G5 Blies (riv.), Fr., Ger.
53/G5 Bliesbruck, Fr.
53/G5 Blieskastel, Ger.
93/Y18 Bligh Water (sound), Fiji
87/F2 Blik (mt.), Phil.
45/G6 Blithfield (res.), Eng,UK
105/L Blizzard (peak), Ant.
50/B4 Bloemendaal, Neth.
102/D3 Bloemfontein, SAfr.
102/D2 Bloemhofdam (res.), SAfr.
56/D3 Blois, Fr.
50/C3 Blokker, Neth.
123/J3 Bloodvein (riv.), Mb, On,Can
43/A3 Bloody Foreland (pt.), Ire.
126/B2 Bloomer, Wi,US
131/F5 Bloomfield, NJ,US
124/F3 Bloomfield, NM,US
132/F6 Bloomfield Hills, Mi,US
132/P16 Bloomingdale, Il,US
131/C2 Bloomington, Ca,US
126/B3 Bloomington, Il,US
126/C4 Bloomington, In,US
123/K4 Bloomington, Mn,US
86/D5 Blora, Indo.
129/G4 Blountstown, Fl,US
105/L Blowaway (peak), Ant.
47/E3 Bloxham, Eng,UK
46/E1 Bloxwich, Eng,UK
57/K1 Blšanka (riv.), Czh.
55/F3 Bludenz, Aus.
85/F3 Blue (mtn.), India
128/D3 Blue (riv.), Ok,US
122/D4 Blue (mts.), Or, Wa,US
123/K5 Blue Earth, Mn,US
126/D4 Bluefield, Va,US
126/D4 Bluefield, WV,US
116/E5 Bluefields, Nic.
132/Q16 Blue Island, Il,US
124/C2 Bluejoint (lake), Or,US
90/D4 Blue Lake Nat'l Park, Austl.
124/F3 Blue Mesa (res.), Co,US
117/F4 Blue Mountain (pk.), Jam.
91/D2 Blue Mountains Nat'l Park, Austl.
97/M5 Blue Nile (riv.), Eth., Sudan
118/E2 Bluenose (lake), NW,Can
129/G3 Blue Ridge, Ga,US
129/H2 Blue Ridge (mts.), NC, Va,US
126/C3 Bluffton, In,US
110/B3 Blumenau, Braz.
45/G1 Blyth, Eng,UK
45/G5 Blyth, Eng,UK
47/H2 Blyth (riv.), Eng,UK
45/F6 Blythe (riv.), Eng,UK
124/D4 Blythe, Ca,US
45/F6 Blythe Bridge, Eng,UK
129/F3 Blytheville, Ar,US
83/D4 B'nom M'hai (peak), Viet.
98/C5 Bo, SLeo.
82/D5 Boac, Phil.
116/D5 Boaco, Nic.
110/C2 Boa Esperança, Braz.
109/J5 Boa Esperança (res.), Braz.
87/G4 Boano (isl.), Indo.
119/H2 Boas (riv.), NW,Can
109/K4 Boa Viagem, Braz.
108/F3 Boa Vista, Braz.
129/G3 Boaz, Al,US
85/J3 Bobai, China
103/J5 Bobaomby (cape), Madg.
84/D4 Bobbili, India
52/B6 Bobigny, Fr.
57/H2 Böblingen, Ger.
98/D4 Bobo Dioulasso, Burk.
62/D4 Bobotov Kuk (peak), Yugo.
62/F4 Bobovdol, Bul.
49/H3 Bóbr (riv.), Pol.
66/G2 Bobrov, Rus.
66/D1 Bobruysk, Bela.
103/H8 Boby (peak), Madg.
108/E5 Boca do Acre, Braz.
110/J7 Bocaina (mts.), Braz.
109/K7 Bocaiúva, Braz.
129/H5 Boca Raton, Fl,US
116/D5 Bocay, Nic.
49/L4 Bochnia, Pol.
53/E1 Bocholt, Belg.
50/D5 Bocholt, Ger.
51/E6 Bochum, Ger.
51/H4 Bockenem, Ger.
47/G3 Bocking, Eng,UK
117/G6 Boconó, Ven.
53/D3 Bocq (riv.), Belg.
96/J7 Boda, CAfr.
69/M4 Bodaybo, Rus.
48/F3 Bode (riv.), Ger.
124/B3 Bodega (bay), Ca,US
50/B4 Bodegraven, Neth.
96/J4 Bodélé (depr.), Chad
42/G2 Boden, Swe.
55/F2 Bodensee (Constance) (lake), Ger., Swi.
84/C4 Bodhan, India
84/C5 Bodināyakkanūr, India
46/B6 Bodmin, Eng,UK
46/B5 Bodmin Moor (upland), Eng,UK
42/E2 Bodø, Nor.
76/C2 Bodonchiyn (riv.), Mong.
62/E1 Bodrog (riv.), Hun.
74/A3 Bodrum, Turk.
83/D4 Bo Duc, Viet.
102/A2 Boegoeberg (peak), Namb.
50/C5 Boekel, Neth.
104/D1 Boende, Zaire
125/K4 Boeuf (riv.), Ar, La,US
129/F4 Bogalusa, La,US
91/C1 Bogan (riv.), Austl.
99/E3 Bogandé, Burk.
62/D3 Bogatić, Yugo.
49/H3 Bogatynia, Pol.
74/C2 Boğazlıyan, Turk.
75/E5 Bogcang (riv.), China
76/E2 Bogd, Mong.
76/B3 Bogda (mts.), China
75/E3 Bogda Feng (peak), China
47/F5 Bognor Regis, Eng,UK
53/D4 Bogny-sur-Meuse, Fr.
82/D5 Bogo, Phil.

144

Bogon - Bueno

91/C3 Bogong (peak), Austl.
91/C3 Bogong Nat'l Park, Austl.
86/C5 Bogor, Indo.
108/D3 Bogotá (cap.), Col.
62/E5 Bogovinje, Macd.
84/E3 Bogra, Bang.
44/E1 Bogrie (hill), Sc,UK
98/B2 Bogué, Mrta.
81/D3 Bohai (bay), China
81/E3 Bohai (str.), China
81/D3 Bo Hai (Chihli) (gulf), China
52/C4 Bohain-en-Vermandois, Fr.
57/K1 Bohemia (reg.), Czh.
51/G3 Böhme (riv.), Ger.
51/F4 Bohmte, Ger.
82/D6 Bohol (isl.), Phil.
85/J4 Bo Ho Su, Viet.
60/D2 Boiano, It.
58/A1 Boiro, Sp.
110/B1 Bois (riv.), Braz.
122/D5 Boise (cap.), Id,US
122/E5 Boise (riv.), Id,US
125/G3 Boise City, Ok,US
52/A5 Bois-Guillaume, Fr.
123/H3 Boissevain, Mb,Can
51/H2 Boizenburg, Ger.
96/C2 Bojador (cape), WSah.
49/J4 Bojkovice, Czh.
73/G1 Bojnūrd, Iran
98/B4 Boké (comm.), Gui.
104/D1 Bokele, Zaire
42/C4 Boknafjorden (fjord), Nor.
101/C2 Bokol (peak), Kenya
96/J5 Bokoro, Chad
102/E2 Boksburg, SAfr.
98/B4 Bolama, GBis.
73/J3 Bolān (pass), Pak.
58/D3 Bolaños de Calatrava, Sp.
56/D2 Bolbec, Fr.
63/H3 Boldeşti-Scăeni, Rom.
45/G2 Boldon, Eng,UK
99/E4 Bole, Gha.
49/H3 Bolesławiec, Pol.
99/E4 Bolgatanga, Gha.
132/P16 Bolingbrook, Il,US
112/E3 Bolívar, Arg.
125/J3 Bolivar, Mo,US
126/B5 Bolivar, Tn,US
117/G6 Bolívar (pk.), Ven.
108/F7 Bolivia
53/F4 Bollendorf, Ger.
56/F4 Bollène, Fr.
54/D4 Bolligen, Swi.
45/F5 Bollin (riv.), Eng,UK
45/F5 Bollington, Eng,UK
42/F3 Bollnäs, Swe.
58/B4 Bollullos Par del Condado, Sp.
47/F5 Bolney, Eng,UK
104/C1 Bolobo, Zaire
57/J4 Bologna, It.
64/G4 Bologoye, Rus.
97/J7 Bolomba, Zaire
77/M2 Bolon' (lake), Rus.
104/C2 Bolongongo, Ang.
83/D3 Bolovens (plat.), Laos
60/B1 Bolsena (lake), It.
67/K2 Bol'shaya Khobda (riv.), Kaz.
67/K1 Bol'shaya Kinel' (riv.), Rus.
65/P2 Bol'shaya Rogovaya (riv.), Rus.
65/N2 Bol'shaya Synya (riv.), Rus.
77/L2 Bol'shaya Ussurka (riv.), Rus.
69/L2 Bol'shevik (isl.), Rus.
65/M2 Bol'shezemel'skaya (tundra), Rus.
68/F2 Bol'shoy Bolvanskiy Nos (pt.), Rus.
67/H2 Bol'shoy Irgiz (riv.), Rus.
69/Q2 Bol'shoy Lyakhovskiy (isl.), Rus.
67/J2 Bol'shoy Uzen' (riv.), Kaz., Rus.
76/D1 Bol'shoy Yenisey (riv.), Rus.
45/G5 Bolsover, Eng,UK
50/C2 Bolsward, Neth.
46/C6 Bolt Head (pt.), Wal,UK
127/Q8 Bolton, On,Can
45/F4 Bolton, Eng,UK
45/G4 Bolton Abbey, Eng,UK
63/K5 Bolu, Turk.
63/K5 Bolu (prov.), Turk.
74/B2 Bolvadin, Turk.
55/H5 Bolzano (Bozen), It.
55/H4 Bolzano-Bozen (prov.), It.
104/B2 Boma, Zaire
91/D2 Bomaderry, Austl.
84/B4 Bombay, India
87/H4 Bomberai (pen.), Indo.
110/C1 Bom Despacho, Braz.
85/G2 Bomi, China
110/J6 Bom Jardim de Minas, Braz.
110/B4 Bom Jesus, Braz.
109/K5 Bom Jesus da Gurguéia (mts.), Braz.
109/K6 Bom Jesus da Lapa, Braz.
110/B1 Bom Jesus de Goiás, Braz.
110/D2 Bom Jesus do Itabapoana, Braz.
110/G8 Bom Jesus dos Perdões, Braz.
51/G3 Bomlitz, Ger.
110/B3 Bom Retiro, Braz.
97/L6 Bomu (riv.), Zaire
60/B4 Bon (cape), Tun.
130/K3 Bona (mtn.), Ak,US
117/H5 Bonaire (isl.), NAnt.
116/C4 Bonampak (ruins), Mex.
117/G4 Bonao, DRep.
92/B6 Bonaparte (arch.), Austl.
130/F3 Bonasila (mtn.), Ak,US
127/H1 Bonaventure, Qu,Can
127/H1 Bonaventure (riv.), Qu,Can
127/L1 Bonavista (bay), Nf,Can
127/L1 Bonavista (cape), Nf,Can
57/J4 Bondeno, It.
90/H8 Bondi, Austl.
97/K7 Bondo, Zaire
98/E4 Bondoukou, IvC.
86/D5 Bondowoso, Indo.
87/F4 Bone (gulf), Indo.
51/E5 Bönen, Ger.
87/F5 Bonerate (isls.), Indo.
75/F5 Bong (lake), China
98/C5 Bong (co.), Libr.
98/C5 Bong (range), Libr.
87/F1 Bongabong, Phil.
97/K7 Bongandanga, Zaire
87/E2 Bongao, Phil.
87/E2 Bonggi (isl.), Malay.
87/F4 Bongka (riv.), Indo.
103/H7 Bongolava (uplands), Madg.
96/J5 Bongor, Chad
97/K6 Bongos (mts.), CAfr.
83/E3 Bong Son, Viet.
128/D3 Bonham, Tx,US
52/D1 Bonheiden, Belg.
60/A2 Bonifacio (str.), Fr., It.
129/G4 Bonifay, Fl,US
92/D2 Bonin (isls.), Japan
129/H5 Bonita Springs, Fl,US
116/D4 Bonito (pk.), Hon.
53/G2 Bonn, Ger.
122/D3 Bonners Ferry, Id,US
122/E4 Bonner-West Riverside, Mt,US
123/K3 Bonnet (lake), Mb,Can
54/C5 Bonneville, Fr.
122/C4 Bonneville (dam), Or, Wa,US
132/C3 Bonney Lake, Wa,US
122/F2 Bonnyville, Ab,Can
102/C4 Bontberg (peak), SAfr.
102/C4 Bontebok Nat'l Park, SAfr.
87/E5 Bonthain, Indo.
98/B5 Bonthe, SLeo.
82/D4 Bontoc, Phil.
62/D2 Bonyhád, Hun.
105/J Bonzare (coast), Ant.
52/D1 Boom, Belg.
123/K5 Boone, Ia,US
129/H2 Boone, NC,US
129/F3 Booneville, Ms,US
131/F5 Boonton, NJ,US
76/D2 Bööntsagaan (lake), Mong.
126/C4 Boonville, In,US
91/C1 Booroondara (peak), Austl.
52/A5 Boos, Fr.
127/G3 Boothbay Harbor, Me,US
105/D Boothby (cape), Ant.
118/G1 Boothia (gulf), NW,Can
118/G1 Boothia (pen.), NW,Can
45/E5 Bootle, Eng,UK
96/H8 Booué, Gabon
53/G3 Boppard, Ger.
91/C1 Boppy (peak), Austl.
112/C4 Boquete (peak), Arg.
101/C2 Bor (dry riv.), Kenya
65/K4 Bor, Rus.
97/M6 Bor, Sudan
74/C3 Bor, Turk.
62/F3 Bor, Yugo.
93/K6 Bora Bora (isl.), FrPol.
122/E4 Borah (peak), Id,US
42/E4 Borås, Swe.
72/F3 Borāzjān, Iran
108/G4 Borba, Braz.
56/D3 Borbonnais (hist. reg.), Fr.
109/L5 Borborema (plat.), Braz.
62/E3 Borča, Yugo.
51/F5 Borchen, Ger.
105/M Borchgrevink (coast), Ant.
74/E2 Borçka, Turk.
50/D4 Borculo, Neth.
110/G7 Borda da Mata, Braz.
56/C4 Bordeaux, Fr.
119/R7 Borden (isl.), NW,Can
119/H2 Borden (pen.), NW,Can
131/F5 Bordentown, NJ,US
45/F1 Borders (reg.), Sc,UK
59/G4 Bordj el Bahri (cape), Alg.
96/G2 Bordj Omar Driss, Alg.
47/F4 Bordon, Eng,UK
47/F3 Borehamwood, Eng,UK
42/E1 Børgefjell Nat'l Park, Nor.
51/G5 Borgentreich, Ger.
50/D3 Borger, Neth.
128/C3 Borger, Tx,US
52/D1 Borgerhout, Belg.
42/F4 Borgholm, Swe.
51/F4 Borgholzhausen, Ger.
51/E4 Borghorst, Ger.
57/G4 Borgo San Dalmazzo, It.
99/F4 Borgou (prov.), Ben.
99/F4 Borgu Game Rsv., Nga.
66/B2 Borislav, Ukr.
67/G2 Borisoglebsk, Rus.
64/F5 Borisov, Bela.
103/H6 Boriziny, Madg.
50/D5 Borken, Ger.
50/D1 Borkum (isl.), Ger.
42/E3 Borlänge, Swe.
57/H4 Bormida (riv.), It.
50/C6 Born, Neth.
48/G3 Borna, Ger.
50/C2 Borndiep (chan.), Neth.
50/D4 Borne, Neth.
52/D1 Bornem, Belg.
86/E3 Borneo (isl.), Asia
53/F2 Bornheim, Ger.
49/H1 Bornholm (co.), Den.
49/H1 Bornholm (isl.), Den.
49/H1 Bornholmsgat (chan.), Swe.
99/H3 Borno (state), Nga.
58/C4 Bornos, Sp.
96/H5 Bornu (plains), Nga.
97/L6 Boro (riv.), Sudan
75/D3 Borohoro (mts.), China, Kaz.
82/E5 Borongan, Phil.
45/G3 Boroughbridge, Eng,UK
64/G4 Borovichi, Rus.
62/D3 Borovo, Cro.
66/B3 Borşa, Rom.
77/H1 Borshchovochnyy (mts.), Rus.
62/E1 Borsod-Abaúj-Zemplén (co.), Hun.
50/A6 Borssele, Neth.
75/D3 Bortala (riv.), China
46/B2 Borth, Wal,UK
72/F2 Borūjen, Iran
72/E2 Borūjerd, Iran
76/D3 Bor Ul (mts.), China
76/H1 Borzya, Rus.
60/A2 Bosa, It.
62/C3 Bosanska Dubica, Bosn.
62/C3 Bosanska Gradiška, Bosn.
62/C3 Bosanska Kostajnica, Bosn.
62/C3 Bosanska Krupa, Bosn.
62/D3 Bosanski Brod, Bosn.
62/C3 Bosanski Petrovac, Bosn.
62/D3 Bosanski Šamac, Bosn.
97/Q5 Bosaso (Bender Cassim), Som.
46/B5 Boscastle, Eng,UK
85/J3 Bose, China
47/F5 Bosham, Eng,UK
50/B4 Boskoop, Neth.
49/J4 Boskovice, Czh.
62/D3 Bosna (riv.), Bosn.
62/C3 Bosnia and Herzegovina
79/G3 Bōsō (pen.), Japan
97/J7 Bosobolo, Zaire
63/J5 Bosporus (str.), Turk.
124/F4 Bosque Farms, NM,US
113/K6 Bosques Petrificados Natural Mon., Arg.
96/J6 Bossangoa, CAfr.
128/E3 Bossier City, La,US
75/E3 Bosten (lake), China
45/H6 Boston, Eng,UK
128/E3 Boston (mts.), Ar,US
127/G3 Boston (cap.), Ma,US
128/E3 Boston, Tx,US
62/D3 Bosut (riv.), Cro.
84/B3 Botād, India
90/H8 Botany (bay), Austl.
129/H3 Boteler (peak), NC,US
103/F2 Botelerpunt (pt.), SAfr.
110/G6 Botelhos, Braz.
61/J1 Botev (peak), Bul.
63/F4 Botevgrad, Bul.
103/E2 Bothaspas (pass), SAfr.
45/E2 Bothel, Eng,UK
132/C2 Bothell, Wa,US
46/D5 Bothenhampton, Eng,UK
42/G2 Bothnia (gulf), Fin., Swe.
66/C3 Botoşani, Rom.
63/H2 Botoşani (co.), Rom.
81/D3 Botou, China
83/D2 Bo Trach, Viet.
53/F3 Botrange (mtn.), Belg.
104/D5 Botswana
60/E3 Botte Donato (peak), It.
45/H4 Bottesford, Eng,UK
45/H6 Bottesford, Eng,UK
123/H3 Bottineau, ND,US
50/D5 Bottrop, Ger.
110/B2 Botucatu, Braz.
127/L1 Botwood, Nf,Can
98/D4 Bou (riv.), IvC.
98/D5 Bouaflé, IvC.
98/D5 Bouaké, IvC.
96/J6 Bouar, CAfr.
57/K2 Boubín (peak), Czh.
97/J6 Bouca, CAfr.
127/P6 Boucherville, Qu,Can
98/C3 Boucle du Baoulé Nat'l Park, Mali
96/E1 Boudenib, Mor.
99/E2 Boû Djébéha (well), Mali
52/B5 Bouffémont, Fr.
90/B1 Bougainville (reef), Austl.
113/N7 Bougainville (cape), Falk.
92/E5 Bougainville (isl.), PNG
98/D4 Bougouni, Mali
98/E4 Bougouriba (prov.), Burk.
56/C3 Bouguenais, Fr.
96/F1 Bouira, Alg.
92/B8 Boulder, Austl.
125/F2 Boulder, Co,US
122/E4 Boulder, Mt,US
124/D4 Boulder City, Nv,US
132/P16 Boulder Hill, Il,US
99/E4 Boulgo (prov.), Burk.
99/E3 Boulkiemde (prov.), Burk.
56/C3 Boulogne (riv.), Fr.
52/B6 Boulogne-Billancourt, Fr.
52/A2 Boulogne-sur-Mer, Fr.
45/F4 Boulsworth (hill), Eng,UK
59/F1 Boumort (mtn.), Sp.
130/K3 Boundary, Yk,Can
124/C3 Boundary (peak), Nv,US
131/F5 Bound Brook, NJ,US
98/D4 Boundiali, IvC.
124/E2 Bountiful, Ut,US
39/T8 Bounty (isls.), NZ
131/B2 Bouquet (canyon), Ca,US
126/C3 Bourbonnais, Il,US
52/B2 Bourbourg, Fr.
99/F2 Bouressa (wadi), Mali
54/B5 Bourg-en-Bresse, Fr.
56/E3 Bourges, Fr.
56/F4 Bourg-lès-Valence, Fr.
56/B3 Bourgneuf (bay), Fr.
52/D5 Bourgogne, Fr.
56/E3 Bourgogne (reg.), Fr.
56/F4 Bourgoin-Jallieu, Fr.
47/F1 Bourne, Eng,UK
47/F3 Bourne End, Eng,UK
47/E5 Bournemouth, Eng,UK
47/E2 Bournville, Eng,UK
43/A4 Bourn-Vincent Mem. Nat'l Park, Ire.
51/E3 Bourtanger Moor (reg.), Ger.
47/E3 Bourton on the Water, Eng,UK
98/B2 Boutilimit, Mrta.
39/K8 Bouvet (isl.), Nor.
52/C5 Bouzy, Fr.
51/G5 Bovenden, Ger.
50/D3 Bovenwijde (lake), Neth.
46/C5 Bovey Tracey, Eng,UK
57/J4 Bovolone, It.
122/E3 Bow (riv.), Ab,Can
123/J4 Bowdle, SD,US
45/F5 Bowdon, Eng,UK
90/C3 Bowen, Austl.
50/C5 Bowen Merwede (can.), Neth.
45/G3 Bowes, Eng,UK
124/E4 Bowie, Az,US
131/K8 Bowie, Md,US
122/F3 Bow Island, Ab,Can
90/B2 Bowling Green (cape), Austl.
126/C4 Bowling Green, Ky,US
125/K3 Bowling Green, Mo,US
126/D3 Bowling Green, Oh,US
90/B2 Bowling Green Bay Nat'l Park, Austl.
105/G Bowman (isl.), Ant.
119/J2 Bowman (bay), NW,Can
123/H4 Bowman, ND,US
127/S8 Bowmanville, Nf,Can
45/E2 Bowness-on-Solway, Eng,UK
87/F4 Bowokan (isls.), Indo.
91/D2 Bowral, Austl.
122/C2 Bowron (riv.), BC,Can
123/H4 Box Elder, SD,US
91/C3 Box Hill, Austl.
91/G5 Box Hill, Austl.
50/C5 Boxmeer, Neth.
50/C5 Boxtel, Neth.
74/C2 Boyabat, Turk.
91/D2 Boyd-Konangra Nat'l Park, Austl.
123/K5 Boyer (riv.), Ia,US
122/E2 Boyle, Ab,Can
44/B4 Boyne (riv.), Ire.
126/C2 Boyne City, Mi,US
129/H5 Boynton Beach, Fl,US
122/F5 Boysen (res.), Wy,US
61/J3 Bozcaada (isl.), Turk.
122/F4 Bozeman, Mt,US
74/C3 Bozkir, Turk.
96/J6 Bozoum, CAfr.
74/B2 Bozüyük, Turk.
57/G4 Bra, It.
52/D2 Brabant (prov.), Belg.
47/G4 Brabourne Lees, Eng,UK
62/C4 Brač (isl.), Cro.
60/B1 Bracciano (lake), It.
126/E2 Bracebridge, On,Can
64/B3 Bräcke, Swe.
128/C4 Brackettville, Tx,US
47/E2 Brackley, Eng,UK
47/F4 Bracknell, Eng,UK
110/B4 Braço do Norte, Braz.
62/F2 Brad, Rom.
60/D2 Bradano (riv.), It.
44/D3 Bradda Head (pt.), IM,UK
129/H5 Bradenton, Fl,US
45/G4 Bradford, Eng,UK
126/E3 Bradford, Pa,US
46/D4 Bradford on Avon, Eng,UK
47/E5 Brading, Eng,UK
131/F5 Bradley Beach, NJ,US
46/C5 Bradninch, Eng,UK
128/D4 Brady, Tx,US
130/L3 Braeburn, Yk,Can
43/D2 Braemar, Sc,UK
58/A2 Braga, Port.
58/A2 Braga (dist.), Port.
112/E2 Bragado, Arg.
109/J4 Bragança, Braz.
58/B2 Bragança, Port.
58/B2 Bragança (dist.), Port.
110/G7 Bragança Paulista, Braz.
71/J7 Brahmaputra (riv.), Asia
44/D6 Braich-y-Pwll (pt.), Wal,UK
44/B2 Braid (riv.), NI,UK
63/H3 Brăila, Rom.
63/H3 Brăila (co.), Rom.
52/D2 Braine-l'Alleud, Belg.
52/D2 Braine-le-Comte, Belg.
123/K4 Brainerd, Mn,US
47/G3 Braintree, Eng,UK
102/C3 Brak (riv.), SAfr.
51/F2 Brake, Ger.
52/C2 Brakel, Belg.
51/G5 Brakel, Ger.
98/B2 Brakna (reg.), Mrta.
127/Q8 Bramalea, On,Can
45/G4 Bramhope, Eng,UK
127/Q8 Brampton, On,Can
45/F2 Brampton, Eng,UK
51/E4 Bramsche, Ger.
108/F4 Branco (riv.), Braz.
104/B5 Brandberg (peak), Namb.
48/G2 Brandenburg, Ger.
48/G2 Brandenburg (state), Ger.
45/H4 Brandesburton, Eng,UK
123/J3 Brandon, Mb,Can
47/G2 Brandon, Eng,UK
129/H5 Brandon, Fl,US
129/F3 Brandon, Ms,US
112/E3 Brandsen, Arg.
49/K1 Braniewo, Pol.
47/E5 Bransgore, Eng,UK
127/J2 Bras d'Or (lake), NS,Can
109/J7 Brasília (cap.), Braz.
109/J7 Brasília Nat'l Park, Braz.
110/D1 Brasil, Planalto do (plat.), Braz.
63/G3 Braşov, Rom.
63/G3 Braşov (co.), Rom.
50/B6 Brasschaat, Belg.
129/H3 Brasstown Bald (peak), Ga,US
49/J4 Bratislava (cap.), Slvk.
49/J4 Bratislava (reg.), Slvk.
69/L4 Bratsk, Rus.
127/F3 Brattleboro, Vt,US
116/E5 Braulio Carrillo, CR
57/K2 Braunau am Inn, Aus.
51/H5 Braunlage, Ger.
51/H4 Braunschweig (Brunswick), Ger.
46/B4 Braunton, Eng,UK
59/G2 Brava (coast), Sp.
113/T12 Brava (pt.), Uru.
108/F7 Bravo (peak), Bol.
124/D4 Brawley, Ca,US
119/J2 Bray (isl.), NW,Can
44/B5 Bray, Ire.
56/D3 Braye (riv.), Fr.
44/B5 Bray Head (pt.), Ire.
52/B4 Bray-sur-Somme, Fr.
107/D3 Brazil
126/C4 Brazil, In,US
107/E4 Brazilian (plat.), Braz.
110/H7 Brazópolis, Braz.
128/D4 Brazos (riv.), Tx,US
113/K7 Brazo Sur (riv.), Arg.
104/C1 Brazzaville (cap.), Congo
62/D3 Brčko, Bosn.
48/J2 Brda (riv.), Pol.
57/K2 Brdy (mts.), Czh.
131/C3 Brea, Ca,US
46/D3 Bream, Eng,UK
63/G3 Breaza, Rom.
43/D2 Brechin, Sc,UK
50/B6 Brecht, Belg.
123/J4 Breckenridge, Mn,US
51/E6 Breckerfeld, Ger.
47/G2 Breckland (reg.), Eng,UK
113/K8 Brecknock (pen.), Chile
49/J4 Břeclav, Czh.
46/C3 Brecon, Wal,UK
46/C3 Brecon Beacons (mts.), Wal,UK
46/C3 Brecon Beacons Nat'l Park, Wal,UK
50/B5 Breda, Neth.
52/B1 Bredene, Belg.
53/E1 Bree, Belg.
102/L10 Breë (riv.), SAfr.
62/F5 Bregalinca (riv.), Macd.
55/F2 Bregenz, Aus.
42/M6 Breidhafjördhur (bay), Ice.
51/F2 Bremen, Ger.
51/F2 Bremen (state), Ger.
90/E7 Bremer (riv.), Austl.
51/F1 Bremerhaven, Ger.
132/B2 Bremerton, Wa,US
51/G2 Bremervörde, Ger.
46/C4 Brendon (hills), Eng,UK
128/D4 Brenham, Tx,US
44/E5 Brenig, Llyn (lake), Wal,UK
54/B4 Brenne (riv.), Fr.
55/H4 Brenner (Brennerpass) (pass), Aus.
57/J4 Brenta (riv.), It.
47/G3 Brentwood, Eng,UK
132/L11 Brentwood, Ca,US
131/G5 Brentwood, NY,US
57/J4 Brescia, It.
55/G5 Brescia (prov.), It.
52/A4 Bresle (riv.), Fr.
57/J3 Bressanone, It.
56/C3 Bressuire, Fr.
49/M2 Brest, Bela.
56/A2 Brest, Fr.
49/M2 Brest Obl., Bela.
56/B2 Bretagne (mts.), Fr.
56/B2 Bretagne (reg.), Fr.
103/R15 Bretagne (pt.), Reun.
122/E2 Breton, Ab,Can
127/K2 Breton (cape), NS,Can
50/B4 Breukelen, Neth.
109/H4 Breves, Braz.
119/K2 Brevoort (isl.), NW,Can
127/G2 Brewer, Me,US
46/D1 Brewood, Eng,UK
125/H2 Brewster, Ne,US
122/D3 Brewster, Wa,US
129/G4 Brewton, Al,US
62/B3 Brežice, Slov.
63/G3 Brezoi, Rom.
97/K6 Bria, CAfr.
57/G4 Briançon, Fr.
46/C2 Brianne, Lyn (res.), Wal,UK
131/F5 Brick, NJ,US
43/A4 Bride (riv.), Ire.
44/D3 Bride, IM,UK
128/E4 Bridge City, Tx,US
46/C4 Bridgend, Wal,UK
124/C3 Bridgeport, Ca,US
127/F3 Bridgeport, Ct,US
125/G2 Bridgeport, Ne,US
126/D4 Bridgeport, WV,US
122/F4 Bridger, Mt,US
117/K5 Bridgetown (cap.), Bar.
91/C4 Bridgewater, Austl.
127/H2 Bridgewater, NS,Can
126/E4 Bridgewater, Va,US
46/D1 Bridgnorth, Eng,UK
127/G2 Bridgton, Me,US
46/D4 Bridgwater, Eng,UK
46/C4 Bridgwater (bay), Eng,UK
45/H3 Bridlington, Eng,UK
45/H3 Bridlington (bay), Eng,UK
46/D5 Bridport, Eng,UK
52/C6 Brie (reg.), Fr.
52/B6 Brie-Comte-Robert, Fr.
49/J3 Brieg Brzeg, Pol.
50/B5 Brielle, Neth.
131/F5 Brielle, NJ,US
45/F4 Brierfield, Eng,UK
45/F4 Brigg, Eng,UK
54/D5 Brig-Glis, Swi.
124/D2 Brigham City, Ut,US
45/G4 Brighouse, Eng,UK
47/E5 Brighstone, Eng,UK
47/H3 Brightlingsea, Eng,UK
90/F6 Brighton, Austl.
91/F5 Brighton, Austl.
47/F5 Brighton, Eng,UK
125/F3 Brighton, Co,US
56/F4 Brignais, Fr.
56/G5 Brignoles, Fr.
98/A3 Brikama, Gam.
47/E3 Brill, Eng,UK
109/H8 Brillante (riv.), Braz.
51/F6 Brilon, Ger.
45/G5 Brimington, Eng,UK
61/E2 Brindisi, It.
46/E3 Brinkworth, Eng,UK
58/A1 Brion, Sp.
132/K11 Briones (res.), Ca,US
90/F6 Brisbane (riv.), Austl.
90/E6 Brisbane For. Park, Austl.
90/E6 Brisbane, Austl.
91/C3 Brisbane Ranges Nat'l Park, Austl.
91/D2 Brisbane Waters Nat'l Park, Austl.
46/B4 Bristol (chan.), UK
46/D4 Bristol, Eng,UK
130/F4 Bristol (bay), Ak,US
131/F5 Bristol, Pa,US
129/H2 Bristol, Tn,US
125/H4 Bristow, Ok,US
130/K2 British (mts.), Yk,Can, Ak,US
118/D3 British Columbia (prov.), Can.
119/S6 British Empire (range), NW,Can
71/G10 British Indian Ocean Terr.
102/P12 Brits, SAfr.
56/B2 Brittany (reg.), Fr.
123/J4 Britton, SD,US
56/D4 Brive-la-Gaillarde, Fr.
46/C6 Brixham, Eng,UK
47/F2 Brixworth, Eng,UK
49/J4 Brno, Czh.
90/C3 Broad (sound), Austl.
130/J3 Broad (pass), Ak,US
129/H3 Broad (riv.), NC, SC,US
126/E1 Broadback (riv.), Qu,Can
43/D3 Broad Law (mtn.), Sc,UK
91/F5 Broadmeadows, Austl.
90/C3 Broad Sound (chan.), Austl.
47/H4 Broadstairs, Eng,UK
47/E5 Broadstone, Eng,UK
123/G4 Broadus, Mt,US
91/E1 Broadwater Nat'l Park, Austl.
47/E2 Broadway, Eng,UK
47/E2 Broadway (hill), Eng,UK
46/D5 Broadwindsor, Eng,UK
119/R7 Brock (isl.), NW,Can
51/H5 Brocken (peak), Ger.
47/E5 Brockenhurst, Eng,UK
127/G3 Brockton, Ma,US
126/F2 Brockville, On,Can
118/G1 Brodeur (pen.), NW,Can
131/E4 Brodhead (cr.), Pa,US
49/K2 Brodnica, Pol.
50/B3 Broek Op Langedijk, Neth.
91/D2 Broken (bay), Austl.
125/J3 Broken Arrow, Ok,US
125/H2 Broken Bow, Ne,US
125/J4 Broken Bow, Ok,US
125/J4 Broken Bow (lake), Ok,US
91/B1 Broken Hill, Austl.
128/B3 Brokeoff (mts.), NM,US
46/D2 Bromsgrove, Eng,UK
46/D2 Bromyard, Eng,UK
56/F4 Bron, Fr.
42/D4 Brønderslev, Den.
99/E5 Brong-Ahafo (reg.), Gha.
57/H4 Broni, It.
46/C3 Bronllys, Wal,UK
42/E2 Brønnøysund, Nor.
127/Q9 Bronte, On,Can
60/D4 Bronte, It.
131/G5 Bronx (co.), NY,US
82/C6 Brooke's Point, Phil.
132/Q16 Brookfield, Il,US
125/J3 Brookfield, Mo,US
132/P13 Brookfield, Wi,US
129/F4 Brookhaven, Ms,US
131/H5 Brookhaven, NY,US
123/J4 Brookings, SD,US
131/G5 Brooklyn (Kings) (co.), NY,US
131/K7 Brooklyn Park, Md,US
47/F3 Brookmans Park, Eng,UK
122/F3 Brooks, Ab,Can
130/E2 Brooks (mtn.), Ak,US
130/F2 Brooks (range), Ak,US
129/H4 Brooksville, Fl,US
131/E6 Broomall, Pa,US
127/P7 Brossard, Qu,Can
45/H2 Brotton, Eng,UK
45/F2 Brough, Eng,UK
127/R8 Brougham, On,Can
44/B2 Broughshane, NI,UK
47/F2 Broughton, Eng,UK
45/E3 Broughton in Furness, Eng,UK
47/G4 Broughton Street, Eng,UK
50/A5 Brouwersdam (dam), Neth.
82/C5 Brown (shoal)
46/D2 Brown Clee (hill), Eng,UK
128/C3 Brownfield, Tx,US
47/E1 Brownhills, Eng,UK
122/E3 Browning, Mt,US
47/E5 Brownsea (isl.), Eng,UK
131/F6 Browns Mills, NJ,US
129/F3 Brownsville, Tn,US
128/D5 Brownsville, Tx,US
46/B5 Brown Willy (hill), Eng,UK
128/D4 Brownwood, Tx,US
52/B3 Bruay-en-Artois, Fr.
52/C3 Bruay-sur-l'Escaut, Fr.
92/A7 Bruce (peak), Austl.
126/D2 Bruce (pen.), On,Can
54/D1 Bruche (riv.), Fr.
53/G5 Bruchmühlbach-Miesau, Ger.
57/H2 Bruchsal, Ger.
51/G5 Brucht (riv.), Ger.
57/K3 Bruck an der Grossglockner-strasse, Aus.
62/C1 Bruck an der Leitha, Aus.
57/L3 Bruck an der Mur, Aus.
48/F5 Bruckmühl, Ger.
46/D4 Brue (riv.), Eng,UK
52/C1 Bruges (Brugge), Belg.
50/D6 Brüggen, Ger.
53/F2 Brühl, Ger.
102/B2 Brukkaros (peak), Namb.
109/K6 Brumado, Braz.
53/G6 Brumath, Fr.
50/D4 Brummen, Neth.
42/D3 Brumunddal, Nor.
60/A2 Bruncu Spina (peak), It.
47/H1 Brundall, Eng,UK
52/D4 Brune (riv.), Fr.
124/D2 Bruneau (riv.), Id, Nv,US
86/D2 Brunei
57/J3 Brunico, It.
51/G1 Brunsbüttel, Ger.
53/E2 Brunssum, Neth.
91/F5 Brunswick, Austl.
113/J8 Brunswick (pen.), Chile
129/H4 Brunswick, Ga,US
127/G3 Brunswick, Me,US
126/D3 Brunswick, Oh,US
51/H4 Brunswick (Braunschweig), Ger.
110/B3 Brusque, Braz.
52/D2 Brussels (Bruxelles) (cap.), Belg.
46/D4 Bruton, Eng,UK
56/C2 Bruz, Fr.
105/U Bryan (coast), Ant.
126/C3 Bryan, Oh,US
128/D4 Bryan, Tx,US
66/E1 Bryansk, Rus.
66/E1 Bryansk Obl., Rus.
124/D3 Bryce Canyon Nat'l Park, Ut,US
45/E5 Brymbo, Wal,UK
46/C2 Bryn Brawd (mtn.), Wal,UK
46/C3 Brynithel, Wal,UK
46/C3 Brynmawr, Wal,UK
49/J3 Brzeg Dolny, Pol.
49/L4 Brzesko, Pol.
49/M4 Brzozów, Pol.
83/C3 Bua Yai, Thai.
98/B4 Buba, GBis.
98/B4 Bubaque, GBis.
72/E3 Būbiyan (isl.), Kuw.
74/B3 Bucak, Turk.
108/D2 Bucaramanga, Col.
59/P10 Bucelas, Port.
119/J1 Buchan (gulf), NW,Can
98/C5 Buchanan, Libr.
125/H5 Buchanan (lake), Tx,US
127/K1 Buchans, Nf,Can
63/H3 Bucharest (Bucureşti) (cap.), Rom.
51/G2 Buchholz in der Nordheide, Ger.
124/B4 Buchon (pt.), Ca,US
45/F3 Buckden Pike (mtn.), Eng,UK
51/G4 Bückeburg, Ger.
46/C6 Buckfastleigh, Eng,UK
126/D4 Buckhannon, WV,US
43/D2 Buckie, Sc,UK
126/F2 Buckingham, Qu,Can
47/F3 Buckingham, Eng,UK
47/F3 Buckinghamshire (co.), Eng,UK
45/E5 Buckley, Wal,UK
46/D2 Bucknell, Eng,UK
43/D2 Bucksburn, Sc,UK
127/H2 Buctouche, NB,Can
63/H3 Bucureşti (Bucharest) (cap.), Rom.
126/D3 Bucyrus, Oh,US
62/D2 Budaörs, Hun.
62/D2 Budapest (cap.), Hun.
84/C2 Budaun, India
105/H Budd (coast), Ant.
132/B3 Budd (inlet), Wa,US
131/F5 Budd Lake, NJ,US
46/B5 Bude, Eng,UK
46/B5 Bude (bay), Eng,UK
50/C6 Budel, Neth.
48/E1 Büdelsdorf, Ger.
57/H1 Büdingen, Ger.
97/J7 Budjala, Zaire
46/C5 Budleigh Salterton, Eng,UK
62/D4 Budva, Yugo.
63/J2 Budzhak (reg.), Mol., Ukr.
96/G7 Buea, Camr.
131/C3 Buena Park, Ca,US
108/C3 Buenaventura, Col.
125/F3 Buena Vista, Co,US
126/E4 Buena Vista, Va,US
112/B4 Bueno (riv.), Chile
113/S12 Buenos Aires (cap.), Arg.
112/C5 Buenos Aires (lake), Arg.

145

Bueno – Cardi

112/E3 **Buenos Aires** (prov.), Arg.
58/A1 **Bueu**, Sp.
91/C3 **Buffalo** (peak), Austl.
122/E2 **Buffalo** (lake), Ab,Can
103/E2 **Buffalo** (riv.), SAfr.
128/E2 **Buffalo** (riv.), Ar,US
123/K4 **Buffalo**, Mn,US
125/J3 **Buffalo**, Mo,US
127/S10 **Buffalo**, NY,US
125/H3 **Buffalo**, Ok,US
123/H4 **Buffalo**, SD,US
129/G3 **Buffalo** (riv.), Tn,US
122/G4 **Buffalo**, Wy,US
132/Q15 **Buffalo Grove**, Il,US
122/F2 **Buffalo Narrows**, Sk,Can
91/B1 **Buffalo Riv. Overflow** (swamp), Austl.
102/B3 **Buffelsrivier** (dry riv.), SAfr.
129/G3 **Buford**, Ga,US
63/G3 **Buftea**, Rom.
66/B1 **Bug** (riv.), Eur.
63/K2 **Bug** (estuary), Ukr.
108/C3 **Buga**, Col.
116/E6 **Bugaba**, Pan.
56/E5 **Bugarach, Pic de** (peak), Fr.
47/E2 **Bugbrooke**, Eng,UK
86/D5 **Bugel** (pt.), Indo.
52/D1 **Buggenhout**, Belg.
62/C3 **Bugojno**, Bosn.
101/B2 **Bugosa** (prov.), Ugan.
87/E2 **Bugsuk** (isl.), Phil.
65/M5 **Bugul'ma**, Rus.
67/K1 **Buguruslan**, Rus.
76/D4 **Buh** (riv.), China
74/D3 **Buhayrat al Asad** (lake), Turk.
72/D2 **Buḩayrat ath Tharthār** (lake), Iraq
122/E5 **Buhl**, Id,US
63/H2 **Buhuşi**, Rom.
99/E4 **Bui** (dam), Gha.
99/E4 **Bui Gorge** (res.), Gha.
46/C2 **Builth Wells**, Wal,UK
112/Q9 **Buin**, Chile
58/C4 **Bujalance**, Sp.
62/E4 **Bujanovac**, Yugo.
63/H3 **Bujor**, Rom.
101/A3 **Bujumbura** (cap.), Buru.
49/J2 **Buk**, Pol.
92/E5 **Buka** (isl.), PNG
76/H1 **Bukachacha**, Rus.
75/F4 **Bukadaban Feng** (peak), China
72/E1 **Būkān**, Iran
101/A3 **Bukavu**, Zaire
83/C5 **Buket Bubat** (peak), Malay.
68/G6 **Bukhara**, Uzb.
76/A2 **Bukhtarma** (riv.), Kaz.
86/B4 **Bukittinggi**, Indo.
62/E1 **Bükki Nat'l Park**, Hun.
101/A3 **Bukoba**, Tanz.
86/B4 **Buku** (cape), Indo.
82/D5 **Bulan**, Phil.
84/C2 **Bulandshahr**, India
74/E2 **Bulanık**, Turk.
87/F3 **Bulawa** (peak), Indo.
104/E5 **Bulawayo**, Zim.
130/B5 **Buldir** (isl.), Ak,US
76/C2 **Bulgan** (riv.), Mong.
63/G4 **Bulgaria**
60/D2 **Bulgheria** (peak), It.
82/C6 **Buliluyan** (cape), Phil.
90/F7 **Bulimba** (cr.), Austl.
47/E2 **Bulkington**, Eng,UK
122/B2 **Bulkley** (riv.), BC,Can
44/B1 **Bull** (pt.), NI,UK
58/E3 **Bullas**, Sp.
91/C3 **Buller** (peak), Austl.
124/D4 **Bullhead City**, Az,US
53/F3 **Büllingen**, Belg.
90/A5 **Bulloo** (riv.), Austl.
125/J3 **Bull Shoals** (lake), Ar, Mo,US
52/B3 **Bully-les-Mines**, Fr.
76/D2 **Bulnayn** (mts.), Mong.
112/B3 **Bulnes**, Chile
92/D5 **Bulolo**, PNG
87/F5 **Bulukumba**, Indo.
104/D2 **Bulungu**, Zaire
97/K7 **Bumba**, Zaire
101/C2 **Buna**, Kenya
79/L9 **Bunaga-take** (peak), Japan
101/A3 **Bunazi**, Tanz.
89/A4 **Bunbury**, Austl.
90/D4 **Bundaberg**, Austl.
51/F4 **Bünde**, Ger.
84/C2 **Būndi**, India
47/H2 **Bungay**, Eng,UK
86/C3 **Bunguran** (isl.), Indo.
101/A2 **Bunia**, Zaire
129/H4 **Bunnell**, Fl,US
50/C4 **Bunnik**, Neth.
59/E3 **Buñol**, Sp.
50/C4 **Bunschoten**, Neth.
47/F3 **Buntingford**, Eng,UK
90/C4 **Bunya Mountains Nat'l Park**, Austl.
74/C2 **Bünyan**, Turk.
90/E6 **Bunya Park**, Austl.
87/E3 **Bunyu** (isl.), Indo.
83/E3 **Buon Me Thuot**, Viet.
83/E3 **Buon Mrong**, Viet.
101/C3 **Bura**, Kenya
97/L5 **Buram**, Sudan
97/M7 **Buranga** (pass), Ugan.
97/Q6 **Burao** (Burco), Som.
129/F4 **Buras-Triumph**, La,US
82/D5 **Burauen**, Phil.
72/D3 **Buraydah**, SAr.
53/H2 **Burbach**, Ger.
131/B2 **Burbank**, Ca,US
132/Q16 **Burbank**, Il,US
97/Q6 **Burco** (Burao), Som.
90/B3 **Burdekin** (riv.), Austl.
132/J10 **Burdell** (mtn.), Ca,US
74/B3 **Burdur**, Turk.
84/E3 **Burdwān**, India
47/H1 **Bure** (riv.), Eng,UK
51/F5 **Büren**, Ger.
50/C5 **Buren**, Neth.
76/E2 **Bürengiyn** (mts.), Mong.
73/K2 **Būrewāla**, Pak.
77/L1 **Bureya** (mts.), Rus.
77/L1 **Bureya** (riv.), Rus.
47/E3 **Burford**, Eng,UK
63/H4 **Burgas**, Bul.
63/H4 **Burgas** (bay), Bul.
63/H4 **Burgas** (reg.), Bul.
51/H4 **Burgdorf**, Ger.
57/M3 **Burgenland** (prov.), Aus.
127/K2 **Burgeo**, Nf,Can
102/D3 **Burgersdorp**, SAfr.
130/L2 **Burgess** (mtn.), Yk,Can
47/F5 **Burgess Hill**, Eng,UK
42/E2 **Burgfjället** (peak), Swe.
45/J5 **Burgh le Marsh**, Eng,UK
57/K2 **Burglengenfeld**, Ger.
58/D1 **Burgos**, Sp.
51/E4 **Burgsteinfurt**, Ger.
54/A3 **Burgundy** (hist. reg.), Fr.
51/G3 **Burgwedel**, Ger.
76/D4 **Burhan Budai** (mts.), China
74/A2 **Burhaniye**, Turk.
84/C3 **Burhānpur**, India
116/E6 **Burica** (pen.), CR, Pan.
116/E6 **Burica** (pt.), Pan.
132/C3 **Burien**, Wa,US
127/L2 **Burin**, Nf,Can
127/K2 **Burin** (pen.), Nf,Can
83/C3 **Buriram**, Thai.
110/B2 **Buritama**, Braz.
110/B1 **Buriti Alegre**, Braz.
110/C1 **Buritizeiro**, Braz.
59/E3 **Burjasot**, Sp.
128/D3 **Burkburnett**, Tx,US
105/S **Burke** (isl.), Ant.
131/J8 **Burke**, Va,US
122/B2 **Burke Channel** (inlet), BC,Can
99/E3 **Burkina Faso**
122/E5 **Burley**, Id,US
132/K11 **Burlingame**, Ca,US
127/Q9 **Burlington**, On,Can
125/G3 **Burlington**, Co,US
123/L5 **Burlington**, Ia,US
125/J3 **Burlington**, Ks,US
129/J2 **Burlington**, NC,US
131/F5 **Burlington**, NJ,US
127/F2 **Burlington**, Vt,US
132/P14 **Burlington**, Wi,US
85/G2 **Burma** (Myanmar)
63/K3 **Burnas** (lake), Ukr.
128/D4 **Burnet**, Tx,US
113/J8 **Burney** (peak), Chile
124/B2 **Burney**, Ca,US
47/G3 **Burnham on Crouch**, Eng,UK
46/D4 **Burnham on Sea**, Eng,UK
91/C4 **Burnie-Somerset**, Austl.
45/F4 **Burnley**, Eng,UK
122/D5 **Burns**, Or,US
118/E2 **Burnside** (riv.), NW,Can
122/B2 **Burns Lake**, BC,Can
123/J2 **Burntwood** (riv.), Mb,Can
47/E1 **Burntwood**, Eng,UK
91/B2 **Buronga**, Austl.
76/B2 **Burqin** (riv.), China
61/G2 **Burrel**, Alb.
91/D2 **Burrendong** (res.), Austl.
91/D2 **Burrewarra** (pt.), Austl.
59/E3 **Burriana**, Sp.
91/D2 **Burrinjuck** (res.), Austl.
90/A2 **Burrowes** (pt.), Austl.
44/D2 **Burrow Head** (pt.), Sc,UK
132/Q16 **Burr Ridge**, Il,US
90/D4 **Burrum River Nat'l Park**, Austl.
46/B3 **Burry** (inlet), Wal,UK
46/B3 **Burry Port**, Wal,UK
63/J5 **Bursa**, Turk.
63/J5 **Bursa** (prov.), Turk.
100/C3 **Būr Safājah**, Egypt
74/J6 **Būr Saʿīd** (gov.), Egypt
74/J6 **Būr Saʿīd** (Port Said), Egypt
51/E6 **Burscheid**, Ger.
45/F4 **Burscough Bridge**, Eng,UK
100/D5 **Būr Sūdān** (Port Sudan), Sudan
127/S9 **Burt**, NY,US
100/C2 **Būr Tawfīq**, Egypt
47/E5 **Burton**, Eng,UK
132/E6 **Burton**, Mi,US
47/F2 **Burton Latimer**, Eng,UK
47/E1 **Burton upon Trent**, Eng,UK
87/G4 **Buru** (isl.), Indo.
74/H6 **Burullus, Buḩayrat al** (lag.), Egypt
101/A3 **Burundi**
76/F2 **Burun Shibertuy** (peak), Rus.
130/L3 **Burwash Landing**, Yk,Can
47/G2 **Burwell**, Eng,UK
125/H2 **Burwell**, Ne,US
47/F5 **Bury**, Eng,UK
69/M4 **Buryat Aut. Rep.**, Rus.
67/J3 **Burynshyk** (pt.), Kaz.
47/G2 **Bury Saint Edmunds**, Eng,UK
57/H4 **Busalla**, It.
44/B1 **Bush** (riv.), NI,UK
76/C2 **Büs Hayrhan** (peak), Mong.
47/F3 **Bushey**, Eng,UK
131/E4 **Bushkill** (falls), Pa,US
102/B3 **Bushmanland** (reg.), SAfr.
44/B1 **Bushmills**, NI,UK
97/K7 **Businga**, Zaire
42/D3 **Buskerud** (co.), Nor.
49/L3 **Busko-Zdrój**, Pol.
89/A4 **Busselton**, Austl.
97/L6 **Busseri** (riv.), Sudan
50/C4 **Bussum**, Neth.
113/K7 **Bustamente** (pt.), Arg.
90/C4 **Bustard** (pt.), Austl.
63/G3 **Buşteni**, Rom.
57/H4 **Busto Arsizio**, It.
82/C5 **Busuanga** (isl.), Phil.
97/K7 **Buta**, Zaire
101/A3 **Butare**, Rwa.
92/G4 **Butaritari** (atoll), Kiri.
122/B3 **Bute** (inlet), BC,Can
43/C3 **Bute** (isl.), Sc,UK
76/E2 **Büteeliyn** (mts.), Mong.
101/A2 **Butembo**, Zaire
110/B4 **Butiá**, Braz.
126/E3 **Butler**, Pa,US
87/F5 **Buton** (isl.), Indo.
122/E4 **Butte**, Mt,US
86/B2 **Butterworth**, Malay.
87/F5 **Butung** (isl.), Indo.
67/G2 **Buturlinovka**, Rus.
57/H1 **Butzbach**, Ger.
48/F2 **Bützow**, Ger.
97/Q7 **Buulo Berde**, Som.
97/P7 **Buur Hakaba**, Som.
51/G2 **Buxtehude**, Ger.
45/G5 **Buxton**, Eng,UK
64/J4 **Buy**, Rus.
67/H4 **Buynaksk**, Rus.
98/D5 **Buyo, Barrage de** (dam), IvC.
77/H2 **Buyr** (lake), Mong.
63/J5 **Büyükçekmece**, Turk.
74/B3 **Büyük Menderes** (riv.), Turk.
81/E2 **Buyun Shan** (peak), China
67/J3 **Buzachi** (pen.), Kaz.
63/H3 **Buzău**, Rom.
63/H3 **Buzău** (co.), Rom.
63/H3 **Buzău** (riv.), Rom.
62/E3 **Buziaş**, Rom.
110/H8 **Búzios** (isl.), Braz.
67/K1 **Buzuluk**, Rus.
63/F4 **Byala Slatina**, Bul.
119/R7 **Byam Martin** (chan.), NW,Can
119/R7 **Byam Martin** (isl.), NW,Can
49/J2 **Bydgoszcz**, Pol.
49/J2 **Bydgoszcz** (prov.), Pol.
47/E2 **Byfield**, Eng,UK
66/D1 **Bykhov**, Bela.
44/E5 **Bylchau**, Wal,UK
119/J1 **Bylot** (isl.), NW,Can
131/G5 **Byram** (pt.), NY,US
105/U **Byrd** (cape), Ant.
105/L **Byrd** (glac.), Ant.
113/J6 **Byron** (isl.), Chile
68/K2 **Byrranga** (mts.), Rus.
49/K4 **Bystrá** (peak), Slvk.
69/N3 **Bytantay** (riv.), Rus.
49/K3 **Bytom**, Pol.
49/J1 **Bytów**, Pol.

C

83/D2 **Ca** (riv.), Viet.
104/C3 **Caála**, Ang.
109/K5 **Caatingas** (reg.), Braz.
82/E6 **Cabadbaran**, Phil.
117/F3 **Cabaiguán**, Cuba
124/F4 **Caballo** (res.), NM,US
58/C1 **Cabañaquinta**, Sp.
82/D4 **Cabanatuan**, Phil.
46/C2 **Caban Coch** (res.), Wal,UK
127/G2 **Cabano**, Qu,Can
56/E5 **Cabestany**, Fr.
58/C3 **Cabeza del Buey**, Sp.
58/C1 **Cabezón de la Sal**, Sp.
117/G5 **Cabimas**, Ven.
104/B2 **Cabinda**, Ang.
96/C2 **Cabo Bojador**, WSah.
101/C5 **Cabo Delgado** (prov.), Moz.
110/D2 **Cabo Frio**, Braz.
126/E2 **Cabonga** (res.), Qu,Can
90/D4 **Caboolture**, Austl.
109/H3 **Cabo Orange Nat'l Park**, Braz.
104/F4 **Cabora Bassa** (lake), Moz.
127/J2 **Cabot** (str.), Nf, NS,Can
110/G6 **Cabo Verde**, Braz.
58/C4 **Cabra**, Sp.
90/G8 **Cabramatta**, Austl.
60/A3 **Cabras**, It.
59/G3 **Cabrera** (isl.), Sp.
122/F3 **Cabri**, Sk,Can
58/E3 **Cabriel** (riv.), Sp.
82/D4 **Cabugao**, Phil.
117/H5 **Cabure**, Ven.
110/B3 **Caçador**, Braz.
62/E4 **Čačak**, Yugo.
110/H8 **Caçapava**, Braz.
60/A2 **Caccia** (cape), It.
108/G7 **Cáceres**, Braz.
58/B3 **Cáceres**, Sp.
112/Q10 **Cachapoal** (riv.), Chile
124/B3 **Cache** (cr.), Ca,US
122/E5 **Cache** (peak), Id,US
122/C3 **Cache Creek**, BC,Can
98/A3 **Cacheu**, GBis.
109/G5 **Cachimbo** (mts.), Braz.
110/A4 **Cachoeira do Sul**, Braz.
110/J7 **Cachoeira Paulista**, Braz.
110/L7 **Cachoeiras de Macacu**, Braz.
110/B4 **Cachoeirinha**, Braz.
110/D2 **Cachoeiro de Itapemirim**, Braz.
110/G6 **Caconde**, Braz.
110/B1 **Caçu**, Braz.
104/B3 **Cacula**, Ang.
109/K6 **Caculé**, Braz.
59/G1 **Cadaques**, Sp.
49/K4 **Čadca**, Slvk.
128/E3 **Caddo** (mts.), Ar,US
46/C1 **Cader Idris** (mtn.), Wal,UK
126/C2 **Cadillac**, Mi,US
82/D5 **Cadiz**, Phil.
58/B4 **Cádiz**, Sp.
58/B4 **Cádiz** (gulf), Sp.
126/C4 **Cadiz**, Ky,US
47/E5 **Cadnam**, Eng,UK
56/C2 **Caen**, Fr.
48/D3 **Caerleon**, Wal,UK
44/D5 **Caernarfon**, Wal,UK
44/D5 **Caernarfon** (bay), Wal,UK
46/C3 **Caerphilly**, Wal,UK
46/C1 **Caersws**, Wal,UK
74/M7 **Caesarea Nat'l Park**, Isr.
52/B2 **Caëstre**, Fr.
111/C2 **Cafayate**, Arg.
82/D6 **Cagayan de Oro**, Phil.
82/C6 **Cagayan Sulu** (isl.), Phil.
60/A3 **Cagliari**, It.
60/A3 **Cagliari** (gulf), It.
57/G5 **Cagnes-sur-Mer**, Fr.
108/D3 **Caguán** (riv.), Col.
117/H4 **Caguas**, PR
104/B4 **Cahama**, Ang.
43/B4 **Cahore** (pt.), Ire.
56/D4 **Cahors**, Fr.
110/B4 **Cai** (riv.), Braz.
109/H7 **Caiapó** (mts.), Braz.
109/H7 **Caiapó** (riv.), Braz.
117/F3 **Caibarién**, Cuba
109/L5 **Caicó**, Braz.
117/G3 **Caicos** (isls.), Trks.
110/G8 **Caieiras**, Braz.
52/A4 **Cailly** (riv.), Fr.
83/D4 **Cai Nuoc**, Viet.
105/Y **Caird** (coast), Ant.
130/G3 **Cairn** (mtn.), Ak,US
91/B3 **Cairn Curran** (dam), Austl.
43/D2 **Cairngorm** (mts.), Sc,UK
44/C2 **Cairn Pat** (hill), Sc,UK
44/C2 **Cairnryan**, Sc,UK
90/B2 **Cairns**, Austl.
44/D1 **Cairnsmore of Carsphairn** (mtn.), Sc,UK
129/G4 **Cairo**, Ga,US
126/B4 **Cairo**, Il,US
100/B2 **Cairo** (Al Qāhirah) (cap.), Egypt
47/H1 **Caister on Sea**, Eng,UK
45/H5 **Caistor**, Eng,UK
127/Q9 **Caistor Centre**, On,Can
127/Q9 **Caistorville**, On,Can
104/B3 **Caitou**, Ang.
104/C4 **Caiundo**, Ang.
81/C5 **Caizi** (lake), China
108/C5 **Cajabamba**, Peru
108/C5 **Cajamarca**, Peru
116/E3 **Cajón** (pt.), Cuba
99/H5 **Calabar**, Nga.
117/H6 **Calabozo**, Ven.
60/E3 **Calabria** (reg.), It.
60/E3 **Calabria Nat'l Park**, It.
58/C4 **Calaburras, Punta de** (pt.), Sp.
62/F4 **Calafat**, Rom.
58/E1 **Calahorra**, Sp.
52/A2 **Calais**, Fr.
127/H2 **Calais**, Me,US
52/A2 **Calais, Canal de** (can.), Fr.
111/C2 **Calalaste** (mts.), Arg.
111/C1 **Calama**, Chile
82/C5 **Calamian Group** (isls.), Phil.
62/F3 **Călan**, Rom.
82/D5 **Calapan**, Phil.
63/H3 **Călăraşi**, Rom.
63/H3 **Călăraşi** (co.), Rom.
58/E3 **Calasparra**, Sp.
58/E2 **Calatayud**, Sp.
132/L12 **Calaveras** (res.), Ca,US
82/D4 **Calayan**, Phil.
82/D4 **Calayan** (isl.), Phil.
82/D5 **Calbayog**, Phil.
112/B4 **Calbuco**, Chile
108/D6 **Calca**, Peru
128/E4 **Calcasieu** (riv.), La,US
126/F2 **Calcium**, NY,US
84/E3 **Calcutta**, India
58/A3 **Caldas da Rainha**, Port.
110/B1 **Caldas Novas**, Braz.
45/E2 **Caldbeck**, Eng,UK
51/G6 **Calden**, Ger.
45/G4 **Calder** (riv.), Eng,UK
130/M4 **Calder** (mtn.), Ak,US
59/L6 **Caldes de Montbui**, Sp.
45/F2 **Caldew** (riv.), Eng,UK
46/D3 **Caldicot**, Wal,UK
122/D5 **Caldwell**, Id,US
128/D4 **Caldwell**, Tx,US
46/B3 **Caldy** (isl.), Wal,UK
102/D3 **Caledon** (riv.), Les., SAfr.
127/Q8 **Caledon East**, On,Can
127/H2 **Caledonia** (hills), NB,Can
59/G2 **Calella**, Sp.
112/Q9 **Calera de Tango**, Chile
117/P9 **Calera Víctor Rosales**, Mex.
117/P10 **Caleta de Campos Chutla**, Mex.
112/D5 **Caleta Olivia**, Arg.
124/D4 **Calexico**, Ca,US
45/F3 **Calf, The** (mtn.), Eng,UK
122/E3 **Calgary**, Ab,Can
59/S12 **Calheta**, Azor.,Port.
59/U15 **Calheta**, Madr.,Port.
129/G3 **Calhoun**, Ga,US
126/C4 **Calhoun**, Ky,US
108/C3 **Cali**, Col.
58/E4 **Calida, Costa** (coast), Sp.
124/D3 **Caliente**, Nv,US
117/M8 **California** (gulf), Mex.
124/B3 **California** (state), US
126/E4 **California**, Md,US
125/J3 **California**, Mo,US
111/D1 **Calilegua Nat'l Park**, Arg.
63/G3 **Călimăneşti**, Rom.
84/C5 **Calimere** (pt.), India
131/C2 **Calimesa**, Ca,US
116/C3 **Calkiní**, Mex.
91/A1 **Callabonna** (lake), Austl.
43/C2 **Callander**, Sc,UK
108/C6 **Callao**, Peru
129/G4 **Callaway**, Fl,US
112/Q9 **Calle Larga**, Chile
46/B6 **Callington**, Eng,UK
59/E3 **Callosa de Ensarriá**, Sp.
59/E3 **Callosa de Segura**, Sp.
46/D4 **Calne**, Eng,UK
52/B3 **Calonne-Ricouart**, Fr.
60/D2 **Calore** (riv.), It.
90/D4 **Caloundra**, Austl.
57/F3 **Calpe**, Sp.
46/B6 **Calstock**, Eng,UK
60/D4 **Caltagirone**, It.
60/D4 **Caltanissetta**, It.
56/F4 **Caluire-et-Cuire**, Fr.
132/Q16 **Calumet** (riv.), Il,US
132/Q16 **Calumet City**, Il,US
104/B3 **Caluquembe**, Ang.
122/A3 **Calvert** (isl.), BC,Can
45/G5 **Calverton**, Eng,UK
131/K7 **Calverton**, Md,US
131/H5 **Calverton**, NY,US
59/G3 **Calvià**, Sp.
102/B3 **Calvinia**, SAfr.
58/C2 **Calvitero** (mtn.), Sp.
47/G2 **Cam** (riv.), Eng,UK
109/L6 **Camaçari**, Braz.
104/C3 **Camacupa**, Ang.
117/F3 **Camagüey**, Cuba
117/F3 **Camagüey** (arch.), Cuba
57/J5 **Camaiore**, It.
108/D7 **Camaná**, Peru
110/B4 **Camaquã**, Braz.
110/A4 **Camaquã** (riv.), Braz.
59/V15 **Câmara de Lobos**, Madr.,Port.
57/G5 **Camarat** (cape), Fr.
58/D1 **Camargo**, Sp.
131/A2 **Camarillo**, Ca,US
58/A1 **Camariñas**, Sp.
116/D4 **Camarón** (cape), Hon.
112/D5 **Camarones** (bay), Arg.
58/B4 **Camas**, Sp.
83/D4 **Ca Mau**, Viet.
83/D4 **Ca Mau** (cape), Viet.
58/A1 **Cambados**, Sp.
110/B2 **Cambará**, Braz.
84/B3 **Cambay**, India
84/B3 **Cambay** (gulf), India
110/B2 **Cambé**, Braz.
47/F4 **Camberley Frimley**, Eng,UK
83/D3 **Cambodia**
110/C3 **Camboriú, Ponta do** (pt.), Braz.
46/A6 **Camborne**, Eng,UK
52/C3 **Cambrai**, Fr.
46/C2 **Cambrian** (mts.), Wal,UK
126/D3 **Cambridge**, On,Can
47/G2 **Cambridge**, Eng,UK
127/G3 **Cambridge**, Ma,US
126/E4 **Cambridge**, Md,US
123/K4 **Cambridge**, Mn,US
126/D3 **Cambridge**, Oh,US
47/G2 **Cambridgeshire** (co.), Eng,UK
59/F2 **Cambrils**, Sp.
110/G7 **Cambuí**, Braz.
110/H6 **Cambuquira**, Braz.
117/E6 **Cambutal** (mt.), Pan.
91/D2 **Camden**, Austl.
129/G4 **Camden**, Al,US
128/E3 **Camden**, Ar,US
127/G2 **Camden**, Me,US
131/E6 **Camden**, NJ,US
129/H3 **Camden**, SC,US
125/J3 **Camdenton**, Mo,US
104/D3 **Cameia Nat'l Park**, Ang.
46/B6 **Camel** (riv.), Eng,UK
131/E4 **Camelback** (mtn.), Pa,US
46/B5 **Camelford**, Eng,UK
119/R7 **Cameron** (isl.), NW,Can
124/E4 **Cameron**, Az,US
128/E4 **Cameron**, La,US
125/J3 **Cameron**, Mo,US
128/D4 **Cameron**, Tx,US
96/H7 **Cameroon**
109/J4 **Cametá**, Braz.
52/A2 **Camiers**, Fr.
82/D4 **Camiguin** (isl.), Phil.
129/G4 **Camilla**, Ga,US
108/F8 **Camiri**, Bol.
104/F5 **Camo-Camo**, Moz.
109/K4 **Camocim**, Braz.
85/F6 **Camorta** (isl.), India
52/A3 **Campagne**, Fr.
112/F2 **Campana**, Arg.
113/J7 **Campana** (isl.), Chile
112/C2 **Campanario** (peak), Arg.
60/D2 **Campanella** (cape), It.
110/H6 **Campanha**, Braz.
60/D2 **Campania** (reg.), It.
39/T8 **Campbell** (isl.), NZ
132/L12 **Campbell**, Ca,US
122/A2 **Campbell Island**, BC,Can
122/B3 **Campbell River**, BC,Can
126/C4 **Campbellsville**, Ky,US
127/H2 **Campbellton**, NB,Can
90/G9 **Campbelltown**, Austl.
127/Q9 **Campbellville**, On,Can
127/R9 **Campden**, On,Can
116/C4 **Campeche**, Mex.
116/C4 **Campeche** (bay), Mex.
116/C4 **Campeche** (state), Mex.
123/H3 **Camperville**, Mb,Can
110/G6 **Campestre**, Braz.
83/D1 **Cam Pha**, Viet.
60/A3 **Campidano** (range), It.
58/C4 **Campillos**, Sp.
109/L5 **Campina Grande**, Braz.
110/F7 **Campinas**, Braz.
110/B1 **Campina Verde**, Braz.
108/C3 **Campoalegre**, Col.
60/D2 **Campobasso**, It.
110/C2 **Campo Belo**, Braz.
58/D3 **Campo de Criptana**, Sp.
117/G5 **Campo de la Cruz**, Col.
109/K6 **Campo Formoso**, Braz.
109/H8 **Campo Grande**, Braz.
111/G2 **Campo Largo**, Braz.
110/G8 **Campo Limpo Paulista**, Braz.
109/K4 **Campo Maior**, Braz.
58/B3 **Campo Maior**, Port.
57/H4 **Campomorone**, It.
110/A3 **Campo Mourão**, Braz.
58/C1 **Camporredondo** (res.), Sp.
110/D2 **Campos**, Braz.
109/J7 **Campos** (reg.), Braz.
110/C1 **Campos Altos**, Braz.
59/G3 **Campos del Puerto**, Sp.
110/H7 **Campos do Jordão**, Braz.
110/C2 **Campos Gerais**, Braz.
110/B3 **Campos Novos**, Braz.
131/K8 **Camp Springs**, Md,US
128/E4 **Campti**, La,US
83/E4 **Cam Ranh**, Viet.
122/E2 **Camrose**, Ab,Can
83/D1 **Cam Thuy**, Viet.
118/* **Canada**
112/E2 **Cañada de Gómez**, Arg.
125/H4 **Canadian** (riv.), US
128/C3 **Canadian**, Tx,US
112/C5 **Cañadon Grande** (mts.), Arg.
117/G6 **Canagua**, Ven.
108/F2 **Canaima Nat'l Park**, Ven.
63/H5 **Çanakkale**, Turk.
63/H5 **Çanakkale** (prov.), Turk.
93/U12 **Canala**, NCal.
112/E2 **Canals**, Arg.
59/E3 **Canals**, Sp.
126/E3 **Canandaigua**, NY,US
117/M7 **Cananea**, Mex.
110/C3 **Cananéia**, Braz.
59/X16 **Canary Islands** (aut. comm.), Sp.
116/D5 **Cañas**, CR
117/P9 **Canatlán**, Mex.
129/H4 **Canaveral** (cape), Fl,US
109/L7 **Canavieiras**, Braz.
91/D2 **Canberra** (cap.), Austl.
52/A3 **Canche** (riv.), Fr.
116/D3 **Cancún**, Mex.
58/C1 **Candás**, Sp.
127/N7 **Candiac**, Qu,Can
110/B2 **Candido Mota**, Braz.
86/D5 **Canding** (cape), Indo.
123/G2 **Candle** (lake), Sk,Can
123/J3 **Cando**, ND,US
82/D4 **Candon**, Phil.
110/B4 **Canela**, Braz.
57/H4 **Canelli**, It.
113/F2 **Canelones**, Uru.
113/F2 **Canelones** (dept.), Uru.
58/A1 **Cangas**, Sp.
58/B1 **Cangas de Narcea**, Sp.
58/C1 **Cangas de Onís**, Sp.
86/C5 **Cangkuang** (cape), Indo.
102/C4 **Cango Caves**, SAfr.
104/D3 **Cangombe**, Ang.
113/J7 **Cangrejo** (peak), Arg.
110/A4 **Canguçu**, Braz.
81/D3 **Cangzhou**, China
83/D1 **Canh Cuoc** (isl.), Viet.
104/B3 **Canhoca**, Ang.
90/C4 **Cania Gorge Nat'l Park**, Austl.
119/K3 **Caniapiscau** (lake), Qu,Can
119/K3 **Caniapiscau** (riv.), Qu,Can
60/C4 **Canicatti**, It.
56/E5 **Canigou, Pic de** (peak), Fr.
74/D2 **Canik** (mts.), Turk.
58/D4 **Caniles**, Sp.
109/L4 **Canindé**, Braz.
109/K5 **Canindé** (riv.), Braz.
74/C2 **Çankırı**, Turk.
87/F1 **Canlaon** (vol.), Phil.
122/E3 **Canmore**, Ab,Can
84/C5 **Cannanore**, India
60/E2 **Canne** (ruins), It.
53/F5 **Canner** (riv.), Fr.
57/G5 **Cannes**, Fr.
43/C2 **Cannich**, Sc,UK
46/D1 **Cannock**, Eng,UK
123/H4 **Cannonball** (riv.), ND,US
123/K4 **Cannon Falls**, Mn,US
110/B4 **Canoas**, Braz.
110/B3 **Canoas** (riv.), Braz.
91/D2 **Canobolas** (peak), Austl.
122/F2 **Canoe** (lake), Sk,Can
110/B3 **Canoinhas**, Braz.
45/F1 **Canonbie**, Sc,UK
125/F3 **Canon City**, Co,US
123/H3 **Canora**, Sk,Can
127/J2 **Canso** (cape), Can.
58/C1 **Cantabria** (aut. comm.), Sp.
56/E4 **Cantal** (plat.), Fr.
58/A2 **Cantanhede**, Port.
117/J6 **Cantaura**, Ven.
90/H8 **Canterbury**, Austl.
47/H4 **Canterbury**, Eng,UK
83/D4 **Can Tho**, Viet.
58/C4 **Cantillana**, Sp.
126/B3 **Canton**, Il,US
132/E7 **Canton**, Mi,US
129/F3 **Canton**, Ms,US
126/F2 **Canton**, NY,US
126/D3 **Canton**, Oh,US
125/H3 **Canton**, Ok,US
123/J5 **Canton**, SD,US
128/E3 **Canton**, Tx,US
93/H5 **Canton** (Abariringa) (atoll), Kiri.
82/B3 **Canton** (Guangzhou), China
57/H4 **Cantù**, It.
112/F2 **Cañuelas**, Arg.
91/B3 **Canunda Nat'l Park**, Austl.
47/G3 **Canvey Island**, Eng,UK
122/G2 **Canwood**, Sk,Can
128/C3 **Canyon**, Tx,US
124/E3 **Canyon de Chelly Nat'l Mon.**, Az,US
124/E3 **Canyonlands Nat'l Park**, Ut,US
83/D1 **Cao Bang**, Viet.
82/A2 **Caodu** (riv.), China
83/D4 **Cao Lanh**, Viet.
108/E2 **Capanaparo** (riv.), Ven.
109/J4 **Capanema**, Braz.
60/B1 **Capanne** (peak), It.
57/J5 **Capannori**, It.
110/B3 **Capão Bonito**, Braz.
110/B3 **Caparaó Nat'l Park**, Braz.
58/A3 **Caparica**, Port.
127/H1 **Cap-Chat**, Qu,Can
127/F2 **Cap-de-la-Madeleine**, Qu,Can
90/B3 **Cape** (riv.), Austl.
91/D4 **Cape Barren** (isl.), Austl.
127/J2 **Cape Breton** (highlands), NS,Can
127/J2 **Cape Breton** (isl.), NS,Can
127/J2 **Cape Breton Highlands Nat'l Park**, NS,Can
90/B2 **Cape Cleveland Nat'l Park**, Austl.
99/E5 **Cape Coast**, Gha.
127/G3 **Cape Cod Nat'l Seashore**, Ma,US
129/H5 **Cape Coral**, Fl,US
129/J3 **Cape Fear** (riv.), NC,US
125/K3 **Cape Girardeau**, Mo,US
129/K3 **Cape Hatteras Nat'l Seashore**, NC,US
130/E2 **Cape Krusenstern Nat'l Mon.**, Ak,US
44/E5 **Capel-Curig**, Wal,UK
110/D1 **Capelinha**, Braz.
59/K6 **Capellades**, Sp.
47/H4 **Capel le Ferne**, Eng,UK
129/J3 **Cape Lookout Nat'l Seashore**, NC,US
47/H2 **Capel Saint Mary**, Eng,UK
90/B1 **Cape Melville Nat'l Park**, Austl.
90/C3 **Cape Palmerston Nat'l Park**, Austl.
131/K7 **Cape Saint Claire**, Md,US
102/B4 **Cape Town** (cap.), SAfr.
90/B2 **Cape Tribulation Nat'l Park**, Austl.
90/B2 **Cape Upstart Nat'l Park**, Austl.
38/H5 **Cape Verde**
90/A1 **Cape York** (pen.), Austl.
117/G4 **Cap-Haïtien**, Haiti
60/A2 **Capicciola** (pt.), Fr.
109/J4 **Capim** (riv.), Braz.
110/B1 **Capinópolis**, Braz.
110/B2 **Capirara** (res.), Braz.
128/B3 **Capitan** (mts.), NM,US
109/J4 **Capitão Poco**, Braz.
124/E3 **Capitol Reef Nat'l Park**, Ut,US
109/H8 **Capivara** (res.), Braz.
110/J6 **Capivari** (riv.), Braz.
62/C4 **Čapljina**, Bosn.
60/D3 **Capo d'Orlando**, It.
60/A3 **Capoterra**, It.
60/A1 **Capraia** (isl.), It.
126/D2 **Capreol**, On,Can
60/D2 **Capri**, It.
90/C3 **Capricorn** (cape), Austl.
90/C3 **Capricorn** (chan.), Austl.
104/D4 **Caprivi Strip** (reg.), Namb.
128/C3 **Cap Rock Escarpment** (cliffs), Tx,US
128/C3 **Caprock, The** (cliffs), NM,US
127/G2 **Cap-Rouge**, Qu,Can
57/G5 **Cap Roux, Pointe du** (pt.), Fr.
125/G3 **Capulin Volcano Nat'l Mon.**, NM,US
108/D4 **Caquetá** (riv.), Col.
59/N9 **Carabanchel** (nrbhd.), Sp.
63/G3 **Caracal**, Rom.
117/H5 **Caracas** (cap.), Ven.
46/B5 **Caradon** (hill), Eng,UK
110/H8 **Caraguatatuba**, Braz.
110/H8 **Caraguatatuba** (bay), Braz.
112/B3 **Carahue**, Chile
109/H5 **Carajás** (mts.), Braz.
110/D1 **Carandaí**, Braz.
110/D2 **Carangola**, Braz.
62/F3 **Caransebeş**, Rom.
60/D2 **Carapelle** (riv.), It.
110/G8 **Carapicuíba**, Braz.
127/H2 **Caraquet**, NB,Can
62/E3 **Caraş-Severin** (co.), Rom.
116/E4 **Caratasca** (lag.), Hon.
110/D1 **Caratinga**, Braz.
108/E4 **Carauari**, Braz.
58/E3 **Caravaca de la Cruz**, Sp.
98/A4 **Caravela** (isl.), GBis.
111/F2 **Carazinho**, Braz.
58/A1 **Carballino**, Sp.
58/A1 **Carballo**, Sp.
123/J3 **Carberry**, Mb,Can
132/C3 **Carbon** (riv.), Wa,US
60/A3 **Carbonara** (cape), It.
60/D4 **Carbonara, Pizzo** (peak), It.
126/B4 **Carbondale**, Il,US
126/F3 **Carbondale**, Pa,US
60/A3 **Carbonia**, It.
59/E3 **Carcagente**, Sp.
112/E2 **Carcaraña**, Arg.
56/E5 **Carcassonne**, Fr.
59/P10 **Carcavelos**, Port.
58/E3 **Carche** (mtn.), Sp.
118/C2 **Carcross**, Yt,Can
59/L6 **Cardedeu**, Sp.
113/K7 **Cardiel** (lake), Arg.
46/C4 **Cardiff** (cap.), Wal,UK
46/B2 **Cardigan**, Wal,UK

Cardo – Chesh

59/F2 **Cardona,** Sp.
110/B2 **Cardoso,** Braz.
122/E3 **Cardston,** Ab,Can
62/F2 **Carei,** Rom.
56/C2 **Carentan,** Fr.
62/F4 **Carev vrh** (peak), Macd.
56/B2 **Carhaix-Plouguer,** Fr.
112/E3 **Carhué,** Arg.
110/D2 **Cariacica,** Braz.
117/J5 **Cariaco,** Ven.
108/C4 **Cariamanga,** Ecu.
60/E3 **Cariati,** It.
117/G5 **Caribbean** (sea)
122/C2 **Cariboo** (mts.), BC,Can
118/E3 **Caribou** (mts.), Ab,Can
126/B1 **Caribou** (lake), On,Can
130/L3 **Caribou,** Yk,Can
122/F5 **Caribou** (range), Id,US
127/G2 **Caribou,** Me,US
82/D5 **Carigara,** Phil.
109/K6 **Carinhanha,** Braz.
60/C3 **Carini,** It.
57/K3 **Carinthia** (prov.), Aus.
117/J5 **Caripito,** Ven.
125/G3 **Carizzo** (cr.), NM, Tx,US
59/E3 **Carlet,** Sp.
127/H2 **Carleton** (peak), NB,Can
127/H2 **Carleton** (riv.), NS,Can
127/H1 **Carleton,** Qu,Can
102/D2 **Carletonville,** SAfr.
124/C2 **Carlin,** Nv,US
90/H8 **Carlingford,** Austl.
44/B3 **Carlingford** (mtn.), Ire.
44/B3 **Carlingford Lough** (inlet), Ire.
126/B4 **Carlinville,** Il,US
127/Q9 **Carlisle,** On,Can
45/F2 **Carlisle,** Eng,UK
56/D5 **Carlit** (peak), Fr.
112/E2 **Carlos Casares,** Arg.
110/D1 **Carlos Chagas,** Braz.
117/F3 **Carlos M. De Cespedes,** Cuba
44/B6 **Carlow,** Ire.
44/B6 **Carlow** (co.), Ire.
125/F4 **Carlsbad,** NM,US
125/F4 **Carlsbad Caverns Nat'l Park,** NM,US
45/G6 **Carlton,** Eng,UK
123/K4 **Carlton,** Mn,US
127/Q9 **Carluke,** On,Can
123/H3 **Carlyle,** Sk,Can
125/K3 **Carlyle** (lake), Il,US
118/C2 **Carmacks,** Yk,Can
57/G4 **Carmagnola,** It.
123/J3 **Carman,** Mb,Can
46/B3 **Carmarthen,** Wal,UK
46/B3 **Carmarthen** (bay), Wal,UK
56/E4 **Carmaux,** Fr.
126/C4 **Carmel,** In,US
44/D5 **Carmel Head** (pt.), Wal,UK
74/K5 **Carmel, Mount** (Har Karmel) (mtn.), Isr.
112/F2 **Carmelo,** Uru.
117/M8 **Carmen** (isl.), Mex.
117/N7 **Carmen** (riv.), Mex.
126/B4 **Carmi,** Il,US
132/M9 **Carmichael,** Ca,US
110/L6 **Carmo,** Braz.
110/C1 **Carmo do Paranaíba,** Braz.
110/C2 **Carmo do Rio Claro,** Braz.
58/C4 **Carmona,** Sp.
44/B1 **Carnanmore** (mtn.), NI,UK
89/A3 **Carnarvon,** Austl.
102/C3 **Carnarvonleegte** (dry riv.), SAfr.
90/B4 **Carnarvon Nat'l Park,** Austl.
59/P10 **Carnaxide,** Port.
44/C2 **Carncastle,** NI,UK
123/H3 **Carnduff,** Sk,Can
44/D5 **Carnedd Dafydd** (mtn.), Wal,UK
44/E5 **Carnedd Llewelyn** (mtn.), Wal,UK
105/S **Carney** (isl.), Ant.
45/F3 **Carnforth,** Eng,UK
52/C3 **Carnières,** Fr.
44/B2 **Carnlough,** NI,UK
96/J7 **Carnot,** CAfr.
58/A1 **Carnota,** Sp.
43/D2 **Carnoustie,** Sc,UK
43/B4 **Carnsore** (pt.), Ire.
118/D2 **Carnwath** (riv.), NW,Can
126/D3 **Caro,** Mi,US
117/H4 **Carolina,** PR
93/K5 **Caroline** (isl.), Kiri.
92/D4 **Caroline** (isls.), Micr.
132/P16 **Carol Stream,** Il,US
41/G4 **Carpathian** (mts.), Eur.
57/J4 **Carpenedolo,** It.
89/C2 **Carpentaria** (gulf), Austl.
132/P15 **Carpentersville,** Il,US
56/F4 **Carpentras,** Fr.
57/J4 **Carpi,** It.
131/A2 **Carpinteria,** Ca,US
132/B3 **Carr** (inlet), Wa,US
129/G4 **Carrabelle,** Fl,US
57/J4 **Carrara,** It.
44/D6 **Carreg Ddu** (pt.), Wal,UK
117/J5 **Carriacou** (isl.), Gren.
44/C2 **Carrickfergus,** NI,UK
44/C2 **Carrickfergus** (dist.), NI,UK
44/A2 **Carrickmore,** NI,UK
52/B6 **Carrières-sous-Poissy,** Fr.
44/B3 **Carrigatuke** (mtn.), NI,UK
123/J4 **Carrington,** ND,US
58/C1 **Carrión** (riv.), Sp.
117/G5 **Carrizal,** Col.
120/E4 **Carrizo** (mts.), Az,US
128/C2 **Carrizo** (cr.), NM,US
128/D4 **Carrizo Springs,** Tx,US
125/F4 **Carrizozo,** NM,US
129/G3 **Carrollton,** Ga,US
126/C4 **Carrollton,** Ky,US
125/J3 **Carrollton,** Mo,US
123/H2 **Carrot** (riv.), Sk,Can
123/H2 **Carrot River,** Sk,Can
44/C2 **Carrowdore,** NI,UK
44/C2 **Carryduff,** NI,UK
74/D2 **Çarşamba,** Turk.
131/B3 **Carson,** Ca,US
124/C3 **Carson** (riv.), Nv,US
124/C3 **Carson** (sink), Nv,US
124/C3 **Carson City** (cap.), Nv,US
44/D1 **Carsphairn,** Sc,UK
122/E3 **Carstairs,** Ab,Can
112/Q9 **Cartagena,** Chile
117/F5 **Cartagena,** Col.
59/E4 **Cartagena,** Sp.
108/C3 **Cartago,** Col.
116/E6 **Cartago,** CR
58/C4 **Cártama,** Sp.
58/A3 **Cartaxo,** Port.
58/B4 **Cartaya,** Sp.
90/A1 **Carter** (peak), Austl.
131/F5 **Carteret,** NJ,US
129/G3 **Cartersville,** Ga,US
47/E3 **Carterton,** Eng,UK
60/B4 **Carthage** (ruins), Tun.
125/J3 **Carthage,** Mo,US
129/F3 **Carthage,** Ms,US
129/G2 **Carthage,** Tn,US
128/E3 **Carthage,** Tx,US
119/L3 **Cartwright,** Nf,Can
109/L5 **Caruaru,** Braz.
108/F1 **Carúpano,** Ven.
125/K3 **Caruthersville,** Mo,US
52/B2 **Carvin,** Fr.
58/A3 **Carvoeiro** (cape), Port.
132/P15 **Cary,** Il,US
129/J3 **Cary,** NC,US
96/D1 **Casablanca,** Mor.
110/F6 **Casa Branca,** Braz.
117/N7 **Casa de Janos,** Mex.
124/E4 **Casa Grande,** Az,US
124/E4 **Casa Grande Nat'l Mon.,** Az,US
60/D2 **Casal di Principe,** It.
57/J4 **Casalecchio di Reno,** It.
57/H4 **Casale Monferrato,** It.
98/A3 **Casamance** (riv.), Sen.
109/L4 **Casa Nova,** Braz.
61/F3 **Casarano,** It.
117/N7 **Casas Grandes** (ruins), Mex.
117/N8 **Cascada de Bassaseachic Nat'l Park,** Mex.
122/C5 **Cascade** (range), Can., US
122/D4 **Cascade** (res.), Id,US
132/C3 **Cascade-Fairwood,** Wa,US
103/R15 **Cascades** (pt.), Reun.
59/P10 **Cascais,** Port.
127/H1 **Cascapédia** (riv.), Qu,Can
57/J5 **Cascina-Navacchio,** It.
132/B3 **Case** (inlet), Wa,US
60/D2 **Caserta,** It.
105/H **Casey,** Ant.
105/D **Casey** (bay), Ant.
97/R5 **Caseyr** (cape), Som.
122/C4 **Cashmere,** Wa,US
112/E2 **Casilda,** Arg.
117/P10 **Casimiro Castillo,** Mex.
91/E1 **Casino,** Austl.
131/A2 **Casitas** (lake), Ca,US
108/C5 **Casma,** Peru
59/E2 **Caspe,** Sp.
123/G5 **Casper,** Wy,US
68/F6 **Caspian** (sea), Eur., Asia
59/G2 **Cassà de la Selva,** Sp.
104/D3 **Cassai** (riv.), Ang.
104/D3 **Cassamba,** Ang.
60/E3 **Cassano allo Ionio,** It.
126/D3 **Cass City,** Mi,US
110/C2 **Cássia,** Braz.
118/C3 **Cassiar** (mts.), BC,Can
110/B1 **Cassilândia,** Braz.
60/C2 **Cassino,** It.
125/J3 **Cassville,** Mo,US
131/B2 **Castaic,** Ca,US
131/B1 **Castaic** (lake), Ca,US
59/E3 **Castalla,** Sp.
109/J4 **Castanhal,** Braz.
60/D4 **Castelbuono,** It.
57/K5 **Castelfidardo,** It.
60/C3 **Castellammare** (gulf), It.
60/D2 **Castellammare di Stabia,** It.
57/G4 **Castellamonte,** It.
59/G2 **Castellar del Vallès,** Sp.
59/K7 **Castelldefels,** Sp.
59/L7 **Castell de Montjuïc,** Sp.
60/D4 **Castello Eurialo** (ruins), It.
59/E3 **Castellón de la Plana,** Sp.
74/N9 **Castel Nat'l Park,** Isr.
56/D5 **Castelnaudary,** Fr.
56/E5 **Castelnau-le-Lez,** Fr.
58/B3 **Castelo Branco,** Port.
58/B2 **Castelo Branco** (dist.), Port.
56/D4 **Castelsarrasin,** Fr.
60/C4 **Castelvetrano,** It.
110/B2 **Castilho,** Braz.
108/B5 **Castilla,** Peru
58/C2 **Castille and León** (aut. comm.), Sp.
58/D3 **Castille-La Mancha** (aut. comm.), Sp.
117/G5 **Castilletes,** Col.
112/C4 **Castillo** (peak), Arg.
129/H4 **Castillo de San Marcos Nat'l Mon.,** Fl,US
113/G2 **Castillos,** Uru.
47/G1 **Castle Acre,** Eng,UK
43/A4 **Castlebar,** Ire.
46/D4 **Castle Cary,** Eng,UK
44/B3 **Castlecaulfield,** NI,UK
46/D4 **Castle Combe,** Eng,UK
124/E3 **Castle Dale,** Ut,US
44/B2 **Castledawson,** NI,UK
45/G6 **Castle Donnington,** Eng,UK
44/E2 **Castle Douglas,** Sc,UK
45/G4 **Castleford,** Eng,UK
122/D3 **Castlegar,** BC,Can
90/H8 **Castle Hill,** Austl.
44/D2 **Castle Kennedy,** Sc,UK
91/C3 **Castlemaine,** Austl.
90/G8 **Castlereagh,** Austl.
44/B1 **Castlerock,** NI,UK
125/F3 **Castle Rock,** Co,US
123/L5 **Castle Rock** (lake), Wi,US
90/C4 **Castle Tower Nat'l Park,** Austl.
44/D3 **Castletown,** IM,UK
44/C3 **Castlewellan,** NI,UK
122/F2 **Castor,** Ab,Can
96/D6 **Castos** (riv.), Libr.
56/E5 **Castres,** Fr.
50/B3 **Castricum,** Neth.
117/J5 **Castries** (cap.), StL.
110/B3 **Castro,** Braz.
112/B4 **Castro,** Chile
58/C4 **Castro del Río,** Sp.
58/B1 **Castro de Rey,** Sp.
51/E5 **Castrop-Rauxel,** Ger.
58/D1 **Castro-Urdiales,** Sp.
132/K11 **Castro Valley,** Ca,US
60/E3 **Castrovillari,** It.
58/C3 **Castuera,** Sp.
117/F3 **Cat** (isl.), Bahm.
123/K3 **Cat** (lake), On,Can
92/B3 **Cataduanes** (isl.), Phil.
110/L6 **Cataguases,** Braz.
82/D5 **Cataiñgan,** Phil.
87/F1 **Cataiñgan,** Phil.
63/K5 **Çatalağzı,** Turk.
110/C1 **Catalão,** Braz.
63/J5 **Çatalca,** Turk.
124/E4 **Catalina,** Az,US
59/F2 **Catalonia** (aut. comm.), Sp.
111/C2 **Catamarca,** Arg.
82/D5 **Catanduanes** (isl.), Phil.
110/B2 **Catanduva,** Braz.
60/D4 **Catania,** It.
60/D4 **Catania** (gulf), It.
60/E3 **Catanzaro,** It.
87/F1 **Catarman,** Indo.
82/D5 **Catarman,** Phil.
59/E3 **Catarroja,** Sp.
117/G6 **Catatumbo** (riv.), Col., Ven.
87/F2 **Catatungan** (mtn.), Phil.
129/H3 **Catawba** (riv.), NC, SC,US
82/D5 **Catbalogan,** Phil.
113/G2 **Catedral** (peak), Uru.
47/F4 **Caterham and Warlingham,** Eng,UK
100/C2 **Catherine, Mount** (Jabal Katrī nah) (mtn.), Egypt
117/F6 **Cativá,** Pan.
126/D4 **Catlettsburg,** Ky,US
116/D3 **Catoche** (cape), Mex.
57/K5 **Catria** (peak), It.
108/F3 **Catrimani** (riv.), Braz.
46/D2 **Catshill,** Eng,UK
126/F3 **Catskill** (mts.), NY,US
53/F5 **Cattenom,** Fr.
45/G3 **Catterick,** Eng,UK
82/D4 **Cauayan,** Phil.
82/D6 **Cauayan,** Phil.
108/C2 **Cauca** (riv.), Col.
109/L4 **Caucaia,** Braz.
108/C2 **Caucasia,** Col.
66/G4 **Caucasus** (mts.), Eur.
59/E3 **Caudete,** Sp.
52/C3 **Caudry,** Fr.
45/F1 **Cauldcleuch** (mtn.), Sc,UK
112/B2 **Cauquenes,** Chile
56/D4 **Caussade,** Fr.
60/D4 **Cava d'Ispica** (ruins), It.
58/B2 **Cávado** (riv.), Port.
56/F5 **Cavaillon,** Fr.
123/J3 **Cavalier,** ND,US
96/D6 **Cavalla** (riv.), IvC., Libr.
98/D5 **Cavalla** (Cavally) (riv.), IvC., Libr.
60/A1 **Cavallo, Capo al** (cape), Fr.
44/A4 **Cavan** (co.), Ire.
124/E4 **Cave Creek,** Az,US
109/J3 **Caviana,** Braz.
63/F2 **Cavnic,** Rom.
82/D5 **Cawayan,** Phil.
91/B2 **Cawndilla** (lake), Austl.
45/G4 **Cawood,** Eng,UK
47/H1 **Cawston,** Eng,UK
110/J6 **Caxambu,** Braz.
109/K4 **Caxias,** Braz.
110/B4 **Caxias do Sul,** Braz.
116/D4 **Caxinas** (pt.), Hon.
104/B2 **Caxito,** Ang.
74/B2 **Çay,** Turk.
108/C3 **Cayambe** (vol.), Ecu.
129/H3 **Cayce,** SC,US
63/L5 **Çaycuma,** Turk.
74/E2 **Çayeli,** Turk.
109/H3 **Cayenne** (cap.), FrG.
117/F4 **Cayman Brac** (isl.), Cay.
116/E4 **Cayman Islands,** UK
116/E4 **Cayos Cajones** (isls.), Hon.
116/E5 **Cayos Miskitos** (isls.), Nic.
62/B3 **Cazin,** Bosn.
58/D4 **Cazorla,** Sp.
58/C1 **Cea** (riv.), Sp.
109/L5 **Ceará-Mirim,** Braz.
113/G2 **Cebollatí** (riv.), Uru.
82/D5 **Cebu,** Phil.
82/D6 **Cebu** (isl.), Phil.
60/C2 **Ceccano,** It.
103/E2 **Cecil Macks** (pass), Swaz.
57/J5 **Cecina,** It.
60/E3 **Cecita** (lake), It.
123/H2 **Cedar** (lake), Mb,Can
126/E2 **Cedar** (lake), On,Can
132/L11 **Cedar** (mtn.), Ca,US
123/L5 **Cedar** (riv.), Ia,US
131/F6 **Cedar** (cr.), NJ,US
132/C3 **Cedar** (riv.), Wa,US
90/B1 **Cedar Bay Nat'l Park,** Austl.
125/G3 **Cedar Bluff** (res.), Ks,US
124/D3 **Cedar Breaks Nat'l Mon.,** Ut,US
124/D3 **Cedar City,** Ut,US
128/D3 **Cedar Creek** (res.), Tx,US
123/K5 **Cedar Falls,** Ia,US
131/F5 **Cedar Grove,** NJ,US
129/H4 **Cedar Key,** Fl,US
123/L5 **Cedar Rapids,** Ia,US
129/G3 **Cedartown,** Ga,US
124/B2 **Cedarville,** Ca,US
58/A1 **Cedeira,** Sp.
109/L5 **Cedro,** Braz.
117/L8 **Cedros** (isl.), Mex.
58/A1 **Cee,** Sp.
97/Q7 **Ceel Dheere,** Som.
97/Q5 **Ceerigaabo** (Erigabo), Som.
60/D3 **Cefalù,** It.
44/D5 **Cefni** (riv.), Wal,UK
45/E6 **Cefn-mawr,** Wal,UK
58/C2 **Cega** (riv.), Sp.
62/D2 **Cegléd,** Hun.
58/E3 **Cehegín,** Sp.
63/F2 **Cehu Silvaniei,** Rom.
45/E6 **Ceiriog** (riv.), Wal,UK
66/F4 **Çekerek** (riv.), Turk.
58/B1 **Celanova,** Sp.
116/D3 **Celarain** (pt.), Mex.
116/A3 **Celaya,** Mex.
44/B5 **Celbridge,** Ire.
87/F3 **Celebes** (sea), Asia
87/E4 **Celebes** (Sulawesi) (isl.), Indo.
126/C3 **Celina,** Oh,US
62/B2 **Celje,** Slov.
62/C2 **Celldömölk,** Hun.
56/E2 **Celle** (riv.), Fr.
51/H3 **Celle,** Ger.
46/A4 **Celtic** (sea), Eur.
46/B2 **Cemaes Head** (pt.), Wal,UK
86/D3 **Cemaru** (peak), Indo.
58/E3 **Cenajo** (res.), Sp.
87/H4 **Cenderawasih** (bay), Indo.
111/C4 **Centenario,** Arg.
110/B2 **Centenario do Sul,** Braz.
124/D4 **Centennial** (wash), Az,US
122/E4 **Centennial** (mts.), Id,US
123/H4 **Center,** ND,US
128/E4 **Center,** Tx,US
131/G5 **Centereach,** NY,US
132/F7 **Center Line,** Mi,US
131/H5 **Center Moriches,** NY,US
129/G3 **Center Point,** Al,US
129/G3 **Centerville,** Tn,US
128/E4 **Centerville,** Tx,US
57/J4 **Cento,** It.
112/C4 **Central** (peak), Arg.
99/E5 **Central** (reg.), Gha.
74/K5 **Central** (dist.), Isr.
101/C3 **Central** (prov.), Kenya
101/A2 **Central** (prov.), Ugan.
97/J6 **Central African Republic**
122/G3 **Central Butte,** Sk,Can
125/H2 **Central City,** Ne,US
108/C5 **Central, Cordillera** (range), SAm.
126/B4 **Centralia,** Il,US
122/C4 **Centralia,** Wa,US
131/G5 **Central Islip,** NY,US
73/H3 **Central Makrān** (range), Pak.
56/E4 **Central, Massif** (plat.), Fr.
109/J7 **Central, Planalto** (plat.), Braz.
122/C5 **Central Point,** Or,US
69/L3 **Central Siberian** (plat.), Rus.
65/N4 **Central Ural** (mts.), Rus.
56/D3 **Centre** (reg.), Fr.
129/G3 **Centreville,** Al,US
56/D4 **Céou** (riv.), Fr.
62/D3 **Čepin,** Cro.
87/G4 **Ceram** (isl.), Indo.
87/G4 **Ceram** (sea), Indo.
60/A2 **Ceraso** (cape), It.
59/L7 **Cerdanyola del Vallès,** Sp.
56/D4 **Cère** (riv.), Fr.
57/J4 **Cerea,** It.
111/D2 **Ceres,** Arg.
109/J7 **Ceres,** Braz.
102/B4 **Ceres,** SAfr.
117/F6 **Cereté,** Col.
52/B5 **Cergy,** Fr.
60/D2 **Cerignola,** It.
63/J5 **Çerkezköy,** Turk.
63/J3 **Cernavodă,** Rom.
46/D5 **Cerne Abbas,** Eng,UK
117/N9 **Cerralvo** (isl.), Mex.
44/E5 **Cerrig-y-Druidion,** Wal,UK
61/F2 **Cërrik,** Alb.
116/A3 **Cerritos,** Mex.
116/B3 **Cerro Azul,** Mex.
112/C3 **Cerro Colorados** (res.), Arg.
117/L7 **Cerro de la Encantada** (peak), Mex.
117/M8 **Cerro Dos Picachos** (peak), Mex.
117/M8 **Cerro Encantada** (peak), Mex.
113/G2 **Cerro Largo** (dept.), Uru.
117/M7 **Cerro Pinacote** (peak), Mex.
60/D2 **Cervaro** (riv.), It.
60/D2 **Cervati** (peak), It.
59/F2 **Cervera,** Sp.
57/K4 **Cervia,** It.
60/D2 **Cervialto** (peak), It.
57/K4 **Cervignano del Friuli,** It.
110/H7 **Cervo** (hills), Braz.
58/B1 **Cervo,** Sp.
117/G5 **César** (riv.), Col.
57/K4 **Cesena,** It.
57/K4 **Cesenatico,** It.
64/E4 **Cēsis,** Lat.
57/L2 **České Budějovice,** Czh.
49/H4 **Českomoravská Vysočina** (upland), Czh.
57/L2 **Český Krumlov,** Czh.
62/C3 **Česma** (riv.), Cro.
61/K3 **Çeşme,** Turk.
74/A2 **Çeşme,** Turk.
56/C2 **Cesson-Sévigné,** Fr.
98/C5 **Cestos** (riv.), Libr.
62/C4 **Cetina** (riv.), Cro.
62/D4 **Cetinje,** Yugo.
58/D2 **Ceurda del Pozo** (res.), Sp.
58/C5 **Ceuta,** Sp.
56/E5 **Cévennes** (mts.), Fr.
56/E4 **Cévennes Nat'l Park,** Fr.
74/C3 **Ceyhan,** Turk.
74/E3 **Ceylânpınar,** Turk.
84/D6 **Ceylon** (isl.), SrL.
56/F4 **Cèze** (riv.), Fr.
56/C5 **Chabarrou** (peak), Fr.
112/E2 **Chacabuco,** Arg.
108/C5 **Chachapoyas,** Peru
83/C3 **Chachoengsao,** Thai.
124/F3 **Chaco** (dry riv.), NM,US
128/B3 **Chaco** (mesa), NM,US
111/D2 **Chaco Austral** (plain), Arg.
108/G8 **Chaco Boreal** (plain), Par.
111/D1 **Chaco Central** (plain), Arg.
111/E2 **Chaco Nat'l Park,** Arg.
116/D4 **Chacujal** (ruins), Guat.
97/J4 **Chad**
96/H5 **Chad** (lake), Afr.
83/E4 **Cha Da** (cape), Viet.
47/E3 **Chadlington,** Eng,UK
125/G2 **Chadron,** Ne,US
63/J2 **Chadyr-Lunga,** Mol.
80/D2 **Chagang-Do** (prov.), NKor.
75/D5 **Chagdo Kangri** (peak), China
71/G10 **Chagos** (arch.), BrIn.
73/H3 **Chāh Behār** (Bandar Beheshtī), Iran
116/C4 **Chahuites,** Mex.
83/C3 **Chainat,** Thai.
83/C3 **Chaiyaphum,** Thai.
84/C5 **Chālakudi,** India
116/D5 **Chalatenango,** ESal.
101/C2 **Chalbi** (des.), Kenya
77/H2 **Chalchyn** (riv.), Mong.
127/H2 **Chaleur** (bay), NB, Qu,Can
47/F3 **Chalfont Saint Peter,** Eng,UK
47/E3 **Chalgrove,** Eng,UK
128/C4 **Chalk** (mts.), Tx,US
56/C3 **Challans,** Fr.
119/T6 **Challenger** (mtn.), NW,Can
53/D5 **Challerange,** Fr.
122/E4 **Challis,** Id,US
47/G4 **Challock,** Eng,UK
52/D6 **Châlons-sur-Marne,** Fr.
54/A4 **Chalon-sur-Saône,** Fr.
72/F1 **Chālūs,** Iran
57/K2 **Cham,** Ger.
124/F3 **Chama** (riv.), Co, NM,US
86/B2 **Chamah** (peak), Malay.
73/J2 **Chaman,** Pak.
73/L2 **Chamba,** India
84/C2 **Chambal** (riv.), India
74/F4 **Chambaran** (plat.), Fr.
127/G2 **Chamberlain** (lake), Me,US
123/J5 **Chamberlain,** SD,US
130/K2 **Chamberlin** (mtn.), Ak,US
126/E4 **Chambersburg,** Pa,US
56/F4 **Chambéry,** Fr.
101/A5 **Chambeshi** (riv.), Zam.
127/P7 **Chambly,** Qu,Can
52/B5 **Chambly,** Fr.
74/F3 **Chamchamāl,** Iraq
56/F4 **Chamechaude** (mtn.), Fr.
111/C3 **Chamical,** Arg.
57/G4 **Chamonix-Mont-Blanc,** Fr.
130/L3 **Champagne,** Yk,Can
52/C6 **Champagne** (reg.), Fr.
56/F2 **Champagne-Ardennes** (reg.), Fr.
52/B5 **Champagne-sur-Oise,** Fr.
126/B3 **Champaign,** Il,US
112/D1 **Champaqui** (peak), Arg.
53/F6 **Champigneulles,** Fr.
126/F2 **Champlain** (lake), Can., US
116/C4 **Champotón,** Mex.
52/B6 **Champs-sur-Marne,** Fr.
111/B2 **Chañaral,** Chile
58/B4 **Chança** (riv.), Port.
108/C5 **Chan Chan** (ruins), Peru
112/B2 **Chanco,** Chile
130/J2 **Chandalar** (riv.), Ak,US
84/C2 **Chandausi,** India
84/C3 **Chanderi,** India
73/L2 **Chandigarh,** India
127/H1 **Chandler,** Qu,Can
130/H2 **Chandler** (riv.), Ak,US
128/D3 **Chandler,** Ok,US
84/C4 **Chandrapur,** India
81/C5 **Chang** (lake), China
81/B8 **Chang** (riv.), China
83/C3 **Chang** (isl.), Thai.
77/K3 **Changbai** (peak), China
80/D2 **Changbai** (mts.), China, NKor.
81/F2 **Changchun,** China
81/D5 **Changdang** (lake), China
82/B2 **Changde,** China
77/K4 **Changgi-ap** (cape), SKor.
82/D3 **Changhua,** Tai.
80/D5 **Changhŭng,** SKor.
81/D3 **Changli,** China
81/D2 **Changping,** China
80/C3 **Changsan-got** (cape), NKor.
82/B2 **Changsha,** China
81/E5 **Changshu,** China
85/J2 **Changshun,** China
80/D5 **Changsŏng,** SKor.
116/E6 **Changuinola,** Pan.
80/E5 **Ch'angwŏn,** SKor.
81/E3 **Changxing** (isl.), China
81/D5 **Chang** (Yangtze) (riv.), China
81/C3 **Changzhi,** China
81/D5 **Changzhou,** China
83/E2 **Chan May Dong** (cape), Viet.
47/H4 **Channel** (tunnel), UK, Fr.
124/C4 **Channel** (isls.), Ca,US
90/A4 **Channel Country** (plain), Austl.
56/B2 **Channel Islands,** UK
124/B4 **Channel Islands Nat'l Park,** Ca,US
127/K2 **Channel-Port aux Basques,** Nf,Can
58/B1 **Chantada,** Sp.
83/C3 **Chanthaburi,** Thai.
52/B5 **Chantilly,** Fr.
118/G2 **Chantrey** (inlet), NW,Can
125/J3 **Chanute,** Ks,US
81/D5 **Chao** (lake), China
77/H4 **Chaobai** (riv.), China
83/C3 **Chao Phraya** (riv.), Thai.
77/J2 **Chaor** (riv.), China
82/C3 **Chaoyang,** China
82/C3 **Chaozhou,** China
109/K6 **Chapada Diamantina Nat'l Park,** Braz.
109/J6 **Chapada dos Veadeiros Nat'l Park,** Braz.
126/F1 **Chapais,** Qu,Can
117/P9 **Chapala** (lake), Mex.
67/J1 **Chapayevsk,** Rus.
110/A3 **Chapecó,** Braz.
45/G5 **Chapel en le Frith,** Eng,UK
45/F2 **Chapelfell Top** (mtn.), Eng,UK
129/J3 **Chapel Hill,** NC,US
52/D3 **Chapelle-Lez-Herlaimont,** Belg.
45/J5 **Chapel Saint Leonards,** Eng,UK
45/G5 **Chapeltown,** Eng,UK
132/D2 **Chaplain** (lake), Wa,US
83/D2 **Chap Le,** Viet.
126/D2 **Chapleau,** On,Can
122/G3 **Chaplin,** Sk,Can
125/G2 **Chappell,** Ne,US
69/M4 **Chara** (riv.), Rus.
108/C3 **Charambirá** (pt.), Col.
61/L6 **Charandra** (riv.), Gre.
111/D2 **Charata,** Arg.
116/A3 **Charcas,** Mex.
105/U **Charcot** (isl.), Ant.
46/D5 **Chard,** Eng,UK
68/G6 **Chardzhou,** Trkm.
56/C4 **Charente** (riv.), Fr.
96/J5 **Chari** (riv.), Chad
73/J1 **Chārīkār,** Afg.
47/G4 **Charing,** Eng,UK
125/J2 **Chariton** (riv.), Ia, Mo,US
47/E3 **Charlbury,** Eng,UK
44/B3 **Charlemont,** NI,UK
52/D3 **Charleroi,** Belg.
52/D2 **Charleroi à Bruxelles, Canal de** (can.), Belg.
119/J2 **Charles** (isl.), NW,Can
126/F4 **Charles** (cape), Va,US
123/K5 **Charles City,** Ia,US
126/B4 **Charleston,** Il,US
125/K3 **Charleston,** Mo,US
129/F3 **Charleston,** Ms,US
124/D2 **Charleston,** Nv,US
129/J3 **Charleston,** SC,US
126/D4 **Charleston** (cap.), WV,US
53/D4 **Charleville-Mézières,** Fr.
126/C2 **Charlevoix,** Mi,US
122/B2 **Charlotte** (lake), BC,Can
126/C3 **Charlotte,** Mi,US
129/H3 **Charlotte,** NC,US
117/J4 **Charlotte Amalie** (cap.), USVI
126/E4 **Charlottesville,** Va,US
127/J2 **Charlottetown** (cap.), PE,Can
117/J5 **Charlotteville,** Trin.
119/H3 **Charlton** (isl.), NW,Can
46/D3 **Charlton Kings,** Eng,UK
56/F3 **Charolais** (mts.), Fr.
75/D2 **Charsk,** Kaz.
90/B3 **Charters Towers,** Austl.
56/D2 **Chartres,** Fr.
75/C3 **Charyn** (riv.), Kaz.
75/D1 **Charysh** (riv.), Rus.
112/F2 **Chascomús,** Arg.
122/D3 **Chase,** BC,Can
56/F4 **Chassezac** (riv.), Fr.
56/C3 **Chassiron, Pointe de** (pt.), Fr.
56/C3 **Châteaubriant,** Fr.
56/C3 **Château-d'Olonne,** Fr.
56/D2 **Châteaudun,** Fr.
127/N7 **Châteauguay,** Qu,Can
56/F5 **Châteaurenard-Provence,** Fr.
56/D3 **Château-Renault,** Fr.
56/D3 **Châteauroux,** Fr.
52/C5 **Château-Thierry,** Fr.
52/D3 **Châtelet,** Belg.
56/D3 **Châtellerault,** Fr.
125/J2 **Chatfield,** Mn,US
127/H2 **Chatham,** NB,Can
126/D3 **Chatham,** On,Can
113/J7 **Chatham** (isl.), Chile
47/G4 **Chatham,** Eng,UK
131/F5 **Chatham,** NJ,US
56/F3 **Châtillon-sur-Seine,** Fr.
84/D4 **Chatrapur,** India
90/H8 **Chatswood,** Austl.
131/B2 **Chatsworth** (res.), Ca,US
129/G3 **Chatsworth,** Ga,US
129/G4 **Chattahoochee,** Fl,US
129/G4 **Chattahoochee** (riv.), Fl, Ga,US
129/G3 **Chattanooga,** Tn,US
47/G2 **Chatteris,** Eng,UK
56/C2 **Chaucey** (isls.), Fr.
53/E2 **Chaudfontaine,** Belg.
127/G2 **Chaudiére** (riv.), Qu,Can
83/D4 **Chau Doc,** Viet.
85/F3 **Chauk,** Burma
85/G2 **Chaukan** (pass), India
52/B4 **Chaulnes,** Fr.
54/B1 **Chaumont,** Fr.
52/A5 **Chaumont-en-Vexin,** Fr.
52/D4 **Chaumont-Porcien,** Fr.
69/T3 **Chaunskaya** (bay), Rus.
52/C4 **Chauny,** Fr.
126/E3 **Chautauqua** (lake), NY,US
56/D3 **Chauvigny,** Fr.
58/B2 **Chaves,** Port.
83/D1 **Chay** (riv.), Viet.
108/E7 **Chayana** (riv.), Bol.
65/M4 **Chaykovskiy,** Rus.
45/G6 **Cheadle,** Eng,UK
129/G3 **Cheaha** (peak), Al,US
57/K1 **Cheb,** Czh.
65/K4 **Cheboksary,** Rus.
65/K4 **Cheboksary** (res.), Rus.
126/C2 **Cheboygan,** Mi,US
67/H4 **Chechen'** (isl.), Rus.
67/H4 **Chechen-Ingush Aut. Rep.,** Rus.
96/D3 **Chech, 'Erg** (des.), Afr.
80/E4 **Chech'ŏn,** SKor.
125/J4 **Checotah,** Ok,US
127/J2 **Chedabucto** (bay), NS,Can
46/D4 **Cheddar,** Eng,UK
85/F4 **Cheduba** (isl.), Burma
127/S10 **Cheektowaga,** NY,US
126/D1 **Cheepash** (riv.), On,Can
126/D1 **Cheepay** (riv.), On,Can
77/L1 **Chegdomyn,** Rus.
104/F4 **Chegutu,** Zim.
122/C4 **Chehalis,** Wa,US
57/G5 **Cheiron, Cime du** (peak), Fr.
77/K5 **Cheju,** SKor.
77/K5 **Cheju** (isl.), SKor.
77/K5 **Cheju** (str.), SKor.
122/C4 **Chelan,** Wa,US
122/C4 **Chelan** (lake), Wa,US
45/F5 **Chelford,** Eng,UK
67/L3 **Chelkar,** Kaz.
49/M3 **Chel'm,** Pol.
49/M3 **Chel'm** (prov.), Pol.
47/G3 **Chelmer** (riv.), Eng,UK
49/K2 **Chel'mno,** Pol.
47/G3 **Chelmsford,** Eng,UK
49/K2 **Chel'mża,** Pol.
91/G6 **Chelsea,** Austl.
127/Q8 **Cheltenham,** On,Can
46/D3 **Cheltenham,** Eng,UK
65/P5 **Chelyabinsk,** Rus.
65/P5 **Chelyabinsk Obl.,** Rus.
69/L2 **Chelyuskina** (cape), Rus.
101/A5 **Chembe,** Zam.
48/G3 **Chemnitz,** Ger.
82/A2 **Chen** (riv.), China
73/K2 **Chenāb** (riv.), India, Pak.
96/E2 **Chenachane** (well), Alg.
122/D4 **Cheney,** Wa,US
81/C3 **Cheng'anpu,** China
81/D2 **Chengde,** China
76/E5 **Chengdu,** China
81/E3 **Chengshan Jiao** (cape), China
54/A3 **Chenôve,** Fr.
82/B2 **Chenzhou,** China
63/G5 **Chepelare,** Bul.
93/V12 **Chépénéhé,** NCal.
112/C2 **Chépica,** Chile
117/F6 **Chepigana,** Pan.
46/D3 **Chepstow,** Wal,UK
65/M4 **Cheptsa** (riv.), Rus.
56/D3 **Cher** (riv.), Fr.
129/J3 **Cheraw,** SC,US
56/C2 **Cherbourg,** Fr.
96/F1 **Cherchell,** Alg.
76/E1 **Cheremkhovo,** Rus.
64/H4 **Cherepovets,** Rus.
66/E2 **Cherkassy,** Ukr.
66/D2 **Cherkassy Obl.,** Ukr.
67/G3 **Cherkessk,** Rus.
90/E6 **Chermside,** Austl.
65/M2 **Chernaya** (riv.), Rus.
66/D2 **Chernigov,** Ukr.
66/D2 **Chernigov Obl.,** Ukr.
63/H4 **Cherni Lom** (riv.), Bul.
63/F4 **Cherni Vrŭkh** (peak), Bul.
66/C2 **Chernovtsy,** Ukr.
66/C2 **Chernovtsy Obl.,** Ukr.
65/N4 **Chernushka,** Rus.
76/H1 **Chernyshevsk,** Rus.
125/H3 **Cherokee,** Ok,US
128/E2 **Cherokees** (lake), Ok,US
85/F2 **Cherrapunjee,** India
124/D3 **Cherry Creek,** Nv,US
131/E6 **Cherry Hill,** NJ,US
131/D3 **Cherry Valley,** Ca,US
69/Q3 **Cherskiy** (range), Rus.
47/F4 **Chertsey,** Eng,UK
63/G4 **Cherven Bryag,** Bul.
66/C2 **Chervonograd,** Ukr.
47/E3 **Cherwell** (riv.), Eng,UK
126/C3 **Chesaning,** Mi,US
126/E4 **Chesapeake** (bay), Md, Va,US
47/F3 **Chesham,** Eng,UK
45/F5 **Cheshire** (co.), Eng,UK
45/F5 **Cheshire** (plain), Eng,UK

147

Chesh – Conce

65/K2 Cheshskaya (bay), Rus.
47/F3 Cheshunt, Eng,UK
45/F5 Chester, Eng,UK
124/B2 Chester, Ca,US
122/F3 Chester, Mt,US
131/F5 Chester, NJ,US
131/E6 Chester, Pa,US
129/H3 Chester, SC,US
118/G2 Chesterfield (inlet), NW,Can
92/E7 Chesterfield (isls.), NCal.
45/G5 Chesterfield, Eng,UK
103/H7 Chesterfield, Nosy (isl.), Madg.
45/G2 Chester-le-Street, Eng,UK
90/B3 Chesterton (range), Austl.
127/G2 Chesuncook (lake), Me,US
116/D4 Chetumal (bay), Belz., Mex.
116/D4 Chetumal, Mex.
122/C2 Chetwynd, BC,Can
46/D4 Chew (riv.), Eng,UK
122/D3 Chewelah, Wa,US
46/D4 Chew Valley (lake), Eng,UK
125/H4 Cheyenne, Ok,US
123/H4 Cheyenne (riv.), SD, Wy,US
123/G5 Cheyenne (cap.), Wy,US
125/G3 Cheyenne Wells, Co,US
84/C3 Chhatarpur, India
84/C3 Chhindwāra, India
83/D3 Chhlong, Camb.
81/D4 Chi (riv.), China
83/C2 Chi (riv.), Thai.
83/B2 Chiang Dao (caves), Thai.
83/B2 Chiang Mai, Thai.
83/B2 Chiang Rai, Thai.
60/C1 Chiani (riv.), It.
116/C4 Chiapas (state), Mex.
67/G4 Chiatura, Geo.
57/H4 Chiavari, It.
55/F5 Chiavenna, It.
82/D3 Chiayi, Tai.
79/G3 Chiba, Japan
79/G3 Chiba (pref.), Japan
126/F1 Chibougamau, Qu,Can
126/F1 Chibougamau (lake), Qu,Can
126/F1 Chibougamau (riv.), Qu,Can
130/D3 Chibukak (pt.), Ak,US
103/F2 Chibuto, Moz.
132/Q16 Chicago, Il,US
132/Q16 Chicago Heights, Il,US
132/Q16 Chicago Ridge, Il,US
130/L4 Chichagof (isl.), Ak,US
73/K2 Chīchāwatni, Pak.
81/C2 Chicheng, China
116/D3 Chichén Itzá (ruins), Mex.
47/F5 Chichester, Eng,UK
79/F3 Chichibu, Japan
79/F3 Chichibu-Tama Nat'l Park, Japan
116/D5 Chichigalpa, Nic.
92/D2 Chichishima (isls.), Japan
129/G3 Chickamauga (lake), Tn,US
125/H4 Chickasha, Ok,US
46/D5 Chickerell, Eng,UK
58/B4 Chiclana de la Frontera, Sp.
108/C5 Chiclayo, Peru
112/C4 Chico (riv.), Arg.
112/D5 Chico (riv.), Arg.
124/B3 Chico, Ca,US
127/F3 Chicopee, Ma,US
104/D4 Chicote, Ang.
127/G1 Chicoutimi, Qu,Can
119/K2 Chidley (cape), Nf,Can
129/H4 Chiefland, Fl,US
83/D1 Chiem Hoa, Viet.
57/K3 Chiemsee (lake), Ger.
60/C1 Chienti (riv.), It.
83/B4 Chieo Lan (res.), Thai.
53/E5 Chiers (riv.), Fr.
55/G6 Chiese (riv.), It.
60/D1 Chieti, It.
47/E4 Chieveley, Eng,UK
77/H3 Chifeng, China
109/K7 Chifre (mts.), Braz.
79/F3 Chigasaki, Japan
130/G4 Chiginagak (mtn.), Ak,US
127/H2 Chignecto (bay), NB,Can
47/G3 Chigwell, Eng,UK
79/L10 Chihayaakasaka, Japan
81/D3 Chihli (Bo Hai) (gulf), China
117/N8 Chihuahua, Mex.
117/N8 Chihuahua (state), Mex.
125/H3 Chikaskia (riv.), Ks,US
84/C5 Chikballāpur, India
84/C3 Chikhli, India
84/C5 Chikmagalūr, India
76/G1 Chikoy (riv.), Rus.
78/B4 Chikugo (riv.), Japan
79/F2 Chikuma (riv.), Japan
79/H8 Chikura, Japan
84/D4 Chilakalūrupet, India
116/B4 Chilapa, Mex.
84/C6 Chilaw, SrL.
122/C3 Chilcotin (riv.), BC,Can
129/G3 Childersburg, Al,US
128/C3 Childress, Tx,US
107/B6 Chile
116/D5 Chile (mt.), Hon.
111/C2 Chilecito, Arg.
104/E3 Chililabombwe, Zam.
84/E4 Chilka (lake), India
122/C3 Chilko (lake), BC,Can
130/L4 Chilkoot (pass), BC,Can, Ak,US
112/B3 Chillán, Chile
126/B3 Chillicothe, Il,US
125/J3 Chillicothe, Mo,US
126/D4 Chillicothe, Oh,US
122/C3 Chilliwack, BC,Can
112/B4 Chiloé (isl.), Chile
112/B4 Chiloé Nat'l Park, Chile
122/C5 Chiloquin, Or,US
116/B4 Chilpancingo, Mex.
47/F3 Chiltern (hills), Eng,UK
104/G4 Chilwa (lake), Malw.
117/F6 Chimán, Pan.
52/D3 Chimay, Belg.
68/F5 Chimbay, Uzb.
108/C4 Chimborazo (vol.), Ecu.
108/C5 Chimbote, Peru
75/A3 Chimkent, Kaz.
117/N7 Chimney (peak), NM.,US
85/F3 Chin (state), Burma
80/D5 Chin (isl.), SKor.
71/J6 China
116/C5 Chinandega, Nic.
128/B4 Chinati (mts.), Tx,US
117/P8 Chinati (peak), Tx.,US
108/C6 Chincha Alta, Peru
118/E3 Chinchaga (riv.), Ab,Can
126/F4 Chincoteague, Va,US
85/F3 Chindwin (riv.), Burma
108/D3 Chingaza Nat'l Park, Col.
84/C5 Chingleput, India
104/E3 Chingola, Zam.
98/B1 Chinguetti, Dhar de (hills), Mrta.
80/E5 Chinhae, SKor.
104/F4 Chinhoyi, Zim.
130/H4 Chiniak (cape), Ak,US
73/K2 Chiniot, Pak.
83/D3 Chinit (riv.), Camb.
97/K6 Chinko (riv.), CAfr.
124/E3 Chinle (dry riv.), Az, Ut,US
47/F3 Chinnor, Eng,UK
79/F3 Chino, Japan
131/C2 Chino, Ca,US
122/F3 Chinook, Mt,US
117/F6 Chinú, Col.
104/F3 Chipata, Zam.
81/D3 Chiping, China
58/B4 Chipiona, Sp.
129/G4 Chipley, Fl,US
84/B4 Chiplūn, India
129/G4 Chipola (riv.), Fl,US
46/D4 Chippenham, Eng,UK
123/K4 Chippewa (riv.), Mn,US
126/B2 Chippewa (riv.), Wi,US
126/B2 Chippewa Falls, Wi,US
47/E2 Chipping Campden, Eng,UK
47/E3 Chipping Norton, Eng,UK
47/G3 Chipping Ongar, Eng,UK
46/D3 Chipping Sodbury, Eng,UK
127/H2 Chiputneticook (lakes), NB,Can, Me,US
116/D5 Chiquimula, Guat.
108/D2 Chiquinquirá, Col.
107/C6 Chiquita, Mar (lake), Arg.
107/A3 Chira (riv.), Peru
84/D4 Chīrāla, India
75/A3 Chirchik, Uzb.
96/H3 Chirfa, Niger
117/N7 Chiricahua (peak), Az.,US
124/E4 Chiricahua Nat'l Mon., Az,US
130/G4 Chirikof (isl.), Ak,US
116/E6 Chiriquí (gulf), Pan.
45/E6 Chirk, Eng,UK
43/D3 Chirnside, Sc,UK
63/G4 Chirpan, Bul.
116/E6 Chirripó Grande (mt.), CR
116/E6 Chirripó Nat'l Park, CR
79/N10 Chiryu, Japan
119/J3 Chisasibi (Fort-George), Qu,Can
116/C4 Chisec, Guat.
47/E3 Chiseldon, Eng,UK
126/A2 Chisholm, Mn,US
73/K3 Chishtiān Mandi, Pak.
97/P8 Chisimayu, Som.
63/J2 Chişinău (cap.), Mol.
62/E2 Chişineu Criş, Rom.
65/L5 Chistopol', Rus.
47/F3 Chiswell Green, Eng,UK
79/M10 Chita, Japan
79/M10 Chita (bay), Japan
79/M10 Chita (pen.), Japan
76/G1 Chita, Rus.
104/B4 Chitado, Ang.
101/B5 Chitipa, Malw.
84/B3 Chitorgarh, India
77/N3 Chitose, Japan
84/C5 Chitradurga, India
84/D2 Chitrakut, India
117/E6 Chitré, Pan.
85/F3 Chittagong, Bang.
84/C5 Chittoor, India
104/D4 Chiume, Ang.
57/G4 Chivasso, It.
117/M8 Chivato (pt.), Mex.
112/E2 Chivilcoy, Arg.
83/D3 Choam Khsant, Camb.
112/C1 Choapa (riv.), Chile
104/D4 Chobe Nat'l Park, Bots.
49/K4 Choč (peak), Slvk.
49/J4 Choceň, Czh.
49/H3 Chocianów, Pol.
124/D4 Chocolate (mts.), Ca,US
57/K1 Chodov, Czh.
49/J2 Chodzież, Pol.
79/F3 Chōfu, Japan
79/H7 Chofū, Japan
92/E5 Choiseul (isl.), Sol.
52/B6 Choisy-le-Roi, Fr.
49/H2 Chojna, Pol.
49/J2 Chojnice, Pol.
49/H3 Chojnów, Pol.
77/N4 Chokai-san (mtn.), Japan
128/D4 Choke Canyon (res.), Tx,US
76/D5 Chola (mts.), China
56/C3 Cholet, Fr.
80/D5 Chŏlla-Bukto (prov.), SKor.
80/D5 Chŏlla-Namdo (prov.), SKor.
47/E3 Cholsey, Eng,UK
116/D5 Choluteca (riv.)
116/D5 Choluteca, Hon.
104/E4 Choma, Zam.
80/E4 Chŏmch'ŏn, SKor.
84/E2 Chomo Lhāri (mtn.), Bhu.
57/K1 Chomutov, Czh.
79/J7 Chōnan, Japan
80/D4 Ch'ŏnan, SKor.
83/C3 Chon Buri, Thai.
112/B4 Chonchi, Chile
108/B4 Chone, Ecu.
80/E2 Ch'ŏngjin, NKor.
80/E2 Ch'ŏngjin-Si (prov.), NKor.
80/D4 Ch'ŏngju, SKor.
83/C3 Chong Kal, Camb.
81/L8 Chongming (isl.), China
82/A2 Chongqing, China
80/E4 Ch'ŏngsong, SKor.
80/D5 Chŏnju, SKor.
112/A5 Chonos (arch.), Chile
83/D4 Chon Thanh, Viet.
45/F4 Chorley, Eng,UK
47/F3 Chorleywood, Eng,UK
66/C2 Chortkov, Ukr.
49/K3 Chorzów, Pol.
79/G3 Chōshi, Japan
49/H2 Choszczno, Pol.
108/C5 Chota, Peru
122/E4 Choteau, Mt,US
102/A2 Chowagasberg (peak), Namb.
129/J2 Chowan (riv.), NC,US
76/G2 Choybalsan, Mong.
89/H7 Christchurch, NZ
47/E5 Christchurch, Eng,UK
47/E5 Christchurch (bay), Eng,UK
130/L4 Christian (sound), Ak,US
102/D2 Christiana, SAfr.
126/D4 Christiansburg, Va,US
122/F2 Christine (riv.), Ab,Can
71/K11 Christmas (isl.), Austl.
93/K4 Christmas (Kiritimati) (atoll), Kiri.
49/H4 Chrudim, Czh.
49/K3 Chrzanów, Pol.
75/B3 Chu (riv.), Kaz.
83/D2 Chu (riv.), Viet.
81/E4 Chuanchang (riv.), China
122/E5 Chubbuck, Id,US
79/F2 Chūbu (prov.), Japan
112/C4 Chubut (prov.), Arg.
112/D4 Chubut (riv.), Arg.
117/F6 Chucanti (mt.), Pan.
78/C3 Chūgoku (mts.), Japan
78/C3 Chūgoku (prov.), Japan
86/B3 Chukai, Malay.
77/M1 Chukchagirskoye (lake), Rus.
69/U3 Chukchi (pen.), Rus.
69/S3 Chukchi Aut. Okr., Rus.
130/D3 Chukotskiy, Mys (pt.), Rus.
124/C4 Chula Vista, Ca,US
108/B5 Chulucanas, Peru
68/J4 Chulym (riv.), Rus.
75/E1 Chulyshman (riv.), Rus.
63/G4 Chumerna (peak), Bul.
83/B4 Chumphon, Thai.
68/K4 Chuna (riv.), Rus.
80/D4 Ch'unch'ŏn, SKor.
80/D4 Ch'ungch'ŏng-Bukto (prov.), SKor.
80/D4 Ch'ungch'ŏng-Namdo (prov.), SKor.
80/D4 Ch'ungju, SKor.
80/E5 Ch'ungmu, SKor.
69/L3 Chunya (riv.), Rus.
111/C1 Chuquicamata, Chile
55/F4 Chur, Swi.
85/F3 Churachandpur, India
45/F4 Church, Eng,UK
118/D3 Churchill (peak), BC,Can
118/G3 Churchill, Mb,Can
118/G3 Churchill (cape), Mb,Can
118/G3 Churchill (riv.), Mb, Sk,Can
119/K3 Churchill (riv.), Nf,Can
122/F1 Churchill (lake), Sk,Can
118/G3 Churchill (riv.), Mb, Sk,Can
91/G5 Churchill Nat'l Park, Austl.
46/D1 Church Stretton, Eng,UK
45/G6 Churnet (riv.), Eng,UK
84/B2 Churu, India
117/H5 Churuguara, Ven.
124/E3 Chuska (mts.), Az, NM,US
65/N4 Chusovaya (riv.), Rus.
65/N4 Chusovoy, Rus.
65/K5 Chuvash Aut. Rep., Rus.
80/E4 Chuwang-san Nat'l Park, SKor.
85/H2 Chuxiong, China
76/B1 Chuya (riv.), Rus.
83/E3 Chu Yang Sin (peak), Viet.
79/M9 Chūzu, Japan
86/C5 Ciamis, Indo.
60/C2 Ciampino, It.
86/C5 Cianjur, Indo.
132/Q16 Cicero, Il,US
109/L6 Cícero Dantas, Braz.
60/C2 Cicero Nat'l Park, It.
74/C2 Cide, Turk.
49/L2 Ciechanów, Pol.
49/K2 Ciechanów (prov.), Pol.
49/K2 Ciechocinek, Pol.
117/F3 Ciego de Avilla, Cuba
117/G5 Ciénaga, Col.
117/E3 Cienfuegos, Cuba
49/H3 Cieplice Śląskie Zdrój, Pol.
49/K4 Cieszyn, Pol.
58/E3 Cieza, Sp.
74/B2 Çifteler, Turk.
58/D3 Cigüela (riv.), Sp.
74/C2 Cihanbeyli, Turk.
117/P10 Cihuatlán, Mex.
58/C3 Cijara (res.), Sp.
86/C5 Cijulang, Indo.
86/C5 Cilacap, Indo.
46/C2 Cilfaesty (hill), Wal,UK
125/G3 Cimarron, Ks,US
125/H3 Cimarron (riv.), Ks, Ok,US
128/B2 Cimarron (range), NM,US
62/F2 Cîmpeni, Rom.
63/F2 Cîmpia Turzii, Rom.
63/G3 Cîmpina, Rom.
63/G3 Cîmpulung, Rom.
63/G2 Cîmpulung Moldovenesc, Rom.
59/F1 Cinca (riv.), Sp.
62/C4 Cincar (peak), Bosn.
126/C4 Cincinnati, Oh,US
112/C3 Cinco Saltos, Arg.
46/D3 Cinderford, Eng,UK
63/F3 Cîndrelu (peak), Rom.
74/B3 Çine, Turk.
53/E3 Ciney, Belg.
131/F6 Cinnaminson, NJ,US
116/C4 Cintalapa, Mex.
60/A1 Cinto (mtn.), Fr.
62/C4 Čiovo (isl.), Cro.
112/D3 Cipolletti, Arg.
123/G4 Circle, Mt,US
126/D4 Circleville, Oh,US
86/C5 Cirebon, Indo.
46/E3 Cirencester, Eng,UK
60/E3 Cirò Marina, It.
56/C4 Ciron (riv.), Fr.
63/G3 Cisnădie, Rom.
112/B5 Cisnes (riv.), Chile
56/D3 Cisse (riv.), Fr.
60/C2 Cisterna di Latina, It.
116/B4 Citlaltépetl (mt.), Mex.
132/M9 Citrus Heights, Ca,US
57/K5 Città di Castello, It.
60/E3 Cittanova, It.
116/A2 Ciudad Acuna, Mex.
117/J6 Ciudad Bolívar, Ven.
117/N8 Ciudad Camargo, Mex.
116/C4 Ciudad del Carmen, Mex.
117/N8 Ciudad Delicias, Mex.
117/P9 Ciudad de Río Grande, Mex.
59/G3 Ciudadela, Sp.
117/J6 Ciudad Guayana, Ven.
117/N8 Ciudad Guerrero, Mex.
117/P10 Ciudad Guzmán, Mex.
117/N7 Ciudad Juárez, Mex.
117/P8 Ciudad Lerdo, Mex.
116/B3 Ciudad Madero, Mex.
116/B3 Ciudad Mante, Mex.
116/B2 Ciudad Miguel Alemán, Mex.
117/N8 Ciudad Obregón, Mex.
117/G5 Ciudad Ojeda, Ven.
58/D3 Ciudad Real, Sp.
116/B2 Ciudad Río Bravo, Mex.
58/B2 Ciudad-Rodrigo, Sp.
116/B3 Ciudad Valles, Mex.
116/B3 Ciudad Victoria, Mex.
66/F4 Civa Burnu (pt.), Turk.
57/K3 Cividale del Friuli, It.
60/C1 Civita Castellana, It.
60/B1 Civitavecchia, It.
74/B2 Çivril, Turk.
81/C3 Ci Xian, China
74/E3 Cizre, Turk.
58/E1 Cizur, Sp.
47/H3 Clacton on Sea, Eng,UK
46/C2 Claerwen (res.), Wal,UK
56/D3 Clain (riv.), Fr.
118/E3 Claire (lake), Ab,Can
124/B2 Clair Engle (lake), Ca,US
56/D3 Claise (riv.), Fr.
47/F5 Clanfield, Eng,UK
129/G3 Clanton, Al,US
127/Q9 Clappison's Corners, On,Can
112/D4 Clara (pt.), Arg.
43/A4 Clare (riv.), Ire.
126/C3 Clare, Mi,US
131/C2 Claremont, Ca,US
127/F3 Claremont, NH,US
125/J3 Claremore, Ok,US
91/E1 Clarence (riv.), Austl.
119/T7 Clarence (pt.), NW,Can
127/S9 Clarence, NY,US
117/G3 Clarence Town, Bahm.
128/C3 Clarendon, Tx,US
122/E3 Claresholm, BC,Can
105/J Clarie (coast), Ant.
123/J4 Clark, SD,US
91/D4 Clarke (isl.), Austl.
90/B3 Clarke (range), Austl.
122/E3 Clark Fork (riv.), Id, Mt,US
129/H3 Clark Hill (lake), Ga, SC,US
126/D4 Clarksburg, WV,US
129/F3 Clarksdale, Ms,US
127/Q8 Clarkson, On,Can
132/F6 Clarkston, Mi,US
122/D4 Clarkston, Wa,US
128/E3 Clarksville, Ar,US
129/G2 Clarksville, Tn,US
128/E3 Clarksville, Tx,US
110/B1 Claro (riv.), Braz.
52/C3 Clary, Fr.
44/D1 Clatteringshaws Loch (lake), Sc,UK
44/A2 Claudy, NI,UK
51/H5 Clausthal-Zellerfeld, Ger.
82/D4 Claveria, Phil.
132/F6 Clawson, Mi,US
125/H3 Clay Center, Ks,US
45/G5 Clay Cross, Eng,UK
47/H2 Claydon, Eng,UK
44/D3 Clay Head (pt.), IM,UK
131/E6 Claymont, De,US
132/L11 Clayton, Ca,US
129/H3 Clayton, Ga,US
125/G3 Clayton, NM,US
125/J4 Clayton, Ok,US
45/F4 Clayton-le-Moors, Eng,UK
113/S11 Clé (stream), Arg.
118/E3 Clear (hills), Ab,Can
43/H8 Clear (cape), Ire.
124/B3 Clear (lake), Ca,US
130/J4 Cleare (cape), Ak,US
123/J4 Clear Lake, SD,US
122/C3 Clearwater, BC,Can
129/H5 Clearwater, Fl,US
122/D4 Clearwater (mts.), Id,US
123/K4 Clearwater (riv.), Mn,US
44/E2 Cleator Moor, Eng,UK
128/D3 Cleburne, Tx,US
45/H4 Cleethorpes, Eng,UK
46/D3 Cleeve (hill), Eng,UK
129/H3 Clemson, SC,US
46/D2 Cleobury Mortimer, Eng,UK
87/E1 Cleopatra Needle (mtn.), Phil.
52/A4 Clères, Fr.
53/E3 Clerf (riv.), Belg., Lux.
52/B5 Clermont, Fr.
46/D4 Clevedon, Eng,UK
90/B2 Cleveland (cape), Austl.
45/G2 Cleveland (co.), Eng,UK
45/G3 Cleveland (hills), Eng,UK
129/F3 Cleveland, Ms,US
122/E3 Cleveland (peak), Mt,US
126/D3 Cleveland, Oh,US
129/G3 Cleveland, Tn,US
128/E4 Cleveland, Tx,US
110/A3 Clevelândia, Braz.
43/A4 Clew (bay), Ire.
129/H5 Clewiston, Fl,US
52/B6 Clichy, Fr.
46/D4 Clifton, Eng,UK
124/E4 Clifton, Az,US
131/F5 Clifton, NJ,US
128/D4 Clifton, Tx,US
129/J2 Clifton Forge, Va,US
46/D2 Clifton upon Teme, Eng,UK
52/C5 Clignon (riv.), Fr.
129/H3 Clingmans (mtn.), Tn,US
122/C3 Clinton, BC,Can
123/L5 Clinton, Ia,US
126/B3 Clinton, Il,US
129/F4 Clinton, La,US
132/G6 Clinton, Mi,US
132/F6 Clinton (riv.), Mi,US
125/J3 Clinton, Mo,US
129/F3 Clinton, Ms,US
129/J3 Clinton, NC,US
131/F5 Clinton, NJ,US
131/F4 Clinton (res.), NJ,US
125/H4 Clinton, Ok,US
129/H3 Clinton, SC,US
118/F2 Clinton-Colden (lake), NW,Can
118/B2 Clinton Creek, Yk,Can
131/K8 Clinton (Surrattsville), Md,US
126/D3 Clio, Mi,US
38/D5 Clipperton (isl.), Fr.
47/F2 Clipston, Eng,UK
45/F4 Clitheroe, Eng,UK
44/B4 Clogherhead, Ire.
44/B4 Clogher Head (pt.), Ire.
44/C3 Cloghy, NI,UK
43/B4 Clonmel, Ire.
51/F3 Cloppenburg, Ger.
123/K4 Cloquet, Mn,US
111/E2 Clorinda, Arg.
44/E1 Closeburn, Sc,UK
122/G4 Cloud (peak), Wy,US
128/B3 Cloudcroft, NM,US
130/G3 Cloudy (mtn.), Ak,US
44/B2 Cloughmills, NI,UK
45/H3 Cloughton, Eng,UK
46/B4 Clovelly, Eng,UK
124/B3 Cloverdale, Ca,US
124/C3 Clovis, Ca,US
125/G4 Clovis, NM,US
43/C2 Clovullin, Sc,UK
45/G5 Clowne, Eng,UK
63/F2 Cluj (co.), Rom.
63/F2 Cluj-Napoca, Rom.
46/C2 Clun, Eng,UK
46/B3 Clunderwen, Wal,UK
54/C5 Cluses, Fr.
57/H4 Clusone, It.
44/E5 Clwyd (co.), Wal,UK
45/E5 Clwyd (riv.), Wal,UK
45/E5 Clwydian (range), Wal,UK
46/C3 Clydach, Wal,UK
127/H2 Clyde (riv.), NS,Can
122/E2 Clyde, NW,Can
43/C3 Clyde (riv.), Sc,UK
43/C3 Clyde, Firth of (inlet), Sc,UK
46/C2 Clywedog (riv.), Wal,UK
127/R8 CN Tower, On,Can
58/B2 Côa (riv.), Port.
124/C4 Coachella, Ca,US
44/B2 Coagh, NI,UK
116/A2 Coahuila (state), Mex.
122/E3 Coaldale, Ab,Can
125/H4 Coalgate, Ok,US
122/E3 Coalhurst, Ab,Can
44/B2 Coalisland, NI,UK
47/E1 Coalville, Eng,UK
124/E2 Coalville, Ut,US
108/F4 Coari, Braz.
108/F5 Coari (riv.), Braz.
118/C2 Coast (mts.), BC, Yk,Can
101/C3 Coast (prov.), Kenya
120/B4 Coast (ranges), Ca,US
129/H4 Coastal (plain), US
116/B4 Coatepec, Mex.
127/G2 Coaticook, Qu,Can
112/H2 Coats (isl.), NW,Can
105/Y Coats Land (reg.), Ant.
116/C4 Coatzacoalcos, Mex.
116/D3 Coba (ruins), Mex.
58/B1 Coba de Serpe, Sierra de (mtn.), Sp.
116/C4 Cobán, Guat.
91/D3 Cobberas (peak), Austl.
131/B1 Cobblestone (mtn.), Ca,US
123/K2 Cobham (riv.), Mb, On,Can
47/F4 Cobham, Eng,UK
89/C2 Cobourg (pen.), Austl.
126/E3 Cobourg, On,Can
112/B3 Cobquecura, Chile
91/F5 Coburg, Austl.
119/T7 Coburg (isl.), NW,Can
57/J1 Coburg, Ger.
59/E3 Cocentaina, Sp.
108/E7 Cochabamba, Bol.
84/C6 Cochin, India
129/H3 Cochran, Ga,US
122/E3 Cochrane, Ab,Can
126/D1 Cochrane, On,Can
113/J8 Cockburn (chan.), Chile
43/D3 Cockburnspath, Sc,UK
45/E2 Cockermouth, Eng,UK
102/D4 Cockscomb (peak), SAfr.
108/A2 Coco (isl.), CR
116/E5 Coco (riv.), Hon.
129/H4 Cocoa, Fl,US
124/D4 Coconino (plat.), Az,US
91/C2 Cocoparra Nat'l Park, Austl.
71/J11 Cocos (Keeling) (isls.), Austl.
119/K3 Cod (isl.), Nf,Can
45/G3 Cod Beck (riv.), Eng,UK
112/C2 Codegua, Chile
63/G3 Codlea, Rom.
109/K4 Codó, Braz.
57/H4 Codogno, It.
117/J4 Codrington, Anti.
57/K4 Codroipo, It.
46/D1 Codsall, Eng,UK
122/F4 Cody, Wy,US
109/K4 Coelho Neto, Braz.
51/E5 Coesfeld, Ger.
39/M6 Coetivy (isl.), Sey.
122/D4 Coeur d'Alene, Id,US
122/D4 Coeur d'Alene (lake), Id,US
50/D3 Coevorden, Neth.
125/J3 Coffeyville, Ks,US
91/E1 Coffs Harbour, Austl.
47/G3 Coggeshall, Eng,UK
60/A2 Coghinas (lake), It.
56/C4 Cognac, Fr.
116/E6 Coiba (isl.), Pan.
113/K7 Coig (riv.), Arg.
112/B5 Coihaique, Chile
112/C3 Coihueco, Chile
84/C5 Coimbatore, India
58/A2 Coimbra, Port.
58/A2 Coimbra (dist.), Port.
58/C4 Coín, Sp.
59/P10 Coina (riv.), Port.
56/F4 Coise (riv.), Fr.
108/E2 Cojedes (riv.), Ven.
117/G5 Cojoro, Ven.
112/C5 Cojudo Blanco (peak), Arg.
116/D5 Cojutepeque, ESal.
122/F5 Cokeville, Wy,US
91/B3 Colac, Austl.
125/H2 Colamus (riv.), Ne,US
59/P10 Colares, Port.
110/D1 Colatina, Braz.
105/P Colbeck (cape), Ant.
112/C2 Colbún, Chile
125/G3 Colby, Ks,US
47/G3 Colchester, Eng,UK
122/F2 Cold (lake), Ab, Sk,Can
45/F2 Cold Fell (mtn.), Eng,UK
122/F2 Cold Lake, Ab,Can
123/K4 Cold Spring, Mn,US
128/E4 Coldspring, Tx,US
125/H3 Coldwater, Ks,US
126/C3 Coldwater, Mi,US
47/E3 Cole (riv.), Eng,UK
46/D3 Coleford, Eng,UK
128/D4 Coleman, Tx,US
74/E3 Çölemerik, Turk.
44/B1 Coleraine, NI,UK
44/B1 Coleraine (dist.), NI,UK
102/D3 Colesberg, SAfr.
47/E2 Coleshill, Eng,UK
131/J7 Colesville, Md,US
122/D4 Colfax, Wa,US
119/S6 Colgate (cape), NW,Can
112/C5 Colhué Huapí (lake), Arg.
83/D2 Co Lieu, Viet.
117/P10 Colima, Mex.
117/P10 Colima (state), Mex.
112/C2 Colina, Chile
109/K5 Colinas, Braz.
58/D2 Collado-Villalba, Sp.
130/J3 College, Ak,US
131/K8 College Park, Md,US
128/D4 College Station, Tx,US
57/G4 Collegno, It.
91/D1 Collie, Austl.
45/G2 Collier Law (hill), Eng,UK
129/F3 Collierville, Tn,US
46/B6 Colliford (res.), Eng,UK
45/G4 Collingham, Eng,UK
126/D2 Collingwood, On,Can
89/H7 Collingwood, NZ
129/F4 Collins, Ms,US
125/J3 Collinsville, Ok,US
126/E4 Collinsville, Va,US
54/D1 Colmar, Fr.
58/D2 Colmenar Viejo, Sp.
113/J7 Colmillo (cape), Chile
44/D1 Colmonell, Sc,UK
47/E3 Coln (riv.), Eng,UK
45/F4 Colne, Eng,UK
47/G3 Colne (riv.), Eng,UK
53/F2 Cologne (Köln), Ger.
108/D3 Colombia
110/B3 Colombo, Braz.
84/C6 Colombo (cap.), SrL.
56/D5 Colomiers, Fr.
112/E2 Colón, Arg.
112/F2 Colón, Arg.
117/F6 Colón, Pan.
92/C4 Colonia, Micro.
113/F2 Colonia (dept.), Uru.
113/F2 Colonia Del Sacramento, Uru.
113/K7 Colorado (peak), Arg.
112/D3 Colorado (riv.), Arg.
110/B2 Colorado, Braz.
124/D4 Colorado (riv.), Mex., US
124/E3 Colorado (plat.), US
124/F3 Colorado (state), US
128/D4 Colorado (riv.), Tx,US
125/F3 Colorado City, Co,US
128/C3 Colorado City, Tx,US
124/E3 Colorado Nat'l Mon., Co,US
111/C2 Colorados, Desagües de los (marsh), Arg.
125/F3 Colorado Springs, Co,US
108/E7 Colquiri, Bol.
122/G4 Colstrip, Mt,US
44/D1 Colt (hill), Sc,UK
112/C2 Coltauco, Chile
47/H1 Coltishall, Eng,UK
131/C2 Colton, Ca,US
131/F5 Colts Neck, NJ,US
107/D4 Coluene (riv.), Braz.
118/E3 Columbia (mtn.), Ab,Can
122/C2 Columbia (mts.), BC,Can
119/T6 Columbia (cape), NW,Can
122/C4 Columbia (riv.), Can., US
122/D4 Columbia (plat.), US
126/C4 Columbia, Ky,US
128/E3 Columbia, La,US
131/K7 Columbia, Md,US
125/J3 Columbia, Mo,US
129/F4 Columbia, Ms,US
129/H3 Columbia (cap.), SC,US
129/G3 Columbia, Tn,US
122/E3 Columbia Falls, Mt,US
102/B4 Columbine (cape), SAfr.
129/G3 Columbus, Ga,US
126/C4 Columbus, In,US
129/F3 Columbus, Ms,US
122/F4 Columbus, Mt,US
125/H2 Columbus, Ne,US
131/F5 Columbus, NJ,US
124/F5 Columbus, NM,US
126/D4 Columbus (cap.), Oh,US
128/D4 Columbus, Tx,US
124/B3 Colusa, Ca,US
118/D2 Colville (lake), NW,Can
130/H2 Colville (riv.), Ak,US
122/D3 Colville, Wa,US
132/B3 Colvos (passg.), Wa,US
46/D2 Colwall, Eng,UK
46/C4 Colwinston, Wal,UK
44/E5 Colwyn Bay, Wal,UK
57/K4 Comacchio, It.
57/K4 Comacchio, Valli di (lag.), It.
128/D4 Comanche, Tx,US
112/F3 Comandante Nicanor Otamendi, Arg.
63/H2 Comăneşti, Rom.
63/G3 Comarnic, Rom.
116/D5 Comayagua, Hon.
111/B3 Combarbalá, Chile
46/B4 Combe Martin, Eng,UK
44/C2 Comber, NI,UK
52/B6 Combs-la-Ville, Fr.
90/C4 Comet (riv.), Austl.
85/F3 Comilla, Bang.
52/B2 Comines, Belg.
52/C2 Comines, Fr.
131/G5 Commack, NY,US
56/E3 Commentry, Fr.
131/B2 Commerce, Ca,US
53/E6 Commercy, Fr.
119/H2 Committee (bay), NW,Can
75/B4 Communism (Kommunizma) (peak), Taj.
57/F4 Como, It.
55/F5 Como (lake), It.
55/F5 Como (prov.), It.
132/P14 Como (lake), Wi,US
112/D5 Comodoro Rivadavia, Arg.
98/D4 Comoé (prov.), Burk.
98/E4 Comoé Nat'l Park, IvC.
84/C6 Comorin (cape), India
103/G5 Comoros
122/B3 Comox, BC,Can
52/B5 Compiègne, Fr.
117/P9 Compostela, Mex.
131/B3 Compton, Ca,US
128/C4 Comstock, Tx,US
98/B4 Conakry (cap.), Gui.
98/B4 Conakry (comm.), Gui.
56/B3 Concarneau, Fr.
110/E1 Conceição da Barra, Braz.
110/B1 Conceição das Alagoas, Braz.
109/J5 Conceição do Araguaia, Braz.
110/D1 Conceição do Mato Dentro, Braz.
110/H6 Conceição do Rio Verde, Braz.
108/F7 Concepción (lake), Bol.
112/B3 Concepción, Chile
111/E1 Concepción, Par.
108/C6 Concepción, Peru
116/A3 Concepción del Oro, Mex.
112/F2 Concepción del Uruguay, Arg.
124/B4 Conception (pt.), Ca,US

148

Conch – Dande

110/F7 **Conchal**, Braz.
125/F4 **Conchas** (lake), NM,US
125/G5 **Concho** (riv.), Tx,US
117/N8 **Conchos** (riv.), Mex.
132/K11 **Concord**, Ca,US
129/H3 **Concord**, NC,US
127/G3 **Concord** (cap.), NH,US
111/E3 **Concordia**, Arg.
110/A3 **Concórdia**, Braz.
125/H3 **Concordia**, Ks,US
122/C3 **Concrete**, Wa,US
83/D2 **Con Cuong**, Viet.
117/F3 **Condado**, Cuba
52/C3 **Condé-sur-L'Escaut**, Fr.
56/C2 **Condé-sur-Noireau**, Fr.
90/C4 **Condomine** (riv.), Austl.
122/C4 **Condon**, Or,US
53/D3 **Condroz** (plat.), Belg.
129/G4 **Conecuh** (riv.), Al,US
57/K4 **Conegliano**, It.
128/B2 **Conejos**, Co,US
52/B6 **Conflans-Sainte-Honorine**, Fr.
131/G4 **Congers**, NY,US
82/B3 **Conghua**, China
45/F5 **Congleton**, Eng,UK
95/D4 **Congo**
97/K7 **Congo** (basin), Afr.
104/C1 **Congo** (riv.), Afr.
110/D2 **Congonhas**, Braz.
112/C3 **Conguillio Nat'l Park**, Chile
112/C4 **Cónico, Cerro** (Nevado) (peak), Arg., Chile
58/B4 **Conil de la Frontera**, Sp.
45/H5 **Coningsby**, Eng,UK
45/G5 **Conisbrough**, Eng,UK
45/E3 **Coniston**, Eng,UK
45/E3 **Coniston Water** (lake), Eng,UK
44/C2 **Conlig**, NI,UK
119/J1 **Conn** (lake), NW,Can
43/A4 **Connacht** (prov.), Ire.
45/E5 **Connah's Quay**, Wal,UK
126/D3 **Conneaut**, Oh,US
127/G2 **Connecticut** (riv.), US
127/F3 **Connecticut** (state), US
43/C2 **Connel**, Sc,UK
126/E3 **Connellsville**, Pa,US
43/H7 **Connemara Nat'l Park**, Ire.
126/C4 **Connersville**, In,US
43/A3 **Conn, Lough** (lake), Ire.
113/K7 **Cono Grande** (peak), Arg.
90/D4 **Conondale Nat'l Park**, Austl.
56/E4 **Conques**, Fr.
122/F3 **Conrad**, Mt,US
116/B1 **Conroe**, Tx.,US
128/E4 **Conroe**, Tx,US
110/D2 **Conselheiro Lafaiete**, Braz.
110/D1 **Conselheiro Pena**, Braz.
45/G2 **Consett**, Eng,UK
131/E5 **Conshohocken**, Pa,US
116/E3 **Consolación del Sur**, Cuba
83/D4 **Con Son** (isl.), Viet.
55/F2 **Constance** (Bodensee) (lake), Ger., Swi.
63/J3 **Constanța**, Rom.
63/J3 **Constanța** (co.), Rom.
59/F2 **Constantí**, Sp.
58/C4 **Constantina**, Sp.
96/G1 **Constantine**, Alg.
130/G4 **Constantine** (cape), Ak,US
112/B2 **Constitución**, Chile
113/T11 **Constitución** (res.), Uru.
117/L7 **Constitución de 1997 Nat'l Park**, Mex.
58/D3 **Consuegra**, Sp.
84/E3 **Contai**, India
57/K4 **Contarina**, It.
109/K6 **Contas** (riv.), Braz.
110/C1 **Contegem**, Braz.
52/B4 **Contigny**, Fr.
122/C2 **Continental** (ranges), Ab, BC,Can
132/L11 **Contra Costa** (can.), Ca,US
117/F3 **Contramaestre**, Cuba
58/E3 **Contreras** (res.), Sp.
130/J3 **Controller** (bay), Ak,US
112/B3 **Contulmo**, Chile
118/E2 **Contwoyto** (lake), NW,Can
52/B4 **Conty**, Fr.
117/G6 **Convención**, Col.
60/E2 **Conversano**, It.
90/C3 **Conway** (cape), Austl.
128/E3 **Conway**, Ar,US
127/G3 **Conway**, NH,US
129/J3 **Conway**, SC,US
90/C3 **Conway Range Nat'l Park**, Austl.
44/E5 **Conway, Vale of** (val.), Wal,UK
44/E5 **Conwy**, Wal,UK
44/D5 **Conwy** (bay), Wal,UK
44/E5 **Conwy** (riv.), Wal,UK
84/E2 **Cooch Behār**, India
90/F7 **Coochiemudlo** (isl.), Austl.
113/K8 **Cook** (bay), Chile
89/H7 **Cook** (str.), NZ
130/H3 **Cook** (inlet), Ak,US
129/G2 **Cookeville**, Tn,US
105/L **Cook Ice Shelf**, Ant.
93/J6 **Cook Islands** (terr.), NZ
44/B2 **Cookstown**, NI,UK
44/B2 **Cookstown** (dist.), NI,UK
91/B3 **Coola Coola** (swamp), Austl.
44/B4 **Cooley** (pt.), Ire.
90/D4 **Cooloola Nat'l Park**, Austl.
91/D3 **Cooma**, Austl.
84/B5 **Coondapoor**, India
84/C5 **Coonoor**, India
128/E3 **Cooper**, Tx,US
123/J4 **Cooperstown**, ND,US
91/A3 **Coorong Nat'l Park**, Austl.
129/G3 **Coosa** (riv.), Al,US
122/B5 **Coos Bay**, Or,US
91/D2 **Cootamundra**, Austl.
131/G5 **Copague**, NY,US
112/C3 **Copahué** (vol.), Chile
116/D5 **Copán** (ruins), Hon.
58/E4 **Cope** (cape), Sp.
44/C2 **Copeland** (isl.), NI,UK
48/G1 **Copenhagen** (København) (cap.), Den.
61/F2 **Copertino**, It.
91/D1 **Copeton** (dam), Austl.
111/B2 **Copiapó**, Chile
57/J4 **Copparo**, It.
51/G4 **Coppenbrügge**, Ger.
128/D4 **Copperas Cove**, Tx,US
118/E2 **Coppermine** (riv.), NW,Can
45/F4 **Coppull**, Eng,UK
63/G2 **Copșa Mică**, Rom.
45/F1 **Coquet** (riv.), Eng,UK
45/G1 **Coquet Dale** (val.), Eng,UK
111/B2 **Coquimbo**, Chile
112/C1 **Coquimbo** (reg.), Chile
63/G4 **Corabia**, Rom.
90/C1 **Coral** (sea)
129/H5 **Coral Gables**, Fl,US
89/E2 **Coral Sea Is.** (terr.), Austl.
129/H5 **Coral Springs**, Fl,US
131/H5 **Coram**, NY,US
56/E2 **Corbeil-Essonnes**, Fr.
52/B4 **Corbie**, Fr.
56/E5 **Corbieres** (mts.), Fr.
126/C4 **Corbin**, Ky,US
45/F2 **Corbridge**, Eng,UK
47/F2 **Corby**, Eng,UK
110/K7 **Corcovado** (mon.), Braz.
112/B4 **Corcovado** (gulf), Chile
112/B4 **Corcovado** (vol.), Chile
116/E6 **Corcovado Nat'l Park**, CR
110/D2 **Cordeiro**, Braz.
129/H4 **Cordele**, Ga,US
125/H4 **Cordell** (New Cordell), Ok,US
57/K4 **Cordenons**, It.
108/D3 **Cordillera de los Picachos Nat'l Park**, Col.
111/D3 **Córdoba**, Arg.
111/D3 **Córdoba** (mts.), Arg.
112/E2 **Córdoba** (prov.), Arg.
116/B4 **Córdoba**, Mex.
58/C4 **Córdoba**, Sp.
130/J3 **Cordova** (peak), Ak,US
58/E1 **Corella**, Sp.
108/G3 **Corentyne** (riv.), Guy.
61/F3 **Corfu** (Kérkira) (isl.), Gre.
58/B3 **Coria**, Sp.
58/B4 **Coria del Río**, Sp.
91/D2 **Coricudgy** (peak), Austl.
60/E3 **Corigliano Calabro**, It.
61/H4 **Corinth** (ruins), Gre.
129/F3 **Corinth**, Ms,US
61/H4 **Corinth** (Kórinthos), Gre.
110/C1 **Corinto**, Braz.
116/D5 **Corinto**, Nic.
58/A1 **Coristanco**, Sp.
61/G2 **Corleone**, It.
63/H5 **Çorlu**, Turk.
52/D5 **Cormontreuil**, Fr.
123/H2 **Cormorant**, Mb,Can
123/H2 **Cormorant** (lake), Mb,Can
46/C1 **Corndon** (hill), Wal,UK
110/B2 **Cornélio Procópio**, Braz.
119/K2 **Cornelius Grinnel** (bay), NW,Can
59/L7 **Cornella**, Sp.
91/C3 **Corner** (inlet), Austl.
127/K1 **Corner Brook**, Nf,Can
126/E3 **Corning**, NY,US
90/B3 **Cornish** (cr.), Austl.
57/J4 **Corno alle Scale** (peak), It.
113/L8 **Cornú** (peak), Arg.
119/S7 **Cornwall** (isl.), NW,Can
126/F2 **Cornwall**, On,Can
127/J2 **Cornwall**, PE,Can
46/B6 **Cornwall** (co.), Eng,UK
119/S7 **Cornwallis** (isl.), NW,Can
117/H5 **Coro**, Ven.
109/K4 **Coroatá**, Braz.
108/E7 **Corocoro**, Bol.
110/C1 **Coromandel**, Braz.
84/D5 **Coromandel** (coast), India
89/H6 **Coromandel**, NZ
82/D5 **Coron**, Phil.
131/C3 **Corona**, Ca,US
125/F4 **Corona**, NM,US
116/E6 **Coronado** (bay), CR
122/F2 **Coronation**, Ab,Can
118/E2 **Coronation** (gulf), NW,Can
112/E1 **Coronda**, Arg.
112/B3 **Coronel**, Chile
112/E3 **Coronel Dorrego**, Arg.
110/D1 **Coronel Fabriciano**, Braz.
112/D2 **Coronel Moldes**, Arg.
111/E2 **Coronel Oviedo**, Par.
112/E3 **Coronel Pringles**, Arg.
112/E3 **Coronel Suárez**, Arg.
110/A3 **Coronel Vivida**, Braz.
108/D7 **Coropuna** (peak), Peru
117/F6 **Corozal**, Col.
116/D4 **Corozal Town**, Belz.
128/D5 **Corpus Christi**, Tx,US
58/D3 **Corral de Almaguer**, Sp.
112/E2 **Corral de Bustos**, Arg.
59/Y16 **Corralejo**, Canl.
91/B3 **Corrangamite** (lake), Austl.
116/E6 **Corredor**, CR
109/J6 **Corrente**, Braz.
110/B1 **Corrente** (riv.), Braz.
43/A4 **Corrib, Lough** (lake), Ire.
111/E2 **Corrientes**, Arg.
116/E3 **Corrientes** (cape), Cuba
108/C4 **Corrientes** (riv.), Ecu., Peru
46/C1 **Corris**, Wal,UK
60/A1 **Corse** (cape), Fr.
60/A1 **Corse** (reg.), Fr.
44/D1 **Corserine** (mtn.), Sc,UK
44/C1 **Corsewall** (pt.), Sc,UK
46/D4 **Corsham**, Eng,UK
60/A1 **Corsica** (Corse) (isl.), Fr.
128/D3 **Corsicana**, Tx,US
60/A1 **Corte**, Fr.
124/E3 **Cortez**, Co,US
57/K3 **Cortina d'Ampezzo**, It.
126/E3 **Cortland**, NY,US
98/B4 **Corubal** (riv.), GBis.
58/A3 **Coruche**, Port.
74/E2 **Çoruh** (riv.), Turk.
108/G7 **Corumbá**, Braz.
110/B1 **Corumbá** (riv.), Braz.
122/C4 **Corvallis**, Or,US
46/D2 **Corve** (riv.), Eng,UK
59/R12 **Corvo** (isl.), Azor.
60/C1 **Corvo** (peak), It.
45/E6 **Corwen**, Wal,UK
60/E3 **Cosenza**, It.
126/D3 **Coshocton**, Oh,US
116/D5 **Cosigüina** (pt.), Nic.
58/D2 **Coslada**, Sp.
110/F7 **Cosmópolis**, Braz.
56/E3 **Cosne-Cours-sur-Loire**, Fr.
58/B1 **Cospeito**, Sp.
111/D3 **Cosquín**, Arg.
56/D3 **Cosson** (riv.), Fr.
131/C3 **Costa Mesa**, Ca,US
116/E5 **Costa Rica**
117/N9 **Costa Rica**, Mex.
47/H1 **Costessey**, Eng,UK
63/G3 **Costești**, Rom.
132/M10 **Cosumnes** (riv.), Ca,US
82/D6 **Cotabato**, Phil.
98/D5 **Côte d'Ivoire** (Ivory Coast)
56/C2 **Cotentin** (pen.), Fr.
98/D5 **Côte d'Ivoire** (Ivory Coast)
54/A3 **Côte d'Or** (dept.), Fr.
127/N7 **Côte-Saint-Luc**, Qu,Can
46/B3 **Cothi** (riv.), Wal,UK
110/G8 **Cotia**, Braz.
99/F5 **Cotonou**, Ben.
46/D4 **Cotswolds** (hills), Eng,UK
122/C5 **Cottage Grove**, Or,US
49/H3 **Cottbus**, Ger.
47/G2 **Cottenham**, Eng,UK
124/D4 **Cottonwood**, Az,US
128/D2 **Cottonwood** (riv.), Ks,US
125/F5 **Cottonwood** (dry riv.), Tx,US
128/D4 **Cotulla**, Tx,US
56/C4 **Coubre, Pointe de la** (pt.), Fr.
52/C5 **Coucy-le-Château-Auffrique**, Fr.
52/B1 **Coudekerque-Branche**, Fr.
56/E5 **Couguille, Pic de** (peak), Fr.
56/D2 **Coulaines**, Fr.
122/D4 **Coulee City**, Wa,US
105/M **Coulman** (isl.), Ant.
52/C6 **Coulommiers**, Fr.
126/E2 **Coulonge** (riv.), Qu,Can
56/D4 **Coulounieix-Chamiers**, Fr.
122/D4 **Council**, Id,US
123/K5 **Council Bluffs**, Ia,US
125/H3 **Council Grove**, Ks,US
43/D2 **Coupar Angus**, Sc,UK
52/D3 **Courcelles**, Belg.
53/F5 **Courcelles-Chaussy**, Fr.
56/E4 **Cournon-d'Auvergne**, Fr.
118/D4 **Courtenay**, BC,Can
127/S8 **Courtice**, On,Can
52/C2 **Courtrai** (Kortrijk), Belg.
56/C2 **Coutances**, Fr.
122/F3 **Coutts**, Ab,Can
52/D3 **Couvin**, Belg.
59/P10 **Cova da Piedade**, Port.
58/C1 **Covadonga Nat'l Park**, Sp.
63/H3 **Covasna**, Rom.
62/G3 **Covasna** (co.), Rom.
47/E2 **Coventry**, Eng,UK
47/E1 **Coventry** (can.), Eng,UK
58/B2 **Covilhã**, Port.
131/C2 **Covina**, Ca,US
129/H3 **Covington**, Ga,US
126/C4 **Covington**, Ky,US
129/F3 **Covington**, Tn,US
126/E4 **Covington**, Va,US
90/H8 **Cowan**, Austl.
46/C4 **Cowbridge**, Wal,UK
47/E5 **Cowes**, Eng,UK
45/F2 **Cow Green** (res.), Eng,UK
122/C4 **Cowlitz** (riv.), Wa,US
129/H3 **Cowpens Nat'l Bfld.**, SC,US
91/D2 **Cowra**, Austl.
45/G2 **Coxhoe**, Eng,UK
109/H7 **Coxim**, Braz.
52/B5 **Coye-la-Forêt**, Fr.
125/H2 **Cozad**, Ne,US
116/D3 **Cozumel**, Mex.
116/D3 **Cozumel** (isl.), Mex.
91/C4 **Cradle** (peak), Austl.
91/C4 **Cradle Mountain-Lake Saint Clair Nat'l Park**, Austl.
102/D4 **Cradock**, SAfr.
130/K3 **Crag** (mtn.), Yk,Can
45/F3 **Crag** (hill), Eng,UK
124/F2 **Craig**, Co,US
44/C2 **Craigavad**, NI,UK
44/B3 **Craigavon**, NI,UK
44/B3 **Craigavon** (dist.), NI,UK
91/F5 **Craigieburn**, Austl.
123/G3 **Craik**, Sk,Can
57/J2 **Crailsheim**, Ger.
63/F3 **Craiova**, Rom.
45/G1 **Cramlington**, Eng,UK
44/A1 **Crana** (riv.), Ire.
123/H2 **Cranberry Portage**, Mb,Can
46/D5 **Cranborne Chase** (for.), Eng,UK
91/C3 **Cranbourne**, Austl.
122/E3 **Cranbrook**, BC,Can
47/G4 **Cranbrook**, Eng,UK
131/F5 **Cranbury**, NJ,US
128/C4 **Crane**, Tx,US
123/J3 **Crane River**, Mb,Can
131/F5 **Cranford**, NJ,US
47/F4 **Cranleigh**, Eng,UK
52/C5 **Craonne**, Fr.
63/F2 **Crasna** (riv.), Rom.
122/C5 **Crater** (lake), Or,US
122/C5 **Crater Lake Nat'l Park**, Or,US
122/E5 **Craters of the Moon Nat'l Mon.**, Id,US
109/K5 **Crateús**, Braz.
60/E3 **Crati** (riv.), It.
109/L5 **Crato**, Braz.
110/C2 **Cravinhos**, Braz.
126/C3 **Crawfordsville**, In,US
129/G4 **Crawfordville**, Fl,US
47/F4 **Crawley**, Eng,UK
122/F4 **Crazy** (mts.), Mt,US
52/A3 **Crécy-en-Ponthieu**, Fr.
46/D2 **Credenhill**, Eng,UK
127/Q8 **Credit** (riv.), On,Can
46/C5 **Crediton**, Eng,UK
118/F3 **Cree** (lake), Sk,Can
118/F3 **Cree** (riv.), Sk,Can
44/D2 **Cree** (riv.), Sc,UK
44/D2 **Creetown**, Sc,UK
123/H2 **Creighton**, Sk,Can
52/B5 **Creil**, Fr.
57/H4 **Crema**, It.
51/H4 **Cremlingen**, Ger.
57/J4 **Cremona**, It.
52/B5 **Crépy-en-Valois**, Fr.
62/B3 **Cres** (isl.), Cro.
124/A2 **Crescent City**, Ca,US
112/E2 **Crespo**, Arg.
56/F4 **Crest**, Fr.
132/P16 **Crest Hill**, Il,US
131/C2 **Crestline**, Ca,US
122/D3 **Creston**, BC,Can
123/K5 **Creston**, Ia,US
129/G4 **Crestview**, Fl,US
45/G5 **Creswell**, Eng,UK
61/J5 **Crete** (isl.), Gre.
61/J5 **Crete** (sea), Gre.
125/H2 **Crete**, Ne,US
52/B6 **Créteil**, Fr.
59/G1 **Creus** (cape), Sp.
56/D3 **Creuse** (riv.), Fr.
53/F5 **Creutzwald-la-Croix**, Fr.
57/J4 **Crevalcore**, It.
59/E3 **Crevillente**, Sp.
45/F5 **Crewe**, Eng,UK
46/D5 **Crewkerne**, Eng,UK
43/C2 **Crianlarich**, Sc,UK
44/D6 **Criccieth**, Wal,UK
110/B4 **Criciúma**, Braz.
46/C3 **Crickhowell**, Wal,UK
47/E3 **Cricklade**, Eng,UK
43/D2 **Crieff**, Sc,UK
52/A3 **Criel-sur-Mer**, Fr.
44/E2 **Criffell** (hill), Eng,UK
66/E3 **Crimean** (pen.), Ukr.
66/E3 **Crimean Obl.**, Ukr.
96/H7 **Cristal** (mts.), Gabon
109/J7 **Cristalina**, Braz.
117/G5 **Cristóbal** (pk.), Col.
62/F2 **Criștul Alb** (riv.), Rom.
63/G2 **Cristuru Secuiesc**, Rom.
62/E2 **Crișul Negru** (riv.), Rom.
109/H6 **Crixás-Açu** (riv.), Braz.
61/G2 **Crna Reka** (riv.), Macd.
91/D3 **Croajingolong Nat'l Park**, Austl.
62/B3 **Croatia**
127/F2 **Croche** (riv.), Qu,Can
86/E3 **Crocker** (range), Malay.
44/E1 **Crocketford**, Sc,UK
128/E4 **Crockett**, Tx,US
91/D2 **Crocodile** (pt.), Austl.
131/K7 **Crofton**, Md,US
46/B3 **Crofty**, Wal,UK
44/B6 **Croghan** (mtn.), Ire.
56/F5 **Croisette** (cape), Fr.
123/L3 **Croix** (lake), Can., US
47/H1 **Cromer**, Eng,UK
89/G7 **Cromwell**, NZ
83/E3 **Crong A Na** (riv.), Viet.
90/H9 **Cronulla**, Austl.
45/G2 **Crook**, Eng,UK
117/G3 **Crooked** (isl.), Bahm.
123/J4 **Crookston**, Mn,US
45/E5 **Crosby**, Eng,UK
123/H3 **Crosby**, ND,US
128/C3 **Crosbyton**, Tx,US
99/H5 **Cross** (riv.), Camr., Nga.
123/J2 **Cross** (lake), Mb,Can
129/H4 **Cross City**, Fl,US
128/F3 **Crossett**, Ar,US
45/F2 **Cross Fell** (mtn.), Eng,UK
122/E3 **Crossfield**, Ab,Can
44/C3 **Crossgar**, NI,UK
46/C2 **Crossgates**, Wal,UK
44/D1 **Crosshill**, Sc,UK
46/C3 **Crosskeys**, Wal,UK
44/B3 **Crossmaglen**, NI,UK
44/E2 **Crossmichael**, Sc,UK
99/H5 **Cross River** (state), Nga.
129/G3 **Crossville**, Tn,US
45/F4 **Croston**, Eng,UK
60/E3 **Crotone**, It.
47/G3 **Crouch** (riv.), Eng,UK
52/C5 **Crouy-sur-Ourq**, Fr.
122/G4 **Crow Agency**, Mt,US
47/G4 **Crowborough**, Eng,UK
91/E1 **Crowdy Bay Nat'l Park**, Austl.
126/E2 **Crowe** (riv.), On,Can
122/F5 **Crowheart**, Wy,US
47/F1 **Crowland**, Eng,UK
45/H4 **Crowle**, Eng,UK
128/E4 **Crowley**, La,US
129/F3 **Crowley's** (ridge), Ar,US
123/K4 **Crow, North Fork** (riv.), Mn,US
126/C3 **Crown Point**, In,US
124/E4 **Crownpoint**, NM,US
119/H1 **Crown Prince Frederik** (isl.), NW,Can
90/D4 **Crows Nest Falls Nat'l Park**, Austl.
47/F4 **Crowthorne**, Eng,UK
47/F3 **Croxley Green**, Eng,UK
91/G5 **Croydon**, Austl.
39/M8 **Crozet** (isls.), FrAnt.
105/M **Crozier** (cape), Ant.
56/A2 **Crozon**, Fr.
43/E2 **Cruden Bay**, Sc,UK
44/B2 **Crumlin**, NI,UK
45/E2 **Crummock Water** (lake), Eng,UK
53/E5 **Crusnes** (riv.), Fr.
117/F4 **Cruz** (cape), Cuba
111/E2 **Cruz Alta**, Arg.
111/F2 **Cruz Alta**, Braz.
59/P10 **Cruz Alta** (mtn.), Port.
109/L6 **Cruz das Almas**, Braz.
111/D3 **Cruz del Eje**, Arg.
110/J7 **Cruzeiro**, Braz.
108/D5 **Cruzeiro do Sul**, Braz.
110/J6 **Cruzília**, Braz.
62/D3 **Crvenka**, Yugo.
45/E5 **Cryn-y-Brain** (mtn.), Wal,UK
124/C3 **Crystal Bay**, Nv,US
128/D4 **Crystal City**, Tx,US
126/B2 **Crystal Falls**, Mi,US
132/P15 **Crystal Lake**, Il,US
62/E2 **Csongrád**, Hun.
62/E2 **Csongrád** (co.), Hun.
62/C2 **Csorna**, Hun.
62/E2 **Csorvás**, Hun.
62/D2 **Csóványos** (peak), Hun.
72/D2 **Ctesiphon** (ruins), Iraq
104/D4 **Cuando** (riv.), Ang.
104/C4 **Cuangar**, Ang.
104/C2 **Cuango** (riv.), Ang.
104/B2 **Cuanza** (riv.), Ang.
59/E3 **Cuart de Poblet**, Sp.
112/D2 **Cuarto** (riv.), Arg.
116/A2 **Cuatrociénagas**, Mex.
117/F3 **Cuba**
125/K3 **Cuba**, Mo,US
104/C4 **Cubango** (riv.), Ang.
110/G8 **Cubatão**, Braz.
74/C2 **Çubuk**, Turk.
131/C2 **Cucamonga** (Rancho Cucamonga), Ca,US
108/E2 **Cuchivero** (riv.), Ven.
47/F4 **Cuckfield**, Eng,UK
47/G5 **Cuckmere** (riv.), Eng,UK
83/D1 **Cuc Phuong Nat'l Park**, Viet.
108/D2 **Cúcuta**, Col.
132/Q14 **Cudahy**, Wi,US
84/C5 **Cuddalore**, India
84/C5 **Cuddapah**, India
45/F5 **Cuddington**, Eng,UK
58/B1 **Cudillero**, Sp.
45/G4 **Cudworth**, Eng,UK
58/C2 **Cuéllar**, Sp.
108/C4 **Cuenca**, Ecu.
58/D2 **Cuenca**, Sp.
58/E2 **Cuenca** (range), Sp.
116/B4 **Cuernavaca**, Mex.
128/D4 **Cuero**, Tx,US
56/G5 **Cuers**, Fr.
108/C3 **Cueva de los Guarcharos Nat'l Park**, Col.
58/E4 **Cuevas del Almanzora**, Sp.
63/F3 **Cugir**, Rom.
56/D5 **Cugnaux-Vignitcasses**, Fr.
109/G7 **Cuiabá**, Braz.
109/G7 **Cuiabá** (riv.), Braz.
50/C5 **Cuijk**, Neth.
104/C2 **Cuilo** (riv.), Ang.
104/C3 **Cuima**, Ang.
104/C3 **Cuito** (riv.), Ang.
104/C4 **Cuito-Cuanavale**, Ang.
108/F4 **Cuiuni** (riv.), Braz.
74/E3 **Çukurca**, Turk.
83/E4 **Cu Lao** (isl.), Viet.
44/A1 **Culdaff** (riv.), Ire.
50/C5 **Culemborg**, Neth.
109/H6 **Culene** (riv.), Braz.
91/C1 **Culgoa** (riv.), Austl.
117/N9 **Culiacán**, Mex.
82/D5 **Culion** (isl.), Phil.
58/D4 **Cúllar Baza**, Sp.
43/D2 **Cullen**, Sc,UK
59/E3 **Cullera**, Sp.
58/A1 **Culleredo**, Sp.
129/G3 **Cullman**, Al,US
46/C5 **Cullompton**, Eng,UK
44/B2 **Cullybackey**, NI,UK
44/A1 **Culmore**, NI,UK
90/B5 **Culoga** (riv.), Austl.
126/E4 **Culpeper**, Va,US
131/B2 **Culver City**, Ca,US
117/J5 **Cumaná**, Ven.
119/K2 **Cumberland** (pen.), NW,Can
119/K2 **Cumberland** (sound), NW,Can
123/H2 **Cumberland** (lake), Sk,Can
129/G3 **Cumberland** (plat.), US
129/H4 **Cumberland** (isl.), Ga,US
129/G2 **Cumberland** (falls), Ky,US
126/C4 **Cumberland** (lake), Ky,US
129/G2 **Cumberland** (riv.), Ky, Tn,US
126/E4 **Cumberland**, Md,US
126/D4 **Cumberland Gap Nat'l Hist. Park**, Tn,US
123/H2 **Cumberland House**, Sk,Can
117/N8 **Cumbres de Majalca Nat'l Park**, Mex.
116/A2 **Cumbres de Monterrey Nat'l Park**, Mex.
45/F2 **Cumbria** (co.), Eng,UK
45/E3 **Cumbrian** (mts.), Eng,UK
84/C4 **Cumbum**, India
74/C3 **Çumra**, Turk.
130/M5 **Cumshewa** (pt.), BC,Can
112/B3 **Cunco**, Chile
104/B4 **Cunene** (riv.), Ang.
57/G4 **Cuneo**, It.
83/E3 **Cung Son**, Viet.
110/J8 **Cunha**, Braz.
42/H1 **Čuokkaraš'ša** (peak), Nor.
57/G4 **Cuorgnè**, It.
43/D2 **Cupar**, Sc,UK
132/K12 **Cupertino**, Ca,US
62/E4 **Ćuprija**, Yugo.
117/H5 **Curaçao** (isl.), NAnt.
112/C3 **Curacautín**, Chile
112/B3 **Curanilahue**, Chile
108/C4 **Curaray** (riv.), Ecu., Peru
112/Q9 **Curaumilla** (pt.), Chile
62/F2 **Curcubăta** (peak), Rom.
56/E3 **Cure** (riv.), Fr.
103/S15 **Curepipe**, Mrts.
112/B2 **Curepto**, Chile
112/C2 **Curicó**, Chile
110/B3 **Curitiba**, Braz.
110/B3 **Curitibanos**, Braz.
44/B5 **Curragh, The**, Ire.
109/L5 **Currais Novos**, Braz.
125/K3 **Current** (riv.), Ar, Mo,US
124/D2 **Currie**, Nv,US
63/G3 **Curtea de Argeș**, Rom.
62/E2 **Curtici**, Rom.
90/C3 **Curtis** (isl.), Austl.
92/H8 **Curtis** (isl.), NZ
109/G4 **Curuá** (riv.), Braz.
109/H5 **Curuá** (riv.), Braz.
108/D5 **Curuçú** (riv.), Braz.
86/B4 **Curup**, Indo.
109/K4 **Cururupu**, Braz.
111/E2 **Curuzú Cuatiá**, Arg.
110/C1 **Curvelo**, Braz.
121/J2 **Curwood** (mtn.), Mi,US
108/D6 **Cusco**, Peru
44/B1 **Cushendall**, NI,UK
44/B3 **Cusher** (riv.), NI,UK
125/H4 **Cushing**, Ok,US
56/E3 **Cusset**, Fr.
129/G3 **Cusseta**, Ga,US
122/G4 **Custer**, Mt,US
123/H5 **Custer**, SD,US
46/C5 **Cut** (hill), Eng,UK
122/E3 **Cut Bank**, Mt,US
108/C5 **Cutervo**, Peru
129/G4 **Cuthbert**, Ga,US
122/F2 **Cut Knife**, Sk,Can
112/C3 **Cutral-Có**, Arg.
84/E3 **Cuttack**, India
51/F1 **Cuxhaven**, Ger.
124/C4 **Cuyama** (riv.), Ca,US
87/F1 **Cuyo**, Phil.
87/F1 **Cuyo** (isls.), Phil.
108/F2 **Cuyuni** (riv.), Guy., Ven.
46/C3 **Cwm**, Wal,UK
46/C3 **Cwmafan**, Wal,UK
46/C3 **Cwmbran**, Wal,UK
123/H5 **C.W. McConaughy** (lake), Ne,US
61/J4 **Cyclades** (isls.), Gre.
126/C4 **Cynthiana**, Ky,US
46/B3 **Cynwyl Elfed**, Wal,UK
122/F3 **Cypress** (hills), Ab, Sk,Can
131/B3 **Cypress**, Ca,US
74/J4 **Cyprus**
97/K1 **Cyrenaica** (reg.), Libya
46/B3 **Cywyn** (riv.), Wal,UK
49/J2 **Czaplinek**, Pol.
49/M2 **Czarna Biał ostocka**, Pol.
49/J2 **Czarnków**, Pol.
49/H4 **Czech Republic**
49/K3 **Częstochowa**, Pol.
49/K3 **Częstochowa** (prov.), Pol.
49/J2 **Czł uchów**, Pol.

D

82/D2 **Da** (riv.), China
81/B4 **Daba** (mts.), China
62/D2 **Dabas**, Hun.
72/C3 **Dabbāgh, Jabal** (mtn.), SAr.
108/C2 **Dabeiba**, Col.
84/B3 **Dabhoi**, India
83/D1 **Da (Black)** (riv.), Viet.
132/B2 **Dabob** (bay), Wa,US
97/Q6 **Daborow**, Som.
98/D5 **Dabou**, IvC.
84/C2 **Dabra**, India
49/M2 **Dąbrowa Biał ostocka**, Pol.
49/K3 **Dąbrowa Górnicza**, Pol.
55/H1 **Dachau**, Ger.
83/D3 **Dac Sut**, Viet.
83/D3 **Dac To**, Viet.
129/H4 **Dade City**, Fl,US
87/H4 **Dadi** (cape), Indo.
84/B4 **Dadra & Nagar Haveli** (terr.), India
73/J3 **Dādu**, Pak.
84/D6 **Daduru** (riv.), SrL.
83/B4 **Daen Noi** (peak), Thai.
82/D5 **Daet**, Phil.
85/J2 **Dafang**, China
98/B2 **Dagana**, Sen.
67/H3 **Dagestan Aut. Rep.**, Rus.
102/D4 **Daggaboersnek** (pass), SAfr.
90/B2 **Dagmar Range Nat'l Park**, Austl.
85/H2 **Daguan**, China
90/E6 **D'Aguilar** (mtn.), Austl.
90/E6 **D'Aguilar** (range), Austl.
77/K2 **Daguokui** (peak), China
82/D4 **Dagupan**, Phil.
75/E5 **Dagzê** (lake), China
81/C2 **Dahaituo Shan** (mtn.), China
71/D7 **Dahana** (des.), SAr.
84/B4 **Dāhānu**, India
84/A2 **Daharki**, Pak.
81/B2 **Dahei** (riv.), China
77/K2 **Daheiding** (peak), China
77/J2 **Da Hinggang** (mts.), China
97/N4 **Dahlak** (arch.), Erit.
129/H3 **Dahlonega**, Ga,US
49/G3 **Dahme** (riv.), Ger.
83/D4 **Da Hoa**, Viet.
81/C5 **Dahong** (mtn.), China
74/E3 **Dahūk**, Iraq
81/C2 **Dai** (lake), China
79/M9 **Daian**, Japan
79/G2 **Daigo**, Japan
84/D2 **Dailekh**, Nepal
44/D1 **Dailly**, Sc,UK
83/E3 **Dai Loc**, Viet.
58/D3 **Daimiel**, Sp.
128/E3 **Daingerfield**, Tx,US
90/B2 **Daintree Nat'l Park**, Austl.
79/E3 **Daiō-zaki** (pt.), Japan
112/E3 **Daireaux**, Arg.
78/C3 **Dai-sen** (mtn.), Japan
78/C3 **Daisen-Oki Nat'l Park**, Japan
79/L10 **Daitō**, Japan
92/C2 **Daitō** (isls.), Japan
98/A3 **Dakar** (cap.), Sen.
98/A3 **Dakar** (reg.), Sen.
100/B3 **Dākhilah, Wāḥāt ad** (oasis), Egypt
96/B3 **Dakhla**, WSah.
98/A1 **Dakhlet Nouadhibou** (reg.), Mrta.
83/D3 **Dak Nhe**, Viet.
99/G3 **Dakoro**, Niger
125/H2 **Dakota City**, Ne,US
62/E4 **Dakovica**, Yugo.
62/D3 **Dakovo**, Yugo.
105/A **Dakshin Gangotri**, Ant.
76/H3 **Dalai** (salt lake), China
74/B3 **Dalaman**, Turk.
76/F2 **Dalanjargalan**, Mong.
42/E3 **Dalarna** (reg.), Swe.
83/E4 **Da Lat**, Viet.
42/Q6 **Dalatangi** (pt.), Ice.
44/E2 **Dalbeattie**, Sc,UK
90/C4 **Dalby**, Austl.
100/B4 **Dal Cataract** (falls), Sudan
50/D4 **Dalfsen**, Neth.
128/C2 **Dalhart**, Tx,US
127/H1 **Dalhousie**, NB,Can
130/N1 **Dalhousie** (cape), NW,Can
85/H2 **Dali**, China
81/B3 **Dali** (riv.), China
58/D4 **Dalías**, Sp.
77/H3 **Daling** (riv.), China
62/D3 **Dalj**, Cro.
130/M4 **Dall** (isl.), Ak,US
130/F3 **Dall** (lake), Ak,US
128/D3 **Dallas**, Tx,US
122/C4 **Dalles, The**, Or,US
99/F3 **Dallol Bosso** (wadi), Mali, Niger
43/C2 **Dalmally**, Sc,UK
62/C4 **Dalmatia** (reg.), Cro.
44/D1 **Dalmellington**, Sc,UK
77/M3 **Dal'negorsk**, Rus.
77/L2 **Dal'nerechensk**, Rus.
98/D5 **Daloa**, IvC.
100/B4 **Dalqū**, Sudan
90/B3 **Dalrymple** (lake), Austl.
43/C3 **Dalrymple**, Sc,UK
129/G3 **Dalton**, Ga,US
84/D3 **Daltonganj**, India
45/E3 **Dalton-in-Furness**, Eng,UK
43/C2 **Dalwhinnie**, Sc,UK
118/H2 **Daly** (bay), NW,Can
132/K11 **Daly City**, Ca,US
75/F5 **Dam** (riv.), China
84/B3 **Damān**, India
84/B3 **Damān & Diu** (terr.), India
74/H6 **Damanhūr**, Egypt
87/G5 **Damar** (isl.), Indo.
131/J7 **Damascus**, Md,US
74/L5 **Damascus** (Dimashq) (cap.), Syria
96/H5 **Damaturu**, Nga.
72/F1 **Damavānd** (mtn.), Iran
83/D4 **Dam Doi**, Viet.
47/E5 **Damerham**, Eng,UK
73/F1 **Dāmghān**, Iran
74/H6 **Damietta** (Dumyāţ), Egypt
81/C3 **Daming**, China
53/D4 **Damion** (mtn.), Fr.
52/B5 **Dammartin-en-Goële**, Fr.
52/C1 **Damme**, Belg.
51/F3 **Damme**, Ger.
84/C3 **Damoh**, India
99/E4 **Damongo**, Gha.
87/H4 **Dampier** (str.), Indo.
83/C4 **Damrei** (mts.), Camb.
50/D2 **Damsterdiep** (riv.), Neth.
53/E5 **Damvillers**, Fr.
81/B4 **Dan** (riv.), China
129/H2 **Dan** (riv.), NC,US
97/P5 **Danakil** (reg.), Djib.
98/C5 **Danané**, IvC.
83/E2 **Da Nang**, Viet.
82/D5 **Danao**, Phil.
47/G3 **Danbury**, Eng,UK
91/G5 **Dandenong**, Austl.
91/G5 **Dandenong** (cr.), Austl.
91/G5 **Dandenong** (mtn.), Austl.

57/K1 **Doupovské Hory** (mts.), Czh.
52/C3 **Dour,** Belg.
109/H8 **Dourados,** Braz.
56/E4 **Dourdou** (riv.), Fr.
58/B2 **Douro** (riv.), Port.
56/F4 **Doux** (riv.), Fr.
56/C4 **Douze** (riv.), Fr.
45/G6 **Dove** (riv.), Eng,UK
45/H3 **Dove** (riv.), Eng,UK
47/H2 **Dove** (riv.), Eng,UK
124/E3 **Dove Creek,** Co,US
52/A2 **Dover** (str.), Fr., UK
47/H4 **Dover,** Eng,UK
126/F4 **Dover** (cap.), De,US
127/G3 **Dover,** NH,US
131/F5 **Dover,** NJ,US
127/G2 **Dover-Foxcroft,** Me,US
45/G6 **Doveridge,** Eng,UK
44/C3 **Down** (dist.), NI,UK
132/P16 **Downers Grove,** Il,US
131/B3 **Downey,** Ca,US
47/G1 **Downham Market,** Eng,UK
124/B3 **Downieville,** Ca,US
44/C3 **Downpatrick,** NI,UK
47/H4 **Downs, The** (har.), Eng,UK
47/E4 **Downton,** Eng,UK
131/E5 **Doylestown,** Pa,US
78/C3 **Dōzen** (isl.), Japan
126/E2 **Dozois** (res.), Qu,Can
96/D2 **Drâa** (plat.), Alg., Mor.
96/D2 **Drâa** (wadi), Alg., Mor.
56/F4 **Drac** (riv.), Fr.
110/B2 **Dracena,** Braz.
50/D2 **Drachten,** Neth.
63/G3 **Drăgăneşti-Olt,** Rom.
63/G3 **Drăgăşani,** Rom.
57/G5 **Draguignan,** Fr.
113/L8 **Drake** (passage), Arg., Chile
104/E6 **Drakensberg** (range), Afr.
42/D4 **Drammen,** Nor.
44/B2 **Draperstown,** NI,UK
57/L3 **Drau** (riv.), Aus.
62/C3 **Drava** (riv.), Eur.
52/B6 **Draveil,** Fr.
49/H2 **Drawa** (riv.), Pol.
49/H2 **Drawsko Pomorskie,** Pol.
123/J3 **Drayton,** ND,US
122/E2 **Drayton Valley,** Ab,Can
87/K4 **Drei Zinnen** (peak), PNG
51/E5 **Drensteinfurt,** Ger.
50/D3 **Drenthe** (prov.), Neth.
50/D3 **Drentse Hoofdvaart** (can.), Neth.
49/G3 **Dresden,** Ger.
52/A6 **Dreux,** Fr.
49/H2 **Drezdenko,** Pol.
50/C4 **Driebergen,** Neth.
122/F5 **Driggs,** Id,US
73/J4 **Drigh Road,** Pak.
61/F2 **Drin** (gulf), Alb.
61/F1 **Drin** (riv.), Alb.
62/D3 **Drina** (riv.), Bosn., Yugo.
62/E5 **Drinizi** (riv.), Alb.
62/F3 **Drobeta-Turnu Severin,** Rom.
51/G1 **Drochtersen,** Ger.
44/B4 **Drogheda,** Ire.
66/B2 **Drogobych,** Ukr.
46/D2 **Droitwich,** Eng,UK
53/G6 **Drolingen,** Fr.
51/E6 **Drolshagen,** Ger.
56/F4 **Drôme** (riv.), Fr.
44/A3 **Dromore** (riv.), Ire.
44/B3 **Dromore,** NI,UK
45/G5 **Dronfield,** Eng,UK
56/D4 **Dronne** (riv.), Fr.
50/C3 **Dronten,** Neth.
56/D4 **Dropt** (riv.), Fr.
52/A6 **Drouette** (riv.), Fr.
126/C1 **Drowning** (riv.), On,Can
44/C3 **Drumaness,** NI,UK
44/C2 **Drumbeg,** NI,UK
122/E3 **Drumheller,** Ab,Can
44/B5 **Drumleck** (pt.), Ire.
90/B4 **Drummond** (peak), Austl.
90/B4 **Drummond** (range), Austl.
127/F2 **Drummondville,** Qu,Can
44/D2 **Drummore,** Sc,UK
44/A2 **Drumnakilly,** NI,UK
50/C5 **Drunen,** Neth.
45/G1 **Druridge** (bay), Eng,UK
49/M1 **Druskininkai,** Lith.
50/C5 **Druten,** Neth.
62/C3 **Drvar,** Bosn.
49/K2 **Drwęca** (riv.), Pol.
63/G4 **Dryanovo,** Bul.
130/K3 **Dry Creek,** Yk,Can
126/A1 **Dryden,** On,Can
128/C4 **Dryden,** Tx,US
46/C2 **Drygarn Fawr** (mtn.), Wal,UK
43/C2 **Drymen,** Sc,UK
99/H5 **Dschang,** Camr.
81/B4 **Du** (riv.), China
46/B3 **Duad** (riv.), Wal,UK
117/H4 **Duarte** (pk.), DRep.
118/F2 **Dubawnt** (lake), NW,Can
118/F2 **Dubawnt** (riv.), NW,Can
73/G3 **Dubayy,** UAE
91/D2 **Dubbo,** Austl.
44/B5 **Dublin** (bay), Ire.
44/B5 **Dublin** (cap.), Ire.
44/B5 **Dublin** (co.), Ire.
132/L11 **Dublin,** Ca,US
129/H3 **Dublin,** Ga,US
64/H4 **Dubna,** Rus.
49/K4 **Dubnica nad Váhom,** Slvk.
66/C2 **Dubno,** Ukr.
126/E3 **Du Bois,** Pa,US
122/F5 **Dubois,** Wy,US
63/J2 **Dubossary** (res.), Mol.
62/D4 **Dubrovnik,** Cro.
123/L5 **Dubuque,** Ia,US
124/E2 **Duchesne,** Ut,US
124/E2 **Duchesne** (riv.), Ut,US
93/N7 **Ducie** (atoll), Pitc.
129/G3 **Duck** (riv.), Tn,US
132/A2 **Duckabush** (riv.), Wa,US
123/G2 **Duck Lake,** Sk,Can
124/D3 **Duckwater,** Nv,US
83/D3 **Duc Lap,** Viet.
83/E3 **Duc Pho,** Viet.
83/D4 **Duc Phong,** Viet.
45/E3 **Dudden** (riv.), Eng,UK
53/F5 **Dudelange,** Lux.
51/H5 **Duderstadt,** Ger.
68/J3 **Dudinka,** Rus.
46/D2 **Dudley,** Eng,UK
58/C2 **Duero** (Douro) (riv.), Sp.
105/W **Dufek Massive** (mtn.), Ant.
92/F5 **Duff** (isl.), Sol.
52/D1 **Duffel,** Belg.
45/G6 **Duffield,** Eng,UK
43/D2 **Dufftown,** Sc,UK
57/G4 **Dufourspitze** (Punta Dufour) (peak), It., Swi.
62/B3 **Dugi Otok** (isl.), Cro.
124/D2 **Dugway,** Ut,US
108/E3 **Duida Marahuaca Nat'l Park,** Ven.
50/D6 **Duisburg,** Ger.
108/D2 **Duitama,** Col.
50/D5 **Duiven,** Neth.
93/L7 **Duke of Gloucester** (isls.), FrPol.
49/L4 **Dukla** (Przełęcz Dukielska) (pass), Pol.
76/D4 **Dulan,** China
111/D2 **Dulce** (riv.), Arg.
124/F3 **Dulce,** NM,US
85/J2 **Duliu** (riv.), China
51/E5 **Dülmen,** Ger.
63/H4 **Dulovo,** Bul.
123/K4 **Duluth,** Mn,US
46/C4 **Dulverton,** Eng,UK
74/L5 **Dūmā,** Syria
131/B2 **Duma** (pt.), Ca,US
82/D6 **Dumaguete,** Phil.
82/D6 **Dumalinao,** Phil.
82/C5 **Dumaran** (isl.), Phil.
91/D1 **Dumaresq** (riv.), Austl.
128/F3 **Dumas,** Ar,US
128/C3 **Dumas,** Tx,US
49/K4 **Ďumbier** (peak), Slvk.
104/C3 **Dumbo,** Ang.
63/G2 **Dumbrăveni,** Rom.
44/E1 **Dumfries,** Sc,UK
44/D1 **Dumfries & Galloway** (reg.), Sc,UK
51/F3 **Dümmer** (lake), Ger.
126/E2 **Dumoine** (lake), Qu,Can
126/E2 **Dumoine** (riv.), Qu,Can
131/F5 **Dumont,** NJ,US
105/K **Dumont d'Urville,** Ant.
74/H6 **Dumyāt** (gov.), Egypt
74/H6 **Dumyāţ** (Damietta), Egypt
49/K5 **Duna** (Danube) (riv.), Hun.
62/D2 **Dunaföldvár,** Hun.
62/D2 **Dunaharaszti,** Hun.
49/K5 **Dunaj** (Danube) (riv.), Slvk.
49/L4 **Dunajec** (riv.), Pol.
49/K5 **Dunakeszi,** Hun.
44/B4 **Dunany** (pt.), Ire.
62/D2 **Dunaújváros,** Hun.
43/D3 **Dunbar,** Sc,UK
43/D2 **Dunblane,** Sc,UK
124/E4 **Duncan,** Az,US
125/H4 **Duncan,** Ok,US
128/D3 **Duncanville,** Tx,US
44/B3 **Dundalk,** Ire.
44/B4 **Dundalk** (bay), Ire.
131/K7 **Dundalk,** Md,US
119/R7 **Dundas** (pen.), NW,Can
127/Q9 **Dundas,** On,Can
103/E3 **Dundee,** SAfr.
43/D2 **Dundee,** Sc,UK
44/C3 **Dundrum,** NI,UK
44/C3 **Dundrum** (bay), NI,UK
122/G3 **Dundurn,** Sk,Can
89/H7 **Dunedin,** NZ
129/H4 **Dunedin,** Fl,US
43/D2 **Dunfermline,** Sc,UK
44/B2 **Dungannon,** NI,UK
44/B3 **Dungannon** (dist.), NI,UK
84/B3 **Dungarpur,** India
43/B4 **Dungarvan,** Ire.
113/K8 **Dungeness** (pt.), Arg.
47/G5 **Dungeness** (pt.), Eng,UK
44/B2 **Dungiven,** NI,UK
101/A2 **Dungu,** Zaire
77/K3 **Dunhua,** China
76/C3 **Dunhuang,** China
46/C4 **Dunkery** (hill), Eng,UK
52/B1 **Dunkirk** (Dunkerque), Fr.
99/E5 **Dunkwa,** Gha.
44/B5 **Dún Laoghaire,** Ire.
44/B2 **Dunloy,** NI,UK
44/B2 **Dunmurry,** NI,UK
129/J3 **Dunn,** NC,US
44/A2 **Dunnamanagh,** NI,UK
44/B2 **Dunnamore,** NI,UK
45/H4 **Dunnington,** Eng,UK
127/Q10 **Dunnville,** On,Can
100/B5 **Dunqulah,** Sudan
44/D2 **Dunragit,** Sc,UK
43/D3 **Duns,** Sc,UK
44/E1 **Dunscore,** Sc,UK
123/H3 **Dunseith,** ND,US
44/B1 **Dunseverick,** NI,UK
124/B2 **Dunsmuir,** Ca,US
47/F3 **Dunstable,** Eng,UK
53/E5 **Dun-sur-Meuse,** Fr.
77/J1 **Duobukur** (riv.), China
132/P16 **Du Page** (riv.), Il,US
123/H4 **Dupree,** SD,US
110/K7 **Duque de Caxias,** Braz.
113/J7 **Duque de York** (isl.), Chile
126/B4 **Du Quoin,** Il,US
56/F5 **Durance** (riv.), Fr.
117/N9 **Durango** (state), Mex.
58/D1 **Durango,** Sp.
124/F3 **Durango,** Co,US
117/P9 **Durango de Victoria,** Mex.
125/H4 **Durant,** Ok,US
113/F2 **Durazno,** Uru.
113/F2 **Durazno** (dept.), Uru.
103/E3 **Durban,** SAfr.
102/L10 **Durbanville,** SAfr.
53/E3 **Durbuy,** Belg.
62/C2 **Đurđevac,** Cro.
53/F2 **Düren,** Ger.
84/D3 **Durg,** India
84/E3 **Durgāpur,** India
45/G2 **Durham,** Eng,UK
45/F2 **Durham** (co.), Eng,UK
129/J3 **Durham,** NC,US
127/G3 **Durham,** NH,US
47/E5 **Durlston Head** (pt.), Eng,UK
52/D1 **Durme** (riv.), Belg.
62/D4 **Durmitor Nat'l Park,** Yugo.
61/F2 **Durrës,** Alb.
47/E4 **Durrington,** Eng,UK
46/D3 **Dursley,** Eng,UK
74/B2 **Dursunbey,** Turk.
87/J4 **D'Urville** (cape), Indo.
126/C1 **Dusey** (riv.), On,Can
81/D2 **Du Shan** (peak), China
68/G6 **Dushanbe** (cap.), Taj.
50/D6 **Düsseldorf,** Ger.
45/H4 **Dutch** (riv.), Eng,UK
51/F4 **Düte** (riv.), Ger.
102/L10 **Dutoitspiek** (peak), SAfr.
85/J2 **Duyun,** China
63/K5 **Düzce,** Turk.
74/D3 **Düzici,** Turk.
64/H2 **Dvina** (bay), Rus.
65/J3 **Dvina, Northern** (riv.), Rus.
64/F5 **Dvina, Western** (riv.), Bel., Rus.
84/A3 **Dwārka,** India
122/D4 **Dworshak** (res.), Id,US
44/D6 **Dwyfor** (riv.), Wal,UK
102/C4 **Dwyka** (riv.), SAfr.
66/E1 **Dyat'kovo,** Rus.
119/K2 **Dyer** (cape), NW,Can
113/J7 **Dyer** (cape), Chile
126/C3 **Dyer,** In,US
129/F2 **Dyersburg,** Tn,US
46/B3 **Dyfed** (co.), Wal,UK
44/D6 **Dyffryn,** Wal,UK
46/C1 **Dyfi** (riv.), Wal,UK
49/J4 **Dyje** (riv.), Czh.
67/G4 **Dykh-tau, Gora** (peak), Rus.
52/D2 **Dyle** (Dijle) (riv.), Belg.
49/K2 **Dylewska Gora** (peak), Pol.
47/G4 **Dymchurch,** Eng,UK
67/H4 **Dyul'tydag, Gora** (peak), Rus.
103/H6 **Dzaoudzi** (cap.), May.
76/C2 **Dzavhan** (riv.), Mong.
66/F3 **Dzenzik, Mys** (pt.), Ukr.
76/C2 **Dzereg,** Mong.
64/J4 **Dzerzhinsk,** Rus.
75/B3 **Dzhalal-Abad,** Kyr.
75/B3 **Dzhambul,** Kaz.
66/E3 **Dzhankoy,** Ukr.
67/M1 **Dzhetygara,** Kaz.
75/A2 **Dzhezkazgan,** Kaz.
68/G5 **Dzhizak,** Uzb.
69/P4 **Dzhugdzhur** (range), Rus.
49/L2 **Działdowo,** Pol.
116/D3 **Dzibilchaltún** (ruins), Mex.
116/D3 **Dzidzantún,** Mex.
49/J3 **Dzierżoniów,** Pol.
76/B3 **Dzungarian** (basin), China
75/D3 **Dzungarian Gate** (pass), China
76/E2 **Dzüünbayan-Ulaan,** Mong.
75/F2 **Dzüüngovĭ,** Mong.
76/D2 **Dzüünhangay,** Mong.
76/F2 **Dzüünharaa,** Mong.

E

125/G3 **Eads,** Co,US
119/L3 **Eagle** (riv.), Nf,Can
126/A1 **Eagle** (lake), On,Can
122/F3 **Eagle** (riv.), Sk,Can
124/B2 **Eagle** (lake), Ca,US
124/F3 **Eagle,** Co,US
123/L4 **Eagle** (peak), Mn,US
132/P14 **Eagle** (lake), Wi,US
123/H4 **Eagle Butte,** SD,US
128/C4 **Eagle Pass,** Tx,US
45/E1 **Eaglesfield,** Sc,UK
45/F4 **Earby,** Eng,UK
126/A1 **Ear Falls,** On,Can
47/G2 **Earith,** Eng,UK
124/C4 **Earlimart,** Ca,US
47/F2 **Earls Barton,** Eng,UK
47/G3 **Earls Colne,** Eng,UK
47/H2 **Earl Stonham,** Eng,UK
128/D4 **Early,** Tx,US
43/D2 **Earn** (riv.), Sc,UK
45/G2 **Easington,** Eng,UK
45/G3 **Easingwold,** Eng,UK
129/H3 **Easley,** SC,US
130/B6 **East** (cape), Ak,US
47/G2 **East Anglia** (reg.), Eng,UK
127/G2 **East Angus,** Qu,Can
47/H3 **East Bergholt,** Eng,UK
123/K4 **East Bethel,** Mn,US
47/G5 **Eastbourne,** Eng,UK
131/F5 **East Brunswick,** NJ,US
45/G1 **East Chevington,** Eng,UK
132/R16 **East Chicago,** In,US
82/D2 **East China** (sea)
46/B3 **East Cleddau** (riv.), Wal,UK
46/C5 **East Dart** (riv.), Eng,UK
47/G1 **East Dereham,** Eng,UK
132/G7 **East Detroit** (East Pointe), Mi,US
93/Q7 **Easter** (isl.), Chile
102/A2 **Easter** (pt.), Namb.
99/E5 **Eastern** (reg.), Gha.
101/C2 **Eastern** (prov.), Kenya
98/C4 **Eastern** (prov.), SLeo.
100/C5 **Eastern** (reg.), Sudan
101/B2 **Eastern** (prov.), Ugan.
45/H4 **Eastern** (plain), Eng,UK
101/B5 **Eastern** (prov.), Zam.
102/D3 **Eastern Cape** (prov.), SAfr.
78/A4 **Eastern Channel** (str.), Japan
84/C5 **Eastern Ghats** (uplands), India
68/K4 **Eastern Sayans** (mts.), Rus.
103/E5 **Eastern Transvaal** (prov.), SAfr.
123/J2 **Easterville,** Mb,Can
113/N8 **East Falkland** (isl.), Falk.
52/C2 **East Flanders** (prov.), Belg.
51/E1 **East Frisian** (isls.), Ger.
47/F1 **East Glen** (riv.), Eng,UK
47/F4 **East Grinstead,** Eng,UK
122/F4 **East Helena,** Mt,US
132/C2 **East Hill-Meridian,** Wa,US
126/C2 **East Jordan,** Mi,US
68/J5 **East Kazakhstan Obl.,** Kaz.
128/D3 **Eastland,** Tx,US
126/C3 **East Lansing,** Mi,US
45/G6 **East Leake,** Eng,UK
47/E5 **Eastleigh,** Eng,UK
126/D3 **East Liverpool,** Oh,US
102/D4 **East London,** SAfr.
131/B2 **East Los Angeles,** Ca,US
126/F1 **Eastmain** (riv.), Qu,Can
129/H3 **Eastman,** Ga,US
131/G5 **East Meadow,** NY,US
127/G2 **East Millinocket,** Me,US
123/K5 **East Nishnabotna** (riv.), Ia,US
46/D5 **Easton,** Eng,UK
131/E5 **Easton,** Pa,US
131/F5 **East Orange,** NJ,US
131/H5 **East Patchogue,** NY,US
129/G3 **East Point,** Ga,US
132/G7 **East Pointe** (East Detroit), Mi,US
127/H2 **Eastport,** Me,US
45/H5 **East Retford,** Eng,UK
45/E2 **Eastriggs,** Sc,UK
47/H4 **Eastry,** Eng,UK
126/B4 **East Saint Louis,** Il,US
69/S2 **East Siberian** (sea), Rus.
131/E5 **East Stroudsburg,** Pa,US
47/G5 **East Sussex** (co.), Eng,UK
126/D2 **East Tawas,** Mi,US
46/B4 **East the Water,** Eng,UK
122/C4 **East Wenatchee,** Wa,US
131/F5 **East Windsor,** NJ,US
47/F5 **East Wittering,** Eng,UK
45/G6 **Eastwood,** Eng,UK
127/R8 **East York,** On,Can
47/E2 **Eatington,** Eng,UK
125/F2 **Eaton,** Co,US
122/F3 **Eatonia,** Sk,Can
47/F2 **Eaton Socon,** Eng,UK
131/F5 **Eatontown,** NJ,US
45/H5 **Eau** (riv.), Eng,UK
119/J3 **Eau Claire** (lake), Qu,Can
126/B2 **Eau Claire,** Wi,US
52/A4 **Eaulne** (riv.), Fr.
92/D4 **Eauripik** (atoll), Micr.
47/E4 **Ebble** (riv.), Eng,UK
46/C3 **Ebbw Vale,** Wal,UK
96/G3 **Ebeggi** (well), Alg.
57/K3 **Ebensee,** Aus.
49/G2 **Eberswalde-Finow,** Ger.
77/N3 **Ebetsu,** Japan
79/H7 **Ebina,** Japan
75/D3 **Ebinur** (lake), China
98/D3 **Ebo** (lake), Mali
60/D2 **Eboli,** It.
96/H7 **Ebolowa,** Camr.
92/F4 **Ebon** (atoll), Mrsh.
59/F2 **Ebro** (riv.), Sp.
116/B4 **Ecatepec,** Mex.
45/E1 **Ecclefechan,** Sc,UK
45/F5 **Eccles,** Eng,UK
45/F6 **Eccleshall,** Eng,UK
99/H3 **Éché Fadadinga** (wadi), Niger
82/B1 **Echeng,** China
79/M9 **Echigawa,** Japan
56/F4 **Echirolles,** Fr.
67/H4 **Echmiadzin,** Arm.
118/E2 **Echo Bay,** NW,Can
123/L2 **Echoing** (riv.), Mb, On,Can
50/C6 **Echt,** Neth.
91/C3 **Echuca,** Austl.
58/C4 **Écija,** Sp.
48/E1 **Eckernförde,** Ger.
46/D2 **Eckington,** Eng,UK
119/H1 **Eclipse** (sound), NW,Can
110/D1 **Ecoporanga,** Braz.
132/F7 **Ecorse,** Mi,US
52/A5 **Écos,** Fr.
56/D2 **Ecouves, Signal d'** (peak), Fr.
108/C4 **Ecuador**
97/P5 **Ēd,** Erit.
43/C2 **Edderton,** Sc,UK
91/D4 **Eddystone** (pt.), Austl.
46/B6 **Eddystone** (rocks), Eng,UK
50/C4 **Ede,** Neth.
99/G5 **Ede,** Nga.
96/H7 **Edéa,** Camr.
52/D1 **Edegem,** Belg.
110/B1 **Edéia,** Braz.
62/E1 **Edelény,** Hun.
51/H4 **Edemissen,** Ger.
45/F2 **Eden** (riv.), Eng,UK
129/J2 **Eden,** NC,US
47/G4 **Edenbridge,** Eng,UK
103/E3 **Edendale,** SAfr.
45/F2 **Edenside** (val.), Eng,UK
51/G6 **Eder** (riv.), Ger.
51/F6 **Eder-Stausee** (res.), Ger.
51/E2 **Edewecht,** Ger.
47/E2 **Edgbaston,** Eng,UK
68/C2 **Edge** (isl.), Sval.
130/L4 **Edgecumbe** (cape), Ak,US
119/K2 **Edgell** (isl.), NW,Can
123/G5 **Edgerton,** Wy,US
132/C3 **Edgewood-North Hill,** Wa,US
46/D1 **Edgmond,** Eng,UK
61/H2 **Édhessa,** Gre.
126/D3 **Edinboro,** Pa,US
128/D5 **Edinburg,** Tx,US
43/D3 **Edinburgh** (cap.), Sc,UK
63/H5 **Edirne,** Turk.
63/H5 **Edirne** (prov.), Turk.
131/F5 **Edison,** NJ,US
129/H3 **Edisto** (riv.), SC,US
129/H3 **Edisto Island,** SC,US
99/F2 **Édjérir** (wadi), Mali
132/C2 **Edmonds,** Wa,US
122/E2 **Edmonton** (cap.), Ab,Can
123/K2 **Edmund** (lake), Mb,Can
90/B2 **Edmund Kennedy Nat'l Park,** Austl.
127/G2 **Edmundston,** NB,Can
128/D4 **Edna,** Tx,US
79/H7 **Edo** (riv.), Japan
74/A2 **Edremit,** Turk.
66/C5 **Edremit** (gulf), Turk.
122/D2 **Edson,** Ab,Can
109/M5 **Eduardo Gomes,** Braz.
101/A3 **Edward** (lake), Ugan., Zaire
125/K2 **Edwards** (riv.), Il,US
128/C4 **Edwards** (plat.), Tx,US
126/B4 **Edwardsville,** Il,US
105/P **Edward VII** (pen.), Ant.
105/D **Edward VIII** (bay), Ant.
43/D2 **Edzell,** Sc,UK
116/C4 **Edzná** (ruins), Mex.
52/C1 **Eeklo,** Belg.
124/B3 **Eel** (riv.), Ca,US
50/D2 **Eelde-Paterswolde,** Neth.
50/C4 **Eem** (riv.), Neth.
50/D2 **Eems** (Ems) (riv.), Neth.
50/D2 **Eemshaven** (har.), Neth.
50/D2 **Eemskanaal** (can.), Neth.
50/C6 **Eersel,** Neth.
92/F6 **Efate** (isl.), Van.
123/L5 **Effigy Mounds Nat'l Mon.,** Ia,US
127/R9 **Effingham,** On,Can
126/B4 **Effingham,** Il,US
63/J3 **Eforie,** Rom.
44/E6 **Efyrnwy, Llyn** (lake), Wal,UK
60/C3 **Egadi** (isls.), It.
124/D3 **Egan** (range), Nv,US
57/K1 **Eger** (riv.), Ger.
62/E2 **Eger,** Hun.
42/C4 **Egersund,** Nor.
51/F5 **Eggegebirge** (ridge), Ger.
45/G3 **Egglescliffe,** Eng,UK
45/G2 **Eggleston,** Eng,UK
47/F4 **Egham,** Eng,UK
53/D2 **Éghezée,** Belg.
76/E1 **Egiyn** (riv.), Mong.
119/R7 **Eglinton** (isl.), NW,Can
44/A1 **Eglinton,** NI,UK
46/C4 **Eglwys Brewis,** Wal,UK
50/B3 **Egmond aan Zee,** Neth.
44/E3 **Egremont,** Eng,UK
74/B3 **Eğridir,** Turk.
100/B3 **Egypt**
78/C4 **Ehime** (pref.), Japan
57/H1 **Ehringshausen,** Ger.
93/L5 **Eiao** (isl.), FrPol.
58/D1 **Eibar,** Sp.
50/D4 **Eibergen,** Neth.
53/G6 **Eichel** (riv.), Fr.
57/J2 **Eichstätt,** Ger.
42/D3 **Eidsvoll,** Nor.
53/F3 **Eifel** (plat.), Ger.
79/M9 **Eigenji,** Japan
84/B6 **Eight Degree** (chan.), India, Mald.
105/T **Eights** (coast), Ant.
50/B2 **Eijerlandsee Gat** (chan.), Neth.
53/E2 **Eijsden,** Neth.
91/C3 **Eildon** (lake), Austl.
90/A2 **Einasleigh** (riv.), Austl.
51/G5 **Einbeck,** Ger.
50/C6 **Eindhoven,** Neth.
108/E5 **Eirunepé,** Braz.
53/E4 **Eisch** (riv.), Lux.
51/H7 **Eisenach,** Ger.
57/L3 **Eisenerz,** Aus.
49/H2 **Eisenhüttenstadt,** Ger.
57/M3 **Eisenstadt,** Aus.
53/G2 **Eiserfeld,** Ger.
51/F3 **Eiter** (riv.), Ger.
53/G2 **Eitorf,** Ger.
59/E1 **Ejea de los Caballeros,** Sp.
117/G6 **Ejido,** Ven.
50/B6 **Ekeren,** Belg.
75/C1 **Ekibastuz,** Kaz.
42/E4 **Eksjö,** Swe.
119/H3 **Ekwan** (riv.), On,Can
98/C2 **El 'Acâba** (reg.), Mrta.
100/B2 **El Alamein** (Al 'Alamayn), Egypt
72/B3 **El Amra** (Abydos) (ruins), Egypt
46/C2 **Elan** (riv.), Wal,UK
52/A6 **Élancourt,** Fr.
102/P12 **Elands** (riv.), SAfr.
102/Q12 **Elandsrivier** (riv.), SAfr.
58/C4 **El Arahal,** Sp.
90/B2 **El Arish,** Austl.
96/F1 **El Asnam,** Alg.
61/H3 **Elassón,** Gre.
58/D1 **El Astillero,** Sp.
100/C2 **Elat,** Isr.
92/D4 **Elato** (atoll), Micr.
74/D2 **Elazığ,** Turk.
60/B1 **Elba** (isl.), It.
129/G4 **Elba,** Al,US
117/G6 **El Banco,** Col.
58/B1 **El Barco,** Sp.
61/G2 **Elbasan,** Alb.
96/F1 **El Bayadh,** Alg.
48/E2 **Elbe** (riv.), Ger.
124/F3 **Elbert** (mtn.), Co,US
129/H3 **Elberton,** Ga,US
51/H2 **Elbe-Seitenkanal** (can.), Ger.
56/D2 **Elbeuf,** Fr.
74/D2 **Elbistan,** Turk.
49/K1 **Elblag,** Pol.
49/K2 **Elblag** (prov.), Pol.
122/G3 **Elbow,** Sk,Can
67/G4 **El'brus, Gora** (peak), Rus.
50/C4 **Elburg,** Neth.
72/E1 **Elburz** (mts.), Iran
124/C4 **El Cajon,** Ca,US
128/D4 **El Campo,** Tx,US
122/E4 **El Capitan** (peak), Mt,US
112/B3 **El Carmen,** Chile
117/F6 **El Carmen,** Col.
59/N8 **El Casar de Talamanca,** Sp.
124/D4 **El Centro,** Ca,US
132/K11 **El Cerrito,** Ca,US
59/E3 **Elche,** Sp.
112/C3 **El Chocón** (res.), Arg.
108/D2 **El Cocuy Nat'l Park,** Col.
111/E2 **El Colorado,** Arg.
59/E3 **Elda,** Sp.
48/G2 **Elde** (riv.), Ger.
131/K7 **Eldersburg,** Md,US
98/C1 **El Djouf** (des.), Mali, Mrta.
111/F2 **Eldorado,** Arg.
117/N9 **Eldorado,** Mex.
128/E3 **El Dorado,** Ar,US
128/D2 **El Dorado,** Ks,US
128/C4 **Eldorado,** Tx,US
101/B2 **Eldoret,** Kenya
120/W13 **Eleao** (peak), Hi,US
96/D2 **El Eglab** (plat.), Alg.
62/E2 **Elek,** Hun.
64/H5 **Elektrostal',** Rus.
63/G4 **Elena,** Bul.
105/W **Elephant** (isl.), Ant.
59/M8 **El Escorial,** Sp.
117/F2 **Eleuthera** (isl.), Bahm.
125/K3 **Eleven Point** (riv.), Ar, Mo,US
61/L6 **Elevsís,** Gre.
58/A1 **El Ferrol,** Sp.
127/Q9 **Elfrida,** On,Can
117/N8 **El Fuerte,** Mex.
43/D2 **Elgin,** Sc,UK
132/P15 **Elgin,** Il,US
123/H4 **Elgin,** ND,US
128/D4 **Elgin,** Tx,US
127/R8 **Elgin Mills,** On,Can
116/A3 **Elgogorrón Nat'l Park,** Mex.
58/D1 **Elgóibar,** Sp.
96/F1 **El Golea,** Alg.
101/B2 **Elgon** (mtn.), Kenya, Ugan.
116/B3 **El Higo,** Mex.
104/D2 **Elias Garcia,** Ang.
125/G4 **Elida,** NM,US
128/C4 **El Indio,** Tx,US
47/E5 **Eling,** Eng,UK
67/H3 **Elista,** Rus.
102/A2 **Elizabeth** (bay), Namb.
131/F5 **Elizabeth,** NJ,US
129/J2 **Elizabeth City,** NC,US
129/H2 **Elizabethton,** Tn,US
126/C4 **Elizabethtown,** Ky,US
96/D1 **El Jadida,** Mor.
49/M2 **Ełk,** Pol.
128/B2 **Elk** (mts.), Co,US
129/H2 **Elk** (riv.), WV,US
125/H4 **Elk City,** Ok,US
132/M10 **Elk Grove,** Ca,US
132/Q15 **Elk Grove Village,** Il,US
126/C3 **Elkhart,** In,US
125/G3 **Elkhart,** Ks,US
96/D3 **El Khatt** (escarp.), Mrta.
123/H3 **Elkhorn,** Mb,Can
125/H2 **Elkhorn** (riv.), Ne,US
63/H4 **Elkhovo,** Bul.
129/H2 **Elkin,** NC,US
126/E4 **Elkins,** WV,US
122/E2 **Elk Island Nat'l Park,** Ab,Can
124/D2 **Elko,** Nv,US
122/F2 **Elk Point,** Ab,Can
126/C2 **Elk Rapids,** Mi,US
131/K7 **Elk Ridge,** Md,US
123/K4 **Elk River,** Mn,US
45/G4 **Elland,** Eng,UK
53/F2 **Elle** (riv.), Ger.
119/R7 **Ellef Ringnes** (isl.), NW,Can
45/E2 **Ellen** (riv.), Eng,UK
123/J4 **Ellendale,** ND,US
122/C4 **Ellensburg,** Wa,US
51/H5 **Eller** (riv.), Ger.
53/G4 **Ellerbach** (riv.), Ger.
91/D3 **Ellery** (peak), Austl.
119/T6 **Ellesmere** (isl.), NW,Can
119/T6 **Ellesmere Island Nat'l Park,** NW,Can
45/F5 **Ellesmere Port,** Eng,UK
112/C2 **El Libertador General Bernardo O'Higgins** (reg.), Chile
118/F2 **Ellice** (riv.), NW,Can
131/K7 **Ellicott City,** Md,US
126/D2 **Elliot Lake,** On,Can
129/J2 **Elliott** (peak), Va,US
104/E5 **Ellisras,** SAfr.
117/F6 **El Llano,** Pan.
43/D2 **Ellon,** Sc,UK
45/H4 **Elloughton,** Eng,UK
105/T **Ellsworth** (mts.), Ant.
125/H3 **Ellsworth,** Ks,US
127/G2 **Ellsworth,** Me,US
126/A2 **Ellsworth,** Wi,US
105/U **Ellsworth Land** (reg.), Ant.
57/J2 **Ellwangen,** Ger.
127/S10 **Elma,** NY,US
74/C2 **Elmadağ,** Turk.
74/B3 **Elmalı,** Turk.
124/F4 **El Malpais Nat'l Mon.,** NM,US
117/M8 **El Marmol,** Mex.
59/L7 **El Masnou,** Sp.
132/P13 **Elm Grove,** Wi,US
132/Q16 **Elmhurst,** Il,US
99/E5 **Elmina,** Gha.
126/E3 **Elmira,** NY,US
108/D7 **El Misti** (vol.), Peru
59/N8 **El Molar,** Sp.
131/G5 **Elmont,** NY,US
59/L6 **El Montcau** (peak), Sp.
131/B2 **El Monte,** Ca,US
112/C1 **El Morrito** (pt.), Chile
124/E4 **El Morro Nat'l Mon.,** NM,US
98/C2 **El Mreyyé** (reg.), Mrta.
51/G1 **Elmshorn,** Ger.
47/G2 **Elmswell,** Eng,UK
132/Q16 **Elmwood Park,** Il,US
131/F5 **Elmwood Park,** NJ,US
96/D3 **El Mzereb** (well), Mali
112/C2 **El Nevado** (peak), Arg.
87/E1 **El Nido,** Phil.
110/H6 **Elói Mendes,** Braz.
56/A2 **Elorn** (riv.), Fr.
96/G1 **El Oued,** Alg.
124/E4 **Eloy,** Az,US
117/J6 **El Palmar,** Ven.
112/F1 **El Palmar Nat'l Park,** Arg.
59/N8 **El Pardo,** Sp.
128/B4 **El Paso,** Tx,US
117/J5 **El Pilar,** Ven.
84/D6 **Elpitiya,** SrL.
116/D4 **El Placer,** Mex.
117/F6 **El Porvenir,** Pan.
116/B3 **El Potosí Nat'l Park,** Mex.
59/G2 **El Prat de Llobregat,** Sp.
116/D4 **El Progreso,** Hon.
58/B4 **El Puerto de Santa María,** Sp.
117/N9 **El Quelite,** Mex.
125/H4 **El Reno,** Ok,US
131/A2 **El Rio,** Ca,US
117/H5 **El Roque,** Ven.
122/F3 **Elrose,** Sk,Can
130/L3 **Elsa,** Yk,Can
57/J5 **Elsa** (riv.), It.
58/B2 **Elsa** (res.), Sp.
58/C1 **Elsa** (riv.), Sp.
117/N9 **El Salado,** Mex.
116/D5 **El Salvador**
117/F3 **El Salvador,** Cuba
116/A3 **El Salvador,** Mex.
117/H6 **El Samán de Apure,** Ven.
51/F4 **Else** (riv.), Ger.
131/B3 **El Segundo,** Ca,US
117/H4 **El Seibo,** DRep.
75/F4 **Elsen** (lake), China
51/F2 **Elsfleth,** Ger.
100/B4 **El Shab** (well), Egypt
131/C3 **Elsinore** (lake), Ca,US
117/L7 **El Socorro,** Mex.
50/C5 **Elst,** Neth.
47/F4 **Elstead,** Eng,UK
116/B3 **El Tajín** (ruins), Mex.
108/D2 **El Tama Nat'l Park,** Ven.
58/B1 **El Teleno** (mtn.), Sp.
117/J6 **El Tigre,** Ven.
67/H2 **El'ton** (lake), Rus.
131/C3 **El Toro,** Ca,US
108/E3 **El Tuparro Nat'l Park,** Col.
57/H1 **Eltville am Rhein,** Ger.
84/D4 **Elūrū,** India
58/B3 **Elvas,** Port.
42/D3 **Elverum,** Nor.
108/D2 **El Viejo** (peak), Col.
117/G6 **El Vigía,** Ven.
117/P8 **El Volcán,** Mex.
101/D2 **El Wak,** Kenya
122/F3 **Elwell** (lake), Mt,US
126/C3 **Elwood,** In,US
44/E5 **Elwy** (riv.), Wal,UK
47/G2 **Ely,** Eng,UK
123/L4 **Ely,** Mn,US
124/D3 **Ely,** Nv,US
47/G2 **Ely, Isle of** (reg.), Eng,UK
126/D3 **Elyria,** Oh,US
53/G3 **Elzbach** (riv.), Ger.
51/G4 **Elze,** Ger.
73/F1 **Emāmshahr,** Iran
109/H7 **Emas Nat'l Park,** Braz.
67/L2 **Emba,** Kaz.
67/K3 **Emba** (riv.), Kaz.
111/D1 **Embarcación,** Arg.
129/E2 **Embarras** (riv.), Il,US
108/D5 **Embira** (riv.), Braz.
110/C1 **Emborcaçao** (res.), Braz.
110/G8 **Embu-Guaçu,** Braz.
51/E2 **Emden,** Ger.
85/H2 **Emei,** China
91/G5 **Emerald,** Austl.
123/J3 **Emerson,** Mb,Can
132/K11 **Emeryville,** Ca,US
74/B2 **Emet,** Turk.
57/J4 **Emilia-Romagna** (reg.), It.
75/D2 **Emin** (riv.), China
125/K3 **Eminence,** Mo,US
63/H4 **Emine, Nos** (cape), Bul.
74/B2 **Emirdağ,** Turk.
74/C3 **Emirgazi,** Turk.
103/E2 **Emlembe** (peak), Swaz.
50/D3 **Emlichheim,** Ger.
42/E4 **Emmaboda,** Swe.
131/E5 **Emmaus,** Pa,US
50/C3 **Emmeloord,** Neth.
50/D3 **Emmen,** Neth.
54/D1 **Emmendingen,** Ger.
51/G5 **Emmer** (riv.), Ger.
51/E5 **Emmerbach** (riv.), Ger.
50/D5 **Emmerich,** Ger.

151

Emmet – Forfa

122/D5 **Emmett**, Id,US
47/G1 **Emneth**, Eng,UK
128/E3 **Emory**, Tx,US
117/P8 **Emory** (peak), Tx.,US
117/M8 **Empalme**, Mex.
103/E3 **Empangeni**, SAfr.
111/E2 **Empedrado**, Arg.
112/B2 **Empedrado**, Chile
125/H3 **Emporia**, Ks,US
126/E4 **Emporia**, Va,US
51/E4 **Emsbüren**, Ger.
51/E4 **Emsdetten**, Ger.
50/D2 **Ems** (Eems) (riv.), Ger., Neth.
51/E2 **Ems-Jade** (can.), Ger.
51/E3 **Emsland** (reg.), Ger.
51/F3 **Emstek**, Ger.
42/H4 **Emumägi** (hill), Est.
77/J1 **Emur** (riv.), China
79/E3 **Ena**, Japan
122/G5 **Encampment**, Wy,US
117/L7 **Encantada** (mt.), Mex.
117/M8 **Encantado** (mt.), Mex.
111/E2 **Encarnación**, Par.
117/P9 **Encarnación de Díaz**, Mex.
98/E5 **Enchi**, Gha.
124/C4 **Encinitas**, Ca,US
91/A2 **Encounter** (bay), Austl.
110/A4 **Encruzilhada do Sul**, Braz.
87/F5 **Ende**, Indo.
90/B1 **Endeavour River Nat'l Park**, Austl.
93/H5 **Enderbury** (atoll), Kiri.
122/D3 **Enderby**, BC,Can
105/D **Enderby Land** (reg.), Ant.
123/J4 **Enderlin**, ND,US
126/E3 **Endicott**, NY,US
108/D6 **Ene** (riv.), Peru
92/F3 **Enewetak** (atoll), Mrsh.
82/D4 **Engaño** (cape), Phil.
67/H2 **Engel's**, Rus.
53/G2 **Engelskirchen**, Ger.
50/D2 **Engelsmanplaat** (isl.), Neth.
110/K7 **Engenheiro Paulo de Froutin**, Braz.
51/F4 **Enger**, Ger.
86/B5 **Enggano** (isl.), Indo.
97/N4 **Enghershatu** (peak), Erit.
52/D2 **Enghien**, Belg.
43/D4 **England**, UK
126/E2 **Englehart**, On,Can
131/F5 **Englewood**, NJ,US
131/G5 **Englewood**, NJ,US
105/V **English** (coast), Ant.
123/K3 **English** (riv.), On,Can
56/B2 **English** (chan.), Eur.
84/E3 **English Bāzār**, India
131/F5 **Englishtown**, NJ,US
125/H3 **Enid**, Ok,US
50/C3 **Enkhuizen**, Neth.
42/F4 **Enköping**, Swe.
60/D4 **Enna**, It.
97/K4 **Ennedi** (plat.), Chad
51/E6 **Ennepe** (riv.), Ger.
51/E6 **Ennepetal**, Ger.
51/F5 **Enningerloh**, Ger.
122/F4 **Ennis**, Mt,US
128/D3 **Ennis**, Tx,US
57/L3 **Enns** (riv.), Aus.
90/E6 **Enoggera** (res.), Austl.
129/H3 **Enoree** (riv.), SC,US
50/D4 **Enschede**, Neth.
51/E6 **Ense**, Ger.
117/L7 **Ensenada**, Mex.
81/B5 **Enshi**, China
101/B2 **Entebbe**, Ugan.
57/K2 **Entenbühl** (peak), Ger.
129/G4 **Enterprise**, Al,US
112/F2 **Entre Ríos** (prov.), Arg.
58/A3 **Entroncamento**, Port.
99/G5 **Enugu**, Nga.
132/D3 **Enumclaw**, Wa,US
79/N10 **Enushū** (sea), Japan
52/A4 **Envermeu**, Fr.
57/H2 **Enz** (riv.), Ger.
79/F3 **Enzan**, Japan
53/F4 **Enzbach** (riv.), Ger.
50/C4 **Epe**, Neth.
52/C5 **Epernay**, Fr.
92/F6 **Epi** (isl.), Van.
61/H4 **Epidaurus** (ruins), Gre.
54/C1 **Epinal**, Fr.
61/G3 **Epirus** (reg.), Gre.
53/F5 **Eppelborn**, Ger.
90/H8 **Epping**, Austl.
47/G3 **Epping**, Eng,UK
90/B3 **Epping Forest Nat'l Park**, Austl.
47/F4 **Epsom and Ewell**, Eng,UK
45/H4 **Epworth**, Eng,UK
96/G7 **Equatorial Guinea**
85/H2 **Er** (lake), China
60/E2 **Eraclea** (ruins), It.
60/C4 **Eraclea Minoa** (ruins), It.
84/D6 **Eravur**, SrL.
83/B3 **Erawan Nat'l Park**, Thai.
57/H4 **Erba**, It.
74/D2 **Erbaa**, Turk.
53/F4 **Erbeskopf** (peak), Ger.
112/B3 **Ercilla**, Chile
74/E2 **Erciş**, Turk.
52/C3 **Erclin** (riv.), Fr.
62/D2 **Érd**, Hun.
77/K3 **Erdao** (riv.), China
63/H5 **Erdek**, Turk.
63/H5 **Erdek** (gulf), Turk.
74/C3 **Erdemli**, Turk.
76/G3 **Erdene**, Mong.
76/E2 **Erdenedalay**, Mong.
97/K4 **Erdi-Ma** (plat.), Chad
57/J2 **Erding**, Ger.
56/C3 **Erdre** (riv.), Fr.
105/M **Erebus** (vol.), Ant.
110/A3 **Erechim**, Braz.
76/G2 **Ereen Davaanī** (mts.), Mong.
63/K5 **Ereğli**, Turk.
74/C3 **Ereğli**, Turk.
75/D3 **Erenhaberga** (mts.), China
76/G3 **Erenhot**, China
63/K5 **Erenler**, Turk.
109/G4 **Erepecu** (lake), Braz.
58/C2 **Eresma** (riv.), Sp.
96/E1 **Erfoud**, Mor.
53/F1 **Erft** (riv.), Ger.
53/F2 **Erftstadt**, Ger.
48/F3 **Erfurt**, Ger.
74/D2 **Ergani**, Turk.
96/D3 **'Erg Chech** (des.), Afr.
96/H4 **'Erg du Ténéré** (des.), Niger
63/H5 **Ergene Nehri** (riv.), Turk.
96/D2 **'Erg Iguidi** (des.), Afr.
97/J5 **Erguig** (riv.), Chad
77/H1 **Ergun** (riv.), China, Rus.
122/D3 **Erickson**, BC,Can
123/J3 **Erickson**, Mb,Can
126/D3 **Erie** (lake), Can., US
127/S9 **Erie** (can.), NY,US
126/D3 **Erie**, Pa,US
97/Q5 **Erigabo**, Som.
123/J3 **Eriksdale**, Mb,Can
92/F4 **Erikub** (atoll), Mrsh.
61/G4 **Erímanthos** (peak), Gre.
77/N3 **Erimo-misaki** (cape), Japan
97/N4 **Eritrea**
50/D6 **Erkelenz**, Ger.
49/G2 **Erkner**, Ger.
50/D6 **Erkrath**, Ger.
57/J2 **Erlangen**, Ger.
81/F2 **Erlongshan** (res.), China
46/C6 **Erme** (riv.), Eng,UK
50/C4 **Ermelo**, Neth.
103/E2 **Ermelo**, SAfr.
74/C3 **Ermenek**, Turk.
61/J4 **Ermoúpolis**, Gre.
53/H2 **Erndtebrück**, Ger.
56/C2 **Ernée** (riv.), Fr.
84/C5 **Erode**, India
52/D3 **Erquelinnes**, Belg.
96/E1 **Er Rachidīa**, Mor.
96/D1 **Er Rif** (mts.), Mor.
43/A3 **Errigal** (mtn.), Ire.
92/F6 **Erromango** (isl.), Van.
51/H4 **Erse** (riv.), Ger.
76/B2 **Ertix** (riv.), China
110/B3 **Erval d'Oeste**, Braz.
126/D4 **Erwin**, Tn,US
51/F5 **Erwitte**, Ger.
61/F2 **Erzen** (riv.), Alb.
57/K1 **Erzgebirge** (Krušné Hory) (mts.), Czh., Ger.
74/D2 **Erzincan**, Turk.
74/E2 **Erzurum**, Turk.
92/D5 **Esa'ala**, PNG
104/D1 **Esambo**, Zaire
77/N3 **Esashi**, Japan
42/D5 **Esbjerg**, Den.
52/B6 **Esbly**, Fr.
42/H3 **Esbo** (Espoo), Fin.
124/E3 **Escalante** (riv.), Ut,US
129/G4 **Escambia** (riv.), Fl,US
126/C2 **Escanaba**, Mi,US
52/C3 **Escaudain**, Fr.
52/C3 **Escaut** (riv.), Belg., Fr.
53/E6 **Esch** (riv.), Fr.
52/B5 **Esches** (riv.), Fr.
53/E5 **Esch-sur-Alzette**, Lux.
51/H6 **Eschwege**, Ger.
53/F2 **Eschweiler**, Ger.
124/C4 **Escondido**, Ca,US
117/N9 **Escuinapa de Hidalgo**, Mex.
116/C5 **Escuintla**, Guat.
74/N7 **Esdraelon, Plain of** (plain), Isr.
96/H7 **Eséka**, Camr.
51/E1 **Esens**, Ger.
59/F1 **Esera** (riv.), Sp.
72/F2 **Eşfahān**, Iran
46/C1 **Esgair Ddu** (mtn.), Wal,UK
45/G2 **Esh**, Eng,UK
47/F4 **Esher**, Eng,UK
104/D2 **Eshimba**, Zaire
45/G2 **Esh Winning**, Eng,UK
45/E2 **Esk** (riv.), Eng,UK
45/H3 **Esk** (riv.), Eng,UK
45/E1 **Eskdale** (val.), Sc,UK
74/C2 **Eskil**, Turk.
42/F4 **Eskilstuna**, Swe.
74/D2 **Eskimalatya**, Turk.
130/M2 **Eskimo** (lakes), NW,Can
74/B2 **Eskişehir**, Turk.
58/C1 **Esla** (riv.), Sp.
72/E2 **Eslāmābād**, Iran
51/F6 **Eslohe**, Ger.
74/B2 **Eşme**, Turk.
108/C3 **Esmeraldas**, Ecu.
53/E2 **Esneux**, Belg.
126/D2 **Espanola**, On,Can
125/F4 **Española**, NM,US
59/K6 **Esparreguera**, Sp.
51/F4 **Espelkamp**, Ger.
89/B4 **Esperance**, Austl.
122/B3 **Esperanza** (inlet), BC,Can
58/A3 **Espichel** (cape), Port.
108/D3 **Espinal**, Col.
95/D1 **Espinhaço** (mts.), Braz.
58/A2 **Espinho**, Port.
113/F2 **Espinillo** (pt.), Uru.
109/K6 **Espinosa**, Braz.
110/D1 **Espírito Santo** (state), Braz.
110/G7 **Espírito Santo do Pinhal**, Braz.
92/F6 **Espiritu Santo** (isl.), Van.
109/L6 **Esplanada**, Braz.
59/L7 **Espluges**, Sp.
42/H3 **Espoo** (Esbo), Fin.
112/C4 **Esquel**, Arg.
111/E3 **Esquina**, Arg.
96/D1 **Essaouira**, Mor.
51/G5 **Esse** (riv.), Ger.
50/B6 **Essen**, Belg.
53/F2 **Essen**, Ger.
50/E6 **Essen**, Ger.
91/F5 **Essendon**, Austl.
108/G2 **Essequibo** (riv.), Guy.
132/G7 **Essex**, On,Can
47/G3 **Essex** (co.), Eng,UK
131/K7 **Essex**, Md,US
57/H2 **Esslingen**, Ger.
52/B6 **Essonne** (dept.), Fr.
113/L8 **Estados** (isl.), Arg.
72/F3 **Eşţahbān**, Iran
109/L6 **Estância**, Braz.
113/L8 **Estancia La Carmen**, Arg.
113/L8 **Estancia La Sera**, Arg.
59/F1 **Estats, Pico de** (peak), Sp.
103/E3 **Estcourt**, SAfr.
116/E3 **Este** (pt.), Cuba
51/G2 **Este** (riv.), Ger.
57/J4 **Este**, It.
110/B4 **Esteio**, Braz.
116/D5 **Estelí**, Nic.
58/D1 **Estella**, Sp.
131/C3 **Estelle** (mtn.), Ca,US
58/C4 **Estepa**, Sp.
58/C4 **Estepona**, Sp.
123/H3 **Esterhazy**, Sk,Can
96/G7 **Esterias** (cape), Gabon
57/G5 **Estéron** (riv.), Fr.
123/H3 **Estevan**, Sk,Can
52/D3 **Estinnes-Au-Mont**, Belg.
45/G2 **Eston**, Eng,UK
64/E4 **Estonia**
58/A3 **Estoril**, Port.
58/B2 **Estrela, Serra da** (mtn.), Port.
58/A3 **Estrela, Serra da** (range), Port.
58/B3 **Estremadura** (aut. comm.), Sp.
58/B3 **Estremoz**, Port.
109/J5 **Estrondo** (mts.), Braz.
62/D2 **Esztergom**, Hun.
92/E4 **Etal** (atoll), Micr.
52/A2 **Étaples**, Fr.
84/C2 **Etāwah**, India
123/H3 **Ethelbert**, Mb,Can
97/N5 **Ethiopia**
97/N6 **Ethiopian** (plat.), Eth.
79/M9 **Eti** (riv.), Japan
60/D4 **Etna, Monte** (Mount Etna) (vol.), It.
127/Q8 **Etobicoke**, On,Can
130/E3 **Etolin** (str.), Ak,US
77/P2 **Etorofu** (isl.), Rus.
104/C4 **Etosha Nat'l Park**, Namb.
104/C4 **Etosha Pan** (salt pan), Namb.
63/G4 **Etropole**, Bul.
79/F2 **Etsu-Joshin Kogen Nat'l Park**, Japan
74/M8 **Et Taiyiba**, Isr.
53/F4 **Ettelbruck**, Lux.
50/B5 **Etten-Leur**, Neth.
52/D2 **Etterbeek**, Belg.
74/M8 **Et Tīra**, Isr.
57/H2 **Ettlingen**, Ger.
45/E1 **Ettrick Pen** (mtn.), Sc,UK
52/A3 **Eu**, Fr.
93/H7 **Eua** (isl.), Tonga
90/B2 **Eubenangee Swamp Nat'l Park**, Austl.
126/D3 **Euclid**, Oh,US
129/F3 **Eudora**, Ar,US
129/G4 **Eufaula**, Al,US
125/J4 **Eufaula**, Ok,US
125/H4 **Eufaula** (lake), Ok,US
122/C4 **Eugene**, Or,US
117/L8 **Eugenia** (pt.), Mex.
58/B1 **Eume** (lake), Sp.
90/C3 **Eungella Nat'l Park**, Austl.
128/E4 **Eunice**, La,US
125/G4 **Eunice**, NM,US
53/F2 **Eupen**, Belg.
71/D6 **Euphrates** (riv.), Asia
56/D2 **Eure** (riv.), Fr.
119/S6 **Eureka**, NW,Can
119/S7 **Eureka** (sound), NW,Can
124/A2 **Eureka**, Ca,US
122/E3 **Eureka**, Mt,US
124/D3 **Eureka**, Nv,US
123/J4 **Eureka**, SD,US
52/B6 **Eurodisney**, Fr.
104/G5 **Europa** (isl.), Reun.
41/* **Europe**
50/B5 **Europoort**, Neth.
53/F2 **Euskirchen**, Ger.
129/H4 **Eustis**, Fl,US
48/F1 **Eutin**, Ger.
101/B5 **Eutini**, Malw.
122/B2 **Eutsuk** (lake), BC,Can
45/F4 **Euxton**, Eng,UK
126/E1 **Évain**, Qu,Can
119/H2 **Evans** (str.), NW,Can
126/E1 **Evans** (lake), Qu,Can
125/F2 **Evans**, Co,US
125/F3 **Evans** (mtn.), Co,US
132/Q15 **Evanston**, Il,US
122/F5 **Evanston**, Wy,US
126/C4 **Evansville**, In,US
125/F2 **Evansville**, Wy,US
126/C3 **Evart**, Mi,US
102/D2 **Evaton**, SAfr.
72/F3 **Evaz**, Iran
123/K4 **Eveleth**, Mn,US
69/L3 **Evenki Aut. Okr.**, Rus.
47/E3 **Evenlode** (riv.), Eng,UK
91/D3 **Everard** (cape), Austl.
46/D4 **Evercreech**, Eng,UK
132/C2 **Everett**, Wa,US
52/C1 **Evergem**, Belg.
129/H5 **Everglades Nat'l Park**, Fl,US
129/G4 **Evergreen**, Al,US
132/Q16 **Evergreen Park**, Il,US
47/F3 **Eversholt**, Eng,UK
51/E5 **Everswinkel**, Ger.
47/E2 **Evesham**, Eng,UK
61/G3 **Évinos** (riv.), Gre.
58/B3 **Évora**, Port.
58/A3 **Évora** (dist.), Port.
52/A5 **Évreux**, Fr.
56/C2 **Évron**, Fr.
61/H4 **Evrótas** (riv.), Gre.
52/B6 **Évry**, Fr.
61/H3 **Évvoia** (gulf), Gre.
61/H3 **Évvoia** (isl.), Gre.
120/V13 **Ewa**, Hi,US
120/V13 **Ewa Beach**, Hi,US
131/F5 **Ewing**, NJ,US
125/J3 **Excelsior Springs**, Mo,US
46/C5 **Exe** (riv.), Eng,UK
46/C5 **Exeter**, Eng,UK
127/G3 **Exeter**, NH,US
46/C5 **Exminster**, Eng,UK
46/C4 **Exmoor Nat'l Park**, Eng,UK
126/F4 **Exmore**, Va,US
113/J7 **Exmouth** (pen.), Chile
46/C5 **Exmouth**, Eng,UK
119/L4 **Exploits** (riv.), Nf,Can
110/G7 **Extrema**, Braz.
117/F3 **Exuma** (sound), Bahm.
45/G5 **Eyam**, Eng,UK
101/B3 **Eyasi** (lake), Tanz.
47/H2 **Eye**, Eng,UK
47/F1 **Eye** (brook), Eng,UK
43/D3 **Eyemouth**, Sc,UK
74/N9 **Eyn Hemed Nat'l Park**, Isr.
47/G4 **Eynsford**, Eng,UK
89/C4 **Eyre** (pen.), Austl.
89/C3 **Eyre North** (lake), Austl.
61/K3 **Ezine**, Turk.
96/H3 **Ezzane** (well), Alg.

F

93/L6 **Faaa**, FrPol.
128/B4 **Fabens**, Tx,US
58/B1 **Fabero**, Sp.
48/F1 **Fåborg**, Den.
57/K5 **Fabriano**, It.
108/D3 **Facatativá**, Col.
52/C2 **Faches-Thumesnil**, Fr.
97/K4 **Fada**, Chad
99/F3 **Fada-N'Gourma**, Burk.
57/J4 **Faenza**, It.
97/J6 **Fafa** (riv.), CAfr.
58/A2 **Fafe**, Port.
97/P6 **Fafen Shet'** (riv.), Eth.
63/G3 **Făgăraş**, Rom.
42/F3 **Fagersta**, Swe.
113/L8 **Fagnano** (lake), Arg.
98/D2 **Faguibine** (lake), Mali
59/S12 **Faial** (isl.), Azor.,Port.
45/F4 **Failsworth**, Eng,UK
130/J3 **Fairbanks**, Ak,US
132/J11 **Fairfax**, Ca,US
131/J8 **Fairfax**, Va,US
90/G8 **Fairfield**, Austl.
132/K10 **Fairfield**, Ca,US
131/G4 **Fairfield**, Ct,US
122/F4 **Fairfield**, Mt,US
126/C4 **Fairfield**, Oh,US
128/D4 **Fairfield**, Tx,US
47/E3 **Fairford**, Eng,UK
127/F3 **Fair Haven**, Vt,US
44/B1 **Fair Head** (pt.), NI,UK
131/K7 **Fairland**, Md,US
131/F5 **Fair Lawn**, NJ,US
131/F5 **Fairless Hills**, Pa,US
47/G5 **Fairlight**, Eng,UK
123/K5 **Fairmont**, Mn,US
126/D4 **Fairmont**, WV,US
132/M9 **Fair Oaks**, Ca,US
128/B2 **Fairplay**, Co,US
122/D1 **Fairview**, Ab,Can
125/H3 **Fairview**, Ok,US
130/L4 **Fairweather** (cape), Ak,US
130/L4 **Fairweather** (mtn.), BC,Can, Ak,US
132/C3 **Fairwood-Cascade**, Wa,US
73/K2 **Faisalabad**, Pak.
61/J5 **Faistós** (ruins), Gre.
84/D2 **Faizābād**, India
93/M6 **Fakahina** (isl.), FrPol.
93/H5 **Fakaofo** (atoll), Tok.
93/L6 **Fakarava** (atoll), FrPol.
47/G1 **Fakenham**, Eng,UK
96/G7 **Fako** (peak), Camr.
48/G1 **Fakse Bugt** (bay), Den.
46/B6 **Fal** (riv.), Eng,UK
128/D5 **Falcon** (res.), Mex., US
57/K5 **Falconara Marittima**, It.
98/C3 **Falémé** (riv.), Mali, Sen.
93/S9 **Faleolo**, WSam.
128/D5 **Falfurrias**, Tx,US
122/D2 **Falher**, Ab,Can
42/E4 **Falkenberg**, Swe.
47/H2 **Falkenham**, Eng,UK
113/M8 **Falkland Islands** (Islas Malvinas) (dpcy.), UK
42/E4 **Falköping**, Swe.
51/G3 **Fallingbostel**, Ger.
124/C3 **Fallon**, Nv,US
127/G3 **Fall River**, Ma,US
131/J8 **Falls Church**, Va,US
125/J2 **Falls City**, Ne,US
46/A6 **Falmouth**, Eng,UK
46/A6 **Falmouth** (bay), Eng,UK
117/G4 **Falso** (cape), DRep.
113/K8 **Falso Cabo de Hornos** (cape), Chile
48/G1 **Falster** (isl.), Den.
63/H2 **Fălticeni**, Rom.
42/E3 **Falun**, Swe.
74/J4 **Famagusta**, Cyp.
53/F5 **Fameck**, Fr.
53/E3 **Famenne** (reg.), Belg.
81/D5 **Fanchang**, China
103/H8 **Fandriana**, Madg.
44/B4 **Fane** (riv.), Ire.
93/L6 **Fangatau** (isl.), FrPol.
93/L7 **Fangataufa** (isl.), FrPol.
82/C2 **Fangcun**, China
82/C2 **Fangdao**, China
82/D3 **Fangliao**, Tai.
82/A2 **Fanjing** (peak), China
93/K4 **Fanning** (Tabuaeran) (atoll), Kiri.
48/E1 **Fanø** (isl.), Den.
57/K5 **Fano**, It.
83/C1 **Fan Si Pan** (peak), Viet.
74/H6 **Fāqūs**, Egypt
101/A2 **Faradje**, Zaire
103/H8 **Farafangana**, Madg.
100/A3 **Farāfirah, Wāḥāt al** (oasis), Egypt
73/H2 **Farāh**, Afg.
73/H2 **Farāh** (riv.), Afg.
124/B3 **Farallon** (isls.), Ca,US
92/D3 **Farallon de Medinilla** (isl.), NMar.
92/D2 **Farallon de Pajaros** (isl.), NMar.
108/C3 **Farallones de Cali Nat'l Park**, Col.
98/C4 **Faranah** (comm.), Gui.
103/H8 **Faraony** (riv.), Madg.
92/D4 **Faraulep** (atoll), Micr.
52/D3 **Farciennes**, Belg.
47/E5 **Fareham**, Eng,UK
123/J4 **Fargo**, ND,US
123/K4 **Faribault**, Mn,US
84/C2 **Farīdābād**, India
84/E3 **Farīdpur**, Bang.
47/E3 **Faringdon**, Eng,UK
74/H6 **Fāriskūr**, Egypt
127/G2 **Farmington**, Me,US
132/F7 **Farmington**, Mi,US
125/K3 **Farmington**, Mo,US
124/E3 **Farmington**, NM,US
132/F7 **Farmington Hills**, Mi,US
126/E4 **Farmville**, Va,US
47/F4 **Farnborough**, Eng,UK
47/F4 **Farnham**, Eng,UK
45/F4 **Farnworth**, Eng,UK
118/C2 **Faro**, Yk,Can
58/B4 **Faro**, Port.
58/B4 **Faro** (dist.), Port.
41/D2 **Faroe** (isls.), Den.
42/F4 **Fårön** (isl.), Swe.
96/H6 **Faro Nat'l Park**, Camr.
39/M6 **Farquhar** (isls.), Sey.
110/B4 **Farroupilha**, Braz.
84/C2 **Farrukhābād**, India
61/H3 **Fársala**, Gre.
122/F5 **Farson**, Wy,US
42/C4 **Farsund**, Nor.
72/F5 **Fartak, Ra's** (pt.), Yem.
115/N4 **Farvel** (cape), Grld.
105/T **Farwell** (isl.), Ant.
72/F3 **Fasā**, Iran
60/E2 **Fasano**, It.
51/H3 **Fassberg**, Ger.
66/D2 **Fastov**, Ukr.
87/H4 **Fatagar Tuting** (cape), Indo.
39/T6 **Fataka** (isl.), Sol.
84/B2 **Fatehpur**, India
84/D2 **Fatehpur**, India
98/A3 **Fatick** (reg.), Sen.
58/A3 **Fátima**, Port.
72/C4 **Fāṭimah** (dry riv.), SAr.
74/D2 **Fatsa**, Turk.
93/M6 **Fatu Hiva** (isl.), FrPol.
54/B1 **Faucilles** (mts.), Fr.
44/A2 **Faughan** (riv.), NI,UK
123/J4 **Faulkton**, SD,US
42/E2 **Fauske**, Nor.
60/C4 **Favara**, It.
47/G4 **Faversham**, Eng,UK
47/E5 **Fawley**, Eng,UK
118/H3 **Fawn** (riv.), On,Can
42/M7 **Faxaflói** (bay), Ice.
110/B2 **Faxinal**, Braz.
97/J4 **Faya-Largeau**, Chad
129/G3 **Fayette**, Al,US
125/J3 **Fayette**, Mo,US
129/F4 **Fayette**, Ms,US
128/E2 **Fayetteville**, Ar,US
129/G3 **Fayetteville**, Ga,US
129/J3 **Fayetteville**, NC,US
129/G3 **Fayetteville**, Tn,US
99/F4 **Fazao** (mts.), Gha., Togo
99/F4 **Fazao Nat'l Park**, Togo
43/A4 **Feale** (riv.), Ire.
129/J3 **Fear** (cape), NC,US
124/B3 **Feather** (riv.), Ca,US
45/G4 **Featherstone**, Eng,UK
56/D2 **Fécamp**, Fr.
132/C3 **Federal Way**, Wa,US
44/A2 **Feeny**, NI,UK
62/F2 **Fehérgyarmat**, Hun.
48/F1 **Fehmarn** (isl.), Ger.
48/F1 **Fehmarn Belt** (str.), Ger., Den.
81/D4 **Fei** (riv.), China
110/D2 **Feia** (lake), Braz.
52/C3 **Feignies**, Fr.
81/D4 **Fei Huang** (riv.), China
109/L6 **Feira de Santana**, Braz.
57/L3 **Feistritz** (riv.), Aus.
62/D2 **Fejér** (co.), Hun.
59/G3 **Felanitx**, Sp.
54/E2 **Feldberg** (peak), Ger.
55/F3 **Feldkirch**, Aus.
57/L3 **Feldkirchen in Kärnten**, Aus.
47/H3 **Felixstowe**, Eng,UK
117/N7 **Félix U. Gómez**, Mex.
45/G2 **Felling**, Eng,UK
51/G6 **Felsberg**, Ger.
47/G2 **Feltwell**, Eng,UK
81/C4 **Fen** (riv.), China
58/A1 **Fene**, Sp.
74/C3 **Fener** (pt.), Turk.
53/G6 **Fénétrange**, Fr.
61/J2 **Fengári** (peak), Gre.
77/J3 **Fengcheng**, China
81/D5 **Fengle** (riv.), China
81/D3 **Fengnan**, China
81/D3 **Fengrun**, China
77/J1 **Fengshui** (peak), China
81/C2 **Fengzhen**, China
130/C5 **Fenimore** (passg.), Ak,US
47/G2 **Fens, The** (reg.), Eng,UK
132/E6 **Fenton**, Mi,US
66/E3 **Feodosiya**, Ukr.
73/G2 **Ferdows**, Iran
60/C2 **Ferentino**, It.
60/C1 **Ferento** (ruins), It.
75/B3 **Fergana**, Uzb.
123/J4 **Fergus Falls**, Mn,US
118/F2 **Ferguson** (lake), NW,Can
98/D4 **Ferkéssédougou**, IvC.
57/L3 **Ferlach**, Aus.
96/C4 **Ferlo** (reg.), Sen.
98/B3 **Ferlo, Vallée du** (wadi), Sen.
44/A3 **Fermanagh** (dist.), NI,UK
131/B3 **Fermin** (pt.), Ca,US
60/C1 **Fermo**, It.
129/H4 **Fernandina Beach**, Fl,US
109/M4 **Fernando de Noronha** (isl.), Braz.
110/B2 **Fernandópolis**, Braz.
58/C4 **Fernán-Núñez**, Sp.
131/K7 **Ferndale**, Md,US
132/F7 **Ferndale**, Mi,US
47/E5 **Ferndown**, Eng,UK
122/E3 **Fernie**, BC,Can
91/G5 **Ferntree Gully Nat'l Park**, Austl.
60/E2 **Ferrandina**, It.
57/J4 **Ferrara**, It.
58/A3 **Ferreira do Alentejo**, Port.
56/C4 **Ferret** (cape), Fr.
128/F4 **Ferriday**, La,US
129/F4 **Ferriday**, La,US
45/G2 **Ferryhill**, Eng,UK
46/B3 **Ferryside**, Wal,UK
57/M3 **Fertő** (Neusiedler See) (lake), Aus., Hun.
50/C2 **Ferwerd**, Neth.
96/E1 **Fès**, Mor.
104/C2 **Feshi**, Zaire
129/F2 **Festus**, Mo,US
47/F4 **Fetcham**, Eng,UK
63/H3 **Feteşti**, Rom.
57/J2 **Feucht**, Ger.
119/J3 **Feuilles** (lake), Qu,Can
119/J3 **Feuilles** (riv.), Qu,Can
56/F4 **Feurs**, Fr.
73/K1 **Feyzābād**, Afg.
96/H2 **Fezzan** (reg.), Libya
44/E6 **Ffestiniog**, Wal,UK
103/H8 **Fianarantsoa**, Madg.
103/H8 **Fianarantsoa** (prov.), Madg.
96/J6 **Fianga**, Chad
102/D3 **Ficksburg**, SAfr.
57/J4 **Fidenza**, It.
98/C4 **Fié** (riv.), Gui., Mali
63/G3 **Fieni**, Rom.
61/F2 **Fier**, Alb.
61/G1 **Fierzë** (lake), Alb.
43/D2 **Fife Ness** (pt.), Sc,UK
56/E4 **Figeac**, Fr.
58/A2 **Figueira da Foz**, Port.
59/G1 **Figueres**, Sp.
96/E1 **Figuig**, Mor.
103/G8 **Fiherenana** (riv.), Madg.
92/G6 **Fiji**
105/X **Filchner Ice Shelf**, Ant.
45/H3 **Filey**, Eng,UK
45/H3 **Filey** (bay), Eng,UK
63/F3 **Filiaşi**, Rom.
60/D3 **Filicudi** (isl.), It.
99/F3 **Filingué**, Niger
61/J2 **Filippoi** (ruins), Gre.
42/E4 **Filipstad**, Swe.
131/B2 **Fillmore**, Ca,US
124/D3 **Fillmore**, Ut,US
93/S9 **Filo** (peak), WSam.
46/D3 **Filton**, Eng,UK
105/Z **Fimbul Ice Shelf**, Ant.
96/J8 **Fimi** (riv.), Zaire
57/H4 **Finale Ligure**, It.
98/C3 **Fina Rsv.**, Mali
43/D2 **Findhorn** (riv.), Sc,UK
126/D3 **Findlay**, Oh,US
91/D4 **Fingal**, Austl.
119/K2 **Finger** (lake), On,Can
126/E3 **Finger** (lakes), NY,US
56/E4 **Finiels, Sommet de** (peak), Fr.
74/B3 **Finike**, Turk.
58/A1 **Finisterre** (cape), Sp.
57/K3 **Finkenstein**, Aus.
42/H2 **Finland**
64/E4 **Finland** (gulf), Eur.
118/D3 **Finlay** (riv.), BC,Can
128/B4 **Finlay** (mts.), Tx,US
51/E6 **Finnentrop**, Ger.
132/C2 **Finn Hill-Inglewood**, Wa,US
90/B1 **Finnigan** (peak), Austl.
42/G1 **Finnmark** (co.), Nor.
42/E4 **Finspång**, Swe.
44/A3 **Fintona**, NI,UK
60/B1 **Fiora** (riv.), It.
57/H4 **Fiorenzuola d'Arda**, It.
132/C2 **Fircrest-Silver Lake**, Wa,US
57/J5 **Firenze** (Florence), It.
112/E2 **Firmat**, Arg.
56/F4 **Firminy**, Fr.
84/C2 **Firozābād**, India
73/K2 **Firozpur**, India
72/F3 **Fīrūzābād**, Iran
57/L3 **Fischbacher** (mts.), Aus.
102/B2 **Fish** (riv.), Namb.
102/C3 **Fish** (riv.), SAfr.
45/G2 **Fishburn**, Eng,UK
105/E **Fisher** (glac.), Ant.
123/J3 **Fisher** (bay), Mb,Can
119/H2 **Fisher** (str.), NW,Can
123/J3 **Fisher Branch**, Mb,Can
90/F6 **Fisherman** (isl.), Austl.
46/B3 **Fishguard**, Wal,UK
66/F4 **Fisht, Gora** (peak), Rus.
45/J6 **Fishtoft**, Eng,UK
93/S8 **Fito** (peak), WSam.
130/L2 **Fitton** (mtn.), Yk,Can
129/H4 **Fitzgerald**, Ga,US
122/B3 **Fitz Hugo** (sound), BC,Can
113/J7 **Fitzroy** (peak), Arg.
90/C3 **Fitzroy** (riv.), Austl.
119/R7 **Fitzwilliam** (str.), NW,Can
60/C2 **Fiumicino**, It.
44/A3 **Fivemiletown**, NI,UK
42/C3 **Fjell**, Nor.
47/F3 **Flackwell Heath**, Eng,UK
125/G3 **Flagler**, Co,US
129/H4 **Flagler Beach**, Fl,US
124/E4 **Flagstaff**, Az,US
126/B2 **Flambeau** (riv.), Wi,US
127/Q9 **Flamborough**, On,Can
45/H3 **Flamborough**, Eng,UK
45/H3 **Flamborough Head** (pt.), Eng,UK
48/G2 **Fläming** (hills), Ger.
122/F5 **Flaming Gorge Nat'l Rec. Area**, Ut, Wy,US
123/K2 **Flanagan** (riv.), On,Can
52/B2 **Flanders** (reg.), Belg., Fr.
123/J4 **Flandreau**, SD,US
130/L3 **Flat Creek**, Yk,Can
122/E4 **Flathead** (lake), Mt,US
122/E3 **Flathead** (riv.), Mt,US
46/C4 **Flat Holm** (isl.), Eng,UK
125/K3 **Flat River**, Mo,US
132/F7 **Flat Rock**, Mi,US
90/B1 **Flattery** (cape), Austl.
122/B3 **Flattery** (cape), Wa,US
47/H4 **Fleet**, Eng,UK
45/E4 **Fleetwood**, Eng,UK
42/C4 **Flekkefjord**, Nor.
131/F5 **Flemington**, NJ,US
48/E1 **Flensburg**, Ger.
53/E2 **Fléron**, Belg.
56/C2 **Flers**, Fr.
52/D3 **Fleurus**, Belg.
56/D3 **Fleury-les-Aubrais**, Fr.
50/C4 **Flevoland** (prov.), Neth.
44/E2 **Flimby**, Eng,UK
91/D3 **Flinders** (isl.), Austl.
90/C2 **Flinders** (reefs), Austl.
90/A2 **Flinders** (riv.), Austl.
123/L3 **Flindt** (riv.), On,Can
123/H2 **Flin Flon**, Mb,Can
119/J2 **Flint** (lake), NW,Can
93/K6 **Flint** (isl.), Kiri.
45/E5 **Flint**, Wal,UK
129/G4 **Flint** (riv.), Ga,US
125/H3 **Flint** (hills), Ks,US
132/E5 **Flint**, Mi,US
47/F3 **Flitwick**, Eng,UK
51/F1 **Flögelner See** (lake), Ger.
49/G3 **Flöha** (riv.), Ger.
126/B4 **Flora**, Il,US
131/G5 **Floral Park**, NY,US
53/F5 **Florange**, Fr.
53/D3 **Floreffe**, Belg.
129/G3 **Florence**, Al,US
124/E4 **Florence**, Az,US
125/F3 **Florence**, Co,US
129/J3 **Florence**, SC,US
57/J5 **Florence** (Firenze), It.
108/C3 **Florencia**, Col.
52/D3 **Florennes**, Belg.
112/E3 **Flores** (riv.), Arg.
122/B3 **Flores** (isl.), BC,Can
116/D4 **Flores**, Guat.
87/F5 **Flores** (isl.), Indo.
87/E5 **Flores** (sea), Indo.
59/R12 **Flores** (isl.), Azor.,Port.
113/F2 **Flores** (dept.), Uru.
109/L5 **Floresta**, Braz.
128/D4 **Floresville**, Tx,US
131/F5 **Florham Park**, NJ,US
109/K5 **Floriano**, Braz.
110/B3 **Florianópolis**, Braz.
117/F3 **Florida**, Cuba
117/E3 **Florida** (str.), NAm.
113/F2 **Florida**, Uru.
113/F2 **Florida** (dept.), Uru.
129/H4 **Florida** (state), US
129/H5 **Florida** (bay), Fl,US
129/H5 **Florida Keys** (isls.), Fl,US
60/D4 **Floridia**, It.
132/M10 **Florin**, Ca,US
61/G2 **Flórina**, Gre.
125/K3 **Florissant**, Mo,US
42/C3 **Florø**, Nor.
128/C3 **Floydada**, Tx,US
50/C3 **Fluessen** (lake), Neth.
60/A3 **Flumendosa** (riv.), It.
126/D3 **Flushing**, Mi,US
50/A6 **Flushing** (Vlissingen), Neth.
92/D5 **Fly** (riv.), PNG
105/T **Flying Fish** (cape), Ant.
42/P6 **Fnjóská** (riv.), Ice.
123/H3 **Foam Lake**, Sk,Can
62/D4 **Foča**, Bosn.
63/H3 **Focşani**, Rom.
60/D2 **Foggia**, It.
57/L3 **Fohnsdorf**, Aus.
48/E1 **Föhr** (isl.), Ger.
56/D5 **Foix**, Fr.
42/C3 **Folarskardnuten** (peak), Nor.
42/D2 **Folda** (fjord), Nor.
61/J4 **Folégandros** (isl.), Gre.
119/J2 **Foley** (isl.), NW,Can
60/C1 **Foligno**, It.
47/H4 **Folkestone**, Eng,UK
129/H4 **Folkston**, Ga,US
60/B1 **Follonica** (gulf), It.
118/F3 **Fond du Lac** (riv.), Sk,Can
126/B3 **Fond du Lac**, Wi,US
60/C2 **Fondi**, It.
42/D3 **Fongen** (peak), Nor.
58/B1 **Fonsagrada**, Sp.
116/D5 **Fonseca** (gulf), NAm.
56/F4 **Fontaine**, Fr.
52/B6 **Fontainebleau**, Fr.
52/D3 **Fontaine-L'Evêque**, Belg.
131/C2 **Fontana**, Ca,US
56/C3 **Fontenay-le-Comte**, Fr.
52/B6 **Fontenay-Trésigny**, Fr.
122/F5 **Fontenelle** (res.), Wy,US
57/G4 **Font Sancte, Pic de la** (peak), Fr.
42/P6 **Fontur** (pt.), Ice.
91/F5 **Footscray**, Austl.
130/H3 **Foraker** (mtn.), Ak,US
53/F5 **Forbach**, Fr.
91/D2 **Forbes**, Austl.
58/A1 **Forcarey**, Sp.
57/J2 **Forchheim**, Ger.
132/E7 **Ford** (lake), Mi,US
47/E5 **Fordingbridge**, Eng,UK
128/E3 **Fordyce**, Ar,US
46/C4 **Foreland** (pt.), Eng,UK
47/E5 **Foreland, The** (pt.), Eng,UK
122/F3 **Foremost**, Ab,Can
47/H4 **Foreness** (pt.), Eng,UK
129/F3 **Forest**, Ms,US
91/D4 **Forestier** (cape), Austl.
127/G1 **Forestville**, Qu,Can
131/K8 **Forestville**, Md,US
56/E4 **Forez** (mts.), Fr.
43/D2 **Forfar**, Sc,UK

152

Foril – Gibra

127/H1 **Forillon Nat'l Park**, Qu,Can
44/B3 **Forkill**, NI,UK
57/K4 **Forlì**, It.
45/E4 **Formby**, Eng,UK
45/E4 **Formby** (pt.), Eng,UK
59/F3 **Formentera** (isl.), Sp.
59/G3 **Formentor, Cabo de** (cape), Sp.
60/C2 **Formia**, It.
110/C2 **Formiga**, Braz.
111/E2 **Formosa**, Arg.
109/J7 **Formosa**, Braz.
109/G6 **Formosa** (mts.), Braz.
98/A4 **Formosa** (isl.), GBis.
102/C4 **Formosa** (peak), SAfr.
109/J6 **Formoso** (riv.), Braz.
57/J5 **Fornacelle**, It.
43/D2 **Forres**, Sc,UK
129/F3 **Forrest City**, Ar,US
42/G3 **Forssa**, Fin.
90/A3 **Forsyth** (range), Austl.
129/H3 **Forsyth**, Ga,US
122/G4 **Forsyth**, Mt,US
73/K3 **Fort Abbās**, Pak.
109/L4 **Fortaleza**, Braz.
113/G2 **Fortaleza Santa Teresa**, Uru.
102/D4 **Fort Beaufort**, SAfr.
122/F4 **Fort Benton**, Mt,US
124/B3 **Fort Bragg**, Ca,US
125/H4 **Fort Cobb** (res.), Ok,US
125/F2 **Fort Collins**, Co,US
128/C4 **Fort Davis**, Tx,US
53/E5 **Fort de Douaumont**, Fr.
117/J5 **Fort-de-France** (cap.), Mart.
53/E5 **Fort de Vaux**, Fr.
123/K5 **Fort Dodge**, Ia,US
104/D3 **Forte Cameia**, Ang.
127/S10 **Fort Erie**, On,Can
92/A7 **Fortescue** (riv.), Austl.
126/A1 **Fort Frances**, On,Can
129/F4 **Fort Gaines**, Al,US
127/R9 **Fort George**, On,Can
119/J3 **Fort-George** (Chisasibi), Qu,Can
125/J4 **Fort Gibson**, Ok,US
128/E2 **Fort Gibson** (lake), Ok,US
96/C3 **Fort-Gouraud**, Mrta.
43/C2 **Forth** (riv.), Sc,UK
43/D2 **Forth, Firth of** (inlet), Sc,UK
127/G2 **Fort Kent**, Me,US
129/H5 **Fort Lauderdale**, Fl,US
131/F5 **Fort Lee**, NJ,US
125/F2 **Fort Lupton**, Co,US
122/E3 **Fort Macleod**, Ab,Can
123/L5 **Fort Madison**, Ia,US
129/H4 **Fort Matanzas Nat'l Mon.**, Fl,US
118/E3 **Fort McMurray**, Ab,Can
126/C2 **Fort Michilimackinac**, Mi,US
125/G2 **Fort Morgan**, Co,US
129/J3 **Fort Moultrie**, SC,US
129/H5 **Fort Myers**, Fl,US
118/D3 **Fort Nelson** (riv.), BC,Can
45/F4 **Forton**, Eng,UK
60/D2 **Fortore** (riv.), It.
129/G3 **Fort Payne**, Al,US
122/G4 **Fort Peck** (lake), Mt,US
129/H5 **Fort Pierce**, Fl,US
123/H4 **Fort Pierre**, SD,US
101/A2 **Fort Portal**, Ugan.
123/H3 **Fort Qu'Appelle**, Sk,Can
123/J5 **Fort Randall** (dam), SD,US
122/B2 **Fort Saint James**, BC,Can
118/D3 **Fort Saint John**, BC,Can
122/E2 **Fort Saskatchewan**, Ab,Can
125/J3 **Fort Scott**, Ks,US
67/J3 **Fort-Shevchenko**, Kaz.
128/E3 **Fort Smith**, Ar,US
128/C4 **Fort Stockton**, Tx,US
125/F4 **Fort Sumner**, NM,US
123/J4 **Fort Totten**, ND,US
127/L2 **Fortune**, Nf,Can
127/L2 **Fortune** (bay), Nf,Can
46/D5 **Fortuneswell**, Eng,UK
125/F4 **Fort Union Nat'l Mon.**, NM,US
129/G4 **Fort Walton Beach**, Fl,US
131/J8 **Fort Washington Park**, Md,US
126/C3 **Fort Wayne**, In,US
43/C2 **Fort William**, Sc,UK
128/D3 **Fort Worth**, Tx,US
123/H4 **Fort Yates**, ND,US
90/B2 **Forty Mile Scrub Nat'l Park**, Austl.
82/B3 **Foshan**, China
119/S7 **Fosheim** (pen.), NW,Can
45/G3 **Foss** (riv.), Eng,UK
57/G4 **Fossano**, It.
52/B5 **Fosses**, Fr.
53/D3 **Fosses-la-Ville**, Belg.
122/C4 **Fossil**, Or,US
122/F5 **Fossil Butte Nat'l Mon.**, Wy,US
126/D3 **Fostoria**, Oh,US
56/C2 **Fougères**, Fr.
97/N3 **Foul** (bay), Egypt, Sudan
47/G3 **Foulness** (isl.), Eng,UK
47/G3 **Foulness** (pt.), Eng,UK
45/H4 **Foulness** (riv.), Eng,UK
47/H1 **Foulsham**, Eng,UK
99/H5 **Foumban**, Camr.
125/F3 **Fountain**, Co,US
131/C3 **Fountain Valley**, Ca,US
128/E3 **Fourche La Fave** (riv.), Ar,US
47/E4 **Four Marks**, Eng,UK
52/D4 **Fourmies**, Fr.
130/D5 **Four Mountains** (isls.), Ak,US
103/R15 **Fournaise, Piton de la** (peak), Reun.
98/B4 **Fouta Djallon** (reg.), Gha.
46/B6 **Fowey**, Eng,UK
46/B6 **Fowey** (riv.), Eng,UK
91/B1 **Fowlers Gap**, Austl.
72/E1 **Fowman**, Iran
130/M3 **Fox** (mtn.), Yk,Can
130/E5 **Fox** (isls.), Ak,US
126/B3 **Fox** (riv.), Il, Wi,US
122/D2 **Fox Creek**, Ab,Can
119/H2 **Foxe** (chan.), NW,Can
119/J2 **Foxe** (pen.), NW,Can
119/J2 **Foxe Basin** (sound), NW,Can
132/P15 **Fox Lake**, Il,US
47/G2 **Foxton**, Eng,UK
122/F3 **Fox Valley**, Sk,Can
44/A2 **Foyle** (riv.), NI,UK
44/A1 **Foyle, Lough** (inlet), Ire., NI,UK
58/B1 **Foz**, Sp.
104/B4 **Foz do Cunene**, Ang.
111/F2 **Foz do Iguaçu**, Braz.
59/F2 **Fraga**, Sp.
110/B3 **Fraiburgo**, Braz.
108/E7 **Frailes** (range), Bol.
52/C3 **Frameries**, Belg.
47/H2 **Framlingham**, Eng,UK
110/C2 **Franca**, Braz.
61/E2 **Francavilla Fontana**, It.
56/D3 **France**
56/E5 **France, Roc de** (mtn.), Fr.
118/C2 **Frances** (lake), Yk,Can
116/E3 **Frances** (cape), Cuba
117/H4 **Francés Viejo** (cape), DRep.
104/B1 **Franceville**, Gabon
54/C3 **Franche-Comté** (reg.), Fr.
123/J5 **Francis Case** (lake), SD,US
116/C4 **Francisco Escárcega**, Mex.
117/P8 **Francisco I. Madero**, Mex.
104/E5 **Francistown**, Bots.
110/G8 **Franco da Rocha**, Braz.
122/B2 **Francois** (lake), BC,Can
52/B6 **Franconville**, Fr.
50/C2 **Franeker**, Neth.
51/F6 **Frankenberg-Eder**, Ger.
126/D3 **Frankenmuth**, Mi,US
126/C3 **Frankfort**, In,US
126/C4 **Frankfort** (cap.), Ky,US
49/H2 **Frankfurt**, Ger.
57/H1 **Frankfurt am Main**, Ger.
57/J2 **Frankische Alb** (mts.), Ger.
57/H1 **Fränkische Saale** (riv.), Ger.
57/J2 **Fränkische Schweiz** (reg.), Ger.
91/C3 **Frankland** (cape), Austl.
105/M **Franklin** (isl.), Ant.
130/N1 **Franklin** (bay), NW,Can
118/D2 **Franklin** (mts.), NW,Can
130/G1 **Franklin** (pt.), Ak,US
126/C4 **Franklin**, In,US
126/C4 **Franklin**, Ky,US
129/H3 **Franklin**, NC,US
129/G3 **Franklin**, Tn,US
128/D4 **Franklin**, Tx,US
126/E4 **Franklin**, Va,US
132/P14 **Franklin**, Wi,US
126/E4 **Franklin**, WV,US
122/D3 **Franklin D. Roosevelt** (lake), Wa,US
131/F4 **Franklin Lakes**, NJ,US
91/C4 **Franklin-Lower Gordon Wild Rivers Nat'l Park**, Austl.
132/Q16 **Franklin Park**, Il,US
131/G5 **Franklin Square**, NY,US
111/F2 **Fransisco Beltrão**, Braz.
110/G8 **Fransisco Morato**, Braz.
68/F2 **Franz Josef Land** (arch.), Rus.
90/D4 **Fraser** (isl.), Austl.
122/B2 **Fraser** (lake), BC,Can
122/C3 **Fraser** (riv.), BC,Can
132/G6 **Fraser**, Mi,US
43/D2 **Fraserburgh**, Sc,UK
122/B2 **Fraser Lake**, BC,Can
91/C3 **Fraser Nat'l Park**, Austl.
55/E2 **Frauenfeld**, Swi.
112/F2 **Fray Bentos**, Uru.
124/C4 **Frazier Park**, Ca,US
53/F2 **Frechen**, Ger.
102/E3 **Fred** (mtn.), SAfr.
48/E1 **Fredericia**, Den.
126/E4 **Frederick**, Md,US
125/H4 **Frederick**, Ok,US
128/D4 **Fredericksburg**, Tx,US
126/E4 **Fredericksburg**, Va,US
127/H2 **Fredericton** (cap.), NB,Can
42/D4 **Frederikshavn**, Den.
124/D3 **Fredonia**, Az,US
125/J3 **Fredonia**, Ks,US
126/E3 **Fredonia**, NY,US
42/D4 **Fredrikstad**, Nor.
125/H3 **Freedom**, Ok,US
131/F5 **Freehold**, NJ,US
91/A1 **Freeling Heights** (peak), Austl.
117/F2 **Freeport**, Bahm.
126/B3 **Freeport**, Il,US
131/G5 **Freeport**, NY,US
128/E4 **Freeport**, Tx,US
128/D5 **Freer**, Tx,US
98/B4 **Freetown** (cap.), SLeo.
56/B2 **Fréhel** (cape), Fr.
48/G3 **Freib** (riv.), Ger.
49/G3 **Freiberg**, Ger.
54/D2 **Freiburg**, Ger.
48/G3 **Freiberger Mulde** (riv.), Ger.
110/D1 **Frei Inocêncio**, Braz.
112/B3 **Freire**, Chile
53/G4 **Freisen**, Ger.
57/J2 **Freising**, Ger.
57/L2 **Freistadt**, Aus.
49/G3 **Freital**, Ger.
57/G5 **Fréjus**, Fr.
46/B4 **Fremington**, Eng,UK
132/L11 **Fremont**, Ca,US
126/C3 **Fremont**, Mi,US
125/H2 **Fremont**, Ne,US
126/D3 **Fremont**, Oh,US
124/E3 **Fremont** (riv.), Ut,US
122/F5 **Fremont** (peak), Wy,US
126/D2 **French** (riv.), On,Can
93/J2 **French Frigate** (shoals), Hi,US
109/H3 **French Guiana** (dpcy.), Fr.
122/G3 **Frenchman** (riv.), Can., US
125/G2 **Frenchman** (cr.), Ne,US
127/R8 **Frenchman's** (bay), On,Can
91/C4 **Frenchmans Cap** (peak), Austl.
93/M6 **French Polynesia** (terr.), Fr.
109/H5 **Fresco** (riv.), Braz.
47/E5 **Freshwater**, Eng,UK
112/B4 **Fresia**, Chile
117/P9 **Fresnillo de González Echeverría**, Mex.
124/C3 **Fresno**, Ca,US
91/D4 **Freycinet Nat'l Park**, Austl.
53/F5 **Freyming-Merlebach**, Fr.
57/K2 **Freyung**, Ger.
104/B4 **Fria** (cape), Namb.
111/C2 **Frías**, Arg.
54/D4 **Fribourg**, Swi.
54/D4 **Fribourg** (canton), Swi.
57/H1 **Friedberg**, Ger.
51/E2 **Friedeburg**, Ger.
57/H1 **Friedrichsdorf**, Ger.
55/F2 **Friedrichshafen**, Ger.
53/G5 **Friedrichsthal**, Ger.
51/G7 **Friedrichsthal**, Ger.
54/D1 **Friesenheim**, Ger.
50/C2 **Friesland** (prov.), Neth.
51/E2 **Friesoythe**, Ger.
47/F4 **Frimley**, Eng,UK
47/H3 **Frinton**, Eng,UK
38/G7 **Frio** (cape), Braz.
125/H5 **Frio** (riv.), Tx,US
51/G6 **Fritzlar**, Ger.
57/K3 **Friuli-Venezia Giulia** (reg.), It.
44/E2 **Frizington**, Eng,UK
119/K2 **Frobisher** (bay), NW,Can
122/F1 **Frobisher** (lake), Sk,Can
45/F5 **Frodsham**, Eng,UK
42/D3 **Frohavet** (bay), Nor.
52/D3 **Froidchapelle**, Belg.
67/G2 **Frolovo**, Rus.
91/B1 **Frome** (lake), Austl.
46/D4 **Frome**, Eng,UK
46/D2 **Frome** (riv.), Eng,UK
46/D5 **Frome** (riv.), Eng,UK
125/F2 **Front** (range), Co,US
56/E5 **Frontignan**, Fr.
126/E4 **Front Royal**, Va,US
60/C2 **Frosinone**, It.
42/E3 **Frösö**, Swe.
105/J **Frost** (glac.), Ant.
53/F6 **Frouard**, Fr.
42/D3 **Frøya** (isl.), Nor.
119/H2 **Frozen** (str.), NW,Can
127/Q9 **Fruitland**, On,Can
62/D3 **Fruška Gora Nat'l Park**, Yugo.
110/B2 **Frutal**, Braz.
112/B4 **Frutillar**, Chile
49/K4 **Frýdek-Místek**, Czh.
81/C5 **Fu** (riv.), China
81/D3 **Fucheng**, China
48/E3 **Fuchskaute** (peak), Ger.
53/H2 **Fuchskauten** (peak), Ger.
78/C3 **Fuchū**, Japan
81/D5 **Fuchun** (riv.), China
87/H4 **Fudi** (mtn.), Indo.
82/D2 **Fuding**, China
59/Y16 **Fuenaventura** (isl.), Canl.
58/C4 **Fuengirola**, Sp.
58/D2 **Fuenlabrada**, Sp.
59/N8 **Fuente**, Sp.
59/E4 **Fuente-Álamo**, Sp.
58/B3 **Fuente del Maestre**, Sp.
58/C3 **Fuente Obejuna**, Sp.
58/E1 **Fuenterrabiá**, Sp.
58/C4 **Fuentes de Andalucía**, Sp.
117/N8 **Fuerte** (riv.), Mex.
82/D4 **Fuga** (isl.), Phil.
48/F3 **Fuhne** (riv.), Ger.
51/H4 **Fuhse** (riv.), Ger.
79/F3 **Fuji**, Japan
79/F3 **Fuji** (riv.), Japan
79/F3 **Fujieda**, Japan
79/F3 **Fuji-Hakone-Izu Nat'l Park**, Japan
79/L10 **Fujiidera**, Japan
79/H7 **Fujimi**, Japan
79/H7 **Fujino**, Japan
79/F3 **Fujinomiya**, Japan
79/F2 **Fujioka**, Japan
79/F3 **Fujisawa**, Japan
79/J7 **Fujishiro**, Japan
79/M9 **Fujiwara**, Japan
79/F3 **Fujiyama** (mtn.), Japan
79/F3 **Fujiyoshida**, Japan
78/D3 **Fukuchiyama**, Japan
78/A4 **Fukue**, Japan
78/A4 **Fukue** (isl.), Japan
78/E2 **Fukui**, Japan
78/E3 **Fukui** (pref.), Japan
78/B4 **Fukuoka**, Japan
78/B4 **Fukuoka** (pref.), Japan
79/E3 **Fukuroi**, Japan
105/C **Fukushima** (peak), Ant.
79/G2 **Fukushima**, Japan
79/F2 **Fukushima** (pref.), Japan
78/C3 **Fukuyama**, Japan
73/J2 **Fūlādī** (mtn.), Afg.
47/G2 **Fulbourn**, Eng,UK
57/H1 **Fulda**, Ger.
45/G4 **Fulford**, Eng,UK
82/A2 **Fuling**, China
131/C3 **Fullerton**, Ca,US
131/E5 **Fullerton** (Whitehall), Pa,US
127/Q9 **Fulton**, On,Can
126/B4 **Fulton**, Ky,US
125/K3 **Fulton**, Mo,US
126/E3 **Fulton**, NY,US
42/E3 **Fulufjället** (peak), Swe.
45/F4 **Fulwood**, Eng,UK
56/D4 **Fumel**, Fr.
79/H7 **Funabashi**, Japan
92/G5 **Funafuti** (atoll), Tuv.
92/G5 **Funafuti** (cap.), Tuv.
117/G5 **Fundación**, Col.
127/H2 **Fundy** (bay), NB, NS,Can
127/H2 **Fundy Nat'l Park**, NB,Can
104/F5 **Funhalouro**, Moz.
64/J4 **Furmanov**, Rus.
43/C2 **Furnace**, Sc,UK
110/H6 **Furnas** (res.), Braz.
91/C4 **Furneaux Group** (isls.), Austl.
51/E3 **Fürstenau**, Ger.
62/C2 **Fürstenfeld**, Aus.
55/H1 **Fürstenfeldbruck**, Ger.
49/H2 **Fürstenwalde**, Ger.
57/K2 **Furth im Wald**, Ger.
77/N4 **Furukawa**, Japan
119/H2 **Fury and Hecla** (str.), NW,Can
81/B4 **Fushan**, China
81/E3 **Fushan**, China
77/J3 **Fushun**, China
79/M9 **Fuso**, Japan
79/H7 **Fussa**, Japan
55/G2 **Füssen**, Ger.
79/M10 **Futami**, Japan
62/D3 **Futog**, Yugo.
112/B4 **Futrono**, Chile
79/F3 **Futtsu**, Japan
92/H6 **Futuna** (isl.), Wall.
74/H6 **Fuwah**, Egypt
85/H3 **Fuxian** (lake), China
77/J3 **Fuxin**, China
81/C4 **Fuyang**, China
82/B2 **Fuyi** (riv.), China
77/J2 **Fuyu**, China
49/L5 **Füzesabony**, Hun.
82/C2 **Fuzhou**, China
48/F1 **Fyn** (co.), Den.
42/D5 **Fyn** (isl.), Den.

G

97/Q6 **Gaalkacyo** (Galcaio), Som.
50/D5 **Gaanderen**, Neth.
50/C2 **Gaast**, Neth.
56/C5 **Gabas** (riv.), Fr.
124/C3 **Gabbs**, Nv,US
104/B3 **Gabela**, Ang.
96/H1 **Gabes** (gulf), Tun.
96/H7 **Gabon**
102/D2 **Gaborone** (cap.), Bots.
63/G4 **Gabrovo**, Bul.
62/D4 **Gacko**, Bosn.
84/C4 **Gadag-Betgeri**, India
129/G3 **Gadsden**, Al,US
63/G3 **Găeşti**, Rom.
60/C2 **Gaeta**, It.
60/C2 **Gaeta** (gulf), It.
129/H3 **Gaffney**, SC,US
64/G5 **Gagarin**, Rus.
98/D5 **Gagnoa**, IvC.
127/G1 **Gagnon**, Qu,Can
52/B6 **Gagny**, Fr.
66/G4 **Gagra**, Geo.
62/A2 **Gail** (riv.), Aus.
56/D5 **Gaillac**, Fr.
57/K3 **Gailtaler Alps** (mts.), Aus.
112/D4 **Gaiman**, Arg.
129/H4 **Gainesville**, Fl,US
129/H3 **Gainesville**, Ga,US
125/J3 **Gainesville**, Mo,US
128/D3 **Gainesville**, Tx,US
45/G2 **Gainford**, Eng,UK
45/H5 **Gainsborough**, Eng,UK
131/J7 **Gaithersburg**, Md,US
64/E4 **Gaizina Kalns** (peak), Lat.
102/C2 **Gakarosa** (peak), SAfr.
58/D2 **Galapagar**, Sp.
43/D3 **Galashiels**, Sc,UK
63/J3 **Galaţi**, Rom.
63/H3 **Galaţi** (co.), Rom.
61/F2 **Galatina**, It.
61/F2 **Galatone**, It.
126/D4 **Galax**, Va,US
61/H3 **Galaxídhiou**, Gre.
87/G3 **Galela**, Indo.
126/B3 **Galena**, Il,US
112/B3 **Galera** (pt.), Chile
108/B3 **Galera** (pt.), Ecu.
117/J5 **Galera** (pt.), Trin.
126/B3 **Galesburg**, Il,US
43/A4 **Galey** (riv.), Ire.
44/B2 **Galgorm**, NI,UK
64/J4 **Galich**, Rus.
49/L3 **Galicia** (reg.), Pol., Ukr.
58/A1 **Galicia** (aut. comm.), Sp.
62/E5 **Galičica Nat'l Park**, Macd.
74/K5 **Galilee, Sea of** (Tiberias) (lake), Isr.
126/D3 **Galion**, Oh,US
129/G2 **Gallatin**, Tn,US
84/D6 **Galle**, SrL.
113/K7 **Gallegos** (riv.), Arg.
117/G5 **Gallinas** (pt.), Col.
128/B3 **Gallinas** (mts.), NM,US
61/E2 **Gallipoli**, It.
63/H5 **Gallipoli** (pen.), Turk.
63/H5 **Gallipoli** (Gelibolu), Turk.
126/D4 **Gallipolis**, Oh,US
42/G2 **Gällivare**, Swe.
60/C3 **Gallo** (cape), It.
44/D2 **Galloway, Mull of** (pt.), Sc,UK
124/E4 **Gallup**, NM,US
76/D2 **Galt**, Mong.
132/M10 **Galt**, Ca,US
43/A4 **Galtymore** (mtn.), Ire.
76/E2 **Galuut**, Mong.
112/B3 **Galvarino**, Chile
128/E4 **Galveston**, Tx,US
128/E4 **Galveston** (bay), Tx,US
128/E4 **Galveston** (isl.), Tx,US
112/E2 **Gálvez**, Arg.
43/A4 **Galway**, Ire.
43/A4 **Galway** (bay), Ire.
83/D1 **Gam** (riv.), Viet.
102/C2 **Gamagara** (dry riv.), SAfr.
79/E3 **Gamagōri**, Japan
84/E2 **Gamba**, China
99/E4 **Gambaga Scarp** (escarp.), Gha., Togo
84/A2 **Gambat**, Pak.
97/M6 **Gambēla**, Eth.
97/M6 **Gambela Nat'l Park**, Eth.
98/B3 **Gambia**
98/A3 **Gambia** (Gambie) (riv.), Afr.
93/M7 **Gambier** (isls.), FrPol.
127/L1 **Gambo**, Nf,Can
104/C1 **Gamboma**, Congo
102/C4 **Gamka** (riv.), SAfr.
102/B3 **Gamkab** (dry riv.), Namb.
47/F2 **Gamlingay**, Eng,UK
64/D2 **Gammelstad**, Swe.
79/M9 **Gamo**, Japan
49/G5 **Gamsfeld** (peak), Aus.
101/C1 **Gamud** (peak), Eth.
82/C2 **Gan** (riv.), China
126/E2 **Gananoque**, On,Can
104/D2 **Gandajika**, Zaire
127/L1 **Gander**, Nf,Can
127/L1 **Gander** (lake), Nf,Can
51/F2 **Ganderkesee**, Ger.
84/B3 **Gāndhīhām**, India
84/B3 **Gandhinagar**, India
84/B3 **Gāndhi Sāgar** (res.), India
59/E3 **Gandía**, Sp.
96/C4 **Ganeb** (well), Mrta.
84/C2 **Gangāpur**, India
84/E2 **Gangārāmpur**, India
75/D5 **Gangdisê** (mts.), China
53/F2 **Gangelt**, Ger.
84/E3 **Ganges** (riv.), India
60/D4 **Gangi**, It.
84/E2 **Gangtok**, India
74/N8 **Gan Hashlosha Nat'l Park**, Isr.
122/F5 **Gannett** (peak), Wy,US
75/F4 **Gansu** (prov.), China
96/H6 **Ganye**, Nga.
82/B2 **Ganzhou**, China
99/E3 **Ganzourgou** (prov.), Burk.
99/E2 **Gao**, Mali
99/E2 **Gao** (reg.), Mali
81/C3 **Gaocheng**, China
82/D2 **Gaojian**, China
98/E4 **Gaoua**, Burk.
81/C3 **Gaoyang**, China
81/D4 **Gaoyou** (lake), China
57/G4 **Gap**, Fr.
76/D5 **Gar** (riv.), China
84/E3 **Garai** (riv.), Bang.
101/A2 **Garamba Nat'l Park**, Zaire
109/L5 **Garanhuns**, Braz.
101/C2 **Garba Tula**, Kenya
48/F2 **Garbsen**, Ger.
110/B2 **Garça**, Braz.
58/C3 **Garcia de Sota** (res.), Sp.
56/F5 **Gard** (riv.), Fr.
57/J4 **Garda** (lake), It.
48/F2 **Gardelegen**, Ger.
131/B3 **Gardena**, Ca,US
129/H3 **Garden City**, Ga,US
125/G3 **Garden City**, Ks,US
132/F7 **Garden City**, Mi,US
131/G5 **Garden City**, NY,US
122/A2 **Gardener Canal** (inlet), BC,Can
131/C3 **Garden Grove**, Ca,US
73/J2 **Gardēz**, Afg.
127/G2 **Gardiner**, Me,US
122/F4 **Gardiner**, Mt,US
93/H5 **Gardner** (Nikumaroro) (atoll), Kiri.
43/C2 **Garelochhead**, Sc,UK
96/G2 **Garet el Djenoun** (peak), Alg.
122/E4 **Garfield** (peak), Mt,US
131/F5 **Garfield**, NJ,US
45/G4 **Garforth**, Eng,UK
56/D4 **Gargan** (mtn.), Fr.
45/F4 **Gargrave**, Eng,UK
84/C3 **Garhākotā**, India
110/B4 **Garibaldi**, Braz.
101/C3 **Garissa**, Kenya
128/D3 **Garland**, Tx,US
44/D2 **Garlieston**, Sc,UK
55/H3 **Garmisch-Partenkirchen**, Ger.
125/J3 **Garnett**, Ks,US
91/B2 **Garnpung** (lake), Austl.
56/D4 **Garonne** (riv.), Fr.
99/E2 **Garou** (lake), Mali
96/H6 **Garoua**, Camr.
96/H6 **Garoua Boulaï**, Camr.
59/K7 **Garraf** (range), Sp.
44/D6 **Garreg**, Wal,UK
51/F3 **Garrel**, Ger.
123/H4 **Garrison**, ND,US
123/H4 **Garrison** (dam), ND,US
44/C1 **Garron** (pt.), NI,UK
119/H2 **Garry** (bay), NW,Can
118/F2 **Garry** (lake), NW,Can
45/F4 **Garstang**, Eng,UK
57/L2 **Garsten**, Aus.
51/H6 **Garte** (riv.), Ger.
56/D3 **Gartempe** (riv.), Fr.
46/C2 **Garth**, Wal,UK
86/C5 **Garut**, Indo.
44/B2 **Garvagh**, NI,UK
49/L3 **Garwolin**, Pol.
132/R16 **Gary**, In,US
108/C3 **Garzón**, Col.
75/F4 **Gas** (lake), China
42/P6 **Gæsafjöll** (peak), Ice.
126/C3 **Gas City**, In,US
125/J3 **Gasconade** (riv.), Mo,US
56/C5 **Gascony** (reg.), Fr.
110/B3 **Gaspar**, Braz.
86/C4 **Gaspar** (riv.), Indo.
127/H1 **Gaspé**, Qu,Can
127/H1 **Gaspé** (pen.), Qu,Can
127/H1 **Gaspé, Cap de** (cape), Qu,Can
127/S9 **Gasport**, NY,US
129/J2 **Gaston** (lake), NC, Va,US
129/H3 **Gastonia**, NC,US
74/J4 **Gata** (cape), Cyp.
58/B2 **Gata** (range), Sp.
58/D4 **Gata, Cabo de** (cape), Sp.
64/F4 **Gatchina**, Rus.
44/D2 **Gatehouse-of-Fleet**, Sc,UK
118/F1 **Gateshead** (isl.), NW,Can
45/G2 **Gateshead**, Eng,UK
130/H2 **Gates of the Arctic Nat'l Pk. & Prsv.**, Ak,US
128/D4 **Gatesville**, Tx,US
131/G5 **Gateway Nat'l Rec. Area**, NJ, NY,US
56/C3 **Gâtine** (hills), Fr.
126/F2 **Gatineau**, Qu,Can
126/F2 **Gatineau** (riv.), Qu,Can
53/H4 **Gau-Bickelheim**, Ger.
85/F2 **Gauhāti**, India
45/G2 **Gaunless** (riv.), Eng,UK
84/E2 **Gauripur**, India
84/E2 **Gauri Sankar** (mtn.), Nepal
42/D4 **Gausta** (peak), Nor.
64/E4 **Gauya Nat'l Park**, Lat.
59/G2 **Gavà**, Sp.
61/J5 **Gávdhos** (isl.), Gre.
58/E1 **Gave de Pau** (riv.), Fr.
52/C2 **Gavere**, Belg.
42/F3 **Gävle**, Swe.
42/E3 **Gävleborg** (co.), Swe.
91/A2 **Gawler**, Austl.
76/D3 **Gaxun** (lake), China
67/L2 **Gay**, Rus.
126/D4 **Gay** (peak), WV,US
77/K3 **Gaya** (riv.), China
84/E3 **Gayā**, India
99/F4 **Gaya**, Niger
126/C2 **Gaylord**, Mi,US
66/D2 **Gaysin**, Ukr.
74/K6 **Gaza** (Ghazzah), Gaza
74/J6 **Gaza Strip**
74/D3 **Gaziantep**, Turk.
77/H1 **Gazimur** (riv.), Rus.
54/C1 **Gazon de Faing** (peak), Fr.
97/K7 **Gbadolite**, Zaire
98/C5 **Gbarnga**, Libr.
49/K1 **Gdańsk**, Pol.
49/K1 **Gdańsk** (prov.), Pol.
49/K1 **Gdańsk** (gulf), Pol., Rus.
49/K1 **Gdynia**, Pol.
81/D5 **Ge** (lake), China
57/J1 **Gebaberg** (peak), Ger.
87/G3 **Gebe** (isl.), Indo.
100/D4 **Gebeit Mine**, Sudan
63/J5 **Gebze**, Turk.
86/C5 **Gede** (peak), Indo.
74/M9 **Gedera**, Isr.
74/B2 **Gediz**, Turk.
74/A2 **Gediz** (riv.), Turk.
53/E1 **Geel**, Belg.
91/C3 **Geelong**, Austl.
51/E3 **Geeste**, Ger.
51/F2 **Geeste** (riv.), Ger.
51/F2 **Geesthacht**, Ger.
75/D5 **Gê'gyai**, China
51/G4 **Gehrden**, Ger.
46/C2 **Geifas** (mtn.), Wal,UK
118/F3 **Geikie** (riv.), Sk,Can
53/F2 **Geilenkirchen**, Ger.
79/M10 **Geinō**, Japan
57/H2 **Geislingen an der Steige**, Ger.
85/H3 **Gejiu**, China
97/L6 **Gel** (riv.), Sudan
60/D4 **Gela**, It.
60/D4 **Gela** (gulf), It.
97/Q6 **Geladī**, Eth.
50/C4 **Gelderland** (prov.), Neth.
50/C5 **Geldermalsen**, Neth.
50/D5 **Geldern**, Ger.
50/C6 **Geldrop**, Neth.
53/E2 **Geleen**, Neth.
66/F3 **Gelendzhik**, Rus.
63/H5 **Gelibolu** (Gallipoli), Turk.
46/C3 **Gelligaer**, Wal,UK
50/E5 **Gelsenkirchen**, Ger.
53/D2 **Gembloux**, Belg.
97/J7 **Gemena**, Zaire
50/C5 **Gemert**, Neth.
63/J5 **Gemlik**, Turk.
63/J5 **Gemlik** (gulf), Turk.
57/K3 **Gemona del Friuli**, It.
102/C2 **Gemsbok-Kalahari Nat'l Park**, SAfr.
102/C2 **Gemsbok Nat'l Park**, Bots.
130/G3 **Gemuk** (mtn.), Ak,US
77/J1 **Gen** (riv.), China
97/N6 **Genalē Wenz** (riv.), Eth.
52/D2 **Genappe**, Belg.
60/A3 **Genargentu** (mts.), It.
74/E2 **Genç**, Turk.
50/D5 **Gendringen**, Neth.
50/C5 **Gendt**, Neth.
50/D3 **Genemuiden**, Neth.
112/D3 **General Acha**, Arg.
112/D2 **General Alvear**, Arg.
112/F2 **General Belgrano**, Arg.
112/E2 **General Cabrera**, Arg.
112/B5 **General Carrera** (lake), Chile
113/F3 **General Juan Madariaga**, Arg.
113/S12 **General Las Heras**, Arg.
111/C1 **General Martín Miguel de Güemes**, Arg.
112/E2 **General Pico**, Arg.
111/D2 **General Pinedo**, Arg.
82/E6 **General Santos**, Phil.
63/J4 **General-Toshevo**, Bul.
112/E2 **General Viamonte**, Arg.
112/E2 **General Villegas**, Arg.
126/E3 **Genesee** (riv.), NY,US
123/L5 **Geneseo**, Il,US
126/E3 **Geneseo**, NY,US
129/G4 **Geneva**, Al,US
132/P16 **Geneva**, Il,US
125/H2 **Geneva**, Ne,US
126/E3 **Geneva**, NY,US
132/P14 **Geneva** (lake), Wi,US
54/C5 **Geneva** (Genève), Swi.
54/C5 **Geneva** (Léman) (lake), Fr., Swi.
54/C5 **Genève** (canton), Swi.
54/E1 **Gengenbach**, Ger.
66/E3 **Genichesk**, Ukr.
58/C4 **Genil** (riv.), Sp.
53/E2 **Genk**, Belg.
50/C5 **Gennep**, Neth.
57/H4 **Genoa** (Genova), It.
57/H4 **Genova** (gulf), It.
52/C1 **Gent-Brugge** (can.), Belg.
86/C5 **Genteng** (cape), Indo.
52/C1 **Gent** (Ghent), Belg.
91/D2 **George** (lake), Austl.
90/C3 **George** (pt.), Austl.
119/K3 **George** (riv.), Qu,Can
102/C4 **George**, SAfr.
129/H4 **George** (lake), Fl,US
68/E1 **George Land** (isl.), Rus.
90/G9 **Georges** (riv.), Austl.
127/Q8 **Georgetown**, On,Can
116/E4 **George Town** (cap.), Cay.
108/G2 **Georgetown** (cap.), Guy.
129/H4 **Georgetown**, Ga,US
126/C4 **Georgetown**, Ky,US
129/J3 **Georgetown**, SC,US
128/D4 **Georgetown**, Tx,US
105/L **George V** (coast), Ant.
105/V **George VI** (sound), Ant.
128/D4 **George West**, Tx,US
67/G4 **Georgia**
122/B3 **Georgia** (str.), Can., US
129/G3 **Georgia** (state), US
126/D2 **Georgian Bay Islands Nat'l Park**, On,Can
63/H4 **Georgi Traykov**, Bul.
51/F4 **Georgsmarienhütte**, Ger.
48/G3 **Gera**, Ger.
52/C2 **Geraardsbergen**, Belg.
109/J6 **Geral de Goiás** (Espigão Mestre) (range), Braz.
89/A3 **Geraldton**, Austl.
126/C1 **Geraldton**, On,Can
56/F4 **Gerbier de Jonc** (mtn.), Fr.
51/H3 **Gerdau** (riv.), Ger.
130/H3 **Gerdine** (mtn.), Ak,US
63/L5 **Gerede**, Turk.
73/H2 **Gereshk**, Afg.
55/H2 **Geretsried**, Ger.
124/C2 **Gerlach**, Nv,US
49/L4 **Gerlachovský Štít** (peak), Slvk.
131/J7 **Germantown**, Md,US
129/F3 **Germantown**, Tn,US
48/E3 **Germany**
55/H1 **Germering**, Ger.
102/E2 **Germiston**, SAfr.
53/F3 **Gerolstein**, Ger.
59/G2 **Gerona** (Girona), Sp.
59/E1 **Ger, Pic du** (peak), Fr.
52/D3 **Gerpinnes**, Belg.
56/D5 **Gers** (riv.), Fr.
53/G5 **Gersheim**, Ger.
50/E5 **Gescher**, Ger.
51/F5 **Geseke**, Ger.
97/P6 **Gestro Wenz** (riv.), Eth.
58/D2 **Getafe**, Sp.
53/E2 **Gete** (riv.), Belg.
123/J4 **Gettysburg**, SD,US
110/A3 **Getúlio Vargas**, Braz.
105/S **Getz Ice Shelf**, Ant.
53/E2 **Geul** (riv.), Belg., Neth.
86/A3 **Geureudong** (peak), Indo.
74/E2 **Gevaş**, Turk.
51/E6 **Gevelsberg**, Ger.
62/F5 **Gevgelija**, Macd.
97/P5 **Gewanē**, Eth.
103/H6 **Geyser** (reef), Madg.
63/K5 **Geyve**, Turk.
75/B4 **Gez** (riv.), China
96/G1 **Ghadāmis**, Libya
100/C3 **Ghadir, Bi'r** (well), Egypt
99/E4 **Ghana**
104/D5 **Ghanzi**, Bots.
100/B5 **Gharb Binna**, Sudan
96/F1 **Ghardaïa**, Alg.
96/H1 **Gharyān**, Libya
96/H3 **Ghāt**, Libya
96/J5 **Ghazal** (riv.), Chad
84/C2 **Ghaziābād**, India
73/J2 **Ghaznī**, Afg.
74/K6 **Ghazzah** (Gaza), Gaza
76/G2 **Ghengis Khan Wall** (ruins), Mong.
52/C1 **Ghent** (Gent), Belg.
63/H2 **Gheorghe Gheorghiu-Dej**, Rom.
63/G2 **Gheorgheni**, Rom.
63/F2 **Gherla**, Rom.
112/C5 **Ghio** (lake), Arg.
84/A2 **Ghotki**, Pak.
73/H2 **Ghūrīān**, Afg.
83/D4 **Gia Nghia**, Viet.
102/E3 **Giant's Castle** (peak), SAfr.
60/D4 **Giarre**, It.
83/E3 **Gia Vuc**, Viet.
122/E2 **Gibbons**, Ab,Can
58/B4 **Gibraleón**, Sp.
58/B4 **Gibraltar** (str.), Afr., Eur.

127/R8 Gibraltar (pt.), On,Can
58/C4 Gibraltar (dpcy.), UK
132/F7 Gibraltar, Mi,US
91/E1 Gibraltar Range Nat'l Park, Austl.
92/B7 Gibson (des.), Austl.
128/D4 Giddings, Tx,US
100/C2 Gidi (pass), Egypt
97/N6 Gīdolē, Eth.
56/E3 Gien, Fr.
57/J2 Giengen an der Brenz, Ger.
56/F4 Gier (riv.), Fr.
57/H1 Giessen, Ger.
50/B5 Giessendam, Neth.
52/B6 Gif, Fr.
119/H1 Gifford (riv.), NW,Can
129/H5 Gifford, Fl,US
51/H4 Gifhorn, Ger.
79/E3 Gifu, Japan
79/E3 Gifu (pref.), Japan
45/F3 Giggleswick, Eng,UK
60/B1 Giglio (isl.), It.
58/C1 Gijón, Sp.
124/D4 Gila (riv.), Az, NM,US
124/D4 Gila Bend, Az,US
124/E4 Gila Cliff Dwellings Nat'l Mon., NM,US
45/H4 Gilberdyke Newport, Eng,UK
90/A2 Gilbert (riv.), Austl.
92/G5 Gilbert (isls.), Kiri.
126/A2 Gilbert, Mn,US
112/C2 Gil de Vilches Nat'l Park, Chile
46/C3 Gilfach Goch, Wal,UK
44/B3 Gilford, NI,UK
131/F6 Gilford Park, NJ,US
73/K1 Gilgit (riv.), Pak.
123/G4 Gillette, Wy,US
122/B3 Gillies Bay, BC,Can
46/D4 Gillingham, Eng,UK
47/G4 Gillingham, Eng,UK
128/E3 Gilmer, Tx,US
73/K1 Gilqit (riv.), Pak.
77/K1 Gilyuy (riv.), Rus.
50/B5 Gilze, Neth.
97/N6 Gīmbī, Eth.
123/J3 Gimli, Mb,Can
51/F3 Gimone (riv.), Fr.
79/M9 Ginan, Japan
53/E2 Gingelom, Belg.
82/E6 Gingoog, Phil.
60/E2 Ginosa, It.
58/B1 Ginzo de Limia, Sp.
97/Q7 Giohar, Som.
60/D3 Gioia (gulf), It.
60/E2 Gioia del Colle, It.
60/D3 Gioia Tauro, It.
61/J3 Gioüra (isl.), Gre.
47/G2 Gipping (riv.), Eng,UK
108/D3 Girardot, Col.
104/B4 Giraul, Ang.
74/D2 Giresun, Turk.
84/E3 Gīrīdīh, India
60/E3 Girifalco, It.
59/G2 Girona (Gerona), Sp.
56/C4 Gironde (riv.), Fr.
91/D1 Girraween Nat'l Park, Austl.
47/G2 Girton, Eng,UK
44/D1 Girvan, Sc,UK
44/D1 Girvan, Water of (riv.), Sc,UK
89/H6 Gisborne, NZ
52/A5 Gisors, Fr.
52/B1 Gistel, Belg.
101/A3 Gitega, Buru.
64/B2 Gittsfjället (peak), Swe.
55/F5 Giubiasco, Swi.
60/C1 Giulianova, It.
63/G4 Giurgiu, Rom.
63/G3 Giurgiu (co.), Rom.
74/M8 Giv'atayim, Isr.
53/D3 Givet, Fr.
56/F4 Givors, Fr.
53/D6 Givry-en-Argonne, Fr.
104/F5 Giyani, SAfr.
97/N6 Giyon, Eth.
100/B2 Giza, Pyramids of (Jīzah) (ruins), Egypt
69/R3 Gizhiga (bay), Rus.
49/L1 Giżycko, Pol.
61/G2 Gjirokastër, Alb.
42/D3 Gjøvik, Nor.
61/F2 Gjuhëzës, Kep i (cape), Alb.
127/K2 Glace Bay, NS,Can
122/D3 Glacier, BC,Can
122/C3 Glacier (peak), Wa,US
130/L4 Glacier Bay Nat'l Park & Prsv., Ak,US
122/D3 Glacier Nat'l Park, Can., US
50/D5 Gladbeck, Ger.
90/C3 Gladstone, Austl.
126/C3 Gladwin, Mi,US
45/H3 Glaisdale, Eng,UK
42/D3 Glåma (riv.), Nor.
53/G4 Glan (riv.), Ger.
82/E6 Glan, Phil.
46/C3 Glanamman, Wal,UK
52/D4 Gland (riv.), Fr.
55/F4 Glarus (canton), Swi.
55/E4 Glarus Alps (range), Swi.
46/C2 Glasbury, Wal,UK
43/C3 Glasgow, Sc,UK
126/C4 Glasgow, Ky,US
122/G3 Glasgow, Mt,US
44/D6 Glaslyn (riv.), Wal,UK
44/D3 Glass (riv.), IM,UK
128/D2 Glass (mts.), Ok,US
128/C4 Glass (mts.), Tx,US
131/K8 Glassmanor-Oxon Hill, Md,US
46/D4 Glastonbury, Eng,UK
65/M4 Glazov, Rus.
47/G2 Glemsford, Eng,UK
45/H6 Glen (riv.), Eng,UK
91/C3 Glenaladale Nat'l Park, Austl.
126/E4 Glen Allen, Va,US
44/C2 Glenarm, NI,UK
44/C2 Glenarm (riv.), NI,UK
44/B2 Glenavy, NI,UK
91/D2 Glenbawn (dam), Austl.
123/J3 Glenboro, Mb,Can
90/G8 Glenbrook, Austl.
131/K7 Glen Burnie, Md,US
124/E3 Glen Canyon Nat'l Rec. Area, Az, Ut,US
44/E1 Glencaple, Sc,UK
103/E3 Glencoe, SAfr.
132/Q15 Glencoe, Il,US
131/G5 Glen Cove, NY,US
124/D4 Glendale, Az,US
131/B2 Glendale, Ca,US
122/C5 Glendale, Or,US
132/P16 Glendale Heights, Il,US
123/G4 Glendive, Mt,US
125/F2 Glendo (res.), Wy,US
131/C2 Glendora, Ca,US
44/B1 Glendun (riv.), NI,UK
91/B3 Glenelg (riv.), Austl.
44/A2 Glenelly (riv.), NI,UK
44/D2 Glenluce, Sc,UK
43/C2 Glen Mòr (val.), Sc,UK
131/E6 Glenolden, Pa,US
130/M4 Glenora, BC,Can
90/H8 Glenorie, Austl.
125/H4 Glenpool, Ok,US
128/D3 Glen Rose, Tx,US
126/F3 Glens Falls, NY,US
44/B2 Glenshane (pass), NI,UK
131/E5 Glenside, Pa,US
44/D1 Glentrool, Sc,UK
123/H4 Glen Ullin, ND,US
132/Q15 Glenview, Il,US
127/Q8 Glen Williams, On,Can
124/F3 Glenwood Springs, Co,US
61/L7 Glifáhda, Gre.
51/H1 Glinde, Ger.
42/D3 Glittertinden (peak), Nor.
49/K3 Gliwice, Pol.
124/E4 Globe, Az,US
49/H5 Gloggnitz, Aus.
49/J3 Głogów, Pol.
49/J3 Głogówek, Pol.
103/H5 Glorieuses, Iles (isls.), Reun.
90/E6 Glorious (mtn.), Austl.
130/D3 Glory of Russia (cape), Ak,US
45/G5 Glossop, Eng,UK
126/F2 Gloucester, On,Can
46/D3 Gloucester, Eng,UK
131/E6 Gloucester City, NJ,US
46/D3 Gloucestershire (co.), Eng,UK
46/D3 Gloucester, Vale of (val.), Eng,UK
127/L1 Glovertown, Nf,Can
49/K3 Głowno, Pol.
49/J3 Głubczyce, Pol.
49/J3 Głuchołazy, Pol.
48/E1 Glücksburg, Ger.
51/G1 Glückstadt, Ger.
66/E2 Glukhov, Ukr.
44/B4 Glyde (riv.), Ire.
46/C3 Glyncorrwg, Wal,UK
44/C2 Glynn, NI,UK
46/C3 Glyn Neath, Wal,UK
49/H4 Gmünd, Aus.
99/E3 Gnagna (prov.), Burk.
51/G2 Gnarrenburg, Ger.
49/J2 Gniezno, Pol.
62/E4 Gnjilane, Yugo.
46/D1 Gnosall, Eng,UK
78/C3 Gō (riv.), Japan
84/B4 Goa (state), India
84/F2 Goālpāra, India
43/C3 Goat Fell (mtn.), Sc,UK
45/H3 Goathland, Eng,UK
97/N6 Goba, Eth.
104/C5 Gobabeb, Namb.
76/E3 Gobi (des.), China, Mong.
78/D4 Gobō, Japan
45/E6 Gobowen, Eng,UK
50/D5 Goch, Ger.
83/D4 Go Cong, Viet.
47/F4 Godalming, Eng,UK
83/D4 Go Dau Ha, Viet.
84/D4 Godāvari (riv.), India
97/P6 Godē, Eth.
62/F3 Godeanu (peak), Rom.
126/D3 Goderich, On,Can
84/B3 Godhra, India
47/G2 Godmanchester, Eng,UK
87/F4 Godo (mtn.), Indo.
79/M9 Gōdo, Japan
62/D2 Gödöllő, Hun.
46/A6 Godolphin Cross, Eng,UK
112/C2 Godoy Cruz, Arg.
123/K2 Gods (lake), Mb,Can
123/K2 Gods (riv.), Mb,Can
119/H2 Gods Mercy (bay), NW,Can
115/M3 Godthåb (Nuuk), Grld.
75/C4 Godwin Austen (K2) (peak), China, Pak.
126/E1 Goéland (lake), Qu,Can
50/A5 Goerce, Neth.
50/A6 Goes, Neth.
126/B2 Gogebic (range), Mi,US
84/D2 Gogra (riv.), India
51/G3 Gohbach (riv.), Ger.
109/M5 Goiana, Braz.
109/J7 Goiânia, Braz.
109/H7 Goiás, Braz.
110/B1 Goiás (state), Braz.
110/B1 Goiatuba, Braz.
50/C5 Goirle, Neth.
78/D3 Gojō, Japan
66/E4 Gök (riv.), Turk.
78/B4 Gokase (riv.), Japan
79/M9 Gokashō, Japan
63/G5 Gökçeada (isl.), Turk.
74/D2 Göksun, Turk.
74/K5 Golan Heights (reg.), Syria
74/C2 Gölbaşı, Turk.
74/D3 Gölbaşı, Turk.
45/F5 Golborne, Eng,UK
132/B2 Gold (mtn.), Wa,US
49/M1 Gołdap, Pol.
122/B5 Gold Beach, Or,US
90/D4 Gold Coast, Austl.
99/E5 Gold Coast (reg.), Gha.
122/D3 Golden, BC,Can
125/F3 Golden, Co,US
122/C4 Goldendale, Wa,US
48/F3 Goldene Aue (reg.), Ger.
132/J11 Golden Gate (chan.), Ca,US
102/E3 Golden Gate Highlands Nat'l Park, SAfr.
122/B3 Golden Hinde (peak), BC,Can
51/F3 Goldenstedt, Ger.
124/C3 Goldfield, Nv,US
122/B3 Gold River, BC,Can
129/J3 Goldsboro, NC,US
128/D4 Goldthwaite, Tx,US
74/E2 Göle, Turk.
49/H2 Goleniów, Pol.
74/B3 Gölhisar, Turk.
128/D4 Goliad, Tx,US
74/D2 Gölköy, Turk.
76/C4 Golmud, China
72/F2 Golpāyegān, Iran
63/K5 Gölpazarı, Turk.
49/K2 Golub-Dobrzyń, Pol.
63/H4 Golyama Kamchiya (riv.), Bul.
63/G5 Golyama Syutkya (peak), Bul.
63/G5 Golyam Perelik (peak), Bul.
101/A3 Goma, Zaire
66/D1 Gomel', Bela.
66/C2 Gomel' Obl., Bela.
59/X16 Gomera (isl.), Canl.
52/B6 Gometz-le-Châtel, Fr.
117/P8 Gómez Palacio, Mex.
48/F2 Gommern, Ger.
47/F4 Gomshall, Eng,UK
73/G2 Gonābād, Iran
104/F5 Gonarezhou Nat'l Park, Zim.
117/G4 Gonâve (gulf), Haiti
73/G1 Gonbad-e Qābūs, Iran
84/D2 Gonda, India
84/B3 Gondal, India
97/N5 Gonder, Eth.
84/D3 Gondia, India
58/A2 Gondomar, Port.
58/A1 Gondomar, Sp.
63/H5 Gönen, Turk.
85/F2 Gongbo'gyamda, China
85/H2 Gongga (peak), China
76/E4 Gonghe, China
99/H4 Gongola (riv.), Nga.
99/H4 Gongola (state), Nga.
91/C1 Gongolgon, Austl.
81/F2 Gongzhuling, China
128/D4 Gonzales, Tx,US
116/B3 González, Mex.
105/J Goodenough (cape), Ant.
102/B4 Good Hope, Cape of (cape), SAfr.
122/E5 Gooding, Id,US
125/G3 Goodland, Ks,US
90/E7 Goodna, Austl.
46/B3 Goodwick, Wal,UK
102/B4 Goodwood, SAfr.
50/C4 Gooimeer (lake), Neth.
45/H4 Goole, Eng,UK
50/D4 Goor, Neth.
123/H2 Goose (lake), Mb,Can
120/B3 Goose (lake), Ca, Or,US
119/K3 Goose Bay-Happy Valley, Nf,Can
45/F5 Goostrey, Eng,UK
57/H2 Göppingen, Ger.
83/D4 Go Quao, Viet.
49/J3 Góra, Pol.
49/L3 Góra Kalwaria, Pol.
84/D2 Gorakhpur, India
62/D4 Goražde, Bosn.
116/E5 Gorda (pt.), Nic.
124/A2 Gorda (pt.), Ca,US
91/C4 Gordon (lake), Austl.
96/J6 Goré, Chad
97/N6 Gorē, Eth.
47/G1 Gore (pt.), Eng,UK
130/H4 Gore (pt.), Ak,US
74/D2 Görele, Turk.
56/B2 Gorey, ChI,UK
73/F1 Gorgān, Iran
53/F4 Gorge du Loup, Lux.
98/B3 Gorgol (reg.), Mrta.
98/B2 Gorgol (riv.), Mrta.
67/H4 Gori, Geo.
50/B5 Gorinchem, Neth.
47/E3 Goring, Eng,UK
47/F5 Goring by Sea, Eng,UK
57/K4 Gorizia, It.
63/F3 Gorj (co.), Rom.
66/D1 Gorki, Bela.
64/J4 Gor'kiy (res.), Rus.
65/K4 Gor'kiy (Nizhniy Novgorod), Rus.
49/L4 Gorlice, Pol.
49/H3 Görlitz, Ger.
46/C2 Gorllwyn (mtn.), Wal,UK
66/F2 Gorlovka, Ukr.
44/B4 Gormanston, Ire.
127/R8 Gormley, On,Can
63/G4 Gorna Oryakhovitsa, Bul.
62/E3 Gornji Milanovac, Yugo.
62/C4 Gornji Vakuf, Bosn.
68/J4 Gorno-Altay Aut. Obl., Rus.
75/E1 Gorno-Altaysk, Rus.
68/H6 Gorno-Badakhstan Aut. Obl., Taj.
65/J4 Gorodets, Rus.
92/D5 Goroka, PNG
87/H4 Gorong (isl.), Indo.
87/F3 Gorontalo, Indo.
46/B3 Gorseinon, Wal,UK
50/D4 Gorssel, Neth.
44/A2 Gortin, NI,UK
66/C2 Goryn' (riv.), Bela., Ukr.
49/H2 Gorzów (prov.), Pol.
49/H2 Gorzów Wielkopolski, Pol.
78/D3 Gōse, Japan
79/F2 Gosen, Japan
45/G2 Gosforth, Eng,UK
77/N3 Goshogawara, Japan
51/H5 Goslar, Ger.
62/B3 Gospić, Cro.
47/E5 Gosport, Eng,UK
62/E5 Gostivar, Maced.
49/J3 Gostyń, Pol.
49/K2 Gostynin, Pol.
42/D4 Göteborg, Swe.
42/D4 Göteborg och Bohus (co.), Swe.
96/H6 Gotel (mts.), Camr., Nga.
79/F3 Gotemba, Japan
51/H7 Gotha, Ger.
125/G2 Gothenburg, Ne,US
42/F4 Gotland (isl.), Swe.
78/A4 Gotō (isls.), Japan
63/F5 Gotse Delchev, Bul.
42/F4 Gotska Sandön Nat'l Park, Swe.
78/C3 Gōtsu, Japan
51/G5 Göttingen, Ger.
50/B4 Gouda, Neth.
38/J8 Gough (isl.), StH.
126/F1 Gouin (res.), Qu,Can
126/C2 Goulais (riv.), On,Can
91/D2 Goulburn, Austl.
91/D2 Goulburn (riv.), Austl.
105/P Gould (coast), Ant.
128/F3 Gould, Ar,US
98/E2 Goundam, Mali
99/H3 Gouré, Niger
102/C4 Gourits (riv.), SAfr.
99/F3 Gourma (prov.), Burk.
99/F3 Gourma (reg.), Burk.
99/E2 Gourma-Rharous, Mali
52/A5 Gournay-en-Bray, Fr.
97/J4 Gouro, Chad
74/D2 Gouşu (riv.), Turk.
110/D1 Gouvêa, Braz.
52/B5 Gouvieux, Fr.
66/C2 Goverla (peak), Ukr.
110/D1 Governador Valadares, Braz.
76/D3 Govĭ Altayn (mts.), Mong.
73/H3 Gowd-e-Zereh (lake), Afg.
46/B3 Gower (pen.), Wal,UK
45/H4 Goxhill, Eng,UK
111/E2 Goya, Arg.
45/F5 Goyt (riv.), Eng,UK
79/M9 Gozaisho-yama (peak), Japan
75/D4 Gozha (lake), China
60/D4 Gozo (isl.), Malta
102/D4 Graaff-Reinet, SAfr.
50/D4 Graafschap (reg.), Neth.
102/B2 Graberberg (peak), Namb.
48/F2 Grabow, Ger.
62/B3 Gračac, Cro.
62/D3 Gračanica, Bosn.
129/G4 Graceville, Fl,US
116/E5 Gracias a Dios (cape), Nic.
59/S12 Graciosa (isl.), Azor.,Port.
62/D3 Gradačac, Bosn.
109/H5 Gradaús, Braz.
58/B1 Grado, Sp.
47/F2 Grafham Water (lake), Eng,UK
91/E1 Grafton, Austl.
90/B2 Grafton (passg.), Austl.
123/J3 Grafton, ND,US
126/D4 Grafton, WV,US
118/C3 Graham (isl.), BC,Can
119/S7 Graham (isl.), NW,Can
117/N7 Graham (peak), Az.,US
128/D3 Graham, Tx,US
132/C3 Graham, Wa,US
68/G1 Graham Bell (isl.), Rus.
105/V Graham Land (reg.), Ant.
102/D4 Grahamstown, SAfr.
47/G4 Grain, Eng,UK
98/C5 Grain Coast (reg.), Libr.
109/J5 Grajaú, Braz.
109/J4 Grajaú (riv.), Braz.
49/M2 Grajewo, Pol.
56/D4 Gramat (plat.), Fr.
43/C2 Grampian (mts.), Sc,UK
91/B3 Grampians Nat'l Park, Austl.
50/D3 Gramsbergen, Neth.
42/D3 Gran, Nor.
108/D3 Granada, Col.
116/D5 Granada, Nic.
58/D4 Granada, Sp.
113/K7 Gran Altiplanicie Central (plat.), Arg.
113/K7 Gran Bajo de San Julián (val.), Arg.
112/C5 Gran Bajo Oriental (val.), Arg.
128/D3 Granbury, Tx,US
125/F2 Granby, Co,US
59/X17 Gran Canaria (isl.), Canl.
107/C5 Gran Chaco (plain), SAm.
127/H2 Grand (lake), NB,Can
127/K1 Grand (lake), Nf,Can
119/J3 Grand (riv.), Qu,Can
81/D4 Grand (can.), China
44/B5 Grand (can.), Ire.
124/D3 Grand (canyon), Az,US
125/J3 Grand (riv.), Ia, Mo,US
125/J5 Grand (lake), La,US
126/C2 Grand (isl.), Mi,US
128/E2 Grand (riv.), Mo,US
127/S9 Grand (isl.), NY,US
123/H4 Grand (riv.), SD,US
117/F2 Grand Bahama (isl.), Bahm.
127/L2 Grand Bank, Nf,Can
98/C5 Grand Bassa (co.), Libr.
98/E5 Grand-Bassam, IvC.
127/H2 Grand Bay, NB,Can
132/E6 Grand Blanc, Mi,US
124/D3 Grand Canyon Nat'l Park, Az,US
98/C5 Grand Cape Mount (co.), Libr.
116/E4 Grand Cayman (isl.), Cay.
122/F2 Grand Centre, Ab,Can
122/D4 Grand Coulee (dam), Wa,US
113/K7 Grande (bay), Arg.
113/K8 Grande (riv.), Arg.
108/F7 Grande (riv.), Bol.
110/K8 Grande (isl.), Braz.
110/J7 Grande (riv.), Braz.
117/F6 Grande (pt.), Pan.
113/T11 Grande (stream), Uru.
122/D2 Grande Cache, Ab,Can
103/G5 Grande Comore (isl.), Com.
60/C1 Grande, Corno (peak), It.
109/H4 Grande de Gurupá, Braz.
60/C4 Grande, Monte (peak), It.
122/D2 Grande Prairie, Ab,Can
96/H4 Grand 'Erg de Bilma (des.), Niger
96/E1 Grand Erg Occidental (des.), Alg.
96/G1 Grand Erg Oriental (des.), Alg.
128/C4 Grande, Rio (riv.), Mex., US
52/B1 Grande-Synthe, Fr.
117/J4 Grande-Terre (isl.), Guad.
127/H2 Grand Falls, NB,Can
127/L1 Grand Falls, Nf,Can
122/D3 Grand Forks, BC,Can
123/J4 Grand Forks, ND,US
52/B2 Grand-Fort-Philippe, Fr.
126/C3 Grand Haven, Mi,US
125/H2 Grand Island, Ne,US
129/F4 Grand Isle, La,US
98/D5 Grand Jide (co.), Libr.
124/E3 Grand Junction, Co,US
125/J3 Grand Lake O'The Cherokees (lake), Ok,US
127/H2 Grand Manan (isl.), NB,Can
123/L4 Grand Marais, Mn,US
52/C6 Grand Marin (riv.), Fr.
127/F2 Grand-Mère, Qu,Can
127/K2 Grand Miquelon (isl.), StP.
54/C5 Grand Mont Ruan (mtn.), Fr.
58/A3 Grândola, Port.
123/L4 Grand Portage Nat'l Mon., Mn,US
53/D5 Grandpré, Fr.
123/J2 Grand Rapids, Mb,Can
126/C3 Grand Rapids, Mi,US
123/K4 Grand Rapids, Mn,US
56/F5 Grand Rhône (riv.), Fr.
122/F5 Grand Teton Nat'l Park, Wy,US
117/G3 Grand Turk, Trks.
47/F3 Grand Union (can.), Eng,UK
123/H3 Grandview, Mb,Can
122/D4 Grandview, Wa,US
112/C2 Graneros, Chile
42/E3 Granfjället (peak), Swe.
45/F3 Grange, Eng,UK
130/L3 Granger (mtn.), Yk,Can
122/D4 Grangeville, Id,US
122/B2 Granisle, BC,Can
122/F4 Granite (peak), Mt,US
126/B4 Granite City, Il,US
109/K4 Granja, Braz.
112/D5 Gran Laguna Salada (lake), Arg.
59/G2 Granollers, Sp.
57/G4 Gran Paradiso Nat'l Park, It.
57/J3 Gran Pilastro (peak), It.
59/Y16 Gran Tarajal, Canl.,Sp.
45/H6 Grantham, Eng,UK
43/D2 Grantown-on-Spey, Sc,UK
124/F4 Grants, NM,US
126/A2 Grantsburg, Wi,US
122/C5 Grants Pass, Or,US
108/C5 Gran Vilaya (ruins), Peru
123/H1 Granville (lake), Mb,Can
56/C2 Granville, Fr.
132/B3 Grapeview-Allyn, Wa,US
51/F2 Grasberg, Ger.
45/E3 Grasmere, Eng,UK
57/G5 Grasse, Fr.
127/Q9 Grassie, On,Can
45/G3 Grassington, Eng,UK
122/G3 Grasslands Nat'l Park, Sk,Can
62/B2 Gratkorn, Aus.
55/F4 Graubünden (canton), Swi.
56/E5 Graulhet, Fr.
50/C5 Grave, Neth.
122/G3 Gravelbourg, Sk,Can
52/B2 Gravelines, Fr.
126/E2 Gravenhurst, On,Can
47/G4 Gravesend, Eng,UK
52/A5 Gravigny, Fr.
60/E2 Gravina di Puglia, It.
117/G4 Gravois (pt.), Haiti
56/B3 Gray, Fr.
126/C2 Grayling, Mi,US
47/G4 Grays, Eng,UK
122/F5 Grays (lake), Id,US
122/B4 Grays (har.), Wa,US
132/P15 Grayslake, Il,US
123/H3 Grayson, Sk,Can
57/L3 Graz, Aus.
91/C4 Great (lake), Austl.
123/G3 Great (plains), Can., US
38/E3 Great (lakes), NAm.
124/C2 Great (basin), US
117/F2 Great Abaco (isl.), Bahm.
49/L5 Great Alföld (plain), Hun.
89/B4 Great Australian (bight), Austl.
117/F3 Great Bahama (bank), Bahm.
47/F2 Great Barford, Eng,UK
90/B2 Great Barrier Reef Marine Park, Austl.
47/G2 Great Barton, Eng,UK
124/D3 Great Basin Nat'l Park, Nv,US
118/D2 Great Bear (lake), NW,Can
125/H3 Great Bend, Ks,US
102/C3 Great Brak (riv.), SAfr.
43/E3 Great Britain (isl.), UK
39/P5 Great Coco (isl.), Burma
47/G2 Great Cornard, Eng,UK
122/F5 Great Divide (basin), Wyo,US
91/B3 Great Dividing (range), Austl.
45/H4 Great Driffield, Eng,UK
47/G3 Great Dunmow, Eng,UK
99/F5 Greater Accra (reg.), Gha.
117/G4 Greater Antilles (arch.), NAm.
67/L3 Greater Barsuki (des.), Kaz.
47/F3 Greater London (co.), Eng,UK
45/F5 Greater Manchester (co.), Eng,UK
86/C4 Greater Sunda (isls.), Indo.
117/F3 Great Exuma (isl.), Bahm.
122/F4 Great Falls, Mt,US
102/D4 Great Fish (pt.), SAfr.
102/D4 Great Fish (riv.), SAfr.
47/F2 Great Gransden, Eng,UK
117/F3 Great Guana Cay (isl.), Bahm.
45/G2 Greatham, Eng,UK
45/F4 Great Harwood, Eng,UK
84/D2 Great Himalaya (range), Asia
117/G3 Great Inagua (isl.), Bahm.
84/A2 Great Indian (des.), India, Pak.
102/C3 Great Karoo (reg.), SAfr.
102/D4 Great Kei (riv.), SAfr.
46/D2 Great Malvern, Eng,UK
47/E3 Great Milton, Eng,UK
46/B5 Great Mis Tor (hill), Eng,UK
131/G5 Great Neck, NY,US
85/F6 Great Nicobar (isl.), India
47/G1 Great Ouse (riv.), Eng,UK
91/C4 Great Oyster (bay), Austl.
129/J3 Great Pee Dee (riv.), SC,US
101/A4 Great Rift (val.), Afr.
101/B4 Great Ruaha (riv.), Tanz.
124/D2 Great Salt (lake), Ut,US
124/D2 Great Salt Lake (des.), Ut,US
125/F3 Great Sand Dunes Nat'l Mon., Co,US
100/A3 Great Sand Sea (des.), Egypt, Libya
92/B6 Great Sandy (des.), Austl.
124/B2 Great Sandy (des.), Or,US
90/D4 Great Sandy Nat'l Park, Austl.
98/B4 Great Scarcies (riv.), Gui., SLeo.
47/G2 Great Shelford, Eng,UK
45/F3 Great Shunner Fell (mtn.), Eng,UK
118/E2 Great Slave (lake), NW,Can
129/H3 Great Smoky Mts. Nat'l Park, NC, Tn,US
131/G5 Great South (bay), NY,US
47/G4 Great Stour (riv.), Eng,UK
83/B3 Great Tenasserim (riv.), Burma
46/B5 Great Torrington, Eng,UK
92/B7 Great Victoria (des.), Austl.
81/B3 Great Wall (ruins), China
91/C4 Great Western Tiers (mts.), Austl.
102/B4 Great Winterhoek (peak), SAfr.
46/D2 Great Witley, Eng,UK
47/H1 Great Yarmouth, Eng,UK
74/F3 Great Zab (riv.), Iraq, Turk.
104/F5 Great Zimbabwe (ruins), Zim.
99/H2 Grébon (peak), Niger
74/K4 Greco (cape), Cyp.
60/D2 Greco (peak), It.
58/C2 Gredos (range), Sp.
41/G5 Greece
125/F2 Greeley, Co,US
119/S6 Greely (fjord), NW,Can
91/D3 Green (cape), Austl.
126/C4 Green (riv.), Ky,US
123/M4 Green (bay), Mi, Wi,US
124/E3 Green (riv.), Ut, Wy,US
127/G3 Green (mts.), Vt,US
126/B2 Green Bay, Wi,US
131/K7 Greenbelt, Md,US
126/C4 Greencastle, In,US
129/H4 Green Cove Springs, Fl,US
132/Q14 Greendale, Wi,US
129/H2 Greeneville, Tn,US
126/C4 Greenfield, In,US
127/F3 Greenfield, Ma,US
132/P14 Greenfield, Wi,US
127/P7 Greenfield Park, Qu,Can
131/K7 Green Haven, Md,US
44/C2 Greenisland, NI,UK
115/R2 Greenland (sea)
115/N2 Greenland (Kalaallit Nunaat) (dpcy.), Den.
43/D3 Greenlaw, Sc,UK
43/C3 Greenock, Sc,UK
130/K2 Greenough (mtn.), Ak,US
127/R8 Green River, On,Can
124/E3 Green River, Ut,US
122/F5 Green River, Wy,US
129/G3 Greensboro, Al,US
129/J2 Greensboro, NC,US
126/C4 Greensburg, In,US
126/E3 Greensburg, Pa,US
127/Q9 Greensville, On,Can
124/E5 Green Valley, Az,US
131/J7 Green Valley, Md,US
98/C5 Greenville, Libr.
129/G4 Greenville, Al,US
124/B2 Greenville, Ca,US
126/C4 Greenville, Ky,US
126/C3 Greenville, Mi,US
129/F3 Greenville, Ms,US
129/J3 Greenville, NC,US
126/C3 Greenville, Oh,US
129/H3 Greenville, SC,US
128/D3 Greenville, Tx,US
132/D3 Greenwater (riv.), Wa,US
131/G4 Greenwich, Ct,US
127/R8 Greenwood, On,Can
129/F3 Greenwood, Ms,US
131/F4 Greenwood (lake), NJ, NY,US
129/H3 Greenwood, SC,US
129/H3 Greenwood (lake), SC,US
125/J4 Greers Ferry (lake), Ar,US
44/B6 Greese (riv.), Ire.
50/D6 Grefrath, Ger.
108/D5 Gregório (riv.), Braz.
90/A2 Gregory (range), Austl.
123/J5 Gregory, SD,US
49/G1 Greifswald, Ger.
49/G1 Greifswalder Bodden (bay), Ger.
62/B2 Greimberg (peak), Aus.
48/G3 Greiz, Ger.
65/N4 Gremyachinsk, Rus.
42/D4 Grenå, Den.
117/J5 Grenada
129/F3 Grenada, Ms,US
54/D3 Grenchen, Swi.
123/H3 Grenfell, Sk,Can
56/F4 Grenoble, Fr.
42/E2 Gressåmoen Nat'l Park, Nor.
45/E2 Greta (riv.), Eng,UK
45/F3 Greta (riv.), Eng,UK
123/J3 Gretna, Mb,Can
45/E2 Gretna, Sc,UK
129/F4 Gretna, La,US
47/F1 Gretton, Eng,UK
52/B6 Gretz-Armainvilliers, Fr.
50/B5 Grevelingendam (dam), Neth.
51/E4 Greven, Ger.
61/G2 Grevená, Gre.
50/D6 Grevenbroich, Ger.
53/F4 Grevenmacher (dist.), Lux.
48/F2 Grevesmühlen, Ger.
50/A5 Grevlingen (chan.), Neth.
90/A5 Grey (range), Austl.
127/K2 Grey (riv.), Nf,Can
44/C2 Grey (pt.), NI,UK
44/C2 Grey Abbey, NI,UK
122/F4 Greybull, Wy,US
130/L3 Grey Hunter (peak), Yk,Can
89/H7 Greymouth, NZ
90/B2 Grey Peaks Nat'l Park, Austl.
45/F2 Greystoke, Eng,UK
44/B5 Greystones, Ire.
103/E3 Greytown, SAfr.
53/D2 Grez-Doiceau, Belg.
46/B6 Gribbin (pt.), Eng,UK
50/C2 Griend (isl.), Neth.
129/G3 Griffin, Ga,US
91/C2 Griffith, Austl.
132/R16 Griffith, In,US
52/B6 Grigny, Fr.
91/C4 Grim (cape), Austl.
52/D2 Grimbergen, Belg.
46/D2 Grimley, Eng,UK
48/G1 Grimmen, Ger.
127/Q9 Grimsby, On,Can
45/H4 Grimsby, Eng,UK
42/N6 Grimsey (isl.), Ice.
42/D4 Grimstad, Nor.
119/S7 Grinnel (pen.), NW,Can
62/B2 Grintavec (peak), Slov.
102/E3 Griqualand East (reg.), SAfr.
102/C2 Griqualand West (reg.), SAfr.
52/A2 Gris Nez (cape), Fr.
132/K10 Grizzly (bay), Ca,US
62/C3 Grmeč (mtn.), Bosn.
53/D1 Grobbendonk, Belg.
49/J3 Grodków, Pol.
49/M2 Grodno, Bela.
64/E5 Grodno Obl., Bela.
49/J2 Grodzisk Wielkopolski, Pol.
50/D4 Groenlo, Neth.
128/D4 Groesbeck, Tx,US
50/C5 Groesbeek, Neth.
56/B3 Groix (isl.), Fr.
49/L3 Grójec, Pol.
48/F1 Grömitz, Ger.
56/E4 Gronau, Ger.
50/D2 Groningen, Neth.
50/D2 Groningen (prov.), Neth.
55/H5 Gronlait (peak), It.
102/C4 Groot (riv.), SAfr.
50/D2 Grootegast, Neth.
104/C4 Grootfontein, Namb.
102/D2 Groot-Marico (riv.), SAfr.
102/C3 Grootvloer (salt pan), SAfr.
117/J5 Gros Islet, StL.
127/K1 Gros Morne (peak), Nf,Can

154

Gros M – Hebd

127/K1 **Gros Morne Nat'l Park,** Nf,Can
56/F3 **Grosne** (riv.), Fr.
51/G6 **Grossalmerode,** Ger.
51/E3 **Grosse Aa** (riv.), Ger.
132/F7 **Grosse Ile,** Mi,US
102/A2 **Grosse Münzenberg** (peak), Namb.
53/G2 **Grosse Nister** (riv.), Ger.
51/F3 **Grossenkneten,** Ger.
132/G7 **Grosse Pointe,** Mi,US
132/G7 **Grosse Pointe Farms,** Mi,US
132/G7 **Grosse Pointe Park,** Mi,US
132/G7 **Grosse Pointe Shores,** Mi,US
132/G7 **Grosse Pointe Woods,** Mi,US
57/K2 **Grosser Arber** (peak), Ger.
51/G3 **Grosser Aue** (riv.), Ger.
48/F3 **Grosser Beer-Berg** (peak), Ger.
57/L3 **Grosser Bösenstein** (peak), Aus.
51/F1 **Grosser Knechtsand** (isl.), Ger.
49/H4 **Grosser Peilstein** (peak), Aus.
57/L3 **Grosser Priel** (peak), Aus.
49/H5 **Grosser Pyhrgas** (peak), Aus.
57/K2 **Grosser Rachel** (peak), Ger.
51/E2 **Grosses Meer** (lake), Ger.
62/A2 **Grosses Wiesbachhorn** (peak), Aus.
60/B1 **Grosseto,** It.
57/H2 **Grossgerau,** Ger.
57/K3 **Grossglockner** (peak), Aus.
51/H1 **Grosshansdorf,** Ger.
57/H5 **Grosso** (cape), Fr.
53/F5 **Grossrosseln,** Ger.
53/E2 **Grote Gete** (riv.), Belg.
53/D1 **Grote Nete** (riv.), Belg.
123/J4 **Groton,** SD,US
60/E2 **Grottaglie,** It.
53/E3 **Grotte de Han,** Belg.
59/E1 **Grottes de Bétharram,** Fr.
122/D2 **Grouard Mission,** Ab,Can
126/D1 **Groundhog** (riv.), On,Can
50/C2 **Grouw,** Neth.
47/E3 **Grove,** Eng,UK
125/J3 **Grove,** Ok,US
124/B4 **Grover City,** Ca,US
128/E4 **Groves,** Tx,US
131/J8 **Groveton,** Va,US
67/H4 **Groznyy,** Rus.
63/H4 **Grudovo,** Bul.
49/K2 **Grudziądz,** Pol.
45/E2 **Grune** (pt.), Eng,UK
66/F1 **Gryazi,** Rus.
49/H2 **Gryfice,** Pol.
49/H2 **Gryfino,** Pol.
112/B4 **Guabun** (pt.), Chile
117/F3 **Guacanayabo** (gulf), Cuba
110/D2 **Guaçuí,** Braz.
117/P9 **Guadalajara,** Mex.
58/D2 **Guadalajara,** Sp.
92/E6 **Guadalcanal** (isl.), Sol.
58/E4 **Guadalentín** (riv.), Sp.
58/D3 **Guadalimlar** (riv.), Sp.
59/N8 **Guadalix** (riv.), Sp.
59/E2 **Guadalope** (riv.), Sp.
58/D4 **Guadalquivir** (riv.), Sp.
117/F6 **Guadalupe,** Pan.
58/C3 **Guadalupe** (range), Sp.
128/B4 **Guadalupe** (peak), Tx,US
128/D4 **Guadalupe** (riv.), Tx,US
128/B4 **Guadalupe Mts. Nat'l Park,** Tx,US
59/M8 **Guadarrama** (pass), Sp.
58/C2 **Guadarrama** (range), Sp.
58/C3 **Guadarrama** (riv.), Sp.
117/J4 **Guadeloupe** (dpcy.), Fr.
117/J4 **Guadeloupe** (passage), NAm.
58/B4 **Guadiana** (riv.), Sp., Port.
58/D4 **Guadiana Menor** (riv.), Sp.
58/D4 **Guadix,** Sp.
112/B4 **Guafo** (chan.), Chile
112/B4 **Guafo** (isl.), Chile
110/B4 **Guaíba,** Braz.
110/B4 **Guaíba** (riv.), Braz.
108/F2 **Guaiquinima** (peak), Ven.
110/B2 **Guaíra,** Braz.
112/B4 **Guaiteca** (isl.), Chile
108/E6 **Guajará-Mirim,** Braz.
117/G5 **Guajira** (pen.), Col., Ven.
124/B3 **Gualala,** Ca,US
60/C1 **Gualdo Tadino,** It.
112/F2 **Gualeguay,** Arg.
112/F2 **Gualeguay** (riv.), Arg.
112/F2 **Gualeguaychú,** Arg.
112/D4 **Gualicho** (val.), Arg.
92/D3 **Guam** (isl.), PacUS
112/B5 **Guamblin** (isl.), Chile
110/K7 **Guanabara** (bay), Braz.
116/A3 **Guanajuato,** Mex.
116/A3 **Guanajuato** (state), Mex.
109/K6 **Guanambi,** Braz.
117/H6 **Guanare,** Ven.
117/H6 **Guanare** (riv.), Ven.
81/C3 **Guancen Shan** (mtn.), China
81/B3 **Guandi Shan** (mtn.), China
85/K3 **Guangdong** (prov.), China
81/D5 **Guangming Ding** (peak), China
85/J3 **Guangxi Zhuangzu Zizhiqu** (aut. reg.), China
82/C2 **Guangze,** China
82/B3 **Guangzhou** (Canton), China
110/D1 **Guanhães,** Braz.
117/J6 **Guanipa** (riv.), Ven.
117/F3 **Guantánamo,** Cuba
81/G6 **Guanting** (res.), China
81/D4 **Guanyun,** China
110/B4 **Guaporé,** Braz.
108/F6 **Guaporé** (riv.), Braz.
59/E1 **Guara** (peak), Sp.
109/L5 **Guarabira,** Braz.
109/J5 **Guaraí,** Braz.
110/B3 **Guaramirim,** Braz.
108/C4 **Guaranda,** Ecu.
110/D2 **Guarapari,** Braz.
110/B3 **Guarapuava,** Braz.
110/B2 **Guararapes,** Braz.
110/G8 **Guararema,** Braz.
110/H7 **Guaratinguetá,** Braz.
110/B3 **Guaratuba,** Braz.
58/B2 **Guarda,** Port.
58/B2 **Guarda** (dist.), Port.
58/B3 **Guareña,** Sp.
108/E2 **Guárico** (res.), Ven.
117/H6 **Guárico** (riv.), Ven.
110/G9 **Guarujá,** Braz.
110/G8 **Guarulhos,** Braz.
117/N8 **Guasave,** Mex.
116/C4 **Guatemala**
116/C5 **Guatemala** (cap.), Guat.
110/G6 **Guaxupé,** Braz.
117/H4 **Guayama,** PR
108/C4 **Guayaquil,** Ecu.
108/B4 **Guayaquil** (gulf), Ecu.
108/E6 **Guayaramerín,** Bol.
117/M8 **Guaymas,** Mex.
65/N4 **Gubakha,** Rus.
49/H3 **Guben,** Ger.
49/H3 **Gubin,** Pol.
66/F2 **Gubkin,** Rus.
76/E2 **Guchin-Us,** Mong.
59/E2 **Gúdar** (range), Sp.
51/G6 **Gudensberg,** Ger.
67/H4 **Gudermes,** Rus.
84/D4 **Gudivāda,** India
84/C5 **Gūdūr,** India
58/D1 **Guecho,** Sp.
98/B1 **Guelb Azefal** (mts.), Mrta.
126/D3 **Guelph,** On,Can
96/C2 **Guelta Zemmur,** WSah.
53/F5 **Guénange,** Fr.
56/B3 **Guérande,** Fr.
56/D3 **Guéret,** Fr.
58/D1 **Guernica y Luno,** Sp.
56/B2 **Guernsey** (isl.), Chl,UK
116/B4 **Guerrero** (state), Mex.
56/F3 **Gueugnon,** Fr.
99/H3 **Guézaoua,** Niger
97/N6 **Gugē** (peak), Eth.
92/D3 **Guguan** (isl.), NMar.
82/B3 **Gui** (riv.), China
59/X16 **Guía de Isora,** Sp.
108/F2 **Guiana Highlands** (mts.), SAm.
116/B4 **Guichicovi,** Mex.
96/H6 **Guidder,** Camr.
98/B3 **Guidimaka** (reg.), Mrta.
60/C2 **Guidonia,** It.
98/D5 **Guiglo,** IvC.
52/B6 **Guignes,** Fr.
52/C5 **Guignicourt,** Fr.
82/D5 **Guihulngan,** Phil.
47/F4 **Guildford,** Eng,UK
56/F4 **Guilherand,** Fr.
85/K2 **Guilin,** China
119/J3 **Guillaume-Delisle** (lake), Qu,Can
58/B4 **Guillena,** Sp.
46/C1 **Guilsfield,** Wal,UK
58/A2 **Guimarães,** Port.
81/D4 **Guimeng Ding** (mtn.), China
98/C4 **Guinea**
96/F7 **Guinea** (gulf), Afr.
98/B3 **Guinea-Bissau**
56/B2 **Guingamp,** Fr.
56/A2 **Guipavas,** Fr.
109/H7 **Guiratinga,** Braz.
117/J5 **Güiria,** Ven.
45/G2 **Guisborough,** Eng,UK
52/C4 **Guise,** Fr.
45/G4 **Guiseley,** Eng,UK
58/B1 **Guitiriz,** Sp.
82/B2 **Guiyang,** China
85/J2 **Guiyang,** China
85/J2 **Guizhou** (prov.), China
56/C4 **Gujan-Mestras,** Fr.
84/B3 **Gujarāt** (state), India
73/K2 **Gūjar Khān,** Pak.
73/K2 **Gujrānwāla,** Pak.
73/K2 **Gujrāt,** Pak.
66/F2 **Gukovo,** Rus.
76/E4 **Gulang,** China
84/C4 **Gulbarga,** India
53/G3 **Guldenbach** (riv.), Ger.
82/C3 **Guleitou,** China
129/F4 **Gulfport,** Ms,US
129/G4 **Gulf Shores,** Al,US
68/G5 **Gulistan,** Uzb.
77/J2 **Guliya** (peak), China
44/B2 **Gulladuff,** NI,UK
122/F3 **Gull Lake,** Sk,Can
74/C3 **Gülnar,** Turk.
53/E2 **Gulpen,** Neth.
101/B2 **Gulu,** Ugan.
63/G4 **Gŭlŭbovo,** Bul.
104/D4 **Gumare,** Bots.
79/F2 **Gumma** (pref.), Japan
51/E6 **Gummersbach,** Ger.
66/E4 **Gümüşhacıköy,** Turk.
74/D2 **Gümüşhane,** Turk.
97/N5 **Guna** (peak), Eth.
84/C3 **Guna,** India
74/E2 **Güneydogu Toroslar** (mts.), Turk.
123/J2 **Gunisao** (lake), Mb,Can
123/J2 **Gunisao** (riv.), Mb,Can
91/D1 **Gunnedah,** Austl.
124/F3 **Gunnison,** Co,US
124/F3 **Gunnison** (riv.), Co,US
124/E3 **Gunnison,** Ut,US
75/B4 **Gunt** (riv.), Taj.
129/G3 **Guntersville,** Al,US
129/G3 **Guntersville** (lake), Al,US
84/D4 **Guntūr,** India
55/G1 **Günz** (riv.), Ger.
57/J2 **Gunzenhausen,** Ger.
81/C4 **Guo** (riv.), China
97/N6 **Gurage** (peak), Eth.
63/G2 **Gura Humorului,** Rom.
111/F2 **Gurai** (mts.), Braz.
76/B2 **Gurbantünggut** (des.), China
73/L2 **Gurdāspur,** India
109/K6 **Gurguéia** (riv.), Braz.
117/J6 **Guri, Embalse de** (res.), Ven.
57/L3 **Gurk** (riv.), Aus.
57/K3 **Gurkthaler** (mts.), Aus.
132/Q15 **Gurnee,** Il,US
63/J5 **Gürsu,** Turk.
109/J6 **Gurupi,** Braz.
109/J4 **Gurupi** (mts.), Braz.
109/J4 **Gurupi** (riv.), Braz.
84/B3 **Guru Sikhar** (mtn.), India
76/G2 **Gurvandzagal,** Mong.
67/J3 **Gur'yev,** Kaz.
67/J3 **Gur'yev Obl.,** Kaz.
64/J5 **Gus'-Khrustal'nyy,** Rus.
60/A3 **Guspini,** It.
48/G2 **Güstrow,** Ger.
51/F5 **Gütersloh,** Ger.
125/H4 **Guthrie,** Ok,US
125/G4 **Guthrie,** Tx,US
42/E3 **Gutulia Nat'l Park,** Nor.
108/G3 **Guyana**
52/B6 **Guyancourt,** Fr.
129/H2 **Guyandotte** (riv.), WV,US
81/B2 **Guyang,** China
56/C4 **Guyenne** (reg.), Fr.
91/E1 **Guy Fawkes Riv. Nat'l Park,** Austl.
47/G1 **Guyhirn,** Eng,UK
125/G3 **Guymon,** Ok,US
76/F4 **Guyuan,** China
76/H3 **Guyuan,** China
117/N7 **Guzmán** (lake), Mex.
73/H3 **Gwādar,** Pak.
84/C2 **Gwalior,** India
104/E5 **Gwanda,** Zim.
47/F1 **Gwash** (riv.), Eng,UK
46/C2 **Gwaunceste** (mtn.), Wal,UK
49/J2 **Gwda** (riv.), Pol.
46/A6 **Gweek,** Eng,UK
46/D3 **Gwent** (co.), Wal,UK
45/E5 **Gwersyllt,** Wal,UK
104/E4 **Gweru,** Zim.
91/D1 **Gwydir** (riv.), Austl.
44/D5 **Gwynedd** (co.), Wal,UK
67/H4 **Gyandzhe,** Azer.
77/D5 **Gyaring** (lake), China
99/F5 **Gyasikan,** Gha.
68/H2 **Gyda** (pen.), Rus.
90/D4 **Gympie,** Austl.
85/G4 **Gyobingauk,** Burma
62/E2 **Gyoma,** Hun.
62/D2 **Gyöngyös,** Hun.
62/C2 **Győr,** Hun.
62/C2 **Győr-Sopron** (co.), Hun.
62/E2 **Gyula,** Hun.

H

52/D2 **Haacht,** Belg.
50/D4 **Haaksbergen,** Neth.
52/D2 **Haaltert,** Belg.
50/E6 **Haan,** Ger.
93/H6 **Ha'apai Group** (isls.), Tonga
42/H2 **Haapavesi,** Fin.
64/D4 **Haapsalu,** Est.
57/J2 **Haar,** Ger.
57/G2 **Haardt** (mts.), Ger.
50/B4 **Haarlem,** Neth.
89/G7 **Haast,** NZ
73/J3 **Hab** (riv.), Pak.
53/E4 **Habay,** Belg.
72/D2 **Habbānīyah,** Iraq
85/F3 **Habiganj,** Bang.
79/L10 **Habikino,** Japan
77/N3 **Haboro,** Japan
77/N5 **Hachijō** (isl.), Japan
79/F3 **Hachiōji,** Japan
131/C3 **Hacienda Heights,** Ca,US
74/C2 **Hacılar,** Turk.
131/F5 **Hackensack,** NJ,US
131/F5 **Hackettstown,** NJ,US
83/D1 **Ha Coi,** Viet.
57/H1 **Hadamar,** Ger.
79/F3 **Hadano,** Japan
100/D4 **Hadarba, Ras** (cape), Sudan
97/J4 **Haddad** (wadi), Chad
47/F3 **Haddenham,** Eng,UK
43/D3 **Haddington,** Sc,UK
131/E6 **Haddonfield,** NJ,US
131/E6 **Haddon** (Westmont), NJ,US
73/G4 **Ḩadd, Ra's al** (pt.), Oman
99/H3 **Hadejia** (riv.), Nga.
51/F1 **Hadelner** (can.), Ger.
74/K5 **Ḩadera,** Isr.
48/E1 **Haderslev,** Den.
74/C3 **Hadım,** Turk.
62/E2 **Hajdú-Bihar** (co.), Hun.
118/F1 **Hadley** (bay), NW,Can
45/F1 **Hadrian's Wall** (ruins), Eng,UK
42/E1 **Hadselfjorden** (fjord), Nor.
80/C3 **Haeju,** NKor.
120/S9 **Haena** (pt.), Hi,US
74/D2 **Hafik,** Turk.
73/K2 **Hāfizābād,** Pak.
42/N7 **Hafnarfjördhur,** Ice.
72/E3 **Ḩafr al Bāţin,** SAr.
72/E2 **Haft Gel,** Iran
97/R5 **Hafun, Ras** (pt.), Som.
130/F4 **Hagemeister** (isl.), Ak,US
51/E6 **Hagen,** Ger.
51/E4 **Hagen am Teutoburger Wald,** Ger.
48/F2 **Hagenow,** Ger.
125/F4 **Hagerman,** NM,US
126/E4 **Hagerstown,** Md,US
78/B3 **Hagi,** Japan
83/D1 **Ha Giang,** Viet.
46/D2 **Hagley,** Eng,UK
53/F5 **Hagondange,** Fr.
43/A4 **Hags Head** (pt.), Ire.
123/G2 **Hague,** Sk,Can
56/C2 **Hague, Cap de la** (cape), Fr.
53/G6 **Haguenau,** Fr.
50/B4 **Hague, The** ('s-Gravenhage) (cap.), Neth.
92/D2 **Hahashima** (isl.), Jap.
51/H6 **Hahle** (riv.), Ger.
53/G3 **Hahnenbach** (riv.), Ger.
81/D3 **Hai** (riv.), China
79/L10 **Haibara,** Japan
77/J3 **Haicheng,** China
83/D1 **Hai Duong,** Viet.
74/K5 **Haifa** (dist.), Isr.
74/K5 **Haifa** (Ḩefa), Isr.
73/H2 **Haiger,** Ger.
83/D1 **Hai Hau,** Viet.
83/B3 **Haikou,** China
77/H2 **Hailar,** China
77/J2 **Hailar** (riv.), China
126/E2 **Haileybury,** On,Can
47/G5 **Hailsham,** Eng,UK
85/J4 **Hainan** (prov.), China
82/B3 **Hainan** (str.), China
52/B2 **Hainaut** (prov.), Belg.
57/H1 **Hainburg,** Ger.
129/H4 **Haines City,** Fl,US
130/L3 **Haines Junction,** Yk,Can
51/H6 **Hainich** (mts.), Ger.
81/L9 **Haining,** China
83/D1 **Haiphong** (Hai Phong), Viet.
117/G4 **Haiti**
83/E2 **Hai Van** (pass), Viet.
85/K3 **Haixia** (str.), China
81/D4 **Haizhou** (bay), China
49/L5 **Hajdú-Bihar** (co.), Hun.
62/E2 **Hajdúböszormény,** Hun.
62/E2 **Hajdúdorog,** Hun.
62/E2 **Hajdúhadház,** Hun.
62/E2 **Hajdúnánás,** Hun.
62/E2 **Hajdúszoboszló,** Hun.
79/F1 **Hajiki-zaki** (pt.), Japan
49/M2 **Hajnówka,** Pol.
85/F2 **Hājo,** India
93/L5 **Hakahau,** Fr.Pol.
78/D3 **Hakken-san** (mtn.), Japan
77/N3 **Hakodate,** Japan
79/H7 **Hakone,** Japan
79/H8 **Hakone-Fuji-Izu Nat'l Park,** Japan
79/E2 **Hakui,** Japan
79/M10 **Hakusan,** Japan
79/E2 **Haku-san** (mtn.), Japan
79/E2 **Hakusan Nat'l Park,** Japan
73/J3 **Hāla,** Pak.
74/D3 **Ḩalab** (Aleppo), Syria
72/E1 **Ḩalabjah,** Iraq
100/D4 **Ḩalā'ib,** Sudan
42/D4 **Halden,** Nor.
48/F2 **Haldensleben,** Ger.
127/Q10 **Haldimand,** On,Can
76/G2 **Haldzan,** Mong.
101/C4 **Hale,** Tanz.
45/F5 **Hale,** Eng,UK
120/T10 **Haleakala Nat'l Park,** Hi,US
53/E2 **Halen,** Belg.
132/P14 **Hales Corners,** Wi,US
46/D2 **Halesowen,** Eng,UK
47/H2 **Halesworth,** Eng,UK
129/G3 **Haleyville,** Al,US
98/E5 **Half Assini,** Gha.
82/C6 **Half Moon** (shoal)
132/K12 **Half Moon Bay,** Ca,US
74/K6 **Ḩalhūl,** WBnk.
126/E2 **Haliburton** (hills), On,Can
90/B2 **Halifax** (bay), Austl.
127/J2 **Halifax** (cap.), NS,Can
45/G4 **Halifax,** Eng,UK
73/G3 **Halīl** (riv.), Iran
130/H1 **Halkett** (cape), Ak,US
119/K2 **Hall** (pen.), NW,Can
92/E4 **Hall** (isls.), Micr.
130/D3 **Hall** (isl.), Ak,US
42/E4 **Halland** (co.), Swe.
77/K5 **Halla-san** (mtn.), SKor.
52/D2 **Halle,** Belg.
51/F4 **Halle,** Ger.
42/E4 **Hällefors,** Swe.
57/K3 **Hallein,** Aus.
52/A4 **Hallencourt,** Fr.
48/F3 **Halle-Neustadt,** Ger.
105/M **Hallett** (cape), Ant.
128/D4 **Hallettsville,** Tx,US
123/J3 **Hallock,** Mn,US
48/B4 **Hallu** (riv.), Fr.
52/B3 **Hallue** (riv.), Fr.
52/C2 **Halluin,** Fr.
80/E5 **Hallyŏ Haesang Nat'l Park,** SKor.
87/G3 **Halmahera** (isl.), Indo.
87/G4 **Halmahera** (sea), Indo.
42/E4 **Halmstad,** Swe.
60/B4 **Ḩalq al Wādī,** Tun.
42/E4 **Hälsingborg,** Swe.
47/G3 **Halstead,** Eng,UK
50/B5 **Halsteren,** Neth.
76/C4 **Haltang** (riv.), China
45/H4 **Haltemprice,** Eng,UK
51/E5 **Haltern,** Ger.
127/Q8 **Halton Hills,** On,Can
45/F2 **Haltwhistle,** Eng,UK
51/E6 **Halver,** Ger.
51/E3 **Halverder Aa** (riv.), Ger.
52/C4 **Ham,** Fr.
78/C3 **Hamada,** Japan
72/E2 **Hamadān,** Iran
74/L4 **Ḩamāh,** Syria
79/M10 **Hamajima,** Japan
79/E3 **Hamakita,** Japan
79/E3 **Hamamatsu,** Japan
42/D3 **Hamar,** Nor.
100/C3 **Ḩamāţah, Jabal** (mtn.), Egypt
84/D6 **Hambantota,** SrL.
47/E5 **Hamble,** Eng,UK
45/G3 **Hambleton** (hills), Eng,UK
51/G3 **Hambühren,** Ger.
51/G1 **Hamburg,** Ger.
51/H1 **Hamburg** (state), Ger.
128/F3 **Hamburg,** Ar,US
126/E3 **Hamburg,** NY,US
42/G3 **Häme** (prov.), Fin.
63/G3 **Hämeenkyrö,** Fin.
42/H3 **Hämeenlinna,** Fin.
51/G4 **Hameln,** Ger.
47/H3 **Hamford Water** (inlet), Eng,UK
80/E2 **Hamgyŏng** (mts.), NKor.
80/E2 **Hamgyŏng-Bukto** (prov.), NKor.
80/D2 **Hamgyŏng-Namdo** (prov.), NKor.
80/D3 **Hamhŭng,** NKor.
80/D3 **Hamhŭng-Si** (prov.), NKor.
76/C3 **Hami,** China
119/L3 **Hamilton** (inlet), Nf,Can
127/Q9 **Hamilton,** On,Can
89/H6 **Hamilton,** NZ
43/C3 **Hamilton,** Sc,UK
129/G3 **Hamilton,** Al,US
132/L12 **Hamilton** (mt.), Ca,US
122/E4 **Hamilton,** Mt,US
126/C4 **Hamilton,** Oh,US
128/D4 **Hamilton,** Tx,US
84/D2 **Hamīrpur,** India
60/B4 **Hammāmāt** (gulf), Tun.
52/D1 **Hamme,** Belg.
51/F2 **Hamme** (riv.), Ger.
42/G1 **Hammerfest,** Nor.
50/D5 **Hamminkeln,** Ger.
132/R16 **Hammond,** In,US
129/F4 **Hammond,** La,US
53/E1 **Hamont-Achel,** Belg.
47/E4 **Hampshire** (co.), Eng,UK
47/E4 **Hampshire Downs** (hills), Eng,UK
126/E4 **Hampton,** Va,US
91/G6 **Hampton Park,** Austl.
96/H1 **Ḩamrā** (upland), Libya
132/F7 **Hamtramck,** Mi,US
79/H7 **Hamura,** Japan
81/C5 **Han** (riv.), China
82/C3 **Han** (riv.), China
80/D4 **Han** (riv.), SKor.
77/N4 **Hanamaki,** Japan
120/U11 **Hanamalo** (pt.), Hi,US
77/M5 **Hanamatsu,** Japan
101/B4 **Hanang** (peak), Tanz.
126/B2 **Hancock,** Mi,US
79/M10 **Handa,** Japan
81/C3 **Handan,** China
47/E1 **Handsworth,** Eng,UK
124/C3 **Hanford,** Ca,US
76/D2 **Hangayn** (mts.), Mong.
46/C5 **Hangingstone** (hill), Eng,UK
102/L11 **Hangklip** (cape), SAfr.
75/B5 **Hangu,** Pak.
81/L9 **Hangzhou,** China
76/C2 **Hanhöhiy** (mts.), Mong.
74/E2 **Hani,** Turk.
123/J4 **Hankinson,** ND,US
123/G3 **Hanley,** Sk,Can
122/F3 **Hanna,** Ab,Can
122/G5 **Hanna,** Wy,US
79/L10 **Hannan,** Japan
125/K3 **Hannibal,** Mo,US
79/H7 **Hannō,** Japan
51/G4 **Hannover,** Ger.
53/E2 **Hannut,** Belg.
42/E5 **Hanöbukten** (bay), Swe.
83/D1 **Hanoi** (Ha Noi) (cap.), Viet.
126/D2 **Hanover,** On,Can
113/J7 **Hanover** (isl.), Chile
127/F3 **Hanover,** NH,US
132/P16 **Hanover Park,** Il,US
84/C2 **Hānsi,** India
75/D3 **Hantengri Feng** (peak), China
119/J2 **Hantzsch** (riv.), NW,Can
84/B2 **Hanumāngarh,** India
76/E2 **Hanuy** (riv.), Mong.
76/F5 **Hanzhong,** China
93/L6 **Hao** (atoll), FrPol.
42/H2 **Haparanda,** Swe.
119/K3 **Happy Valley-Goose Bay,** Nf,Can
76/D4 **Har** (lake), China
76/C2 **Har** (lake), Mong.
76/F2 **Haraa** (riv.), Mong.
79/G2 **Haramachi,** Japan
73/K2 **Harappa** (ruins), Pak.
104/F4 **Harare** (cap.), Zim.
76/F2 **Har-Ayrag,** Mong.
98/C5 **Harbel,** Libr.
77/K2 **Harbin,** China
127/L2 **Harbour Breton,** Nf,Can
47/E2 **Harbury,** Eng,UK
84/C3 **Harda,** India
42/C3 **Hardangervidda Nat'l Park,** Nor.
102/B2 **Hardap** (dam), Namb.
51/H3 **Hardau** (riv.), Ger.
51/G5 **Hardegsen,** Ger.
50/D3 **Hardenberg,** Neth.
50/C4 **Harderwijk,** Neth.
122/G4 **Hardin,** Mt,US
73/L3 **Hardwār,** India
113/K8 **Hardy** (pen.), Chile
127/L1 **Hare** (bay), Nf,Can
52/C2 **Harelbeke,** Belg.
51/E3 **Haren,** Ger.
50/D2 **Haren,** Neth.
97/P6 **Hārer,** Eth.
74/N8 **Har Eval** (Jabal 'Aybāl) (mtn.), WBnk.
97/P6 **Hargeysa,** Som.
63/G2 **Harghita** (co.), Rom.
63/G2 **Harghita** (peak), Rom.
86/B4 **Hari** (riv.), Indo.
84/C5 **Harihar,** India
78/D3 **Harima** (sound), Japan
50/B5 **Haringvliet** (chan.), Neth.
73/H2 **Harī rūd** (riv.), Afg.
126/D4 **Harlan,** Ky,US
44/D6 **Harlech,** Wal,UK
47/H2 **Harleston,** Eng,UK
50/C2 **Harlingen,** Neth.
128/D5 **Harlingen,** Tx,US
47/F3 **Harlington,** Eng,UK
122/F4 **Harlowton,** Mt,US
50/B4 **Harmelen,** Neth.
52/B3 **Harnes,** Fr.
122/D5 **Harney** (lake), Or,US
122/D5 **Harney** (val.), Or,US
123/H5 **Harney** (peak), SD,US
42/F3 **Härnösand,** Swe.
117/M8 **Haro** (cape), Mex.
58/D1 **Haro,** Sp.
47/F3 **Harpenden,** Eng,UK
130/L3 **Harper** (mtn.), Yk,Can
98/D5 **Harper,** Libr.
130/K3 **Harper** (mtn.), Ak,US
128/D2 **Harper,** Ks,US
132/G7 **Harper Woods,** Mi,US
126/E1 **Harricana** (riv.), Qu,Can
129/G3 **Harriman,** Tn,US
126/B4 **Harrisburg,** Il,US
125/G2 **Harrisburg,** Ne,US
126/E3 **Harrisburg** (cap.), Pa,US
48/E1 **Harrislee,** Ger.
102/E3 **Harrismith,** SAfr.
122/C3 **Harrison** (lake), BC,Can
119/L3 **Harrison** (cape), Nf,Can
130/H1 **Harrison** (bay), Ak,US
128/E2 **Harrison,** Ar,US
125/G2 **Harrison,** Ne,US
131/G5 **Harrison,** NY,US
126/E4 **Harrisonburg,** Va,US
126/C4 **Harrodsburg,** Ky,US
45/G4 **Harrogate,** Eng,UK
125/J3 **Harry S Truman** (res.), Mo,US
51/G2 **Harsefeld,** Ger.
51/F5 **Harsewinkel,** Ger.
42/F1 **Harstad,** Nor.
118/C2 **Hart** (riv.), Yk,Can
124/C2 **Hart** (lake), Or,US
102/C3 **Hartbeesrivier** (dry riv.), SAfr.
42/C3 **Hårteigen** (peak), Nor.
50/B5 **Hartelkanaal** (can.), Neth.
127/F3 **Hartford** (cap.), Ct,US
126/C3 **Hartford City,** In,US
125/H2 **Hartington,** Ne,US
46/B5 **Hartland,** Eng,UK
46/B4 **Hartland** (pt.), Eng,UK
46/D2 **Hartlebury,** Eng,UK
45/G2 **Hartlepool,** Eng,UK
47/G4 **Hartley,** Eng,UK
123/H3 **Hartney,** Mb,Can
102/D3 **Harts** (riv.), SAfr.
131/G4 **Hartsdale,** NY,US
129/G3 **Hartselle,** Al,US
47/E1 **Hartshill,** Eng,UK
132/B3 **Hartstene** (isl.), Wa,US
129/H3 **Hartwell,** Ga,US
129/H3 **Hartwell** (lake), Ga, SC,US
91/C4 **Hartz Mtn. Nat'l Park,** Austl.
53/G6 **Hartzviller,** Fr.
73/K3 **Hārūnābād,** Pak.
87/E3 **Harun, Bukit** (peak), Indo.
75/F2 **Har Us** (lake), Mong.
76/D2 **Har-Us** (riv.), Mong.
73/H2 **Hārūt** (riv.), Afg.
132/Q16 **Harvey,** Il,US
123/J4 **Harvey,** ND,US
47/H3 **Harwich,** Eng,UK
45/G5 **Harworth,** Eng,UK
84/C2 **Haryana** (state), India
51/H5 **Harz** (mts.), Ger.
51/E3 **Hase** (riv.), Ger.
51/E3 **Haselünne,** Ger.
79/M9 **Hashima,** Japan
78/D3 **Hashimoto,** Japan
96/D2 **Hasi el Farsía** (well), WSah.
73/K3 **Hāsilpur,** Pak.
128/D3 **Haskell,** Tx,US
47/F4 **Haslemere,** Eng,UK
45/F4 **Haslingden,** Eng,UK
45/F5 **Haslington,** Eng,UK
84/C5 **Hassan,** India
119/S7 **Hassel** (sound), NW,Can
53/E2 **Hasselt,** Belg.
50/D3 **Hasselt,** Neth.
57/J1 **Hassfurt,** Ger.
96/G1 **Hassi Messaoud,** Alg.
42/E4 **Hässleholm,** Swe.
89/H6 **Hastings,** NZ
47/G5 **Hastings,** Eng,UK
126/C3 **Hastings,** Mi,US
123/K4 **Hastings,** Mn,US
125/H2 **Hastings,** Ne,US
131/G4 **Hastings-on-Hudson,** NY,US
79/H7 **Hasuda,** Japan
79/M9 **Hatashō,** Japan
131/E5 **Hatboro,** Pa,US
125/F4 **Hatch,** NM,US
83/B5 **Hat Chao Mai Nat'l Park,** Thai.
113/J7 **Hatcher** (peak), Arg.
62/F3 **Haţeg,** Rom.
47/F3 **Hatfield,** Eng,UK
91/E1 **Hat Head Nat'l Park,** Austl.
45/G5 **Hathersage,** Eng,UK
84/C2 **Hāthras,** India
72/C4 **Ḩāţibah, Ra's** (pt.), SAr.
83/D4 **Ha Tien,** Viet.
83/D2 **Ha Tinh,** Viet.
83/B5 **Hat Nai Yang Nat'l Park,** Thai.
79/H7 **Hatogaya,** Japan
117/H4 **Hato Mayor,** DRep.
79/H7 **Hatoyama,** Japan
84/C3 **Hatta,** India
91/B2 **Hattah-Kulkyne Nat'l Park,** Austl.
50/D4 **Hattem,** Neth.
51/F2 **Hatten,** Ger.
129/K3 **Hatteras** (cape), NC,US
129/F4 **Hattiesburg,** Ms,US
51/E6 **Hattingen,** Ger.
45/G6 **Hatton,** Eng,UK
62/D2 **Hatvan,** Hun.
83/C5 **Hat Yai,** Thai.
83/E3 **Hau Bon,** Viet.
52/B2 **Haubourdin,** Fr.
97/Q6 **Haud** (reg.), Eth., Som.
42/C4 **Haugesund,** Nor.
83/D4 **Hau Giang** (riv.), Viet.
42/H2 **Haukipudas,** Fin.
131/G5 **Hauppauge,** NY,US
59/E1 **Hauskoa** (mtn.), Fr.
96/D1 **Haut Atlas** (mts.), Mor.
54/B1 **Haute-Marne** (dept.), Fr.
56/D2 **Haute-Normandie** (reg.), Fr.
127/G1 **Hauterive,** Qu,Can
54/B2 **Haute-Saône** (dept.), Fr.
54/C5 **Haute-Savoie** (dept.), Fr.
53/E3 **Hautes Fagnes** (uplands), Belg.
52/C3 **Hautmont,** Fr.
54/D2 **Haut-Rhin** (dept.), Fr.
52/B6 **Hauts-de-Seine** (dept.), Fr.
101/A2 **Haut-Zaire** (reg.), Zaire
116/E3 **Havana** (La Habana) (cap.), Cuba
93/V13 **Havannah** (chan.), NCal.
47/F5 **Havant,** Eng,UK
124/D4 **Havasu** (lake), Az, Ca,US
49/G2 **Havel** (riv.), Ger.
48/G2 **Havelland** (reg.), Ger.
129/J3 **Havelock,** NC,US
47/G3 **Havengore** (isl.), Eng,UK
46/B3 **Haverfordwest,** Wal,UK
47/G2 **Haverhill,** Eng,UK
127/G3 **Haverhill,** Ma,US
49/K4 **Havířov,** Czh.
51/E5 **Havixbeck,** Ger.
49/H4 **Havlíčkuv Brod,** Czh.
122/F3 **Havre,** Mt,US
127/J1 **Havre-Saint-Pierre,** Qu,Can
63/H5 **Havsa,** Turk.
120/S10 **Hawaii** (state), US
120/U11 **Hawaii** (isl.), Hi,US
93/H2 **Hawaiian** (isls.), Hi,US
120/U11 **Hawaii Volcanoes Nat'l Park,** Hi,US
72/E3 **Ḩawallī,** Kuw.
45/E5 **Hawarden,** Wal,UK
123/J5 **Hawarden,** Ia,US
89/H6 **Hawera,** NZ
45/F3 **Hawes,** Eng,UK
45/F2 **Haweswater** (res.), Eng,UK
43/D3 **Hawick,** Sc,UK
91/E2 **Hawke** (cape), Austl.
90/G8 **Hawkesbury** (riv.), Austl.
122/A2 **Hawkesbury** (isl.), BC,Can
126/F2 **Hawkesbury,** On,Can
72/E2 **Hawr al Ḩammār** (lake), Iraq
74/H6 **Ḩawsh 'Īsá,** Egypt
131/B3 **Hawthorne,** Ca,US
124/C3 **Hawthorne,** Nv,US
45/G3 **Haxby,** Eng,UK
90/C3 **Hay** (pt.), Austl.
118/E3 **Hay** (riv.), Ab, NW,Can
79/H7 **Hayama,** Japan
53/F5 **Hayange,** Fr.
45/F5 **Haydock,** Eng,UK
45/F2 **Haydon Bridge,** Eng,UK
118/G3 **Hayes** (riv.), Mb,Can
118/G2 **Hayes** (riv.), NW,Can
119/T7 **Hayes** (pen.), Grld.
130/J3 **Hayes** (mtn.), Ak,US
46/A6 **Hayle,** Eng,UK
46/A6 **Hayle** (riv.), Eng,UK
47/F5 **Hayling** (isl.), Eng,UK
128/E3 **Haynesville,** La,US
46/C2 **Hay on Wye,** Wal,UK
63/H5 **Hayrabolu,** Turk.
125/H3 **Hays,** Ks,US
125/H3 **Haysville,** Ks,US
132/K11 **Hayward,** Ca,US
126/B2 **Hayward,** Wi,US
47/F5 **Haywards Heath,** Eng,UK
73/G3 **Hazār** (mtn.), Iran
126/D4 **Hazard,** Ky,US
84/E3 **Hazāribag,** India
52/B2 **Hazebrouck,** Fr.
45/F5 **Hazel Grove,** Eng,UK
132/F7 **Hazel Park,** Mi,US
119/R7 **Hazen** (str.), NW,Can
130/E3 **Hazen** (bay), Ak,US
50/B4 **Hazerswoude-Dorp,** Neth.
129/F4 **Hazlehurst,** Ms,US
47/F3 **Hazlemere,** Eng,UK
131/F5 **Hazlet,** NJ,US
122/B2 **Hazleton** (mts.), BC,Can
126/F3 **Hazleton,** Pa,US
79/N10 **Hazu,** Japan
47/G1 **Heacham,** Eng,UK
47/G4 **Headcorn,** Eng,UK
45/G4 **Headingley,** Eng,UK
124/B3 **Healdsburg,** Ca,US
91/G5 **Healesville,** Austl.
45/G6 **Heanor,** Eng,UK
39/P8 **Heard** (isl.), Austl.
128/D4 **Hearne,** Tx,US
105/V **Hearst** (isl.), Ant.
126/D1 **Hearst,** On,Can
123/H4 **Heart** (riv.), ND,US
127/J1 **Heath** (pt.), Qu,Can
90/G9 **Heathcote Nat'l Park,** Austl.
47/G5 **Heathfield,** Eng,UK
128/D5 **Hebbronville,** Tx,US
45/F4 **Hebden Bridge,** Eng,UK

81/G6 **Hebei** (prov.), China
128/E3 **Heber Springs**, Ar,US
81/C4 **Hebi**, China
43/B2 **Hebrides** (isls.), Sc,UK
43/A2 **Hebrides, Outer** (isls.), Sc,UK
125/H2 **Hebron**, Ne,US
74/K6 **Hebron** (Al Khalīl), WBnk.
130/M5 **Hecate** (str.), BC,Can
85/J3 **Hechi**, China
53/E1 **Hechtel**, Belg.
45/H6 **Heckington**, Eng,UK
123/J4 **Hecla**, SD,US
119/R7 **Hecla and Griper** (bay), NW,Can
122/D3 **Hector** (peak), Ab,Can
42/E3 **Hedemora**, Swe.
42/D3 **Hedmark** (co.), Nor.
45/H4 **Hedon**, Eng,UK
51/E4 **Heek**, Ger.
50/B3 **Heemskerk**, Neth.
50/B4 **Heemstede**, Neth.
50/D4 **Heerde**, Neth.
50/C3 **Heerenveen**, Neth.
50/B3 **Heerhugowaard**, Neth.
53/E2 **Heerlen**, Neth.
53/E2 **Heers**, Belg.
52/F5 **Heesch**, Neth.
50/C6 **Heeze**, Neth.
74/K5 **Hefa** (Haifa), Isr.
81/D5 **Hefei**, China
77/L2 **Hegang**, China
55/E2 **Hegau** (reg.), Ger.
79/L10 **Heguri**, Japan
76/D4 **Hei** (riv.), China
81/B3 **Heicha Shan** (mtn.), China
48/E1 **Heide**, Ger.
91/G5 **Heidelberg**, Austl.
57/H2 **Heidelberg**, Ger.
103/E2 **Heidelberg**, SAfr.
129/F4 **Heidelberg**, Ms,US
50/D5 **Heiden**, Ger.
77/K1 **Heihe**, China
48/F1 **Heikendorf**, Ger.
102/D2 **Heilbron**, SAfr.
57/H2 **Heilbronn**, Ger.
48/F1 **Heiligenhafen**, Ger.
50/D6 **Heiligenhaus**, Ger.
51/H6 **Heiligenstadt**, Ger.
77/L2 **Heilong** (Amur) (riv.), China
50/B3 **Heiloo**, Neth.
42/N7 **Heimaey** (isl.), Ice.
50/D4 **Heino**, Neth.
42/H3 **Heinola**, Fin.
50/D6 **Heinsberg**, Ger.
81/C3 **Heituo Shan** (mtn.), China
79/M9 **Heiwa**, Japan
81/D3 **Hejian**, China
74/D2 **Hekimhan**, Turk.
79/M10 **Hekinan**, Japan
42/N7 **Hekla** (vol.), Ice.
76/F4 **Helan** (mts.), China
50/D6 **Helden**, Neth.
129/F3 **Helena**, Ar,US
122/E4 **Helena** (cap.), Mt,US
48/D1 **Helgoland** (isl.), Ger.
48/D1 **Helgoländer Bucht** (bay), Ger.
72/F3 **Helleh** (riv.), Iran
50/D4 **Hellendoorn**, Neth.
53/F3 **Hellenthal**, Ger.
50/B5 **Hellevoetsluis**, Neth.
58/E3 **Hellín**, Sp.
122/D4 **Hells Canyon Nat'l Rec. Area**, Id, Or,US
73/H2 **Helmand** (riv.), Afg.
48/F3 **Helme** (riv.), Ger.
130/K2 **Helmet** (mtn.), Ak,US
50/C6 **Helmond**, Neth.
45/G3 **Helmsley**, Eng,UK
48/F2 **Helmstedt**, Ger.
124/E3 **Helper**, Ut,US
45/F5 **Helsby**, Eng,UK
42/E4 **Helsingør**, Den.
42/H3 **Helsinki** (Helsingfors) (cap.), Fin.
46/A6 **Helston**, Eng,UK
42/G3 **Helvetinjärven Nat'l Park**, Fin.
52/C2 **Hem**, Fr.
52/B2 **Hem** (riv.), Fr.
47/F3 **Hemel Hempstead**, Eng,UK
51/E6 **Hemer**, Ger.
131/D3 **Hemet**, Ca,US
51/G4 **Hemmingen**, Ger.
51/G1 **Hemmoor**, Ger.
128/E4 **Hemphill**, Tx,US
131/G5 **Hempstead**, NY,US
47/H1 **Hemsby**, Eng,UK
45/G4 **Hemsworth**, Eng,UK
81/B4 **Henan** (prov.), China
58/D2 **Henares** (riv.), Sp.
56/C5 **Hendaye**, Fr.
63/K5 **Hendek**, Turk.
112/E3 **Henderson**, Arg.
93/N7 **Henderson** (isl.), Pitc.
126/C4 **Henderson**, Ky,US
129/J2 **Henderson**, NC,US
124/D3 **Henderson**, Nv,US
129/F3 **Henderson**, Tn,US
128/E3 **Henderson**, Tx,US
129/H3 **Hendersonville**, NC,US
129/G2 **Hendersonville**, Tn,US
50/B5 **Hendrik-Ido-Ambacht**, Neth.
102/D3 **Hendrik Verwoerdam** (res.), SAfr.
47/F5 **Henfield**, Eng,UK
81/L8 **Heng** (isl.), China
85/G2 **Hengduan** (mts.), China
50/D4 **Hengelo**, Neth.
81/C3 **Heng Shan** (mtn.), China
81/C3 **Hengshui**, China
82/B2 **Hengyang**, China
52/B3 **Hénin-Beaumont**, Fr.
47/E2 **Henley-in-Arden**, Eng,UK
47/F3 **Henley-on-Thames**, Eng,UK
56/B3 **Hennebont**, Fr.
53/G2 **Hennef**, Ger.
53/E2 **Henri-Chapelle**, Belg.
128/D3 **Henrietta**, Tx,US
119/H3 **Henrietta Maria** (cape), On,Can
130/M5 **Henry** (cape), BC,Can
124/E3 **Henry** (mts.), Ut,US
125/J4 **Henryetta**, Ok,US
52/C3 **Hensies**, Belg.
76/F2 **Hentiyn** (mts.), Mong.
85/G4 **Henzada**, Burma
42/N6 **Heradhsvötn** (riv.), Ice.
73/H2 **Herāt**, Afg.
59/G1 **Hérault** (riv.), Fr.
90/B2 **Herbert** (riv.), Austl.
122/G3 **Herbert**, Sk,Can
90/B2 **Herbert Riv. Falls Nat'l Park**, Austl.
52/B5 **Herblay**, Fr.
62/D4 **Hercegnovi**, Yugo.
132/K10 **Hercules**, Ca,US
51/E6 **Herdecke**, Ger.
53/G2 **Herdorf**, Ger.
116/E6 **Heredia**, CR
46/D2 **Hereford**, Eng,UK
128/C3 **Hereford**, Tx,US
46/D2 **Hereford & Worcester** (co.), Eng,UK
93/L6 **Hereheretue** (isl.), FrPol.
63/J5 **Hereke**, Turk.
58/C3 **Herencia**, Sp.
53/D1 **Herentals**, Belg.
51/F4 **Herford**, Ger.
125/H3 **Herington**, Ks,US
55/F3 **Herisau**, Swi.
53/E2 **Herk** (riv.), Belg.
53/E2 **Herk-de-Stad**, Belg.
76/G2 **Herlen** (riv.), Mong.
129/F2 **Hermann**, Mo,US
51/H3 **Hermannsburg**, Ger.
52/B5 **Hermes**, Fr.
122/D4 **Hermiston**, Or,US
74/K5 **Hermon** (mtn.), Leb., Syria
131/B3 **Hermosa Beach**, Ca,US
117/M8 **Hermosillo**, Mex.
112/E2 **Hernando**, Arg.
129/F3 **Hernando**, Ms,US
58/E1 **Hernani**, Sp.
52/D2 **Herne**, Belg.
51/E5 **Herne**, Ger.
47/H4 **Herne Bay**, Eng,UK
42/D4 **Herning**, Den.
74/N9 **Herodian** (ruins), WBnk.
74/N9 **Herodion Nat'l Park**, WBnk.
117/M7 **Heroica Caborca**, Mex.
117/M7 **Heroica Nogales**, Mex.
116/D4 **Herrero** (pt.), Mex.
56/D5 **Hers** (riv.), Fr.
51/E6 **Herscheid**, Ger.
130/L2 **Herschel**, Yk,Can
53/D1 **Herselt**, Belg.
53/E2 **Herstal**, Belg.
47/G5 **Herstmonceux**, Eng,UK
51/E5 **Herten**, Ger.
47/F3 **Hertford**, Eng,UK
47/F3 **Hertfordshire** (co.), Eng,UK
53/E2 **Herve**, Belg.
90/D4 **Hervey Bay**, Austl.
51/H5 **Herzberg am Harz**, Ger.
51/F5 **Herzebrock-Clarholz**, Ger.
52/C2 **Herzele**, Belg.
74/M8 **Herzliyya**, Isr.
57/J2 **Herzogenaurach**, Ger.
62/B1 **Herzogenburg**, Aus.
53/F2 **Herzogenrath**, Ger.
53/D3 **Hesbaye** (plat.), Belg.
85/J3 **Heshan**, China
53/F4 **Hesperange**, Lux.
131/C2 **Hesperia**, Ca,US
130/M3 **Hess** (riv.), Yk,Can
51/G6 **Hesse** (state), Ger.
51/F5 **Hessel** (riv.), Ger.
51/G6 **Hessisch Lichtenau**, Ger.
51/G4 **Hessisch Oldendorf**, Ger.
45/H4 **Hessle**, Eng,UK
45/E5 **Heswall**, Eng,UK
123/H4 **Hettinger**, ND,US
45/G2 **Hetton-le-Hole**, Eng,UK
51/E5 **Heubach** (riv.), Ger.
49/H5 **Heukuppe** (peak), Aus.
53/E1 **Heusden-Zolder**, Belg.
53/F5 **Heusweiler**, Ger.
56/D2 **Hève, Cap de la** (cape), Fr.
62/E2 **Heves**, Hun.
49/L5 **Heves** (co.), Hun.
131/G5 **Hewlett** (pt.), NY,US
45/F2 **Hexham**, Eng,UK
77/H3 **Hexigten Qi**, China
102/L10 **Hex River** (mts.), SAfr.
102/L10 **Hex River** (pass), SAfr.
45/F3 **Heysham**, Eng,UK
50/C6 **Heythuysen**, Neth.
45/F4 **Heywood**, Eng,UK
81/C4 **Heze**, China
129/H5 **Hialeah**, Fl,US
125/J3 **Hiawatha**, Ks,US
123/K4 **Hibbing**, Mn,US
91/C4 **Hibbs** (pt.), Austl.
130/M4 **Hickman** (mtn.), BC,Can
126/B4 **Hickman**, Ky,US
129/H3 **Hickory**, NC,US
131/G5 **Hicksville**, NY,US
79/E3 **Hida** (riv.), Japan
79/H7 **Hidaka**, Japan
78/D4 **Hidaka** (riv.), Japan
116/B3 **Hidalgo** (state), Mex.
117/N8 **Hidalgo del Parral**, Mex.
51/F4 **Hiddenhausen**, Ger.
59/W17 **Hierro** (isl.), Canl.
51/E2 **Hieve** (lake), Ger.
79/H7 **Higashikurume**, Japan
79/H7 **Higashimurayama**, Japan
79/G1 **Higashine**, Japan
79/L10 **Higashi-Ōsaka**, Japan
79/K10 **Higashiura**, Japan
79/H7 **Higashiyamato**, Japan
122/C5 **High** (des.), Or,US
47/F2 **Higham Ferrers**, Eng,UK
46/D4 **Highbridge**, Eng,UK
131/F5 **High Bridge**, NJ,US
128/E4 **High Island**, Tx,US
131/C2 **Highland**, Ca,US
132/R16 **Highland**, In,US
132/Q15 **Highland Park**, Il,US
132/F7 **Highland Park**, Mi,US
131/F5 **Highland Park**, NJ,US
46/D2 **Highley**, Eng,UK
123/J4 **Highmore**, SD,US
129/H3 **High Point**, NC,US
122/D2 **High Prairie**, Ab,Can
123/H2 **Highrock** (lake), Mb,Can
45/F3 **High Street** (mtn.), Eng,UK
45/E4 **Hightown**, Eng,UK
131/F5 **Hightstown**, NJ,US
46/B5 **High Willhays** (hill), Eng,UK
47/E3 **Highworth**, Eng,UK
47/F3 **High Wycombe**, Eng,UK
117/H4 **Higüey**, DRep.
74/H6 **Hihyā**, Egypt
42/J3 **Hiidenportin Nat'l Park**, Fin.
64/D4 **Hiiumaa** (isl.), Est.
72/C3 **Hijāz, Jabal al** (mts.), SAr.
78/B4 **Hiji**, Japan
112/Q9 **Hijuelas de Conchali**, Chile
79/L9 **Hikami**, Japan
78/E3 **Hikone**, Japan
93/L6 **Hikueru** (atoll), FrPol.
53/H2 **Hilchenbach**, Ger.
57/J1 **Hildburghausen**, Ger.
50/D6 **Hilden**, Ger.
51/G4 **Hildesheim**, Ger.
105/L **Hillary** (coast), Ant.
125/H3 **Hill City**, Ks,US
131/F4 **Hillcrest**, NY,US
51/F4 **Hille**, Ger.
50/B4 **Hillegom**, Neth.
42/E5 **Hillerød**, Den.
44/B2 **Hillhall**, NI,UK
43/D2 **Hill of Fearn**, Sc,UK
123/J4 **Hillsboro**, ND,US
124/F4 **Hillsboro**, NM,US
126/D4 **Hillsboro**, Oh,US
122/C4 **Hillsboro**, Or,US
128/D3 **Hillsboro**, Tx,US
90/C3 **Hillsborough** (chan.), Austl.
44/B3 **Hillsborough**, NI,UK
132/K11 **Hillsborough**, Ca,US
131/F5 **Hillsborough**, NJ,US
126/C3 **Hillsdale**, Mi,US
131/F5 **Hillside**, NJ,US
44/B3 **Hilltown**, NI,UK
120/U11 **Hilo**, Hi,US
82/D5 **Hilongos**, Phil.
45/E3 **Hilpsford** (pt.), Eng,UK
129/H3 **Hilton Head Island**, SC,US
50/C6 **Hilvarenbeek**, Neth.
50/C4 **Hilversum**, Neth.
75/C5 **Himachal Pradesh** (state), India
84/D2 **Himalaya, Great** (range), Asia
82/D5 **Himamaylan**, Phil.
78/D3 **Himeji**, Japan
79/E2 **Himi**, Japan
97/N5 **Himora**, Eth.
74/L4 **Ḩimş**, Syria
130/J3 **Hinchinbrook** (chan.), Ak,US
90/B2 **Hinchinbrook I. Nat'l Park**, Austl.
47/E1 **Hinckley**, Eng,UK
45/H2 **Hinderwell**, Eng,UK
45/F4 **Hindley**, Eng,UK
91/B2 **Hindmarsh** (lake), Austl.
73/J1 **Hindu Kush** (mts.), Afg., Pak.
84/C5 **Hindupur**, India
129/H4 **Hinesville**, Ga,US
84/C3 **Hinganghāt**, India
73/J3 **Hingol** (riv.), Pak.
84/C4 **Hingoli**, India
73/J3 **Hingorja**, Pak.
74/E2 **Hınıs**, Turk.
79/H7 **Hino**, Japan
79/M9 **Hino** (riv.), Japan
79/H7 **Hinode**, Japan
58/C3 **Hinojosa del Duque**, Sp.
78/C3 **Hino-misaki** (cape), Japan
132/Q16 **Hinsdale**, Il,US
45/F6 **Hinstock**, Eng,UK
51/E2 **Hinte**, Ger.
122/D2 **Hinton**, Ab,Can
126/D4 **Hinton**, WV,US
50/B3 **Hippolytushoef**, Neth.
45/G3 **Hipswell**, Eng,UK
79/L9 **Hira** (mts.), Japan
78/A4 **Hirado**, Japan
78/D3 **Hirakata**, Japan
84/D3 **Hirakud** (res.), India
78/C3 **Hirata**, Japan
79/H7 **Hiratsuka**, Japan
63/H2 **Hîrlău**, Rom.
77/N3 **Hirosaki**, Japan
78/C3 **Hiroshima**, Japan
78/C3 **Hiroshima** (pref.), Japan
57/J2 **Hirschau**, Ger.
52/D4 **Hirson**, Fr.
63/H3 **Hîrşova**, Rom.
42/D4 **Hirtshals**, Den.
46/C3 **Hirwaun**, Wal,UK
78/E3 **Hisai**, Japan
84/C2 **Hisār**, India
76/E2 **Hishig-Öndör**, Mong.
117/G4 **Hispaniola** (isl.), DRep., Haiti
79/G2 **Hitachi**, Japan
79/G2 **Hitachi-ōta**, Japan
47/F3 **Hitchin**, Eng,UK
78/B4 **Hitoyoshi**, Japan
42/C3 **Hitra** (isl.), Nor.
93/M5 **Hiva Oa** (isl.), FrPol.
64/B2 **Hjartfjellet** (peak), Nor.
83/B1 **Hka** (riv.), Burma
85/G2 **Hkakabo** (peak), Burma
49/J4 **Hlohovec**, Slvk.
90/G8 **Hmas-Nirimba**, Austl.
85/G4 **Hmawbi**, Burma
99/F5 **Ho**, Gha.
83/D1 **Hoa Bin**, Viet.
83/E4 **Hoa Da**, Viet.
83/C1 **Hoang Lien** (mts.), Viet.
119/K2 **Hoare** (bay), NW,Can
79/G2 **Hobara**, Japan
91/C4 **Hobart**, Austl.
125/H4 **Hobart**, Ok,US
105/Q **Hobbs** (coast), Ant.
125/G4 **Hobbs**, NM,US
52/D1 **Hoboken**, Belg.
131/F5 **Hoboken**, NJ,US
97/Q6 **Hobyo**, Som.
62/A2 **Hochalmspitze** (peak), Aus.
83/D4 **Ho Chi Minh City** (Saigon), Viet.
57/K3 **Hochkönig** (peak), Aus.
57/L3 **Hochschwab** (peak), Aus.
53/G3 **Hochsimmer** (peak), Ger.
47/G3 **Hockley**, Eng,UK
45/F4 **Hodder** (riv.), Eng,UK
47/F3 **Hoddesdon**, Eng,UK
122/G3 **Hodgeville**, Sk,Can
98/C2 **Hodh** (reg.), Mrta.
74/M8 **Hod HaSharon**, Isr.
98/D2 **Hodh ech Chargui** (reg.), Mrta.
98/C2 **Hodh el Gharbi** (reg.), Mrta.
62/E2 **Hódmezővásárhely**, Hun.
45/F6 **Hodnet**, Eng,UK
49/J4 **Hodonín**, Czh.
53/E2 **Hoegnel** (riv.), Belg.
50/B5 **Hoekse Waard** (polder), Neth.
53/G6 **Hoenheim**, Fr.
53/E2 **Hoensbroek**, Neth.
53/E2 **Hoeselt**, Belg.
50/C4 **Hoevelaken**, Neth.
50/B5 **Hoeven**, Neth.
57/J1 **Hof**, Ger.
132/P15 **Hoffman Estates**, Il,US
51/G6 **Hofgeismar**, Ger.
81/B3 **Hofong Qagan** (salt lake), China
42/P6 **Hofsá** (riv.), Ice.
42/N7 **Hofsjökull** (glac.), Ice.
78/B3 **Hōfu**, Japan
50/C4 **Hoge Veluwe Nat'l Park**, Neth.
57/G6 **Hohegrass** (peak), Ger.
55/F3 **Hohenems**, Aus.
51/H4 **Hohenhameln**, Ger.
57/H2 **Hohenloher Ebene** (plain), Ger.
57/K3 **Hoher Dachstein** (peak), Aus.
57/K3 **Hohe Tauern** (mts.), Aus.
57/K3 **Hohe Tauern Nat'l Park**, Aus.
81/B2 **Hohhot**, China
54/C1 **Hohneck** (mtn.), Fr.
53/G3 **Höhr-Grenzhausen**, Ger.
75/F4 **Hoh Sai** (lake), China
75/F4 **Hoh Xil** (lake), China
75/E4 **Hoh Xil** (mts.), China
83/E3 **Hoi An**, Viet.
128/D2 **Hoisington**, Ks,US
83/D1 **Hoi Xuan**, Viet.
78/C4 **Hōjō**, Japan
89/H7 **Hokitika**, NZ
77/N3 **Hokkaidō** (isl.), Japan
79/G2 **Hokota**, Japan
79/K10 **Hokudan**, Japan
79/M9 **Hokusei**, Japan
45/J6 **Holbeach**, Eng,UK
47/H3 **Holbrook**, Eng,UK
124/E4 **Holbrook**, Az,US
125/H4 **Holdenville**, Ok,US
45/H4 **Holderness** (pen.), Eng,UK
125/H2 **Holdrege**, Ne,US
117/F3 **Holguín**, Cuba
130/G3 **Holitna** (riv.), Ak,US
126/C3 **Holland**, Mi,US
129/F3 **Hollandale**, Ms,US
50/B4 **Hollandse IJssel** (riv.), Neth.
47/H2 **Hollesley**, Eng,UK
125/H4 **Hollis**, Ok,US
124/B3 **Hollister**, Ca,US
53/E2 **Hollogne-aux-Pierres**, Belg.
42/H3 **Hollola**, Fin.
129/F3 **Holly Springs**, Ms,US
129/H5 **Hollywood**, Fl,US
42/F3 **Holm**, Swe.
118/E1 **Holman**, NW,Can
131/F5 **Holmdel**, NJ,US
90/C2 **Holmes** (reefs), Austl.
122/F4 **Holmes** (peak), Wy,US
45/F5 **Holmes Chapel**, Eng,UK
45/H4 **Holme upon Spalding Moor**, Eng,UK
45/G4 **Holmfirth**, Eng,UK
105/C **Holm-Lützow** (bay), Ant.
42/F3 **Holmsjön** (lake), Swe.
74/K5 **Holon**, Isr.
42/D4 **Holstebro**, Den.
129/H2 **Holston** (riv.), Tn,US
46/B5 **Holsworthy**, Eng,UK
47/H1 **Holt**, Eng,UK
50/D4 **Holten**, Neth.
125/J3 **Holton**, Ks,US
131/G5 **Holtsville**, NY,US
44/D5 **Holy** (isl.), Wal,UK
44/D5 **Holyhead**, Wal,UK
44/D5 **Holyhead** (bay), Wal,UK
43/E3 **Holy** (Lindisfarne) (isl.), Eng,UK
125/G2 **Holyoke**, Co,US
127/F3 **Holyoke**, Ma,US
45/E5 **Holywell**, Wal,UK
44/C2 **Holywood**, NI,UK
48/F5 **Holzkirchen**, Ger.
51/G5 **Holzminden**, Ger.
51/E6 **Holzwickede**, Ger.
102/B3 **Hom** (dry riv.), Namb.
50/D6 **Homberg**, Ger.
51/G6 **Homberg**, Ger.
99/E3 **Hombori Tondo** (peak), Mali
53/F5 **Hombourg-Haut**, Fr.
53/G5 **Homburg**, Ger.
119/K2 **Home** (bay), NW,Can
53/E5 **Homécourt**, Fr.
128/E3 **Homer**, La,US
129/H5 **Homestead**, Fl,US
129/G3 **Homewood**, Al,US
132/Q16 **Homewood**, Il,US
129/F4 **Homochitto** (riv.), Ms,US
84/B5 **Honāvar**, India
83/D4 **Hon Chong**, Viet.
46/C3 **Honddu** (riv.), Wal,UK
78/B4 **Hondo**, Japan
125/F4 **Hondo** (dry riv.), NM,US
128/D4 **Hondo**, Tx,US
50/D3 **Hondsrug** (reg.), Neth.
116/D4 **Honduras**
116/D4 **Honduras** (gulf), NAm.
124/B2 **Honey** (lake), Ca,US
47/E2 **Honeybourne**, Eng,UK
81/C5 **Hong** (lake), China
81/C4 **Hong** (riv.), China
85/J2 **Hongdu** (riv.), China
83/D1 **Hong Gai**, Viet.
81/C5 **Honghu**, China
85/J2 **Hongjiang**, China
82/B3 **Hong Kong** (dpcy.), UK
81/B3 **Hongliu** (riv.), China
83/C1 **Hong** (Red) (riv.), Viet.
85/J3 **Hongshui** (riv.), China
81/C3 **Hongtao Shan** (mtn.), China
127/H1 **Honguedo** (passg.), Qu,Can
81/D4 **Hongze** (lake), China
92/E5 **Honiara** (cap.), Sol.
46/C5 **Honiton**, Eng,UK
120/T10 **Honolulu** (cap.), Hi,US
83/D4 **Hon Quan**, Viet.
77/M5 **Honshu** (isl.), Japan
132/J10 **Hood** (mt.), Ca,US
122/C4 **Hood** (mt.), Or,US
122/C4 **Hood Canal** (inlet), Wa,US
50/B4 **Hoofddorp**, Neth.
50/C6 **Hoogeloon**, Neth.
50/B6 **Hoogerheide**, Neth.
50/D3 **Hoogeveen**, Neth.
50/D3 **Hoogeveense Vaart** (can.), Neth.
50/D2 **Hoogezand**, Neth.
84/E3 **Hooghly-Chinsura**, India
52/C2 **Hooglede**, Belg.
50/B6 **Hoogstraten**, Belg.
90/C3 **Hook** (isl.), Austl.
47/F4 **Hook**, Eng,UK
43/B4 **Hook Head** (pt.), Ire.
126/C3 **Hoopeston**, Il,US
50/C3 **Hoorn**, Neth.
50/C3 **Hoornse Hop** (bay), Neth.
124/D3 **Hoover** (dam), Az,US
74/E2 **Hopa**, Turk.
131/F5 **Hopatcong**, NJ,US
131/F5 **Hopatcong** (lake), NJ,US
122/C3 **Hope**, BC,Can
45/E5 **Hope**, Wal,UK
128/E3 **Hope**, Ar,US
119/K2 **Hopes Advance** (cape), Qu,Can
46/C6 **Hope's Nose** (pt.), Eng,UK
46/D2 **Hope under Dinmore**, Eng,UK
131/F5 **Hopewell**, NJ,US
126/E4 **Hopewell**, Va,US
91/B3 **Hopkins** (riv.), Austl.
126/C4 **Hopkinsville**, Ky,US
51/F6 **Hoppecke** (riv.), Ger.
51/E4 **Hopsten**, Ger.
122/C4 **Hoquiam**, Wa,US
130/J2 **Horace** (mtn.), Ak,US
79/L9 **Hōrai-san** (peak), Japan
74/E2 **Horasan**, Turk.
74/K5 **Horbat Qesari** (ruins), Isr.
45/G4 **Horbury**, Eng,UK
42/C3 **Hordaland** (co.), Nor.
45/G2 **Horden**, Eng,UK
63/G3 **Horezu**, Rom.
76/F3 **Hörh** (peak), Mong.
39/S6 **Horiara** (cap.), Sol.
47/F4 **Horley**, Eng,UK
57/L2 **Horn**, Aus.
42/M6 **Horn** (pt.), Ice.
49/L4 **Hornád** (riv.), Slvk.
42/E2 **Hornavan** (lake), Swe.
51/F5 **Horn-Bad Meinberg**, Ger.
127/Q8 **Hornby**, On,Can
45/H5 **Horncastle**, Eng,UK
126/E3 **Hornell**, NY,US
126/C1 **Hornepayne**, On,Can
113/L8 **Horn** (Hornos) (cape), Chile
113/L8 **Hornos Nat'l Park, Cabo de**, Chile
52/A4 **Hornoy-le-Bourg**, Fr.
90/H8 **Hornsby**, Austl.
45/H4 **Hornsea**, Eng,UK
48/E1 **Hornum Odde** (cape), Ger.
77/N3 **Horoshiri-dake** (mtn.), Japan
46/B6 **Horrabridge**, Eng,UK
125/F2 **Horse** (cr.), Ne, Wy,US
126/C4 **Horse Cave**, Ky,US
122/C2 **Horsefly** (lake), BC,Can
42/D5 **Horsens**, Den.
47/H3 **Horsey** (isl.), Eng,UK
45/G4 **Horsforth**, Eng,UK
91/B3 **Horsham**, Austl.
47/F4 **Horsham**, Eng,UK
131/E5 **Horsham**, Pa,US
50/D6 **Horst**, Neth.
51/E4 **Hörstel**, Ger.
51/E4 **Horstmar**, Ger.
59/S12 **Horta**, Azor.,Port.
59/N9 **Hortaleza**, Sp.
62/E2 **Hortobágyi Nat'l Park**, Hun.
130/N2 **Horton** (riv.), NW,Can
74/K6 **Horvot 'Avedat** (ruins), Isr.
74/K6 **Horvot Mezada** (Masada) (ruins), Isr.
45/F4 **Horwich**, Eng,UK
126/D2 **Horwood** (lake), On,Can
84/C3 **Hoshangābād**, India
84/C4 **Hospet**, India
113/K8 **Hoste** (isl.), Chile
79/E2 **Hotaka**, Japan
79/E2 **Hotaka-dake** (mtn.), Japan
75/D4 **Hotan** (riv.), China
123/H5 **Hot Springs**, SD,US
128/E3 **Hot Springs Nat'l Park**, Ar,US
118/E2 **Hottah** (lake), NW,Can
102/A2 **Hottentot** (bay), Namb.
102/A2 **Hottentots** (pt.), Namb.
52/B3 **Houdain**, Fr.
98/D4 **Houet** (prov.), Burk.
126/B2 **Houghton**, Mi,US
126/C2 **Houghton Lake**, Mi,US
45/G2 **Houghton-le-Spring**, Eng,UK
127/H2 **Houlton**, Me,US
81/B4 **Houma**, China
129/F4 **Houma**, La,US
52/B2 **Houplines**, Fr.
52/A3 **Hourdel, Pointe du** (pt.), Fr.
124/D3 **House** (range), Ut,US
122/B2 **Houston**, BC,Can
125/K3 **Houston**, Mo,US
129/F3 **Houston**, Ms,US
128/E4 **Houston**, Tx,US
50/C4 **Houten**, Neth.
52/B2 **Houthulst**, Belg.
50/C3 **Houtribdijk** (dam), Neth.
47/F5 **Hove**, Eng,UK
51/F5 **Hövelhof**, Ger.
124/E3 **Hovenweep Nat'l Mon.**, Co,US
47/H1 **Hoveton**, Eng,UK
42/E3 **Hovfjället** (peak), Swe.
45/H3 **Hovingham**, Eng,UK
76/E1 **Hövsgöl** (lake), Mong.
130/H2 **Howard** (hill), Ak,US
130/G2 **Howard** (pass), Ak,US
45/H4 **Howden**, Eng,UK
91/D3 **Howe** (cape), Austl.
126/D3 **Howell**, Mi,US
131/F5 **Howell**, NJ,US
103/E3 **Howick**, SAfr.
93/H4 **Howland** (isl.), PacUS
84/E3 **Howrah**, India
48/E3 **Höxter**, Ger.
49/H3 **Hoyerswerda**, Ger.
45/E5 **Hoylake**, Eng,UK
45/G5 **Hoyland Nether**, Eng,UK
59/N8 **Hoyo-de-Manzanares**, Sp.
53/E3 **Hoyoux** (riv.), Belg.
76/E2 **Hoyt Tamir** (riv.), Mong.
79/M9 **Hozumi**, Japan
49/H3 **Hradec Králové**, Czh.
62/D4 **Hrasnica**, Bosn.
62/B2 **Hrastnik**, Slov.
42/M6 **Hrolleifsborg** (peak), Ice.
49/K4 **Hron** (riv.), Slvk.
49/J3 **Hronov**, Czh.
49/M3 **Hrubieszów**, Pol.
49/J3 **Hrubý Jeseník** (mts.), Czh.
42/P6 **Hrútafjöll** (peak), Ice.
76/G5 **Hua** (peak), China
108/C6 **Huacho**, Peru
83/B3 **Hua Hin**, Thai.
93/K6 **Huahine** (isl.), FrPol.
81/C4 **Huai** (riv.), China
81/D4 **Huai'an**, China
76/H5 **Huaibei**, China
82/A2 **Huaihua**, China
81/C2 **Huailai**, China
81/D4 **Huainan**, China
81/C3 **Huairen**, China
81/D4 **Huaiyin**, China
116/B4 **Huajuapan de León**, Mex.
112/C2 **Hualañé**, Chile
82/D3 **Hualien**, Tai.
108/C5 **Huallaga** (riv.), Peru
108/C5 **Huamachuco**, Peru
104/C3 **Huambo**, Ang.
81/C5 **Huan** (riv.), China
108/C6 **Huancavelica**, Peru
108/C6 **Huancayo**, Peru
108/E8 **Huanchaca** (peak), Bol.
83/C2 **Huang** (riv.), Laos, Thai.
81/C4 **Huangchuan**, China
82/C2 **Huanggang** (peak), China
81/C2 **Huangqi** (lake), China
81/D5 **Huangshan**, China
81/C5 **Huangshi**, China
81/C5 **Huangtang** (lake), China
81/B4 **Huangtu** (plat.), China
77/H4 **Huang** (Yellow) (riv.), China
108/C5 **Huánuco**, Peru
108/E7 **Huanuni**, Bol.
108/C6 **Huaral**, Peru
108/C5 **Huaráz**, Peru
108/C5 **Huarmey**, Peru
108/C5 **Huascarán** (peak), Peru
108/C5 **Huascarán Nat'l Park**, Peru
81/B4 **Hua Shan** (peak), China
117/N8 **Huatabampo**, Mex.
108/E6 **Huatunas** (lake), Bol.
82/A1 **Huaying**, China
130/L3 **Hubbard** (mtn.), Ak,US, Yk,Can
125/H4 **Hubbard Creek** (res.), Tx,US
81/C5 **Hubei** (prov.), China
81/B4 **Hubei Kou** (pass), China
84/C4 **Hubli-Dhārwār**, India
50/D6 **Hückelhoven**, Ger.
51/E6 **Hückeswagen**, Ger.
45/G5 **Hucknall Torkard**, Eng,UK
52/A2 **Hucqueliers**, Fr.
45/G4 **Huddersfield**, Eng,UK
64/C4 **Huddinge**, Swe.
51/F2 **Hude**, Ger.
42/F3 **Hudiksvall**, Swe.
105/L **Hudson** (cape), Ant.
119/H2 **Hudson** (bay), Can.
119/J2 **Hudson** (str.), NW, Qu,Can
127/M7 **Hudson**, Qu,Can
126/F3 **Hudson** (riv.), NJ, NY,US
126/F3 **Hudson**, NY,US
123/H2 **Hudson Bay**, Sk,Can
118/D3 **Hudson's Hope**, BC,Can
83/D2 **Hue**, Viet.
62/F2 **Huedin**, Rom.
116/C4 **Huehuetenango**, Guat.
116/B3 **Huejutla**, Mex.
58/B4 **Huelva**, Sp.
58/B3 **Huelva** (riv.), Sp.
112/B4 **Huequi** (vol.), Chile
58/E4 **Huercal-Overa**, Sp.
125/F3 **Huerfano** (riv.), Co,US
59/E1 **Huesca**, Sp.
58/D4 **Huéscar**, Sp.
112/F3 **Huesos** (riv.), Arg.
116/A4 **Huetamo de Nuñez**, Mex.
84/E3 **Hugli** (riv.), India
125/G3 **Hugo**, Co,US
125/J4 **Hugo**, Ok,US
125/G3 **Hugoton**, Ks,US
76/H2 **Hui** (riv.), China
102/B2 **Huib-Hock** (plat.), Namb.
104/B4 **Huila** (plat.), Ang.
112/D2 **Huinca Renancó**, Arg.
81/E5 **Hui Shan** (mtn.), China
56/D2 **Huisne** (riv.), Fr.
50/C5 **Huissen**, Neth.
64/D3 **Huittinen**, Fin.
116/C4 **Huixtla**, Mex.
50/C4 **Huizen**, Neth.
82/B3 **Huizhou**, China
80/C5 **Hŭksan** (arch.), SKor.
76/K2 **Hulan** (riv.), China
76/F2 **Hulan**, Mong.
123/G4 **Hulett**, Wy,US
126/F2 **Hull**, Qu,Can
45/H4 **Hull**, Eng,UK
45/H4 **Hull** (riv.), Eng,UK
51/F4 **Hüllhorst**, Ger.
93/H5 **Hull** (Orona) (atoll), Kiri.
50/B6 **Hulst**, Neth.
81/B3 **Hulu** (riv.), China
76/H2 **Hulun** (lake), China
77/K1 **Huma** (riv.), China
108/F5 **Humaitá**, Braz.
117/N8 **Humaya** (riv.), Mex.
104/B4 **Humbe**, Ang.
127/K2 **Humber** (riv.), Nf,Can
127/R8 **Humber** (bay), On,Can
127/Q8 **Humber** (riv.), On,Can
45/H4 **Humber** (riv.), Eng,UK
45/H4 **Humberside** (co.), Eng,UK
45/H4 **Humberston**, Eng,UK
128/E4 **Humble**, Tx,US
123/G2 **Humboldt**, Sk,Can
92/F7 **Humboldt** (peak), NCal.
124/C2 **Humboldt** (range), Nv,US
124/D2 **Humboldt** (riv.), Nv,US
129/F3 **Humboldt**, Tn,US
91/C2 **Hume** (lake), Austl.
49/L4 **Humenné**, Slvk.
130/K2 **Humphrey** (pt.), Ak,US
124/E4 **Humphreys** (peak), Az,US
45/F1 **Humshaugh**, Eng,UK
77/J3 **Hun** (riv.), China
77/K3 **Hun** (riv.), China
42/N6 **Húnaflói** (bay), Ice.
85/K2 **Hunan** (prov.), China
77/L3 **Hunchun**, China
62/F3 **Hunedoara**, Rom.
62/F2 **Hunedoara** (co.), Rom.
48/E3 **Hünfeld**, Ger.
62/D2 **Hungary**
57/H1 **Hungen**, Ger.
47/E4 **Hungerford**, Eng,UK
76/C2 **Hüngüy** (riv.), Mong.
83/D1 **Hung Yen**, Viet.
77/K3 **Hunjiang**, China
45/H3 **Hunmanby**, Eng,UK
53/G1 **Hunspatch**, Fr.
53/G4 **Hunsrück** (mts.), Ger.
47/G1 **Hunstanton**, Eng,UK
51/F2 **Hunte** (riv.), Ger.
91/C4 **Hunter** (isl.), Austl.
91/D2 **Hunter** (riv.), Austl.
122/A3 **Hunter** (isl.), BC,Can
130/H3 **Hunter** (mtn.), Ak,US
126/C4 **Huntingburg**, In,US
47/F2 **Huntingdon**, Eng,UK
45/G4 **Huntington**, Eng,UK
126/C3 **Huntington**, In,US
131/G5 **Huntington**, NY,US
126/D4 **Huntington**, WV,US
131/C3 **Huntington Beach**, Ca,US
131/B3 **Huntington Park**, Ca,US
132/F7 **Huntington Woods**, Mi,US
43/D2 **Huntly**, Sc,UK
130/M4 **Hunts Inlet**, BC,Can
126/E2 **Huntsville**, On,Can
129/G3 **Huntsville**, Al,US
128/E4 **Huntsville**, Tx,US
50/D5 **Hünxe**, Ger.
77/H2 **Huolin Gol**, China
83/D2 **Huong Hoa**, Viet.
83/D2 **Huong Khe**, Viet.

Huong – Jarāb

83/D2 Huong Son, Viet.
85/J4 Huong Thuy, Viet.
81/B3 Huo Shan (mtn.), China
97/R5 Hurdiyo, Som.
124/E4 Hurley, NM,US
126/D2 Huron (lake), Can., US
132/F7 Huron (riv.), Mi,US
123/J4 Huron, SD,US
126/D4 Hurricane, WV,US
47/F5 Hurstpierpoint, Eng,UK
52/D4 Hurtaut (riv.), Fr.
53/F2 Hürth, Ger.
45/G3 Hurworth, Eng,UK
84/D3 Husainābād, India
47/E2 Husbands Bosworth, Eng,UK
63/J2 Huşi, Rom.
48/E1 Husum, Ger.
125/H3 Hutchinson, Ks,US
123/K4 Hutchinson, Mn,US
45/J5 Huttoft, Eng,UK
90/C4 Hutton (peak), Austl.
45/H4 Hutton Cranswick, Eng,UK
45/G3 Hutton Rudby, Eng,UK
127/Q8 Huttonville, On,Can
81/C3 Hutuo (riv.), China
53/E2 Huy, Belg.
45/F5 Huyton-with-Roby, Eng,UK
81/E5 Huzhou, China
42/P7 Hvannadalshnúkur (peak), Ice.
62/C4 Hvar (isl.), Cro.
42/N7 Hvítá (riv.), Ice.
104/E4 Hwange, Zim.
104/E4 Hwange (Wankie) Nat'l Park, Zim.
80/D3 Hwanghae-Bukto (prov.), NKor.
80/C3 Hwanghae-Namdo (prov.), NKor.
112/B5 Hyades (peak), Chile
76/C2 Hyargas, Mong.
76/C2 Hyargas (lake), Mong.
131/K8 Hyattsville, Md,US
45/F5 Hyde, Eng,UK
84/C4 Hyderābād, India
73/J3 Hyderābād, Pak.
57/G5 Hyères, Fr.
57/G5 Hyères (isls.), Fr.
118/D2 Hyland (riv.), Yk,Can
78/D3 Hyōgo (pref.), Japan
78/D3 Hyō-no-sen (mtn.), Japan
124/E2 Hyrum, Ut,US
47/E5 Hythe, Eng,UK
47/H4 Hythe, Eng,UK
78/B4 Hyūga, Japan
42/H3 Hyvinkää, Fin.

I

62/A2 Iâf di Montasio (peak), It.
63/H3 Ialomiţa (riv.), Rom.
110/D1 Iapu, Braz.
63/H2 Iaşi, Rom.
63/H2 Iaşi (co.), Rom.
82/C4 Iba, Phil.
99/F5 Ibadan, Nga.
108/C3 Ibagué, Col.
110/B2 Ibaiti, Braz.
82/D5 Ibajay, Phil.
124/D2 Ibapah, Ut,US
62/E4 Ibar (riv.), Yugo.
78/C3 Ibara, Japan
79/L10 Ibaraki, Japan
79/F2 Ibaraki (pref.), Japan
108/C3 Ibarra, Ecu.
111/E2 Ibarreta, Arg.
97/L6 Ibba (riv.), Sudan
51/E4 Ibbenbüren, Ger.
99/F2 Ibdekhene (wadi), Mali
111/E2 Ibera, Esteros de (marshes), Arg.
58/D2 Ibérico, Sistema (range), Sp.
127/P7 Iberville, Qu,Can
78/E3 Ibi (riv.), Japan
59/E3 Ibi, Sp.
110/C1 Ibiá, Braz.
109/L6 Ibicaraí, Braz.
110/B2 Ibitinga, Braz.
110/F8 Ibiúna, Braz.
59/F3 Ibiza, Sp.
59/F3 Ibiza (isl.), Sp.
78/D3 Ibo (riv.), Japan
109/K6 Ibotirama, Braz.
96/H8 Iboundji (peak), Gabon
49/L4 Ibrány, Hun.
100/B2 Ibshawāy, Egypt
47/E1 Ibstock, Eng,UK
87/G3 Ibu (mtn.), Indo.
79/M9 Ibuki, Japan
79/M9 Ibuki-yama (peak), Japan
108/C6 Ica, Peru
42/N7 Iceland
84/B4 Ichalkaranji, India
84/D4 Ichchāpuram, India
79/J7 Ichihara, Japan
79/L9 Ichijima, Japan
79/H7 Ichikawa, Japan
78/E3 Ichinomiya, Japan
77/N4 Ichinoseki, Japan
79/M10 Ichishi, Japan
52/C1 Ichtegem, Belg.
109/L5 Icó, Braz.
130/K4 Icy (bay), Ak,US
130/F1 Icy (cape), Ak,US
130/L4 Icy (str.), Ak,US
125/J4 Idabel, Ok,US
122/E5 Idaho (state), US
122/E5 Idaho Falls, Id,US
84/B3 Idar, India
53/G4 Idarkopf (peak), Ger.
53/G4 Idar-Oberstein, Ger.
79/L10 Ide, Japan
76/D2 Ider (riv.), Mong.
100/C3 Idfū, Egypt
61/J5 Ídhi (peak), Gre.
74/H6 Idkū, Egypt
45/H5 Idle (riv.), Eng,UK
74/D3 Idlib, Syria
62/B3 Idrija, Slov.
52/B2 Ieper, Belg.
61/J5 Ierápetra, Gre.
101/C5 Ifakara, Tanz.
92/D4 Ifalik (isl.), Micr.
103/H8 Ifanadiana, Madg.
99/G5 Ife, Nga.
79/M10 Iga, Japan
79/M10 Iga (riv.), Japan
110/C2 Igarapava, Braz.
109/J4 Igarapé-Miri, Braz.
68/J3 Igarka, Rus.
84/B4 Igatpuri, India
74/F2 Iğdır, Turk.
130/H2 Igikpak (mtn.), Ak,US
60/A3 Iglesias, It.
126/B1 Ignace, On,Can
63/J5 İğneada (cape), Turk.
65/M4 Igra, Rus.
110/B3 Iguaçu (riv.), Braz.
111/F2 Iguaçu Nat'l Park, Braz.
116/B4 Iguala, Mex.
59/F2 Igualada, Sp.
111/E2 Iguapa (riv.), Braz.
110/C3 Iguape, Braz.
110/C3 Iguape (riv.), Braz.
109/L5 Iguatu, Braz.
111/F2 Iguazu Nat'l Park, Arg.
96/D2 Iguidi, 'Erg (des.), Afr.
103/H8 Ihosy, Madg.
103/G8 Ihotry (lake), Madg.
68/C3 Ii (riv.), Fin.
79/E3 Iida, Japan
79/F2 Iide-san (mtn.), Japan
64/E2 Iijoki (riv.), Fin.
79/M10 Iinan, Japan
42/H3 Iisalmi, Fin.
79/M10 Iitaka, Japan
64/E3 Iitti, Fin.
79/F2 Iiyama, Japan
78/B4 Iizuka, Japan
96/C3 Ijill (peak), Mrta.
50/C4 IJmeer (bay), Neth.
50/B4 IJmuiden, Neth.
98/B2 Ijnaoun (well), Mrta.
42/H2 Ijoki (riv.), Fin.
50/C4 IJssel (riv.), Neth.
50/C3 IJsselmeer (lake), Neth.
50/C3 IJsselmuiden, Neth.
50/C4 IJsselstein, Neth.
111/F2 Ijuí, Braz.
78/B5 Ijūin, Japan
52/B2 Ijzer (riv.), Belg.
65/M5 Ik (riv.), Rus.
103/H7 Ikahavo (plat.), Madg.
61/J4 Ikaría (isl.), Gre.
104/D1 Ikela, Zaire
79/M10 Ikenokoya-yama (peak), Japan
63/F4 Ikhtiman, Bul.
78/A4 Iki (chan.), Japan
78/A4 Iki (isl.), Japan
79/L10 Ikoma, Japan
103/H7 Ikopa (riv.), Madg.
82/D4 Ilagan, Phil.
72/E2 Īlām, Iran
84/E2 Ilam, Nepal
82/D3 Ilan, Tai.
49/K2 Iława, Pol.
97/M4 'Ilay, Sudan
46/D4 Ilchester, Eng,UK
122/G2 Ile-à-la-Crosse, Sk,Can
123/G2 Ile-à-la-Crosse (lake), Sk,Can
104/D1 Ilebo, Zaire
56/E2 Ile-de-France (reg.), Fr.
67/K2 Ilek (riv.), Kaz., Rus.
127/N7 Ile-Perrot, Qu,Can
98/E5 Iles Ehotilés Nat'l Park, IvC.
99/G5 Ilesha, Nga.
90/B3 Ilfracombe, Austl.
46/B4 Ilfracombe, Eng,UK
66/E4 Ilgaz, Turk.
74/B2 Ilgın, Turk.
110/H8 Ilhabela, Braz.
110/J8 Ilha Grande (bay), Braz.
110/B1 Ilha Solteira (res.), Braz.
58/A2 Ílhavo, Port.
109/L6 Ilhéus, Braz.
75/C3 Ili (riv.), China, Kaz.
130/G4 Iliamna (lake), Ak,US
130/H3 Iliamna (vol.), Ak,US
82/D6 Iligan, Phil.
74/E3 Ilisu (res.), Turk.
63/H6 Ilium (Troy) (ruins), Turk.
45/G6 Ilkeston, Eng,UK
45/G4 Ilkley, Eng,UK
55/F3 Ill (riv.), Aus.
54/D1 Ill (riv.), Fr.
112/C1 Illapel, Chile
99/G3 Illéla, Niger
55/F1 Iller (riv.), Ger.
58/D2 Illescas, Sp.
108/E7 Illimani (peak), Bol.
53/G5 Illingen, Ger.
126/B4 Illinois (state), US
126/B3 Illinois (riv.), Il,US
46/A6 Illogan, Eng,UK
58/D4 Illora, Sp.
54/D2 Illzach, Fr.
57/J2 Ilm (riv.), Ger.
42/G3 Ilmajoki, Fin.
51/G5 Ilme (riv.), Ger.
64/F4 Il'men' (lake), Rus.
48/F3 Ilmenau, Ger.
51/H2 Ilmenau (riv.), Ger.
46/D5 Ilminster, Eng,UK
108/D7 Ilo, Peru
82/D5 Iloilo, Phil.
99/G4 Ilorin, Nga.
67/H2 Ilovlya (riv.), Rus.
51/H4 Ilse (riv.), Ger.
51/H4 Ilsede, Ger.
51/H5 Ilsenburg, Ger.
63/H5 Ilyas (pt.), Turk.
65/N3 Ilych (riv.), Rus.
57/K2 Ilz (riv.), Ger.
78/C3 Imabari, Japan
79/F2 Imaichi, Japan
103/H8 Imaloto (riv.), Madg.
74/C3 Imamoğlu, Turk.
64/F2 Imandra (lake), Rus.
78/A4 Imari, Japan
42/J3 Imatra, Fin.
78/E3 Imazu, Japan
79/J7 Imba, Japan
110/B4 Imbituba, Braz.
97/P6 Īmī, Eth.
67/J5 Imishli, Azer.
61/L7 Imittós (mtn.), Gre.
124/C2 Imlay, Nv,US
51/G6 Immenhausen, Ger.
55/G2 Immenstadt im Allgäu, Ger.
45/H4 Immingham, Eng,UK
129/H5 Immokalee, Fl,US
130/J2 Imnavait (mtn.), Ak,US
99/G5 Imo (state), Nga.
57/J4 Imola, It.
109/J5 Imperatriz, Braz.
57/H5 Imperia, It.
123/G3 Imperial, Sk,Can
125/G2 Imperial, Ne,US
96/J7 Impfondo, Congo
85/F3 Imphāl, India
63/J5 İmralı (isl.), Turk.
74/D2 İmranlı, Turk.
55/G3 Imst, Aus.
79/E3 Ina, Japan
79/L10 Ina (riv.), Japan
49/H2 Ina (riv.), Pol.
79/M9 Inabe, Japan
79/L10 Inagawa, Japan
79/H7 Inagi, Japan
98/G2 I-n-Amenas, Alg.
79/K10 Inami, Japan
42/H1 Inari (lake), Fin.
63/G2 Inău (peak), Rom.
79/G2 Inawashiro (lake), Japan
79/M9 Inazawa, Japan
59/G3 Inca, Sp.
99/F2 I-n-Chaouâg (wadi), Mali
43/C3 Inchinnan, Sc,UK
98/B2 Inchiri (reg.), Mrta.
80/D4 Inch'ŏn, SKor.
80/D4 Inch'on-Jikhalsi (prov.), SKor.
96/E3 I-n-Dagouber (well), Mali
110/C1 Indaiá (riv.), Braz.
110/C2 Indaiatuba, Braz.
82/D6 Indanan, Phil.
53/F2 Inde (riv.), Ger.
53/F2 Inden, Ger.
116/D4 Independence, Belz.
124/C3 Independence, Ca,US
125/J3 Independence, Ks,US
125/J3 Independence, Mo,US
124/C2 Independence (mts.), Nv,US
131/E6 Independence Nat'l Hist. Park, Pa,US
67/J2 Inder (lake), Kaz.
71/G7 India
39/N6 Indian (ocean)
126/C3 Indiana (state), US
126/E3 Indiana, Pa,US
132/R16 Indiana Dunes Nat'l Lakesh., In,US
126/C4 Indianapolis (cap.), In,US
123/H3 Indian Head, Sk,Can
129/F3 Indianola, Ms,US
129/H5 Indiantown, Fl,US
110/B1 Indiaporã, Braz.
69/Q3 Indigirka (riv.), Rus.
62/E3 Indija, Yugo.
124/C4 Indio, Ca,US
83/C1 Indochina (reg.), Asia
87/E4 Indonesia
90/E6 Indooroopilly, Austl.
84/C3 Indore, India
86/B4 Indragiri (riv.), Indo.
86/C5 Indramayu (cape), Indo.
84/D4 Indrāvati (riv.), India
56/D3 Indre (riv.), Fr.
56/D3 Indrois (riv.), Fr.
71/F7 Indus (riv.), Asia
73/J4 Indus, Mouths of the, Pak.
74/C2 Inebolu, Turk.
99/E1 I-n-Echaï (well), Mali
74/B2 İnegöl, Turk.
62/E2 Ineu, Rom.
96/D1 Inezgane, Mor.
102/C4 Infanta (cape), SAfr.
116/A4 Infiernillo (res.), Mex.
58/C1 Infiesto, Sp.
108/C4 Ingapirca, Ecu.
52/C2 Ingelmunster, Belg.
90/G8 Ingleburn, Austl.
45/G2 Ingleton, Eng,UK
127/Q8 Inglewood, On,Can
131/B3 Inglewood, Ca,US
132/C2 Inglewood-Finn Hill, Wa,US
129/H4 Inglis, Fl,US
76/G1 Ingoda (riv.), Rus.
45/J5 Ingoldmells, Eng,UK
57/J2 Ingolstadt, Ger.
105/E Ingrid Christianson (coast), Ant.
99/G2 I-n-Guezzâm, Alg.
66/E3 Ingulets (riv.), Ukr.
67/G4 Inguri (riv.), Geo.
109/J7 Inhumas, Braz.
44/A1 Inishowen (pen.), Ire.
44/B1 Inishowen Head (pt.), Ire.
57/K2 Ilz (riv.), Ger.
132/F7 Inkster, Mi,US
78/C3 Inland (sea), Japan
85/G3 Inle (lake), Burma
99/E2 I-n-Milach (well), Mali
57/K2 Inn (riv.), Eur.
76/G3 Inner Mongolia (reg.), China
51/H4 Innerste (riv.), Ger.
57/K3 Innichen (San Candido), It.
90/B2 Innisfail, Austl.
122/E2 Innisfail, Ab,Can
130/G3 Innoko (riv.), Ak,US
55/H3 Innsbruck, Aus.
46/B5 Inny (riv.), Eng,UK
78/C4 Ino, Japan
104/C1 Inongo, Zaire
49/K4 Inovec (peak), Slvk.
49/K2 Inowrocław, Pol.
99/E1 I-n-Sâkâne, Erg (des.), Mali
96/F2 I-n-Salah, Alg.
43/D2 Insch, Sc,UK
85/G4 Insein, Burma
122/A2 Inside (passg.), BC,Can
65/P2 Inta, Rus.
99/F2 I-n-Tassik (well), Mali
122/B2 Interior (plat.), BC,Can
123/K3 International Falls, Mn,US
83/B2 Inthanon (peak), Thai.
63/H3 Întorsura Buzăului, Rom.
79/G3 Inubō-zaki (pt.), Japan
119/J3 Inukjuak, Qu,Can
113/K8 Inútil (bay), Chile
79/E3 Inuyama, Japan
43/C2 Inveraray, Sc,UK
89/G7 Invercargill, NZ
91/D1 Inverell, Austl.
43/C2 Invergarry, Sc,UK
43/D2 Inverkeilor, Sc,UK
123/H3 Invermay, Sk,Can
127/J2 Inverness, NS,Can
43/C2 Inverness, Sc,UK
129/G3 Inverness, Al,US
129/H4 Inverness, Fl,US
43/D2 Inverurie, Sc,UK
82/B6 Investigator (shoal)
104/F4 Inyangani (peak), Zim.
130/D2 Inymney, Gora (mtn.), Rus.
124/C3 Inyo (mts.), Ca,US
67/H1 Inza, Rus.
79/J7 Inzai, Japan
61/G3 Ioánnina, Gre.
125/J3 Iola, Ks,US
73/H1 Iolotan', Trkm.
104/B4 Iona Nat'l Park, Ang.
126/C3 Ionia, Mi,US
61/F3 Ionian (sea), Eur.
61/F3 Ionian (isls.), Gre.
61/J4 Íos (isl.), Gre.
98/A2 Iouîk (cape), Mrta.
123/K5 Iowa (state), US
123/L5 Iowa (riv.), Ia,US
123/L5 Iowa City, Ia,US
123/K5 Iowa Falls, Ia,US
110/B1 Ipameri, Braz.
112/B5 Ipan (isl.), Chile
110/D1 Ipanema, Braz.
110/D1 Ipatinga, Braz.
49/K4 Ipel' (Ipoly) (riv.), Hun., Slvk.
108/C3 Ipiales, Col.
109/L6 Ipiaú, Braz.
86/B3 Ipoh, Malay.
49/K4 Ipoly (Ipel') (riv.), Hun., Slvk.
109/H7 Iporá, Braz.
61/K2 Ipsala, Turk.
90/E7 Ipswich, Austl.
47/H2 Ipswich, Eng,UK
123/J4 Ipswich, SD,US
109/K4 Ipu, Braz.
110/B2 Ipuã, Braz.
108/D8 Iquique, Chile
108/D4 Iquitos, Peru
79/M10 Irago (chan.), Japan
79/E3 Irago-misaki (cape), Japan
61/J4 Iráklia (isl.), Gre.
61/J5 Iráklion, Gre.
72/F2 Iran
86/D3 Iran (mts.), Indo., Malay.
73/H3 Irānshahr, Iran
116/A3 Irapuato, Mex.
72/D2 Iraq
110/B3 Irati, Braz.
87/H4 Irau (mtn.), Indo.
74/K5 Irbid, Jor.
74/L5 Irbid (gov.), Jor.
74/F3 Irbīl, Iraq
109/K6 Irecê, Braz.
43/A4 Ireland
43/B3 Ireland, Northern, UK
44/B5 Ireland's Eye (isl.), Ire.
65/N5 Iremel', Gora (peak), Rus.
46/C2 Irfon (riv.), Wal,UK
99/G2 Irhazer Oua-n-Agadez (wadi), Niger
80/D5 Iri, SKor.
87/H4 Irian Jaya (reg.), Indo.
98/D2 Irîgui (reg.), Mali, Mrta.
67/L2 Iriklinskiy (res.), Rus.
101/B4 Iringa, Tanz.
101/B5 Iringa (prov.), Tanz.
82/D3 Iriomote (isl.), Japan
109/H4 Iriri (riv.), Braz.
44/C4 Irish (sea), Ire., UK
76/E1 Irkut (riv.), Rus.
76/E1 Irkutsk, Rus.
47/F5 Irlam, Eng,UK
46/D1 Iron Bridge, Eng,UK
62/F3 Iron Gate (gorge), Eur.
126/B2 Iron Mountain, Mi,US
126/B2 Iron River, Mi,US
126/D4 Ironton, Oh,US
126/B2 Ironwood, Mi,US
126/D1 Iroquois Falls, On,Can
79/F3 Irō-zaki (pt.), Japan
66/E1 Irput' (riv.), Bela., Rus.
85/G4 Irrawaddy (riv.), Burma
53/F4 Irrel, Ger.
53/F3 Irsen (riv.), Ger.
45/E3 Irt (riv.), Eng,UK
45/F1 Irthing (riv.), Eng,UK
47/F2 Irthlingborough, Eng,UK
68/G4 Irtysh (riv.), Kaz., Rus.
79/H7 Iruma, Japan
101/A2 Irumu, Zaire
58/E1 Irún, Sp.
43/C3 Irvine, Sc,UK
131/C3 Irvine, Ca,US
128/D3 Irving, Tx,US
131/F5 Irvington, NJ,US
90/C3 Isaac (riv.), Austl.
82/D6 Isabela, Phil.
119/K2 Isabella (bay), NW,Can
119/R7 Isachsen (cape), NW,Can
42/M6 Ísafjardhardjúp (fjord), Ice.
78/B4 Isahaya, Japan
103/H8 Isalo Nat'l Park, Madg.
103/H8 Isalo Ruiniform, Massif (plat.), Madg.
48/G4 Isar (riv.), Aus., Ger.
55/H4 Isarco (Eisack) (riv.), It.
60/C2 Ischia, It.
51/H3 Ise (riv.), Ger.
79/E3 Ise, Japan
79/M10 Ise (bay), Japan
47/F2 Ise (riv.), Eng,UK
79/F3 Isehara, Japan
131/F5 Iselin, NJ,US
57/K2 Isen (riv.), Ger.
57/J4 Iseo (lake), It.
56/F4 Isère (riv.), Fr.
51/E6 Iserlohn, Ger.
60/D2 Isernia, It.
79/F2 Isesaki, Japan
79/E3 Ise-Shima Nat'l Park, Japan
65/Q4 Iset' (riv.), Rus.
99/F5 Iseyin, Nga.
79/L10 Ishi (riv.), Japan
79/F2 Ishibashi, Japan
79/M9 Ishibe, Japan
92/B2 Ishigaki, Japan
82/D3 Ishigaki (isl.), Japan
79/F2 Ishige, Japan
79/G2 Ishikawa, Japan
79/E2 Ishikawa (pref.), Japan
79/N10 Ishiki, Japan
68/H4 Ishim (riv.), Kaz., Rus.
65/R4 Ishim, Rus.
67/L1 Ishimbay, Rus.
79/G1 Ishinomaki, Japan
79/G2 Ishioka, Japan
78/C4 Ishizuchi-san (mtn.), Japan
126/C2 Ishpeming, Mi,US
108/E7 Isiboro Securé Nat'l Park, Bol.
113/G1 Isidoro, Uru.
68/H4 Isil'kul', Rus.
101/A2 Isiro, Zaire
100/C4 Is, Jabal (peak), Sudan
74/D3 İskenderun, Turk.
74/C2 İskilip, Turk.
61/H1 Iskŭr (res.), Bul.
61/H1 Iskŭr (riv.), Bul.
43/D2 Isla (riv.), Sc,UK
58/B4 Isla Cristina, Sp.
112/Q9 Isla de Maipo, Chile
90/C4 Isla Gorge Nat'l Park, Austl.
117/N9 Isla Isabella Nat'l Park, Mex.
73/K2 Islāmābād (cap.), Pak.
112/B5 Isla Magdalena Nat'l Park, Chile
84/E2 Islāmpur, India
116/D3 Isla Mujeres, Mex.
123/K2 Island Lake, Mb,Can
127/K1 Islands (bay), Nf,Can
56/D4 Isle (riv.), Fr.
47/G2 Isleham, Eng,UK
44/D3 Isle of Man, UK
44/D2 Isle of Whithorn, Sc,UK
126/B2 Isle Royale Nat'l Park, Mi,US
131/G5 Islip, NY,US
65/X9 Ismailovo Park, Rus.
100/C2 Ismailia (Al Ismāʻīlīyah), Egypt
100/C3 Isnā, Egypt
55/G2 Isny, Ger.
79/M10 Isobe, Japan
42/H3 Isojärven Nat'l Park, Fin.
101/B5 Isoka, Zam.
60/C2 Isola del Liri, It.
60/E3 Isola di Capo Rizzuto, It.
74/B3 Isparta, Turk.
56/C5 Ispéguy, Col d' (pass), Fr.
63/H4 Isperikh, Bul.
74/E2 Ispir, Turk.
74/J5 Israel
132/C2 Issaquah, Wa,US
50/D5 Issel (riv.), Ger.
50/D5 Isselburg, Ger.
98/D5 Issia, IvC.
56/E4 Issoire, Fr.
56/E3 Issoudun, Fr.
50/D5 Issum, Ger.
75/C3 Issyk-Kul' (lake), Kyr.
52/B6 Issy-les-Moulineaux, Fr.
62/E1 Istállós-kő (peak), Hun.
63/J5 İstanbul, Turk.
63/J5 İstanbul (prov.), Turk.
63/H5 Istranca (mts.), Turk.
56/F5 Istres, Fr.
62/A3 Istria (pen.), Cro.
87/F2 Isulan, Phil.
109/L6 Itabaiana, Braz.
110/D2 Itabapoana (riv.), Braz.
109/K6 Itaberaba, Braz.
110/D1 Itabira, Braz.
110/D2 Itabirito, Braz.
110/L7 Itaboraí, Braz.
109/L7 Itabuna, Braz.
109/H5 Itacaiunas (riv.), Braz.
108/G4 Itacoatiara, Braz.
108/D5 Itacuaí (riv.), Braz.
110/K7 Itaguaí, Braz.
108/C2 Itagüí, Col.
110/B2 Itaí, Braz.
110/B3 Itaiópolis, Braz.
111/F1 Itaipu (res.), Braz., Par.
109/G4 Itaituba, Braz.
110/B3 Itajaí, Braz.
110/B3 Itajaí (riv.), Braz.
110/H7 Itajubá, Braz.
79/G3 Itako, Japan
41/F4 Italy
109/L7 Itamaraju, Braz.
110/D1 Itamarandiba, Braz.
110/D1 Itambacuri, Braz.
110/D1 Itambé (peak), Braz.
79/L10 Itami, Japan
85/F2 Itanagar, India
110/G9 Itanhaém, Braz.
110/C2 Itanhandu, Braz.
110/D1 Itanhém (riv.), Braz.
110/D1 Itanhomi, Braz.
109/K7 Itaobim, Braz.
110/D2 Itaocara, Braz.
109/L4 Itapagé, Braz.
110/C2 Itapecerica, Braz.
109/K4 Itapecuru-Mirim, Braz.
110/D2 Itapemirim, Braz.
110/D2 Itaperuna, Braz.
109/K7 Itapetinga, Braz.
110/B2 Itapetininga, Braz.
110/B2 Itapeva, Braz.
110/B2 Itapeví, Braz.
109/K6 Itapicuru (riv.), Braz.
109/L4 Itapipoca, Braz.
110/G7 Itapira, Braz.
110/B2 Itaporanga, Braz.
110/G8 Itaquaquecetuba, Braz.
110/B2 Itararé, Braz.
84/C3 Itārsi, India
110/C2 Itatiaia Nat'l Park, Braz.
110/G8 Itatiba, Braz.
110/C2 Itatinga (res.), Braz.
109/K5 Itaueira (riv.), Braz.
110/C2 Itaúna, Braz.
77/N3 Itayanagi, Japan
82/D3 Itbayat (isl.), Phil.
47/E4 Itchen (riv.), Eng,UK
97/K7 Itembiri (riv.), Zaire
108/F6 Iténez (riv.), Bol.
104/E4 Itezhi-Tezhi (dam), Zam.
126/E3 Ithaca, NY,US
61/G3 Ithaca (Itháki) (isl.), Gre.
51/G5 Ith Hils (ridge), Ger.
46/C2 Ithon (riv.), Wal,UK
101/B4 Itigi, Tanz.
79/F3 Itō, Japan
79/E2 Itoigawa, Japan
56/D2 Iton (riv.), Fr.
79/H7 Itsukaichi, Japan
51/F6 Itter (riv.), Ger.
60/A2 Ittiri, It.
110/C2 Itu, Braz.
108/D5 Ituí (riv.), Braz.
110/B1 Ituiutaba, Braz.
110/B1 Itumbiara, Braz.
110/B1 Itumbiara (res.), Braz.
123/H3 Ituna, Sk,Can
110/B3 Ituporanga, Braz.
110/B1 Iturama, Braz.
110/J6 Itutinga (res.), Braz.
110/C2 Ituverava, Braz.
108/E5 Ituxi (riv.), Braz.
74/H6 Ityāy al Bārūd, Egypt
48/E2 Itzehoe, Ger.
130/C2 Iul'tin, Gora (mtn.), Rus.
110/D2 Iuna, Braz.
110/B3 Ivaí (riv.), Braz.
110/B3 Ivaiporã, Braz.
42/H1 Ivalojoki (riv.), Fin.
57/M2 Ivančice, Czh.
62/D4 Ivangrad, Yugo.
126/D1 Ivanhoe (riv.), On,Can
62/E4 Ivanjica, Yugo.
66/C2 Ivano-Frankovsk, Ukr.
66/C2 Ivano-Frankovsk Obl., Ukr.
64/J4 Ivanovo, Rus.
65/J4 Ivanovo Obl., Rus.
61/J2 Ivaylovgrad (res.), Bul.
65/P3 Ivdel, Rus.
96/H7 Ivindo (riv.), Gabon
103/H8 Ivohibe, Madg.
103/J7 Ivondro (riv.), Madg.
57/G4 Ivrea, It.
52/B6 Ivry-sur-Seine, Fr.
46/C6 Ivybridge, Eng,UK
79/F2 Iwai, Japan
79/G2 Iwaki, Japan
78/C3 Iwakuni, Japan
79/M9 Iwakura, Japan
78/D3 Iwami, Japan
77/N3 Iwamizawa, Japan
79/G1 Iwanuma, Japan
79/E3 Iwata, Japan
77/N4 Iwate-san (mtn.), Japan
79/H7 Iwatsuki, Japan
99/G5 Iwo, Nga.
92/D2 Iwo Jima (isl.), Japan
48/C3 Ixelles, Belg.
116/B4 Ixtaltepec, Mex.
117/P9 Ixtlán del Río, Mex.
47/G2 Ixworth, Eng,UK
76/D1 Iya (riv.), Rus.
78/C4 Iyo, Japan
78/C4 Iyo (sea), Japan
116/D4 Izabal (lake), Guat.
67/H4 Izberbash, Rus.
52/C2 Izegem, Belg.
130/F4 Izembek Nat'l Wild. Ref., Ak,US
65/M4 Izhevsk, Rus.
65/M2 Izhma (riv.), Rus.
130/E5 Izigan (cape), Ak,US
73/G4 Izkī, Oman
63/J3 Izmail, Ukr.
74/A2 İzmir, Turk.
63/J5 İzmit, Turk.
63/J5 İzmit (gulf), Turk.
58/C4 Iznájar, Sp.
63/J5 İznik, Turk.
63/H5 İznik (lake), Turk.
74/L5 Izra', Syria
62/D2 Izsák, Hun.
77/M5 Izu (isls.), Japan
79/F3 Izu (pen.), Japan
116/B4 Izúcar de Matamoros, Mex.
79/H8 Izu-Fuji-Hakone Nat'l Park, Japan
78/A3 Izuhara, Japan
78/D3 Izumi, Japan
79/L10 Izumi-ōtsu, Japan
78/D3 Izumi-Sano, Japan
78/C3 Izumo, Japan
66/F2 Izyum, Ukr.

J

100/B5 Jabal Abyad (plat.), Sudan
74/K4 Jabal Lubnān (gov.), Leb.
58/D3 Jabalón (riv.), Sp.
84/C3 Jabalpur, India
74/K6 Jabālyah, Gaza
52/C1 Jabbeke, Belg.
100/C4 Jabjabah, Wādī (dry riv.), Egypt, Sudan
74/K4 Jablah, Syria
61/G2 Jablanica (mts.), Alb.
49/H3 Jablonec nad Nisou, Czh.
109/L5 Jaboatão, Braz.
110/B2 Jaboticabal, Braz.
62/E3 Jabuka, Yugo.
86/B4 Jabung (cape), Indo.
59/E1 Jaca, Sp.
110/C2 Jacareí, Braz.
97/Q5 Jaceel (riv.), Som.
127/G2 Jackman, Me,US
124/D2 Jackpot, Nv,US
128/D3 Jacksboro, Tx,US
129/G4 Jackson, Al,US
124/B3 Jackson, Ca,US
126/C3 Jackson, Mi,US
123/K5 Jackson, Mn,US
125/K3 Jackson, Mo,US
129/F3 Jackson (cap.), Ms,US
122/D5 Jackson (mts.), Nv,US
126/D4 Jackson, Oh,US
129/F3 Jackson, Tn,US
122/F5 Jackson, Wy,US
122/F4 Jackson (lake), Wy,US
129/G3 Jacksonville, Al,US
128/E3 Jacksonville, Ar,US
129/H4 Jacksonville, Fl,US
126/B4 Jacksonville, Il,US
129/J3 Jacksonville, NC,US
128/E4 Jacksonville, Tx,US
129/H4 Jacksonville Beach, Fl,US
117/G4 Jacmel, Haiti
73/J3 Jacobābād, Pak.
109/K6 Jacobina, Braz.
127/H1 Jacques-Cartier (mtn.), Qu,Can
127/G2 Jacques-Cartier (riv.), Qu,Can
111/F2 Jacuí (riv.), Braz.
109/L6 Jacuipe (riv.), Braz.
110/C3 Jacupiranga, Braz.
73/H3 Jaddi (pt.), Pak.
48/E2 Jade (bay), Ger.
51/F2 Jade (riv.), Ger.
51/F2 Jadebusen (bay), Ger.
58/D4 Jaén, Sp.
91/A3 Jaffa (cape), Austl.
84/D6 Jaffna, SrL.
84/D4 Jagdalpur, India
84/D2 Jagdīspur, India
82/D6 Jagna, Phil.
75/C5 Jagraon, India
57/J2 Jagst (riv.), Ger.
84/C4 Jagtiāl, India
109/K6 Jaguaquara, Braz.
113/G2 Jaguarão, Braz.
113/G2 Jaguarão (riv.), Braz.
110/G7 Jaguari (riv.), Braz.
110/B3 Jaguariaíva, Braz.
109/L5 Jaguaribe (riv.), Braz.
110/G7 Jaguariúna, Braz.
91/D3 Jagungal (peak), Austl.
72/F3 Jahrom, Iran
87/G3 Jailolo, Indo.
84/C2 Jaipur, India
84/B2 Jaisalmer, India
62/C3 Jajce, Bosn.
84/E3 Jājpur, India
86/C5 Jakarta (cap.), Indo.
42/G3 Jakobstad, Fin.
125/G4 Jal, NM,US
73/K2 Jalālābād, Afg.
42/G3 Jalasjärvi, Fin.
110/B2 Jales, Braz.
84/C3 Jālgaon, India
96/H6 Jalingo, Nga.
117/P9 Jalisco (state), Mex.
60/A4 Jāliţah, Jazīrat (isl.), Tun.
84/C4 Jālna, India
58/E2 Jalon (riv.), Sp.
84/B2 Jālor, India
84/E2 Jalpaiguri, India
97/K2 Jālū, Libya
92/F4 Jaluit (atoll), Mrsh.
72/E2 Jalūlā', Iraq
97/P7 Jamaame, Som.
99/H4 Jamaare (riv.), Nga.
117/F4 Jamaica
117/F4 Jamaica (chan.), NAm.
84/E3 Jamālpur, Bang.
84/E3 Jamālpur, India
109/G5 Jamanxim (riv.), Braz.
108/F5 Jamari (riv.), Braz.
86/B4 Jambi, Indo.
86/A2 Jambuair (cape), Indo.
121/K1 James (lake), On,Can
119/H3 James (bay), On, Qu,Can
112/B5 James (pt.), Chile
123/J4 James (riv.), ND, SD,US
126/E4 James (riv.), Va,US
131/F5 Jamesburg, NJ,US
118/G1 James Ross (str.), NW,Can
123/J4 Jamestown, ND,US
126/E3 Jamestown, NY,US
129/G2 Jamestown, Tn,US
116/B4 Jamiltepec, Mex.
75/B5 Jammu, India
75/C5 Jammu and Kashmīr (state), India
84/B3 Jāmnagar, India
73/K3 Jāmpur, Pak.
42/H3 Jämsä, Fin.
84/E3 Jamshedpur, India
42/E3 Jämtland (co.), Swe.
84/E3 Jamūi, India
123/H2 Jan (lake), Sk,Can
64/E3 Janakkala, Fin.
109/K7 Janaúba, Braz.
109/J3 Janaucu (isl.), Braz.
110/B2 Jandaia do Sul, Braz.
58/C4 Jándula (riv.), Sp.
126/B3 Janesville, Wi,US
84/C4 Jangaon, India
84/E3 Jangipur, India
49/K2 Janikowo, Pol.
74/K5 Janīn, WBnk.
62/D3 Janja, Bosn.
41/D1 Jan Mayen (isl.), Nor.
62/D2 Jánoshalma, Hun.
49/M3 Janów Lubelski, Pol.
109/K7 Janúaria, Braz.
100/C2 Janūb Sīnā' (gov.), Egypt
84/C3 Jaora, India
77/M4 Japan
77/L4 Japan (sea), Asia
79/E3 Japanese Alps (range), Japan
79/E2 Japanese Alps Nat'l Park, Japan
108/E4 Japurá (riv.), Braz.
74/D3 Jarābulus, Syria

157

Jaraí – Kasim

58/C2 **Jaraíz de la Vera**, Sp.
74/K5 **Jarash**, Jor.
96/H1 **Jarbah** (isl.), Tun.
111/E2 **Jardín América**, Arg.
110/C2 **Jardinópolis**, Braz.
109/H3 **Jari** (riv.), Braz.
84/E3 **Jaridih**, India
96/H1 **Jarjīs**, Tun.
53/E5 **Jarny**, Fr.
49/J3 **Jarocin**, Pol.
49/H3 **Jaroměř**, Czh.
49/M3 **Jarosław**, Pol.
45/G2 **Jarrow**, Eng,UK
83/C2 **Jars** (plain), Laos
53/F6 **Jarville-la-Malgrange**, Fr.
93/J5 **Jarvis** (isl.), PacUS
49/L4 **Jasło**, Pol.
122/D2 **Jasper**, Ab,Can
129/G3 **Jasper**, Al,US
129/H4 **Jasper**, Fl,US
129/G3 **Jasper**, Ga,US
126/C4 **Jasper**, In,US
128/E4 **Jasper**, Tx,US
122/D2 **Jasper Nat'l Park**, Ab, BC,Can
84/C2 **Jaspur**, India
49/J2 **Jastrowie**, Pol.
49/K4 **Jastrzębie Zdroj**, Pol.
62/E2 **Jászapáti**, Hun.
62/D2 **Jászárokszállás**, Hun.
62/D2 **Jászberény**, Hun.
62/E2 **Jászladány**, Hun.
62/E2 **Jász-Nagykun-Szolnok** (co.), Hun.
110/B1 **Jataí**, Braz.
108/G4 **Jatapu** (riv.), Braz.
59/E3 **Játiva**, Sp.
110/B2 **Jaú**, Braz.
108/F4 **Jaú** (riv.), Braz.
108/F3 **Jauaperi** (riv.), Braz.
109/H4 **Jauaru** (mts.), Braz.
108/F3 **Jaua Sarisarinama Nat'l Park**, Ven.
108/C6 **Jauja**, Peru
54/D4 **Jaunpass** (pass), Swi.
86/C5 **Java** (isl.), Indo.
86/D5 **Java** (sea), Indo.
108/D5 **Javari** (riv.), Braz.
59/F3 **Jávea**, Sp.
113/J6 **Javier** (isl.), Chile
62/D1 **Javorie** (peak), Slvk.
97/Q7 **Jawhar** (Giohar), Som.
49/J3 **Jawor**, Pol.
87/J4 **Jaya** (peak), Indo.
87/K4 **Jayapura**, Indo.
128/C3 **Jayton**, Tx,US
47/H3 **Jaywick**, Eng,UK
72/D5 **Jazā'ir Farasān** (isls.), SAr.
49/L3 **Jędrzejów**, Pol.
48/F2 **Jeetze** (riv.), Ger.
122/C4 **Jefferson** (peak), Or,US
128/E3 **Jefferson**, Tx,US
125/J3 **Jefferson City** (cap.), Mo,US
126/C4 **Jeffersonville**, In,US
122/G5 **Jeffrey City**, Wy,US
112/B5 **Jeinemeni** (peak), Chile
64/E4 **Jēkabpils**, Lat.
49/J3 **Jelcz-Laskowice**, Pol.
49/H3 **Jelenia Góra**, Pol.
49/H3 **Jelenia Góra** (prov.), Pol.
84/E2 **Jelep** (pass), China
64/D4 **Jelgava**, Lat.
52/C3 **Jemappes**, Belg.
86/D5 **Jember**, Indo.
124/F4 **Jemez Pueblo**, NM,US
87/E4 **Jempang** (riv.), Indo.
100/C3 **Jemsa**, Egypt
48/F3 **Jena**, Ger.
128/E4 **Jena**, La,US
87/E5 **Jeneponto**, Indo.
128/E4 **Jennings**, La,US
118/F2 **Jenny Lind** (isl.), NW,Can
119/H2 **Jens Muck** (isl.), NW,Can
109/L6 **Jequié**, Braz.
109/K7 **Jequitinhonha**, Braz.
109/K7 **Jequitinhonha** (riv.), Braz.
117/G4 **Jérémie**, Haiti
117/P9 **Jerez de García Salinas**, Mex.
58/B4 **Jerez de la Frontera**, Sp.
58/B3 **Jerez de los Caballeros**, Sp.
131/G5 **Jericho**, NY,US
74/K6 **Jericho** (Arīḩā), WBnk.
122/E5 **Jerome**, Id,US
131/F5 **Jersey City**, NJ,US
126/B4 **Jerseyville**, Il,US
74/M9 **Jerusalem** (dist.), Isr.
74/N9 **Jerusalem Walls Nat'l Park**, Isr.
74/K6 **Jerusalem** (Yerushalayim) (cap.), Isr.
122/C3 **Jervis** (inlet), BC,Can
62/B2 **Jesenice**, Slov.
57/K5 **Jesi**, It.
84/E3 **Jessore**, Bang.
129/H4 **Jesup**, Ga,US
127/N6 **Jésus** (isl.), Qu,Can
111/D3 **Jesús María**, Arg.
117/F3 **Jesús Menéndez**, Cuba
98/A4 **Jeta** (isl.), GBis.
125/H3 **Jetmore**, Ks,US
84/B3 **Jetpur**, India
52/D3 **Jeumont**, Fr.
51/E1 **Jever**, Ger.
123/G5 **Jewel Cave Nat'l Mon.**, SD,US
84/D4 **Jeypore**, India
61/F1 **Jezerce** (peak), Alb.
49/K2 **Jeziorák** (lake), Pol.
84/E3 **Jhā Jhā**, India
84/C3 **Jhālawār**, India
73/K2 **Jhang Sadar**, Pak.
84/C2 **Jhānsi**, India
84/D3 **Jhārsuguda**, India
73/K2 **Jhelum** (riv.), India, Pak.
73/K2 **Jhelum**, Pak.
84/E3 **Jiāganj**, India
76/F5 **Jialing** (riv.), China
81/C4 **Jialu** (riv.), China
77/L2 **Jiamusi**, China
82/B2 **Ji'an**, China
82/B3 **Jian** (riv.), China
83/E1 **Jiang** (riv.), China
82/B3 **Jiangmen**, China
81/D4 **Jiangsu** (prov.), China
81/D5 **Jiangxi** (prov.), China
81/E5 **Jiangyin**, China
82/C2 **Jianyang**, China
82/D2 **Jiaojiang**, China
77/J3 **Jiaolai** (riv.), China
81/C4 **Jiaozuo**, China
75/C4 **Jiashi**, China
81/E5 **Jiaxing**, China
76/D4 **Jiayuguan**, China
63/F2 **Jibou**, Rom.
73/G4 **Jibsh, Ra's** (pt.), Oman
49/H3 **Jičín**, Czh.
72/C4 **Jiddah**, SAr.
49/H4 **Jihlava**, Czh.
57/L2 **Jihočeský** (reg.), Czh.
49/J4 **Jihomoravský** (reg.), Czh.
96/G1 **Jijel**, Alg.
63/H2 **Jijia** (riv.), Rom.
97/P6 **Jijiga**, Eth.
59/E3 **Jijona**, Sp.
100/A4 **Jilf al Kabīr, Hadabat al** (upland), Egypt
110/B2 **Jilhá** (res.), Braz.
49/J4 **Jihlava** (riv.), Czh.
75/E2 **Jili** (lake), China
77/K3 **Jilin**, China
77/J1 **Jiliu** (riv.), China
59/E2 **Jiloca** (riv.), Sp.
97/N6 **Jīma**, Eth.
62/E3 **Jimbolia**, Rom.
58/C4 **Jimena de la Frontera**, Sp.
76/B3 **Jimsar**, China
82/C2 **Jin** (riv.), China
85/K2 **Jin** (riv.), China
81/D3 **Jinan**, China
84/C2 **Jīnd**, India
49/H4 **Jindřichuv Hradec**, Czh.
81/B4 **Jing** (riv.), China
82/C2 **Jingdezhen**, China
82/B2 **Jinggangshan**, China
81/D3 **Jinghai**, China
81/C5 **Jingmen**, China
82/C2 **Jinhua**, China
81/C2 **Jining**, China
81/D4 **Jining**, China
101/B2 **Jinja**, Ugan.
116/D5 **Jinotega**, Nic.
116/D5 **Jinotepe**, Nic.
81/B4 **Jinqian** (riv.), China
81/E5 **Jinshan**, China
85/K2 **Jinshi**, China
82/D5 **Jintotlo** (chan.), Phil.
84/C4 **Jintūr**, India
81/E2 **Jinxi**, China
82/C2 **Jinxi**, China
81/E2 **Jinzhou**, China
108/F6 **Ji-Paraná**, Braz.
108/F5 **Jiparaná** (riv.), Braz.
108/B4 **Jipijapa**, Ecu.
100/B3 **Jirgā**, Egypt
82/A2 **Jishou**, China
74/D3 **Jisr ash Shughūr**, Syria
63/F4 **Jiu** (riv.), Rom.
82/C2 **Jiujiang**, China
82/A2 **Jiuwan** (mts.), China
81/D5 **Jixi**, China
81/C4 **Ji Xian**, China
81/D2 **Ji Xian**, China
100/B2 **Jīzah, Pyramids of** (Giza) (ruins), Egypt
81/C3 **Jize**, China
57/L1 **Jizera** (riv.), Czh.
78/C3 **Jizō-zaki** (pt.), Japan
72/F5 **Jiz', Wādī al** (dry riv.), Yem.
110/B3 **Joaçaba**, Braz.
110/D1 **João Monlevade**, Braz.
109/M5 **João Pessoa**, Braz.
110/C1 **João Pinheiro**, Braz.
111/D2 **Joaquín V. González**, Arg.
117/F3 **Jobabo**, Cuba
58/D4 **Jódar**, Sp.
84/B2 **Jodhpur**, India
53/D2 **Jodoigne**, Belg.
42/J3 **Joensuu**, Fin.
79/F2 **Jōetsu**, Japan
53/F5 **Joeuf**, Fr.
102/E2 **Johannesburg**, SAfr.
124/C4 **Johannesburg**, Ca,US
122/D4 **John Day**, Or,US
122/C4 **John Day** (riv.), Or,US
122/C4 **John Day Fossil Beds Nat'l Mon.**, Or,US
128/C2 **John Martin** (res.), Co,US
129/H2 **Johnson City**, Tn,US
128/D4 **Johnson City**, Tx,US
125/G3 **Johnson** (Johnson City), Ks,US
130/M3 **Johnsons Crossing**, Yk,Can
93/J3 **Johnston** (atoll), PacUS
46/B3 **Johnston**, Wal,UK
126/E3 **Johnstown**, Pa,US
86/B3 **Johor Baharu**, Malay.
56/E3 **Joigny**, Fr.
110/B3 **Joinvile**, Braz.
105/W **Joinville** (isl.), Ant.
97/M6 **Jokau**, Sudan
42/F2 **Jokkmokk**, Swe.
42/P6 **Jökulsargljufur Nat'l Park**, Ice.
132/P16 **Joliet**, Il,US
126/F2 **Joliette**, Qu,Can
128/D4 **Jollyville**, Tx,US
82/D6 **Jolo**, Phil.
82/D6 **Jolo** (isl.), Phil.
86/D5 **Jombang**, Indo.
55/E3 **Jona**, Swi.
49/N1 **Jonava**, Lith.
119/S7 **Jones** (sound), NW,Can
129/F3 **Jonesboro**, Ar,US
128/E3 **Jonesboro**, La,US
44/B3 **Jonesborough**, NI,UK
42/E4 **Jönköping**, Swe.
42/E4 **Jönköping** (co.), Swe.
127/G1 **Jonquière**, Qu,Can
125/J3 **Joplin**, Mo,US
72/C2 **Jordan**
127/R9 **Jordan**, On,Can
74/K6 **Jordan** (riv.), Jor., WBnk.
122/G4 **Jordan**, Mt,US
124/E2 **Jordan** (riv.), Ut,US
127/R9 **Jordan Station**, On,Can
122/D5 **Jordan Valley**, Or,US
113/J7 **Jorge** (cape), Chile
85/F2 **Jorhāt**, India
51/G1 **Jork**, Ger.
128/B3 **Jornada del Muerto** (val.), NM,US
99/H4 **Jos** (plat.), Nga.
82/E6 **Jose Abad Santos**, Phil.
110/B2 **José Bonifacio**, Braz.
79/F2 **Joshin-Etsu Kogen Nat'l Park**, Japan
124/D4 **Joshua Tree Nat'l Mon.**, Ca,US
42/C3 **Jotunheimen Nat'l Park**, Nor.
56/C2 **Jouanne** (riv.), Fr.
52/C6 **Jouarre**, Fr.
56/D3 **Joué-lès-Tours**, Fr.
90/B2 **Joumna Falls Nat'l Park**, Austl.
128/D4 **Jourdanton**, Tx,US
50/C3 **Joure**, Neth.
42/J3 **Joutseno**, Fin.
72/G1 **Joveyn** (riv.), Iran
85/F2 **Jowai**, India
130/M3 **Joy** (mtn.), Yk,Can
79/L10 **Jōyō**, Japan
98/A2 **Jreïda**, Mrta.
81/B5 **Ju** (riv.), China
117/P9 **Juan Aldama**, Mex.
122/B3 **Juan de Fuca** (str.), Can., US
103/G7 **Juan de Nova** (isl.), Reun.
107/A6 **Juan Fernández** (isls.), Chile
117/J5 **Juangriego**, Ven.
108/C5 **Juanjuí**, Peru
113/T12 **Juan L. Lacaze**, Uru.
112/F3 **Juárez**, Arg.
110/J8 **Juatinga** (pt.), Braz.
109/K5 **Juazeiro**, Braz.
109/L5 **Juazeiro do Norte**, Braz.
97/M7 **Juba**, Sudan
97/P7 **Jubba** (riv.), Eth., Som.
59/Y17 **Juby** (cape), Mor.
58/D3 **Júcar** (riv.), Sp.
50/D6 **Jüchen**, Ger.
74/N9 **Judaea** (reg.), WBnk.
57/L3 **Judenburg**, Aus.
122/F4 **Judith** (riv.), Mt,US
100/B3 **Juhaynah**, Egypt
116/D5 **Juigalpa**, Nic.
56/E2 **Juine** (riv.), Fr.
82/D3 **Juishui**, Tai.
50/D1 **Juist** (isl.), Ger.
110/K6 **Juiz de Fora**, Braz.
125/G2 **Julesburg**, Co,US
108/D7 **Juliaca**, Peru
57/K3 **Julian Alps** (mts.), It., Slov.
53/F2 **Jülich**, Ger.
117/F3 **Julio A. Mella**, Cuba
73/L2 **Jullundur**, India
81/C3 **Juma** (riv.), China
58/E3 **Jumilla**, Sp.
84/D2 **Jumla**, Nepal
51/E2 **Jümme** (riv.), Ger.
84/B3 **Junāgadh**, India
112/C2 **Juncal** (peak), Arg., Chile
128/D4 **Junction**, Tx,US
124/D3 **Junction**, Ut,US
125/H3 **Junction City**, Ks,US
122/C4 **Junction City**, Or,US
110/G8 **Jundiaí**, Braz.
81/H6 **Jundu** (mts.), China
130/M4 **Juneau** (cap.), Ak,US
54/D4 **Jungfrau** (peak), Swi.
108/C6 **Junín**, Peru
52/D5 **Juniville**, Fr.
81/C3 **Junji Guan** (pass), China
129/H5 **Juno Beach**, Fl,US
110/B2 **Junqueirópolis**, Braz.
110/E1 **Juparanã** (lake), Braz.
127/J1 **Jupiter** (riv.), Qu,Can
129/H5 **Jupiter**, Fl,US
132/A2 **Jupiter** (mtn.), Wa,US
110/C3 **Juquiá**, Braz.
110/F8 **Juquitiba**, Braz.
97/L6 **Jur** (riv.), Sudan
54/B4 **Jura** (dept.), Fr.
54/B4 **Jura** (mts.), Fr.
54/D3 **Jura** (canton), Swi.
56/C5 **Jurançon**, Fr.
52/C2 **Jurbise**, Belg.
44/D3 **Jurby Head** (pt.), IM,UK
64/D4 **Jūrmala**, Lat.
108/E4 **Juruá** (riv.), Braz.
108/G6 **Juruena** (riv.), Braz.
109/G4 **Juruti**, Braz.
79/M9 **Jushiyama**, Japan
112/D2 **Justo Daract**, Arg.
108/E4 **Jutaí** (riv.), Braz.
116/D5 **Jutiapa**, Guat.
116/D5 **Juticalpa**, Hon.
42/D4 **Jutland** (pen.), Den.
42/H3 **Juva**, Fin.
116/E3 **Juventud** (Pinos) (isl.), Cuba
81/D4 **Juye**, China
81/C5 **Juzhang** (riv.), China
62/E4 **Južna Morava** (riv.), Yugo.
42/H3 **Jyväskylä**, Fin.

K

75/C4 **K2** (Godwin Austen) (mtn.), China, Pak.
96/F5 **Ka** (riv.), Nga.
102/C3 **Kaap** (plat.), SAfr.
64/D3 **Kaarina**, Fin.
50/D6 **Kaarst**, Ger.
62/E2 **Kaba**, Hun.
87/F5 **Kabaena** (isl.), Indo.
116/D3 **Kabah** (ruins), Mex.
101/A3 **Kabale**, Ugan.
101/A2 **Kabalega Nat'l Park**, Ugan.
104/E2 **Kabalo**, Zaire
104/E2 **Kabamba** (lake), Zaire
87/F2 **Kabankalan**, Phil.
67/G4 **Kabardin-Balkar Aut. Rep.**, Rus.
126/C1 **Kabinakagami** (lake), On,Can
104/D2 **Kabinda**, Zaire
60/A5 **Kabīyah** (lag.), Tun.
104/D3 **Kabompo** (riv.), Zam.
104/D2 **Kabongo**, Zaire
73/J2 **Kabul** (riv.), Afg.
73/J2 **Kābul** (Kābol) (cap.), Afg.
87/G3 **Kaburuang** (isl.), Indo.
104/E3 **Kabwe**, Zam.
62/E4 **Kačanik**, Yugo.
130/H4 **Kachemak** (bay), Ak,US
85/G2 **Kachin** (state), Burma
84/C6 **Kadaianallur**, India
83/B3 **Kadan** (isl.), Burma
57/K1 **Kadaň**, Czh.
92/G6 **Kadavu** (isl.), Fiji
96/J7 **Kadéï** (riv.), CAfr., Congo
63/H5 **Kadıköy**, Turk.
74/C2 **Kadınhanı**, Turk.
99/E3 **Kadiogo** (prov.), Burk.
84/C5 **Kadiri**, India
74/D3 **Kadirli**, Turk.
123/H5 **Kadoka**, SD,US
79/L10 **Kadoma**, Japan
104/E4 **Kadoma**, Zim.
99/G4 **Kaduna**, Nga.
99/G4 **Kaduna** (riv.), Nga.
99/G4 **Kaduna** (state), Nga.
97/L5 **Kāduqlī**, Sudan
98/B2 **Kaédi**, Mrta.
96/H5 **Kaélé**, Camr.
83/C2 **Kaeng Khlo**, Thai.
83/B3 **Kaeng Krachan Nat'l Park**, Thai.
80/D3 **Kaesŏng**, NKor.
80/D4 **Kaesŏng-Si** (prov.), NKor.
67/H5 **Kafan**, Arm.
73/J2 **Kafar Jar Ghar** (mts.), Afg.
104/D2 **Kaffraria** (reg.), SAfr.
98/B3 **Kaffrine**, Sen.
97/K6 **Kafia Kingi**, Sudan
61/J3 **Kafirévs, Akra** (cape), Gre.
74/H6 **Kafr ad Dawwār**, Egypt
74/H6 **Kafr ash Shaykh**, Egypt
74/H6 **Kafr ash Shaykh** (gov.), Egypt
74/H6 **Kafr az Zayyāt**, Egypt
74/N8 **Kafr Qarī'**, Isr.
74/M8 **Kafr Qāsim**, Isr.
104/E4 **Kafue**, Zam.
104/E4 **Kafue** (riv.), Zam.
104/E4 **Kafue Nat'l Park**, Zam.
78/E2 **Kaga**, Japan
96/J6 **Kaga Bandoro**, CAfr.
68/G6 **Kagan**, Uzb.
78/D3 **Kagawa** (pref.), Japan
63/J5 **Kağıthane**, Turk.
72/E2 **Kağızman**, Turk.
78/B5 **Kagoshima**, Japan
78/B5 **Kagoshima** (bay), Japan
78/B5 **Kagoshima** (pref.), Japan
63/J3 **Kagul**, Mol.
120/W12 **Kahana**, Hi,US
86/D4 **Kahayan** (riv.), Indo.
104/C2 **Kahemba**, Zaire
76/D1 **Kahmsara** (riv.), Rus.
125/K2 **Kahoka**, Mo,US
120/T10 **Kahoolawe** (isl.), Hi,US
42/G1 **Kahperusvaara** (peak), Fin.
74/D3 **Kahramanmaraş**, Turk.
73/K3 **Kahror Pakka**, Pak.
74/D3 **Kâhta**, Turk.
120/T10 **Kahuku** (pt.), Hi,US
120/T10 **Kahului**, Hi,US
104/E1 **Kahuzi-Biega Nat'l Park**, Zaire
87/H5 **Kai** (isls.), Indo.
124/D3 **Kaibab** (plat.), Az,US
79/L9 **Kaibara**, Japan
87/H5 **Kai Besar** (isl.), Indo.
75/E3 **Kaidu** (riv.), China
76/G5 **Kaifeng**, China
78/D4 **Kaifu**, Japan
87/H5 **Kai Kecil** (isl.), Indo.
89/H7 **Kaikoura**, NZ
85/J2 **Kaili**, China
120/U11 **Kailua**, Hi,US
102/B2 **Kainab** (dry riv.), Namb.
62/B2 **Kainach** (riv.), Aus.
78/D3 **Kainan**, Japan
99/G4 **Kainji** (lake), Nga.
79/H7 **Kaisei**, Japan
53/G5 **Kaiserslautern**, Ger.
89/H6 **Kaitaia**, NZ
75/C6 **Kaithal**, India
120/T10 **Kaiwi** (chan.), Hi,US
81/F2 **Kaiyuan**, China
85/H3 **Kaiyuan**, China
79/M9 **Kaizu**, Japan
79/L10 **Kaizuka**, Japan
42/H2 **Kajaani**, Fin.
80/E5 **Kaji-san** (mtn.), SKor.
97/M5 **Kākā**, Sudan
42/G3 **Kakaanpää**, Fin.
101/B2 **Kakamega**, Kenya
79/E3 **Kakamigahara**, Japan
62/D3 **Kakanj**, Bosn.
130/M4 **Kaketsa** (mtn.), BC,Can
66/E3 **Kakhovka**, Ukr.
66/E3 **Kakhovka** (res.), Ukr.
84/D4 **Kākināda**, India
79/L9 **Kako** (riv.), Japan
98/B4 **Kakrima** (riv.), Gui.
79/G2 **Kakuda**, Japan
101/B2 **Kakuma**, Kenya
101/A3 **Kakuto**, Ugan.
60/B5 **Kalaa-Kebia**, Tun.
115/N2 **Kalaallit Nunaat** (Greenland) (dpcy.), Den.
104/D3 **Kalabo**, Zam.
67/G2 **Kalach**, Rus.
68/H4 **Kalachinsk**, Rus.
67/G2 **Kalach-na-Donu**, Rus.
85/F3 **Kaladan** (riv.), Burma
120/U11 **Ka Lae** (cape), Hi,US
104/D5 **Kalahari** (des.), Afr.
102/C2 **Kalahari-Gemsbok Nat'l Park**, SAfr.
61/L7 **Kalamáki**, Gre.
96/H5 **Kalamaloué Nat'l Park**, Camr.
61/H2 **Kalamariá**, Gre.
61/H4 **Kalamáta**, Gre.
126/C3 **Kalamazoo**, Mi,US
83/C2 **Kalasin**, Thai.
73/J3 **Kalāt**, Pak.
60/B5 **Kalbīyah** (lake), Tun.
42/N7 **Kaldakvísl** (riv.), Ice.
51/H5 **Kalefeld**, Ger.
101/A4 **Kalemie**, Zaire
49/K3 **Kalety**, Pol.
89/B4 **Kalgoorlie-Boulder**, Austl.
63/J4 **Kaliakra, Nos** (pt.), Bul.
86/C5 **Kalianda**, Indo.
82/D5 **Kalibo**, Phil.
104/E1 **Kalima**, Zaire
86/D4 **Kalimantan** (reg.), Indo.
74/A3 **Kálimnos**, Gre.
49/L1 **Kaliningrad**, Rus.
64/H5 **Kaliningrad**, Rus.
49/K1 **Kaliningrad** (lag.), Rus.
64/D5 **Kaliningrad Obl.**, Rus.
67/H2 **Kalininsk**, Rus.
66/D1 **Kalinkovichi**, Bela.
101/A3 **Kalisizo**, Ugan.
122/E3 **Kalispell**, Mt,US
49/K3 **Kalisz**, Pol.
49/J3 **Kalisz** (prov.), Pol.
42/G2 **Kalix**, Swe.
42/G2 **Kalixälv** (riv.), Swe.
84/E2 **Kāliyāganj**, India
126/C2 **Kalkaska**, Mi,US
61/L7 **Kallithea**, Gre.
42/E3 **Kallsjön** (lake), Swe.
42/F4 **Kalmar**, Swe.
42/E4 **Kalmar** (co.), Swe.
50/B6 **Kalmthout**, Belg.
67/H3 **Kalmyk Aut. Rep.**, Rus.
62/D2 **Kalocsa**, Hun.
120/T10 **Kalohi** (chan.), Hi,US
84/B3 **Kālol**, India
104/E4 **Kalomo**, Zam.
84/C2 **Kālpi**, India
48/E2 **Kaltenkirchen**, Ger.
57/F4 **Kaltern** (Caldaro), It.
84/D6 **Kalu** (riv.), SrL.
64/H5 **Kaluga**, Rus.
64/G5 **Kaluga Obl.**, Rus.
48/F1 **Kalundborg**, Den.
66/C2 **Kalush**, Ukr.
84/C6 **Kalutara**, SrL.
84/B4 **Kalyān**, India
65/M4 **Kama** (res.), Rus.
65/M3 **Kama** (riv.), Rus.
104/E1 **Kama**, Zaire
79/J7 **Kamagaya**, Japan
77/N4 **Kamaishi**, Japan
120/T10 **Kamakou** (peak), Hi,US
79/H7 **Kamakura**, Japan
75/B5 **Kamālia**, Pak.
74/C2 **Kaman**, Turk.
98/E2 **Kamango** (lake), Mali
84/C4 **Kāmāreddi**, India
84/E3 **Kāmārhāti**, India
84/A2 **Kambar**, Pak.
104/E3 **Kambove**, Zaire
87/F4 **Kambuno** (peak), Indo.
69/R4 **Kamchatka** (pen.), Rus.
69/R4 **Kamchatka Obl.**, Rus.
63/H4 **Kamchiya** (riv.), Bul.
51/E5 **Kamen**, Ger.
66/C2 **Kamenets-Podol'skiy**, Ukr.
62/A3 **Kamenjak, Rt** (cape), Cro.
67/H1 **Kamenka**, Rus.
75/D1 **Kamen'-na-Obi**, Rus.
66/G2 **Kamensk-Shakhtinskiy**, Rus.
65/P4 **Kamensk-Ural'skiy**, Rus.
78/D3 **Kameoka**, Japan
79/M10 **Kameyama**, Japan
122/D4 **Kamiah**, Id,US
49/H2 **Kamień Pomorski**, Pol.
79/H7 **Kamifukuoka**, Japan
77/N3 **Kamiisco**, Japan
79/M9 **Kamiishizu**, Japan
120/U11 **Kamilo** (pt.), Hi,US
104/E2 **Kamina**, Zaire
79/G1 **Kaminoyama**, Japan
130/H4 **Kamishak** (bay), Ak,US
78/B5 **Kamiyaku**, Japan
122/C3 **Kamloops**, BC,Can
83/C4 **Kamlot**, Camb.
79/L10 **Kammaki**, Japan
62/B2 **Kamnik**, Slov.
79/J7 **Kamo** (riv.), Japan
79/G3 **Kamogawa**, Japan
78/D3 **Kamojima**, Japan
57/L2 **Kamp** (riv.), Aus.
101/B2 **Kampala** (cap.), Ugan.
86/B3 **Kampar** (riv.), Indo.
86/B3 **Kampar**, Malay.
50/C3 **Kampen**, Neth.
83/B2 **Kamphaeng Phet**, Thai.
49/L2 **Kampinoski Nat'l Park**, Pol.
50/D6 **Kamp-Lintfort**, Ger.
83/D4 **Kampong Cham**, Camb.
83/D3 **Kampong Chhnang**, Camb.
83/D3 **Kampong Khleang**, Camb.
83/C4 **Kampong Saom**, Camb.
83/C4 **Kampong Saom** (bay), Camb.
83/D4 **Kampong Spoe**, Camb.
83/D3 **Kampong Thum**, Camb.
83/D4 **Kampong Trabek**, Camb.
83/D4 **Kampot**, Camb.
87/H4 **Kamrau** (bay), Indo.
123/H3 **Kamsack**, Sk,Can
123/H1 **Kamuchawie** (lake), Sk,Can
116/E6 **Kámuk** (mt.), CR
67/H2 **Kamyshin**, Rus.
119/J3 **Kanaaupscow** (riv.), Qu,Can
124/D3 **Kanab** (riv.), Az, Ut,US
124/D3 **Kanab**, Ut,US
130/C6 **Kanaga** (isl.), Ak,US
130/C6 **Kanaga** (vol.), Ak,US
79/F3 **Kanagawa** (pref.), Japan
119/K3 **Kanairiktok** (riv.), Nf,Can
79/L10 **Kanan**, Japan
104/D2 **Kananga**, Zaire
65/K5 **Kanash**, Rus.
126/D4 **Kanawha** (riv.), WV,US
79/E2 **Kanazawa**, Japan
83/B3 **Kanchanaburi**, Thai.
84/C5 **Kānchīpuram**, India
64/G2 **Kandalaksha**, Rus.
64/G2 **Kandalaksha** (gulf), Rus.
93/Y18 **Kandavu** (passg.), Fiji
73/J3 **Kandhkot**, Pak.
84/E3 **Kāndi**, India
87/F3 **Kandi** (cape), Indo.
63/K5 **Kandıra**, Turk.
84/C4 **Kandukūr**, India
84/D6 **Kandy**, SrL.
119/T7 **Kane Basin** (sound), NW,Can
96/H5 **Kanem** (reg.), Chad
120/W13 **Kaneohe**, Hi,US
120/W13 **Kaneohe** (bay), Hi,US
104/D5 **Kang**, Bots.
74/D2 **Kangal**, Turk.
86/B2 **Kangar**, Malay.
72/E2 **Kangāvar**, Iran
87/E5 **Kangean** (isls.), Indo.
119/K3 **Kangiqsualujjuaq**, Qu,Can
119/J2 **Kangiqsujuaq**, Qu,Can
119/J2 **Kangirsuk**, Qu,Can
80/E4 **Kangnŭng**, SKor.
75/D5 **Kangrinboqê Feng** (peak), China
85/F2 **Kangto** (peak), China
80/D3 **Kangwŏn-Do** (prov.), NKor.
80/D4 **Kangwŏn-Do** (prov.), SKor.
84/C3 **Kanhān** (riv.), India
79/N9 **Kani**, Japan
79/M9 **Kanie**, Japan
65/K2 **Kanin** (pen.), Rus.
64/J1 **Kanin Nos** (pt.), Rus.
62/E2 **Kanjiža**, Yugo.
126/C3 **Kankakee**, Il,US
126/C3 **Kankakee** (riv.), Il, In,Us
98/C4 **Kankan**, Gui.
98/C4 **Kankan** (comm.), Gui.
84/D3 **Kānker**, India
78/C3 **Kanmuri-yama** (mtn.), Japan
129/H3 **Kannapolis**, NC,US
84/C2 **Kannauj**, India
79/H7 **Kannon-zaki** (pt.), Japan
99/H4 **Kano**, Nga.
99/H3 **Kano** (state), Nga.
78/C3 **Kan'onji**, Japan
78/B5 **Kanoya**, Japan
84/D2 **Kānpur**, India
125/H3 **Kansas** (state), US
125/H3 **Kansas** (riv.), Ks,US
125/J3 **Kansas City**, Ks, Mo,US
68/K4 **Kansk**, Rus.
84/D3 **Kantābānji**, India
79/F2 **Kantō** (prov.), Japan
79/F2 **Kanuma**, Japan
108/G3 **Kanuku** (mts.), Guy.
130/H2 **Kanuti Nat'l Wild. Ref.**, Ak,US
102/D2 **Kanye**, Bots.
83/D3 **Kaoh Nhek**, Camb.
82/D3 **Kaohsiung**, Tai.
104/B4 **Kaokoveld** (reg.), Namb.
98/A3 **Kaolack**, Sen.
98/B3 **Kaolack** (reg.), Sen.
104/D3 **Kaoma**, Zam.
120/S9 **Kapaa**, Hi,US
82/E6 **Kapalong**, Phil.
104/D2 **Kapanga**, Zaire
62/E4 **Kapaonik** (upland), Yugo.
75/C3 **Kapchagay**, Kaz.
75/C3 **Kapchagay** (res.), Kaz.
50/B6 **Kapellen**, Belg.
57/L3 **Kapfenberg**, Aus.
63/H5 **Kapıdağı** (pen.), Turk.
92/E4 **Kapingamarangi** (isl.), Micr.
104/E3 **Kapiri Mposhi**, Zam.
119/H3 **Kapiskau** (riv.), On,Can
97/M7 **Kapoeta**, Sudan
62/C2 **Kapos** (riv.), Hun.
62/C2 **Kaposvár**, Hun.
49/M1 **Kapsukas**, Lith.
86/C4 **Kapuas** (riv.), Indo.
86/D3 **Kapuas Hulu** (mts.), Indo., Malay.
126/D1 **Kapuskasing**, On,Can
126/D1 **Kapuskasing** (riv.), On,Can
62/C2 **Kapuvár**, Hun.
67/H5 **Kapydzhik, Gora** (peak), Azer.
65/Q1 **Kara** (riv.), Rus.
68/G2 **Kara** (sea), Rus.
67/K4 **Kara-Bogaz-Gol** (gulf), Trkm.
87/H4 **Karabra** (riv.), Indo.
74/C2 **Karabük**, Turk.
74/D3 **Karaca** (peak), Turk.
74/B2 **Karacabey**, Turk.
67/G4 **Karachay-Cherkass Aut. Obl.**, Rus.
66/E1 **Karachev**, Rus.
73/J4 **Karāchi**, Pak.
84/B4 **Karād**, India
75/B2 **Karaganda**, Kaz.
71/R4 **Karaginskiy** (isl.), Rus.
75/E1 **Karagoš** (peak), Rus.
84/C5 **Kāraikkudi**, India
72/F1 **Karaj**, Iran
67/L3 **Karakalpak Aut. Rep.**, Uzb.
75/C4 **Karakax** (riv.), China
74/D2 **Karakaya** (res.), Turk.
87/G3 **Karakelong** (isl.), Indo.
76/E3 **Karakhoto** (ruins), China
74/E2 **Karakoçan**, Turk.
75/C4 **Karakoram** (range), Asia
75/C4 **Karakoram** (pass), China, India
98/C3 **Karakoro** (riv.), Mali, Mrta.
76/E2 **Karakorum** (ruins), Mong.
74/E2 **Karaköse**, Turk.
75/B4 **Karakul'** (lake), Taj.
67/L5 **Karakumy** (des.), Trkm.
67/K4 **Karakyon, Gora** (peak), Trkm.
73/H1 **Karakyr** (peak), Trkm.
87/E4 **Karam** (riv.), Indo.
74/C3 **Karaman**, Turk.
75/D2 **Karamay**, China
75/D4 **Karamiran** (riv.), China
75/E4 **Karamiran Shankou** (pass), China
101/B2 **Karamoja** (prov.), Ugan.
63/J5 **Karamürsel**, Turk.
85/G4 **Karan** (state), Burma
87/E5 **Karangasem**, Indo.
69/S4 **Karanginskiy** (bay), Rus.
69/S4 **Karanginskiy** (isl.), Rus.
84/C3 **Kāranja**, India
83/B2 **Karan** (Kayin) (state), Burma
74/C3 **Karapınar**, Turk.
78/A3 **Kara-saki** (pt.), Japan
79/M10 **Karasu**, Japan
63/K5 **Karasu**, Turk.
75/C1 **Karasuk**, Rus.
75/C2 **Karatal** (riv.), Kaz.
75/B3 **Karatau**, Kaz.
75/A3 **Karatau** (mts.), Kaz.
78/A4 **Karatsu**, Japan
61/G3 **Karáva** (peak), Gre.
75/B2 **Karazhal**, Kaz.
100/C5 **Karbaka**, Sudan
72/D2 **Karbalā'**, Iraq
62/E2 **Karcag**, Hun.
61/G3 **Kardhítsa**, Gre.
68/D3 **Karelian Aut. Rep.**, Rus.
101/A4 **Karema**, Tanz.
76/H1 **Karenga** (riv.), Rus.
104/E4 **Kariba** (lake), Zam., Zim.
104/E4 **Kariba**, Zim.
86/C4 **Karimata** (isl.), Indo.
86/C4 **Karimata** (str.), Indo.
84/C4 **Karīmnagar**, India
101/A3 **Karisimbi** (vol.), Rwa.
79/M10 **Kariya**, Japan
97/Q6 **Karkaar** (mts.), Som.
84/B5 **Kārkāl**, India
92/D5 **Karkar** (isl.), PNG
66/E3 **Karkinitsk** (gulf), Ukr.
75/B4 **Karla Marksa, Pik** (peak), Taj.
62/B3 **Karlovac**, Slov.
63/G4 **Karlovo**, Bul.
57/K1 **Karlovy Vary** (Karlsbad), Czh.
42/E4 **Karlshamn**, Swe.
42/E4 **Karlskoga**, Swe.
42/E4 **Karlskrona**, Swe.
57/H2 **Karlsruhe**, Ger.
42/E4 **Karlstad**, Swe.
100/B5 **Karmah**, Sudan
84/C4 **Karmāla**, India
74/K5 **Karmel, Har** (Mount Carmel) (mtn.), Isr.
84/C2 **Karnāl**, India
84/C4 **Karnātaka** (state), India
128/D4 **Karnes City**, Tx,US
63/H4 **Karnobat**, Bul.
62/A2 **Kärnten** (prov.), Aus.
101/B5 **Karonga**, Malw.
102/C4 **Karoo Nat'l Park**, SAfr.
73/K2 **Karor**, Pak.
87/E5 **Karoso** (cape), Indo.
74/A3 **Kárpathos** (isl.), Gre.
102/M11 **Kars** (riv.), SAfr.
74/E2 **Kars**, Turk.
68/G6 **Karshi**, Uzb.
67/M1 **Kartaly**, Rus.
63/L3 **Kartinitsk** (gulf), Ukr.
49/K1 **Kartuzy**, Pol.
72/E2 **Karūn** (riv.), Iran
49/K4 **Karviná**, Czh.
84/B5 **Karwar**, India
123/L2 **Kasabonika** (lake), On,Can
84/E3 **Kāsai** (riv.), India
78/D3 **Kasai**, Japan
104/C1 **Kasai** (riv.), Zaire
79/G2 **Kasama**, Japan
101/A5 **Kasama**, Zam.
79/M9 **Kasamatsu**, Japan
104/E4 **Kasane**, Bots.
78/C3 **Kasaoka**, Japan
84/C5 **Kāsaragod**, India
100/D5 **Kasar, Ras** (cape), Sudan
79/M10 **Kasartori-yama** (peak), Japan
118/F2 **Kasba** (lake), NW,Can
78/B5 **Kaseda**, Japan
84/C2 **Kāsganj**, India
73/H1 **Kashaf** (riv.), Iran
72/F2 **Kāshān**, Iran
75/C4 **Kashi**, China
79/L10 **Kashiba**, Japan
78/D3 **Kashihara**, Japan
78/B4 **Kashima**, Japan
79/G3 **Kashima**, Japan
64/H4 **Kashin**, Rus.
79/H7 **Kashiwa**, Japan
79/L10 **Kashiwara**, Japan
79/F2 **Kashiwazaki**, Japan
73/G1 **Kashmar**, Iran
84/A2 **Kashmor**, Pak.
64/J5 **Kasimov**, Rus.

Kasir – Kohtl

159
Kohŭn – Lake

80/D5 Kohŭng, SKor.
116/D4 Kohunlich (ruins), Mex.
102/A2 Koichab (dry riv.), Namb.
130/K3 Koidern, Yk,Can
80/E5 Kŏje (isl.), SKor.
49/L4 Kojšovská Hol'a (peak), Slvk.
83/B1 Kok (riv.), Burma
79/M10 Kōka, Japan
79/J7 Kokai (riv.), Japan
75/B3 Kokand, Uzb.
75/A1 Kokchetav, Kaz.
42/G3 Kokkola, Fin.
98/C3 Kokofata, Mali
120/W13 Koko Head (crater), Hi,US
101/A2 Kokola, Zaire
126/C3 Kokomo, In,US
84/F2 Kokrajhar, India
75/C3 Kokshaal-Tau (mts.), Kyr.
52/B1 Koksijde, Belg.
119/K3 Koksoak (riv.), Qu,Can
102/E3 Kokstad, SAfr.
78/B5 Kokubu, Japan
64/H1 Kola (pen.), Rus.
64/G1 Kola (riv.), Rus.
87/F4 Kolaka, Indo.
84/C5 Kolār, India
62/D4 Kolašin, Yugo.
48/G5 Kolbermoor, Ger.
49/L3 Kolbuszowa, Pol.
98/B3 Kolda, Sen.
98/B3 Kolda (reg.), Sen.
48/E1 Kolding, Den.
42/E2 Kölen (Kjølen) (mts.), Nor., Swe.
92/C5 Kolepom (isl.), Indo.
64/F4 Kolgompya (cape), Rus.
65/K1 Kolguyev (isl.), Rus.
84/B4 Kolhāpur, India
98/B3 Koliba (riv.), Gui.
49/H3 Kolín, Czh.
64/D4 Kolkasrags (pt.), Lat.
50/D2 Kollum, Neth.
50/D7 Köln (Cologne), Ger.
49/L2 Kolno, Pol.
66/A1 Koło, Pol.
101/B4 Kolo, Tanz.
49/H1 Kołobrzeg, Pol.
98/C3 Kolokani, Mali
66/F1 Kolomna, Rus.
66/C2 Kolomyya, Ukr.
92/E4 Kolonia (cap.), Micr.
84/C6 Kolonnawa, SrL.
98/D3 Kolossa (riv.), Mali
68/J4 Kolpashevo, Rus.
64/F4 Kolpino, Rus.
62/E3 Kolubara (riv.), Yugo
49/K3 Koluszki, Pol.
75/A1 Koluton (riv.), Kaz.
65/N2 Kolva (riv.), Rus.
104/E3 Kolwezi, Zaire
69/R2 Kolyma (lowland), Rus.
69/R3 Kolyma (range), Rus.
69/R3 Kolyma (riv.), Rus.
62/F4 Kom (peak), Bul.
79/H7 Koma (riv.), Japan
62/E2 Komádi, Hun.
99/H4 Komadugu Gana (riv.), Nga.
99/H3 Komadugu Yobé (riv.), Nga.
79/H7 Komae, Japan
79/E3 Komagane, Japan
79/M9 Komaki, Japan
69/S4 Komandorskiye (isls.), Rus.
49/K5 Komárno, Slvk.
62/D2 Komárom, Hun.
62/D2 Komárom-Esztergom (co.), Hun.
78/E2 Komatsu, Japan
78/D4 Komatsushima, Japan
65/L2 Komi Aut. Rep., Rus.
65/M3 Komi-Permyak Aut. Okr., Rus.
62/D2 Komló, Hun.
66/F2 Kommunarsk, Ukr.
75/B4 Kommunizma (Communism) (peak), Taj.
87/E5 Komodo Isl. Nat'l Park, Indo.
98/E5 Komoé (riv.), IvC.
78/E3 Komono, Japan
61/J2 Komotiní, Gre.
102/D3 Kompasberg (peak), SAfr.
63/J2 Komrat, Mol.
69/L1 Komsomolets (isl.), Rus.
65/P2 Komsomol'skiy, Rus.
77/M1 Komsomol'sk-na-Amure, Rus.
61/K3 Kömür (pt.), Turk.
75/A2 Kon (riv.), Kaz.
64/H4 Konakovo, Rus.
79/M10 Kōnan, Japan
79/M9 Kōnan, Japan
91/D2 Konangra-Boyd Nat'l Park, Austl.
87/F4 Konaweha (riv.), Indo.
76/G1 Konda (riv.), Rus.
64/G3 Kondopoga, Rus.
73/J1 Kondūz, Afg.
83/C4 Kong (isl.), Camb.
83/D3 Kong (riv.), Laos
80/D4 Kongju, SKor.
104/E2 Kongolo, Zaire
79/L10 Kongō-zan (peak), Japan
42/D4 Kongsberg, Nor.
42/E3 Kongsvinger, Nor.
75/C4 Kongur Shan (peak), China
101/C4 Kongwa, Tanz.
49/K3 Koniecpol, Pol.
51/H4 Königslutter am Elm, Ger.
53/G2 Königswinter, Ger.
49/G2 Königs Wusterhausen, Ger.
49/K2 Konin, Pol.
49/K2 Konin (prov.), Pol.
54/D4 Köniz, Swi.
62/C4 Konjic, Bosn.
102/B2 Konkiep (dry riv.), Namb.
98/B4 Konkouré (riv.), Gui.
66/E2 Konotop, Ukr.
75/E3 Konqi (riv.), China
49/L3 Końskie, Pol.
49/L2 Konstancin-Jeziorna, Pol.
66/F2 Konstantinovka, Ukr.
49/K3 Konstantynów Łódzki, Pol.
55/F2 Konstanz, Ger.
52/D1 Kontich, Belg.
42/J3 Kontiolahti, Fin.
83/E3 Kon Tum, Viet.
74/C3 Konya, Turk.
53/F4 Konz, Ger.
122/E3 Koocanusa (lake), Can., US
122/D3 Kootenai (riv.), Id, Mt,US
122/D3 Kootenay (lake), BC,Can
122/D3 Kootenay Nat'l Park, BC,Can
84/B4 Kopargaon, India
42/N7 Kópavogur, Ice.
98/D5 Kope (peak), IvC.
49/G2 Köpenick, Ger.
65/P5 Kopeysk, Rus.
66/G4 Kop Geçidi (pass), Turk.
97/K7 Kopia, Zaire
64/C4 Köping, Swe.
87/F5 Kopondei (cape), Indo.
42/E3 Kopparberg (co.), Swe.
77/M2 Koppi (riv.), Rus.
62/C2 Koprivnica, Cro.
72/F2 Kor (riv.), Iran
79/M9 Kōra, Japan
61/G2 Korab (peak), Alb.
57/L4 Korana (riv.), Bosn., Cro.
84/D4 Koraput, India
84/D3 Korba, India
51/F6 Korbach, Ger.
61/G2 Korçë, Alb.
62/C4 Korčula (isl.), Cro.
62/C4 Korčulanski (chan.), Cro.
72/F1 Kord Kūy, Iran
80/B3 Korea (bay), China, NKor.
78/A4 Korea (str.), Japan, SKor.
80/D2 Korea, North
80/D4 Korea, South
66/F3 Korenovsk, Rus.
98/D4 Korhogo, IvC.
61/H4 Kórinthos (Corinth), Gre.
62/C2 Kőris-hegy (peak), Hun.
79/G2 Kōriyama, Japan
96/J3 Korizo, Passe de (pass), Chad
69/R3 Korkodon (riv.), Rus.
74/B3 Korkuteli, Turk.
75/E3 Korla, China
74/J4 Kormakiti (cape), Cyp.
62/B4 Kornat (isl.), Cro.
93/Z18 Koro (isl.), Fiji
92/G6 Koro (sea), Fiji
63/K5 Köroğlu (peak), Turk.
101/C4 Korogwe, Tanz.
82/E6 Koronadal, Phil.
61/H2 Korónia (lake), Gre.
49/J2 Koronowo, Pol.
61/L7 Koropí, Gre.
92/C4 Koror (cap.), Palau
62/E2 Körös (riv.), Hun.
66/D2 Korosten', Ukr.
66/D2 Korostyshev, Ukr.
65/P1 Korotaikha (riv.), Rus.
96/J4 Koro Toro, Chad
130/D5 Korovin (vol.), Ak,US
77/N2 Korsakov, Rus.
50/D6 Korschenbroich, Ger.
48/F1 Korsør, Den.
52/C1 Kortemark, Belg.
53/E2 Kortenaken, Belg.
52/D2 Kortenberg, Belg.
53/E2 Kortessem, Belg.
52/C2 Kortrijk, Belg.
99/H5 Korup Nat'l Park, Camr.
71/R3 Koryak (range), Rus.
69/S3 Koryak Aut. Okr., Rus.
65/K3 Koryazhma, Rus.
79/L10 Kōryō, Japan
74/A3 Kós (isl.), Gre.
79/E3 Kosai, Japan
78/A3 Ko-saki (pt.), Japan
83/C3 Ko Samut Nat'l Park, Thai.
49/J2 Kościan, Pol.
49/J1 Kościerzyna, Pol.
91/D3 Kosciusko (mt.), Austl.
129/F3 Kosciusko, Ms,US
91/D3 Kosciusko Nat'l Park, Austl.
79/M10 Kosei, Japan
100/B4 Kosha, Sudan
79/F3 Koshigaya, Japan
73/H2 Koshk, Afg.
84/E2 Kosi (riv.), India
49/L4 Košice, Slvk.
75/C2 Kosoba, Gora (peak), Kaz.
62/E4 Kosovo (aut. reg.), Yugo.
62/E4 Kosovo Polje, Yugo.
62/E4 Kosovska Mitrovica, Yugo.
92/F4 Kosrae (isl.), Micr.
98/D3 Kossi (prov.), Burk.
98/D5 Kossou (lake), IvC.
63/F4 Kostinbrod, Bul.
66/C2 Kostopol', Ukr.
64/J4 Kostroma, Rus.
64/J4 Kostroma (riv.), Rus.
64/J4 Kostroma Obl., Rus.
49/H2 Kostrzyn, Pol.
49/J2 Kostrzyn, Pol.
65/N4 Kos'va (riv.), Rus.
65/N2 Kos'yu (riv.), Rus.
49/J1 Koszalin, Pol.
49/H2 Koszalin (prov.), Pol.
84/C2 Kota, India
79/N10 Kōta, Japan
86/B5 Kotaagung, Indo.
86/B2 Kota Baharu, Malay.
87/E4 Kotabaru, Indo.
86/C4 Kotabumi, Indo.
73/K2 Kot Addu, Pak.
63/H4 Kotel, Bul.
65/L4 Kotel'nich, Rus.
67/G3 Kotel'nikovo, Rus.
69/P2 Kotel'nyy (isl.), Rus.
48/F3 Köthen, Ger.
42/H3 Kotka, Fin.
64/E3 Kotka, Fin.
73/K2 Kot Kapūra, India
65/K3 Kotlas, Rus.
79/M9 Kotō, Japan
62/D4 Kotor, Yugo.
67/H2 Kotovo, Rus.
67/G1 Kotovsk, Rus.
73/J3 Kotri, Pak.
84/D4 Kottagūdem, India
84/C6 Kottayam, India
84/C6 Kotte, SrL.
97/K6 Kotto (riv.), CAfr.
69/L3 Kotuy (riv.), Rus.
130/E2 Kotzebue (sound), Ak,US
127/H2 Kouchibouguac Nat'l Park, NB,Can
99/E3 Koudougou, Burk.
61/J5 Koufonísion (isl.), Gre.
130/E2 Kougarok (mtn.), Ak,US
82/D3 Kouhu, Tai.
119/J2 Koukdjuak (riv.), NW,Can
104/B1 Koula-Moutou, Gabon
98/D3 Koulikoro, Mali
98/B3 Koulountou (riv.), Gui., Sen.
98/D3 Koumbi Saleh (ruins), Mrta.
96/J6 Koumra, Chad
75/C2 Kounradskiy, Kaz.
128/E4 Kountze, Tx,US
99/H5 Koupé (peak), Camr.
99/E3 Koupela, Burk.
99/E3 Kouritenga (prove.), Burk.
109/H2 Kourou, FrG.
96/J4 Koussi (peak), Chad
98/D3 Koutiala, Mali
42/H3 Kouvola, Fin.
62/E3 Kovačica, Yugo.
64/F2 Kovdozero (lake), Rus.
66/C2 Kovel', Ukr.
84/C6 Kovilpatti, India
64/J4 Kovrov, Rus.
84/C5 Kovūr, India
67/G1 Kovylkino, Rus.
73/J1 Kowkcheh (riv.), Afg.
73/H2 Kowl-e Namaksār (lake), Afg., Iran
82/B3 Kowloon, HK
78/B5 Kōyama, Japan
63/G4 Koynare, Bul.
130/H2 Koyukuk (riv.), Ak,US
79/N10 Kozakai, Japan
74/C3 Kozan, Turk.
61/G2 Kozáni, Gre.
62/C3 Kozara Nat'l Park, Bosn.
84/C5 Kozhikode, India
64/H3 Kozhozero (lake), Rus.
65/M2 Kozhva (riv.), Rus.
49/L3 Kozienice, Pol.
63/F4 Kozloduy, Bul.
74/E2 Kozluk, Turk.
49/J3 Koźmin, Pol.
63/F4 Koznitsa (peak), Bul.
49/H3 Kożuchów, Pol.
99/F5 Kpalimé, Togo
99/F5 Kpandu, Gha.
83/B4 Kra (isth.), Burma, Thai.
102/D3 Kraai (riv.), SAfr.
102/L10 Kraaifontein, SAfr.
83/B4 Krabi, Thai.
83/D3 Kracheh, Camb.
42/D4 Kragerø, Nor.
62/E3 Kragujevac, Yugo.
57/H2 Kraichgau (reg.), Ger.
86/C5 Krakatoa (vol.), Indo.
83/D3 Krakor, Camb.
49/K3 Kraków, Pol.
49/K3 Kraków (prov.), Pol.
83/C3 Kralanh, Camb.
117/H5 Kralendijk, NAnt.
62/E4 Kraljevo, Yugo.
57/L1 Kralupy nad Vltavou, Czh.
66/F2 Kramatorsk, Ukr.
42/F3 Kramfors, Swe.
50/B5 Krammer (chan.), Neth.
50/D5 Kranenburg, Ger.
62/B2 Kranj, Slov.
49/J3 Krapkowice, Pol.
49/M3 Kraśnik, Pol.
49/M3 Kraśnik Fabryczny, Pol.
67/H2 Krasnoarmeysk, Rus.
66/F3 Krasnodar, Rus.
66/F3 Krasnodar (kray), Rus.
66/F1 Krasnogorsk, Rus.
66/E2 Krasnograd, Ukr.
77/H1 Krasnokamensk, Rus.
65/M4 Krasnokamsk, Rus.
67/H2 Krasnoslobodsk, Rus.
68/G4 Krasnotur'insk, Rus.
65/P4 Krasnoural'sk, Rus.
67/K5 Krasnovodsk, Trkm.
68/K4 Krasnoyarsk, Rus.
49/M3 Krasnystaw, Pol.
67/H2 Krasnyy Kut, Rus.
66/F3 Krasnyy Luch, Ukr.
66/G3 Krasnyy Sulin, Rus.
83/C4 Kravanh (mts.), Camb.
86/C5 Krawang, Indo.
50/D6 Krefeld, Ger.
51/G5 Kreiensen, Ger.
61/G3 Kremastón (lake), Gre.
66/E2 Kremenchug, Ukr.
66/E2 Kremenchug (res.), Ukr.
124/F2 Kremmling, Co,US
57/L2 Krems an der Donau, Aus.
69/T3 Kresta (gulf), Rus.
42/G5 Kretinga, Lith.
53/F2 Kreuzau, Ger.
53/G2 Kreuztal, Ger.
96/G7 Kribi, Camr.
66/D1 Krichev, Bela.
77/N2 Kril'on, Mys (cape), Rus.
50/B5 Krimpen aan de IJssel, Neth.
84/D4 Krishna (riv.), India
84/C5 Krishnagiri, India
42/C4 Kristiansand, Nor.
42/E4 Kristianstad, Swe.
49/H1 Kristianstad (co.), Swe.
42/C3 Kristiansund, Nor.
42/E4 Kristinehamn, Swe.
62/F4 Kriva Palanka, Macd.
66/E3 Krivoy Rog, Ukr.
62/B3 Krk, Cro.
62/C3 Krka (riv.), Cro.
49/J3 Krnov, Czh.
103/E2 Krokodil (riv.), SAfr.
102/D2 Krokodilrivier (riv.), SAfr.
66/E2 Krolevets, Ukr.
49/J4 Kroměříž, Czh.
57/J1 Kronach, Ger.
83/C4 Krong Kaoh Kong, Camb.
83/D4 Krong Keb, Camb.
42/E4 Kronoberg (co.), Swe.
64/F4 Kronshtadt, Rus.
90/C4 Kroombit Tops Nat'l Park, Austl.
102/D2 Kroonstad, SAfr.
67/G3 Kropotkin, Rus.
49/L4 Krosno, Pol.
49/L4 Krosno (prov.), Pol.
49/H2 Krosno Odrzańskie, Pol.
49/J3 Krotoszyn, Pol.
62/B3 Krško, Slov.
51/G1 Kruckau (riv.), Ger.
104/F5 Kruger Nat'l Park, SAfr.
102/P13 Krugersdorp, SAfr.
65/N5 Kruglitsa, Gora (peak), Rus.
130/A5 Kruglof (pt.), Ak,US
50/B6 Kruibeke, Belg.
62/D5 Krujë, Alb.
63/G5 Krumovgrad, Bul.
83/C3 Krung Thep (Bangkok) (cap.), Thai.
49/K4 Krupina, Slvk.
130/F2 Krusenstern (cape), Ak,US
62/E4 Kruševac, Yugo.
57/K1 Krušné Hory (Erzgebirge) (mts.), Czh., Ger.
49/K2 Kruszwica, Pol.
130/L4 Kruzof (isl.), Ak,US
66/F3 Krymsk, Rus.
49/L4 Krynica, Pol.
49/M3 Krzna (riv.), Pol.
49/J2 Krzyż, Pol.
81/D4 Kuai (riv.), China
86/D3 Kuala Belait, Bru.
86/B3 Kuala Dungun, Malay.
86/B3 Kuala Lipis, Malay.
86/B3 Kuala Lumpur (cap.), Malay.
86/B3 Kuala Pilah, Malay.
86/B2 Kuala Terengganu, Malay.
86/B3 Kuantan, Malay.
67/J4 Kuba, Azer.
66/F3 Kuban' (riv.), Rus.
64/H4 Kubenskoye (lake), Rus.
78/C4 Kubokawa, Japan
63/H4 Kubrat, Bul.
86/D3 Kuching, Malay.
61/F2 Kuçovë, Alb.
78/B4 Kudamatsu, Japan
86/D5 Kudus, Indo.
65/M4 Kudymkar, Rus.
97/K3 Kufrah (oasis), Libya
74/K5 Kufrinjah, Jor.
57/K3 Kufstein, Aus.
42/J2 Kuhmo, Fin.
50/D3 Kuinder of Tjonger (riv.), Neth.
83/E1 Kuishan (mtn.), China
104/C3 Kuito, Ang.
130/M4 Kuiu (isl.), Ak,US
99/E5 Kujani Game Rsv., Gha.
49/K2 Kujawy (reg.), Pol.
77/N3 Kuji, Japan
78/B4 Kujū-san (mtn.), Japan
61/G1 Kukës, Alb.
79/F2 Kuki, Japan
79/J7 Kukizaki, Japan
73/G3 Kūl (riv.), Iran
62/D3 Kula, Yugo.
86/B3 Kulai, Malay.
67/J3 Kulaly (isl.), Kaz.
67/K4 Kulandag (mts.), Trkm.
67/G4 Kulashi, Geo.
64/D4 Kuldīga, Lat.
64/J5 Kulebaki, Rus.
83/D3 Kulen, Camb.
91/B2 Kulkyne-Hattah Nat'l Park, Austl.
73/L2 Kullu, India
57/J1 Kulmbach, Ger.
65/J2 Kuloy (riv.), Rus.
67/K3 Kul'sary, Kaz.
74/C2 Kulu, Turk.
68/H4 Kulunda, Rus.
75/C1 Kulunda (lake), Rus.
75/D1 Kulunda (riv.), Rus.
75/C1 Kulunda Steppe (grsld.), Kaz., Rus.
73/J1 Kulyab, Taj.
67/H3 Kuma (riv.), Rus.
79/F2 Kumagaya, Japan
78/B4 Kumamoto, Japan
78/B4 Kumamoto (pref.), Japan
78/E4 Kumano, Japan
78/D4 Kumano (riv.), Japan
62/E4 Kumanovo, Macd.
99/E5 Kumasi, Gha.
79/L10 Kumatori, Japan
67/G4 Kumayri, Arm.
99/H5 Kumba, Camr.
99/H5 Kumbo, Camr.
67/K5 Kum-Dag, Trkm.
82/E5 Kumé (isl.), Japan
67/K1 Kumertau, Rus.
80/E4 Kumi, SKor.
79/L10 Kumiyama, Japan
42/E4 Kumla, Swe.
74/B3 Kumluca, Turk.
85/G2 Kumon (range), Burma
84/B5 Kumta, India
120/U11 Kumukahi (cape), Hi,US
77/P3 Kunashiri (isl.), Rus.
84/C2 Kūnch, India
104/E3 Kundelungu Nat'l Park, Zaire
73/K2 Kundiān, Pak.
84/B3 Kundla, India
42/E4 Kungsbacka, Swe.
97/J7 Kungu, Zaire
65/N4 Kungur, Rus.
62/E2 Kunhegyes, Hun.
78/B4 Kunimi-dake (mtn.), Japan
86/C5 Kuningan, Indo.
79/H7 Kunitachi, Japan
75/C4 Kunjirap Daban (pass), China
75/C4 Kunlun (mts.), China
62/E2 Kunmadaras, Hun.
85/H2 Kunming, China
80/D5 Kunsan, SKor.
81/E5 Kunshan, China
62/E2 Kunszentmárton, Hun.
81/E3 Kunyu Shan (mtn.), China
42/H3 Kuopio, Fin.
42/H3 Kuopio (prov.), Fin.
62/B3 Kupa (riv.), Cro., Slov.
87/F6 Kupang, Indo.
68/H4 Kupino, Rus.
130/M4 Kupreanof (isl.), Ak,US
66/F2 Kupyansk, Ukr.
77/L1 Kur (riv.), Rus.
67/J5 Kura (riv.), Azer., Geo.
79/L9 Kurama-yama (peak), Japan
78/C3 Kurashiki, Japan
100/B5 Kurayimah, Sudan
78/C3 Kurayoshi, Japan
72/D1 Kurdistan (reg.), Asia
63/G5 Kŭrdzhali, Bul.
61/J2 Kŭrdzhali (res.), Bul.
78/C3 Kure, Japan
74/C2 Küre (mts.), Turk.
92/H2 Kure (isl.), Hi,US
64/D4 Kuressaare, Est.
68/K3 Kureyka (riv.), Rus.
65/Q5 Kurgan, Rus.
65/Q5 Kurgan Obl., Rus.
73/J1 Kurgan-Tyube, Taj.
92/G4 Kuria (isl.), Kiri.
72/G5 Kuria Muria (isls.), Oman
69/Q5 Kuril (isls.), Rus.
90/H8 Ku-Ring-Gai Nat'l Park, Austl.
97/M5 Kurmuk, Sudan
84/C4 Kurnool, India
79/K9 Kurodashō, Japan
79/G2 Kuroiso, Japan
79/M10 Kuroso-yama (peak), Japan
73/K2 Kurram (riv.), Pak.
64/D5 Kuršėnai, Lith.
84/E2 Kurseong, India
66/F2 Kursk, Rus.
49/L1 Kurskaya (spit), Lith., Rus.
49/L1 Kurskiy (lag.), Rus.
66/E2 Kursk Obl., Rus.
62/E4 Kuršumlija, Yugo.
74/E3 Kurtalan, Turk.
51/E6 Kürten, Ger.
100/B5 Kūrtī, Sudan
97/L6 Kuru (riv.), Sudan
67/G4 Kuruçay (riv.), Turk.
75/E3 Kuruktag (mts.), China
78/B4 Kurume, Japan
84/D6 Kurunegala, SrL.
100/B4 Kurur, Jabal (peak), Sudan
90/E6 Kurwongbah (lake), Austl.
74/A3 Kuşadası, Turk.
83/C2 Ku Sathan (peak), Thai.
79/L9 Kusatsu, Japan
79/M9 Kusatsu, Japan
79/M10 Kushida (riv.), Japan
78/B5 Kushikino, Japan
78/B5 Kushima, Japan
78/D4 Kushimoto, Japan
77/N3 Kushiro, Japan
65/Q5 Kushmurun (lake), Kaz.
76/F4 Kushui (riv.), China
67/J2 Kushum (riv.), Kaz.
130/F4 Kuskokwim (bay), Ak,US
130/G3 Kuskokwim (mts.), Ak,US
130/F3 Kuskokwim (riv.), Ak,US
67/M1 Kustanay, Kaz.
67/M2 Kustanay Obl., Kaz.
97/M5 Kūstī, Sudan
79/M10 Kusu, Japan
83/C4 Kut (isl.), Thai.
74/B2 Kütahya, Turk.
67/G4 Kutaisi, Geo.
84/A3 Kutch (gulf), India
84/A3 Kutch (reg.), India
73/J4 Kutch, Rann of (swamp), India, Pak.
49/H4 Kutná Hora, Czh.
49/K2 Kutno, Pol.
104/C1 Kutu, Zaire
97/K5 Kutum, Sudan
118/E1 Kuujjua (riv.), NW,Can
119/K3 Kuujjuaq (Fort-Chimo), Qu,Can
119/J3 Kuujjuarapik, Qu,Can
42/J2 Kuusamo, Fin.
42/H3 Kuusankoski, Fin.
42/H4 Kuutse Mägi (mt.), Est.
67/L2 Kuvandyk, Rus.
72/E3 Kuwait
72/E3 Kuwait (Al Kuwait) (cap.), Kuw.
84/D2 Kuwānā (riv.), India
78/E3 Kuwana, Japan
65/L5 Kuybyshev (res.), Rus.
81/B3 Kuye (riv.), China
74/F3 Küysanjaq, Iraq
64/F2 Kuyto (lake), Rus.
75/E3 Kuytun, China
75/D2 Kuytun (riv.), China
116/E5 Kuyu Tingni, Nic.
130/E2 Kuzitrin (riv.), Ak,US
67/H1 Kuznetsk, Rus.
42/F1 Kvaløy (isl.), Nor.
62/B3 Kvarner (chan.), Cro.
62/B3 Kvarnerić (chan.), Cro.
42/E2 Kvigtinden (peak), Nor.
42/C4 Kvinnherad, Nor.
104/C1 Kwa (riv.), Zaire
83/B3 Kwai, River (bridge), Thai.
92/F4 Kwajelein (atoll), Mrsh.
80/D5 Kwangju, SKor.
80/D5 Kwangju-Jikhalsi (prov.), SKor.
104/C1 Kwango (riv.), Zaire
101/B2 Kwania (lake), Ugan.
99/G4 Kwara (state), Nga.
126/D1 Kwataboahegan (riv.), On,Can
103/E7 KwaZulu Natal (prov.), SAfr.
104/E4 Kwekwe, Zim.
49/K2 Kwidzyn, Pol.
97/N5 Kwīha, Eth.
96/J6 Kyabé, Chad
83/B2 Kyaikkami, Burma
83/B2 Kyaikto, Burma
76/F1 Kyakhta, Rus.
85/G4 Kyangin, Burma
83/D2 Ky Anh, Viet.
83/B1 Kyaukme, Burma
85/F4 Kyaukpyu, Burma
83/B1 Kyaukse, Burma
49/J4 Kyjov, Czh.
122/F3 Kyle, Sk,Can
53/F3 Kyll (riv.), Ger.
53/F3 Kyllburg, Ger.
47/F2 Kym (riv.), Eng,UK
42/H3 Kymi (prov.), Fin.
84/C3 Kymore, India
101/B2 Kyoga (lake), Ugan.
78/D3 Kyōga-misaki (cape), Japan
79/F3 Kyonan, Japan
80/C4 Kyŏnggi (bay), SKor.
80/D4 Kyŏnggi-Do (prov.), SKor.
80/E5 Kyŏngju, SKor.
80/E5 Kyŏngju Nat'l Park, SKor.
80/E4 Kyŏngsang-bukto (prov.), SKor.
80/E5 Kyŏngsang-namdo (prov.), SKor.
78/D3 Kyōto, Japan
78/D3 Kyōto (pref.), Japan
74/J4 Kyrenia (dist.), Cyp.
75/B3 Kyrgyzstan
48/G2 Kyritz, Ger.
85/H4 Ky Son, Viet.
78/B5 Kyūshū (isl.), Japan
78/B4 Kyūshū (mts.), Japan
78/B4 Kyūshū (prov.), Japan
62/F4 Kyustendil, Bul.
75/F1 Kyzyl, Rus.
68/G5 Kyzylkum (des.), Kaz.,Uzb.
68/G5 Kzyl-Orda, Kaz.

L

48/G2 Laage, Ger.
57/K3 Laakirchen, Aus.
58/B4 La Algaba, Sp.
116/E6 La Amistad Int'l Park
112/B3 La Araucanía (reg.), Chile
52/C1 Laarne, Belg.
117/N7 La Ascensión, Mex.
117/J5 La Asunción, Ven.
51/G4 Laatzen, Ger.
96/C2 Laayoune, WSah.
127/G1 La Baie, Qu,Can
58/A1 La Baña, Sp.
111/D2 La Banda, Arg.
58/C1 La Bañeza, Sp.
82/D6 Labason, Phil.
52/B2 La Bassée, Fr.
56/B3 La Baule-Escoublac, Fr.
60/B1 Labbro (peak), It.
96/H1 Labdah (Leptis Magna) (ruins), Libya
98/B4 Labé, Gui.
98/B4 Labé (comm.), Gui.
49/H3 Labe (Elbe) (riv.), Czh.
129/H5 La Belle, Fl,US
62/B3 Labin, Cro.
67/G3 Labinsk, Rus.
59/G2 La Bisbal, Sp.
116/D3 Labná (ruins), Mex.
49/L4 Laborec (riv.), Slvk.
112/E2 Laboulaye, Arg.
119/K3 Labrador (reg.), Nf,Can
115/M4 Labrador (sea), Can., Grld.
119/K3 Labrador City, Nf,Can
108/F5 Lábrea, Braz.
87/E2 Labuk (bay), Malay.
87/E2 Labuk (riv.), Malay.
85/F4 Labutta, Burma
61/F2 Laç, Alb.
112/C2 La Calera, Chile
127/N6 Lac-Alouette, Qu,Can
112/C2 La Campana Nat'l Park, Chile
131/B2 La Cañada-Flintridge, Ca,US
112/E2 La Carlota, Arg.
58/C4 La Carlota, Sp.
58/D3 La Carolina, Sp.
84/B5 Laccadive (sea), India
123/J3 Lac du Bonnet, Mb,Can
116/D4 La Ceiba, Hon.
91/A3 Lacepede (bay), Austl.
132/B3 Lacey, Wa,US
64/H3 Lacha (lake), Rus.
52/A5 Lachapelle-aux-Pots, Fr.
56/F2 La Chapelle-Saint-Luc, Fr.
56/C3 La Chapelle-sur-Erdre, Fr.
127/N6 Lachenaie, Qu,Can
127/N7 Lachine, Qu,Can
91/C2 Lachlan (riv.), Austl.
117/F6 La Chorrera, Pan.
51/H3 Lachte (riv.), Ger.
125/F4 La Cienega, NM,US
58/A1 La Ciñiza, Sp.
56/F5 La Ciotat, Fr.
117/N9 La Ciudad Nat'l Park, Mex.
127/S10 Lackawanna, NY,US
122/F2 Lac La Biche, Ab,Can
127/G2 Lac-Mégantic, Qu,Can
46/D4 Lacock, Eng,UK
122/E2 Lacombe, Ab,Can
116/E6 La Concepción, Pan.
117/G5 La Concepción, Ven.
123/G3 Laconia, NH,US
58/A1 La Coruña, Sp.
56/D4 La Couronne, Fr.
123/L5 La Crescent, Mn,US
131/B2 La Crescenta-Montrose, Ca,US
126/B3 La Crosse, Wi,US
112/Q9 La Cruz, Chile
116/D5 La Cruz, CR
117/N9 La Cruz, Mex.
83/D1 Lac Son, Viet.
86/C1 Lac Thien, Viet.
73/L2 Ladakh (mts.), Pak., India
91/B3 Laddon (riv.), Austl.
49/J3 Lądek-Zdrój, Pol.
60/C2 Ladispoli, It.
64/F3 Ladoga (lake), Rus.
108/D2 La Dorada, Col.
113/J8 Ladrillero (mtn.), Chile
102/D3 Ladybrand, SAfr.
103/E3 Ladysmith, SAfr.
126/B2 Ladysmith, Wi,US
92/F4 Lae (atoll), Mrsh.
92/D5 Lae, PNG
116/D5 La Esperanza, Hon.
117/J6 La Esperanza, Ven.
58/B1 La Estaca de Bares, Punta de (cape), Sp.
58/A1 La Estrada, Sp.
111/D3 La Falda, Arg.
132/K11 Lafayette, Ca,US
129/G3 La Fayette, Ga,US
126/C3 Lafayette, In,US
128/E4 Lafayette, La,US
56/D2 La Ferté-Bernard, Fr.
56/C2 La Ferté-Macé, Fr.
52/C6 La Ferté-sous-Jouarre, Fr.
126/E1 Laflamme (riv.), Qu,Can
56/C3 La Flèche, Fr.
57/L3 Lafnitz (riv.), Aus.
127/M6 Lafontaine, Qu,Can
57/G4 La Font Sancte, Pic de (peak), Fr.
117/G6 La Fría, Ven.
85/F6 Lāfūl, India
44/B3 Lagan (riv.), NI,UK
128/B2 La Garita (mts.), Co,US
59/L6 La Garriga, Sp.
109/L6 Lagarto, Braz.
82/D4 Lagawe, Phil.
96/H6 Lagdo (riv.), Camr.
51/F5 Lage, Ger.
110/B3 Lages, Braz.
50/C4 Lage Vaart (can.), Neth.
96/F1 Laghouat, Alg.
52/B5 Lagny-le-Sec, Fr.
52/B6 Lagny-sur-Marne, Fr.
110/C2 Lagoa da Prata, Braz.
110/C1 Lagoa Formosa, Braz.
110/B4 Lagoa Vermelha, Braz.
112/C4 Lago Puelo Nat'l Park, Arg.
99/F5 Lagos, Nga.
99/F5 Lagos (state), Nga.
58/A4 Lagos, Port.
116/A3 Lagos de Moreno, Mex.
115/K4 La Grande (riv.), Can.
122/D4 La Grande, Or,US
57/G4 La Grande Ruine (mtn.), Fr.
129/G3 La Grange, Ga,US
126/C4 La Grange, Ky,US
128/D4 La Grange, Tx,US
108/F2 La Gran Sabana (plain), Ven.
58/A2 La Guardia, Sp.
112/D3 La Guerra (peak), Arg.
110/B4 Laguna, Braz.
132/M10 Laguna (cr.), Ca,US
112/C3 Laguna Blanca Nat'l Park, Arg.
58/C2 Laguna de Duero, Sp.
112/C3 Laguna del Laja Nat'l Park, Chile
131/C3 Laguna Hills, Ca,US
113/J6 Laguna San Rafael Nat'l Park, Chile
116/C4 Lagunas de Montebello Nat'l Park, Mex.
117/G6 Lagunillas, Ven.
131/C3 La Habra, Ca,US
86/B4 Lahat, Indo.
127/H2 La Have (riv.), NS,Can
111/B2 La Higuera, Chile
72/F1 Lāhījān, Iran
48/E3 Lahn (riv.), Ger.
53/G3 Lahnstein, Ger.
42/E4 Laholm, Swe.
73/K2 Lahore, Pak.
54/D1 Lahr, Ger.
42/H3 Lahti, Fin.
96/J6 Laï, Chad
83/C1 Lai Chau, Viet.
82/D2 Laifeng Tujiazu Zizhixian, China
56/D2 L'Aigle, Fr.
42/G3 Laihia, Fin.
42/G2 Lainioälven (riv.), Swe.
42/G3 Laitila, Fin.
55/H5 Laives (Leifers), It.
81/D3 Laiwu, China
81/D3 Laizhou (bay), China
112/C3 Laja (lake), Chile
110/B4 Lajeado, Braz.
59/S12 Lajes do Pico, Azor.,Port.
110/D2 Lajinha, Braz.
62/D2 Lajosmizse, Hun.
125/G3 La Junta, Co,US
123/J5 Lake Andes, SD,US

Lake – Liffe

93/V12 **Lifou** (isl.), NCal.
46/B5 **Lifton**, Eng,UK
87/F1 **Ligao**, Phil.
57/H4 **Ligure, Appenino** (mts.), It.
57/H4 **Liguria** (reg.), It.
57/H5 **Ligurian** (sea), Eur.
85/H2 **Lijiang** (Lijiang Naxizu Zizhixian), China
104/E3 **Likasi**, Zaire
122/C2 **Likely**, BC,Can
104/F3 **Likoma** (isl.), Malw.
96/J8 **Likouala** (riv.), Congo
60/A1 **L'Ile-Rousse**, Fr.
51/F2 **Lilienthal**, Ger.
85/K2 **Liling**, China
53/D1 **Lille**, Belg.
52/C2 **Lille**, Fr.
42/D3 **Lillehammer**, Nor.
52/B2 **Lillers**, Fr.
42/D4 **Lillestrøm**, Nor.
122/C3 **Lillooet**, BC,Can
122/C3 **Lillooet** (riv.), BC,Can
104/F3 **Lilongwe** (cap.), Malw.
91/G5 **Lilydale**, Austl.
62/D4 **Lim** (riv.), Yugo.
108/C6 **Lima** (cap.), Peru
58/A2 **Lima** (riv.), Port.
123/L4 **Lima** (peak), Mn,US
126/C3 **Lima**, Oh,US
112/Q9 **Limache**, Chile
110/K6 **Lima Duarte**, Braz.
49/L4 **Limanowa**, Pol.
74/J4 **Limassol**, Cyp.
44/B1 **Limavady**, NI,UK
44/A2 **Limavady** (dist.), NI,UK
112/C4 **Limay** (riv.), Arg.
52/A6 **Limay**, Fr.
60/A2 **Limbara** (peak), It.
84/B3 **Limbdi**, India
53/E2 **Limburg** (prov.), Belg.
53/E1 **Limburg** (prov.), Neth.
57/H1 **Limburg an der Lahn**, Ger.
127/Q8 **Limehouse**, On,Can
110/C2 **Limeira**, Braz.
43/A4 **Limerick**, Ire.
58/B2 **Limia** (riv.), Sp.
61/J3 **Límnos** (isl.), Gre.
56/D4 **Limoges**, Fr.
56/D4 **Limogne** (plat.), Fr.
116/E5 **Limón**, CR
125/G3 **Limon**, Co,US
56/D4 **Limousin** (mts.), Fr.
56/D4 **Limousin** (reg.), Fr.
56/E5 **Limoux**, Fr.
104/F5 **Limpopo** (riv.), Afr.
47/G4 **Limpsfield**, Eng,UK
83/E2 **Limu** (mtn.), China
82/C5 **Linapacan** (isl.), Phil.
112/C2 **Linares**, Chile
116/B3 **Linares**, Mex.
58/D3 **Linares**, Sp.
82/C2 **Linchuan**, China
112/E2 **Lincoln**, Arg.
127/R9 **Lincoln**, On,Can
115/L1 **Lincoln** (sea), Can., Grld.
45/H5 **Lincoln**, Eng,UK
126/B3 **Lincoln**, Il,US
127/G2 **Lincoln**, Me,US
125/H2 **Lincoln** (cap.), Ne,US
122/B4 **Lincoln Beach**, Or,US
122/B4 **Lincoln City**, Or,US
45/H5 **Lincoln Heath** (woodl.), Eng,UK
132/F7 **Lincoln Park**, Mi,US
131/F5 **Lincoln Park**, NJ,US
45/H5 **Lincolnshire** (co.), Eng,UK
45/H5 **Lincolnshire Wolds** (hills), Eng,UK
129/H3 **Lincolnton**, NC,US
131/F5 **Lincroft**, NJ,US
60/A2 **L'Incudine, Mont** (mtn.), Fr.
50/D3 **Linde** (riv.), Neth.
90/C3 **Lindeman** (isl.), Austl.
108/G2 **Linden**, Guy.
129/G3 **Linden**, Al,US
131/F5 **Linden**, NJ,US
55/F2 **Lindenberg im Allgäu**, Ger.
132/P15 **Lindenhurst**, Il,US
131/G5 **Lindenhurst**, NY,US
131/F6 **Lindenwold**, NJ,US
64/B4 **Lindesberg**, Swe.
101/C5 **Lindi**, Tanz.
101/C5 **Lindi** (prov.), Tanz.
43/E3 **Lindisfarne** (Holy) (isl.), Eng,UK
51/E6 **Lindlar**, Ger.
91/D3 **Lind Nat'l Park**, Austl.
126/E2 **Lindsay**, On,Can
124/C3 **Lindsay**, Ca,US
128/D2 **Lindsborg**, Ks,US
93/K4 **Line** (isls.), Kiri.
81/B3 **Linfen**, China
81/C4 **Lingchuan**, China
82/B2 **Lingchuan**, China
50/C5 **Linge** (riv.), Neth.
51/E3 **Lingen**, Ger.
47/F4 **Lingfield**, Eng,UK
86/B3 **Lingga** (isls.), Indo.
53/G6 **Lingolsheim**, Fr.
98/B3 **Linguère**, Sen.
81/D3 **Ling Xian**, China
82/B2 **Ling Xian**, China
81/E5 **Lingyang Shan** (mtn.), China
81/L8 **Lingyen Shan** (mtn.), China
81/E5 **Lingyin Si**, China
82/D2 **Linhai**, China
110/D1 **Linhares**, Braz.
42/E4 **Linköping**, Swe.
81/C3 **Linliu Shan** (mtn.), China
42/J3 **Linnansaaren Nat'l Park**, Fin.
46/A3 **Linney Head** (pt.), Wal,UK
43/C2 **Linnhe, Loch** (inlet), Sc,UK
53/F2 **Linnich**, Ger.
60/C5 **Linosa** (isl.), It.
81/C3 **Linqing**, China
110/B2 **Lins**, Braz.
103/H9 **Linta** (riv.), Madg.
47/G2 **Linton**, Eng,UK
126/C4 **Linton**, In,US
123/H4 **Linton**, ND,US
45/H5 **Linwood**, Eng,UK
81/B4 **Linyi**, China
81/D3 **Linyi**, China
81/D4 **Linyi**, China
57/L2 **Linz**, Aus.
56/E5 **Lions** (gulf), Fr.
60/D3 **Lipari** (isls.), It.
42/J3 **Liperi**, Fin.
66/F1 **Lipetsk**, Rus.
66/F1 **Lipetsk Obl.**, Rus.
108/E8 **Lípez** (range), Bol.
108/E8 **Lípez** (riv.), Bol.
47/F4 **Liphook**, Eng,UK
62/E4 **Ljiljan**, Yugo.
49/K2 **Lipno**, Pol.
62/E2 **Lipova**, Rom.
50/E5 **Lippe** (riv.), Ger.
51/F5 **Lippetal**, Ger.
51/F5 **Lippstadt**, Ger.
49/K4 **Liptovský Mikuláš**, Slvk.
91/C3 **Liptrap** (cape), Austl.
75/D5 **Lipu La** (pass), India
75/D5 **Lipu Lehk Shankou** (pass), China
101/B2 **Lira**, Ugan.
104/C1 **Liranga**, Congo
60/C2 **Liri** (riv.), It.
59/E3 **Liria**, Sp.
97/K7 **Lisala**, Zaire
59/P10 **Lisboa** (dist.), Port.
127/G2 **Lisbon**, Me,US
123/J4 **Lisbon**, ND,US
59/P10 **Lisbon** (Lisboa) (cap.), Port.
44/B2 **Lisburn**, NI,UK
44/B3 **Lisburn** (dist.), NI,UK
130/E2 **Lisburne** (cape), Ak,US
81/B4 **Li Shan** (mtn.), China
85/H2 **Lishe** (riv.), China
82/C2 **Lishui**, China
93/H2 **Lisianski** (isl.), Hi,US
66/F2 **Lisichansk**, Ukr.
56/D2 **Lisieux**, Fr.
46/B6 **Liskeard**, Eng,UK
132/P16 **Lisle**, Il,US
52/B5 **L'Isle-Adam**, Fr.
56/F5 **L'Isle-sur-la-Sorgue**, Fr.
91/E1 **Lismore**, Austl.
44/B3 **Lisnacree**, NI,UK
47/F4 **Liss**, Eng,UK
50/B4 **Lisse**, Neth.
51/E6 **Lister** (riv.), Ger.
126/D3 **Listowel**, On,Can
85/H2 **Litang** (riv.), China
74/K5 **Līţanī** (riv.), Leb.
126/B4 **Litchfield**, Il,US
123/K4 **Litchfield**, Mn,US
50/C5 **Lith**, Neth.
45/F5 **Litherland**, Eng,UK
91/D2 **Lithgow**, Austl.
64/D5 **Lithuania**
64/E5 **Litovskiy Nat'l Park**, Lith.
90/D4 **Littabella Nat'l Park**, Austl.
129/H4 **Little** (riv.), Ga,US
125/J4 **Little** (riv.), La,US
129/J3 **Little** (riv.), NC,US
125/J4 **Little** (riv.), Ok,US
128/D4 **Little** (riv.), Tx,US
126/D1 **Little Abitibi** (riv.), On,Can
49/J5 **Little Alföld** (plain), Hun.
85/F5 **Little Andaman** (isl.), India
122/F4 **Little Belt** (mts.), Mt,US
122/G4 **Little Bighorn Nat'l Mon.**, Mt,US
125/H2 **Little Blue** (riv.), Ks, Ne,US
45/F4 **Littleborough**, Eng,UK
117/E4 **Little Cayman** (isl.), Cay.
124/E4 **Little Colorado** (riv.), Az,US
126/D2 **Little Current**, On,Can
126/C1 **Little Current** (riv.), On,Can
46/C5 **Little Dart** (riv.), Eng,UK
91/B3 **Little Desert Nat'l Park**, Austl.
130/E2 **Little Diomede** (isl.), Ak,US
123/K4 **Little Falls**, Mn,US
128/C3 **Littlefield**, Tx,US
123/K4 **Little Fork** (riv.), Mn,US
47/F5 **Littlehampton**, Eng,UK
117/G3 **Little Inagua** (isl.), Bahm.
102/C4 **Little Karoo** (reg.), SAfr.
127/K2 **Little Miquelon** (isl.), StP.
125/J4 **Little Missouri** (riv.), Ar,US
123/H4 **Little Missouri** (riv.), ND, SD,US
85/F6 **Little Nicobar** (isl.), India
47/G2 **Little Ouse** (riv.), Eng,UK
47/G2 **Littleport**, Eng,UK
125/J4 **Little Red** (riv.), Ar,US
128/E3 **Little Rock** (cap.), Ar,US
130/L3 **Little Salmon**, Yk,Can
98/B4 **Little Scarcies** (riv.), Gui., SLeo.
123/K5 **Little Sioux** (riv.), Ia,US
130/B5 **Little Sitkin** (isl.), Ak,US
122/D2 **Little Smoky** (riv.), Ab,Can
124/E2 **Little Snake** (riv.), Co, Wy,US
47/G4 **Little Stour** (riv.), Eng,UK
47/F2 **Little Stukeley**, Eng,UK
127/G2 **Littleton**, NH,US
126/B4 **Little Wabash** (riv.), Il,US
125/G2 **Little White** (riv.), SD,US
122/E5 **Little Wood** (riv.), Id,US
74/F3 **Little Zab** (riv.), Iraq
77/J3 **Liu** (riv.), China
77/K3 **Liu** (riv.), China
82/A3 **Liu** (riv.), China
104/D3 **Liuwa Pan Nat'l Park**, Zam.
85/J3 **Liuzhou**, China
129/H4 **Live Oak**, Fl,US
53/F6 **Liverdun**, Fr.
132/L11 **Livermore**, Ca,US
128/B4 **Livermore** (peak), Tx,US
90/G8 **Liverpool**, Austl.
127/H2 **Liverpool**, NS,Can
130/M2 **Liverpool** (bay), NW,Can
119/J1 **Liverpool** (cape), NW,Can
45/F5 **Liverpool**, Eng,UK
45/E5 **Liverpool** (bay), Eng,UK
45/H2 **Liverton**, Eng,UK
122/F4 **Livingston**, Mt,US
131/F5 **Livingston**, NJ,US
128/E4 **Livingston**, Tx,US
125/J5 **Livingston** (lake), Tx,US
122/E3 **Livingstone** (range), Ab,Can
104/E4 **Livingstone**, Zam.
104/B1 **Livingstone, Chutes de** (Livingstone) (falls), Congo
62/C4 **Livno**, Bosn.
66/F1 **Livny**, Rus.
42/H2 **Livojoki** (riv.), Fin.
132/F7 **Livonia**, Mi,US
57/J5 **Livorno**, It.
56/F4 **Livron-sur-Drôme**, Fr.
52/B6 **Livry-Gargan**, Fr.
101/C5 **Liwale**, Tanz.
46/A7 **Lizard**, Eng,UK
46/A7 **Lizard** (pt.), Eng,UK
46/A6 **Lizard, The** (pen.), Eng,UK
62/B2 **Ljubljana** (cap.), Slov.
62/C4 **Ljubuški**, Cro.
42/F3 **Ljungan** (riv.), Swe.
42/E4 **Ljungby**, Swe.
64/C3 **Ljusdal**, Swe.
42/E3 **Ljusnan** (riv.), Swe.
112/C2 **Llaillay**, Chile
112/C3 **Llaima** (vol.), Chile
108/E7 **Llallagua**, Bol.
46/B2 **Llanarth**, Wal,UK
44/D5 **Llanberis**, Wal,UK
44/D5 **Llanberis, Pass of** (pass), Wal,UK
112/C2 **Llancañelo** (lake), Arg.
46/C3 **Llandeilo**, Wal,UK
46/D3 **Llandogo**, Wal,UK
46/C3 **Llandovery**, Wal,UK
44/E6 **Llandrillo**, Wal,UK
46/C2 **Llandrindod Wells**, Wal,UK
44/E5 **Llandudno**, Wal,UK
46/C3 **Llandybie**, Wal,UK
46/B2 **Llandyssul**, Wal,UK
46/B3 **Llanelli**, Wal,UK
46/C1 **Llanelltyd**, Wal,UK
44/D6 **Llanenddwyn**, Wal,UK
44/D5 **Llanerchymedd**, Wal,UK
58/C1 **Llanes**, Sp.
46/C1 **Llanfair Caereinion**, Wal,UK
44/E5 **Llanfairfechan**, Wal,UK
44/D5 **Llanfair-Pwllgwyngyll**, Wal,UK
46/C1 **Llanfyllin**, Wal,UK
46/C2 **Llangammarch Wells**, Wal,UK
46/C3 **Llangattock**, Wal,UK
45/E6 **Llangollen**, Wal,UK
46/C2 **Llangurig**, Wal,UK
46/C2 **Llanidloes**, Wal,UK
44/D5 **Llanllyfni**, Wal,UK
46/B3 **Llannon**, Wal,UK
128/D4 **Llano**, Tx,US
125/H5 **Llano** (riv.), Tx,US
124/G4 **Llano Estacado** (plain), NM, Tx,US
46/B2 **Llanon**, Wal,UK
108/D3 **Llanos** (plain), Col., Ven.
112/B4 **Llanquihue** (lake), Chile
45/E5 **Llanrhaeadr**, Wal,UK
46/B2 **Llanrhystyd**, Wal,UK
46/A3 **Llanrian**, Wal,UK
44/E5 **Llanrwst**, Wal,UK
46/C3 **Llanthony**, Wal,UK
46/C3 **Llantrisant**, Wal,UK
46/C4 **Llantwit Major**, Wal,UK
44/E6 **Llanuwchllyn**, Wal,UK
46/C1 **Llanwnog**, Wal,UK
46/C2 **Llanwrtyd Wells**, Wal,UK
45/E5 **Llay**, Wal,UK
46/C2 **Lledrod**, Wal,UK
59/F2 **Lleida** (Lérida), Sp.
116/B3 **Llera**, Mex.
44/D6 **Lleyn** (pen.), Wal,UK
59/F1 **Llobregat** (riv.), Sp.
58/D1 **Llodio**, Sp.
59/G2 **Lloret de Mar**, Sp.
116/E6 **Llorona** (pt.), CR
131/G5 **Lloyd** (pt.), NY,US
122/F2 **Lloydminster**, Ab, Sk,Can
127/K1 **Lloyds** (riv.), Nf,Can
59/G3 **Lluchmayor**, Sp.
111/C1 **Llullaillaco** (vol.), Chile
46/C3 **Llynfi** (riv.), Wal,UK
83/D1 **Lo** (riv.), Viet.
111/C1 **Loa** (riv.), Chile
124/E3 **Loa**, Ut,US
129/H4 **Loano**, It.
59/N8 **Loaoya** (can.), Sp.
102/D2 **Lobatse**, Bots.
112/F3 **Lobería**, Arg.
104/B3 **Lobito**, Ang.
98/D5 **Lobo** (riv.), IvC.
112/F3 **Lobos**, Arg.
108/B5 **Lobos de Tierra** (isl.), Peru
112/B2 **Lobos, Punta de** (pt.), Chile
55/E5 **Locarno**, Swi.
44/D2 **Lochans**, Sc,UK
44/E1 **Locharbriggs**, Sc,UK
50/D4 **Lochem**, Neth.
43/C2 **Lochgilphead**, Sc,UK
44/E1 **Lochmaben**, Sc,UK
52/C1 **Lochristi**, Belg.
43/C2 **Lochy, Loch** (lake), Sc,UK
45/E1 **Lockerbie**, Sc,UK
128/D4 **Lockhart**, Tx,US
126/E3 **Lock Haven**, Pa,US
91/C3 **Lockington**, Austl.
132/P16 **Lockport**, Il,US
127/S9 **Lockport**, NY,US
83/D4 **Loc Ninh**, Viet.
60/E3 **Locri**, It.
125/J3 **Locust** (cr.), Ia, Mo,US
74/M9 **Lod**, Isr.
47/H1 **Loddon**, Eng,UK
47/E4 **Loddon** (riv.), Eng,UK
56/E5 **Lodève**, Fr.
64/G3 **Lodeynoye Pole**, Rus.
122/F3 **Lodge** (cr.), Mt,US
125/G2 **Lodgepole** (cr.), Ne, Wy,US
57/H4 **Lodi**, It.
132/M10 **Lodi**, Ca,US
131/F5 **Lodi**, NJ,US
104/D1 **Lodja**, Zaire
101/B2 **Lodwar**, Kenya
49/K3 **Łódź**, Pol.
49/K3 **Łódź** (prov.), Pol.
59/N9 **Loeches**, Sp.
83/C2 **Loei**, Thai.
50/C4 **Loenen**, Neth.
98/C5 **Lofa** (co.), Libr.
98/C5 **Lofa** (riv.), Libr.
42/D2 **Lofoten** (isls.), Nor.
45/H2 **Loftus**, Eng,UK
91/C4 **Lofty** (range), Austl.
90/F7 **Logan**, Austl.
130/K3 **Logan** (mtn.), Yk,Can
125/G4 **Logan**, NM,US
126/D4 **Logan**, Oh,US
124/E2 **Logan**, Ut,US
126/D4 **Logan**, WV,US
44/D2 **Logan, Mull of** (pt.), Sc,UK
126/C3 **Logansport**, In,US
96/J6 **Logone** (riv.), Camr., Chad
58/D1 **Logroño**, Sp.
51/G6 **Lohfelden**, Ger.
64/E3 **Lohja**, Fin.
53/G2 **Lohmar**, Ger.
48/E2 **Lohne**, Ger.
51/F3 **Löhne**, Ger.
85/G3 **Loi Lun** (range), Burma, China
56/E2 **Loing** (riv.), Fr.
56/C3 **Loir** (riv.), Fr.
56/C3 **Loire** (riv.), Fr.
53/E5 **Loisin** (riv.), Fr.
101/B3 **Loita** (hills), Kenya
108/C4 **Loja**, Ecu.
58/C4 **Loja**, Sp.
52/D1 **Lokeren**, Belg.
104/D1 **Lokolia**, Zaire
97/K8 **Lokolo** (riv.), Zaire
97/J8 **Lokoro** (riv.), Zaire
119/K2 **Loks** (isl.), NW,Can
97/L6 **Lol** (riv.), Sudan
48/F1 **Lolland** (isl.), Den.
122/E4 **Lolo** (peak), Mt,US
104/E1 **Lolo**, Zaire
92/G5 **Lolua**, Tuv.
63/F4 **Lom**, Bul.
98/C4 **Loma** (mts.), Gui., SLeo.
116/B4 **Loma Bonita**, Mex.
131/C2 **Loma Linda**, Ca,US
98/C4 **Loma Mansa** (peak), SLeo.
97/K8 **Lomami** (riv.), Zaire
113/S12 **Lomas de Zamora**, Arg.
132/P16 **Lombard**, Il,US
109/H3 **Lombarda** (mts.), Braz.
57/J4 **Lombardy** (reg.), It.
87/F5 **Lomblen** (isl.), Indo.
87/E5 **Lombok** (isl.), Indo.
99/F5 **Lomé** (cap.), Togo
104/D1 **Lomela**, Zaire
97/K8 **Lomela** (riv.), Zaire
131/B3 **Lomita**, Ca,US
56/E1 **Lomme**, Fr.
53/E1 **Lommel**, Belg.
43/C2 **Lomond, Loch** (lake), Sc,UK
87/E5 **Lompobatang** (peak), Indo.
124/B4 **Lompoc**, Ca,US
83/C2 **Lom Sak**, Thai.
49/M2 **Łomża**, Pol.
49/M2 **Łomża** (prov.), Pol.
84/B4 **Lonāvale**, India
112/B3 **Loncoche**, Chile
52/D2 **Londerzeel**, Belg.
52/A4 **Londinières**, Fr.
126/D3 **London**, On,Can
47/F3 **London** (cap.), Eng,UK
126/C4 **London**, Ky,US
47/F3 **London Colney**, Eng,UK
113/J8 **Londonderry** (isl.), Chile
44/A2 **Londonderry**, NI,UK
44/A2 **Londonderry** (dist.), NI,UK
110/B2 **Londrina**, Braz.
125/H4 **Lone Grove**, Ok,US
90/E7 **Lone Pine Sanct.**, Austl.
90/C4 **Lonesome Nat'l Park**, Austl.
117/F3 **Long** (isl.), Bahm.
123/J2 **Long** (pt.), Mb,Can
126/C1 **Long** (lake), On,Can
82/A3 **Long** (riv.), China
46/C1 **Long** (mtn.), Wal,UK
127/F3 **Long** (isl.), NY,US
69/T2 **Long** (str.), Rus.
112/C2 **Longaví**, Chile
127/R10 **Long Beach**, On,Can
131/B3 **Long Beach**, Ca,US
131/F6 **Long Beach** (isl.), NJ,US
131/G5 **Long Beach**, NY,US
45/G1 **Longbenton**, Eng,UK
129/H5 **Longboat Key**, Fl,US
131/G5 **Long Branch**, NJ,US
47/E2 **Long Buckby**, Eng,UK
83/D1 **Long Chau**, Viet.
82/C3 **Longchuan**, China
85/G3 **Longchuan**, China
47/F3 **Long Crendon**, Eng,UK
45/G6 **Long Eaton**, Eng,UK
53/E5 **Longeau** (riv.), Fr.
127/G2 **Longfellow** (mts.), Me,US
43/B4 **Longford**, Ire.
82/B2 **Longhui**, China
131/G5 **Long Island** (sound), Ct,NY,US
126/C1 **Longlac**, On,Can
46/D4 **Longleat House**, Eng,UK
81/B4 **Longmen Shan** (mtn.), China
81/C4 **Longmen Shiyao** (caves), China
125/F2 **Longmont**, Co,US
46/D1 **Long Mynd, The** (hill), Eng,UK
45/G5 **Longnor**, Eng,UK
83/D4 **Long Phu**, Viet.
127/K2 **Long Range** (mts.), Nf,Can
45/F4 **Longridge**, Eng,UK
76/E4 **Longshou** (mts.), China
45/J6 **Long Sutton**, Eng,UK
45/F2 **Longtown**, Eng,UK
52/B2 **Longuenesse**, Fr.
127/N6 **Longueuil**, Qu,Can
53/E5 **Longuyon**, Fr.
54/B3 **Longvic**, Fr.
128/E3 **Longview**, Tx,US
122/C4 **Longview**, Wa,US
53/E4 **Longwy**, Fr.
83/D4 **Long Xuyen**, Viet.
82/C2 **Longyan**, China
51/E3 **Löningen**, Ger.
56/C5 **Lons**, Fr.
54/B4 **Lons-le-Saunier**, Fr.
46/B6 **Looe**, Eng,UK
46/B6 **Looe** (isl.), Eng,UK
90/B1 **Lookout** (pt.), Austl.
129/J3 **Lookout** (cape), NC,US
101/B3 **Loolmalasin** (peak), Tanz.
122/F2 **Loon Lake**, Sk,Can
50/C5 **Loon op Zand**, Neth.
43/G7 **Loop Head** (pt.), Ire.
52/C2 **Loos**, Fr.
75/F3 **Lop** (lake), China
69/R4 **Lopatka, Mys** (cape), Rus.
83/C3 **Lop Buri**, Thai.
96/G8 **Lopez** (cape), Gabon
50/B5 **Lopik**, Neth.
97/K7 **Lopori** (riv.), Zaire
42/G1 **Lopphavet** (bay), Nor.
73/J3 **Lora** (riv.), Pak.
58/C4 **Lora del Río**, Sp.
73/J3 **Lora, Hāmūn-i-** (lake), Pak.
126/D3 **Lorain**, Oh,US
73/J2 **Loralai**, Pak.
59/E4 **Lorca**, Sp.
92/E8 **Lord Howe** (isl.), Austl.
124/E4 **Lordsburg**, NM,US
53/G3 **Lorelei** (cliff), Ger.
110/H7 **Lorena**, Braz.
87/J5 **Lorentz** (riv.), Indo.
50/C2 **Lorentzsluizen** (dam), Neth.
123/J3 **Lorette**, Mb,Can
97/N7 **Lorian** (swamp), Kenya
117/F6 **Lorica**, Col.
56/B3 **Lorient**, Fr.
118/G2 **Lorillard** (riv.), NW,Can
62/D2 **Lorinci**, Hun.
127/Q8 **Lorne Park**, On,Can
54/D2 **Lörrach**, Ger.
53/F6 **Lorrain** (plat.), Fr.
127/N6 **Lorraine**, Qu,Can
54/C1 **Lorraine** (reg.), Fr.
45/E2 **Lorton**, Eng,UK
131/J8 **Lorton**, Va,US
131/B3 **Los Alamitos** , Ca,US
124/B4 **Los Alamos**, Ca,US
125/F4 **Los Alamos**, NM,US
112/C4 **Los Alerces Nat'l Park**, Arg.
132/K12 **Los Altos**, Ca,US
112/C2 **Los Andes**, Chile
112/B3 **Los Ángeles**, Chile
131/B2 **Los Angeles**, Ca,US
131/B2 **Los Angeles** (riv.), Ca,US
124/B3 **Los Banos**, Ca,US
58/C4 **Los Barrios**, Sp.
107/B7 **Los Chonos** (arch.), Chile
58/C1 **Los Corrales de Buelna**, Sp.
113/J7 **Los Glaciares Nat'l Park**, Arg.
53/F4 **Losheim**, Ger.
117/N8 **Los Herreras**, Mex.
49/M2 **Łosice**, Pol.
62/B3 **Lošinj** (isl.), Cro.
112/B3 **Los Lagos**, Chile
112/B4 **Los Lagos** (reg.), Chile
124/F4 **Los Lunas**, NM,US
117/N8 **Los Mochis**, Mex.
112/B4 **Los Muermos**, Chile
108/C2 **Los Orquídeas Nat'l Park**, Col.
58/C4 **Los Palacios y Villafranca**, Sp.
113/J8 **Los Pingüinos Nat'l Park**, Chile
116/A4 **Los Reyes**, Mex.
117/H5 **Los Roques** (isls.), Ven.
58/B3 **Los Santos de Maimona**, Sp.
112/B3 **Los Sauces**, Chile
50/E4 **Losser**, Neth.
117/H5 **Los Teques**, Ven.
124/D1 **Lost River** (range), Id,US
46/B6 **Lostwithiel**, Eng,UK
112/C1 **Los Vilos**, Chile
58/D3 **Los Yébenes**, Sp.
56/D4 **Lot** (riv.), Fr.
112/B3 **Lota**, Chile
73/G1 **Lotfābād**, Trkm.
51/E4 **Lotte**, Ger.
81/B5 **Lou** (riv.), China
83/C2 **Louangphrabang**, Laos
104/B1 **Loubomo**, Congo
56/B2 **Loudéac**, Fr.
82/B2 **Loudi**, China
56/D3 **Loudun**, Fr.
54/B3 **Loue** (riv.), Fr.
98/A3 **Louga**, Sen.
98/B3 **Louga** (reg.), Sen.
45/G6 **Loughborough**, Eng,UK
44/B3 **Loughbrickland**, NI,UK
119/R7 **Lougheed** (isl.), NW,Can
44/B3 **Loughgall**, NI,UK
126/E4 **Louisa**, Va,US
92/E6 **Louisiade** (arch.), PNG
128/E4 **Louisiana** (state), US
126/C4 **Louisville**, Ky,US
129/F3 **Louisville**, Ms,US
119/J3 **Louis XIV** (pt.), Qu,Can
58/A4 **Loulé**, Port.
57/K1 **Louny**, Czh.
125/H2 **Loup** (riv.), Ne,US
44/B2 **Loup, The**, NI,UK
56/C5 **Lourdes**, Fr.
59/P10 **Loures**, Port.
58/A3 **Louriçal**, Port.
58/A3 **Lourinhã**, Port.
58/A2 **Lousã**, Port.
59/P10 **Lousa**, Port.
44/B4 **Louth** (co.), Ire.
45/H5 **Louth**, Eng,UK
61/H4 **Loutrákion**, Gre.
53/D2 **Louvain** (Leuven), Belg.
110/G8 **Louveira**, Braz.
52/A5 **Louviers**, Fr.
52/B5 **Louvres**, Fr.
52/C3 **Louvroil**, Fr.
52/B2 **Lovaart** (can.), Belg.
64/F4 **Lovat'** (riv.), Bela., Rus.
62/D4 **Lovćen Nat'l Park**, Yugo.
63/G4 **Lovech**, Bul.
63/G4 **Lovech** (reg.), Bul.
125/F2 **Loveland**, Co,US
122/F4 **Lovell**, Wy,US
124/C2 **Lovelock**, Nv,US
57/J4 **Lovere**, It.
125/F4 **Loving**, NM,US
125/G4 **Lovington**, NM,US
64/G2 **Lovozero** (lake), Rus.
119/H2 **Low** (cape), NW,Can
97/L8 **Lowa** (riv.), Zaire
45/H6 **Lowdham**, Eng,UK
127/G3 **Lowell**, Ma,US
102/B2 **Löwen** (dry riv.), Namb.
122/D3 **Lower Arrow** (lake), BC,Can
57/L2 **Lower Austria** (prov.), Aus.
47/E2 **Lower Brailes**, Eng,UK
91/B3 **Lower Glenelg Nat'l Park**, Austl.
91/C4 **Lower Gordon-Franklin Wild Rivers Nat'l Park**, Austl.
47/E3 **Lower Heyford**, Eng,UK
123/K4 **Lower Red** (lake), Mn,US
48/E2 **Lower Saxony** (state), Ger.
68/K3 **Lower Tunguska** (riv.), Rus.
104/E4 **Lower Zambezi Nat'l Park**, Zam.
47/H2 **Lowestoft**, Eng,UK
104/E1 **Lowi** (riv.), Zaire
49/K2 **Łowicz**, Pol.
44/E1 **Lowther** (hills), Sc,UK
127/Q9 **Lowville**, On,Can
51/F2 **Loxstedt**, Ger.
93/V12 **Loyalty** (isls.), NCal.
62/D3 **Loznica**, Yugo.
66/F2 **Lozovaya**, Ukr.
62/E3 **Lozovik**, Yugo.
81/C5 **Lu** (riv.), China
104/D2 **Luachimo**, Ang.
104/E1 **Lualaba** (riv.), Zaire
81/J6 **Luam** (riv.), China
120/T10 **Lua Makika** (crater), Hi,US
81/D5 **Lu'an**, China
81/D2 **Luan** (riv.), China
58/C1 **Luanco**, Sp.
104/B2 **Luanda** (cap.), Ang.
83/C5 **Luang** (lag.), Thai.
83/B4 **Luang** (peak), Thai.
83/C2 **Luang Prabang** (range), Laos
101/B5 **Luangwa** (riv.), Moz., Zam.
104/E3 **Luanshya**, Zam.
81/D3 **Luan Xian**, China
104/D3 **Luao**, Ang.
101/A5 **Luapula** (prov.), Zam.
58/B1 **Luarca**, Sp.
104/D3 **Luashi**, Zaire
96/G7 **Luba**, EqG.
116/D4 **Lubaantun** (ruins), Belz.
49/M3 **Lubaczów**, Pol.
49/H3 **Lubań**, Pol.
104/B3 **Lubango**, Ang.
49/M3 **Lubartów**, Pol.
49/K2 **Lubawa**, Pol.
51/F4 **Lübbecke**, Ger.
53/D2 **Lubbeek**, Belg.
128/C3 **Lubbock**, Tx,US
48/F2 **Lübeck**, Ger.
104/D1 **Lubefu**, Zaire
49/M3 **Lubelska** (upland), Pol.
101/A4 **Lubero**, Zaire
49/J3 **Lubin**, Pol.
49/M3 **Lublin**, Pol.
49/M3 **Lublin** (prov.), Pol.
49/K3 **Lubliniec**, Pol.
66/E2 **Lubny**, Ukr.
49/J2 **Luboń**, Pol.
49/H3 **Lubsko**, Pol.
104/E2 **Lubudi**, Zaire
86/B4 **Lubuklinggau**, Indo.
86/B3 **Lubuksikaping**, Indo.
104/E3 **Lubumbashi**, Zaire
104/E2 **Lubunda**, Zaire
104/C2 **Lucala**, Ang.
44/B5 **Lucan**, Ire.
83/D1 **Luc An Chau**, Viet.
130/K3 **Lucania** (mtn.), Yk,Can
104/D2 **Lucapa**, Ang.
57/J5 **Lucca**, It.
44/D2 **Luce** (bay), Sc,UK
129/F4 **Lucedale**, Ms,US
110/B2 **Lucélia**, Braz.
82/D5 **Lucena**, Phil.
58/C4 **Lucena**, Sp.
49/K4 **Lučenec**, Slvk.
55/E3 **Lucerne** (Vierwaldstättersee) (lake), Swi.
48/F2 **Lüchow**, Ger.
49/G2 **Luckenwalde**, Ger.
84/D2 **Lucknow**, India
122/G3 **Lucky Lake**, Sk,Can
117/F3 **Lucrecia** (cape), Cuba
104/D3 **Lucusse**, Ang.
63/H4 **Luda Kamchiya** (riv.), Bul.
51/E6 **Lüdenscheid**, Ger.
102/A2 **Lüderitz**, Namb.
47/E4 **Ludgershall**, Eng,UK
73/L2 **Ludhiāna**, India
51/E5 **Ludinghausen**, Ger.
126/C3 **Ludington**, Mi,US
46/D2 **Ludlow**, Eng,UK
63/H4 **Ludogorie** (reg.), Bul.
63/G2 **Luduş**, Rom.
42/E3 **Ludvika**, Swe.
57/H2 **Ludwigsburg**, Ger.
49/G2 **Ludwigsfelde**, Ger.
48/F2 **Ludwigslust**, Ger.
104/D2 **Luebo**, Zaire
128/E4 **Lufkin**, Tx,US
64/F4 **Luga**, Rus.
55/E6 **Lugano**, Swi.
66/F2 **Lugansk**, Ukr.
66/F2 **Lugansk Obl.**, Ukr.
51/G5 **Lügde**, Ger.
104/G3 **Lugenda** (riv.), Moz.
46/D2 **Lugg** (riv.), Eng,UK
44/B6 **Lugnaquillia** (mtn.), Ire.
58/B1 **Lugo**, Sp.
62/E3 **Lugoj**, Rom.
51/H2 **Lühe** (riv.), Ger.
104/D4 **Luiana**, Ang.
57/H4 **Luino**, It.
105/X **Luitpold** (coast), Ant.
62/D3 **Lukavac**, Bosn.
104/C1 **Lukenie** (riv.), Zaire
63/G4 **Lukovit**, Bul.
49/M3 **Łuków**, Pol.
92/E4 **Lukunor** (atoll), Micr.
42/G2 **Luleå**, Swe.
42/G2 **Luleälv** (riv.), Swe.
63/H5 **Lüleburgaz**, Turk.
81/B4 **Luling Guan** (pass), China
92/G5 **Lulua**, Tuv.
104/D2 **Lulua** (riv.), Zaire
104/D3 **Lumai**, Ang.
75/D5 **Lumajamgdong** (lake), China
129/J3 **Lumberton**, NC,US
128/E4 **Lumberton**, Tx,US
104/H4 **Lumbo**, Moz.
122/D3 **Lumby**, BC,Can
85/F2 **Lumding**, India
53/E2 **Lummen**, Belg.
83/D3 **Lumphat**, Camb.
123/G3 **Lumsden**, Sk,Can
89/G7 **Lumsden**, NZ
104/D3 **Lunache**, Ang.
49/G1 **Lund**, Swe.
124/D3 **Lund**, Nv,US
104/F5 **Lundi** (riv.), Zim.
46/B4 **Lundy** (isl.), Eng,UK
51/F2 **Lune** (riv.), Ger.
45/F3 **Lune** (riv.), Eng,UK
51/H2 **Lüneburg**, Ger.
51/G2 **Lüneburger Heide** (reg.), Ger.
56/F5 **Lunel**, Fr.
51/E5 **Lünen**, Ger.
127/H2 **Lunenburg**, NS,Can
104/E3 **Lunga** (riv.), Zam.
85/F3 **Lunglei**, India
104/D3 **Lungue-Bungo** (riv.), Ang.
84/B3 **Luni** (riv.), India
81/B3 **Luo** (riv.), China
81/B4 **Luo** (riv.), China
81/C4 **Luohe**, China
81/D4 **Luoma** (lake), China
83/C1 **Luong** (mts.), Viet.
81/C4 **Luoyang**, China
104/B1 **Luozi**, Zaire
104/E4 **Lupane**, Zim.
85/H2 **Lupanshui**, China
63/F3 **Lupeni**, Rom.
85/H2 **Luquan**, China
73/J2 **Lūrah** (riv.), Afg.
126/E4 **Luray**, Va,US
44/B3 **Lurgan**, NI,UK
104/H3 **Lúrio**, Moz.
104/G3 **Lúrio** (riv.), Moz.
104/E4 **Lusaka** (cap.), Zam.
104/E1 **Lusamba**, Zaire
104/D1 **Lusambo**, Zaire
81/D3 **Lu Shan** (mtn.), China
81/C5 **Lu Shan** (peak), China
61/F2 **Lushnje**, Alb.
123/G5 **Lusk**, Wy,US
97/J7 **Lutanga** (riv.), Zaire
131/K7 **Lutherville**, Md,US
50/D1 **Lütjehorn** (isl.), Ger.
47/F3 **Luton**, Eng,UK
66/C2 **Lutsk**, Ukr.
51/F5 **Lutter** (riv.), Ger.
105/C **Lützow-Holm** (bay), Ant.
97/P7 **Luuq**, Som.
123/J5 **Luverne**, Mn,US
53/E4 **Luxembourg**
53/E4 **Luxembourg** (prov.), Belg.
53/F4 **Luxembourg** (cap.), Lux.
53/F4 **Luxembourg** (dist.), Lux.
85/J2 **Lu Xian**, China
100/C3 **Luxor** (Al Uqşur), Egypt
56/C5 **Luy** (riv.), Fr.
81/B3 **Luya Shan** (mtn.), China
110/C1 **Luz**, Braz.
65/L3 **Luza** (riv.), Rus.
54/E3 **Luzern** (canton), Swi.
55/E3 **Luzern** (Lucerne), Swi.
85/J2 **Luzhou**, China
109/J7 **Luziânia**, Braz.

Luzon – Marie

82/D4 Luzon (isl.), Phil.
66/C2 L'viv, Ukr.
66/B2 L'viv Obl., Ukr.
83/C1 Lwi (riv.), Burma
65/P3 Lyapin (riv.), Rus.
63/G4 Lyaskovets, Bul.
42/F2 Lycksele, Swe.
47/G5 Lydd, Eng,UK
105/Y Lyddan (isl.), Ant.
103/E2 Lydenburg, SAfr.
46/D3 Lydney, Eng,UK
122/F5 Lyman, Wy,US
46/C5 Lyme (bay), Eng,UK
46/D5 Lyme Regis, Eng,UK
47/E5 Lymington, Eng,UK
45/F5 Lymm, Eng,UK
49/L1 Łyna (riv.), Pol.
44/D5 Lynas (pt.), Wal,UK
131/G5 Lynbrook, NY,US
126/E4 Lynchburg, Va,US
129/H3 Lynches (riv.), SC,US
90/A2 Lynd (riv.), Austl.
47/E5 Lyndhurst, Eng,UK
131/F5 Lyndhurst, NJ,US
45/F1 Lyne (riv.), Eng,UK
42/G1 Lyngen (fjord), Nor.
127/G3 Lynn, Ma,US
129/G4 Lynn Haven, Fl,US
132/C2 Lynnwood, Wa,US
46/C4 Lynton, Eng,UK
131/B3 Lynwood, Ca,US
118/F2 Lynx (lake), NW,Can
56/F4 Lyon, Fr.
125/H3 Lyons, Ks,US
46/C4 Lype (hill), Eng,UK
92/E5 Lyra (reef), PNG
52/B2 Lys (riv.), Fr.
49/K4 Lysá (peak), Czh.
64/E5 Lysaya, Gora (hill), Bela.
49/L3 Łysica (peak), Pol.
52/C2 Lys-lez-Lannoy, Fr.
65/N4 Lys'va, Rus.
46/D5 Lytchett Matravers, Eng,UK
45/E4 Lytham Saint Anne's, Eng,UK
65/X9 Lytkarino, Rus.
122/C3 Lytton, BC,Can
66/F1 Lyubertsy, Rus.
63/H5 Lyubimets, Bul.
66/E2 Lyubotin, Ukr.
66/E1 Lyudinovo, Rus.
46/C3 Lywd (riv.), Wal,UK

M

83/C1 Ma (riv.), Laos, Viet.
74/K5 Ma'alot, Isr.
64/F2 Maanselkä (mts.), Fin.
81/D5 Ma'anshan, China
50/C6 Maarheeze, Neth.
50/C4 Maarssen, Neth.
48/D3 Maas (riv.), Eur.
50/C6 Maasbracht, Neth.
50/D6 Maasbree, Neth.
53/E1 Maaseik, Belg.
82/D5 Maasin, Phil.
53/E2 Maasmechelen, Belg.
50/B5 Maassluis, Neth.
53/E2 Maastricht, Neth.
74/N7 Ma'ayan Harod Nat'l Park, Isr.
82/D4 Mabalacat, Phil.
104/F5 Mabalane, Moz.
45/J5 Mablethorpe, Eng,UK
104/F5 Mabote, Moz.
112/B5 Macá (peak), Chile
110/D2 Macaé, Braz.
109/L5 Macaíba, Braz.
109/H3 Macapá, Braz.
108/C4 Macará, Ecu.
109/L5 Macau, Braz.
82/B3 Macau (cap.), Macau
82/B3 Macau (dpcy.), Port.
92/H7 Macauley (isl.), NZ
108/D3 Macaya (riv.), Col.
117/G4 Macaya (pk.), Haiti
129/H4 Macclenny, Fl,US
45/F5 Macclesfield, Eng,UK
45/F5 Macclesfield (can.), Eng,UK
102/D3 Macdhui (peak), SAfr.
43/D2 Macduff, Sc,UK
61/G2 Macedonia
61/G2 Macedonia (reg.), Gre., Macd.
109/L5 Maceió, Braz.
60/C1 Macerata, It.
105/E Macey (peak), Ant.
102/D3 Machache (peak), Les.
110/H6 Machado, Braz.
101/C3 Machakos, Kenya
108/C4 Machala, Ecu.
108/B4 Machalilla Nat'l Park, Ecu.
104/F5 Machanga, Moz.
44/D2 Machars, The (pen.), Sc,UK
104/F5 Machaze, Moz.
104/E5 Machemma (ruins), SAfr.
46/C3 Machen, Wal,UK
81/C5 Macheng, China
127/H2 Machias, Me,US
58/D1 Machichaco (cape), Sp.
59/V15 Machico, Madr.,Port.
79/H7 Machida, Japan
84/D4 Machilipatnam, India
117/G5 Machiques, Ven.
108/D6 Machu Picchu (ruins), Peru
108/F6 Machupo (riv.), Bol.
46/C1 Machynlleth, Wal,UK
63/J3 Măcin, Rom.
98/D3 Macina (reg.), Mali
91/D1 Macintyre (riv.), Austl.
124/E3 Mack, Co,US
90/C3 Mackay, Austl.
105/E MacKenzie (bay), Ant.
90/C3 Mackenzie (riv.), Austl.
122/C2 Mackenzie, BC,Can
130/N2 Mackenzie (riv.), NW,Can
119/C2 Mackenzie (bay), NW, Yk,Can
118/C2 Mackenzie (mts.), NW, Yk,Can
119/R7 Mackenzie King (isl.), NW,Can
126/C2 Mackinac Island, Mi,US
129/F1 Mackinaw (riv.), Il,US
126/C2 Mackinaw City, Mi,US
122/F2 Macklin, Sk,Can
90/F7 Macleay (isl.), Austl.
130/L3 Macmillan (riv.), Yk,Can
60/A2 Macomer, It.
54/A5 Mâcon, Fr.
125/K4 Macon (bayou), Ar, La,US
129/H3 Macon, Ga,US
125/J3 Macon, Mo,US
44/B1 Macosquin, NI,UK
91/C4 Macquarie (har.), Austl.
39/S8 Macquarie (isl.), Austl.
91/C1 Macquarie (riv.), Austl.
105/D Mac-Robertson Land (reg.), Ant.
108/F5 Macuim (riv.), Braz.
122/C5 Mad (riv.), Ca,US
74/K6 Ma'dabā, Jor.
103/H8 Madagascar
96/H3 Madama, Niger
63/G5 Madan, Bul.
84/C5 Madanapalle, India
92/D5 Madang, PNG
96/H1 Madanīyīn, Tun.
99/G3 Madaoua, Niger
84/F3 Mādārīpur, Bang.
126/E2 Madawaska (riv.), On,Can
127/G2 Madawaska, Me,US
108/F5 Madeira (riv.), Braz.
59/V15 Madeira (isl.), Madr., Port.
59/U14 Madeira (aut. reg.), Port.
123/L4 Madelin (isl.), Wi,US
117/N8 Madera, Mex.
116/D5 Madera (vol.), Nic.
84/E2 Madhipura, India
84/C3 Madhya Pradesh (state), India
108/E6 Madidi (riv.), Bol.
125/H4 Madill, Ok,US
104/B1 Madingo-Kayes, Congo
129/G3 Madison, Al,US
129/H4 Madison, Fl,US
126/C4 Madison, In,US
129/F3 Madison, Ms,US
122/F4 Madison (riv.), Mt,US
125/H2 Madison, Ne,US
131/F5 Madison, NJ,US
123/J4 Madison, SD,US
126/B3 Madison (cap.), Wi,US
126/D4 Madison, WV,US
132/F6 Madison Heights, Mi,US
126/C4 Madisonville, Ky,US
128/E4 Madisonville, Tx,US
86/D5 Madiun, Indo.
76/D5 Madoi, China
54/C1 Madon (riv.), Fr.
60/C4 Madonie Nebrodi (mts.), It.
73/G5 Madrakah, Ra's al (pt.), Oman
84/D5 Madras, India
122/C4 Madras, Or,US
116/B2 Madre (lag.), Mex.
128/D5 Madre (lag.), Tx,US
107/C4 Madre de Dios (riv.), Bol., Peru
113/J7 Madre de Dios (isl.), Chile
56/E5 Madrès (mtn.), Fr.
58/C2 Madrid (aut. comm.), Sp.
59/N9 Madrid (cap.), Sp.
58/D3 Madridejos, Sp.
84/D4 Madugula, India
84/C6 Madurai, India
79/F2 Maebashi, Japan
83/C2 Mae Charim, Thai.
83/B2 Mae Ping Nat'l Park, Thai.
46/C3 Maesteg, Wal,UK
83/B2 Mae Tho (peak), Thai.
92/F6 Maewo (isl.), Van.
83/B2 Mae Ya (mtn.), Thai.
101/C4 Mafia (isl.), Tanz.
102/D2 Mafikeng, SAfr.
98/C4 Mafou (riv.), Gui.
110/B3 Mafra, Braz.
58/A3 Mafra, Port.
69/R4 Magadan, Rus.
101/C3 Magadi, Kenya
102/P12 Magalies Berg (range), SAfr.
113/K8 Magallanes (Magellan) (str.), Arg., Chile
113/K8 Magallanes y Antártica Chilena (reg.), Chile
117/G6 Magangué, Col.
82/D6 Maganoy, Phil.
99/H3 Magaria, Niger
82/D4 Magat (riv.), Phil.
125/J4 Magazine (peak), Ar,US
77/K1 Magdagachi, Rus.
127/J2 Magdalen (isls.), Qu,Can
113/T12 Magdalena, Arg.
108/D3 Magdalena (riv.), Col.
117/M7 Magdalena de Kino, Mex.
87/E3 Magdalena, Gunung (peak), Malay.
48/F2 Magdeburg, Ger.
48/F2 Magdeburger Börde (plain), Ger.
110/K7 Magé, Braz.
129/F4 Magee, Ms,US
44/C2 Magee, Island (pen.), NI,UK
86/C5 Magelang, Indo.
113/K8 Magellan (Magallanes) (str.), Arg., Chile
42/H1 Magerøya (isl.), Nor.
57/H4 Maggiore (lake), It., Swi.
100/B2 Maghāghah, Egypt
44/B2 Maghera, NI,UK
44/B2 Magherafelt, NI,UK
44/B2 Magherafelt (dist.), NI,UK
60/A5 Maghīla (peak), Tun.
45/F4 Maghull, Eng,UK
44/B1 Magilligan, NI,UK
44/B1 Magilligan (pt.), NI,UK
62/D3 Maglaj, Bosn.
62/D4 Maglić (peak), Yugo.
61/F2 Maglie, It.
126/D2 Magnetawan (riv.), On,Can
90/B2 Magnetic (passg.), Austl.
90/B2 Magnetic I. Nat'l Park, Austl.
65/N5 Magnitogorsk, Rus.
128/E3 Magnolia, Ar,US
127/F2 Magog, Qu,Can
97/N6 Mago Nat'l Park, Eth.
46/D3 Magor, Wal,UK
127/H1 Magpie (riv.), Qu,Can
85/F3 Magwe, Burma
85/F4 Magwe (div.), Burma
72/E1 Mahābād, Iran
84/B4 Mahād, India
93/X15 Mahaena, FrPol.
108/G2 Mahaica, Guy.
103/H6 Mahajamba (bay), Madg.
103/H7 Mahajamba (riv.), Madg.
103/H6 Mahajanga (prov.), Madg.
103/H7 Mahajilo (riv.), Madg.
87/E3 Mahakam (riv.), Indo.
104/E5 Mahalapye, Bots.
72/F2 Maḥallāt, Iran
73/G2 Māhān, Iran
84/D3 Mahānadī (riv.), India
98/D4 Mahandiabani (riv.), IvC.
84/C2 Mahārājpur, India
84/B4 Mahārāshtra (state), India
84/D3 Mahāsamund, India
83/C2 Maha Sarakham, Thai.
103/H7 Mahavavy (riv.), Madg.
84/C4 Mahbubnagar, India
73/L2 Mahe, India
39/M6 Mahé (isl.), Sey.
103/S15 Mahébourg, Mrts.
85/G3 Mahlaing, Burma
84/C2 Mahoba, India
59/H3 Mahón, Sp.
84/B3 Mahuva, India
131/F4 Mahwah, NJ,US
90/E6 Maiala Nat'l Park, Austl.
92/G4 Maiana (atoll), Kiri.
93/W15 Maiao (isl.), FrPol.
108/D1 Maicao, Col.
109/H3 Maicuru (riv.), Braz.
47/G3 Maidenhead, Eng,UK
46/D5 Maiden Newton, Eng,UK
44/D1 Maidens, Sc,UK
132/G7 Maidstone, On,Can
122/F2 Maidstone, Sk,Can
47/G4 Maidstone, Eng,UK
96/H5 Maiduguri, Nga.
52/B4 Maignelay-Montigny, Fr.
43/A4 Maigue (riv.), Ire.
84/D3 Maihar, India
78/E3 Maihara, Japan
97/L8 Maiko Nat'l Park, Zaire
120/V13 Maili, Hi,US
73/K3 Mailsi, Pak.
57/H2 Main (riv.), Ger.
44/B2 Main (riv.), NI,UK
104/C1 Mai-Ndombe (lake), Zaire
127/G3 Maine (gulf), Can., US
56/C2 Maine (hills), Fr.
43/A4 Maine (riv.), Ire.
127/G2 Maine (state), US
90/C5 Main Range Nat'l Park, Austl.
57/H2 Mainz, Ger.
112/C2 Maipo (vol.), Arg., Chile
112/Q9 Maipo (riv.), Chile
112/F3 Maipú, Arg.
112/C2 Maipú, Chile
57/G4 Maira (riv.), It.
110/G8 Mairiporã, Braz.
117/G3 Maisí (cape), Cuba
126/D3 Maitland (riv.), On,Can
53/F5 Maizières-lès-Metz, Fr.
78/D3 Maizuru, Japan
59/N9 Majadahonda, Sp.
61/G2 Maja e Zezë (peak), Alb.
60/A4 Majardah (riv.), Tun.
62/E3 Majdanpek, Yugo.
96/J2 Majdūl, Libya
87/E4 Majene, Indo.
97/N6 Majī, Eth.
81/D3 Majia (riv.), China
59/G3 Majorca (Mallorca) (isl.), Sp.
92/G4 Majuro (atoll), Mrsh.
92/G4 Majuro (cap.), Mrsh.
104/B1 Makabana, Congo
120/V13 Makaha, Hi,US
120/V13 Makakilo City, Hi,US
77/N2 Makarov, Rus.
62/C4 Makarska, Cro.
86/E4 Makassar (str.), Indo.
93/L6 Makatea (isl.), FrPol.
103/H8 Makay (massif), Madg.
93/L6 Makemo (atoll), FrPol.
98/B4 Makeni, SLeo.
66/F2 Makeyevka, Ukr.
104/D5 Makgadikgadi (salt pans), Bots.
67/H4 Makhachkala, Rus.
87/G3 Makian (isl.), Indo.
92/G4 Makin (atoll), Kiri.
75/B1 Makinsk, Kaz.
72/C4 Makkah (Mecca), SAr.
62/E2 Makó, Hun.
96/H7 Makokou, Gabon
49/L2 Maków Mazowiecki, Pol.
73/H3 Makran (reg.), Iran, Pak.
73/K3 Makrāna, India
74/F2 Mākū, Iran
101/B5 Makumbako, Tanz.
78/B5 Makurazaki, Japan
130/E5 Makushin (vol.), Ak,US
108/C6 Mala, Peru
84/B5 Malabar (coast), India
96/G7 Malabo (cap.), EqG.
110/D1 Malacacheta, Braz.
83/B5 Malacca (str.), Malay., Thai.
49/J4 Malacky, Slvk.
122/E5 Malad City, Id,US
58/C4 Málaga, Sp.
58/D3 Malagón, Sp.
44/B5 Malahide, Ire.
92/F5 Malaita (isl.), Sol.
97/M6 Malakāl, Sudan
84/D4 Malakangiri, India
117/G5 Malambo, Col.
86/D5 Malang, Indo.
104/C2 Malange, Ang.
112/C2 Malargüe, Arg.
126/E1 Malartic, Qu,Can
87/E5 Malasoro (pt.), Indo.
74/D2 Malatya, Turk.
104/F3 Malawi
83/B5 Malay (pen.), Malay.
64/G4 Malaya Vishera, Rus.
82/E6 Malaybalay, Phil.
72/E2 Malāyer, Iran
86/C2 Malaysia
65/L2 Malazemel'skaya (tundra), Rus.
74/E2 Malazgirt, Turk.
127/G2 Malbaie (riv.), Qu,Can
99/G3 Malbaza-Usine, Niger
49/K1 Malbork, Pol.
56/D5 Malcaras, Pic de (peak), Fr.
48/G2 Malchin, Ger.
76/C2 Malchin, Mong.
52/C1 Maldegem, Belg.
93/K5 Malden (isl.), Kiri.
126/B4 Malden, Mo,US
71/G9 Maldives
48/D3 Malden, Eng,UK
113/G2 Maldonado, Uru.
113/G2 Maldonado (dept.), Uru.
71/G9 Male (cap.), Mald.
61/H4 Maléa, Ákra (cape), Gre.
84/B3 Mālegaon, India
92/F6 Malekula (isl.), Van.
56/D4 Malemort-sur-Corrèze, Fr.
48/F1 Malente, Ger.
73/L2 Māler Kotla, India
67/H4 Malgobek, Rus.
59/G2 Malgrat de Mar, Sp.
97/L4 Malha Wells, Sudan
122/D5 Malheur (lake), Or,US
122/D5 Malheur (riv.), Or,US
103/S14 Malheureux (cape), Mrts.
98/E2 Mali
83/B3 Mali (isl.), Burma
76/F4 Malian (riv.), China
131/B2 Malibu, Ca,US
97/L4 Malik (wadi), Sudan
66/D2 Malin, Ukr.
87/E3 Malinau, Indo.
101/D3 Malindi, Kenya
52/D1 Malines (Mechelen), Belg.
81/C3 Maling Guan (pass), China
103/H8 Malio (riv.), Madg.
83/D1 Malipo, China
73/J4 Malīr Cantonment, Pak.
82/E6 Malita, Phil.
97/P7 Malka Mari Nat'l Park, Kenya
63/H5 Malkara, Turk.
99/H3 Mallammaduri, Nga.
100/B3 Mallawī, Egypt
91/B2 Mallee Cliffs Nat'l Park, Austl.
112/Q10 Malloa, Chile
59/G3 Mallorca (Majorca) (isl.), Sp.
43/A4 Mallow, Ire.
42/G2 Malmberget, Swe.
53/F3 Malmédy, Belg.
102/B4 Malmesbury, SAfr.
46/D3 Malmesbury, Eng,UK
48/G1 Malmö, Swe.
49/G1 Malmöhus (co.), Swe.
65/L4 Malmyzh, Rus.
109/H5 Maloca, Braz.
92/G4 Maloelap (atoll), Mrsh.
126/F2 Malone, NY,US
49/L3 Małopolska (upland), Pol.
42/C3 Måløy, Nor.
45/F5 Malpas, Eng,UK
108/B3 Malpelo (isl.), Col.
58/A1 Malpica, Sp.
60/D5 Malta
60/D5 Malta (isl.), Malta
122/G3 Malta, Mt,US
45/G2 Maltby, Eng,UK
45/G5 Maltby, Eng,UK
127/Q8 Malton, On,Can
45/H3 Malton, Eng,UK
104/C1 Maluku, Zaire
42/E3 Malung, Swe.
84/B4 Malvan, India
59/P10 Malveira, Port.
91/G5 Malvern, Austl.
128/E3 Malvern, Ar,US
46/D2 Malvern (Great Malvern), Eng,UK
113/M8 Malvinas, Islas (Falkland Islands) (dpcy.), UK
67/J2 Malyy Uzen' (riv.), Kaz.
76/D1 Malyy Yenisey (riv.), Rus.
53/F6 Malzéville, Fr.
109/M5 Mamanguape, Braz.
131/G5 Mamaroneck, NY,US
104/E4 Mamba, Zam.
82/D6 Mambajao, Phil.
97/A2 Mambasa, Zaire
87/J4 Mamberamo (riv.), Indo.
96/J6 Mambéré (riv.), CAfr.
74/D3 Mambij, Syria
82/D5 Mamburao, Phil.
53/F4 Mamer, Lux.
56/D2 Mamers, Fr.
52/B2 Mametz, Fr.
99/H5 Mamfé, Camr.
126/C4 Mammoth Cave Nat'l Park, Ky,US
129/F2 Mammoth Spring, Ar,US
108/E6 Mamoré (riv.), Bol.
99/E5 Mampong, Gha.
49/L1 Mamry (lake), Pol.
87/E4 Mamuju, Indo.
104/D5 Mamuno, Bots.
109/G4 Mamurí (riv.), Braz.
81/C5 Man (riv.), China
98/D5 Man, IvC.
108/F4 Manacapuru, Braz.
46/A6 Manacle (pt.), UK
59/G3 Manacor, Sp.
87/F3 Manado, Indo.
116/D5 Managua (cap.), Nic.
116/D5 Managua (lake), Nic.
103/J8 Manakara, Madg.
131/F5 Manalapan, NJ,US
72/F3 Manama (Al Manāmah) (cap.), Bahr.
103/H7 Manambaho (riv.), Madg.
103/H7 Manambolo (riv.), Madg.
103/J7 Mananara, Madg.
103/H8 Mananara (riv.), Madg.
103/J8 Mananjary, Madg.
103/H8 Mananjary (riv.), Madg.
75/D2 Manas (lake), China
75/E3 Manas (riv.), China
84/D2 Manāslu (mtn.), Nepal
131/F5 Manasquan, NJ,US
131/F5 Manasquan (riv.), NJ,US
125/F3 Manassa, Co,US
126/E4 Manassas, Va,US
61/G1 Manastir Dečani, Yugo.
61/G1 Manastir Gračanica, Yugo.
61/G1 Manastir Sopoćani, Yugo.
79/H7 Manatsuru, Japan
108/F4 Manaus, Braz.
74/B3 Manavgat, Turk.
123/H2 Manawan (lake), Sk,Can
79/H7 Manazuru-misaki (cape), Japan
44/D3 Man, Calf of (isl.), IM,UK
58/D4 Mancha Real, Sp.
84/C4 Mancherāl, India
90/E6 Manchester (lake), Austl.
45/F5 Manchester, Eng,UK
126/D4 Manchester, Ky,US
127/G3 Manchester, NH,US
129/G3 Manchester, Tn,US
77/J3 Manchuria (reg.), China
72/F3 Mand (riv.), Iran
101/B5 Manda, Tanz.
110/B2 Mandaguari, Braz.
42/C4 Mandal, Nor.
87/K4 Mandala (peak), Indo.
83/B1 Mandalay, Burma
83/A1 Mandalay (div.), Burma
69/L5 Mandalgovĭ, Mong.
72/E2 Mandalī, Iraq
123/H4 Mandan, ND,US
97/J6 Manda Nat'l Park, Chad
81/D4 Mandang Shan (mtn.), China
87/F5 Mandasavu (peak), Indo.
82/D5 Mandaue, Phil.
57/H4 Mandello del Lario, It.
53/F3 Manderscheid, Ger.
117/F4 Mandeville, Jam.
73/L2 Mandi, India
104/F4 Mandié, Moz.
87/G4 Mandiola (isl.), Indo.
84/D3 Mandla, India
48/E1 Mandø (isl.), Den.
61/L6 Mándra, Gre.
103/H9 Mandrare (riv.), Madg.
103/J6 Mandritsara, Madg.
84/C3 Mandsaur, India
89/A4 Mandurah, Austl.
61/E2 Manduria, It.
84/A3 Māndvi, India
84/C5 Mandya, India
84/D2 Mane (pass), Nepal
47/G2 Manea, Eng,UK
84/D3 Manendragarh, India
99/H5 Manéngouba, Massif du (peak), Camr.
57/J4 Manerbio, It.
72/B3 Manfalūt, Egypt
60/D2 Manfredonia, It.
60/E2 Manfredonia (gulf), It.
81/B4 Mang (riv.), China
109/J6 Mangabeiras (hills), Braz.
104/C1 Mangai, Zaire
93/K7 Mangaia (isl.), Cookls.
85/F2 Mangaldai, India
82/D4 Mangaldan, Phil.
63/J4 Mangalia, Rom.
84/B5 Mangalore, India
93/M7 Mangareva (isl.), FrPol.
67/K4 Mangistauz Obl., Kaz.
87/E3 Mangkalihat (cape), Indo.
73/K2 Mangla, Pak.
108/C3 Manglares (pt.), Col.
99/F4 Mango, Togo
104/G3 Mangoche, Malw.
103/H8 Mangoky (riv.), Madg.
87/G4 Mangole (isl.), Indo.
103/J7 Mangoro (riv.), Madg.
46/D4 Mangotsfield, Eng,UK
84/B3 Māngrol, India
113/G2 Mangueira (lake), Braz.
125/H4 Mangum, Ok,US
67/J3 Mangyshlak (pen.), Kaz.
67/K4 Mangyshlak (plat.), Kaz.
125/H3 Manhattan, Ks,US
122/F4 Manhattan, Mt,US
131/B3 Manhattan Beach, Ca,US
110/D2 Manhuaçu, Braz.
110/D2 Manhumirim, Braz.
61/H4 Máni (pen.), Gre.
103/H7 Mania (riv.), Madg.
104/F4 Manica, Moz.
108/F5 Manicoré, Braz.
108/F5 Manicoré (riv.), Braz.
123/J3 Manicouagan, Mb,Can
127/G1 Manicouagan (res.), Qu,Can
127/G1 Manicouagan (riv.), Qu,Can
127/H1 Manicouagan, Petit Lac (lake), Qu,Can
90/C3 Manifold (cape), Austl.
93/L6 Manihi (isl.), FrPol.
93/J6 Manihiki (atoll), Cookls.
82/D5 Manila (cap.), Phil.
124/E2 Manila, Ut,US
103/J7 Maningory (riv.), Madg.
87/G4 Manipa (str.), Indo.
85/F3 Manipur (state), India
74/A2 Manisa, Turk.
44/D3 Man, Isle of (isl.), UK
126/C2 Manistee, Mi,US
126/C2 Manistee (riv.), Mi,US
118/G3 Manitoba (prov.), Can.
123/J3 Manitoba (lake), Mb,Can
127/H1 Manitou (riv.), Qu,Can
126/D2 Manitoulin (isl.), On,Can
128/B2 Manitou Springs, Co,US
126/C1 Manitouwadge, On,Can
126/C2 Manitowoc, Wi,US
126/F2 Maniwaki, Qu,Can
108/C2 Manizales, Col.
84/C4 Manjlegaon, India
73/L5 Mānjra (riv.), India
123/K4 Mankato, Mn,US
98/D4 Mankono, IvC.
76/F3 Manlay, Mong.
58/D2 Manlleu, Sp.
90/H8 Manly, Austl.
84/B3 Manmād, India
83/B4 Man Mia (peak), Thai.
84/C6 Mannar (gulf), India, SrL.
84/C6 Mannar, SrL.
84/C5 Mannārgudi, India
102/C4 Mannetjiesberg (peak), SAfr.
57/H2 Mannheim, Ger.
119/Q7 Manning (cape), NW,Can
129/H3 Manning, SC,US
47/H3 Manningtree, Eng,UK
98/C5 Mano (riv.), Libr., SLeo.
104/E2 Manono, Zaire
131/H5 Manorville, NY,US
56/F5 Manosque, Fr.
127/G1 Manouane (lake), Qu,Can
127/G1 Manouane (riv.), Qu,Can
93/H5 Manra (Sydney) (atoll), Kiri.
59/F2 Manresa, Sp.
101/A5 Mansa, Zam.
98/B3 Mansa Konko, Gam.
87/F1 Mansalay, Phil.
119/H2 Mansel (isl.), NW,Can
49/G5 Mansfield, Eng,UK
128/E3 Mansfield, La,US
126/D3 Mansfield, Oh,US
45/G5 Mansfield Woodhouse, Eng,UK
108/B4 Manta, Ecu.
87/E2 Mantalingajan (mt.), Phil.
108/C6 Mantaro (riv.), Peru
124/B3 Manteca, Ca,US
110/D1 Mantena, Braz.
52/A6 Mantes-la-Jolie, Fr.
52/A6 Mantes-la-Ville, Fr.
84/C4 Manthani, India
124/E3 Manti, Ut,US
131/G5 Manticock (pt.), NY,US
110/C2 Mantiquiera (range), Braz.
81/C3 Mantou Shan (mtn.), China
57/J4 Mantova, It.
116/E3 Mantua, Cuba
65/K4 Manturovo, Rus.
42/H3 Mäntyharju, Fin.
108/E6 Manú (riv.), Peru
93/J6 Manua (isls.), ASam.
93/K6 Manuae (atoll), Cookls.
120/W13 Manuawili, Hi,US
109/J6 Manuel Alves (riv.), Braz.
86/C5 Manuk (riv.), Indo.
89/H6 Manukau, NZ
108/D6 Manu Nat'l Park, Peru
108/E6 Manuripe (riv.), Bol.
92/D5 Manus (isl.), PNG
131/F5 Manville, NJ,US
128/E4 Many, La,US
67/G3 Manych (riv.), Rus.
67/G3 Manych-Gudilo (lake), Rus.
124/E3 Many Farms, Az,US
101/B4 Manyoni, Tanz.
58/D3 Manzanares, Sp.
59/N8 Manzanares (riv.), Sp.
117/P10 Manzanillo, Mex.
128/B3 Manzano (mts.), NM,US
77/H2 Manzhouli, China
100/C2 Manzilah, Buḥayrat al (lake), Egypt
60/A4 Manzil bū Ruqaybah, Tun.
60/B4 Manzil Tamīn, Tun.
103/E2 Manzini, Swaz.
117/G4 Mao, DRep.
87/J4 Maoke (mts.), Indo.
82/B3 Maoming, China
75/D5 Mapam (lake), China
116/C4 Mapastepec, Mex.
117/P8 Mapimí, Bolsón de (val.), Mex.
127/Q8 Maple, On,Can
123/K5 Maple (riv.), Ia,US
123/J4 Maple (riv.), ND,US
122/F3 Maple Creek, Sk,Can
131/F6 Maple Shade, NJ,US
131/F5 Maplewood, NJ,US
108/G4 Mapuera (riv.), Braz.
84/B4 Mapusa, India
103/F2 Maputo (cap.), Moz.
100/D5 Maqdam, Ras (cape), Sudan
73/J2 Maqor, Afg.
75/D5 Maquan (riv.), China
104/C2 Maquela do Zombo, Ang.
125/K2 Maquoketa (riv.), Ia,US
110/B3 Mar (range), Braz.
101/B3 Mara (prov.), Tanz.
109/J5 Marabá, Braz.
109/J3 Maracá (isl.), Braz.
117/G5 Maracaibo, Ven.
117/G6 Maracaibo (lake), Ven.
109/H7 Maracaju (mts.), Braz.
117/H5 Maracay, Ven.
58/D4 Maracena, Sp.
99/G3 Maradi, Niger
99/G3 Maradi (dept.), Niger
72/E1 Marāgheh, Iran
108/E3 Marahuaca (peak), Ven.
125/J3 Marais des Cygnes (riv.), Ks, Mo,US
109/J4 Marajó, Braz.
109/J4 Marajó (bay), Braz.
107/D3 Marajó (isl.), Braz.
82/E6 Maramag, Phil.
110/K8 Marambaia (isl.), Braz.
129/F2 Maramec (riv.), Mo,US
63/F2 Maramureş (co.), Rom.
124/E4 Marana, Az,US
109/L4 Maranguape, Braz.
109/J6 Maranhão (riv.), Braz.
90/C4 Maranoa (riv.), Austl.
108/C4 Marañón (riv.), Peru
98/D5 Maraoue Nat'l Park, IvC.
86/B4 Marapi (peak), Indo.
86/C4 Maras (peak), Indo.
63/H3 Mărăşeşti, Rom.
126/C1 Marathon, On,Can
129/H5 Marathon, Fl,US
128/C4 Marathon, Tx,US
110/A4 Marau, Braz.
82/D6 Marawi, Phil.
100/B5 Marawī, Sudan
46/A6 Marazion, Eng,UK
58/C4 Marbella, Sp.
122/F5 Marbleton, Wy,US
48/E3 Marburg, Ger.
62/C2 Marcali, Hun.
104/B4 Marca, Ponta da (pt.), Ang.
47/G1 March, Eng,UK
56/D3 Marche (mts.), Fr.
57/K5 Marche (reg.), It.
53/E3 Marche-en-Famenne, Belg.
58/C4 Marchena, Sp.
111/D3 Mar Chiquita (lake), Arg.
52/A2 Marck, Fr.
129/H5 Marco, Fl,US
108/C7 Marcona, Peru
122/E3 Marconi (peak), BC,Can
112/E2 Marcos Juárez, Arg.
52/C2 Marcq-en-Baroeul, Fr.
130/J3 Marcus Baker (mtn.), Ak,US
126/F2 Marcy (peak), NY,US
73/K2 Mardān, Pak.
113/F3 Mar del Plata, Arg.
47/G4 Marden, Eng,UK
74/E3 Mardin, Turk.
93/W12 Maré (isl.), NCal.
90/B2 Mareeba, Austl.
43/C2 Maree, Loch (lake), Sc,UK
45/H5 Mareham le Fen, Eng,UK
47/G5 Maresfield, Eng,UK
128/B4 Marfa, Tx,US
46/C3 Margam, Wal,UK
66/E3 Marganets, Ukr.
84/B4 Margao, India
117/J5 Margarita (isl.), Ven.
47/H4 Margate, Eng,UK
56/E4 Margeride (mts.), Fr.
101/A2 Margherita (peak), Ugan.
62/F2 Marghita, Rom.
75/B3 Margilan, Uzb.
75/E5 Margog Caka (lake), China
82/D6 Margosatubig, Phil.
53/E2 Margraten, Neth.
105/V Marguerite (bay), Ant.
91/D4 Maria (peak), Austl.
93/K7 Maria (isl.), FrPol.
91/D4 Maria Island Nat'l Park, Austl.
129/F3 Marianna, Ar,US
129/G4 Marianna, Fl,US
116/E3 Mariano, Cuba
57/K2 Mariánské Lázně (Marienbad), Czh.
122/F3 Marias (riv.), Mt,US
62/B2 Maribor, Slov.
110/L7 Maricá, Braz.
108/E4 Marié (riv.), Braz.
105/S Marie Byrd Land (reg.), Ant.
117/J4 Marie-Galante (isl.), Guad.
42/F3 Mariehamn, Fin.
57/K2 Marienbad (Mariánské Lázně), Czh.
51/E6 Marienheide, Ger.
42/E4 Mariestad, Swe.
129/G3 Marietta, Ga,US
126/D4 Marietta, Oh,US

163

Marig – Middl

56/F5 Marignane, Fr.
110/B2 Marília, Braz.
58/A1 Marín, Sp.
131/B3 Marina del Rey, Ca,US
52/A5 Marines, Fr.
126/C2 Marinette, Wi,US
110/B2 Maringá, Braz.
58/A3 Marinha Grande, Port.
129/G3 Marion, Al,US
126/B4 Marion, Il,US
126/C3 Marion, In,US
126/B4 Marion, Ky,US
126/C2 Marion, Mi,US
126/D3 Marion, Oh,US
129/H3 Marion (lake), SC,US
126/D4 Marion, Va,US
124/C3 Mariposa, Ca,US
63/H5 Maritsa (riv.), Bul., Turk.
66/F3 Mariupol', Ukr.
65/K4 Mariy Aut. Rep., Rus.
74/K5 Marj 'Uyūn, Leb.
50/B6 Mark (riv.), Belg.
76/B2 Markakol (lake), Kaz.
42/E4 Markaryd, Swe.
50/C4 Marken (isl.), Neth.
50/C4 Markerwaard (polder), Neth.
47/E1 Market Bosworth, Eng,UK
47/F1 Market Deeping, Eng,UK
45/F6 Market Drayton, Eng,UK
47/F2 Market Harborough, Eng,UK
44/B3 Markethill, NI,UK
45/H5 Market Rasen, Eng,UK
45/H4 Market Weighton, Eng,UK
119/J2 Markham (bay), NW,Can
127/R8 Markham, On,Can
49/L2 Marki, Pol.
124/C3 Markleeville, Ca,US
61/L7 Markópoulon, Gre.
67/H2 Marks, Rus.
128/E4 Marksville, La,US
57/K2 Marktredwitz, Ger.
125/J3 Mark Twain (lake), Mo,US
51/E5 Marl, Ger.
131/F5 Marlboro, NJ,US
47/E4 Marlborough, Eng,UK
52/B3 Marles-les-Mines, Fr.
47/F3 Marlow, Eng,UK
131/F6 Marlton, NJ,US
52/C3 Marly, Fr.
52/B5 Marly-la-Ville, Fr.
52/B5 Marly-le-Roi, Fr.
53/F5 Marly-sur-Seille, Fr.
56/D4 Marmande, Fr.
63/H5 Marmara (isl.), Turk.
63/J5 Marmara (sea), Turk.
74/B3 Marmaris, Turk.
108/F5 Marmelos (riv.), Braz.
126/A1 Marmion (lake), On,Can
57/J3 Marmolada (peak), It.
58/C3 Marmolejo, Sp.
52/C6 Marne (dept.), Fr.
56/E2 Marne (riv.), Fr.
53/D6 Marne au Rhin, Canal de la (can.), Fr.
46/D5 Marnhull, Eng,UK
96/J6 Maro, Chad
93/H2 Maro (reef), Hi,US
103/J6 Maroantsetra, Madg.
93/L6 Marokau (atoll), FrPol.
103/J8 Marolambo, Madg.
103/J6 Maromokotro (peak), Madg.
104/F4 Marondera, Zim.
109/H3 Maroni (riv.), FrG., Sur.
90/D4 Maroochydore-Mooloolaba, Austl.
96/H5 Maroua, Camr.
103/H7 Marovoay, Madg.
53/G5 Marpingen, Ger.
45/F5 Marple, Eng,UK
76/D5 Marqên Gangri (peak), China
92/D8 Marquarie (riv.), Austl.
93/M5 Marquesas (isls.), FrPol.
126/C2 Marquette, Mi,US
97/K5 Marrah (mts.), Sudan
96/D1 Marrakech, Mor.
101/C2 Marsabit, Kenya
60/C4 Marsala, It.
97/L1 Marsá Matrūh, Egypt
51/F6 Marsberg, Ger.
60/C1 Marsciano, It.
45/G4 Marsden, Eng,UK
50/B3 Marsdiep (chan.), Neth.
56/F5 Marseille, Fr.
128/E4 Marsh (isl.), La,US
122/F2 Marshall, Sk,Can
123/K4 Marshall, Mn,US
125/J3 Marshall, Mo,US
128/E3 Marshall, Tx,US
92/G3 Marshall Islands
123/K5 Marshalltown, Ia,US
125/J3 Marshfield, Mo,US
126/B2 Marshfield, Wi,US
47/E3 Marsh Gibbon, Eng,UK
45/G2 Marske-by-the-Sea, Eng,UK
83/B2 Martaban (gulf), Burma
122/G2 Martensville, Sk,Can
127/G3 Martha's Vineyard (isl.), Ma,US
54/D5 Martigny, Swi.
56/F5 Martigues, Fr.
105/S Martin (pen.), Ant.
49/K4 Martin, Slvk.
129/G3 Martin (lake), Al,US
123/H5 Martin, SD,US
129/F2 Martin, Tn,US
60/E2 Martina Franca, It.
132/K10 Martinez, Ca,US
129/H3 Martinez, Ga,US
116/B3 Martínez de la Torre, Mex.
117/J4 Martinique (passage), Dom., Mart.
117/J5 Martinique (isl.), Fr.
110/B2 Martinópolis, Braz.
126/E4 Martinsburg, WV,US
126/C4 Martinsville, In,US
126/E4 Martinsville, Va,US
38/H7 Martin Vaz (isls.), Braz.
46/D2 Martley, Eng,UK
46/D5 Martock, Eng,UK
59/F2 Martorell, Sp.
58/D4 Martos, Sp.
126/F1 Martre (riv.), Qu,Can
123/J5 Marty, SD,US
78/C3 Marugame, Japan
79/F2 Maruko, Japan
50/D2 Marum, Neth.
78/E2 Maruoka, Japan
93/M7 Marutea (atoll), FrPol.
79/H7 Maruyama, Japan
72/F3 Marv Dasht, Iran
90/D4 Mary (riv.), Austl.
73/H1 Mary, Trkm.
90/D4 Maryborough, Austl.
91/B3 Maryborough, Austl.
129/G4 Mary Esther, Fl,US
123/H3 Maryfield, Sk,Can
98/C5 Maryland (co.), Libr.
126/E4 Maryland (state), US
131/K7 Maryland City, Md,US
44/E2 Maryport, Eng,UK
127/L2 Marystown, Nf,Can
125/H3 Marysville, Ks,US
132/H6 Marysville, Mi,US
132/C1 Marysville, Wa,US
125/J2 Maryville, Mo,US
129/H3 Maryville, Tn,US
60/D2 Marzano (peak), It.
96/H2 Marzūq, Libya
96/H3 Marzūq, Ṣaḩrā (des.), Libya
74/K6 Masada (Ḩorvot Meẕada) (ruins), Isr.
101/C4 Masai Steppe (grsld.), Tanz.
101/A3 Masaka, Ugan.
60/B5 Masākin, Tun.
59/E3 Masamagrell, Sp.
87/F4 Masamba, Indo.
80/E5 Masan, SKor.
101/C5 Masasi, Tanz.
116/D5 Masaya, Nic.
82/D5 Masbate, Phil.
82/D5 Masbate (isl.), Phil.
96/F1 Mascara, Alg.
103/S15 Mascarene (isls.), Mrts., Reun.
117/P9 Mascota, Mex.
127/N6 Mascouche, Qu,Can
102/D3 Maseru (cap.), Les.
71/E6 Mashad, Iran
45/G3 Masham, Eng,UK
73/G1 Mashhad, Iran
73/H3 Māshkel, Hāmūn-i- (lake), Pak.
73/H3 Māshkīd (riv.), Iran
67/L1 Masim (peak), Rus.
73/G5 Masira (gulf), Oman
73/G4 Maşīrah (isl.), Oman
72/E2 Masjed-e Soleymān, Iran
43/A4 Mask, Lough (lake), Ire.
103/J6 Masoala (cape), Madg.
103/J6 Masoala (pen.), Madg.
126/C3 Mason, Mi,US
128/D4 Mason, Tx,US
132/A3 Mason (lake), Wa,US
123/K5 Mason City, Ia,US
59/X17 Maspalomas, Canl.,Sp.
59/K6 Masquefa, Sp.
57/J4 Massa, It.
127/F3 Massachusetts (state), US
127/G3 Massachusetts (bay), Ma,US
60/E2 Massafra, It.
131/G5 Massapequa, NY,US
126/F2 Massena, NY,US
119/S7 Massey (sound), NW,Can
104/D3 Massibi, Ang.
56/E4 Massif Central (plat.), Fr.
126/D3 Massillon, Oh,US
105/G Masson (isl.), Ant.
52/B6 Massy, Fr.
50/B5 Mastgat (chan.), Neth.
131/H5 Mastic, NY,US
73/J3 Mastung, Pak.
78/B3 Masuda, Japan
86/B4 Masurai (peak), Indo.
104/F5 Masvingo, Zim.
74/L4 Maşyāf, Syria
61/F2 Mat (riv.), Alb.
104/B2 Matadi, Zaire
128/C3 Matador, Tx,US
116/D5 Matagalpa, Nic.
126/E1 Matagami (lake), Qu,Can
128/D4 Matagorda (bay), Tx,US
128/D4 Matagorda (isl.), Tx,US
84/D6 Matale, SrL.
98/B3 Matam, Sen.
116/A2 Matamoros, Mex.
116/B2 Matamoros, Mex.
97/K3 Ma'ṭan as Sarra (well), Libya
127/H1 Matane, Qu,Can
127/H1 Matane (riv.), Qu,Can
116/E3 Matanzas, Cuba
110/B2 Matão, Braz.
127/H1 Matapedia (riv.), Qu,Can
112/C2 Mataquito (riv.), Chile
72/C6 Matara (ruins), Egypt
84/D6 Matara, SrL.
87/E5 Mataram, Indo.
59/G2 Mataró, Sp.
93/L7 Mataura, FrPol.
92/H6 Mata Utu (cap.), Wall.
131/F5 Matawan, NJ,US
116/A3 Matehuala, Mex.
60/E2 Matera, It.
117/F3 Maternillos (pt.), Cuba
62/F2 Mátészalka, Hun.
131/C3 Mathews (lake), Ca,US
128/D4 Mathis, Tx,US
84/C2 Mathurā, India
82/E6 Mati, Phil.
110/K6 Matias Barbosa, Braz.
116/B4 Matías Romero, Mex.
60/A4 Mātir, Tun.
45/G5 Matlock, Eng,UK
108/G7 Mato Grosso, Braz.
109/G6 Mato Grosso (plat.), Braz.
110/A1 Mato Grosso do Sul (state), Braz.
104/E5 Matopos, Zim.
58/A2 Matosinhos, Port.
73/G4 Maţraḩ, Oman
102/B4 Matroosberg (peak), SAfr.
100/A2 Maţrūḩ, Egypt
100/B2 Maţrūḩ (gov.), Egypt
103/H8 Matsiatra (riv.), Madg.
79/L10 Matsubara, Japan
79/H7 Matsubushi, Japan
79/H7 Matsudo, Japan
78/C3 Matsue, Japan
77/N3 Matsumae, Japan
79/E2 Matsumoto, Japan
78/E3 Matsusaka, Japan
79/G1 Matsushima, Japan
78/E2 Matsutō, Japan
78/C4 Matsuyama, Japan
126/D1 Mattagami (riv.), On,Can
126/E2 Mattawa, On,Can
57/G4 Matterhorn (pk.), It., Swi.
132/Q16 Matteson, Il,US
130/H2 Matthews (mtn.), Ak,US
117/G3 Matthew Town, Bahm.
78/E2 Mattō, Japan
44/B4 Mattock (riv.), Ire.
126/B4 Mattoon, Il,US
117/J6 Maturín, Ven.
104/E4 Matusadona Nat'l Park, Zim.
87/F2 Matutum (mt.), Phil.
108/G3 Maú (riv.), Braz., Guy.
110/C2 Mauá, Braz.
52/C3 Maubeuge, Fr.
85/G4 Ma-ubin, Burma
43/D2 Maud, Sc,UK
84/D2 Maudaha, India
108/G4 Maués, Braz.
108/G4 Maués Açu (riv.), Braz.
92/D3 Maug (isls.), NMar.
44/D3 Maughold, IM,UK
44/D3 Maughold Head (pt.), IM,UK
56/F5 Mauguio, Fr.
120/T10 Maui (isl.), Hi,US
93/K7 Mauke (isl.), Cookls.
52/A6 Mauldre (riv.), Fr.
112/B2 Maule (reg.), Chile
112/C1 Maule (riv.), Chile
56/C3 Mauléon, Fr.
112/B4 Maullín, Chile
126/C3 Maumee (riv.), In, Oh,US
104/D4 Maun, Bots.
120/U11 Mauna Kea (vol.), Hi,US
120/U11 Mauna Loa (vol.), Hi,US
93/K6 Maupiti (isl.), FrPol.
84/C2 Mau Rānīpur, India
52/A6 Maurepas, Fr.
127/F2 Mauricie Nat'l Park, Qu,Can
98/B2 Mauritania
103/S15 Mauritius
126/B3 Mauston, Wi,US
62/E5 Mavrovo Nat'l Park, Macd.
83/B4 Maw Daung (pass), Thai.
105/D Mawson (coast), Ant.
105/E Mawson (sta.), Ant.
116/D3 Maxcanú, Mex.
53/F6 Maxéville, Fr.
126/F4 May (cape), NJ,US
86/C4 Maya (isl.), Indo.
69/P4 Maya (riv.), Rus.
117/G3 Mayaguana (isl.), Bahm.
117/H4 Mayagüez, PR
73/K1 Mayakovskogo (peak), Taj.
117/F3 Mayarí, Cuba
79/L10 Maya-san (peak), Japan
44/D1 Maybole, Sc,UK
97/N5 Maych'ew, Eth.
53/G3 Mayen, Ger.
56/C2 Mayenne, Fr.
56/C3 Mayenne (riv.), Fr.
122/E2 Mayerthorpe, Ab,Can
126/B4 Mayfield, Ky,US
66/G3 Maykop, Rus.
47/G3 Mayland, Eng,UK
85/G3 Maymyo, Burma
112/C5 Mayo (riv.), Arg.
130/L3 Mayo, Yk,Can
117/N8 Mayo (riv.), Mex.
58/D1 Mayor (cape), Sp.
103/H6 Mayotte (terr.), Fr.
117/F4 May Pen, Jam.
126/D4 Maysville, Ky,US
123/J4 Mayville, ND,US
132/Q16 Maywood, Il,US
104/E4 Mazabuka, Zam.
56/E5 Mazamet, Fr.
60/C4 Mazara (val.), It.
60/C4 Mazara del Vallo, It.
73/J1 Mazār-e Sharīf, Afg.
58/A1 Mazaricos, Sp.
58/E4 Mazarrón, Sp.
108/G2 Mazaruni (riv.), Guy.
116/C5 Mazatenango, Guat.
117/N9 Mazatlán, Mex.
64/D4 Mažeikiai, Lith.
90/B3 Mazeppa Nat'l Park, Austl.
44/B3 Mazetown, NI,UK
52/B3 Mazingarbe, Fr.
104/C2 Mazingu, Zaire
76/D3 Mazong (peak), China
49/L2 Mazury (reg.), Pol.
100/C2 Ma'ān, Jor.
103/E2 Mbabane (cap.), Swaz.
96/H6 Mbabo (peak), Camr.
96/J7 Mbaïki, CAfr.
97/H6 Mbakaou (lake), Camr.
101/A5 Mbala, Zam.
96/H7 Mbalam, Camr.
101/B2 Mbale, Ugan.
96/H7 Mbalmayo, Camr.
99/H5 Mbam (riv.), Camr.
99/H5 Mbam, Massif du (peak), Camr.
97/J7 Mbandaka, Zaire
101/A3 Mbarara, Ugan.
97/J7 Mbata, CAfr.
93/Y18 Mbengga (isl.), Fiji
101/B5 Mbeya, Tanz.
101/B5 Mbeya (prov.), Tanz.
101/B5 Mbeya (range), Tanz.
104/B1 M'Bigou, Gabon
96/G7 Mbini, EqG.
96/H7 Mbini (riv.), EqG.
97/L6 Mbomou (riv.), CAfr.
98/B3 Mboune, Vallée du (wadi), Sen.
98/A3 M'Bour, Sen.
104/D2 Mbuji-Mayi, Zaire
125/J4 McAlester, Ok,US
128/D5 McAllen, Tx,US
122/C2 McBride, BC,Can
122/D4 McCall, Id,US
128/C4 McCamey, Tx,US
132/C3 McChord A.F.B., Wa,US
132/M9 McClellan A.F.B., Ca,US
123/H4 McClusky, ND,US
129/F4 McComb, Ms,US
125/G2 McConaughy (lake), Ne,US
125/G2 McCook, Ne,US
129/H3 McCormick, SC,US
123/J3 McCreary, Mb,Can
124/C2 McDermitt, Nv,US
39/N8 McDonald (isls.), Austl.
130/F3 McDonald (mtn.), Ak,US
130/L2 McDougall (pass), NW, Yk,Can
128/F3 McGehee, Ar,US
129/F3 McGehee, Ar,US
122/C2 McGregor (riv.), BC,Can
132/G7 McGregor, On,Can
132/P15 McHenry, Il,US
93/H5 McKean (atoll), Kiri.
119/K2 McKeand (riv.), NW,Can
126/E3 McKeesport, Pa,US
129/F2 McKenzie, Tn,US
130/H3 McKinley (mtn.), Ak,US
130/J3 McKinley Park, Ak,US
122/B5 McKinleyville, Ca,US
128/D3 McKinney, Tx,US
123/H4 McLaughlin, SD,US
131/J8 McLean, Va,US
122/D2 McLennan, Ab,Can
122/D2 McLeod (riv.), Ab,Can
118/E2 McLeod (bay), NW,Can
122/C2 McLeod Lake, BC,Can
118/F1 M'Clintock (chan.), NW,Can
119/Q7 M'Clure (str.), NW,Can
122/C4 McMinnville, Or,US
129/G3 McMinnville, Tn,US
105/M McMurdo, Ant.
132/B3 McNeil (isl.), Wa,US
104/F3 Mcocha, Malw.
125/H3 McPherson, Ks,US
76/E5 Mê (riv.), China
124/D3 Mead (lake), Az, Nv,US
130/G2 Meade (riv.), Ak,US
122/F2 Meadow Lake, Sk,Can
127/Q8 Meadowvale, On,Can
124/D3 Meadow Valley (riv.), Nv,US
129/F4 Meadville, Ms,US
126/D3 Meadville, Pa,US
109/J5 Mearim (riv.), Braz.
47/E1 Measham, Eng,UK
130/F2 Meat (mtn.), Ak,US
44/B4 Meath (co.), Ire.
123/G2 Meath Park, Sk,Can
52/B6 Meaux, Fr.
72/C4 Mecca (Makkah), SAr.
52/D1 Mechelen (Malines), Belg.
48/F1 Mecklenburger Bucht (bay), Ger.
48/F2 Mecklenburg-Western Pomerania (state), Ger.
104/G3 Mecuia (peak), Moz.
84/C4 Medak, India
86/A3 Medan, Indo.
113/L7 Medanosa (pt.), Arg.
47/F1 Medbourne, Eng,UK
51/F6 Medebach, Ger.
108/C2 Medellín, Col.
50/C3 Medemblik, Neth.
45/G5 Meden (riv.), Eng,UK
131/H5 Medford, NY,US
122/C5 Medford, Or,US
126/B2 Medford, Wi,US
63/J3 Medgidia, Rom.
63/G2 Mediaş, Rom.
122/D4 Medical Lake, Wa,US
124/F2 Medicine Bow (range), Co, Wy,US
123/G5 Medicine Bow, Wy,US
122/F3 Medicine Hat, Ab,Can
47/E5 Medina (riv.), Eng,UK
123/J4 Medina, ND,US
126/D3 Medina, Oh,US
125/H5 Medina, Tx,US
72/C4 Medina (Al Madīnah), SAr.
58/C2 Medina del Campo, Sp.
58/C4 Medina-Sidonia, Sp.
39/K4 Mediterranean (sea)
122/F2 Medley, Ab,Can
67/L2 Mednogorsk, Rus.
67/H2 Medveditsa, Gora (riv.), Rus.
69/S2 Medvezh'i (isls.), Rus.
64/G3 Medvezh'yegorsk, Rus.
124/F2 Meeker, Co,US
51/G3 Meerbach (riv.), Ger.
50/D6 Meerbusch, Ger.
53/E1 Meerhout, Belg.
53/E2 Meerssen, Neth.
84/C2 Meerut, India
47/E1 Meese (riv.), Eng,UK
122/F4 Meeteetse, Wy,US
97/N7 Mēga, Eth.
97/P6 Megalo, Eth.
127/G2 Megantic (peak), Qu,Can
61/H3 Mégara, Gre.
85/F2 Meghalaya (state), India
74/N7 Megiddo (ruins), Isr.
126/E1 Mégiscane (lake), Qu,Can
126/E1 Mégiscane (riv.), Qu,Can
74/B3 Megista (isl.), Gre.
53/E2 Mehaigne (riv.), Belg.
51/G1 Mehe (riv.), Ger.
84/C3 Mehkar, India
73/F3 Mehrān (riv.), Iran
72/F2 Mehriz, Iran
84/B3 Mehsāna, India
82/C2 Mei (riv.), China
82/C3 Mei (riv.), China
110/B1 Meia Ponte (riv.), Braz.
96/H6 Meiganga, Camr.
119/R6 Meighen (isl.), NW,Can
77/K3 Meihekou, China
83/A1 Meiktila, Burma
51/H4 Meine, Ger.
51/E6 Meinerzhagen, Ger.
57/J1 Meiningen, Ger.
81/C5 Meishan (res.), China
49/G3 Meissen, Ger.
51/G6 Meissner (peak), Ger.
79/M10 Meiwa, Japan
82/C3 Meizhou, China
96/H7 Mekambo, Gabon
97/N5 Mek'elē, Eth.
96/D1 Meknès, Mor.
71/K8 Mekong (riv.), Asia
87/F4 Mekongga (peak), Indo.
83/D4 Mekong, Mouths of the, Viet.
86/B3 Melaka, Malay.
92/E5 Melanesia (reg.)
84/C6 Melappālaiyam, India
86/D4 Melawi (riv.), Indo.
47/G2 Melbourn, Eng,UK
91/F5 Melbourne, Austl.
118/F2 Melbourne (isl.), NW,Can
45/G6 Melbourne, Eng,UK
129/H4 Melbourne, Fl,US
112/B5 Melchor (isl.), Chile
116/D4 Melchor de Mencos, Mex.
116/A2 Melchor Múzquiz, Mex.
46/D5 Melcombe Regis, Eng,UK
48/E1 Meldorf, Ger.
62/E3 Melenci, Yugo.
64/J5 Melenki, Rus.
67/K1 Meleuz, Rus.
119/J3 Mélèzes (riv.), Qu,Can
96/J5 Melfi, Chad
60/D2 Melfi, It.
123/G2 Melfort, Sk,Can
42/D3 Melhus, Nor.
96/E1 Melilla, Sp.
112/B5 Melimoyu (peak), Chile
112/Q9 Melipilla, Chile
61/F3 Melissano, It.
123/H3 Melita, Mb,Can
60/D4 Melito di Porto Salvo, It.
66/E3 Melitopol', Ukr.
57/L2 Melk, Aus.
97/P7 Melka Meri, Eth.
46/D4 Melksham, Eng,UK
52/C2 Melle, Belg.
51/F4 Melle, Ger.
42/E4 Mellerud, Swe.
58/B1 Mellid, Sp.
45/F3 Melling, Eng,UK
113/J7 Mellizo Sur (peak), Chile
57/J1 Mellrichstadt, Ger.
51/F1 Mellum (isl.), Ger.
57/L1 Mělník, Czh.
113/G2 Melo, Uru.
132/Q16 Melrose Park, Il,US
51/G6 Melsungen, Ger.
45/G4 Meltham, Eng,UK
91/C3 Melton, Austl.
45/H6 Melton Mowbray, Eng,UK
56/E2 Melun, Fr.
90/B1 Melville (cape), Austl.
92/B6 Melville (isl.), Austl.
119/L3 Melville (lake), Nf,Can
119/R7 Melville (isl.), NW,Can
119/H2 Melville (pen.), NW,Can
123/H3 Melville, Sk,Can
82/D5 Melville (cape), Phil.
131/G5 Melville, NY,US
132/F7 Melvindale, Mi,US
62/D2 Mélykút, Hun.
75/D5 Mêmar (lake), China
50/D1 Memmert (isl.), Ger.
55/G2 Memmingen, Ger.
83/D4 Memot, Camb.
86/B2 Memphis (ruins), Egypt
132/G6 Memphis, Mi,US
125/J2 Memphis, Mo,US
129/F3 Memphis, Tn,US
128/C3 Memphis, Tx,US
128/E3 Mena, Ar,US
44/D5 Menai (str.), Wal,UK
44/D5 Menai Bridge, Wal,UK
50/C2 Menaldum, Neth.
103/H9 Menarandra (riv.), Madg.
128/D4 Menard, Tx,US
126/B2 Menasha, Wi,US
103/H7 Menavava (riv.), Madg.
86/D4 Mendawai (riv.), Indo.
56/E4 Mende, Fr.
51/E6 Menden, Ger.
130/E4 Mendenhall (cape), Ak,US
74/B3 Menderes, Büyük (riv.), Turk.
110/K7 Mendes, Braz.
97/N6 Mendī, Eth.
53/G3 Mendig, Ger.
46/D4 Mendip (hills), Eng,UK
124/B3 Mendocino, Ca,US
120/B3 Mendocino (cape), Ca,US
112/C2 Mendoza, Arg.
112/C2 Mendoza (prov.), Arg.
103/H9 Mendrare (riv.), Madg.
62/F3 Menedinți (co.), Rom.
117/G6 Mene Grande, Ven.
74/A2 Menemen, Turk.
52/C2 Menen, Belg.
101/C3 Menengai Crater, Kenya
76/H2 Menengiyn (plain), Mong.
60/C4 Menfi, It.
86/C4 Menggala, Indo.
58/D4 Mengibar, Sp.
81/D4 Menglianggu (mtn.), China
91/B2 Menindee (lake), Austl.
112/B5 Menlolat (peak), Chile
132/K12 Menlo Park, Ca,US
126/C2 Menominee, Mi,US
126/B3 Menomonee Falls, Wi,US
126/B2 Menomonie, Wi,US
59/H3 Menorca (Minorca) (isl.), Sp.
86/A4 Mentawai (isls.), Indo.
86/A4 Mentawai (str.), Indo.
131/C2 Mentone, Ca,US
128/C4 Mentone, Tx,US
126/D3 Mentor, Oh,US
87/E3 Menyapa (peak), Indo.
130/M3 Menzie (mtn.), Yk,Can
47/E5 Meon (riv.), Eng,UK
117/N8 Meoquí, Mex.
87/H4 Meos Waar (isl.), Indo.
104/B2 Mepala, Ang.
67/G4 Mepistskaro (peak), Geo.
50/D3 Meppel, Neth.
51/E3 Meppen, Ger.
59/E2 Mequinenzo (res.), Sp.
125/K3 Meramec (riv.), Mo,US
55/H4 Merano, It.
86/D4 Meratus (mts.), Indo.
92/D5 Merauke, Indo.
97/P7 Merca, Som.
57/G4 Mercantour Nat'l Park, Fr.
124/B3 Merced, Ca,US
124/C3 Merced (riv.), Ca,US
112/C1 Mercedario (peak), Arg.
112/D2 Mercedes, Arg.
112/F2 Mercedes, Arg.
113/F2 Mercedes, Uru.
132/C2 Mercer Island, Wa,US
131/F5 Mercerville-Hamilton Square, NJ,US
52/D2 Merchtem, Belg.
127/N7 Mercier, Qu,Can
122/D2 Mercoal, Ab,Can
124/D3 Mercury, Nv,US
119/K2 Mercy (cape), Yk,Can
56/E5 Merdellou (mtn.), Fr.
46/D4 Mere, Eng,UK
113/M8 Meredith (cape), Falk.
128/C3 Meredith (lake), Tx,US
66/F2 Merefa, Ukr.
52/C2 Merelbeke, Belg.
83/D3 Mereuch, Camb.
77/J2 Mergel (riv.), China
83/B3 Mergui, Burma
83/B4 Mergui (arch.), Burma
52/B3 Méricourt, Fr.
116/D3 Mérida, Mex.
58/B3 Mérida, Sp.
117/G6 Mérida, Ven.
108/D2 Mérida, Ven.
129/F3 Meridian, Ms,US
128/D4 Meridian, Tx,US
132/C2 Meridian-East Hill, Wa,US
56/C4 Mérignac, Fr.
52/D1 Merksem, Belg.
50/B6 Merksplas, Belg.
97/M4 Meroe (ruins), Sudan
74/K5 Meron, Har (mtn.), Isr.
91/F5 Merri (cr.), Austl.
131/G5 Merrick, NY,US
126/B2 Merrill, Wi,US
127/G3 Merrimack, NH,US
46/D5 Merriott, Eng,UK
122/C3 Merritt, BC,Can
129/H4 Merritt Island, Fl,US
45/F5 Mersey (riv.), Eng,UK
45/F5 Merseyside (co.), Eng,UK
74/C3 Mersin, Turk.
86/B3 Mersing, Malay.
53/F5 Merten, Fr.
46/C3 Merthyr Tydfil, Wal,UK
105/K Mertz (glac.), Ant.
128/C4 Mertzon, Tx,US
52/B5 Méru, Fr.
101/C2 Meru, Kenya
52/B2 Merville, Fr.
50/C5 Merwedekanaal (can.), Neth.
53/F2 Merzenich, Ger.
74/C2 Merzifon, Turk.
53/F5 Merzig, Ger.
113/K7 Mesa (peak), Arg.
130/G3 Mesa (mtn.), Ak,US
124/E4 Mesa, Az,US
123/K4 Mesabi (range), Mn,US
117/M8 Mesa del Seri, Mex.
61/E2 Mesagne, It.
61/J5 Mesarás (gulf), Gre.
124/E3 Mesa Verde Nat'l Park, Co,US
128/C3 Mescalero (ridge), NM,US
51/F6 Meschede, Ger.
57/H4 Mesco, Punta di (pt.), It.
126/F1 Mesgouez (lake), Qu,Can
61/G3 Mesolóngion, Gre.
112/F2 Mesopotamia (reg.), Arg.
72/D2 Mesopotamia (reg.), Iraq
60/E3 Mesoraca, It.
128/D3 Mesquite, Tx,US
96/E1 Mesrouh (peak), Mor.
96/F1 Messaad, Alg.
113/J7 Messier (chan.), Chile
60/D3 Messina, It.
60/D4 Messina (str.), It.
104/F5 Messina, SAfr.
61/H4 Messíni, Gre.
61/H4 Messíni (gulf), Gre.
63/F5 Mesta (riv.), Bul.
57/K4 Mestre, It.
98/C5 Mesurado (cape), Libr.
127/G1 Métabetchouan, Qu,Can
127/G1 Métabetchouane (riv.), Qu,Can
119/K2 Meta Incognita (pen.), NW,Can
129/F4 Metairie, La,US
111/D2 Metán, Arg.
60/E2 Metapontum (ruins), It.
61/G3 Metéora, Gre.
45/H5 Metheringham, Eng,UK
61/G4 Methóni, Gre.
62/C4 Metković, Cro.
126/B4 Metropolis, Il,US
53/D3 Mettet, Belg.
51/E4 Mettingen, Ger.
53/F5 Mettlach, Ger.
50/D6 Mettmann, Ger.
97/N6 Metu, Eth.
131/F5 Metuchen, NJ,US
53/F5 Metz, Fr.
52/C2 Meulebeke, Belg.
53/E6 Meurthe-et-Moselle (dept.), Fr.
53/E3 Meuse (riv.), Belg., Fr.
52/E6 Meuse (dept.), Fr.
53/E5 Meuse, Cotes de (uplands), Fr.
74/N9 Mevasseret Ẕiyyon, Isr.
45/G5 Mexborough, Eng,UK
128/D4 Mexia, Tx,US
109/J3 Mexiana, Braz.
117/L7 Mexicali, Mex.
116/A3 Mexico
116/B4 México (state), Mex.
125/J5 Mexico (gulf), NAm
125/K3 Mexico, Mo,US
116/B4 Mexico City (cap.), Mex.
72/F2 Meybod, Iran
102/Q13 Meyerton, SAfr.
73/H1 Meymaneh, Afg.
74/K6 Meẕada, Ḩorvot (Masada) (ruins), Isr.
63/F4 Mezdra, Bul.
64/J2 Mezen' (bay), Rus.
65/K2 Mezen' (riv.), Rus.
68/J4 Mezhdurechensk, Rus.
68/E2 Mezhdusharskiy (isl.), Rus.
62/E2 Mezoberény, Hun.
62/E2 Mezokovácsháza, Hun.
62/E2 Mezőkövesd, Hun.
62/E2 Mezőtúr, Hun.
84/C3 Mhow, India
81/D3 Mi (riv.), China
116/B4 Miahuatlán, Mex.
58/C3 Miajadas, Sp.
124/E4 Miami, Az,US
129/H5 Miami, Fl,US
125/J3 Miami, Ok,US
129/H5 Miami Beach, Fl,US
81/B4 Mianchi, China
72/E1 Mīāndoāb, Iran
72/E1 Mīāneh, Iran
131/G4 Mianus (riv.), Ct,US
73/K2 Miānwāli, Pak.
76/E5 Mianyang, China
82/B2 Miao'er (peak), China
81/E3 Miaodao (isls.), China
81/H6 Miaofeng Shan (mtn.), China
65/P5 Miass, Rus.
65/Q5 Miass (riv.), Rus.
49/J2 Miastko, Pol.
100/C5 Miberika, Sudan
122/D2 Mica Creek, BC,Can
49/L4 Michalovce, Slvk.
130/K2 Michelson (mtn.), Ak,US
126/C3 Michigan (lake), Can., US
126/C2 Michigan (state), US
126/C3 Michigan City, In,US
126/C2 Michipicoten (isl.), On,Can
116/A4 Michoacán (state), Mex.
67/G1 Michurinsk, Rus.
45/F2 Mickle Fell (mtn.), Eng,UK
45/F2 Mickleton, Eng,UK
116/E5 Mico (riv.), Nic.
117/J5 Micoud, StL.
92/E3 Micronesia (reg.)
92/D4 Micronesia, Fed. States of
99/G2 Midal (well), Niger
123/H3 Midale, Sk,Can
50/A6 Middelburg, Neth.
102/D3 Middelburg, SAfr.
103/E2 Middelburg, SAfr.
48/E1 Middelfart, Den.
50/B5 Middelharnis, Neth.
52/B1 Middelkerke, Belg.
124/C2 Middle Alkali (lake), Ca,US
85/F5 Middle Andaman (isl.), India
127/F2 Middlebury, Vt,US

164

Middl – Morri

128/C4 **Middle Concho** (riv.), Tx,US
45/G3 **Middleham**, Eng,UK
125/G2 **Middle Loup** (riv.), Ne,US
125/J2 **Middle Raccoon** (riv.), Ia,US
131/K7 **Middle River**, Md,US
126/D4 **Middlesboro**, Ky,US
45/G2 **Middlesbrough**, Eng,UK
47/F4 **Middlesex** (reg.), Eng,UK
131/F5 **Middlesex**, NJ,US
122/C4 **Middle Sister** (peak), Or,US
45/F4 **Middleton**, Eng,UK
47/E2 **Middleton Cheney**, Eng,UK
45/F2 **Middleton-in-Teesdale**, Eng,UK
44/B3 **Middletown**, NI,UK
131/F5 **Middletown**, NJ,US
45/F5 **Middlewich**, Eng,UK
46/C3 **Mid Glamorgan** (co.), Wal,UK
47/F5 **Midhurst**, Eng,UK
56/D5 **Midi** (can.), Fr.
56/D4 **Midi-Pyrénées** (reg.), Fr.
126/E2 **Midland**, On,Can
126/C3 **Midland**, Mi,US
128/C4 **Midland**, Tx,US
132/Q16 **Midlothian**, Il,US
56/C5 **Midou** (riv.), Fr.
82/D6 **Midsayap**, Phil.
46/D4 **Midsomer Norton**, Eng,UK
92/H2 **Midway** (isls.), PacUS
91/C4 **Midway Point-Sorell**, Austl.
125/H4 **Midwest City**, Ok,US
72/C3 **Midyan** (reg.), SAr.
74/E3 **Midyat**, Turk.
66/B4 **Midzhur** (peak), Bul.
62/F4 **Midžor** (peak), Yugo.
78/B4 **Mie**, Japan
78/E3 **Mie** (pref.), Japan
49/H2 **Międzychód**, Pol.
49/M3 **Międzyrzec Podlaski**, Pol.
49/H2 **Międzyrzecz**, Pol.
49/L3 **Mielec**, Pol.
96/J7 **Miéle I**, Congo
63/G2 **Miercurea Ciuc**, Rom.
58/C1 **Mieres**, Sp.
57/J3 **Miesbach**, Ger.
97/P6 **Mī'ēso**, Eth.
56/E3 **Migennes**, Fr.
116/A3 **Miguel Auza**, Mex.
110/B2 **Miguelópolis**, Braz.
110/K7 **Miguel Pereira**, Braz.
58/D3 **Miguelturra**, Sp.
78/D3 **Mihama**, Japan
78/C3 **Mihara**, Japan
79/G2 **Miharu**, Japan
73/J3 **Mihrābpur**, Pak.
59/E2 **Mijares** (riv.), Sp.
58/C4 **Mijas**, Sp.
50/B4 **Mijdrecht**, Neth.
79/N10 **Mikawa** (bay), Japan
79/N9 **Mikawa-Mino** (mts.), Japan
67/G4 **Mikha Tskhakaya**, Geo.
63/F4 **Mikhaylovgrad**, Bul.
62/F4 **Mikhaylovgrad** (reg.), Bul.
67/G2 **Mikhaylovka**, Rus.
79/K10 **Miki**, Japan
42/H3 **Mikkeli**, Fin.
42/H3 **Mikkeli** (prov.), Fin.
61/J4 **Míkonos** (isl.), Gre.
61/G2 **Mikri Prespa** (lake), Gre.
79/M10 **Mikuma**, Japan
101/C4 **Mikumi**, Tanz.
101/C4 **Mikumi Nat'l Park**, Tanz.
78/E2 **Mikuni**, Japan
79/F2 **Mikuni-tōge** (pass), Japan
108/C4 **Milagro**, Ecu.
57/H4 **Milan** (Milano), It.
74/A3 **Milas**, Turk.
60/D3 **Milazzo**, It.
46/D5 **Milborne Port**, Eng,UK
47/G2 **Mildenhall**, Eng,UK
91/B2 **Mildura**, Austl.
128/C4 **Miles**, Tx,US
123/G4 **Miles City**, Mt,US
57/K1 **Milešovka** (peak), Czh.
123/G3 **Milestone**, Sk,Can
60/D2 **Miletto** (peak), It.
47/F4 **Milford**, Eng,UK
44/B3 **Milford**, NI,UK
128/D2 **Milford** (lake), Ks,US
124/D3 **Milford**, Ut,US
46/A3 **Milford Haven**, Wal,UK
47/E5 **Milford on Sea**, Eng,UK
92/G4 **Mili** (atoll), Mrsh.
49/J3 **Milicz**, Pol.
120/V13 **Mililani Town**, Hi,US
122/F3 **Milk** (riv.), Can., US
47/E4 **Milk** (hill), Eng,UK
122/E3 **Milk River**, Ab,Can
105/G **Mill** (isl.), Ant.
119/J2 **Mill** (isl.), NW,Can
56/E4 **Millau**, Fr.
132/K11 **Millbrae**, Ca,US
46/B6 **Millbrook**, Eng,UK
129/H3 **Milledgeville**, Ga,US
127/N6 **Mille Iles** (riv.), Qu,Can
126/B1 **Mille Lacs** (lake), On,Can
123/K4 **Mille Lacs** (lake), Mn,US
123/J4 **Miller**, SD,US
67/G2 **Millerovo**, Rus.
44/C1 **Milleur** (pt.), Sc,UK
56/D4 **Millevaches** (plat.), Fr.
127/Q9 **Millgrove**, On,Can
127/R8 **Milliken**, On,Can
127/G2 **Millinocket**, Me,US
44/C2 **Millisle**, NI,UK
45/E3 **Millom**, Eng,UK
123/G5 **Mills**, Wy,US
131/F5 **Millstone** (riv.), NJ,US
45/F3 **Millthrop**, Eng,UK
132/J11 **Mill Valley**, Ca,US
128/E3 **Millwood** (lake), Ar,US
92/E5 **Milne** (bay), PNG
45/F4 **Milnrow**, Eng,UK
98/C4 **Milo** (riv.), Gui.
127/G2 **Milo**, Me,US
61/J4 **Mílos** (isl.), Gre.
132/L12 **Milpitas**, Ca,US
57/H1 **Milseburg** (peak), Ger.
127/Q8 **Milton**, On,Can
45/F2 **Milton**, Eng,UK
47/G4 **Milton**, Eng,UK
129/G4 **Milton**, Fl,US
127/G3 **Milton**, NH,US
122/D4 **Milton-Freewater**, Or,US
127/Q8 **Milton Heights**, On,Can
47/F2 **Milton Keynes**, Eng,UK
43/H7 **Miltown Malbay**, Ire.
82/B2 **Miluo**, China
46/C4 **Milverton**, Eng,UK
132/Q13 **Milwaukee**, Wi,US
78/B4 **Mimi** (riv.), Japan
56/C4 **Mimizan**, Fr.
82/C2 **Min** (riv.), China
85/H2 **Min** (riv.), China
124/C3 **Mina**, Nv,US
87/F3 **Minahasa** (pen.), Indo.
79/M10 **Minakuchi**, Japan
78/B4 **Minamata**, Japan
79/F3 **Minami-Alps Nat'l Park**, Japan
79/M10 **Minamichita**, Japan
92/D2 **Minamiiō** (isl.), Japan
92/E2 **Minami-Tori-Shima** (isl.), Japan
113/G2 **Minas**, Uru.
116/E3 **Minas de Matahambre**, Cuba
58/B4 **Minas de Ríotinto**, Sp.
110/H6 **Minas Gerais** (state), Braz.
85/F3 **Minbu**, Burma
112/C1 **Mincha**, Chile
46/D3 **Minchinhampton**, Eng,UK
112/B4 **Minchinmávida** (vol.), Chile
82/D6 **Mindanao** (isl.), Phil.
82/D6 **Mindanao** (sea), Phil.
55/G1 **Mindel** (riv.), Ger.
51/F4 **Minden**, Ger.
128/E3 **Minden**, La,US
125/H2 **Minden**, Ne,US
82/D5 **Mindoro** (isl.), Phil.
82/D5 **Mindoro** (str.), Phil.
46/C4 **Minehead**, Eng,UK
109/H7 **Mineiros**, Braz.
131/G5 **Mineola**, NY,US
67/G3 **Mineral'nye Vody**, Rus.
128/D3 **Mineral Wells**, Tx,US
57/H5 **Minerbio** (pt.), Fr.
81/C3 **Ming** (riv.), China
127/J1 **Mingan** (riv.), Qu,Can
73/K2 **Mingāora**, Pak.
67/H4 **Mingechaur**, Azer.
67/H4 **Mingechaur** (res.), Azer.
83/A1 **Mingun** (ruins), Burma
58/B1 **Minho** (riv.), Sp.
123/L3 **Miniss** (lake), On,Can
123/H2 **Minitonas**, Mb,Can
123/K4 **Minneapolis**, Mn,US
123/J3 **Minnedosa**, Mb,Can
123/K4 **Minnesota** (state), US
123/K4 **Minnesota** (riv.), Mn,US
44/D2 **Minnigaff**, Sc,UK
126/B1 **Minnis** (lake), On,Can
126/A1 **Minnitaki** (lake), On,Can
79/E3 **Mino**, Japan
79/F3 **Minobu**, Japan
79/N9 **Mino-Mikawa** (mts.), Japan
79/L10 **Mino'o**, Japan
79/L10 **Mino'o** (riv.), Japan
59/G3 **Minorca** (Menorca) (isl.), Sp.
123/H3 **Minot**, ND,US
82/C2 **Minqing**, China
51/F1 **Minsener Oog** (isl.), Ger.
66/C1 **Minsk** (cap.), Bela.
49/L2 **Mińsk Mazowiecki**, Pol.
66/C1 **Minsk Obl.**, Bela.
47/G4 **Minster**, Eng,UK
75/B4 **Mintaka** (pass), China
127/H2 **Minto**, NB,Can
118/E1 **Minto** (inlet), NW,Can
130/L3 **Minto**, Yk,Can
60/C2 **Minturno**, It.
100/B2 **Minūf**, Egypt
68/K4 **Minusinsk**, Rus.
127/K2 **Miquelon**, StP.
108/C3 **Mira** (riv.), Col., Ecu.
58/A2 **Mira**, Port.
58/A4 **Mira** (riv.), Port.
127/M6 **Mirabel**, Qu,Can
110/D2 **Miracema**, Braz.
109/J5 **Miracema do Norte**, Braz.
112/C4 **Mirador** (pass), Chile
84/B4 **Miraj**, India
131/C2 **Mira-Loma**, Ca,US
61/J5 **Mirambéllou** (gulf), Gre.
131/A2 **Mira Monte**, Ca,US
109/G8 **Miranda** (riv.), Braz.
58/D1 **Miranda de Ebro**, Sp.
57/J4 **Mirandola**, It.
110/B2 **Mirandópolis**, Braz.
110/B2 **Mirante do Paranapanema**, Braz.
110/B2 **Mirassol**, Braz.
116/D5 **Miravalles** (vol.), CR
58/B1 **Miravalles** (mtn.), Sp.
54/C1 **Mirecourt**, Fr.
45/G4 **Mirfield**, Eng,UK
66/E2 **Mirgorod**, Ukr.
113/G2 **Mirim** (lake), Braz., Uru.
73/H3 **Mirjāveh**, Iran
105/G **Mirnyy**, Ant.
69/M3 **Mirnyy**, Rus.
123/H2 **Mirond** (lake), Sk,Can
61/H4 **Mirtóön** (sea), Gre.
80/E5 **Miryang**, SKor.
84/D2 **Mirzāpur**, India
97/M7 **Misa**, Zaire
100/A4 **Misāha, Bi'r** (well), Egypt
78/D3 **Misaki**, Japan
126/C3 **Mishawaka**, In,US
130/F2 **Misheguk** (mtn.), Ak,US
79/F3 **Mishima**, Japan
60/C3 **Misilmeri**, It.
117/L7 **Misión del Rosario**, Mex.
111/F2 **Misiones** (mts.), Arg.
117/L8 **Misión San Fernando**, Mex.
62/E1 **Miskolc**, Hun.
79/M10 **Misono**, Japan
87/H4 **Misool** (isl.), Indo.
123/L4 **Misquah** (hills), Mn,US
96/J1 **Mişrātah**, Libya
97/L1 **Mişrātah** (pt.), Libya
126/D1 **Missinaibi** (lake), On,Can
126/D1 **Missinaibi** (riv.), On,Can
128/D5 **Mission**, Tx,US
124/C4 **Mission Viejo**, Ca,US
123/M2 **Missisa** (lake), On,Can
126/E1 **Missisicabi** (riv.), Qu,Can
127/Q8 **Mississauga**, On,Can
121/J6 **Mississippi** (delta), US
121/H5 **Mississippi** (riv.), US
129/F3 **Mississippi** (state), US
92/C5 **Missol** (isl.), Indo.
122/E4 **Missoula**, Mt,US
121/G3 **Missouri** (riv.), US
125/J3 **Missouri** (state), US
128/E4 **Missouri City**, Tx,US
123/H3 **Missouri, Coteau du** (upland), Can., US
90/B3 **Mistake** (cr.), Austl.
127/L2 **Mistaken** (pt.), Can.
127/F1 **Mistassibi** (riv.), Qu,Can
126/F1 **Mistassini**, Qu,Can
126/F1 **Mistassini** (lake), Qu,Can
127/F1 **Mistassini** (riv.), Qu,Can
49/J4 **Mistelbach an der Zaya**, Aus.
47/H3 **Mistley**, Eng,UK
61/H4 **Mistrás** (ruins), Gre.
60/D4 **Mistretta**, It.
130/M4 **Misty Fjords Nat'l Mon.**, Ak,US
79/M10 **Misugi**, Japan
117/N9 **Mita** (pt.), Mex.
79/H7 **Mitaka**, Japan
46/D3 **Mitcheldean**, Eng,UK
90/A1 **Mitchell** (riv.), Austl.
129/H3 **Mitchell** (mtn.), NC,US
125/G2 **Mitchell**, Ne,US
123/J5 **Mitchell**, SD,US
90/A1 **Mitchell & Alice Rivers Nat'l Park**, Austl.
74/H6 **Mīt Ghamr**, Egypt
84/B2 **Mithankot**, Pak.
73/J4 **Mithi**, Pak.
93/K6 **Mitiaro** (isl.), CookIs.
61/K3 **Mitilíni**, Gre.
100/C2 **Mitla** (pass), Egypt
116/B4 **Mitla** (ruins), Mex.
79/G2 **Mito**, Japan
96/G7 **Mitra** (peak), EqG.
113/L8 **Mitre** (pen.), Arg.
52/B6 **Mitry-Mory**, Fr.
103/H7 **Mitsinjo**, Madg.
103/J6 **Mitsio, Nosy** (isl.), Madg.
97/N4 **Mits'iwa**, Erit.
79/F2 **Mitsukaidō**, Japan
79/F2 **Mitsuke**, Japan
51/F4 **Mittelland** (can.), Ger.
51/E3 **Mittelradde** (riv.), Ger.
48/G3 **Mittweida**, Ger.
101/A4 **Mitumba** (mts.), Zaire
104/E2 **Mitwaba**, Zaire
79/H7 **Miura**, Japan
79/H7 **Miura** (pen.), Japan
116/C5 **Mixco Viejo** (ruins), Guat.
79/M10 **Miya** (riv.), Japan
79/G1 **Miyagi** (pref.), Japan
77/N4 **Miyako**, Japan
82/E3 **Miyako** (isl.), Japan
78/B5 **Miyakonojō**, Japan
78/B5 **Miyanojō**, Japan
79/H6 **Miyashiro**, Japan
78/B4 **Miyazaki** (pref.), Japan
78/D3 **Miyazu**, Japan
81/D2 **Miyun**, China
81/D2 **Miyun** (res.), China
44/B6 **Mizen Head** (pt.), Ire.
63/H3 **Mizil**, Rom.
85/F3 **Mizoram** (state), India
79/E3 **Mizunami**, Japan
42/F4 **Mjölby**, Swe.
42/D3 **Mjøsa** (lake), Nor.
96/D1 **Mkorn** (peak), Mor.
103/F2 **Mkuze** (riv.), SAfr.
57/L1 **Mladá Boleslav**, Czh.
62/E3 **Mladenovac**, Yugo.
101/B4 **Mlala** (hills), Tanz.
49/L2 **Mława**, Pol.
62/C4 **Mljet** (isl.), Cro.
62/C4 **Mljet Nat'l Park**, Cro.
42/E2 **Mo**, Nor.
87/G5 **Moa** (isl.), Indo.
98/C5 **Moa** (riv.), Libr., SLeo.
124/E3 **Moab**, Ut,US
92/H6 **Moala Group** (isls.), Fiji
58/A1 **Moaña**, Sp.
104/B1 **Moanda**, Gabon
72/F2 **Mobārakeh**, Iran
125/J3 **Moberly**, Mo,US
122/C2 **Moberly Lake**, BC,Can
129/F4 **Mobile**, Al,US
123/H4 **Mobridge**, SD,US
109/J4 **Mocajuba**, Braz.
104/B4 **Moçâmedes**, Ang.
83/D4 **Moc Hoa**, Viet.
102/D2 **Mochudi**, Bots.
108/C3 **Mocoa**, Col.
110/G6 **Mococa**, Braz.
84/B3 **Modāsa**, India
46/C6 **Modbury**, Eng,UK
102/D3 **Modderrivier** (riv.), SAfr.
57/J4 **Modena**, It.
57/G2 **Moder** (riv.), Fr., Ger.
124/B3 **Modesto**, Ca,US
60/D4 **Modica**, It.
96/H4 **Modjigo** (reg.), Niger
49/J4 **Mödling**, Aus.
62/D3 **Modriča**, Bosn.
83/E3 **Mo Duc**, Viet.
60/E2 **Modugno**, It.
91/C3 **Moe**, Austl.
102/A2 **Moeb** (bay), Namb.
56/B3 **Moëlan-sur-Mer**, Fr.
45/E5 **Moel Fammau** (mtn.), Wal,UK
45/E6 **Moel Fferna** (mtn.), Wal,UK
46/C1 **Moelfre** (mtn.), UK
46/C2 **Moel Hywel** (mtn.), Wal,UK
45/E6 **Moel Sych** (mtn.), Wal,UK
46/C2 **Moel y Llyn** (mtn.), UK
92/E4 **Moen**, Micr.
124/E3 **Moenkopi** (dry riv.), Az,US
93/K7 **Moerai**, FrPol.
50/D6 **Moers**, Ger.
52/C1 **Moervaart** (can.), Belg.
44/E1 **Moffat**, Sc,UK
73/L2 **Moga**, India
97/Q7 **Mogadishu** (cap.), Som.
79/G2 **Mogami** (riv.), Japan
59/L6 **Mogent** (riv.), Sp.
110/G8 **Mogi das Cruzes**, Braz.
110/G7 **Mogi-Guaçu**, Braz.
66/D1 **Mogilëv**, Bela.
66/D1 **Mogilëv Obl.**, Bela.
66/C2 **Mogilev-Podol'skiy**, Ukr.
49/J2 **Mogilno**, Pol.
110/F7 **Mogi-Mirim**, Braz.
77/H1 **Mogocha**, Rus.
85/G3 **Mogok**, Burma
113/F3 **Mogotes** (pt.), Arg.
58/B4 **Moguer**, Sp.
62/D3 **Mohács**, Hun.
123/H3 **Mohall**, ND,US
126/F3 **Mohawk** (riv.), NY,US
103/G6 **Mohéli** (isl.), Com.
104/D4 **Mohembo**, Bots.
130/E3 **Mohican** (cape), Ak,US
51/F6 **Möhne** (riv.), Ger.
51/F6 **Möhnestausee** (res.), Ger.
63/H2 **Moineşti**, Rom.
75/A3 **Moinkum** (des.), Kaz.
99/E5 **Moinsi** (hills), Gha.
126/E2 **Moira** (riv.), On,Can
56/F4 **Moirans**, Fr.
119/K3 **Moisie** (riv.), Qu,Can
56/D4 **Moissac**, Fr.
59/Q10 **Moita**, Port.
124/C4 **Mojave** (des.), Ca,US
110/G7 **Moji-Guaçu** (riv.), Braz.
123/L3 **Mojikit** (lake), On,Can
108/E6 **Mojos** (plain), Bol.
109/J4 **Moju** (riv.), Braz.
79/F2 **Mōka**, Japan
120/W13 **Mokapu** (pt.), Hi,US
124/B3 **Mokelumne** (riv.), Ca,US
132/Q16 **Mokena**, Il,US
92/F4 **Mokil** (atoll), Micr.
83/B3 **Mokochu** (peak), Thai.
85/F2 **Mokokchūng**, India
96/H5 **Mokolo**, Camr.
80/D5 **Mokp'o**, SKor.
62/E3 **Mokrin**, Yugo.
67/G1 **Moksha** (riv.), Rus.
53/E1 **Mol**, Belg.
62/E3 **Mol**, Yugo.
60/E2 **Mola di Bari**, It.
62/B3 **Molat** (isl.), Cro.
58/E3 **Molatón** (mtn.), Sp.
45/E5 **Mold**, Wal,UK
63/H2 **Moldavia** (reg.), Rom.
63/G2 **Moldavian Carpathians** (range), Rom.
42/C3 **Molde**, Nor.
66/C3 **Moldova**
63/H2 **Moldova** (riv.), Rom.
62/E3 **Moldova Nouă**, Rom.
63/G3 **Moldoveanu** (peak), Rom.
47/F4 **Mole** (riv.), Eng,UK
102/D2 **Molepolole**, Bots.
60/E2 **Molfetta**, It.
81/F2 **Molihong Shan** (peak), China
112/C2 **Molina**, Chile
58/E3 **Molina de Segura**, Sp.
126/B3 **Moline**, Il,US
60/D2 **Molise** (reg.), It.
57/K3 **Möll** (riv.), Aus.
42/D5 **Møllebjerg** (peak), Den.
108/D7 **Mollendo**, Peru
59/F2 **Mollerussa**, Sp.
112/C2 **Molles** (pt.), Chile
59/L6 **Mollet del Vallès**, Sp.
59/L7 **Mollins de Rei**, Sp.
48/F2 **Mölln**, Ger.
64/E5 **Molodechno**, Bela.
105/D **Molodezhnaya**, Ant.
64/H4 **Mologa** (riv.), Rus.
120/T10 **Molokai** (isl.), Hi,US
65/L4 **Moloma** (riv.), Rus.
102/C2 **Molopo** (Moloporivier) (dry riv.), Bots., SAfr.
96/J7 **Moloundou**, Camr.
123/J2 **Molson** (lake), Mb,Can
87/H5 **Molu** (isl.), Indo.
87/G4 **Molucca** (sea), Indo.
87/G3 **Moluccas** (isls.), Indo.
109/K5 **Mombaça**, Braz.
101/C4 **Mombasa**, Kenya
77/N3 **Mombetsu**, Japan
63/G5 **Momchilgrad**, Bul.
87/H4 **Momfafa** (cape), Indo.
117/G6 **Mompós**, Col.
85/F3 **Mon** (riv.), Burma
83/B3 **Mon** (state), Burma
48/G1 **Møn** (isl.), Den.
117/H4 **Mona** (passage), DRep., PR
57/G5 **Monaco**
57/G5 **Monaco** (cap.), Mona.
44/B3 **Monaghan**, Ire.
44/A3 **Monaghan** (co.), Ire.
117/E6 **Monagrillo** (ruins), Pan.
128/C4 **Monahans**, Tx,US
122/D3 **Monashee** (mts.), BC,Can
90/H8 **Mona Vale**, Austl.
59/E3 **Moncada**, Sp.
57/G4 **Moncalieri**, It.
82/E6 **Moncayo**, Phil.
58/D2 **Moncayo** (range), Sp.
64/G2 **Monchegorsk**, Rus.
50/D6 **Mönchengladbach**, Ger.
58/A4 **Monchique**, Port.
58/A4 **Monchique** (range), Port.
129/H3 **Moncks Corner**, SC,US
116/A2 **Monclova**, Mex.
127/H2 **Moncton**, NB,Can
58/A2 **Mondego** (cape), Port.
58/A2 **Mondego** (riv.), Port.
58/B1 **Mondoñedo**, Sp.
53/F5 **Mondorf-les-Bains**, Lux.
57/G4 **Mondovì**, It.
58/D1 **Mondragón**, Sp.
60/C2 **Mondragone**, It.
58/B3 **Monesterio**, Sp.
125/J3 **Monett**, Mo,US
44/C2 **Money Head** (pt.), Sc,UK
44/B2 **Moneymore**, NI,UK
44/C2 **Moneyreagh**, NI,UK
57/K4 **Monfalcone**, It.
57/H4 **Monferrato** (reg.), It.
58/B1 **Monforte**, Sp.
110/G9 **Mongaguá**, Braz.
83/D1 **Mong Cai**, Viet.
84/E2 **Monghyr**, India
97/J5 **Mongo**, Chad
98/C4 **Mongo** (riv.), Gui., SLeo.
76/D2 **Mongolia**
97/K5 **Mongororo**, Chad
104/B1 **Mongoungou**, Gabon
104/D4 **Mongu**, Zam.
75/F2 **Mönh Hayrhan Uul** (peak), Mong.
76/E1 **Mönh Sarīdag** (peak), Mong.
44/E1 **Moniaive**, Sc,UK
59/K6 **Monistrol de Montserrat**, Sp.
124/C3 **Monitor** (range), Nv,US
49/M2 **Mońki**, Pol.
104/D1 **Monkoto**, Zaire
46/D3 **Monmouth**, Eng,UK
126/B3 **Monmouth**, Il,US
122/C4 **Monmouth**, Or,US
131/G5 **Monmouth Beach**, NJ,US
46/D2 **Monmow** (riv.), UK
50/C4 **Monnickendam**, Neth.
99/F5 **Mono** (prov.), Ben.
99/F5 **Mono** (riv.), Ben., Togo
124/C3 **Mono** (lake), Ca,US
60/E2 **Monopoli**, It.
62/D2 **Monor**, Hun.
127/Q8 **Mono Road**, On,Can
59/E3 **Monóvar**, Sp.
60/C3 **Monreale**, It.
129/H3 **Monroe**, Ga,US
128/E3 **Monroe**, La,US
126/D3 **Monroe**, Mi,US
129/H3 **Monroe**, NC,US
124/D3 **Monroe**, Ut,US
126/B3 **Monroe**, Wi,US
129/G4 **Monroeville**, Al,US
98/C5 **Monrovia** (cap.), Libr.
131/C2 **Monrovia**, Ca,US
52/C3 **Mons**, Belg.
53/F2 **Monschau**, Ger.
57/J4 **Monselice**, It.
131/F4 **Monsey**, NY,US
50/B4 **Monster**, Neth.
42/F4 **Mönsteras**, Swe.
103/J6 **Montagne d'Ambre Nat'l Park**, Madg.
127/J2 **Montague**, PE,Can
130/L3 **Montague**, Yk,Can
130/J4 **Montague** (isl.), Ak,US
130/J4 **Montague** (str.), Ak,US
128/D3 **Montague**, Tx,US
60/E2 **Montalbano Jonico**, It.
122/F4 **Montana** (state), US
110/D1 **Montanha**, Braz.
56/E3 **Montargis**, Fr.
52/B5 **Montataire**, Fr.
56/D4 **Montauban**, Fr.
104/E6 **Mont aux Sources** (peak), Les.
56/F3 **Montbard**, Fr.
54/C2 **Montbéliard**, Fr.
59/L7 **Montcada i Reixac**, Sp.
56/F3 **Montceau-les-Mines**, Fr.
131/C2 **Montclair**, Ca,US
56/C5 **Mont-de-Marsan**, Fr.
52/B4 **Montdidier**, Fr.
116/B4 **Monte Albán** (ruins), Mex.
109/H4 **Monte Alegre**, Braz.
110/B1 **Monte Alegre de Minas**, Braz.
110/B2 **Monte Alto**, Braz.
109/K7 **Monte Azul**, Braz.
131/B2 **Montebello**, Ca,US
111/F2 **Montecarlo**, Arg.
110/C1 **Monte Carmelo**, Braz.
117/G6 **Monte Carmelo**, Ven.
111/E3 **Monte Caseros**, Arg.
117/G4 **Monte Cristo**, DRep.
60/B1 **Montecristo** (isl.), It.
58/C4 **Montefrío**, Sp.
117/F4 **Montego Bay**, Jam.
59/P10 **Montelavar**, Port.
56/F4 **Montélimar**, Fr.
58/C4 **Montellano**, Sp.
124/D2 **Montello**, Nv,US
112/D5 **Montemayor** (plat.), Arg.
116/B2 **Montemorelos**, Mex.
58/A3 **Montemor-o-Novo**, Port.
58/A2 **Montemuro** (mtn.), Port.
110/B4 **Montenegro**, Braz.
62/D4 **Montenegro** (rep.), Yugo.
60/D2 **Montenero di Bisaccia**, It.
48/B5 **Montenoison, Butte de** (mtn.), Fr.
109/L7 **Monte Pascoal Nat'l Park**, Braz.
56/E2 **Montereau-faut-Yonne**, Fr.
124/B3 **Monterey**, Ca,US
124/B3 **Monterey** (bay), Ca,US
131/B2 **Monterey Park**, Ca,US
117/F6 **Montería**, Col.
108/F7 **Montero**, Bol.
111/C2 **Monteros**, Arg.
60/C1 **Monterotondo**, It.
116/A2 **Monterrey**, Mex.
113/K7 **Montes** (pt.), Arg.
60/D2 **Monte Sant'Angelo**, It.
60/E2 **Montescaglioso**, It.
109/K7 **Montes Claros**, Braz.
60/D1 **Montesilvano Marina**, It.
56/F4 **Monteux**, Fr.
113/F2 **Montevideo** (cap.), Uru.
113/T12 **Montevideo** (dept.), Uru.
123/K4 **Montevideo**, Mn,US
53/E5 **Montfaucon**, Fr.
50/B4 **Montfoort**, Neth.
52/B6 **Montgeron**, Fr.
46/C1 **Montgomery**, Wal,UK
129/G3 **Montgomery** (cap.), Al,US
126/D4 **Montgomery**, WV,US
131/J7 **Montgomery Village**, Md,US
131/E5 **Montgomeryville**, Pa,US
56/E5 **Montgrand** (mtn.), Fr.
54/C5 **Monthey**, Swi.
128/F3 **Monticello**, Ar,US
132/K9 **Monticello** (dam), Ca,US
129/H4 **Monticello**, Fl,US
126/C3 **Monticello**, In,US
126/C4 **Monticello**, Ky,US
125/K2 **Monticello**, Mo,US
124/E3 **Monticello**, Ut,US
126/E4 **Monticello**, Va,US
52/B3 **Montigny-en-Gohelle**, Fr.
52/B6 **Montigny-le-Bretonneux**, Fr.
53/F5 **Montigny-lès-Metz**, Fr.
52/D3 **Montigny-le-Tilleul**, Belg.
58/A3 **Montijo**, Port.
58/B3 **Montijo**, Sp.
58/C4 **Montilla**, Sp.
56/D2 **Montivilliers**, Fr.
127/G1 **Mont-Joli**, Qu,Can
126/F2 **Mont-Laurier**, Qu,Can
56/E3 **Montluçon**, Fr.
127/G2 **Montmagny**, Qu,Can
56/D3 **Montmorillon**, Fr.
58/C3 **Montoro**, Sp.
98/D5 **Mont Peko Nat'l Park**, IvC.
122/F5 **Montpelier**, Id,US
127/F2 **Montpelier** (cap.), Vt,US
56/E5 **Montpellier**, Fr.
126/C2 **Montreal** (riv.), On,Can
127/N7 **Montréal**, Qu,Can
123/G2 **Montreal** (lake), Sk,Can
52/A3 **Montreuil**, Fr.
54/C5 **Montreux**, Swi.
43/D2 **Montrose**, Sc,UK
124/F3 **Montrose**, Co,US
127/N6 **Mont-Royal**, Qu,Can
52/B6 **Montry**, Fr.
127/P6 **Mont-Saint-Hilaire**, Qu,Can
53/E4 **Mont-Saint-Martin**, Fr.
126/F2 **Mont-Saint-Michel**, Qu,Can
56/C2 **Mont-Saint-Michel**, Fr.
56/C2 **Mont-Saint-Michel** (bay), Fr.
98/D4 **Mont Sangbé Nat'l Park**, IvC.
59/L6 **Montseny Nat'l Park**, Sp.
98/C5 **Montserrado** (co.), Libr.
59/F2 **Montserrat** (mtn.), Sp.
117/J4 **Montserrat** (isl.), UK
131/F5 **Montville**, NJ,US
125/G4 **Monument Draw** (cr.), NM, Tx,US
85/G3 **Monywa**, Burma
57/H4 **Monza**, It.
104/E4 **Monze**, Zam.
59/F2 **Monzón**, Sp.
102/P13 **Mooi** (riv.), SAfr.
90/D4 **Mooloolaba-Maroochydore**, Austl.
91/G5 **Moorabbin**, Austl.
123/G4 **Moorcroft**, Wy,US
127/R8 **Moore** (pt.), On,Can
125/H4 **Moore**, Ok,US
93/K6 **Moorea** (isl.), FrPol.
129/H5 **Moore Haven**, Fl,US
131/F6 **Moorestown**, NJ,US
129/H3 **Mooresville**, NC,US
123/J4 **Moorhead**, Mn,US
52/C2 **Moorslede**, Belg.
57/J2 **Moosburg**, Ger.
126/D1 **Moose** (riv.), On,Can
123/H3 **Moose** (mtn.), Sk,Can
126/D1 **Moose Factory**, On,Can
127/G2 **Moosehead** (lake), Me,US
130/H3 **Mooseheart** (mtn.), Ak,US
123/G3 **Moose Jaw**, Sk,Can
123/H3 **Moosomin**, Sk,Can
126/D1 **Moosonee**, On,Can
98/D3 **Mopti**, Mali
98/E3 **Mopti** (reg.), Mali
108/D7 **Moquegua**, Peru
62/D2 **Mór**, Hun.
96/H5 **Mora**, Camr.
58/D3 **Mora**, Sp.
42/E3 **Mora**, Swe.
125/F4 **Mora**, NM,US
125/F4 **Mora** (riv.), NM,US
61/F1 **Morača** (riv.), Yugo.
84/C2 **Morādābād**, India
109/L5 **Morada Nova**, Braz.
110/C1 **Morada Nova de Mina**, Braz.
112/C2 **Morado Nat'l Park**, Chile
103/H7 **Morafenobe**, Madg.
49/K2 **Morąg**, Pol.
132/K11 **Moraga**, Ca,US
112/B5 **Moraleda** (chan.), Chile
58/B2 **Moraleja**, Sp.
116/D4 **Morales**, Guat.
124/E2 **Moran**, Wy,US
90/C3 **Moranbah**, Austl.
93/M7 **Morane** (isl.), FrPol.
58/E3 **Moratalla**, Sp.
49/J4 **Morava** (riv.), Czh.
61/G1 **Morava** (riv.), Yugo.
49/J4 **Moravia** (reg.), Czh.
49/J4 **Moravská Třebová**, Czh.
49/H4 **Moravské Budějovice**, Czh.
53/G4 **Morbach**, Ger.
52/B2 **Morbecque**, Fr.
55/F5 **Morbegno**, It.
42/F4 **Mörbylanga**, Swe.
123/J3 **Morden**, Mb,Can
91/G6 **Mordialloc**, Austl.
67/G1 **Mordvian Aut. Rep.**, Rus.
123/H4 **Moreau** (riv.), SD,US
43/D3 **Morebattle**, Sc,UK
45/F3 **Morecambe**, Eng,UK
45/E3 **Morecambe** (bay), Eng,UK
91/D1 **Moree**, Austl.
126/D4 **Morehead**, Ky,US
129/J3 **Morehead City**, NC,US
116/A4 **Morelia**, Mex.
116/B4 **Morelos** (state), Mex.
84/C2 **Morena**, India
58/C3 **Morena** (range), Sp.
63/G3 **Moreni**, Rom.
131/C3 **Moreno Valley**, Ca,US
42/C3 **Møre og Romsdal** (co.), Nor.
131/B2 **Morepack**, Ca,US
118/C3 **Moresby** (isl.), BC,Can
90/F6 **Moreton** (bay), Austl.
90/D4 **Moreton** (cape), Austl.
46/C5 **Moretonhampstead**, Eng,UK
90/D4 **Moreton I. Nat'l Park**, Austl.
47/E3 **Moreton in Marsh**, Eng,UK
65/N2 **Moreyu** (riv.), Rus.
54/C4 **Morez**, Fr.
129/F4 **Morgan City**, La,US
126/C4 **Morganfield**, Ky,US
60/D4 **Morgantina** (ruins), It.
129/H3 **Morganton**, NC,US
126/C4 **Morgantown**, Ky,US
126/E4 **Morgantown**, WV,US
56/E3 **Morge** (riv.), Fr.
54/C4 **Morges**, Swi.
73/H1 **Morghāb** (riv.), Afg.
112/B3 **Morguilla** (pt.), Chile
76/C3 **Mori**, China
57/J4 **Mori**, It.
125/F4 **Moriarty**, NM,US
122/B2 **Morice** (lake), BC,Can
79/L10 **Moriguchi**, Japan
55/G5 **Moringen**, Ger.
122/E2 **Morinville**, Ab,Can
77/N4 **Morioka**, Japan
79/H7 **Moriya**, Japan
78/D3 **Moriyama**, Japan
56/B2 **Morlaix**, Fr.
52/D3 **Morlanwelz**, Belg.
45/G4 **Morley**, Eng,UK
84/B4 **Mormugao**, India
90/F6 **Morningside**, Austl.
113/J7 **Mornington** (isl.), Chile
73/J3 **Moro**, Pak.
82/D6 **Moro** (gulf), Phil.
96/C1 **Morocco**
101/C4 **Morogoro**, Tanz.
101/C4 **Morogoro** (prov.), Tanz.
91/C3 **Moroka-Wonnangatta Nat'l Park**, Austl.
103/G8 **Morombe**, Madg.
112/F2 **Morón**, Arg.
117/F3 **Morón**, Cuba
108/C4 **Morona** (riv.), Ecu., Peru
103/H8 **Morondara** (riv.), Madg.
103/H8 **Morondava**, Madg.
58/C4 **Morón de la Frontera**, Sp.
103/G5 **Moroni** (cap.), Com.
87/G3 **Morotai** (isl.), Indo.
87/G3 **Morotai** (str.), Indo.
101/B2 **Moroto**, Ugan.
79/H7 **Moroyama**, Japan
67/G2 **Morozovsk**, Rus.
45/G1 **Morpeth**, Eng,UK
74/J4 **Morphou**, Cyp.
74/J4 **Morphou** (bay), Cyp.
50/C3 **Morra** (lake), Neth.
125/G2 **Morrill**, Ne,US
110/B1 **Morrinhos**, Braz.
123/J3 **Morris**, Mb,Can
126/B3 **Morris**, Il,US
123/K4 **Morris**, Mn,US
115/P1 **Morris Jesup** (cape), Grld.

165

Morri – Néa Al

131/F5 **Morris Plains**, NJ,US
46/C3 **Morriston**, Wal,UK
131/F5 **Morristown**, NJ,US
129/H2 **Morristown**, Tn,US
131/F5 **Morrisville**, Pa,US
124/B4 **Morro Bay**, Ca,US
104/C3 **Morro de Môco** (peak), Ang.
110/B3 **Morro do Capão Doce** (hill), Braz.
109/K6 **Morro do Chapéu**, Braz.
53/G2 **Morsbach**, Ger.
67/G1 **Morshansk**, Rus.
67/J3 **Morskoy** (isl.), Kaz.
46/B4 **Morte** (pt.), UK
109/H6 **Mortes** (riv.), Braz.
47/E4 **Mortimer**, Eng,UK
46/D2 **Mortimers Cross**, Eng,UK
126/B3 **Morton**, Il,US
132/Q15 **Morton Grove**, Il,US
91/D2 **Morton Nat'l Park**, Austl.
52/D1 **Mortsel**, Belg.
56/E3 **Morvan** (plat.), Fr.
84/B3 **Morvi**, India
91/C3 **Morwell**, Austl.
58/A1 **Mos**, Sp.
57/H2 **Mosbach**, Ger.
59/P10 **Moscavide**, Port.
64/G5 **Moscow** (upland), Rus.
122/D4 **Moscow**, Id,US
65/X9 **Moscow** (Moskva) (cap.), Rus.
64/H5 **Moscow Obl.**, Rus.
105/H **Moscow Univ. Ice Shelf**, Ant.
53/F4 **Mosel** (riv.), Ger.
52/F5 **Moselle** (dept.), Fr.
53/F5 **Moselle** (riv.), Fr.
122/D4 **Moses Lake**, Wa,US
102/C2 **Moshaweng** (dry riv.), SAfr.
101/C3 **Moshi**, Tanz.
49/J2 **Mosina**, Pol.
42/E2 **Mosjøen**, Nor.
64/G5 **Moskva** (riv.), Rus.
65/X9 **Moskva** (Moscow) (inset) (cap.), Rus.
62/C2 **Mosonmagyaróvár**, Hun.
125/G4 **Mosquero**, NM,US
116/E6 **Mosquitos** (gulf), Pan.
116/E5 **Mosquitos, Costa de** (coast), Nic.
42/D4 **Moss**, Nor.
98/E4 **Mossi Highlands** (upland), Burk.
57/H2 **Mössingen**, Ger.
45/F4 **Mossley**, Eng,UK
44/C2 **Mossley**, NI,UK
109/L5 **Mossoró**, Braz.
129/F4 **Moss Point**, Ms,US
44/B1 **Moss-side**, NI,UK
57/K1 **Most**, Czh.
96/E1 **Mostaganem**, Alg.
62/C4 **Mostar**, Bosn.
58/D2 **Móstoles**, Sp.
45/E5 **Mostyn**, Wal,UK
74/E3 **Mosul** (Al Mawşil), Iraq
116/D4 **Motagua** (riv.), Guat.
42/E4 **Motala**, Swe.
81/E2 **Motian Ling** (mtn.), China
84/D2 **Motīhāri**, India
79/G2 **Motomiya**, Japan
42/K1 **Motovskiy** (gulf), Rus.
58/D4 **Motril**, Sp.
123/H4 **Mott**, ND,US
116/D3 **Motul**, Mex.
68/K4 **Motygino**, Rus.
98/B2 **Mougris** (well), Mrta.
98/E3 **Mouhoun** (prov.), Burk.
104/B1 **Mouila**, Gabon
96/H4 **Moul** (well), Niger
91/C2 **Moulamein** (riv.), Austl.
45/F5 **Mouldsworth**, Eng,UK
56/E3 **Moulins**, Fr.
83/B2 **Moulmein**, Burma
96/E1 **Moulouya** (riv.), Mor.
47/G2 **Moulton**, Eng,UK
129/H4 **Moultrie**, Ga,US
129/H3 **Moultrie** (lake), SC,US
125/J3 **Mound City**, Ks,US
96/J6 **Moundou**, Chad
126/D4 **Moundsville**, WV,US
83/C3 **Moung Roessei**, Camb.
83/D3 **Mounlapamok**, Laos
90/B3 **Mount Aberdeen Nat'l Park**, Austl.
84/B3 **Mount Abu**, India
118/D2 **Mountain** (riv.), NW,Can
46/C3 **Mountain Ash**, Wal,UK
129/G3 **Mountain Brook**, Al,US
125/J3 **Mountain Grove**, Mo,US
128/E2 **Mountain Home**, Ar,US
122/E5 **Mountain Home**, Id,US
128/E3 **Mountain View**, Ar,US
132/K12 **Mountain View**, Ca,US
102/D4 **Mountain Zebra Nat'l Park**, SAfr.
129/H2 **Mount Airy**, NC,US
89/A4 **Mount Barker**, Austl.
91/A2 **Mount Barker**, Austl.
90/C5 **Mount Barney Nat'l Park**, Austl.
91/C3 **Mount Buffalo Nat'l Park**, Austl.
126/C4 **Mount Carmel**, Il,US
97/M2 **Mount Catherine** (peak), Egypt
132/G6 **Mount Clemens**, Mi,US
90/E6 **Mount Coot'tha**, Austl.
104/F4 **Mount Darwin**, Zim.
91/B3 **Mount Eccles Nat'l Park**, Austl.
90/B2 **Mount Elliot Nat'l Park**, Austl.
91/B3 **Mount Emu** (cr.), Austl.
91/C4 **Mount Field Nat'l Park**, Austl.
91/B3 **Mount Gambier**, Austl.
92/D5 **Mount Hagen**, PNG
131/F6 **Mount Holly**, NJ,US
127/Q9 **Mount Hope**, On,Can
91/D3 **Mount Imlay Nat'l Park**, Austl.
89/C3 **Mount Isa**, Austl.
91/D1 **Mount Kaputar Nat'l Park**, Austl.
131/G4 **Mount Kisco**, NY,US
132/C2 **Mountlake Terrace**, Wa,US
131/F6 **Mount Laurel**, NJ,US
90/D4 **Mount Mistake Nat'l Park**, Austl.
126/D3 **Mount Morris**, Mi,US
90/E6 **Mount Nebo**, Austl.
129/J3 **Mount Olive**, NC,US
61/H3 **Mount Parnes Nat'l Park**, Gre.
127/L2 **Mount Pearl**, Nf,Can
123/L5 **Mount Pleasant**, Ia,US
126/C3 **Mount Pleasant**, Mi,US
128/E3 **Mount Pleasant**, Tx,US
124/E3 **Mount Pleasant**, Ut,US
132/Q15 **Mount Prospect**, Il,US
131/K8 **Mount Rainier**, Md,US
122/C4 **Mount Rainier Nat'l Park**, Wa,US
122/D3 **Mount Revelstoke Nat'l Park**, BC,Can
91/B3 **Mount Richmond Nat'l Park**, Austl.
125/G2 **Mount Rushmore Nat'l Mem.**, SD,US
46/A6 **Mount's** (bay), Eng,UK
90/B2 **Mount Spec Nat'l Park**, Austl.
126/D4 **Mount Sterling**, Ky,US
126/B4 **Mount Vernon**, Il,US
126/C4 **Mount Vernon**, In,US
131/G5 **Mount Vernon**, NY,US
126/D3 **Mount Vernon**, Oh,US
131/J8 **Mount Vernon**, Va,US
122/C3 **Mount Vernon**, Wa,US
90/C4 **Mount Walsh Nat'l Park**, Austl.
91/E1 **Mount Warning Nat'l Park**, Austl.
91/D4 **Mount William Nat'l Park**, Austl.
58/B3 **Moura**, Port.
56/C5 **Mourenx**, Fr.
44/B3 **Mourne** (dist.), NI,UK
44/B3 **Mourne** (mts.), NI,UK
52/C2 **Mouscron**, Belg.
96/J5 **Moussoro**, Chad
52/B5 **Moussy-le-Neuf**, Fr.
52/C2 **Mouvaux**, Fr.
44/B3 **Moy**, NI,UK
101/C2 **Moyalē**, Eth.
96/D1 **Moyen Atlas** (mts.), Mor.
53/F5 **Moyeuvre-Grande**, Fr.
44/B2 **Moygashel**, NI,UK
44/B1 **Moyle** (dist.), NI,UK
87/E5 **Moyo** (isl.), Indo.
75/C4 **Moyu**, China
104/G4 **Mozambique**
104/G5 **Mozambique** (chan.), Afr.
64/H5 **Mozhaysk**, Rus.
65/M4 **Mozhga**, Rus.
66/D1 **Mozyr'**, Bela.
101/A4 **Mpanda**, Tanz.
104/C4 **Mpangu**, Namb.
101/A5 **Mpika**, Zam.
101/A5 **Mporokoso**, Zam.
99/E5 **Mpraeso**, Gha.
49/L2 **Mrągowo**, Pol.
62/C3 **Mrkonjić Grad**, Bosn.
64/G4 **Msta** (riv.), Rus.
49/L4 **Mszana Dolna**, Pol.
66/F1 **Mtsensk**, Rus.
101/D5 **Mtwara**, Tanz.
101/C5 **Mtwara** (prov.), Tanz.
104/G4 **Mualama**, Moz.
83/D2 **Muang Gnommarat**, Laos
83/C2 **Muang Kenthao**, Laos
83/D3 **Muang Khong**, Laos
83/D3 **Muang Khongxedon**, Laos
83/D3 **Muang Lakhonpheng**, Laos
83/D1 **Muang Soy**, Laos
83/C2 **Muang Thathom**, Laos
83/D2 **Muang Xamteu**, Laos
83/D2 **Muang Xepon**, Laos
86/B3 **Muar**, Malay.
86/B4 **Muarabungo**, Indo.
73/J4 **Muāri** (pt.), Pak.
96/H5 **Mubi**, Nga.
108/F3 **Mucajaí** (riv.), Braz.
53/G2 **Much**, Ger.
101/A5 **Muchinga** (mts.), Zam.
46/D1 **Much Wenlock**, Eng,UK
44/B2 **Muckamore Abbey**, NI,UK
104/H3 **Mucojo**, Moz.
74/C2 **Mucur**, Turk.
110/D1 **Mucuri** (riv.), Braz.
104/D3 **Mucussueje**, Ang.
77/K3 **Mudanjiang**, China
63/J5 **Mudanya**, Turk.
77/K2 **Muddan** (riv.), China
42/F2 **Muddas Nat'l Park**, Swe.
124/E3 **Muddy** (riv.), Ut,US
125/H4 **Muddy Boggy** (cr.), Ok,US
53/G2 **Mudersbach**, Ger.
91/D2 **Mudgee**, Austl.
122/G1 **Mudjatik** (riv.), Sk,Can
132/D3 **Mud Mountain** (lake), Wa,US
83/B2 **Mudon**, Burma
113/J8 **Muela** (peak), Chile
74/N8 **Mufjir, Nahr** (dry riv.), WBnk.
104/E3 **Mufulira**, Zam.
58/A1 **Mugardos**, Sp.
57/K4 **Muggia**, It.
58/A1 **Mugia**, Sp.
74/B3 **Muğla**, Turk.
67/L2 **Mugodzharskoye** (mts.), Kaz.
101/A4 **Mugombazi**, Tanz.
100/D4 **Muḩammad Qawl**, Sudan
100/C3 **Muḩammad, Ra's** (pt.), Egypt
104/E2 **Muhila** (mts.), Zaire
57/K2 **Mühlviertel** (reg.), Aus.
42/H2 **Muhos**, Fin.
72/C2 **Mūḩ, Sabkhat al** (lake), Syria
64/D4 **Muhu** (isl.), Est.
50/C4 **Muiden**, Neth.
43/C3 **Muirkirk**, Sc,UK
43/C2 **Muir of Ord**, Sc,UK
132/J11 **Muir Woods Nat'l Mon.**, Ca,US
80/D5 **Muju**, SKor.
66/B2 **Mukachevo**, Ukr.
100/D4 **Mukawwar** (isl.), Sudan
123/M2 **Muketei** (riv.), On,Can
74/L5 **Mukhayyam al Yarmūk**, Syria
132/C2 **Mukilteo**, Wa,US
79/L10 **Mukō**, Japan
92/D2 **Mukoshima** (isls.), Japan
83/B4 **Mu Ko Similan Nat'l Park**, Thai.
83/B4 **Mu Ko Surin Nat'l Park**, Thai.
73/K2 **Muktsar**, India
58/E3 **Mula**, Sp.
104/G4 **Mulanje**, Malw.
130/G4 **Mulchatna** (riv.), Ak,US
113/B3 **Mulchén**, Chile
48/G3 **Mulde** (riv.), Ger.
105/D **Mule** (pt.), Ant.
58/D4 **Mulhacén, Cerro de** (mtn.), Sp.
48/F3 **Mülhausen**, Ger.
50/D6 **Mülheim an der Ruhr**, Ger.
54/D2 **Mulhouse**, Fr.
81/D3 **Muling** (pass), China
77/L2 **Muling** (riv.), China
93/R9 **Mulinu'u** (cape), WSam.
73/L2 **Mulkila** (mtn.), India
44/B5 **Mullaghcleevaun** (mtn.), Ire.
44/B2 **Mullaghmore** (mtn.), NI,UK
125/G2 **Mullen**, Ne,US
86/D4 **Muller** (mts.), Indo.
54/D2 **Müllheim**, Ger.
43/B4 **Mullingar**, Ire.
129/J3 **Mullins**, SC,US
46/A6 **Mullion**, Eng,UK
104/C4 **Mulondo**, Ang.
73/K2 **Multān**, Pak.
122/C3 **Multnomah** (falls), Or,US
86/D3 **Mulu, Gunung** (peak), Malay.
100/B5 **Mulwad**, Sudan
104/C3 **Mumbué**, Ang.
104/E3 **Mumbwa**, Zam.
83/B5 **Mum Nauk** (pt.), Thai.
83/C3 **Mun** (riv.), Thai.
87/F4 **Muna** (isl.), Indo.
42/H4 **Munamägi** (hill), Est.
126/C3 **Muncie**, In,US
132/P15 **Mundelein**, Il,US
99/H5 **Mundemba**, Camr.
48/E3 **Munden**, Ger.
51/G6 **Münden**, Ger.
47/H1 **Mundesley**, Eng,UK
47/G2 **Mundford**, Eng,UK
84/C3 **Mungaolī**, India
91/B2 **Mungo Nat'l Park**, Austl.
75/F1 **Mungun-Tayga, Gora** (peak), Rus.
55/H1 **Munich** (München), Ger.
126/C2 **Munising**, Mi,US
69/L4 **Munku-Sardyk** (peak), Rus.
76/D1 **Munku-Sasan** (peak), Rus.
113/J8 **Muñoz Gamero** (pen.), Chile
51/E5 **Münster**, Ger.
51/H3 **Munster**, Ger.
43/A4 **Munster** (prov.), Ire.
132/Q16 **Munster**, In,US
51/E4 **Münsterland** (reg.), Ger.
63/F2 **Muntele Mare** (peak), Rom.
86/C4 **Muntok**, Indo.
83/D1 **Muong Khuong**, Viet.
42/G1 **Muonioälv** (riv.), Swe.
42/G1 **Muoniojoki** (riv.), Fin.
104/C4 **Mupa Nat'l Park**, Moz.
97/Q7 **Muqdisho** (Mogadishu) (cap.), Som.
57/L3 **Mur** (riv.), Aus.
62/C2 **Mura** (riv.), Slvk.
74/E2 **Muradiye**, Turk.
79/F1 **Murakami**, Japan
113/J7 **Murallón** (peak), Chile
101/C3 **Murang'a**, Kenya
74/E2 **Murat** (riv.), Turk.
66/D5 **Murat Dağı** (peak), Turk.
59/E4 **Murcia**, Sp.
58/E4 **Murcia** (aut. comm.), Sp.
127/H1 **Murdochville**, Qu,Can
90/B1 **Murdock** (pt.), Austl.
63/G2 **Mureş** (co.), Rom.
63/G2 **Mureş** (riv.), Rom.
56/D5 **Muret**, Fr.
128/E3 **Murfreesboro**, Ar,US
129/G3 **Murfreesboro**, Tn,US
73/H1 **Murgab** (riv.), Trkm.
86/D5 **Muria** (peak), Indo.
110/D2 **Muriaé**, Braz.
73/G3 **Mūrīān, Hāmūn-e Jaz** (lake), Iran
48/G2 **Müritz See** (lake), Ger.
97/N6 **Murle**, Eth.
64/G1 **Murmansk**, Rus.
64/G2 **Murmansk Obl.**, Rus.
79/M10 **Muro**, Japan
59/G3 **Muro**, Sp.
64/J5 **Murom**, Rus.
77/N3 **Muroran**, Japan
58/A1 **Muros**, Sp.
78/D4 **Muroto**, Japan
78/D4 **Muroto-zaki** (pt.), Japan
49/J2 **Murowana Goślina**, Pol.
129/G3 **Murphy**, NC,US
126/B4 **Murphysboro**, Il,US
91/D2 **Murramarang Nat'l Park**, Austl.
91/A2 **Murray** (riv.), Austl.
92/D5 **Murray** (lake), PNG
126/B4 **Murray**, Ky,US
129/H3 **Murray** (lake), SC,US
91/A2 **Murray Bridge**, Austl.
91/C2 **Murrumbidgee** (riv.), Austl.
62/C2 **Murska Sobota**, Slov.
45/G2 **Murton**, Eng,UK
93/M7 **Mururoa** (isl.), FrPol.
84/D3 **Murwāra**, India
91/E1 **Murwillumbah**, Austl.
49/H5 **Mürz** (riv.), Aus.
57/L3 **Mürzzuschlag**, Aus.
74/E2 **Muş**, Turk.
63/F4 **Musala** (peak), Bul.
73/G3 **Musandam** (pen.), Oman
79/H7 **Musashino**, Japan
73/G4 **Muscat** (Musqaţ) (cap.), Oman
131/E5 **Musconetcong** (riv.), NJ,US
131/C2 **Muscoy**, Ca,US
104/E5 **Musekwapoort** (pass), SAfr.
92/C7 **Musgrave** (ranges), Austl.
127/L1 **Musgrave Harbour**, Nf,Can
84/E3 **Mushābani**, India
74/N9 **Mushāsh, Wādī** (dry riv.), WBnk.
104/C1 **Mushie**, Zaire
86/B4 **Musi** (riv.), Indo.
132/P14 **Muskego**, Wi,US
126/C3 **Muskegon**, Mi,US
126/C3 **Muskegon** (riv.), Mi,US
126/D4 **Muskingum** (riv.), Oh,US
125/J4 **Muskogee**, Ok,US
126/E2 **Muskoka** (lake), On,Can
101/B3 **Musoma**, Tanz.
73/G4 **Musqaţ** (Muscat) (cap.), Oman
127/J1 **Musquaro** (riv.), Qu,Can
92/D5 **Mussau** (isl.), PNG
122/F4 **Musselshell** (riv.), Mt,US
60/C4 **Mussomeli**, It.
74/B2 **Mustafakemalpaşa**, Turk.
84/D2 **Mustāng**, Nepal
125/H4 **Mustang**, Ok,US
57/K2 **Můstek** (peak), Czh.
112/C5 **Musters** (lake), Arg.
80/E2 **Musu-dan** (pt.), NKor.
116/D5 **Musún** (mt.), Nic.
91/D2 **Muswellbrook**, Austl.
100/B3 **Mūt**, Egypt
74/C3 **Mut**, Turk.
104/F4 **Mutare**, Zim.
87/F5 **Mutis** (peak), Indo.
103/H6 **Mutsamudu**, Com.
77/N3 **Mutsu**, Japan
110/D1 **Mutum**, Braz.
67/L4 **Muynak**, Uzb.
73/K2 **Muzaffargarh**, Pak.
84/C2 **Muzaffarnagar**, India
84/E2 **Muzaffarpur**, India
110/G6 **Muzambinho**, Braz.
75/D3 **Muzat** (riv.), China
75/D4 **Muztag** (peak), China
75/E4 **Muztag** (peak), China
75/C4 **Muztagata** (peak), China
104/C2 **Mwadi-Kalumbu**, Zaire
101/B3 **Mwanza**, Tanz.
101/B3 **Mwanza** (prov.), Tanz.
43/H7 **Mweelrea** (mtn.), Ire.
104/D1 **Mweka**, Zaire
104/D2 **Mwene-Ditu**, Zaire
101/A5 **Mweru** (lake), Zaire, Zam.
91/E2 **Myall Lakes Nat'l Park**, Austl.
85/G4 **Myanaung**, Burma
76/C2 **Myangad**, Mong.
85/G2 **Myanmar** (Burma)
85/F4 **Myaungmya**, Burma
85/G3 **Myingyan**, Burma
85/G2 **Myitkyina**, Burma
49/J4 **Myjava**, Slvk.
46/C2 **Mynydd Eppynt** (mts.), Wal,UK
46/B2 **Mynydd Pencarreg** (mtn.), Wal,UK
85/F3 **Myohaung**, Burma
79/F2 **Myōkō-san** (mtn.), Japan
129/J3 **Myrtle Beach**, SC,US
122/C5 **Myrtle Creek**, Or,US
42/D4 **Mysen**, Nor.
49/K4 **Myślenice**, Pol.
49/H2 **Myślibórz**, Pol.
83/E3 **My Son** (ruins), Viet.
84/C5 **Mysore**, India
49/K3 **Myszków**, Pol.
83/D4 **My Tho**, Viet.
64/H5 **Mytishchi**, Rus.
57/K2 **Mže** (riv.), Czh.
101/B5 **Mzuzu**, Malw.

N

83/C1 **Na** (riv.), Viet.
57/J2 **Naab** (riv.), Ger.
50/B5 **Naaldwijk**, Neth.
50/C4 **Naarden**, Neth.
44/B5 **Naas**, Ire.
102/B3 **Nababeep**, SAfr.
84/E3 **Nabadwīp**, India
78/E3 **Nabari**, Japan
79/M10 **Nabari** (riv.), Japan
65/M5 **Naberezhnye Chelny**, Rus.
72/D5 **Nabī Shu'ayb, Jabal an** (mtn.), Yem.
127/J1 **Nabisipi** (riv.), Qu,Can
82/D5 **Nabua**, Phil.
60/B4 **Nābul**, Tun.
60/B4 **Nābul** (gov.), Tun.
74/K5 **Nābulus**, WBnk.
78/D4 **Nachi-Katsuura**, Japan
49/J3 **Náchod**, Czh.
51/E6 **Nachrodt-Wiblingwerde**, Ger.
112/B3 **Nacimiento**, Chile
128/E4 **Nacogdoches**, Tx,US
46/D4 **Nadder** (riv.), Eng,UK
92/G6 **Nadi**, Fiji
84/B3 **Nadiād**, India
62/E2 **Nădlac**, Rom.
45/H3 **Nafferton**, Eng,UK
73/J3 **Nag**, Pak.
82/D5 **Naga**, Phil.
78/C4 **Nagahama**, Japan
78/E3 **Nagahama**, Japan
79/G1 **Nagai**, Japan
85/F2 **Nāgāland** (state), India
79/F2 **Nagano**, Japan
79/E3 **Nagano** (pref.), Japan
79/F2 **Nagaoka**, Japan
78/D3 **Nagaokakyō**, Japan
79/J7 **Nagara**, Japan
79/E3 **Nagara** (riv.), Japan
79/H7 **Nagareyama**, Japan
84/B4 **Nagar Haveli, Dadrak** (terr.), India
84/C4 **Nāgārjuna Sāgar** (res.), India
116/D5 **Nagarote**, Nic.
130/M5 **Nagas** (pt.), BC,Can
78/A4 **Nagasaki**, Japan
78/A4 **Nagasaki** (pref.), Japan
79/M9 **Nagashima**, Japan
78/B3 **Nagato**, Japan
84/B2 **Nāgaur**, India
84/C3 **Nāgda**, India
84/C6 **Nāgercoil**, India
75/F2 **Nagoonnuur**, Mong.
67/H5 **Nagorno-Karabakh Aut. Obl.**, Azer.
79/E3 **Nagoya**, Japan
84/C3 **Nāgpur**, India
76/C5 **Nagqu** (riv.), China
62/C2 **Nagyatád**, Hun.
62/E1 **Nagyhalász**, Hun.
62/E2 **Nagykálló**, Hun.
62/C2 **Nagykanizsa**, Hun.
62/D2 **Nagykáta**, Hun.
62/D2 **Nagykőrös**, Hun.
62/E1 **Nagy-Milic** (peak), Hun.
82/E2 **Naha**, Japan
118/D2 **Nahanni Nat'l Park**, NW,Can
74/K5 **Nahariyya**, Isr.
92/D2 **Nahashima** (isls.), Japan
72/E2 **Nahāvand**, Iran
53/G4 **Nahe** (riv.), Ger.
99/E4 **Nahouri** (prov.), Burk.
112/B3 **Nahuelbuta Nat'l Park**, Chile
112/C4 **Nahuel Huapí Nat'l Park**, Arg.
117/N8 **Naica**, Mex.
76/C4 **Naij Gol** (riv.), China
78/C3 **Naikai-Seto Nat'l Park**, Japan
46/D4 **Nailsea**, Eng,UK
46/D3 **Nailsworth**, Eng,UK
84/D3 **Nainpur**, India
43/D2 **Nairn**, Sc,UK
43/D2 **Nairn** (riv.), Sc,UK
101/C3 **Nairobi** (cap.), Kenya
101/C3 **Nairobi Nat'l Park**, Kenya
72/F2 **Najafābād**, Iran
72/D3 **Najd** (des.), SAr.
58/D1 **Nájera**, Sp.
84/C2 **Najībābād**, India
79/K9 **Naka**, Japan
78/D4 **Naka** (riv.), Japan
79/G2 **Naka** (riv.), Japan
79/H7 **Nakai**, Japan
79/F1 **Nakajō**, Japan
120/T10 **Nakalele** (pt.), Hi,US
79/G2 **Nakaminato**, Japan
78/C4 **Nakamura**, Japan
79/F2 **Nakano**, Japan
78/C3 **Nakano** (lake), Japan
78/B5 **Nakatane**, Japan
79/E3 **Nakatsugawa**, Japan
97/N4 **Nak'fa**, Erit.
67/H5 **Nakhichevan'**, Azer.
67/H5 **Nakhichevan Aut. Rep.**, Azer.
77/L3 **Nakhodka**, Rus.
83/C3 **Nakhon Nayok**, Thai.
83/C3 **Nakhon Pathom**, Thai.
83/D2 **Nakhon Phanom**, Thai.
83/C3 **Nakhon Ratchasima**, Thai.
83/C3 **Nakhon Sawan**, Thai.
83/B4 **Nakhon Si Thammarat**, Thai.
42/G3 **Nakkila**, Fin.
49/J2 **Nakło nad Notecią**, Pol.
48/F1 **Nakskov**, Den.
80/E5 **Naktong** (riv.), SKor.
101/C3 **Nakuru**, Kenya
122/D3 **Nakusp**, BC,Can
73/J3 **Nāl** (riv.), Pak.
76/F2 **Nalayh**, Mong.
53/F5 **Nalbach**, Ger.
85/F2 **Nalbāri**, India
91/D3 **Nalbaugh Nat'l Park**, Austl.
67/G4 **Nal'chik**, Rus.
83/C2 **Nale**, Laos
84/C4 **Nalgonda**, India
63/K5 **Nallıhan**, Turk.
58/B1 **Nalón** (riv.), Sp.
96/H1 **Nālūt**, Libya
72/F2 **Namak** (lake), Iran
73/G2 **Namakzār-e Shadād** (salt dep.), Iran
75/B3 **Namangan**, Uzb.
102/B3 **Namaqualand** (reg.), SAfr.
87/J4 **Namaripi** (cape), Indo.
53/G4 **Namborn**, Ger.
90/D4 **Nambour**, Austl.
83/D4 **Nam Can**, Viet.
83/C1 **Nam Cum**, Viet.
83/D1 **Nam Dinh**, Viet.
126/B2 **Namekagon** (riv.), Wi,US
99/E3 **Namemtenga** (prov.), Burk.
79/E2 **Namerikawa**, Japan
104/B5 **Namib** (des.), Namb.
104/C5 **Namibia**
102/A2 **Namib-Naukluft Park**, Namb.
79/G2 **Namie**, Japan
84/D2 **Namja** (pass), Nepal
85/G2 **Namjagbarwa** (peak), China
83/C2 **Nam Nao Nat'l Park**, Thai.
83/B4 **Namnoi** (peak), Burma
91/D1 **Namoi** (riv.), Austl.
92/E4 **Namonuito** (atoll), Micr.
92/F4 **Namorik** (atoll), Mrsh.
122/D5 **Nampa**, Id,US
80/C3 **Namp'o**, NKor.
104/G4 **Nampula**, Moz.
75/D6 **Namsê Shankou** (pass), China
42/D2 **Namsos**, Nor.
83/B2 **Nam Tok Mae Surin Nat'l Park**, Thai.
92/F4 **Namu** (atoll), Mrsh.
83/C2 **Nam Un** (res.), Thai.
53/D3 **Namur**, Belg.
53/D3 **Namur** (prov.), Belg.
49/J3 **Namysłów**, Pol.
81/B4 **Nan** (riv.), China
83/C2 **Nan**, Thai.
83/C2 **Nan** (riv.), Thai.
122/C3 **Nanaimo**, BC,Can
120/V13 **Nanakuli**, Hi,US
79/E2 **Nanao**, Japan
108/D4 **Nanay** (riv.), Peru
112/C2 **Nancagua**, Chile
82/C2 **Nanchang**, China
82/C2 **Nancheng**, China
53/F6 **Nancy**, Fr.
84/C4 **Nānded**, India
85/G3 **Nanding** (riv.), China
82/A4 **Nandu** (riv.), China
84/B3 **Nandurbār**, India
84/C4 **Nandyāl**, India
73/K1 **Nanga Parbat** (mtn.), Pak.
86/D4 **Nangapinoh**, Indo.
81/C3 **Nangong**, China
87/F1 **Nangtud** (mt.), Phil.
81/D4 **Nanjing**, China
78/C4 **Nankoku**, Japan
85/J3 **Nanliu** (riv.), China
77/K3 **Nanlou** (peak), China
85/J3 **Nanning**, China
79/M9 **Nannō**, Japan
44/B4 **Nanny** (riv.), Ire.
84/D2 **Nānpāra**, India
82/C2 **Nanping**, China
79/M10 **Nansei**, Japan
119/S6 **Nansen** (sound), NW,Can
101/B3 **Nansio**, Tanz.
79/F2 **Nantai-san** (mtn.), Japan
52/B6 **Nanterre**, Fr.
56/C3 **Nantes**, Fr.
52/B5 **Nanteuil-le-Haudouin**, Fr.
126/D3 **Nanticoke**, On,Can
122/E3 **Nanton**, Ab,Can
81/E4 **Nantong**, China
127/G3 **Nantucket** (isl.), MA,US
45/F5 **Nantwich**, Eng,UK
46/C3 **Nantyglo**, Wal,UK
131/F4 **Nanuet**, NY,US
93/Z18 **Nanuku** (chan.), Fiji
92/G5 **Nanumanga** (atoll), Tuv.
92/G5 **Nanumea** (isl.), Tuv.
110/D1 **Nanuque**, Braz.
81/C4 **Nanwon** (res.), China
81/B4 **Nanwutai** (mtn.), China
81/D4 **Nanyang**, China
81/D4 **Nanyang** (lake), China
101/C2 **Nanyuki**, Kenya
119/J3 **Naococane** (lake), Qu,Can
84/A3 **Naokot**, Pak.
77/L2 **Naoli** (riv.), China
98/D5 **Naoua** (falls), IvC.
132/K10 **Napa**, Ca,US
132/K10 **Napa** (riv.), Ca,US
126/E2 **Napanee**, On,Can
100/B5 **Napata** (ruins), Sudan
132/P16 **Naperville**, Il,US
89/H6 **Napier**, NZ
102/L11 **Napier**, SAfr.
129/H5 **Naples**, Fl,US
60/D2 **Naples** (Napoli), It.
60/D2 **Napoli** (gulf), It.
90/A4 **Nappa Merrie**, Austl.
47/E2 **Napton on the Hill**, Eng,UK
93/L6 **Napuka** (isl.), FrPol.
78/D3 **Nara**, Japan
78/D3 **Nara** (pref.), Japan
98/D3 **Nara**, Mali
73/J3 **Nāra** (riv.), Pak.
75/D5 **Nara Logna** (pass), Nepal
84/D4 **Narasannapeta**, India
79/J7 **Narashino**, Japan
83/C5 **Narathiwat**, Thai.
84/F3 **Nārāyanganj**, Bang.
84/C4 **Nārāyanpet**, India
46/B3 **Narberth**, Wal,UK
56/E5 **Narbonne**, Fr.
58/B1 **Narcea** (riv.), Sp.
61/F2 **Nardò**, It.
46/B6 **Nare** (pt.), UK
119/T7 **Nares** (str.), NW,Can
49/L2 **Narew** (riv.), Pol.
117/F6 **Narganá**, Pan.
103/H6 **Narinda** (bay), Madg.
113/K8 **Nariz** (peak), Chile
84/D2 **Narkatiāganj**, India
84/C3 **Narmada** (riv.), India
74/E2 **Narman**, Turk.
60/C1 **Narni**, It.
65/P2 **Narodnaya** (peak), Rus.
58/A1 **Narón**, Sp.
73/K2 **Nārowāl**, Pak.
42/G3 **Närpes**, Fin.
82/C6 **Narra**, Phil.
91/D1 **Narrabri**, Austl.
84/C3 **Narsimhapur**, India
84/C3 **Narsingarh**, India
78/D3 **Naruto**, Japan
64/F4 **Narva**, Est.
64/E4 **Narva** (riv.), Est., Rus.
82/D4 **Narvacan**, Phil.
42/F1 **Narvik**, Nor.
65/M2 **Nar'yan-Mar**, Rus.
75/C3 **Naryn**, Kyr.
75/B3 **Naryn** (riv.), Kyr.
63/G2 **Năsăud**, Rom.
47/F3 **Nash**, Eng,UK
46/C4 **Nash** (pt.), Wal,UK
127/G3 **Nashua**, NH,US
128/E3 **Nashville**, Ar,US
129/G2 **Nashville** (cap.), Tn,US
62/D3 **Našice**, Cro.
49/L2 **Nasielsk**, Pol.
84/B4 **Nāsik**, India
97/M6 **Nāşir**, Sudan
84/B2 **Nasīrābād**, India
73/J3 **Nasīrābād**, Pak.
87/F1 **Naso** (pt.), Phil.
93/Z17 **Nasorolevu** (peak), Fiji
130/N4 **Nass** (riv.), BC,Can
117/F2 **Nassau** (cap.), Bahm.
113/L8 **Nassau** (bay), Chile
93/J6 **Nassau** (isl.), Cookls.
100/C4 **Nasser** (res.), Egypt
42/E4 **Nässjö**, Swe.
119/J3 **Nastapoka** (isls.), NW,Can
48/F1 **Næstved**, Den.
79/F2 **Nasu-dake** (mtn.), Japan
83/B2 **Nat** (peak), Burma
104/E5 **Nata**, Bots.
126/C1 **Natagani** (riv.), On,Can
109/L5 **Natal**, Braz.
127/J1 **Natashquan** (riv.), Qu,Can
129/F4 **Natchez**, Ms,US
128/E4 **Natchitoches**, La,US
54/D5 **Naters**, Swi.
93/Z17 **Natewa** (bay), Fiji
84/B3 **Nāthdwāra**, India
122/B2 **Nation** (riv.), BC,Can
124/C4 **National City**, Ca,US
85/G4 **Nattaung** (peak), Burma
86/C3 **Natuna** (isls.), Indo.
124/E3 **Natural Bridges Nat'l Mon.**, Ut,US
91/D4 **Naturaliste** (cape), Austl.
116/B4 **Naucalpan**, Mex.
102/E3 **Naudesnek** (pass), SAfr.
82/D5 **Naujan**, Phil.
64/D4 **Naujoji-Akmenė**, Lith.
102/A2 **Naukluft-Namib Game Rsv.**, Namb.
92/F5 **Nauru**
59/N8 **Navacarrada** (pass), Sp.
124/E3 **Navajo Nat'l Mon.**, Az,US
59/M9 **Navalcarnero**, Sp.
58/C3 **Navalmoral de la Mata**, Sp.
44/B4 **Navan**, Ire.
69/T3 **Navarin** (cape), Rus.
113/L8 **Navarino** (isl.), Chile
58/D1 **Navarre** (aut. comm.), Sp.
112/F2 **Navarro**, Arg.
46/A6 **Navax** (pt.), UK
58/B1 **Navia**, Sp.
58/B1 **Navia** (riv.), Sp.
112/C2 **Navidad**, Chile
109/H8 **Naviraí**, Braz.
63/J3 **Năvodari**, Rom.
68/G5 **Navoi**, Uzb.
117/N8 **Navojoa**, Mex.
117/N9 **Navolato**, Mex.
61/G3 **Návpaktos**, Gre.
61/H4 **Návplion**, Gre.
84/B3 **Navsāri**, India
119/H1 **Navy Board** (inlet), NW,Can
84/E3 **Nawābganj**, Bang.
84/D2 **Nawābganj**, India
73/J3 **Nawābshāh**, Pak.
73/G5 **Nawş, Ra's** (pt.), Oman
61/J4 **Náxos** (isl.), Gre.
117/P9 **Nayarit** (state), Mex.
47/G3 **Nayland**, Eng,UK
76/B2 **Nayramadlīn** (peak), Mong.
75/B4 **Nayzatash, Pereval** (pass), Taj.
58/A3 **Nazaré**, Port.
52/C2 **Nazareth**, Belg.
74/K5 **Nazareth** (Nazerat), Isr.
117/P8 **Nazas** (riv.), Mex.
108/D6 **Nazca**, Peru
108/C6 **Nazca Lines** (ruins), Peru
92/B2 **Naze**, Japan
47/H3 **Naze, The** (pt.), Eng,UK
74/B3 **Nazilli**, Turk.
97/N6 **Nazrēt**, Eth.
68/H4 **Nazyvayevsk**, Rus.
101/A5 **Nchelenge**, Zam.
101/A5 **Ncheu**, Malw.
104/B2 **Ndalatando**, Ang.
97/K6 **Ndele**, CAfr.
92/F6 **Ndende** (isl.), Sol.
96/J5 **N'Djamena** (cap.), Chad
96/H8 **N'Djolé**, Gabon
104/E3 **Ndola**, Zam.
99/H5 **Ndop**, Camr.
98/B2 **Ndrhamcha, Sebkha de** (dry lake), Mrta.
56/C4 **Né** (riv.), Fr.
61/J5 **Néa Alikarnassós**, Gre.

Neagh – North

44/B2 **Neagh, Lough** (lake), NI,UK
61/H3 **Néa Ionía,** Gre.
63/H2 **Neamţ** (co.), Rom.
130/A6 **Near** (isls.), Ak,US
46/C3 **Neath,** Wal,UK
46/C3 **Neath** (riv.), Wal,UK
44/D3 **Neb** (riv.), IM,UK
67/K5 **Nebit-Dag,** Trkm.
90/E6 **Nebo** (mtn.), Austl.
125/G2 **Nebraska** (state), US
125/J2 **Nebraska City,** Ne,US
60/C4 **Nebrodi, Madonie** (mts.), It.
122/B2 **Nechako** (riv.), BC,Can
128/E4 **Neches** (riv.), Tx,US
97/N6 **Nechisar Nat'l Park,** Eth.
55/E1 **Neckar** (riv.), Ger.
93/J2 **Necker** (isl.), Hi,US
112/F3 **Necochea,** Arg.
60/C1 **Necropoli** (ruins), It.
58/A1 **Neda,** Sp.
50/C6 **Nederweert,** Neth.
50/D4 **Neede,** Neth.
47/H2 **Needham Market,** Eng,UK
47/F2 **Needingworth,** Eng,UK
124/D4 **Needles,** Ca,US
47/E5 **Needles, The** (seastacks), UK
126/B2 **Neenah,** Wi,US
123/J3 **Neepawa,** Mb,Can
53/E1 **Neerpelt,** Belg.
51/H2 **Neetze** (riv.), Ger.
53/F2 **Neffelbach** (riv.), Ger.
65/M4 **Neftekamsk,** Rus.
71/C7 **Nefud** (des.), SAr.
44/D6 **Nefyn,** Wal,UK
126/C2 **Negaunee,** Mi,US
97/N6 **Negēlē,** Eth.
100/D2 **Negev** (phys. reg.), Isr.
63/G3 **Negoiu** (peak), Rom.
84/C6 **Negombo,** SrL.
62/F3 **Negotin,** Yugo.
62/F5 **Negotino,** Macd.
108/B5 **Negra** (pt.), Peru
85/F4 **Negrais** (cape), Burma
58/A1 **Negreira,** Sp.
63/H2 **Negreşti,** Rom.
112/C3 **Negro** (peak), Arg.
112/D3 **Negro** (riv.), Arg.
108/F7 **Negro** (riv.), Bol.
109/G7 **Negro** (riv.), Braz.
108/F4 **Negro** (riv.), Braz., Ven.
113/F2 **Negro** (riv.), Uru., Braz.
82/D6 **Negros** (isl.), Phil.
117/G4 **Neiba,** DRep.
103/R15 **Neiges, Piton des** (peak), Reun.
81/C4 **Neihuang,** China
81/B2 **Nei Monggol** (aut. reg.), China
76/G3 **Nei Monggol** (plat.), China
108/C3 **Neiva,** Col.
118/G3 **Nejanilini** (lake), Mb,Can
97/N6 **Nejo,** Eth.
97/N6 **Nek'emtē,** Eth.
64/G4 **Nelidovo,** Rus.
125/H2 **Neligh,** Ne,US
84/C5 **Nellore,** India
91/B3 **Nelson** (cape), Austl.
122/D3 **Nelson,** BC,Can
118/G3 **Nelson** (riv.), Mb,Can
113/J7 **Nelson** (str.), Chile
89/H7 **Nelson,** NZ
45/F4 **Nelson,** Eng,UK
46/C3 **Nelson,** Wal,UK
130/F3 **Nelson** (isl.), Ak,US
91/E2 **Nelson Bay,** Austl.
103/E2 **Nelspruit,** SAfr.
98/D2 **Néma,** Mrta.
98/D2 **Néma, Dhar** (hills), Mrta.
57/H4 **Nembro,** It.
63/H2 **Nemira** (peak), Rom.
77/J2 **Nemor** (riv.), China
56/E2 **Nemours,** Fr.
77/P3 **Nemuro,** Japan
77/J2 **Nen** (riv.), China
47/G1 **Nene** (riv.), Eng,UK
65/M2 **Nenets Aut. Okr.,** Rus.
125/J3 **Neosho** (riv.), Ks, Mo,US
125/J3 **Neosho,** Mo,US
71/H7 **Nepal**
84/D2 **Nepālganj,** Nepal
84/C3 **Nepanagar,** India
90/G8 **Nepean** (riv.), Austl.
126/F2 **Nepean,** Can.
124/E3 **Nephi,** Ut,US
43/A3 **Nephin** (mtn.), Ire.
127/H2 **Nepisiguit** (riv.), NB,Can
76/H1 **Nercha** (riv.), Rus.
64/J4 **Nerekhta,** Rus.
62/D4 **Neretva** (riv.), Bosn., Cro.
64/E5 **Neris** (riv.), Lith.
58/D4 **Nerja,** Sp.
58/B4 **Nerva,** Sp.
66/C4 **Nesebür,** Bul.
125/H3 **Ness City,** Ks,US
51/H6 **Nesse** (riv.), Ger.
130/M4 **Nesselrode** (mtn.), Ak,US
43/C2 **Ness, Loch** (lake), Sc,UK
45/E5 **Neston,** Eng,UK
61/J2 **Néstos** (riv.), Gre.
74/M9 **Nes Ziyyona,** Isr.
74/K5 **Netanya,** Isr.
131/F5 **Netcong,** NJ,US
51/G5 **Nethe** (riv.), Ger.
46/D3 **Netherend,** Eng,UK
50/B5 **Netherlands**
117/H5 **Netherlands Antilles** (isls.), Neth.
47/E5 **Netley,** Eng,UK
60/E3 **Neto** (riv.), It.
53/H2 **Netphen,** Ger.
50/D6 **Nette** (riv.), Ger.
51/H5 **Nette** (riv.), Ger.
53/G3 **Nettebach** (riv.), Ger.
53/F3 **Nettersheim,** Ger.
50/D6 **Nettetal,** Ger.
119/J2 **Nettilling** (lake), NW,Can
45/H5 **Nettleham,** Eng,UK
60/C2 **Nettuno,** It.
49/G2 **Neubrandenburg,** Ger.
54/C4 **Neuchâtel,** Swi.
54/C4 **Neuchâtel** (canton), Swi.
54/C4 **Neuchâtel** (lake), Swi.
49/G2 **Neuenhagen,** Ger.
50/D4 **Neuenhaus,** Ger.
51/E4 **Neuenkirchen,** Ger.
51/F3 **Neuenkirchen,** Ger.
51/E6 **Neuenrade,** Ger.
53/E4 **Neufchâteau,** Belg.
54/B1 **Neufchâteau,** Fr.
52/B5 **Neuilly-en-Thelle,** Fr.
52/C5 **Neuilly-Saint-Front,** Fr.
52/B6 **Neuilly-sur-Seine,** Fr.
57/J2 **Neumarkt in der Oberpfalz,** Ger.
48/E1 **Neumünster,** Ger.
62/C2 **Neunkirchen,** Aus.
53/G5 **Neunkirchen,** Ger.
53/H2 **Neunkirchen,** Ger.
53/G2 **Neunkirchen-Seelscheid,** Ger.
112/C3 **Neuquén,** Arg.
112/C3 **Neuquén** (prov.), Arg.
112/C3 **Neuquén** (riv.), Arg.
48/G2 **Neuruppin,** Ger.
129/J3 **Neuse** (riv.), NC,US
50/D6 **Neuss,** Ger.
51/G4 **Neustadt am Rübenberge,** Ger.
57/J2 **Neustadt an der Donau,** Ger.
57/H2 **Neustadt an der Weinstrasse,** Ger.
57/J1 **Neustadt bei Coburg,** Ger.
48/F1 **Neustadt in Holstein,** Ger.
48/G2 **Neustrelitz,** Ger.
55/G1 **Neu-Ulm,** Ger.
56/G2 **Neuves-Maisons,** Fr.
51/F1 **Neuwerk** (isl.), Ger.
53/G3 **Neuwied,** Ger.
67/V7 **Neva** (riv.), Rus.
58/D4 **Nevada** (mts.), Sp.
124/C3 **Nevada** (state), US
125/J3 **Nevada,** Mo,US
112/C4 **Nevado Cónico** (peak), Chile
111/C1 **Nevado de Chañi** (peak), Arg.
117/P10 **Nevado de Colima Nat'l Park,** Mex.
111/C2 **Nevado del Candado** (peak), Arg.
108/C3 **Nevado del Huila** (peak), Col.
105/C3 **Nevado del Huila Nat'l Park,** Col.
112/C2 **Nevado, Sierra del** (mts.), Arg.
64/F4 **Nevel',** Rus.
52/C1 **Nevele,** Belg.
77/N2 **Nevel'sk,** Rus.
56/E3 **Nevers,** Fr.
62/D4 **Nevesinje,** Bosn.
67/G3 **Nevinnomyssk,** Rus.
117/J4 **Nevis** (isl.), StK.
74/C2 **Nevşehir,** Turk.
108/G3 **New** (riv.), Guy.
47/E5 **New** (for.), Eng,UK
126/D4 **New** (riv.), WV,US
44/E2 **New Abbey,** Sc,UK
126/C4 **New Albany,** In,US
129/F3 **New Albany,** Ms,US
47/E4 **New Alfresford,** Eng,UK
109/G2 **New Amsterdam,** Guy.
45/H5 **New Ancholme** (riv.), Eng,UK
132/K11 **Newark,** Ca,US
131/F5 **Newark,** NJ,US
126/D3 **Newark,** Oh,US
45/H5 **Newark-on-Trent,** Eng,UK
132/G6 **New Baltimore,** Mi,US
127/G3 **New Bedford,** Ma,US
132/P14 **New Berlin,** Wi,US
129/J3 **New Bern,** NC,US
126/C2 **Newberry,** Mi,US
129/H3 **Newberry,** SC,US
45/G1 **Newbiggin-by-the-Sea,** Eng,UK
128/D4 **New Braunfels,** Tx,US
46/C2 **Newbridge on Wye,** Wal,UK
92/D5 **New Britain** (isl.), PNG
127/F3 **New Britain,** Ct,US
127/H2 **New Brunswick** (prov.), Can.
131/F5 **New Brunswick,** NJ,US
44/A2 **New Buildings,** NI,UK
45/G2 **Newburn,** Eng,UK
47/E4 **Newbury,** Eng,UK
45/F3 **Newby Bridge,** Eng,UK
92/F6 **New Caledonia** (terr.), Fr.
93/U12 **New Caledonia** (isl.), NCal.
131/G4 **New Canaan,** Ct,US
91/D2 **Newcastle,** Austl.
127/H2 **Newcastle,** NB,Can
127/S8 **Newcastle,** On,Can
103/E2 **Newcastle,** SAfr.
44/C3 **Newcastle,** NI,UK
126/C4 **New Castle,** In,US
126/D3 **New Castle,** Pa,US
123/G5 **Newcastle,** Wy,US
46/B2 **Newcastle Emlyn,** Wal,UK
45/F1 **Newcastleton,** Sc,UK
45/F5 **Newcastle-under-Lyme,** Eng,UK
45/G2 **Newcastle upon Tyne,** Eng,UK
131/G4 **New City,** NY,US
43/C3 **New Cumnock,** Sc,UK
84/C2 **New Delhi** (cap.), India
122/D3 **New Denver,** BC,Can
131/F5 **New Egypt,** NJ,US
91/E1 **New England Nat'l Park,** Austl.
130/F4 **Newenham** (cape), Ak,US
46/D3 **Newent,** Eng,UK
127/S9 **Newfane,** NY,US
119/K3 **Newfoundland** (prov.), Can.
127/L1 **Newfoundland** (isl.), Nf,Can
44/D1 **New Galloway,** Sc,UK
92/E5 **New Georgia** (isls.), Sol.
92/E5 **New Georgia** (sound), Sol.
127/J2 **New Glasgow,** NS,Can
127/N6 **New Glasgow,** Qu,Can
92/C5 **New Guinea** (isl.), Indo., PNG
127/G3 **New Hampshire** (state), US
92/D5 **New Hanover** (isl.), PNG
47/F5 **Newhaven,** Eng,UK
126/F3 **New Haven,** Ct,US
132/G6 **New Haven,** Mi,US
92/F6 **New Hebrides** (isls.), Van.
131/F5 **New Hope,** Pa,US
128/F4 **New Iberia,** La,US
47/G5 **Newick,** Eng,UK
92/E5 **New Ireland** (isl.), PNG
126/F3 **New Jersey** (state), US
126/E3 **New Kensington,** Pa,US
128/D2 **Newkirk,** Ok,US
132/Q16 **New Lenox,** Il,US
126/E2 **New Liskeard,** On,Can
127/F3 **New London,** Ct,US
126/B2 **New London,** Wi,US
46/A6 **Newlyn,** Eng,UK
125/K3 **New Madrid,** Mo,US
90/F6 **Newmarket,** Austl.
126/E2 **Newmarket,** On,Can
47/G2 **Newmarket,** Eng,UK
126/D4 **New Martinsville,** WV,US
122/D4 **New Meadows,** Id,US
124/F4 **New Mexico** (state), US
45/F5 **New Mills,** Eng,UK
129/G3 **Newnan,** Ga,US
46/D3 **Newnham,** Eng,UK
91/C4 **New Norfolk,** Austl.
129/F4 **New Orleans,** La,US
126/D3 **New Philadelphia,** Oh,US
89/H6 **New Plymouth,** NZ
45/F6 **Newport,** Eng,UK
47/E5 **Newport,** Eng,UK
46/B2 **Newport,** Wal,UK
46/D3 **Newport,** Wal,UK
129/F3 **Newport,** Ar,US
126/C4 **Newport,** Ky,US
122/B4 **Newport,** Or,US
127/G3 **Newport,** RI,US
126/D5 **Newport,** Tn,US
127/F2 **Newport,** Vt,US
122/D3 **Newport,** Wa,US
131/C3 **Newport Beach,** Ca,US
126/E4 **Newport News,** Va,US
47/F2 **Newport Pagnell,** Eng,UK
129/H4 **New Port Richey,** Fl,US
117/F3 **New Providence** (isl.), Bahm.
46/A6 **Newquay,** Eng,UK
46/B2 **New Quay,** Wal,UK
46/C2 **New Radnor,** Wal,UK
127/H1 **New Richmond,** Qu,Can
131/G5 **New Rochelle,** NY,US
123/J4 **New Rockford,** ND,US
47/G5 **New Romney,** Eng,UK
45/G5 **New Rossington,** Eng,UK
44/B3 **Newry,** NI,UK
44/B3 **Newry** (can.), NI,UK
105/Z **New Schwabenland** (reg.), Ant.
69/P2 **New Siberian** (isls.), Rus.
129/H4 **New Smyrna Beach,** Fl,US
91/C2 **New South Wales** (state), Austl.
46/D2 **Newton,** Eng,UK
45/E1 **Newton,** Sc,UK
125/H3 **Newton,** Ks,US
127/G3 **Newton,** Ma,US
131/F4 **Newton,** NJ,US
128/E4 **Newton,** Tx,US
46/C5 **Newton Abbot,** Eng,UK
45/G2 **Newton Aycliffe,** Eng,UK
46/B6 **Newton Ferrers,** Eng,UK
45/F5 **Newton-le-Willows,** Eng,UK
43/C2 **Newtonmore,** Sc,UK
45/G1 **Newton on the Moor,** Eng,UK
44/D2 **Newton Stewart,** Sc,UK
91/B3 **Newtown,** Austl.
46/C1 **Newtown,** Wal,UK
123/H4 **New Town,** ND,US
131/F5 **Newtown,** Pa,US
44/C2 **Newtownabbey,** NI,UK
44/C2 **Newtownards,** NI,UK
43/B3 **Newtownbutler,** NI,UK
44/B3 **Newtownhamilton,** NI,UK
43/D3 **Newtown Saint Boswells,** Sc,UK
44/A2 **Newtownstewart,** NI,UK
46/C3 **New Tredegar,** Wal,UK
123/K4 **New Ulm,** Mn,US
127/J2 **New Waterford,** NS,Can
122/C3 **New Westminster,** BC,Can
126/F3 **New York** (state), US
131/G5 **New York,** NY,US
89/H6 **New Zealand**
105/L **New Zealand** (peak), Ant.
79/L10 **Neyagawa,** Japan
46/B3 **Neyland,** Wal,UK
73/F3 **Neyrīz,** Iran
73/G1 **Neyshābūr,** Iran
65/P4 **Neyva** (riv.), Rus.
84/C5 **Neyveli,** India
84/C6 **Neyyāttinkara,** India
66/D2 **Nezhin,** Ukr.
122/D4 **Nezperce,** Id,US
86/C3 **Ngabang,** Indo.
87/H5 **Ngabordamlu** (cape), Indo.
104/F4 **Ngabu,** Malw.
96/H5 **Ngala,** Nga.
75/D5 **Ngangla Ringco** (lake), China
75/E5 **Ngangzê** (lake), China
96/H6 **Ngaoundéré,** Camr.
91/B2 **Ngarkat Consv. Park,** Austl.
92/E4 **Ngatik** (isl.), Micr.
93/Z18 **Ngau** (isl.), Fiji
83/D2 **Nghia Dan,** Viet.
83/D1 **Nghia Lo,** Viet.
104/C4 **Ngiva,** Ang.
104/C1 **Ngo,** Congo
83/E4 **Ngoan Muc** (pass), Viet.
85/J4 **Ngoc Linh** (peak), Viet.
104/D4 **Ngonye** (falls), Zam.
77/D5 **Ngoring** (lake), China
96/H8 **Ngounié** (riv.), Gabon
96/H5 **Nguigmi,** Niger
92/C4 **Ngulu** (atoll), Micr.
83/C2 **Ngum** (riv.), Laos
83/D1 **Nguyen Binh,** Viet.
103/E2 **Ngwenya** (peak), Swaz.
108/G4 **Nhamundá** (riv.), Braz.
83/E3 **Nha Trang,** Viet.
98/E3 **Niafounké,** Mali
127/R9 **Niagara** (riv.), Can., US
127/R9 **Niagara Falls,** On,Can
127/R9 **Niagara Falls,** NY,US
99/F3 **Niamey** (cap.), Niger
99/F3 **Niamey** (dept.), Niger
98/C4 **Niandan** (riv.), Gui.
97/L7 **Niangara,** Zaire
98/E3 **Niangay** (lake), Mali
81/C3 **Niangzi Guan** (pass), China
86/A3 **Nias** (isl.), Indo.
101/B5 **Niassa** (prov.), Moz.
116/D5 **Nicaragua**
116/E5 **Nicaragua** (lake), Nic.
60/E3 **Nicastro-Sambiase,** It.
57/G5 **Nice,** Fr.
129/G4 **Niceville,** Fl,US
78/B5 **Nichinan,** Japan
85/F6 **Nicobar** (isls.), India
127/F2 **Nicolet,** Qu,Can
74/J4 **Nicosia** (cap.), Cyp.
60/D4 **Nicosia,** It.
116/D5 **Nicoya,** CR
116/D6 **Nicoya** (gulf), CR
116/D6 **Nicoya** (pen.), CR
45/G4 **Nidd** (riv.), Eng,UK
57/H1 **Nidda,** Ger.
53/F2 **Nideggen,** Ger.
53/G6 **Niderviller,** Fr.
55/E4 **Nidwalden** (canton), Swi.
49/L2 **Nidzica,** Pol.
48/E1 **Niebüll,** Ger.
57/G2 **Nied** (riv.), Fr.
53/F5 **Nied** (riv.), Ger.
57/K3 **Niedere Tauern** (mts.), Aus.
49/G3 **Niederlausitz** (reg.), Ger.
53/H4 **Nieder-Olm,** Ger.
51/E1 **Niedersächsisches Wattenmeer Nat'l Park,** Ger.
62/B1 **Niederüsterreich** (prov.), Aus.
53/F2 **Niederzier,** Ger.
49/L2 **Niegocin** (lake), Pol.
51/G5 **Nieheim,** Ger.
49/J3 **Niemodlin,** Pol.
51/G3 **Nienburg,** Ger.
98/D5 **Niénokoué** (peak), IvC.
52/B2 **Nieppe,** Fr.
98/B3 **Niéri Ko** (riv.), Sen.
50/D5 **Niers** (riv.), Ger.
83/D4 **Niet Ban Tinh Xa,** Viet.
50/D5 **Nieuw-Bergen,** Neth.
50/C4 **Nieuwegein,** Neth.
50/B5 **Nieuwerkerk aan de IJssel,** Neth.
50/B4 **Nieuwkoop,** Neth.
50/D3 **Nieuwleusen,** Neth.
50/C4 **Nieuw-Loosdrecht,** Neth.
109/G2 **Nieuw-Nickerie,** Sur.
52/B1 **Nieuwpoort,** Belg.
50/D3 **Nieuw-Schoonebeek,** Neth.
74/C3 **Niğde,** Turk.
102/E2 **Nigel,** SAfr.
99/G2 **Niger**
99/G5 **Niger** (riv.), Afr.
99/G4 **Niger** (state), Nga.
99/G4 **Nigeria**
99/G5 **Niger, Mouths of the** (delta), Nga.
126/D1 **Nighthawk** (lake), On,Can
58/A1 **Nigrán,** Sp.
61/H2 **Nigrita,** Gre.
93/J2 **Nihoa** (isl.), Hi,US
79/G2 **Nihonmatsu,** Japan
79/F3 **Nii** (isl.), Japan
79/F2 **Niigata,** Japan
79/F2 **Niigata** (pref.), Japan
79/E4 **Niihama,** Japan
120/R10 **Niihau** (isl.), Hi,US
78/C3 **Niimi,** Japan
79/F2 **Niitsu,** Japan
79/H7 **Niiza,** Japan
58/D4 **Nijar,** Sp.
50/C4 **Nijkerk,** Neth.
52/D1 **Nijlen,** Belg.
50/C5 **Nijmegen,** Neth.
64/F1 **Nikel',** Rus.
79/F2 **Nikkō,** Japan
79/F2 **Nikkō Nat'l Park,** Japan
66/E3 **Nikolayev,** Ukr.
66/D3 **Nikolayev Obl.,** Ukr.
69/Q4 **Nikolayevsk-na-Amure,** Rus.
67/H1 **Nikol'sk,** Rus.
66/E3 **Nikopol',** Ukr.
74/D2 **Niksar,** Turk.
62/D4 **Nikšić,** Yugo.
93/H5 **Nikumaroro** (Gardner) (atoll), Kiri.
92/G5 **Nikunau** (isl.), Kiri.
97/M2 **Nile** (riv.), Afr.
74/H6 **Nile** (delta), Egypt
101/A2 **Nile** (prov.), Ugan.
132/Q15 **Niles,** Il,US
126/C3 **Niles,** Mi,US
126/D3 **Niles,** Oh,US
110/K7 **Nilópolis,** Braz.
42/J3 **Nilsiä,** Fin.
84/B3 **Nīmach,** India
77/L1 **Niman** (riv.), Rus.
98/C5 **Nimba** (peak), IvC.
98/C5 **Nimba** (co.), Libr.
56/F5 **Nîmes,** Fr.
105/L **Nimrod** (glac.), Ant.
53/F4 **Nimsbach** (riv.), Ger.
101/A2 **Nimule Nat'l Park,** Sudan
72/D1 **Nineveh** (ruins), Iraq
112/D4 **Ninfas** (pt.), Arg.
82/D2 **Ningbo,** China
81/C4 **Ningling,** China
81/B3 **Ningxia Huizu Zizhiqu** (aut. reg.), China
83/D1 **Ninh Binh,** Viet.
83/E3 **Ninh Hoa,** Viet.
92/D5 **Niningo** (isl.), PNG
105/K **Ninnis** (glac.), Ant.
79/H7 **Ninomiya,** Japan
52/D2 **Ninove,** Belg.
125/G2 **Niobrara** (riv.), Ne,US
98/B3 **Niokolo-Koba Nat'l Park,** Sen.
98/D3 **Niono,** Mali
98/B3 **Nioro-du-Rip,** Sen.
98/C3 **Nioro du Sahel,** Mali
56/C3 **Niort,** Fr.
123/H2 **Nipawin,** Sk,Can
126/B1 **Nipigon,** On,Can
126/B1 **Nipigon** (lake), On,Can
126/E2 **Nipissing** (lake), On,Can
112/C3 **Ñiquén,** Chile
79/F3 **Nirasaki,** Japan
90/H8 **Nirimba-Hmas,** Austl.
84/C4 **Nirmal,** India
62/E4 **Niš,** Yugo.
58/B3 **Nisa,** Port.
61/H1 **Nišava** (riv.), Yugo.
60/D4 **Niscemi,** It.
79/M9 **Nishiharu,** Japan
78/C3 **Nishiki** (riv.), Japan
79/L10 **Nishinomiya,** Japan
78/B5 **Nishino'omote,** Japan
79/E3 **Nishio,** Japan
78/D3 **Nishiwaki,** Japan
49/M3 **Nisko,** Pol.
132/B3 **Nisqually Reach** (str.), Wa,US
92/E5 **Nissan** (isl.), PNG
79/N9 **Nisshin,** Japan
123/K4 **Nisswa,** Mn,US
110/K7 **Niterói,** Braz.
44/E1 **Nith** (riv.), Sc,UK
44/E1 **Nithsdale** (val.), Sc,UK
75/C5 **Niti** (pass), India
49/K4 **Nitra,** Slvk.
49/K4 **Nitra** (riv.), Slvk.
65/P4 **Nitsa** (riv.), Rus.
93/H6 **Niuafo'ou** (isl.), Tonga
93/H6 **Niuatoputapu Group** (isls.), Tonga
93/J7 **Niue** (terr.), NZ
92/G6 **Niulakita** (isl.), Tuv.
85/H2 **Niulan** (riv.), China
86/C3 **Niut** (peak), Indo.
92/G5 **Niutau** (isl.), Tuv.
52/D2 **Nivelles,** Belg.
56/E3 **Nivernais** (hills), Fr.
123/J3 **Niverville,** Mb,Can
124/C3 **Nixon,** Nv,US
75/D4 **Niya** (riv.), China
78/C4 **Niyodo** (riv.), Japan
84/C4 **Nizāmābād,** India
65/K4 **Nizhegorod Obl.,** Rus.
65/M4 **Nizhnekama** (res.), Rus.
65/L5 **Nizhnekamsk,** Rus.
69/K4 **Nizhneudinsk,** Rus.
68/H3 **Nizhnevartovsk,** Rus.
67/G1 **Nizhniy Lomov,** Rus.
65/K4 **Nizhniy Novgorod** (Gor'kiy), Rus.
65/N4 **Nizhniy Tagil,** Rus.
74/D3 **Nizip,** Turk.
49/K4 **Nízke Tatry Nat'l Park,** Slvk.
101/B5 **Njombe,** Tanz.
99/H5 **Nkambe,** Camr.
104/B1 **Nkayi,** Congo
101/B3 **Nkhata Bay,** Malw.
99/H5 **Nkogam, Massif du** (peak), Camr.
99/H5 **N'Kongsamba,** Camr.
85/G2 **Nmai** (riv.), Burma
52/B5 **Noailles,** Fr.
84/F3 **Noākhāli,** Bang.
84/E3 **Noāmundi,** India
130/F2 **Noatak** (riv.), Ak,US
130/F2 **Noatak Nat'l Prsv.,** Ak,US
78/B4 **Nobeoka,** Japan
125/H4 **Noble,** Ok,US
126/C3 **Noblesville,** In,US
127/Q8 **Nobleton,** On,Can
77/N3 **Noboribetsu,** Japan
62/C5 **Noci,** It.
79/H7 **Noda,** Japan
52/B3 **Noeux-les-Mines,** Fr.
124/E5 **Nogales,** Az,US
56/D2 **Nogent-le-Rotrou,** Fr.
52/B5 **Nogent-sur-Oise,** Fr.
64/H5 **Noginsk,** Rus.
90/B4 **Nogoa** (riv.), Austl.
76/C2 **Nogoonuur,** Mong.
112/F2 **Nogoyá,** Arg.
49/K5 **Nógrád** (co.), Hun.
59/F1 **Noguera Pallarosa** (riv.), Sp.
80/E4 **Nogwak-san** (mtn.), SKor.
84/B2 **Nohar,** India
53/G4 **Nohfelden,** Ger.
126/E2 **Noire** (riv.), Qu,Can
56/B2 **Noires** (mts.), Fr.
56/B3 **Noirmoutier** (isl.), Fr.
52/B6 **Noisiel,** Fr.
52/B6 **Noisy-le-Sec,** Fr.
79/F3 **Nojima-zaki** (pt.), Japan
42/G3 **Nokia,** Fin.
87/F4 **Nokilalaki** (peak), Indo.
73/H3 **Nok Kundi,** Pak.
96/J7 **Nola,** CAfr.
91/D2 **Nomadgi Nat'l Park,** Austl.
130/F3 **Nome** (cape), Ak,US
78/B5 **Nomo-misaki** (cape), Japan
78/A4 **Nomo-zaki** (pt.), Japan
76/D2 **Nömrög,** Mong.
118/F2 **Nonacho** (lake), NW,Can
57/G4 **None,** It.
52/B5 **Nonette** (riv.), Fr.
81/F1 **Nong'an,** China
83/D2 **Nong Han** (res.), Thai.
83/C2 **Nong Het,** Laos
83/C2 **Nong Khai,** Thai.
83/C2 **Nong Pet,** Laos
53/F4 **Nonnweiler,** Ger.
92/G5 **Nonouti** (atoll), Kiri.
81/E5 **Nonri** (isl.), China
80/D4 **Nonsan,** SKor.
50/A5 **Noordbeveland** (isl.), Neth.
50/B3 **Noorderhaaks** (isl.), Neth.
50/B3 **Noordhollandsch** (can.), Neth.
50/C3 **Noordostpolder** (polder), Neth.
50/B4 **Noordwijk aan Zee,** Neth.
50/B4 **Noordwijkerhout,** Neth.
50/B4 **Noordzeekanaal** (can.), Neth.
90/D4 **Noosa-Tewantin,** Austl.
122/B3 **Nootka** (isl.), BC,Can
122/B3 **Nootka** (sound), BC,Can
116/B4 **Nopala,** Mex.
77/L1 **Nora** (riv.), Rus.
64/B4 **Nora,** Swe.
87/F2 **Norala,** Phil.
131/C3 **Norco,** Ca,US
127/M6 **Nord** (riv.), Qu,Can
52/C3 **Nord** (dept.), Fr.
52/B3 **Nord, Canal du** (can.), Fr.
51/E1 **Norden,** Ger.
51/F2 **Nordenham,** Ger.
68/K2 **Nordenskjöld** (arch.), Rus.
51/E1 **Norderney,** Ger.
51/E1 **Norderney** (isl.), Ger.
51/G1 **Norderstedt,** Ger.
48/F3 **Nordhausen,** Ger.
51/F1 **Nordholz,** Ger.
51/E4 **Nordhorn,** Ger.
42/H1 **Nordkapp** (North) (cape), Nor.
42/H1 **Nordkinn** (pt.), Nor.
51/E5 **Nordkirchen,** Ger.
42/E2 **Nordland** (co.), Nor.
42/F3 **Nordmaling,** Swe.
48/E1 **Nord-Ostsee** (can.), Ger.
99/H5 **Nord-Ouest** (prov.), Camr.
56/D1 **Nord-Pas-de-Calais** (reg.), Fr.
51/E3 **Nord-Radde** (riv.), Ger.
51/E3 **Nord-Sud** (can.), Ger.
42/E2 **Nord-Trøndelag** (co.), Nor.
51/E4 **Nordwalde,** Ger.
43/B4 **Nore** (riv.), Ire.
56/E5 **Nore, Pic de** (peak), Fr.
92/F7 **Norfolk** (isl.), Austl.
91/C4 **Norfolk** (peak), Austl.
47/G1 **Norfolk** (co.), Eng,UK
125/H2 **Norfolk,** Ne,US
126/E4 **Norfolk,** Va,US
47/H1 **Norfolk Broads** (swamp), Eng,UK
125/J3 **Norfork** (lake), Ar, Mo,US
50/D2 **Norg,** Neth.
79/E2 **Norikura-dake** (mtn.), Japan
68/J3 **Noril'sk,** Rus.
126/B3 **Normal,** Il,US
90/A2 **Norman** (riv.), Austl.
125/H4 **Norman,** Ok,US
92/E6 **Normanby** (isl.), PNG
132/C3 **Normandy Park,** Wa,US
45/G4 **Normanton,** Eng,UK
102/B3 **Norotshama** (peak), Namb.
123/H3 **Norquay,** Sk,Can
42/F2 **Norrbotten** (co.), Swe.
58/B1 **Norrea** (riv.), Sp.
52/B2 **Norrent-Fontes,** Fr.
132/Q16 **Norridge,** Il,US
129/H2 **Norris** (lake), Tn,US
131/E5 **Norristown,** Pa,US
42/F4 **Norrköping,** Swe.
42/F2 **Norrland** (reg.), Swe.
42/F4 **Norrtälje,** Swe.
112/E4 **Norte** (pt.), Arg.
113/F3 **Norte** (pt.), Arg.
108/G6 **Norte** (mts.), Braz.
109/J3 **Norte, Cabo do** (cape), Braz.
113/J6 **Norte, Campo de Hielo** (glacier), Chile
109/G6 **Nortelândia,** Braz.
51/G5 **Nörten-Hardenberg,** Ger.
91/C3 **North** (pt.), Austl.
91/C4 **North** (pt.), Austl.
126/D2 **North** (chan.), On,Can
127/J2 **North** (cape), PE,Can
41/E3 **North** (sea), Eur.
89/H6 **North** (cape), NZ
89/H6 **North** (isl.), NZ
44/C1 **North** (chan.), UK
130/D5 **North** (cape), Ak,US
130/F3 **North** (peak), Ak,US
62/D4 **North Albanian Alps** (mts.), Alb., Yugo.
45/G3 **Northallerton,** Eng,UK
89/A4 **Northam,** Austl.
46/B4 **Northam,** Eng,UK
115/* **North America**
47/F2 **Northampton,** Eng,UK
47/E2 **Northampton** (uplands), Eng,UK
126/F3 **Northampton,** Ma,US
131/E5 **Northampton,** Pa,US
47/F2 **Northamptonshire** (co.), Eng,UK
85/F5 **North Andaman** (isl.), India
119/K3 **North Aulatsivik** (isl.), Nf,Can
43/C2 **North Ballachulish,** Sc,UK
44/D3 **North Barrule** (mtn.), IM,UK
122/F2 **North Battleford,** Sk,Can
126/E2 **North Bay,** On,Can
122/B5 **North Bend,** Or,US
131/F5 **North Bergen,** NJ,US
43/D2 **North Berwick,** Sc,UK
50/C5 **North Brabant** (prov.), Neth.
132/Q15 **Northbrook,** Il,US
131/F5 **North Brunswick,** NJ,US
101/A2 **North Buganda** (prov.), Ugan.
125/H3 **North Canadian** (riv.), Ok,US
123/L2 **North Caribou** (lake), On,Can
129/H3 **North Carolina** (state), US
122/C3 **North Cascades Nat'l Park,** Wa,US
129/J3 **North Charleston,** SC,US
132/Q15 **North Chicago,** Il,US
45/H5 **North Collingham,** Eng,UK
122/C3 **North Cowichan,** BC,Can
123/H4 **North Dakota** (state), US
46/D5 **North Dorset Downs** (uplands), Eng,UK
44/C2 **North Down** (dist.), NI,UK
47/F4 **North Downs** (hills), Eng,UK
90/C3 **North East** (pt.), Austl.
117/G3 **Northeast** (pt.), Bahm.
130/E3 **Northeast** (cape), Ak,US
101/D2 **North Eastern** (prov.), Kenya
68/C2 **Northeast Land** (isl.), Sval.
51/G5 **Northeim,** Ger.
47/G1 **North Elmham,** Eng,UK
89/C2 **Northern** (terr.), Austl.
99/E4 **Northern** (reg.), Gha.
74/K5 **Northern** (dist.), Isr.
101/B5 **Northern** (reg.), Malw.
98/B4 **Northern** (prov.), SLeo.
100/B4 **Northern** (reg.), Sudan
101/B2 **Northern** (prov.), Ugan.
101/A5 **Northern** (prov.), Zam.
75/B4 **Northern Areas** (terr.), Pak.
102/C3 **Northern Cape** (prov.), SAfr.
93/J6 **Northern Cook** (isls.), CookIs.
41/J2 **Northern Dvina** (riv.), Rus.
43/B3 **Northern Ireland,** UK
126/B1 **Northern Light** (lake), On,Can, Mn,US
92/D3 **Northern Marianas,** US
68/G3 **Northern Sos'va** (riv.), Rus.
61/J3 **Northern Sporades** (isls.), Gre.
103/E6 **Northern Transvaal** (prov.), SAfr.
65/N3 **Northern Ural** (mts.), Rus.
65/K4 **Northern Uval** (hills), Rus.
68/E4 **Northern Wals** (upland), Rus.
130/K2 **Northern Yukon Nat'l Park,** Yk,Can
123/K4 **Northfield,** Mn,US
47/G4 **Northfleet,** Eng,UK
47/H4 **North Foreland** (pt.), Eng,UK
129/H5 **North Fort Myers,** Fl,US
126/D1 **North French** (riv.), On,Can
48/E1 **North Frisian** (isls.), Den., Ger.
127/F2 **North Hero,** Vt,US
132/M9 **North Highlands,** Ca,US
132/C3 **North Hill-Edgewood,** Wa,US
50/B3 **North Holland** (prov.), Neth.
45/H5 **North Hykeham,** Eng,UK
65/Q5 **North Kazakhstan Obl.,** Rus.
80/D2 **North Korea**
85/F2 **North Lakhimpur,** India
124/D3 **North Las Vegas,** Nv,US
128/E3 **North Little Rock,** Ar,US
101/B5 **North Luangwa Nat'l Park,** Zam.
119/R7 **North Magnetic Pole,** NAm

167

North – Orjen

123/J2 **North Moose** (lake), Mb,Can
129/J3 **North Myrtle Beach**, SC,US
42/H1 **North** (Nordkapp) (cape), Nor.
67/G4 **North Ossetian Aut. Rep.**, Rus.
127/R9 **North Pelham**, On,Can
46/C4 **North Petherton**, Eng,UK
90/E6 **North Pine** (riv.), Austl.
131/F5 **North Plainfield**, NJ,US
125/G2 **North Platte** (riv.), US
125/G2 **North Platte**, Ne,US
129/G3 **Northport**, Al,US
131/G5 **Northport** (Old Northport), NY,US
131/J7 **North Potomac**, Md,US
48/E3 **North Rhine-Westphalia** (state), Ger.
124/D3 **North Rim**, Az,US
122/F2 **North Saskatchewan** (riv.), Ab, Sk,Can
45/G2 **North Shields**, Eng,UK
68/K2 **North Siberian** (plain), Rus.
45/J5 **North Somercotes**, Eng,UK
90/D4 **North Stradbroke** (isl.), Austl.
131/G4 **North Tarrytown**, NY,US
45/H5 **North Thoresby**, Eng,UK
47/E4 **North Tidworth**, Eng,UK
127/S9 **North Tonawanda**, NY,US
45/F1 **North Tyne** (riv.), Eng,UK
127/J2 **Northumberland** (str.), Can.
45/F1 **Northumberland** (co.), Eng,UK
45/F1 **Northumberland Nat'l Park**, Eng,UK
124/B2 **North Umpqua** (riv.), Or,US
118/D4 **North Vancouver**, BC,Can
132/F7 **Northville**, Mi,US
47/H1 **North Walsham**, Eng,UK
89/A3 **North West** (cape), Austl.
102/D2 **North-West** (prov.), SAfr.
75/B4 **Northwest Frontier** (prov.), Pak.
127/L1 **North West Gander** (riv.), Nf,Can
43/C2 **North West Highlands** (mts.), Sc,UK
118/E2 **Northwest Territories** (terr.), Can.
45/H5 **North Wheatley**, Eng,UK
45/F5 **Northwich**, Eng,UK
45/G5 **North Wingfield**, Eng,UK
123/J4 **Northwood**, ND,US
127/R8 **North York**, On,Can
45/H3 **North York Moors Nat'l Park**, Eng,UK
45/G3 **North Yorkshire** (co.), Eng,UK
130/F3 **Norton** (bay), Ak,US
130/E3 **Norton** (sound), Ak,US
125/H3 **Norton**, Ks,US
126/D4 **Norton**, Va,US
45/F6 **Norton Bridge**, Eng,UK
126/C3 **Norton Shores**, Mi,US
48/E1 **Nortorf**, Ger.
127/Q8 **Norval**, On,Can
105/Z **Norvegia** (cape), Ant.
53/F2 **Nörvenich**, Ger.
131/B3 **Norwalk**, Ca,US
131/G4 **Norwalk**, Ct,US
126/D3 **Norwalk**, Oh,US
42/B3 **Norway**
123/J2 **Norway House**, Mb,Can
119/S7 **Norwegian** (bay), NW,Can
41/D2 **Norwegian** (sea), Eur.
47/H1 **Norwich**, Eng,UK
126/F3 **Norwich**, NY,US
79/L10 **Nose**, Japan
73/K1 **Noshaq** (mtn.), Pak.
77/N3 **Noshiro**, Japan
63/H4 **Nos Maslen Nos** (pt.), Bul.
86/E2 **Nosong** (cape), Malay.
102/C2 **Nosop** (dry riv.), Bots.
66/D2 **Nosovka**, Ukr.
73/G3 **Noşratābād**, Iran
113/J7 **Notch** (cape), Chile
49/J2 **Notec** (riv.), Pol.
60/D4 **Noto**, It.
60/D4 **Noto** (gulf), It.
79/E2 **Noto** (pen.), Japan
60/D4 **Noto Antica** (ruins), It.
79/M9 **Notogawa**, Japan
127/L1 **Notre Dame** (bay), Nf,Can
127/G1 **Notre Dame** (mts.), Qu,Can
127/N7 **Notre-Dame-de-l'Ile-Perrot**, Qu,Can
126/E1 **Nottaway** (riv.), Qu,Can
119/H2 **Nottingham** (isl.), NW,Can
45/G6 **Nottingham**, Eng,UK
45/H5 **Nottinghamshire** (co.), Eng,UK
51/E5 **Nottuln**, Ger.
96/B3 **Nouadhibou**, Mrta.
98/B2 **Nouakchott** (cap.), Mrta.
93/V13 **Nouméa** (cap.), NCal.
102/D3 **Noupoort**, SAfr.
52/A3 **Nouvion**, Fr.
53/D4 **Nouzonville**, Fr.
109/H8 **Nova Andradina**, Braz.
63/F3 **Novaci**, Rom.
109/L5 **Nova Cruz**, Braz.
49/K4 **Nová Dubnica**, Slvk.
110/L7 **Nova Friburgo**, Braz.
62/C3 **Nova Gradiška**, Cro.
110/K7 **Nova Iguaçu**, Braz.
108/G4 **Nova Olinda do Norte**, Braz.
62/E3 **Nova Pazova**, Yugo.
110/B4 **Nova Prata**, Braz.
57/H4 **Novara**, It.
55/E5 **Novara** (prov.), It.
127/J2 **Nova Scotia** (prov.), Can.
132/J10 **Novato**, Ca,US
62/D4 **Nova Varoš**, Yugo.
110/D1 **Nova Venécia**, Braz.
109/H6 **Nova Xavantina**, Braz.
66/E3 **Novaya Kakhovka**, Ukr.
69/R2 **Novaya Sibir'** (isl.), Rus.
68/E2 **Novaya Zemlya** (isl.), Rus.
63/H4 **Nova Zagora**, Bul.
59/E3 **Novelda**, Sp.
49/J4 **Nové Mesto nad Váhom**, Slvk.
49/K5 **Nové Zámky**, Slvk.
64/F4 **Novgorod**, Rus.
64/G4 **Novgorod Obl.**, Rus.
132/F7 **Novi**, Mi,US
62/E3 **Novi Bečej**, Yugo.
63/F4 **Novi Iskŭr**, Bul.
57/H4 **Novi Ligure**, It.
63/H4 **Novi Pazar**, Bul.
62/E4 **Novi Pazar**, Yugo.
62/D3 **Novi Sad**, Yugo.
110/K6 **Novo** (riv.), Braz.
67/G2 **Novoanninskiy**, Rus.
108/F5 **Novo Aripuanã**, Braz.
65/K4 **Novocheboksarsk**, Rus.
66/G3 **Novocherkassk**, Rus.
66/C2 **Novograd-Volynskiy**, Ukr.
64/E5 **Novogrudok**, Bela.
110/B4 **Novo Hamburgo**, Braz.
110/B2 **Novo Horizonte**, Braz.
68/G5 **Novokazalinsk**, Kaz.
67/J1 **Novokuybyshevsk**, Rus.
68/J4 **Novokuznetsk**, Rus.
105/A **Novolazarevskaya**, Ant.
62/B3 **Novo Mesto**, Slov.
62/E3 **Novo Miloševo**, Yugo.
66/F1 **Novomoskovsk**, Rus.
66/E3 **Novomoskovsk**, Ukr.
64/F5 **Novopolotsk**, Bela.
66/F3 **Novorossiysk**, Rus.
66/F3 **Novoshakhtinsk**, Rus.
68/J4 **Novosibirsk**, Rus.
67/L2 **Novotroitsk**, Rus.
66/D2 **Novoukrainka**, Ukr.
66/C2 **Novovolynsk**, Ukr.
65/L4 **Novovyatsk**, Rus.
66/D1 **Novozybkov**, Rus.
62/C3 **Novska**, Cro.
49/K4 **Nový Jičín**, Czh.
67/K4 **Novyy Uzen'**, Kaz.
49/L3 **Nowa Dęba**, Pol.
49/J3 **Nowa Ruda**, Pol.
49/M3 **Nowa Sarzyna**, Pol.
49/H3 **Nowa Sól**, Pol.
125/J3 **Nowata**, Ok,US
49/K2 **Nowe**, Pol.
49/K2 **Nowe Miasto Lubawskie**, Pol.
84/C2 **Nowgong**, India
85/F2 **Nowgong**, India
130/H3 **Nowitna** (riv.), Ak,US
130/H3 **Nowitna Nat'l Wild. Ref.**, Ak,US
49/H2 **Nowogard**, Pol.
124/F1 **Nowood** (riv.), Wy,US
73/K2 **Nowshera**, Pak.
49/K1 **Nowy Dwór Gdański**, Pol.
49/L4 **Nowy Sącz**, Pol.
49/L4 **Nowy Sącz** (prov.), Pol.
49/L4 **Nowy Targ**, Pol.
49/J2 **Nowy Tomyśl**, Pol.
58/A1 **Noya**, Sp.
52/B5 **Noye** (riv.), Fr.
52/C4 **Noyon**, Fr.
104/G4 **Nsanje**, Malw.
99/E5 **Nsawam**, Gha.
76/D5 **Nu** (riv.), China
97/M5 **Nūbah** (mts.), Sudan
100/C4 **Nubian** (des.), Sudan
124/E3 **Nucla**, Co,US
128/D4 **Nueces** (riv.), Tx,US
118/G2 **Nueltin** (lake), NW,Can
50/C6 **Nuenen**, Neth.
81/E2 **Nü'er** (riv.), China
116/C5 **Nueva Concepción**, Guat.
116/E3 **Nueva Gerona**, Cuba
113/F2 **Nueva Helvecia**, Uru.
112/B3 **Nueva Imperial**, Chile
108/C3 **Nueva Loja**, Ecu.
113/S11 **Nueva Palmira**, Uru.
116/A2 **Nueva Rosita**, Mex.
117/F3 **Nuevitas**, Cuba
112/D4 **Nuevo** (gulf), Arg.
117/N7 **Nuevo Casas Grandes**, Mex.
117/N9 **Nuevo Ideal**, Mex.
116/B2 **Nuevo Laredo**, Mex.
116/A2 **Nuevo León** (state), Mex.
113/S11 **Nuevo Palmira**, Uru.
92/E5 **Nuguria** (isls.), PNG
93/J2 **Nuhau** (isl.), Hi,US
51/F6 **Nuhne** (riv.), Ger.
92/G5 **Nui** (atoll), Tuv.
79/N10 **Nukata**, Japan
130/F4 **Nuklunek** (mtn.), Ak,US
93/H7 **Nuku'alofa** (cap.), Tonga
92/G5 **Nukufetau** (atoll), Tuv.
93/L5 **Nuku Hiva** (isl.), FrPol.
92/H5 **Nukulaelae** (isl.), Tuv.
92/F5 **Nukumanu** (atoll), PNG
93/H5 **Nukunonu** (atoll), Tok.
92/E4 **Nukuoro** (isl.), Micr.
68/F5 **Nukus**, Uzb.
93/M6 **Nukutavake** (isl.), FrPol.
59/E3 **Nules**, Sp.
92/B8 **Nullarbor** (plain), Austl.
96/H6 **Numan**, Nga.
50/B5 **Numansdorp**, Neth.
79/F2 **Numata**, Japan
79/F3 **Numazu**, Japan
53/G2 **Nümbrecht**, Ger.
87/H4 **Numfoor** (isl.), Indo.
91/G5 **Nunawading**, Austl.
47/E1 **Nuneaton**, Eng,UK
91/D3 **Nungatta Nat'l Park**, Austl.
130/E4 **Nunivak** (isl.), Ak,US
50/C4 **Nunspeet**, Neth.
45/G2 **Nunthorpe**, Eng,UK
77/J1 **Nuomin** (riv.), China
98/C5 **Nuon** (riv.), IvC., Libr.
60/A2 **Nuoro**, It.
75/B2 **Nura** (riv.), Kaz.
53/F3 **Nürburgring**, Ger.
74/D3 **Nurhak**, Turk.
100/B5 **Nuri** (ruins), Sudan
57/J2 **Nürnberg**, Ger.
91/C1 **Nurri** (peak), Austl.
57/H2 **Nürtingen**, Ger.
74/L4 **Nuşari'yah, Jabal an** (mts.), Syria
74/E3 **Nusaybin**, Turk.
130/G4 **Nushagak** (riv.), Ak,US
73/J3 **Nushki**, Pak.
53/E2 **Nuth**, Neth.
131/F5 **Nutley**, NJ,US
115/M3 **Nuuk** (Godthåb), Grld.
93/X15 **Nuupere** (pt.), FrPol.
100/C2 **Nuwaybi'**, Egypt
102/L10 **Nuy** (riv.), SAfr.
104/E4 **Nxai Pan Nat'l Park**, Bots.
131/G4 **Nyack**, NY,US
101/B4 **Nyahua**, Tanz.
75/F5 **Nyainqêntanglha Feng** (peak), China
97/K5 **Nyala**, Sudan
97/L6 **Nyamlell**, Sudan
64/J3 **Nyandoma**, Rus.
101/B3 **Nyanza** (prov.), Kenya
101/A4 **Nyanza-Lac**, Buru.
101/B5 **Nyasa** (Malawi) (lake), Afr.
48/F1 **Nyborg**, Den.
42/E4 **Nybro**, Swe.
49/L5 **Nyíradony**, Hun.
62/F2 **Nyírbátor**, Hun.
62/E2 **Nyíregyháza**, Hun.
101/C2 **Nyiru** (peak), Kenya
48/F1 **Nykøbing**, Den.
42/F4 **Nyköping**, Swe.
102/E2 **Nylstroom**, SAfr.
42/F4 **Nynäshamn**, Swe.
54/C5 **Nyon**, Swi.
57/K2 **Nýřany**, Czh.
49/J3 **Nysa**, Pol.
122/D5 **Nyssa**, Or,US
77/M4 **Nyūdo-zaki** (pt.), Japan
64/F2 **Nyuk** (lake), Rus.
104/E2 **Nyunzu**, Zaire
79/E2 **Nyūzen**, Japan
98/C5 **Nzérékoré**, Gui.
98/C4 **Nzérékoré** (comm.), Gui.
98/D5 **Nzi** (riv.), IvC.

O

47/E1 **Oadby**, Eng,UK
123/H4 **Oahe** (lake), ND, SD,US
120/V13 **Oahu** (isl.), Hi,US
123/J3 **Oakbank**, Mb,Can
132/Q14 **Oak Creek**, Wi,US
123/J4 **Oakes**, ND,US
132/Q16 **Oak Forest**, Il,US
47/F1 **Oakham**, Eng,UK
126/D4 **Oak Hill**, WV,US
124/C3 **Oakhurst**, Ca,US
132/K11 **Oakland**, Ca,US
131/F4 **Oakland**, NJ,US
132/A3 **Oakland** (bay), Wa,US
132/Q16 **Oak Lawn**, Il,US
47/E3 **Oakley**, Eng,UK
47/F2 **Oakley**, Eng,UK
132/L11 **Oakley**, Ca,US
125/G3 **Oakley**, Ks,US
132/Q16 **Oak Park**, Il,US
132/F7 **Oak Park**, Mi,US
122/C5 **Oakridge**, Or,US
126/C4 **Oak Ridge**, Tn,US
127/R8 **Oak Ridges**, On,Can
46/D3 **Oaksey**, Eng,UK
131/A2 **Oak View**, Ca,US
127/Q9 **Oakville**, On,Can
89/H7 **Oamaru**, NZ
116/B4 **Oaxaca**, Mex.
116/B4 **Oaxaca** (state), Mex.
68/H3 **Ob'** (gulf), Rus.
68/G3 **Ob'** (riv.), Rus.
92/F6 **Oba** (isl.), Van.
126/D2 **Obabika** (lake), On,Can
78/D3 **Obama**, Japan
99/H5 **Oban** (hills), Camr., Nga.
89/G7 **Oban**, NZ
126/D1 **Obasatika** (riv.), On,Can
79/M10 **Obata**, Japan
111/E2 **Oberá**, Arg.
50/D6 **Oberhausen**, Ger.
49/H3 **Oberlausitz** (reg.), Ger.
125/G3 **Oberlin**, Ks,US
55/E1 **Oberndorf am Neckar**, Ger.
51/G4 **Obernkirchen**, Ger.
53/G4 **Oberthal**, Ger.
57/L3 **Oberwölz**, Aus.
87/G4 **Obi** (isls.), Indo.
87/G4 **Obi** (str.), Indo.
109/G4 **Óbidos**, Braz.
77/N3 **Obihiro**, Japan
62/E4 **Obilić**, Yugo.
79/J7 **Obitsu** (riv.), Japan
83/B2 **Ob Luang Gorge**, Thai.
77/L2 **Obluch'ye**, Rus.
64/H5 **Obninsk**, Rus.
97/P5 **Obock**, Djib.
49/J2 **Oborniki**, Pol.
49/J3 **Oborniki Śląskie**, Pol.
49/J2 **Obra** (riv.), Pol.
62/E3 **Obrenovac**, Yugo.
79/M10 **Ōbu**, Japan
99/E5 **Obuasi**, Gha.
55/E4 **Obwalden** (canton), Swi.
129/H4 **Ocala**, Fl,US
56/C5 **Occabe, Sommet d'** (peak), Fr.
108/E7 **Occidental, Cordillera** (range), SAm.
130/L4 **Ocean** (cape), Ak,US
131/G5 **Ocean Beach**, NY,US
126/F4 **Ocean City**, Md,US
122/B2 **Ocean Falls**, BC,Can
131/F5 **Ocean Grove**, NJ,US
92/* **Oceania**
124/C4 **Oceanside**, Ca,US
131/G5 **Oceanside**, NY,US
83/D4 **Oc-Eo** (ruins), Viet.
67/G4 **Ochamchira**, Geo.
77/P3 **Ochiishi-misaki** (cape), Japan
117/F4 **Ocho Rios**, Jam.
51/E4 **Ochtrup**, Ger.
51/F2 **Ochtum** (riv.), Ger.
47/E3 **Ock** (riv.), Eng,UK
64/C3 **Ockelbo**, Swe.
129/H4 **Ocmulgee** (riv.), Ga,US
63/F2 **Ocna Mureş**, Rom.
129/H3 **Oconee** (lake), Ga,US
129/H3 **Oconee** (riv.), Ga,US
116/D5 **Ocotal**, Nic.
116/A3 **Ocotlán**, Mex.
116/B4 **Ocotlán**, Mex.
56/C2 **Octeville**, Fr.
69/L1 **October Revolution** (isl.), Rus.
99/E5 **Oda**, Gha.
78/C3 **Oda**, Japan
79/M10 **Ōdai**, Japan
78/E3 **Ōdaigahara-san** (mtn.), Japan
100/D4 **Oda, Jabal** (peak), Sudan
77/N3 **Ōdate**, Japan
79/F3 **Odawara**, Japan
42/C3 **Odda**, Nor.
97/P7 **Oddur**, Som.
51/F6 **Odeborn** (riv.), Ger.
48/A4 **Odemira**, Port.
74/A2 **Ödemiş**, Turk.
102/D2 **Odendaalsrus**, SAfr.
48/F1 **Odense**, Den.
51/E6 **Odenthal**, Ger.
131/K7 **Odenton**, Md,US
49/H2 **Oderhaff** (lag.), Ger., Pol.
49/H2 **Oder** (Odra) (riv.), Ger., Pol.
57/K4 **Oderzo**, It.
66/D3 **Odessa**, Ukr.
128/C4 **Odessa**, Tx,US
122/D4 **Odessa**, Wa,US
63/J2 **Odessa Obl.**, Ukr.
56/B2 **Odet** (riv.), Fr.
98/D4 **Odienné**, IvC.
64/H5 **Odintsovo**, Rus.
82/D5 **Odiongan**, Phil.
59/P10 **Odivelas**, Port.
63/H3 **Odobeşti**, Rom.
56/C2 **Odon** (riv.), Fr.
83/D4 **Odongk**, Camb.
50/D3 **Odoorn**, Neth.
63/G2 **Odorheiu Secuiesc**, Rom.
49/H2 **Odra** (Oder) (riv.), Ger., Pol.
62/D3 **Odžaci**, Yugo.
96/J7 **Odzala Nat'l Park**, Congo
79/L9 **Ōe**, Japan
50/B4 **Oegstgeest**, Neth.
109/K5 **Oeiras**, Braz.
51/F5 **Oelde**, Ger.
57/K1 **Oelsnitz**, Ger.
93/M7 **Oeno** (atoll), Pitc.,UK
51/E5 **Oer-Erkenschwick**, Ger.
53/E4 **Oesling** (mts.), Lux.
50/B6 **Oesterdam** (dam), Neth.
57/H2 **Oestrich-Winkel**, Ger.
61/H3 **Oeta Nat'l Park**, Gre.
74/E2 **Of**, Turk.
60/D2 **Ofanto** (riv.), It.
74/K6 **Ofaqim**, Isr.
44/A5 **Offaly** (co.), Ire.
57/H1 **Offenbach**, Ger.
54/D1 **Offenburg**, Ger.
57/G3 **Oftringen**, Swi.
77/M4 **Oga**, Japan
97/P6 **Ogadēn** (reg.), Eth.
78/E3 **Ōgaki**, Japan
125/G2 **Ogallala**, Ne,US
92/D2 **Ogasawara**, Japan
99/G4 **Ogbomosho**, Nga.
124/E2 **Ogden**, Ut,US
126/F2 **Ogdensburg**, NY,US
129/H3 **Ogeechee** (riv.), Ga,US
126/D2 **Ogidaki** (mtn.), On,Can
130/L3 **Ogilvie** (mts.), Yk,Can
118/C2 **Ogilvie** (riv.), Yk,Can
57/J4 **Oglio** (riv.), It.
46/C4 **Ogmore by Sea**, Wal,UK
54/B3 **Ognon** (riv.), Fr.
87/F3 **Ogoamas** (peak), Indo.
123/M3 **Ogoki**, On,Can
123/L3 **Ogoki** (res.), On,Can
123/M3 **Ogoki** (riv.), On,Can
96/G8 **Ogooué** (riv.), Gabon
79/H7 **Ogose**, Japan
63/F4 **Ogosta** (riv.), Bul.
64/E4 **Ogre**, Lat.
79/M9 **Oguchi**, Japan
62/B3 **Ogulin**, Cro.
99/F5 **Ogun** (riv.), Nga.
99/F5 **Ogun** (state), Nga.
67/K5 **Ogurchinskiy** (isl.), Trkm.
96/G2 **Ohanet**, Alg.
90/G8 **O'Hares** (cr.), Austl.
74/E1 **Ohe** (riv.), Ger.
113/J7 **O'Higgins** (lake), Chile
126/B4 **Ohio** (riv.), US
126/D3 **Ohio** (state), US
45/F1 **Oh Me Edge** (hill), Eng,UK
129/H3 **Ohoopee** (riv.), Ga,US
57/K1 **Ohře** (riv.), Czh.
48/F2 **Ohre** (riv.), Ger.
62/E5 **Ohrid** (lake), Alb., Macd.
62/E5 **Ohrid**, Macd.
85/G2 **Oi** (riv.), China
79/H7 **Ōi**, Japan
79/F3 **Ōi** (riv.), Japan
109/H3 **Oiapoque** (riv.), Braz.
59/P10 **Oieras**, Port.
53/D5 **Oignies**, Fr.
126/E3 **Oil City**, Pa,US
50/C5 **Oirschot**, Neth.
52/B5 **Oise** (dept.), Fr.
52/B5 **Oise** (riv.), Fr.
52/C5 **Oise à l'Aisne, Canal de** (can.), Fr.
52/A4 **Oisemont**, Fr.
79/H7 **Ōiso**, Japan
50/C5 **Oisterwijk**, Neth.
52/C3 **Oisy-le-Verger**, Fr.
78/B4 **Ōita**, Japan
78/B4 **Ōita** (pref.), Japan
78/B4 **Ōita** (riv.), Japan
131/A2 **Ojai**, Ca,US
49/K3 **Ojcowski Nat'l Park**, Pol.
79/L10 **Ōji**, Japan
117/P8 **Ojinaga**, Mex.
79/F2 **Ojiya**, Japan
116/A3 **Ojocaliente**, Mex.
111/C2 **Ojos del Salado** (peak), Arg., Chile
117/L7 **Ojos Negros**, Mex.
65/J4 **Oka** (riv.), Rus.
119/K3 **Okak** (isl.), Nf,Can
122/C3 **Okanagan** (lake), BC,Can
122/D3 **Okanagan Falls**, BC,Can
104/B1 **Okanda Nat'l Park**, Gabon
122/D3 **Okanogan**, Wa,US
122/D3 **Okanogan** (riv.), Wa,US
73/K2 **Okāra**, Pak.
104/C4 **Okaukuejo**, Namb.
104/D4 **Okavango Delta** (reg.), Bots.
78/B4 **Ōkawa**, Japan
79/F2 **Okaya**, Japan
78/C3 **Okayama**, Japan
78/C3 **Okayama** (pref.), Japan
79/E3 **Okazaki**, Japan
129/H5 **Okeechobee**, Fl,US
129/H5 **Okeechobee** (lake), Fl,US
79/H7 **Okegawa**, Japan
46/C5 **Okehampton**, Eng,UK
46/B5 **Okement** (riv.), Eng,UK
51/H4 **Oker** (riv.), Ger.
69/Q4 **Okha**, Rus.
61/J3 **Ókhi** (peak), Gre.
69/Q4 **Okhotsk** (sea), Japan, Rus.
78/C2 **Oki** (isls.), Japan
78/C2 **Oki-Daisen Nat'l Park**, Japan
82/E2 **Okinawa** (isls.), Japan
92/C2 **Okino-Tori-Shima** (Parece Vela) (isl.), Japan
85/G4 **Okkan**, Burma
125/H4 **Oklahoma** (state), US
125/H4 **Oklahoma City** (cap.), Ok,US
129/H4 **Oklawaha** (riv.), Fl,US
125/J4 **Okmulgee**, Ok,US
123/K5 **Okoboji** (lakes), Ia,US
129/F3 **Okolona**, Ms,US
122/E3 **Okotoks**, Ab,Can
100/C4 **Oko, Wādī** (dry riv.), Sudan
42/E2 **Oksskolten** (peak), Nor.
67/J1 **Oktyabr'sk**, Rus.
65/M5 **Oktyabr'skiy**, Rus.
64/G4 **Okulovka**, Rus.
77/M3 **Okushiri** (isl.), Japan
79/H7 **Okutama**, Japan
104/D5 **Okwa** (riv.), Bots.
124/C3 **Olancha**, Ca,US
116/D4 **Olanchito**, Hon.
42/F4 **Öland** (isl.), Swe.
42/F4 **Ölands södra udde** (pt.), Swe.
57/G4 **Olan, Pic d'** (peak), Fr.
60/D2 **Olanto** (riv.), It.
124/F3 **Olathe**, Co,US
125/J3 **Olathe**, Ks,US
112/E3 **Olavarría**, Arg.
49/J3 **Oława**, Pol.
51/F5 **Ölbach** (riv.), Ger.
60/A2 **Olbia**, It.
55/H1 **Olching**, Ger.
127/S9 **Olcott**, NY,US
132/D3 **Old Baldy** (mtn.), Wa,US
131/F5 **Old Bridge**, NJ,US
130/L2 **Old Crow**, Yk,Can
50/C4 **Oldebroek**, Neth.
51/F2 **Oldenburg**, Ger.
50/D4 **Oldenzaal**, Neth.
45/F4 **Oldham**, Eng,UK
122/E3 **Oldman** (riv.), Ab,Can
44/E3 **Old Man of Coolston, The** (mtn.), Eng,UK
47/F2 **Old Nene** (riv.), Eng,UK
131/G5 **Old Northport** (Northport), NY,US
51/F1 **Oldoog** (isl.), Ger.
127/G2 **Old Town**, Me,US
47/F4 **Old Windsor**, Eng,UK
123/G3 **Old Wives** (lake), Sk,Can
126/E3 **Olean**, NY,US
49/M1 **Olecko**, Pol.
58/A1 **Oleiros**, Sp.
69/N4 **Olekma** (riv.), Rus.
132/B2 **Olele** (pt.), Wa,US
64/G1 **Olenegorsk**, Rus.
69/N2 **Olenek** (bay), Rus.
69/N2 **Olenëk** (riv.), Rus.
75/B1 **Olenty** (riv.), Kaz.
56/C4 **Oléron** (isl.), Fr.
59/K6 **Olesa de Montserrat**, Sp.
49/J3 **Oleśnica**, Pol.
49/K3 **Olesno**, Pol.
51/E5 **Olfen**, Ger.
76/B2 **Ölgiy**, Mong.
58/B4 **Olhão**, Port.
57/L4 **Olib** (isl.), Cro.
60/A2 **Oliena**, It.
102/B2 **Olifants** (dry riv.), Namb.
102/B3 **Olifants** (riv.), SAfr.
102/E2 **Olifantsrivier** (riv.), SAfr.
92/D4 **Olimarao** (atoll), Micr.
61/H2 **Ólimbos** (Mount Olympus) (peak), Gre.
110/B2 **Olímpia**, Braz.
109/M5 **Olinda**, Braz.
112/E2 **Oliva**, Arg.
59/E3 **Oliva**, Sp.
58/B3 **Oliva de la Frontera**, Sp.
58/A3 **Olivais**, Port.
110/C2 **Oliveira**, Braz.
58/B3 **Olivenza**, Sp.
122/D3 **Oliver**, BC,Can
56/D3 **Olivet**, Fr.
108/E8 **Ollagüe** (vol.), Bol.
59/E3 **Olleria**, Sp.
84/C5 **Ollūr**, India
112/Q9 **Olmué**, Chile
47/F2 **Olney**, Eng,UK
126/B4 **Olney**, Il,US
131/J7 **Olney**, Md,US
127/J1 **Olomane** (riv.), Qu,Can
49/J4 **Olomouc**, Czh.
82/D5 **Olongapo**, Phil.
56/C3 **Olonne-sur-Mer**, Fr.
56/C5 **Oloron-Sainte-Marie**, Fr.
59/G1 **Olot**, Sp.
69/S3 **Oloy** (range), Rus.
51/E6 **Olpe**, Ger.
51/F6 **Olsberg**, Ger.
50/D4 **Olst**, Neth.
49/L2 **Olsztyn**, Pol.
49/L2 **Olsztyn** (prov.), Pol.
49/L2 **Olsztynek**, Pol.
63/G3 **Olt** (co.), Rom.
63/G4 **Olt** (riv.), Rom.
112/C4 **Olte** (mts.), Arg.
54/D3 **Olten**, Swi.
63/H3 **Olteniţa**, Rom.
63/F3 **Olteţ** (riv.), Rom.
74/E2 **Oltu**, Turk.
74/E2 **Oltu** (riv.), Turk.
82/D3 **Oluanpi**, Tai.
58/C4 **Olvera**, Sp.
132/B3 **Olympia** (cap.), Wa,US
61/G4 **Olympia** (Olimbía) (ruins), Gre.
122/B4 **Olympic** (mts.), Wa,US
122/B4 **Olympic Nat'l Park**, Wa,US
74/J4 **Olympus** (mtn.), Cyp.
122/C4 **Olympus** (peak), Wa,US
61/H2 **Olympus, Mount** (Ólimbos) (peak), Gre.
61/H2 **Olympus Nat'l Park**, Gre.
69/S3 **Olyutorskiy** (bay), Rus.
65/K2 **Oma** (riv.), Rus.
79/E2 **Ōmachi**, Japan
79/F3 **Omae-zaki** (pt.), Japan
44/A2 **Omagh**, NI,UK
44/A2 **Omagh** (dist.), NI,UK
125/J2 **Omaha**, Ne,US
122/D3 **Omak**, Wa,US
73/G4 **Oman**
73/G4 **Oman** (gulf), Asia
104/C4 **Omatako** (riv.), Namb.
87/F5 **Ombai** (str.), Indo.
46/D2 **Ombersley**, Eng,UK
104/B4 **Ombombo**, Namb.
104/A1 **Omboué**, Gabon
60/B1 **Ombrone** (riv.), It.
97/M4 **Omdurman** (Umm Durmān), Sudan
79/H7 **Ōme**, Japan
57/H4 **Omegna**, It.
116/B4 **Ometepec**, Mex.
79/M9 **Ōmihachiman**, Japan
60/E1 **Omiš**, Cro.
79/G2 **Ōmiya**, Japan
130/M4 **Ommaney** (cape), Ak,US
50/D3 **Ommen**, Neth.
76/F2 **Ömnödelger**, Mong.
76/C2 **Ömnögovĭ**, Mong.
60/A2 **Omodeo** (lake), It.
71/Q3 **Omolon** (riv.), Rus.
97/N6 **Omo Nat'l Park**, Eth.
97/N6 **Omo Wenz** (riv.), Eth.
68/H4 **Omsk**, Rus.
63/G3 **Omul** (peak), Rom.
63/H4 **Omurtag**, Bul.
78/B4 **Ōmuta**, Japan
65/M4 **Omutninsk**, Rus.
79/G1 **Onagawa**, Japan
125/J5 **Onalaska**, Tx,US
58/D1 **Oñate**, Sp.
126/C2 **Onaway**, Mi,US
112/E1 **Oncativo**, Arg.
44/D3 **Onchan**, IM,UK
104/B4 **Oncócua**, Ang.
59/E3 **Onda**, Sp.
104/C4 **Ondangua**, Namb.
49/L4 **Ondava** (riv.), Slvk.
104/C4 **Ondjiva**, Ang.
99/G5 **Ondo** (state), Nga.
76/G2 **Öndörhaan**, Mong.
76/C2 **Öndorhangay**, Mong.
64/H3 **Onega**, Rus.
64/H2 **Onega** (bay), Rus.
64/G3 **Onega** (lake), Rus.
64/H2 **Onega** (pen.), Rus.
64/H3 **Onega** (riv.), Rus.
122/C3 **One Hundred Mile House**, BC,Can
126/F3 **Oneida**, NY,US
125/H2 **O'Neill**, Ne,US
126/F3 **Oneonta**, NY,US
76/E2 **Ongiyn** (riv.), Mong.
84/D4 **Ongole**, India
123/H4 **Onida**, SD,US
59/E3 **Onil**, Sp.
103/G8 **Onilahy** (riv.), Madg.
99/G5 **Onitsha**, Nga.
103/H7 **Onive** (riv.), Madg.
52/C3 **Onnaing**, Fr.
46/D2 **Onny** (riv.), Eng,UK
78/D3 **Ono**, Japan
78/E3 **Ōno**, Japan
78/B4 **Onoda**, Japan
78/C3 **Onomichi**, Japan
76/G1 **Onon** (riv.), Mong., Rus.
92/G5 **Onotoa** (atoll), Kiri.
79/E3 **Ontake-san** (mtn.), Japan
118/H3 **Ontario** (prov.), Can.
126/E3 **Ontario** (lake), Can., US
131/C2 **Ontario**, Ca,US
122/D4 **Ontario**, Or,US
59/E3 **Onteniente**, Sp.
126/B2 **Ontonagon**, Mi,US
92/F5 **Ontong Java** (isl.), Sol.
128/E2 **Oologan** (lake), Ok,US
50/A6 **Oostburg**, Neth.
50/C4 **Oostelijk Flevoland** (polder), Neth.
52/B1 **Oostende**, Belg.
50/B5 **Oosterhout**, Neth.
50/A5 **Oosterschelde** (chan.), Neth.
52/C2 **Oosterzele**, Belg.
52/C1 **Oostkamp**, Belg.
50/C4 **Oostvaarderplassen** (lake), Neth.
50/B4 **Oostzaan**, Neth.
84/C5 **Ootacamund**, India
123/B2 **Ootsa** (lake), BC,Can
104/D1 **Opala**, Zaire
49/J2 **Opalenica**, Pol.
62/B3 **Opatija**, Cro.
49/L3 **Opatów**, Pol.
49/J4 **Opava**, Czh.
129/G3 **Opelika**, Al,US
128/E4 **Opelousas**, La,US
126/E2 **Opeongo** (lake), On,Can
53/E1 **Opglabbeek**, Belg.
50/C5 **Oploo**, Neth.
50/B3 **Opmeer**, Neth.
49/L3 **Opoczno**, Pol.
49/J3 **Opole**, Pol.
49/J3 **Opole** (prov.), Pol.
49/L3 **Opole Lubelskie**, Pol.
129/G4 **Opp**, Al,US
42/D3 **Oppdal**, Nor.
42/D3 **Oppland** (co.), Nor.
122/D4 **Opportunity**, Wa,US
52/D2 **Opwijk**, Belg.
62/E2 **Oradea**, Rom.
62/E4 **Orahovac**, Yugo.
84/C2 **Orai**, India
96/E1 **Oran**, Alg.
102/B3 **Orange** (riv.), Afr.
91/D2 **Orange**, Austl.
56/F4 **Orange**, Fr.
109/H3 **Orange** (mts.), Sur.
131/C3 **Orange**, Ca,US
131/F5 **Orange**, NJ,US
128/E4 **Orange**, Tx,US
126/E4 **Orange**, Va,US
129/H3 **Orangeburg**, SC,US
102/D3 **Orange Free State** (prov.), SAfr.
129/H4 **Orange Park**, Fl,US
126/D3 **Orangeville**, On,Can
116/D4 **Orange Walk**, Belz.
98/A4 **Orango** (isl.), GBis.
49/G2 **Oranienburg**, Ger.
50/D3 **Oranjekanaal** (can.), Neth.
117/G5 **Oranjestad** (cap.), Aru.
104/E5 **Orapa**, Bots.
74/M8 **Or 'Aqiva**, Isr.
82/E5 **Oras**, Phil.
63/F3 **Orăştie**, Rom.
62/E3 **Oravița**, Rom.
56/E5 **Orb** (riv.), Fr.
58/C1 **Orbigo** (riv.), Sp.
128/B2 **Orchard City**, Co,US
122/E4 **Orchard Homes**, Mt,US
132/F6 **Orchard Lake Village**, Mi,US
82/D3 **Orchid** (isl.), Tai.
57/G4 **Orco** (riv.), It.
56/F3 **Or, Côte d'** (uplands), Fr.
125/H2 **Ord**, Ne,US
58/A1 **Ordenes**, Sp.
59/F1 **Ordesa y Monte Perdido Nat'l Park**, Sp.
81/B3 **Ordos** (des.), China
74/D2 **Ordu**, Turk.
125/G3 **Ordway**, Co,US
42/E4 **Örebro**, Swe.
42/E4 **Örebro** (co.), Swe.
122/C4 **Oregon** (state), US
124/B2 **Oregon Caves Nat'l Mon.**, Or,US
122/C4 **Oregon City**, Or,US
66/F1 **Orël**, Rus.
66/E2 **Orel'** (riv.), Ukr.
66/E1 **Orel Obl.**, Rus.
124/E2 **Orem**, Ut,US
67/K2 **Orenburg**, Rus.
67/K1 **Orenburg Obl.**, Rus.
58/B1 **Orense**, Sp.
61/K2 **Orestiás**, Gre.
47/H2 **Orford**, Eng,UK
47/H2 **Orford Ness** (pt.), UK
124/D4 **Organ Pipe Cactus Nat'l Mon.**, Az,US
110/L7 **Órgãos** (mts.), Braz.
63/J2 **Orgeyev**, Mol.
66/D5 **Orhaneli**, Turk.
63/J5 **Orhangazi**, Turk.
76/F2 **Orhon** (riv.), Mong.
56/C5 **Orhy, Pic d'** (peak), Fr.
111/C6 **Oriental** (val.), Arg.
108/D6 **Oriental, Cordillera** (range), SAm.
59/E3 **Orihuela**, Sp.
126/E2 **Orillia**, On,Can
132/K11 **Orinda**, Ca,US
108/F2 **Orinoco** (riv.), Col., Ven.
117/J6 **Orinoco** (delta), Ven.
126/C3 **Orion** (lake), Mi,US
84/D3 **Orissa** (state), India
60/A3 **Oristano**, It.
60/A3 **Oristano** (gulf), It.
42/H3 **Orivesi**, Fin.
109/G4 **Oriximiná**, Braz.
116/B4 **Orizaba**, Mex.
62/D4 **Orjen** (peak), Yugo.

51/F6 **Orke** (riv.), Ger.
41/D3 **Orkney** (isls.), Sc,UK
128/C4 **Orla,** Tx,US
110/C2 **Orlândia,** Braz.
129/H4 **Orlando,** Fl,US
60/D3 **Orlando, Capo d'** (cape), It.
132/Q16 **Orland Park,** Il,US
56/D2 **Orléanais** (hist. reg.), Fr.
56/D3 **Orléans,** Fr.
124/B2 **Orleans,** Ca,US
49/K4 **Orlová,** Czh.
82/D5 **Ormoc,** Phil.
129/H4 **Ormond Beach,** Fl,US
45/F4 **Ormskirk,** Eng,UK
56/F2 **Ornain** (riv.), Fr.
53/F5 **Orne** (riv.), Fr.
42/E2 **Ørnes,** Nor.
49/L1 **Orneta,** Pol.
42/F3 **Örnsköldsvik,** Swe.
117/N8 **Oro** (riv.), Mex.
55/F6 **Orobie, Alpi** (range), It.
98/D4 **Orodara,** Burk.
59/E1 **Oroel** (peak), Sp.
122/D4 **Orofino,** Id,US
93/L6 **Orohena** (peak), FrPol.
92/E4 **Oroluk** (atoll), Micr.
127/H2 **Oromocto,** NB,Can
60/A1 **Oro, Monte d'** (mtn.), Fr.
93/H5 **Orona** (Hull) (atoll), Kiri.
127/G2 **Orono,** Me,US
74/L4 **Orontes** (riv.), Asia
77/J1 **Oroqen Zizhiqi,** China
87/F2 **Oroquieta,** Phil.
60/A2 **Orosei** (gulf), It.
62/E2 **Orosháza,** Hun.
62/D2 **Oroszlány,** Hun.
124/C2 **Orovada,** Nv,US
124/E4 **Oro Valley,** Az,US
124/B3 **Oroville,** Ca,US
122/D3 **Oroville,** Wa,US
45/F4 **Orrell,** Eng,UK
52/B5 **Orry-la-Ville,** Fr.
42/E3 **Orsa,** Swe.
52/B6 **Orsay,** Fr.
64/F5 **Orsha,** Bela.
67/L2 **Orsk,** Rus.
62/F3 **Orşova,** Rom.
42/C3 **Ørsta,** Nor.
57/H4 **Orta** (lake), It.
74/C2 **Orta,** Turk.
74/B3 **Ortaca,** Turk.
60/D2 **Orta Nova,** It.
58/B1 **Ortegal** (cape), Sp.
56/C5 **Orthez,** Fr.
58/B1 **Ortigueira,** Sp.
55/G5 **Ortles** (mts.), It., Swi.
108/E6 **Ortón** (riv.), Bol.
77/H2 **Orton** (riv.), China
60/D1 **Ortona,** It.
132/F6 **Ortonville,** Mi,US
123/J4 **Ortonville,** Mn,US
51/H3 **Örtze** (riv.), Ger.
74/F3 **Orūmīyeh,** Iran
108/E7 **Oruro,** Bol.
60/C1 **Orvieto,** It.
105/V **Orville** (coast), Ant.
47/H2 **Orwell** (riv.), Eng,UK
76/H2 **Orxon** (riv.), China
63/F4 **Oryakhovo,** Bul.
74/M8 **Or Yehuda,** Isr.
65/M4 **Osa,** Rus.
125/J3 **Osage** (riv.), Mo,US
125/J3 **Osage Beach,** Mo,US
78/L10 **Ōsaka,** Japan
79/L10 **Osaka** (bay), Japan
78/D3 **Ōsaka** (pref.), Japan
80/D4 **Osan,** SKor.
110/G8 **Osasco,** Braz.
130/E3 **Osborn** (mtn.), Ak,US
125/H3 **Osborne,** Ks,US
129/F3 **Osceola,** Ar,US
48/F2 **Oschersleben,** Ger.
128/B3 **Oscura** (mts.), NM,US
75/B3 **Osh,** Kyr.
104/C4 **Oshakati,** Namb.
127/S8 **Oshawa,** On,Can
77/M3 **Oshima** (pen.), Japan
104/C4 **Oshivelo,** Namb.
123/H5 **Oshkosh,** Ne,US
126/B2 **Oshkosh,** Wi,US
74/F3 **Oshnovīyeh,** Iran
99/G5 **Oshogbo,** Nga.
104/C1 **Oshwe,** Zaire
62/D3 **Osijek,** Cro.
57/K5 **Osimo,** It.
66/D1 **Osipovichi,** Bela.
123/K5 **Oskaloosa,** Ia,US
42/F4 **Oskarshamn,** Swe.
66/F2 **Oskol** (riv.), Rus., Ukr.
42/D4 **Oslo** (cap.), Nor.
84/C4 **Osmānābād,** India
74/C2 **Osmancık,** Turk.
63/K5 **Osmaneli,** Turk.
74/D3 **Osmaniye,** Turk.
51/F4 **Osnabrück,** Ger.
52/B5 **Osny,** Fr.
110/B4 **Osório,** Braz.
112/B4 **Osorno,** Chile
122/D3 **Osoyoos,** BC,Can
90/B1 **Osprey** (reef), Austl.
50/C5 **Oss,** Neth.
91/C4 **Ossa** (peak), Austl.
61/H3 **Ossa** (mtn.), Gre.
48/B3 **Ossa** (range), Port.
99/G5 **Osse** (riv.), Nga.
45/G4 **Ossett,** Eng,UK
131/G4 **Ossining,** NY,US
64/G4 **Ostashkov,** Rus.
51/E4 **Ostbevern,** Ger.
51/G1 **Oste** (riv.), Ger.
52/B1 **Ostend** (Oostende), Belg.
48/F2 **Osterburg,** Ger.
51/F4 **Ostercappeln,** Ger.
50/D1 **Osterems** (chan.), Neth.
42/E4 **Östergötland** (co.), Swe.
57/K2 **Osterhofen,** Ger.
51/F2 **Osterholz-Scharmbeck,** Ger.
51/H5 **Osterode,** Ger.
48/F3 **Osterode am Harz,** Ger.
42/E3 **Östersund,** Swe.
42/D4 **Østfold** (co.), Nor.
51/E2 **Ostfriesland** (reg.), Ger.
42/F3 **Östhammar,** Swe.
60/C2 **Ostia Antica** (ruins), It.
57/J4 **Ostiglia,** It.
49/K4 **Ostrava,** Czh.
51/E2 **Ostrhauderfehn,** Ger.
52/C3 **Ostricourt,** Fr.
62/D4 **Oštri Rt** (cape), Yugo.
49/K2 **Ostróda,** Pol.
66/F2 **Ostrogozhsk,** Rus.
49/L2 **Ostroľęka,** Pol.
49/L2 **Ostroľęka** (prov.), Pol.
57/K1 **Ostrov,** Czh.
64/F4 **Ostrov,** Rus.
49/L3 **Ostrowiec Świętokrzyski,** Pol.
49/L2 **Ostrów Mazowiecka,** Pol.
49/J3 **Ostrów Wielkopolski,** Pol.
49/J3 **Ostrzeszów,** Pol.
51/H1 **Oststeinbek,** Ger.
60/E2 **Ostuni,** It.
61/G2 **Osum** (riv.), Alb.
63/G4 **Osŭm** (riv.), Bul.
78/B5 **Ōsumi** (isls.), Japan
78/B5 **Ōsumi** (pen.), Japan
78/B5 **Ōsumi** (str.), Japan
58/C4 **Osuna,** Sp.
110/B2 **Osvaldo Cruz,** Braz.
45/G3 **Oswaldkirk,** Eng,UK
45/F4 **Oswaldtwistle,** Eng,UK
126/E3 **Oswego,** NY,US
45/E6 **Oswestry,** Eng,UK
49/K3 **Oświęcim** (Auschwitz), Pol.
78/F2 **Ota,** Japan
78/C3 **Ōta** (riv.), Japan
78/C3 **Ōtake,** Japan
79/G2 **Ōtakine-yama** (mtn.), Japan
57/K2 **Otava** (riv.), Czh.
79/G2 **Ōtawara,** Japan
62/F3 **Oţelu Roşu,** Rom.
93/L6 **Otepa,** FrPol.
117/N8 **Oteros** (riv.), Mex.
76/D2 **Otgon,** Mong.
76/D2 **Otgon Tenger** (peak), Mong.
122/D4 **Othello,** Wa,US
52/B5 **Othis,** Fr.
61/F3 **Othonoí** (isl.), Gre.
99/F4 **Oti** (riv.), Gui.
104/C5 **Otjikango,** Namb.
104/C5 **Otjinene,** Namb.
104/C5 **Otjiwarongo,** Namb.
104/B4 **Otjokavare,** Namb.
45/G4 **Otley,** Eng,UK
81/A3 **Otog Qi,** China
123/L3 **Otoskwin** (riv.), On,Can
79/N10 **Otowa,** Japan
42/C4 **Otra** (riv.), Nor.
67/J1 **Otradnyy,** Rus.
61/F2 **Otranto** (str.), Alb., It.
49/J4 **Otrokovice,** Czh.
78/D3 **Ōtsu,** Japan
42/D3 **Otta,** Nor.
126/F2 **Ottawa** (cap.), Can.
119/H3 **Ottawa** (isls.), NW,Can
126/E2 **Ottawa** (riv.), On, Qu,Can
126/B3 **Ottawa,** Il,US
125/J3 **Ottawa,** Ks,US
126/C3 **Ottawa,** Oh,US
46/C5 **Otter** (riv.), Eng,UK
45/F1 **Otterburn,** Eng,UK
51/F1 **Otterndorf,** Ger.
51/G2 **Ottersberg,** Ger.
46/C5 **Ottery Saint Mary,** Eng,UK
52/D2 **Ottignies-Louvain-La-Neuve,** Belg.
57/J2 **Ottobrunn,** Ger.
123/K5 **Ottumwa,** Ia,US
53/G5 **Ottweiler,** Ger.
91/B3 **Otway** (cape), Austl.
113/J8 **Otway** (bay), Chile
113/K8 **Otway** (sound), Chile
91/B3 **Otway Nat'l Park,** Austl.
49/L2 **Otwock,** Pol.
55/G4 **Ötztal Alps** (mts.), Aus., It.
83/C1 **Ou** (riv.), Laos
128/E3 **Ouachita** (riv.), Ar, La,US
125/J4 **Ouachita** (mts.), Ar, Ok,US
96/C3 **Ouadane,** Mrta.
97/J5 **Ouaddaï** (reg.), Chad
99/E3 **Ouagadougou** (cap.), Burk.
97/K6 **Ouaka** (riv.), CAfr.
98/D2 **Oualâta, Dhar** (hills), Mrta.
56/E3 **Ouanne** (riv.), Fr.
96/C3 **Ouarane** (reg.), Mrta.
96/G1 **Ouargla,** Alg.
96/D1 **Ouarzazate,** Mor.
127/F1 **Ouasiemsca** (riv.), Qu,Can
97/J6 **Oubangui** (riv.), CAfr.
99/E3 **Oubritenga** (prov.), Burk.
79/L10 **Ōuda,** Japan
99/E3 **Oudalan** (prov.), Burk.
50/B5 **Oud-Beijerland,** Neth.
50/A5 **Ouddorp,** Neth.
50/D5 **Oude IJssel** (riv.), Neth.
52/C2 **Oudenaarde,** Belg.
50/B5 **Oudenbosch,** Neth.
52/B1 **Oudenburg,** Belg.
50/E2 **Oude Pekela,** Neth.
56/C3 **Oudon** (riv.), Fr.
102/C4 **Oudtshoorn,** SAfr.
50/B6 **Oud-Turnhout,** Belg.
98/E2 **Oued el Hadjar** (well), Mali
96/D1 **Oued Zem,** Mor.
99/F5 **Ouémé** (prov.), Ben.
99/F4 **Ouémé** (riv.), Ben.
93/V13 **Ouen** (isl.), NCal.
56/A2 **Ouessant** (isl.), Fr.
96/J7 **Ouesso,** Congo
99/H5 **Ouest** (prov.), Camr.
117/G4 **Ouest** (pt.), Haiti
96/D1 **Ouezzane,** Mor.
97/J6 **Ouham** (riv.), CAfr., Chad
52/C5 **Ouichy-le-Château,** Fr.
96/E1 **Oujda,** Mor.
42/J2 **Oulangan Nat'l Park,** Fin.
91/A2 **Oulnina** (peak), Austl.
42/H2 **Oulu,** Fin.
42/H2 **Oulu** (prov.), Fin.
42/H2 **Oulujärvi** (lake), Fin.
96/D1 **Oum er Rhia** (riv.), Mor.
97/J5 **Oum Hadjer,** Chad
64/E2 **Ounasjoki** (riv.), Fin.
47/F2 **Oundle,** Eng,UK
97/K4 **OuniangaKebir,** Chad
53/E2 **Oupeye,** Belg.
53/F4 **Our** (riv.), Eur.
54/A2 **Ource** (riv.), Fr.
52/C5 **Ourcq** (riv.), Fr.
42/H1 **Øure Anarjokka Nat'l Park,** Nor.
42/F1 **Øure Dividal Nat'l Park,** Nor.
97/J3 **Ouri,** Chad
109/K5 **Ouricuri,** Braz.
110/B2 **Ourinhos,** Braz.
99/H3 **Ourofané,** Niger
110/G7 **Ouro Fino,** Braz.
110/D2 **Ouro Preto,** Braz.
53/E3 **Ourthe** (riv.), Belg.
45/H4 **Ouse** (riv.), Eng,UK
47/G5 **Ouse** (riv.), Eng,UK
56/B3 **Oust** (riv.), Fr.
59/Q11 **Outão,** Port.
126/E2 **Outaouais** (riv.), Qu,Can
127/G1 **Outardes** (riv.), Qu,Can
127/G1 **Outardes Quatre** (res.), Qu,Can
98/D2 **Outeid Arkas** (well), Mali
43/A2 **Outer Hebrides** (isls.), Sc,UK
58/A1 **Outes,** Sp.
122/G3 **Outlook,** Sk,Can
52/A2 **Outreau,** Fr.
127/N6 **Outremont,** Qu,Can
93/V12 **Ouvéa** (atoll), NCal.
57/H4 **Ovada,** It.
93/Y18 **Ovalau** (isl.), Fiji
111/B3 **Ovalle,** Chile
58/A2 **Ovar,** Port.
53/G2 **Overath,** Ger.
50/B5 **Overflakkee** (isl.), Neth.
52/D2 **Overijse,** Belg.
50/D3 **Overijssel** (prov.), Neth.
50/D4 **Overijssels** (can.), Neth.
125/J3 **Overland Park,** Ks,US
131/K7 **Overlea,** Md,US
112/C5 **Overo** (peak), Arg.
53/E1 **Overpelt,** Belg.
47/E1 **Overseal,** Eng,UK
47/H1 **Overstrand,** Eng,UK
47/E4 **Overton,** Eng,UK
45/F6 **Overton,** Wal,UK
124/D3 **Overton,** Nv,US
42/G2 **Övertorneå,** Swe.
58/C1 **Oviedo,** Sp.
42/J1 **Øvre Pasvik Nat'l Park,** Nor.
104/C1 **Owando,** Congo
79/N9 **Owariasahi,** Japan
78/E3 **Owase,** Japan
125/J3 **Owasso,** Ok,US
123/K4 **Owatonna,** Mn,US
126/E3 **Owego,** NY,US
82/B6 **Owen** (shoal)
44/A2 **Owenkillew** (riv.), NI,UK
124/C3 **Owens** (riv.), Ca,US
126/C4 **Owensboro,** Ky,US
126/D2 **Owen Sound,** On,Can
124/C2 **Owhyee** (mts.), Id,US
131/K7 **Owings Mills,** Md,US
122/F4 **Owl Creek** (mts.), Wy,US
126/C3 **Owosso,** Mi,US
122/D5 **Owyhee** (riv.), Id, Or,US
124/C2 **Owyhee,** Nv,US
124/C2 **Owyhee** (lake), Or,US
72/E1 **Owzan** (riv.), Iran
123/H3 **Oxbow,** Sk,Can
123/K2 **Oxford** (lake), Mb,Can
47/E3 **Oxford,** Eng,UK
47/E3 **Oxford** (can.), Eng,UK
132/F6 **Oxford,** Mi,US
129/F3 **Oxford,** Ms,US
126/C4 **Oxford,** Oh,US
47/E3 **Oxfordshire** (co.), Eng,UK
90/E7 **Oxley** (cr.), Austl.
131/A2 **Oxnard,** Ca,US
131/K8 **Oxon Hill-Glassmanor,** Md,US
47/F4 **Oxted,** Eng,UK
79/E2 **Oyabe,** Japan
79/F2 **Oyama,** Japan
79/M10 **Ōyamada,** Japan
79/L10 **Ōyamazaki,** Japan
109/H3 **Oyapock** (riv.), FrG.
96/H7 **Oyem,** Gabon
122/F3 **Oyen,** Ab,Can
99/F5 **Oyo,** Nga.
99/F4 **Oyo** (state), Nga.
79/L10 **Ōyodo,** Japan
78/B5 **Ōyodo** (riv.), Japan
131/G5 **Oyster Bay,** NY,US
51/G2 **Oyten,** Ger.
82/D6 **Ozamiz,** Phil.
56/D2 **Ozanne** (riv.), Fr.
125/J3 **Ozark** (plat.), US
129/G4 **Ozark,** Al,US
128/E3 **Ozark,** Ar,US
128/E3 **Ozark** (mts.), Ar, Mo,US
125/J3 **Ozarks, Lake of the** (lake), Mo,US
62/E1 **Ózd,** Hun.
69/S4 **Ozernoy** (cape), Rus.
122/B3 **Ozette** (lake), Wa,US
123/L3 **Ozhiski** (lake), On,Can
60/A2 **Ozieri,** It.
49/K3 **Ozimek,** Pol.
52/B6 **Ozoir-la-Ferrière,** Fr.
128/C4 **Ozona,** Tx,US
49/K3 **Ozorków,** Pol.
78/C4 **Ōzu,** Japan

P

55/H1 **Paar** (riv.), Ger.
102/B4 **Paarl,** SAfr.
49/K3 **Pabianice,** Pol.
84/E3 **Pābna,** Bang.
108/F6 **Pacaás Novos** (mts.), Braz.
108/F6 **Pacaás Novos Nat'l Park,** Braz.
109/H4 **Pacajá** (riv.), Braz.
108/C5 **Pacasmayo,** Peru
60/C4 **Paceco,** It.
108/C6 **Pachacamac** (ruins), Peru
60/D4 **Pachino,** It.
84/C3 **Pachmarhī,** India
38/B4 **Pacific** (ocean)
122/B3 **Pacific** (ranges), BC,Can
132/K11 **Pacifica,** Ca,US
131/B2 **Pacifico** (mtn.), Ca,US
118/D4 **Pacific Rim Nat'l Park,** BC,Can
86/D5 **Pacinan** (cape), Indo.
86/D5 **Pacitan,** Indo.
59/P10 **Paço de Arcos,** Port.
86/B4 **Padang,** Indo.
86/B4 **Padangpanjang,** Indo.
86/A3 **Padangsidempuan,** Indo.
47/G4 **Paddock Wood,** Eng,UK
51/F5 **Paderborn,** Ger.
73/J3 **Pad Īdan,** Pak.
45/F4 **Padiham,** Eng,UK
62/E3 **Padina,** Yugo.
42/E2 **Padjelanta Nat'l Park,** Swe.
57/J4 **Padova** (Padua), It.
104/B2 **Padrão, Ponta do** (pt.), Ang.
128/D5 **Padre Island Nat'l Seashore,** Tx,US
58/A1 **Padrón,** Sp.
102/D4 **Padrone** (cape), SAfr.
46/B5 **Padstow,** Eng,UK
57/J4 **Padua** (Padova), It.
126/B4 **Paducah,** Ky,US
128/C3 **Paducah,** Tx,US
80/E4 **Paektŏk-san** (mtn.), SKor.
80/D2 **Paektu-San** (mtn.), NKor.
80/C4 **Paengnyŏng** (isl.), SKor.
62/B3 **Pag** (isl.), Cro.
82/D6 **Pagadian,** Phil.
86/B4 **Pagai Selatan** (isl.), Indo.
86/A4 **Pagai Utara** (isl.), Indo.
92/D3 **Pagan** (isl.), NMar.
124/E3 **Page,** Az,US
93/H6 **Pago Pago** (cap.), ASam.
124/F3 **Pagosa Springs,** Co,US
126/C1 **Pagwachuan** (riv.), On,Can
86/B3 **Pahang** (riv.), Malay.
124/D3 **Pahrump,** Nv,US
124/C3 **Pahute Mesa** (upland), Nv,US
81/C5 **Pai** (lake), China
61/L7 **Paiania,** Gre.
46/C6 **Paignton,** Eng,UK
42/H3 **Päijänne** (lake), Fin.
83/C3 **Pailin,** Camb.
120/T10 **Pailolo** (chan.), Hi,US
64/D3 **Paimio,** Fin.
112/C2 **Paine,** Chile
113/J7 **Paine** (peak), Chile
126/D3 **Painesville,** Oh,US
46/C2 **Painscastle,** Wal,UK
123/J2 **Paint** (lake), Mb,Can
124/E4 **Painted** (des.), Az,US
128/D4 **Paint Rock,** Tx,US
126/D4 **Paintsville,** Ky,US
43/C3 **Paisley,** Sc,UK
84/C4 **Paithan,** India
42/G2 **Pajala,** Swe.
49/K3 **Pajęczno,** Pol.
117/E6 **Pajonal Abajo,** Pan.
86/B3 **Pakanbaru,** Indo.
91/G6 **Pakenham,** Austl.
113/J7 **Pakenham** (cape), Chile
61/J5 **Pákhnes** (peak), Gre.
65/X9 **Pakhra** (riv.), Rus.
73/H3 **Pakistan**
62/B3 **Paklenica Nat'l Park,** Cro.
85/G3 **Pakokku,** Burma
122/F3 **Pakowki** (lake), Ab,Can
73/K2 **Pākpattan,** Pak.
85/H6 **Pak Phanang,** Thai.
62/C3 **Pakrac,** Cro.
62/D2 **Paks,** Hun.
83/D3 **Pakxe,** Laos
96/H6 **Pala,** Chad
59/N9 **Palacio Real,** Sp.
59/G2 **Palafrugell,** Sp.
60/D4 **Palagonia,** It.
60/E1 **Palagruža** (isls.), Cro.
61/F3 **Palaiokastritsa,** Gre.
84/D4 **Pālakolla,** India
59/G2 **Palamós,** Sp.
86/D4 **Palangkaraya,** Indo.
84/B3 **Pālanpur,** India
120/T10 **Palaoa** (pt.), Hi,US
104/E5 **Palapye,** Bots.
84/C5 **Palar** (riv.), India
58/B1 **Palas de Rey,** Sp.
132/P15 **Palatine,** Il,US
129/H4 **Palatka,** Fl,US
92/C4 **Palau**
82/C6 **Palawan** (isl.), Phil.
82/C5 **Palawan** (passage), Phil.
84/C6 **Pālayankottai,** India
60/D4 **Palazzolo Acreide,** It.
96/G8 **Palé,** EqG.
87/F3 **Paleleh,** Indo.
86/B4 **Palembang,** Indo.
112/B4 **Palena** (riv.), Chile
58/C1 **Palencia,** Sp.
127/Q9 **Palermo,** On,Can
60/C3 **Palermo,** It.
128/E4 **Palestine,** Tx,US
128/E3 **Palestine** (lake), Tx,US
73/K5 **Pālghar,** India
80/E4 **P'algong-san** (mtn.), SKor.
110/B3 **Palhoça,** Braz.
84/B2 **Pāli,** India
113/K8 **Pali Aike Nat'l Park,** Chile
62/D2 **Palić,** Yugo.
120/V13 **Palikea** (peak), Hi,US
61/H3 **Palioúrion, Ákra** (cape), Gre.
131/F5 **Palisades Park,** NJ,US
84/B3 **Pālitāna,** India
62/C3 **Paljenik** (peak), Bosn.
84/C6 **Palk** (str.), India, SrL.
42/H1 **Pallas-Ounastunturin Nat'l Park,** Fin.
42/H1 **Pallastunturi** (peak), Fin.
109/J6 **Palma** (riv.), Braz.
59/G3 **Palma,** Sp.
58/C4 **Palma del Río,** Sp.
60/C4 **Palma di Montechiaro,** It.
109/L5 **Palmares,** Braz.
110/B3 **Palmas,** Braz.
98/D5 **Palmas** (cape), Libr.
117/F3 **Palma Soriano,** Cuba
129/H4 **Palm Bay,** Fl,US
90/H8 **Palm Beach,** Austl.
131/B1 **Palmdale,** Ca,US
110/B3 **Palmeira,** Braz.
109/L5 **Palmeira dos Índios,** Braz.
104/B2 **Palmeirinhas, Ponta das** (pt.), Ang.
59/Q10 **Palmela,** Port.
105/V **Palmer** (arch.), Ant.
105/V **Palmer Land** (reg.), Ant.
90/C3 **Palmerston** (cape), Austl.
93/J6 **Palmerston** (atoll), CookIs.
89/H7 **Palmerston,** NZ
90/B2 **Palmerston Nat'l Park,** Austl.
89/H7 **Palmerston North,** NZ
129/H5 **Palmetto,** Fl,US
129/H4 **Palm Harbor,** Fl,US
60/D3 **Palmi,** It.
112/C2 **Palmilla,** Chile
108/C3 **Palmira,** Col.
124/C4 **Palm Springs,** Ca,US
93/J4 **Palmyra** (isl.), PacUS
72/C2 **Palmyra** (ruins), Syria
84/E3 **Palmyras** (pt.), India
44/E2 **Palnackie,** Sc,UK
84/C5 **Palni,** India
82/D5 **Palo,** Phil.
132/K12 **Palo Alto,** Ca,US
117/M8 **Palo Bola,** Mex.
125/G3 **Palo Duro** (cr.), Ok, Tx,US
57/J4 **Palon** (peak), It.
128/D3 **Palo Pinto,** Tx,US
59/E4 **Palos, Cabo de** (cape), Sp.
132/Q16 **Palos Hills,** Il,US
131/B3 **Palos Verdes Estates,** Ca,US
116/D5 **Palo Verde Nat'l Park,** Mex.
84/D2 **Pālpa,** Nepal
111/C1 **Palpalá,** Arg.
87/G4 **Palpetu** (cape), Indo.
74/D2 **Palu,** Turk.
82/D5 **Paluan,** Phil.
86/C3 **Pamangkat,** Indo.
56/D5 **Pamiers,** Fr.
75/B4 **Pamir** (riv.), Afg., Taj.
75/B4 **Pamir** (reg.), China, Taj.
129/J3 **Pamlico** (riv.), NC,US
129/J3 **Pamlico** (sound), NC,US
128/C3 **Pampa,** Tx,US
112/E2 **Pampa Humida** (plain), Arg.
112/E3 **Pampas** (plain), Arg.
112/D3 **Pampa Seca** (plain), Arg.
108/D2 **Pamplona,** Col.
58/E1 **Pamplona,** Sp.
63/K5 **Pamukova,** Turk.
82/E6 **Panabo,** Phil.
124/D3 **Panaca,** Nv,US
84/C6 **Panadura,** SrL.
63/G4 **Panagyurishte,** Bul.
86/B5 **Panaitan** (isl.), Indo.
84/B4 **Pānāji,** India
117/E6 **Panama**
117/E6 **Panama** (can.), Pan.
117/F6 **Panamá** (cap.), Pan.
117/F6 **Panama** (gulf), Pan.
117/F6 **Panama** (isth.), Pan.
129/G4 **Panama City,** Fl,US
124/C3 **Panamint** (range), Ca,US
57/J4 **Panaro** (riv.), It.
82/D5 **Panay** (isl.), Phil.
124/C3 **Pancake** (range), Nv,US
62/E3 **Pančevo,** Yugo.
62/E4 **Pančicev vrh** (peak), Yugo.
63/H3 **Panciu,** Rom.
104/E4 **Pandamatenga,** Bots.
111/B2 **Pan de Azúcar Nat'l Park,** Chile
84/C4 **Pandharpur,** India
113/G2 **Pando,** Uru.
85/F2 **Pandu,** India
64/E5 **Panevėžys,** Lith.
75/D3 **Panfilov,** Kaz.
83/B1 **Pang** (riv.), Burma
93/H7 **Pangai,** Tonga
61/J2 **Pangaíon** (peak), Gre.
101/C3 **Pangani** (riv.), Tanz.
47/E4 **Pangbourne,** Eng,UK
86/A3 **Pangkalanberandan,** Indo.
87/F4 **Pangkalaseang** (cape), Indo.
86/C4 **Pangkalpinang,** Indo.
124/D3 **Panguitch,** Ut,US
87/F2 **Pangutaran,** Phil.
82/D6 **Pangutaran** (isl.), Phil.
128/C3 **Panhandle,** Tx,US
87/J4 **Paniai** (lake), Indo.
120/R10 **Paniau** (peak), Hi,US
92/F7 **Panié** (peak), NCal.
84/C2 **Pānīpat,** India
73/K1 **Panj** (Pyandzh) (riv.), Afg., Taj.
84/D3 **Panna,** India
90/F7 **Pannikin** (isl.), Austl.
110/B2 **Panorama,** Braz.
45/E6 **Pant,** Eng,UK
47/G3 **Pant** (riv.), Eng,UK
109/G7 **Pantanal Matogrossense Nat'l Park,** Braz.
60/B4 **Pantelleria** (isl.), It.
52/B5 **Pantin,** Fr.
58/B1 **Pantón,** Sp.
116/B3 **Pánuco,** Mex.
116/B3 **Pánuco** (riv.), Mex.
85/H2 **Panzhihua,** China
60/E3 **Paola,** It.
125/J3 **Paola,** Ks,US
124/F3 **Paonia,** Co,US
96/J6 **Paoua,** CAfr.
83/C3 **Paoy Pet,** Camb.
62/C2 **Pápa,** Hun.
116/D5 **Papagayo** (gulf), CR
116/B3 **Papantla de Olarte,** Mex.
93/X15 **Papara,** FrPol.
93/X15 **Papeete** (cap.), FrPol.
51/E2 **Papenburg,** Ger.
50/B5 **Papendrecht,** Neth.
93/X15 **Papenoo,** FrPol.
93/X15 **Papetoai,** FrPol.
74/J4 **Paphos,** Cyp.
125/H2 **Papillion,** Ne,US
61/G2 **Papingut, Maj'e** (peak), Alb.
87/H4 **Papisoi** (cape), Indo.
92/D5 **Papua** (gulf), PNG
92/D5 **Papua New Guinea**
110/C1 **Pará** (riv.), Braz.
110/K7 **Paracambi,** Braz.
109/J7 **Paracatu,** Braz.
82/B4 **Paracel** (isls.)
71/N7 **Parace Vela** (Okino-Tori-Shima) (isl.), Japan
62/E4 **Paraćin,** Yugo.
59/N8 **Paracuellos,** Sp.
110/C1 **Pará de Minas,** Braz.
84/E3 **Paradip,** India
122/F2 **Paradise Hill,** Sk,Can
109/J4 **Paragominas,** Braz.
129/F2 **Paragould,** Ar,US
108/F6 **Paraguá** (riv.), Bol.
108/F2 **Paragua** (riv.), Ven.
110/H6 **Paraguaçu,** Braz.
109/L6 **Paraguaçu** (riv.), Braz.
110/B2 **Paraguaçu Paulista,** Braz.
109/G6 **Paraguai** (riv.), Braz.
117/G5 **Paraguaná** (pen.), Ven.
111/E2 **Paraguarí,** Par.
107/D5 **Paraguay**
110/D2 **Paraíba do Sul** (riv.), Braz.
110/H8 **Paraibuna** (riv.), Braz.
109/J6 **Paraíso do Norte de Goiás,** Braz.
110/G7 **Paraisópolis,** Braz.
99/F4 **Parakou,** Ben.
109/G2 **Paramaribo** (cap.), Sur.
108/C2 **Paramillo Nat'l Park,** Col.
109/K6 **Paramirim** (riv.), Braz.
131/B3 **Paramount,** Ca,US
131/F5 **Paramus,** NJ,US
69/R4 **Paramushir** (isl.), Rus.
110/B3 **Paraná** (state), Braz.
107/D5 **Paraná** (riv.), SAm.
110/B3 **Paranaguá,** Braz.
110/B1 **Paranaíba,** Braz.
110/B1 **Paranaiba** (riv.), Braz.
110/B2 **Paranapanema** (riv.), Braz.
110/B3 **Paranapiacaba** (range), Braz.
107/D4 **Paranatinga** (riv.), Braz.
109/H8 **Paranavai,** Braz.
87/F2 **Parang,** Phil.
110/C1 **Paraopeba,** Braz.
109/J8 **Parapanema** (riv.), Braz.
108/F7 **Parapetí** (riv.), Bol.
110/J8 **Parati,** Braz.
110/H8 **Paratinga** (riv.), Braz.
84/C4 **Parbhani,** India
48/F2 **Parchim,** Ger.
49/M3 **Parczew,** Pol.
74/M8 **Pardes Hanna-Kardur,** Isr.
84/B3 **Pārdi,** India
110/G6 **Pardo** (riv.), Braz.
49/H3 **Pardubice,** Czh.
86/D5 **Pare,** Indo.
108/F6 **Parecis** (mts.), Braz.
59/P10 **Parede,** Port.
112/C2 **Paredones,** Chile
126/E1 **Parent** (lake), Qu,Can
87/E4 **Parepare,** Indo.
59/L6 **Parets del Vallès,** Sp.
61/G3 **Párga,** Gre.
117/J5 **Paria** (gulf), Trin., Ven.
124/E3 **Paria** (riv.), Az, Ut,US
117/J5 **Paria** (pen.), Ven.
117/J6 **Pariaguán,** Ven.
86/B4 **Pariaman,** Indo.
108/E7 **Parinacota** (peak), Bol.
109/G4 **Parintins,** Braz.
52/B6 **Paris** (cap.), Fr.
128/E3 **Paris,** Ar,US
126/B4 **Paris,** Tn,US
128/E3 **Paris,** Tx,US
124/F2 **Park** (range), Co,US
124/D4 **Parker,** Az,US
125/F3 **Parker,** Co,US
126/D4 **Parkersburg,** WV,US
91/D2 **Parkes,** Austl.
47/H3 **Parkeston,** Eng,UK
126/B2 **Park Falls,** Wi,US
44/B2 **Parkgate,** NI,UK
46/A5 **Park Head** (pt.), UK
47/E5 **Parkhurst,** Eng,UK
132/C3 **Parkland,** Wa,US
123/K4 **Park Rapids,** Mn,US
132/Q15 **Park Ridge,** Il,US
131/F4 **Park Ridge,** NJ,US
123/J3 **Park River,** ND,US
131/K7 **Parkville,** Md,US
132/L9 **Parkway-Sacramento,** Ca,US
58/D2 **Parla,** Sp.
84/D4 **Parlakhemundi,** India
84/C4 **Parli,** India
57/J4 **Parma,** It.
126/D3 **Parma,** Oh,US
109/K4 **Parnaíba,** Braz.
109/K4 **Parnaíba** (riv.), Braz.
61/H3 **Parnassos Nat'l Park,** Gre.
61/H3 **Párnis** (peak), Gre.
61/H4 **Párnon** (mts.), Gre.
64/E4 **Pärnu,** Est.
91/C1 **Paroo** (riv.), Austl.
61/J4 **Páros** (isl.), Gre.
102/B4 **Parow,** SAfr.
124/D3 **Parowan,** Ut,US
112/C3 **Parral,** Chile
90/H8 **Parramatta,** Austl.
116/A2 **Parras de la Fuente,** Mex.
46/D4 **Parrett** (riv.), Eng,UK
116/E6 **Parrita,** CR
119/H2 **Parry** (bay), NW,Can
118/F1 **Parry** (chan.), NW,Can
119/R7 **Parry** (isls.), NW,Can
126/D2 **Parry Sound,** On,Can
55/G3 **Parseierspitze** (peak), Aus.
123/H4 **Parshall,** ND,US
131/F5 **Parsippany,** NJ,US
122/C2 **Parsnip** (riv.), BC,Can
125/J3 **Parsons,** Ks,US
64/C2 **Pårtefjället** (peak), Swe.
56/C3 **Parthenay,** Fr.
60/C3 **Partinico,** It.
77/L3 **Partizansk,** Rus.
126/D1 **Partridge** (riv.), On,Can
84/C4 **Partūr,** India
109/H4 **Paru** (riv.), Braz.
84/D4 **Pārvathīpuram,** India
45/G5 **Parwich,** Eng,UK
102/D2 **Parys,** SAfr.
127/K1 **Pasadena,** Nf,Can
131/B2 **Pasadena,** Ca,US
131/K7 **Pasadena,** Md,US
128/E4 **Pasadena,** Tx,US
108/C4 **Pasaje,** Ecu.
83/C3 **Pa Sak** (riv.), Thai.
86/B3 **Pasaman** (peak), Indo.
129/F4 **Pascagoula,** Ms,US
63/H2 **Paşcani,** Rom.
122/D4 **Pasco,** Wa,US
113/J7 **Pascua** (riv.), Chile
52/A3 **Pas-de-Calais** (dept.), Fr.
52/B3 **Pas-en-Artois,** Fr.
82/D5 **Pasig,** Phil.
85/G2 **Pāsighāt,** India
74/E2 **Pasinler,** Turk.
49/K1 **Pasľęk,** Pol.
49/L2 **Pasľęka** (riv.), Pol.
62/B4 **Pašman** (isl.), Cro.
73/H3 **Pasni,** Pak.
111/E2 **Paso de Los Libres,** Arg.
112/C2 **Paso del Planchón** (peak), Chile
124/B4 **Paso Robles** (El Paso de Robles), Ca,US
130/M3 **Pass** (peak), Yk,Can
131/F5 **Passaic,** NJ,US
131/F5 **Passaic** (riv.), NJ,US
110/J7 **Passa Quatro,** Braz.
57/K2 **Passau,** Ger.
52/C2 **Passendale,** Belg.
60/D4 **Passero** (pt.), It.
111/F2 **Passo Fundo,** Braz.
110/A3 **Passo Fundo** (res.), Braz.
99/E3 **Passoré** (prov.), Burk.
110/C2 **Passos,** Braz.
57/G4 **Passy,** Fr.
108/C4 **Pastaza** (riv.), Ecu., Peru
108/C3 **Pasto,** Col.
130/F3 **Pastol** (bay), Ak,US
86/D5 **Pasuruan,** Indo.
62/D2 **Pásztó,** Hun.
112/D4 **Patagonia** (reg.), Arg.
86/B4 **Patah** (peak), Indo.
84/B3 **Pātan,** India
131/K7 **Patapsco** (riv.), Md,US
131/G5 **Patchogue,** NY,US
46/D3 **Patchway,** Eng,UK
45/G3 **Pateley Bridge,** Eng,UK
59/E3 **Paterna,** Sp.
131/F5 **Paterson,** NJ,US
73/L2 **Pathānkot,** India
122/G5 **Pathfinder** (res.), Wy,US
86/D5 **Pati,** Indo.
108/C3 **Patía** (riv.), Col.
73/L2 **Patiāla,** India
87/F2 **Patikul,** Phil.
84/E2 **Patna,** India
44/D1 **Patna,** Sc,UK
87/F1 **Patnongon,** Phil.
74/E2 **Patnos,** Turk.
110/A3 **Pato Branco,** Braz.
129/G2 **Patoka** (riv.), In,US
61/F2 **Patos,** Alb.
109/L5 **Patos,** Braz.
110/B4 **Patos** (lake), Braz.
110/C1 **Patos de Minas,** Braz.
61/G3 **Pátrai,** Gre.
61/G3 **Patrai** (gulf), Gre.
113/J7 **Patricio Lynch** (isl.), Chile
45/H4 **Patrington,** Eng,UK
110/C1 **Patrocínio,** Braz.
83/C5 **Pattani,** Thai.
83/C3 **Pattaya,** Thai.
51/G4 **Pattensen,** Ger.
60/D3 **Patti,** It.
46/D1 **Pattingham,** Eng,UK
84/C5 **Pattukkottai,** India
130/N4 **Pattullo** (mtn.), BC,Can
116/E4 **Patuca** (pt.), Hon.
116/D5 **Patuca** (riv.), Hon.
131/K8 **Patuxent** (riv.), Md,US
56/C5 **Pau,** Fr.
109/L7 **Pau Brasil,** Braz.
108/E5 **Pauini** (riv.), Braz.
110/F7 **Paulínia,** Braz.
109/L5 **Paulo Afonso,** Braz.
109/L5 **Paulo Afonso Nat'l Park,** Braz.
131/E6 **Paulsboro,** NJ,US
125/H4 **Pauls Valley,** Ok,US
46/D4 **Paulton,** Eng,UK
85/G4 **Paungde,** Burma
75/C5 **Pauri,** India
57/H4 **Pavia,** It.
63/G4 **Pavlikeni,** Bul.

Pomba – Queen

110/D2 **Pomba** (riv.), Braz.
109/L5 **Pombal**, Braz.
58/A3 **Pombal**, Port.
49/H2 **Pomerania** (reg.), Pol.
49/H1 **Pomeranian** (bay), Ger., Pol.
110/B3 **Pomerode**, Braz.
44/B2 **Pomeroy**, NI,UK
122/D4 **Pomeroy**, Wa,US
92/E5 **Pomio**, PNG
131/C2 **Pomona**, Ca,US
63/H4 **Pomorie**, Bul.
129/H5 **Pompano Beach**, Fl,US
60/D2 **Pompei** (ruins), It.
110/C1 **Pompeu**, Braz.
131/F4 **Pompton Lakes**, NJ,US
99/E4 **Pô Nat'l Park**, Burk.
125/H3 **Ponca City**, Ok,US
117/H4 **Ponce**, PR
126/E1 **Poncheville** (lake), Qu,Can
119/J1 **Pond** (inlet), NW,Can
84/B5 **Pondicherry** (terr.), India
84/C5 **Pondicherry** (terr.), India
84/D4 **Pondicherry** (terr.), India
58/B1 **Ponferrada**, Sp.
103/E2 **Pongolo** (riv.), SAfr.
98/E4 **Poni** (prov.), Burk.
49/M3 **Poniatowa**, Pol.
122/E2 **Ponoka**, Ab,Can
64/H2 **Ponoy** (riv.), Rus.
52/D3 **Pont-à-Celles**, Belg.
109/L7 **Ponta da Baleia** (pt.), Braz.
59/S12 **Ponta da Pico** (mtn.), Azor.,Port.
59/T13 **Ponta Delgada**, Azor.,Port.
59/U15 **Ponta do Sol**, Madr.,Port.
110/B3 **Ponta Grossa**, Braz.
110/B1 **Pontalina**, Braz.
53/F6 **Pont-à-Mousson**, Fr.
109/G8 **Ponta Porã**, Braz.
46/C3 **Pontardawe**, Wal,UK
46/B3 **Pontardulais**, Wal,UK
54/C4 **Pontarlier**, Fr.
52/B6 **Pontault-Combault**, Fr.
126/E1 **Pontax** (riv.), Qu,Can
129/F4 **Pontchartrain** (lake), La,US
56/B3 **Pontchâteau**, Fr.
56/F4 **Pont-du-Château**, Fr.
60/C2 **Pontecorvo**, It.
58/A3 **Ponte de Sor**, Port.
45/G4 **Pontefract**, Eng,UK
45/G1 **Ponteland**, Eng,UK
110/D2 **Ponte Nova**, Braz.
46/C2 **Ponterwyd**, Wal,UK
46/D1 **Pontesbury**, Eng,UK
108/G7 **Pontes e Lacerda**, Braz.
58/A1 **Pontevedra**, Sp.
126/B3 **Pontiac**, Il,US
132/F6 **Pontiac**, Mi,US
86/C4 **Pontianak**, Indo.
56/B2 **Pontivy**, Fr.
52/B5 **Pontoise**, Fr.
129/F3 **Pontotoc**, Ms,US
46/C2 **Pontrhydfendigaid**, Wal,UK
46/D3 **Pontrilas**, Eng,UK
52/B5 **Pont-Sainte Maxence**, Fr.
56/F4 **Pont-Saint-Esprit**, Fr.
46/B3 **Pontyates**, Wal,UK
46/C3 **Pontyclun**, Wal,UK
46/C3 **Pont y Cymmer**, Wal,UK
46/C3 **Pontypool**, Wal,UK
46/C3 **Pontypridd**, Wal,UK
60/C2 **Ponziane** (isls.), It.
46/E5 **Poole**, Eng,UK
47/E5 **Poole** (bay), Eng,UK
84/B4 **Poona**, India
108/F7 **Poopó** (lake), Bol.
108/C3 **Popayán**, Col.
52/B2 **Poperinge**, Belg.
91/B2 **Popilta** (lake), Austl.
91/B2 **Popio** (lake), Austl.
123/K2 **Poplar** (riv.), Mb, On,Can
123/G3 **Poplar**, Mt,US
123/G3 **Poplar** (riv.), Mt,US
125/K3 **Poplar Bluff**, Mo,US
129/F4 **Poplarville**, Ms,US
96/J6 **Popokabaka**, Zaire
92/D5 **Popondetta**, PNG
63/H4 **Popovo**, Bul.
49/L4 **Poprad**, Slvk.
49/L4 **Poprad** (riv.), Slvk.
109/J6 **Porangatu**, Braz.
84/A3 **Porbandar**, India
58/C4 **Porcuna**, Sp.
130/K2 **Porcupine** (riv.), Yk,Can, Ak,US
90/B3 **Porcupine Gorge Nat'l Park**, Austl.
123/H2 **Porcupine Plain**, Sk,Can
57/K4 **Pordenone**, It.
64/F5 **Pori**, Fin.
89/H7 **Porirua**, NZ
64/E4 **Porkhov**, Rus.
117/J5 **Porlamar**, Ven.
46/C4 **Porlock**, Eng,UK
77/N2 **Poronaysk**, Rus.
105/J **Porpoise** (bay), Ant.
58/A1 **Porriño**, Sp.

42/H1 **Porsangen** (fjord), Nor.
42/D4 **Porsgrunn**, Nor.
74/B2 **Porsuk** (riv.), Turk.
108/F7 **Portachuelo**, Bol.
44/B3 **Portadown**, NI,UK
44/C3 **Portaferry**, NI,UK
126/C3 **Portage**, Mi,US
126/B3 **Portage**, Wi,US
123/J3 **Portage la Prairie**, Mb,Can
122/B3 **Port Alberni**, BC,Can
58/B3 **Portalegre**, Port.
58/B3 **Portalegre** (dist.), Port.
125/G4 **Portales**, NM,US
102/D4 **Port Alfred**, SAfr.
122/B3 **Port Alice**, BC,Can
45/E6 **Port Angeles**, Wa,US
117/F4 **Port Antonio**, Jam.
43/C2 **Port Appin**, Sc,UK
128/E4 **Port Arthur**, Tx,US
127/K1 **Port au Choix**, Nf,Can
89/C4 **Port Augusta**, Austl.
117/G4 **Port-au-Prince** (cap.), Haiti
44/C3 **Portavogie**, NI,UK
51/F4 **Porta Westfalica**, Ger.
85/F5 **Port Blair**, India
128/E4 **Port Bolivar**, Tx,US
98/E5 **Port-Bouët**, IvC.
117/K2 **Port Charlotte**, Fl,US
127/H1 **Port-Cartier**, Qu,Can
129/H5 **Port Charlotte**, Fl,US
131/G5 **Port Chester**, NY,US
126/D3 **Port Clinton**, Oh,US
127/R10 **Port Colborne**, On,Can
127/Q8 **Port Credit**, On,Can
127/S8 **Port Darlington**, On,Can
91/C4 **Port Davey** (har.), Austl.
117/G4 **Port-de-Paix**, Haiti
86/B3 **Port Dickson**, Malay.
130/M4 **Port Edward**, BC,Can
109/H4 **Portel**, Braz.
126/D2 **Port Elgin**, Can.
102/D4 **Port Elizabeth**, SAfr.
44/D3 **Port Erin**, IM,UK
102/L10 **Porterville**, SAfr.
56/F4 **Porterville**, Ca,US
56/F4 **Portes-lès-Valence**, Fr.
96/B3 **Port-Étienne**, Mrta.
56/D5 **Portet-sur-Garonne**, Fr.
46/B3 **Port Eynon**, Wal,UK
46/B3 **Port Eynon** (pt.), Wal,UK
104/A1 **Port-Gentil**, Gabon
43/C2 **Port Glasgow**, Sc,UK
44/B2 **Portglenone**, NI,UK
46/C3 **Porth**, Wal,UK
99/G5 **Port Harcourt**, Nga.
122/B3 **Port Hardy**, BC,Can
127/J2 **Port Hawkesbury**, NS,Can
46/C4 **Porthcawl**, Wal,UK
89/A3 **Port Hedland**, Austl.
46/A6 **Porthleven**, Eng,UK
44/D6 **Porthmadog**, Wal,UK
131/N2 **Port Hueneme**, Ca,US
132/H6 **Port Huron**, Mi,US
58/A4 **Portimão**, Port.
46/D4 **Port Isaac**, Eng,UK
46/D4 **Portishead**, Eng,UK
131/G5 **Port Jefferson**, NY,US
91/C4 **Portland** (cape), Austl.
117/F4 **Portland** (pt.), Jam.
45/G1 **Portland** (pt.), Eng,UK
130/N4 **Portland** (inlet), BC,Can, Ak,US
126/C3 **Portland**, In,US
127/G3 **Portland**, Me,US
127/G2 **Portland**, Or,US
129/G2 **Portland**, Tn,US
46/D5 **Portland, Isle of** (pen.), Eng,UK
128/D4 **Port Lavaca**, Tx,US
89/C4 **Port Lincoln**, Austl.
103/S15 **Port Louis** (cap.), Mrts.
91/E1 **Port Macquarie**, Austl.
44/B5 **Portmarnock**, Ire.
44/B5 **Port McNeill**, BC,Can
127/H1 **Port-Menier**, Qu,Can
92/D5 **Port Moresby** (cap.), PNG
127/G1 **Portneuf** (riv.), Qu,Can
58/A2 **Porto**, Port.
58/A2 **Porto** (dist.), Port.
110/B4 **Pôrto Alegre**, Braz.
104/B3 **Porto Amboim**, Ang.
109/H7 **Pôrto Artur**, Braz.
108/F5 **Porto Esperidião**, Braz.
110/B1 **Pôrto Ferreira**, Braz.
117/J5 **Port-of-Spain** (cap.), Trin.
57/K4 **Portogruaro**, It.
57/J4 **Portomaggiore**, It.
109/J6 **Porto Nacional**, Braz.
99/F5 **Porto-Novo** (cap.), Ben.
129/H4 **Port Orange**, Fl,US
60/C1 **Porto San Giorgio**, It.
60/B1 **Porto Santo Stefano**, It.
60/A2 **Porto Torres**, It.
110/B3 **Porto União**, Braz.
108/F5 **Porto Velho**, Braz.
108/B4 **Portoviejo**, Ecu.
44/C2 **Portpatrick**, Sc,UK

91/C3 **Port Phillip** (bay), Austl.
89/C4 **Port Pirie**, Austl.
44/B1 **Portrush**, NI,UK
100/C2 **Port Said** (Bûr Sa'îd), Egypt
129/G4 **Port Saint Joe**, Fl,US
56/F5 **Port-Saint-Louis-du-Rhône**, Fr.
129/H5 **Port Saint Lucie**, Fl,US
44/C3 **Port Saint Mary**, IM,UK
47/E5 **Portsea** (isl.), Eng,UK
130/M4 **Port Simpson**, BC,Can
47/F5 **Portslade by Sea**, Eng,UK
47/E5 **Portsmouth**, Eng,UK
127/G3 **Portsmouth**, NH,US
126/D3 **Portsmouth**, Oh,US
126/E4 **Portsmouth**, Va,US
91/E2 **Port Stephens** (bay), Austl.
44/B1 **Portstewart**, NI,UK
100/D5 **Port Sudan** (Bûr Südân), Sudan
46/C3 **Port Talbot**, Wal,UK
122/C3 **Port Townsend**, Wa,US
58/A3 **Portugal**
58/A3 **Portugalete**, Sp.
117/H6 **Portuguesa** (riv.), Ven.
131/G5 **Port Washington**, NY,US
126/C3 **Port Washington**, Wi,US
44/D2 **Port William**, Sc,UK
111/E2 **Posadas**, Arg.
58/C4 **Posadas**, Sp.
62/C3 **Posavina** (val.), Bosn., Cro.
87/F4 **Poso** (lake), Indo.
80/D5 **Posŏng**, SKor.
132/C2 **Possession** (sound), Wa,US
125/F3 **Post**, Tx,US
64/E5 **Postavy**, Bela.
96/F3 **Poste Maurice Cortier** (ruins), Alg.
96/F3 **Poste Weygand** (ruins), Alg.
122/D4 **Post Falls**, Id,US
102/C3 **Postmasburg**, SAfr.
62/B3 **Postojna**, Slov.
102/D2 **Potchefstroom**, SAfr.
125/J4 **Poteau**, Ok,US
60/D2 **Potenza**, It.
60/C1 **Potenza** (riv.), It.
122/D4 **Potholes** (res.), Wa,US
109/H5 **Poti** (riv.), Braz.
67/G4 **Poti**, Geo.
57/J5 **Poti, Alpe di** (peak), It.
131/H2 **Potomac**, Md,US
126/E4 **Potomac** (riv.), Md, Va,US
108/E7 **Potosí**, Bol.
125/K3 **Potosi**, Mo,US
111/C2 **Potrerillos**, Chile
48/G2 **Potsdam**, Ger.
127/J2 **Potsdam**, NY,US
47/F3 **Potters Bar**, Eng,UK
47/F3 **Potterspury**, Eng,UK
84/D6 **Pottuvil**, SrL.
126/F3 **Poughkeepsie**, NY,US
44/B5 **Poulaphouca** (res.), Ire.
45/G5 **Poulter** (riv.), Eng,UK
45/F4 **Poulton-le-Fylde**, Eng,UK
57/G4 **Pourri** (mtn.), Fr.
110/H7 **Pouso Alegre**, Braz.
83/C3 **Pouthisat**, Camb.
83/C3 **Pouthisat** (riv.), Camb.
49/K4 **Považská Bystrica**, Slvk.
58/A2 **Póvoa de Varzim**, Port.
67/G2 **Povorino**, Rus.
77/L3 **Povorotnyy, Mys** (cape), Rus.
119/J2 **Povungnituk** (riv.), Qu,Can
123/G4 **Powder** (riv.), Mt, Wy,US
124/E3 **Powell** (lake), Az, Ut,US
122/F4 **Powell**, Wy,US
122/B3 **Powell River**, BC,Can
127/R9 **Power** (res.), NY,US
46/C1 **Powys, Vale** (val.), Wal,UK
109/H7 **Poxoréo**, Braz.
82/C2 **Poyang** (lake), China
45/F5 **Poynton**, Eng,UK
58/A1 **Poyo**, Sp.
62/E3 **Požarevac**, Yugo.
116/B3 **Poza Rica**, Mex.
63/F3 **Požega**, Yugo.
49/J2 **Poznań**, Pol.
49/J2 **Poznań** (prov.), Pol.
58/D4 **Pozo Alcón**, Sp.
58/C3 **Pozoblanco**, Sp.
59/N9 **Pozuelo de Alarcón**, Sp.
60/D4 **Pozzallo**, It.
60/D1 **Pozzoni** (peak), It.
49/K2 **Prabuty**, Pol.
83/B4 **Pracham Hiang** (pt.), Thai.
57/J2 **Prachatice**, Czh.
83/C3 **Prachin Buri**, Thai.

83/C3 **Prachin Buri** (riv.), Thai.
83/B4 **Prachuap Khiri Khan**, Thai.
49/J3 **Praděd** (peak), Czh.
109/L7 **Prado**, Braz.
131/C3 **Prado** (dam), Ca,US
57/L1 **Prague** (Praha) (cap.), Czh.
57/L1 **Praha** (reg.), Czh.
63/G3 **Prahova** (co.), Rom.
59/S12 **Praia de Victória**, Azor.,Port.
110/G9 **Praia Grande**, Braz.
126/B3 **Prairie du Chien**, Wi,US
127/N6 **Prairies** (riv.), Qu,Can
123/J4 **Prairies, Coteau des** (upland), US
128/E4 **Prairie View**, Tx,US
83/B3 **Pran Buri** (res.), Thai.
84/D4 **Prānhita** (riv.), India
86/A3 **Prapat**, Indo.
83/D3 **Prasat Preah Vihear**, Camb.
49/K3 **Praszka**, Pol.
110/B1 **Prata**, Braz.
57/J5 **Prato**, It.
60/C1 **Pratola Peligna**, It.
113/J7 **Pratt** (isl.), Chile
125/H3 **Pratt**, Ks,US
129/G3 **Prattville**, Al,US
58/B1 **Pravia**, Sp.
46/C6 **Prawle** (pt.), Eng,UK
87/E5 **Praya**, Indo.
63/G3 **Predeal**, Rom.
123/H3 **Preeceville**, Sk,Can
45/F6 **Prees**, Eng,UK
45/F4 **Preesall**, Eng,UK
48/F1 **Preetz**, Ger.
49/L1 **Pregolya** (riv.), Rus.
126/E1 **Preissac** (lake), On,Can
83/D4 **Prek Pouthi**, Camb.
58/A2 **Premià de Mar**, Sp.
49/G2 **Prenzlau**, Ger.
49/J4 **Přerov**, Czh.
55/G5 **Presanella** (peak), It.
45/F5 **Prescot**, Eng,UK
126/F2 **Prescott**, On,Can
124/D4 **Prescott**, Az,US
62/E4 **Preševo**, Yugo.
111/D2 **Presidencia Roque Sáenz Peña**, Arg.
109/K5 **Presidente Dutra**, Braz.
110/A2 **Presidente Epitácio**, Braz.
110/B2 **Presidente Prudente**, Braz.
112/B5 **Presidente Ríos** (lake), Chile
110/B2 **Presidente Venceslau**, Braz.
128/B4 **Presidio**, Tx,US
63/H4 **Preslav**, Bul.
52/B6 **Presles-en-Brie**, Fr.
49/L4 **Prešov**, Slvk.
62/E4 **Prespa** (lake), Eur.
127/G2 **Presque Isle**, Me,US
45/E5 **Prestatyn**, Wal,UK
99/E5 **Prestea**, Gha.
90/D2 **Presteigne**, Wal,UK
57/K2 **Přeštice**, Czh.
91/G5 **Preston**, Austl.
45/F4 **Preston**, Eng,UK
48/D5 **Preston**, Eng,UK
122/F5 **Preston**, Id,US
126/D4 **Prestonsburg**, Ky,US
45/F4 **Prestwich**, Eng,UK
43/C3 **Prestwick**, Sc,UK
47/F4 **Prestwood**, Eng,UK
109/J6 **Prêto** (riv.), Braz.
102/E2 **Pretoria** (cap.), SAfr.
102/E2 **Pretoria-Witwatersrand-Vereeniging** (prov.), SAfr.
51/F4 **Preussisch Oldendorf**, Ger.
49/G3 **Préveza**, Gre.
130/D4 **Pribilof** (isls.), Ak,US
57/L2 **Příbram**, Czh.
124/E3 **Price**, Ut,US
124/E3 **Price** (riv.), Ut,US
129/F4 **Prichard**, Al,US
58/C4 **Priego de Córdoba**, Sp.
102/C3 **Prieska**, SAfr.
122/D3 **Priest** (lake), Id,US
122/D3 **Priest River**, Id,US
58/C1 **Prieta** (mtn.), Sp.
49/K4 **Prievidza**, Slvk.
62/D3 **Prijedor**, Bosn.
62/D4 **Prijepolje**, Yugo.
67/H3 **Prikaspian** (plain), Kaz., Rus.
67/H3 **Prikumsk**, Rus.
62/E5 **Prilep**, Macd.
66/E2 **Priluki**, Ukr.
60/C2 **Prima Porta**, It.
113/J7 **Primero** (cape), Chile
47/E1 **Primethorpe**, Eng,UK
69/P5 **Primorsk Kray**, Rus.
66/F3 **Primorsko-Akhtarsk**, Rus.
122/F2 **Primrose** (lake), Ab, Sk,Can
53/F5 **Prims** (riv.), Ger.
118/E1 **Prince Albert** (pen.), NW,Can
118/E1 **Prince Albert** (sound), NW,Can
123/G2 **Prince Albert**, Sk,Can
123/G2 **Prince Albert Nat'l Park**, Sk,Can

118/D1 **Prince Alfred** (cape), NW,Can
119/J2 **Prince Charles** (isl.), NW,Can
39/L8 **Prince Edward** (isls.), SAfr.
127/J2 **Prince Edward Island** (prov.), Can.
127/J2 **Prince Edward Island Nat'l Park**, PE,Can
122/C2 **Prince George**, BC,Can
119/R7 **Prince Gustav Adolf** (sea), NW,Can
105/C **Prince Harold** (coast), Ant.
118/G2 **Prince Leopold** (isl.), NW,Can
50/C2 **Princenhof** (lake), Neth.
118/G1 **Prince of Wales** (isl.), NW,Can
118/E1 **Prince of Wales** (str.), NW,Can
130/M4 **Prince of Wales** (isl.), Ak,US
105/C **Prince Olav** (coast), Ant.
119/R7 **Prince Patrick** (isl.), NW,Can
118/G1 **Prince Regent** (inlet), NW,Can
130/M4 **Prince Rupert**, BC,Can
47/F3 **Princes Risborough**, Eng,UK
105/A **Princess Astrid** (coast), Ant.
90/A1 **Princess Charlotte** (bay), Austl.
119/S6 **Princess Margaret** (range), NW,Can
105/Z **Princess Martha** (coast), Ant.
105/B **Princess Ragnhild** (coast), Ant.
122/A2 **Princess Royal** (isl.), BC,Can
122/J5 **Princes Town**, Trin.
122/B3 **Princeton**, BC,Can
126/B3 **Princeton**, Il,US
126/C4 **Princeton**, In,US
123/K4 **Princeton**, Ky,US
131/F5 **Princeton**, Mn,US
126/D4 **Princeton**, NJ,US
126/D4 **Princeton**, WV,US
130/J3 **Prince William** (sound), Ak,US
96/G7 **Príncipe** (isl.), SaoT.
130/K3 **Prindle** (vol.), Ak,US
122/C4 **Prineville**, Or,US
50/B5 **Prinsenbeek**, Neth.
50/C2 **Prinses Margriet** (can.), Neth.
116/E5 **Prinzapolka**, Nic.
60/D4 **Priolo di Gargallo**, It.
58/A1 **Prior** (cape), Sp.
64/F3 **Priozersk**, Rus.
66/C2 **Pripet** (marshes), Bela., Ukr.
62/E4 **Priština**, Yugo.
48/G2 **Pritzwalk**, Ger.
56/F4 **Privas**, Fr.
67/H2 **Privolzhskiy**, Rus.
67/K1 **Priyutovo**, Rus.
62/E4 **Prizren**, Yugo.
62/C3 **Prnjavor**, Bosn.
86/D5 **Probolinggo**, Indo.
128/D3 **Proctor** (lake), Tx,US
84/C5 **Proddatūr**, India
53/D3 **Profondeville**, Belg.
116/E6 **Progreso**, Pan.
113/T12 **Progreso**, Uru.
77/K2 **Progress**, Rus.
67/H4 **Prokhladnyy**, Rus.
75/E1 **Prokop'yevsk**, Rus.
62/E4 **Prokuplje**, Yugo.
85/G4 **Prome**, Burma
110/B2 **Promissão**, Braz.
110/B2 **Promissão** (res.), Braz.
109/L6 **Propriá**, Braz.
49/J3 **Prosna** (riv.), Pol.
130/L3 **Prospector** (mtn.), Yk,Can
93/J6 **Prosperidad**, Phil.
49/J4 **Prostějov**, Czh.
49/J3 **Prószowice**, Pol.
63/H4 **Provadiya**, Bul.
57/G5 **Provence** (reg.), Fr.
56/F5 **Provence** (mts.), Fr.
57/G4 **Provence-Alpes-Côte d'Azur** (reg.), Fr.
108/F6 **Providência** (mts.), Braz.
116/E5 **Providencia** (isl.), Col.
49/L3 **Provins**, Fr.
124/E2 **Provo**, Ut,US
59/T13 **Provoação**, Azor.,Port.
122/F2 **Provost**, Ab,Can
62/C4 **Prozor**, Bosn.
110/B3 **Prudentópolis**, Braz.
45/G2 **Prudhoe**, Eng,UK
130/J1 **Prudhoe** (bay), Ak,US
49/J3 **Prudnik**, Pol.
53/F3 **Prüm** (riv.), Ger.
49/K2 **Pruszcz Gdański**, Pol.
49/K2 **Pruszków**, Pol.
63/J2 **Prut** (riv.), Eur.
105/F **Prydz** (bay), Ant.
128/E2 **Pryor**, Ok,US
49/K2 **Przasnysz**, Pol.
49/H3 **Przemków**, Pol.
49/M4 **Przemyśl**, Pol.

49/M4 **Przemyśl** (prov.), Pol.
49/M3 **Przeworsk**, Pol.
75/C3 **Przheval'sk**, Kyr.
64/C5 **Przylądek Rozewie** (cape), Pol.
49/L3 **Przysucha**, Pol.
61/J3 **Psará** (isl.), Gre.
64/F4 **Pskov** (lake), Est., Rus.
64/F4 **Pskov**, Rus.
64/F4 **Pskov Obl.**, Rus.
49/K4 **Pszczyna**, Pol.
62/B2 **Ptuj**, Slov.
83/C2 **Pua**, Thai.
108/D5 **Pucallpa**, Peru
81/B4 **Pucheng**, China
112/Q9 **Puchuncaví**, Chile
63/G3 **Pucioasa**, Rom.
49/K1 **Puck**, Pol.
47/G3 **Puckeridge**, Eng,UK
112/Q10 **Pucón**, Chile
42/H2 **Pudasjärvi**, Fin.
46/D5 **Puddletown**, Eng,UK
45/G4 **Pudsey**, Eng,UK
85/H2 **Pudu** (riv.), China
84/C5 **Pudukkottai**, India
116/B4 **Puebla**, Mex.
58/A1 **Puebla** (state), Mex.
58/A1 **Puebla del Caramiñal**, Sp.
125/F3 **Pueblo**, Co,US
116/E5 **Pueblo Nuevo Tiquisate**, Guat.
112/C2 **Puente Alto**, Chile
58/A1 **Puenteareas**, Sp.
58/A1 **Puente Caldelas**, Sp.
58/A1 **Puente-Ceso**, Sp.
112/C2 **Puente del Inca**, Arg.
58/A1 **Puentedeume**, Sp.
58/B1 **Puente-Genil**, Sp.
58/B1 **Puentes de García Rodríguez**, Sp.
120/R10 **Pueo** (pt.), Hi,US
124/E4 **Puerco** (riv.), Az, NM,US
122/A2 **Puerto Aisén**, Chile
112/B5 **Puerto Asís**, Col.
108/E2 **Puerto Ayacucho**, Ven.
116/D4 **Puerto Barrios**, Guat.
117/H5 **Puerto Cabello**, Ven.
116/E5 **Puerto Cabezas**, Nic.
117/H5 **Puerto Cumarebo**, Ven.
59/X16 **Puerto de la Cruz**, Canl.
81/B3 **Puerto del Son**, Sp.
116/B4 **Puerto Escondido**, Mex.
111/F2 **Puerto Iguazú**, Arg.
117/J5 **Puerto La Cruz**, Ven.
116/E4 **Puerto Lempira**, Hon.
58/C3 **Puertollano**, Sp.
58/E4 **Puerto Lumbreras**, Sp.
112/B4 **Puerto Madryn**, Arg.
108/E6 **Puerto Maldonado**, Peru
112/B4 **Puerto Montt**, Chile
116/B4 **Puerto Morelos**, Mex.
113/J7 **Puerto Natales**, Chile
117/F6 **Puerto Obaldía**, Pan.
117/G4 **Puerto Plata**, DRep.
82/C6 **Puerto Princesa**, Phil.
112/B4 **Puerto Quellón**, Chile
112/B4 **Puerto Real**, Sp.
117/H4 **Puerto Rico** (commonwealth), US
116/C5 **Puerto San José**, Guat.
108/G7 **Puerto Suárez**, Bol.
117/N9 **Puerto Vallarta**, Mex.
112/B4 **Puerto Varas**, Chile
124/B5 **Puget** (sound), Wa,US
60/E2 **Puglia** (reg.), It.
56/E5 **Puigmal** (mtn.), Fr.
59/G1 **Puigcerdà** (mtn.), Sp.
86/C5 **Pujut** (cape), Indo.
94/A5 **Pukapuka** (isl.), Cooki.
93/M6 **Puka Puka** (atoll), FrPol.
93/M6 **Pukarua** (isl.), FrPol.
126/C2 **Pukaskwa Nat'l Park**, On,Can
87/F1 **Pulanduta** (pt.), Phil.
92/D4 **Pulap** (atoll), Micr.
129/G3 **Pulaski**, Tn,US
126/D4 **Pulaski**, Va,US
49/L3 **Puf awy**, Pol.
47/F5 **Pulborough**, Eng,UK
50/D7 **Pulheim**, Ger.
87/G3 **Pulisan** (cape), Indo.
122/D4 **Pullman**, Wa,US
54/C5 **Pully**, Swi.
49/G3 **Pulsnitz** (riv.), Ger.
84/D2 **Punakha**, Bhu.
110/B3 **Punata**, Bol.
73/K2 **Punch**, India
86/B3 **Punggai** (cape), Malay.
104/E3 **Punia**, Zaire
75/C5 **Punjab** (state), India
72/B1 **Punjab** (plains), Pak.
73/K3 **Punjab** (plains), Pak.
108/D7 **Puno**, Peru

116/D4 **Punta Allen**, Mex.
113/K8 **Punta Arenas**, Chile
117/G5 **Punta Cardón**, Ven.
117/J6 **Punta de Mata**, Ven.
116/D4 **Punta Gorda**, Belz.
116/E5 **Punta Gorda** (bay), Nic.
129/H5 **Punta Gorda**, Fl,US
117/M7 **Punta Peñasco**, Mex.
116/E6 **Puntarenas**, CR
58/A1 **Punta Umbría**, Sp.
120/S10 **Puolo** (pt.), Hi,US
108/D6 **Puquio**, Peru
68/H3 **Pur** (riv.), Rus.
108/C3 **Puracé Nat'l Park**, Col.
46/D5 **Purbeck, Isle of** (pen.), Eng,UK
125/H4 **Purcell**, Ok,US
112/B3 **Purén**, Chile
125/G3 **Purgatoire** (riv.), Co,US
84/D3 **Puri**, India
64/E4 **Purikari** (pt.), Est.
50/B3 **Purmerend**, Neth.
84/C4 **Pūrna**, India
84/C3 **Pūrna** (riv.), India
111/B5 **Purranque**, Chile
47/E3 **Purton**, Eng,UK
108/F4 **Purús** (riv.), Braz.
63/G4 **Pūrvomay**, Bul.
86/C5 **Purwokerto**, Indo.
84/C4 **Pusad**, India
80/E5 **Pusan**, SKor.
80/D5 **Pusan-Jikhalsi** (prov.), SKor.
86/A2 **Pusat Gayo** (mts.), Indo.
64/F4 **Pushkin**, Rus.
62/E2 **Püspökladány**, Hun.
112/C2 **Putaendo**, Chile
86/D4 **Puting** (cape), Indo.
116/B4 **Putla**, Mex.
112/B4 **Putomayo** (riv.), Col.
68/K3 **Putorana** (mts.), Rus.
112/C4 **Putrachoique** (peak), Arg.
84/C6 **Puttalam**, SrL.
52/D1 **Putte**, Belg.
50/C4 **Putten**, Neth.
50/B5 **Putten** (isl.), Neth.
53/F5 **Püttlingen**, Ger.
98/C5 **Putu** (range), Libr.
110/A4 **Putumayo** (riv.), SAm.
86/D3 **Putussibau**, Indo.
120/T10 **Puu Kukui** (peak), Hi,US
52/D1 **Puurs**, Belg.
81/B3 **Pu Xian**, China
132/C3 **Puyallup**, Wa,US
132/C3 **Puyallup** (riv.), Wa,US
81/C4 **Puyang**, China
56/E4 **Puy de Barbier** (peak), Fr.
56/F4 **Puy de Sancy** (peak), Fr.
112/B4 **Puyehué** (vol.), Chile
112/B4 **Puyehué Nat'l Park**, Chile
56/D5 **Puymorens, Col de** (pass), Fr.
101/C4 **Pwani** (prov.), Tanz.
101/A5 **Pweto**, Zaire
44/D6 **Pwllheli**, Wal,UK
73/J1 **Pyandzh** (Panj) (riv.), Afg., Taj.
64/F2 **Pyaozero** (lake), Rus.
85/G4 **Pyapon**, Burma
68/J2 **Pyasina** (riv.), Rus.
56/F4 **Pyatigorsk**, Rus.
56/F4 **Pyfara** (mtn.), Fr.
42/H3 **Pyhä-Häkin Nat'l Park**, Fin.
42/H3 **Pyhäjärvi**, Fin.
42/H2 **Pyhätunturi** (peak), Fin.
83/B2 **Pyinmana**, Burma
46/C3 **Pyle**, Wal,UK
80/C2 **P'yŏngan-Bukto** (prov.), NKor.
80/C3 **P'yŏngan-Namdo** (prov.), NKor.
80/D4 **P'yŏngt'aek**, SKor.
80/C3 **P'yŏngyang** (cap.), NKor.
80/C3 **P'yŏngyang-Si** (prov.), NKor.
119/K2 **Pyramid** (mtn.), BC,Can
124/C3 **Pyramid** (lake), Nv,US
59/E1 **Pyrenees** (range), Eur.
49/H2 **Pyrzyce**, Pol.
65/Q4 **Pyshma** (riv.), Rus.
83/B3 **Pyu**, Burma

Q

74/M8 **Qalansuwa**, Isr.
74/F3 **Qal'at Dizah**, Iraq
74/H6 **Qalīl**, Egypt
74/K5 **Qalqīlyah**, WBnk.
72/F5 **Qamar, Ghubbat al** (bay), Yem.
74/N8 **Qanah, Wādī** (dry riv.), WBnk.
73/J2 **Qandahār**, Afg.
74/F3 **Qarah Qōsh**, Iraq
97/Q6 **Qardho**, Som.
72/E2 **Qareh Chāy** (riv.), Iran
75/F4 **Qarqan** (riv.), China
61/G2 **Qarrit, Qaf'e** (pass), Alb.
60/B4 **Qarţājannah** (ruins), Tun.
100/B2 **Qārūn, Birkat** (lake), Egypt
72/E2 **Qaşr-e-Shīrīn**, Iran
100/A3 **Qaşr Farāfirah**, Egypt
74/L5 **Qaţanā**, Syria
72/F3 **Qatar**
100/A2 **Qattara** (depr.), Egypt
74/L4 **Qaţţīnah** (lake), Syria
84/A2 **Qāzi Ahmad**, Pak.
72/F1 **Qazvīn**, Iran
61/F2 **Qendrevica** (peak), Alb.
73/G3 **Qeshm** (isl.), Iran
72/E1 **Qezel** (riv.), Iran
85/J2 **Qi** (riv.), China
81/D4 **Qian** (can.), China
81/B5 **Qian** (riv.), China
81/D5 **Qianjiang Guan** (pass), China
81/E2 **Qian Shan** (peak), China
81/B5 **Qifeng Guan** (pass), China
76/D4 **Qilian** (mts.), China
76/D4 **Qilian** (mts.), China
74/N9 **Qilt, Wādī** (dry riv.), WBnk.
75/F4 **Qimantag** (mts.), China
81/B4 **Qin** (mts.), China
81/D4 **Qin** (riv.), China
100/C3 **Qinā**, Egypt
100/C3 **Qinā** (gov.), Egypt
81/E3 **Qingdao**, China
76/D4 **Qinghai** (lake), China
76/D4 **Qinghai** (mts.), China
82/C2 **Qingjiang**, China
82/A2 **Qingshui** (riv.), China
77/H4 **Qingzhou**, China
81/D3 **Qinhuangdao**, China
81/C3 **Qinyuan**, China
82/B4 **Qiongshan**, China
77/J2 **Qiqihar**, China
74/K5 **Qiryat Ata**, Isr.
74/K5 **Qiryat Bialik**, Isr.
74/K6 **Qiryat Gat**, Isr.
74/M9 **Qiryat Mal'akhi**, Isr.
74/K5 **Qiryat Shemona**, Isr.
74/K5 **Qiryat Yam**, Isr.
81/C4 **Qi Xian**, China
77/L2 **Qixing** (riv.), China
72/F2 **Qom**, Iran
72/F2 **Qom**, Iran
84/E2 **Qomolangma** (Everest) (peak), China
73/J1 **Qondūz** (riv.), Afg.
82/C2 **Qu** (riv.), China
127/F3 **Quabbin** (res.), Ma,US
47/F3 **Quainton**, Eng,UK
51/E3 **Quakenbrück**, Ger.
131/E5 **Quakertown**, Pa,US
76/H5 **Quan** (riv.), China
128/D3 **Quanah**, Tx,US
81/B4 **Quanbao Shan** (mtn.), China
83/E3 **Quang Ngai**, Viet.
83/D2 **Quang Trach**, Viet.
83/D2 **Quang Tri**, Viet.
46/C4 **Quantocks** (hills), Eng,UK
82/B2 **Quanzhou**, China
123/G3 **Qu'Appelle** (riv.), Mb, Sk,Can
123/G3 **Qu'Appelle**, Sk,Can
123/G3 **Qu'Appelle** (dam), Sk,Can
119/K2 **Quaqtaq**, Qu,Can
52/C3 **Quaregnon**, Belg.
86/E4 **Quarles** (mts.), Indo.
57/J5 **Quarrata**, It.
60/A3 **Quartu Sant'Elena**, It.
131/B1 **Quartz Hill**, Ca,US
60/A4 **Quballāţ**, Tun.
73/G1 **Qūchān**, Iran
91/D2 **Queanbeyan**, Austl.
119/J3 **Québec** (prov.), Qu,Can
127/G2 **Québec** (cap.), Qu,Can
110/J7 **Quebra-Cangalha** (mts.), Braz.
112/B4 **Quedal** (pt.), Chile
46/D3 **Quedgeley**, Eng,UK
118/C3 **Queen Charlotte** (isls.), BC,Can
118/C3 **Queen Charlotte** (sound), BC,Can
122/B3 **Queen Charlotte** (str.), BC,Can
128/E3 **Queen City**, Tx,US
119/R7 **Queen Elizabeth**
105/G **Queen Mary** (coast), Ant.
105/P **Queen Maud** (mts.), Ant.
118/F2 **Queen Maud** (gulf), NW,Can

171

Queen – Rockp

105/Z **Queen Maud Land** (reg.), Ant.
119/S7 **Queens** (chan.), NW,Can
44/E1 **Queensberry** (mtn.), Sc,UK
45/G4 **Queensbury,** Eng,UK
45/E5 **Queensferry,** Wal,UK
90/B3 **Queensland** (state), Austl.
127/R9 **Queenston,** On,Can
102/D3 **Queenstown,** SAfr.
112/B4 **Queilén,** Chile
109/H4 **Queimada,** Braz.
104/G4 **Quelimane,** Moz.
58/A3 **Queluz,** Port.
47/E3 **Quenington,** Eng,UK
112/F3 **Quequén,** Arg.
112/F3 **Quequén Grande** (riv.), Arg.
116/A3 **Querétaro,** Mex.
116/A3 **Querétaro** (state), Mex.
116/E5 **Quesada,** CR
58/D4 **Quesada,** Sp.
81/C4 **Queshan,** China
122/C2 **Quesnel,** BC,Can
122/C2 **Quesnel** (lake), BC,Can
83/E3 **Que Son,** Viet.
125/F3 **Questa,** NM,US
73/J2 **Quetta,** Pak.
112/B5 **Queulat Nat'l Park,** Chile
108/C4 **Quevedo,** Ecu.
116/C5 **Quezaltenango,** Guat.
82/E6 **Quezon,** Phil.
82/D5 **Quezon City,** Phil.
81/D4 **Qufu,** China
104/B3 **Quibala,** Ang.
108/C2 **Quibdó,** Col.
56/B3 **Quiberon** (bay), Fr.
104/B2 **Quiçama Nat'l Park,** Ang.
51/G1 **Quickborn,** Ger.
53/G5 **Quierschied,** Ger.
124/D4 **Quijotoa,** Az,US
112/B4 **Quilán** (cape), Chile
112/Q9 **Quilicura,** Chile
123/G2 **Quill** (lakes), Sk,Can
108/D6 **Quillabamba,** Peru
108/E7 **Quillacollo,** Bol.
112/B4 **Quillagua** (pt.), Chile
112/C3 **Quilleco,** Chile
112/C2 **Quillota,** Chile
84/C6 **Quilon,** India
112/C2 **Quilpué,** Chile
56/A3 **Quimper,** Fr.
129/G4 **Quincy,** Fl,US
126/B4 **Quincy,** Il,US
127/G3 **Quincy,** Ma,US
122/D4 **Quincy,** Wa,US
83/E3 **Qui Nhon,** Viet.
124/C2 **Quinn** (riv.), Nv,US
58/D3 **Quintanar de la Orden,** Sp.
116/D4 **Quintana Roo** (state), Mex.
112/Q9 **Quintero,** Chile
112/D2 **Quinto** (riv.), Arg.
117/N8 **Quiriego,** Mex.
112/B3 **Quirihue,** Chile
101/D5 **Quirimba** (arch.), Moz.
110/B1 **Quirinópolis,** Braz.
117/J6 **Quiriquire,** Ven.
127/H2 **Quispamsis,** NB,Can
111/D2 **Quitilipi,** Arg.
129/H4 **Quitman,** Ga,US
129/F3 **Quitman,** Ms,US
128/E3 **Quitman,** Tx,US
108/C4 **Quito** (cap.), Ecu.
109/L4 **Quixadá,** Braz.
109/L5 **Quixeramobim,** Braz.
85/H2 **Qujing,** China
76/C4 **Qumar** (riv.), China
118/G2 **Quoich** (riv.), NW,Can
44/C3 **Quoile** (riv.), NI,UK
102/B4 **Quoin** (pt.), SAfr.
74/L4 **Qurnat as Sawdā'** (mtn.), Leb.
100/C3 **Qūş,** Egypt
76/F4 **Quwu** (mts.), China
83/C1 **Quynh Nhai,** Viet.
81/C3 **Quzhou,** China
82/C2 **Quzhou,** China
62/D5 **Qyteti Stalin,** Alb.

R

57/L3 **Raab** (riv.), Aus.
42/H2 **Raahe,** Fin.
50/D4 **Raalte,** Neth.
50/B5 **Raamsdonk,** Neth.
74/M8 **Ra'ananna,** Isr.
119/S7 **Raanes** (pen.), NW,Can
101/D3 **Raas Jumbo,** Som.
62/B3 **Rab** (isl.), Cro.
62/C2 **Rába** (riv.), Hun.
60/D5 **Rabat,** Malta
96/D1 **Rabat** (cap.), Mor.
92/E5 **Rabaul,** PNG
57/K4 **Rabbi** (riv.), It.
49/K4 **Rabka,** Pol.
84/C4 **Rabkavi,** India
127/S8 **Raby** (pt.), On,Can
57/G4 **Racconigi,** It.
129/F4 **Raccoon** (pt.), La,US
119/L4 **Race** (cape), Nf,Can
83/D4 **Rach Gia,** Viet.
83/D4 **Rach Gia** (bay), Viet.
49/K3 **Racibórz,** Pol.
132/Q14 **Racine,** Wi,US
62/D2 **Ráckeve,** Hun.
63/G2 **Rădăuți,** Rom.
57/K2 **Radbuza** (riv.), Czh.
45/F4 **Radcliffe,** Eng,UK
45/G6 **Radcliffe on Trent,** Eng,UK
62/A2 **Radenthein,** Aus.
51/E6 **Radevormwald,** Ger.
126/D4 **Radford,** Va,US
84/B3 **Rādhanpur,** India
122/G2 **Radisson,** Sk,Can
47/F3 **Radlett,** Eng,UK
63/G4 **Radnevo,** Bul.
49/L3 **Radom,** Pol.
49/L3 **Radom** (prov.), Pol.
62/F4 **Radomir,** Bul.
49/K3 **Radomsko,** Pol.
62/F5 **Radoviš,** Macd.
46/D4 **Radstock,** Eng,UK
64/D5 **Radviliškis,** Lith.
46/C3 **Radyr,** Wal,UK
49/K2 **Radziejów,** Pol.
49/L2 **Radzymin,** Pol.
49/M3 **Radzyń Podlaski,** Pol.
119/H3 **Rae** (isth.), NW,Can
118/E2 **Rae** (riv.), NW,Can
84/D2 **Rāe Bareli,** India
129/J3 **Raeford,** NC,US
53/F2 **Raeren,** Belg.
50/D5 **Raesfeld,** Ger.
111/D3 **Rafaela,** Arg.
74/K6 **Rafaḩ,** Gaza
73/G2 **Rafsanjān,** Iran
122/E5 **Raft** (riv.), Id, Ut,US
97/L6 **Raga,** Sudan
113/J8 **Ragged** (pt.), Chile
44/A1 **Raghtin More** (mtn.), Ire.
46/D3 **Raglan,** Wal,UK
42/E2 **Rago Nat'l Park,** Nor.
60/D4 **Ragusa,** It.
51/F4 **Rahden,** Ger.
73/K3 **Rahīmyār Khān,** Pak.
131/F5 **Rahway,** NJ,US
93/K6 **Raiatea** (isl.), FrPol.
84/C4 **Raichūr,** India
84/D3 **Raigarh,** India
124/E3 **Rainbow Bridge Nat'l Mon.,** Ut,US
45/F4 **Rainford,** Eng,UK
122/C4 **Rainier** (mt.), Wa,US
129/G3 **Rainsville,** Al,US
45/G5 **Rainworth,** Eng,UK
123/K3 **Rainy** (lake), Can., US
123/K3 **Rainy** (riv.), Can., US
126/A1 **Rainy River,** On,Can
84/D3 **Raipur,** India
48/F1 **Raisdorf,** Ger.
132/E8 **Raisin** (riv.), Mi,US
42/G3 **Raisio,** Fin.
52/C3 **Raismes,** Fr.
93/L7 **Raivavae** (isl.), FrPol.
86/A3 **Raja** (pt.), Indo.
84/D4 **Rājahmundry,** India
84/C5 **Rājampet,** India
86/D3 **Rajang** (riv.), Malay.
73/K3 **Rājanpur,** Pak.
84/C6 **Rājapālaiyam,** India
84/B4 **Rājāpur,** India
84/B2 **Rājasthān** (state), India
73/L3 **Rajgarh,** India
84/C3 **Rājgarh,** India
84/B3 **Rājkot,** India
84/D3 **Rāj-Nāndagaon,** India
73/L2 **Rājpura,** India
84/E3 **Rājshāhi,** Bang.
84/B3 **Rājula,** India
93/J5 **Rakahanga** (atoll), Cookls.
73/K1 **Rakaposhi** (mtn.), Pak.
85/F4 **Rakhine** (state), Burma
73/H3 **Rakhshān** (riv.), Pak.
104/D5 **Rakops,** Bots.
63/G4 **Rakovski,** Bul.
64/E4 **Rakvere,** Est.
129/J3 **Raleigh** (cap.), NC,US
92/F4 **Ralik Chain** (arch.), Mrsh.
122/F3 **Ralston,** Ab,Can
109/K6 **Ramalho** (mts.), Braz.
74/K6 **Rām Allāh,** WBnk.
84/B4 **Ramas** (cape), India
74/K5 **Ramat Gan,** Isr.
74/M8 **Ramat HaSharon,** Isr.
93/Z17 **Rambi** (isl.), Fiji
52/A6 **Rambouillet,** Fr.
46/B6 **Rame** (pt.), Eng,UK
84/E2 **Rāmechhāp,** Nepal
84/C6 **Rāmeswaram,** India
72/E2 **Rāmhormoz,** Iran
74/K6 **Ramla,** Isr.
100/C2 **Ramm, Jabal** (mt.), Jor.
44/A4 **Ramor, Lough** (lake), Ire.
85/F4 **Ramree** (isl.), Burma
72/F1 **Ramsar** (Sakht Sar), Iran
45/F4 **Ramsbottom,** Eng,UK
47/E4 **Ramsbury,** Eng,UK
126/D2 **Ramsey** (lake), On,Can
47/F2 **Ramsey,** Eng,UK
44/D3 **Ramsey,** IM,UK
46/A3 **Ramsey** (isl.), Wal,UK
47/H4 **Ramsgate,** Eng,UK
53/G5 **Ramstein-Miesenbach,** Ger.
92/D5 **Ramu** (riv.), PNG
84/E3 **Rānāghāt,** India
112/C2 **Rancagua,** Chile
56/B2 **Rance** (riv.), Fr.
110/B2 **Rancharia,** Braz.
122/G4 **Ranchester,** Wy,US
84/E3 **Rānchī,** India
132/M9 **Rancho Cordova,** Ca,US
131/C2 **Rancho Cucamonga** (Cucamonga), Ca,US
131/B3 **Rancho Palos Verdes,** Ca,US
112/B4 **Ranco** (lake), Chile
97/P5 **Randa,** Djib.
131/K7 **Randallstown,** Md,US
44/B2 **Randalstown,** NI,UK
60/D4 **Randazzo,** It.
102/P13 **Randburg,** SAfr.
42/D4 **Randers,** Den.
131/F5 **Randolph,** NJ,US
49/H2 **Randow** (riv.), Ger.
90/H8 **Randwick,** Austl.
83/C2 **Rang** (peak), Thai.
85/F3 **Rāngāmāti,** Bang.
87/E4 **Rangasa** (cape), Indo.
124/E2 **Rangely,** Co,US
128/D3 **Ranger,** Tx,US
93/L6 **Rangiroa** (atoll), FrPol.
83/B2 **Rangoon** (div.), Burma
83/B2 **Rangoon** (Yangon) (cap.), Burma
84/E2 **Rangpur,** Bang.
84/C5 **Rānībennur,** India
128/C4 **Rankin,** Tx,US
83/B4 **Ranong,** Thai.
53/G3 **Ransbach-Baumbach,** Ger.
127/S9 **Ransomville,** NY,US
52/D1 **Ranst,** Belg.
87/F4 **Rantekombola** (peak), Indo.
126/B3 **Rantoul,** Il,US
83/D2 **Rao Co** (peak), Laos
54/C1 **Raon-L'Etape,** Fr.
92/H7 **Raoul** (isl.), NZ
81/C3 **Raoyang,** China
93/L7 **Rapa** (isl.), FrPol.
112/Q10 **Rapel** (lake), Chile
112/B5 **Raper** (cape), Chile
123/H4 **Rapid City,** SD,US
126/E4 **Rappahannock** (riv.), Va,US
84/D2 **Rapti** (riv.), India
131/F5 **Raritan** (bay), NJ,US
131/F5 **Raritan** (riv.), NJ,US
93/L6 **Raroia** (atoll), FrPol.
93/J7 **Rarotonga** (isl.), Cookls.
112/E4 **Rasa** (pt.), Arg.
74/E3 **Ra's al 'Ayn,** Syria
97/J7 **Ra's al Unūf,** Libya
100/C2 **Ras Gharib,** Egypt
44/B2 **Rasharkin,** NI,UK
74/K5 **Rāshayyā,** Leb.
74/H6 **Rashīd** (Rosetta), Egypt
72/E1 **Rasht,** Iran
62/E4 **Raška,** Yugo.
118/G2 **Rasmussen** (basin), NW,Can
59/P10 **Raso** (cape), Port.
67/G1 **Rasskazovo,** Rus.
57/H2 **Rastatt,** Ger.
51/F2 **Rastede,** Ger.
130/B6 **Rat** (isls.), Ak,US
86/B5 **Rata** (cape), Indo.
84/B2 **Ratangarh,** India
83/B3 **Rat Buri,** Thai.
84/C2 **Rāth,** India
123/K5 **Rathbun** (lake), Ia,US
48/G2 **Rathenow,** Ger.
44/B3 **Rathfriland,** NI,UK
44/B1 **Rathlin** (isl.), NI,UK
44/B1 **Rathlin** (sound), NI,UK
92/F4 **Ratik Chain** (arch.), Mrsh.
50/D6 **Ratingen,** Ger.
84/C3 **Ratlām,** India
84/B4 **Ratnāgiri,** India
84/D6 **Ratnapura,** SrL.
125/F3 **Raton,** NM,US
42/E3 **Rättvik,** Swe.
48/F2 **Ratzeburg,** Ger.
86/B3 **Raub,** Malay.
112/F3 **Rauch,** Arg.
42/D3 **Raufoss,** Nor.
110/D2 **Raul Soares,** Braz.
84/D3 **Raurkela,** India
60/C4 **Ravanusa,** It.
50/C6 **Ravels,** Belg.
45/E3 **Ravenglass,** Eng,UK
57/K4 **Ravenna,** It.
57/F2 **Ravensburg,** Ger.
45/G5 **Ravenshead,** Eng,UK
126/D4 **Ravenswood,** WV,US
73/K2 **Rāvi** (riv.), India, Pak.
62/B2 **Ravne na Koroškem,** Slov.
93/H5 **Rawaki** (Phoenix) (atoll), Kiri.
73/K2 **Rāwalpindi,** Pak.
49/L3 **Rawa Mazowiecka,** Pol.
49/J3 **Rawicz,** Pol.
122/G5 **Rawlins,** Wy,US
45/G5 **Rawmarsh,** Eng,UK
112/D4 **Rawson,** Arg.
45/F4 **Rawtenstall,** Eng,UK
127/K2 **Ray** (cape), Nf,Can
86/D4 **Raya** (peak), Indo.
84/C5 **Rāyadrug,** India
84/D4 **Rāyagada,** India
77/K2 **Raychikhinsk,** Rus.
47/G3 **Rayleigh,** Eng,UK
123/F3 **Raymond,** Ab,Can
128/D5 **Raymondville,** Tx,US
123/G3 **Raymore,** Sk,Can
83/C3 **Rayong,** Thai.
67/H4 **Razdan,** Arm.
63/J3 **Razelm** (lake), Rom.
63/H4 **Razgrad,** Bul.
61/K1 **Razgrad** (reg.), Bul.
63/F5 **Razlog,** Bul.
56/A2 **Raz, Pointe du** (pt.), Fr.
56/C3 **Ré** (isl.), Fr.
46/D2 **Rea** (riv.), Eng,UK
47/F4 **Reading,** Eng,UK
83/C3 **Reang Kesei,** Camb.
93/M6 **Reao** (atoll), FrPol.
77/N2 **Rebun** (isl.), Japan
57/K5 **Recanati,** It.
53/F6 **Réchicourt-le-Château,** Fr.
66/D1 **Rechitsa,** Bela.
109/M5 **Recife,** Braz.
102/D4 **Recife** (cape), SAfr.
51/E4 **Recke,** Ger.
51/E5 **Recklinghausen,** Ger.
48/G2 **Recknitz** (riv.), Ger.
83/B2 **Reclining Buddha** (Shwethalyaung) (ruins), Burma
111/E2 **Reconquista,** Arg.
72/C4 **Red** (sea), Afr., Asia
85/H3 **Red** (riv.), China, Viet.
44/B1 **Red** (bay), NI,UK
125/J5 **Red** (riv.), US
128/D2 **Red** (hills), Ks,US
49/K1 **Reda,** Pol.
131/F5 **Red Bank,** NJ,US
124/B2 **Red Bluff,** Ca,US
125/G4 **Red Bluff** (lake), NM, Tx,US
47/F3 **Redbourn,** Eng,UK
45/G2 **Redcar,** Eng,UK
122/F3 **Redcliff,** Ab,Can
90/F6 **Redcliffe,** Austl.
125/H2 **Red Cloud,** Ne,US
122/E2 **Red Deer,** Ab,Can
122/F3 **Red Deer** (riv.), Ab,Can
123/H2 **Red Deer** (lake), Mb,Can
123/H2 **Red Deer** (riv.), Mb, Sk,Can
124/B2 **Redding,** Ca,US
47/E2 **Redditch,** Eng,UK
45/F1 **Rede** (riv.), Eng,UK
123/J4 **Redfield,** SD,US
132/F7 **Redford,** Mi,US
47/F4 **Redhill,** Eng,UK
120/T10 **Red Hill** (peak), Hi,US
127/K1 **Red Indian** (lake), Nf,Can
53/G6 **Réding,** Fr.
123/K3 **Red Lake,** On,Can
123/K3 **Red Lake** (riv.), Mn,US
131/J7 **Redland,** Md,US
90/F7 **Redland Bay,** Austl.
131/C2 **Redlands,** Ca,US
122/F4 **Red Lodge,** Mt,US
122/C4 **Redmond,** Or,US
132/C2 **Redmond,** Wa,US
56/B3 **Redon,** Fr.
58/A1 **Redondela,** Sp.
58/B3 **Redondo,** Port.
131/B3 **Redondo Beach,** Ca,US
130/H3 **Redoubt** (vol.), Ak,US
123/J3 **Red River of the North** (riv.), Can., US
123/K5 **Red Rock** (lake), Ia,US
46/A6 **Redruth,** Eng,UK
100/D4 **Red Sea** (hills), Sudan
118/D2 **Redstone** (riv.), NW,Can
123/K2 **Red Sucker** (lake), Mb,Can
123/H3 **Redvers,** Sk,Can
99/E4 **Red Volta** (riv.), Burk., Gui.
122/E2 **Redwater,** Ab,Can
124/B2 **Redway,** Ca,US
125/G2 **Red Willow** (cr.), Ne,US
126/A2 **Red Wing,** Mn,US
132/K12 **Redwood City,** Ca,US
123/K4 **Redwood Falls,** Mn,US
124/A2 **Redwood Nat'l Park,** Ca,US
126/C3 **Reed City,** Mi,US
47/H1 **Reedham,** Eng,UK
124/C3 **Reedley,** Ca,US
126/B3 **Reedsburg,** Wi,US
122/B5 **Reedsport,** Or,US
91/B3 **Reedy** (cr.), Austl.
92/F6 **Reef** (isls.), Sol.
89/H7 **Reefton,** NZ
44/A4 **Ree, Lough** (lake), Ire.
47/H1 **Reepham,** Eng,UK
50/D5 **Rees,** Ger.
124/C3 **Reese** (riv.), Nv,US
50/D3 **Reest** (riv.), Neth.
45/G3 **Reeth,** Eng,UK
50/B4 **Reeuwijk,** Neth.
128/D4 **Refugio,** Tx,US
49/H2 **Rega** (riv.), Pol.
110/E1 **Regência, Pontal de** (pt.), Braz.
109/K5 **Regeneração,** Braz.
57/K2 **Regensburg,** Ger.
57/K2 **Regenstauf,** Ger.
90/H8 **Regents Park,** Austl.
96/F2 **Reggane,** Alg.
50/D4 **Regge** (riv.), Neth.
60/D3 **Reggio di Calabria,** It.
57/J4 **Reggio nell'Emilia,** It.
62/G2 **Reghin,** Rom.
123/G3 **Regina** (cap.), Sk,Can
124/F3 **Regina,** NM,US
123/G3 **Regina Beach,** Sk,Can
110/C3 **Registro,** Braz.
57/J2 **Regnitz** (riv.), Ger.
58/B3 **Reguengos de Monsaraz,** Port.
51/G4 **Rehburg-Loccum,** Ger.
53/F5 **Rehlingen-Siersburg,** Ger.
104/C5 **Rehoboth,** Namb.
74/M9 **Reḥovot,** Isr.
53/G2 **Reichshof,** Ger.
122/F3 **Reid** (lake), Sk,Can
129/J2 **Reidsville,** NC,US
47/F4 **Reigate,** Eng,UK
52/D5 **Reims,** Fr.
113/J7 **Reina Adelaida** (arch.), Chile
51/H1 **Reinbek,** Ger.
123/J2 **Reindeer** (isl.), Mb,Can
123/H1 **Reindeer** (lake), Mb, Sk,Can
123/H1 **Reindeer** (riv.), Sk,Can
58/C1 **Reinosa,** Sp.
42/G1 **Reisduoddarhal'di** (peak), Nor.
50/D2 **Reitdiep** (riv.), Neth.
122/F5 **Reliance,** Wy,US
96/F1 **Relizane,** Alg.
51/G1 **Rellingen,** Ger.
53/G2 **Remagen,** Ger.
109/K5 **Remanso,** Braz.
86/D5 **Rembang,** Indo.
109/H3 **Rémire,** FrG.
57/H2 **Rems** (riv.), Ger.
51/E6 **Remscheid,** Ger.
81/B5 **Ren** (riv.), China
112/C2 **Renca,** Chile
129/F2 **Rend** (lake), Il,US
48/E1 **Rendsburg,** Ger.
54/C4 **Renens,** Swi.
126/E2 **Renfrew,** On,Can
86/B4 **Rengat,** Indo.
112/C2 **Rengo,** Chile
66/D3 **Reni,** Ukr.
50/C5 **Renkum,** Neth.
92/F6 **Rennell** (isl.), Sol.
56/C2 **Rennes,** Fr.
57/J4 **Reno** (riv.), It.
124/C3 **Reno,** Nv,US
102/C3 **Renoster** (riv.), SAfr.
102/D2 **Renoster** (riv.), SAfr.
81/D3 **Renqiu,** China
126/C3 **Rensselaer,** In,US
58/E1 **Rentería,** Sp.
132/C3 **Renton,** Wa,US
127/P6 **Repentigny,** Qu,Can
45/G6 **Repton,** Eng,UK
122/D3 **Republic,** Wa,US
125/H2 **Republican** (riv.), Ks, Ne,US
90/C3 **Repulse** (bay), Austl.
108/D4 **Requena,** Peru
59/E3 **Requena,** Sp.
112/C2 **Requiñoa,** Chile
112/B5 **Rescue** (pt.), Chile
62/E5 **Resen,** Macd.
110/J7 **Resende,** Braz.
124/E4 **Reserve,** NM,US
111/E2 **Resistencia,** Arg.
62/E3 **Reşiţa,** Rom.
118/G1 **Resolute,** NW,Can
119/K2 **Resolution** (isl.), NW,Can
46/C3 **Resolven,** Wal,UK
110/D1 **Resplendor,** Braz.
52/B4 **Ressons-sur-Matz,** Fr.
127/H2 **Restigouche** (riv.), NB,Can
123/H3 **Reston,** Mb,Can
131/J8 **Reston,** Va,US
132/C2 **Restoration** (pt.), Wa,US
116/C5 **Retalhuleu,** Guat.
52/D4 **Rethel,** Fr.
61/J5 **Réthimnon,** Gre.
53/E1 **Retie,** Belg.
62/F3 **Retrezap Nat'l Park,** Rom.
103/R15 **Réunion** (dpcy.), Fr.
59/F2 **Reus,** Sp.
50/C6 **Reusel,** Neth.
48/G2 **Reuterstadt Stavenhagen,** Ger.
55/F1 **Reutlingen,** Ger.
64/H5 **Reutov,** Rus.
56/D5 **Revel,** Fr.
122/D3 **Revelstoke,** BC,Can
90/H8 **Revesby,** Austl.
52/D4 **Revin,** Fr.
75/B4 **Revolyutsii, Pik** (peak), Taj.
42/G1 **Revsbotn** (fjord), Nor.
84/D3 **Rewa,** India
84/C2 **Rewāri,** India
130/J3 **Rex** (mtn.), Ak,US
122/F5 **Rexburg,** Id,US
52/B2 **Rexpoëde,** Fr.
117/F6 **Rey** (isl.), Pan.
47/H2 **Reydon,** Eng,UK
124/B3 **Reyes** (pt.), Ca,US
74/D3 **Reyhanlı,** Turk.
42/N7 **Reykjavík** (cap.), Ice.
116/B2 **Reynosa,** Mex.
56/C3 **Rezé,** Fr.
64/E4 **Rēzekne,** Lat.
55/F4 **Rhaetian Alps** (mts.), It., Swi.
55/F3 **Rhätikon** (mts.), Aus., Swi.
46/C2 **Rhayader,** Wal,UK
51/F5 **Rheda-Wiedenbrück,** Ger.
50/D5 **Rheden,** Neth.
47/F2 **Rhee** (Cam) (riv.), Eng,UK
53/F2 **Rheinbach,** Ger.
50/D5 **Rheinberg,** Ger.
51/E4 **Rheine,** Ger.
96/E2 **Rhemiles** (well), Alg.
50/C5 **Rhenen,** Neth.
48/D3 **Rhine** (riv.), Eur.
51/E5 **Rhine-Herne** (can.), Ger.
126/B2 **Rhinelander,** Wi,US
53/F3 **Rhineland-Palatinate** (state), Ger.
53/D3 **Rhisnes,** Belg.
46/C1 **Rhiw** (riv.), Wal,UK
127/G3 **Rhode Island** (state), US
74/B3 **Rhodes** (isl.), Gre.
74/B3 **Rhodes** (Ródhos), Gre.
63/F4 **Rhodope** (mts.), Bul.
46/C3 **Rhondda,** Wal,UK
56/F4 **Rhône** (riv.), Fr., Swi.
56/F4 **Rhône-Alpes** (reg.), Fr.
52/C3 **Rhonelle** (riv.), Fr.
45/E6 **Rhosllanerchrugog,** Wal,UK
46/B3 **Rhossili,** Wal,UK
44/E5 **Rhuddlan,** Wal,UK
51/H5 **Rhume** (riv.), Ger.
46/C2 **Rhyddhywel** (mtn.), Wal,UK
46/B2 **Rhydowen,** Wal,UK
44/E5 **Rhyl,** Wal,UK
46/C3 **Rhymney,** Wal,UK
109/K6 **Riacho de Santana,** Braz.
131/C2 **Rialto,** Ca,US
58/A1 **Rianjo,** Sp.
86/B3 **Riau** (isls.), Indo.
58/A1 **Ribadavia,** Sp.
58/B1 **Ribadeo,** Sp.
58/C1 **Ribadesella,** Sp.
103/H8 **Ribaṅ'i Manamby** (mts.), Madg.
45/F4 **Ribble** (riv.), Eng,UK
48/E1 **Ribe,** Den.
48/E1 **Ribe** (co.), Den.
110/B3 **Ribeira** (riv.), Braz.
109/L6 **Ribeira do Pombal,** Braz.
59/T13 **Ribeira Grande,** Azor.
110/B2 **Ribeirão do Pinha,** Braz.
110/C2 **Ribeirão Preto,** Braz.
52/C4 **Ribemont,** Fr.
60/C4 **Ribera,** It.
108/E6 **Riberalta,** Bol.
48/G1 **Ribnitz-Damgarten,** Ger.
126/E2 **Rice** (lake), On,Can
126/B2 **Rice Lake,** Wi,US
118/C2 **Richards** (isl.), NW,Can
127/G2 **Richardson** (lakes), Me,US
50/C2 **Richel** (isl.), Neth.
124/D3 **Richfield,** Ut,US
44/B3 **Richhill,** NI,UK
122/D4 **Richland,** Wa,US
129/H3 **Richland Balsam** (peak), NC,US
126/B3 **Richland Center,** Wi,US
128/D4 **Richland Creek** (res.), Tx,US
91/D2 **Richmond,** Austl.
127/F2 **Richmond,** Qu,Can
45/G3 **Richmond,** Eng,UK
132/K11 **Richmond,** Ca,US
126/C4 **Richmond,** In,US
126/C4 **Richmond,** Ky,US
128/E4 **Richmond,** Tx,US
126/E4 **Richmond** (cap.), Va,US
132/C2 **Richmond Beach-Innis Arden,** Wa,US
127/R8 **Richmond Hill,** On,Can
90/G8 **Richmond-Raaf,** Austl.
47/F3 **Rickmansworth,** Eng,UK
50/B5 **Ridderkerk,** Neth.
126/E2 **Rideau** (lake), On,Can
124/C4 **Ridgecrest,** Ca,US
131/F5 **Ridgewood,** NJ,US
45/G2 **Riding Mill,** Eng,UK
123/H3 **Riding Mtn. Nat'l Park,** Mb,Can
57/K2 **Ried im Innkreis,** Aus.
53/F5 **Riegelsberg,** Ger.
53/E2 **Riemst,** Belg.
49/G3 **Riesa,** Ger.
113/J8 **Riesco** (isl.), Chile
102/D3 **Riet** (riv.), SAfr.
51/F5 **Rietberg,** Ger.
60/C1 **Rieti,** It.
45/G3 **Rievaulx,** Eng,UK
122/C4 **Riffe** (lake), Wa,US
124/F3 **Rifle,** Co,US
42/N6 **Rifsnes** (pt.), Ice.
101/B2 **Rift Valley** (prov.), Kenya
64/E4 **Riga** (Rīga) (cap.), Lat.
122/F5 **Rigby,** Id,US
73/H2 **Rīgestan** (reg.), Afg.
122/D4 **Riggins,** Id,US
84/D3 **Rihand Sāgar** (res.), India
42/H3 **Riihimäki,** Fin.
105/C **Riiser-Larsen** (pen.), Ant.
42/J2 **Riisitunturin Nat'l Park,** Fin.
62/B3 **Rijeka,** Cro.
50/B4 **Rijnsburg,** Neth.
50/D4 **Rijssen,** Neth.
50/B4 **Rijswijk,** Neth.
93/M7 **Rikitea,** FrPol.
63/F4 **Rila** (mts.), Bul.
61/H1 **Rilski Manastir,** Bul.
93/K7 **Rimatara** (isl.), FrPol.
49/L4 **Rimavská Sobota,** Slvk.
72/D3 **Rīma, Wādi** (dry riv.), SAr.
122/E2 **Rimbey,** Ab,Can
97/J5 **Rimé** (wadi), Chad
57/K4 **Rimini,** It.
63/H3 **Rîmnicu Sărat,** Rom.
63/G3 **Rîmnicu Vîlcea,** Rom.
127/G1 **Rimouski,** Qu,Can
76/D1 **Rinchinlhümbe,** Mong.
58/C4 **Rincón de la Victoria,** Sp.
116/D5 **Rincon de la Vieja Nat'l Park,** CR
117/P9 **Rincón de Romos,** Mex.
44/C3 **Ringboy** (pt.), NI,UK
42/D4 **Ringkøbing,** Den.
47/G5 **Ringmer,** Eng,UK
131/F5 **Ringoes,** NJ,US
44/B1 **Ringsend,** NI,UK
48/F1 **Ringsted,** Den.
50/B4 **Ringvaart** (can.), Neth.
42/F1 **Ringvassøy** (isl.), Nor.
91/G5 **Ringwood,** Austl.
47/E5 **Ringwood,** Eng,UK
131/F4 **Ringwood,** NJ,US
61/J4 **Rínia** (isl.), Gre.
44/C2 **Rinns, The** (pen.), Sc,UK
51/G4 **Rinteln,** Ger.
108/C5 **Río Abiseo Nat'l Park,** Peru
108/C4 **Riobamba,** Ecu.
110/L7 **Rio Bonito,** Braz.
108/E5 **Rio Branco,** Braz.
113/G2 **Río Branco,** Uru.
110/B3 **Rio Branco do Sul,** Braz.
126/C4 **Río Bravo del Norte** (Río Grande) (riv.), Mex., US
112/B4 **Río Bueno,** Chile
110/D2 **Rio Casca,** Braz.
113/T12 **Riochuelo,** Uru.
112/C2 **Río Clarillo Nat'l Park,** Chile
110/J7 **Rio Claro,** Braz.
112/D3 **Río Colorado,** Arg.
112/D2 **Río Cuarto,** Arg.
110/K7 **Rio de Janeiro,** Braz.
110/K7 **Rio de Janeiro** (state), Braz.
122/B5 **Rio Dell,** Ca,US
110/B3 **Rio do Sul,** Braz.
59/Q10 **Rio Frio,** Port.
113/K7 **Río Gallegos,** Arg.
113/L8 **Río Grande,** Arg.
110/A5 **Rio Grande,** Braz.
128/C4 **Rio Grande** (riv.), Mex., US
128/D5 **Rio Grande City,** Tx,US
110/G8 **Rio Grande da Serra,** Braz.
116/E5 **Río Grande de Matagalpa** (riv.), Nic.
110/A4 **Rio Grande do Sul** (state), Braz.
117/G5 **Riohacha,** Col.
117/E6 **Río Hato,** Pan.
108/C5 **Rioja,** Peru
108/F4 **Rio Jaú Nat'l Park,** Braz.
109/L5 **Rio Largo,** Braz.
56/E4 **Riom,** Fr.
58/A3 **Rio Maior,** Port.
122/D3 **Riondel,** BC,Can
112/C4 **Río Negro** (prov.), Arg.
113/F2 **Río Negro** (dept.), Uru.
113/F2 **Río Negro** (res.), Uru.
60/D2 **Rionero in Vulture,** It.
110/C1 **Rio Paranaíba,** Braz.
110/A4 **Rio Pardo,** Braz.
111/E2 **Río Pilcomayo Nat'l Park,** Arg.
124/F4 **Rio Rancho,** NM,US
56/F3 **Riorges,** Fr.
112/E1 **Río Segundo,** Arg.
112/B5 **Río Simpson Nat'l Park,** Chile
112/D2 **Río Tercero,** Arg.
110/B1 **Rio Verde,** Braz.
116/B3 **Rioverde,** Mex.
109/H7 **Rio Verde de Mato Grosso,** Braz.
62/E3 **Ripanj,** Yugo.
129/F3 **Ripley,** Ms,US
129/F3 **Ripley,** Tn,US
59/G1 **Ripoll,** Sp.
59/L6 **Ripoll** (riv.), Sp.
59/L6 **Ripollet,** Sp.
45/G3 **Ripon,** Eng,UK
123/L5 **Ripon,** Wi,US
60/D4 **Riposto,** It.
45/G4 **Ripponden,** Eng,UK
46/C3 **Risca,** Wal,UK
77/N2 **Rishiri** (isl.), Japan
74/K6 **Rishon LeZiyyon,** Isr.
56/D2 **Risle** (riv.), Fr.
62/B3 **Risnjak** (peak), Cro.
62/B3 **Risnjak Nat'l Park,** Cro.
63/G3 **Rîşnov,** Rom.
128/E3 **Rison,** Ar,US
42/D4 **Risør,** Nor.
108/D2 **Ritacuba** (peak), Col.
92/C2 **Ritaiō** (isl.), Japan
51/F2 **Ritterhude,** Ger.
79/L9 **Rittō,** Japan
122/D4 **Ritzville,** Wa,US
57/J4 **Riva,** It.
112/E2 **Rivadavia,** Arg.
57/G4 **Rivarolo Canavese,** It.
116/D5 **Rivas,** Nic.
56/F4 **Rive-de-Gier,** Fr.
112/B5 **Rivera** (isl.), Chile
111/E3 **Rivera,** Uru.
113/G1 **Rivera** (dept.), Uru.
132/F7 **River Rouge,** Mi,US
122/B3 **Rivers** (inlet), BC,Can
123/H3 **Rivers,** Mb,Can
99/G5 **Rivers** (state), Nga.
102/C4 **Riversdale,** SAfr.
131/C3 **Riverside,** Ca,US
90/G8 **Riverstone,** Austl.
123/J3 **Riverton,** Mb,Can
122/F5 **Riverton,** Wy,US
127/H2 **Riverview,** NB,Can
132/F7 **Riverview,** Mi,US
129/H5 **Riviera Beach,** Fl,US
131/K7 **Riviera Beach,** Md,US
127/G2 **Rivière-du-Loup,** Qu,Can
102/L11 **Riviersonderendreeks** (mts.), SAfr.
57/G4 **Rivoli,** It.
52/D2 **Rixensart,** Belg.
72/E4 **Riyadh** (Ar Riyāḑ) (cap.), SAr.
74/E2 **Rize,** Turk.
81/D4 **Rizhao,** China
60/E3 **Rizzuto** (cape), It.
42/D4 **Rjukan,** Nor.
98/B2 **Rkîz** (lake), Mrta.
42/D3 **Roa,** Nor.
47/F2 **Roade,** Eng,UK
43/D2 **Roadside,** Sc,UK
117/J4 **Road Town** (cap.), BVI
124/E3 **Roan** (plat.), Co,US
45/F1 **Roan Fell** (hill), Sc,UK
129/H2 **Roan High** (peak), NC,US
56/F3 **Roanne,** Fr.
129/G3 **Roanoke,** Al,US
129/J2 **Roanoke** (riv.), NC, Va,US
126/E4 **Roanoke,** Va,US
129/J2 **Roanoke Rapids,** NC,US
116/D4 **Roatán** (isl.), Hon.
91/C4 **Robbins** (isl.), Austl.
91/B1 **Robe** (peak), Austl.
43/A4 **Robe** (riv.), Ire.
53/E6 **Robert-Espagne,** Fr.
128/C4 **Robert Lee,** Tx,US
130/E4 **Roberts** (mtn.), Ak,US
47/G5 **Robertsbridge,** Eng,UK
42/G2 **Robertsfors,** Swe.
84/D3 **Robertsganj,** India
102/B4 **Robertson,** SAfr.
127/F1 **Roberval,** Qu,Can
45/H3 **Robin Hood's Bay,** Eng,UK
126/C4 **Robinson,** Il,US
132/C3 **Robinson** (pt.), Wa,US
107/B6 **Robinson Crusoe** (isl.), Chile
90/C4 **Robinson Gorge Nat'l Park,** Austl.
123/H3 **Roblin,** Mb,Can
108/G7 **Roboré,** Bol.
122/D2 **Robson** (peak), BC,Can
128/D5 **Robstown,** Tx,US
128/C3 **Roby,** Tx,US
58/A3 **Roca, Cabo da** (cape), Port.
116/B4 **Roca Partida** (pt.), Mex.
109/M4 **Rocas,** Braz.
57/G4 **Rocciamelone** (peak), It.
56/E5 **Roc de France** (mtn.), Fr.
113/G2 **Rocha,** Uru.
113/G2 **Rocha** (dept.), Uru.
45/F4 **Rochdale,** Eng,UK
46/B6 **Roche,** Eng,UK
56/C4 **Rochefort,** Fr.
47/G4 **Rochester,** Eng,UK
126/C3 **Rochester,** In,US
132/F6 **Rochester,** Mi,US
123/K4 **Rochester,** Mn,US
127/G3 **Rochester,** NH,US
126/E3 **Rochester,** NY,US
132/F6 **Rochester Hills,** Mi,US
47/G3 **Rochford,** Eng,UK
126/B3 **Rock** (riv.), Il, Wi,US
122/C4 **Rock** (cr.), Or,US
41/C3 **Rockall** (isl.), UK
130/L3 **Rock Creek,** Yk,Can
90/H8 **Rockdale,** Austl.
105/R **Rockefeller** (plat.), Ant.
126/B3 **Rockford,** Il,US
127/G2 **Rock Forest,** Qu,Can
123/G3 **Rockglen,** Sk,Can
90/C3 **Rockhampton,** Austl.
129/H3 **Rock Hill,** SC,US
89/A4 **Rockingham,** Austl.
129/J3 **Rockingham,** NC,US
126/B3 **Rock Island,** Il,US
126/F2 **Rockland,** On,Can
127/G2 **Rockland,** Me,US
91/B3 **Rocklands** (res.), Austl.
129/H4 **Rockledge,** Fl,US
128/D4 **Rockport,** Tx,US

Rocks – Saint

173

Saint – Santa

47/F2 Saint Neots, Eng,UK
53/E2 Saint-Nicolas, Belg.
52/B2 Saint-Omer, Fr.
52/A4 Saint-Omer-en-Chaussée, Fr.
127/G2 Saint-Pamphile, Qu,Can
127/G2 Saint-Pascal, Qu,Can
38/H5 Saint Paul (isls.), Braz.
122/F2 Saint Paul, Ab,Can
39/N7 Saint Paul (isl.), FrAnt.
99/F5 Saint Paul (cape), Gha.
98/C5 Saint Paul (riv.), Gui., Libr.
103/R15 Saint-Paul, Reun.
130/E4 Saint Paul (isl.), Ak,US
125/J3 Saint Paul, Ks,US
123/K4 Saint Paul (cap.), Mn,US
56/C5 Saint-Paul-lès-Dax, Fr.
90/B1 Saint Pauls (peak), Austl.
56/F4 Saint-Paul-Trois-Châteaux, Fr.
123/K4 Saint Peter, Mn,US
109/M3 Saint Peter and Saint Paul (rocks), Braz.
56/B2 Saint Peter Port, Chl,UK
47/H4 Saint Peter's, Eng,UK
65/V7 Saint Petersburg (Leningrad), Rus.
129/H5 Saint Petersburg, Fl,US
64/G3 Saint Petersburg Obl., Rus.
127/P7 Saint-Philippe-de-La Prairie, Qu,Can
117/J5 Saint-Pierre, Mart.
103/R15 Saint-Pierre, Reun.
127/K2 Saint Pierre & Miquelon (dpcy.), Fr
56/D3 Saint-Pierre-des-Corps, Fr.
56/C5 Saint-Pierre-du-Mont, Fr.
123/J3 Saint Pierre-Jolys, Mb,Can
56/B2 Saint-Pol-de-Léon, Fr.
52/B1 Saint-Pol-sur-Mer, Fr.
56/E5 Saint-Pons (mtn.), Fr.
52/B5 Saint-Prix, Fr.
52/C4 Saint-Quentin, Fr.
57/G5 Saint-Raphaël, Fr.
56/F5 Saint-Rémy-de-Provence, Fr.
52/A3 Saint-Riquier, Fr.
56/B2 Saint Sampson's, Chl,UK
52/C3 Saint-Saulve, Fr.
129/H4 Saint Simons Island, Ga,US
127/H2 Saint Stephen, NB,Can
46/B6 Saint Stephen in Brannel, Eng,UK
126/D3 Saint Thomas, On,Can
117/H4 Saint Thomas (isl.), USVI
127/N7 Saint-Urbain-Premier, Qu,Can
56/F3 Saint-Vallier, Fr.
52/B2 Saint-Venant, Fr.
91/C4 Saint Vincent (pt.), Austl.
117/J5 Saint Vincent & the Grenadines
53/F3 Saint Vith, Belg.
122/F2 Saint Walburg, Sk,Can
84/D2 Sāipal (mtn.), Nepal
92/D3 Saipan (isl.), NMar.
79/F2 Saitama (pref.), Japan
78/B4 Saito, Japan
83/B3 Sai Yok Nat'l Park, Thai.
108/E7 Sajama Nat'l Park, Bol.
62/E1 Sajószentpéter, Hun.
102/C3 Sak (riv.), SAfr.
79/H7 Sakado, Japan
79/J7 Sakae, Japan
79/M9 Sakahogi, Japan
79/F2 Sakai, Japan
78/C3 Sakaide, Japan
78/C3 Sakaiminato, Japan
123/H3 Sakakawea (lake), ND,US
119/J3 Sakami (lake), Qu,Can
63/K5 Sakarya (prov.), Turk.
74/B2 Sakarya (riv.), Turk.
77/M4 Sakata, Japan
78/C4 Sakawa, Japan
69/Q4 Sakhalin (gulf), Rus.
69/Q4 Sakhalin (isl.), Rus.
72/F1 Sakht Sar (Ramsar), Iran
66/E3 Saki, Ukr.
82/D3 Sakishima (isls.), Japan
67/L1 Sakmara (riv.), Rus.
83/D2 Sakon Nakhon, Thai.
73/J3 Sakrand, Pak.
79/F2 Saku, Japan
79/J7 Sakura, Japan
79/L10 Sakurai, Japan
67/G3 Sal (riv.), Rus.
49/J4 Šal'a, Slvk.
42/F4 Sala, Swe.
60/D2 Sala Consilina, It.
111/E2 Saladas, Arg.
112/F2 Saladillo, Arg.
112/D3 Salado (riv.), Arg.
112/F2 Salado (riv.), Arg.
116/B2 Salado (riv.), Mex.
107/C5 Salado del Norte (riv.), Arg.
99/E4 Salaga, Gha.
87/G4 Salahatu (mtn.), Indo.
62/F2 Sălaj (co.), Rom.
96/J5 Salal, Chad
100/D4 Şalālah, Sudan
112/D5 Salamanca (plain), Arg.
112/C1 Salamanca, Chile
116/A3 Salamanca, Mex.
58/C2 Salamanca, Sp.
126/E3 Salamanca, NY,US
97/J6 Salamat (riv.), Chad
61/H3 Salamís, Gre.
61/L7 Salamís (isl.), Gre.
74/L4 Salamīyah, Syria
83/C1 Sala Mok, Laos
58/B1 Salas, Sp.
67/K1 Salavat, Rus.
92/B5 Salayar (isl.), Indo.
38/D7 Sala y Gomez (isls.), Chile
56/E3 Salbris, Fr.
46/C6 Salcombe, Eng,UK
91/C3 Sale, Austl.
96/D1 Salé, Mor.
45/F5 Sale, Eng,UK
87/G3 Salebabu (isl.), Indo.
68/G3 Salekhard, Rus.
84/C5 Salem, India
126/C4 Salem, In,US
125/K3 Salem, Mo,US
127/G3 Salem, NH,US
122/C4 Salem (cap.), Or,US
126/D4 Salem, Va,US
60/C4 Salemi, It.
60/F2 Salentina (pen.), It.
60/D2 Salerno, It.
60/D2 Salerno (gulf), It.
47/G3 Sales (pt.), UK
45/F5 Salford, Eng,UK
62/D1 Salgótarján, Hun.
109/L5 Salgueiro, Braz.
125/F3 Salida, Co,US
74/B2 Salihli, Turk.
104/F3 Salima, Malw.
100/B4 Salīmah (oasis), Sudan
58/B1 Salime (res.), Sp.
117/G3 Salina (pt.), Bahm.
60/D3 Salina (isl.), It.
125/H3 Salina, Ks,US
124/E3 Salina, Ut,US
116/B4 Salina Cruz, Mex.
109/K7 Salinas, Braz.
116/A3 Salinas, Mex.
124/B3 Salinas, Ca,US
124/B3 Salinas (riv.), Ca,US
59/G3 Salinas, Cabo de (cape), Sp.
125/F4 Salinas Nat'l Mon., NM,US
60/D2 Saline (marsh), It.
125/J4 Saline (riv.), Ar,US
125/G3 Saline (riv.), Ks,US
109/J4 Salinópolis, Braz.
119/J2 Salisbury (isl.), NW,Can
47/E4 Salisbury, Eng,UK
46/D4 Salisbury (plain), Eng,UK
126/F4 Salisbury, Md,US
129/H3 Salisbury, NC,US
42/J2 Salla, Fin.
57/G4 Sallanches, Fr.
50/D4 Salland (reg.), Neth.
98/B4 Sallatouk (pt.), Gui.
52/B3 Sallaumines, Fr.
59/F2 Sallent, Sp.
125/J4 Sallisaw, Ok,US
100/D5 Sallūm, Sudan
84/D2 Sallyāna, Nepal
44/B5 Sally Gap (pass), Ire.
53/F3 Salm (riv.), Ger.
74/F2 Salmās, Iran
122/D4 Salmon (riv.), Id,US
122/D3 Salmon Arm, BC,Can
124/D2 Salmon Falls (riv.), Id, Nv,US
122/E4 Salmon River (mts.), Id,US
42/G3 Salo, Fin.
54/B2 Salon (riv.), Fr.
56/F5 Salon-de-Provence, Fr.
97/K8 Salonga Nat'l Park, Zaire
61/H3 Salonika (Thermaic) (gulf), Gre.
61/H2 Salonika (Thessaloníki), Gre.
62/E2 Salonta, Rom.
58/B3 Salor (riv.), Sp.
98/B3 Saloum, Vallée du (wadi), Sen.
67/G3 Sal'sk, Rus.
60/C4 Salso (riv.), It.
102/C3 Salt (riv.), SAfr.
124/E4 Salt (riv.), Az,US
111/C1 Salta, Arg.
46/B6 Saltash, Eng,UK
45/H2 Saltburn, Eng,UK
43/B4 Saltee (isls.), Ire.
42/E2 Saltfjorden (fjord), Nor.
46/D4 Saltford, Eng,UK
129/H4 Saltilla (riv.), Ga,US
116/A2 Saltillo, Mex.
124/E2 Salt Lake City (cap.), Ut,US
112/E2 Salto, Arg.
110/C2 Salto, Braz.
60/C1 Salto (riv.), It.
111/E3 Salto, Uru.
113/F1 Salto (dept.), Uru.
111/E3 Salto Grande (res.), Arg., Uru.
124/C4 Salton Sea (lake), Ca,US
110/A3 Salto Santiago (res.), Braz.
129/H3 Saluda (riv.), SC,US
82/D6 Salug, Phil.
84/D4 Sālūr, India
109/H2 Salut (isls.), FrG.
57/G4 Saluzzo, It.
113/J7 Salvación (bay), Chile
109/L6 Salvador, Braz.
58/A3 Salvaterra de Magos, Port.
58/A1 Salvatierra de Miño, Sp.
71/J8 Salween (riv.), Asia
126/D4 Salyersville, Ky,US
67/J5 Sal'yany, Azer.
49/H5 Salza (riv.), Aus.
51/E4 Salzbergen, Ger.
57/K3 Salzburg, Aus.
57/K3 Salzburg (prov.), Aus.
51/H4 Salzgitter, Ger.
51/G4 Salzhemmendorf, Ger.
51/F5 Salzkotten, Ger.
48/F2 Salzwedel, Ger.
58/C1 Sama, Sp.
86/C4 Samak (cape), Indo.
87/F2 Samales (isls.), Phil.
84/D4 Sāmalkot, India
100/B2 Samālūt, Egypt
117/H4 Samaná (cape), DRep.
74/C3 Samandağı, Turk.
74/H6 Samannūd, Egypt
82/E5 Samar (isl.), Phil.
67/J1 Samara, Rus.
67/K1 Samara (riv.), Rus.
67/J1 Samara Obl., Rus.
77/M2 Samarga (riv.), Rus.
74/N8 Samaria (reg.), WBnk.
74/N8 Samaria Nat'l Park, WBnk.
61/H5 Samarias Gorge Nat'l Park, Gre.
87/E4 Samarinda, Indo.
68/G6 Samarkand, Uzb.
72/D2 Sāmarrā', Iraq
73/K3 Samasata, Pak.
84/D3 Sambalpur, India
104/C2 Samba Lucala, Ang.
103/H7 Sambao (riv.), Madg.
86/D4 Sambar (cape), Indo.
86/C3 Sambas, Indo.
103/J6 Sambava, Madg.
66/B2 Sambor, Ukr.
113/F2 Samborombón (bay), Arg.
83/D3 Sambor Prei Kuk (ruins), Camb.
52/C3 Sambre (riv.), Belg.,Fr.
52/C4 Sambre à l'Oise, Canal de (can.), Fr.
80/E4 Samch'ŏk, SKor.
101/C4 Same, Tanz.
83/C4 Samit (cape), Camb.
83/C3 Samkos (peak), Camb.
132/C2 Sammamish (lake), Wa,US
80/E5 Samnangjin, SKor.
62/B3 Samobor, Cro.
63/F4 Samokov, Bul.
59/Q10 Samora Correia, Port.
74/A3 Sámos, Gre.
61/J2 Samothráki (isl.), Gre.
112/D2 Sampacho, Arg.
86/D4 Sampit, Indo.
86/D4 Sampit (riv.), Indo.
128/E4 Sam Rayburn (res.), Tx,US
83/C1 Sam Sao (mts.), Laos, Viet.
90/E6 Samson (mtn.), Austl.
83/D2 Sam Son, Viet.
90/E6 Samsonvale (lake), Austl.
74/D2 Samsun, Turk.
83/B4 Samui (isl.), Thai.
79/H7 Samukawa, Japan
67/J4 Samur (riv.), Azer., Rus.
83/C3 Samut Prakan, Thai.
83/C3 Samut Sakhon, Thai.
83/C3 Samut Songkhram, Thai.
83/D3 San (riv.), Camb.
77/H5 San (riv.), China
98/D3 San, Mali
49/M3 San (riv.), Pol.
62/C3 Sana (riv.), Bosn.
72/D5 Sanaa (Şan'a) (cap.), Yemen
58/A1 San Adrián, Cabo de (cape), Sp.
82/E6 San Agustín (cape), Phil.
59/N8 San Agustín de Guadalix, Sp.
130/F5 Sanak (isl.), Ak,US
87/G4 Sanana (isl.), Indo.
107/B5 San Ambrosio (isl.), Chile
72/E1 Sanandaj, Iran
132/K11 San Andreas (lake), Ca,US
116/E5 San Andrés, Col.
116/E5 San Andrés (isl.), Col.
124/F4 San Andres (mts.), NM,US
113/S12 San Andrés de Giles, Arg.
58/C1 San Andrés del Rabanedo, Sp.
116/B4 San Andrés Tuxtla, Mex.
128/C4 San Angelo, Tx,US
132/J11 San Anselmo, Ca,US
113/F3 San Antonio (cape), Arg.
112/C2 San Antonio, Chile
117/M9 San Antonio, Mex.
131/C2 San Antonio (mt.), Ca,US
124/F4 San Antonio, NM,US
128/D4 San Antonio, Tx,US
128/D4 San Antonio (riv.), Tx,US
59/F3 San Antonio Abad, Sp.
112/F2 San Antonio de Areco, Arg.
117/J5 San Antonio del Golfo, Ven.
112/D4 San Antonio Oeste, Arg.
128/E4 San Augustine, Tx,US
84/C3 Sānāwad, India
60/D2 San Bartolomeo in Galdo, It.
60/C1 San Benedetto del Tronto, It.
131/C2 San Bernardino, Ca,US
131/C2 San Bernardino (mts.), Ca,US
112/C2 San Bernardo, Chile
117/F6 San Bernardo (pt.), Col.
117/N8 San Blas, Mex.
129/G4 San Blas (cape), Fl,US
128/E3 San Bois (mts.), Ok,US
57/J4 San Bonifacio, It.
108/E6 San Borja, Bol.
127/S9 Sanborn, NY,US
132/K11 San Bruno, Ca,US
116/A2 San Buenaventura, Mex.
131/A2 San Buenaventura (Ventura), Ca,US
112/C3 San Carlos, Chile
116/A2 San Carlos, Mex.
116/E5 San Carlos, Nic.
82/D4 San Carlos, Phil.
113/G2 San Carlos, Uru.
124/E4 San Carlos (lake), Az,US
132/K11 San Carlos, Ca,US
117/H6 San Carlos, Ven.
112/C4 San Carlos de Bariloche, Arg.
117/G6 San Carlos del Zulia, Ven.
61/F2 San Cataldo, It.
112/C2 San Clemente, Chile
58/D3 San Clemente, Sp.
124/C4 San Clemente (isl.), Ca,US
111/D3 San Cristóbal, Arg.
116/E3 San Cristóbal, Cuba
116/D5 San Cristobal (vol.), Nic.
92/F6 San Cristobal (isl.), Sol.
108/D2 San Cristóbal, Ven.
116/C4 San Cristóbal de las Casas, Mex.
117/F3 Sancti Spíritus, Cuba
122/F2 Sand (riv.), Ab,Can
102/D3 Sand (riv.), SAfr.
125/G2 Sand (hills), Ne,US
78/D3 Sanda, Japan
44/C1 Sanda (isl.), Sc,UK
83/D3 Sandan, Camb.
63/F5 Sandanski, Bul.
45/F5 Sandbach, Eng,UK
51/F2 Sande, Ger.
42/D4 Sandefjord, Nor.
105/Q Sanders (coast), Ant.
128/C4 Sanderson, Tx,US
129/H3 Sandersville, Ga,US
90/F6 Sandgate, Austl.
44/D2 Sandhead, Sc,UK
127/Q8 Sandhill, On,Can
47/F4 Sandhurst, Eng,UK
113/L8 San Diego (cape), Arg.
124/C4 San Diego, Ca,US
128/D5 San Diego, Tx,US
74/B2 Sandıklı, Turk.
131/C2 San Dimas, Ca,US
60/D4 San Dimitri, Ras (pt.), Malta
116/E3 Sandino, Cuba
87/E3 Sandkan, Malay.
42/C4 Sandnes, Nor.
42/E2 Sandnessjøen, Nor.
104/D2 Sandoa, Zaire
49/L3 Sandomierz, Pol.
57/K4 San Donà di Piave, It.
98/B3 Sandougou (riv.), Gam., Sen.
47/E5 Sandown, Eng,UK
122/D3 Sandpoint, Id,US
91/F5 Sandringham, Austl.
47/G1 Sandringham, Eng,UK
126/D3 Sandusky, Mi,US
126/D3 Sandusky, Oh,US
42/D4 Sandvika, Nor.
42/F3 Sandviken, Swe.
90/B2 Sandwich (cape), Austl.
47/H4 Sandwich, Eng,UK
90/D4 Sandy (cape), Austl.
123/K2 Sandy (lake), On,Can
47/F2 Sandy, Eng,UK
124/E2 Sandy, Ut,US
123/H2 Sandy Bay, Sk,Can
131/F5 Sandy Hook (bay), NJ,US
129/G3 Sandy Springs, Ga,US
53/E4 Sanem, Lux.
60/C2 San Felice Circeo, It.
112/C2 San Felipe, Chile
117/M7 San Felipe, Mex.
108/E1 San Felipe, Ven.
107/A5 San Félix (isl.), Chile
113/S12 San Fernando, Arg.
112/C2 San Fernando, Chile
116/B3 San Fernando, Mex.
82/D4 San Fernando, Phil.
58/B4 San Fernando, Sp.
131/B2 San Fernando, Ca,US
117/H6 San Fernando de Apure, Ven.
59/N9 San Fernando-de-Henares, Sp.
42/E3 Sånfjällets Nat'l Park, Swe.
130/K3 Sanford (mtn.), Ak,US
129/H4 Sanford, Fl,US
127/G3 Sanford, Me,US
129/J3 Sanford, NC,US
111/D3 San Francisco, Arg.
117/M7 San Francisco, Mex.
82/E6 San Francisco, Phil.
124/E4 San Francisco (riv.), Az, NM,US
132/K11 San Francisco, Ca,US
132/K11 San Francisco (bay), Ca,US
117/G5 San Francisco, Ven.
116/D5 San Francisco de la Paz, Hon.
117/N8 San Francisco del Oro, Mex.
117/G4 San Francisco de Macorís, DRep.
112/C2 San Francisco de Mostazal, Chile
131/B2 San Gabriel, Ca,US
131/B2 San Gabriel (mts.), Ca,US
131/C2 San Gabriel (riv.), Ca,US
84/B4 Sangamner, India
126/B3 Sangamon (riv.), Il,US
73/H2 Sangān (mtn.), Afg.
108/C4 Sangay Nat'l Park, Ecu.
58/A1 Sangenjo, Sp.
81/C2 Sanggan (riv.), China
86/D3 Sanggau, Indo.
96/J7 Sangha (riv.), CAfr., Congo
73/J3 Sanghar, Pak.
87/F3 Sangihe (isls.), Indo.
108/D2 San Gil, Col.
60/E2 San Giorgio Ionico, It.
60/C4 San Giovanni Gemini, It.
60/E3 San Giovanni in Fiore, It.
57/J4 San Giovanni in Persiceto, It.
76/D2 Sangiyn Dalay (lake), Mong.
80/E4 Sangju, SKor.
87/E3 Sangkulirang, Indo.
84/B4 Sāngli, India
96/H7 Sangmélima, Camr.
79/L10 Sangō, Japan
124/C4 San Gorgonio (peak), Ca,US
125/F3 Sangre de Cristo (mts.), Co, NM,US
117/J5 Sangre Grande, Trin.
60/D2 Sangro (riv.), It.
108/G6 Sangue (riv.), Braz.
99/E4 Sanguie (prov.), Burk.
117/M8 San Hipólito (pt.), Mex.
102/E3 Sani (pass), SAfr.
116/D4 San Ignacio, Belz.
108/E6 San Ignacio, Bol.
108/F7 San Ignacio, Bol.
112/B3 San Ignacio, Chile
117/M8 San Ignacio, Mex.
117/N9 San Ignacio, Mex.
78/D3 San'in Kaigin Nat'l Park, Japan
117/F6 San Jacinto, Col.
131/C3 San Jacinto (riv.), Ca,US
112/C2 San Javier, Chile
59/E4 San Javier, Sp.
79/F2 Sanjō, Japan
108/F6 San Joaquín, Bol.
124/B3 San Joaquin (val.), Ca,US
112/E1 San Jorge, Arg.
112/D5 San Jorge (cape), Arg.
112/D5 San Jorge (gulf), Arg.
117/M7 San Jorge (bay), Mex.
59/F2 San Jorge (gulf), Sp.
112/D4 San José (gulf), Arg.
116/D4 San Jose, Belz.
116/E6 San José (cap.), CR
117/M8 San José (isl.), Mex.
82/D4 San Jose, Phil.
59/F3 San José, Sp.
113/F2 San José (dept.), Uru.
113/T11 San José (riv.), Uru.
132/L12 San Jose, Ca,US
117/G5 San José, Ven.
117/J6 San José de Amacuro, Ven.
82/D5 San Jose de Buenavista, Phil.
108/F7 San José de Chiquitos, Bol.
117/M8 San José de Gracia, Mex.
117/J6 San José de Guanipa, Ven.
117/H6 San José de Guaribe, Ven.
111/C3 San José de Jáchal, Arg.
117/N9 San José del Cabo, Mex.
112/Q9 San José de Maipo, Chile
113/F2 San José de Mayo, Uru.
117/M8 San José de Pimas, Mex.
112/C1 San Juan, Arg.
113/M8 San Juan (cape), Arg.
112/C1 San Juan (prov.), Arg.
111/C3 San Juan (riv.), Arg.
116/E5 San Juan (riv.), CR, Nic.
117/G4 San Juan, DRep.
117/H4 San Juan (cap.), PR
124/F3 San Juan (mts.), Co,US
124/E3 San Juan (riv.), Co, Ut,US
128/A2 San Juan (basin), NM,US
111/E2 San Juan Bautista, Par.
59/E3 San Juan de Alicante, Sp.
58/B4 San Juan de Aznalfarache, Sp.
117/P10 San Juan de Lima (pt.), Mex.
116/E5 San Juan del Norte, Nic.
117/P9 San Juan de los Lagos, Mex.
117/H6 San Juan de los Morros, Ven.
113/K7 San Julián, Gran Bajo de (val.), Arg.
111/D3 San Justo, Arg.
98/C4 Sankanbiriwa (peak), SLeo.
98/C4 Sankoroni (riv.), Gui., Mali
57/L3 Sankt Andrä, Aus.
53/G2 Sankt Augustin, Ger.
55/F3 Sankt Gallen, Swi.
55/F3 Sankt Gallen (canton), Swi.
53/G5 Sankt Ingbert, Ger.
57/K3 Sankt Johann im Pongau, Aus.
57/K3 Sankt Johann in Tirol, Aus.
57/L2 Sankt Pölten, Aus.
57/L3 Sankt Veit an der Glan, Aus.
53/G5 Sankt Wendel, Ger.
117/M9 San Lázaro (cape), Mex.
132/K11 San Leandro, Ca,US
108/E6 San Lorenzo, Bol.
113/J6 San Lorenzo (peak), Chile
108/C3 San Lorenzo, Ecu.
108/B4 San Lorenzo (cape), Ecu.
60/A3 San Lorenzo (cape), It.
117/N8 San Lorenzo, Mex.
132/K11 San Lorenzo, Ca,US
58/C2 San Lorenzo de El Escorial, Sp.
58/B4 Sanlúcar de Barrameda, Sp.
117/N9 San Lucas, Mex.
117/N9 San Lucas (cape), Mex.
112/D2 San Luis, Arg.
112/D2 San Luis (mts.), Arg.
112/D2 San Luis (prov.), Arg.
117/F3 San Luis, Cuba
116/D4 San Luis, Guat.
128/B2 San Luis (val.), Co,US
124/B4 San Luis Obispo, Ca,US
116/A3 San Luis Potosi, Mex.
116/A3 San Luis Potosí (state), Mex.
117/M7 San Luis Río Colorado, Mex.
124/E4 San Manuel, Az,US
117/F6 San Marcos, Col.
116/B4 San Marcos, Mex.
128/D4 San Marcos, Tx,US
82/D4 San Mariano, Phil.
57/K5 San Marino
57/K5 San Marino (cap.), SMar.
112/C2 San Martín, Arg.
113/J7 San Martín (lake), Arg.
108/F6 San Martín (riv.), Bol.
112/C4 San Martín de los Andes, Arg.
99/E3 Sanmatenga (prov.), Burk.
132/K11 San Mateo, Ca,US
128/B3 San Mateo (mts.), NM,US
112/D4 San Matías (gulf), Arg.
108/G7 San Matías, Bol.
81/B4 Sanmenxia, China
108/F6 San Miguel (riv.), Bol.
116/D5 San Miguel, ESal.
116/A3 San Miguel de Allende, Mex.
112/F2 San Miguel del Monte, Arg.
111/C2 San Miguel de Tucumán, Arg.
82/C2 Sanming, China
79/L9 Sannan, Japan
97/M5 Sannār, Sudan
60/D2 Sannicandro Garganico, It.
124/C4 San Nicolas (isl.), Ca,US
112/E2 San Nicolás de los Arroyos, Arg.
116/A2 San Nicolás de los Garzas, Mex.
69/P2 Sannikova (str.), Rus.
79/F2 Sano, Japan
49/M4 Sanok, Pol.
112/B4 San Pablo, Chile
82/D5 San Pablo, Phil.
132/K11 San Pablo, Ca,US
132/K10 San Pablo (bay), Ca,US
112/F2 San Pedro, Arg.
116/D4 San Pedro, Belz.
112/C2 San Pedro, Chile
111/C1 San Pedro (vol.), Chile
98/D5 San Pédro, IvC.
111/E1 San Pedro, Par.
58/B3 San Pedro (range), Sp.
124/E4 San Pedro (riv.), Az,US
131/B3 San Pedro (bay), Ca,US
116/C4 San Pedro Carchá, Guat.
116/A2 San Pedro de las Colinas, Mex.
108/C5 San Pedro de Lloc, Peru
59/E4 San Pedro del Pinatar, Sp.
117/H4 San Pedro de Macorís, DRep.
116/B4 San Pedro Pochutla, Mex.
116/D4 San Pedro Sula, Hon.
60/A3 San Pietro (isl.), It.
44/E1 Sanquhar, Sc,UK
108/C3 Sanquianga Nat'l Park, Col.
117/L7 San Quintín, Mex.
117/L7 San Quintín (cape), Mex.
112/C2 San Rafael, Arg.
132/J11 San Rafael, Ca,US
124/E3 San Rafael (riv.), Ut,US
117/G5 San Rafael, Ven.
113/G2 San Ramón, Uru.
132/L11 San Ramon, Ca,US
111/D1 San Ramón de la Nueva Orán, Arg.
57/G5 San Remo, It.
58/C4 San Roque, Sp.
112/B3 San Rosendo, Chile
128/D4 San Saba, Tx,US
125/H5 San Saba (riv.), Tx,US
116/D5 San Salvador (cap.), ESal.
113/S11 San Salvador (riv.), Uru.
111/C1 San Salvador de Jujuy, Arg.
117/G3 San Salvador (Watling) (isl.), Bahm.
60/D1 San Salvo, It.
58/E1 San Sebastián, Sp.
58/D2 San Sebastián de los Reyes, Sp.
57/J4 San Sebastiano, It.
60/D2 San Severo, It.
76/F2 Sant, Mong.
116/D5 Santa Ana, ESal.
117/M7 Santa Ana, Mex.
131/C3 Santa Ana, Ca,US
131/C3 Santa Ana (mts.), Ca,US
117/H5 Santa Ana, Ven.
110/D1 Santa Bárbara, Braz.
112/B3 Santa Bárbara, Chile
116/D5 Santa Bárbara, Hon.
117/N8 Santa Bárbara, Mex.
131/A2 Santa Barbara, Ca,US
131/A2 Santa Barbara (chan.), Ca,US
108/E3 Santa Bárbara, Ven.
110/C2 Santa Bárbara d'Oeste, Braz.
82/D6 Santa Catalina, Phil.
124/C4 Santa Catalina (gulf), Ca,US
124/C4 Santa Catalina (isl.), Ca,US
110/B3 Santa Catarina (isl.), Braz.
110/B3 Santa Catarina (state), Braz.
110/B3 Santa Cecília, Braz.
117/F3 Santa Clara, Cuba
58/A4 Santa Clara (res.), Port.
132/L12 Santa Clara, Ca,US
131/B2 Santa Clara (riv.), Ca,US
117/J6 Santa Clara, Ven.
131/B2 Santa Clarita, Ca,US
59/G2 Santa Coloma de Farners, Sp.
59/L7 Santa Coloma de Gramanet, Sp.
58/A1 Santa Comba, Sp.
113/K7 Santa Cruz (prov.), Arg.
113/K7 Santa Cruz (riv.), Arg.
108/F7 Santa Cruz, Bol.
112/C2 Santa Cruz, Chile
116/D5 Santa Cruz, CR
82/D5 Santa Cruz, Phil.
82/E6 Santa Cruz, Phil.
92/F6 Santa Cruz (isls.), Sol.
124/B3 Santa Cruz, Ca,US
131/A2 Santa Cruz (isl.), Ca,US
59/S12 Santa Cruz da Graciosa, Azor.,Port.
59/R12 Santa Cruz das Flores, Azor.,Port.
116/C4 Santa Cruz del Quiché, Guat.
117/F3 Santa Cruz del Sur, Cuba
59/X16 Santa Cruz de Tenerife, Canl.
110/B2 Santa Cruz do Rio Pardo, Braz.
111/F2 Santa Cruz do Sul, Braz.
59/L7 Sant Adrià de Besòs, Sp.
112/D5 Santa Elena (peak), Arg.
116/D5 Santa Elena (cape), CR
58/A1 Santa Eugenia de Ribeira, Sp.
59/F3 Santa Eulalia del Río, Sp.
112/E1 Santa Fé, Arg.
112/E2 Santa Fé (prov.), Arg.
58/D4 Santa Fé, Sp.
129/H4 Santa Fe (riv.), Fl,US
125/F4 Santa Fe (cap.), NM,US
110/B2 Santa Fe do Sul, Braz.
60/D3 Sant'Agata di Militello, It.
110/B1 Santa Helena de Goiás, Braz.
109/J4 Santa Inês, Braz.
113/J8 Santa Inés (isl.), Chile
110/G8 Santa Isabel, Braz.
116/E5 Santa Isabel, Col.
92/E5 Santa Isabel (isl.), Sol.
96/G7 Santa Isabel, Pico de (peak), EqG.
113/F2 Santa Lucía, Uru.
113/G2 Santa Lucía (riv.), Uru.
109/J4 Santa Luzia, Braz.
110/D1 Santa Luzia, Braz.
112/E2 Santa Magdalena, Arg.
117/M8 Santa Magdalena (isl.), Mex.
117/M9 Santa Margarita (isl.), Mex.
111/F2 Santa Maria, Braz.
112/C2 Santa María, Chile
112/B3 Santa María (isl.), Chile
59/T13 Santa Maria (isl.), Azor.,Port.
124/B4 Santa Maria, Ca,US
58/B4 Santa Maria, Cabo de (cape), Port.
60/D2 Santa Maria Capua Vetere, It.
109/K6 Santa Maria da Vitória, Braz.
61/F3 Santa Maria di Leuca (cape), It.
110/D1 Santa Maria do Suaçí, Braz.
117/G5 Santa Marta, Col.
110/B4 Santa Marta Grande, Cabo de (cape), Braz.
131/B2 Santa Monica, Ca,US
131/B3 Santa Monica (bay), Ca,US
131/B2 Santa Monica Mts. Nat'l Rec. Area, Ca,US
109/K6 Santana, Braz.
59/P11 Santana, Port.
59/V15 Santana, Madr.,Port.
111/E3 Santana do Livramento, Braz.
108/C3 Santander, Col.
58/D1 Santander, Sp.
60/A3 Sant'Antioco, It.
131/A2 Santa Paula, Ca,US
59/E3 Santa Pola, Sp.
59/E3 Santa Pola, Cabo de (cape), Sp.
109/H4 Santarém, Braz.
58/A3 Santarém, Port.
58/A3 Santarém (dist.), Port.
109/L5 Santa Rita, Braz.
110/H7 Santa Rita do Sapucaí, Braz.
112/D3 Santa Rosa, Arg.
112/D4 Santa Rosa (val.), Arg.
111/F2 Santa Rosa, Braz.
108/C4 Santa Rosa, Ecu.
124/B3 Santa Rosa, Ca,US
124/B4 Santa Rosa (isl.), Ca,US
125/F4 Santa Rosa, NM,US
124/C2 Santa Rosa (range), Nv,US
112/D2 Santa Rosa de Calamuchita, Arg.
116/D5 Santa Rosa de Copán, Hon.
110/C2 Santa Rosa de Viterbo, Braz.

Santa – Shang

175
Shang – Somer

81/C4 Shangqiu, China
82/C2 Shangrao, China
47/E5 Shanklin, Eng,UK
43/A4 Shannon (riv.), Ire.
69/P4 Shantar (isls.), Rus.
82/C3 Shantou, China
82/B3 Shaoguan, China
82/D2 Shaoxing, China
82/B2 Shaoyang, China
45/F2 Shap, Eng,UK
105/L Shapeless (peak), Ant.
65/M2 Shapkina (riv.), Rus.
74/F3 Shaqlāwah, Iraq
73/G5 Sharbatāt, Ra's ash (pt.), Oman
100/C3 Sharm ash Shaykh, Egypt
47/F2 Sharnbrook, Eng,UK
126/D3 Sharon, Pa,US
123/K2 Sharpe (lake), Mb,Can
123/J4 Sharpe (lake), SD,US
65/K4 Shar'ya, Rus.
97/N6 Shashemenē, Eth.
81/C5 Shashi, China
124/B2 Shasta (dam), Ca,US
124/B2 Shasta (peak), Ca,US
66/B2 Shatskiy Nat'l Park, Ukr.
96/G1 Shaṭṭ al Jarīd (dry lake), Tun.
125/H3 Shattuck, Ok,US
122/F3 Shaunavon, Sk,Can
47/E4 Shaw, Eng,UK
126/B2 Shawano, Wi,US
127/M6 Shawbridge, Qu,Can
46/D1 Shawbury, Eng,UK
127/F2 Shawinigan, Qu,Can
125/H4 Shawnee, Ok,US
74/E3 Shaykhān, Iraq
66/C1 Shchara (riv.), Bela.
66/F1 Shchekino, Rus.
65/X9 Shchelkovo, Rus.
66/F2 Shchigry, Rus.
75/B1 Shchuchinsk, Kaz.
97/P6 Shebelē Wenz (riv.), Eth.
73/J1 Sheberghān, Afg.
126/C3 Sheboygan, Wi,US
127/H2 Shediac, NB,Can
44/A4 Sheelin, Lough (lake), Ire.
130/F2 Sheep (mtn.), Ak,US
50/D5 's-Heerenberg, Neth.
45/G5 Sheffield, Eng,UK
129/G3 Sheffield, Al,US
47/F2 Shefford, Eng,UK
97/P6 Shēh Husēn, Eth.
113/K7 Shehuen (riv.), Arg.
126/C1 Shekak (riv.), On,Can
73/K2 Shekhūpura, Pak.
67/H4 Sheki, Azer.
69/T2 Shelagskiy (cape), Rus.
127/H3 Shelburne, NS,Can
129/F3 Shelby, Ms,US
122/F3 Shelby, Mt,US
129/H3 Shelby, NC,US
129/F2 Shelbyville (lake), Il,US
126/C4 Shelbyville, In,US
129/G3 Shelbyville, Tn,US
69/R3 Shelekhov (gulf), Rus.
130/H4 Shelikof (str.), Ak,US
123/G2 Shellbrook, Sk,Can
126/B2 Shell Lake, Wi,US
123/K5 Shell Rock (riv.), Ia,US
132/A3 Shelton, Wa,US
67/J4 Shemakha, Azer.
130/A5 Shemya (isl.), Ak,US
123/K5 Shenandoah, Ia,US
126/E4 Shenandoah Nat'l Park, Va,US
98/B5 Shenge (pt.), SLeo.
75/E3 Shengli Daban (pass), China
81/B5 Shennongjia, China
47/E1 Shenstone, Eng,UK
77/J3 Shenyang, China
85/K3 Shenzhen, China
84/B2 Sheoganj, India
84/C2 Sheopur, India
66/C2 Shepetovka, Ukr.
128/E4 Shepherd, Tx,US
92/F6 Shepherd (isls.), Van.
47/G4 Sheppey (isl.), Eng,UK
47/E1 Shepshed, Eng,UK
46/D4 Shepton Mallet, Eng,UK
119/H1 Sherard (cape), NW,Can
46/D5 Sherborne, Eng,UK
98/B5 Sherbro (isl.), SLeo.
127/G2 Sherbrooke, Qu,Can
45/G2 Sherburn, Eng,UK
99/H4 Shere (hill), Nga.
84/D3 Sherghāti, India
128/E3 Sheridan, Ar,US
122/G4 Sheridan, Wy,US
47/H1 Sheringham, Eng,UK
128/D3 Sherman, Tx,US
50/C5 's-Hertogenbosch, Neth.
122/E2 Sherwood Park, Ab,Can
41/D2 Shetland (isls.), Sc,UK
67/J4 Shevchenko, Kaz.
81/D4 Sheyang (riv.), China
123/J4 Sheyenne (riv.), ND,US
81/C4 Shi (riv.), China
132/E6 Shiawassee (riv.), Mi,US
79/F2 Shibata, Japan
100/B2 Shibīn al Kaum, Egypt
123/L2 Shibogama (lake), On,Can
78/B5 Shibushi (bay), Japan
75/B1 Shiderty (riv.), Kaz.
78/D3 Shido, Japan
46/D1 Shifnal, Eng,UK
79/L9 Shiga, Japan
78/E3 Shiga (pref.), Japan
79/M10 Shigaraki, Japan
81/C3 Shigu Shan (mtn.), China
75/E3 Shihezi, China
61/F2 Shijak, Alb.
81/C3 Shijiazhuang, China
73/J3 Shikārpur, Pak.
79/M9 Shikatsu, Japan
79/H7 Shiki, Japan
78/C4 Shikoku (isl.), Japan
78/C4 Shikoku (mts.), Japan
77/P3 Shikotan (isl.), Rus.
45/G2 Shildon, Eng,UK
76/H1 Shilka, Rus.
77/H1 Shilka (riv.), Rus.
73/L2 Shilla (mtn.), India
74/N8 Shillo, Naḥal (dry riv.), WBnk.
85/F2 Shillong, India
76/D2 Shilüüstey, Mong.
79/M10 Shima (pen.), Japan
78/B4 Shimabara, Japan
78/D3 Shimamoto, Japan
78/C3 Shimane (pref.), Japan
77/K1 Shimanovsk, Rus.
79/M9 Shimasahi, Japan
97/Q5 Shimber Berris (peak), Som.
85/H2 Shimian, China
79/F3 Shimizu, Japan
79/F3 Shimoda, Japan
79/F2 Shimodate, Japan
84/C5 Shimoga, India
79/L10 Shimoichi, Japan
78/A5 Shimo-koshiki (isl.), Japan
78/B4 Shimonoseki, Japan
79/F2 Shinano (riv.), Japan
73/H2 Shindand, Afg.
78/D4 Shingū, Japan
78/C3 Shinji (lake), Japan
77/N4 Shinjō, Japan
79/M9 Shinkawa, Japan
79/F2 Shinminato, Japan
79/M9 Shinsei, Japan
101/B3 Shinyanga, Tanz.
101/B3 Shinyanga (prov.), Tanz.
79/G1 Shiogama, Japan
78/D4 Shio-no-misaki (cape), Japan
45/G4 Shipley, Eng,UK
127/H2 Shippegan, NB,Can
79/M9 Shippo, Japan
124/E3 Shiprock, NM,US
47/E2 Shipston on Stour, Eng,UK
75/C5 Shipuqi Shankou (pass), China
72/F2 Shīr (mtn.), Iran
79/H8 Shirahama, Japan
78/E3 Shirakawa-tōge (pass), Japan
79/F3 Shirane-san (mtn.), Japan
79/H6 Shiraoka, Japan
72/F3 Shīrāz, Iran
74/H6 Shirbīn, Egypt
45/G1 Shiremoor, Eng,UK
81/C5 Shirjiu (lake), China
79/J7 Shiroi, Japan
79/G2 Shiroishi, Japan
79/G2 Shirone, Japan
79/H7 Shiroyama, Japan
73/G1 Shīrvān, Iran
81/D2 Shi San Ling, China
130/F5 Shishaldin (vol.), Ak,US
76/D1 Shishhid (riv.), Mong.
81/C5 Shishou, China
79/J7 Shisui, Japan
84/C2 Shivpurī, India
81/B4 Shiyan, China
76/F4 Shizuishan, China
77/N3 Shizunai, Japan
79/F3 Shizuoka, Japan
79/F3 Shizuoka (pref.), Japan
61/F1 Shkodër, Alb.
61/G2 Shkumbin (riv.), Alb.
130/C2 Shmidta, Mys (pt.), Rus.
91/D2 Shoalhaven (riv.), Austl.
123/H3 Shoal Lake, Mb,Can
90/C3 Shoalwater (bay), Austl.
78/C3 Shōbara, Japan
78/D3 Shōdo (isl.), Japan
47/G3 Shoeburyness, Eng,UK
84/C4 Sholāpur, India
74/N8 Shomron (ruins), WBnk.
79/M9 Shonai (riv.), Japan
79/J7 Shōnan, Japan
84/C4 Shorāpur, India
47/F5 Shoreham by Sea, Eng,UK
132/P16 Shorewood, Il,US
132/Q13 Shorewood, Wi,US
73/K2 Shorkot, Pak.
90/F6 Shorncliffe, Austl.
129/G3 Short (peak), Tn,US
92/E5 Shortland (isl.), Sol.
47/E5 Shorwell, Eng,UK
124/C3 Shoshone (mts.), Nv,US
122/F4 Shoshone (riv.), Wy,US
122/F5 Shoshoni, Wy,US
66/E2 Shostka, Ukr.
47/H3 Shotley, Eng,UK
45/G2 Shotton, Eng,UK
79/H7 Shōwa, Japan
124/E4 Show Low, Az,US
66/D2 Shpola, Ukr.
128/E3 Shreveport, La,US
46/D1 Shrewsbury, Eng,UK
46/D1 Shropshire (co.), Eng,UK
45/F6 Shropshire Union (can.), Eng,UK
81/D4 Shu (riv.), China
81/D5 Shu (riv.), China
77/K3 Shuangyang, China
77/L2 Shuangyashan, China
74/H6 Shubrā Khīt, Egypt
74/K6 Shu'fāṭ, WBnk.
81/D5 Shuiyang (riv.), China
73/K3 Shujāābād, Pak.
76/D4 Shule (riv.), China
130/G4 Shumagin (isls.), Ak,US
63/H4 Shumen, Bul.
65/K5 Shumerlya, Rus.
75/B2 Shunak, Gora (peak), Kaz.
81/C3 Shuo Xian, China
73/G2 Shūr (riv.), Iran
104/F4 Shurugwi, Zim.
75/F1 Shushenskoye, Rus.
72/E2 Shūshtar, Iran
122/D3 Shuswap (lake), BC,Can
97/N5 Shuwak, Sudan
64/J4 Shuya, Rus.
83/A1 Shwebo, Burma
83/B2 Shwemawdaw Pagoda (ruins), Burma
75/C5 Shyok (riv.), India
73/H2 Siāh (mts.), Afg.
86/B3 Siak (riv.), Indo.
73/K2 Siālkot, Pak.
82/E6 Siargao (isl.), Phil.
82/D6 Siasi, Phil.
87/F2 Siaton (pt.), Phil.
87/G3 Siau (isl.), Indo.
64/D5 Šiauliai, Lith.
82/D5 Sibalom, Phil.
67/L1 Sibay, Rus.
62/B4 Šibenik, Cro.
68/K3 Siberia (reg.), Rus.
73/J3 Sibi, Pak.
101/C1 Sibiloi Nat'l Park, Kenya
104/B1 Sibiti, Congo
63/G3 Sibiu, Rom.
63/G2 Sibiu (co.), Rom.
47/G3 Sible Hedingham, Eng,UK
86/A3 Sibolga, Indo.
85/F2 Sibsāgar, India
87/F2 Sibuco, Phil.
87/F2 Sibuko, Phil.
87/F1 Sibuyan (isl.), Phil.
82/D5 Sibuyan (sea), Phil.
122/D3 Sicamous, BC,Can
85/H2 Sichuan (prov.), China
60/C4 Sicilia (reg.), It.
60/C3 Sicily (isl.), It.
60/B4 Sicily (str.), It., Tun.
116/D4 Sico (riv.), Hon.
108/D6 Sicuani, Peru
62/D3 Šid, Yugo.
84/C4 Siddipet, India
60/E3 Siderno Marina, It.
110/B4 Siderópolis, Braz.
131/C1 Sidewinder (mtn.), Ca,US
61/G3 Sidhári, Gre.
84/D3 Sidhi, India
61/H2 Sidhirókastron, Gre.
84/B3 Sidhpur, India
100/A2 Sīdī Barrānī, Egypt
96/E1 Sidi Bel-Abbes, Alg.
60/A5 Sīdī Bū Zayd (gov.), Tun.
96/C2 Sidi Ifni, Mor.
74/H6 Sīdī Sālim, Egypt
105/R Sidley (mtn.), Ant.
90/A1 Sidmouth (cape), Austl.
46/C5 Sidmouth, Eng,UK
122/C3 Sidney, BC,Can
123/G4 Sidney, Mt,US
125/G2 Sidney, Ne,US
126/C3 Sidney, Oh,US
129/G3 Sidney Lanier (lake), Ga,US
74/K5 Sidon (Şaydā), Leb.
96/J1 Sidra (gulf), Libya
51/F3 Siede (riv.), Ger.
49/M2 Siedlce, Pol.
49/L2 Siedlce (prov.), Pol.
53/G2 Sieg (riv.), Ger.
53/G2 Siegburg, Ger.
53/H2 Siegen, Ger.
49/M2 Siemianówka (lake), Pol.
49/M2 Siemiatycze, Pol.
83/D3 Siempang, Camb.
83/C3 Siemreab, Camb.
57/J5 Siena, It.
56/C2 Sienne (riv.), Fr.
49/K3 Sieradz, Pol.
49/K3 Sieradz (prov.), Pol.
53/F5 Sierk-les-Bains, Fr.
49/K2 Sierpc, Pol.
128/B4 Sierra Blanca, Tx,US
108/D3 Sierra de la Macarena Nat'l Park, Col.
116/A2 Sierra del Carmen Nat'l Park, Mex.
117/M7 Sierra de San Pedro Mártir, Mex.
112/D4 Sierra Grande, Arg.
98/B4 Sierra Leone
98/B4 Sierra Leone (cape), SLeo.
131/B2 Sierra Madre, Ca,US
116/B4 Sierra Madre del Sur (mts.), Mex.
117/N8 Sierra Madre Occidental (range), Mex.
116/B3 Sierra Madre Oriental (mts.), Mex.
116/A2 Sierra Mojada, Mex.
124/B3 Sierra Nevada (range), Ca,US
117/G5 Sierra Nevada de Santa Marta, Col.
117/G6 Sierra Nevada Nat'l Park, Ven.
124/E5 Sierra Vista, Az,US
52/E5 Sierre, Swi.
59/M8 Siete (peak), Sp.
112/C2 Siete Tazas Nat'l Park, Chile
61/J4 Sífnos (isl.), Gre.
63/F2 Sighetu Marmaţiei, Rom.
63/G2 Sighişoara, Rom.
45/F1 Sighty Crag (hill), Eng,UK
86/A2 Sigli, Indo.
55/F1 Sigmaringen, Ger.
64/C4 Sigtuna, Swe.
84/D3 Sihorā, India
42/H3 Siilinjärvi, Fin.
74/E3 Siirt, Turk.
118/D3 Sikanni Chief (riv.), BC,Can
84/C2 Sīkar, India
98/D4 Sikasso, Mali
98/D4 Sikasso (reg.), Mali
125/K3 Sikeston, Mo,US
77/M2 Sikhote-Alin' (mts.), Rus.
61/J4 Síkinos (isl.), Gre.
84/E2 Sikkim (state), India
62/D3 Siklós, Hun.
58/B1 Sil (riv.), Sp.
55/G4 Silandro (Schlanders), It.
116/A3 Silao, Mex.
82/D5 Silay, Phil.
85/F3 Silchar, India
63/J5 Şile, Turk.
47/E1 Sileby, Eng,UK
49/H3 Silesia (reg.), Pol.
96/F3 Silet, Alg.
74/C3 Silifke, Turk.
84/E2 Silīguri, India
75/E5 Siling (lake), China
93/H6 Silisili (peak), WSam.
63/H3 Silistra, Bul.
63/J5 Silivri, Turk.
42/D4 Silkeborg, Den.
45/G2 Silksworth, Eng,UK
59/E3 Silla, Sp.
42/E4 Sillamäe, Est.
58/A1 Silleda, Sp.
45/E2 Silloth, Eng,UK
128/E2 Siloam Springs, Ar,US
72/D1 Silopi, Turk.
128/E4 Silsbee, Tx,US
45/G4 Silsden, Eng,UK
96/J4 Siltou (well), Chad
49/L1 Šilutė, Lith.
47/E2 Silvan, Turk.
84/B3 Silvassa, India
122/D5 Silver (cr.), Or,US
124/B2 Silver (lake), Or,US
123/L4 Silver Bay, Mn,US
124/E4 Silver City, NM,US
130/L3 Silver Creek, Yk,Can
45/F3 Silverdale, Eng,UK
132/B2 Silverdale, Wa,US
132/C2 Silver Lake-Fircrest, Wa,US
131/J8 Silver Spring, Md,US
47/E2 Silverstone, Eng,UK
46/C5 Silverton, Eng,UK
124/F3 Silverton, Co,US
122/C4 Silverton, Or,US
128/C3 Silverton, Tx,US
58/A4 Silves, Port.
60/D1 Silvi, It.
124/C2 Silvies (riv.), Or,US
55/G4 Silvretta (mts.), Aus., Swi.
60/A4 Silyānah (gov.), Tun.
86/D3 Simanggang, Malay.
126/E2 Simard (lake), Qu,Can
74/B2 Simav, Turk.
67/J1 Simbirsk, Rus.
67/H1 Simbirsk Obl., Rus.
126/D3 Simcoe, On,Can
126/E2 Simcoe (lake), On,Can
97/N5 Simēn (mts.), Eth.
62/F3 Simeria, Rom.
86/A3 Simeulue (isl.), Indo.
66/E3 Simferopol', Ukr.
81/E5 Siming (mtn.), China
63/F5 Simitli, Bul.
131/B2 Simi Valley, Ca,US
73/L2 Simla, India
62/F2 Şimleu Silvaniei, Rom.
55/D4 Simme (riv.), Swi.
53/F2 Simmerath, Ger.
53/G4 Simmerbach (riv.), Ger.
116/C4 Simojovel, Mex.
122/D2 Simonette (riv.), Ab,Can
102/B4 Simonstown, SAfr.
50/D1 Simonszand (isl.), Neth.
86/A3 Simpang-kiri (riv.), Indo.
53/E2 Simpelveld, Neth.
118/H2 Simpson (pen.), NW,Can
118/G2 Simpson (riv.), NW,Can
49/H1 Simrishamn, Swe.
87/E3 Simunul, Phil.
97/Q6 Sinadhago, Som.
72/B3 Sinafir (isl.), SAr.
100/C2 Sinai (pen.), Egypt
117/N8 Sinaloa (state), Mex.
117/F6 Sincelejo, Col.
129/H3 Sinclair (lake), Ga,US
122/G5 Sinclair, Wy,US
84/C2 Sind (riv.), India
73/J3 Sind (prov.), Pak.
82/D6 Sindañgan, Phil.
86/C5 Sindangbarang, Indo.
57/H2 Sindelfingen, Ger.
58/A4 Sines, Port.
58/A4 Sines, Cabo de (cape), Port.
98/D5 Sinfra, IvC.
86/B3 Singapore
86/B3 Singapore (cap.), Sing.
83/C3 Sing Buri, Thai.
55/E2 Singen, Ger.
63/G2 Sîngeorz-Băi, Rom.
101/B4 Singida, Tanz.
101/B4 Singida (prov.), Tanz.
61/H2 Singitic (gulf), Gre.
87/F4 Singkang, Indo.
86/C3 Singkawang, Indo.
86/B4 Singkep (isl.), Indo.
91/D2 Singleton, Austl.
60/A2 Siniscola, It.
97/M5 Sinjah, Sudan
74/E3 Sinjār, Iraq
100/D5 Sinkāt, Sudan
52/C3 Sin-le-Noble, Fr.
84/B4 Sinnar, India
60/E2 Sinni (riv.), It.
62/E2 Sînnicolau Mare, Rom.
100/B2 Sinnūris, Egypt
98/C5 Sino (co.), Libr.
63/J3 Sinoe (lake), Rom.
109/G6 Sinop, Braz.
74/C1 Sinop, Turk.
86/D3 Sintang, Indo.
52/D2 Sint-Genesius-Rode, Belg.
52/D1 Sint-Gillis-Waas, Belg.
52/D1 Sint-Katelijne-Waver, Belg.
52/C1 Sint-Laureins, Belg.
117/J4 Sint Maarten (isl.), NAnt.
50/C5 Sint-Michielsgestel, Neth.
52/D1 Sint-Niklaas, Belg.
50/C5 Sint-Oedenrode, Neth.
128/D4 Sinton, Tx,US
52/D2 Sint-Pieters-Leeuw, Belg.
58/A3 Sintra, Port.
59/P10 Sintra (mts.), Port.
53/E2 Sint-Truiden, Belg.
117/F6 Sinú (riv.), Col.
80/D2 Sinŭiju, NKor.
53/G2 Sinzig, Ger.
62/D2 Sió (riv.), Hun.
87/F2 Siocon, Phil.
62/D2 Siófok, Hun.
104/D4 Sioma Ngwezi Nat'l Park, Zam.
54/D5 Sion, Swi.
56/E4 Sioule (riv.), Fr.
123/J5 Sioux City, Ia,US
123/J5 Sioux Falls, SD,US
126/B1 Sioux Lookout, On,Can
60/E1 Šipan (isl.), Cro.
81/F2 Siping, China
123/J2 Sipiwesk (lake), Mb,Can
105/Q Siple (coast), Ant.
105/R Siple (isl.), Ant.
129/G3 Sipsey (riv.), Al,US
84/A4 Sipura (isl.), Indo.
110/B2 Siqueira Campos, Braz.
116/E5 Siquia (riv.), Nic.
42/C4 Sira (riv.), Nor.
60/D4 Siracusa (Syracuse), It.
84/E3 Sirājganj, Bang.
122/C2 Sir Alexander (peak), BC,Can
74/D2 Şiran, Turk.
63/H2 Siret, Rom.
63/H3 Siret (riv.), Rom.
86/D3 Sirik (cape), Malay.
83/C2 Sirikit (res.), Thai.
85/H4 Sirit (res.), Thai.
130/B5 Sirius (pt.), Ak,US
118/D2 Sir James MacBrien (peak), NW,Can
73/G3 Sīrjān, Iran
91/D4 Sir John (cape), Austl.
74/E3 Şırnak, Turk.
84/B3 Sirohi, India
84/C3 Sironj, India
61/J4 Síros (isl.), Gre.
84/C2 Sirsa, India
84/B5 Sirsi, India
62/C3 Sisak, Cro.
83/D3 Sisaket, Thai.
85/H4 Si Sa Ket, Thai.
83/B2 Si Satchanalai (ruins), Thai.
123/H2 Sisipuk (lake), Mb, Sk,Can
83/C3 Sisophon, Camb.
123/J4 Sisseton, SD,US
99/E4 Sissili (prov.), Burk.
129/H2 Sissonville, WV,US
85/F3 Sitākunda, Bang.
59/F2 Sitges, Sp.
61/H2 Sithoniá (pen.), Gre.
61/K5 Sitía, Gre.
130/M2 Sitidgi (lake), NW,Can
130/L4 Sitka, Ak,US
49/K4 Sitno (peak), Slvk.
83/B2 Sittang (riv.), Burma
50/C7 Sittard, Neth.
47/G4 Sittingbourne, Eng,UK
85/F3 Sittwe (Akyab), Burma
62/D3 Sivac, Yugo.
84/C6 Sivakāsi, India
74/D2 Sivas, Turk.
74/D3 Siverek, Turk.
74/B2 Sivrihisar, Turk.
52/D3 Sivry-Rance, Belg.
97/L2 Sīwah, Egypt
84/D2 Siwān, India
44/A2 Sixmilecross, NI,UK
130/K3 Sixtymile, Yk,Can
76/G3 Siziwang, China
42/D5 Sjælland (isl.), Den.
62/E4 Sjenica, Yugo.
42/M6 Sjónfridh (peak), Ice.
42/P7 Skaftafell Nat'l Park, Ice.
42/D4 Skagen, Den.
42/D4 Skagens (cape), Den.
42/D4 Skagerrak (str.), Eur.
42/P6 Skálfandafljót (riv.), Ice.
49/J4 Skalica, Slvk.
57/K2 Skalice (riv.), Czh.
61/J3 Skantzoura (isl.), Gre.
42/E4 Skaraborg (co.), Swe.
49/L3 Skarżysko-Kamienna, Pol.
49/K4 Skawina, Pol.
118/D3 Skeena (range), BC,Can
122/A2 Skeena (riv.), BC,Can
45/J5 Skegness, Eng,UK
42/G2 Skellefteå, Swe.
42/F2 Skellefteälv (riv.), Swe.
45/G4 Skelmanthorpe, Eng,UK
45/F4 Skelmersdale, Eng,UK
45/H2 Skelton, Eng,UK
45/G2 Skerne (riv.), Eng,UK
44/B4 Skerries, Ire.
61/G4 Skhiza (isl.), Gre.
125/H3 Skiatook, Ok,US
45/E2 Skiddaw (mtn.), Eng,UK
42/D4 Skien, Nor.
49/L3 Skierniewice, Pol.
49/K3 Skierniewice (prov.), Pol.
96/G1 Skikda, Alg.
61/G4 Skinári, Ákra (cape), Gre.
45/H4 Skipsea, Eng,UK
45/F4 Skipton, Eng,UK
45/F3 Skirfare (riv.), Eng,UK
61/J3 Skíros (isl.), Gre.
42/D4 Skjeberg, Nor.
64/B2 Skjelåtinden (peak), Nor.
42/D5 Skjern, Den.
46/A3 Skokholm (isl.), Wal,UK
132/Q15 Skokie, Il,US
46/A3 Skomer (isl.), Wal,UK
83/D3 Skon, Camb.
61/H3 Skópelos (isl.), Gre.
66/F1 Skopin, Rus.
62/E5 Skopje (cap.), Macd.
42/E4 Skövde, Swe.
77/J1 Skovorodino, Rus.
127/G2 Skowhegan, Me,US
130/L3 Skukum (mtn.), Yk,Can
125/K2 Skunk (riv.), Ia,US
49/H2 Skwierzyna, Pol.
132/D2 Skykomish (riv.), Wa,US
113/J8 Skyway (sound), Chile
42/D5 Slagelse, Den.
45/F4 Slaidburn, Eng,UK
49/L4 Slaná (riv.), Slvk.
43/B4 Slaney (riv.), Ire.
64/F4 Slantsy, Rus.
63/G3 Slatina, Rom.
115/F3 Slave (riv.), Can.
99/F5 Slave Coast (reg.), Afr.
122/E2 Slave Lake, Ab,Can
75/C1 Slavgorod, Rus.
62/C3 Slavonia (reg.), Cro.
62/D3 Slavonska Požega, Cro.
62/D3 Slavonski Brod, Cro.
66/C2 Slavuta, Ukr.
66/F2 Slavyansk, Ukr.
66/F3 Slavyansk-na-Kubani, Rus.
49/J1 Sławno, Pol.
123/K5 Slayton, Mn,US
45/H6 Sleaford, Eng,UK
50/D3 Sleen, Neth.
119/H3 Sleeper (isls.), NW,Can
123/K4 Sleepy Eye, Mn,US
44/A4 Sliabh na Caillighe (mtn.), Ire.
129/F4 Slidell, La,US
50/B5 Sliedrecht, Neth.
60/D5 Sliema, Malta
44/A3 Slieve Beagh (mtn.), NI,UK
44/C3 Slieve Binnian (mtn.), NI,UK
44/C3 Slieve Croob (mtn.), NI,UK
44/C3 Slieve Donard (mtn.), NI,UK
44/B3 Slieve Gullion (mtn.), NI,UK
44/A1 Slieve Snaght (mtn.), Ire.
43/A3 Sligo, Ire.
43/A3 Sligo (bay), Ire.
63/H4 Sliven, Bul.
62/F4 Slivnitsa, Bul.
127/S10 Sloan, NY,US
65/L4 Slobodskoy, Rus.
63/H3 Slobozia, Rom.
50/D2 Slochteren, Neth.
66/C1 Slonim, Bela.
50/C3 Slotermeer (lake), Neth.
47/F4 Slough, Eng,UK
49/K4 Slovakia
62/B3 Slovenia
62/B2 Slovenska Bistrica, Slov.
49/L4 Slovenské Rudohorie (mts.), Slvk.
49/J1 Słowiński Nat'l Park, Pol.
49/H2 Słubice, Pol.
66/C2 Sluch' (riv.), Ukr.
49/J2 Słupca, Pol.
49/J1 Słupia (riv.), Pol.
49/J1 Słupsk, Pol.
49/J1 Słupsk (prov.), Pol.
66/C1 Slutsk, Bela.
76/E1 Slyudyanka, Rus.
47/F4 Smallfield, Eng,UK
119/K3 Smallwood (res.), Nf,Can
123/G2 Smeaton, Sk,Can
62/E3 Smederevo, Yugo.
62/E3 Smederevska Palanka, Yugo.
42/E3 Smedjebacken, Swe.
66/D2 Smela, Ukr.
50/D3 Smilde, Neth.
105/V Smith (pen.), Ant.
122/B3 Smith (inlet), BC,Can
119/J2 Smith (isl.), NW,Can
122/F4 Smith (riv.), Mt,US
122/B2 Smithers, BC,Can
129/J3 Smithfield, NC,US
124/E2 Smithfield, Ut,US
126/E4 Smith Mtn. (lake), Va,US
126/E2 Smiths Falls, On,Can
131/G5 Smithtown, NY,US
127/Q9 Smithville, On,Can
125/J4 Smithville, Ok,US
91/E1 Smoky (cape), Austl.
122/D2 Smoky (riv.), Ab,Can
125/H3 Smoky (hills), Ks,US
125/G3 Smoky Hill (riv.), Ks,US
122/E2 Smoky Lake, Ab,Can
42/C3 Smøla (isl.), Nor.
64/G5 Smolensk, Rus.
64/F5 Smolensk Obl., Rus.
61/G2 Smólikas (peak), Gre.
63/G5 Smolyan, Bul.
105/U Smyley (isl.), Ant.
129/G3 Smyrna, Ga,US
44/D3 Snaefell (mtn.), IM,UK
130/M2 Snake (riv.), Yk,Can
122/D4 Snake (riv.), US
125/G2 Snake (riv.), Ne,US
50/C2 Sneek, Neth.
50/C2 Sneekermeer (lake), Neth.
102/D3 Sneeuberg (mts.), SAfr.
102/B4 Sneeuberg (peak), SAfr.
127/Q8 Snelgrove, On,Can
47/G1 Snettisham, Eng,UK
49/H3 Sněžka (peak), Czh.
62/B3 Snežnik (peak), Yugo.
49/L2 Śniardwy (lake), Pol.
47/G4 Snodland, Eng,UK
42/D3 Snøhetta (peak), Nor.
132/C2 Snohomish, Wa,US
132/C2 Snohomish (riv.), Wa,US
132/D2 Snoqualmie (riv.), Wa,US
42/E2 Snøtind (peak), Nor.
44/D5 Snowdon (mtn.), Wal,UK
44/D5 Snowdonia Nat'l Park, Wal,UK
124/E4 Snowflake, Az,US
123/H2 Snow Lake, Mb,Can
130/K2 Snowy (peak), Ak,US
91/D3 Snowy River Nat'l Park, Austl.
128/C3 Snyder, Tx,US
103/H7 Soalala, Madg.
103/J7 Soanierana-Ivongo, Madg.
45/G6 Soar (riv.), Eng,UK
57/L2 Soběslav, Czh.
87/K4 Sobger (riv.), Indo.
73/J3 Sobhādero, Pak.
109/K6 Sobradinho (res.), Braz.
109/K4 Sobral, Braz.
79/M9 Sobue, Japan
49/L2 Sochaczew, Pol.
66/F4 Sochi, Rus.
93/K6 Society (isls.), FrPol.
110/G7 Socorro, Braz.
124/F4 Socorro, NM,US
128/B4 Socorro, Tx,US
71/E8 Socotra (isl.), Yem.
83/D4 Soc Trang, Viet.
58/D3 Socuéllamos, Sp.
42/H2 Sodankylä, Fin.
122/F5 Soda Springs, Id,US
79/H7 Sodegaura, Japan
42/F3 Söderhamn, Swe.
42/F4 Södertälje, Swe.
97/N6 Sodo, Eth.
51/F5 Soest, Ger.
50/C4 Soest, Neth.
51/E3 Soeste (riv.), Ger.
103/J6 Sofia (riv.), Madg.
62/F4 Sofia (Sofiya) (cap.), Bul.
62/F4 Sofiya (reg.), Bul.
108/D2 Sogamoso, Col.
42/B3 Sognafjorden (fjord), Nor.
42/C3 Sogn og Fjordane (co.), Nor.
96/J4 Sogollé (well), Chad
77/K5 Sŏgwip'o, SKor.
47/G2 Soham, Eng,UK
52/D2 Soignies, Belg.
52/C5 Soissons, Fr.
78/C3 Sōja, Japan
84/B2 Sojat, India
80/C3 Sŏjosŏn (bay), NKor.
67/J1 Sok (riv.), Rus.
83/C3 Sok (pt.), Thai.
79/H7 Sōka, Japan
80/E3 Sokch'o, SKor.
74/A3 Söke, Turk.
76/F1 Sokhor (peak), Rus.
62/E4 Sokobanja, Yugo.
99/F4 Sokodé, Togo
64/J4 Sokol, Rus.
49/M2 Sokółka, Pol.
57/K1 Sokolov, Czh.
49/M2 Sokołów Podlaski, Pol.
99/G4 Sokoto (plains), Nga.
99/G4 Sokoto (riv.), Nga.
99/G3 Sokoto (state), Nga.
42/C4 Sola, Nor.
82/D4 Solana, Phil.
108/C2 Solano (pt.), Col.
58/C4 Sol, Costa del (coast), Sp.
59/P10 Sol, Costa do (reg.), Port.
125/J2 Soldier (riv.), Ia,US
117/G5 Soledad, Col.
131/B2 Soledad (canyon), Ca,US
117/J6 Soledad, Ven.
116/A3 Soledad Diez Gutierrez, Mex.
110/A4 Soledade, Braz.
47/E5 Solent (chan.), Eng,UK
53/E4 Soleuvre (mtn.), Lux.
74/E2 Solhan, Turk.
66/C1 Soligorsk, Bela.
47/E2 Solihull, Eng,UK
65/N4 Solikamsk, Rus.
67/K2 Sol'-Iletsk, Rus.
51/E6 Solingen, Ger.
42/F3 Sollefteå, Swe.
59/G3 Sóller, Sp.
51/G5 Solling (mts.), Ger.
42/D3 Søln (peak), Nor.
54/B5 Solnan (riv.), Fr.
86/D5 Solo (riv.), Indo.
86/B4 Solok, Indo.
116/C5 Sololá, Guat.
92/E5 Solomon (sea), PNG, Sol.
128/D2 Solomon (riv.), Ks,US
92/E6 Solomon Islands
67/L4 Solonchak Goklenkui (salt marsh), Trkm.
54/D3 Solothurn, Swi.
54/D3 Solothurn (canton), Swi.
64/G2 Solovetskiy (isls.), Rus.
59/F2 Solsona, Sp.
62/D2 Solt, Hun.
62/B4 Šolta (isl.), Cro.
51/G3 Soltau, Ger.
62/D2 Soltvadkert, Hun.
62/E5 Solunska (peak), Macd.
46/A3 Solva (riv.), Wal,UK
124/B4 Solvang, Ca,US
42/E4 Sölvesborg, Swe.
44/E2 Solway Firth (inlet), Eng, Sc,UK
104/E3 Solwezi, Zam.
79/G2 Sōma, Japan
74/A2 Soma, Turk.
52/C3 Somain, Fr.
97/Q6 Somalia
127/F1 Somaqua (riv.), Qu,Can
62/D3 Sombor, Cro.
117/P9 Sombrerete, Mex.
110/B4 Sombrio, Braz.
45/G5 Somercotes, Eng,UK
50/C6 Someren, Neth.
42/G3 Somero, Fin.
122/E3 Somers, Mt,US
118/G1 Somerset (isl.), NW,Can
46/D4 Somerset (co.), Eng,UK
126/C4 Somerset, Ky,US
131/F5 Somerset, NJ,US

176

Somer – Sunsh

127/S9 **Somerset**, NY,US
91/C4 **Somerset-Burnie**, Austl.
102/D4 **Somerset East**, SAfr.
102/B4 **Somerset West**, SAfr.
47/F2 **Somersham**, Eng,UK
127/G3 **Somersworth**, NH,US
46/D4 **Somerton**, Eng,UK
124/D4 **Somerton**, Az,US
131/F5 **Somerville**, NJ,US
125/H5 **Somerville** (lake), Tx,US
63/F2 **Someş** (riv.), Rom.
63/G2 **Someşul Mare** (riv.), Rom.
56/D1 **Somme** (bay), Fr.
52/B4 **Somme** (dept.), Fr.
52/A3 **Somme** (riv.), Fr.
52/D6 **Somme** (riv.), Fr.
52/D5 **Somme-Soude** (riv.), Fr.
62/C2 **Somogy** (co.), Hun.
116/D5 **Somoto**, Nic.
47/F5 **Somptin**, Eng,UK
42/D5 **Sønderborg**, Den.
102/L11 **Sonderend** (riv.), SAfr.
48/E1 **Sønderjylland** (co.), Den.
55/F5 **Sondrio**, It.
84/C2 **Sonepat**, India
84/D3 **Sonepur**, India
83/E3 **Song Cau**, Viet.
83/D4 **Song Dinh**, Viet.
55/F5 **Sondrio** (prov.), It.
101/B5 **Songea**, Tanz.
81/F1 **Songhua** (riv.), China
75/B3 **Song-Kel'** (lake), Kyr.
83/C5 **Songkhla**, Thai.
83/C2 **Songkhram** (riv.), Thai.
77/J2 **Songling**, China
83/C1 **Song Ma**, Viet.
104/F4 **Songo**, Moz.
81/C4 **Song Shan** (peak), China
80/D4 **Songt'an**, SKor.
81/C5 **Songzi Guan** (pass), China
83/E3 **Son Ha**, Viet.
76/G3 **Sonid Youqi**, China
76/G3 **Sonid Zuoqi**, China
83/C1 **Son La**, Viet.
73/J3 **Sonmiāni** (bay), Pak.
57/J1 **Sonneberg**, Ger.
47/F4 **Sonning**, Eng,UK
48/G5 **Sonntagshorn** (peak), Ger.
109/J5 **Sono** (riv.), Braz.
78/D3 **Sonobe**, Japan
132/K10 **Sonoma**, Ca,US
132/J10 **Sonoma** (mts.), Ca,US
117/M8 **Sonora** (riv.), Mex.
117/M8 **Sonora** (state), Mex.
124/B3 **Sonora**, Ca,US
128/C4 **Sonora**, Tx,US
117/M7 **Sonoyta** (riv.), Mex.
72/E2 **Sonqor**, Iran
50/D5 **Sonsbeck**, Ger.
58/D3 **Sonseca**, Sp.
116/D5 **Sonsonate**, ESal.
92/C4 **Sonsorol** (isls.), Palau
62/D3 **Sonta**, Yugo.
83/D1 **Son Tay**, Viet.
51/G6 **Sontra**, Ger.
87/G3 **Sopi** (cape), Indo.
83/C1 **Sopka**, Laos
73/K2 **Sopore**, India
63/G4 **Sopot**, Bul.
49/K1 **Sopot**, Pol.
62/C2 **Sopron**, Hun.
46/D3 **Sôr** (riv.), Wal,UK
60/C2 **Sora**, It.
80/E3 **Sŏrak-san** (mtn.), SKor.
127/F2 **Sorel**, Qu,Can
74/M9 **Soreq, Nabel** (dry riv.), Isr.
57/H4 **Soresina**, It.
56/F5 **Sorgues**, Fr.
74/C2 **Sorgun**, Turk.
58/D2 **Soria**, Sp.
113/F2 **Soriano** (dept.), Uru.
86/A3 **Sorikmerapi** (peak), Indo.
67/K3 **Sor Karatuley** (salt pan), Kaz.
67/K3 **Sor Kaydak** (salt marsh), Kaz.
67/K3 **Sor Mertvyy Kultuk** (salt marsh), Kaz.
52/D4 **Sormonne** (riv.), Fr.
48/F1 **Sorø**, Den.
110/C2 **Sorocaba**, Braz.
67/K1 **Sorochinsk**, Rus.
63/J1 **Soroki**, Mol.
92/D4 **Sorol** (atoll), Micr.
87/H4 **Sorong**, Indo.
101/B2 **Soroti**, Ugan.
42/G1 **Sørøya** (isl.), Nor.
42/G1 **Sørøysundet** (chan.), Nor.
51/E6 **Sorpestausee** (res.), Ger.
58/A3 **Sorraia** (riv.), Port.
60/D2 **Sorrento**, It.
104/B5 **Sorris-Sorris**, Namb.
60/A2 **Sorso**, It.
82/D5 **Sorsogon**, Phil.
64/F3 **Sortavala**, Rus.
64/D4 **Sõrve** (pt.), Est.
51/H5 **Söse** (riv.), Ger.
66/F1 **Sosna** (riv.), Rus.
112/C2 **Sosneado** (peak), Arg.
65/M3 **Sosnogorsk**, Rus.
65/L4 **Sosnovka**, Rus.
49/K3 **Sosnowiec**, Pol.
117/G4 **Sosúa**, DRep.
52/D6 **Soude** (riv.), Fr.
117/J4 **Soufrière** (mt.), Guad.
117/J5 **Soufrière** (mt.), StV.
96/G1 **Souk Ahras**, Alg.
53/G1 **Soultz-sous-Forets**, Fr.
99/E3 **Soum** (prov.), Burk.
53/E2 **Soumagne**, Belg.
102/E3 **Sources, Mont aux** (peak), Les.
109/J4 **Soure**, Braz.
58/A2 **Soure**, Port.
123/H3 **Souris**, Mb,Can
127/J2 **Souris**, PE,Can
123/H3 **Souris** (riv.), Can., US
98/E3 **Sourou** (prov.), Burk.
96/D2 **Sous** (wadi), Mor.
109/L5 **Sousa**, Braz.
58/B3 **Sousel**, Port.
102/C3 **Sout** (riv.), SAfr.
90/G8 **South** (cr.), Austl.
127/H2 **South** (mts.), NS,Can
119/H2 **South** (bay), NW,Can
89/G7 **South** (cape), NZ
89/H7 **South** (isl.), NZ
104/D6 **South Africa**
47/E2 **Southam**, Eng,UK
107/* **South America**
119/H2 **Southampton** (cape), NW,Can
119/H2 **Southampton** (isl.), NW,Can
126/D2 **Southampton**, On,Can
47/E5 **Southampton**, Eng,UK
85/F5 **South Andaman** (isl.), India
129/J2 **South Anna** (riv.), Va,US
129/H3 **South Augusta**, Ga,US
119/K3 **South Aulatsivik** (isl.), Nf,Can
89/C3 **South Australia** (state), Austl.
129/F3 **Southaven**, Ms,US
44/D3 **South Barrule** (mtn.), IM,UK
126/C3 **South Bend**, In,US
47/G4 **Southborough**, Eng,UK
126/E4 **South Boston**, Va,US
47/F5 **Southbourne**, Eng,UK
46/C6 **South Brent**, Eng,UK
101/A3 **South Buganda** (prov.), Ugan.
127/F2 **South Burlington**, Vt,US
129/H3 **South Carolina** (state), US
71/L8 **South China** (sea), Asia
123/H4 **South Dakota** (state), US
46/D5 **South Dorset Downs** (uplands), Eng,UK
47/F5 **South Downs** (hills), Eng,UK
39/S8 **South East** (cape), Austl.
91/C3 **South East** (pt.), Austl.
117/G3 **Southeast** (pt.), Bahm.
130/E3 **Southeast** (cape), Ak,US
132/P16 **South Elgin**, Il,US
45/G4 **South Elmsall**, Eng,UK
44/C1 **Southend**, Sc,UK
47/G3 **Southend-on-Sea**, Eng,UK
74/K6 **Southern** (dist.), Isr.
98/B5 **Southern** (prov.), SLeo.
101/A3 **Southern** (prov.), Ugan.
93/J6 **Southern Cook** (isls.), CookIs.
118/G3 **Southern Indian** (lake), Mb,Can
129/J3 **Southern Pines**, NC,US
44/D1 **Southern Uplands** (mts.), Sc,UK
47/G1 **Southery**, Eng,UK
91/C4 **South Esk** (riv.), Austl.
132/F7 **Southfield**, Mi,US
47/H4 **South Foreland** (pt.), Eng,UK
124/F3 **South Fork**, Co,US
129/F2 **South Fulton**, Tn,US
131/B3 **South Gate**, Ca,US
132/F7 **Southgate**, Mi,US
105/X **South Georgia** (isl.), UK
46/C4 **South Glamorgan** (co.), Wal,UK
46/C6 **South Hams** (plain), Eng,UK
47/F5 **South Hayling**, Eng,UK
126/E4 **South Hill**, Va,US
50/B5 **South Holland** (prov.), Neth.
132/Q16 **South Holland**, Il,US
45/G4 **South Kirkby**, Eng,UK
80/D4 **South Korea**
124/C3 **South Lake Tahoe**, Ca,US
104/F3 **South Luangwa Nat'l Park**, Zam.
105/K **South Magnetic Pole**, Ant.
132/Q14 **South Milwaukee**, Wi,US
47/G3 **Southminster**, Eng,UK
46/C4 **South Molton**, Eng,UK
123/J2 **South Moose** (lake), Mb,Can
130/M5 **South Moresby Nat'l Park Rsv.**, BC,Can
45/G5 **South Normanton**, Eng,UK
105/W **South Orkney** (isls.), UK
67/G4 **South Ossetian Aut. Obl.**, Geo.
47/F3 **South Oxhey**, Eng,UK
46/D5 **South Petherton**, Eng,UK
90/E6 **South Pine** (riv.), Austl.
131/F5 **South Plainfield**, NJ,US
125/G2 **South Platte** (riv.), Co, Ne,US
105/A **South Pole**, Ant.
45/E4 **Southport**, Eng,UK
129/J3 **Southport**, NC,US
131/F5 **South River**, NJ,US
105/Y **South Sandwich** (isls.), UK
132/K11 **South San Francisco**, Ca,US
122/F3 **South Saskatchewan** (riv.), Ab, Sk,Can
105/W **South Shetland** (isls.), UK
45/G2 **South Shields**, Eng,UK
125/H2 **South Sioux City**, Ne,US
84/E3 **South Suburban**, India
45/F2 **South Tyne** (riv.), Eng,UK
87/F2 **South Ubian**, Phil.
45/H5 **Southwell**, Eng,UK
91/C4 **South West** (cape), Austl.
91/C4 **South West Nat'l Park**, Austl.
47/H2 **Southwold**, Eng,UK
47/G3 **South Woodham Ferrers**, Eng,UK
90/C4 **Southwood Nat'l Park**, Austl.
45/G5 **South Yorkshire** (co.), Eng,UK
63/G2 **Sovata**, Rom.
60/E3 **Soverato Marina**, It.
49/L1 **Sovetsk**, Rus.
64/D5 **Sovetsk**, Rus.
64/L4 **Sovetsk**, Rus.
77/N2 **Sovetskaya Gavan'**, Rus.
45/G4 **Sowerby Bridge**, Eng,UK
102/D2 **Soweto**, SAfr.
64/J2 **Soyana** (riv.), Rus.
80/D4 **Soyang** (lake), SKor.
56/D4 **Soyaux**, Fr.
105/E **Soyuz**, Ant.
66/D1 **Sozh** (riv.), Eur.
53/E3 **Spa**, Belg.
105/U **Spaatz** (isl.), Ant.
58/C2 **Spain**
45/H6 **Spalding**, Eng,UK
132/C3 **Spanaway**, Wa,US
117/F4 **Spanish Town**, Jam.
124/C3 **Sparks**, Nv,US
129/H2 **Sparta**, NC,US
131/F4 **Sparta**, NJ,US
129/G3 **Sparta**, Tn,US
126/B3 **Sparta**, Wi,US
129/H3 **Spartanburg**, SC,US
61/H4 **Sparta** (Spárti), Gre.
60/A3 **Spartivento** (cape), It.
60/E4 **Spartivento** (cape), It.
122/E3 **Sparwood**, BC,Can
77/L3 **Spassk-Dal'niy**, Rus.
61/H5 **Spátha, Ákra** (cape), Gre.
43/C2 **Spean** (riv.), Sc,UK
43/C2 **Spean Bridge**, Sc,UK
123/H4 **Spearfish**, SD,US
45/F5 **Speke**, Eng,UK
92/C8 **Spencer** (gulf), Austl.
130/E2 **Spencer** (pt.), Ak,US
123/K5 **Spencer**, Ia,US
51/F4 **Spenge**, Ger.
45/G2 **Spennymoor**, Eng,UK
61/H3 **Sperkhiós** (riv.), Gre.
44/A2 **Sperrin** (mts.), NI,UK
43/D2 **Spey** (riv.), Sc,UK
57/H2 **Speyer**, Ger.
127/Q8 **Speyside**, On,Can
60/E3 **Spezzano Albanese**, It.
119/H2 **Spicer** (isl.), NW,Can
51/E1 **Spiekeroog** (isl.), Ger.
54/D4 **Spiez**, Swi.
50/B5 **Spijkenisse**, Neth.
130/K2 **Spike** (mtn.), Ak,US
62/A2 **Spilimbergo**, It.
45/J5 **Spilsby**, Eng,UK
60/A2 **Spina, Bruncu** (peak), It.
73/J2 **Spin Būldak**, Afg.
53/E5 **Spincourt**, Fr.
122/D2 **Spirit River**, Ab,Can
122/G2 **Spiritwood**, Sk,Can
49/L4 **Spišská Nová Ves**, Slvk.
47/E5 **Spithead** (chan.), Eng,UK
68/B2 **Spitsbergen** (isl.), Sval.
57/K3 **Spittal an der Drau**, Aus.
123/K2 **Split** (lake), Mb,Can
62/C4 **Split**, Cro.
55/F4 **Splugenpass** (pass), It., Swi.
122/D4 **Spokane** (riv.), Id, Wa,US
122/D4 **Spokane**, Wa,US
60/C1 **Spoleto**, It.
126/B3 **Spoon** (riv.), Il,US
126/B2 **Spooner**, Wi,US
123/K3 **Sprague**, Mb,Can
50/C5 **Sprang-Capelle**, Neth.
82/B5 **Spratly** (isls.)
49/H2 **Spree** (riv.), Ger.
57/K4 **Spresiano**, It.
53/E3 **Sprimont**, Belg.
129/G4 **Spring** (cr.), Ga,US
128/E4 **Spring**, Tx,US
127/K1 **Springdale**, Nf,Can
128/E2 **Springdale**, Ar,US
51/G4 **Springe**, Ger.
125/F3 **Springer**, NM,US
124/E4 **Springerville**, Az,US
125/G3 **Springfield**, Co,US
126/B4 **Springfield** (cap.), Il,US
127/F3 **Springfield**, Ma,US
125/J3 **Springfield**, Mo,US
126/D4 **Springfield**, Oh,US
122/C4 **Springfield**, Or,US
129/G2 **Springfield**, Tn,US
131/J8 **Springfield**, Va,US
127/F3 **Springfield**, Vt,US
127/H2 **Springhill**, NS,Can
128/E3 **Springhill**, La,US
102/E2 **Springs**, SAfr.
123/H3 **Springside**, Sk,Can
91/G5 **Springvale**
123/K5 **Spring Valley**, Mn,US
131/F4 **Spring Valley**, NY,US
51/E6 **Sprockhövel**, Ger.
47/H1 **Sprowston**, Eng,UK
126/E4 **Spruce** (peak), WV,US
131/E5 **Spruce Run** (res.), NJ,US
50/B5 **Spui** (riv.), Neth.
45/J4 **Spurn Head** (pt.), Eng,UK
122/C3 **Squamish**, BC,Can
60/E3 **Squillace** (gulf), It.
61/F2 **Squinzano**, It.
62/D3 **Srbobran**, Yugo.
83/C4 **Sre Ambel**, Camb.
62/D3 **Srebrenica**, Bosn.
63/G4 **Sredna** (mts.), Bul.
63/G4 **Srednogorie**, Bul.
83/D3 **Sre Khtum**, Camb.
49/J2 **Śrem**, Pol.
62/E3 **Sremčica**, Yugo.
62/D3 **Sremska Mitrovica**, Yugo.
83/C3 **Sreng** (riv.), Camb.
83/D3 **Sre Noy**, Camb.
83/D3 **Srepok** (riv.), Camb.
77/H1 **Sretensk**, Rus.
73/K3 **Sri Dungargarh**, India
73/K3 **Sri Gangānagar**, India
84/D4 **Srikākulam**, India
84/D6 **Sri Lanka**
73/K2 **Srīnagar**, India
84/B4 **Srīvardhan**, India
49/J3 **Środa Śląska**, Pol.
49/J2 **Środa Wielkopolska**, Pol.
90/A2 **Staaten River Nat'l Park**, Austl.
42/H1 **Stabbursdalen Nat'l Park**, Nor.
50/B6 **Stabroek**, Belg.
51/G1 **Stade**, Ger.
52/C2 **Staden**, Belg.
50/D3 **Stadskanaal**, Neth.
51/G4 **Stadthagen**, Ger.
50/D5 **Stadtlohn**, Ger.
55/E3 **Stäfa**, Swi.
49/G1 **Staffanstorp**, Swe.
45/F6 **Stafford**, Eng,UK
46/D2 **Stafford & Worcester** (can.), Eng,UK
45/F5 **Staffordshire** (co.), Eng,UK
60/B4 **Stagnone** (isls.), It.
45/G2 **Staindrop**, Eng,UK
47/F4 **Staines**, Eng,UK
132/M12 **Stakes** (mtn.), Ca,US
66/F2 **Stakhanov**, Ukr.
46/D5 **Stalbridge**, Eng,UK
47/H1 **Stalham**, Eng,UK
119/S6 **Stallworthy** (cape), NW,Can
49/M3 **Stalowa Wola**, Pol.
45/F5 **Stalybridge**, Eng,UK
63/G4 **Stamboliyski**, Bul.
47/F1 **Stamford**, Eng,UK
131/G4 **Stamford**, Ct,US
45/H4 **Stamford Bridge**, Eng,UK
42/E1 **Stamsund**, Nor.
44/B4 **Stamullin**, Ire.
102/E2 **Standerton**, SAfr.
45/F4 **Standish-with-Langtree**, Eng,UK
47/G4 **Stanford le Hope**, Eng,UK
42/D3 **Stange**, Nor.
103/E3 **Stanger**, SAfr.
45/F2 **Stanhope**, Eng,UK
131/F5 **Stanhope**, NJ,US
124/B3 **Stanislaus** (riv.), Ca,US
63/F4 **Stanke Dimitrov**, Bul.
91/C4 **Stanley** (peak), Austl.
127/H2 **Stanley**, NB,Can
84/C5 **Stanley** (res.), India
45/G2 **Stanley**, Eng,UK
123/H3 **Stanley**, ND,US
97/L8 **Stanley** (falls), Zaire
62/E4 **Stanovo**, Yugo.
69/N4 **Stanovoy** (range), Rus.
47/G3 **Stansted Mountfitchet**, Eng,UK
47/G2 **Stanton**, Eng,UK
131/C3 **Stanton**, Ca,US
126/D4 **Stanton**, Ky,US
128/C3 **Stanton**, Tx,US
50/D3 **Staphorst**, Neth.
47/E4 **Stapleford**, Eng,UK
47/G4 **Staplehurst**, Eng,UK
49/L3 **Starachowice**, Pol.
62/E3 **Stara Pazova**, Yugo.
62/F3 **Stara Planina** (mts.), Yugo.
64/F4 **Staraya Russa**, Rus.
63/G4 **Stara Zagora**, Bul.
93/K5 **Starbuck** (isl.), Kiri.
90/B1 **Starcke Nat'l Park**, Austl.
49/H2 **Stargard Szczeciński**, Pol.
129/H4 **Starke**, Fl,US
129/F3 **Starkville**, Ms,US
66/F3 **Staroderevyan-kovskaya**, Rus.
66/E1 **Starodub**, Rus.
49/K2 **Starogard Gdański**, Pol.
66/F3 **Staroshcher-binovskaya**, Rus.
46/C6 **Start** (bay), Eng,UK
46/C6 **Start** (pt.), Eng,UK
49/L3 **Staszów**, Pol.
126/E3 **State College**, Pa,US
131/F5 **Staten** (isl.), NY,US
129/H3 **Statesboro**, Ga,US
129/H3 **Statesville**, NC,US
48/E3 **Staufenberg**, Ger.
46/D3 **Staunton**, Eng,UK
126/E4 **Staunton**, Va,US
46/D2 **Staunton on Wye**, Eng,UK
42/C4 **Stavanger**, Nor.
45/F3 **Staveley**, Eng,UK
45/G5 **Staveley**, Eng,UK
67/G3 **Stavropol'**, Rus.
67/G3 **Stavropol' Kray**, Rus.
91/B3 **Stawell**, Austl.
122/C4 **Stayton**, Or,US
124/F2 **Steamboat Springs**, Co,US
51/H3 **Stederau** (riv.), Ger.
91/F5 **Steele** (cr.), Austl.
123/J4 **Steele**, ND,US
103/E2 **Steelpoortrivier** (riv.), SAfr.
50/B5 **Steenbergen**, Neth.
124/C2 **Steens** (mtn.), Or,US
119/J1 **Steensby** (inlet), NW,Can
50/D3 **Steenwijk**, Neth.
123/G1 **Steephill** (lake), Sk,Can
46/C4 **Steep Holm** (isl.), Eng,UK
45/J5 **Steeping** (riv.), Eng,UK
130/J2 **Steese Nat'l Rec. Area**, Ak,US
118/F1 **Stefansson** (isl.), NW,Can
112/C5 **Steffen** (peak), Chile
54/D4 **Steffisburg**, Swi.
62/A2 **Steiermark** (prov.), Aus.
57/J2 **Steigerwald** (for.), Ger.
48/F4 **Stein**, Ger.
53/E2 **Stein**, Neth.
123/J3 **Steinbach**, Mb,Can
51/F5 **Steinhagen**, Ger.
51/G5 **Steinheim**, Ger.
51/G4 **Steinhuder Meer** (lake), Ger.
42/D2 **Steinkjer**, Nor.
52/D1 **Stekene**, Belg.
127/J2 **Stellarton**, NS,Can
51/H2 **Stelle**, Ger.
102/B4 **Stellenbosch**, SAfr.
57/H5 **Stello** (mtn.), Fr.
55/G4 **Stelvio Nat'l Park**, It.
48/F2 **Stendal**, Ger.
63/G4 **Steneto Nat'l Park**, Bul.
42/D4 **Stenungsund**, Swe.
67/H5 **Stepanakert**, Azer.
91/B1 **Stephens Creek**, Austl.
127/K1 **Stephenville**, Nf,Can
128/D3 **Stephenville**, Tx,US
125/G2 **Sterling**, Co,US
128/C4 **Sterling City**, Tx,US
132/F6 **Sterling Heights**, Mi,US
67/K1 **Sterlitamak**, Rus.
122/E2 **Stettler**, Ab,Can
126/D3 **Steubenville**, Oh,US
47/F3 **Stevenage**, Eng,UK
123/J2 **Stevenson** (lake), Mb,Can
130/H4 **Stevenson** (str.), Ak,US
126/B2 **Stevens Point**, Wi,US
122/E4 **Stevensville**, Mt,US
50/C3 **Stevinsluizen** (dam), Neth.
130/L3 **Stewart** (riv.), Yk,Can
130/L3 **Stewart Crossing**, Yk,Can
130/L3 **Stewart River**, Yk,Can
44/B2 **Stewartstown**, NI,UK
123/K5 **Stewartville**, Mn,US
47/F5 **Steyning**, Eng,UK
57/L2 **Steyr**, Aus.
57/L3 **Steyr** (riv.), Aus.
50/C2 **Stiens**, Neth.
125/J4 **Stigler**, Ok,US
130/M4 **Stikine** (riv.), BC,Can
123/K4 **Stillwater**, Mn,US
124/C3 **Stillwater** (range), Nv,US
125/H3 **Stillwater**, Ok,US
125/J4 **Stilwell**, Ok,US
44/D1 **Stinchar** (riv.), Sc,UK
128/C3 **Stinnett**, Tx,US
62/F5 **Štip**, Macd.
53/F5 **Stiring-Wendel**, Fr.
43/D2 **Stirling**, Sc,UK
127/L2 **St. John's** (cap.), Nf,Can
42/D3 **Stjørdal**, Nor.
47/E4 **Stockbridge**, Eng,UK
49/J4 **Stockerau**, Aus.
42/F4 **Stockholm** (cap.), Swe.
45/F5 **Stockport**, Eng,UK
45/F4 **Stocks** (res.), Eng,UK
45/G5 **Stocksbridge**, Eng,UK
132/M11 **Stockton**, Ca,US
125/J3 **Stockton** (lake), Mo,US
128/C4 **Stockton** (plat.), Tx,US
45/G2 **Stockton-on-Tees**, Eng,UK
83/D3 **Stoeng Treng**, Camb.
46/B6 **Stoke** (pt.), Eng,UK
45/F5 **Stoke-on-Trent**, Eng,UK
91/B4 **Stokes** (pt.), Austl.
62/C4 **Stolac**, Bosn.
53/F2 **Stolberg**, Ger.
69/P2 **Stolbovoy** (isl.), Rus.
102/K10 **Stompneuspunt** (pt.), SAfr.
45/F6 **Stone**, Eng,UK
43/D2 **Stonehaven**, Sc,UK
47/E4 **Stonehenge** (ruins), Eng,UK
46/D3 **Stonehouse**, Eng,UK
123/J3 **Stonewall**, Mb,Can
127/Q9 **Stoney Creek**, On,Can
123/J2 **Stony** (pt.), Mb,Can
131/G5 **Stony Brook**, NY,US
123/J3 **Stony Mountain**, Mb,Can
131/G4 **Stony Point**, NY,US
68/K3 **Stony Tunguska** (riv.), Rus.
126/D1 **Stooping** (riv.), On,Can
119/S7 **Stor** (isl.), NW,Can
51/G1 **Stör** (riv.), Ger.
42/F2 **Stora Sjöfallets Nat'l Park**, Swe.
42/F2 **Storavan** (lake), Swe.
48/F1 **Store Bælt** (chan.), Den.
42/D3 **Støren**, Nor.
91/C4 **Storm** (bay), Austl.
123/K5 **Storm Lake**, Ia,US
44/C2 **Stormont**, NI,UK
47/F5 **Storrington**, Eng,UK
42/F1 **Storsteinsfjellet** (peak), Nor.
48/F1 **Storstrøm** (co.), Den.
47/G3 **Stort** (riv.), Eng,UK
42/F2 **Storuman**, Swe.
122/G4 **Story**, Wy,US
113/J7 **Stosch** (isl.), Chile
47/F2 **Stotfold**, Eng,UK
123/H3 **Stoughton**, Sk,Can
46/D5 **Stour** (riv.), Eng,UK
47/E2 **Stour** (riv.), Eng,UK
47/H3 **Stour** (riv.), Eng,UK
47/H4 **Stour** (riv.), Eng,UK
46/D2 **Stourbridge**, Eng,UK
47/G4 **Stour, Great** (riv.), Eng,UK
46/D2 **Stourport on Severn**, Eng,UK
47/G2 **Stowmarket**, Eng,UK
47/E3 **Stow on the Wold**, Eng,UK
44/A2 **Strabane** (dist.), NI,UK
43/D2 **Strachan**, Sc,UK
43/C2 **Strachur**, Sc,UK
57/H4 **Stradella**, It.
50/D6 **Straelen**, Ger.
57/K2 **Strakonice**, Czh.
63/H4 **Straldzha**, Bul.
48/G1 **Stralsund**, Ger.
102/B4 **Strand**, SAfr.
44/C3 **Strangford**, NI,UK
44/C3 **Strangford Lough** (inlet), NI,UK
64/C4 **Strängnäs**, Swe.
44/B1 **Stranocum**, NI,UK
44/C2 **Stranraer**, Sc,UK
123/G3 **Strasbourg**, Sk,Can
54/D1 **Strasbourg**, Fr.
126/D3 **Stratford**, On,Can
89/H6 **Stratford**, NZ
131/E6 **Stratford**, NJ,US
47/E2 **Stratford upon Avon**, Eng,UK
43/C3 **Strathaven**, Sc,UK
44/D1 **Strathclyde** (reg.), Sc,UK
122/E3 **Strathmore**, Ab,Can
46/B5 **Stratton**, Eng,UK
57/K2 **Straubing**, Ger.
42/M6 **Straumnes** (pt.), Ice.
49/G2 **Strausberg**, Ger.
131/B2 **Strawberry** (peak), Ca,US
132/P15 **Streamwood**, Il,US
47/E3 **Streatley**, Eng,UK
126/B3 **Streator**, Il,US
57/L2 **Středočeská Žulová Vrchovina** (mts.), Czh.
57/L2 **Středočeský** (reg.), Czh.
49/K4 **Středoslovenský** (reg.), Slvk.
46/D4 **Street**, Eng,UK
127/Q8 **Streetsville**, On,Can
63/F3 **Strehaia**, Rom.
64/H2 **Strel'na** (riv.), Rus.
45/F5 **Stretford**, Eng,UK
47/G2 **Stretham**, Eng,UK
50/B5 **Strijen**, Neth.
61/H2 **Strimón** (gulf), Gre.
61/H2 **Strimónas** (riv.), Gre.
113/K7 **Strobel** (lake), Arg.
61/G4 **Strofádhes** (isls.), Gre.
60/D3 **Stromboli** (isl.), It.
42/D3 **Strømmen**, Nor.
42/D4 **Strömstad**, Swe.
42/E3 **Strömsund**, Swe.
49/J3 **Stronie Śląskie**, Pol.
46/D3 **Stroud**, Eng,UK
62/E5 **Struga**, Macd.
102/C4 **Struisbaai** (bay), SAfr.
44/A2 **Strule** (riv.), NI,UK
61/H2 **Struma** (riv.), Bul., Gre.
46/A2 **Strumble Head** (pt.), UK
62/F5 **Strumica**, Macd.
42/C3 **Stryn**, Nor.
49/J3 **Strzegom**, Pol.
49/H2 **Strzelce Krajeńskie**, Pol.
90/A5 **Strzelecki** (cr.), Austl.
91/D4 **Strzelecki** (peak), Austl.
49/J3 **Strzelin**, Pol.
49/L4 **Strzyżów**, Pol.
122/B2 **Stuart** (lake), BC,Can
122/B2 **Stuart** (riv.), BC,Can
129/H5 **Stuart**, Fl,US
126/E4 **Stuarts Draft**, Va,US
49/G1 **Stubbenkammer** (pt.), Ger.
47/E5 **Studland**, Eng,UK
47/E2 **Studley**, Eng,UK
49/J4 **Stupava**, Slvk.
64/H5 **Stupino**, Rus.
123/J3 **Sturgeon** (bay), Mb,Can
126/B1 **Sturgeon** (lake), On,Can
126/C2 **Sturgeon Bay**, Wi,US
126/E2 **Sturgeon Falls**, On,Can
126/C3 **Sturgis**, Mi,US
123/H4 **Sturgis**, SD,US
46/D5 **Sturminster Newton**, Eng,UK
47/H4 **Sturry**, Eng,UK
90/A5 **Sturt** (des.), Austl.
91/B1 **Sturt** (peak), Austl.
91/B1 **Sturt Nat'l Park**, Austl.
102/D4 **Stutterheim**, SAfr.
57/H2 **Stuttgart**, Ger.
129/F3 **Stuttgart**, Ar,US
66/C2 **Styr** (riv.), Ukr.
57/L3 **Styria** (prov.), Aus.
110/D1 **Suaçui Grande** (riv.), Braz.
100/D5 **Suakin** (arch.), Sudan
82/D3 **Suao**, Tai.
86/C5 **Subang**, Indo.
60/C1 **Subasio** (peak), It.
86/C3 **Subi** (isl.), Indo.
62/D2 **Subotica**, Yugo.
131/F5 **Succasunna-Kenvil**, NJ,US
63/H2 **Suceava**, Rom.
63/G2 **Suceava** (co.), Rom.
49/L3 **Suchedniów**, Pol.
43/A4 **Suck** (riv.), Ire.
108/E7 **Sucre** (cap.), Bol.
108/G5 **Sucunduri** (riv.), Braz.
110/B2 **Sucuriú** (riv.), Braz.
64/H4 **Suda** (riv.), Rus.
97/L5 **Sudan**
96/H5 **Sudan** (phys. reg.), Afr.
126/D2 **Sudbury**, On,Can
47/G2 **Sudbury**, Eng,UK
51/F2 **Sude** (riv.), Ger.
49/H3 **Sudeten** (mts.), Czh., Pol.
50/D5 **Südlohn**, Ger.
99/H5 **Sud-Ouest** (prov.), Camr.
97/L6 **Sue** (riv.), Sudan
59/E3 **Sueca**, Sp.
63/G4 **Sŭedinenie**, Bul.
100/C2 **Suez** (can.), Egypt
100/C2 **Suez** (gulf), Egypt
100/C2 **Suez** (As Suways), Egypt
74/K5 **Sūf**, Jor.
131/F4 **Suffern**, NY,US
47/G2 **Suffolk** (co.), Eng,UK
126/E4 **Suffolk**, Va,US
125/K2 **Sugar** (riv.), Il, Wi,US
128/E4 **Sugar Land**, Tx,US
46/C3 **Sugar Loaf** (mtn.), Wal,UK
129/H2 **Sugarloaf** (peak), Ky,US
76/F1 **Sühbaatar**, Mong.
57/J1 **Suhl**, Ger.
74/B2 **Şuhut**, Turk.
82/B3 **Sui** (riv.), China
83/B4 **Sui** (pt.), Thai.
109/H6 **Suia-Missu** (riv.), Braz.
77/L2 **Suibin**, China
77/L2 **Suifenhe**, China
77/K2 **Suihua**, China
77/K2 **Suileng**, China
52/D5 **Suippe** (riv.), Fr.
43/B4 **Suir** (riv.), Ire.
132/K10 **Suisun City**, Ca,US
79/L10 **Suita**, Japan
131/K8 **Suitland-Silver Hill**, Md,US
76/G5 **Suizhou**, China
84/B2 **Sūjāngarh**, India
86/C5 **Sukabumi**, Indo.
86/C4 **Sukadana**, Indo.
86/C4 **Sukadana** (bay), Indo.
79/G2 **Sukagawa**, Japan
66/E1 **Sukhinichi**, Rus.
64/J4 **Sukhona** (riv.), Rus.
83/B2 **Sukhothai**, Thai.
67/G4 **Sukhumi**, Geo.
73/J3 **Sukkur**, Pak.
78/C4 **Sukumo**, Japan
87/G4 **Sula** (isls.), Indo.
65/L2 **Sula** (riv.), Rus.
73/J3 **Sulaimān** (range), Pak.
87/E4 **Sulawesi** (Celebes) (isl.), Indo.
100/B4 **Sulb Temple** (ruins), Sudan
44/D3 **Sulby** (riv.), IM,UK
49/H2 **Sulechów**, Pol.
49/H2 **Sulęcin**, Pol.
49/L2 **Sulejówek**, Pol.
51/F3 **Sulingen**, Ger.
76/D4 **Sulin Gol** (riv.), China
42/F2 **Sulitjelma** (peak), Nor.
108/B4 **Sullana**, Peru
122/F3 **Sullivan** (lake), Ab,Can
126/C4 **Sullivan**, In,US
126/E1 **Sullivan Mines**, Qu,Can
46/C4 **Sully**, Wal,UK
60/C1 **Sulmona**, It.
125/J4 **Sulphur** (riv.), Ar, Tx,US
128/E4 **Sulphur**, La,US
125/H4 **Sulphur**, Ok,US
128/E3 **Sulphur Springs**, Tx,US
87/E2 **Sulu** (sea), Malay., Phil.
82/D6 **Sulu** (arch.), Phil.
74/C2 **Suluova**, Turk.
97/K1 **Sulūq**, Libya
53/G2 **Sülz** (riv.), Ger.
53/G5 **Sulzbach**, Ger.
57/J2 **Sulzbach-Rosenberg**, Ger.
105/P **Sulzberger** (bay), Ant.
105/Q **Sulzberger Ice Shelf**, Ant.
62/E3 **Šumadija** (reg.), Yugo.
108/D3 **Sumapaz Nat'l Park**, Col.
86/A3 **Sumatra** (isl.), Indo.
86/E5 **Sumba** (isl.), Indo.
87/E5 **Sumba** (str.), Indo.
67/L5 **Sumbar** (riv.), Trkm.
86/E5 **Sumbawa** (isl.), Indo.
87/E5 **Sumbawa Besar**, Indo.
101/A5 **Sumbawanga**, Tanz.
104/B3 **Sumbe**, Ang.
76/F2 **Sümber**, Mong.
130/M4 **Sumdum** (mtn.), Ak,US
62/C2 **Sümeg**, Hun.
86/D5 **Sumenep**, Indo.
67/J4 **Sumgait**, Azer.
45/G3 **Summer Bridge**, Eng,UK
122/D3 **Summerland**, BC,Can
127/J2 **Summerside**, PE,Can
126/D4 **Summersville**, WV,US
129/G3 **Summerville**, Ga,US
129/H3 **Summerville**, SC,US
131/F5 **Summit**, NJ,US
132/C3 **Sumner**, Wa,US
78/D3 **Sumoto**, Japan
49/J4 **Šumperk**, Czh.
129/H3 **Sumter**, SC,US
66/E2 **Sumy**, Ukr.
66/E2 **Sumy Obl.**, Ukr.
122/E4 **Sun** (riv.), Mt,US
79/M9 **Sunami**, Japan
91/C3 **Sunbury**, Austl.
47/F4 **Sunbury on Thames**, Eng,UK
80/D5 **Sunch'ŏn**, SKor.
124/D4 **Sun City**, Az,US
131/C3 **Sun City**, Ca,US
127/G3 **Suncook**, NH,US
86/B5 **Sunda** (str.), Indo.
123/G4 **Sundance**, Wy,US
84/E3 **Sundarbans** (reg.), Bang., India
84/D3 **Sundargarh**, India
73/L2 **Sundarnagar**, India
102/D4 **Sundays** (riv.), SAfr.
45/G2 **Sunderland**, Eng,UK
51/F6 **Sundern**, Ger.
91/D1 **Sundown Nat'l Park**, Austl.
122/E3 **Sundre**, Ab,Can
42/F3 **Sundsvall**, Swe.
86/B4 **Sungaipenuh**, Indo.
86/B2 **Sungai Petani**, Malay.
74/C2 **Sungurlu**, Turk.
128/B4 **Sunland Park**, NM,US
42/D3 **Sunndalsøra**, Nor.
42/E4 **Sunne**, Swe.
47/F4 **Sunninghill**, Eng,UK
132/K12 **Sunnyvale**, Ca,US
79/H8 **Su-no-saki** (cape), Japan
126/B3 **Sun Prairie**, Wi,US
131/B3 **Sunset Beach**, Ca,US
91/B2 **Sunset Country** (reg.), Austl.
124/E4 **Sunset Crater Nat'l Mon.**, Az,US
91/F5 **Sunshine**, Austl.

177
Sunta – Tenoj

69/P3 Suntar-Khayata (mts.), Rus.
51/G4 Süntel (mts.), Ger.
99/E5 Sunyani, Gha.
101/A5 Sunzu (peak), Zam.
78/B4 Suo (sea), Japan
83/D1 Suoi Rut, Viet.
42/H3 Suomenselkä (reg.), Fin.
83/D4 Suong, Camb.
108/C6 Supe, Peru
126/C2 Superior (lake), Can., US
124/E4 Superior, Az,US
122/E4 Superior, Mt,US
126/A2 Superior, Wi,US
126/B2 Superior (upland), Wi,US
83/C3 Suphan Buri, Thai.
87/J4 Supiori (isl.), Indo.
72/E2 Sūq ash Shuyūkh, Iraq
74/L4 Şuqaylabīyah, Syria
81/D4 Suqian, China
113/F3 Sur (pt.), Arg.
53/E4 Sûr (riv.), Belg.
124/B3 Sur (pt.), Ca,US
67/H1 Sura (riv.), Rus.
86/D5 Surabaya, Indo.
84/D4 Surada, India
86/D5 Surakarta, Indo.
86/D6 Surallah, Phil.
49/K4 Šurany, Slvk.
84/B3 Surat, India
84/B2 Suratgarh, India
83/B4 Surat Thani, Thai.
53/G6 Surbourg, Fr.
113/J7 Sur, Campo de Hielo (glacier), Chile
62/E3 Surčin, Yugo.
62/F4 Surdulica, Yugo.
53/E4 Sûre (riv.), Belg., Lux.
84/B3 Surendranagar, India
56/C3 Surgères, Fr.
68/H3 Surgut, Rus.
84/E3 Sūri, India
59/F2 Súria, Sp.
82/E6 Surigao, Phil.
83/C3 Surin, Thai.
109/G3 Suriname
75/A4 Surkhob (riv.), Taj.
131/K8 Surrattsville (Clinton), Md,US
122/C3 Surrey, BC,Can
47/F4 Surrey (co.), Eng,UK
96/J1 Surt, Libya
42/D3 Sur-Trøndelag (co.), Nor.
74/K5 Şūr (Tyre), Leb.
74/D3 Sürüç, Turk.
79/F3 Suruga (bay), Japan
60/B5 Sūsah, Tun.
60/B5 Sūsah (gov.), Tun.
78/C4 Susaki, Japan
72/E2 Sūsangerd, Iran
124/B2 Susanville, Ca,US
74/D2 Suşehri, Turk.
81/B4 Sushui (riv.), China
130/J3 Susitna (riv.), Ak,US
79/F3 Susono, Japan
126/E3 Susquehanna (riv.), US
127/H2 Sussex, NB,Can
47/F4 Sussex, Vale of (val.), Eng,UK
50/C6 Susteren, Neth.
69/Q3 Susuman, Rus.
90/H9 Sutherland, Austl.
62/D4 Sutjeska Nat'l Park, Bosn.
73/K2 Sutlej (riv.), India, Pak.
45/H6 Sutterton, Eng,UK
45/J6 Sutton Bridge, Eng,UK
47/E1 Sutton Coldfield, Eng,UK
45/G5 Sutton in Ashfield, Eng,UK
45/J5 Sutton on Sea, Eng,UK
45/H5 Sutton on Trent, Eng,UK
102/D4 Suurberge (mts.), SAfr.
92/G6 Suva (cap.), Fiji
79/F2 Suwa, Japan
49/M1 Suwałki, Pol.
49/M2 Suwałki (prov.), Pol.
129/H4 Suwannee (riv.), Fl,US
93/J6 Suwarrow (atoll), Cookls.
74/K5 Şuwaylih, Jor.
81/D4 Suzhou, China
81/E5 Suzhou, China
79/E2 Suzu, Japan
78/E3 Suzuka, Japan
79/M10 Suzuka (range), Japan
79/E2 Suzu-misaki (cape), Japan
57/J4 Suzzara, It.
68/C2 Svalbard (arch.), Nor.
83/D4 Svay Rieng, Camb.
42/E4 Svealand (reg.), Swe.
48/F1 Svendborg, Den.
119/S7 Svendsen (pen.), NW,Can
42/E4 Svenljunga, Swe.
65/P4 Sverdlovsk (Yekaterinburg), Rus.
119/S7 Sverdrup (chan.), NW,Can
119/R7 Sverdrup (isls.), NW,Can
68/H2 Sverdrup (isl.), Rus.
66/D1 Svetlogorsk, Bela.
67/G3 Svetlograd, Rus.
62/E4 Svetozarevo, Yugo.
42/P7 Svíahnúkar (peak), Ice.
62/E3 Svilajnac, Yugo.
63/H5 Svilengrad, Bul.
63/G4 Svishtov, Bul.
49/J4 Svitavy, Czh.
77/K1 Svobodnyy, Rus.
63/F4 Svoge, Bul.
42/E1 Svolvær, Nor.
69/Q2 Svyatyy Nos (cape), Rus.
47/E1 Swadlincote, Eng,UK
47/G1 Swaffham, Eng,UK
90/D3 Swain (reefs), Austl.
129/H3 Swainsboro, Ga,US
93/H5 Swains Island (atoll), ASam.
104/C2 Swa-Kibula, Zaire
104/B5 Swakopmund, Namb.
45/G3 Swale (riv.), Eng,UK
47/H4 Swalecliffe, Eng,UK
47/G4 Swale, The (chan.), Eng,UK
50/D6 Swalmen, Neth.
122/D2 Swan (hills), Ab,Can
123/H2 Swan (riv.), Mb, Sk,Can
116/E4 Swan (isls.), Hon.
47/E5 Swanage, Eng,UK
91/B2 Swan Hill, Austl.
47/G4 Swanley-Hextable, Eng,UK
123/H2 Swan River, Mb,Can
46/C3 Swansea, Wal,UK
46/C3 Swansea (bay), Wal,UK
131/E6 Swarthmore, Pa,US
102/D3 Swart Kei (riv.), SAfr.
49/J2 Swarzędz, Pol.
102/B2 Swarzrand (mts.), Namb.
44/B2 Swatragh, NI,UK
47/E5 Sway, Eng,UK
103/E2 Swaziland
42/E3 Sweden
122/C4 Sweet Home, Or,US
128/C3 Sweetwater, Tx,US
122/F5 Sweetwater (riv.), Wy,US
102/C4 Swellendam, SAfr.
49/J3 Świdnica, Pol.
49/M3 Świdnik, Pol.
49/H2 Świdwin, Pol.
49/J3 Świebodzice, Pol.
49/H2 Świebozin, Pol.
49/K2 Świecie, Pol.
122/G3 Swift Current, Sk,Can
47/E3 Swindon, Eng,UK
45/H6 Swineshead, Eng,UK
49/H2 Świnoujście, Pol.
45/G5 Swinton, Eng,UK
54/D4 Swiss (plat.), Swi.
53/F2 Swist Bach (riv.), Ger.
54/D4 Switzerland
44/B5 Swords, Ire.
64/G3 Syamozero (lake), Rus.
49/J3 Syców, Pol.
90/H8 Sydney, Austl.
127/J2 Sydney, NS,Can
93/H5 Sydney (Manra) (atoll), Kiri.
127/J2 Sydney Mines, NS,Can
51/F3 Syke, Ger.
65/L3 Syktyvkar, Rus.
129/G3 Sylacauga, Al,US
42/E3 Sylarna (peak), Swe.
85/F3 Sylhet, Bang.
48/E1 Sylt (isl.), Ger.
65/N4 Sylva (riv.), Rus.
126/D3 Sylvania, Oh,US
132/F6 Sylvan Lake, Mi,US
61/L6 Syntagma Square, Gre.
131/G5 Syosset, NY,US
105/C Syowa, Ant.
125/G3 Syracuse, Ks,US
126/E3 Syracuse, NY,US
60/D4 Syracuse (Siracusa), It.
68/G5 Syrdar'ya (riv.), Asia
72/C1 Syria
64/G4 Syriam, Burma
65/L3 Sysola (riv.), Rus.
47/E1 Syston, Eng,UK
67/J1 Syzran', Rus.
62/E1 Szabolcs-Szatmár-Bereg (co.), Hun.
49/J2 Szamotuły, Pol.
62/E2 Szarvas, Hun.
62/D2 Százhalombatta, Hun.
49/H2 Szczecin, Pol.
49/H2 Szczecin (prov.), Pol.
49/J2 Szczecinek, Pol.
49/L2 Szczytno, Pol.
62/E2 Szeged, Hun.
62/E2 Szeghalom, Hun.
62/E2 Szegvár, Hun.
62/D2 Székesfehérvár, Hun.
62/D2 Szekszárd, Hun.
62/D2 Szentendre, Hun.
62/E2 Szentes, Hun.
62/E1 Szerencs, Hun.
49/M1 Szeskie (peak), Pol.
62/C2 Szigetvár, Hun.
62/E2 Szolnok, Hun.
62/C2 Szombathely, Hun.
49/H3 Szprotawa, Pol.
49/K2 Sztum, Pol.
49/J2 Szubin, Pol.
49/L3 Szydłowiec, Pol.

T

82/D5 Tabaco, Phil.
73/G2 Ţabas, Iran
116/C4 Tabasco (state), Mex.
109/K6 Tabatinga (mts.), Braz.
122/E3 Taber, Ab,Can
59/E3 Tabernes de Valldigna, Sp.
92/G5 Tabiteuea (atoll), Kiri.
82/D5 Tablas (isl.), Phil.
102/B4 Table (bay), SAfr.
102/L10 Table (mtn.), SAfr.
125/J3 Table Rock (lake), Ar, Mo,US
58/B1 Taboada, Sp.
57/L2 Tábor, Czh.
101/B4 Tabora, Tanz.
101/B4 Tabora (prov.), Tanz.
98/D5 Tabou, IvC.
93/K4 Tabuaeran (Fanning) (atoll), Kiri.
82/D4 Tabuk, Phil.
72/C3 Tabūk, SAr.
92/F6 Tabwemasana (mtn.), Van.
117/F6 Tacarcuna (mt.), Pan.
75/D2 Tacheng, China
82/D3 Tachia (riv.), Tai.
78/A4 Tachibana (bay), Japan
79/F3 Tachikawa, Japan
82/D3 Tachoshui, Tai.
57/K2 Tachov, Czh.
82/E5 Tacloban, Phil.
108/D7 Tacna, Peru
132/C3 Tacoma, Wa,US
108/E7 Tacora (vol.), Chile
59/X16 Tacoronte, Canl.,Sp.
113/G1 Tacuarembó, Uru.
113/G2 Tacuarembó (dept.), Uru.
79/F2 Tadami (riv.), Japan
79/L10 Tadaoka, Japan
45/G4 Tadcaster, Eng,UK
96/F2 Tademaït (plat.), Alg.
84/D4 Tādepallegūdem, India
93/V12 Tadine, NCal.
47/E4 Tadley, Eng,UK
72/C2 Tadmur, Syria
79/M9 Tado, Japan
78/C3 Tadotsu, Japan
84/C5 Tādpatri, India
96/H2 Tadrart (mts.), Alg., Libya
80/D3 T'aebaek (mts.), NKor., SKor.
80/D4 Taech'ŏn, SKor.
80/D3 Taegang-got (pt.), NKor.
80/E5 Taegu, SKor.
80/E5 Taegu-Jikhalsi (prov.), SKor.
80/D4 Taejŏn, SKor.
46/B3 Taf (riv.), Wal,UK
58/E1 Tafalla, Sp.
46/C3 Taff (riv.), Wal,UK
111/C2 Tafí Viejo, Arg.
72/F2 Taft, Iran
73/H3 Taftān (mtn.), Iran
79/M9 Taga, Japan
66/F3 Taganrog, Rus.
66/F3 Taganrog (gulf), Rus., Ukr.
98/C2 Tagant (reg.), Mrta.
73/G1 Tagarav (peak), Trkm.
78/B4 Tagawa, Japan
82/D6 Tagbilaran, Phil.
57/G5 Taggia, It.
96/E1 Taghit, Alg.
130/M3 Tagish, Yk,Can
57/K3 Tagliamento (riv.), It.
52/D5 Tagnon, Fr.
87/F2 Tagolo (pt.), Phil.
109/J7 Taguatinga, Braz.
92/E6 Tagula (isl.), PNG
82/E6 Tagum, Phil.
65/P4 Tagun (riv.), Rus.
58/B3 Tagus (riv.), Port., Sp.
86/B3 Tahan (peak), Malay.
79/N10 Tahara, Japan
96/G3 Tahat (peak), Alg.
93/L6 Tahenea (atoll), FrPol.
93/L6 Tahiti (isl.), FrPol.
128/E3 Tahlequah, Ok,US
130/J3 Tahneta (pass), Ak,US
124/C3 Tahoe (lake), Ca, Nv,US
128/C3 Tahoka, Tx,US
99/G3 Tahoua, Niger
99/G3 Tahoua (dept.), Niger
122/B3 Tahsis, BC,Can
100/B3 Taḥtā, Egypt
93/L6 Tahuata (isl.), FrPol.
87/G3 Tahulandang (isl.), Indo.
81/L8 Tai (lake), China
77/H4 Tai'an, China
93/X15 Taiarapu (pen.), FrPol.
81/C3 Taibai Shan (mtn.), China
82/D3 Taichung, Tai.
81/C3 Taihang (mts.), China
82/D3 Taihsi, Tai.
79/L10 Taima, Japan
82/D3 Tainan, Tai.
61/H4 Tainaron, Akra (cape), Gre.
98/D5 Taï Nat'l Park, IvC.
93/L5 Taiohae, FrPol.
82/D2 Taipei (cap.), Tai.
77/J2 Taiping (peak), China
86/B3 Taiping, Malay.
78/C3 Taisha, Japan
79/L10 Taishi, Japan
82/C2 Taishun, China
112/B5 Taitao (pen.), Chile
82/D3 Taitung, Tai.
82/D3 Taiwan
82/C3 Taiwan (str.), China, Tai.
61/H4 Taíyetos (mts.), Gre.
81/C3 Taiyuan, China
81/D4 Taizhou, China
81/E2 Taizi (riv.), China
86/C4 Tajam (peak), Indo.
96/H3 Tajarhī, Libya
68/H6 Tajikistan
79/F2 Tajima, Japan
79/E3 Tajimi, Japan
79/L10 Tajiri, Japan
58/C3 Tajo (Tagus) (riv.), Sp.
72/F1 Tajrīsh, Iran
116/C4 Tajumulco (vol.), Guat.
58/D2 Tajuña (riv.), Sp.
83/B2 Tak, Thai.
79/G2 Takahagi, Japan
78/D3 Takahama, Japan
78/C3 Takahashi, Japan
78/C3 Takahashi (riv.), Japan
79/G2 Takahata, Japan
79/L10 Takaishi, Japan
78/D3 Takamatsu, Japan
79/M10 Takami-yama (peak), Japan
78/B4 Takanabe, Japan
79/E2 Takaoka, Japan
89/H6 Takapuna, NZ
79/L10 Takarazuka, Japan
93/L6 Takaroa (isl.), FrPol.
79/F2 Takasaki, Japan
79/M9 Takashima, Japan
79/L10 Takatori, Japan
78/D3 Takatsuki, Japan
79/E2 Takayama, Japan
78/E3 Takefu, Japan
78/C3 Takehara, Japan
72/E1 Tākestān, Iran
78/B4 Taketa, Japan
79/M10 Taketoyo, Japan
83/D4 Takev, Camb.
85/H4 Ta Khli, Thai.
97/R2 Takht-e Jamshīd (Persepolis) (ruins), Iran
79/M10 Taki, Japan
118/E2 Takijuq (lake), NW,Can
77/N3 Takikawa, Japan
79/K10 Takino, Japan
122/B2 Takla (lake), BC,Can
75/D4 Takla Makan (des.), China
99/E5 Takoradi, Gha.
74/H6 Talā, Egypt
45/E5 Talacre, Wal,UK
112/Q9 Talagante, Chile
84/B3 Talāja, India
99/G2 Talak (reg.), Niger
104/C2 Tala Mugongo, Ang.
86/B4 Talang (peak), Indo.
75/F3 Talange, Fr.
54/A3 Talant, Fr.
108/B4 Talara, Peru
75/B3 Talas (riv.), Kaz.
74/C2 Talas, Turk.
87/G3 Talaud (isls.), Indo.
58/C3 Talavera de la Reina, Sp.
84/D6 Talawakele, SrL.
97/M5 Talawdī, Sudan
58/C3 Talayuela, Sp.
112/C2 Talca, Chile
112/B3 Talcahuano, Chile
84/E3 Tālcher, India
75/C3 Taldy-Kurgan, Kaz.
56/C4 Talence, Fr.
68/H5 Talgar, Kaz.
46/C3 Talgarth, Wal,UK
87/F4 Taliabu (isl.), Indo.
97/M6 Tali Post, Sudan
87/E5 Taliwang, Indo.
74/H6 Talkhā, Egypt
129/G3 Talladega, Al,US
74/E3 Tall 'Afar, Iraq
129/G4 Tallahassee (cap.), Fl,US
129/F3 Tallahatchie (riv.), Ms,US
74/N9 Tall 'Āsūr (Ba'al Hazor) (mtn.), WBnk.
131/E6 Talleyville, De,US
64/E4 Tallinn (cap.), Est.
74/E3 Tall Kayf, Iraq
129/H3 Tallulah (falls), Ga,US
129/F3 Tallulah, La,US
97/N5 Talo (peak), Eth.
84/B3 Taloda, India
73/J1 Tāloqān, Afg.
111/B2 Taltal, Chile
118/E2 Taltson (riv.), NW,Can
83/C4 Talumphuk (pt.), Thai.
73/L2 Talwāra, India
79/H7 Tama, Japan
79/H7 Tama (riv.), Japan
79/M10 Tamaki, Japan
99/E4 Tamale, Gha.
92/G5 Tamana (atoll), Kiri.
96/G3 Tamanghasset, Alg.
46/B5 Tamar (riv.), Eng,UK
62/D2 Tamási, Hun.
116/B3 Tamazunchale, Mex.
79/L9 Tamba, Japan
79/L9 Tamba (hills), Japan
98/B3 Tambacounda, Sen.
98/B3 Tambacounda (reg.), Sen.
98/C3 Tambaoura, Falaise de (escarp.), Mali
86/C3 Tambelan (isls.), Indo.
87/E5 Tambora (peak), Indo.
91/C3 Tamboritha (peak), Austl.
67/G1 Tambov, Rus.
67/G1 Tambov Obl., Rus.
58/A1 Tambre (riv.), Sp.
97/L6 Tambura, Sudan
47/E1 Tame (riv.), Eng,UK
58/B2 Tâmega (riv.), Port.
99/H2 Tamgak (peak), Niger
98/B3 Tamgue, Massif du (reg.), Gui., Sen.
84/C5 Tamil Nadu (state), India
83/E3 Tam Ky, Viet.
83/D2 Tam Le, Viet.
129/H5 Tampa, Fl,US
42/G3 Tampere, Fin.
116/B3 Tampico, Mex.
86/A3 Tampulonanjing (peak), Indo.
116/B3 Tamuín, Mex.
116/B3 Tamulipas (state), Mex.
91/D1 Tamworth, Austl.
47/E1 Tamworth, Eng,UK
85/K3 Tan (riv.), China
97/N5 Tana (lake), Eth.
101/C3 Tana (riv.), Kenya
42/H1 Tana (riv.), Nor.
78/D4 Tanabe, Japan
110/B2 Tanabi, Braz.
42/J1 Tanafjorden (fjord), Nor.
130/C6 Tanaga (isl.), Ak,US
60/D2 Tanagro (riv.), It.
79/G2 Tanagura, Japan
83/C5 Tanah Merah, Malay.
83/D4 Tan An, Viet.
130/J3 Tanana (riv.), Ak,US
57/H4 Tanaro (riv.), It.
84/C2 Tānda, India
84/D2 Tāndā, India
98/D3 Tanda (lake), Mali
97/M5 Tandaltī, Sudan
63/H3 Ţăndărei, Rom.
112/F3 Tandil, Arg.
73/J3 Tando Ādam, Pak.
73/J3 Tando Allāhyār, Pak.
73/J3 Tando Muhammad Khān, Pak.
91/B2 Tandou (lake), Austl.
44/B3 Tandragee, NI,UK
78/B5 Tanega (isl.), Japan
83/B2 Tanem (range), Burma, Thai.
96/E3 Tanezrouft (des.), Alg., Mali
81/C3 Tang (riv.), China
81/C4 Tang (riv.), China
101/C4 Tanga, Tanz.
101/C4 Tanga (prov.), Tanz.
103/H8 Tangainony, Madg.
101/A4 Tanganyika (lake), Afr.
109/G6 Tangará da Serra, Braz.
130/G1 Tangent (pt.), Ak,US
48/F2 Tangerhütte, Ger.
75/E5 Tanggula (mts.), China
75/F5 Tanggula Shankou (pass), China
96/D1 Tangier (Tanger), Mor.
132/B3 Tanglewilde-Thompson Place, Wa,US
75/E5 Tangra (lake), China
82/D6 Tangub, Phil.
87/H5 Tanimbar (isls.), Indo.
82/D6 Tanjay, Phil.
86/A3 Tanjungbalai, Indo.
86/C5 Tanjungkarang-Telukbetung, Indo.
86/C4 Tanjungpandan, Indo.
86/A3 Tanjungpura, Indo.
73/K2 Tānk, Pak.
92/F6 Tanna (isl.), Van.
79/L9 Tannan, Japan
75/F1 Tannu-Ola (mts.), Mong., Rus.
99/E5 Tano (riv.), Ghana, IvC.
74/H6 Ţanţā, Egypt
97/M1 Ţanţā, Egypt
96/C2 Tan-Tan, Mor.
116/B3 Tantoyuca, Mex.
84/D4 Tanuku, India
101/B4 Tanzania
79/H7 Tanzawa-yama (peak), Japan
82/B2 Tao (riv.), China
83/B4 Tao (isl.), Thai.
77/J2 Tao'er (riv.), China
60/D4 Taormina, It.
125/F3 Taos, NM,US
96/E3 Taoudenni, Mali
82/B2 Taoyuan, China
82/D3 Taoyuan, Tai.
64/E4 Tapa, Est.
116/C5 Tapachula, Mex.
109/G4 Tapajós (riv.), Braz.
109/G3 Tapanahoni (riv.), Sur.
108/E5 Tapauá (riv.), Braz.
82/D5 Tapaz, Phil.
110/B4 Tapejara, Braz.
110/B4 Tapes, Braz.
86/B3 Tapis (peak), Malay.
99/F3 Tapoa (prov.), Burk.
62/C2 Tapolca, Hun.
126/E4 Tappahannock, Va,US
131/G4 Tappan, NY,US
131/G4 Tappan Zee (reach), NY,US
132/C3 Tapps (lake), Wa,US
84/B3 Tāpti (riv.), India
100/B5 Taqab, Sudan
100/D5 Taqātu' Hayyā, Sudan
110/B4 Taquara, Braz.
110/B4 Taquari, Braz.
109/G7 Taquari (riv.), Braz.
110/B2 Taquaritinga, Braz.
110/B2 Taquarituba, Braz.
75/B3 Tar (riv.), Kyr.
62/D4 Tara (riv.), Bosn., Yugo.
68/H4 Tara, Rus.
99/H4 Taraba (riv.), Nga.
74/K4 Ţarābulus (Tripoli), Leb.
96/H1 Ţarābulus (Tripoli) (cap.), Libya
44/B4 Tara, Hill of (hill), Ire.
87/E3 Tarakan, Indo.
58/D2 Tarancón, Sp.
101/B3 Tarangire Nat'l Park, Tanz.
60/E2 Taranto, It.
60/E3 Taranto (gulf), It.
108/C5 Tarapoto, Peru
56/F4 Tarare, Fr.
56/F5 Tarascon, Fr.
108/D5 Tarauacá, Braz.
93/M7 Taravai (isl.), FrPol.
92/G4 Tarawa (atoll), Kiri.
58/E2 Tarazona, Sp.
58/E3 Tarazona de la Mancha, Sp.
75/D2 Tarbagatay (mts.), Kaz.
73/K2 Tarbela (res.), Pak.
56/D5 Tarbes, Fr.
129/J3 Tarboro, NC,US
62/A2 Tarcento, It.
56/E3 Tardes (riv.), Fr.
56/D4 Tardoire (riv.), Fr.
77/M2 Tardoki-Jani (peak), Rus.
91/E1 Taree, Austl.
100/C2 Ţarfā', Wādī al (dry riv.), Egypt
100/B4 Tarfâwi, Bîr (well), Egypt
44/D2 Tarf Water (riv.), Sc,UK
96/H1 Tarhūnah, Libya
58/C4 Tarifa, Sp.
108/F8 Tarija, Bol.
87/J4 Tariku (riv.), Indo.
87/J4 Tariku-taritatu (plain), Indo.
76/B4 Tarim (basin), China
75/D3 Tarim (riv.), China
73/J2 Tarin (riv.), Afg.
87/J4 Taritatu (riv.), Indo.
66/E3 Tarkhankut, Mys (cape), Ukr.
99/E5 Tarkwa, Gha.
82/D4 Tarlac, Phil.
108/C6 Tarma, Peru
56/D5 Tarn (riv.), Fr.
76/E2 Tarna (riv.), Mong.
73/J2 Tarnak (riv.), Afg.
49/L3 Tarnobrzeg, Pol.
49/L3 Tarnobrzeg (prov.), Pol.
49/L3 Tarnów, Pol.
49/L3 Tarnów (prov.), Pol.
75/D5 Taro (lake), China
57/J4 Taro (riv.), It.
96/D1 Taroudannt, Mor.
129/H4 Tarpon Springs, Fl,US
45/F5 Tarporley, Eng,UK
60/B1 Tarquinia, It.
59/F2 Tarragona, Sp.
59/F2 Tàrrega, Sp.
131/G4 Tarrytown, NY,US
74/C3 Tarsus, Turk.
64/E4 Tartu, Est.
74/K4 Ţarţūs, Syria
74/K4 Ţarţūs (dist.), Syria
79/M9 Tarui, Japan
78/B5 Tarumizu, Japan
83/B5 Tarutao Nat'l Park, Thai.
76/D2 Tarvagatay (mts.), Mong.
45/F5 Tarvin, Eng,UK
83/D3 Ta Seng, Camb.
75/E2 Tashanta, Rus.
68/F5 Tashauz, Trkm.
67/L4 Tashauz Obl., Trkm.
75/A3 Tashkent (cap.), Uzb.
75/B3 Tash-Kumyr, Kyr.
86/C5 Tasikmalaya, Indo.
74/C3 Taşkent, Turk.
74/C2 Taşköprü, Turk.
92/E8 Tasman (sea)
91/C4 Tasman (pen.), Austl.
91/C4 Tasman Head (cape), Austl.
91/C4 Tasmania (state), Austl.
62/F2 Tăşnad, Rom.
62/D2 Tata, Hun.
96/D2 Tata, Mor.
62/D2 Tatabánya, Hun.
126/D2 Tatachikapika (riv.), On,Can
93/M6 Tatakoto (isl.), FrPol.
76/D4 Tatalin (riv.), China
77/N2 Tatar (str.), Rus.
65/L5 Tatar Aut. Rep., Rus.
68/H4 Tatarsk, Rus.
96/H1 Taṭāwīn, Tun.
79/F3 Tateyama, Japan
79/E2 Tate-yama (mtn.), Japan
118/E2 Tathlina (lake), NW,Can
98/B2 Tatilt (well), Mrta.
118/G3 Tatnam (cape), Mb,Can
99/H3 Tatokou, Niger
49/K4 Tatranský Nat'l Park, Slvk.
49/K4 Tatrzański Nat'l Park, Pol.
47/G4 Tatsfield, Eng,UK
79/E3 Tatsuno, Japan
45/H5 Tattershall, Eng,UK
74/E2 Tatvan, Turk.
109/K5 Tauá, Braz.
110/H8 Taubaté, Braz.
57/H2 Tauberbischofsheim, Ger.
57/K3 Tauern, Hohe (mts.), Aus.
57/K2 Taufkirchen, Ger.
125/K3 Taum Sauk (peak), Mo,US
85/G3 Taungdwingyi, Burma
83/B1 Taunggyi, Burma
73/K2 Taunsa, Pak.
127/S8 Taunton, On,Can
46/C4 Taunton, Eng,UK
127/G3 Taunton, Ma,US
57/H1 Taunusstein, Ger.
89/H6 Taupo, NZ
49/M1 Tauragė, Lith.
89/H6 Tauranga, NZ
56/D3 Taurion (riv.), Fr.
74/C3 Taurus (mts.), Turk.
58/E2 Tauste, Sp.
56/C2 Taute (riv.), Fr.
93/X15 Tautira, FrPol.
92/E5 Tauu (isls.), PNG
124/E3 Tavaputs (plat.), Ut,US
129/H4 Tavares, Fl,US
74/B3 Tavas, Turk.
65/Q4 Tavda (riv.), Rus.
47/H1 Taverham, Eng,UK
52/B5 Taverny, Fr.
93/Z17 Taveuni (isl.), Fiji
58/B4 Tavira, Port.
46/B5 Tavistock, Eng,UK
83/B3 Tavoy, Burma
77/L3 Tavrichanka, Rus.
74/B2 Tavşanlı, Turk.
46/B5 Tavy (riv.), Eng,UK
46/B4 Taw (riv.), Eng,UK
79/L10 Tawaramoto, Japan
126/D2 Tawas City, Mi,US
87/E3 Tawau, Malay.
46/C3 Tawe (riv.), Wal,UK
82/C6 Tawi-tawi (isl.), Phil.
100/D5 Tawkar, Sudan
96/G1 Tawzar, Tun.
116/B4 Taxco, Mex.
73/K2 Taxila (ruins), Pak.
75/C4 Taxkorgan (Taxkorgan Tajik Zizhixian), China
43/D2 Tay (riv.), Sc,UK
43/C2 Tay, Loch (lake), Sc,UK
125/H2 Taylor, Ne,US
126/B4 Taylorville, Il,US
69/L2 Taymyr (isl.), Rus.
68/K2 Taymyr (pen.), Rus.
68/K2 Taymyr (riv.), Rus.
68/J2 Taymyr Aut. Okr., Rus.
83/D4 Tay Ninh, Viet.
68/K4 Tayshet, Rus.
82/C5 Taytay, Phil.
68/J3 Taz (riv.), Rus.
96/B1 Taza, Mor.
129/H2 Tazewell, Tn,US
126/D4 Tazewell, Va,US
97/K2 Tāzirbū (oasis), Libya
116/D5 Tazumal (ruins), ESal.
67/H4 Tbilisi (cap.), Geo.
104/B1 Tchibanga, Gabon
96/H6 Tcholliré, Camr.
49/K1 Tczew, Pol.
108/E4 Tea (riv.), Braz.
45/H5 Tealby, Eng,UK
89/G7 Te Anau, NZ
131/F5 Teaneck, NJ,US
116/C4 Teapa, Mex.
86/B4 Tebak (peak), Indo.
96/G1 Tébessa, Alg.
99/F2 Tebesselamane (well), Mali
111/E2 Tebicuary (riv.), Par.
86/A3 Tebingtinggi, Indo.
67/H4 Tebulos-mta (peak), Rus.
59/E5 Tech (riv.), Fr.
63/J3 Techirghiol, Rom.
112/C4 Tecka (riv.), Arg.
117/P10 Tecomán, Mex.
117/N9 Tecuala, Mex.
63/H3 Tecuci, Rom.
132/G7 Tecumseh, On,Can
126/D3 Tecumseh, Mi,US
125/H2 Tecumseh, Ne,US
73/H1 Tedzhen, Trkm.
68/G6 Tedzhen (riv.), Trkm.
45/G2 Tees (bay), Eng,UK
45/G2 Tees (riv.), Eng,UK
108/F4 Tefé, Braz.
108/E4 Tefé (riv.), Braz.
86/C5 Tegal, Indo.
50/D6 Tegelen, Neth.
96/H2 Tegheri (well), Libya
44/E6 Tegid, Llyn (lake), Wal,UK
99/H3 Tégouma (wadi), Niger
116/D5 Tegucigalpa (cap.), Hon.
118/G2 Tehek (lake), NW,Can
72/F1 Tehrān (cap.), Iran
75/C5 Tehri, India
116/B4 Tehuacán, Mex.
116/C4 Tehuantepec (gulf), Mex.
116/C4 Tehuantepec (isth.), Mex.
59/X16 Teide (peak), Canl.,Sp.
46/B2 Teifi (riv.), Wal,UK
97/L4 Teiga (plat.), Sudan
46/C5 Teignmouth, Eng,UK
58/B3 Tejo (Tagus) (riv.), Port.
125/H2 Tekamah, Ne,US
89/H6 Te Kao, NZ
116/D3 Tekax, Mex.
75/C3 Tekeli, Kaz.
75/D3 Tekes (riv.), China
72/C6 Tekezē Wenz (reg.), Eth.
97/N5 Tekezē Wenz (riv.), Eth., Sudan
75/D4 Tekiliktag (peak), China
63/H5 Tekirdağ, Turk.
84/D4 Tekkali, India
84/D3 Tel (riv.), India
116/D4 Tela, Hon.
67/H4 Telavi, Geo.
74/K5 Tel Aviv (dist.), Isr.
74/K5 Tel Aviv-Yafo, Isr.
59/X17 Telde, Canl.
98/E2 Télé (lake), Mali
75/G2 Telem (lake), Mong.
110/B3 Telemaco Borba, Braz.
42/D4 Telemark (co.), Nor.
87/E3 Telen (riv.), Indo.
63/G4 Teleorman (co.), Rom.
96/G3 Telertheba (peak), Alg.
109/G5 Teles Pires (riv.), Braz.
46/D1 Telford, Eng,UK
54/H3 Telfs, Aus.
51/E5 Telgte, Ger.
98/B4 Télimélé, Gui.
74/N9 Tel Jericho Nat'l Park, WBnk.
122/B2 Telkwa, BC,Can
126/C4 Tell City, In,US
84/C5 Tellicherry, India
124/F3 Telluride, Co,US
74/N7 Tel Megiddo Nat'l Park, Isr.
76/D2 Telmen (lake), Mong.
86/B3 Telok Anson, Malay.
75/E1 Telotskoye (lake), Rus.
64/D5 Telšiai, Lith.
49/G2 Teltow (reg.), Ger.
99/E5 Tema, Gha.
126/D2 Temagami (lake), On,Can
102/E2 Tembisa, SAfr.
117/J6 Temblador, Ven.
104/C2 Tembo, Zaire
46/D2 Teme (riv.), Eng,UK
62/D3 Temerin, Yugo.
86/B3 Temerloh, Malay.
75/B1 Temirtau, Kaz.
127/F1 Témiscamie (riv.), Qu,Can
126/E2 Témiscaming, Qu,Can
76/E1 Temnik (riv.), Rus.
93/M7 Temoe (isl.), FrPol.
124/E4 Tempe, Az,US
60/A2 Tempio Pausania, It.
128/D4 Temple, Tx,US
44/B2 Templepatrick, NI,UK
91/G5 Templestowe, Austl.
49/G2 Templin, Ger.
116/B3 Tempoal, Mex.
104/C3 Tempué, Ang.
66/F3 Temryuk, Rus.
52/D1 Temse, Belg.
112/B3 Temuco, Chile
96/D5 Tena Kourou (peak), Burk.
84/D4 Tenāli, India
83/B3 Tenasserim (range), Burma
83/B4 Tenasserim (Thanintharyi) (div.), Burma
50/D2 Ten Boer, Neth.
46/D2 Tenbury, Eng,UK
46/B3 Tenby, Wal,UK
97/P5 Tendaho, Eth.
79/G1 Tendō, Japan
96/G3 Ténéré du Tafassasset (des.), Niger
99/H2 Ténéré, 'Erg du (des.), Niger
59/X16 Tenerife (isl.), Canl.
59/L6 Tenes (riv.), Sp.
83/B1 Teng (riv.), Burma
87/E4 Tenggarong, Indo.
76/E4 Tengger (des.), China
75/A1 Tengiz (lake), Kaz.
57/G4 Tenibres (peak), It.
111/D1 Teniente Enciso Nat'l Park, Par.
62/D3 Tenja, Cro.
99/E4 Tenkodogo, Burk.
129/F2 Tennessee (riv.), US
129/G3 Tennessee (state), US
112/C2 Teno, Chile
42/H1 Tenojoki (riv.), Fin.

Tenos – Trail

116/C4 Tenosique, Mex.
79/L10 Tenri, Japan
79/E3 Tenryū (riv.), Japan
47/G4 Tenterden, Eng,UK
83/B2 Ten Thousand Buddhas, Cave of, Burma
87/F3 Tentolomatinan (peak), Indo.
58/A1 Teo, Sp.
116/A3 Teocaltiche, Mex.
110/A2 Teodoro Sampaio, Braz.
110/D1 Teófilo Otoni, Braz.
117/P9 Tepatitlán de Morelos, Mex.
117/P9 Tepic, Mex.
49/G3 Teplice, Czh.
117/M7 Tepoca (cape), Mex.
93/L6 Tepoto (isl.), FrPol.
117/P9 Tequila, Mex.
59/G1 Ter (riv.), Sp.
99/F3 Téra, Niger
58/B1 Tera (riv.), Sp.
50/B4 Ter Aar, Neth.
93/K4 Teraina (Washington) (atoll), Kiri.
60/C1 Teramo, It.
74/E2 Tercan, Turk.
59/S12 Terceira (isl.), Azor.,Port.
112/E2 Tercero (riv.), Arg.
63/K2 Terderovsk (bay), Ukr.
67/H4 Terek (riv.), Rus.
109/K5 Teresina, Braz.
110/L7 Teresópolis, Braz.
52/C4 Tergnier, Fr.
76/D4 Tergun Daba (mts.), China
50/B5 Terheijden, Neth.
64/G1 Teriberskiy, Mys (pt.), Rus.
50/C2 Terkaplesterpoelen (lake), Neth.
63/H5 Terkirdağ (prov.), Turk.
73/J1 Termez, Uzb.
60/C4 Termini Imerese, It.
116/C4 Términos (lag.), Mex.
124/B2 Termo, Ca,US
60/D1 Termoli, It.
46/D1 Tern (riv.), Eng,UK
87/G3 Ternate, Indo.
50/A6 Terneuzen, Neth.
60/C1 Terni, It.
56/F3 Ternin (riv.), Fr.
52/B3 Ternoise (riv.), Fr.
66/C2 Ternopol', Ukr.
66/C2 Ternopol' Obl., Ukr.
77/N2 Terpeniya (bay), Rus.
122/A2 Terrace, BC,Can
126/C1 Terrace Bay, On,Can
60/C2 Terracina, It.
127/Q8 Terra Cotta, On,Can
60/A3 Terralba, It.
127/L1 Terra Nova Nat'l Park, Nf,Can
59/G2 Terrassa, Sp.
56/D4 Terrasson-la-Villedieu, Fr.
127/N6 Terrebonne, Qu,Can
129/G2 Terre Haute, In,US
90/H8 Terrey Hills, Austl.
47/G1 Terrington Saint Clement, Eng,UK
123/G4 Terry, Mt,US
75/A1 Tersakkan (riv.), Kaz.
50/C2 Terschelling (isl.), Neth.
59/E2 Teruel, Sp.
83/B5 Terutao (isl.), Thai.
63/H4 Tervel, Bul.
57/K3 Terza Grande (peak), It.
76/C1 Tes, Mong.
76/D2 Tes, Mong.
56/D5 Tescou (riv.), Fr.
130/G1 Teshekpuk (lake), Ak,US
77/N3 Teshio-dake (mtn.), Japan
76/D2 Tesiyn (riv.), Mong.
76/C1 Tes-Khem (riv.), Rus.
62/C3 Teslić, Bosn.
118/C3 Teslin (lake), BC,Can
130/M3 Teslin, Yk,Can
118/C2 Teslin (riv.), Yk,Can
99/G3 Tessaoua, Niger
53/E1 Tessenderlo, Belg.
47/E4 Test (riv.), Eng,UK
59/G1 Têt (riv.), Fr.
46/D3 Tetbury, Eng,UK
57/G4 Tête de l'Estrop (peak), Fr.
63/G4 Teteven, Bul.
45/H5 Tetford, Eng,UK
93/L6 Tetiaroa (isl.), FrPol.
53/F5 Teting-sur-Nied, Fr.
130/K3 Tetlin Nat'l Wild. Ref., Ak,US
122/F4 Teton (riv.), Mt,US
96/D1 Tétouan, Mor.
62/E4 Tetovo, Macd.
59/N9 Tetuan, Sp.
111/D1 Teuco (riv.), Arg.
60/A3 Teulada (cape), It.
123/J3 Teulon, Mb,Can
51/F4 Teutoburger Wald (for.), Ger.
57/K5 Tevere (Tiber) (riv.), It.
74/K5 Teverya (Tiberias), Isr.
43/D3 Teviot (riv.), Sc,UK
90/D4 Tewantin-Noosa, Austl.
46/D3 Tewkesbury, Eng,UK
128/E3 Texarkana, Ar, Tx,US
128/C4 Texas (state), US
128/E4 Texas City, Tx,US
50/B2 Texel (isl.), Neth.
125/G3 Texoma, Ok,US
64/J4 Teykovo, Rus.
116/B4 Teziutlán, Mex.
85/F2 Tezpur, India
83/C1 Tha (riv.), Laos
118/G2 Tha-anne (riv.), NW,Can
102/E3 Thabana-Ntlenyana (peak), Les.
103/E2 Thabankulu (peak), SAfr.
102/D2 Thabazimbi, SAfr.
83/B3 Tha Chin (riv.), Thai.
83/B4 Thaen (pt.), Thai.
83/D1 Thai Binh, Viet.
83/C3 Thailand
83/C4 Thailand (gulf), Thai.
83/D1 Thai Nguyen, Viet.
73/K2 Thal, Pak.
75/B5 Thal (des.), Pak.
83/C5 Thaleban Nat'l Park, Thai.
72/E6 Thamar, Jabal (mtn.), Yem.
47/F3 Thame, Eng,UK
47/F3 Thame (riv.), Eng,UK
126/D3 Thames (riv.), On,Can
47/G3 Thames (riv.), Eng,UK
84/B4 Thāna, India
47/H4 Thanet, Isle of (isl.), Eng,UK
85/J5 Thang Duc, Viet.
83/D2 Thanh Hoa, Viet.
85/J4 Thanh Lang Xa, Viet.
83/D4 Thanh Phu, Viet.
83/D4 Thanh Tri, Viet.
83/B4 Thanintharyi (Tenasserim) (div.), Burma
84/C5 Thanjavur, India
73/J3 Thar (des.), India, Pak.
84/B3 Tharād, India
85/G4 Tharrawaddy, Burma
61/J2 Thásos (isl.), Gre.
47/E4 Thatcham, Eng,UK
83/D1 That Khe, Viet.
83/B2 Thaton, Burma
85/H4 Tha Uthen, Thai.
47/G3 Thaxted, Eng,UK
49/H4 Thaya (riv.), Aus.
85/G4 Thayetmyo, Burma
85/G3 Thazi, Burma
47/E4 Theale, Eng,UK
100/C3 Thebes (ruins), Egypt
128/C3 The Caprock (cliffs), NM,US
122/C4 The Dalles, Or,US
91/B3 The Grampians (mts.), Austl.
50/B4 The Hague ('s-Gravenhage) (cap.), Neth.
91/C3 The Lakes Nat'l Park, Austl.
118/F2 Thelon (riv.), NW,Can
44/B2 The Loup, NI,UK
123/H3 Theodore, Sk,Can
124/E4 Theodore Roosevelt (lake), Az,US
123/G4 Theodore Roosevelt Nat'l Park, ND,US
123/H2 The Pas, Mb,Can
52/B5 Thérain (riv.), Fr.
61/H3 Thermaic (Salonika) (gulf), Gre.
61/H3 Thermopílai (Thermopylae) (pass), Gre.
122/F5 Thermopolis, Wy,US
126/D2 Thessalon, On,Can
61/H2 Thessaloníki (Salonika), Gre.
61/H3 Thessaly (reg.), Gre.
47/G2 Thet (riv.), Eng,UK
47/G2 Thetford, Eng,UK
127/G2 Thetford Mines, Qu,Can
53/E2 Theux, Belg.
117/J4 The Valley (cap.), Angu.
47/G1 The Wash (bay), Eng,UK
47/G4 The Weald (reg.), Eng,UK
128/E4 The Woodlands, Tx,US
46/D1 The Wrekin (hill), Eng,UK
61/G3 Thiamis (riv.), Gre.
129/F4 Thibodaux, La,US
123/J3 Thief River Falls, Mn,US
122/C5 Thielsen (peak), Or,US
83/D4 Thien Ngon, Viet.
56/E4 Thiers, Fr.
98/A3 Thiès, Sen.
98/A3 Thiès (reg.), Sen.
101/C3 Thika, Kenya
84/E2 Thimphu (cap.), Bhu.
42/N7 Thingvellir Nat'l Park, Ice.
53/F5 Thionville, Fr.
61/J4 Thíra (isl.), Gre.
45/E2 Thirlmere (lake), Eng,UK
45/G3 Thirsk, Eng,UK
42/D4 Thisted, Den.
42/P6 Thistilfjördhur (bay), Ice.
130/L3 Thistle (mtn.), Yk,Can
93/Z18 Thithia (isl.), Fiji
82/B5 Thitu (isl.)
61/H3 Thívai, Gre.
42/N7 Thjórsa (riv.), Ice.
118/G2 Thlewiaza (riv.), NW,Can
83/D4 Thoi Binh, Viet.
50/B5 Tholen, Neth.
50/B5 Tholen (isl.), Neth.
53/G5 Tholey, Ger.
129/G3 Thomaston, Ga,US
129/G4 Thomasville, Al,US
129/H4 Thomasville, Ga,US
129/H3 Thomasville, NC,US
122/C3 Thompson (riv.), BC,Can
123/J2 Thompson, Mb,Can
125/J2 Thompson (riv.), Ia, Mo,US
122/E4 Thompson Falls, Mt,US
132/B3 Thompson Place-Tanglewilde, Wa,US
118/E1 Thomsen (riv.), NW,Can
90/A4 Thomson (riv.), Austl.
129/H3 Thomson, Ga,US
83/C3 Thon Buri, Thai.
85/J4 Thon Cam Lo, Viet.
83/B2 Thongwa, Burma
83/E4 Thon Lac Nghiep, Viet.
54/C5 Thonon-les-Bains, Fr.
83/E4 Thon Song Pha, Viet.
124/E4 Thoreau, NM,US
122/E2 Thorhild, Ab,Can
52/B6 Thorigny, Fr.
45/G2 Thornaby-on-Tees, Eng,UK
46/D3 Thornbury, Eng,UK
45/H4 Thorne, Eng,UK
127/R8 Thornhill, On,Can
44/E1 Thornhill, Sc,UK
45/G2 Thornley, Eng,UK
45/G3 Thornthwaite, Eng,UK
45/E4 Thornton Cleveleys, Eng,UK
45/H3 Thornton Dale, Eng,UK
127/R9 Thorold, On,Can
47/H3 Thorpe le Soken, Eng,UK
45/G2 Thorpe Thewles, Eng,UK
56/C3 Thouars, Fr.
56/C3 Thouet (riv.), Fr.
131/B2 Thousand Oaks, Ca,US
66/C4 Thracian (sea), Gre., Turk.
122/F4 Three Forks, Mt,US
130/L4 Three Guardsmen (mtn.), BC,Can
122/E3 Three Hills, Ab,Can
91/C4 Three Hummock (isl.), Austl.
92/G8 Three Kings (isls.), NZ
83/B3 Three Pagodas (pass), Burma
99/E5 Three Points (cape), Gha.
126/C3 Three Rivers, Mi,US
128/D3 Throckmorton, Tx,US
46/B5 Thrushel (riv.), Eng,UK
46/D2 Thruxton, Eng,UK
83/D4 Thu Dau Mot, Viet.
83/D4 Thu Duc, Viet.
52/D3 Thuin, Belg.
56/E5 Thuir, Fr.
119/T7 Thule Air Base, Grld.
54/D4 Thun, Swi.
126/B1 Thunder Bay, On,Can
83/C2 Thung Salaeng Luang Nat'l Park, Thai.
55/E2 Thur (riv.), Swi.
55/F2 Thurgau (canton), Swi.
57/H1 Thüringer Wald (for.), Ger.
48/F3 Thuringia (state), Ger.
47/E2 Thurlaston, Eng,UK
43/B4 Thurles, Ire.
105/T Thurston (isl.), Ant.
116/B4 Tiacolula, Mex.
108/E7 Tiahuanco (ruins), Bol.
130/M5 Tian (pt.), BC,Can
109/K4 Tianguá, Braz.
81/D3 Tianjin, China
81/D3 Tianjin (prov.), China
81/C5 Tianmen, China
81/K9 Tianmu (mts.), China
68/H5 Tian Shan (range), Asia
76/F5 Tianshui, China
81/C5 Tiantangzhai (mtn.), China
96/F1 Tiaret, Alg.
93/S9 Tiavea, WSam.
110/B2 Tibaji (riv.), Braz.
96/H6 Tibati, Camr.
45/F6 Tibberton, Eng,UK
98/C4 Tibé, Pic de (peak), Gui.
74/K5 Tiberias (Sea of Galilee) (lake), Isr., Syria
74/K5 Tiberias (Teverya), Isr.
57/K5 Tiber (Tevere) (riv.), It.
96/J3 Tibesti (mts.), Chad, Libya
75/D5 Tibet (Xizang) Aut. Reg., China
59/L7 Tibidabo (peak), Sp.
96/H1 Ţīb, Ra's aţ (Cape Bon) (cape), Tun.
45/G5 Tibshelf, Eng,UK
117/G4 Tiburon (cape), Haiti
117/M8 Tiburón (isl.), Mex.
132/K11 Tiburon, Ca,US
47/G4 Ticehurst, Eng,UK
132/P14 Tichigan (lake), Wi,US
98/C2 Tichît, Dhar (hills), Mrta.
96/C3 Tichla, WSah.
57/H4 Ticino (riv.), It.
55/E5 Ticino (canton), Swi.
45/G5 Tickhill, Eng,UK
126/F3 Ticonderoga, NY,US
116/D3 Ticul, Mex.
42/E4 Tidaholm, Swe.
45/G5 Tideswell, Eng,UK
96/F2 Tidikelt (plain), Alg.
98/C2 Tidjikdja, Mrta.
87/G3 Tidore (isl.), Indo.
98/A2 Tidra (isl.), Mrta.
59/X16 Tiede Nat'l Park, Canl.
50/C5 Tiel, Neth.
77/J3 Tieling, China
59/N9 Tielmes, Sp.
52/C1 Tielt, Belg.
53/D2 Tielt-Winge, Belg.
98/D4 Tiemba (riv.), IvC.
75/E3 Tiemen Guan (pass), China
53/D2 Tienen, Belg.
71/H5 Tien Shan (range), China
83/D1 Tien Yen, Viet.
83/D2 Tien Yen, Viet.
96/J3 Tieroko (peak), Chad
42/F3 Tierp, Swe.
124/F3 Tierra Amarilla, NM,US
113/L8 Tierra del Fuego (isl.), Arg., Chile
113/L8 Tierra del Fuego, Antártida e Islas del Atlántico Sur (prov.), Arg.
113/K8 Tierra del Fuego Nat'l Park, Arg.
58/C2 Tiétar (riv.), Sp.
110/B2 Tietê (riv.), Braz.
96/C2 Tifariti, WSah.
126/D3 Tiffin, Oh,US
129/H4 Tifton, Ga,US
93/V12 Tiga (isl.), NCal.
96/H6 Tignère, Camr.
113/S12 Tigre, Arg.
122/F4 Tigre (riv.), Peru
117/J6 Tigre (riv.), Ven.
72/D1 Tigris (riv.), Iraq, Turk.
96/J4 Tigui (well), Chad
99/G2 Tiguidit, Falaise de (escarp.), Niger
116/B3 Tihuatlán, Mex.
42/J3 Tiilikkajärven Nat'l Park, Fin.
98/B1 Tijirît (reg.), Mrta.
117/L7 Tijuana, Mex.
110/K8 Tijuca Nat'l Park, Braz.
110/B3 Tijucas, Braz.
110/B1 Tijuco (riv.), Braz.
116/C4 Tikal Nat'l Park, Guat.
84/C3 Tīkamgarh, India
130/G3 Tikchik (lakes), Ak,US
93/L6 Tikehau (atoll), FrPol.
66/G3 Tikhoretsk, Rus.
64/G4 Tikhvin, Rus.
61/H2 Tikveš (lake), Macd.
50/C5 Tilburg, Neth.
47/G4 Tilbury, Eng,UK
128/D4 Tilden, Tx,US
45/H5 Till (riv.), Eng,UK
122/C4 Tillamook, Or,US
54/B3 Tille (riv.), Fr.
42/D4 Tilst, Den.
43/D2 Tilt (riv.), Sc,UK
112/Q9 Tiltil, Chile
65/L2 Timan (ridge), Rus.
89/H7 Timaru, NZ
66/F3 Timashevsk, Rus.
109/L5 Timbaúba, Braz.
123/H4 Timber Lake, SD,US
110/B3 Timbó, Braz.
98/E2 Timbuktu (Tombouctou), Mali
87/H4 Timbuni (riv.), Indo.
61/G3 Timfristós (peak), Gre.
96/F2 Timimoun, Alg.
98/A2 Timiris (cape), Mrta.
62/E3 Timiş (co.), Rom.
62/E3 Timiş (riv.), Rom.
62/E3 Timişoara, Rom.
99/G2 Ti-m-Mershoï (wadi), Niger
126/D1 Timmins, On,Can
126/B2 Timms (hill), Wi,US
109/K5 Timon, Braz.
131/K7 Timonium, Md,US
89/B2 Timor (sea)
87/F5 Timor (isl.), Indo.
110/D1 Timóteo, Braz.
69/N4 Timpton (riv.), Rus.
42/F3 Timrå, Swe.
129/G3 Tims Ford (lake), Tn,US
102/E3 Tina (riv.), SAfr.
82/E6 Tinaca (pt.), Phil.
84/C5 Tindivanam, India
96/D2 Tindouf, Alg.
58/B1 Tineo, Sp.
82/C2 Ting (riv.), China
90/F7 Tingalpa (res.), Austl.
91/D3 Tingaringy Nat'l Park, Austl.
96/H2 Tinghert (upland), Libya
98/C4 Tingi (mts.), Gui., SLeo.
130/F2 Tingmerkpuk (mtn.), Ak,US
108/C5 Tingo María, Peru
112/C2 Tinguirrica (vol.), Chile
109/L6 Tinharé, Braz.
109/L6 Tinharé (isl.), Braz.
83/D2 Tinh Gia, Viet.
92/D3 Tinian (isl.), NMar.
98/C4 Tinkisso (riv.), Gui.
132/Q16 Tinley Park, Il,US
111/C2 Tinogasta, Arg.
61/J4 Tínos (isl.), Gre.
52/C5 Tinqueux, Fr.
96/G2 Tinrhert (plat.), Alg.
96/D1 Tinrhir, Mor.
85/G2 Tinsukia, India
46/B5 Tintagel, Eng,UK
58/B4 Tinto (riv.), Sp.
131/F5 Tinton Falls, NJ,US
45/G5 Tintwistle, Eng,UK
96/F4 Ti-n-Zaouâten, Alg.
123/H3 Tioga, ND,US
86/B3 Tioman (isl.), Malay.
47/G3 Tiptree, Eng,UK
84/C5 Tiptūr, India
93/L6 Tiputa, FrPol.
109/J4 Tiracambu (mts.), Braz.
100/C2 Tiran (str.), Egypt
61/F2 Tiranë (cap.), Alb.
100/C3 Tiran, Jazīrat (isl.), Egypt
55/G5 Tirano, It.
63/J2 Tiraspol', Mol.
74/A2 Tire, Turk.
66/F4 Tirebolu, Turk.
99/F1 Tirest (well), Mali
63/G3 Tîrgovişte, Rom.
63/H3 Tîrgu Bujor, Rom.
63/F3 Tîrgu Cărbuneşti, Rom.
63/H2 Tîrgu Frumos, Rom.
63/F3 Tîrgu Jiu, Rom.
63/F2 Tîrgu Lăpuş, Rom.
63/G2 Tîrgu Mureş, Rom.
63/H2 Tîrgu Neamţ, Rom.
63/H2 Tîrgu Ocna, Rom.
63/H3 Tîrgu Secuiesc, Rom.
73/K1 Tirich Mīr (mtn.), Pak.
63/G2 Tîrnava Mare (riv.), Rom.
63/G2 Tîrnava Mică (riv.), Rom.
63/G2 Tîrnăveni, Rom.
61/H3 Tírnavos, Gre.
55/G3 Tirol (prov.), Aus.
46/C1 Tir Rhiwiog (mtn.), Wa,UK
57/K2 Tirschenreuth, Ger.
60/A2 Tirso (riv.), It.
84/C5 Tiruchchendūr, India
84/C5 Tiruchchirāppalli, India
84/C6 Tiruchendūr, India
84/C6 Tirunelveli, India
84/C5 Tirupati, India
84/C5 Tiruppattūr, India
84/C5 Tiruppūr, India
84/C5 Tirūr, India
84/C5 Tiruvannāmalai, India
66/B2 Tisa (riv.), Eur.
46/D4 Tisbury, Eng,UK
123/G2 Tisdale, Sk,Can
125/H4 Tishomingo, Ok,US
62/E2 Tisza (riv.), Hun.
62/E2 Tiszaföldvár, Hun.
62/E2 Tiszafüred, Hun.
62/E2 Tiszakécske, Hun.
62/E2 Tiszalök, Hun.
62/E2 Tiszavasvári, Hun.
62/E3 Titel, Yugo.
108/E7 Titicaca (lake), Bol., Peru
84/D3 Titlagarh, India
55/E4 Titlis (peak), Swi.
62/D4 Titograd, Yugo.
62/D4 Titovo Užice, Yugo.
62/E5 Titov Veles, Macd.
62/E5 Titov vrh (peak), Macd.
63/G3 Titu, Rom.
129/H4 Titusville, Fl,US
98/A3 Tivaouane, Sen.
62/D4 Tivat, Yugo.
46/C5 Tiverton, Eng,UK
116/D3 Tizimín, Mex.
73/L1 Tiznap (riv.), China
96/D2 Tiznit, Mor.
50/C3 Tjeukemeer (lake), Neth.
117/P8 Tlahualilo de Zaragoza, Mex.
116/B4 Tlalnepantla, Mex.
116/B4 Tlapa, Mex.
116/B4 Tlaxcala, Mex.
116/B4 Tlaxcala (state), Mex.
96/E1 Tlemcen, Alg.
96/J2 Tmassah, Libya
63/G2 Toaca (peak), Rom.
103/J7 Toamasina, Madg.
103/J7 Toamasina (prov.), Madg.
132/B2 Toandos (pen.), Wa,US
93/L6 Toau (atoll), FrPol.
122/B3 Toba (inlet), BC,Can
76/D5 Toba, China
86/A3 Toba (lake), Indo.
79/E3 Toba, Japan
117/J5 Tobago (isl.), Trin.
73/J2 Toba Kākar (range), Pak.
58/E3 Tobarra, Sp.
75/B5 Toba Tek Singh, Pak.
44/B2 Tobermore, NI,UK
109/L6 Tobias Barreto, Braz.
123/H2 Tobin (lake), Sk,Can
127/H2 Tobique (riv.), NB,Can
65/Q4 Tobol (riv.), Kaz., Rus.
68/G4 Tobol'sk, Rus.
97/K1 Tobruk, Libya
131/E4 Tobyhanna (lake), Pa,US
65/L2 Tobysh (riv.), Rus.
109/J5 Tocantinópolis, Braz.
109/J5 Tocantins (riv.), Braz.
129/H3 Toccoa, Ga,US
55/E5 Toce (riv.), It.
79/F2 Tochigi, Japan
79/F2 Tochigi (pref.), Japan
79/F2 Tochio, Japan
58/C4 Tocina, Sp.
111/B1 Tocopilla, Chile
117/F6 Tocumen, Pan.
117/H5 Tocuyito, Ven.
117/H5 Tocuyo (riv.), Ven.
79/H7 Toda, Japan
84/C2 Toda Bhīm, India
47/F3 Toddington, Eng,UK
60/C1 Todi, It.
45/F4 Todmorden, Eng,UK
94/C4 Todos os Santos (bay), Braz.
109/G3 Toekomstig (res.), Sur.
122/E2 Tofield, Ab,Can
42/E3 Töfsingdalens Nat'l Park, Swe.
93/H6 Tofua (isl.), Tonga
98/C2 Togba (well), Mrta.
130/G4 Togiak Nat'l Wild. Ref., Ak,US
99/F4 Togo
79/N9 Tōgō, Japan
124/E4 Tohatchi, NM,US
93/X15 Tohivea (peak), FrPol.
79/F2 Tōhoku (prov.), Japan
79/F3 Toi, Japan
79/M9 Tōin, Japan
124/C3 Toiyabe (range), Nv,US
78/C3 Tojō, Japan
79/L10 Tōjō, Japan
79/E3 Tōkai, Japan
79/F2 Tōkamachi, Japan
100/D5 Tokar, Sudan
92/B1 Tokara (isls.), Japan
100/D5 Tokar Game Rsv., Sudan
74/D2 Tokat, Turk.
93/H5 Tokelau (terr.), NZ
79/N9 Toki, Japan
79/N9 Toki (riv.), Japan
79/H6 Tokigawa, Japan
79/M10 Tokoname, Japan
89/H6 Tokoroa, NZ
79/F3 Tokorozawa, Japan
76/B2 Toksun, China
75/B3 Toktogul (res.), Kyr.
78/D3 Tokushima, Japan
78/C4 Tokushima (pref.), Japan
79/H7 Tokyo (bay), Japan
79/F3 Tōkyō (cap.), Japan
103/H9 Tôlañaro, Madg.
63/H4 Tolbukhin, Bul.
111/F1 Toledo, Braz.
82/D5 Toledo, Phil.
58/C3 Toledo, Sp.
58/C3 Toledo (mts.), Sp.
126/D3 Toledo, Oh,US
128/E4 Toledo Bend (res.), La, Tx,US
60/C1 Tolentino, It.
112/C3 Tolhuaca Nat'l Park, Chile
75/D2 Toli, China
103/G8 Toliara, Madg.
103/H8 Toliara (prov.), Madg.
87/F3 Tolitoli, Indo.
44/B5 Tolka (riv.), Ire.
62/A2 Tolmezzo, It.
62/D2 Tolna, Hun.
62/D2 Tolna (co.), Hun.
87/F4 Tolo (gulf), Indo.
58/D1 Tolosa, Sp.
132/D2 Tolt (riv.), Wa,US
112/B3 Toltén, Chile
112/B3 Toltén (riv.), Chile
116/B4 Toluca, Mex.
67/J1 Tol'yatti, Rus.
68/J4 Tom' (riv.), Rus.
126/B3 Tomah, Wi,US
77/N3 Tomakomai, Japan
92/G6 Tomanivi (peak), Fiji
58/A3 Tomar, Port.
61/G3 Tómaros (peak), Gre.
49/M3 Tomaszów Lubelski, Pol.
49/L3 Tomaszów Mazowiecki, Pol.
43/D2 Tomatin, Sc,UK
108/G6 Tombador (mts.), Braz.
97/M6 Tombe, Sudan
129/F4 Tombigbee (riv.), Al, Ms,US
104/B2 Tomboco, Ang.
98/E2 Tombouctou (Timbuktu), Mali
124/E5 Tombstone, Az,US
104/B4 Tombua, Ang.
112/B3 Tomé, Chile
56/B2 Tomé (isl.), Fr.
49/G1 Tomelilla, Swe.
58/D3 Tomelloso, Sp.
87/F4 Tomini (gulf), Indo.
58/A2 Tomiño, Sp.
79/H7 Tomiura, Japan
69/N4 Tommot, Rus.
108/E2 Tomo (riv.), Col.
126/C4 Tompkinsville, Ky,US
68/J4 Tomsk, Rus.
131/F6 Toms River, NJ,US
130/K3 Tom White (mtn.), Ak,US
122/D3 Tonasket, Wa,US
127/S9 Tonawanda, NY,US
47/G4 Tonbridge, Eng,UK
79/L10 Tondabayashi, Japan
87/F3 Tondano, Indo.
42/D5 Tönder, Den.
97/K6 Tondou (mts.), CAfr.
79/J7 Tone, Japan
79/G3 Tone (riv.), Japan
46/C4 Tone (riv.), Eng,UK
72/F1 Tonekābon, Iran
76/F5 Tong (riv.), China
93/H7 Tonga
93/K5 Tongareva (Penrhyn) (atoll), CookIs.
93/H7 Tonga-tapu (isl.), Tonga
76/F4 Tongchuan, China
53/E2 Tongeren, Belg.
82/B2 Tonggu, China
77/K3 Tonghua, China
87/E5 Tongo (peak), Indo.
85/J2 Tongren, China
84/F2 Tongsa (riv.), Bhu.
76/D5 Tongtian (riv.), China
122/G4 Tongue (riv.), Mt, Wy,US
50/D6 Tönisvorst, Ger.
97/L6 Tonj, Sudan
84/C2 Tonk, India
125/H3 Tonkawa, Ok,US
83/D1 Tonkin (gulf), China, Viet.
98/D5 Tonkoui (peak), IvC.
83/C3 Tonle Sap (lake), Camb.
56/D4 Tonneins, Fr.
124/D4 Tonopah, Az,US
124/C3 Tonopah, Nv,US
78/D3 Tonoshō, Japan
104/E5 Tonota, Bots.
42/D4 Tønsberg, Nor.
124/E4 Tonto Nat'l Mon., Az,US
124/D2 Tooele, Ut,US
91/G6 Toomuc (cr.), Austl.
90/C4 Toowoomba, Austl.
131/B2 Topanga, Ca,US
125/J3 Topeka (cap.), Ks,US
122/B2 Topley, BC,Can
63/G2 Toplița, Rom.
49/K4 Topoľčany, Slvk.
63/G3 Topoloveni, Rom.
63/H4 Topolovgrad, Bul.
64/F2 Topozero (lake), Rus.
122/C4 Toppenish, Wa,US
46/C5 Topsham, Eng,UK
97/M6 Tor, Eth.
79/M9 Torahime, Japan
108/D7 Torata, Peru
87/G3 Torawitan (cape), Indo.
74/A2 Torbalı, Turk.
73/G1 Torbat-e Ḩeydarīyeh, Iran
56/B1 Torbay, Eng,UK
130/H3 Torbert (mtn.), Ak,US
48/E1 Tørder, Den.
59/L6 Tordera (riv.), Sp.
58/C2 Tordesillas, Sp.
59/G1 Torelló, Sp.
49/G2 Torgelow, Ger.
52/C1 Torhout, Belg.
79/J7 Toride, Japan
79/E3 Torii-tōge (pass), Japan
58/A1 Toriñana (cape), Sp.
57/G4 Torino (Turin), It.
92/D1 Tori-Shima (isl.), Japan
97/M7 Torit, Sudan
73/H1 Torkestān (mts.), Afg.
58/C2 Tormes (riv.), Sp.
45/H4 Torne (riv.), Eng,UK
51/G1 Tornesch, Ger.
62/D4 Tornik (peak), Yugo.
42/G2 Torniojoki (Torneälven) (riv.), Fin., Swe.
58/C2 Toro, Sp.
111/C2 Toro, Cerro del (peak), Arg.
62/E2 Törökszentmiklós, Hun.
61/H2 Toronaic (gulf), Gre.
127/R8 Toronto (cap.), On,Can
64/F4 Toropets, Rus.
101/B2 Tororo, Ugan.
59/N8 Torote (riv.), Sp.
46/B6 Torpoint, Eng,UK
46/C6 Torquay, Eng,UK
131/B3 Torrance, Ca,US
58/D4 Torre del Campo, Sp.
58/D4 Torredonjimeno, Sp.
58/D2 Torrejón de Ardoz, Sp.
58/C1 Torrelavega, Sp.
59/N8 Torrelodones, Sp.
90/B3 Torrens (cr.), Austl.
89/C4 Torrens (lake), Austl.
59/E3 Torrente, Sp.
117/P8 Torreón, Mex.
59/E4 Torre-Pacheco, Sp.
58/D3 Torreperogil, Sp.
92/D6 Torres (str.), Austl.
110/B4 Tôrres, Braz.
92/F6 Torres (isls.), Van.
113/J7 Torres del Paine Nat'l Park, Chile
58/A3 Torres Novas, Port.
58/A3 Torres Vedras, Port.
59/E4 Torrevieja, Sp.
44/B1 Torr Head (pt.), NI,UK
46/B5 Torridge (riv.), Eng,UK
58/C3 Torrijos, Sp.
123/G5 Torrington, Wy,US
58/D4 Torrox, Sp.
41/D2 Tórshavn, Den.
56/B2 Torteval, Chl,UK
117/J4 Tortola (isl.), BVI
60/A3 Tortolì, It.
57/H4 Tortona, It.
59/F2 Tortosa, Sp.
59/F2 Tortosa (cape), Sp.
75/C3 Torugart, Pereval (pass), Kyr.
49/K2 Toruń, Pol.
49/K2 Toruń (prov.), Pol.
43/A3 Tory (isl.), Ire.
49/L4 Torysa (riv.), Slvk.
64/G4 Torzhok, Rus.
78/C4 Tosa, Japan
78/C4 Tosa (bay), Japan
78/C4 Tosashimizu, Japan
104/B5 Toscanini, Namb.
57/J4 Tosco-Emiliano (range), It.
76/D4 Toson (lake), China
76/D2 Tosontsengel, Mong.
55/E3 Töss (riv.), Swi.
45/G1 Tosson (hill), Eng,UK
111/D2 Tostado, Arg.
51/G2 Tostedt, Ger.
78/B4 Tosu, Japan
74/C2 Tosya, Turk.
58/E4 Totana, Sp.
47/E5 Totland, Eng,UK
46/C6 Totnes, Eng,UK
116/A4 Totolapan, Mex.
112/E2 Totoras, Arg.
105/H Totten (glac.), Ant.
45/F4 Tottington, Eng,UK
47/E5 Totton, Eng,UK
78/D3 Tottori, Japan
78/C3 Tottori (pref.), Japan
96/D1 Toubkal, Jebel (peak), Mor.
82/D3 Toucheng, Tai.
123/G3 Touchwood (hills), Sk,Can
98/E3 Tougan, Burk.
96/G1 Touggourt, Alg.
53/E6 Toul, Fr.
127/H1 Toulnustouc (riv.), Qu,Can
56/F5 Toulon, Fr.
56/D5 Toulouse, Fr.
96/H3 Toumo (well), Niger
98/D5 Toumodi, IvC.
82/D3 Tounan, Tai.
83/B2 Toungoo, Burma
98/D5 Toura (mts.), IvC.
52/C2 Tourcoing, Fr.
56/C5 Tourettes, Pic de (peak), Fr.
58/A1 Touriñan (cape), Sp.
56/C2 Tourlaville, Fr.
52/C2 Tournai, Belg.
54/A4 Tournus, Fr.
56/D3 Tours, Fr.
59/E3 Tous (res.), Sp.
56/B2 Toussaines, Signal de (peak), Fr.
96/J3 Toussidé (peak), Chad
97/K6 Toussoro (peak), CAfr.
102/C4 Touws (riv.), SAfr.
117/G6 Tovar, Ven.
47/E2 Tove (riv.), Eng,UK
76/E2 Tövshrüüleh, Mong.
79/G2 Towada, Japan
47/F2 Towcester, Eng,UK
45/G2 Tow Law, Eng,UK
123/H3 Towner, ND,US
122/F4 Townsend, Mt,US
132/A2 Townsend (mt.), Wa,US
90/C3 Townshend (cape), Austl.
90/B2 Townsville, Austl.
73/H1 Towraghondi, Afg.
131/K7 Towson, Md,US
87/F4 Towuti (lake), Indo.
75/C3 Toxkan (riv.), China, Kyr.
128/C4 Toyah, Tx,US
128/C4 Toyahvale, Tx,US
79/E2 Toyama, Japan
79/E2 Toyama (bay), Japan
79/E2 Toyama (pref.), Japan
79/N9 Toyoake, Japan
79/E3 Toyohashi, Japan
79/E3 Toyokawa, Japan
79/L10 Toyonaka, Japan
79/L10 Toyono, Japan
78/D3 Toyo'oka, Japan
79/M9 Toyosato, Japan
79/E2 Toyoshina, Japan
79/E3 Toyota, Japan
79/M9 Toyoyama, Japan
130/H2 Tozi (mtn.), Ak,US
83/E3 Tra Bong, Viet.
74/D2 Trabzon, Turk.
127/H2 Tracadie, NB,Can
83/D4 Tra Cu, Viet.
127/F2 Tracy, QU,Can
132/M11 Tracy, Ca,US
58/B4 Trafalgar (cape), Sp.
59/P10 Trafaria, Port.
112/B3 Traiguén, Chile
122/D3 Trail, BC,Can

179

Trais – Vaasa

57/L3 **Traisen** (riv.), Aus.
49/J4 **Traiskirchen,** Aus.
43/A4 **Tralee,** Ire.
83/D1 **Tra Linh,** Viet.
110/B4 **Tramandaí,** Braz.
83/E3 **Tra Mi,** Viet.
125/G3 **Tramperos** (cr.), NM, Tx,US
42/E4 **Tranås,** Swe.
53/D4 **Tranet** (mtn.), Fr.
83/B5 **Trang,** Thai.
87/H5 **Trangan** (isl.), Indo.
60/E2 **Trani,** It.
105/W **Transantarctic** (mts.), Ant.
63/F1 **Trans-Carpathian Obl.,** Ukr.
62/F2 **Transylvania** (reg.), Rom.
62/F3 **Transylvanian Alps** (range), Rom.
83/D4 **Tra On,** Viet.
60/C3 **Trapani,** It.
83/D3 **Trapeang Veng,** Camb.
122/E4 **Trapper** (peak), Mt,US
52/B6 **Trappes,** Fr.
91/C3 **Traralgon,** Austl.
98/B2 **Trarza** (reg.), Mrta.
60/C1 **Trasimeno** (lake), It.
58/B2 **Trás-os-Montes e Alto Douro** (dist.), Port.
102/E2 **Trasvaal** (prov.), SAfr.
83/C3 **Trat,** Thai.
57/L2 **Traun,** Aus.
57/L2 **Traun** (riv.), Aus.
57/K3 **Traunreut,** Ger.
57/K3 **Traunsee** (lake), Aus.
57/K3 **Traunstein,** Ger.
48/F2 **Trave** (riv.), Ger.
91/B2 **Travellers** (lake), Austl.
130/G2 **Traverse** (peak), Ak,US
123/J4 **Traverse** (lake), SD,US
126/C2 **Traverse City,** Mi,US
83/D4 **Tra Vinh,** Viet.
128/D4 **Travis** (lake), Tx,US
62/C3 **Travnik,** Bosn.
46/C2 **Trawsalt** (mtn.), Wal,UK
44/E6 **Trawsfynydd,** Wal,UK
44/E6 **Trawsfynydd, Llyn** (lake), Wal,UK
62/B2 **Trbovlje,** Slov.
57/H4 **Trebbia** (riv.), It.
48/G1 **Trebel** (riv.), Ger.
49/H4 **Třebíč,** Czh.
62/D4 **Trebinje,** Bosn.
60/E3 **Trebisacce,** It.
57/L2 **Třeboň,** Czh.
58/B4 **Trebujena,** Sp.
46/C3 **Tredegar,** Wal,UK
46/C2 **Trefeglwys,** Wal,UK
44/E5 **Trefnant,** Wal,UK
46/C2 **Tregaron,** Wal,UK
113/G2 **Treinta y Tres,** Uru.
113/G2 **Treinta y Tres** (dept.), Uru.
57/G4 **Tré-la-Tête** (mtn.), Fr.
56/C3 **Trélazé,** Fr.
46/B3 **Trelech,** Wal,UK
112/D4 **Trelew,** Arg.
56/D4 **Trélissac,** Fr.
48/G1 **Trelleborg,** Swe.
44/D6 **Tremadoc** (bay), Wal,UK
44/B4 **Tremblestown** (riv.), Ire.
122/B2 **Trembleur** (lake), BC,Can
53/D2 **Tremelo,** Belg.
60/D1 **Tremiti** (isls.), It.
124/D2 **Tremonton,** Ut,US
127/F1 **Trenche** (riv.), Qu,Can
49/K4 **Trenčín,** Slvk.
112/E2 **Trenque Lauquen,** Arg.
45/H5 **Trent** (riv.), Eng,UK
45/F6 **Trent and Mersey** (can.), Eng,UK
57/J3 **Trentino-Alto Adige** (reg.), It.
55/H5 **Trento,** It.
55/H5 **Trento** (prov.), It.
126/E2 **Trenton,** On,Can
129/H4 **Trenton,** Fl,US
129/G3 **Trenton,** Ga,US
132/F7 **Trenton,** Mi,US
125/J2 **Trenton,** Mo,US
131/F5 **Trenton** (cap.), NJ,US
129/F3 **Trenton,** Tn,US
46/C3 **Treorchy,** Wal,UK
61/F2 **Trepuzzi,** It.
113/T11 **Tres Arboles,** Uru.
112/E3 **Tres Arroyos,** Arg.
110/H6 **Três Corações,** Braz.
110/B2 **Trés Irmáos** (res.), Braz.
111/D2 **Tres Isletas,** Arg.
110/B2 **Três Lagoas,** Braz.
110/C1 **Três Marias,** Braz.
110/C1 **Três Marias** (res.), Braz.
117/N9 **Tres Marías** (isls.), Mex.
112/B5 **Tres Montes** (cape), Chile
112/C4 **Tres Picos** (peak), Arg.
112/E3 **Tres Picos** (peak), Arg.
110/H6 **Três Pontas,** Braz.
112/D5 **Tres Puntas** (cape), Arg.
110/K7 **Três Rios,** Braz.
57/J2 **Treuchtlingen,** Ger.
48/G2 **Treuenbrietzen,** Ger.
57/H4 **Treviglio,** It.
57/K4 **Treviso,** It.
46/A5 **Trevose Head** (pt.), Eng,UK
131/J7 **Triadelphia** (res.), Md,US
90/B2 **Tribulation** (cape), Austl.
61/F3 **Tricase,** It.
84/C5 **Trichūr,** India
87/J4 **Tricora** (peak), Indo.
82/B5 **Trident** (shoal)
52/A5 **Trie-Château,** Fr.
53/F4 **Trier,** Ger.
60/E2 **Triggiano,** It.
63/G4 **Triglav** (peak), Bul.
62/A2 **Triglav** (peak), Slov.
62/A2 **Triglav Nat'l Park,** Slov.
60/D2 **Trigno** (riv.), It.
58/B4 **Trigueros,** Sp.
61/G3 **Tríkala,** Gre.
61/G3 **Trikhonís** (lake), Gre.
54/D3 **Trimbach,** Swi.
45/G2 **Trimdon,** Eng,UK
84/D6 **Trincomalee,** SrL.
109/J7 **Trindade,** Braz.
49/K4 **Třinec,** Czh.
47/F3 **Tring,** Eng,UK
112/E3 **Trinidad** (isl.), Arg.
108/F6 **Trinidad,** Bol.
113/J7 **Trinidad** (gulf), Chile
113/F2 **Trinidad,** Uru.
125/F3 **Trinidad,** Co,US
117/J5 **Trinidad and Tobago**
109/N8 **Trinidade,** Braz.
127/L2 **Trinity** (bay), Nf,Can
130/H4 **Trinity** (isls.), Ak,US
124/B2 **Trinity** (riv.), Ca,US
124/C2 **Trinity** (range), Nv,US
128/E4 **Trinity** (riv.), Tx,US
100/D5 **Trinkitat,** Sudan
103/S15 **Triolet,** Mrts.
61/H4 **Trípolis,** Gre.
96/H1 **Tripolitania** (reg.), Libya
74/K4 **Tripoli** (Ţarābulus), Leb.
96/H1 **Tripoli** (Ţarābulus) (cap.), Libya
84/C6 **Tripunittura,** India
85/F3 **Tripura** (state), India
38/J7 **Tristan da Cunha** (isls.), StH.
98/B4 **Tristao** (isls.), Guin.
112/D4 **Triste** (peak), Arg.
83/D4 **Tri Ton,** Viet.
51/H1 **Trittau,** Ger.
84/C6 **Trivandrum,** India
49/J4 **Trnava,** Slvk.
92/E5 **Trobriand** (isls.), PNG
52/A5 **Troesne** (riv.), Fr.
57/L3 **Trofaiach,** Aus.
60/D2 **Troia,** It.
59/Q11 **Tróia,** Port.
53/G2 **Troisdorf,** Ger.
53/G6 **Troisfontaines,** Fr.
127/G1 **Trois-Pistoles,** Qu,Can
127/F2 **Trois-Rivières,** Qu,Can
65/P5 **Troitsk,** Rus.
42/E4 **Trollhättan,** Swe.
109/G4 **Trombetas** (riv.), Braz.
39/M6 **Tromelin** (isl.), Reu.
42/F1 **Troms** (co.), Nor.
42/F1 **Tromsø,** Nor.
112/C4 **Tronador** (peak), Arg., Chile
42/D3 **Trondheim,** Nor.
60/C1 **Tronto** (riv.), It.
74/J4 **Troodos** (mts.), Cyp.
44/D1 **Trool, Loch** (lake), Sc,UK
43/C3 **Troon,** Sc,UK
60/D3 **Tropea,** It.
124/D3 **Tropic,** Ut,US
44/B1 **Trostan** (mtn.), NI,UK
118/D2 **Trout** (lake), NW,Can
123/K3 **Trout** (lake), On,Can
45/F3 **Troutbeck,** Eng,UK
122/E1 **Trout Lake,** BC,Can
46/D4 **Trowbridge,** Eng,UK
129/G4 **Troy,** Al,US
132/F6 **Troy,** Mi,US
126/F3 **Troy,** NY,US
129/G1 **Troy,** Oh,US
63/G4 **Troyan,** Bul.
63/G4 **Troyanski Prokhod** (pass), Bul.
56/F2 **Troyes,** Fr.
61/K3 **Troy** (Ilium) (ruins), Turk.
62/E4 **Trstenik,** Yugo.
130/M3 **Truitt** (peak), Yk,Can
116/D4 **Trujillo,** Hon.
108/C5 **Trujillo,** Peru
58/C3 **Trujillo,** Sp.
117/G6 **Trujillo,** Ven.
92/E4 **Truk** (isls.), Micr.
131/G4 **Trumbull,** Ct,US
46/D2 **Trumpet,** Eng,UK
83/D1 **Trung Khanh,** Viet.
127/J2 **Truro,** NS,Can
46/A6 **Truro,** Eng,UK
124/F4 **Truth Or Consequences,** NM,US
49/H3 **Trutnov,** Czh.
56/E4 **Truyère** (riv.), Fr.
44/D6 **Trwyn Cilan** (pt.), Wal,UK
63/G4 **Tryavna,** Bul.
42/E3 **Trysil,** Nor.
49/J2 **Trzcianka,** Pol.
49/H1 **Trzebiatów,** Pol.
49/J3 **Trzebnica,** Pol.
49/J2 **Trzemeszno,** Pol.
62/B2 **Tržič,** Slov.
76/D3 **Tsagaan Bogd** (peak), Mong.
76/G2 **Tsagaan-Ovoo,** Mong.
76/E1 **Tsagaan-Üür,** Mong.
103/J6 **Tsaratanana Massif** (plat.), Madg.
102/B2 **Tsarisberge** (mts.), Namb.
75/F2 **Tsast Uul** (peak), Mong.
102/E3 **Tsatsana** (peak), Les.
104/D5 **Tsau,** Bots.
101/C3 **Tsavo,** Kenya
101/C3 **Tsavo East Nat'l Park,** Kenya
101/C3 **Tsavo West Nat'l Park,** Kenya
76/F2 **Tsenhermandal,** Mong.
76/D2 **Tsetsen-Uul,** Mong.
104/B1 **Tshela,** Zaire
104/D2 **Tshibwika,** Zaire
104/D2 **Tshikapa,** Zaire
97/K8 **Tshuapa** (riv.), Zaire
65/L2 **Tsil'ma** (riv.), Rus.
67/G2 **Tsimlyansk** (res.), Rus.
103/H9 **Tsiombe,** Madg.
103/H7 **Tsiribihina** (riv.), Madg.
103/H7 **Tsiroanomandidy,** Madg.
102/C4 **Tsitsikamma Forest & Coastal Nat'l Park,** SAfr.
67/G4 **Tskhinvali,** Geo.
64/G4 **Tsna** (riv.), Rus.
76/D2 **Tsogt,** Mong.
76/F3 **Tsogt-Ovoo,** Mong.
76/F3 **Tsogttsetsiy,** Mong.
76/F2 **Tsöh** (riv.), Mong.
102/D3 **Tsomo** (riv.), SAfr.
78/E3 **Tsu,** Japan
78/A3 **Tsu** (isls.), Japan
79/F2 **Tsubame,** Japan
78/E2 **Tsubata,** Japan
79/G2 **Tsuchiura,** Japan
79/M10 **Tsuchiyama,** Japan
77/M3 **Tsugaru** (str.), Japan
79/L10 **Tsuge,** Japan
79/H7 **Tsukui,** Japan
78/B4 **Tsukumi,** Japan
104/C4 **Tsumeb,** Namb.
79/K10 **Tsuna,** Japan
79/F3 **Tsuru,** Japan
78/E3 **Tsuruga,** Japan
79/H7 **Tsurugashima,** Japan
79/E2 **Tsurugi,** Japan
78/D4 **Tsurugi-san** (mtn.), Japan
79/M9 **Tsushima,** Japan
78/D3 **Tsuyama,** Japan
86/C5 **Tua** (cape), Indo.
58/B2 **Tua** (riv.), Port.
112/B4 **Tuamapu** (chan.), Chile
93/L6 **Tuamotu** (arch.), FrPol.
81/B4 **Tuan** (riv.), China
86/A3 **Tuan** (pt.), Indo.
83/C1 **Tuan Giao,** Viet.
86/A3 **Tuangku** (isl.), Indo.
83/D2 **Tuan Thuong,** Viet.
82/D4 **Tuao,** Phil.
66/F3 **Tuapse,** Rus.
124/E3 **Tuba City,** Az,US
86/D5 **Tuban,** Indo.
72/D6 **Tuban** (riv.), Yem.
110/B4 **Tubarão,** Braz.
50/D4 **Tubbergen,** Neth.
55/E1 **Tübingen,** Ger.
52/D2 **Tubize,** Belg.
98/C5 **Tubmanburg,** Libr.
92/H6 **Tubou,** Fiji
97/K1 **Ţubruq** (Tobruk), Libya
93/K7 **Tubuaä** (isls.), FrPol.
93/K7 **Tubuaï** (isl.), FrPol.
49/J2 **Tuchola,** Pol.
124/E4 **Tucson,** Az,US
125/G4 **Tucumcari,** NM,US
117/H6 **Tucupido,** Ven.
117/J6 **Tucupita,** Ven.
109/J4 **Tucuruí,** Braz.
109/H4 **Tucuruí** (res.), Braz.
58/E1 **Tudela,** Sp.
56/E5 **Tude, Rochers de la** (mtn.), Fr.
102/E3 **Tugela** (falls), SAfr.
103/E3 **Tugela** (riv.), SAfr.
129/H2 **Tug Fork** (riv.), WV,US
82/D4 **Tuguegarao,** Phil.
87/F5 **Tukangbesi** (isls.), Indo.
64/D4 **Tukums,** Lat.
86/D4 **Tukung** (peak), Indo.
132/C3 **Tukwila,** Wa,US
116/B3 **Tula,** Mex.
66/F1 **Tula,** Rus.
75/F4 **Tulagt Ar** (riv.), China
116/B3 **Tulancingo,** Mex.
66/F1 **Tula Obl.,** Rus.
124/C3 **Tulare,** Ca,US
125/F4 **Tularosa,** NM,US
125/F4 **Tularosa** (val.), NM,US
102/L10 **Tulbagh,** SAfr.
108/C3 **Tulcán,** Ecu.
63/J3 **Tulcea,** Rom.
63/J3 **Tulcea** (co.), Rom.
128/C3 **Tulia,** Tx,US
130/E5 **Tulik** (vol.), Ak,US
92/E5 **Tulin** (isls.), PNG
74/K5 **Ţūlkarm,** WBnk.
129/G3 **Tullahoma,** Tn,US
43/B4 **Tullamore,** Ire.
56/D4 **Tulle,** Fr.
49/J4 **Tulln,** Aus.
64/G1 **Tuloma** (riv.), Rus.
125/J3 **Tulsa,** Ok,US
108/C3 **Tuluá,** Col.
69/L4 **Tulun,** Rus.
116/D5 **Tuma** (riv.), Nic.
124/E5 **Tumacacori Nat'l Mon.,** Az,US
109/H3 **Tumac-Humac** (mts.), Braz.
108/C3 **Tumaco,** Col.
82/D4 **Tumauini,** Phil.
97/J8 **Tumba** (lake), Zaire
108/B4 **Tumbes,** Peru
83/C3 **Tumbot** (peak), Camb.
77/K3 **Tumen,** China
117/J6 **Tumeremo,** Ven.
84/C5 **Tumkūr,** India
43/C2 **Tummel** (riv.), Sc,UK
77/M1 **Tumnin** (riv.), Rus.
86/B2 **Tumpat,** Malay.
87/F4 **Tumpu** (peak), Indo.
91/D2 **Tumut,** Austl.
132/B3 **Tumwater,** Wa,US
74/D2 **Tunceli,** Turk.
101/B5 **Tunduma,** Tanz.
101/C5 **Tunduru,** Tanz.
75/C1 **Tundyk** (riv.), Kaz.
62/H4 **Tundzha** (riv.), Bul., Turk.
84/C4 **Tungabhadra** (res.), India
84/C4 **Tungabhadra** (riv.), India
91/C3 **Tungamah,** Austl.
68/K3 **Tunguska, Lower** (riv.), Rus.
68/K3 **Tunguska, Stony** (riv.), Rus.
60/B4 **Tūnis** (cap.), Tun.
60/B4 **Tunis** (gov.), Tun.
60/B4 **Tunis** (gulf), Tun.
96/G1 **Tunisia**
108/D2 **Tunjá,** Col.
119/K3 **Tunungayualuk** (isl.), Nf,Can
112/C2 **Tunuyán,** Arg.
112/C2 **Tunuyán** (riv.), Chile
124/B3 **Tuolumne** (riv.), Ca,US
83/D2 **Tuong Duong,** Viet.
85/J3 **Tuoniang** (riv.), China
75/F5 **Tuotuo** (riv.), China
110/B2 **Tupã,** Braz.
110/B1 **Tupaciguara,** Braz.
93/K6 **Tupai** (isl.), FrPol.
129/F3 **Tupelo,** Ms,US
110/B2 **Tupi Paulista,** Braz.
108/E8 **Tupiza,** Bol.
126/F2 **Tupper Lake,** NY,US
112/C2 **Tupungato** (peak), Arg., Chile
84/F2 **Tura,** India
65/Q4 **Tura** (riv.), Rus.
77/L1 **Turana** (mts.), Rus.
68/G5 **Turan Lowland** (plain), Uzb.
117/F5 **Turbaco,** Col.
73/H3 **Turbat,** Pak.
117/F6 **Turbo,** Col.
63/F2 **Turda,** Rom.
93/M7 **Tureia** (atoll), FrPol.
49/K2 **Turek,** Pol.
68/G4 **Turgay Obl.,** Kaz.
126/E1 **Turgeon** (riv.), Qu,Can
63/H4 **Tŭrgovishte,** Bul.
74/A2 **Turgutlu,** Turk.
74/D2 **Turhal,** Turk.
59/E3 **Turia** (riv.), Sp.
57/G4 **Turin** (Torino), It.
101/C2 **Turkana** (lake), Eth., Kenya
75/A3 **Turkestan,** Kaz.
62/E2 **Túrkeve,** Hun.
74/C2 **Turkey**
68/F6 **Turkmenistan**
117/G3 **Turks and Caicos** (isls.), UK
42/G3 **Turku** (Åbo), Fin.
42/G3 **Turku Ja Pori** (prov.), Fin.
124/B3 **Turlock,** Ca,US
117/H5 **Turmero,** Ven.
44/D1 **Turnberry,** Sc,UK
116/D4 **Turneffe** (isls.), Belz.
50/B6 **Turnhout,** Belg.
122/F1 **Turnor Lake,** Sk,Can
49/H3 **Turnov,** Czh.
63/G4 **Turnu Măgurele,** Rom.
76/B3 **Turpan,** China
75/E3 **Turpan** (depr.), China
116/F4 **Turquino** (pk.), Cuba
43/D2 **Turriff,** Sc,UK
98/B5 **Turtle** (isls.), SLeo.
122/F2 **Turtleford,** Sk,Can
45/F4 **Turton,** Eng,UK
75/C3 **Turugart Shankou** (pass), China
110/J6 **Turvo** (riv.), Braz.
129/G3 **Tuscaloosa,** Al,US
60/B1 **Tuscano** (arch.), It.
57/J5 **Tuscany** (reg.), It.
124/C2 **Tuscarora,** Nv,US
129/G3 **Tuskegee,** Al,US
131/C3 **Tustin,** Ca,US
49/K3 **Tuszyn,** Pol.
64/H4 **Tutayev,** Rus.
45/G6 **Tutbury,** Eng,UK
84/C6 **Tuticorin,** India
62/E4 **Tutin,** Yugo.
86/D3 **Tutong,** Bru.
63/H3 **Tutrakan,** Bul.
125/H3 **Tuttle Creek** (lake), Ks,US
93/H6 **Tutuila** (isl.), ASam.
130/F2 **Tututalak** (mtn.), Ak,US
76/F2 **Tuul** (riv.), Mong.
42/H3 **Tuusula,** Fin.
68/K4 **Tuva Aut. Rep.,** Rus.
92/G5 **Tuvalu**
72/E4 **Ţuwayq, Jabal** (mts.), SAr.
45/H5 **Tuxford,** Eng,UK
117/N9 **Tuxpan,** Mex.
116/B4 **Tuxtepec,** Mex.
116/C4 **Tuxtla Gutiérrez,** Mex.
58/A1 **Túy,** Sp.
83/D2 **Tuyen Hoa,** Viet.
83/D1 **Tuyen Quang,** Viet.
83/E3 **Tuy Hoa,** Viet.
65/M5 **Tuymazy,** Rus.
72/E2 **Tūysarkān,** Iran
74/C2 **Tuz** (lake), Turk.
124/D4 **Tuzigoot Nat'l Mon.,** Az,US
72/D2 **Ţūz Khurmātū,** Iraq
62/D3 **Tuzla,** Bosn.
64/G4 **T'ver,** Rus.
64/G4 **T'ver Obl.,** Rus.
64/G4 **Tvertsa** (riv.), Rus.
63/G4 **Tvŭrditsa,** Bul.
49/J3 **Twardogóra,** Pol.
43/D3 **Tweed** (riv.), UK
91/E1 **Tweed Heads,** Austl.
50/D4 **Twente** (can.), Neth.
50/D4 **Twente** (reg.), Neth.
127/Q9 **Twenty Mile** (riv.), On,Can
125/G5 **Twin Buttes** (res.), Tx,US
122/E5 **Twin Falls,** Id,US
51/G6 **Twiste** (riv.), Ger.
51/F3 **Twistringen,** Ger.
125/G3 **Two Buttes** (riv.), Co,US
91/D3 **Twofold** (bay), Austl.
123/L4 **Two Harbors,** Mn,US
122/F2 **Two Hills,** Ab,Can
126/C2 **Two Rivers,** Wi,US
47/E1 **Twycross,** Eng,UK
47/F4 **Twyford,** Eng,UK
46/C1 **Twymyn** (riv.), Wal,UK
44/D2 **Twynholm,** Sc,UK
49/K3 **Tychy,** Pol.
47/G1 **Tydd Saint Giles,** Eng,UK
126/E2 **Tyendinaga,** On,Can
129/H3 **Tyger** (riv.), SC,US
45/F4 **Tyldesley,** Eng,UK
128/E3 **Tyler,** Tx,US
77/N1 **Tymovskoye,** Rus.
57/L2 **Týn,** Czh.
125/H2 **Tyndall,** SD,US
43/C2 **Tyndrum,** Sc,UK
45/F2 **Tyne** (riv.), Eng,UK
45/G2 **Tyne & Wear** (co.), Eng,UK
45/G1 **Tynemouth,** Eng,UK
72/C2 **Tyre,** Leb.
74/K5 **Tyre** (Şūr), Leb.
77/L2 **Tyrma** (riv.), Rus.
67/G4 **Tyrnyauz,** Rus.
91/B2 **Tyrrell** (cr.), Austl.
91/B2 **Tyrrell** (lake), Austl.
60/B2 **Tyrrhenian** (sea), It.
131/J8 **Tysons Corner,** Va,US
67/J3 **Tyub-Karagan** (pt.), Kaz.
67/J3 **Tyulen'i** (isls.), Kaz.
67/H3 **Tyuleniy** (isl.), Rus.
65/Q4 **Tyumen',** Rus.
65/Q4 **Tyumen' Obl.,** Rus.
75/C3 **Tyup,** Kyr.
46/B3 **Tywi** (riv.), Wal,UK
46/B1 **Tywyn,** Wal,UK
104/F5 **Tzaneen,** SAfr.

U

93/M5 **Ua Huka** (isl.), FrPol.
93/L5 **Ua Pou** (isl.), FrPol.
108/G4 **Uatumã** (riv.), Braz.
108/E3 **Uaupés** (riv.), Braz.
62/E3 **Ub,** Yugo.
110/D2 **Ubá,** Braz.
53/F2 **Übach-Palenberg,** Ger.
65/Q5 **Ubagan** (riv.), Kaz.
97/J7 **Ubangi** (riv.), Zaire
109/L6 **Ubatã,** Braz.
110/H8 **Ubatuba,** Braz.
82/D5 **Ubay,** Phil.
57/G4 **Ubaye** (riv.), Fr.
50/C5 **Ubbergen,** Neth.
78/B4 **Ube,** Japan
58/D3 **Úbeda,** Sp.
108/G7 **Uberaba** (lake), Bol.
110/C1 **Uberaba,** Braz.
53/F5 **Überherrn,** Ger.
110/B1 **Uberlândia,** Braz.
87/J4 **Ubia** (peak), Indo.
83/D3 **Ubon Ratchathani,** Thai.
58/C4 **Ubrique,** Sp.
108/D5 **Ucayali** (riv.), Peru
48/C3 **Uccle,** Belg.
65/N5 **Uchaly,** Rus.
65/X8 **Uchinskoye,** Rus.
77/N3 **Uchiura** (bay), Japan
48/F2 **Uchte** (riv.), Ger.
69/P4 **Uchur** (riv.), Rus.
53/F5 **Uckange,** Fr.
49/G2 **Uckermark** (reg.), Ger.
47/G5 **Uckfield,** Eng,UK
122/B3 **Ucluelet,** BC,Can
76/F1 **Uda** (riv.), Rus.
84/B3 **Udaipur,** India
42/D4 **Uddevalla,** Swe.
42/F2 **Uddjaure** (lake), Swe.
50/C5 **Uden,** Neth.
50/C5 **Udenhout,** Neth.
84/C4 **Udgīr,** India
73/L2 **Udhampur,** India
57/K3 **Udine,** It.
84/B5 **Udipi,** India
65/L4 **Udmurt Aut. Rep.,** Rus.
83/C2 **Udon Thani,** Thai.
49/H2 **Ueckermünde,** Ger.
79/F2 **Ueda,** Japan
97/K7 **Uele** (riv.), Zaire
51/H3 **Uelzen,** Ger.
79/F3 **Uenohara,** Japan
51/G1 **Uetersen,** Ger.
51/H4 **Uetze,** Ger.
65/M5 **Ufa,** Rus.
65/N5 **Ufa** (riv.), Rus.
47/E3 **Uffington,** Eng,UK
101/B2 **Uganda**
61/F3 **Ugento,** It.
57/G4 **Ugine,** Fr.
77/N2 **Uglegorsk,** Rus.
64/H4 **Uglich,** Rus.
57/L4 **Ugljan** (isl.), Cro.
66/E1 **Ugra** (riv.), Rus.
76/F2 **Ugtaaltsaydam,** Mong.
49/J4 **Uherské Hradiště,** Czh.
57/K2 **Úhlava** (riv.), Czh.
104/C2 **Uíge,** Ang.
67/K2 **Uil** (riv.), Kaz.
102/L11 **Uilkraal** (riv.), SAfr.
67/G4 **Uilpata, Gora** (peak), Rus.
124/E2 **Uinta** (mts.), Ut,US
80/E4 **Ŭisŏng,** SKor.
102/D4 **Uitenhage,** SAfr.
50/B3 **Uitgeest,** Neth.
50/B4 **Uithoorn,** Neth.
92/F4 **Ujae** (atoll), Mrsh.
92/F4 **Ujelang** (atoll), Mrsh.
62/E2 **Újfehértó,** Hun.
79/L10 **Uji,** Japan
79/L10 **Ujitawara,** Japan
84/C3 **Ujjain,** India
87/E5 **Ujung Pandang,** Indo.
65/M3 **Ukhta,** Rus.
124/B3 **Ukiah,** Ca,US
64/E5 **Ukmergė,** Lith.
66/D2 **Ukraine**
76/F2 **Ulaanbaatar** (cap.), Mong.
76/C2 **Ulaangom,** Mong.
76/B2 **Ulaanhus,** Mong.
76/F1 **Ulan-Burgasy** (mts.), Rus.
77/J2 **Ulanhot,** China
76/F1 **Ulan-Ude,** Rus.
75/F5 **Ulan Ul** (lake), China
101/C4 **Ulaya,** Tanz.
80/E4 **Ulchin,** SKor.
62/D5 **Ulcinj,** Yugo.
76/G2 **Uldz** (riv.), Mong.
77/H2 **Ulgain** (riv.), China
84/B4 **Ulhāsnagar,** India
76/D2 **Uliastay,** Mong.
97/L8 **Ulindi** (riv.), Zaire
92/D3 **Ulithi** (atoll), Micr.
58/A1 **Ulla** (riv.), Sp.
91/D2 **Ulladulla,** Austl.
42/F1 **Ullsfjorden** (fjord), Nor.
45/F2 **Ullswater** (lake), Eng,UK
78/B2 **Ullŭng** (isl.), SKor.
55/F1 **Ulm,** Ger.
80/E5 **Ulsan,** SKor.
44/A3 **Ulster** (reg.), Ire.
116/D4 **Ulúa** (riv.), Hon.
72/D1 **Uludoruk** (peak), Turk.
74/C3 **Ulukışla,** Turk.
76/B2 **Ulungur** (lake), China
76/B2 **Ulungur** (riv.), China
92/C7 **Uluru** (Ayers Rock) (peak), Austl.
75/A2 **Ulutau, Gora** (peak), Kaz.
45/E3 **Ulverston,** Eng,UK
91/C4 **Ulverstone,** Austl.
64/F4 **Ul'yanovka,** Rus.
128/C2 **Ulysses,** Ks,US
116/D3 **Umán,** Mex.
66/D2 **Uman',** Ukr.
84/D4 **Umarkot,** India
73/L2 **Umāsi La** (pass), India
92/D5 **Umboi** (isl.), PNG
60/C1 **Umbria** (reg.), It.
57/K5 **Umbro-Marchigiano, Appenino** (range), It.
68/B3 **Ume** (riv.), Swe.
42/G3 **Umeå,** Swe.
42/F2 **Umeälv** (riv.), Swe.
103/E3 **Umfolozi** (riv.), SAfr.
103/E3 **Umgeni** (riv.), SAfr.
73/F4 **Umm as Samīm** (salt dep.), Oman
97/M4 **Umm Durmān** (Omdurman), Sudan
74/K5 **Umm el Fahm,** Isr.
100/C4 **Umm Hibal, Bi'r** (well), Egypt
97/M5 **Umm Ruwābah,** Sudan
130/E5 **Umnak** (isl.), Ak,US
122/C5 **Umpqua** (riv.), Or,US
102/E3 **Umtata,** SAfr.
111/F1 **Umuarama,** Braz.
102/E3 **Umzimvubu** (riv.), SAfr.
62/B3 **Una** (riv.), Bosn., Cro.
109/J7 **Unaí,** Braz.
130/E5 **Unalaska** (isl.), Ak,US
72/C2 **'Unāzah, Jabal** (mtn.), SAr.
124/E3 **Uncompahgre** (plat.), Co,US
123/H4 **Underwood,** ND,US
93/Z17 **Undu** (pt.), Fiji
66/E1 **Unecha,** Rus.
130/F4 **Unga** (isl.), Ak,US
101/D3 **Ungama** (bay), Kenya
119/K3 **Ungava** (bay), Qu,Can
119/J2 **Ungava** (pen.), Qu,Can
66/C3 **Ungeny,** Mol.
109/K4 **União,** Braz.
110/B3 **União da Vitória,** Braz.
109/L5 **União dos Palmares,** Braz.
130/E4 **Unimak** (isl.), Ak,US
108/F4 **Unini** (riv.), Braz.
125/K3 **Union,** Mo,US
131/F5 **Union,** NJ,US
122/D4 **Union,** Or,US
129/H3 **Union,** SC,US
132/K11 **Union City,** Ca,US
131/F5 **Union City,** NJ,US
129/F2 **Union City,** Tn,US
116/E3 **Unión de Reyes,** Cuba
129/G3 **Union Springs,** Al,US
126/E4 **Uniontown,** Pa,US
127/R8 **Unionville,** On,Can
125/J2 **Unionville,** Mo,US
72/F4 **United Arab Emirates**
43/* **United Kingdom**
118/* **United States**
119/T6 **United States** (range), NW,Can
122/F2 **Unity,** Sk,Can
128/D4 **Universal City,** Tx,US
84/B3 **Unjha,** India
51/E5 **Unna,** Ger.
84/D2 **Unnāo,** India
48/F3 **Unstruct** (riv.), Ger.
54/E4 **Unterwalden** (canton), Swi.
74/D2 **Ünye,** Turk.
78/A4 **Unzen-Amakusa Nat'l Park,** Japan
78/B4 **Unzen-dake** (mtn.), Japan
65/K4 **Unzha** (riv.), Rus.
79/E2 **Uozu,** Japan
117/J6 **Upata,** Ven.
104/E2 **Upemba Nat'l Park,** Zaire
102/C3 **Upington,** SAfr.
84/B3 **Upleta,** India
120/U10 **Upolu** (pt.), Hi,US
93/H6 **Upolu** (isl.), WSam.
124/C2 **Upper** (lake), Ca,US
129/H1 **Upper Arlington,** Oh,US
122/D3 **Upper Arrow** (lake), BC,Can
57/K2 **Upper Austria** (prov.), Aus.
131/E6 **Upper Darby,** Pa,US
47/G5 **Upper Dicker,** Eng,UK
99/E4 **Upper East** (reg.), Gha.
89/H7 **Upper Hutt,** NZ
125/J2 **Upper Iowa** (riv.), Ia,US
122/C5 **Upper Klamath** (lake), Or,US
44/B2 **Upperlands,** NI,UK
126/C2 **Upper Peninsula** (pen.), Mi,US
123/L5 **Upper Peoria** (lake), Il,US
123/K3 **Upper Red** (lake), Mn,US
47/E3 **Upper Thames** (val.), Eng,UK
99/E4 **Upper West** (reg.), Gha.
47/F1 **Uppingham,** Eng,UK
42/F4 **Uppsala,** Swe.
42/F3 **Uppsala** (co.), Swe.
130/D3 **Upright** (cape), Ak,US
90/B2 **Upstart** (bay), Austl.
123/G4 **Upton,** Wy,US
46/D2 **Upton upon Severn,** Eng,UK
72/E2 **Ur** (ruins), Iraq
79/H7 **Uraga** (chan.), Japan
68/F3 **Ural** (mts.), Rus.
68/F5 **Ural** (riv.), Rus., Kaz.
67/J2 **Ural'sk,** Kaz.
67/J2 **Ural'sk Obl.,** Kaz.
118/F3 **Uranium City,** Sk,Can
108/F3 **Uraricoera** (riv.), Braz.
79/F3 **Urawa,** Japan
68/G3 **Uray,** Rus.
79/H7 **Urayasu,** Japan
126/B3 **Urbana,** Il,US
126/D3 **Urbana,** Oh,US
45/G3 **Ure** (riv.), Eng,UK
116/E6 **Ureña,** CR
124/E5 **Ures,** Mex.
79/M10 **Ureshino,** Japan
74/D3 **Urfa,** Turk.
51/G6 **Urft** (riv.), Ger.
68/G5 **Urgench,** Uzb.
42/H1 **Urho Kekkosen Nat'l Park,** Fin.
55/E4 **Uri** (canton), Swi.
108/F2 **Urimáan,** Ven.
117/N8 **Urique** (riv.), Mex.
50/C3 **Urk,** Neth.
74/A2 **Urla,** Turk.
63/H3 **Urlaţi,** Rom.
77/L2 **Urmi** (riv.), Rus.
72/D1 **Urmia** (lake), Iran
45/F5 **Urmston,** Eng,UK
62/E4 **Uroševac,** Yugo.
44/E1 **Urr Water** (riv.), Sc,UK
109/J6 **Uruaçu,** Braz.
116/A4 **Uruapan,** Mex.
108/D6 **Urubamba** (riv.), Peru
108/G4 **Urubu** (riv.), Braz.
109/K5 **Uruçuí** (mts.), Braz.
109/J7 **Uruçuía** (riv.), Braz.
111/E2 **Uruguaiana,** Braz.
111/E3 **Uruguay**
111/E2 **Uruguay** (riv.), SAm.
76/B3 **Ürümqi,** China
69/R5 **Urup** (isl.), Rus.
110/B4 **Urussanga,** Braz.
77/H1 **Uryumkan** (riv.), Rus.
67/G2 **Uryupinsk,** Rus.
63/H3 **Urziceni,** Rom.
78/B4 **Usa,** Japan
65/N2 **Usa** (riv.), Rus.
74/B2 **Uşak,** Turk.
113/N7 **Usborne** (peak), Falk.
78/B4 **Ushibuka,** Japan
79/J7 **Ushiku,** Japan
75/C2 **Ushtobe,** Kaz.
113/K8 **Ushuaia,** Arg.
84/C6 **Usilampatti,** India
46/D3 **Usk,** Wal,UK
46/D3 **Usk** (riv.), Wal,UK
63/J5 **Üsküdar,** Turk.
51/G5 **Uslar,** Ger.
66/F1 **Usman',** Rus.
76/E1 **Usol'ye-Sibirskoye,** Rus.
82/D5 **Uson,** Phil.
112/C2 **Uspallata** (pass), Arg., Chile
54/C5 **Ussel,** Fr.
54/C5 **Usses** (riv.), Fr.
77/L2 **Ussuri** (Wusuli) (riv.), Rus., China
77/L3 **Ussuriysk,** Rus.
60/C3 **Ustica** (isl.), It.
69/L4 **Ust'-Ilimsk,** Rus.
49/H3 **Ústí nad Labem,** Czh.
49/J1 **Ustka,** Pol.
69/S4 **Ust'-Kamchatsk,** Rus.
75/D2 **Ust'-Kamenogorsk,** Kaz.
69/L4 **Ust'-Kut,** Rus.
76/E1 **Ust'-Ordynskiy,** Rus.
49/M4 **Ustrzyki Dolne,** Pol.
65/K3 **Ust'ya** (riv.), Rus.
67/K4 **Ustyurt** (plat.), Kaz., Uzb.
75/D3 **Usu,** China
78/B4 **Usuki,** Japan
116/D5 **Usulután,** ESal.
116/C4 **Usumacinta** (riv.), Mex.
124/E3 **Utah** (state), US
124/D2 **Utah** (lake), Ut,US
79/L10 **Utano,** Japan
125/G3 **Ute** (cr.), NM,US
64/E5 **Utena,** Lith.
83/C3 **Uthai Thani,** Thai.
126/F3 **Utica,** NY,US
58/E3 **Utiel,** Sp.
123/K2 **Utik** (lake), Mb,Can
122/E2 **Utikuma** (lake), Ab,Can
92/G3 **Utirik** (atoll), Mrsh.
92/G5 **Utiroa,** Kiri.
84/D2 **Utraulā,** India
50/C4 **Utrecht,** Neth.
50/C4 **Utrecht** (prov.), Neth.
58/C4 **Utrera,** Sp.
79/F2 **Utsunomiya,** Japan
83/C2 **Uttaradit,** Thai.
75/C5 **Uttarkashi,** India
84/C2 **Uttar Pradesh** (state), India
45/G6 **Uttoxeter,** Eng,UK
117/H4 **Utuado,** PR
92/F6 **Utupua** (isl.), Sol.
93/K6 **Uturoa,** FrPol.
76/G2 **Uulbayan,** Mong.
76/E1 **Üür** (riv.), Mong.
76/C1 **Üüreg** (lake), Mong.
76/C1 **Uus** (lake), Mong.
42/H3 **Uusimaa** (prov.), Fin.
108/E3 **Uva** (riv.), Col.
128/D4 **Uvalde,** Tx,US
65/K4 **Uval, Northern** (hills), Rus.
67/G2 **Uvarovo,** Rus.
75/F1 **Uvs Nuur** (lake), Mong.
78/C4 **Uwajima,** Japan
97/L6 **Uwayl,** Sudan
81/B3 **Uxin Qi,** China
116/D3 **Uxmal** (ruins), Mex.
65/P5 **Uy** (riv.), Kaz., Rus.
76/E2 **Uyanga,** Mong.
76/C2 **Üyench,** Mong.
108/E8 **Uyuni,** Bol.
68/G5 **Uzbekistan**
66/B2 **Uzhgorod,** Ukr.
66/F1 **Uzlovaya,** Rus.
63/H5 **Uzunköprü,** Turk.

V

102/C3 **Vaal** (riv.), SAfr.
102/E2 **Vaaldam** (res.), SAfr.
53/F2 **Vaals,** Neth.
53/E2 **Vaalsberg** (hill), Neth.
42/G3 **Vaasa** (prov.), Fin.
42/G3 **Vaasa** (Vasa), Fin.

180

Vaass – Waddā

50/C4 **Vaassen**, Neth.
62/D2 **Vác**, Hun.
132/K10 **Vaca** (mts.), Ca,US
110/B4 **Vacaria**, Braz.
132/L10 **Vacaville**, Ca,US
119/J2 **Vachon** (riv.), Qu,Can
55/F3 **Vaduz** (cap.), Lcht.
64/J3 **Vaga** (riv.), Rus.
62/B3 **Vaganski vrh** (peak), Cro.
65/R4 **Vagay** (riv.), Rus.
42/E4 **Vaggeryd**, Swe.
49/J4 **Vah** (riv.), Slvk.
93/M6 **Vahitahi** (isl.), FrPol.
73/K5 **Vaijāpur**, India
125/F3 **Vail**, Co,US
52/C5 **Vailly-sur-Aisnes**, Fr.
92/G5 **Vaitupu** (isl.), Tuv.
74/D2 **Vakfıkebir**, Turk.
68/J3 **Vakh** (riv.), Rus.
73/K1 **Vākhān** (mts.), Afg.
73/J1 **Vakhsh** (riv.), Trkm.
54/D5 **Valais** (canton), Swi.
50/C5 **Valburg**, Neth.
64/G4 **Valdai** (hills), Rus.
53/F6 **Val-de-Bide**, Fr.
58/C3 **Valdecañas** (res.), Sp.
52/B6 **Val-de-Marne** (dept.), Fr.
42/F4 **Valdemarsvik**, Swe.
59/M8 **Valdemorillo**, Sp.
58/D3 **Valdepeñas**, Sp.
58/C2 **Valderaduey** (riv.), Sp.
112/E4 **Valdés** (pen.), Arg.
112/B3 **Valdivia**, Chile
52/A5 **Val-d'Oise** (dept.), Fr.
126/E1 **Val d'Or**, Qu,Can
129/H4 **Valdosta**, Ga,US
58/A1 **Valdoviño**, Sp.
122/D5 **Vale**, Or,US
122/D2 **Valemount**, BC,Can
110/K7 **Valença**, Braz.
59/E3 **Valencia**, Sp.
59/E3 **Valencia** (aut. comm.), Sp.
59/F3 **Valencia** (gulf), Sp.
117/H5 **Valencia**, Ven.
58/B3 **Valencia de Alcántara**, Sp.
52/C3 **Valenciennes**, Fr.
63/H3 **Vălenii de Munte**, Rom.
125/G2 **Valentine**, Ne,US
128/B4 **Valentine**, Tx,US
57/H4 **Valenza**, It.
117/G6 **Valera**, Ven.
64/E4 **Valga**, Est.
110/G7 **Valhinos**, Braz.
56/D5 **Valier** (mtn.), Fr.
60/A2 **Valinco** (gulf), Fr.
62/D3 **Valjevo**, Yugo.
53/E2 **Valkenburg**, Neth.
50/C6 **Valkenswaard**, Neth.
116/D3 **Valladolid**, Mex.
58/C2 **Valladolid**, Sp.
59/E3 **Vall de Uxó**, Sp.
59/N9 **Vallecas**, Sp.
57/G5 **Vallecrosia**, It.
57/G4 **Valle d'Aosta** (reg.), It.
117/L7 **Valle de Guadalupe**, Mex.
117/H6 **Valle de la Pascua**, Ven.
59/M8 **Valle de los Caídos**, Sp.
117/N8 **Valle de Zaragoza**, Mex.
117/G5 **Valledupar**, Col.
108/F7 **Vallegrande**, Bol.
59/X16 **Vallehermoso**, Canl.,Sp.
50/C4 **Valleikanaal** (can.), Neth.
132/K10 **Vallejo**, Ca,US
111/B2 **Vallenar**, Chile
53/G3 **Vallendar**, Ger.
117/L7 **Valle San Telmo**, Mex.
60/D5 **Valletta** (cap.), Malta
123/J4 **Valley City**, ND,US
131/G4 **Valley Cottage**, NY,US
126/D2 **Valley East**, On,Can
127/M7 **Valleyfield**, Qu,Can
131/E5 **Valley Forge Nat'l Hist. Park**, Pa,US
131/G5 **Valley Stream**, NY,US
122/D2 **Valleyview**, Ab,Can
112/E3 **Vallimanca** (riv.), Arg.
59/F2 **Valls**, Sp.
122/G3 **Val Marie**, Sk,Can
59/M8 **Valmayor** (res.), Sp.
51/F6 **Valme** (riv.), Ger.
64/E4 **Valmiera**, Lat.
61/F2 **Valona** (bay), Alb.
84/C5 **Vālpārai**, India
112/C2 **Valparaíso**, Chile
112/C2 **Valparaíso** (reg.), Chile
117/P9 **Valparaíso**, Mex.
124/C3 **Valparaiso**, Fl,US
126/C3 **Valparaiso**, In,US
62/D3 **Valpovo**, Cro.
56/F4 **Valréas**, Fr.
102/D2 **Vals** (riv.), SAfr.
84/B3 **Valsād**, India
102/B4 **Valsbaai** (bay), SAfr.
66/F2 **Valuyki**, Rus.
131/B2 **Val Verde**, Ca,US
58/B4 **Valverde del Camino**, Sp.
42/G3 **Vammala**, Fin.
74/E2 **Van**, Turk.
74/E2 **Van** (lake), Turk.
93/L7 **Vanavaro** (isl.), FrPol.
128/E3 **Van Buren**, Ar,US
127/H2 **Van Buren**, Me,US
125/K3 **Van Buren**, Mo,US
122/C3 **Vancouver**, BC,Can
122/B3 **Vancouver** (isl.), BC,Can
122/C4 **Vancouver**, Wa,US
130/L3 **Vancouver** (mtn.), Yk,Can, Ak,US
105/L **Vanda**, Ant.
126/B4 **Vandalia**, Il,US
125/K3 **Vandalia**, Mo,US
102/D2 **Vanderbijl Park**, SAfr.
122/B2 **Vanderhoof**, BC,Can
53/F6 **Vandoeuvre-lès-Nancy**, Fr.
42/E4 **Vänern** (lake), Swe.
42/E4 **Vänersborg**, Swe.
103/H8 **Vangaindrano**, Madg.
50/C2 **Van Harinxmakanaal** (can.), Neth.
83/D1 **Van Hoa**, Viet.
128/B4 **Van Horn**, Tx,US
119/R7 **Vanier** (isl.), NW,Can
92/F6 **Vanikoro** (isl.), Sol.
87/K4 **Vanimo**, PNG
77/N2 **Vanino**, Rus.
42/F3 **Vännäs**, Swe.
56/E2 **Vanne** (riv.), Fr.
56/B3 **Vannes**, Fr.
83/E3 **Van Ninh**, Viet.
57/G4 **Vanoise Nat'l Park**, Fr.
102/E3 **Vanreenenpas** (pass), SAfr.
87/J4 **Van Rees** (mts.), Indo.
119/H2 **Vansittart** (isl.), NW,Can
42/H3 **Vantaa**, Fin.
92/G6 **Vanua Levu** (isl.), Fiji
92/F6 **Vanuatu**
126/C3 **Van Wert**, Oh,US
83/D1 **Van Yen**, Viet.
57/G5 **Var** (riv.), Fr.
72/F1 **Varāmīn**, Iran
84/D2 **Vārānāsi**, India
42/J1 **Varangerfjorden** (fjord), Nor.
42/J1 **Varangerhalvøya** (pen.), Nor.
60/D2 **Varano** (lake), It.
62/C2 **Varaždin**, Cro.
57/H4 **Varazze**, It.
42/E4 **Varberg**, Swe.
62/E5 **Vardar** (riv.), Macd.
48/E1 **Varde**, Den.
51/F2 **Varel**, Ger.
127/P6 **Varennes**, Qu,Can
52/A4 **Varennes** (riv.), Fr.
56/E3 **Varennes-Vauzelles**, Fr.
62/D3 **Vareš**, Bosn.
57/H4 **Varese**, It.
110/G6 **Vargem do Sul**, Braz.
109/K5 **Vargem Grande**, Braz.
110/H6 **Varginha**, Braz.
42/C4 **Varhaug**, Nor.
42/H3 **Varkaus**, Fin.
42/E3 **Värmland** (co.), Swe.
63/H4 **Varna**, Bul.
63/H4 **Varna** (reg.), Bul.
42/E4 **Värnamo**, Swe.
62/D2 **Várpalota**, Hun.
74/E2 **Varto**, Turk.
44/B5 **Vartry** (res.), Ire.
44/B5 **Vartry** (riv.), Ire.
110/C1 **Várzea da Palma**, Braz.
109/G7 **Várzea Grande**, Braz.
64/H2 **Varzuga** (riv.), Rus.
62/C2 **Vas** (co.), Hun.
109/L5 **Vasa Barris** (riv.), Braz.
49/M4 **Vásárosnamény**, Hun.
42/G3 **Vasa** (Vaasa), Fin.
65/K2 **Vashka** (riv.), Rus.
132/C3 **Vashon** (isl.), Wa,US
66/D2 **Vasil'kov**, Ukr.
63/H2 **Vaslui**, Rom.
63/H2 **Vaslui** (co.), Rom.
126/D3 **Vassar**, Mi,US
61/G4 **Vassés** (Bassae) (ruins), Gre.
110/K7 **Vassouras**, Braz.
42/F4 **Västerås**, Swe.
42/F2 **Västerbotten** (co.), Swe.
42/F4 **Västerhaninge**, Swe.
42/F3 **Västernorrland** (co.), Swe.
42/F4 **Västervik**, Swe.
42/E3 **Västmanland** (co.), Swe.
64/C3 **Vastmanland** (co.), Swe.
60/D1 **Vasto**, It.
57/J2 **Vaterstetten**, Ger.
60/C2 **Vatican City**
42/P7 **Vatnajökull** (glac.), Ice.
63/G2 **Vatra Dornei**, Rom.
42/E4 **Vättern** (lake), Swe.
93/Y18 **Vatukoula**, Fiji
54/C4 **Vaud** (canton), Swi.
127/M7 **Vaudreuil**, Qu,Can
127/Q8 **Vaughan**, On,Can
125/F4 **Vaughn**, NM,US
56/F4 **Vaulx-en-Velin**, Fr.
56/F5 **Vauvert**, Fr.
52/D4 **Vaux** (riv.), Fr.
122/E3 **Vauxhall**, Ab,Can
52/B3 **Vaux-Vraucourt**, Fr.
93/H6 **Vava'u Group** (isls.), Tonga
84/D6 **Vavuniya**, SrL.
42/E4 **Växjö**, Swe.
68/F3 **Vaygach** (isl.), Rus.
110/C1 **Vazante**, Braz.
110/G8 **Vázea Paulista**, Braz.
64/G5 **Vazuza** (res.), Rus.
50/D4 **Vecht** (riv.), Neth.
51/F3 **Vechta**, Ger.
51/E4 **Vechte** (riv.), Ger.
62/D2 **Vecsés**, Hun.
63/G3 **Vedea** (riv.), Rom.
112/E2 **Vedia**, Arg.
50/D2 **Veendam**, Neth.
50/C4 **Veenendaal**, Neth.
50/A5 **Veerse Meer** (res.), Neth.
42/D2 **Vega** (isl.), Nor.
130/B6 **Vega** (pt.), Ak,US
42/D2 **Vegafjorden** (fjord), Nor.
50/C5 **Veghel**, Neth.
61/G2 **Vegorítis** (lake), Gre.
122/E2 **Vègreville**, Ab,Can
42/H3 **Vehkalahti**, Fin.
58/C4 **Vejer de la Frontera**, Sp.
48/E1 **Vejle**, Den.
48/E1 **Vejle** (co.), Den.
117/G5 **Vela** (cape), Col.
59/S12 **Velas**, Azor,Port.
50/E6 **Velbert**, Ger.
57/L3 **Velden am Wörthersee**, Aus.
50/C6 **Veldhoven**, Neth.
50/D5 **Velen**, Ger.
62/B2 **Velenje**, Slov.
58/C4 **Vélez-Málaga**, Sp.
58/D4 **Vélez-Rubio**, Sp.
110/C1 **Velhas** (Araguari) (riv.), Braz.
62/C3 **Velika Gorica**, Cro.
62/E3 **Velika Plana**, Yugo.
64/F4 **Velikaya** (riv.), Rus.
64/F4 **Velikiye Luki**, Rus.
64/K3 **Velikiy Ustyug**, Rus.
63/G4 **Veliko Tŭrnovo**, Bul.
63/G4 **Velingrad**, Bul.
49/J4 **Velké Meziříčí**, Czh.
49/K4 **Veľký Krtiš**, Slvk.
60/C2 **Velletri**, It.
51/G6 **Vellmar**, Ger.
59/N8 **Vellón** (res.), Sp.
84/C5 **Vellore**, India
64/J3 **Vel'sk**, Rus.
50/C4 **Veluwe** (reg.), Neth.
50/C4 **Veluwemeer** (lake), Neth.
50/C4 **Veluwezoom Nat'l Park**, Neth.
123/H3 **Velva**, ND,US
112/E2 **Venado Tuerto**, Arg.
60/D2 **Venafro**, It.
110/A4 **Venâncio Aires**, Braz.
57/G4 **Venaria**, It.
57/G5 **Vence**, Fr.
110/B2 **Venceslau Brás**, Braz.
58/A3 **Vendas Novas**, Port.
56/D3 **Vendôme**, Fr.
59/F2 **Vendrell**, Sp.
57/J4 **Veneto** (reg.), It.
57/K4 **Venezia** (gulf), It.
57/K4 **Venezia** (Venice), It.
108/E2 **Venezuela**
117/G5 **Venezuela** (gulf), Col., Ven.
84/B4 **Vengurla**, India
130/G4 **Veniaminof** (vol.), Ak,US
129/H5 **Venice**, Fl,US
57/K4 **Venice** (Venezia), It.
56/F4 **Vénissieux**, Fr.
84/C5 **Venkatagiri**, India
50/D6 **Venlo**, Neth.
42/C4 **Vennesla**, Nor.
60/D2 **Venosa**, It.
50/C5 **Venray**, Neth.
64/D4 **Venta** (riv.), Lat., Lith.
58/C2 **Venta de Baños**, Sp.
93/L6 **Vent, Iles du** (isls.), FrPol.
93/K6 **Vent, Iles sous le** (isls.), FrPol.
47/E5 **Ventnor**, Eng,UK
64/D4 **Ventspils**, Lat.
131/A2 **Ventura** (San Buenaventura), Ca,US
60/B1 **Venturina**, It.
93/X15 **Vénus** (pt.), FrPol.
116/C4 **Venustiano Carranza**, Mex.
111/D2 **Vera**, Arg.
116/B4 **Veracruz**, Mex.
116/B3 **Veracruz** (state), Mex.
110/B4 **Veranópolis**, Braz.
84/B3 **Verāval**, India
57/H4 **Verbania**, It.
57/H4 **Vercelli**, It.
42/D3 **Verdal**, Nor.
110/B1 **Verdão** (riv.), Braz.
112/E3 **Verde** (bay), Arg.
110/H6 **Verde** (riv.), Braz.
117/N8 **Verde** (riv.), Mex.
111/E1 **Verde** (riv.), Par.
96/B5 **Verde** (cape), Sen.
124/E4 **Verde** (riv.), Az,US
58/B1 **Verde, Costa** (coast), Sp.
109/K7 **Verde Grande** (riv.), Braz.
51/G3 **Verden**, Ger.
125/J3 **Verdigris** (riv.), Ks, Ok,US
110/B1 **Verdinho** (riv.), Braz.
56/F5 **Verdon** (riv.), Fr.
127/N7 **Verdun**, Qu,Can
53/E5 **Verdun-sur-Meuse**, Fr.
102/D2 **Vereeniging**, SAfr.
65/M4 **Vereshchagino**, Rus.
49/M4 **Veretskiy Pereval** (pass), Ukr.
98/B4 **Verga** (cape), Gui.
58/D1 **Vergara**, Sp.
127/F2 **Vergennes**, Vt,US
61/H2 **Vergína** (ruins), Gre.
58/B2 **Verín**, Sp.
64/F1 **Verkhnetulomskiy** (res.), Rus.
69/N3 **Verkhoyansk** (range), Rus.
51/F5 **Verl**, Ger.
52/C4 **Vermand**, Fr.
122/F2 **Vermilion**, Ab,Can
122/F2 **Vermilion** (riv.), Ab,Can
125/K2 **Vermilion** (riv.), Il,US
123/K4 **Vermillion** (range), Mn,US
123/J5 **Vermillion**, SD,US
125/H2 **Vermillion** (riv.), SD,US
127/F2 **Vermont** (state), US
124/E2 **Vernal**, Ut,US
56/D2 **Verneuil-sur-Avre**, Fr.
102/C3 **Verneukpan** (salt pan), SAfr.
122/D3 **Vernon**, BC,Can
52/A5 **Vernon**, Fr.
128/D3 **Vernon**, Tx,US
132/Q15 **Vernon Hills**, Il,US
53/F5 **Verny**, Fr.
129/H5 **Vero Beach**, Fl,US
61/H2 **Véroia**, Gre.
57/J4 **Verona**, It.
52/B6 **Verrières-le-Buisson**, Fr.
52/B6 **Versailles**, Fr.
126/C4 **Versailles**, Ky,US
66/E2 **Verskla** (riv.), Rus., Ukr.
51/F4 **Versmold**, Ger.
58/E1 **Vert** (riv.), Fr.
55/G4 **Vertana** (peak), It.
56/C3 **Vertou**, Fr.
53/E2 **Verviers**, Belg.
47/E5 **Verwood**, Eng,UK
46/B6 **Veryan** (bay), Eng,UK
53/F2 **Vesdre** (riv.), Belg.
67/G3 **Veselyy** (res.), Rus.
52/D5 **Vesle** (riv.), Fr.
54/C2 **Vesoul**, Fr.
42/C4 **Vest-Agder** (co.), Nor.
42/E1 **Vesterålen** (isls.), Nor.
42/E2 **Vestfjorden** (fjord), Nor.
42/D4 **Vestfold** (co.), Nor.
48/F1 **Vest-Sjælland** (co.), Den.
42/E1 **Vestvågøya** (isl.), Nor.
62/C2 **Veszprém**, Hun.
62/C2 **Veszprém** (co.), Hun.
62/E2 **Vészto**, Hun.
102/D3 **Vet** (riv.), SAfr.
42/E4 **Vetlanda**, Swe.
65/K4 **Vetluga** (riv.), Rus.
60/C1 **Vetralla**, It.
56/D3 **Veude** (riv.), Fr.
52/B1 **Veurne**, Belg.
54/C5 **Vevey**, Swi.
53/F2 **Veybach** (riv.), Ger.
56/D4 **Vézère** (riv.), Fr.
74/C2 **Vezirköprü**, Turk.
108/E7 **Viacha**, Bol.
109/K4 **Viana**, Braz.
58/B1 **Viana del Bollo**, Sp.
58/A2 **Viana do Castelo**, Port.
58/A2 **Viana do Castelo** (dist.), Port.
50/C5 **Vianen**, Neth.
83/C2 **Viangchan** (Vientiane) (cap.), Laos
58/C4 **Viar** (riv.), Sp.
57/J5 **Viareggio**, It.
56/E4 **Viaur** (riv.), Fr.
42/D4 **Viborg**, Den.
60/E3 **Vibo Valentia**, It.
59/G2 **Vic**, Sp.
58/D4 **Vícar**, Sp.
113/S12 **Vicente López**, Arg.
57/J4 **Vicenza**, It.
64/J4 **Vichuga**, Rus.
56/E3 **Vichy**, Fr.
129/F3 **Vicksburg**, Ms,US
60/C1 **Vico** (lake), It.
110/D2 **Viçosa**, Braz.
61/G3 **Vicou Gorge Nat'l Park**, Gre.
52/C5 **Vic-sur-Aisne**, Fr.
53/F6 **Vic-sur-Seille**, Fr.
101/B3 **Victoria** (lake), Afr.
112/E2 **Victoria**, Arg.
91/C3 **Victoria** (state), Austl.
116/D4 **Victoria** (peak), Belz.
85/F3 **Victoria** (peak), Burma
122/C3 **Victoria** (cap.), BC,Can
118/E1 **Victoria** (isl.), NW,Can
118/F2 **Victoria** (str.), NW,Can
127/Q8 **Victoria**, On,Can
112/B3 **Victoria**, Chile
82/B3 **Victoria** (cap.), HK
87/E2 **Victoria** (peak), Phil.
63/G3 **Victoria**, Rom.
128/D4 **Victoria**, Tx,US
117/F3 **Victoria de las Tunas**, Cuba
105/L **Victoria Land** (reg.), Ant.
101/B2 **Victoria Nile** (riv.), Ugan.
127/G2 **Victoriaville**, Qu,Can
131/C1 **Victorville**, Ca,US
103/F3 **Vidal** (cape), SAfr.
129/H3 **Vidalia**, Ga,US
129/F4 **Vidalia**, La,US
110/B3 **Videira**, Braz.
63/G3 **Videle**, Rom.
62/F4 **Vidin**, Bul.
84/C3 **Vidisha**, India
128/E4 **Vidor**, Tx,US
56/E5 **Vidourle** (riv.), Fr.
56/C3 **Vie** (riv.), Fr.
112/E4 **Viedma**, Arg.
113/J7 **Viedma** (lake), Arg.
58/C1 **Vieja** (mtn.), Sp.
128/B4 **Vieja** (mts.), Tx,US
53/E3 **Vielsalm**, Belg.
51/H5 **Vienenburg**, Ger.
131/J8 **Vienna**, Va,US
126/D4 **Vienna**, WV,US
49/J4 **Vienna** (Wien) (cap.), Aus.
56/F4 **Vienne**, Fr.
56/D3 **Vienne** (riv.), Fr.
83/C2 **Vientiane** (Viangchan) (cap.), Laos
53/D6 **Viere** (riv.), Fr.
50/D5 **Vierlingsbeek**, Neth.
53/E4 **Vierre** (riv.), Fr.
50/D6 **Viersen**, Ger.
56/E3 **Vierzon**, Fr.
60/E2 **Vieste**, It.
83/D2 **Vietnam**
83/D1 **Viet Tri**, Viet.
52/C3 **Vieux-Condé**, Fr.
117/J5 **Vieux Fort**, StL.
82/D5 **Viga**, Phil.
82/D4 **Vigan**, Phil.
57/H4 **Vigevano**, It.
109/J4 **Vigia**, Braz.
60/C2 **Viglio** (peak), It.
56/C5 **Vignemale** (mtn.), Fr.
52/B6 **Vigneux**, Fr.
57/J4 **Vignola**, It.
58/A1 **Vigo**, Sp.
53/F5 **Vigy**, Fr.
73/K2 **Vihāri**, Pak.
42/H3 **Viitasaari**, Fin.
84/D4 **Vijayawada**, India
61/F2 **Vijosë** (riv.), Alb.
42/D4 **Vikersund**, Nor.
63/F5 **Vikhren** (peak), Bul.
122/F2 **Viking**, Ab,Can
92/F6 **Vila** (cap.), Van.
59/G2 **Viladecans**, Sp.
59/V14 **Vila de Porto Santo**, Madr.,Port.
104/G4 **Vila de Sena**, Moz.
58/A2 **Vila do Conde**, Port.
59/T13 **Vila do Porto**, Azor,Port.
59/K7 **Vilafranca del Penedès**, Sp.
58/A3 **Vila Franca de Xira**, Port.
59/T13 **Vila Franca do Campo**, Azor.,Port.
56/B3 **Vilaine** (riv.), Fr.
103/H7 **Vilanandro** (cape), Madg.
58/A2 **Vila Nova de Gaia**, Port.
59/F2 **Vilanova i la Geltrú**, Sp.
59/K7 **Vilanova i la Geltru**, Sp.
58/B2 **Vila Real**, Port.
58/B2 **Vila Real** (dist.), Port.
58/B4 **Vila Real de Santo António**, Port.
110/D2 **Vila Velha Argolas**, Braz.
63/F3 **Vîlcea** (co.), Rom.
42/F2 **Vilhelmina**, Swe.
108/F6 **Vilhena**, Braz.
64/E5 **Viliya** (riv.), Bela.
64/E4 **Viljandi**, Est.
69/K2 **Vil'kitsogo** (str.), Rus.
112/Q9 **Villa Alemana**, Chile
111/D2 **Villa Angela**, Arg.
58/E1 **Villaba**, Sp.
58/D1 **Villablino**, Sp.
117/H6 **Villa Bruzual**, Ven.
112/E2 **Villa Cañas**, Arg.
58/D3 **Villacañas**, Sp.
111/D3 **Villa Carlos Paz**, Arg.
58/D3 **Villacarrillo**, Sp.
57/K3 **Villach**, Aus.
112/E2 **Villa Constitución**, Arg.
58/A1 **Villa de Cruces**, Sp.
58/C4 **Villa del Río**, Sp.
111/C3 **Villa Dolores**, Arg.
116/C4 **Villa Flores**, Mex.
58/B3 **Villafranca de los Barros**, Sp.
116/A2 **Villa Frontera**, Mex.
58/A1 **Villagarcía**, Sp.
128/E4 **Village Mills**, Tx,US
113/F3 **Villa Gesell**, Arg.
112/F1 **Villaguay**, Arg.
116/C4 **Villahermosa**, Mex.
117/N7 **Villa Hidalgo**, Mex.
59/E3 **Villajoyosa**, Sp.
58/B1 **Villalba**, Sp.
58/B2 **Villalcampo** (res.), Sp.
112/E2 **Villa María**, Arg.
58/C4 **Villamartín**, Sp.
108/F8 **Villa Montes**, Bol.
116/D4 **Villanueva**, Hon.
58/A1 **Villanueva de Arosa**, Sp.
58/C3 **Villanueva de Córdoba**, Sp.
58/D3 **Villanueva del Arzobispo**, Sp.
58/C3 **Villanueva de la Serena**, Sp.
58/D3 **Villanueva de los Infantes**, Sp.
131/C3 **Villa Park**, Ca,US
132/Q16 **Villa Park**, Il,US
112/D3 **Villa Regina**, Arg.
59/E3 **Villarreal de los Infantes**, Sp.
112/B3 **Villarrica**, Chile
112/B3 **Villarrica** (lake), Chile
111/E2 **Villarrica**, Par.
112/C3 **Villarrica Nat'l Park**, Chile
58/D3 **Villarrobledo**, Sp.
58/D3 **Villarrubia de los Ojos**, Sp.
112/F2 **Villa San José**, Arg.
108/F7 **Villa Serrano**, Bol.
111/C2 **Villa Unión**, Arg.
117/N9 **Villa Unión**, Mex.
108/D3 **Villavicencio**, Col.
58/C1 **Villaviciosa**, Sp.
59/N9 **Villaviciosa de Odon**, Sp.
108/E8 **Villazón**, Bol.
56/E4 **Villefranche-de-Rouergue**, Fr.
56/F4 **Villefranche-sur-Saône**, Fr.
52/B6 **Villejuif**, Fr.
59/E3 **Villena**, Sp.
52/C2 **Villeneuve-d'Ascq**, Fr.
56/F5 **Villeneuve-lès-Avignon**, Fr.
52/B6 **Villeneuve-Saint-Georges**, Fr.
56/D4 **Villeneuve-sur-Lot**, Fr.
56/D5 **Villeneuve-Tolosane**, Fr.
52/B6 **Villeparisis**, Fr.
128/E4 **Ville Platte**, La,US
52/C5 **Villers-Cotterêts**, Fr.
53/F6 **Villers-lès-Nancy**, Fr.
52/C3 **Villers-Outreaux**, Fr.
53/E5 **Villerupt**, Fr.
55/E1 **Villingen-Schwenningen**, Ger.
84/C5 **Villupuram**, India
49/N1 **Vilnius** (cap.), Lith.
42/H3 **Vilppula**, Fin.
57/K2 **Vils** (riv.), Ger.
57/K2 **Vilshofen**, Ger.
52/D2 **Vilvoorde**, Belg.
69/M3 **Vilyuy** (range), Rus.
69/N3 **Vilyuy** (riv.), Rus.
55/H4 **Vipiteno** (Sterzing), It.
58/B1 **Vimianzo**, Sp.
42/E4 **Vimmerby**, Swe.
52/B3 **Vimy**, Fr.
96/H6 **Vina** (riv.), Camr.
112/C2 **Viña del Mar**, Chile
57/G5 **Vinaigre** (mtn.), Fr.
59/F2 **Vinaroz**, Sp.
105/H **Vincennes** (bay), Ant.
52/B6 **Vincennes**, Fr.
126/C4 **Vincennes**, In,US
131/B2 **Vincent**, Ca,US
42/F2 **Vindeln**, Swe.
127/R9 **Vineland**, On,Can
126/F4 **Vineland**, NJ,US
83/D2 **Vinh**, Viet.
110/G8 **Vinhedo**, Braz.
83/D4 **Vinh Long**, Viet.
83/D4 **Vinh Quoi**, Viet.
83/E3 **Vinh Thanh**, Viet.
83/D1 **Vinh Yen**, Viet.
62/F5 **Vinica**, Macd.
125/J3 **Vinita**, Ok,US
62/F3 **Vînju Mare**, Rom.
62/D3 **Vinkovci**, Cro.
66/D2 **Vinnitsa**, Ukr.
66/D2 **Vinnitsa Obl.**, Ukr.
66/B2 **Vinogradov**, Ukr.
28/E9 **Vinson** (peak), Ant.
52/A5 **Viosne** (riv.), Fr.
55/H4 **Vipiteno** (Sterzing), It.
82/D5 **Virac**, Phil.
74/D3 **Viranşehir**, Turk.
84/B4 **Virār**, India
123/H3 **Virden**, Mb,Can
56/C2 **Vire**, Fr.
104/B4 **Virei**, Ang.
111/C7 **Vírgenes** (cape), Arg.
127/R9 **Virgil**, On,Can
117/J4 **Virgin** (isls.), UK, US
124/D3 **Virgin** (riv.), US
126/E5 **Virginia** (state), US
123/K4 **Virginia**, Mn,US
126/F4 **Virginia Beach**, Va,US
124/C3 **Virginia City**, Nv,US
83/D3 **Virochey**, Camb.
52/D3 **Viroin** (riv.), Belg.
126/B3 **Viroqua**, Wi,US
62/C3 **Virovitica**, Cro.
53/E4 **Virton**, Belg.
84/C6 **Virudunagar**, India
52/B6 **Viry-Châtillon**, Fr.
60/D1 **Vis** (isl.), Cro.
84/D4 **Visākhapatnam**, India
124/C3 **Visalia**, Ca,US
82/D5 **Visayan** (sea), Phil.
51/F3 **Visbek**, Ger.
42/F4 **Visby**, Swe.
110/D2 **Visconde do Rio Branco**, Braz.
119/R7 **Viscount Melville** (sound), NW,Can
53/E2 **Visé**, Belg.
62/D4 **Višegrad**, Bosn.
58/B2 **Viseu**, Port.
58/B2 **Viseu** (dist.), Port.
63/G2 **Vişeu de Sus**, Rom.
65/N3 **Vishera** (riv.), Rus.
102/B4 **Vishoek**, SAfr.
84/B3 **Visnagar**, India
62/D3 **Višnjevac**, Cro.
62/D4 **Visoko**, Bosn.
51/G3 **Visselhövede**, Ger.
124/C4 **Vista**, Ca,US
61/J2 **Vistonís** (lake), Gre.
49/K2 **Vistula** (Wisła) (riv.), Pol.
63/G4 **Vit** (riv.), Bul.
123/J3 **Vita**, Mb,Can
57/J5 **Vitalba** (peak), It.
64/F5 **Vitebsk**, Bela.
64/E5 **Vitebsk Obl.**, Bela.
60/C1 **Viterbo**, It.
83/D4 **Vi Thanh**, Viet.
92/G6 **Viti Levu** (isl.), Fiji
76/G1 **Vitim** (plat.), Rus.
76/G1 **Vitim** (riv.), Rus.
110/D2 **Vitória**, Braz.
58/D1 **Vitoria**, Sp.
109/K6 **Vitória da Conquista**, Braz.
109/L5 **Vitória de Santo Antão**, Braz.
63/F4 **Vitosha Nat'l Park**, Bul.
56/C2 **Vitré**, Fr.
56/F5 **Vitrolles**, Fr.
52/D6 **Vitry-le-François**, Fr.
52/B6 **Vitry-sur-Seine**, Fr.
60/D4 **Vittoria**, It.
57/K4 **Vittorio Veneto**, It.
56/F4 **Vivarais** (mts.), Fr.
58/B1 **Vivero**, Sp.
63/H5 **Vize**, Turk.
65/K2 **Vizhas** (riv.), Rus.
84/D4 **Vizianagaram**, India
50/B5 **Vlaardingen**, Neth.
62/F2 **Vlădeasa** (peak), Rom.
67/H4 **Vladikavkaz**, Rus.
64/J4 **Vladimir**, Rus.
64/J5 **Vladimir Obl.**, Rus.
66/C2 **Vladimir-Volynskiy**, Ukr.
77/L3 **Vladivostok**, Rus.
51/E2 **Vlagtwedde**, Neth.
63/G2 **Vlăhiţa**, Rom.
62/E4 **Vlajna** (peak), Yugo.
62/D3 **Vlasenica**, Bosn.
49/H4 **Vlašim**, Czh.
62/F4 **Vlasotince**, Yugo.
50/B2 **Vlieland** (isl.), Neth.
50/C2 **Vliestroom** (chan.), Neth.
50/C5 **Vlijmen**, Neth.
50/A6 **Vlissingen**, Neth.
61/F2 **Vlorë**, Alb.
51/F4 **Vlotho**, Ger.
57/L1 **Vltava** (riv.), Czh.
57/K2 **Vöcklabruck**, Aus.
64/H3 **Vodlozero** (lake), Rus.
50/D5 **Voerde**, Ger.
57/H1 **Vogelsberg** (mts.), Ger.
57/H4 **Voghera**, It.
62/D4 **Vogošća**, Bosn.
57/J1 **Vogtland** (reg.), Ger.
93/U12 **Voh**, NCal.
57/K2 **Vohenstrauss**, Ger.
103/H9 **Vohimena** (cape), Madg.
103/G7 **Vohipeno**, Madg.
101/C3 **Voi**, Kenya
56/F4 **Voiron**, Fr.
56/D2 **Voise** (riv.), Fr.
119/K3 **Voisey** (bay), Nf,Can
52/B5 **Voisne** (riv.), Fr.
62/D5 **Vojosë** (riv.), Alb.
62/D3 **Vojvodina** (aut. prov.), Yugo.
53/F5 **Vöklingen**, Ger.
92/C2 **Volcano** (isls.), Japan
42/C3 **Volda**, Nor.
50/C4 **Volendam**, Neth.
41/J3 **Volga** (riv.), Rus.
64/H3 **Volga-Baltic Wtwy.**, Rus.
67/G3 **Volgodonsk**, Rus.
67/H2 **Volgograd**, Rus.
67/H2 **Volgograd** (res.), Rus.
67/G2 **Volgograd Obl.**, Rus.
50/B5 **Volkerakdam** (dam), Neth.
57/L3 **Völkermarkt**, Aus.
64/G4 **Volkhov**, Rus.
64/F4 **Volkhov** (riv.), Rus.
53/F5 **Völklingen**, Ger.
51/G6 **Volkmarsen**, Ger.
49/N2 **Volkovysk**, Bela.
103/E2 **Volksrust**, SAfr.
53/G5 **Volmunster**, Fr.
64/H4 **Vologda**, Rus.
64/J3 **Vologda Obl.**, Rus.
54/C1 **Vologne** (riv.), Fr.
61/H3 **Vólos**, Gre.
61/H3 **Vólos** (gulf), Gre.
67/H1 **Vol'sk**, Rus.
99/E4 **Volta** (lake), Gha.
99/F5 **Volta** (reg.), Gha.
99/F5 **Volta** (riv.), Gha.
110/J7 **Volta Redonda**, Braz.
57/J5 **Volterra**, It.
60/D2 **Volturno** (riv.), It.
61/H2 **Vólvi** (lake), Gre.
65/L5 **Volzhsk**, Rus.
67/H2 **Volzhskiy**, Rus.
130/H3 **Von Frank** (mtn.), Ak,US
56/D3 **Vonne** (riv.), Fr.
50/B4 **Voorburg**, Neth.
50/B5 **Voorne** (isl.), Neth.
50/B4 **Voorschoten**, Neth.
50/D4 **Voorst**, Neth.
55/F3 **Vorarlberg** (prov.), Aus.
50/D4 **Vorden**, Neth.
55/E4 **Vorderrhein** (riv.), Swi.
56/F4 **Voreppe**, Fr.
65/Q2 **Vorkuta**, Rus.
67/G1 **Vorona** (riv.), Rus.
66/F2 **Voronezh**, Rus.
66/F1 **Voronezh** (riv.), Rus.
67/G2 **Voronezh Obl.**, Rus.
64/G1 **Voron'ya** (riv.), Rus.
53/E1 **Vorst**, Belg.
64/E4 **Võru**, Est.
54/C1 **Vosges** (dept.), Fr.
54/C2 **Vosges** (mts.), Fr.
64/H5 **Voskresensk**, Rus.
42/C3 **Voss**, Nor.
105/V **Vostock** (cape), Ant.
105/H **Vostok**, Ant.
93/K6 **Vostok** (isl.), Kiri.
65/M4 **Votkinsk**, Rus.
65/M4 **Votkinsk** (res.), Rus.
110/C2 **Votorantim**, Braz.
110/B2 **Votuporanga**, Braz.
58/B2 **Vouga** (riv.), Port.
61/H5 **Voúxa, Akra** (cape), Gre.
123/K3 **Voyageurs Nat'l Park**, Mn,US
105/J **Voyeykov Ice Shelf**, Ant.
65/M3 **Voy-Vozh**, Rus.
64/H3 **Vozhe** (lake), Rus.
66/D3 **Voznesensk**, Ukr.
63/H3 **Vrancea** (co.), Rom.
71/S2 **Vrangelya** (isl.), Rus.
62/E4 **Vranje**, Yugo.
49/L4 **Vranov nad Teplou**, Slvk.
63/F4 **Vratsa**, Bul.
62/C3 **Vrbas** (riv.), Bosn.
62/D3 **Vrbas**, Yugo.
102/E2 **Vrede**, SAfr.
50/D4 **Vreden**, Ger.
102/B4 **Vredenburg**, SAfr.
57/L4 **Vrhnika**, Slov.
50/D2 **Vries**, Neth.
50/D4 **Vriezenveen**, Neth.
48/B5 **Vrin** (riv.), Fr.
84/C2 **Vrindāban**, India
62/E4 **Vrnjačka Banja**, Yugo.
62/E3 **Vršac**, Yugo.
102/D2 **Vryburg**, SAfr.
103/E2 **Vryheid**, SAfr.
49/K4 **Vsetín**, Czh.
130/E5 **Vsevidof** (mtn.), Ak,US
49/K4 **Vtáčnik** (peak), Slvk.
62/E4 **Vučitrn**, Yugo.
50/C5 **Vught**, Neth.
62/D3 **Vukovar**, Cro.
122/E3 **Vulcan**, Ab,Can
63/F3 **Vulcan**, Rom.
60/D3 **Vulcano** (isl.), It.
63/F4 **Vŭlchedrŭm**, Bul.
60/B1 **Vulci** (ruins), It.
83/D2 **Vu Liet**, Viet.
83/D4 **Vung Tau**, Viet.
92/G7 **Vunisea**, Fiji
64/E1 **Vuotso**, Fin.
63/F4 **Vŭrshets**, Bul.
84/B3 **Vyāra**, India
65/L4 **Vyatka**, Rus.
65/L4 **Vyatka** (riv.), Rus.
65/L4 **Vyatka Obl.**, Rus.
65/L4 **Vyatskiye Polyany**, Rus.
77/L2 **Vyazemskiy**, Rus.
64/G5 **Vyaz'ma**, Rus.
64/F3 **Vyborg**, Rus.
65/K3 **Vychegda** (riv.), Rus.
49/H3 **Východočeský** (reg.), Czh.
49/L4 **Východoslovenský** (reg.), Slvk.
64/G3 **Vygozero** (lake), Rus.
49/M4 **Vyhorlat** (peak), Slvk.
64/J5 **Vyksa**, Rus.
65/L3 **Vym'** (riv.), Rus.
46/C1 **Vyrnwy** (riv.), Wal,UK
64/G4 **Vyshniy Volochek**, Rus.
49/J4 **Vyškov**, Czh.

W

99/E4 **Wa**, Gha.
50/C5 **Waal** (riv.), Neth.
50/C6 **Waalre**, Neth.
50/C5 **Waalwijk**, Neth.
52/C1 **Waarschoot**, Belg.
122/E2 **Wabasca**, Ab,Can
118/E3 **Wabasca** (riv.), Ab,Can
126/C4 **Wabash** (riv.), Il, In,US
126/C3 **Wabash**, In,US
51/G6 **Wabern**, Ger.
123/K3 **Wabigoon** (lake), On,Can
123/J2 **Wabowden**, Mb,Can
49/K2 **Wąbrzeźno**, Pol.
81/D4 **Wabu** (lake), China
79/L9 **Wachi**, Japan
52/C1 **Wachtebeke**, Belg.
50/D6 **Wachtendonk**, Ger.
128/D4 **Waco**, Tx,US
128/D2 **Waconda** (lake), Ks,US
123/K4 **Waconia**, Mn,US
91/D3 **Wadbilliga Nat'l Park**, Austl.
96/J2 **Waddān**, Libya

182

Wilmi – Zafra

131/E6 **Wilmington,** De,US
129/J3 **Wilmington,** NC,US
126/D4 **Wilmington,** Oh,US
129/H4 **Wilmington Island,** Ga,US
45/F5 **Wilmslow,** Eng,UK
53/H2 **Wilnsdorf,** Ger.
50/B6 **Wilrijk,** Belg.
51/G2 **Wilseder Berg** (peak), Ger.
119/H2 **Wilson** (cape), NW,Can
131/B2 **Wilson** (mt.), Ca,US
129/J3 **Wilson,** NC,US
127/S9 **Wilson,** NY,US
131/E5 **Wilson,** Pa,US
91/C3 **Wilsons Promontory Nat'l Park,** Austl.
47/E4 **Wilton,** Eng,UK
47/E4 **Wiltshire** (co.), Eng,UK
46/E5 **Wimborne Minster,** Eng,UK
52/A2 **Wimereux,** Fr.
102/D3 **Winburg,** SAfr.
46/D4 **Wincanton,** Eng,UK
47/E3 **Winchcombe,** Eng,UK
47/G5 **Winchelsea,** Eng,UK
47/E4 **Winchester,** Eng,UK
126/C4 **Winchester,** Ky,US
129/G3 **Winchester,** Tn,US
126/E4 **Winchester,** Va,US
122/F5 **Wind** (riv.), Wy,US
123/G5 **Wind Cave Nat'l Park,** SD,US
129/H3 **Winder,** Ga,US
45/F3 **Windermere,** Eng,UK
45/F3 **Windermere** (lake), Eng,UK
104/C5 **Windhoek** (cap.), Namb.
123/K5 **Windom,** Mn,US
124/E4 **Window Rock,** Az,US
122/F5 **Wind River** (range), Wy,US
47/E3 **Windrush** (riv.), Eng,UK
90/G8 **Windsor,** Austl.
127/L1 **Windsor,** NF,Can
127/H2 **Windsor,** NS,Can
132/F7 **Windsor,** On,Can
127/G2 **Windsor,** Qu,Can
47/F4 **Windsor,** Eng,UK
117/K5 **Windward** (isls.), NAm.
117/G4 **Windward** (passage), NAm.
122/D3 **Winfield,** BC,Can
125/H3 **Winfield,** Ks,US
47/F3 **Wing,** Eng,UK
45/G2 **Wingate,** Eng,UK
52/C1 **Wingene,** Belg.
127/R10 **Winger,** On,Can
47/H4 **Wingham,** Eng,UK
123/M2 **Winisk,** On,Can
123/M2 **Winisk** (lake), On,Can
123/M2 **Winisk** (riv.), On,Can
123/J3 **Winkler,** Mb,Can
99/E5 **Winneba,** Gha.
126/B3 **Winnebago** (lake), Wi,US
124/C2 **Winnemucca,** Nv,US
123/J5 **Winner,** SD,US
132/Q15 **Winnetka,** Il,US
122/F4 **Winnett,** Mt,US
128/E4 **Winnfield,** La,US
123/J3 **Winnipeg** (cap.), Mb,Can
123/J2 **Winnipeg** (lake), Mb,Can
123/K3 **Winnipeg** (riv.), Mb, On,Can
123/J3 **Winnipeg Beach,** Mb,Can
123/J3 **Winnipegosis,** Mb,Can
123/H2 **Winnipegosis** (lake), Mb,Can
128/F3 **Winnsboro,** La,US
129/H3 **Winnsboro,** SC,US
127/Q9 **Winona,** On,Can
123/L4 **Winona,** Mn,US
50/E2 **Winschoten,** Neth.
46/D4 **Winscombe,** Eng,UK
45/F5 **Winsford,** Eng,UK
46/D4 **Winsley,** Eng,UK
47/F3 **Winslow,** Eng,UK
124/E4 **Winslow,** Az,US
129/H2 **Winston-Salem,** NC,US
50/D2 **Winsum,** Neth.
51/F6 **Winterberg,** Ger.
102/D4 **Winterberge** (mts.), SAfr.
46/D3 **Winterbourne,** Eng,UK
129/H4 **Winter Haven,** Fl,US
129/H4 **Winter Park,** Fl,US
50/D5 **Winterswijk,** Neth.
55/E2 **Winterthur,** Swi.
127/G2 **Winthrop,** Me,US
132/Q15 **Winthrop Harbor,** Il,US
48/F3 **Wipper** (riv.), Ger.
51/H2 **Wipperau** (riv.), Ger.
51/E6 **Wipperfürth,** Ger.
45/G5 **Wirksworth,** Eng,UK
45/E5 **Wirral** (pen.), Eng,UK
47/G1 **Wisbech,** Eng,UK
126/B2 **Wisconsin** (state), US
126/B2 **Wisconsin Rapids,** Wi,US
123/J4 **Wishek,** ND,US
49/K4 **Wisła,** Pol.
49/K1 **Wiślany** (lag.), Pol.
49/K2 **Wisła** (Vistula) (riv.), Pol.
49/L4 **Wisłok** (riv.), Pol.
49/L4 **Wisłoka** (riv.), Pol.
48/F2 **Wismar,** Ger.
53/G5 **Wissembourg,** Fr.
53/G2 **Wissen,** Ger.
47/G1 **Wissey** (riv.), Eng,UK
102/E2 **Witbank,** SAfr.
102/A2 **Witberg** (peak), Namb.
47/G3 **Witham,** Eng,UK
45/H5 **Witham** (riv.), Eng,UK
46/C5 **Witheridge,** Eng,UK
45/J4 **Withernsea,** Eng,UK
130/J3 **Witherspoon** (mtn.), Ak,US
129/H4 **Withlacoochee** (riv.), Fl, Ga,US
45/F4 **Withnell,** Eng,UK
102/D3 **Wit Kei** (riv.), SAfr.
49/J2 **Witkowo,** Pol.
47/E3 **Witney,** Eng,UK
49/H2 **Witnica,** Pol.
53/E2 **Wittem,** Neth.
51/E6 **Witten,** Ger.
48/G3 **Wittenberg,** Ger.
48/F2 **Wittenberge,** Ger.
54/D2 **Wittenheim,** Fr.
47/F1 **Wittering,** Eng,UK
51/H3 **Wittingen,** Ger.
53/F4 **Wittlich,** Ger.
51/E1 **Wittmund,** Ger.
49/G1 **Witton** (pen.), Ger.
48/G2 **Wittstock,** Ger.
102/P12 **Witwatersrand** (reg.), SAfr.
51/G6 **Witzenhausen,** Ger.
46/C4 **Wiveliscombe,** Eng,UK
47/G3 **Wivenhoe,** Eng,UK
132/E6 **Wixom,** Mi,US
49/L2 **Wkra** (riv.), Pol.
49/K1 **Władysławowo,** Pol.
49/K2 **Włocławek,** Pol.
49/K2 **Włocławek** (prov.), Pol.
49/K2 **Włocławskie** (lake), Pol.
49/M3 **Włodawa,** Pol.
49/K3 **Włoszczowa,** Pol.
46/C1 **Wnion** (riv.), Wal,UK
47/F2 **Woburn Sands,** Eng,UK
91/C3 **Wodonga,** Austl.
49/K4 **Wodzisław Śląski,** Pol.
50/B4 **Woerden,** Neth.
53/G6 **Woerth,** Fr.
50/C3 **Wognum,** Neth.
53/F5 **Woippy,** Fr.
87/H5 **Wokam** (isl.), Indo.
77/K2 **Woken** (riv.), China
47/F4 **Woking,** Eng,UK
47/F4 **Wokingham,** Eng,UK
127/S9 **Wolcottsville,** NY,US
92/D4 **Woleai** (atoll), Micr.
130/H2 **Wolf** (mtn.), Ak,US
125/G3 **Wolf** (cr.), Ok, Tx,US
126/B2 **Wolf** (riv.), Wi,US
130/F3 **Wolf Creek** (mtn.), Ak,US
122/E4 **Wolf Creek,** Mt,US
48/G3 **Wolfen,** Ger.
51/H4 **Wolfenbüttel,** Ger.
51/G6 **Wolfhagen,** Ger.
123/G3 **Wolf Point,** Mt,US
51/H4 **Wolfsburg,** Ger.
49/G1 **Wolgast,** Ger.
49/H2 **Woliński Nat'l Park,** Pol.
118/E2 **Wollaston** (pen.), NW,Can
118/F3 **Wollaston** (lake), Sk,Can
113/L8 **Wollaston** (isl.), Chile
47/F2 **Wollaston,** Eng,UK
91/D2 **Wollemi Nat'l Park,** Austl.
91/D2 **Wollongong,** Austl.
102/D2 **Wolmaransstad,** SAfr.
57/J3 **Wolnzach,** Ger.
96/C6 **Wologizi** (range), Libr.
49/L2 **Wołomin,** Pol.
49/J3 **Wołów,** Pol.
102/L10 **Wolseley,** SAfr.
45/G2 **Wolsingham,** Eng,UK
49/J2 **Wolsztyn,** Pol.
52/D2 **Woluwé-Saint-Lambert,** Belg.
50/D3 **Wolvega,** Neth.
46/D1 **Wolverhampton,** Eng,UK
47/F2 **Wolverton,** Eng,UK
126/D2 **Woman** (riv.), On,Can
46/D1 **Wombourne,** Eng,UK
45/G4 **Wombwell,** Eng,UK
132/P15 **Wonder** (lake), Il,US
91/C1 **Wongalarroo** (lake), Austl.
91/C3 **Wonnangatta-Moroka Nat'l Park,** Austl.
80/D3 **Wŏnsan,** NKor.
123/H2 **Wood** (lake), Sk,Can
122/G3 **Wood** (mtn.), Sk,Can
130/K3 **Wood** (mtn.), Yk,Can
127/Q8 **Woodbridge,** On,Can
47/H2 **Woodbridge,** Eng,UK
131/F5 **Woodbridge,** NJ,US
118/E2 **Wood Buffalo Nat'l Park,** Ab, Yk,Can
127/Q9 **Woodburn,** On,Can
44/C2 **Woodburn,** NI,UK
122/C4 **Woodburn,** Or,US
131/E6 **Woodbury,** NJ,US
132/Q16 **Wood Dale,** Il,US
90/D4 **Woodgate Nat'l Park,** Austl.
45/H5 **Woodhall Spa,** Eng,UK
132/F7 **Woodhaven,** Mi,US
132/L9 **Woodland,** Ca,US
125/F3 **Woodland Park,** Co,US
92/E5 **Woodlark** (isl.), PNG
131/K7 **Woodlawn,** Md,US
47/F4 **Woodley,** Eng,UK
131/G5 **Woodmere,** NY,US
132/P16 **Woodridge,** Il,US
45/F6 **Woodseaves,** Eng,UK
127/H2 **Woodstock,** NB,Can
47/E3 **Woodstock,** Eng,UK
132/P15 **Woodstock,** Il,US
126/E4 **Woodstock,** Va,US
129/F4 **Woodville,** Ms,US
128/E4 **Woodville,** Tx,US
125/H3 **Woodward,** Ok,US
46/D5 **Wool,** Eng,UK
46/D4 **Woolavington,** Eng,UK
45/G1 **Woolsington,** Eng,UK
125/H1 **Woonsocket,** SD,US
45/F6 **Woore,** Eng,UK
126/D3 **Wooster,** Oh,US
47/E3 **Wootton Basset,** Eng,UK
102/B4 **Worcester,** SAfr.
46/D2 **Worcester,** Eng,UK
127/G3 **Worcester,** Ma,US
46/D2 **Worcester & Birmingham** (can.), Eng,UK
57/K3 **Wörgl,** Aus.
44/E2 **Workington,** Eng,UK
45/G5 **Worksop,** Eng,UK
122/G4 **Worland,** Wy,US
38/* **World**
50/B4 **Wormer,** Neth.
57/H2 **Worms,** Ger.
57/J2 **Wörnitz** (riv.), Ger.
51/F2 **Worpswede,** Ger.
45/G4 **Worsbrough,** Eng,UK
132/Q16 **Worth,** Il,US
47/F5 **Worthing,** Eng,UK
123/K5 **Worthington,** Mn,US
92/F3 **Wotho** (atoll), Mrsh.
92/G4 **Wotje** (atoll), Mrsh.
46/D3 **Wotton under Edge,** Eng,UK
50/C4 **Woudenberg,** Neth.
50/C5 **Woudrichem,** Neth.
50/B5 **Wouw,** Neth.
87/F4 **Wowoni** (isl.), Indo.
45/H5 **Wragby,** Eng,UK
69/T2 **Wrangel** (isl.), Rus.
130/A5 **Wrangell** (cape), Ak,US
130/K3 **Wrangell** (mts.), Ak,US
130/K3 **Wrangell-Saint Elias Nat'l Park & Prsv.,** Ak,US
45/J5 **Wrangle,** Eng,UK
125/G2 **Wray,** Co,US
45/H6 **Wreake** (riv.), Eng,UK
102/B3 **Wreck** (pt.), SAfr.
46/D1 **Wrekin, The** (hill), Eng,UK
45/F5 **Wrenbury,** Eng,UK
45/F5 **Wrexham,** Wal,UK
123/G5 **Wright,** Wy,US
131/F5 **Wrightstown,** NJ,US
131/C2 **Wrightwood,** Ca,US
47/G3 **Writtle,** Eng,UK
49/J3 **Wrocław,** Pol.
49/J3 **Wrocław** (prov.), Pol.
118/D1 **Wrottesley** (cape), NW,Can
46/D1 **Wroxeter,** Eng,UK
47/H1 **Wroxham,** Eng,UK
49/J2 **Września,** Pol.
49/J3 **Wschowa,** Pol.
85/K2 **Wu** (riv.), China
81/C3 **Wu'an,** China
81/C5 **Wuchang** (lake), China
77/K2 **Wudalianchi,** China
81/B4 **Wudang Shan** (mtn.), China
81/B3 **Wuding** (riv.), China
81/C5 **Wuhan,** China
81/D5 **Wuhu,** China
76/F3 **Wujia** (riv.), China
50/E6 **Wülfrath,** Ger.
82/B2 **Wuling** (mts.), China
99/H5 **Wum,** Camr.
51/F2 **Wümme** (riv.), Ger.
84/C3 **Wūn,** India
51/F5 **Wünnenberg,** Ger.
51/G4 **Wunstorf,** Ger.
124/E4 **Wupatki Nat'l Mon.,** Az,US
51/E6 **Wüpper** (riv.), Ger.
51/E6 **Wuppertal,** Ger.
75/C4 **Wuqia,** China
53/F2 **Würm** (riv.), Ger.
99/G3 **Wurno,** Nga.
53/F2 **Würselen,** Ger.
57/H2 **Würzburg,** Ger.
77/H5 **Wushan** (lake), China
81/C5 **Wusheng Guan** (pass), China
75/C3 **Wushi,** China
51/G6 **Wüstegarten** (peak), Ger.
77/L2 **Wusuli** (Ussuri) (riv.), China, Rus.
81/C3 **Wutai Shan** (peak), China
98/C4 **Wuteve** (peak), Libr.
50/B6 **Wuustwezel,** Belg.
81/D5 **Wuwei,** China
81/E5 **Wuxi,** China
81/C5 **Wuxue,** China
82/C2 **Wuyi** (mts.), China
77/K2 **Wuyur** (riv.), China
83/E2 **Wuzhi** (mts.), China
81/D2 **Wuzhi Shan** (peak), China
85/K3 **Wuzhou,** China
132/F7 **Wyandotte,** Mi,US
91/D2 **Wyangale** (dam), Austl.
131/F4 **Wyckoff,** NJ,US
46/D3 **Wye** (riv.), UK
46/D4 **Wylye** (riv.), Eng,UK
45/G6 **Wymeswold,** Eng,UK
47/H1 **Wymondham,** Eng,UK
129/F3 **Wynne,** Ar,US
90/F6 **Wynnum,** Austl.
123/G3 **Wynyard,** Sk,Can
122/F5 **Wyoming** (state), US
126/C3 **Wyoming,** Mi,US
122/F5 **Wyoming** (peak), Wy,US
124/E2 **Wyoming** (range), Wy,US
91/B2 **Wyperfeld Nat'l Park,** Austl.
45/F4 **Wyre** (riv.), Eng,UK
49/L2 **Wyszków,** Pol.
126/D4 **Wytheville,** Va,US

X

83/D4 **Xa Binh Long,** Viet.
116/B4 **Xadani,** Mex.
75/E5 **Xainza,** China
84/E2 **Xaitongmoin,** China
103/F2 **Xai-Xai,** Moz.
83/D1 **Xam Nua,** Laos
83/D3 **Xan** (riv.), Viet.
50/D5 **Xanten,** Ger.
61/J2 **Xánthi,** Gre.
110/A3 **Xanxerê,** Braz.
97/Q7 **Xarardheere,** Som.
83/E4 **Xa Song Luy,** Viet.
104/C3 **Xassengue,** Ang.
83/D3 **Xa Tho Thanh,** Viet.
109/J6 **Xavantes** (mts.), Braz.
110/B2 **Xavantes** (res.), Braz.
83/D4 **Xa Vo Dat,** Viet.
75/D3 **Xayar,** China
116/D3 **Xel-há** (ruins), Mex.
126/D4 **Xenia,** Oh,US
83/D2 **Xeno,** Laos
81/E2 **Xi** (lake), China
77/E3 **Xi** (riv.), China
77/F5 **Xi** (riv.), China
77/H5 **Xi** (riv.), China
82/B3 **Xi** (riv.), China
85/H2 **Xiaguan,** China
82/C3 **Xiamen,** China
81/B4 **Xi'an,** China
82/B2 **Xiang** (riv.), China
81/C4 **Xiangfan,** China
83/C2 **Xiang Khoang** (plat.), Laos
82/B2 **Xiangtan,** China
82/B2 **Xiangxiang,** China
81/C5 **Xianning,** China
81/C5 **Xiantao,** China
76/F5 **Xianyang,** China
81/C3 **Xiao** (riv.), China
82/B2 **Xiao** (riv.), China
85/H2 **Xiao** (riv.), China
77/J1 **Xiaobole** (peak), China
81/C5 **Xiaogan,** China
77/K2 **Xiao Hinggang** (mts.), China
81/D3 **Xiaoqing** (riv.), China
81/L9 **Xiaoshan,** China
81/C3 **Xiaowutai Shan** (peak), China
85/F2 **Xibaxa** (riv.), China
81/C4 **Xicheng Shan** (mtn.), China
116/B3 **Xicohténcatl,** Mex.
116/B3 **Xicotepec,** Mex.
81/C4 **Xifei** (riv.), China
76/F4 **Xifeng,** China
77/J3 **Xifeng,** China
82/A2 **Xifeng,** China
84/E2 **Xigazê,** China
76/E5 **Xihan** (riv.), China
75/F4 **Xijir Ulan** (lake), China
81/E2 **Xiliao** (riv.), China
82/C2 **Xin** (riv.), China
81/D5 **Xin'an** (riv.), China
81/D5 **Xin'anjiang** (res.), China
82/B3 **Xinfengjiang** (res.), China
81/E2 **Xingcheng,** China
104/C2 **Xinge,** Ang.
81/D4 **Xinghua,** China
75/D3 **Xingjiang Uygur Aut. Reg.,** China
77/L3 **Xingkai** (lake), China
105/H6 **Xingo Nat'l Park,** Braz.
81/C3 **Xingtai,** China
109/H4 **Xingu** (riv.), Braz.
81/C4 **Xingyang,** China
76/E4 **Xining** (Xining Shi), China
81/C3 **Xinji,** China
71/J5 **Xinjiang** (reg.), China
81/D4 **Xintai,** China
81/C4 **Xinxiang,** China
81/C4 **Xinyang,** China
82/B2 **Xinyu,** China
75/D3 **Xinyuan,** China
76/E5 **Xiqing** (mts.), China
109/K6 **Xique-Xique,** Braz.
82/B2 **Xiu** (riv.), China
84/E2 **Xixabangma** (peak), China
85/J3 **Xiyang** (riv.), China
81/E3 **Xizhong** (isl.), China
82/C2 **Xu** (riv.), China
81/C2 **Xuanhua,** China
81/C4 **Xuchang,** China
81/E5 **Xuedou** (peak), China
76/D4 **Xugin Gol** (riv.), China
81/B4 **Xun** (riv.), China
82/B3 **Xun** (riv.), China
77/K2 **Xunke,** China
81/D4 **Xuyi,** China
81/D4 **Xuzhou,** China

Y

76/E6 **Ya'an,** China
96/G7 **Yabassi,** Camr.
97/N7 **Yabēlo,** Eth.
116/E5 **Yablis,** Nic.
76/F1 **Yablonovyy** (ridge), Rus.
79/G2 **Yabuki,** Japan
82/A2 **Yachi** (riv.), China
79/J7 **Yachiyo,** Japan
110/A4 **Yacuí** (riv.), Braz.
108/F8 **Yacuiba,** Bol.
84/C4 **Yādgīr,** India
79/L9 **Yagi,** Japan
96/J5 **Yagoua,** Camr.
76/D4 **Yagradagzê** (peak), China
113/G2 **Yaguarón** (riv.), Uru.
79/N10 **Yahagi** (riv.), Japan
74/C2 **Yahyalı,** Turk.
79/F2 **Yaita,** Japan
79/F3 **Yaizu,** Japan
77/J2 **Yakeshi,** China
122/C4 **Yakima,** Wa,US
122/C4 **Yakima** (riv.), Wa,US
99/E3 **Yako,** Burk.
97/K7 **Yakoma,** Zaire
63/F4 **Yakoruda,** Bul.
78/B5 **Yaku-Kirishima Nat'l Park,** Japan
79/K9 **Yakuno,** Japan
130/K4 **Yakutat** (bay), Ak,US
69/N3 **Yakut Aut. Rep.,** Rus.
69/N3 **Yakutsk,** Rus.
83/C5 **Yala,** Thai.
125/K4 **Yalobusha** (riv.), Ms,US
96/J6 **Yaloké,** CAfr.
85/H2 **Yalong** (riv.), China
66/E3 **Yalta,** Ukr.
80/C2 **Yalu** (riv.), China, NKor.
78/B4 **Yamaga,** Japan
79/G1 **Yamagata,** Japan
79/F1 **Yamagata** (pref.), Japan
78/B3 **Yamaguchi** (pref.), Japan
68/G2 **Yamal** (pen.), Rus.
68/G3 **Yamal-Nenets Aut. Okr.,** Rus.
79/F3 **Yamanashi** (pref.), Japan
90/B2 **Yamanie Falls Nat'l Park,** Austl.
65/N5 **Yamantau, Gora** (peak), Rus.
79/N9 **Yamaoka,** Japan
79/L10 **Yamashiro,** Japan
79/L10 **Yamato-Kōriyama,** Japan
78/D3 **Yamatotakada,** Japan
79/M10 **Yamazoe,** Japan
97/L7 **Yambio,** Sudan
63/H4 **Yambol,** Bul.
83/B1 **Yamethin,** Burma
87/K4 **Yamin** (peak), Indo.
90/A4 **Yamma Yamma** (lake), Austl.
79/G1 **Yamoto,** Japan
98/D5 **Yamoussoukro** (cap.), IvC.
124/F2 **Yampa** (riv.), Co,US
84/C2 **Yamuna** (riv.), India
73/L2 **Yamunānagar,** India
85/E2 **Yamzho Yumco** (lake), China
81/B3 **Yan** (riv.), China
84/D6 **Yan** (riv.), SrL.
69/P3 **Yana** (riv.), Rus.
78/B4 **Yanagawa,** Japan
78/C4 **Yanai,** Japan
65/M4 **Yanaul,** Rus.
81/C4 **Yancheng,** China
81/E4 **Yancheng,** China
93/T12 **Yandé** (isl.), NCal.
85/G4 **Yandoon,** Burma
97/K7 **Yangambi,** Zaire
85/G2 **Yangbi** (riv.), China
81/L8 **Yangcheng** (lake), China
82/C2 **Yangdang** (mts.), China
80/D2 **Yanggang-Do** (prov.), NKor.
81/C2 **Yanggao,** China
80/E3 **Yanggu,** SKor.
83/B2 **Yangon** (Rangoon) (cap.), Burma
81/C3 **Yangquan,** China
85/K3 **Yangshan,** China
85/K3 **Yangshuo,** China
81/D5 **Yangtze** (Chang) (riv.), China
97/P5 **Yangudi Rassa Nat'l Park,** Eth.
80/E3 **Yangyang,** SKor.
81/C2 **Yangyuan,** China
81/D4 **Yangzhou,** China
77/K3 **Yanji,** China
99/H4 **Yankari Game Rsv.,** Nga.
123/J5 **Yankton,** SD,US
81/C3 **Yanmen Guan** (pass), China
81/E3 **Yantai,** China
81/C2 **Yantong Shan** (mtn.), China
91/G5 **Yan Yean** (res.), Austl.
78/D3 **Yao,** Japan
96/H7 **Yaoundé** (cap.), Camr.
92/C4 **Yap** (isls.), Micr.
108/E3 **Yapacana Nat'l Park,** Ven.
87/J4 **Yapen** (isl.), Indo.
87/J4 **Yapen** (str.), Indo.
131/H5 **Yaphank,** NY,US
117/M8 **Yaqui,** Mex.
117/N8 **Yaqui** (riv.), Mex.
47/E5 **Yar** (riv.), Eng,UK
117/F3 **Yara,** Cuba
87/J4 **Yaramaniapuka** (mtn.), Indo.
65/K4 **Yaransk,** Rus.
74/B3 **Yardımcı** (pt.), Turk.
47/H1 **Yare** (riv.), Eng,UK
79/E2 **Yari-ga-take** (mtn.), Japan
63/J5 **Yarımca,** Turk.
75/C4 **Yarkant** (riv.), China
127/H3 **Yarmouth,** NS,Can
64/H4 **Yaroslavl',** Rus.
64/H4 **Yaroslavl' Obl.,** Rus.
91/G5 **Yarra** (riv.), Austl.
108/C2 **Yarumal,** Col.
92/G6 **Yasawa Group** (isls.), Fiji
66/C1 **Yasel'da** (riv.), Bela.
79/H7 **Yashio,** Japan
79/K10 **Yashiro,** Japan
67/L2 **Yasnyy,** Rus.
83/D3 **Yasothon,** Thai.
72/F4 **Yas, Sir Bani** (isl.), UAE
79/M9 **Yasu,** Japan
79/M10 **Yasu** (riv.), Japan
78/C3 **Yasugi,** Japan
108/C4 **Yasuni Nat'l Park,** Ecu.
79/G2 **Yatabe,** Japan
74/B3 **Yatağan,** Turk.
46/D3 **Yate,** Eng,UK
47/F4 **Yateley,** Eng,UK
99/E3 **Yatenga** (prov.), Burk.
125/J3 **Yates Center,** Ks,US
118/G2 **Yathkyed** (lake), NW,Can
79/M9 **Yatomi,** Japan
79/E2 **Yatsuo,** Japan
78/B4 **Yatsushiro,** Japan
74/K6 **Yaṭṭah,** WBnk.
46/D4 **Yatton,** Eng,UK
108/D5 **Yavari** (riv.), Peru
84/C3 **Yavatmāl,** India
68/H2 **Yavay** (pen.), Rus.
117/F6 **Yaviza,** Pan.
74/M9 **Yavne,** Isr.
79/J7 **Yawahara,** Japan
79/L10 **Yawata,** Japan
78/C4 **Yawatahama,** Japan
116/C4 **Yaxchilán** (ruins), Mex.
47/F2 **Yaxley,** Eng,UK
73/F2 **Yazd,** Iran
129/F3 **Yazoo** (riv.), Ms,US
129/F3 **Yazoo City,** Ms,US
57/L2 **Ybbs** (riv.), Aus.
83/B3 **Ye,** Burma
45/G4 **Yeadon,** Eng,UK
46/B6 **Yealmpton,** Eng,UK
83/C4 **Yeay Sen** (cape), Camb.
75/C4 **Yecheng,** China
59/E3 **Yecla,** Sp.
66/F1 **Yefremov,** Rus.
67/G3 **Yegorlak** (riv.), Rus.
74/M8 **Yehud,** Isr.
97/M7 **Yei,** Sudan
65/P4 **Yekaterinburg Obl.,** Rus.
65/P4 **Yekaterinburg** (Sverdlovsk), Rus.
65/M5 **Yelabuga,** Rus.
67/G2 **Yelan',** Rus.
66/F1 **Yelets,** Rus.
69/Q4 **Yelizavety** (cape), Rus.
69/R4 **Yelizovo,** Rus.
77/J4 **Yellow** (sea), Asia
129/G4 **Yellow** (riv.), Al, Fl,US
123/G3 **Yellow Grass,** Sk,Can
77/H4 **Yellow** (Huang) (riv.), China
118/E2 **Yellowknife** (cap.), NW,Can
118/E2 **Yellowknife** (riv.), NW,Can
123/G4 **Yellowstone** (riv.), Mt,US
122/F4 **Yellowstone** (lake), Wy,US
122/F4 **Yellowstone Nat'l Park,** Wy,US
128/E2 **Yellville,** Ar,US
46/B6 **Yelverton,** Eng,UK
76/D4 **Yema** (riv.), China
72/E5 **Yemen**
66/F2 **Yenakiyevo,** Ukr.
85/F3 **Yenangyaung,** Burma
83/D1 **Yen Bai,** Viet.
99/E4 **Yendi,** Gha.
75/C4 **Yengisar,** China
66/E4 **Yenice** (riv.), Turk.
74/C2 **Yeniceoba,** Turk.
63/J5 **Yenişehir,** Turk.
68/J3 **Yenisey** (riv.), Rus.
68/K4 **Yeniseysk,** Rus.
83/D1 **Yen Minh,** Viet.
46/D5 **Yeo** (riv.), Eng,UK
73/K4 **Yeola,** India
46/D5 **Yeovil,** Eng,UK
90/C3 **Yeppoon,** Austl.
61/H3 **Yerakovoúni** (peak), Gre.
52/A4 **Yères** (riv.), Fr.
67/H4 **Yerevan** (cap.), Arm.
124/C3 **Yerington,** Nv,US
74/C2 **Yerköy,** Turk.
75/C1 **Yermak,** Kaz.
68/H4 **Yermentau,** Kaz.
74/K6 **Yeroḫam,** Isr.
52/B6 **Yerres,** Fr.
108/C6 **Yerupaja** (peak), Peru
74/K6 **Yerushalayim** (Jerusalem) (cap.), Isr.
85/G3 **Yesagyo,** Burma
75/A1 **Yesil',** Kaz.
74/D2 **Yeşilirmak** (riv.), Turk.
67/G3 **Yessentuki,** Rus.
46/D5 **Yetminster,** Eng,UK
56/B3 **Yeu** (isl.), Fr.
84/B3 **Yevla,** India
67/H4 **Yevlakh,** Azer.
66/E3 **Yevpatoriya,** Ukr.
66/G3 **Yeya** (riv.), Rus.
66/F3 **Yeysk,** Rus.
81/C4 **Yi** (riv.), China
113/G2 **Yi** (riv.), Uru.
61/H2 **Yiannitsá,** Gre.
61/J4 **Yíaros** (isl.), Gre.
81/B5 **Yichang,** China
82/B2 **Yichun,** China
82/C2 **Yihuang,** China
77/K2 **Yilan,** China
74/D2 **Yıldızeli,** Turk.
77/J1 **Yilehuli** (mts.), China
81/B4 **Yima,** China
77/J2 **Yimin** (riv.), China
76/F3 **Yin** (mts.), China
76/F4 **Yinchuan,** China
81/C4 **Ying** (riv.), China
81/C5 **Yingcheng,** China
77/J3 **Yingkou,** China
82/C2 **Yingtan,** China
75/D3 **Yining,** China
97/M6 **Yirol,** Sudan
81/F2 **Yitong** (riv.), China
81/C4 **Yiyang,** China
82/B2 **Yiyang,** China
81/D4 **Yizheng,** China
44/E6 **Y Llethr** (mtn.), Wal,UK
42/G3 **Ylöjärvi,** Fin.
128/D4 **Yoakum,** Tx,US
78/D3 **Yodo** (riv.), Japan
69/P4 **Yoduma** (riv.), Rus.
96/J4 **Yogoum** (well), Chad
86/D5 **Yogyakarta,** Indo.
122/D3 **Yoho Nat'l Park,** BC,Can
96/J7 **Yokadouma,** Camr.
78/E3 **Yōkaichi,** Japan
78/D3 **Yokawa,** Japan
78/E3 **Yokkaichi,** Japan
79/H7 **Yokohama,** Japan
79/F3 **Yokosuka,** Japan
96/H6 **Yola,** Nga.
83/C2 **Yom** (riv.), Thai.
104/B1 **Yombi,** Gabon
82/A3 **Yon** (riv.), China
56/C3 **Yon** (riv.), Fr.
78/C3 **Yonago,** Japan
79/G2 **Yonezawa,** Japan
82/C2 **Yong'an,** China
80/E5 **Yŏngch'ŏn,** SKor.
85/G3 **Yongde,** China
81/H7 **Yongding** (riv.), China
80/E4 **Yŏngdŏk,** SKor.
85/J3 **Yongfu,** China
80/E4 **Yŏngju,** SKor.
81/C3 **Yongnian,** China
80/E4 **Yŏngwŏl,** SKor.
82/B2 **Yongzhou,** China
131/G5 **Yonkers,** NY,US
56/E2 **Yonne** (riv.), Fr.
79/H7 **Yono,** Japan
75/C4 **Yopurga,** China
131/C3 **Yorba Linda,** Ca,US
89/D2 **York** (cape), Austl.
127/R8 **York,** On,Can
127/H1 **York** (riv.), Qu,Can
45/G4 **York,** Eng,UK
129/F3 **York,** Al,US
125/H2 **York,** Ne,US
129/H3 **York,** SC,US
126/E4 **York** (riv.), Va,US
89/C4 **Yorke** (pen.), Austl.
123/J1 **York Landing,** Mb,Can
45/G4 **York Minster,** Eng,UK
45/F3 **Yorkshire Dales Nat'l Park,** Eng,UK
45/H3 **Yorkshire Wolds** (hills), Eng,UK
123/H3 **Yorkton,** Sk,Can
45/G3 **York, Vale of** (val.), Eng,UK
116/D4 **Yoro,** Hon.
79/M9 **Yorō,** Japan
79/J7 **Yōrō** (riv.), Japan
79/M10 **Yoroi-zaki** (pt.), Japan
76/F2 **Yöröö,** Mong.
45/F6 **Yorton,** Eng,UK
99/F4 **Yorubaland** (plat.), Nga.
124/C3 **Yosemite Nat'l Park,** Ca,US
78/C4 **Yoshida,** Japan
78/D3 **Yoshii** (riv.), Japan
79/H7 **Yoshikawa,** Japan
78/D3 **Yoshimo** (riv.), Japan
79/L10 **Yoshino,** Japan
78/E3 **Yoshino-Kumano Nat'l Park,** Japan
65/L4 **Yoshkar-Ola,** Rus.
80/D5 **Yŏsu,** SKor.
77/N3 **Yōtei-san** (mtn.), Japan
79/J7 **Yotsukaidō,** Japan
82/A2 **You** (riv.), China
82/A3 **You** (riv.), China
91/D2 **Young,** Austl.
113/F2 **Young,** Uru.
127/R9 **Youngstown,** NY,US
126/D3 **Youngstown,** Oh,US
77/L2 **Youyi,** China
108/E2 **Yoví** (peak), Ven.
74/C2 **Yozgat,** Turk.
132/E7 **Ypsilanti,** Mi,US
44/D6 **Yr Eifl** (mtn.), Wal,UK
124/B2 **Yreka,** Ca,US
52/B2 **Yser** (riv.), Fr.
49/G1 **Ystad,** Swe.
46/C3 **Ystalyfera,** Wal,UK
46/C3 **Ystradgynlais,** Wal,UK
46/C3 **Ystrad Mynach,** Wal,UK
46/C2 **Ystwyth** (riv.), Wal,UK
43/D2 **Ythan** (riv.), Sc,UK
85/J3 **Yu** (riv.), China
82/D3 **Yū** (peak), Tai.
81/C5 **Yuan** (lake), China
82/B2 **Yuan** (riv.), China
85/H3 **Yuan** (riv.), China
81/C3 **Yuanping,** China
124/B3 **Yuba City,** Ca,US
77/N3 **Yūbari,** Japan
131/C2 **Yucaipa,** Ca,US
116/D4 **Yucatan** (pen.), Mex.
116/D3 **Yucatan** (state), Mex.
116/D3 **Yucatan** (chan.), NAm.
124/D4 **Yucca,** Az,US
81/C3 **Yuci,** China
81/D5 **Yuexi,** China
85/H2 **Yuexi,** China
82/B2 **Yueyang,** China
65/K3 **Yug** (riv.), Rus.
65/P1 **Yugorskiy** (pen.), Rus.
62/D3 **Yugoslavia**
81/L9 **Yuhang,** China
79/F2 **Yūki,** Japan
118/B2 **Yukon** (riv.), Can., US
130/K2 **Yukon-Charley Rivers Nat'l Prsv.,** Ak,US
130/L3 **Yukon Crossing,** Yk,Can
118/C2 **Yukon Territory** (terr.), Can.
74/F3 **Yüksekova,** Turk.
72/D1 **Yüksekova,** Turk.
78/B4 **Yukuhashi,** Japan
83/E2 **Yulin,** China
85/K3 **Yulin,** China
81/B3 **Yulin** (riv.), China
81/D5 **Yuling Guan** (pass), China
124/D4 **Yuma,** Az,US
125/G2 **Yuma,** Co,US
112/B3 **Yumbel,** Chile
104/E1 **Yumbi,** Zaire
108/C3 **Yumbo,** Col.
76/D4 **Yumen,** China
81/C5 **Yun** (riv.), China
74/B2 **Yunak,** Turk.
108/E7 **Yungas** (reg.), Bol.
112/B3 **Yungay,** Chile
85/H3 **Yunnan** (prov.), China
81/D4 **Yuntai Shan** (peak), China
81/D2 **Yunwu Shan** (peak), China
81/D4 **Yunyan** (riv.), China
81/C3 **Yunzhong Shan** (mtn.), China
85/J2 **Yuping,** China
81/H7 **Yuqiao** (res.), China
78/D3 **Yura** (riv.), Japan
68/J4 **Yurga,** Rus.
108/C5 **Yurimaguas,** Peru
75/C4 **Yurungkax** (riv.), China
65/N5 **Yuryuzan'** (riv.), Rus.
81/D3 **Yutian,** China
53/F5 **Yutz,** Fr.
81/C3 **Yu Xian,** China
81/C4 **Yu Xian,** China
82/D1 **Yuyao,** China
77/N2 **Yuzhno-Sakhalinsk,** Rus.
66/D2 **Yuzhnyy Bug** (riv.), Ukr.
52/A6 **Yvelines** (dept.), Fr.
54/C4 **Yverdon,** Swi.
53/D3 **Yvoir,** Belg.
56/E3 **Yzeure,** Fr.

Z

50/B4 **Zaandam,** Neth.
49/L2 **Ząbki,** Pol.
49/J3 **Ząbkowice Śląskie,** Pol.
73/H2 **Zābol,** Iran
49/J4 **Zábřeh,** Czh.
49/K3 **Zabrze,** Pol.
116/D5 **Zacapa,** Guat.
116/A4 **Zacapú,** Mex.
116/A3 **Zacatecas,** Mex.
117/P9 **Zacatecas,** Mex.
116/A3 **Zacatecas** (state), Mex.
116/D5 **Zacatecoluca,** ESal.
129/F4 **Zachary,** La,US
116/B3 **Zacualtipán,** Mex.
62/B3 **Zadar,** Cro.
83/B4 **Zadetkyi** (isl.), Burma
76/D5 **Zadoi,** China
58/B3 **Zafra,** Sp.

Żagań – Żywie

Acknowledgements

Several years ago, we saw an opportunity to create a radically new map-making system. Advances in technology put within our grasp a means of producing maps more efficiently and more accurately than ever before. At the heart of our plan was a computerized geographic database – one which would enable maps to be created and changed at whim.

This world atlas is one of the first products of our new system. Behind it hums another world, a bustling, close-knit family of talented and innovative cartographers, researchers, editors, artists, technicians and scholars. In the five years it has taken to create our new system, their world has seen almost as many upheavals as our own planet. For their constancy and faith in a project which sometimes seemed so daunting, for their patience and creativity to explore new technologies, and for the teamwork which enabled us to realize such an ambitious goal, we are deeply grateful.

We are especially grateful for the support of our many contributors, whose efforts made this volume better. In particular, we wish to thank Mitchell Feigenbaum, a brilliant scientist and dear friend, whose illumination of the world around him extends to the art – and science – of cartography. His genius is ever-present in this atlas, from his revolutionary map projection to his pioneering software, which was crucial to the success of our computer mapping system.

At last, a map-making system that moves as fast as the world is changing. As new technology continues to redefine what is possible, we will continue to push the envelope, to pioneer a better way. We are committed to maintaining the highest level of quality – in accuracy and timeliness, in design and printing, and in service to our clients and readers. It is our goal to ensure that you can always turn to Hammond for the very best in map and atlas design and geographic information.

C. Dean and Kathleen Hammond

COMPUTERIZED CARTOGRAPHIC ADVISORY BOARD

Mitchell J. Feigenbaum, Ph.D
Chief Technical Consultant
Toyota Professor, The Rockefeller University
Wolf Prize in Physics, 1986
Member, The National Academy of Sciences

Judson G. Rosebush, Ph.D
Computer Graphics Animation
Producer, Director and Author

Gary Martin Andrew, Ph.D
Consultant in Operations Research,
Planning and Management

Warren E. Schmidt, B.A.
Former U.S. Geological Survey,
Chief of the Branch of Geographic
and Cartographic Research

HAMMOND PUBLICATIONS ADVISORY BOARD

LATIN AND MIDDLE AMERICA
John P. Augelli
Professor and Chairman,
Department of Geography-Meteorology,
University of Kansas

WESTERN AND SOUTHERN EUROPE
Norman J. W. Thrower
Professor, Department of Geography,
University of California, Los Angeles

NORTHERN AND CENTRAL EUROPE
Vincent H. Malmstrom
Professor, Department of Geography,
Dartmouth College

SOUTH AND SOUTHEAST ASIA
P. P. Karan
Professor, Department of Geography,
University of Kentucky

EAST ASIA
Christopher L. Salter
Professor and Chairman,
Department of Geography,
University of Missouri

AUSTRALIA, NEW ZEALAND
& THE PACIFIC AREA
Tom L. McKnight
Professor, Department of Geography,
University of California, Los Angeles

POPULATION AND DEMOGRAPHY
Kingsley Davis
Distinguished Professor of Sociology,
University of Southern California
and Senior Research Fellow,
The Hoover Institution,
Stanford University

BIBLICAL ARCHAEOLOGY
Roger S. Boraas
Professor of Religion,
Upsala College

FLAGS
Whitney Smith
Executive Director,
The Flag Research Center,
Winchester, Massachusetts

LIBRARY CONSULTANT
Alice C. Hudson
Chief, Map Division,
The New York Public Library

SPECIAL ADVISORS

DESIGN CONSULTANT
Pentagram

CONTRIBUTING WRITER
Frederick A. Shamlian

HAMMOND INCORPORATED

Charles G. Lees, Jr., V.P.
Editor in Chief, Cartography

William L. Abel, V.P.
Graphic Services

Phil Giouvanos
Director, Computer Cartography

Michael E. Agishtein, Ph.D
Director, Research and Development

Ernst G. Hofmann
Manager Emeritus, Topographic Arts

Martin A. Bacheller
Editor in Chief, Emeritus

Joseph F. Kalina, Jr.
Managing Editor